AUSTRALIAN DICTIONARY
OF BIOGRAPHY

General Editor
JOHN RITCHIE

AUSTRALIAN
DICTIONARY
OF BIOGRAPHY

VOLUME 13 : 1940-1980

A - De

General Editor
JOHN RITCHIE

Deputy General Editor
CHRISTOPHER CUNNEEN

MELBOURNE UNIVERSITY PRESS

First published 1993
Reprinted 1994

Typeset by Abb-typesetting Pty Ltd, Collingwood, Victoria
Printed in Australia by Brown Prior Anderson Pty Ltd, Burwood, Victoria, for
Melbourne University Press, Carlton, Victoria 3053

National Library of Australia Cataloguing-in-Publication entry

Australian dictionary of biography. Volume 13, 1940–1980, A–De.
Includes bibliographical references.
ISBN 0 522 84512 6.
ISBN 0 522 84236 4 (set).

1. Australia—Biography—Dictionaries. 2. Australia—History—
1945-   —Biography. I. Ritchie, John, 1941-   . II. Cunneen,
Christopher, 1940-   .
920.094

PREFACE

In January 1940 cheering crowds farewelled soldiers of the 6th Division as they sailed to do battle in the deserts of the Middle East. In December 1980 an inquest into the death of Azaria Chamberlain began at Alice Springs. Many of the events that occurred and the people who rose to prominence in the intervening years provide the subject matter for volume 13 of the *Australian Dictionary of Biography*. It contains 670 entries by 537 authors and is the first of four in the 1940-1980 section which will include some 2700 lives.

Spanning the years from 1940 to 1980, volumes 13 to 16 illuminate the themes of immigration, accelerating industrialism, urbanization and suburbanization, and war (World War II, Korea, Malaya and Vietnam). While other themes are also reflected— material progress, increasing cultural maturity, conservative and radical politics, conflict and harmony, loss of isolation and innocence—the emphasis of the biographies is on the individuals. The entries throw light on the complexity of the human situation, and on the greatness and the littleness of moral response and actual behaviour which this can evoke. In volume 13 the subjects range from Robert Davies, a midshipman who died at the age of 18, to the pharmacist Henry Cox who lived until he was 104 years old. Although the majority of the men and women included in these volumes flourished in the 1940-1980 period, a minority of the lives, like that of the explorer Caroline Barnett, who was born in 1860, reveal facets of Australian history long before 1940.

The two volumes of the 1788-1850 section, the four of the 1851-1890 section and the six of the 1891-1939 section were published from 1966 to 1990. The late Douglas Pike was general editor for volumes 1 to 5, Bede Nairn for volume 6, Nairn and Geoffrey Serle for volumes 7 to 10, Serle for volume 11 and John Ritchie for volume 12. An index to volumes 1-12 was published in 1991. The chronological division was designed to simplify production, for 7211 entries have been included in volumes 1-12 (volumes 1-2, for 1788-1850, had 1116 entries; volumes 3-6, for 1851-1890, 2053; volumes 6-12, for 1891-1939, 4042). For the period from 1788 to 1939, the placing of each individual's name in the appropriate section was determined by when he/she did his/her most important work (*floruit*). By contrast, the 1940-1980 section only includes individuals who died in this period. Volume 13 thus marks a change from the *floruit* to the 'date of death' principle. When volumes 13-16 have been completed, the A.D.B. will begin work on the period 1981-1990.

The choice of names for inclusion required prolonged consultation. After quotas were estimated, working parties in each State, and the Armed Services and Commonwealth working parties, prepared provisional lists which were widely circulated and carefully amended. Many of the names were obviously significant and worthy of inclusion as leaders in politics, business, the armed services, the church, the professions, the arts and the labour movement. Some have been included as representatives of ethnic and social minorities, and of a wide range of occupations; others have found a place as innovators, notorieties or eccentrics. A number had to be omitted through pressure of space or lack of material, and thereby joined the great mass whose members richly deserve a more honoured place, but thousands of these names, and information about them, have accumulated in the biographical register at the A.D.B. headquarters in the Australian National University.

Most authors were nominated by working parties. The burden of writing has been shared almost equally by the staff of universities and by a variety of other specialists.

The *A.D.B.* is a project based on consultation and co-operation. The Research School of Social Sciences at the A.N.U. has borne the cost of the headquarters staff, of much research and of occasional special contingencies, while other Australian universities have supported the project in numerous ways. The *A.D.B.*'s policies were originally determined by a national committee composed mainly of representatives from the departments of history in each Australian university. In Canberra the editorial board has kept in touch with these representatives, and with working parties, librarians, archivists and other local experts, as well as with research assistants in each Australian capital city and correspondents overseas. With such varied support, the *A.D.B.* is truly a national project.

ACKNOWLEDGMENTS

The *Australian Dictionary of Biography* is a programme fully supported by the Research School of Social Sciences at the Australian National University. Special thanks are due to Professor K. S. Inglis for guidance as chairman of the editorial board, and to Professor H. G. Brennan, director of the R.S.S.S., and his predecessor Professor P. F. Bourke, and Mr P. J. Grimshaw, the school's business manager. Those who helped in planning the shape of the work have been mentioned in earlier volumes.

Within Australia the *A.D.B.* is indebted to many librarians and archivists, schools, colleges, universities, institutes, historical and genealogical societies, and numerous other organizations; to the editors of the *Northern Territory Dictionary of Biography*; to the Australian War Memorial, the Commonwealth Scientific and Industrial Research Organization, the Australian Institute of Aboriginal and Torres Strait Islander Studies, and the Australian Archives; to the archives and public records offices in the various States and Territories, and registrars of probates and of the Supreme and Family courts, whose co-operation has solved many problems; to various town and shire clerks; to the Police Department, the Australian Dental Association, Big Brother Movement Ltd, the Powerhouse Museum, the Royal Australasian College of Physicians, the Royal Humane Society of New South Wales, the Royal Society of New South Wales, the Institute of Chartered Accountants and the Technical and Further Education History Unit, all in Sydney; to the Royal Humane Society of Australasia, the Australian Society of Certified Practising Accountants, the Royal Melbourne Institute of Technology, the State Electricity Commission of Victoria, the Association of Professional Engineers Australia and the Victorian Artists Society, all in Melbourne; to the Australian College of Veterinary Scientists, Queensland; to the company historian, Qantas Airways Ltd; and to the Australian Department of Defence for authenticating a host of details. Warm thanks for the free gift of their time and talents are due to contributors, to members of the editorial board and to the working parties. For particular advice the *A.D.B.* owes much to Stuart W. Alldritt, Cecily Close, Chris Coulthard-Clark, Mary Eagle, Bill Gammage, Bryan Gandevia, Joan Hughes, Oliver MacDonagh, Norm Neill, Hank Nelson, Greg Pemberton, Bill Ramson, Caroline Simpson, Kenneth Smith, F. B. Smith, R. J. M. Tolhurst, Peter Yeend, Norbert Zmijewski, and the staff of the National Library of Australia.

Essential assistance with birth, death and marriage certificates has been provided by the co-operation of registrars in New South Wales, Queensland, South Australia, Tasmania, Victoria, Western Australia, the Northern Territory and the Australian Capital Territory; by the General Register offices in Edinburgh and in London; by the registrars general of the Bahamas, Bermuda and Papua New Guinea; by the registrar of births and deaths, Singapore; by Bureaux of Vital Statistics in State Health departments in California, Florida, Michigan and New York, United States of America; by the Ministry of Health, British Columbia, Canada; by the Public Registry, Valletta, Malta; by the State Archive, Kristiansand, and the Office of the Population Register, Larvik, Norway; by the mayors of Nice, Sablons, and 14e, 16e and 19e Arrondissements, Paris, France; by civil status officers in Altivole, Cagliari, Grumo Appula, Verona and Venice, Italy; by the citizens records officer in Nova Gorica, Slovenia; by the state archives in Bonn, Bremen, Charlottenburg von Berlin and Schmalkalden, and the Evangelisch Lutherische Landeskirche,

ACKNOWLEDGMENTS

Mecklenburg, Germany; by the State Archives, Basel, and the civil registration offices in Lucerne, Meyrin and Neuchâtel, Switzerland; by the State Archive in Cracow, Poland, and the consul general for Poland, Sydney; and by the German, Hungarian and South African embassies, Canberra.

For other assistance overseas, thanks are due to Oonagh Walsh, Dublin, and Betty Iggo, Edinburgh; to Susan Luensmann of Remote Control, Virginia, U.S.A.; to the archives and libraries of the universities of Cambridge, Durham, Liverpool, London, Manchester, Oxford, and Reading, Imperial College, London, the London School of Economics and Political Science, University College London, Stonyhurst College, Lancashire, and the Haberdashers' Aske's School, Elstree, England; to the University of Edinburgh, Scotland; to the University of Wales, Aberystwyth; to the University of Toronto, Canada; to the New Zealand Vice-Chancellors' Committee and the universities of Auckland and Canterbury, and Victoria University of Wellington, New Zealand; to the universities of Geneva and Zurich, Switzerland; to Albert-Ludwigs-Universität Freiburg, Ernst-Moritz-Arndt-Universität Greifswald, Ludwig-Maximilians-Universität Munich, Germany; and to New York University, Columbia University, New York, University of Rochester, New York, Harvard University, Louisiana State University, Queens College, New York, and Bryn Mawr College, Pennsylvania, U.S.A.

Gratitude is also due to the Royal Anthropological Institute, the Royal College of Music, the Royal College of Physicians, the Royal College of Surgeons of England, the Royal Geographical Society, the Royal Society for the Encouragement of Arts, the Royal Society of Chemistry, the Royal Society of Health, the British Association of Paediatric Surgeons, the Church Missionary Society, the Institute of Physics, the Institution of Electrical Engineers, the Wiener Library, and the Worshipful Company of Butchers, all in London; the British Association of Social Workers, Birmingham, the Old Bedfordians Club, Bedford, the Institute of Chartered Accountants in England and Wales, Milton Keynes, and the Ministry of Defence, Hayes and Innsworth, England; to the Royal College of Surgeons of Edinburgh and the Royal Scottish Academy, Edinburgh; the General Register and Record Office of Shipping and Seamen, Cardiff, Wales; to Kenya National Archives, Nairobi; to Deutscher Alpenverein E.V., Munich, Germany; to the staffs of the *Österreichisches Biographisches Lexikon*, Vienna, *Dictionary of Canadian Biography*, Toronto, and *Dictionary of New Zealand Biography*, Wellington; to Auckland Grammar School, the reference librarian, Alexander Turnbull Library, and the New Zealand Defence Force, Wellington, New Zealand; to the Leo Baeck Institute, New York, U.S.A.; and to other individuals and institutions who have co-operated with the *A.D.B.*

The *A.D.B.* deeply regrets the deaths of such notable contributors as Richard E. Apperly, A. G. Austin, E. A. Beever, E. K. Braybrooke, W. L. Calov, Catherine Cameron, Manning Clark, Peter Cook, Arthur Corbett, R. M. Crawford, David Dexter, E. A. Dunphy, Diana Dyason, Malcolm S. S. Earlam, Brian Eaton, J. W. Evans, L. M. Field, Kathleen Fitzpatrick, L. R. Gardiner, Dorothy Green, Guy B. Gresford, Peter Harrison, Helen Heney, Wilfrid E. Henn, Ian Hogbin, Ronald Hopkins, E. J. H. Howard, J. C. Irwin, Prue Joske, M. J. B. Kenny, Coral Lansbury, T. J. Linane, Joan Lynravn, Arthur McMartin, I. W. Morley, Ada M. Norris, W. M. O'Neil, J. Percival, W. R. Ray, Gordon Rimmer, E. M. Robertson, A. de Q. Robin, G. H. Stephens, S. E. Stephens, G. Sturgeon, S. G. Tomlin, V. A. Wardell, P. Wardle, Alan Watt, Rowan Webb and Harley Wood.

Grateful acknowledgment is due, as well, to the director and staff of Melbourne University Press, and to former *A.D.B.* staff members—Helen Boxall, Lindie Davey, Kathleen Dermody, Vicky Fairhall, Emma Grahame, Jenny Holmes, Hilary Kent and Jenny Newell—who worked on volume 13.

EDITORIAL BOARD

SECTION EDITORS

STAFF

WORKING PARTIES

Armed Services
F. H. Brown, P. Burness, C. D. Coulthard-Clark, B. Eaton*, P. G. Edwards, W. D. H. Graham, A. J. Hill (chair), D. M. Horner, J. McCarthy, Perditta McCarthy, A. L. Morrison, A. J. Sweeting.

Commonwealth
Patricia Clarke, C. Hazlehurst (chair), J. Ann Hone, C. Hughes, Anthea Hyslop, R. Hyslop, Margot Kerley, C. J. Lloyd, G. Powell, J. Thompson.

New South Wales
J. M. Bennett, K. J. Cable, J. J. Carmody, Alison Crook (chair), C. Cunneen, R. Curnow, Ann Curthoys, F. Farrell, S. Garton, E. M. Goot, Beverley Kingston, A. J. Moore, N. B. Nairn, Heather Radi, Jill Roe, G. Souter, G. P. Walsh.

Queensland
Nancy Bonnin, M. D. Cross, J. C. H. Gill, Helen Gregory, I. F. Jobling, W. R. Johnston (chair), G. N. Logan, R. I. Longhurst, Lorna McDonald, Dawn May, Margaret O'Hagan, S. J. Routh, C. G. Sheehan, V. T. Vallis.

South Australia
W. L. Gammage, Joyce Gibberd, R. M. Gibbs, P. A. Howell, Helen Jones, J. H. Love, Susan Marsden, J. D. Playford (chair), Patricia Stretton, R. E. Thornton.

Tasmania
G. P. R. Chapman, Shirley Eldershaw, R. A. Ferrall, Margaret Glover, Elizabeth McLeod, F. M. Neasey, S. Petrow, Anne Rand, O. M. Roe (chair), G. T. Stilwell.

Victoria
W. A. Bate, Judith Brett, G. R. Browne, Mimi Colligan, G. J. Davison, F. J. Kendall, J. F. Lack, Marilyn Lake, J. R. Poynter (chair), J. D. Rickard, A. G. Serle, Judith Smart, F. Strahan.

Western Australia
Wendy Birman (chair), D. Black, G. C. Bolton, P. J. Boyce, Dorothy Erickson, Jenny Gregory, Mary Anne Jebb, Lenore Layman, Margaret Medcalf, C. Mulcahy, R. H. W. Reece, A. C. Staples.

* deceased

AUTHORS

ADAMS, Bruce:
Balson.
ALEXANDER, Fred:
Beasley, F.
ALLPORT, Carolyn:
Burke, P.
AMPT, C. R.:
Callinan.
ANDERSON, D. J.:
Armstrong, Sir A.
ANDERSON, Derek:
Barber, H.
ANDREW, R. R.:
Corkill.
APPERLY, Richard E.*:
Ancher; Baldwinson; Dellit.
ASHTON, Paul:
Blake, R.
ATCHISON, John:
Allen, A. M.; Clews.
ATKINSON, H. F.:
Adamson, Sir K.; Amies.
ATTWOOD, H. D.:
Butler, H.

BAILEY, R. G.:
Davies, C.
BAKER, D. W. A.:
Andronicus.
BALLARD, B. A.:
Archer, C.
BALMFORD, Peter:
Burt.
BARNES, Geoffrey:
Campbell, A. P.; Cockett.
BARTER, Margaret:
Chowne.
BARTLETT, Margaret E.:
Crespin.
BARTROP, Paul R.:
Barkman.
BASSETT, Jan:
Bowe.
BECKETT, Jeremy:
Biggs.
BENNET, Darryl:
Bowden, V.; Brodribb; Callaway; Cowper;
Davies, R.
BENNETT, J. M.:
Currey.
BENNETT, Scott:
Binney.
BEST, Alleyn:
Coull.
BHATHAL, R.:
Bolliger; Bosworth.
* deceased

BILINSKY, Bohdan:
Benjafield.
BIRMAN, Wendy:
Carter; Cummins.
BISHOP, P. O.:
Davies, H.
BISSET, Andrew:
Coughlan, F.
BLAAZER, David:
Breen.
BLACK, David:
Brand, Sir D.; Cardell-Oliver.
BLACKMORE, Kate:
Armstrong, M.
BLAINEY, Ann:
Bassett, F.
BLANDEN, John B.:
Davison, A.
BOLTON, G. C.:
Boyer; Burke, T.; Button; Collins, H.;
Courtney; Davidson, D.
BOLTON, H. C.:
Colechin.
BOOT, H. M.:
Collins, T.
BOSWORTH, Michal:
Bindi.
BOXALL, Helen:
Boyle.
BOYES, Jeffery:
Batt.
BRANAGAN, D. F.:
Black, A.; Cameron, K.
BRAZIER, Jan:
Allsop; Beatty; Dawes, E.
BREGU, Bahri:
Cuni.
BRIGNELL, Lyn:
Boelke.
BRISSENDEN, Alan:
Bishop.
BRODRICK, Lloyd:
Anthony.
BROOMHAM, Rosemary:
Boyd, E.
BROUGHTON, Lindsay:
Carington Smith.
BROWN, Elaine:
Corser; Courtice.
BROWN, Nicholas:
Brown, G.; Davies, E.
BROWN, Paula:
Agaundo.
BROWN, Tasman:
Campbell, T.
BROWNE, Elspeth:
Davies, S.

BROWNE, Geoff:
Allnutt, A.; Barry, W.; Cremean.
BRUNTON, Paul:
Appleroth.
BUCKLEY, Ken:
Burns.
BURNESS, Peter:
Connely; Cox, G.
BYRNE, Dianne:
Corones.

CABLE, K. J.:
Allman; Clark-Duff.
CAIN, Frank:
Crawford, J.
CAMERON, Clyde:
Chambers.
CAMPION, Edmund:
Armstrong, J.; Davey, G.
CANTRELL, Carol:
David.
CARMENT, David:
Abbott, C.
CARMODY, John:
Conley; Dew.
CARNELL, Ian:
Barrenger; Chippindall.
CARROLL, Brian:
Derham, F. J.
CARRON, L. T.:
Dadswell.
CASHMAN, R. I.:
Alderson.
CASSIDY, Jill:
Chung Gon.
CATTANI, Licia:
Coleman, L.
CHAMBERS, Don:
Darwin.
CHAPMAN, Ivan:
Cousens.
CHAPMAN, R. J. K.:
Barnard, H. C.; Cole, G.
CHAPPELL, Louise:
Beveridge, D.; Brown, L.
CHARLWOOD, Don:
Barker, H.
CHIPPENDALE, George M.:
Burbidge.
CHURCH, Judith:
Deen.
CHURCHWARD, M. S.:
Burnell.
CLARKE, Patricia:
Dalgarno.
CLEREHAN, Brian:
Burston, Sir S.
CLEREHAN, Neil:
Boyd, R.
CLOSE, Cecily:
Chamberlin.
CLUNE, David:
Cahill, J.

COLLIGAN, Mimi:
Darbyshire.
COLLINS, Hugh:
Cooke.
COLLINS PERSSE, Michael D. de B.:
Connal.
COLTHEART, Lenore:
Beveridge, D.
COMBE, Diana R.:
Dearth.
CONNELL, W. F.:
Brown, M. S.; Browne, G.
CONNORS, Jane:
Bedford.
CONROY, Denise K.:
Bulcock.
CONSANDINE, Marion:
Barclay, E.
COOPER, Jan:
Cronin, M.
CORCORAN, Kristine:
Burge.
CORKERY, J. F.:
Alderman.
CORNISH, Selwyn:
Chapman, J. L.
COSTAR, B. J.:
Barnes, J.; Bowden, G.; Byrnes, Sir T.
COULTHARD-CLARK, C. D.:
Anderson, W. H.; Charlesworth;
Coleman, P.; Crace; De La Rue.
COWEN, Zelman:
Ashkanasy; Coppel.
CRIBB, Margaret Bridson:
Adermann; Bell, C.; Cooper, Sir W.
CROFT, Julian:
Clune.
CROSS, J. J.:
Behrend; Cherry.
CROSS, Manfred:
Cooper, F.; Dawson, G.
CRYLE, Denis:
Amiet.
CUCKSON, Marie:
Bodenwieser.
CUNNEEN, Chris:
Chamberlain; Charles; Craig, D.
CURDIE, John:
Aston.
CURNOW, Ross:
Bland.

DALKIN, R. N.:
Bladin.
DANIELS, Louis V.:
Cranswick, G. F.
DARBY, Robert:
Adamson, G.; Davison, F.
DAVIS, R. P.:
Brooker.
DAVISON, Graeme:
Coleman, J.
DE SERVILLE, P. H.:
Brooks.

DEER, A. F.:
Alder.
DENHOLM, David:
Clowes.
DENHOLM, Decie:
Cooper, C.
DENING, Greg:
Adam, L.
DENOON, Donald:
Davidson, J.
DERMODY, Kathleen:
Daley, H.
DETTMANN, Mary E.:
Cookson.
DEWAR, Mickey:
Alngindabu.
DICKER, George:
Boase.
DICKIE, Phil:
Brifman.
DIGNAN, Don:
Castellano.
DINGLE, Tony:
Borrie.
DIX, Warwick:
Barunga.
DOHERTY, R. L.:
Derrick, E. H.
DONAGHY, Gerald:
Dalziel, A.
DREYFUS, Kay:
Davis, H.
DUNCAN, Alan T.:
Blair.
DUNSTAN, David:
Connelly; de Castella.
DURDIN, Joan:
Carroll, D.

EASTMAN, Berenice:
Chauncy.
EATHER, Warwick:
Clegg.
EATON, Brian*:
Brill; Cole, A.
EDGAR, Suzanne:
Angwin; Birdseye; Cotton, L.
EDMONDS, Leigh:
Brownell.
EGAN, Bryan:
de Gruchy.
ELMSLIE, Ronald:
Abbie.
ELSE-MITCHELL, R.:
Brewster.

FAHEY, Charles:
Buckland, E.
FAIRWEATHER, D. F.:
Anderson, F.; Bradford.
FERGUSON, Anthony:
Casey, G.

* deceased

FERRALL, R. A.:
Denny.
FINLAY, H. A.:
Baker, Sir H.
FINLAY, Ric:
Bushby.
FINNIMORE, Christine:
Campbell, R.
FISCHER, Pat:
Cavill.
FLETCHER, B. H.:
Bateson.
FLETCHER, Daina:
Allcot.
FOLEY, Meredith:
Blomfield.
FOTHERINGHAM, Richard:
Dann.
FOX, Charlie:
Connolly, P.
FRAME, Tom:
Becher.
FRANCES, Raelene:
Brodney.
FRASER, Alan:
Curr.
FREDMAN, L. E.:
Berrick.
FRENCH, Eric L.:
Bull.
FREUDENBERG, Graham:
Calwell.
FULLOON, Gillian:
Abbott, J. S.

GAMMAGE, Bill:
Derrick, T.
GARDINER, Lyndsay:
Collins, V.; de Neeve.
GARRICK, Phyl:
Bennett, A.
GARRISSON, A. D.:
Bostock.
GARTON, Stephen:
Bradley, S.; Dawson, W.
GAUDRY, Anne-Marie:
Banvard.
GEORGE, W. I.:
Axon.
GIBBERD, Joyce:
Bonython; Cade, W.; Deacon.
GILL, J. C. H.:
Adair; Boyd, W.
GILL, K. E.:
Craig, E.
GILLMAN, Ian:
Bardon.
GODDEN, Judith:
Blomfield.
GOLDRICK, J. V. P.:
Buchanan.
GOLLAN, Robin:
Baracchi.

INDER, Stuart:
Ashton, H.
INGRAM, Glen:
Barnard, H. G.
IRONSIDE, Wallace:
Cade, J.
ISAACS, Keith:
Broadbent; Clark, James.

JAMES, G. F.:
Addison.
JAMIESON, Ronda:
Black, E.
JARRETT, Hugh:
Band.
JENKIN, John:
Brose.
JENNINGS, Margaret J.:
Benham.
JOHNSON, L. A. S.:
Anderson, R.
JOHNSON, Lesley:
Davey, J.
JOHNSTON, W. Ross:
Bischof; Carroll, C.
JONES, Barry O.:
Dease.
JONES, David J.:
Bertles.
JONES, Helen:
Allnutt, M.; Baker, M.; Beeston;
Davies, N.
JONES, Philip:
Aiston.

KELLY, Shay Ann:
Callaghan, E.
KEMP, D. H.:
Butt.
KEMSLEY, James:
Cross, S.
KENDALL, F. J.:
Chapman, L.
KENT, Hilary:
Brophy; Cross, Sir R.
KERLEY, Margot:
Boniwell; Brown, H.; Carver.
KERR, John D.:
Bennett, N.; Curlewis.
KERR, Ruth S.:
Binnie.
KING, Hugh:
Denning, A.
KINGSTON, Beverley:
Buckingham.
KINNANE, Stephen:
Argyle.
KIRBY, Michael:
Conybeare.
KLOOT, Tess:
Chandler, L.; Chisholm, A.
KNIGHT, Ken G.:
Affleck.

KNIGHT, Kenneth W.:
Bourke.
KNOTT, John:
Birchell.
KRAMER, Leonie:
Campbell, D. W. I.
KYLE, Noeline J.:
Allan, M.

LABY, Betty:
Belz.
LANCASTER, H. O.:
Baldwin.
LANGMORE, Diane:
Arek; Biddlecombe; Cawthorn, M.;
Creswick.
LAVERTY, John:
Chandler, Sir J.
LAWRENCE, T. F. C.:
Boswell.
LAWRIE, Margaret:
Corran.
LAWRIE, Robert:
Charlton.
LAWSON, Valerie:
Baume.
LE MAISTRE, Barbara:
Anderson, A. W.
LEE, David:
Ashley; Cotton, T.
LEMON, Andrew:
Basser.
LEVETT, John:
Collier, J. & J.
LINCOLN, Merrilyn:
Best, K.
LINN, R. W.:
Angas.
LISTON, Carol:
Bain.
LLOYD, C. J.:
Clarey; Connor.
LLOYD, Peter L.:
Bell, A.
LODGE, A. B.:
Bennett, H.
LOEWALD, Klaus:
Broughton.
LOMAS, L.:
Carmody, T.
LOUGHEED, A. L.:
Campbell, A. W.
LOVE, J. H.:
Blanchard.
LUDLOW, Christa:
Bailey, E.

McARTHUR, T. J.:
Connell, R.
MacAULAY, Bettina:
Annand.
McAULAY, Lex:
Clisby.

McBURNIE, Grant:
  Booth, A.
McCALMAN, Iain:
  Bendrodt.
McCALMAN, Janet:
  Bell, H.
McCARTHY, John:
  Balmer; Cotton, F.
McDONALD, G. L.:
  Belisario; Collins, Sir A.
McDONALD, Jan:
  Andrew.
McDONALD, Lorna:
  Anderson, A. C.; Archer, A.; Archer, D.;
  Beak.
McEVEY, Allan:
  Coleman, E.
McGRATH, Joyce:
  Buckmaster.
MACINTYRE, Eileen:
  Deasey.
McKINNON, Julie:
  Carroll, G.
McLAREN, Alex C.:
  Bowden, F.
McLAUGHLIN, John Kennedy:
  Cantor; Cassidy.
McLENNAN, Graham:
  Colvin.
McMICHAEL, D. F.:
  Allan, C.
McMULLIN, Ross:
  Cunningham, L.
McNEILL, Ian:
  Badcoe.
McNICOLL, Ronald:
  Chapman, W.
McPHERSON, Albert B.:
  Cranswick, G. H.
MAFF, Winsome J. M.:
  Barnett.
MAHER, Brian:
  Cahill, T.
MAMMINO, Rosemary:
  Adamson, M. & A.
MANDLE, W. F.:
  Burke, J.
MANSFIELD, Joan:
  Coughlan, W.
MARCHANT, Sylvia:
  Butler, C.
MARGINSON, B.:
  Condon.
MARKS, Horace B.:
  Cornwall.
MARSDEN, Susan:
  Cartledge; Cleggett;
  Crawford, S.
MARSHALL, Norman J.:
  Andersen.
MARTIN, A. W.:
  Curthoys.
MARTIN, N. D.:
  Arnott.

MARTINUZZI, A. L.:
  Cotter.
MAUGHAN, Jill E.:
  Bennetts, H.
MAVOR, John E.:
  Alcorn.
MAXWELL, Helen:
  Dangar.
MEDCALF, M.:
  Battye.
MELLICK, J. S. D.:
  Byrnes, R.
MENGHETTI, Diane:
  Arida.
MILEY, Caroline:
  Cumming.
MINCHAM, Hans:
  Cooper, H.
MISSEN, Mollie:
  Dacomb.
MITCHELL, Bruce:
  Booth, E.
MIZZI, Jillian:
  Clark, F.
MOFFAT, Angelika G. I.:
  Allen, Sir W.
MOIGNARD, Kathy:
  Ackland.
MOORE, Andrew:
  Clayton.
MOORE, Bryce:
  Brisbane.
MORAN, John Michael:
  Boland.
MORGAN, George:
  Blumenthal.
MORGAN, Patrick:
  Bednall.
MORISON, Patricia:
  Cameron, Sir G.
MORRIS, Deirdre:
  Dalley.
MORRIS, Ewan:
  Clint.
MULCAHY, Clement:
  Catalan.
MURRAY, Robert:
  Anderson, Sir W.; Broadby; Cain.

NAIRN, Bede:
  Beasley, J.; Browne, J.
NANCE, Susan:
  Abbie.
NAPPER, D. H.:
  Alexander.
NEASEY, F. M.:
  Clark, A.
NELSON, H. N.:
  Cleland; Dawes, A.
NEWTON, Gael:
  Cato.
NIALL, Brenda:
  Boyd, M.

NORTHEY, R. E.:
Dawson, C.

O'BRIEN, Anne:
Baker, A.; Bradley, C.
O'BRIEN, Ilma Martinuzzi:
Cantamessa.
O'BRIEN, Laurie:
Coaldrake.
O'FARRELL, Virginia:
Anderson, J.
O'HAGAN, M. D.:
Devaney.
O'NEIL, W. M.*:
Clark, J. F.
O'NEILL, Robert:
Burnett.
O'NEILL, Sally:
Cardus.
OSBORN, E. F.:
Barber, G.
OTTAVI, Dino:
Bini.

PARNABY, Owen:
Brown, M.
PARSONS, A. D.:
Butler, A.
PATMORE, Greg:
Cranwell.
PEARN, John H.:
Adam, G.
PEEK, Jane:
Dechaineux.
PEMBERTON, Gregory J.:
Dalziel, A. J.
PEMBERTON, P. A.:
Carson.
PENNAY, Bruce:
Agostini.
PERKINS, John:
Becker, J.; Davis, L.
PHILLIPS, Julian:
Cohen, S.
PLAYFORD, John:
Aunger; Barclay-Harvey; Cameron, Archie.
POOLE, Max:
Boas.
POPE, David:
Armstrong, T.
PORTER, Anne:
Birtwistle.
PORTER, Q. N.:
Davies, W.
POWELL, J. M.:
Aird.
POYNTER, J. R.:
Brookes; Cowan, R.
PRENTICE, S. A.:
Barton; Corbett.

* deceased

PRIOR, Robin:
Cook.
PROUDFOOT, Helen:
Brown, A. J. & D.
PROUDLEY, Ray:
Andrews.
PULLAR, Margaret:
Cobb.

QUARTERMAINE, M. K.:
Compton.
QUICK, Aubrey:
Daws.
QUINN, Michael P.:
Cecil.

RADI, Heather:
Bradley, E. & J.; Bryant; Byles; Campbell, P.
RADIC, Maureen Thérèse:
Collier, M.
RAMSON, W. S.:
Baker, S.
RAND, A.:
Baudinet.
RASMUSSEN, Carolyn:
Blackburn; Borrie.
RASZEJA, V. M.:
Dennis.
RAYNER, S. A.:
Connell, C.
READ, Peter:
Coe.
REECE, R. H. W.:
de Burgh.
REED, M. P.:
Clark, C.
REFSHAUGE, W. D.:
Bell, G.
REGAN, Kerry:
Anton.
REID, Rex:
Church.
REITTERER, H.:
Bodenwieser.
REYNOLDS, Peter:
Ancher; Baldwinson; Dellit.
RICHARDS, Duncan:
Clifton.
RICHARDSON, Jack E.:
Bailey, Sir K.
RICHMOND, Mark:
Burne.
RICKARD, John:
Alden.
RIDDETT, Lyn Anne:
Carrodus.
RITCHIE, John:
Angles; Cole, L.
ROE, J. I.:
Bennett, E.
ROGERS, Ruth:
Campbell, T.

ROLLEY, Ailsa:
Beet.
ROSS, F. J.:
Bowmaker.
ROUTH, S. J.:
Bowhay.
RUBINSTEIN, Hilary L.:
Brodie.
RUTLAND, Suzanne D.:
Brand, W. L.; Cohen, R.
RUTLEDGE, Martha:
Allen, A. D.; Anderson, E.; Basser;
Bergman; Bligh; Brunton; Carr-Glyn.
RYAN, Jan:
Craig, L. & F.
RYAN, K. W.:
Anderson, H.
RYAN, Peter:
Conlon, A.

ST LEON, Mark Valentine:
Bullen, A. & L.; Colleano.
SAMUEL, Merran:
Allison.
SAYERS, Stuart:
Campbell, Sir H.
SCARLETT, Ken:
Anderson, W. W.
SCHEDVIN, C. B.:
Butlin; Clunies Ross.
SCHWIEGER, Arthur:
Cox, L.
SCOTT, Margaret:
Davis, N.
SEMMLER, Clement:
Barry, K.; Bronner.
SERLE, Geoffrey:
Brake; Curtin.
SHAMSULLAH, Ardel:
Barclay, N.
SHARP, Allan McL.:
Baile.
SHARWOOD, R. L.:
Dean.
SHAW, J. W.:
Clancy.
SILSBURY, Elizabeth:
Chinner.
SIMPSON, Caroline:
Chisholm, M.
SIMPSON, John P.:
Briggs.
SINCLAIR, E. K.:
Booth, Sir C.
SITSKY, Larry:
Banks; Burston, W.
SKEWES, Edna M.:
Ackman.
SMITH, Neil:
Cremor.
SOUTER, Gavin:
Banning; Deamer.
SOUTHERN, R. L.:
Akeroyd.

SOUTHEY, R. J.:
Algeranoff.
SPAULL, Andrew:
Dedman.
SPEARRITT, Gordon D.:
Day.
SPEARRITT, Peter:
Bunning; Deering.
SPINK, J. A.:
Bastow; Bowden, F.
STATHAM, Pamela:
Bell, D.
STAUNTON, Anthony:
Cartwright.
STEADMAN, Margaret:
Campbell, C.
STEPHENS, Alan:
Crombie.
STEPHENS, F. Douglas:
Browne, Sir D.
STEPHENS, Jack:
Devanny.
STEVEN, Margaret:
Brett, J.
STEVENSON, Brian F.:
Brand, Sir W. A.; Bryan, S.;
Delamothe.
STEWART, Elizabeth:
Cerutty, C.
STILWELL, G. T.:
Allport.
STOCK, Jenny Tilby:
Blesing.
STODDART, Brian:
Barnes, S.; Cremin.
STOKES, H. J. W.:
Beattie.
STONE, Jonathan:
Burkitt.
STRAHAN, Frank:
Brain, Sir H.; Colman.
SUMERLING, Patricia:
Bean.
SUTTON, R.:
Callaghan, C.
SWAIN, Shurlee:
Derrick, E. M.
SWAN, Geoffrey:
Ashburn; Bryan, E.
SWANTON, Bruce:
Barge.
SWEETING, A. J.:
Allen, A. S.; Bazley; Cameron, Allan;
Derbyshire.
SYDENHAM, Diane:
Coles.

TATE, Audrey:
Dale.
TAYLOR, Helen:
Berry.
TEAGUE, Bernard:
Barry, Sir J.

AUTHORS

TEALE, Ruth:
Davidson, E.
THOMAS, Daniel:
Crowley.
THOMAS, Joanne W.:
Brownbill.
THOMPSON, Roger C.:
Chapman, J. A.
THOMSON, Joyce:
Bell, J.
THORNTON, Harold:
Bukowski.
TIFFIN, Chris:
Connolly, R.
TILBROOK, John D.:
Beavis.
TILSE, Sheila:
Cohen, I.
TOLLEY, Michael J.:
Afford.
TOWNSLEY, W. A.:
Cosgrove.
TSOKHAS, Kosmas:
Abbott, J. P.
TUCCERI, Anne:
Casimaty.
TUCKER, Doug:
Behan; Chuter.

UPTON, Murray S.:
Clark, John.

VALE, Gill E.:
Crosby.
VALLANCE, Sarah:
Conde.
VALLANCE, T. G.:
Browne, W.
VARVARESSOS, Maria S.:
Bannan.
VINCENT, David:
Atkinson, R.
VON STURMER, John:
Arkwookerum.

WAITE, Marjorie:
Beggs; Boyd, D.; Dahlenburg.
WALL, Barbara:
Biaggini.
WALLER, Louis:
Brett, P.
WALSH, G. P.:
Ashton, J.; Barrett; Burke-Gaffney;
Chapman, G.; Copeley; Debenham.
WATERFORD, Jack:
Bennetts, R.
WATERHOUSE, Jill:
Blake, F.; Cumpston.

WATERSON, D. B.:
Chifley.
WATSON, A. O.:
Best, Sir J.
WATSON, Don:
Conrad.
WATSON, Jack:
Cochran.
WEATHERBURN, Hilary:
Charley; Croft.
WEBB, Rowan*:
Coates.
WEBBER, Kimberley:
Burke, E.
WEICKHARDT, L. W.:
Begg.
WHEATLEY, Nadia:
Clift.
WHITE, Isobel:
Atkinson, E.
WHITE, Kate:
Cain.
WHITE, M. W. D.:
Butts.
WHITE, Richard:
Athaldo.
WHITMORE, Raymond L.:
Binnie; Darker.
WHITTON, Evan:
Allan, N.
WHYTE, Jean P.:
Archer, M.
WILLIAMS, Brian:
Cunningham, K.
WILLIAMS, Rosemary:
Callanan.
WILSON, David:
Brennan.
WINCH, Denis E.:
Bullen, K.
WINDSCHUTTLE, Elizabeth:
Conlon, P.
WINZENRIED, Arthur:
Camm.
WOODRUFF, Philip:
Cowan, Sir D.
WOTHERSPOON, Garry C.:
Delaney.

YORK, Barry:
Ciantar; Curmi.

ZELLING, Howard:
Campbell, A. L.
ZERNER, M. E.:
Barker, G.
ZIMMER, Jenny:
Baldessin.

* deceased

A NOTE ON SOME PROCEDURES

Differences of opinion exist among our authors, readers and the editorial board as to whether certain information should normally be included—such as cause of death, burial or cremation details, and value of estate. In this volume our practices have been as follows:

Cause of death: usually included, except in the case of those aged over 70.

Burial/cremation: included when details available.

Value of estate: included where possible for categories such as businessmen, and if the amount is unusually high or low. In recent years, when the practice developed of distributing assets early in order to avoid estate and probate duties, the sum is not always meaningful; moreover, at times it is impossible to ascertain full details. Hence we have resorted to discretionary use.

Some other procedures require explanation:

Measurements: as the least unsatisfactory solution we have used imperial system measurements (as historically appropriate), followed by the metric equivalent in brackets.

Money: we have retained £ for pounds for references prior to 14 February 1966 (when the conversion rate was A£1 = A$2).

Religion: stated whenever information is available, but there is often no good evidence of actual practice, e.g. the information is confined to marriage and funeral rites.

[q.v.]: the particular volume is given for those included in volumes 1-12, but not for those in this volume. Note that the cross-reference [q.v.] now accompanies the names of all who have separate articles in the *A.D.B.* In volumes 1-6 it was not shown for royal visitors, governors, lieutenant-governors and those Colonial Office officials who were included.

Small capitals: used for relations and others when they are of substantial importance, though not included in their own right; these people are also q.v.'d.

Floruit and 'date of death': for the period 1788 to 1939, the placing of subjects in volumes 1 to 12 was determined by when they flourished; in contrast, volumes 13 to 16 (for the period 1940 to 1980) only include people who died in those years.

CORRIGENDA

Every effort is made to check every detail in every article, but a work of the *A.D.B.*'s size and complexity is bound to contain some errors.

Corrigenda have been published with each volume. A consolidated list, including corrections made after the publication of volume 12 (1990), forms part of the *Index* (1991). A list of corrigenda compiled since 1991 accompanies volume 13.

Only corrections are shown; additional information is not included; nor is any reinterpretation attempted. The exception to this procedure occurs when new details about parents, births, marriages and deaths become available.

Documented corrections are welcomed. Additional information, with sources, is also invited, and will be placed in the appropriate files for future use. In both cases, readers should write to:

> The General Editor
> Australian Dictionary of Biography
> Research School of Social Sciences
> Australian National University
> CANBERRA ACT 0200
> Australia.

REFERENCES

The following and other standard works of reference have been widely used, though not usually acknowledged in individual biographies:

Australian Encyclopaedia, 1-2 (Syd, 1925), 1-10 (1958), 1-12 (1983)

Biographical register for various Australian parliaments: (A. W. Martin & P. Wardle *and* H. Radi, P. Spearritt & E. Hinton *and* C. N. Connolly—New South Wales; G. C. Bolton & A. Mozley—Western Australia; K. Thomson & G. Serle *and* G. Browne—Victoria; D. B. Waterson *and* D. B. Waterson & J. Arnold—Queensland; H. Coxon, J. Playford & R. Reid—South Australia; S. & B. Bennett—Tasmania; and J. Rydon—Commonwealth)

B. Burke, *A Genealogical and Heraldic History of the Colonial Gentry*, 1-2 (Lond, 1891, 1895)

O'M. Creagh and E. M. Humphris (eds), *The V.C. and D.S.O.: a complete record* . . . 1-3 (Lond, 1934)

Dictionary of National Biography (Lond, 1885-1990)

H. M. Green, *A History of Australian Literature*, 1-2 (Syd, 1961, 2nd edn 1971), revised by D. Green (Syd, 1984-85)

C. A. Hughes and B. D. Graham, *A Handbook of Australian Government and Politics 1890-1964* (Canb, 1968); *Voting for the Australian House of Representatives 1901-1964*, with corrigenda (Canb, 1975), for *Queensland Legislative Assembly 1890-1964* (Canb, 1974), for *New South Wales* . . . (1975), *Victoria* . . . (1975), and *South Australian, Western Australian and Tasmanian Lower Houses* . . . (1976)

F. Johns, *Johns's Notable Australians* (Melb, 1906), *Fred Johns's Annual* (Lond, 1914); *An Australian Biographical Dictionary* (Melb, 1934)

A. McCulloch, *Encyclopedia of Australian Art* (Lond, 1968), 1-2 (Melb, 1984)

E. M. Miller, *Australian Literature* . . . *to 1935* (Melb, 1940), extended to 1950 by F. T. Macartney (Syd, 1956)

W. Moore, *The Story of Australian Art*, 1-2 (Syd, 1934), (Syd, 1980)

P. C. Mowle, *A Genealogical History of Pioneer Families in Australia* (Syd, 1939; 5th edn Adel, 1978)

P. Serle, *Dictionary of Australian Biography*, 1-2 (Syd, 1949)

Who's Who (Lond), and *Who's Who in Australia* (Syd, Melb, present and past edns)

W. H. Wilde, J. Hooton & B. Andrews, *The Oxford Companion to Australian Literature* (Melb, 1985)

ABBREVIATIONS USED IN BIBLIOGRAPHIES

AA	Australian Archives	Dept	Department
AAA	*All About Australians*	*DNB*	*Dictionary of National Biography*
AAA	Amateur Athletic Association		
ABC	Australian Broadcasting Commission/Corporation	ed	editor
ACT	Australian Capital Territory	edn	edition
Adel	Adelaide	Edinb	Edinburgh
Agr	Agriculture, Agricultural	Eng	England
AIF	Australian Imperial Force		
AJCP	Australian Joint Copying Project	Fr	Father (priest)
ALP	Australian Labor Party	Geog	Geographical
AMPA (SLV)	Arts, Music and Performing Arts Library, State Library of Victoria	Govt	Government
ANU	Australian National University, Canberra	HA	House of Assembly
		Hist	History, Historical
ANUABL	ANU Archives of Business and Labour	Hob	Hobart
		HR	House of Representatives
ANZAAS	Australian and New Zealand Association for the Advancement of Science	HSSA	Historical Society of South Australia
A'sia/n	Australasia/n	*IAN*	*Illustrated Australian News*
Assn	Association	Inc	Incorporated
Aust	Australia/n	Inst	Institute, Institution
AWM	Australian War Memorial, Canberra	intro	introduction, introduced by
		ISN	*Illustrated Sydney News*
		J	*Journal*
Basser L	Adolph Basser Library, Australian Academy of Science, Canberra	JCU	James Cook University of North Queensland, Townsville
Bd	Board	LA	Legislative Assembly
BHP	Broken Hill Proprietary Co. Ltd	LaTL	La Trobe Library, Melbourne
		Launc	Launceston
bib	bibliography	LC	Legislative Council
biog	biography, biographical	L	Library
BL	J. S. Battye Library of West Australian History, Perth	Lond	London
Brisb	Brisbane	*Mag*	*Magazine*
		Melb	Melbourne
c	circa	MDHC	Melbourne Diocesan Historical Commission (Catholic), Fitzroy
CAE	College of Advanced Education		
Canb	Canberra	mf	microfilm/s
cat	catalogue	*MJA*	*Medical Journal of Australia*
CO	Colonial Office, London	ML	Mitchell Library, Sydney
co	company	Mort L	Mortlock Library of South Australiana
C of E	Church of England		
Col Sec	Colonial Secretary	ms/s	manuscript/s
Com	Commission/er	mthly	monthly
comp	compiler		
Corp	Corporation/s	nd	date of publication unknown
CSIRO	Commonwealth Scientific and Industrial Research Organization	NFSA	National Film and Sound Archive, Canberra
		NG	New Guinea
cte	committee	NL	National Library of Australia, Canberra
Cwlth	Commonwealth		

no	number		1st S	First Session
np	place of publication unknown		2nd S	Second Session
NSW	New South Wales		2nd s	second series
NSWA	The Archives Authority of New South Wales, Sydney		SA	South Australia/n
			Sel	Select
NT	Northern Territory		SLNSW	State Library of New South Wales
NY	New York			
NZ	New Zealand		SLSA	State Library of South Australia
OL	John Oxley Library, Brisbane		SLT	State Library of Tasmania
			SLV	State Library of Victoria
p, pp	page, pages		*SMH*	*Sydney Morning Herald*
pc	photocopy		Soc	Society
PD	*Parliamentary Debates*		SRSA	State Records Office, South Australia
PIM	*Pacific Islands Monthly*			
PP	*Parliamentary Papers*		supp	supplement
PRGSSA	*Proceedings of the Royal Geographical Society of Australasia (South Australian Branch)*		Syd	Sydney
			TA	Tasmanian State Archives, Hobart
priv pub	private publication			
PRO	Public Record Office		*T&CJ*	*Australian Town and Country Journal*
Procs	*Proceedings*			
pt	part/s		Tas	Tasmania/n
PTHRA	*Papers and Proceedings of the Tasmanian Historical Research Association*		*Trans*	*Transactions*
			ts	typescript
pub	publication, publication number		UK	United Kingdom
			UNE	University of New England, Armidale
Q	*Quarterly*			
QA	Queensland State Archives, Brisbane		Univ	University
			UNSW	University of New South Wales
Qld	Queensland		UPNG	University of Papua New Guinea
RAHS	Royal Australian Historical Society (Sydney)		US	United States of America
RG	Registrar General's Office		v, vol	volume
RGS	Royal Geographical Society		*V&P*	*Votes and Proceedings*
RHSQ	Royal Historical Society of Queensland (Brisbane)		*VHM(J)*	*Victorian Historical Magazine (Journal)*
RHSV	Royal Historical Society of Victoria (Melbourne)		Vic	Victoria/n
RMIT	Royal Melbourne Institute of Technology		WA	Western Australia/n
			WAA	Western Australian State Archives
Roy	Royal			
RWAHS	Royal Western Australian Historical Society (Perth)		*	deceased

A

ABBIE, ANDREW ARTHUR (1905-1976), anatomist and anthropologist, and FREIDA RUTH HEIGHWAY (1907-1963), gynaecologist, were husband and wife. Andrew was born on 8 February 1905 at Gillingham, Kent, England, only son and eldest child of William Christie Abbie, engine-room artificer, R.N., and his wife Minnie Catherine, née Baylis. Educated at Sir Joseph Williamson's Mathematical School, Rochester, he held a Kent County scholarship and matriculated at the University of London in 1922. The family migrated to New South Wales and in 1924 Andrew enrolled at the University of Sydney (B.Sc., M.B., B.S., 1929) where he won several prizes and graduated with second-class honours. The university awarded him an M.D. in 1936 and, for two papers published in the *Journal of Comparative Neurology*, a D.Sc. in 1941.

On completing his training, Abbie had been appointed to Royal Prince Alfred Hospital as resident medical officer to (Sir) Hugh Poate and (Sir) Charles Blackburn [qq.v.11,7]. In 1930 Abbie published his first paper dealing with the treatment of a patient with diabetic coma. Two years later he took up a Walter and Eliza Hall [qq.v.9] travelling fellowship, enabling him to work under (Sir) Grafton Elliot Smith [q.v.11] at University College, London (Ph.D., 1934), where he won the Johnston Symington prize of the Anatomical Society of Great Britain and Ireland. On 7 November 1934 in Moore Theological College chapel, Newtown, Sydney, Abbie married Freida Ruth Heighway. Next year he became senior lecturer in anatomy at the University of Sydney. He continued his researches on neuroanatomy, and wrote and illustrated two undergraduate texts, *The Principles of Anatomy* (1940) and *Human Physiology* (1941).

Ruth had been born on 2 June 1907 in Sydney. Educated at Methodist Ladies' College, Burwood, she graduated from the University of Sydney (M.B., B.S., 1930; M.D., 1939). In 1932 she travelled to Britain where she spent some months in Edinburgh before obtaining a resident appointment at St Mary's Hospital, Manchester, England. Having completed two years training in obstetrics and gynaecology, she became a member (fellow 1958) of the Royal College of Obstetricians and Gynaecologists. In 1934 she returned to Sydney and entered general practice at Burwood; she then took rooms in Macquarie Street and obtained honorary appointments at the Rachel Forster Hospital for Women and Children, and the Women's Hospital, Crown Street. During World War II Ruth raised the three daughters of her marriage.

In December 1941 Abbie was called up for full-time duty in the Australian Military Forces with the rank of captain. On 11 August 1942 he transferred to the Australian Imperial Force and in September, as a major, was selected for training at the Chemical Warfare Physiology School, University of Melbourne. From March 1943 he trained medical personnel in methods of treating chemical warfare casualties; early in 1944 he moved with the school to Townsville, Queensland, to investigate the physiological effects of war gases under tropical conditions. Briefly at Port Moresby, Papua, he relinquished his A.I.F. appointment in December 1944 to take up the Elder [q.v.4] chair of anatomy and histology at the University of Adelaide.

Although Abbie continued his interest in neuroanatomy and neurophysiology, the appointment required prodigious effort in planning a new medical school building and in preparing for postwar enrolments. For years he did much of the lecturing; in making blackboard illustrations, he used both hands simultaneously and built up the components with such skill that students long remembered his classes, particularly those in neuroanatomy. An erect, somewhat aloof man, he was fastidious in dress and meticulous in every matter. He was an assiduous worker, spurred on, perhaps by early deprivations, to succeed in a field which then attracted some of the best medical graduates. As in other small university departments with long-serving staff and limited resources, opportunities for postgraduate research were limited. He was associate dean (1949 and 1955-59) and dean (1950-52) of his faculty at a time when the clinical and para-clinical departments were expanding and modernizing.

In 1950 Abbie wrote his first paper on the anatomical features of the Australian Aborigines. Thereafter he concentrated on gathering information about the social and physical characteristics of these people for whom he had high regard. In 1951-64 his department mounted expeditions to Aboriginal communities in South Australia and the Northern Territory. Abbie and his colleagues collected anthropomorphic data which formed the basis of his book, *The Original Australians* (1969): it was a personal account for the general reader and quickly ran to a second edition. He retired from the university in 1970.

Abbie had been president of the Anthropological Society of South Australia (1948 and

1959) and of the anthropological section of the Australian and New Zealand Association for the Advancement of Science (1951). In 1963-72 he was chairman of the South Australian Board of Aboriginal Affairs. His concern for integration led him to propose two scholarships for Aborigines at Presbyterian Girls' College, Adelaide, where he chaired (1951-66) the council. He was a foundation and life member of the Anatomical Society of Australia and New Zealand (acting-president 1964; president 1965-67), and was, as well, a life member (1971) of the Anatomical Society of Great Britain and Ireland. During his academic career Abbie published over 120 papers, mostly as sole author.

When she had moved with her family to Adelaide in 1945, Ruth found her specialty entirely served by men. Undaunted, she set up a solo specialist practice which grew quickly. While her honorary work was centred on the Queen Victoria Maternity Hospital, she also held appointments at the Royal Adelaide and Queen Elizabeth hospitals. Tall, gracious and commanding, Dr Heighway was dedicated to her patients and allowed neither personal activities nor twelve years of physical illness to divert her attention from them. Somewhat uncompromising in earlier years, she grew more tolerant at a time when age sometimes renders the reverse. She died of ovarian cancer on 30 December 1963 in the Memorial Hospital, North Adelaide, and was cremated. A prize given by the University of Adelaide commemorates her.

On 14 February 1967 in the Unitarian Christian Church, Adelaide, Abbie married a physiotherapist Audrey Katherine Allen Simpson. Survived by her, and by the three daughters of his first marriage, he died on 22 July 1976 at his Unley Park home and was cremated. A memorial lecture at the university was endowed by his widow. Many of Abbie's papers and books are held in the university's Barr Smith [q.v.11] Library; another 1615 items are housed at the Australian Institute of Aboriginal and Torres Strait Islander Studies, Canberra.

MJA, 4 June 1977; Aust Council, Roy College of Obstetricians and Gynaecologists, Council Minutes, 14 Mar 1964 (held at the College, Syd); Abbie family papers (held by Mrs A. A. Abbie, Burnside, Adel); Archives, Univ Adel *and* Univ Syd; information from Aust Inst of Aboriginal and Torres Strait Islander Studies, Canb.

RONALD ELMSLIE
SUSAN NANCE

ABBOTT, CHARLES LYDIARD AUBREY (1886-1975), politician and administrator of the Northern Territory, was born on 4 May 1886 at St Leonards, Sydney, son of Thomas Kingsmill Abbott, stipendiary magistrate, and his wife Marion, née Lydiard, both native-born. Aubrey's uncles—(Sir) Joseph and William [qq.v.3,7]—served in the New South Wales Legislative Assembly and his cousins —Joseph [q.v.] and Macartney—were to enter Federal parliament. Educated at The King's School, Parramatta, at 14 Aubrey left to work as a jackeroo near Gunnedah; after attempting to become an actor in Sydney, he took jobs as a stockman on stations at Mitchell and Roma, Queensland. Having been employed in driving horses that pulled trucks of sugarcane to Pleystowe mill, near Mackay, he joined the New South Wales Police Force and in 1908-14 was a confidential clerk at headquarters in Sydney.

On 11 August 1914 Abbott enlisted in the Australian Naval and Military Expeditionary Force which captured German New Guinea. Transferring to the Australian Imperial Force in March 1915, he embarked for Egypt with the 12th Light Horse Regiment. He was commissioned at Gallipoli on 28 October. While serving at Sinai in July 1916, he fell ill and was invalided to England. On 24 October in Westminster Cathedral, London, he married with Catholic rites HILDA GERTRUDE (1890-1984), daughter of John Joseph Harnett, an Australian grazier. Rejoining the 12th L.H.R. in June 1917, Abbott took part in the charge at Beersheba (31 October) during the Egyptian Expeditionary Force's advance to Damascus. He was wounded in action in May 1918 and promoted captain later that month; his A.I.F. appointment terminated in Australia on 13 February 1920.

Financial assistance from William Abbott enabled Aubrey to buy Echo Hills, a property at Kootingal, near Tamworth. Active in the Graziers' Association of New South Wales and the Northern New State League, he joined the Country Party and stood unsuccessfully for the Legislative Assembly seat of Namoi in 1925, but in November won Gwydir at the Federal elections. He soon established himself as one of the promising younger members of parliament, serving effectively on the joint committee of public accounts in 1926-28. As minister for home affairs (1928-29), he was responsible for the Northern Territory which he visited in June 1929, taking 'particular notice of conditions in the pastoral industry'.

Defeated in the 1929 general elections, Abbott was concerned by economic collapse and social disorder: next year he became paid secretary of the Primary Producers' Advisory Council and evidence exists to suggest that he was an organizer of the paramilitary Old Guard. The conservative victory in 1931 saw him again returned as member for Gwydir; he remained in parliament until his appointment on 29 March 1937 as administrator of the Northern Territory. Vigorous and frequently authoritarian, he had immediate impact. His intervention in an industrial dispute on the Darwin wharf in July alienated the union movement. Town dwellers regarded him as insensitive and arrogant; he reciprocated by treating them with contempt. In contrast, he forged close links with the pastoral industry and attended meetings of the executive committee of the Northern Territory Pastoral Lessees Association. In 1938 he played a part in removing Dr Cecil Cook—long a target of pastoralists' criticism—as chief protector of Aborigines. While Abbott had good relations with his personal Aboriginal staff and a paternalistic solicitude for the general welfare of the 'natives', they were to him little more than a resource in the development of the cattle industry.

During the Japanese bombing attack on Darwin on 19 February 1942, Abbott and his wife were lucky to survive a blast which damaged their shelter. (Sir) Charles Lowe's [q.v.] first report (March) of his commission of inquiry into the events of that day criticized the administrator for lack of leadership. The finding was unfair: Abbott had been denied counsel, and many of the witnesses heard were unionists and others biased against him. Unlike a number of his detractors, he had remained in the town until 2 March to offer assistance and to organize the evacuation of the civil administration to Alice Springs. There he had limited powers and came into conflict with the local military commander. Abbott reoccupied Government House, Darwin, in July 1945, supervising the return of the public service. On 26 May 1946 he left the Territory on sick leave and was superseded next day.

Tall, handsome and powerfully built, Abbott could be a charming companion and host. He was an effective speaker and had been a hard-working administrator. His interest in and concern for the Northern Territory were deep and sustained. In 1947 he presented a paper on the region to the Royal Geographical Society in London and his well-received book, *Australia's Frontier Province* (Sydney, 1950), offered a perceptive survey of the Territory's development. A member of the Imperial Service Club, Sydney, he retired to Bowral where he continued writing. Survived by his wife and two daughters, Abbott died on 30 April 1975 in St Luke's Hospital, Darlinghurst; following a state funeral at St Mark's Anglican Church, Darling Point, he was buried in South Head cemetery.

Hilda Abbott was born on 9 September 1890 at Eucumbene station, near Adaminaby, New South Wales. Trained as a secretary, in 1916 she worked in the office of the Australian Red Cross Society in Cairo before being invalided to England. She was president of the society's Northern Territory division in 1937-46. With Gladys Owen [q.v.10 J. D. Moore], she had written *Life on the Land* (Sydney, 1932); a children's book, *Among the Hills* (1948), followed. In the 1950s she became well known as a broadcaster and her work as an interior designer included a commission to redecorate the bedrooms of the Wentworth Hotel in Sydney. She died on 26 May 1984 at Bowral and was buried with Catholic rites in South Head cemetery.

P. F. Donovan, *At the Other End of Australia* (Brisb, 1984); A. Powell, *The Shadow's Edge* (Melb, 1988); A. Moore, *The Secret Army and the Premier* (Syd, 1989); D. Carment, R. Maynard and A. Powell (eds), *Northern Territory Dictionary of Biography*, 1 (Darwin, 1990); *PP* (Cwlth), 1945-46 (40), 1946-47 (48); *SMH*, 2 May 1975; H. de Berg, Hilda Abbott *and* M. Pratt, C. L. A. Abbott (taped interviews) *and* Abbott papers (NL).

DAVID CARMENT

ABBOTT, JOAN STEVENSON (1899-1975), nursing sister and army matron, was born on 11 December 1899 at Normanby Hill, Brisbane, fourth surviving daughter of John William Abbott, a native-born engine driver, and his Scottish wife Isabella, née Stevenson. Entering Brisbane General Hospital as a probationer in 1920, Joan won the 1923 gold medal for theoretical and practical work, gained her general certificate in 1924 and obtained her midwifery certificate at Lady Bowen Hospital, Wickham Terrace. She completed the State child-welfare course, worked in baby clinics in 1926-28 and later at a private hospital, and was engaged as tutor sister in 1929 by the Brisbane and South Coast Hospitals Board. A strict disciplinarian, she expected much from her trainees and endeavoured to improve nursing standards. Abbott worked briefly in Canberra Community Hospital in 1937 before travelling to England.

Back in Brisbane, on 7 August 1940 she joined the (Royal) Australian Army Nursing Service and was appointed matron, 2nd/6th Australian General Hospital. Embarking for the Middle East in December, she took her fifty-five nurses and masseuses to Greece on 31 March 1941. With the German advance, the women sheltered at Kifisiá, Athens, until ordered to be evacuated to Alexandria, Egypt, on 20 April. While they were boarding ship, there was an air raid; only Abbott and twenty-four nurses managed to leave. The remainder rejoined them at Gaza Ridge, Palestine, in May. Temporarily located at Jerusalem (October 1941 - March 1942), the 2nd/6th A.G.H. returned to Gaza Ridge. Matron Abbott was awarded the Royal Red Cross, 1st Class, for her leadership when the hospital was expanded from 600 to 1500 beds between May and August 1942. She and her staff worked long hours: on one day in November they handled 615 admissions and 235 discharges. Repatriated in February 1943, Abbott was promoted temporary lieutenant colonel on 12 April and posted to the Queensland Lines of Communication Area. In January 1944 she became principal matron; she ceased full-time duty on 21 June 1946 in the substantive rank of lieutenant colonel.

A 1946 Florence Nightingale International Foundation scholarship winner, Abbott studied for eighteen months at the Royal College of Nursing, London. On 1 July 1948 she was appointed principal matron, Citizen Military Forces, headquarters Northern Command. She returned to the tutorial staff of Brisbane Hospital that year. During the Korean War she briefly served in the 1st Camp Hospital, Brisbane. Elected president of the Queensland branch of the Australasian Trained Nurses' Association in 1954, Abbott was a member (1955-58) of the State's Nurses and Masseurs Registration Board. She resigned as A.T.N.A. president in 1956, disappointed that she could not improve nurses' training and working conditions. Next year she was awarded a Florence Nightingale medal and in 1962 was appointed honorary colonel of the Royal Australian Army Nursing Corps.

'Judy' Abbott was a Methodist, 5 ft 4 ins (162.6 cm) tall, with hazel eyes and brown hair. Her rather gruff manner concealed her inner warmth and her sense of fun; many were inspired by her energy and enthusiasm. She served as a staff nurse with the Commonwealth Savings Bank for five years and then worked in a doctors' surgery until 1970. Early in 1975 she fractured her spine and suffered quadriplegia; she died on 27 November that year in the Bethesda Hospital, Corinda; her body was given to the school of anatomy, University of Queensland.

A. S. Walker, *Middle East and Far East* (Canb, 1953) and *Medical Services of the R.A.N. and R.A.A.F.* (Canb, 1961); T. Wilkinson, *History of 2/6th Australian General Hospital 1940-1946* (priv pub, Syd, 1978?); R. Goodman (ed), *Queensland Nurses* (Brisb, 1985) and *Our War Nurses* (Brisb, 1988); H. Gregory, *A Tradition of Care* (Brisb, 1988); *Aust Nurses J*, Aug 1937, Apr, Dec 1948, Jan 1951, Nov 1952, Oct 1954; *RANF Review* (Brisb), 7, no 1, Jan 1976; *Courier-Mail*, 24 Mar 1943, 15 June 1946, 7 June, 20 Sept 1957; AWM records; information from Miss B. Schultz, Auchenflower, Brisb.   GILLIAN FULLOON

ABBOTT, JOSEPH PALMER (1891-1965), grazier and politician, was born on 18 October 1891 in North Sydney, fourth child of (Sir) Joseph Palmer Abbott [q.v.3], solicitor and politician, and his native-born wife Edith,

née Solomon. Educated at The Armidale School and the University of Sydney (B.A., 1913), young Joseph enlisted in the Australian Imperial Force on 8 February 1915. He served in the 1st Field Ambulance on Gallipoli from July to September. Invalided to England next month, he was discharged from the A.I.F. prior to taking a commission in the Royal Field Artillery Special Reserve on 14 December. While serving on the Western Front, he leapt into a burning gun-pit and extinguished a fire started by enemy shelling; for this action he was awarded the Military Cross in September 1918.

After the war he acquired Murrulla, a property near Wingen, New South Wales, formerly owned by his uncle W. E. Abbott [q.v.7]. On 26 February 1924 in St James's Anglican Church, Sydney, Joe married Katherine Bliss Wilkinson. Having expanded his involvement in the affairs of the wool industry, he was elected president of the Graziers' Association of New South Wales in 1935. He opposed the creation of a price-support scheme for wool, fearing that the measure would lead to greater use of synthetics. In 1936-37 he headed his industry's campaign against the imposition of restrictions on imports of Japanese textiles. Japan's retaliatory boycott of Australian wool auctions concerned Abbott, but he was also worried that Japan might be tempted to pursue economic power by means of war, were she to be denied access to British Empire markets. A member (1935-37) of the royal commission on monetary and banking systems, Abbott was deputy-chairman (1936-51) of the Australian Wool Board which administered wool publicity and research funds. His twelve months in office as president of the Graziers' Federal Council of Australia began in June 1937.

Before the outbreak of World War II, the Australian and British governments agreed that Britain would buy all of Australia's wool, at a guaranteed price, during the period of hostilities; as a member (1939-40) of the Central Wool Committee, Abbott helped to counter criticism of the arrangement. He had been a Country Party organizer during the 1930s and won the House of Representatives seat of New England in 1940. Minister for home security (June to August 1941) in the government of (Sir) Robert Menzies [q.v.], he was responsible for civil defence. At Prime Minister John Curtin's [q.v.] request, in 1942 Abbott became chairman of the Administrative Planning Committee which was set up to expedite logistics support for forces of the United States of America stationed in Australia. In the immediate postwar years Abbott was quick to warn politicians of communist espionage, and of the party's influence within the trade unions and the scientific community. Ill health obliged him to retire from parliament in 1949; he was appointed O.B.E. in 1951.

Strong minded, hearty and forthright, Abbott was a tall, powerfully-built man, said to have 'the voice of a bull'. He belonged to the Australian Club, was a prominent lay Anglican in the Diocese of Newcastle and vented in public his views on all manner of subjects. The 1951 proposal to establish a reserve-price scheme for wool attracted his strenuous opposition. Survived by his wife and son, he died on 7 May 1965 at Camperdown, Sydney, and was buried in the private cemetery at Murrulla.

S. J. Butlin, *War Economy 1939-1942* (Canb, 1955); P. Hasluck, *The Government and the People 1942-1945* (Canb, 1970); K. Tsokhas, *Markets, Money and Empire* (Melb, 1990); *SMH*, 24 July 1935, 8 June 1937, 8 Aug 1951, 8 May 1965; Abbott papers (NL).   KOSMAS TSOKHAS

ABERCROMBIE, RALPH (1881-1957), public servant, was born on 19 July 1881 at Mount Duneed, Victoria, ninth child of Andrew Thomson Abercrombie, a schoolteacher from Scotland, and his English wife Mary Anna, née Kenshole. Educated probably at government schools in his father's charge, on 2 September 1896 Ralph became a pupil-teacher at South Melbourne State School. A wish to remain in the city prompted him to transfer to clerical duties in the public service and he joined the Department of the Treasurer in July 1901. At the Victorian Amateur Athletic Association meeting in April 1907 he won the 100-yards (10.1 seconds) and 220-yards (23.2 seconds) championships. On 1 August 1911 he was appointed a receiver of public moneys and paying officer in the Navy Office of the Commonwealth Department of Defence.

Originally second-in-charge to Honorary Fleet Paymaster Albert Martin, director of navy accounts, Abercrombie became acting D.N.A. when Martin departed for London in late 1914. Naval accounting functions expanded markedly during the war. The Naval Board became responsible for a fleet of seventy-four merchant ships, each of which was requisitioned and fitted out to transport troops, horses, stores and—when expedient—commercial cargoes; the board also operated twelve seized enemy vessels in a mercantile role. Claims arising between the Australian government and shipping companies, merchants, ship-fitters and the Imperial authorities were brought to account in the D.N.A.'s office. Abercrombie worked long hours. Though critical of some procedures, a report (September 1918) of the royal commission into navy and defence administration was favourable overall and rec-

ommended that Abercrombie be confirmed in his position: the appointment was effected on 1 April 1919.

In 1923 he travelled to England to settle accounts concerning the repatriation of Australian troops. While attached to the Admiralty, he gained experience in Imperial accountancy organization. Appointed O.B.E. in 1935, he joined the Naval Board next year as finance and civil member. On 1 September 1938 he succeeded H. C. Brown as auditor-general for the Commonwealth. During World War II Abercrombie maintained government accounting and administrative standards in the face of daunting shortages of experienced staff. It was not a time for innovation, but in his final report (1946) he recommended an amendment (passed in 1948) to the Audit Act because the Naval Charter Rates Board had refused him access to its papers. The destruction of non-current records during his term was a loss to Australian administrative history. He retired on 18 July 1946.

Tall, slim, quietly spoken, modest and a bachelor, he had seemed remote in the office; away from officialdom, he was a keen golfer, merry companion and cheerful *habitué* of the billiards-room of the Hotel Canberra. Abercrombie was an associate member of the Commonwealth Institute of Accountants and a member of the Naval and Military Club, Melbourne. He died on 3 May 1957 at Hawthorn and was buried in Melbourne general cemetery with the forms of the Churches of Christ. His estate was sworn for probate at £43 898.

A. W. Jose, *The Royal Australian Navy 1914-18* (Syd, 1928); W. Perry, *The Naval and Military Club, Melbourne* (Melb, 1981); *PP* (Cwlth), 1917-19, 4 (105), 1945-46, 4 (55); *Herald* (Melb), 6 July 1938; information from Messrs V. J. W. Skermer, K. W. Major and T. R. Rees, Canb, and Mrs E. M. Rankine, Glen Iris, Melb.   ROBERT HYSLOP

ACKLAND, ESSIE ADELE (1896-1975), singer, was born on 27 March 1896 at Woollahra, Sydney, eldest daughter of Henry James Ackland, licensed victualler, and his wife Marea, née Bassetti, both native-born. A grand-daughter of 'the silvery tenor' Harry Ackland, Essie had a lifelong ambition to sing, but did well at school and acquired basic secretarial skills before studying at the New South Wales State Conservatorium of Music under Roland Foster [q.v.8] who found her modest, unassuming and diligent. Despite being plagued with throat trouble, she took further lessons from Joseph Bradley [q.v.7] and Madame Emily Marks.

In 1921 Miss Ackland was invited to sing in Handel's *Messiah* on Christmas Eve with the local Welsh Choral Society. She performed in 1922 with the Royal Sydney Apollo Club and the Royal Philharmonic Society of Sydney, and also toured Queensland. Encouraged by Henri Verbrugghen [q.v.12] and Dame Clara Butt, Essie was chosen as solo vocalist to accompany the Belgian cellist Jean Gerardy on his 1923 tour of Australasia. In ninety-five performances over six months she won unanimous critical acclaim.

Although Gerardy had advised her to study in Vienna, she eventually sailed for London on 21 March 1925, following a farewell concert at the town hall, stage-managed by Reginald Joseph Morphew, a baritone and fellow student. Having studied in Italy, he joined her in London and married her at St Saviour's parish church, Paddington, on 24 February 1926; they were to remain childless. Both obtained work in the concert field, yet seldom appeared together; Essie later attributed their long and happy marriage to their independent, successful careers.

Befriended by Ada Crossley [q.v.8], Essie became a prominent oratorio and concert performer. She was introduced to the Gramophone Co. by Browning Mummery [q.v.10] and made forty His Master's Voice discs, often with organ accompaniment, but became best known as a ballad singer. Tall and dark, with a contralto voice of 'phenomenal range and power' once described by Verbrugghen as 'liquid gold', she was regarded as an 'unaffected, genial Australian' of 'natural simplicity and charm'. In 1936 she was soloist in Queen's Hall and National Sunday League concerts, gave two *Messiah* performances, broadcast for the British Broadcasting Corporation, made gramophone records, and toured the provinces and Scotland.

When Essie came to Sydney with her husband in March 1937, radio had made her name a household word. Her triumphant four-month concert tour for the Australian Broadcasting Commission was followed by eight weeks in New Zealand. Critics praised the lustrous quality of her voice, her sincerity and her grace. In Britain during World War II she joined the Entertainments National Service Association's first concert party and appeared in 1300 concerts in army camps, hospitals, factory canteens and air-raid shelters throughout the country. She entertained Australian soldiers in London at her Edgware home, and enjoyed gardening and golf.

Accompanied by Reginald, in November 1947 Essie Ackland returned to Sydney. Next year she toured the State's coalfields, Queensland, South Australia and Western Australia; she announced her retirement in February 1949 and afterwards lived quietly at Gosford, New South Wales. Predeceased by her husband, she died on 14 February 1975 at Mosman and was cremated.

Aust Musical News, 1 June 1923, 2 Feb 1925, 1 July 1929, 1 Dec 1936, 1 Jan, 1 Apr 1937, 2 Aug 1948; *Radio Pictorial*, 1 Feb 1937; *Wireless Weekly*, 19 Feb 1937, p viii; *ABC Weekly*, 12 June 1948, p 17; *Herald* (Melb), 2 Mar 1937; *Courier-Mail*, 2 Apr 1937; *Age*, 24 Nov 1947; *SMH*, 15 Feb 1975; taped interviews, 1972, made and held by Mr P. Burgis, Port Macquarie, NSW; Ackland papers (NL); Ackland press-clippings and brochures (ABC Archives, Syd); ABC papers (AA, Syd).

KATHY MOIGNARD

ACKMAN, AMY VERA (1886-1966), Sister of Charity and hospital administrator, was born on 3 July 1886 at Randwick, Sydney, only child of native-born parents Michael Ackman, furniture-dealer, and his wife Annie, née Conway. The family returned to Melbourne where Michael died before Amy was 3 years old. Annie later opened a needlework shop at Kyneton. Amy was sent to St Mary's Convent School, Malmsbury, run by the Sisters of Mercy, with the stipulation that—as her family was Jewish—she should not attend classes in religion. Having matriculated, she qualified as an optometrist by completing a London correspondence course. In 1912 she set up practice at 151 Collins Street, Melbourne, and also attended out-patients at St Vincent's Hospital, Fitzroy. Having been received into the Catholic Church when she was aged about 21, after the death of her mother Amy was admitted to the novitiate of the Sisters of Charity on 15 August 1914. She made her vows in April 1917 and, as Sister Giovanni, trained at St Vincent's Hospital, Darlinghurst, Sydney; from early 1922 she worked in its admissions office.

Sister Giovanni was administrator and superior of the Order's hospitals at Bathurst (1932-37) and at Lismore (1938-41); she went in 1942 to St Vincent's Private Hospital, Darlinghurst, and in 1947 transferred to the Order's main hospital next door. As Mother Giovanni, she was elected in 1949 to the general council of the Sisters of Charity. After it was decided to found a hospice at Kangaroo Point, Brisbane, on land formerly belonging to Lilian Violet Cooper [q.v.8] and Mary Josephine Bedford, Mother Giovanni was asked to oversee the project.

When she arrived in Queensland in March 1953, Archbishop (Sir) James Duhig [q.v.8] inquired how much money she already had towards the building. The reply was, 'Nothing'. Serene, humble, but immensely capable, she established a city office and negotiated with the banks; fund-raising committees were formed, and she began door-to-door collecting in the city, suburbs and country towns. Wearing her long, black, serge habit, she endured fierce summer heat, sometimes receiving only a few shillings, but the little, smiling woman with a keen sense of fun enlivened these 'begging days' for her companions.

So successfully did she organize the appeal that the Mount Olivet Hospital for the incurably sick and dying was opened on 8 September 1957. The 176-bed building cost £428 000, to which the State government contributed £176 000. The need for further funds was met by a one-day, house-to-house appeal held on 8 March 1959 that provided £57 000. Mother Giovanni was appointed first superior and administrator of the hospital. Indefatigable and practical, renowned for her sewing-box of tricks and her fund of well-told stories, she recovered her remarkable vitality through an occasional, solitary day of fishing on Bribie Island.

At the end of her term of office in 1963, she volunteered to go with a missionary group to New Guinea. For a year after her arrival in August, she helped to care for the health of three hundred children at Bundi, before returning to take charge of a convalescent home at Darling Point, Sydney. In 1966 Mother Giovanni returned to Mount Olivet where she died on 23 August and was buried in Nudgee cemetery.

E. M. Skewes, *Life Comes to Newness* (Brisb, 1982); S. Baldwin (ed), *Unsung Heroes and Heroines of Australia* (Melb, 1988); *Catholic Leader*, 1 Sept 1966; Memoirs of Mother Giovanni Ackman, ms and ts, c.1963, *and* Ackman papers (Archives of Sisters of Charity, St Vincent's Convent, Potts Point, Syd); Annals *and* records of Mount Olivet Hospital, Kangaroo Point, Brisb; personal information.   EDNA M. SKEWES

ADAIR, JOHN RONALD SHAFTO (1893–1960), aviator and businessman, was born on 22 May 1893 at Maryborough, Queensland, son of Victorian-born parents John Hamilton Adair, surveyor, and his wife Constance Ada, née Smith. Educated at Maryborough Grammar School, Ron completed an engineering apprenticeship and attained sergeant's rank in the Australian Military Forces. On 21 February 1916 he enlisted in the Australian Imperial Force and was posted to No. 1 Squadron, Australian Flying Corps, as a fitter. He reached Egypt in April and was reclassified air mechanic in November; after training as a pilot, he rejoined his original squadron in February 1918 and was promoted lieutenant in March. Adair saw action in the Middle East until the Armistice. On 10 February 1919 he married Rose Ethel Ellis at the British Consulate, Cairo; they were later to be divorced. His A.I.F. appointment terminated in Sydney on 29 September.

Like a number of his contemporaries, Adair spent some years 'barnstorming': to promote air travel in outback Queensland, he flew to centres without landing fields and endeavoured to persuade local councils to provide facilities. In 1920 he ran a newspaper-delivery service from Brisbane to Toowoomba and carried passengers on the return flights. He demonstrated exceptional airmanship, safely landing an Avro Avian biplane near Bowen in 1928 after its engine had fallen out. On 24 March he registered his own commercial airline, Aircrafts Pty Ltd, which provided regular services between Brisbane and Toowoomba, and extended its reach to coastal and outback centres. Though he increased his original issued capital of £1400 to £5900 by October 1931, the company stagnated in the Depression. In May 1934 Adair flew from Brisbane to Darwin whence he escorted the New Zealand aviatrix Jean Batten to Sydney, thereby completing a 5000-mile (8047 km) trip. That year he joined Qantas Empire Airways and by 1938 was captaining Empire flying boats on the Sydney-Singapore run. He married a divorcee Bertha Ella, née Savery, late Kither, on 16 January 1937 at St Andrew's Presbyterian Church, Brisbane. On a Q.E.A. flight from Karachi to Sydney in December 1941, with Major General Gordon Bennett [q.v.] on board, Adair carried out refuelling at Mergui, Burma, while Japanese aircraft flew overhead. During that year he had ferried Catalina flying boats from San Diego, California, to Sydney for the Royal Australian Air Force; he remained on the R.A.A.F. active list throughout World War II.

Quiet, thoughtful and popular, Adair was not tall, but had presence; in his mattter-of-fact manner he told reporters of his sole ambition—to be 'the oldest living aviator'. After the war he was chairman of Coachcraft Pty Ltd, a Ford motor agency (1946-51), and of Airstream Ltd, refrigerator manufacturers (1946-53). Meanwhile, he remained managing director of Aircrafts Pty Ltd which became Queensland Airlines Pty Ltd in January 1949 and operated under charter arrangements with Butler [q.v.] Air Transport Pty Ltd. The company suffered a crushing blow on 10 March when one of its chartered aircraft, a Lockheed Lodestar, crashed at Coolangatta, Queensland, with the loss of twenty-one lives. By 1958 almost all of the company's shares had been acquired by Butler; that year, when (Sir) Reginald Ansett (Bungana Investments Pty Ltd) took over Butler Air Transport, including Queensland Airlines, Adair received stock worth £2300 and was employed by Ansett Transport Industries Ltd.

Adair had been appointed O.B.E. in 1955. He died of a coronary occlusion on 27 June 1960 at Ascot, Brisbane, and was cremated with Anglican rites. His wife and their adopted daughter survived him, as did the son of his first marriage.

F. M. Cutlack, *The Australian Flying Corps* (Syd, 1923); H. Fysh, *Qantas at War* (Syd, 1968); H. Holthouse, *Illustrated History of Queensland* (Adel, 1978); N. Parnell and T. Boughton, *Flypast* (Canb, 1988); *SMH*, 25 Sept 1926, 22 Oct 1940, 17 Dec 1961; *Queenslander*, 1 Jan, 9 June 1927; *Courier-Mail*, 2 June 1934, 28 June 1960; CAC (Q), Companies, 104A/1927, 38/1945 (QA).

J. C. H. GILL

ADAM, GEOFFREY WILLIAM SHEDDEN (1908-1973), obstetrician and gynaecologist, was born on 29 February 1908 at Turramurra, Sydney, sixth child of John Shedden Adam, architect, and his wife Ruth Eliza, née Harris, both native-born. Geoffrey was educated at Sydney Church of England Grammar School (Shore) and the University of Sydney (M.B., B.S., 1933). Aged 17, he had been involved in a bicycle accident which had led to the amputation of his leg; in later years this handicap was to become part of his image as one of the identities of Australian medicine. He worked as a resident medical officer at Royal Prince Alfred Hospital (1933) and at the Royal Hospital for Women, Paddington (1934), before becoming a registrar in obstetrics and gynaecology at Newcastle Hospital (1935). This appointment influenced the direction of his professional life by leading him to undertake postgraduate studies in these fields at Hammersmith Hospital, London, and in Edinburgh and Vienna. He was then employed as a medical officer by the London County Council. Returning to New South Wales, on 30 April 1938 he married Mary Lenore Brent Rodd with Anglican rites at Christ Church Cathedral, Newcastle.

In May 1938 Adam was appointed foundation professor (half-time) of obstetrics and gynaecology in the recently established faculty of medicine at the University of Queensland; as a joint appointment he was also to be the first medical superintendent of the new Women's Hospital, Brisbane. For thirty years he made significant contributions to the practice of obstetrics, while teaching thousands of medical students and scores of postgraduate specialists-in-training. Always known as 'Sheddie', but noted for his formality, he had a stilted and didactic manner of lecturing and teaching which led to much clandestine ribaldry at his expense: students and staff alike mimicked his phrases, particularly the often-quoted 'Anchor my prosthesis' when he was about to undertake a difficult forceps delivery. During World War II he worked as a medical officer in army camps in Brisbane. Throughout the war and during its 'baby boom' aftermath he co-ordinated services for the city's only midwifery hospital. Unlike many of his contemporaries who in their subsequent careers left obstetrics for the more ordered life of gynaecology, Adam remained foremost a clinical obstetrician and teacher. After his retirement as superintendent of the Women's Hospital in 1947, he built up a large private practice at Wickham Terrace, and was especially concerned with complicated obstetrics cases and with the investigation of infertility.

Respected for his clinical skills, his integrity and his scholarship, Adam served on the editorial board of the *Australian and New Zealand Journal of Obstetrics and Gynaecology*. He contributed numerous articles and reviews to professional journals, and published *Manipulative and Operative Obstetrics* (1962). A fellow (1937) of the Royal College of Surgeons, Edinburgh, he was a member (1937) and fellow (1945) of the Royal College of Obstetricians and Gynaecologists, London, a member (1947-56) of its Australian regional council and chairman (1951-60) of its Queensland committee; he was also a member (1940-70) of the Postgraduate Medical Education Committee and a life-governor (appointed 1970) of the Australian Postgraduate Federation in Medicine; he was, as well, a foundation member (1961) of the Queensland maternal mortality committee and chairman (1957) of the Queensland Marriage Council. Survived by his wife and two sons, Adam died of sudden myocardial infarction on 21 November 1973 in his home at Hamilton, Brisbane, and was cremated with Presbyterian forms.

H. Gregory, *Vivant Professores* (Brisb, 1987); *Roy Women's Hospital (Brisb) Medical News Bulletin*, Apr 1980, p 2; *Courier-Mail*, 23 Aug 1973; staff files, Univ Qld Archives.   JOHN H. PEARN

ADAM, LEONHARD (1891-1960), anthropologist and lawyer, was born on 16 December 1891 in Berlin, son of Meinhardt Michael Adam and his wife Katharina Clare Rosa, née Schmidt. Part Jewish in extraction, Leonhard studied at the Royal Frederick William Gymnasium and the Ethnological Museum. Ethnology (the passion of his life), law, economics and Sinology were his chosen subjects at the universities of Berlin and Greifswald (LL.D., 1916). Having completed a degree in practising law in 1920, he was appointed assistant judge (later district judge) in the provincial court, Berlin. Adam had already studied and published extensively in primitive law; his first field-work was among prisoners of war in Rumanian camps. He edited (1919-38) *Zeitschrift für Vergleichende Rechtswissenschaft* (*Journal of Comparative Jurisprudence*). In 1931-33 he lectured in ethnological jurisprudence and primitive law at the Institute of Foreign Laws and was a member of the board of experts of the Ethnographical Museum, Berlin.

The Nazis' anti-Semitic laws stripped Adam of all official positions in 1933. Five years later he sought refuge in England where he taught at the University of London and published *Primitive Art* (1940). His academic haven was shattered when he was interned on 16 May 1940 as an 'enemy alien' and dispatched to Australia. Among the most eminent of the gifted collectivity of scholars who arrived aboard the *Dunera* in September, he became pro-rector of 'Collegium Taturense' in the internment camp at Tatura, Victoria, and gave lessons on primitive religion and ethnology.

Letters from Bronislaw Malinowski alerted Margaret Holmes, of the Australian Student Christian Movement, and Lady Masson [q.v.10] to Adam's fate. On 29 May 1942 he was released on parole to the National Museum of Victoria, given residence at Queen's College, University of Melbourne, and placed under the supervision of Professor Max Crawford to embark upon a research project on the Aborigines' use of stone. At Christ Church, South Yarra, on 5 June 1943 he married a musician Julia Mary Baillie with Anglican rites.

As research scholar (1943-47), lecturer (1947-56) and part-time curator (1958-60) of the ethnological collection, Adam was always on the edge of the university's establishment. Mystified at the politics of an institution which had refused to introduce anthropology for sixty years, he poured out proposals which never came to pass. Then he made a *fait accompli* of an ethnological museum by exchange of artefacts on a picayune budget through an Australian and worldwide network. It was subsequently named the Leonhard Adam Ethnological Collection.

Naturalized on 21 February 1956, he travelled to Germany in 1957 to receive a doctorate from the University of Bonn and to have a volume of the journal he had edited dedicated to him. In 1960 he again returned to Europe as the University of Melbourne's delegate to the International Congress of Anthropological and Ethnological Sciences in Paris. Survived by his wife and daughter, he died suddenly of heart disease on 9 September 1960 in Bonn.

Adam's seminal work in primitive law and art had been completed before his coming to Australia. He was elected a fellow of the Royal Anthropological Institute of Great Britain and Ireland in 1945. Poor health, the trauma of imprisonment and the ambivalence of his status at the University of Melbourne distracted him from further research and from converting his studies of Aboriginal artefacts into a major work. An unpublished list of his publications is in the university's archives.

The Leonhard Adam Ethnological Collection in the University of Melbourne, pt 1, *Groote Eylandt Art* (Melb, 1973) and pt 2, *Warfare in Melanesia* (Melb, 1975); B. Patkin, *The Dunera Internees* (Syd, 1979); C. Pearl, *The Dunera Scandal* (Syd, 1983); *Oceania*, 31, 1960-61, p 161; *Univ Melb Gazette*, 19 Apr 1957, p 14, Dec 1960, p 4; Collegium Taturense. No 4 Internment Camp, Tatura (Vic). First Anniversary 1940-41: 26 Oct 1941 (ts copies, Univ Melb Archives); Dept of the Army, MP 1103/1, Registers containing Service and Casualty Forms (Form A.112) of Internees and Prisoners of War held in Australia, Aug 1939-Dec 1947, File no E 35000: Leonard [sic] Adam *and* MP 1103/2, Prisoners of War Information Bureau, Reports of POW and Internees, 1939-1945, Report no: Adam, Leonard [sic] (AA, Vic); Adam files (Museum of Art *and* Registry *and* Archives, Univ Melb).

GREG DENING

ADAMSON, GEORGE ERNEST BARTLETT (1884-1951), journalist, was born on 22 December 1884 at Cascade, Ringarooma, Tasmania, son of George Adamson, a miner from Scotland, and his English wife Jane, née Bartlett. The Adamsons shifted to the west coast where Bartlett attended primary schools at Zeehan and Dundas, then worked as a clerk at a mine. About 1914 the family moved to New Zealand. There Adamson became a clerk with the Wellington publishers Whitcombe & Tombs Ltd and later publicity manager for New Zealand Picture Supplies Ltd. On 16 November 1917 he married with Methodist forms Scottish-born Mary Anna McLachlan in her mother's home at Brooklyn; they were to have three sons. Always interested in literature, particularly the English Romantics, he published a volume of verse, *Twelve Sonnets* (1918).

He was encouraged by its favourable reception in Australia and sailed with his wife for Sydney. Arriving in April 1919, he joined the staff of *Smith's Weekly* and wrote feature articles, topical verse, jokes and light fiction. In 1923 Adamson left the paper to do freelance work, notably a regular feature in the *Sunday News*, as well as syndicated crime stories and adventure serials; he also grew fruit at Arcadia and in 1924 helped to establish a packing co-operative for local orchardists. He later founded the slightly salacious *Sydneysider* which crashed during the Depression, leaving him without a regular income until he rejoined *Smith's Weekly* in 1935; he was to remain with the paper until it closed in 1950.

Rejected for military service in 1914 on medical grounds, Adamson had been pro-war and anti-Bolshevik. In the 1930s he became an active executive-member of the Fellowship of Australian Writers. In the mid-1930s he promoted the communist-sponsored Writers' League (later Association) which amalgamated with the fellowship in 1938. Although subsequently accused by Miles Franklin and Jean Devanny [qq.v.8] of factionalism in his activities on the F.A.W. executive, as its president Adamson persuaded the government to increase the vote for the Commonwealth Literary Fund in 1938 and was to suggest liberal changes embodied in the Obscene and Indecent Publications (Amendment) Act of 1946. His experience in the Depression, his relationsip with other writers (especially Devanny), and his alarm at fascist triumphs in Europe and authoritarian trends in his own country had led him to join the Communist Party of Australia by 1943.

Adamson's publications included two collections of leftist political verse, a long erotic poem, *Beyond the Sun* (privately printed in 1942), bushranger stories, an adventure book for boys and miscellaneous works. Most of his vast journalistic output remains uncollected. As a poet, he was old-fashioned. He typified the survivor on Sydney's Grub Street, the working journalist who could turn his pen to whatever copy was required: in 1939-40 he wrote a poem in praise of airmen for *Smith's Weekly* and another denouncing the national register for the *Workers' Weekly*.

Genial, passionate and sometimes obstinate, Adamson was a fighter for civil liberties, a hater of wowsers, an indulgent and often delightful father, and a man who wanted his writing to improve the lot of ordinary people. He was tall and swarthy, with a magnificent voice, and revelled in fresh air, surfing and stonework. Survived by his wife and sons, he died suddenly on 4 November 1951 in Sydney while speaking at the Domain on behalf of the Australian-Soviet Friendship Society. He was cremated after a secular ceremony.

L. P. Fox, *Bartlett Adamson* (Syd, 1963); J. Devanny, *Point of Departure*, C. Ferrier ed (Brisb, 1986); *Barjai*, 22, 1947, p 28; *Journalist*, Dec 1951; *Southerly*, 13, no 3, 1952; *SMH*, 27 Oct 1924; *Tribune* (Syd), 7 Nov 1951; information from and Adamson scrap-book held by Dr D. Adamson, Northwood, Syd; Adamson *and* Franklin papers (ML); F. D. Davison *and* Ryland papers (NL).

ROBERT DARBY

ADAMSON, SIR KENNETH THOMAS (1904-1976), orthodontist and academic, was born on 19 June 1904 at Prahran, Melbourne, son of Thomas Cartwright Adamson, dentist, and his wife Gertrude Jane, née Thompson, both Victorian born. Educated at Wesley College and the University of Melbourne (B.D.Sc., 1927), he was appointed a house surgeon at the (Royal) Dental Hospital of Melbourne where he engaged in research which led to a D.D.Sc. in 1929. He was to become lecturer, senior lecturer and head of the department of orthodontics in the Australian College of Dentistry, while continuing as honorary consultant in orthodontics to the Dental Hospital. On 4 February 1932 at the Presbyterian Church, Toorak, he married Jean Isobel King Scott.

Joining the faculty of dental science at the university as a senior lecturer in 1935, Adamson held a commission as honorary captain in the Reserve of Officers, Australian Military Forces, during World War II. He was a member of the council of the Australian College of Dentistry (until 1963) and of the council of the Dental Hospital (from 1947). President (1935), honorary secretary (1944) and permanent vice-president (from 1962) of the Victorian branch of the Australian Dental Association, he was federal president in 1954-60 and made a life member in 1970. He was president (1954-57) of the Australian Society of Orthodontists and a founding member of the (Royal) Australian College of Dental Surgeons (president 1968-70). His professional honours included life membership of the American Dental Association, the British Society for the Study of Orthodontics and the R.A.C.D.S. In 1956 he became a fellow of dental surgery of the Royal College of Surgeons, England. He was appointed C.M.G. in 1963 and knighted in 1968.

Broad shouldered and well built, Adamson saw the dental fraternity much as an extended family: he was often called upon for his leadership, his knowledge and his connexions, both social and political. Within the Australian Dental Association his approach helped to weld the State delegates into a body with a like-minded professional outlook. An excellent teacher who freely shared his knowledge and enjoyed the one-to-one relationship in surgery or clinic, from 1930 he had published regularly in the *Australian Dental Journal*. He was patient and skilful in the design and fabrication of orthodontic appliances, and his practice flourished. His concern with the general and dental health of Victorians was revealed on the council of the Dental Hospital where his wisdom in balancing the competing needs of the hospital, university and profession frequently produced an outcome satisfactory to all parties. Under Adamson's chairmanship, the Dental Alumni Research Foundation (formed in 1963) collected funds to build a research centre within the grounds of the hospital for use by the university; in 1975 he also played a central role in combining the university and hospital departments of orthodontics into a single, self-contained unit for treatment, teaching and research, which was named in his honour.

Known as Kenny by his close friends, Adamson was a keen fisherman and golfer. He was fond of music, played the piano, organ and violin, and supported the Melbourne Symphony Orchestra. Survived by his wife, son and two daughters, he died at his Toorak home on 19 July 1976 and was cremated. A portrait by Harley Griffiths is held by Sir Kenneth's son Thomas.

Aust Dental J, Aug 1976; *Univ Melb Gazette*, Dec 1976; Minutes, Faculty of Dental Science, Univ Melb, *and* Council of Roy Dental Hospital of Melb *and* Aust College of Dentistry *and* Adamson papers and correspondence (held by L, Roy Dental Hospital of Melb); information from Dr M. Adamson, Kooyong, Melb.   H. F. ATKINSON

ADAMSON, MAY MABEL (1891-1966) and AMY HANNAH (1893-1963), headmistresses, were born on 28 March 1891 and 4 August 1893, respectively at Rockhampton and Cooktown, Queensland, fourth and fifth daughters of John Adamson [q.v.7], a Primitive Methodist clergyman who later became a politician, and his wife, Caroline, née Jones, both English born. Committed to the emancipation of women, John placed a high value on the academic achievement of his six surviving children.

May was educated at Maryborough Girls' Grammar School where she won a medal for botany at the senior examination. She began a teaching career as an assistant on probation at Maryborough East State School. By 1927, when she was appointed to her fifth school, at Roma, she had begun to suffer ill health that obliged her to take periods of leave. Her former principal at Brisbane Central School described her as 'a most conscientious teacher. Her work is always well-prepared. She gives much thought to the organization of subject matter. She is cultured and has a good influence on trainees'. After almost five years of country service, May returned to Brisbane to teach at Milton (1932-35) and from 1936 at the Central Technical College's Domestic Science High School. In 1927 she had commenced part-time study and later graduated from the University of Queensland (B.A., 1940).

The life sciences were her great forte. An innovative teacher of physiology and zoology, she took her pupils on regular field-trips and instructed student-teachers in physical training. She was tall and slim, with dark hair and a commanding gaze, and always well groomed. A strict but fair teacher, whose students both feared and admired her, she was also an active member of the Queensland Teachers' Union. In October 1953 she was appointed principal of the Domestic Science High School; strong willed and determined, she did not find it easy to delegate authority. May retired on 30 June 1957. She died on 3 October 1966 at Wahroonga, Sydney, and was cremated with Presbyterian forms.

Educated at Maryborough Girls' Grammar School, on 15 November 1912 Amy was appointed assistant-teacher on probation at Eagle Junction State School. In the next three years she regularly resigned from teaching— in February or March—to attend the University of Queensland (B.A., 1916) on a government scholarship and just as regularly was re-engaged. After graduating, she successively served as a secondary teacher, senior instructor and principal at seven other schools in southern Queensland. Following the foundation in 1933 of the State Commercial High School and College, Brisbane, Amy was one of three teachers selected as floormaster, a position involving control over large numbers of students. In 1943, while still a teacher, she was officer-in-charge of the commercial section of the State's Juvenile Employment Bureau.

Both Misses Adamson were particularly interested in the education of girls and in equal employment opportunities. Amy regarded herself as 'the problem child of the Department' because she saw no reason why women should have limited promotion in the Department of Public Instruction. In 1947 she applied for the post of senior instructor, general branch, State Commercial High School and College: although unsuccessful, she won her subsequent appeal against the appointment of a male colleague. Within eight months, however, she was transferred to Maryborough State High and Intermediate School (Girls) as acting-principal and on 7 July 1949 became principal. There she encouraged relationships between the school and the community, and initiated improvements for both pupils and teachers. Despite suffering coronary disease from 1953, she did not retire until 31 December 1959.

Very short and rather plump, with dark eyes and hair, and a lively personality, Amy was held in high esteem by her colleagues and remembered with affection by her students. She died of myocardial infarction on 19 June 1963 at Clayfield, Brisbane, and was cremated with Presbyterian forms.

R. Bonnin (ed), *Dazzling Prospects* (Brisb, 1988); Dept of Education, staff cards of A. and M. Adamson (Dept of Education Archives, Brisb); Dept of Education, personnel files of A. and M. Adamson, *and* Domestic Science High School files, *and* Maryborough State High School (Girls) files (QA); information from Mrs J. Zahnleiter, Sherwood, and Mrs C. Tomlinson, Kenmore, and Miss R. Don, Chapel Hill, Brisb.   ROSEMARY MAMMINO

ADDISON, STANLEY SIMPSON (1880-1972), administrator and publisher, was born on 14 October 1880 at Aldinga, South Australia, second son of Charley Addison, baker, and his wife Fanny, née Butterworth. Educated at the local state school, Stanley worked on a farm and as a doctor's coachman; in 1901 he became a workshop assistant and eventually laboratory assistant to Professor (Sir) William Henry Bragg [q.v.7] at the University of Adelaide. There, Addison studied mathematics and physics (B.Sc., 1908), joined the tennis and lacrosse teams, and was treasurer of the Scientific Society, vice-chairman of the Student Christian Movement and editor of the *Intercollegian*.

Appointed general secretary of the Australian Student Christian Movement in 1908, Addison developed its publications and, on its behalf in 1910 and 1913, visited the United States of America, Britain, Europe, the Middle East and India. Having been declared medically unfit to enlist in 1914, he joined the Australian branch of the British Red Cross Society in October 1915, and was among those selected and trained to inquire after missing soldiers. He served on Lemnos, at Gallipoli, in Egypt and France, and was mentioned in dispatches. On 8 January 1917 he married Minnie Vera Elizabeth Staley at the parish church, Brondesbury, Middlesex, England; they were to remain childless.

In March 1918 Addison was commissioned temporary sub-lieutenant in the Royal Naval Volunteer Reserve. Briefly attached to the personal staff of his former 'chief' Bragg—then professor of physics at University College, London, who was applying sound-range recording to submarine detection—Addison was directly involved in setting up bases for hydrophone-equipped patrol boats. Invalided from the navy in October 1918, he joined the staff of Professor (Sir) Henry Barraclough [q.v.7] and helped to oversee the welfare of some five thousand Australian munitions workers in Britain. While assisting with their repatriation, Addison was transferred in 1919 to the Department of Defence, Melbourne. In 1920 he was appointed O.B.E.

That year he was selected for the new position of assistant-registrar at the University of Melbourne. He established a student employment bureau and, according to W. Macmahon Ball, excited interest in his informal study groups. After council approved the establishment of a bookroom, Addison became an *ex officio* director and part-time manager in October 1921. A reporter saw him as tall, clean shaven and slightly stooped, with 'round, beaming glasses' and a mild, scholarly face. Seeking further income-producing amenities, Addison found space for a university post-and-telegraph office, for hoods and gowns hire, and for a formalized lecture-note

service. The post office, however, was an error of judgement: the small commission on stamp sales met but a fraction of the staffing cost.

Directors agreed that publication of 'university works' was to be the ultimate objective of the bookroom, to which all other activities would contribute. An appeal for funds was disappointing; most early publications depended on authors' assistance. Myra Willard's *History of the White Australia Policy to 1920* opened the list of Melbourne University Press publications in 1923. When Addison resigned in 1931 following continued ill health, almost forty items had been issued. The *Economic Record* was appearing biannually on behalf of the Economic Society of Australia and New Zealand, and agreement had been reached with the Australian Council for Educational Research for publication of its reports and monographs. Both the establishment and the early growth of Melbourne University Press owed much to Addison's initiative and sustained interest.

Secretary (from 1932) of the Victorian division of the Sound Finance League, Addison wrote reviews and broadcast on monetary policy and international affairs. In 1937 he rejoined the Australian Red Cross Society. As secretary-general in 1938-39, he played a major role in preparing its early wartime organization and emergency services. He was assistant-director, Central Bureau for Prisoners of War, in 1940, chief controller of Voluntary Aid Detachments for the Commonwealth in 1942-47, research officer for postwar reconstruction in 1943 and joint secretary of the Australian Council for United Nations Relief and Rehabilitation Administration in 1944.

Having concluded his Red Cross service on 15 August 1947, Addison moved to Kangaroo Ground and in 1949-56 served on the Eltham Shire Council (president, 1952). He was appointed president of the local war memorial trust in 1957. Survived by his wife, he died on 1 January 1972 at North Balwyn and was cremated.

H. Dow (ed), *Memories of Melbourne University* (Melb, 1983); Aust Red Cross Soc, *Annual Report*, 1915-18, 1947-48; *SMH*, 28 Sept 1915, 29 Dec 1938, 17 July 1944; *Punch* (Melb), 4 Dec 1924; S. S. Addison, Brief Outline of M.U.P. Development, 1930, *and* L. Scott, Outline History of M.U.P., 1960 (Melb Univ Press Archives); Univ Melb Archives.   G. F. JAMES

ADERMANN, SIR CHARLES FREDERICK (1896-1979), farmer and politician, was born on 3 August 1896 at Vernor Siding, near Lowood, Queensland, eighth child of Carl Friederich Adermann, farmer, and his wife Emilie, née Litzow, both migrants from Germany. Having settled at Wooroolin, in 1909 the Adermanns founded the first congregation of the Churches of Christ in the Kingaroy district. Educated at Lowood and Wooroolin State schools to age 13, Charles later took correspondence courses in farm management. He tried to join the Australian Imperial Force in 1916 when he learned that his brother Robert had been killed in action, but was rejected on medical grounds.

Working on his parents' farm, Adermann emerged as a primary industry leader. Farmers in the South Burnett region had turned to peanut-growing, seeking an alternative cash crop to maize. Increased production led to a sharp reduction in price during the 1924 season. The farmers refused to sell and approached the State government under the terms of the Primary Products Pools Act (1922-23) to form a Peanut (later Peanut Marketing) Board. Chairman of the board in 1925-31 and 1934-52, Adermann presided over the gradual stabilization of the industry: through a compulsory collective marketing system, the board treated, stored and sold annual crops on behalf of growers. On 7 April 1926 at St Andrew's Anglican Church, Wooroolin, Adermann had married Mildred Turner. From 1931 they worked their own farm in the district. In 1938, as 'Uncle John', Adermann began his popular Sunday-School broadcasts on radio 4SB, hoping that 'a children's session of this type . . . would have a tendency to encourage others to read the word of God'. He was chairman of the local wartime patriotic fund and of Kingaroy Shire Council in 1939-46.

Convinced that farmers needed their own political representation, in 1943 Adermann had won the Federal seat of Maranoa for the Country Party. After a redistribution in 1949, his electorate was Fisher. His parliamentary appointments included deputy-speaker (1950 and 1955-56) and chairman of committees (1950-58), before he was chosen in 1958 to be minister for primary industry in the coalition government of (Sir) Robert Menzies [q.v.]. In this role Adermann became prominent in his party's successful push for further subsidies, grants and other assistance to rural producers. One beneficiary was the ailing Queensland ginger industry. Deputy-leader of the parliamentary Country Party for three years from 1964, he was appointed a privy counsellor in 1966 and K.B.E. in 1971. His ministerial term had ended in 1967 and he retired from parliament in 1972; his son Albert Evan succeeded him as member for Fisher. Charles's brother Ernest Philip had represented New Plymouth in the New Zealand parliament in 1943-66.

'Lean and with lanky dark hair', his face lined and tanned in middle age, Adermann was devoted to his family. He gave practical expression to two powerful forces: his staunch Christian faith, which ever buoyed him, and his love of the land and farming. He continued his 'Uncle John' programmes until late in life and had been president of the Queensland and federal conferences of the Churches of Christ. As a farmer, he was typical of the best of his era: honest, loyal, efficient and hard working. His achievements in politics had been solid, although he was not overly ambitious. A robust fighter in committee and party rooms, he recalled with pride the fifty Acts he had helped to place on the statute books on behalf of Australia's primary producers. Energetic, kind and compassionate, he was a dedicated community worker and became a life member of Kingaroy Rotary Club; he enjoyed watching Test cricket and was a competent lawn bowler. Sir Charles died on 9 May 1979 at Dalby; after a state funeral he was buried in Taabinga cemetery, Kingaroy; his wife, two sons and two daughters survived him. Paying tribute to him, Queensland Premier (Sir) Joh Bjelke-Petersen credited Adermann's encouragement as the stimulus for his own political career.

J. E. Murphy and E. W. Easton, *Wilderness to Wealth* (Brisb, 1950); Hist Soc of Qld, *J*, 5, no 1, 1953, p 833; *Bulletin*, 30 Dec 1959; *Qld Country Life*, 16 May 1968, 27 Sept 1979; *Sunday Mail* (Brisb), 29 Aug 1943, 3 Oct 1971; *Townsville Daily Bulletin*, 10 May 1979; *South Burnett Times*, 16 May 1979; information from Mr and Mrs E. Adermann, Nambour, Qld.

MARGARET BRIDSON CRIBB

AFFLECK, ARTHUR HERBERT (1903-1966), aviator, was born on 3 July 1903 at Brighton, Melbourne, second son of Alfred Stow Affleck, a Victorian-born shipping clerk, and his English wife Alice, née Buckley. Educated at Wesley College, Arthur worked as a bank officer for two years before entering the Royal Australian Air Force in 1923. His wider ambition was for a career in commercial aviation. Selected as one of three civil aviation cadets in November that year, he passed his pilot's course and on 18 July 1925 was discharged from the R.A.A.F. In 1925-26 he flew the route between Melbourne and Hay, New South Wales, for Australian Aerial Services Ltd. He joined Queensland and Northern Territory Aerial Services Ltd in 1927.

On 27 March 1928 QANTAS agreed to provide a pilot and aircraft for a one-year trial of Rev. John Flynn's [q.v.8] proposed aerial medical service to be based at Cloncurry in north-west Queensland. Affleck piloted the D.H.50A plane which carried Dr Kenyon St

Vincent Welch, an experienced surgeon from Sydney, to the scene of medical emergencies and transported patients from remote areas to hospital. Through his skilful flying, concern for safety, and bluff, hearty nature, Affleck did much to ensure the success of a service which quickly caught the imagination of Australians. On 30 September 1930 in St Andrew's Anglican Church, Cloncurry, he married Jane Alice Stewart (d. 1945); they were to have two sons. Quitting aviation in September 1931, Affleck settled at Mareeba as a tobacco-grower. The venture failed and in 1932-33 he worked as a pilot for Pacific Aerial Transport Ltd which operated in Papua and the mandated Territory of New Guinea.

Defeated in a second attempt at farming, Affleck moved to Perth in 1934. During the next two years he flew for West Australian Airways Ltd and MacRobertson-[q.v.11 Robertson] Miller [q.v.10] Aviation Co. Ltd, completing a number of medical missions in addition to his commercial flights. In 1936 he became a flying inspector in the civil aviation branch, Department of Defence, Melbourne. Granted an honorary commission as flying officer in the Citizen Air Force, in 1944-45 he flew transport aircraft for No. 37 Squadron, R.A.A.F. He led a party to the Territory of Papua-New Guinea in April 1947 to survey airfields and report on requirements for the resumption of civil air operations; his recommendations were adopted by the Department of Civil Aviation.

At the Presbyterian Church, Sandringham, Melbourne, Affleck had married Myra Ruth Roberts on 16 January 1946. Promoted regional superintendent of air navigation, D.C.A., Sydney, in 1948, he developed a heart disease which was to end his flying. In 1959 he transferred to Port Moresby as regional director of civil aviation. Retiring to Sydney in 1963, he published his lively, anecdotal autobiography, *The Wandering Years* (Melbourne, 1964). He died of pulmonary embolism on 11 September 1966 while cruising off Vancouver, Canada, in the liner *Orsova*; his wife survived him, as did the sons of his first marriage.

M. Page, *The Flying Doctor Story, 1928-78* (Adel, 1977); J. Behr, *Aviation History of the Royal Flying Doctor Service of Australia* (Syd, priv pub, 1979); J. Gunn, *The Defeat of Distance* (Brisb, 1985); *Sth Pacific Post*, 18 Dec 1959; Affleck papers (NL); information from Capt V. Cover, Surfers Paradise, Qld.   KEN G. KNIGHT

AFFORD, MALCOLM (MAX) (1906-1954), playwright and novelist, was born on 8 April 1906 at Parkside, Adelaide, fifth surviving child of Robert Daniel Afford, grocer, and his second wife Mary Ann, née Crundell.

Known as Max, he was educated at Parkside Public and Unley High schools, and held various jobs before working as a reporter at the *News* and *Mail* in 1926-31. Having published his first story in *Smith's Weekly* in 1928, he freelanced in the 'ear-phone and cat's whisker days' of wireless and mastered the new technology. His first play to be broadcast was macabre: it included a thunderstorm, a wronged mistress, a maniac who believed himself to be a cat, a number of slit throats and a suicide. In 1935 Afford joined radio 5DN as a producer and continuity writer. Next year he won the *Advertiser*'s centenary play competition with *William Light—The Founder* (later *Awake My Love*). His Jeffery Blackburn novels, *Blood On His Hands!* (London, 1936) and *Death's Mannikins* (London, 1937), achieved several reprintings. By eventually writing more than sixty radio and stage plays and eight crime novels—usually employing English settings—Afford was to gain international repute.

He moved to Sydney in 1936, on contract to the Australian Broadcasting Commission as a playwright and producer. A tall man, tanned from swimming, with penetrating blue eyes, a heavy jaw, and prematurely white hair, Afford was witty, ebullient and captivating. On 16 April 1938 at St Michael's Anglican Church, Vaucluse, he married Thelma May Thomas, a costume designer; they were to remain childless. Tired of churning out radio dialogue and thrillers, Afford stated in 1939 that he wanted to write a book expressing 'the helpless antagonism of the average person trapped in this sticky web of international affairs'; his wish was never realized. From 1941 he again freelanced, selling children's and adult serials like *Hagen's Circus* (800 episodes) to radio 2GB and 2UE. These programmes proved so popular that his name was emblazoned on roadside hoardings and city billboards.

Afford's comedy thriller *Lady in Danger* (published in Sydney, 1944; New York, 1945) was originally produced by (Dame) Doris Fitton for Sydney's Independent Theatre (March 1942); it was also staged (1944) by J. C. Williamson [q.v.6] Ltd. Taken in 1945 to Broadway's Broadhurst Theatre, New York, the play closed after twelve performances and poor box office: 'wordy, dull, and gimcrack', wrote the *New York Times*. Afford enjoyed success with *Mischief in the Air* (Theatre Royal, Sydney, October 1944) and co-wrote with Ken G. Hall the story for the Columbia Film Corporation's film, *Smithy*, in 1944. Max was president of the Sydney P.E.N. Club in 1950. While his play, *Dark Enchantment*, toured England's provincial theatres that year, he studied television with the British Broadcasting Corporation in London.

Returning home, he used Australian settings and subjects in such radio plays as *Lazy in the Sun* and *Out of This Nettle*, and in the long-running 1951 A.B.C. serial, *Stranger Come In*, which explored the subject of immigration. Believing that radio was more personal than the stage and more manageable than the cinema, he rejoined the A.B.C. Survived by his wife, Afford died of cancer on 2 November 1954 at Mosman, Sydney, and was cremated. The A.B.C. continued to serialize his *It Walks by Night* and in 1959 televised *Lady in Danger*. *Mischief in the Air*, a selection of Afford's plays, was published in Brisbane in 1974. Ivor Hele's and Vincent Juradovitch's portraits of Afford are held by his widow.

L. Rees, *The Making of Australian Drama* (Syd, 1973); *Listener In*, 25 Feb-3 Mar 1939; *Teleradio*, 25 Jan 1941; *ABC Weekly*, 20 Nov 1954; *SMH*, 15, 28 July 1944, 31 Mar 1945; *Herald* (Melb), 31 Mar 1945; H. de Berg, Thelma Afford (taped interview, NL); Performing Arts Collection (Fulton L, Univ Adel); ABC Archives (Syd); Afford collections (Fryer L, Univ Qld, *and* Barr-Smith L, Univ Adel); PRG 689/1 (Mort L); film scripts and home movies (NFSA); information from and ms held by Mrs T. Afford, Balmoral, Syd.   MICHAEL J. TOLLEY

AGAUNDO, KONDOM (c.1917-1966), tribal leader and politician, was born probably about 1917 near Kundiawa, Eastern Highlands, New Guinea, son of Agaundo, a war leader. Kondom's rise to prominence corresponded to the early period of Australian colonial control of his country. Orphaned in childhood, he sought a close association with the newly-arrived government and mission: his first job was to carry milk from Mingende Catholic mission to the government station at Kundiawa.

In 1943, realizing that Arime, his tribe's *luluai* (government-appointed headman), was experiencing difficulties in his conflicting allegiances to government and mission, Kondom grasped the opportunity to impress the Australian officer with his abilities and his loyalty. He became one of the youngest Chimbu *luluais*, an impressive orator and a progressive leader, and was taken on visits to conferences and development projects. An enthusiast for government-sponsored advancement, he directed coffee-planting throughout his tribal region, built a timber-frame home for himself and a community meeting-house, and installed a coffee-pulper at Wandi which he wanted to become a showcase for the district. He had at least eight wives and took care of widows and children in his clan.

Kondom's tribe, with three others of the Waiye area close to the Chimbu subdistrict headquarters at Kundiawa, formed an early highlands local government council; with the *kiap*'s support, Kondom was elected its first president in 1959. He soon mastered the procedures of council leadership and was active in promoting economic programmes, as well as schools and health facilities in the council area. In 1961 he was elected to the Legislative Council of Papua and New Guinea as representative of almost one million highlanders. In his speeches he made persistent demands for developing the highlands and emphasized the need for continuing dependence on Australia. Defeated in the 1964 elections for the new national House of Assembly, he found an outlet for his energies through the Chimbu Coffee Cooperative. He was also a member of the Eastern Highlands District Advisory Council.

On 28 August 1966 Kondom was killed in a traffic accident on the precipitous Daulo Pass in the Eastern Highlands; he was buried at Wandi. His death was mourned by thousands; years after the accident the tribe to which his car-driver belonged paid Kondom's family a vast sum. The Kundiawa provincial office-building is named Kondom Agaundo House. Although he had received no formal education and was illiterate, he was one of the few 'big men' whose influence extended beyond his locality. He is remembered by the Chimbu as the person who brought coffee, cash crops, business and local government to the highlands, as one who directed the building of roads, bridges, airstrips, schools and clinics, as a peacemaker and a great man.

M. Williams, *Stone Age Island* (Syd, 1964); D. G. Bettison *et al* (eds), *The Papua-New Guinea 1964 Elections* (Canb, 1965); J. L. Whittaker *et al* (eds), *Documents and Readings in New Guinea History* (Brisb, 1975); P. Brown, 'Kondom', *J of the PNG Soc*, 1, no 2, 1967, p 26, *and* 'Big Man, Past and Present', *Ethnology*, 29, 1990, p 97; *Sth Pacific Post*, 29 Aug, 5 Sept 1966.   PAULA BROWN

AGOSTINI, ANTONIO (1903-1969), waiter, and LINDA (1905-1934), hairdresser, were husband and wife. Antonio was born on 20 May 1903 at Altivole, Treviso, Italy, son of Mario Agostini and his wife Madalena, née Bernardi. He migrated to Australia in 1927 and leased the cloakroom at Romano's [q.v.11]. In 1928 he met Linda Platt, a cinema usherette. Born on 12 September 1905 at Forest Hill, London, Linda had migrated to New Zealand in 1926 and to Australia next year. They were married at the registrar general's office, Sydney, on 22 April 1930.

Tony and Linda were a popular couple. He was 5 ft 7 ins (170.2 cm) tall, trim and dark haired; she was only five feet (152.4 cm) tall, attractive and well liked. Yet, according to Tony, their relationship was not an easy one. Linda sometimes left him for long periods and drank too much which shamed him within the Italian community. In 1933 the couple moved to Carlton, Melbourne, where he worked on the newspaper, *Il Giornale Italiano*, and she took a job at Ferrari's hairdressing salon in the Manchester Unity Building. Agostini later claimed that there were frequent altercations. During one quarrel in bed, Linda was fatally shot with a pistol which Tony alleged she had held. To avoid a police investigation, he carried her body by car across the New South Wales border to the Howlong road, five miles (8 km) west of Albury, where he hid it in a culvert and attempted to set fire to it.

The charred remains of the body, clad in Oriental-style pyjamas, and wrapped in a sack and towel, were found on 1 September 1934. Police were unable to establish the identity of 'the Pyjama Girl'. The crime became a *cause célèbre*. Agostini was questioned, but claimed that his wife had left him. In 1936 he moved to Perth and in January 1938 to Sydney. Interned as an alien in June 1940, he was released in February 1944 and returned to Romano's as a waiter.

Linda's body had been preserved in formalin in a zinc-lined bath at the University of Sydney and shown to hundreds of people, including Agostini. In 1938 a coroner's inquest failed to establish identity. Although several witnesses had declared the corpse to be that of Linda, police were misled by an inaccurate dental record. Errors made in plotting the dental work were discovered in February 1944 and new charts were matched to those of Linda Agostoni, on whom police had a file as a missing person. Several of her acquaintances confirmed the body's identity. As corroboration, freckles on an upper arm were found to match those in earlier photographs of her.

On 4 March 1944 Agostini was interviewed by the police commissioner William John MacKay [q.v.10], a regular patron at Romano's, who had known him in the 1930s. Tony confessed his involvement in Linda's death. Taken to Melbourne, he was arrested on 6 March and committed in April to stand trial for murder. In June the jury returned a verdict of manslaughter. The judge (Sir) Charles Lowe [q.v.] sentenced Agostini to six years imprisonment with hard labour.

Released from Pentridge gaol under a general amnesty, Agostini was deported to Italy on 21 August 1948. He married a widow Giuseppina Gasoni in December 1952 at Cagliari, Sardinia; he died there in 1969 and was buried in San Michele cemetery. Linda had been given a funeral at state expense and was buried in Preston cemetery on 13 July 1944.

R. Coleman, *The Pyjama Girl* (Melb, 1978); *Border Morning Mail*, Sept 1934, Jan 1938, Apr 1939, 13 Jan, 7-10 Nov 1941, 10 Dec 1942, Apr 1943, Apr-June 1944; *Argus*, 3 Sept 1934, 7, 28, 29 Mar, 1, 14 July 1944, 23 Aug 1948; transcripts of evidence of coroner's inquest, Melb, Mar 1944 *and* trial of A. Agostini, Melb, June 1944 (Justice and Police Museum, Syd).   BRUCE PENNAY

AINSLIE, JAMES PERCIVAL (1899-1973), surgeon, was born on 14 August 1899 in South Perth, son of James Walter Ainslie, company secretary, and his wife Marion Agnes, née Inglis, both Melbourne born. Educated at the local state school and at the High School, Perth, in 1918 Jim enrolled at the University of Western Australia, taking units of science as prerequisites for medical studies at the University of Melbourne where he entered Trinity College next year. Graduating with first-class honours (M.B., B.S., 1923; M.D., 1924), Ainslie successively appointed resident medical officer (1923), registrar (1924) and medical superintendent (1925) at Melbourne Hospital. He completed postgraduate studies in surgery in London and became a fellow of the Royal College of Surgeons in 1927. Establishing himself in private practice in Perth, Ainslie was honorary assistant surgeon to out-patients from 1928 and honorary consulting surgeon to in-patients from 1935 at the city's only public hospital. He was appointed a fellow (1929) of the (Royal) Australasian College of Surgeons and won respect from his patients for his skills. On 15 October 1930 he married a medical practitioner Jean Wilmore Clemons at St John's Anglican Church, Launceston, Tasmania.

Having served with the Australian Army Medical Corps Reserve from 1929, Ainslie volunteered for full-time duty in World War II and was stationed with the 110th Australian General Hospital at Hollywood, Perth. After training in neurosurgery in 1948, mainly at the Radcliffe Infirmary, Oxford, England, he helped to found the Royal Perth Hospital's clinical research unit in 1952 and became director of R.P.H.'s neurosurgery unit next year. As a member (from 1933) of the senate of the University of Western Australia, he played a key role in the long and complex negotiations that led to the establishment of the university's medical school in 1956. A niggling perfectionist and a 'surgeon of the old school' who hated humbug, he brooked no opposition. A former colleague recalled how Ainslie sometimes hurled his instruments on the floor of the operating theatre during his tantrums over mishaps. While formidable and abrasive to subordinates, he was also helpful to those students who sought his advice.

A director (1960-73) of the Western Australian Medical Board, Ainslie served on the board of management of R.P.H. from 1966. He also lectured in the faculty of medicine and, as a foundation member (1970) of the Advisory Medical Council of Australia, proposed standards for postgraduate education in medicine and sat on accreditation committees. His beloved domestic life was sacrificed to prodigiously long working hours. Unhappy with the university convocation election campaign in 1958, Ainslie retired from the senate and next year from the practising staff of the hospital. In 1962 he was appointed C.M.G. Some 5 ft 10 ins (177.8 cm) tall, balding in later life, he had played competitive cricket, continued to be a keen fisherman and turned in his retirement to golf and bowls. He died on 14 January 1973 at Subiaco, and was cremated; his wife, son and two daughters survived him.

F. Alexander, *Campus at Crawley* (Melb, 1963); G. C. Bolton and P. Joske, *History of Royal Perth Hospital* (Perth, 1982); Roy Perth Hospital, *Annual Report*, 1973, p 32; *MJA*, 20 Oct 1973, p 786; *West Australian*, 15 Jan 1973; personal information.

HELGA M. GRIFFIN

AIRD, JOHN ALLAN (1892-1959), irrigation commissioner, was born on 17 October 1892 at Clifton Hill, Melbourne, second son of Andrew Aird, a storeman from Scotland, and his native-born wife Augustine, née Baum. Educated at Scotch College, Jock joined the State Rivers and Water Supply Commission, and in 1913 was sponsored by that agency— then under the leadership of the controversial American engineer Elwood Mead [q.v.10]— to study in the United States of America. In 1915 Aird completed a B.S. (Agriculture) at the University of California, Berkeley. He enlisted in the Australian Imperial Force on 11 October 1916 and served in the 1st Divisional Ammunition Column on the Western Front. Promoted lieutenant in February 1919, he studied briefly in England at the University of Leeds before returning to Australia in 1920 and resuming his former employment. On 3 October 1922 he married Jessie Alice Adam at the Presbyterian Church, Brunswick, Melbourne.

His career in Victoria's celebrated water management commission spanned its early years, the booms and busts of rural settlement expansion, and the commencement of the great surge of dam building under Premier (Sir) Henry Bolte. While rising in the commission's ranks, Aird graduated from the University of Melbourne (B.Ag.Sc., 1922; Dip.Comm., 1932) and was a member (1931-58) of the faculty of agriculture. His senior career appointments included superintendent of irrigation settlements (1927-33), closer settlement commissioner (1933-49) and chief irrigation officer (1939-49). Appointed commissioner (one of three top executives) in 1949, he held that post until his retirement in 1958.

A large, genial man, Jock Aird had a temperament and an expertise which complemented those of his fellow executives. In a powerful monopolistic agency dominated by engineering perspectives (though less so than related bodies in other States) his training had given him insights into the complex spectrum of water uses and the changing demands made by rural consumers. With forceful Chief Commissioner (Sir) Ronald East and Commissioner Harold Hanslow [q.v.], he persuaded the Victorian cabinet to introduce novel legislation dealing with soil conservation, despite the machinations of Premier (Sir) Albert Dunstan [q.v.8]. Under East's instructions, Aird prepared important review material, accompanied government advisers on a well-prepared, fact-finding tour of New South Wales and carefully drafted their main recommendations. The 1940 legislation, amended by successive governments after the war, owed much to the commission's efforts.

Aird's principal technical publications derived from his work with the commission and for the most part enjoyed only limited circulation. They included practical papers on the economics of erosion, and on representative costs on pioneer irrigated blocks and the efficient control of irrigation water; economic studies of water conservation in the Campaspe, Goulburn and Werribee catchments; and a survey of soldier settlement after World War I. He also contributed to the growing debate on the wisdom of continuing public investment in irrigation and to arguments for new and augmented dams. In a wider arena, his simple paper on the relationships between rainfall, productivity and the distribution of population was frequently consulted and cribbed in Victoria's secondary schools.

In the commission, an institution that was synonymous with the development of Victoria, Aird won the affection and loyalty of subordinates. An honorary life member of the Royal Institute of Public Administration, England, he served as secretary of the local body for many years. He died of myocardial infarction on 25 January 1959 at his East Malvern home and was cremated; his wife, son and daughter survived him. The J. A. Aird prize in public administration is awarded annually at the University of Melbourne.

J. M. Powell, *Watering the Garden State* (Syd, 1989); *Age* (Melb), 3 Feb 1933, 30 Jan 1959.

J. M. POWELL

AISTON, GEORGE (1879-1943), policeman and ethnographer, was born on 11 October 1879 at Burnside, South Australia, only son of native-born parents James Albert Aiston, blacksmith, and his wife Rebecca, née Perry. George's mother died in his infancy and his stepmother Amelia treated him coldly. He left school at 11, but read keenly and widely. In 1897 he joined the South Australian Military Forces, becoming an orderly in the Chief Secretary's Office and at Government House. Enlisting in the South Australian First (Mounted Rifles) Contingent in 1899, he served in the South African War. As a constable (from April 1901) in the South Australian Mounted Police, in 1901-03 he worked at Yorketown, Kooringa and Port Germein where he first encountered Aborigines. On 12 April 1905 at Holy Trinity Church, Adelaide, he married Mabel Agnes Maud Mary White; they were to remain childless.

In 1904 Aiston had been posted to the west coast and was to spend five years at Tarcoola and Tumby Bay. He had an imposing physical presence. While patrolling the Nullarbor Plain and Gawler Ranges, he developed an interest in the culture of the Aborigines, earned their respect and friendship by enforcing the law without a gun, and sent documented stone tools to the South Australian Museum. From 1912 to 1923 he was based at the Birdsville Track outpost of Mungeranie and was also a sub-protector of Aborigines. He distributed rations, levied bore fees, inspected stock, collected dingo scalps, registered births, deaths and marriages, processed mail and issued licences. In addition, he studied the customs, beliefs and technology of the local people, and was assigned the Red Ochre *mura* (Dreaming). An authority on Central Australian Aborigines, particularly the Wangkangurru of eastern Lake Eyre, he photographed secular and ceremonial activities, as well as Birdsville Track life and landscapes.

In 1920 he wrote to the Melbourne art dealer W. H. Gill, through whom he contacted amateur anthroplogists and archaeologists, among them Dr George Horne, Alfred Kenyon [q.v.9], Stanley Mitchell and Thomas Campbell [qq.v.]. Aiston's extensive newspaper articles and correspondence encouraged the view that Aboriginal stone-tool technology was an entirely indigenous development. He supplied individuals and museums with his stone-tool series, fossils, tektites and natural history specimens, and guided expeditions through the Lake Eyre region. In 1922 he collaborated with Horne and Dr Brooke-Nicholls on an early ethnographic film, and with Horne on *Savage Life in Central Australia* (London, 1924): Aiston contributed most of the text and all the photographs. He published papers and contributed to the work of other researchers.

Resigning from the police force in 1923, 'Poddy' Aiston bought the Mulka store and leased the government bore to sell water at a penny a drink. He had ridden with Aboriginal trackers throughout the State's north-east and buried over thirty 'perishers'. Despite his legendary hospitality, Aiston valued his solitude. He enjoyed meetings of the Anthropological Society of South Australia, and belonged to the Bread and Cheese, and Savage clubs in Melbourne, but preferred the company of bush travellers, drovers and Aborigines, supplemented by correspondence which was delivered by camel-train until the late 1920s. His mail also brought Indian swords, Japanese armour and a Persian helmet. In 1931 in Canberra Aiston catalogued the Commonwealth's Horne-Bowie collection of Aboriginal implements, a laborious task which was alleviated by his phenomenal memory.

George and Mabel saw the remoteness of the Birdsville Track diminished by the aeroplane, the motorcar and the pedal wireless. He bought a Dodge buckboard in 1933 and they also began operating a base for the National Aerial Medical Service of Australia. Drought in the late 1920s and the Depression of the 1930s affected business, but he continued to sell everything from petrol to his hand-made spurs. Aiston had visited Melbourne in 1929 for an exhibition of 'Primitive Art' and in 1934 for the Outback Australia Centenary Exhibition: on each occasion he escorted tribesmen from Mulka who demonstrated tool-making and performed ceremonies.

He belonged to a generation of scientists and self-taught natural historians who gathered material objects for data. His ethnographic collection and knowledge increased as the local Aboriginal population dwindled; he retained the Aborigines' trust and fought for their interests. While coveting their sacred objects, he bought only what they offered.

Aiston died of cancer on 25 September 1943 at Broken Hill and was buried with Anglican rites in the local cemetery. In 1953 his widow donated his ethnographica and his collection of arms and armour to the South Australian Museum which later acquired many of his photographs. His papers and correspondence are in the National Museum of Australia, Canberra, the Mitchell Library, Sydney, and the South Australian Museum.

Willochran, 1 Jan 1944; *Wild Life*, Feb 1944; SA Police Dept records (PRO, SA); Aiston papers (SA Museum Archives); Aiston to W. H. Gill, Correspondence 1920-40 (ML); information from Mrs J. Reynolds, Croydon Park, Adel.   PHILIP JONES

AKEROYD, ARTHUR GORDON (1890-1948), meteorologist, was born on 29 May 1890 at Shepparton, Victoria, son of William Akeroyd, a skin merchant from England, and his Irish-born wife Elizabeth Anne, née Gordon. Educated locally, and at Hamilton State School and Mr Krome's [q.v.9] University High School, from 1905 Arthur worked as a telegraph messenger at Mooroopna Post Office. He moved with his widowed mother to Melbourne in 1907 and joined the Department of Home Affairs as a clerk next year. In 1915 he topped an Australia-wide, competitive examination for a position as an assistant (meteorologist) in the meteorological branch. As a sculler, he competed for the Melbourne Rowing Club and won several prizes. On 23 October 1920 he married Alice Lister Smith at St Andrew's Anglican Church, Clifton Hill.

Early in his career Akeroyd specialized in marine meteorology and assisted the planning of Antarctic expeditions; he later headed a forecasting section in the meteorological branch's head office and studied at the University of Melbourne (B.Comm., 1930). Placed in charge of the weather bureau's climatological section, Akeroyd was appointed divisional meteorologist in charge of the Western Australia division in 1937. He held the honorary rank of wing commander in the Royal Australian Air Force during World War II, and, as part of the meteorological division's activities, supervised the provision of weather forecasts for long-range aircraft, mostly Catalina flying-boats which maintained a strategic, non-stop air link between Perth and Ceylon. In this task he was aided by the young John Hogan [q.v.]. Referring to Akeroyd's introduction of accurate, daily, maximum temperature forecasts in 1945, an editorial in *Wadaja* (the bulletin of the Western Australian branch of the Australian Journalists' Association) rated him as the hero of Perth. Akeroyd's service spanned the period in which weather forecasting gradually changed from an intuitive, observational art (at which he excelled) to a soundly-based, predictive science.

A burly, balding man, Akeroyd impressed his colleagues with his business acumen, impeccable prose, personal idiosyncrasies and wit. He was an inveterate pipe-smoker who twiddled a pencil while spinning a yarn or dictating a forecast. His keen sense of individual rights reputedly sprang from resentment at being passed over for early promotions, apparently because of his youth. With a compassionate interest in his staff, he was a foundation member of the Professional Officers' Association of the Commonwealth Public Service.

Akeroyd collapsed in William Street, Perth, and died of 'coronary sclerosis' on 25 March 1948; he was buried in the Presbyterian section of Karrakatta cemetery; his wife and daughter survived him. Although he left no published work, Akeroyd had made his mark as a spokesman for the weather bureau in the daily press and as an advocate of the application of weather science to everyday affairs.

Wadaja, 1, no 7, Jan 1945; *West Australian*, 27 Mar 1948; *Shepparton News*, 5 Apr 1948; information from and papers held by Mrs C. A. Nettle, Torrens, Canb; personal information based on the reminiscences of long-serving officers of the Cwlth Weather Bureau.   R. L. SOUTHERN

ALCORN, CYRIL DAVID (1911-1972) and IVAN WELLS (1912-1972), Methodist ministers, were born on 16 July 1911 and 28 November 1912 at Mutdapilly, near Ipswich, Queensland, eldest of nine children of David Ebenezer Alcorn, farmer, and his wife Mary Ellen, née Wells, both Queenslanders. The family later moved to Tingalpa where David took up poultry farming. Cyril was educated at Normanby and Tingalpa State schools, Brisbane State High School and the Teachers' Training College. Sent as a teacher to Greenup, in south-west Queensland, he lived in a tent in the school grounds to save money for a theological training, but was known to swagmen during the Depression as one who would provide them with food. In 1935 he was accepted as a candidate for the Methodist ministry; he entered King's College, University of Queensland (B.A., 1940; M.A., 1964), and was ordained on 3 March 1941.

At the Albert Street Methodist Church, Brisbane, Cyril married Joyce Carmichael, a domestic science teacher, on 29 March 1941. The couple had intended to go to India as missionaries, but their plan was frustrated by Japan's entry into World War II. From December 1942 until 1946 Cyril served as a chaplain in the Royal Australian Navy: he was initially stationed in Darwin and later sailed in H.M.A.S. *Shropshire* in 1944-45. While in Darwin he had made friends with Rev. Arch Grant, a former padre with the Australian Inland Mission; after the war he and Alcorn worked together in Darwin to help set up a United Church in Northern Australia. As principal (1947-55) of Blackheath and Thornburgh Colleges at Charters Towers, North Queensland, Cyril improved the property and introduced a new course in agriculture, as well as another in home science (run by his wife Joyce). In 1956 he became superintendent minister of the Ashgrove circuit and was senior naval chaplain at the Port of Brisbane. He received a bachelor degree from the Melbourne College of Divinity in 1958.

With his brother Ivan, in 1960 he established the Methodist Training College and

Bible School at Kangaroo Point, Brisbane, where students were prepared for the ministry. Cyril was its foundation principal and the institution was subsequently named Alcorn College (1976) in recognition of the brothers' work. When he was appointed M.B.E. in 1966, Cyril's citation acknowledged the pastoral care he had given after the sinking of H.M.A.S. *Voyager* in 1964. He was respected as 'a great preacher and a compassionate man', and in 1969 was elected president of the Queensland Methodist Conference. Survived by his wife, daughter and three of his four sons, Cyril Alcorn died of ruptured abdominal aneurysm on 15 May 1972 at Parkville, Melbourne and was cremated in Brisbane.

Ivan was educated at Tingalpa State School, but left to help his father before following Cyril into the ministry. Quick and energetic, in 1934 Ivan became a home missionary at Malanda, North Queensland, where he needed a string of horses to maintain his far-flung preaching commitments. As a student at King's College where he received his licentiate of theology in 1940, he developed a commitment to education that was to be manifested in his efforts to establish what became Alcorn College. On 5 May 1941 at the Methodist Church, Kingaroy, he married a schoolteacher Iris Sarah Simpson. In September Ivan was appointed chaplain in the Australian Imperial Force and embarked for the Middle East in November; he returned to Australia in February 1943. Having served on Horn Island in Torres Strait, he was in Papua and New Guinea, mostly with the 2nd/2nd Battalion, in 1944-45.

As director (1949-70) of the Queensland Methodist Young People's Department, Ivan extended its camping movement and developed Christian tourism and stewardship. Sensitive, but humorous and optimistic, he preceded Cyril as president (1967) of the Queensland Methodist Conference, and in 1970 became director of the social welfare and pastoral care department. Having organized the Brisbane centre for Lifeline in 1966, he became its director-general (1972); he was Queensland's 'Father of the Year' (1969) and was appointed M.B.E. in 1972. That year he unsuccessfully contested the Legislative Assembly seat of Ashgrove as an Independent, opposing the Liberal minister for health S. D. Tooth over social welfare and the government's handling of the drug problem.

Survived by his wife, son and two of his three daughters, Ivan Alcorn died of hypertensive coronary vascular disease on 28 September 1972 at St Johns Wood, Brisbane, and was cremated. As embodiments of robust Christianity the brothers had strikingly similar careers, but, whereas Cyril was a teacher, scholarly, thoughtful and without guile, Ivan

was a lively visionary and an inspirer of action.

A. Grant, *Palmerston to Darwin* (Syd, 1990); Methodist Church of A'sia (Qld), *Minutes of 1972 Conference*, Brisb, 1972; *Methodist Times*, 16 Oct 1969, 18 May, 1 June, 5, 12, 19 Oct 1972; *Telegraph* (Brisb), 16 May, 29 Sept 1972; *Courier-Mail*, 29 Sept 1972; I. Alcorn, God's Work First, My Life with Ivan Alcorn (ms, 1991, held by its author, Enoggera, Brisb).   JOHN E. MAVOR

ALDEN, JOHN (1908-1962), actor-manager, was born on 17 January 1908 at Taree, New South Wales, third son of native-born parents George Nathaniel Buchanan, storekeeper, and his wife Elizabeth Malina, née Lee; named Gordon Henry, he was a great-nephew of Nathaniel and William Buchanan [qq.v.3]. He was educated at Taree Intermediate High School, Teachers' College, Sydney, and the University of Sydney (B.A., 1930), and began schoolteaching in 1927. Following several city postings Buchanan taught at Maclean (1930-32) and was transferred to Sutherland Intermediate High School, Sydney, in January 1933. Intent on becoming an actor, in 1934 he approached (Dame) Doris Fitton, founder of the Independent Theatre, but first sought experience backstage. He adopted the stage-name 'John Alden' and in 1935 made an impact as King Magnus in George Bernard Shaw's *The Apple Cart*.

Resigning from the Department of Education in September 1937 to make the pilgrimage to England, Alden spent some time in repertory, toured with (Sir) Donald Wolfit and joined the Old Vic Theatre Company; although playing 'bits and pieces', he gained valuable experience. Back in Sydney in 1940, he earned a living as a radio actor. He also directed repertory-style productions for J. C. Williamson [q.v.6] Ltd at the Theatre Royal and introduced school audiences to Shakespeare's *Twelfth Night* and *The Tempest*. In 1944 Alden and Birrell Moss unsuccessfully sought support from the Department of Education for a 'state touring dramatic company'.

Returning to Sydney in 1947 after a year playing to army of occupation audiences in Japan, Alden embarked on a Shakespeare season on Wednesday nights at the Independent Theatre, North Sydney. For these essentially amateur productions, to which leading professionals donated their services, he trained a pool of young supporting actors and paid meticulous attention to detail. His 1948 production of *Measure for Measure*, in which he played Angelo, attracted attention; it was followed by *The Merry Wives of Windsor*, *The Tempest*, *The Winter's Tale* and *The*

Merchant of Venice. In 1950 Alden brought his company to St James Hall, Sydney, where next year his powerful production of *King Lear* was hailed by the *Sydney Morning Herald* critic Lindsey Browne as 'a rare and enthralling experience'. Pondering on whether the play was 'actable', Alden concluded that 'the modern mind tempered by two world wars does not find "Lear" too unbearably cruel'.

In 1951-52 the John Alden Company made a national tour, modestly supported by the Commonwealth as a jubilee event, and was soon being lauded by (Sir) Charles Moses as 'the beginning of a true national theatre'. Although the company had acquired the experienced business manager Elsie Beyer, protracted negotiations for an annual Commonwealth grant collapsed when Alden resisted any erosion of his personal control. The company disbanded.

While playing King Creon opposite (Dame) Judith Anderson in the Australian Elizabethan Theatre Trust production of *Medea* in 1955, Alden suffered a heart attack. Little more than a year later he was again directing at the Independent. The 1958 production of *Titus Andronicus* launched his second campaign for a national theatre company which led next year to the J. C. Williamson Shakespeare Company. In July 1961 he organized the Sydney Shakespeare Festival, but his angina continued to distress him. He died of a coronary occlusion on 10 November 1962 at his Mosman home and was cremated with Anglican rites. Homosexual, Alden did not marry, and invested his own earnings as well as his energy in his company; his estate was sworn for probate at £3758. Despite some mannerisms, he had a commanding stage presence, matched by impressive interpretive skills. As a director and teacher, he introduced a generation of Australian actors to the techniques of classical theatre.

D. Fitton, *Not Without Dust and Heat* (Syd, 1981); *People* (Syd), 28 Mar 1961; *SMH*, 7 Sept 1940, 17, 18 Feb 1951, 26 July 1955, 21 Mar 1959, 4, 7, 11 July 1961; *Sun-Herald*, 11 Nov 1962; J. Andrews, Subsidy for the Performing Arts in Australia, 1942-1970 (Ph.D. thesis, Monash Univ, 1988); teachers' records, Dept of Education (NSW) archives; theatre programmes, Performing Arts Museum (Vic Arts Centre, Melb); Alden papers (ML).   JOHN RICKARD

ALDER, MILTON CROMWELL (1887-1961), insurance general manager, was born on 5 May 1887 at Marrickville, Sydney, fourth of seven children of Alfred Keen Alder, portrait-painter, and his wife Charlotte Eliza, née Barnes, both English born. Educated at Petersham Superior Public School and Syd-

ney Boys' High School on a scholarship, Milton won the university prize for general proficiency and medals for algebra and geometry at the 1903 junior public examinations. In August he joined the Citizens' Life Assurance Co. (Mutual Life & Citizens Assurance Co. Ltd from 1908). Alder soon qualified as an associate of the Institute of Actuaries, London. On 22 February 1913 at the Newtown Methodist Church he married Pearl Roberts Anderson; they lived at Marrickville for twenty years and he played for the Kingston Methodist cricket team.

Appointed assistant-secretary to the M.L.C. in 1923, he worked closely with its managing director (Sir) John Garvan [q.v.8]. Alder rose from secretary (1927) to assistant to the managing director (1938) and was general manager from 1941. He was president of the Actuarial Society of Australia and New Zealand (1921), of the Insurance Institute of New South Wales (1924) and later of the Incorporated Australian Insurance Institute. Founding joint-secretary (1925) and president (1929-30) of the State branch of the Economic Society of Australia and New Zealand, he was, as well, president of the Council of Social Service of New South Wales, honorary treasurer of Toc H and of the Sydney group of Round Table, a trustee of the Institute of Public Affairs, chairman of the Rochdale Pastoral Co. and director of Alliance Holdings Ltd. In addition, he served on the appointments board of the University of Sydney (1935-49) and for twelve years on the standing committee of the International Chamber of Commerce.

For one so energetic, Alder was unusually shy and modest. All who knew him found in him uncompromising integrity, absolute honesty of thought and extraordinary quickness of mind. He disliked 'cant, humbug, any sort of hypocrisy or bluff', but he was stirred by emotion, sentiment and compassion.

A member of the standing committee of the Diocese of Sydney, Alder was involved with Church of England property and finances: he was honorary treasurer of the Home Mission Society, a churchwarden and honorary treasurer of his parish church, St Mark's, Darling Point, and a member (1959) of the Archbishop's Commission. He was also interested in the problems of the elderly: while he was its president (1956-57), the Rotary Club of Sydney, with the Council of Social Service and Sydney City Council, launched the Old People's Welfare Council; Alder became vice-chairman.

On retiring as general manager in 1955, Alder was made deputy-chairman of M.L.C.'s board. He belonged to the Australian Club, studied etymology and enjoyed gardening at his Point Piper home. Survived by his wife, son and three daughters, he died on 23 March

1961 in St Luke's Hospital, Darlinghurst, and was cremated with Anglican rites; his estate was sworn for probate at £41 625. The Alder memorial wing of the Chesalon Church of England Parish Nursing Home, Harris Park, was named after him.

L. Foster, *High Hopes* (Melb, 1986); R. H. Scott, *The Economic Society of Australia, its History 1925-1985*, (Melb, 1990); Rotary Club of Syd, *Annual Report*, 1956-57; *A'sian Insurance and Banking Record*, May 1961, p 242; *MLC News*, May 1961; Univ Syd Union, *Union Recorder*, 11 May 1961; *SMH*, 12 Apr 1929, 26 Mar 1954; *Anglican*, 14 Apr 1961; family information.   A. F. DEER

ALDERMAN, SIR HARRY GRAHAM (1895-1962), lawyer, was born on 24 September 1895 at Parkside, Adelaide, son of Thomas John Alderman (d. 1916), bootmaker, and his Scottish wife Annie, née Graham. Harry attended Christian Brothers' College, even then inscribing 'H. G. Alderman Q.C.' on the flyleaves of his schoolbooks. Encouraged in his ambition by his mother, he was articled to Paris Nesbit [q.v.11] and admitted to the Bar on 21 April 1917; another mentor and Alderman's first partner was Francis Villeneuve Smith [q.v.11]. On 29 October 1919 Alderman married a civil servant Mary Philomena Farrelly in St Francis Xavier's Cathedral, Adelaide.

By 1928 the firm of Alderman, Brazel, Clark & Ligertwood [q.v.] (now Piper Alderman) was established. Alderman's clients included (Sir) Arthur Fadden, (Field Marshal Sir) Thomas Blamey [qq.v.] and Rupert Murdoch. Alderman took silk in 1943, becoming the fourth Catholic to do so in the State. He assisted the labour movement in South Australia and became the confidant of powerful people, among them Ben Chifley [q.v.]: in Canberra the two enjoyed long walks together, the prime minister smoking a pipe and Alderman his perennial cigar. H. V. Evatt [q.v.], attorney-general in the Curtin [q.v.] and Chifley governments, briefed Alderman several times and was also a close, if fair-weather, friend.

Following Japanese attacks on Darwin, in 1942-43 Alderman led a government inquiry into compensation claims made by those from the evacuated areas against the Department of the Army. He had strong links with the military, was an unofficial adviser to the wartime Commonwealth government and had been involved in negotiations to mend the breach between Blamey and (Sir) Sydney Rowell [q.v.]. President (1945-47) of the Law Society of South Australia, Alderman became president of the Law Council of Australia in 1950 and next year ran a successful National Law Council convention which established his prominence beyond the State.

An able barrister, he often appeared before the High Court of Australia. His most notable case before the Privy Council was *O'Sullivan v Noarlunga Meat Ltd* No. 1 (1954), on the scope and interpretation of sections 51(i) and 109 of the Commonwealth of Australia Constitution Act. Alderman's expertise extended to taxation law and he successfully argued the taxpayer's case in *Quarries Ltd v Federal Commissioner of Taxation* (1961) which concerned depreciation of 'plant and articles' under s. 54 of the Income Tax Assessment Act. In 1959 Alderman's partner J. F. Brazel was senior counsel assisting the royal commission into the case of Rupert Max Stuart who was sentenced to hang for the sexual attack on and killing of a child. Next year, with John Bray, Q.C., Alderman successfully defended the Adelaide *News* in defamation proceedings arising from alleged sensational reporting of the affair.

Alderman's gregariousness, professional skills, national influence and 'folksy' wisdom ensured him a place in Australian legal history. He coined the term 'luck follows the good player', and himself exemplified the aphorism. A generous friend, a loyal colleague and a meticulous counsel, he was also renowned as a legal draftsman and helped to frame South Australian statutes on matrimonial causes, religious education and compulsory third-party insurance.

In 1961 Alderman developed bronchial cancer. After an operation he kept working, his clerks trundling oxygen cylinders with him to court. Survived by his wife, two daughters and three sons, he died on 15 June 1962 and was buried in Mitcham cemetery. Thirteen days before his death he had been knighted.

J. A. Hetherington, *Blamey* (Melb, 1954); S. F. Rowell, *Full Circle* (Melb, 1974); J. A. Cassidy and J. F. Corkery, *Aldermans, Barristers & Solicitors* (Adel, 1988); *Aust Law J*, 28 June 1963; *SMH*, 21, 27 Sept 1944; *Herald* (Melb), 29 Sept 1944, 17 Oct 1947; *Advertiser* (Adel), 2 June 1962; *Age*, 18 June 1962.   J. F. CORKERY

ALDERSON, SIR HAROLD GEORGE (1890-1978), sports administrator, was born on 18 August 1890 at Balmain, Sydney, second child of James Bull Alderson, architect, and his wife Lilias Maud, née Smith, both Sydneysiders. Educated at Mosman Public and Fort Street Model schools, Harold was a clerk when he married Rose Stella Wills on 14 December 1915 in St James's Anglican Church, Sydney. By 1919 he was operating his own business as a public accountant and stock and station agent in O'Connell Street. Having joined the Mosman Rowing Club in

1911 and been a member of the crew which won the maiden IVs at the club's inaugural appearance that season, Alderson became captain of the M.R.C. by 1915. He was secretary (1918-20), chairman (1920-70) and president (1970-78) of the New South Wales Rowing Association, and served several terms as chairman of the Australian Rowing Council. For some time he coached the State's King's Cup VIII, managed the oarsmen in 1920 and 1924, and was secretary of the Anniversary Regatta Committee for over fifty years from 1920. A publicist for rowing, Alderson contributed to the *Sydney Morning Herald* and wrote extensively on the history of the sport. His meticulous and forthright articles also helped to focus debate on such issues as the physical effect of rowing on youth and the 1935 controversy over moving the 'head of the river' race from the Parramatta to the Nepean River.

His interest in rowing attracted him to the Olympic movement: emerging as an outstanding administrator, he was dubbed 'Mr Olympics' by one journalist. President of the New South Wales Olympic Council in 1926-70 and of the Australian Olympic Federation in 1946-73, he served on the committees for the British Empire (and Commonwealth) Games in 1938, 1962 and 1966. He was appointed M.B.E. for managing the Australian team at the 1936 Berlin Olympics. His leadership of the federation helped Melbourne to secure and to make a success of the 1956 Olympic Games. Alderson was knighted that year.

An unashamed and frank exponent of amateur sport, he admired Jesse Owens and criticized the excessive nationalism and quasi-professionalism at the 1936 games; Alderson even argued that Australia should consider withdrawing from the Olympics to concentrate on the British Empire Games which he regarded as less tainted. In an era when there were few tangible rewards Sir Harold was one of a small band willing to work hard and long for amateur sport. He was respected for his down-to-earth approach and preferred to be known as Harry.

As honorary treasurer for some three decades of the executive committee of the St John Ambulance Association, New South Wales, Alderson put its finances on a secure basis, and was appointed a knight of grace of the Order of St John in 1959. He was also chairman of the Rothmans National Sport Foundation from 1966 and a member of the New South Wales Council of National Fitness from 1970. A widower, he had married Hilda Nancy Buddee at Mosman on 18 August 1966 with Presbyterian forms. Sir Harry died on 4 October 1978 at Mosman and was cremated; his wife and the daughter of his first marriage survived him.

A. L. May, *Sydney Rows* (Syd, 1970); *Sun-Herald*, 18 July 1976; *SMH*, 5 Oct 1978; NSW Rowing Assn, Annual Reports 1920-78 (ML).

R. I. CASHMAN

ALEXANDER, ALBERT ERNEST (1914-1970), professor of chemistry, was born on 5 January 1914 at Ringwood, Southampton, England, youngest of six children of William Albert Alexander, master builder, and his wife Beatrice, née Daw. Educated at Brockenhurst County School and the University of Reading (B.Sc., 1934), Bert gained first-class honours in chemistry and won an open scholarship to King's College, Cambridge (B.A., 1936; Ph.D., 1938; Sc.D., 1951), where he was awarded first-class honours in the natural science tripos. A King's College senior scholarship and a Ramsay memorial fellowship enabled him to undertake doctoral research under the supervision of Professor (Sir) Eric Rideal in the department of colloid science.

This milieu had such a profound impact on Alexander that he devoted all of his scientific life to the study of colloids and surfaces. From Rideal he also learned to apply the principles of colloid and surface chemistry to biological contexts, a theme in much of his subsequent research. Having completed his doctorate, he was awarded a Rockefeller travelling fellowship to work from December 1938 at the University of Uppsala, Sweden. In September 1939 he returned to a fellowship at King's and to work in Rideal's department on classified war projects. On 17 May 1940 Alexander married Catherine Robson at the register office, Cambridge. In 1944 he became an assistant-director of research. After the war he resumed full-time research activities which led to the publication, with his colleague Paley Johnson, of the influential text book, *Colloid Science* (Oxford, 1949).

The direction of Alexander's burgeoning career in Britain—recognized in 1947 by the award of the Tilden lectureship of the Chemical Society of London—was altered by his appointment in 1949 to the foundation chair of applied chemistry at the New South Wales University of Technology (later the University of New South Wales). While he was prompted by his wife's need to escape the rigours of European winters, he was also sympathetic to the university's objectives, which included the promotion of the application of science to the development of industry and commerce. Alexander presided enthusiastically over the rapid expansion of his school and its outposts at Newcastle, Wollongong and Broken Hill, became dean of the faculty of science and was active in the Royal Australian Chemical Institute (State president 1955).

Nonetheless, by 1956 Alexander was completely disillusioned with the governance of the university. Impressed by the academic traditions of Cambridge, he had fought stubbornly to ensure that these basic values would be incorporated into the new university as it endeavoured to free itself from what he saw as the public service mentality from which it had emerged. His hopes were dashed with the appointment as vice-chancellor of (Sir) Philip Baxter, professor of chemical engineering, with whom Alexander had conflicted on university organization.

In November that year Alexander became professor of physical chemistry at the University of Sydney, which he had long believed embodied a more enlightened approach. He persisted in his criticism of university governance in Australia. In his 1965 A. D. Ross [q.v.11] lecture at the University of Western Australia, entitled 'University organization and government: a century out-of-date?', he advocated many of the democratic and devolutionary reforms that were to be widely implemented by Australian universities in the 1980s. His reforming zeal, however, was increasingly directed towards improving the teaching of science in government high schools.

At the University of Sydney, Alexander expanded the breadth of his research programmes, collaborating with industry and with the Commonwealth Scientific and Industrial Research Organization, on whose advisory council he served in 1959-64. He published some 140 scientific papers in internationally recognized journals. Many of his research students (referred to irreverently as 'Alexander's ragtime band') were to contribute significantly to the pre-eminent international position of Australian colloid and surface science. He was elected a fellow of the Australian Academy of Science in 1960.

'Alex', as he was known outside his family, was a man of considerable warmth, compassion and humility, yet it was not easy to get close to him. He was friendly and even tempered, with a ready smile and a distinctive, plangent laugh. His latter years were clouded by personal tragedy with the death of his wife (1963) and daughter (1966). On 11 December 1965 he married a widow Gisela Gudrum Baker, née Zutavern, at the Presbyterian Church, Pymble. Stricken by a brain tumour in 1969 when serving as dean of science, he died at his Mosman home on 23 May 1970 and was cremated. His wife, and the son of his first marriage, survived him.

Aust Chemical Inst, *Procs*, 37, no 8, Aug 1970, p 211; King's College, Cambridge, *Annual Report*, 1970, p 17; *Records of Aust Academy of Science*, 2, no 2, Nov 1971, p 61.   D. H. NAPPER

ALGERANOFF, HARCOURT (1903-1967), dancer, ballet master and teacher, was born on 18 April 1903 in London, son of Thomas Richard Essex, sculptor, and his wife Alice, née Kendall, and registered as Harcourt Algernon Leighton Essex. Encouraged by a mother with theatrical inclinations, he attended a day school, took weekly dancing classes and by the age of 18 had performed in musical comedy. He joined Anna Pavlova's company in 1921 and, as the adoption of a Russianized name was a condition of his engagement, was thenceforward known as Algeranoff.

With Pavlova, he toured North America (1921-22, 1923-24 and 1924-25), the Far East (1922 and 1928-29) and Europe (1925): the repertoire, apart from Pavlova's celebrated *Coppélia* and *Giselle*, was based on short ballets and *divertissements* which offered scope for his developing talent. While in Asia, Algeranoff was encouraged to study the dances of Japan and India. Well read in English, with some colloquial Japanese and facility in five European languages, he carried out research for Pavlova in the British and the Victoria and Albert museums, London.

During their visit to Australia in 1926, his partnering of Pavlova in *Russian Dance* received favourable notice and the young (Sir) Robert Helpmann sought Algeranoff's assistance with his career. On Pavlova's 1929 visit the company performed in the mainland State capitals and at Mackay, Rockhampton and Bundaberg, Queensland. Algeranoff recorded these experiences in his happy, gossipy *My Years with Pavlova* (1957). He returned to Australia with the Dandré-Levitoff Company in 1934. In the following year he became a member of the Markova-Dolin Ballet.

It was with De Basil's Ballets Russes (1933-34 and 1937-42), however, that his gifts as a character dancer flowered: on that company's tours in 1938-39 and 1939-40 he enchanted Australian audiences in such roles as the astrologer (*Le Coq d'Or*) and Pierrot (*Carnaval*). In 1943 he joined the International Ballet where his colleague Nicholas Sergeyev gave further authority to his knowledge of classical ballet, but the work Algeranoff choreographed for that company (*For Love or Money*) was not a success.

On 10 April 1945 at the parish church in Newton Nottage, Glamorgan, Wales, Algeranoff married the French dancer Claude Leonard and in 1953 accompanied her to Australia where she appeared with Edouard Borovansky [q.v.]. While she danced, Algeranoff studied Aboriginal music and legends, and taught at the National Theatre Ballet School in Melbourne. In 1955-56 Algeranoff and Claudie, with New Zealand dancer Ronald Reay, took ballet to Central and Northern Australia under the auspices of the Australian

Children's Theatre; they performed excerpts from the classical repertoire and traditional Japanese dances. The marriage did not survive the propinquity of three dancers in a caravan; Claudie left her husband for Ronald Reay, whom she married. The Algeranoffs' only child Nöel remained with his father and was to become a sculptor.

Algeranoff's confidence was shaken by the divorce and his subsequent career seemed to lose direction. Appointments followed as choreographer with the Carl Rosa Opera Company, as ballet master (1957-58) with the Norwegian State Opera and Ballet Company, and in Australia as ballet master (1959) with the Borovansky Ballet Company. On Borovansky's untimely death, Algeranoff helped William Akers to keep the company operating until the appointment of (Dame) Peggy van Praagh. After the Borovansky company's final performance in February 1961, Algeranoff briefly revisited Europe, but was back in Australia later that year, lecturing to schools and speaking on radio for the Australian Broadcasting Commission.

He took part in the first performances of the newly formed Australian Ballet as a guest artist in 1962-63, but was not used by van Praagh to the extent he had hoped. The profession was then insufficiently established in Australia either to provide continuous and secure employment, or to exploit Algeranoff's knowledge of the classical repertoire, his sensitivity to Asian civilization and his growing interest in Aboriginal culture. In February 1962 he moved to Mildura as ballet master of the North-West Victorian Ballet Society. Although he had always been something of a gipsy, he was determined to provide a stable and healthy background for his son. Algeranoff's literacy, his humour, his love of music, his ability to communicate with children and his whimsical kindness all contributed to his popularity as a teacher and to his success in civilizing young Australians.

Only 5 ft 4 ins (162.6 cm) tall, with clear, blue eyes and thick, straight, neatly-parted, fair hair, Algeranoff possessed noticeable good looks and charm. He wore well-cut suits, but preferred to relax in the pale corduroys, cream shirt and paisley scarf of the period. Survived by his son, he died on 7 April 1967 in a motor accident near Robinvale, Victoria, and was cremated.

M. T. Clark, *Strolling Players* (Melb, 1972); E. H. Pask, *Enter the Colonies, Dancing* (Melb, 1979) and *Ballet in Australia* (Melb, 1982); *DNB*, 1961-70; K. S. Walker, *De Basil's Ballets Russes* (Lond, 1982); *Walkabout*, May 1966, p 22; *Sunraysia Daily*, 10 Apr 1967; Algeranoff papers (NL); information from Mr N. Essex, Ocean Grove, Vic, Miss Y. Gates, Flemington, Melb, Mr W. Akers, Westgarth, Melb, and Mrs D. A. Nolan, Irymple, Vic; personal information.　　　　　R. J. SOUTHEY

ALLAN, CATHERINE MABEL JOYCE (1896-1966), conchologist and museum curator, was born on 8 April 1896 at Balmain, Sydney, eighth of nine children of Joseph Stuart Allan, an artist from New Zealand, and his English wife Florence Fountain, née Hesketh. Educated privately and at Fort Street Girls' High School, Joyce intended to study medicine, but in February 1917 became temporary assistant to Charles Hedley [q.v.9], conchologist at the Australian Museum, Sydney; she helped to sort collections, drew shells to illustrate his scientific writings and was appointed permanently to the museum staff in 1920. She signed her drawings and scientific articles as 'Joyce K. Allan'. When Hedley resigned in 1924, she had temporary charge of the conchology section before working under Tom Iredale [q.v.9]; she was appointed scientific assistant in 1931.

Her principal talent was as an artist: she worked in oils, water-colour, pen-and-ink and lamp-black wash, producing some excellent drawings and paintings of molluscs, but she could be careless when rushed. Art was Miss Allan's profession and her hobby, and she exhibited paintings with the Royal Art Society of New South Wales.

While working with Iredale, she began to publish popular articles on molluscs and soon progressed to writing scientific papers, especially about the colourful, soft-bodied molluscs of the sub-class *Opisthobranchia.* She produced some twenty papers that added to scientific knowledge, wrote articles in the *Australian Museum Magazine* and contributed to the *Australian Encyclopaedia* (1925-26, 1958). Seconded to the Department of National Emergency Services in 1942 as assistant to the superintendent of air-raid precautions, she lectured and showed films on training, and was in charge of the information bureau at Air Force House, Sydney.

The first woman to be elected a fellow (1943) of the Royal Zoological Society of New South Wales, Allan succeeded Iredale in 1944 and on 1 February 1949 was appointed curator (of shells, later molluscs). She attended meetings of the Australian and New Zealand Association for the Advancement of Science, the Pacific Science Congress in New Zealand (1949) and the International Congress of Zoology in Copenhagen (1953). Her most notable collecting trips were to Lord Howe Island and to the mouth of the Clarence River in northern New South Wales where opisthobranch molluscs abounded. She belonged to the Linnean Society of New South Wales, the (Royal) Over-Seas League and the Society of Women Writers of New South Wales, and was patroness of the Malacological Club of Victoria (Society of Australia from 1956).

Allan's major achievement was her monumental book on Australian molluscs, *Aus-*

tralian Shells (Melbourne, 1950, revised 1959, reprinted 1962), the first, comprehensive work to attempt to describe the bulk of the Australian molluscan fauna and to illustrate in line, half-tone and colour a substantial proportion of them. Despite some poor illustrations, and an inadequate index to the scientific and popular names of the shells, the book remains invaluable to collectors.

Dark haired and attractive, Joyce enjoyed an active social life and played at Manly Golf Club. On 18 May 1949 at St Clement's Anglican Church, Mosman, she married a close friend Hector Walker Kirkpatrick, a retired cable officer. Accompanied by her husband, in 1953 she visited Europe and, to her satisfaction as a royalist, reached England at the time of Queen Elizabeth II's coronation celebrations.

Having studied shell collections in overseas museums, Joyce returned to Sydney, but began to suffer ill health and retired in June 1956. Appointed an honorary zoologist, she continued to work with the museum collections until 1962 and produced two more books, *Cowry Shells of World Seas* (Melbourne, 1956) and *The Sea-Horse and its Relatives* (with Gilbert Whitley [q.v.], Melbourne, 1958). Survived by her husband, she died of cerebrovascular disease on 31 August 1966 at Mosman and was cremated. Three shells, a fish and an insect were named after her.

J. H. Prince, *The First One Hundred Years of the Royal Zoological Society of N.S.W., 1879-1979* (Syd, 1979); *People* (Syd), 10 Sept 1952; Malacological Soc of Aust, *J*, 11, Mar 1968, p 50; Roy Zoological Soc of NSW, *Procs*, Feb 1967, p 12; *SMH*, 2 Dec 1950; *Daily Telegraph (Saturday Mag)*, 16 June 1956.   D. F. McMICHAEL

ALLAN, FRANCES ELIZABETH (1905-1952), statistician, was born on 11 July 1905 at St Kilda, Melbourne, third daughter of Edwin Frank Allan, journalist, and his wife Stella May [q.v.7 Allan], née Henderson. Educated at Melbourne Church of England Girls' Grammar School and the University of Melbourne (B.A., 1926; Dip.Ed., M.A., 1928), Betty shared the Dixson and Wyselaskie [q.v.6] scholarships for mathematics in 1926. Under the supervision of J. H. Michell [q.v.10], she did postgraduate work on solitary waves at the common boundary of two liquids, for which she won the Professor Nanson [q.v.10] prize and a Fred Knight research scholarship. In 1928 Allan arranged to attend Newnham College, Cambridge, and, before leaving Australia, applied for a Council for Scientific and Industrial Research studentship in 'the study of statistical methods applied to agriculture'. Tenable for two years and able to be taken abroad, a studentship

would obviate her need to live on borrowed money. News of her success and the concomitant lifting of her financial burden greeted her when she reached London.

At Cambridge, Allan studied mathematics, statistics, applied biology and general agriculture. In late 1929 she proceeded to Rothamsted Experimental Station, Harpenden, Hertfordshire, to learn the methods used by (Sir) Ronald Fisher in his pioneering statistical work. Of the three papers she produced at Rothamsted, the best known was written jointly with John Wishart and concerned the estimation of the yield of a missing plot in field experiments. Fisher found her 'helpful and congenial in co-operative work', and noted her 'rare gift for first-class mathematics'. C.S.I.R. did not hesitate to take up its option on Allan's services and on 29 September 1930 she was provisionally appointed to the division of plant industry in Canberra as the council's first biometrician. Allan was soon giving mathematical and statistical assistance to all six divisions of C.S.I.R., as well as to outside organizations.

Consulting and collaborating on a broad range of projects, she used novel statistical techniques which had a marked effect on research programmes. Among her tasks was the collection and collating of climatic data. She also contributed to research on plant diseases, noxious weeds, control of blowflies and dietary supplements for sheep. Committed to teaching, she lectured on statistical theory at Canberra University College in 1932 and gave classes in pure mathematics there in 1935-37. The C.S.I.R.'s chief executive officer (Sir) David Rivett [q.v.11] had observed in 1933: 'we need more people of her type'. Reclassified as a research officer in 1935, Allan became a foundation member that year of the Australian Institute of Agricultural Science. In 1936 she wrote a set of four instructional papers for the institute on the application of statistical methods to agriculture, delivered sixteen lectures to officers of the Canberra-based C.S.I.R. divisions, trained the first of two students from the Queensland Department of Agriculture and Stock, and lectured part time at the Australian Forestry School.

On 22 April 1940 in Trinity College chapel, Parkville, Melbourne, Allan married with Anglican rites Dr Patrick Joseph Calvert, an assistant research officer in C.S.I.R.'s division of plant industry. Although subject to government regulations requiring her to resign on marriage, Mrs Calvert was given ministerial approval to work until the end of the year. She had resumed her lectures at the forestry school in 1938 and continued them after her marriage, along with part-time research for the Commonwealth Bureau of Census and Statistics. After the birth of her son, she became secretary (1943-44) of the Canberra Nursery Kindergarten Society and president (1944-46) of the Canberra Mothercraft Society. Family commitments prevented her from accepting Rivett's offer of six months work in 1945 at Proserpine, Queensland, on chemical warfare.

Survived by her husband and 11-year-old son, Betty Calvert died of hypertensive cerebral haemorrhage on 6 August 1952 in Canberra Community Hospital and was buried in Canberra cemetery with Presbyterian forms; students from the forestry school were pallbearers at the funeral. She was remembered as having been 'kind-hearted and considerate, easy to work with, and always willing to help'. The scientific community recorded the loss occasioned by the early death of one of Canberra's best-known mathematicians.

Aust J of Statistics, 30, no 1, Apr 1988, p 15, 30B, Aug 1988, p 54; *Canb Times*, 8 Aug 1952; CSIRO records, Canb.
C. C. HEYDE

ALLAN, HERBERT TRANGMAR (1895-1967), army officer, was born on 5 January 1895 at Woolwich, Sydney, second son of Percy Allan [q.v.7], civil engineer, and his wife Alice Mary, née Trangmar, both nativeborn. Educated at St Ignatius' College, Riverview, where he shone as a scholar and an athlete, Herbert enrolled at the University of Sydney in 1914. He was commissioned in the 38th Battalion, Australian Military Forces, on 16 June; transferring to the Australian Imperial Force, in February 1917 he joined the 17th Battalion on the Western Front.

In the attack on Passchendaele Ridge, Belgium, on 9 October 1917 Allan found himself the sole surviving officer of two companies and successfully controlled them both: for his leadership in the action, he was awarded the Military Cross. 'Blue' Allan (he had fiery, red hair) was promoted captain on 24 November. At the storming of Mont St Quentin, France, in August 1918, he boldly altered the axis of his company's advance when he saw that the battalion's flank would be exposed. He was gassed in October. His A.I.F. appointment terminated in Sydney on 26 May 1919. Allan's brothers Myron and Keith had served in the 20th Battalion; Myron died from wounds in 1916. 'Blue' returned to university and studied law before completing a bachelor of arts degree (1920). Seeking a more adventurous life, he went to the mandated Territory of New Guinea and worked as a goldminer and plantation overseer. On 19 February 1929 he married Gertrude May Hodge (d. 1957) in St Mary's Catholic Church, North Sydney, and also at Randwick with Presbyterian forms; they were to remain childless.

While at Wau, New Guinea, in 1934-39, Allan was a leading member of the Returned Sailors' and Soldiers' Imperial League of Australia and president of the New Guinea Mining Association. In March 1939 he visited Canberra to persuade the government to build a road between Wau and Salamaua; he also impressed on W. M. Hughes [q.v.9] the strategic and economic importance of the Territory to Australia, and suggested that it be annexed. When World War II broke out in September, Allan hastened to Sydney where he served in the 2nd Garrison Battalion until seconded to the A.I.F. in May 1940. He embarked for the Middle East in October as a company commander in the 2nd/17th Battalion. Promoted major on 7 January 1941, he became the battalion's second-in-command in Libya. After the withdrawal to Tobruk in April, he was made brigade major, 20th Infantry Brigade. His performance during the German and Italian siege of Tobruk led to his being appointed O.B.E. in 1942. At El Alamein, Egypt, he was on headquarters staff, 9th Division.

Back in Australia by February 1943, Allan proved especially useful during training for jungle warfare. In June he was promoted temporary lieutenant colonel and proceeded to Papua as Australian army representative, Staff of Co-ordination, Milne Bay. It was probably a private arrangement that enabled him to accompany the 20th Brigade in the landing at Finschhafen, New Guinea, on 22 September. He quickly made contact with the *luluai* (headman) of Tareko to arrange for carriers and observers to report on Japanese movements. As the army advanced along the northern coast, base sub-areas were established and Allan successively took charge of several. Promoted temporary colonel, he commanded the Pacific Islands Regiment from October 1945 to February 1946; he was mentioned four times in dispatches for his service in World War II and transferred to the Reserve of Officers on 7 May with the rank of honorary colonel. 'A burly, muscular man who radiated confidence', Allan was 5 ft 11 ins (180.3 cm) tall. He was a courageous and practical leader, with a 'strong personality concealed under a cloak of irresponsibility'; he loved whisky and smoked heavily.

With two partners, after the war Allan operated a transport company at Rabaul, New Britain. As a delegate to the 1947 national congress of the R.S.L., he criticized Australian policy towards the Territory of Papua-New Guinea and again urged its annexation. In 1951 he warned of the possibility of a local, communist, guerilla movement. A devoted couple, 'Blue' and Gertrude lived in Sydney, travelled in Europe and finally settled on a banana-farm at Mullaway, near Woolgoolga, New South Wales. Allan died there on 23 May

1967 and was buried in the Catholic section of Coffs Harbour cemetery.

C. E. W. Bean, *The A.I.F. in France*, 1917-18 (Syd, 1933, 1942); K. W. Mackenzie, *The Story of the Seventeenth Battalion A.I.F. in the Great War, 1914-1918* (Syd, 1946); D. Dexter, *The New Guinea Offensives* (Canb, 1961); B. Maughan, *Tobruk and El Alamein* (Canb, 1966); *PIM*, July, Oct 1967; *SMH*, 14, 22 Mar, 4, 17 Apr 1939, 29, 30 Oct 1947, 14 May 1951; *Sunday Herald*, 21 May 1950; information from Lieut Col A. J. Newton, Dickson, ACT.   A. J. HILL

ALLAN, MARGARET THEADORA (1889-1968), community worker, was born on 2 June 1889 at the Manse, Charters Towers, Queensland, third child of Rev. Alexander McWatt Allan, Presbyterian minister, and his second wife Margaret Jane, née Menzies, both Scottish born. McWatt was transferred to Brisbane about 1893 and to New South Wales in 1903; after several pastorates, in December 1908 he was appointed to Tweed Heads where he was killed in a sulky accident on 9 May 1909. His daughter Margaret was a secretary for the Young Women's Christian Association in Colombo before being employed in 1936 by the Travellers' Aid Society of New South Wales, which had been a branch of the Y.W.C.A. in Sydney since 1900. She was appointed secretary in 1938 when the society became a separate organization and opened a room at Central Railway Station.

Appointed organizing secretary in 1940, from the outset Miss Allan insisted on full control of the office, staff, policy decisions and financial arrangements. She steered the society through its early years of fund-raising and was the major force behind the welfare work which she directed from the travellers' aid rest-room at Central Station. She publicized the society through her talks, canvassed for large donations and negotiated with affiliated societies, among them the Country Women's Association, the National Council of Women and the Good Neighbour Council. Although supported by an executive of women volunteers and a small committee who applauded her energy, it was Margaret who made the decisions.

The major objective of the organization was to give aid and protection to travellers, especially to women and children; as the society came to encompass all travellers—irrespective of sex, age or background, and whether they went by aeroplane, ship or train—the work of Margaret Allan became more widely known and appreciated. In 1966 the T.A.S. provided accommodation for a total of 1762 women and children at the Lodge in Elizabeth Street (which it had purchased in 1952), many school children were met at Central Railway Station and employment was found for young women. From a staff of two who assisted 1147 travellers in 1938, the society had a staff of ten to assist 33 073 travellers in 1968.

At the T.A.S. annual meeting in 1963 the patron Lady Cutler paid tribute to Miss Allan for her long, loyal and cheerful service: her personality and dedication had made the society a success. Living in North Sydney, Margaret belonged to the Daughters of the Manse Association; for her services to the community, she was awarded the British Empire medal in January 1968. She died on 14 December that year in St Vincent's Hospital, Darlinghurst, and was cremated; her estate was sworn for probate at $14 792.

The Story of the Sydney Young Women's Christian Association (Syd, nd); Travellers' Aid Soc (NSW), Annual Meeting Reports, 1 July 1938-3 Sept 1968, *and* Cttee Meeting Reports, 21 May 1936-5 May 1941, *and* Executive Minutes, 6 June 1941-13 Sept 1948 (Travellers' Aid Soc rooms, Central Railway Station, Syd); information from Miss A. Buchanan, Ferguson Memorial L, Syd.   NOELINE J. KYLE

ALLAN, NORMAN THOMAS WILLIAM (1909-1977), police commissioner, was born on 3 June 1909 at Lithgow, New South Wales, son of Thomas Sorbie Allan, an ironroller from Scotland, and his native-born wife Florence Gertrude Lewis, née Price. The family moved to Sydney where Norman was educated at Haberfield Public School and became a junior telephone technician. Having been retrenched, he joined the State police force on probation on 18 September 1929 and was formally accepted the day after he had married Elsie Lillian Wild on 17 September 1930 at St David's Presbyterian Church, Haberfield.

With grey eyes and a strong nose, Allan was 5 ft 11½ ins (181.6 cm) tall and weighed 11 st. 11 lb. (74.8 kg). Following a brief spell on the beat at Redfern, he prosecuted at Central Criminal Court from 1932 until transferred to headquarters in 1938. A Protestant and a Freemason, he was assistant from 1944 to three police commissioners, W. J. MacKay [q.v.10] (1935-48), J. F. Scott (1948-52) and C. J. Delaney [q.v.] (1952-62). Promoted to the rank of inspector in 1948 and superintendent in 1956, he was commended for 'exceptional skill and ability' in securing the extradition and conviction of Stephen Leslie Bradley [q.v.] for the kidnapping and murder of Graeme Thorn.

A competent administrator, known as 'Norman the Foreman', Allan was acting deputy-commissioner in 1959 and became chief commissioner of police on 28 February

1962. With command over 5000 men, he could be paternalistic and charming, but also autocratic, pedantic and inconsiderate; he maddened his secretaries by changing his mind, found it difficult to delegate responsibility and was increasingly unable to cope with the media. He showed pride in his force, but his assertion—later that year—that the local police would not tolerate breaches of the liquor and gambling laws at Broken Hill engendered scepticism in parliament and the press. Allan believed that, by working with his men in the field, he kept in touch with underlying problems: he took personal charge of the investigation into the bizarre deaths of Gilbert Bogle and Margaret Chandler [qq.v.] during the night of 31 December 1962, only to be as baffled as everyone else.

Considering them to be the nearest approach to the man on the beat, Allan introduced additional motorcycle police who remained in radio contact with headquarters. He planned to have the finest equipment available, with every type of electronic device for crime detection, and secretly initiated illegal telephone interceptions about 1967. He upgraded police training and encouraged his men to take degrees or diplomas in law and criminology at the University of Sydney.

Physically courageous, Allan personally negotiated with a petty criminal Wallace George Mellish who defied police in a siege at Glenfield in July 1968 by holding his girlfriend Beryl Muddle and their baby as hostages. Having persuaded Allan to arrange his marriage to Beryl, and to provide the wedding ring and the feast, Mellish refused to surrender as promised. Allan, by then the subject of international media attention, acceded at gunpoint to Mellish's demand to be furnished with an Armalite rifle and 200 bullets. The marriage celebrant Rev. Clyde John Paton persuaded Mellish to surrender five days later. Both Allan and Paton were commended by the Queen for bravery.

In November 1971 Sergeant Philip Arantz of the computer section declared that Allan was party to falsifying official statistics on 'solved' crimes. Although an attempt failed to have Arantz declared insane, he was dismissed without a pension in January 1972. Allan was not charged with any offence and negotiated early retirement in May, with a pension and two years salary. He recommended Frederick John Hanson [q.v.] as his successor.

A member of Manly Bowling Club, Allan lived at Balgowlah. In 1963 he had shared a £30 000 winning lottery ticket with a friend. Awarded Queen Elizabeth II's coronation and police good conduct medals, as well as the Queen's medal for distinguished service (1957), he was appointed M.V.O. in 1963 and C.M.G in 1973. Survived by his wife and son,

Allan died of a cerebral neoplasm on 28 January 1977 at Manly and was accorded a state funeral. When the hearse stopped suddenly as it left St Andrew's Anglican Cathedral *en route* to Northern Suburbs crematorium, an inspector remarked: 'He's changed his mind again'. Some observers later alleged that a long-established culture of corruption had become more deeply entrenched during Allan's term as chief commissioner, and that Premier (Sir) Robert Askin had continued to support his police chief because they had 'established an arrangement under which thousands of dollars weekly in bribes and payments were handed over by the gambling clubs'.

D. Hickie, *The Prince and the Premier* (Syd, 1985); B. Swanton and G. Hannigan, *Police Source Book 2* (Canb, 1985); D. Stewart, *Royal Commission of Inquiry into Alleged Telephone Interceptions* (Canb, 1986); E. Whitton, *Can of Worms*, 1-2 (Syd, 1986, 1987); *Aust Security J*, June 1969, p 13; *NSW Police News*, Aug, Nov 1990; *SMH*, 1 Jan 1957, 30 July 1963, 27 Jan 1966, 16 July 1969, 1 Mar 1972, 29 Jan 1977, 9 Dec 1990; *Daily Telegraph* (Syd), 3 Feb 1977; Allan service record (NSW Police Dept); information from Sergt A. Small, NSW Police Media Unit, Syd.   EVAN WHITTON

ALLCOT, JOHN CHARLES (1888-1973), artist, was born on 14 November 1888 at Liverpool, Lancashire, England, son of George Allcot, mariner, and his wife Mary Elizabeth, née Phillips. Educated at Arnot Street Board School, at the age of 14 John was apprenticed to Tillotson & Son Ltd, lithographers, and attended classes at the Liverpool Institute and School of Art. In 1906 he worked in the Mersey tugboats and next year sailed as a deck-boy in the barque, *Invermark*. He loved painting and would scrounge ship's paint, sailcloth and handkerchiefs with which to depict the sea, ships and life on board.

Arriving in Sydney in the *Miltiades* in 1909, Allcot signed on with the old clipper, *Antiope*. He worked in coastal, island and intercolonial vessels out of Sydney before giving up the sea in 1912. At the Pitt Street Congregational Church on 13 September 1915 he married Elsie Alma Johnson, but they later became estranged. Supporting himself by painting theatre sets, he obtained commissions for ship paintings from Sydney photographers and toured the countryside, completing landscapes which he exhibited regularly with the Royal Art Society of New South Wales from 1920. About this time he formed an enduring friendship with Phyllis Zanker.

He gained widespread recognition in the 1920s with a series of oil paintings (on the founding of the Australian colonies) which were later acquired by the Australasian Pioneers' Club. Other commissions followed.

Allcot also worked as an illustrator and wrote articles about the sea for the *Sydney Mail*. In the 1940s he painted the seas for ship-models built by the sculptor Robert Klippel. Allcot's painting of the *Cutty Sark* was presented to the Duke of Edinburgh in 1954.

Allcot was dark and diminutive, less than five feet (152.4 cm) tall. His studio became a meeting-place for those interested in ships, paintings and models. Regular visitors included maritime artists Oswald Brett and Ian Hansen who watched him work and listened to his colourful stories of seafaring. Allcot exhibited landscapes and still lifes at Beard, Watson [q.v.12] & Co. Ltd (1962); his paintings of ships were shown at Underwood Galleries (1965) and those of twelve windjammers at the San Francisco Maritime Museum, United States of America (1969). In Sydney he held a successful exhibition (1970) at Proud's [q.v.11] Art Gallery to celebrate the bicentenary of James Cook's [q.v.1] landing in Australia; Allcot's last showing took place at the Copperfield Gallery (1973).

Painting to tried and tested conventions, with impeccable attention to detail, Allcot used water-colour and gouache, and oils. His work was prolific and romantic. At a time of great change in the shipping industry, he specialized in nostalgic views of sailing ships and steamers, and found an appreciative market of ship-owners, captains, crews and their families. While best known for his ships, he continued to enjoy painting landscapes. A fellow (1956) of the local Royal Art Society, Allcot was a member of the League of Ancient Mariners and of the Shiplovers' Society. He was elected an honorary life member (1962) of the Australasian Pioneers' Club and appointed O.B.E. in 1970. Survived by his wife, son and daughter, he died on 13 July 1973 at North Sydney and was cremated with Anglican rites. His work is represented in private and public collections in Australia and abroad.

John Allcot, Marine Artist (Syd, 1978); P. D. Lark and R. McKenzie, *A History of the Australasian Pioneers' Club, Sydney, 1910-1988* (Brisb, 1988); *People* (Syd), 3 Oct 1956; *Pix*, 29 Mar 1969; *Sea History*, Summer 1984; *Aust Sea Heritage*, no 28, Autumn 1991; *SMH*, 2 Mar 1970; Allcot papers held by and information from Mr O. Brett, Levittown, NY; Collection of Roy Art Soc of NSW exhibition cats, 1920-67 (Roy Art Soc of NSW, Syd); information from Mr R. Allcot, Harbord, and Mr I. Hansen, Hunters Hill, Syd.   DAINA FLETCHER

ALLEN, ARTHUR DENIS WIGRAM (1894-1967), solicitor and aviator, was born on 19 August 1894 at Burwood, Sydney, second of four children of native-born parents Arthur Wigram Allen, solicitor, and his wife Ethel Grace, née Lamb. Belonging to one of Sydney's oldest and most respected families, Denis was educated at Tudor House school, Moss Vale, and from 1906 in England at Summer Fields school, Oxford, and St Peter's College, Radley, Berkshire (1908-12). From boyhood, he was a close friend of his cousins Dundas Allen (later his partner) and (Sir) George ('Gubby') Allen who was to captain the 1936-37 English cricket team.

Back home, Denis was articled on 16 July 1913 to Alfred Macartney Hemsley, a solicitor in the family firm. Denis was a skilled horseman and a successful amateur rider at picnic race meetings. When he joined the Royal Naval Air Service in England in June 1916, he brought 'the same delicate touch to an aeroplane'. Cool and courageous as an acting flight commander, he served in France and won the Distinguished Service Cross that year. Transferring to the Royal Air Force as an 'aeroplane and seaplane officer', he was promoted captain in April 1918. He was appointed technical officer on the staff of the director-general of aircraft production, flew as a test-pilot and was awarded the Air Force Cross in November. Later he did similar work for Thomas Sopwith; Allen's British commercial flying licence was No. 2.

Returning to Sydney in 1919 to carry on the family tradition, he resumed his articles on 12 December, was admitted as a solicitor on 21 October 1922 and became a partner in Allen, Allen [qq.v.1,3] & Hemsley. He would have preferred to continue flying. At All Saints Anglican Church, Singleton, on 9 November that year he married Mary Beatrice Dangar, a grand-daughter of H. C. Dangar [q.v.4]. Molly had worked with a voluntary aid detachment in London. She died on 4 April 1934, leaving three sons.

Allen was chairman of New England Airways Ltd and from 1935 of its successor, Airlines of Australia Ltd. He served on a committee of veteran airmen appointed in 1940 to recruit 50 000 men for the Empire Air Training Scheme and was a founder of Air Force House in Sydney. During World War II he drove his father's 1916 Detroit electric brougham which he was to present to the Museum of Applied Arts and Sciences in 1947. Allen did much to hold the law firm together while many of its partners were on active service. He won the confidence of clients by his common sense and meticulous attention to detail. Modest about his own ability as a lawyer among more gifted men, after the war he restructured the firm to divide the equity among all the partners. He retired late in 1963. Allen was chairman of Mount Kembla Collieries Ltd, and a director of Australian Mutual Fire Insurance Society Ltd and of Butler [q.v.] Air Transport Ltd; he strongly opposed B.A.T.'s takeover by Ansett Transport Industries Ltd.

Tall and rather loose-limbed, with the pale-blue eyes of his family, Allen was extremely conservative in his habits. He belonged to the Union, Royal Sydney Golf and Australian Jockey clubs. On 20 February 1943 at St Mark's Church, Darling Point, he had married Philippa Nancy, daughter of Sir Colin Stephen [q.v.12]. She shared Denis's love of horses and owned Advocate, winner of the 1952 Victoria Derby. Survived by his wife, and by the sons of his first marriage, Allen died on 4 June 1967 at his Double Bay home and was cremated. His youngest son Patrick, deputy fleet training manager with the British Overseas Airways Corporation, was to pilot the supersonic Concorde on her early development flights.

M. Gifford, *I Can Hear the Horses* (Lond, 1975); *SMH*, 5 June 1967; Maj-Gen the Rev C. A. Osborne, Funeral oration (ts, ADB, Canb); information from and papers held by Mr D. W. Allen, Birchgrove, Syd, and information from Mrs B. M. Allen, Edgecliff, Syd.   MARTHA RUTLEDGE

ALLEN, ARTHUR MAX (1891-1979), surveyor-general and soldier, was born on 21 February 1891 at Leichhardt, Sydney, son of Arthur Allen, railways clerk, and his wife Ethel Beatrice, née Primrose, both native-born. Educated at public schools and privately while his father was district superintendent of railways at Murrurundi, Max joined the Department of Lands in 1908 as a cadet draughtsman and was stationed at Tamworth and Armidale. He was licensed in 1913 and worked as a temporary salaried surveyor at Orange and Goulburn.

Fair haired, grey eyed, of middle height and medium build, Allen was commissioned in June 1915 in the Australian Imperial Force. From March 1916 he fought in Palestine and Syria with the 1st Field Squadron, Anzac Mounted Division, and met his future patron (Sir) Michael Bruxner [q.v.7]. Promoted lieutenant (1916), captain (1917) and major (1918), Allen was awarded the Military Cross in 1918 and twice mentioned in dispatches. After serving at A.I.F. Headquarters, Cairo, in 1919 he gained experience in forestry at University College of North Wales, Bangor, and in technology with Troughton & Simms, mathematical instrument makers, London. He returned to New South Wales in November, was placed on the Reserve of Officers and in March 1920 became staff surveyor at Cooma.

Appointed State migration officer at the Commonwealth government's Migration and Settlement Office, London, in January 1924, Allen travelled extensively in Britain and Germany. On 4 September in the parish church of St Clement Danes, Middlesex, he married Hazel May Stone. Back home in 1928, he was attached to the Metropolitan Land Board and rose to senior surveyor in 1931. He was a councillor (from 1931), vice-president (1935-37), fellow (1934) and life member (1949) of the Institution of Surveyors, New South Wales, a fellow (1938) of the Commonwealth Institute of Valuers and a foundation member of the State branch of the Town and Country Planning Institute of Australia.

Capable and conscientious, formidable and gruff, Allen was promoted surveyor-general in 1937; he was also chief mining surveyor and president of the Board of Surveyors. In 1940 he organized the raising of No. 1 Field Survey Unit, soon to be incorporated with No. 2 Australian Field Survey Company under H. P. G. Clews [q.v.]. From October Major Allen served as deputy assistant-director of survey, headquarters, Eastern Command. He remained surveyor-general, but additionally acted as State survey liaison officer, co-ordinating civilian and military programmes to produce urgently needed maps of Australia's strategic areas. When Japan entered the war and General MacArthur [q.v.] assumed his command, in June 1942 Allen (as temporary lieutenant colonel) became deputy-director of survey at First Australian Army headquarters, Toowoomba, Queensland.

By March 1943 the direct threat to Australia had receded and Allen returned to New South Wales as State director of postwar reconstruction and development. His transfer excited parliamentary questions from J. T. Lang [q.v.9] who alleged that Allen had previously been connected with the New Guard. In 1945 Allen was appointed chairman of the Closer Settlement Advisory Board. By and large he succeeded in the difficult task of acquiring, designating and disposing of land under the War Service Land Settlement Act (1941), but faced the Pye brothers' legal challenge (1945-56) to the resumption of Ghoolendaadi which was eventually taken to the Privy Council.

Having retired in 1956, Allen remained on the Metropolitan Land Board and focussed his energies on the Lane Cove National Park Trust, of which he was a foundation member and president (1957-61): the trust was to name Max Allen Drive after him. He was a great talker, an idiosyncratic golfer and a member of the Imperial Service Club. Survived by his wife and daughter, he died on 28 November 1979 in Concord Repatriation General Hospital and was cremated.

H. P. G. Clews, *Memories of 2 Australian Field Survey Company 1940-1944* (np, 1966); *PD* (NSW), 172, 1943, p 235; *NSW Valuer*, Apr 1930; *Aust Surveyor*, Mar 1932, June 1934, Sept 1937, Dec

1943, Mar 1980; Survey Ex-Servicemen's Assn (NSW), *Bulletin*, 66, 1980, 67, 1981; *SMH*, 12, 13 Oct, 22 Nov 1943, 8 Jan 1944, 8 Dec 1979; No 1 Field Survey Unit, Engineers, AIF, records (AWM); information from Mrs M. Booth, Bayview, Syd, Mr L. N. Fletcher and Brig D. Macdonald, Syd, and Col J. Hillier, Canb.   JOHN ATCHISON

ALLEN, ARTHUR SAMUEL (1894-1959), army officer and accountant, was born on 10 March 1894 at Hurstville, Sydney, fifth child of John Allen, a native-born engine driver, and his English wife Annie, née Hadfield. Educated at Hurstville Superior Public School, Arthur worked as an audit clerk in the New South Wales Government Railways. He served in the cadets and in the 39th Battalion, Australian Military Forces; commissioned in September 1913, he transferred to the 38th Battalion. On 24 June 1915 he was appointed to the Australian Imperial Force and in August embarked for Egypt with reinforcements for the 13th Battalion. In March 1916 he became a platoon commander and was promoted captain in the newly-formed 45th Battalion.

Arriving in France on 8 June, Allen survived the terrible German artillery barrage at Pozières in August and endured the severe winter of 1916-17 on the Somme. In the battle of Messines, Belgium, from 7 to 11 June 1917, he led repeated bombing attacks on enemy trenches, capturing 120 prisoners and two machine-guns. So intense was the fighting that the battalion lost 16 officers and 552 soldiers; for much of the time it was organized as one company with Allen as its front-line commander. For his deeds, he was awarded the Distinguished Service Order. Promoted major in July, he commanded the 45th during the fighting at Dernancourt, France, in April 1918. Next month, as temporary lieutenant colonel, he had charge of the 48th Battalion in the costly attempt to seize Monument Wood, near Villers Bretonneux. From June to October he attended the senior officers' course at Aldershot, England. On 20 November he was promoted substantive lieutenant colonel and, at the age of 24, given command of the 13th Battalion. A buoyant leader, he was mentioned in dispatches and awarded the French Croix de Guerre for his service on the Western Front.

Although Allen's A.I.F. appointment terminated in Australia on 10 November 1919, he remained active in the Militia. On 7 December 1921 at Rollands Plains, New South Wales, he married Agnes Mona Blair Mackay with Presbyterian forms. Establishing himself as an accountant, he became a partner in the firm of Truman Harrison & Co., Sydney, and a fellow (1932) of the Institute of Chartered Accountants in Australia. Allen successively

commanded the 13th, 41st, 18th and 36th battalions until 1933 when he was promoted colonel and took charge of the 14th Brigade. On 1 May 1938 he was made brigadier and in October 1939 chosen to command the 16th Brigade, 6th Division, A.I.F. He was blunt, honest, 'choleric yet kindly', and 'completely without affectation or pomposity'. His military lore stemmed from experience rather than study, and 'was based on a wide and sympathetic knowledge of men in battle'. Short, thickset and powerfully built, he was affectionately known as 'Tubby'.

Having sailed in the first Australian-New Zealand convoy to the Middle East, on 13 February 1940 Allen and his staff proceeded to Palestine to establish the nucleus of a divisional headquarters. He forged good relations with British troops, government officials and the local community, and ensured the comfort of future A.I.F. contingents by improving camps, services and amenities; for his efforts, he was appointed C.B.E. in 1941. During the British advance into Libya the 16th Brigade breached the Italian defences at Bardia (3-5 January) and Tobruk (21-22 January). Allen's organization, enthusiasm and attention to detail contributed to the defeat of the enemy in both engagements, and he was to be appointed C.B. later that year.

He left on 18 March 1941 for Greece. There he was confronted by a powerful German army which had the crucial advantage of air superiority. The Anzac Corps fought a series of rearguard actions, enabling each part of the force to withdraw in ordered sequence. At the Piniós Gorge on 17 April, Allen coolly held his ground until the pre-arranged time to fall back; he called it 'a fantastic battle'. He embarked with his troops from the port of Kalámai (Kalamáta) on 27 April and was awarded the Greek Military Cross for his part in the campaign.

On 18 June Allen took command of the 7th Division, then engaged against Vichy-French forces in Syria; his temporary promotion to major general was to be made permanent in August. Following the defeat of the French in July, he spent the next five months preparing the Tripoli fortress for a possible German attack. Mentioned in dispatches, he returned to Australia in March 1942.

Allen arrived in Port Moresby, Papua, on 13 August to take charge of operations against Japanese units advancing over the Owen Stanley Range. His division halted the Japanese at Ioribaiwa and moved on the offensive, but harsh terrain and logistical problems impeded progress. From 11 October Allen became the target of galling messages from General Douglas MacArthur and General Sir Thomas Blamey [qq.v.], criticizing the slowness of the advance. The complaints were based on ignorance of the conditions and were not justified. Though his forces broke through at Eora Creek on 28 October, throwing open the mountain paths to Kokoda, Allen was relieved of his command next day. He later served in appointments of lesser operational importance in Port Moresby and the Northern Territory.

At a subsequent interview with Allen, MacArthur expressed real or feigned surprise that his messages had distressed him, and claimed to have nothing but praise for Allen and his troops, whom he had merely been urging to greater efforts. Allen replied: 'Well, that's not the way to urge Australians'. He was further vindicated in October 1944 when Blamey recommended that he be appointed K.B.E. Allen was transferred to the Reserve of Officers on 30 April 1945. He possessed experience of front-line warfare rare among generals in any army. A knighthood, which would have been automatic in World War I, did not eventuate.

After the war he became senior partner in the firm of A. S. Allen & Co., chartered accountants of Sydney. His recreations were golf and bowls. Survived by his wife and two sons, he died of hypertensive cerebrovascular disease on 25 January 1959 at Concord; following a military funeral, he was cremated. Allen's portrait by (Sir) William Dargie is in the Australian War Memorial, Canberra.

C. E. W. Bean, *The A.I.F. in France*, 4-6 (Syd, 1933, 1937, 1942); J. E. Lee, *The Chronicle of the 45th Battalion, A.I.F.* (Syd, 1924); T. A. White, *The History of the Thirteenth Battalion, A.I.F.* (Syd, 1924); G. Long, *To Benghazi* (Canb, 1952) and *Greece, Crete and Syria* (Canb, 1953); L. Wigmore, *The Japanese Thrust* (Canb, 1957); D. McCarthy, *South-West Pacific Area—First Year* (Canb, 1959); D. M. Horner, *Crisis of Command* (Canb, 1978); *Reveille* (Syd), 1 Nov 1939; AWM records.

A. J. SWEETING

ALLEN, SIR WILLIAM GUILDFORD (1897-1977), grazier and businessman, was born on 26 April 1897 at Boobera, near Moree, New South Wales, youngest of ten children of Robert Cornelius Allen, a grazier from the United States of America, and his native-born wife Margaret Anne, née Allen, a cousin. William was educated at St Joseph's College, Sydney, and at Nudgee College, Brisbane. He worked on the family property, Carbucky, at Goondiwindi, New South Wales; with his four elder brothers, he engaged in stock and land dealings until 1923 when he bought Limbri Downs at Hughenden in North Queensland. On 13 July 1927 he married Mona Maria Nolan (d. 1956) at the Sacred Heart Church, Pymble, Sydney.

Over the next fifty years Allen put together a pastoral empire of sheep and cattle properties, beginning in 1931 when he bought Elvira and Whitewood at Hughenden and Glenallen at Morella. Acquiring Bexley in 1945, he established Bexreach Shorthorn Stud and the Bexley Merino Stud in 1949. The latter was to become the biggest, privately-owned merino stud in the State: at times its flocks exceeded 150 000. In 1948 and 1949 Allen purchased Westbury and Elmore at Longreach, then Ludgate and Ohio at Prairie in 1951; North Yanburra followed in 1952 and Alice Downs, Blackall, in 1959; Nukinenda at Esk was added in 1963. By consolidating his properties, Allen eventually acquired a twenty-five-mile (40.2 km) frontage on the Thomson River. Intensive development methods dramatically increased productivity and his wool consignments constituted one of the largest, privately-owned clips in Australia. A senior partner in the pastoral company, Allen, Allen & Crawshaw, he also served as a member and deputy-chairman (1948-58) of the Longreach Shire Council.

Having taken a radio receiver to Hughenden in 1925, Allen recognized the importance of communications for Queensland's sparsely populated north-western region. As a director of the Longreach Printing Co. from the mid-1950s, he helped to improve the *Longreach Leader* newspaper. In 1957 he founded the Central Queensland Broadcasting Corporation Pty Ltd and acquired the Longreach-based radio station 4LG; by 1962 the network included 4LM Mount Isa, 4VL Charleville, 4WK Warwick and 4IP Brisbane. Some 6 ft 1 in. (185.4 cm) tall, with penetrating hazel eyes, an olive complexion and thin lips, 'W. G.' was persuaded that being the youngest in a large family instilled the desire to excel: his achievements were regarded as 'not normally associated with those of an individual but more that of a corporate body'. During the 1960s Allen was actively involved in the central council of the State branch of the Australian Country Party and was to become a life member of the National Party. Appointed C.B.E. in 1970, he was knighted in 1973.

On 18 March 1961 he had married a nurse Josephine Agnes Peacock in St Francis's Catholic Church, West End, Brisbane. Sir William suffered a stroke in 1974; he died on 3 January 1977 at Benowa and was buried in Nudgee cemetery. His wife survived him, as did the daughter and two sons of his first marriage; his Queensland estate was sworn for probate at $400 001.

Notable Queenslanders (Brisb, 1975); M. McCosker, *Heritage Merino* (Brisb, 1988); *Qld Country Life*, 18 June 1970, 6 Jan 1977; *Longreach Leader*, 19 June 1970; *Courier-Mail*, 4 Jan 1977; family papers (held by Sir W. G. Allen, jnr, Hamilton, Brisb).

ANGELIKA G. I. MOFFAT

ALLISON, SIR WILLIAM JOHN (1903-1966), businessman, was born on 7 March 1903 in South Melbourne, son of Victorian-born parents Alfred James Allison, carpenter, and his wife Florence Nightingale, née Gray. John left Middle Park State School at the age of 13 to work as an office-boy with Permewan [q.v.5] Wright Ltd, operators of retail grocery chain-stores. He studied accountancy at night, passing the examinations of both the Commonwealth and Federal institutes of accountants: on the basis of his results, he gained admission to the faculty of commerce at the University of Melbourne. Transferred to Sydney, he did not complete his degree. On 8 February 1930 he married a clerk Olive Dorothy Becroft at St John's Anglican Church, Glebe; they were to have two sons and a daughter.

Fascinated by accountancy, Allison rose rapidly in the firm, with the support of its New South Wales manager W. R. Williams whom he succeeded in 1939. In 1940 Allison returned to Melbourne as general manager. He became managing director in 1947 and chairman in 1952. A stickler for accurate accounting, he allowed no hint of insider-trading or nepotism, demanded punctuality from employees and forbade alcohol at the workplace. In later years he envisaged the company becoming a broadly-based chain of supermarkets and moved towards this end as architect of the merger with Grocery & General Merchants Ltd.

He served on the council of the Melbourne Chamber of Commerce from 1946 (vice-president, 1948; president, 1952-55) and was president of the Associated Chambers of Commerce of Australia in 1951-53. The latter position provided a public platform for his views. At the prime minister's national conference on inflation in 1951, Allison's call to the government to fight inflation by monetary and fiscal measures made a profound impression on Federal ministers. A close relationship developed with Prime Minister (Sir) Robert Menzies [q.v.] and Allison was invited to join the elite, eccentric, power-broking and very private West Brighton Club. Menzies frequently visited his home where the two men talked for long hours into the night. When import restrictions were imposed in March 1952, Allison was appointed a member of the Commonwealth Consultative Committee on Imports and served on that body for six years. Although theoretically a 'free trader', he recognized that pockets of industry required protection.

Government concern for the necessity to be prepared for war led to Allison's appointment in 1953 as chairman of the board of business administration, Department of Defence. Among the issues it considered were the purchase of a Jindivic pilotless aircraft,

the need to maintain a submarine capacity and whether to buy Mirage aeroplanes. He subsequently became chairman of a committee that reviewed rates of pay, allowances and retirement benefits for servicemen. His concern to establish superannuation for workers, in the defence forces and elsewhere, arose from his family's suffering after his father's death.

In 1955 Allison was appointed a member of the business advisory group of the Australian Atomic Energy Commission. He believed that the potential advantages of atomic power for peaceful use far outweighed its potential as a 'destroyer of mankind'; he also thought that, as coal and water were freely available in the south-eastern States, the development of atomic power would probably occur in such places as South Australia and the Northern Territory. As a policy-shaping body, the business advisory group initially made a strong contribution, but by 1958 had been reduced to being a 'rubber stamp' for the commission's policies.

Having been persuaded to stand for the Melbourne City Council in 1954, Allison was elected unopposed for the Lonsdale Ward and became chairman of the finance committee. Somewhat over-extended and disillusioned with council politics, he resigned in 1958. Duty to government continued to attract him and he served as chairman (1958-65) of the Export Development Council. He considered exports to be crucial in determining the rate of Australia's economic growth and recommended taxation rebates as incentives for producers.

His lifelong commitment to education and training led to Allison's appointment as a member of the council of the University of Melbourne in 1955. He played an influential part in the establishment of the university's summer school of business administration, and was chairman of its board of management and principal from 1956. Keen to establish a professional status for businessmen, he was foundation president (1964) of the Victorian Institute of Directors. He was knighted in 1954 and elevated to K.B.E. in 1959.

Generally good humoured, with a pleasant voice, engaging smile and erect carriage, Sir John had great managerial ability, as well as a quality of friendship and an ability to delegate which partly accounted for his success. People were inspired by him and worked hard for him. On occasions he would be applauded by his exhausted friends as he handed to charity a cheque, the funds of which had been raised by them. A number of worthy causes attracted his interest. He was treasurer (1944-48) and president (1949-50) of the 'Uncle Bob's Club' which collected money for the orthopaedic hospital at Frankston; he was also chairman (1955-56) of the annual Red Cross appeal.

A gregarious man who often enjoyed a drink with his many friends, Allison belonged to numerous clubs, among them the Australian, Hawthorn and Commonwealth. He was a director of Murray Shipping Ltd, Robert Harper [q.v.9] & Co. Ltd, Holeproof Industries Ltd and Peters [q.v.11] Ice Cream (Vic.) Ltd (Petersville Australia Ltd). His family life was unpretentious, his private interests simple—reading and early-morning swimming year-round at the Middle Park baths. Survived by his wife and sons, he died of a coronary occlusion on 20 September 1966 at his Kew home and was buried in Boroondara cemetery. Menzies, Harold Holt and (Sir) John McEwen [qq.v.] paid tribute to his public service and his contribution towards the encouragement of exports. Allison's portrait by Paul Fitzgerald hangs in the graduate school of management, University of Melbourne; another is held by the family.

Melb Chamber of Commerce, *Record*, June 1951, June 1952, Jan 1954, Apr 1954; *Univ Melb Gazette*, Oct 1966; *VHM*, Nov 1966; *Search* (Syd), 6, no 9, 1975; *Argus*, 6 Oct 1949, 18 Apr 1951, 13 Jan, 18 May, 1 June 1954; *Age* (Melb), 12 Aug, 25 Sept, 11-16 Dec 1954, 31 May 1955, 10 Apr 1958, 13 June 1959, 9 Feb 1960, 4 Feb 1961, 22 Oct 1964, 20 Jan, 1 Apr, 26 May 1965, 22 Sept 1966; *Herald* (Melb), 26-28 May, 20 June 1953, 1, 21 Jan, 6 June 1954, 21 Sept 1966; *Sun News-Pictorial*, 26 May, 1 July, 8 Oct 1965; Dept of Defence, Personal correspondence, A 595459/3 (AA); information from Mr J. B. Allison, Kew, and Mr J. Shaw, Glen Iris, Melb.

MERRAN SAMUEL

ALLMAN, GEORGE FAUNCE (1883-1967), organist, choirmaster and music teacher, was born on 27 December 1883 at Yass, New South Wales, eldest of four children of native-born parents Edward McCarthy Allman, road superintendent, and his wife Henrietta Elizabeth, née Faunce. Two of George's great-grandfathers were Francis Allman and Alured Tasker Faunce [qq.v.1]. As a civil engineer, Edward moved about and George attended five schools before completing his education in 1897-98 at Sydney Church of England Grammar School (Shore) where his musical talent was encouraged. He worked as an accounts clerk with Burns, Philp [qq.v.7,11] & Co. Ltd for five years and hated it. Rather than accept a transfer to the South Pacific, he resigned to face the uncertainties of being a full-time musician and teacher.

When his mentor Arthur Mason went to England in 1907, Allman took over temporarily as organist at St James's Church, Sydney; his appointment (which was to last for fifty-three years) became permanent when Mason did not return. Allman found a popular church, with a choral tradition dating back to 1827 and a developing Anglo-Catholic liturgy. Introducing new English music for the elaborate choral settings, he maintained a sizeable voluntary choir, made St James's a centre for church music and taught a large band of pupils. A devout man, he was active as a trustee, warden and councillor. The simplicity and other-worldliness of his character enabled him to weather the theological storms which sometimes beset the parish, even if his endearing attributes did not fit him for managing practical affairs.

On 7 January 1911, at St James's, Allman married a violinist EDITH DORA RANCLAUD (1885-1960); they were to remain childless. The marriage was an ideal union of two dedicated musicians. Dora taught at the New South Wales State Conservatorium of Music and played in its orchestra; she toured (1919-21) with the State Orchestra under Henri Verbrugghen [q.v.12]. George was engaged by the Australian Music Examinations Board from 1915, joined the conservatorium staff in 1924 and was president for twelve terms of the Musical Association of New South Wales (which he and Dora had helped to found in 1912). He taught at Presbyterian Ladies' College, Croydon; she at Ascham, Darling Point; they occasionally taught together, as at Shore (1947-57).

Their partnership was best exemplified in the field of choral music. In all his choir work, Dora acted as Allman's assistant and general factotum, arranging the music and mothering the younger choristers. At St James's, they were 'Sir' and 'Miss' to generations of choirboys. Allman also conducted the Sydney University Musical Society for thirty years from 1928; appointed the university's organist in 1936, he began to conduct its graduates' choir in 1952. Mindful of the educational role of the musician, Allman championed Bach's choral work for Sydney audiences, held lunchhour recitals at St James's, and played and conducted for wartime concerts. Unassuming and almost hesitant in mundane matters, he was courteously forceful when conducting any kind of choir. For him, the rendition of a choral work was a spiritual and ennobling experience.

Dora Allman died on 22 September 1960. Next year Allman retired from St James's. He had been awarded King George V's jubilee (1935) medal, as well as King George VI's and Queen Elizabeth II's coronation (1937 and 1953) medals. In 1961 the University of Sydney conferred an honorary doctorate of letters upon him. Allman's final years were clouded by illness at his North Sydney home, where his sister acted as housekeeper. He died on 16 February 1967 at Mosman and was cremated after a hugely-attended funeral service at St James's; his ashes, as those of Dora, were interred in its crypt.

W. Orchard, *Music in Australia* (Melb, 1952); G. D. Rushworth, *Historic Organs of New South Wales* (Syd, 1988); *St James's Church Parish Messenger*, Nov 1957, Oct 1960, Sept-Oct 1961, Mar-Apr 1967; *SMH*, 25 Oct 1957, 31 Oct 1961; *Anglican*, 31 Oct 1957.   K. J. CABLE

ALLNUTT, ALBERT GEORGE (1892-1963), farmer and politician, was born on 29 April 1892 at Cheltenham, Melbourne, third child of George Thomas Allnutt, market gardener, and his wife Josephine, née Cameron, both Victorian born. Educated at Cheltenham and Moorabbin State schools, Albert worked with his father and became prominent in local organizations. He enlisted in the Australian Imperial Force in 1917, but was discharged medically unfit. Next year he took up wheat-growing and road-contracting in the Mallee town of Carwarp. On 11 February 1922 at the Denholm Street Methodist Church, Hawthorn, he married Robina Elizabeth Marchbank (d. 1926); on 28 September 1929 at St Matthew's Anglican Church, Albury, he married Wilhelmina Redenbach: they were to move to Red Cliffs in 1933.

A founding member of the Victorian Farmers' Union in 1916, Allnutt had convened a meeting at Ouyen in April 1926 which saw a split with the V.F.U. and the formation of a new political body, the Country Progressive Party led by (Sir) Albert Dunstan [q.v.8]. Standing for the seat of Mildura, Allnutt was one of four C.P.P. candidates returned to the Legislative Assembly at the 1927 elections. In 1930 the C.P.P. merged with the Victorian Country Party (formerly the V.F.U.). Allnutt was a firm supporter of Dunstan; in 1935 he seconded the latter's successful bid for party leadership and, during Dunstan's first ministry, served as government whip (1936-37). As a diligent local member whose electorate was farthest from Melbourne, he had few recreations. He enjoyed watching football, and bred horses and pigs. His one extravagance was his Cazare Beraut car.

Dunstan was to see Allnutt emerge as his most bitter opponent. Late in 1936 Allnutt thwarted government plans to push a night trotting bill through the assembly and subsequently denounced his leader as an untrustworthy, time-serving 'Iscariot'. In 1939 he was equally vehement in opposing the removal of A. E. Hocking [q.v.] as a commissioner of the State Savings Bank. A staunch Methodist and 'wowser', with a pronounced stammer, Allnutt was a parliamentary maverick whose uncompromising opinions and caustic tongue made him for a time 'the most despised member of his party'.

From 1940 he had allies in the assembly, but found himself opposed in his electorate by pro-Dunstan candidates who were backed by the local press. Dunstan then promised benefits to Mildura which Allnutt had previously sought and been denied. In September 1945, speaking against his expulsion from the Country Party for having supported a no-confidence motion against the Dunstan-Hollway [q.v.] ministry, Allnutt declared: 'I have tried to be as outspoken as I dare . . . when you are attacked I find it best to hit to kill'. At the ensuing elections in November he lost his seat to Labor.

A commissioner (1947-50) of the Melbourne Harbor Trust, Allnutt unsuccessfully contested the Legislative Assembly seat of Mornington as an Independent in 1950 and was defeated for the Legislative Council's North Western Province in 1958. He later farmed at Mount Eliza, Research and Kerang. Throughout his career fire plagued him: his properties at Carwarp, Red Cliffs and Research were burnt out. Allnutt died of cancer on 18 March 1963 at Kerang. Survived by his wife and daughter, and by the son of his first marriage, he was buried in Carwarp cemetery.

F. Beaton, *Carwarp* (Carwarp, Vic, nd, 1968?); P. Hocking, *Stormy Petrel* (Melb, 1990); *Sunraysia Daily*, 14 Feb, 8 Apr 1927, 19 Mar 1963; J. B. Paul, The Premiership of Sir Albert Dunstan (M.A. thesis, Univ Melb, 1961); information from Mrs G. Thorne, Kerang, Vic.   GEOFF BROWNE

ALLNUTT, MARION ELLEN LEA (1896-1980), welfare worker, was born on 8 September 1896 at Woodville Park, Adelaide, daughter of Earnest Allnutt, merchant, and his wife Marion Anderson, née Fowler. The family moved to Fremantle, Western Australia, in Marion's infancy and returned to Adelaide in 1914. Nicknamed 'Polly', she studied piano at the Elder [q.v.4] Conservatorium of Music and accompanied soloists in concerts at the Adelaide Town Hall: her wealthy father refused to allow his daughters to work. Dark haired, with a broad smile and strong features, she was confident, quietly spoken and a devout Anglican.

Following a broken engagement, Marion cared for her mother and did voluntary social work, especially for children. She served on the committee of the Walkerville Church of England Boys' Home (1927-52) and on the executive of the Kindergarten Union of South Australia (1928-38), and acted as a transport officer in 1939-41 for the South Australian division of the Australian Red Cross Society. In 1949 she became a charter member of the Soroptomist Club of Adelaide (president 1951-53).

Marion had been a founder in 1941 of the South Australian unit of the Women's Australian National Services whose motto was 'Pledged to unity and service'. As its full-time secretary and commanding officer (from 1942), she proved a natural leader. During World War II she directed women in pre-enlistment training for the armed services, and instructed members in air-raid precautions work and fire-fighting; she also supported the dispatch of food parcels to victims of the Blitz in Britain. Wearing blue uniforms and peaked caps, some three thousand members of the South Australian W.A.N.S. worked for the St John Ambulance Brigade, undertook transport duties for police and military authorities, performed secretarial tasks, and cared for elderly people and those in hospitals and children's homes. They financed their own operations. In July 1944 Commander Allnutt answered the Royal Adelaide Hospital's call for the W.A.N.S. to replace striking domestic workers. At a few hours notice, she arranged a complete service for nine days, despite accusations of 'scab' labour.

Next month she proposed that the W.A.N.S. should establish Wanslea, an emergency home for children, on a Western Australian model. Fund-raising began with the renovation of a yellow, horse-drawn pie-cart that traded briskly in the city; Marion stoked the fire daily to heat pies and drinks. Through money from badge days, catering enterprises and the support of other women's groups, the W.A.N.S. opened Wanslea at Payneham in March 1947; the home was later moved to Kingswood. The matron and staff cared for about thirty children in times of family crises; girls were trained as 'Wanslea aids' to take over the mothers' home duties when necessary.

Miss Allnutt continued her work on Wanslea's council (1947-69 and 1975-80), on management and training committees, and in fund-raising. In 1951 she was appointed M.B.E. She died on 10 November 1980 at Wynwood Nursing Home, Norwood, and was cremated. Her relations donated funds for a rose garden at St Andrew's Anglican Church, Walkerville, in her memory. Marion had bequeathed a generous legacy to Wanslea. In 1991 Marion Allnutt House at Wanslea Child Care Centre, Kingswood, was named after her.

A. S. Angus, *History of the Women's Australian National Services* (Adel, 1981); C of E Boys' Home, Walkerville, *Annual Reports*, 1927-52; Kindergarten Union of SA, *Annual Reports*, 1928-38; Wanslea Inc, *Annual Reports*, 1946-47, 1980-81; *Advertiser* (Adel), 28 Apr 1917, 1 Jan 1951; Soroptomist Club of Adel, Executive cte minutes, 1949-58 (held by the club); WANS, SA unit, Minute-book, 22 May 1941, 1, 8 Aug, 5 Sept 1944, and Wanslea news-cuttings (Mort L); information from Dr D. S. Muecke, Walkerville, and Miss J. Farmer, Glenelg, Adel.
HELEN JONES

ALLPORT, HENRY (1890-1965), lawyer and public benefactor, was born on 14 July 1890 in Hobart, second son of MORTON JOHN CECIL ALLPORT (1858-1926) and his wife Annie, née Campbell. Henry was a great-grandson of Joseph Allport and a grandson of Morton Allport [qq.v.1,3]. Admitted to the Bar in 1881, Cecil became senior partner in Dobson, Mitchell & Allport and a director of several prominent Tasmanian companies; a bibliophile and author of numerous articles on the island's history, he published *A Page From the Past* (1924), a centenary history of the Cascade estate. He also treasured Australian paintings, books and manuscripts, building up an impressive collection which was to be inherited by his sole surviving son.

Henry was educated at the King's Grammar School, The Hutchins School and the University of Tasmania (LL.B., 1914). The legacy of rheumatic fever which he had suffered in boyhood prevented him from enlisting during World War I and he was admitted to the Bar in 1914. He joined his father's firm, practised conveyancing and commercial law, and was made a partner in 1923. At St Aidan's Anglican Church, Launceston, on 4 April 1929 he married Claudine Miriam 'Daisy' Hawker; they were to remain childless.

Stimulated from childhood by his father's interests, Allport had developed a passion for history, antiques and colonial art. He studied the work of local artists and was an authority on early Tasmanian literature. His interests were reflected in his membership of the organizing committee of the Art, Antique, and Historical Exhibition (held to raise funds for unemployment relief in Hobart in August 1931) and in his pamphlet, *Early Art in Tasmania*, published to mark the occasion. With his wife, he built up a diverse and valuable collection of antiques and *objets d'art* at Cedar Court, their Sandy Bay home. A number of their pieces were bought locally, but most were purchased on visits to England. Acquisitions included a small collection of antique glass, a selection of eighteenth- and nineteenth-century English porcelain, domestic silverware dating from the late Elizabethan era, and individual pieces representative of three centuries of the furniture-maker's craft. Other purchases augmented Cecil's collection of books, pictures, manuscripts and documents.

Henry Allport was golf champion (1910, 1911 and 1930) of Southern Tasmania, and club champion, captain and secretary of the (Royal) Hobart Golf Club; he was also a keen tennis player and a camping enthusiast. Vice-president (1941-42 and 1945-47) of the Royal Society of Tasmania, he lectured on art and antiques, and wrote for the *Australian Dictionary of Biography*. He was, as well, chairman of the Cascade Brewery Co. Ltd, deputy chairman of the Hobart Gas Co. and a founding director of Richardson's Meat Industries Ltd.

Predeceased by his wife, Allport died on 21 May 1965 at Sandy Bay. His will directed that his estate be used to establish a library 'on the lines of the Mitchell [q.v.5] Library ... with a small fine arts museum attached' as a memorial to the family of which he was the last male descendant. Originally housed at Cedar Court, but transferred to a permanent home in the State Library of Tasmania after the passage of legislation to alter the terms of Henry's will, the Allport Library and Museum of Fine Arts was opened on 27 October 1972.

The Allport Library and Museum of Fine Arts (Hob, 1972); *Illustrated Tas Mail*, 9 June 1921; *Weekly Courier*, 8 Apr 1926; *Australian*, 23 Nov 1965; *Examiner* (Launc), 9 June, 17 Sept 1966; *Mercury* (Hob), 22 May, 4, 9 Nov 1965, 4, 28 Oct 1972, 26 July 1980; *Sunday Tasmanian*, 30 June 1985; personal information.   G. T. STILWELL

ALLSOP, RAYMOND COTTAM (1898-1972), radio pioneer and engineer, was born on 11 March 1898 at Randwick, Sydney, sixth child of native-born parents John Allsop, horse-trainer, and his wife Harriet Rebecca, née Cottam. Young Ray haunted Father Shaw's [q.v.11] wireless telegraph station, received an experimental licence on 3 June 1911 and joined the Wireless Institute of Australia. On leaving Sydney Grammar School in 1913, he was apprenticed at Shaw's Maritime Wireless Co. From 1916 Allsop served as a senior wireless telegraph operator in transports, among them the *Argyllshire* and *Indarra*; between ships, he was employed at the Naval (formerly Shaw) Wireless Works.

After the war Allsop experimented in the emerging field of radio telephony, made possible by the development of the triode valve. He married Emily Tebbutt Rodda, granddaughter of John Tebbutt [q.v.6], on 30 September 1922 at St Jude's Anglican Church, Randwick. Next year he was appointed radio engineer of New Systems Telephones Pty Ltd which, as part of Broadcasters (Sydney) Ltd, was preparing for the introduction of radio broadcasting. Allsop worked on experimental transmissions at 2BL, the first station in Australia to go to air (on 23 November). He redesigned and rebuilt the transmitter, and from June 1925 was engineer-in-charge until the Postmaster General's Department took over all A-class stations in July 1929. From his private station, 2YG, Allsop had continued experimental work since 1922 and used a landline to 2BL to achieve a number of long-distance radio 'firsts', including a triple transmission via 2LO London-PCJJ Holland-2BL by which Australian listeners heard Big Ben live in 1927. Through 2YG-2BL he charted (Sir) Charles Kingsford Smith's [q.v.9] flight across the Pacific in the *Southern Cross* in 1928.

Reviving an earlier interest, on 10 June 1929 Allsop publicly demonstrated his 'Raycophone' system of synchronized sound for motion pictures at the Wintergarden Theatre, Rose Bay. Raycophone Ltd (from RAYmond COttam) was set up to produce the apparatus which at £1700 was far cheaper than the competing American system that cost £11 000. Following a short 'Talkie war' when United States interests threatened to stop supplying theatres fitted with Allsop's equipment, the Raycophone system was installed in 375 Australian theatres by 1938. Raycophone had been acquired in 1930 by Harringtons Ltd which was taken over by Kodak (Australasia) Pty Ltd by 1933; Allsop remained a director and chief engineer, and continued research into stereo recording and reproduction. During the World Radio Convention he demonstrated his stereo equipment at the Plaza Theatre, Sydney, on 10 April 1938.

From August 1940 Allsop served as an engineer lieutenant (acting lieutenant commander, June 1941), Royal Australian Naval Volunteer Reserve, at the Anti-Submarine School, H.M.A.S. *Rushcutter*, where he produced Asdic (submarine detection) equipment and tested radar. He returned to Raycophone in August 1943 and retired in 1945. Employed as a private consultant until 1957, he campaigned for the introduction of television and FM broadcasting.

A foundation member (1932), fellow (1940) and president of the Institution of Radio Engineers, Australia, Allsop was a fellow (1934) of the Society of Motion Picture and Television Engineers, United States of America; he was also a member of the American (1946) and British (1947) institutions of Radio Engineers, and of the Australian Broadcasting Control Board (1953-54). He was appointed O.B.E. in 1971. A brilliant inventor and practical engineer, Allsop was proud of Australian ingenuity in the early development of radio electronics, but regretted the postwar loss of impetus and world standing. Survived by his wife and two daughters, he died on 19 March 1972 at his Roseville home and was cremated.

A'sian Wireless Review, May 1923, p 24; *World Radio Convention, Complete Procs*, 4-14 Apr 1938, p 27; *Radio Active*, Apr 1972; *Electronics Aust*,

May-Aug 1974; *Cinema Papers,* 78, Mar 1990; *Sun* (Syd), 9, 12, 27 June 1929; *SMH,* 9 June 1927, 11 Apr 1953, 30 Dec 1954; Allsop papers (NL); Allsop's Oral History transcript (ABC Radio Archives, Syd).   JAN BRAZIER

ALNGINDABU (LUCY McGINNESS) (1874?-1961), Aboriginal elder, was born probably in 1874 at Chapana, near the Finniss River, Northern Territory, and belonged to the Kungarakany language group whom Europeans called the Paperbark People. Trained as a domestic servant in her girlhood, Alngindabu (Alyandabu) became an expert cook and seamstress. The Whites named her Lucy. About 1900 she married Stephen Joseph McGuinness [*sic*]; they were to have five children—Bernard, John, Margaret, Valentine and Joseph—all of whom were baptized as Catholics. A ganger on the North Australia Railway, Stephen was stationed at the 'Thirty-Four Mile', outside Darwin.

After an accident in which one of his men was killed, Stephen was dismissed and the family left for Bynoe Harbour to look for work. *En route,* Lucy found what her brother Maranda identified as tin ore. The Lucy Mine was officially taken up in October 1908 and became the McGinness's home. Alngindabu baked bread for her family and used an old sewing-machine to make them clothes from bleached, calico flour-sacks. Having learned Scottish folk-songs from her husband, she sang them to her children; she also taught them the Kungarakany language and told them about kinship, the land and the *Kurduk* (spirits) who controlled it. She passed on to them stories of the ancestral Dreaming: of the *Kewen* (sand-goanna women) and *Kulutuk* (doves) that protected Kungarakany land.

When Stephen died in 1918, Alngindabu and the youngest two children were taken to Darwin to live in the Kahlin Aboriginal Compound. In 1918-22 Margaret and her husband operated the Lucy Mine; thereafter, it was not worked by the family until 1960 when Val re-pegged the lease. Employed as a laundress and housemaid, Alngindabu was described by Ted Egan as 'around six feet tall, straight as a gun barrel, black, proud, barefooted, wearing a simple cotton frock and a wide-brimmed stockman's hat. In her hand she carried a few items tied in a red handkerchief, and she puffed contentedly on a pipe as she walked'. Fiercely independent, she was known for her generosity and esteemed for her devotion to her family. She became an *almiyuk*—a female elder, a custodian of special knowledge and a bestower of names to children—and her brother Maranda was a *namiyuk* (elder).

Survived by her daughter and three sons, Alngindabu died on 23 September 1961 in Darwin and was buried in the local cemetery with Catholic rites. To ensure the maintenance of spiritual obligations, a shade-laying ceremony was held for her at Humpty Doo station in 1963. Her son Jack was president of the North Australian Workers' Union in the 1950s. Another son Joe was president of the Federal Council for the Advancement of Aborigines and Torres Strait Islanders for most of the period 1961-78; he campaigned for the removal of constitutional limitations on Aboriginal citizenship which was achieved through a referendum in 1967. Alngindabu's grand-daughter Mimbingal (Vai Stanton) inherited the role of *almiyuk* and worked to secure justice, education and political representation for Aborigines.

D. W. Lockwood, *The Front Door* (Adel, 1968); T. Egan, *A Drop of Rough Ted* (Syd, 1979); R. Layton and N. Williams (comps), *The Finniss River Land Claim* (Darwin, 1980); S. Baldwin (ed), *Unsung Heroes and Heroines of Australia* (Melb, 1988); J. McGinness, *Son of Alyandabu* (Brisb, 1991); *NT Times,* 26 Oct 1918; *NT News,* 28, 30 Sept 1961; I. M. Bishop, Lucy McGuinness (ms, 1981, Malak School, Darwin); V. McGuiness, transcript of interview 1984, NT Archives, Darwin; information from Mrs V. Stanton, Darwin.   MICKEY DEWAR

ALYANDABU; *see* ALNGINDABU

AMIES, SIR ARTHUR BARTON PILGRIM (1902-1976), professor of dental science, was born on 17 October 1902 in Perth, son of Arthur Pilgrim Amies, business manager, and his wife Sarah Ann, née Presland, both native-born. Educated at Perth Modern School and the University of Melbourne (B.D.Sc., 1924), he went in 1926 to Edinburgh where he qualified L.R.C.P., L.R.C.S. (1928). After visiting London, Vienna and the United States of America, he returned on a part-time basis to the (Royal) Dental Hospital of Melbourne and entered private practice, while also studying for a D.D.Sc. (1929) and a diploma of laryngology and otology (1933). In 1934 he became a fellow of the Royal Australasian College of Surgeons.

On 27 May 1930 at Scots Church, Adelaide, Amies married GERALDINE CHRISTEIN WILHELMINA COLLEE (1906-1982). He was appointed professor of dental science (later dental medicine and surgery) at the University of Melbourne in 1934, an appointment which simultaneously made him dean of the faculty, principal of the Australian College of Dentistry and dean of the Dental Hospital. Having served that year on the Dental Board of Victoria, he became president (1936-37) of the Victorian branch of the Australian Dental Association and federal president (1938-39).

Elected a fellow (1939) of Queen's College, he was a councillor in 1945-76; he chaired the professorial board in 1956 and twice acted as vice-chancellor. During his presidency (1944-70) the Victorian College of Optometry became a department in the faculty of science.

Amies joined the Australian Imperial Force on 19 June 1940. As a major in the dental service, he served with the 4th Australian General Hospital at Tobruk, and in a facio-maxillary and plastic unit attached to the 2nd A.G.H. in Egypt, before returning to university duties in 1942. He was nominated to Legacy in 1945, was president in 1955 and did much to advance its aims.

Throughout his career Amies received many academic distinctions: he became a fellow of both the Royal Society of Edinburgh and of the American College of Dentists in 1938, a fellow in dental surgery of both the Royal College of Surgeons, England (1948), and Edinburgh (1951), and a fellow in surgery of the latter institution in 1949. He was awarded an honorary LL.D. by the University of Glasgow in 1963 and became a fellow of the (Royal) Australian College of Dental Surgeons in 1965; he was appointed C.M.G. in 1949 and knighted in 1957.

As a teacher, Amies was a disciplinarian who instilled in his students a sense of responsibility and professional pride. Though not a committed researcher, he encouraged others to undertake advanced studies. From his appointment in 1934, his main interest was the pursuit of a new and independent dental hospital and school: in spite of constant opposition from the State Department of Health, he steadfastly maintained the need for in-patient accommodation in such an establishment. The new institution opened in 1963 and in 1967 Sir Robert Menzies [q.v.] named the Arthur Amies ward in recognition of his contribution. At his retirement that year Amies was presented with a portrait by Paul Fitzgerald which now hangs in the foyer of the (Sir William) Anderson [q.v.] Auditorium at the Royal Dental Hospital of Melbourne; another, by John Heath, is also held by the university.

There were two sides to Sir Arthur. Besides the ambitious professional there was the public figure, a member of the establishment who achieved much and who basked in the glow of success. He was a popular speaker, with a powerful delivery that was clear and precise. Amies did not take kindly to criticism, attacking the critic rather than the substance of his argument, as in the debate on fluoridation, to which he was resolutely opposed. A big man, he stood out in a crowd by his bearing and appearance. He was happiest in full academic dress, or in white tie and decorations, and when in the presence of

royalty would almost burst with pride. He pursued publicity: leading an academic procession, presenting candidates and attending receptions were meat and drink to him. His knowledge of protocol was impressive. He and his wife, to whom he was devoted, were meticulous in manner and dress, and overtly conscious of status. Predeceased by his daughter, he died in his home at Christmas Hills, Victoria, on 4 December 1976 and was cremated.

Lady Amies had a distinguished medical career. Born on 26 August 1906 at Delft, Holland, she was educated in Europe, and in Edinburgh where she qualified L.D.S.R.C.S. (1928); L.R.C.P., L.R.C.S. (1938). Prior to her marriage she had practised dentistry in Scotland and in Harley Street, London. After she came to Melbourne she established a medical practice and in 1946 became honorary medical officer in charge of the diabetic clinic at the (Royal) Children's Hospital. She died on 13 November 1982.

Univ Melb Gazette, Jan 1968; *Aust Dental J*, Feb 1968, Feb 1977; *Herald* (Melb), 23 Dec 1933, 18 Sept 1964; Minutes, Faculty of Dental Science, Univ Melb, *and* Council of Roy Dental Hospital of Melb, *and* Aust College of Dentistry *and* Roy Dental Hospital of Melb, Correspondence and papers (held by L, Roy Dental Hospital of Melb); Amies papers *and* Queen's College records (Univ Melb Archives); Hospitals and Charities Com, Minutes (PRO, Vic).   H. F. ATKINSON

AMIET, WILLIAM ALBERT (1890-1959), writer and barrister, was born on 3 June 1890 at Murgheboluc, near Geelong, Victoria, son of native-born parents Edward William Amiet, farmer, and his wife Mary Ann, née Begley. William was educated at the local state school and Ormond [q.v.5] College, University of Melbourne (B.A., 1911; M.A., 1913), where he excelled in modern and classical languages. Moving to Queensland, he organized Young Men's Christian Association concerts for railway workers at Dawson River valley in 1912, before taking up his appointment as a master at Maryborough Grammar School. Having studied law, he moved to Brisbane in 1915 and was called to the Bar in 1916. On 2 May he enlisted in the Australian Imperial Force and embarked for England in October with reinforcements for the 26th Battalion. In June 1917 he joined his unit in France and was commissioned on 1 August 1918. He was wounded in October at Bellicourt and mentioned in dispatches.

After briefly attending King's College, London, Amiet returned to Brisbane where his appointment terminated on 30 December 1919. Next year he entered into partnership with the solicitor Vincent Macrossan at

Mackay. There, in the Catholic presbytery, on 17 December 1923 Amiet married Agnes May Hurley, a 22-year-old civil servant. In demand as a speaker, Amiet became a founding president of the Mackay Rotary Club and a patron of local business, sporting and social organizations. In November 1929 he unsuccessfully contested the Federal seat of Herbert as a Coalitionist candidate. He contributed reviews and a Saturday article to the Mackay *Daily Mercury* for more than thirty years and helped to establish its weekend issue as an intellectual forum. By the 1930s he had formed the 'Mercredian Munchers', a small circle which discussed matters literary and scientific. As its acknowledged luminary, he undertook an encyclopaedic survey of world literature in *Literature by Languages: a roll call* (Sydney, 1932). A popularizer of contemporary British scientific writing who combined Wellsian speculation with flashes of humour, Amiet was an assiduous star-gazer and regarded astronomy as the 'queen of sciences'. He republished some of his columns from the *Daily Mercury* in *Starry Pages* (Sydney, 1932) and *Starry Ages* (Sydney, 1937).

Most of his sources were drawn from his voluminous personal library. Amiet published *A Shakespeare or Two* (Sydney, 1935) which was followed by *The Practice of Literary History* (Sydney, 1936) and *Courses in Literary History* (Sydney, 1938). His cosmopolitanism did not preclude him from supporting Australian literature in criticism and reviews. He opposed restrictive racial and immigration policies in the 1930s, was active in local recruiting campaigns during World War II and became involved in the postwar activities of the air-training corps at Mackay. *Metrical Diversions of a Sexagenarian* (Brisbane, 1952) included poetry that he had written from World War I to the early 1950s and revealed his deep affection for friends and family; one of the poems was in memory of his eldest daughter Berenice who had been killed in a motorcar accident. Amiet's *Scrambled Scrutinies* (Brisbane, 1949) had proclaimed the vanity of scientific knowledge and embraced the 'here and now' of existence; in later life he adopted a calm agnosticism.

Survived by his wife and two daughters, Amiet died of cardiorenal failure on 13 April 1959 at the Mater Hospital, Mackay, and was cremated. An eclectic rather than a specialist, he has been described as a 'charming and witty writer of prose', though somewhat lacking in 'philosophical substance'. The Amiet Memorial Library at Mackay commemorates him.

Literature in North Qld, 5, no 3, 1977, p 27; Amiet collection, including diaries, 1903-59, and correspondence, 1941-55 (Fryer L, Univ Qld); information from Mr H. A. Moore, Brisb, Mr G. Nos-

cov and Mrs A. Gilbert, Amiet Memorial L, Mackay, Sr C. Amiet, Duchesne College, Brisb, and Mrs L. McFarlane, Syd.   DENIS CRYLE

ANCHER, SYDNEY EDWARD CAMBRIAN (1904-1979), architect, was born on 25 February 1904 at Woollahra, Sydney, son of Edward Albert Ancher, a journalist from New Zealand, and his Australian-born wife Ethel Puah, née Parsons. Educated at Mosman Superior Public, North Sydney Boys' High and Sydney Technical High schools, young Ancher was articled (1924-26) to the architect E. W. S. Wakeley and in 1926-30 gained experience with Wunderlich [q.v.12] Ltd, Prevost, Synnot & Ruwald, and Ross & Rowe. From 1924 he attended Sydney Technical College at night and qualified as an architect in 1929. Next year he was awarded the Australian medallion and travelling scholarship of the Board of Architects of New South Wales.

In July Ancher arrived in London where he worked in the offices of leading architects, among them Cyril Farey, a perspectivist, and Joseph Emberton, a modernist. Travelling extensively in Europe, Ancher first saw the work of Mies van der Rohe at the Weissenhof-Siedlung housing colony at Stuttgart, Germany, and the 1931 building exhibition in Berlin. Van der Rohe and Le Corbusier became his idols.

Arriving home in January 1936, Ancher married a stenographer Aaletha Ethel Hasemer on 26 November at the Presbyterian Church, Mosman. He worked for Emil Sodersten [q.v.] and then with Reginald A. de T. Prevost. Ancher made a major contribution to the design of an *avant-garde* house for the Prevost family at Bellevue Hill. Completed in 1937, it was a rare Australian example of the radical International Style. He put the rigorous ideology into practice by using abstract geometric elevations, circular windows as a counterpoint to rectangular ones, curved walls in contrast to rectilinear shapes, and 'open planning' by means of the interrelated spaces on the ground floor adjacent to the entrance. Elsewhere, the house was conventional. In his typical, self-deprecatory way, he later dismissed this design as 'pretty ghastly', but the Prevost house revealed how Ancher was moving towards the kind of architecture which he would help to establish in his own country after World War II.

The partnership of Prevost & Ancher, begun in 1937, thrived on a steady stream of designs for hotels. Acknowledging that it was 'considered madness', in January 1939 Ancher sailed with his wife for England to seek more creative outlets for his talent. In London he was impressed by four lectures given by Frank Lloyd Wright; he also travelled in Denmark, Sweden and Finland, where he was 'bowled over' by some of the modern building. With the outbreak of war, he returned to Sydney late in 1939. He worked for three months for the Commonwealth government and subsequently with John D. Moore [q.v.10].

On 3 June 1940 Ancher enlisted in the Australian Imperial Force as a sapper in the 2nd/6th Field Company. He embarked for the Middle East in October. Commissioned lieutenant in March 1941, he was posted to the Garrison Engineers, A.I.F. Base Area. Back in Australia in March 1942, he performed engineering and architectural duties, mainly at Land Headquarters, Melbourne. He was transferred to the Reserve of Officers with the rank of major on 28 July 1944 and appointed technical officer at the Commonwealth experimental building station.

Resuming private practice in 1945, Ancher designed about ten houses a year until 1951, all in his mature, modern style, and made alterations and additions to numerous hotels. His own home at Killara, Sydney, was awarded the (Sir John) Sulman [q.v.12] medal for 1945, despite postwar restrictions and shortages, and in the face of obstructions from a conservative local council which required amendments to be made to some of his designs. W. M. Farley's house at North Curl Curl also aroused the ire of Warringah Shire Council. When building approval was refused for Ancher's proposed flat-roofed house with large areas of glass, his determined client took the matter to court and the council's ruling was overturned in a landmark judgement in 1948. Among the other important homes which followed were the English house at St Ives (1949) and a house that Ancher built for himself at Neutral Bay (1956), the latter having a modular plan derived from its post-and-beam construction.

In 1952 Ancher took two of his assistants into partnership as Ancher, Mortlock & Murray. The flow of domestic and hotel work continued. From 1960 the practice expanded to take commissions for council chambers, municipal libraries and university buildings, and was joined by Ken Woolley in 1964. Ancher retired from the firm in 1966 and moved to Coffs Harbour where he completed a house for himself in 1968. His wife died in 1970. Two years later he moved to another self-designed home near Camden, and later to Fosterton, near Dungog. He had been a councillor of the State chapter of the Royal Australian Institute of Architects and was awarded its gold medal in 1975. Survived by his two sons, he died on 8 December 1979 in hospital at Waratah and was cremated.

With Arthur Baldwinson, Robin Boyd [qq.v.], Roy Grounds and Harry Seidler,

Ancher had pioneered modern domestic architecture in Australia. His houses of the late 1940s and 1950s became widely known and demonstrated to others the possibilities of a new approach to the field. Their appeal lay in their subtlety, their suitability for Sydney's temperate climate and their encouragement of a freer life-style for their occupants. Ancher was an unassuming man who firmly rejected the tags of 'intellectual' and 'rationalist'. Many of his planning ideas evolved from a response to simple functional demands, tempered by his penchant for doing things 'his way'. His houses, which have a quality 'rather like a hard-edged painting', demonstrate his conviction that the beauty of the natural environment could be sensitively complemented by the man-made precision of his structures. The rigorous simplicity which characterizes his architecture is tempered by understatement, and by a certain relaxed quality which may be seen as expressing something of the Australian ethos.

D. Saunders and C. Burke, *Ancher, Mortlock, Murray, Woolley* (Syd, 1976); J. Taylor, *An Australian Identity, Houses for Sydney, 1953-63* (Syd, 1972, 1984) and *Australian Architecture Since 1960* (Syd, 1986); *Architecture Aust*, 69, no 1, Mar 1980; *SMH*, 8 May 1930, 27 June 1944, 29 Oct, 11 Dec 1946, 2 Mar 1948, 12 Dec 1979; *National Times*, 16-21 Feb 1976; R. Apperly, Sydney Houses 1914-1939 (M.Arch. thesis, Univ NSW, 1972); C. Boesen, Sydney Ancher: A Profile (B.Sc.(Arch.) Hons thesis, Univ Syd, 1979).

RICHARD E. APPERLY*
PETER REYNOLDS

ANDERSEN, CLIFFORD WERLIN (1906-1972), accountant, was born on 23 May 1906 in Adelaide, ninth child of Danish parents Adolph Otto Andersen, corporation ganger, and his wife Marie Emilie Augustus, née Werlin. The family was closely knit, but poor. Clifford left school at an early age and could only study part time at Adelaide Technical High School and at the University of Adelaide (Dip.Comm., 1927) where he was president of the Students' Representative Council. In 1928 he was admitted to membership of the Commonwealth Institute of Accountants. At St Augustine's Anglican Church, Unley, on 26 December 1932 he married a teacher Caroline Everard Verco.

In that year he moved to Melbourne to take up an appointment as assistant-registrar of the Commonwealth Institute which co-operated with the Institute of Chartered Accountants to hold the first Australasian Congress on Accounting in Melbourne in 1936: as its secretary, Andersen established his reputation as a first-rate administrator. The congress kindled his lifelong interest in furthering the professional development of accounting in Australia. In 1938 he succeeded R. J. Oehr as general registrar of the Commonwealth Institute. Having been declared unfit for military service, Andersen was seconded in 1942-44 to the Department of War Organisation of Industry.

Convinced that the profession was being weakened by the proliferation of accounting bodies, he played a major role in moves which led to the amalgamation of the Commonwealth Institute with the Federal Institute of Accountants to form the Australian Society of Accountants in 1953. Andersen was appointed first general registrar of the A.S.A. and became executive director in 1968. In response to the Martin and Vatter reports, in the 1960s he supported wide-ranging changes in the society's membership policy. Largely as a result of his interest, the society gradually built up what was to be named the C. W. Andersen Library, one of the best accounting repositories outside Britain and the United States of America. In 1957-69 Andersen also served as general registrar of the Australasian Institute of Cost Accountants and was instrumental in its merger with the A.S.A.

During this time he became increasingly involved in advancing the international standing of the profession. As part of the Colombo Plan, he had been invited by the Commonwealth government in 1957 to lead a mission to promote the development of accounting bodies in South East Asia. In 1961 he assisted in drafting legislation to establish the Singapore Society of Accountants. Andersen regularly represented Australia at regional conferences and presented papers at international conferences in Manila (1957), Canberra (1960), Tokyo (1962), New Delhi (1965) and New Zealand (1968). A delegate to the eighth and ninth international congresses of accountants in New York and Paris, he did much to secure the tenth congress (1972) for Australia.

Of middle height and medium build, with dark, straight hair parted in the middle, Andersen dressed neatly and conservatively; in his dealings with people he had an easy manner, and was tactful and a good listener. He was a devout member of the Catholic Apostolic Church, Carlton. His interests included tennis, classical music, carpentry and debating. President of the council of the Royal Dental Hospital of Melbourne and a life member of the Bush Nursing Association of Victoria, Andersen was appointed O.B.E. in 1971. On his retirement that year, he was made a life member of the A.S.A. He died of complications of aortic stenosis on 29 April 1972 at Parkville and was buried in Springvale cemetery. His wife, two sons and two daughters survived him.

N. J. Marshall, *A Jubilee History, The Institute of Chartered Accountants in Australia (Victorian Branch), 1928-1978* (Melb, 1978); *Aust Accountant*, Dec 1971, June 1972; *Chartered Accountant in Aust*, June 1972; information from Mrs F. Sienkowski, Canb.
                                                    NORMAN J. MARSHALL

ANDERSON, ALFRED WILLIAM (1888-1956), butcher and entrepreneur, was born on 4 June 1888 at East Brighton, Melbourne, third child of John Charles Anderson, butcher, and his wife Elizabeth, née Jervis, both Victorian born. Raised as a Methodist, he was aged 8 when John moved the family to Western Australia and took up market-gardening. Alf attended half a dozen schools before leaving Jandacot State School at 14. Having tried various jobs, about 1911 he opened a butchery in Perth; because he lacked refrigeration, he gave away leftover meat on Saturdays to gain customers. He married Elizabeth Maud Gilbert on 22 June 1912 at St Luke's Anglican Church, Cottesloe; they were to have six children.

Moving to Sydney, in April 1918 Anderson set up as a sausages and smallgoods manufacturer on the corner of George and Bathurst streets, and registered two companies, A. W. Anderson Pty Ltd and Anderson's Sausages Pty Ltd. He opened branches in the suburbs and later at Newcastle; by 1923 he also had wholesaling interests at the Homebush Bay abattoirs. In 1924 he set up freezing and canning works at Lismore, and next at Tuncester. To overcome the wholesalers' monopoly at Pyrmont, in 1925 he developed meat-chilling at rural Byron Bay for the Sydney market, leasing premises and improvising rolling-stock by packing ice into ordinary railway-vans. During the Depression he developed the veal trade on the north coast, produced fertilizer by-products from 1933, and acquired meatworks in Queensland at Wallangarra and Karumba.

Becoming dissatisfied with wartime policies and dreaming of government by Independents, Anderson launched his own political party, the One Parliament for Australia, at Sydney Town Hall in June 1943; for the occasion he sang a comic song and impersonated a Norwegian sea-captain. He contested the Federal seat of Richmond at the August elections; though defeated, he received 20 per cent of the primary vote.

In the late 1940s A. W. Anderson Pty Ltd became large wholesale butchers, specializing in beef, veal and pork, meatworks proprietors, meat exporters, and manufacturers of 'Anderson's Famous Sausages and Smallgoods'; the firm's annual turnover was about £4 million. Anderson acquired grazing interests in Queensland through Euroka Springs Pastoral Co., and bought refrigerated ships and barges at army disposal sales. Concentrating on exports to the Territory of Papua-New Guinea, he established a retail butchery at Rabaul and another in a refrigerated barge in Port Moresby. In 1950 he founded Andersons Island Industries Ltd in the Territory (where he spent much time) and in 1953 a holding company, Andersons Meat Industries Ltd. He also helped to set up the Byron Whaling Co. Pty Ltd in 1954.

Unconventional, with a streak of showmanship and a grassroots mentality, Anderson liked a gamble: he owned racehorses and bred them at his Warema stud near Cabramatta, Sydney, raced ponies and invested heavily in night trotting until the sport was banned. He called one of his horses Sausajax, but had to rename it (Flax) when the Australian Jockey Club objected. Although he lived for many years in 'Bookmakers Row' (Lang Road, Centennial Park), his lack of pretension sometimes dismayed those around him. Known as 'Big Ando' (which he detested), he was over six feet (182.9 cm) tall and weighed almost twenty stone (127 kg). With wide cheeks, 'a knobby nose', arched eyebrows and 'bright hazel eyes', he was talkative and down-to-earth: he attributed the success of his sausages simply to using the best meat. A diabetic, Anderson died of heart disease on 6 August 1956 at his Strathfield home and was buried in Waverley cemetery. His wife, three sons and three daughters survived him.

Meat Trades J, 1947; *People* (Syd), 14 Mar 1951; *Sunday Herald*, 26 Mar 1950; *SMH*, 12 June, 6 Aug 1943, 8 Aug 1956.   BARBARA LE MAISTRE

ANDERSON, ANDREW CANNING (1873-1957), publisher and journalist, was born on 29 September 1873 at Dunfermline, Fife, Scotland, son of William Anderson, power-loom tenter, and his wife Elspit, née Birrell. Educated at the local Carnegie Institute, in 1884 he came with his parents to Maryborough, Queensland, where he assisted his father who had taken work as a mail contractor. At 14 Andrew was apprenticed in the printing trade; he served his articles with the Maryborough *Chronicle* and later joined the staff of the Bundaberg *Patriot*. On 9 September 1902 he married Emma Johnston with Presbyterian forms in her father's house at Bundaberg; they were to have eight children.

Moving to Rockhampton, in 1903 Anderson founded a weekly paper, the *Critic*, in partnership with J. C. Kerr, formerly editor of the *Patriot*: its first issue appeared on Labour Day. Anderson became sole proprietor in 1905. There were then two dailies and another weekly at Rockhampton, but the *Critic* confounded its critics by surviving until the Depression led to its demise in 1931. A lively paper which initially supported Labor policy and retained sympathy for the party, it was the vehicle for Anderson's promotion of the eight-hour day and other working-class reforms. His leading article on the 1907 Labour Day procession referred to labour displaying itself 'to the public gaze in all its lusty manhood'. The *Critic* sold 5000 copies a week. Through constructive criticism, it influenced the social and industrial life of the city. Although its tone was facetious and its columns included 'Candid and Critical', 'Personal Peeps' and 'Sportlets', Anderson never resorted to slander. On 8 May 1907 'Politicomania' described William Kidston's [q.v.9] Independent candidates as 'so flat they need an awful lot of blowing up'.

An active supporter of local business and industry, Anderson was a member of the executive of the Central Queensland Advancement League. Setting an example to combat the high unemployment of 1933, he expanded the printing, bookbinding and office-systems sections of his City Printing Works. By 1957 it was the largest Queensland printery outside Brisbane, with thirty employees, including three of his sons, all trained through his own apprenticeship system. One of his last requests to a son was, 'Jack, look after the business'.

Anderson's commitment to Queensland's central region included membership (1925-48) of the Rockhampton Harbour Board. While he was its wartime chairman (from 1939) he persuaded the Commonwealth government to build two small naval craft at Rockhampton, using the board's workforce. He resigned in 1948 to visit relations in Scotland for the first time since his emigration.

In his earlier years the 6 ft 3 ins (190.5 cm) Anderson (predictably nicknamed 'Lofty') had been an outstanding sportsman, representing Queensland in Rugby Union and rowing. He was also a first-class cricketer and golfer, and in his later years promoted sport as an administrator. Although he never owned a racehorse, he was chairman (1925-33) of the Rockhampton Jockey Club and subsequently of the trustees of Callaghan Park Racecourse. As a footballer, it was said that 'he ran straight, played straight and spoke straight'; the description fairly summed up the character of 'a dour Scot' whose actions spoke louder than others' words. Survived by four sons and three daughters, Anderson died on 6 February 1957 at Rockhampton and was buried in North Rockhampton cemetery. 'Few men have played a bigger part in the commercial and sporting life of Rockhampton . . . and none have been held in higher regard', commented the *Morning Bulletin*, a onetime rival of the *Critic*.

Queensland and Queenslanders (Brisb, 1936); L. McDonald, *Rockhampton* (Brisb, 1981); *Critic* (Rockhampton), 8 May 1907; *Morning Bulletin,* 18 June 1932, 8, 20 Feb 1957; *Bulletin,* 3 Apr 1957; information from Mr J. B. Anderson, City Printing Works, Rockhampton, and Mr F. Stewart, Nth Rockhampton; news-cuttings (held by author, West Rockhampton).   LORNA MCDONALD

ANDERSON, SIR DONALD GEORGE (1917-1975), public servant, was born on 1 March 1917 at Waikerie, South Australia, son of Alex Gibb Anderson, labourer, and his wife Clara Catherine, née Nash, both native-born. Educated at Adelaide High School, Adelaide Teachers' College and the University of Adelaide, Don qualified in 1938 to teach in primary schools; the four subjects he passed at university earned him an appointment next year at Minlaton Higher Primary School. He had also worked in journalism and played cricket, football and tennis. Enlisting in the Citizen Air Force, Royal Australian Air Force, in 1940, he appeared to contemporaries on his pilot's training course as a tall (some 6 ft 3 ins, 190.5 cm), seemingly amiable and slow-moving young man. On 4 April 1941 in St George's Anglican Cathedral, Perth, he married Monica Mary Porker, a telephonist. Commissioned on 25 January 1942, he flew transport aircraft in the South-West Pacific Area and the United States of America, and was mentioned in dispatches for services between 1 July and 30 September 1945. He held the rank of temporary flight lieutenant on his demobilization in 1946.

Joining the Department of Civil Aviation as an examiner of airmen, Anderson was appointed an airway surveyor (flying), air navigation branch, directorate of air navigation, D.C.A., on 19 June 1947. Promoted next year to the new office of superintendent, air traffic control branch, Melbourne, he was a member of the Australian delegation to the International Civil Aviation Organization conference at Montreal, Canada, and chaired a session on the rules of the air and air traffic control. He continued to indulge his passion for cricket and became a stodgy opener for the Essendon first-grade XI. In 1951 he rose to be assistant director-general (personnel and establishments) and in 1954 assistant director-general (administration, personnel and establishments). On 1 January 1956 he succeeded Sir Richard Williams [q.v.12] as director-general of civil aviation. Domestic commercial aviation was in crisis and Anderson's major task was to study the industry's problems. His proposals in May 1957 revitalized the government's two-airline policy, by which the main trunk routes were reserved for two major carriers, one government owned and the other privately owned. Hold-

ing concurrently the posts of rationalization co-ordinator and departmental head, he was judge and jury in the disputes between the two airlines which were referred to him; that appeals against his decisions were rare seemed further 'proof of his accepted detachment'.

In 1957 Anderson led a mission to Washington to negotiate a route across the U.S.A. to Europe for Qantas Empire Airways Ltd. The agreement assured the viability of Q.E.A. and marked a personal triumph, but, in subsequent international haggling over traffic rights, he was to gain mixed results. Awarded the Oswald Watt [q.v.12] medal in 1957 for his contribution to Australian aviation, Anderson was appointed C.B.E. in 1959 and knighted in 1967. His responsibilities for ground facilities and safety presented problems of increasing complexity as the domestic and international civil aviation industry grew, bringing with it advanced technology, and he fought strenuously for the funds necessary for capital investment in infrastructure that ranged from radar to runways.

Called 'the Longfella' in his department, Sir Donald dressed untidily, smoked heavily and belonged to the Savage Club. His height combined with his increasing weight (over sixteen stone, 101.6 kg) to give him a commanding presence. He travelled widely, and frequently, and his shuffling gait became well known. Some of his staff were allowed to see his humour and keen sense of the ridiculous; those who worked close to him generally considered him tough and ruthless; most people in the aviation industry accepted him as a benevolent dictator. With his ambition, drive and innovative organizing ability, he influenced every facet of civil aviation policy until his retirement in 1973. He then became chairman of Qantas Airways Ltd.

In his new post, located in Sydney, Anderson advocated low-cost travel, served on the executive committee of the International Air Transport Association, and joined the board of the Royal New South Wales Institution for Deaf and Blind Children. Having suffered from diabetes for five years, he again retired in August 1975. He died of cardiac failure on 30 November that year at Heidelberg, Melbourne, and was cremated. His wife and two daughters survived him. In recognition of his achievements the International Civil Aviation Organization in 1978 honoured Anderson posthumously with its thirteenth Edward Warner award.

D. Corbett, *Politics and the Airlines* (Lond, 1965); S. Brogden, *Australia's Two-Airline Policy* (Melb, 1968); H. Fysh, *Wings to the World* (Syd, 1970); J. Gunn, *High Corridors* (Brisb, 1988); *Aircraft* (Melb), July 1969; *ICAO Bulletin* (Montreal, Canada), Sept 1978; information from Lady Anderson, Toorak, Melb, Mr K. M. Barclay, Coromandel Valley, Adel, Mr J. E. Schofield, Kensington Gardens, Adel, and Mr A. F. Rainbird, Civil Aviation Authority, Canb.   JOHN GUNN

ANDERSON, ETHEL CAMPBELL LOUISE (1883-1958), writer, was born on 16 March 1883 at Lillington, Warwickshire, England, eldest of four children of Cyrus Mason, squatter, and his wife Louise Campbell, née Scroggie, both Australian born. Ethel was brought up in Sydney and on her grandfather's station, Rangamatty, near Picton. With her two sisters, she was educated at home by Miss Piggott, and at Sydney Church of England Grammar School for Girls (1897-1900) under Edith Badham [q.v.7] who recommended that she become a professional musician.

Small and dark, with green eyes 'flecked with brown', Ethel was endowed with charm, a sense of humour and a zest for living. On 8 October 1904 at Christ Church, Ahmednagar, Bombay, India, she married 36-year-old Major AUSTIN THOMAS ANDERSON (1868-1949), Royal Artillery. Born on 28 August 1868 on Mauritius, he studied at Eton and served in India and Queensland (1899-1902). Ethel adored many things about India. She accompanied Austin (usually riding)—whether he was shooting bears or marching with his battery—from the remote North-West Frontier to the Himalayan foothills. Their daughter was born in 1907.

On the outbreak of war, in 1914 Anderson sailed with the 7th (Meerut) Division for France, and his family for England. Ethel lived at Cambridge and attended drawing classes at Downing College. She exhibited with a modern group, and mixed with the Darwins and their connexions. Appointed C.M.G. in 1918, Austin commanded the 48th (South Midland) Division's artillery in 1920-24. The Andersons lived in a very old house at White Ladies Aston, Worcestershire, where she decorated the whitewashed walls with murals in tempera and did the same to a nearby Saxon church.

Retiring from the army in 1924, in September Brigadier Anderson settled with his family in Sydney; they bought a house, Ball Green, at Turramurra, which Ethel filled with Indian bric-à-brac. From 1927 he was successively private secretary to Governors Sir Dudley de Chair and Sir Philip Game [qq.v.8], and to Sir Alexander Hore-Ruthven [q.v.9 Lord Gowrie] as governor and governor-general. Austin was appointed comptroller and assistant military officer in 1939. For many years chairman of the Boys' Brigade, he published several military works, and articles and letters in the Sydney Morning Herald. His wife was a member (1929-48) of the general council of the Girl Guides' Association.

Ethel 'delighted in a life which was made up of a macedoine of governors, artists and writers'. Despite slender means, she kept open house. She joined the Contemporary Group of artists and exhibited with them. Having met the modernists Roi de Mestre, Grace Cossington Smith and Roland Wakelin [qq.v.8,11, 12], she promoted their work in such magazines as Art in Australia and the Home, and in 1930 cleared her house of furniture to show Wakelin's paintings. Assisted by others, she also painted jewel-coloured frescoes in the crypt of St James's, Sydney.

Drawing on her experiences in Australia, India and Worcestershire, Ethel Anderson contributed to the Pioneer and the Civil & Military Gazette in India, the Spectator, Punch and the Cornhill Magazine in England, the American Atlantic Monthly, and the Sydney Morning Herald and Bulletin. She published two volumes of verse, Squatter's Luck (Melbourne, 1942) and Sunday at Yarralumla (1947), four collections of essays and short stories, Adventures in Appleshire (1944), Timeless Garden (1945), Indian Tales (1948) and The Little Ghosts (posthumously, 1959), and edited the letters of Patrick Hore-Ruthven, Joy of Youth (London, 1950).

Although Ethel Anderson's love for Australia was deep and complex, she was too sophisticated and too individual to fit comfortably into any stream of Australian writing. Steeped in English, French and classical literature, Ethel also appreciated the moderns. She collected 'words as a naturalist collects butterflies' and experimented constantly with metre and form. Her verse is polished, glittering, and deceptively fresh and simple; her prose a mixture of fantasy and comedy, permeated with wit and delicate irony. She saw the world with a painter's eye. Her metaphors are visual and often sensuous: 'Odours of fading hawthorne, cloying as warm honey, potent as hops'. She loved gardens and lyrically described trees, flowers and fruit. Yet, she could also write with power and restraint, as in her story, 'Mrs James Greene'. Her poem, The Song of Hagar (1957), was set to music as an oratorio by John Antill.

Somewhat formidable in later life, Ethel became quite deaf and brandished an immense, silver ear-trumpet, adorned with chiffon to match her dresses. She retained a wide circle of friends and belonged to the Queen's Club, Sydney. Austin died at Turramurra on 22 February 1949, leaving his wife virtually penniless. Ethel, always thoroughly professional in her writing, managed to earn enough to survive: her novella, At Parramatta (1956), first appeared in the Bulletin. Survived by her daughter, she died on 4

August 1958 at Ball Green and was cremated with Anglican rites.

J. D. Pringle (ed), foreword, *The Best of Ethel Anderson* (Syd, 1973); B. Foott, *Ethel and the Governors' General* (Syd, 1992); *Aust Q*, Sept 1960, p 23; *Hemisphere*, 19, no 4, Apr 1975, p 9; *SMH*, 2 Sept 1924, 7 May 1927, 19 Aug 1929, 11 Sept 1936, 19 Aug, 20 Nov 1939, 13 Sept 1940, 6 Feb 1945, 23 Feb 1949, 3 Aug 1958, 1 Dec 1973, 3 May 1975; *The Times*, 8 Aug 1958; *Bulletin*, 27 Aug 1958; H. de Berg, Roland Wakelin (taped interview, NL); Anderson family papers (ML); information from Mrs B. Ogden, Cirencester, Gloucestershire, Eng.
                                        MARTHA RUTLEDGE

ANDERSON, FRANK STRUAN (1909-1976), mining engineer, was born on 11 July 1909 at Cheshunt, Victoria, eldest son of Gerald Struan Evans Anderson, a farmer from New Zealand, and his native-born wife Olive Carr, née Best. Having attended country state schools and Melbourne Church of England Grammar School (1924-26), he enrolled in 1927 at the University of Melbourne (B.Mech.Eng., 1934). On 17 December 1937 he married Elisabeth Marian Moline at Melbourne Grammar chapel.

After gaining mining experience in South Australia, Tasmania and Victoria, in 1937 Anderson joined the Zinc Corporation Ltd as assistant underground manager at its Broken Hill operations. He was appointed general superintendent of mines in 1951. Next year he was transferred to the Melbourne headquarters of the Consolidated Zinc Pty Ltd group with which he spent terms as managing director of such enterprises as timber milling, zinc smelting, and heavy mineral sands and uranium mining. He became chairman of directors of Blair Athol Coal Pty Ltd and Australian Fluorine Chemicals Pty Ltd, and a director of several other associated or subsidiary companies, including Interstate Oil Ltd and Kembla Coal and Coke Pty Ltd. In 1952-62 he was a director of Consolidated Zinc Pty Ltd and from 1962 of the newly-formed Conzinc Riotinto of Australia Ltd. Following his retirement in 1971, he served as a non-executive director of C.R.A. and remained a director until his death.

In 1953 Struan Anderson had been appointed to the Australian Atomic Energy Commission's advisory committee on uranium mining. For his dynamic and innovative leadership in the rapid development of the Rum Jungle uranium mine in the Northern Territory on behalf of the A.A.E.C., he was appointed C.B.E. in 1955.

From 1962 Anderson was managing director of Hamersley Iron Pty Ltd and Hamersley Holdings Ltd. His major contribution to the Australian mining industry was his direction of the Hamersley Iron project in the remote Pilbara region of Western Australia, a major pioneering enterprise described as 'world scale', 'bold' and 'imaginative' by the premier of Western Australia (Sir) Charles Court. The project included the design and completion of a large mine, a heavy-duty 182-mile (293 km) railway, a major port and two complete towns; it was to cost $126 million. Construction began in January 1965 and the first ship departed in August 1966. The key factor in the achievement was Anderson's leadership —his sound engineering perceptions, his selection of able subordinates and his relentless drive. Far-sighted and courageous, he fought for high-quality engineering design and equipment. He was convinced that cutting capital expenditure was 'usually a certain route to high total costs'.

As managing director of Hamersley Iron Pty Ltd, Anderson was also responsible for negotiating Western Australian government approvals and sales contracts with the Japanese steel mills. His directness, impatience and lack of tact were resented by the Japanese, as well as by some American and English directors of H.I.'s parent companies. In 1966, when work was at a peak, he was replaced as managing director by (Sir) Russel Madigan. Anderson was then appointed director of development for the C.R.A. group, with responsiblity for research. In 1968 he was appointed a director of the Commercial Bank of Australia Ltd.

Most subordinates found Anderson to be extremely demanding, but fair, and capable of mixing freely with them after work. They appreciated his strengths: clarity of instruction, the ability to get quickly to the heart of a problem, dedication to the job, engineering judgement, vision, courage, energy and will to succeed. To others, however, he appeared aloof, even arrogant, secretive, humourless, ruthless and insensitive to people's needs. Although he served as a director (1959-68) and president (1969-71) of the Australian Mines and Metals Association (Inc.), he took no official role in the Australasian Institute of Mining and Metallurgy which he had joined in 1934 and attained its then top grade of member in 1946.

Rather tall, good looking and lean in his earlier years, he became somewhat thicker in girth with middle age. His eyes were hazel, his complexion olive, his hair brown. He dressed conservatively. Anderson belonged to the Melbourne and Athenaeum clubs in Melbourne, the Union in Sydney, the Queensland in Brisbane, the Weld in Perth and the Broken Hill Club, as well as the Melbourne Cricket and Victoria Racing clubs. While retaining membership of the Metropolitan Golf Club in Melbourne, he rarely graced its course. His work and status required a deal of first-class travel abroad. Fond of high living, he found little time for exercise, but enjoyed retreating to his farm in south Gippsland. He died suddenly of hypertensive cardiovascular disease on 6 October 1976 at South Yarra and was cremated. His wife, son and two of his three daughters survived him. Anderson's estate was sworn for probate at $297 454.

A. Trengove, *Adventure in Iron* (Melb, 1976); G. W. Hills, Engineering History, HI Project to 1966 (Internal Report, Hamersley Iron, Melb); records of A'sian Inst of Mining and Metallurgy *and* Aust Mines and Metals Assn (Melb); Univ Melb Archives.   D. F. FAIRWEATHER

ANDERSON, GEORGE (1878-1969) and **WILLIAM GEORGE** (1889-1974), printers, were born on 12 August 1878 in Edinburgh and 22 April 1889 at Footscray, Melbourne, first and fourth sons of Thomas Anderson, shipwright, and his wife Elizabeth Ogilvy, née McDonald, both Scottish born. Thomas and Elizabeth migrated to Victoria with their family in the late 1880s. On leaving school, George worked for a Melbourne printer, to whom he was probably apprenticed. He later joined another printer, Bryam Rutter Gowan, whom he eventually bought out. Trading as Keystone Printing Co., he took Herbert Du Rieu, a jobbing printer, into partnership in 1912 and printed many books for George Robertson [q.v.6] & Co., publishers. In 1916 Keystone became Anderson, Gowan & Du Rieu Pty Ltd, following Gowan's return as sleeping partner; George was managing director. When Du Rieu retired in 1918 the company was named Anderson, Gowan Pty Ltd: it concentrated on coloured brochures after Robertson & Co. curtailed publishing activities.

On 23 December 1901 George married Emily Sarah Green at Fitzroy with Methodist forms; they were to have three daughters and a son. Although he had received only a basic education, he was an avid reader with a thirst for knowledge and had a prodigious memory. Having matriculated in 1907 at the University of Melbourne, he graduated B.A. (1918), M.A. (1920), LL.B. (1922), LL.M. (1923), B.Comm. (1927), M.Comm. (1928) and Litt.D. (1949). He wrote *Fixation of Wages* (1929) and was honorary lecturer in industrial relations at the university in 1930-54. His personal library of seven thousand volumes included incunabula and fine editions.

President (1921-23 and 1931-32) of the Master Printers' Association of Victoria, he organized its jubilee exhibition of 1932 in the Melbourne Town Hall. In 1924-25 he had been foundation president of the Printing and Allied Trades Employers' Federation of Australia. Called to the Bar in 1924, George Anderson served as the federation's indus-

trial advocate in 1924-41. He was active in the Economic Society of Australia and New Zealand and a fellow (1941) of the Advertising Association of Australia; he often spoke on fiscal and printing matters, besides contributing to journals and symposiums. A fellow of the Royal Astronomical Society, he was president of the Victorian branch of the British Astronomical Association in 1953-55 and 1961-62, and also belonged to Rotary and the Melbourne Club. Survived by his daughters, he died on 3 May 1969 in East Melbourne and was buried in Burwood cemetery; his estate, which contained no realty, was sworn for probate at $154 000.

After attending Williamstown and South Melbourne State schools, Bill Anderson was apprenticed to Varley Bros, printers; from 1908 he completed his apprenticeship with Francis A. Brown and Henry E. Prior. On 12 May 1914 at Park Street Methodist Church, South Melbourne, Bill married Martha Ann Waite. They went to New Zealand where he was employed by Whitcombe & Tombs Ltd at Christchurch. In 1918 he returned to Brown, Prior & Co. They prospered and by 1925 were able to build their own premises, Printcraft House, 430 Little Bourke Street. From 1922 the firm printed most of Robertson & Mullens's [q.v.5] publications: the list grew and Brown, Prior & Co. produced many attractive volumes for them, including some limited editions. Bill was in charge of production; his high standards attracted other publishers to the house in a period when many local books were poorly produced. The firm became Brown, Prior, Anderson Pty Ltd in 1937, with Bill its managing director; in 1966, when he was chairman of directors, it moved to Burwood.

President of the Master Printers' and Allied Trades' Association in 1935-36 and 1941-42, and of the Printing and Allied Trades Employers' Federation of Australia in 1945-46, Bill represented the trade on the Apprenticeship Commission, and served on book publication and manpower committees in World War II. His recreations were gardening and lawn bowls. Survived by his four daughters and two of his three sons, he died on 13 June 1974 at Hampton and was cremated; his estate was sworn for probate at $140 610.

Sun News-Pictorial, 15 June 1974; Anderson papers (LaTL); records, Univ Melb; personal information.   J. P. HOLROYD

ANDERSON, GEORGE HERBERT (1897-1974), broadcasting executive and market researcher, was born on 20 March 1897 in Hobart, son of Rev. Henry Hudson Anderson and his wife Catherine Margaret, née Dakin. Educated at The Hutchins School (where his father was headmaster for fifteen years) and at Zeehan and Stanley state schools, from 1912 George worked on the survey and construction of Tasmanian railways.

When he enlisted in the Australian Imperial Force on 13 July 1915, Anderson was 5 ft 7¼ ins (170.8 cm) tall and weighed 10 st. 6 lb. (66.2 kg). He served in Egypt and France with the 13th Field Company, Engineers; commissioned in March 1918, he was posted to the 5th Pioneer Battalion. By the time he sailed for home in May 1919, he had matriculated through the Australian Corps Central School and had met Helen Lana Anderson. They married on 9 December 1920 at St Matthew's Anglican Church, New Norfolk, Tasmania. He became a local orchardist, farmer and grazier, and a director of the Derwent Valley Fruitgrowers Co-operative Co. Ltd.

Moving to Sydney in 1925, Anderson was assistant general secretary (1926-35) of the Graziers' Association of New South Wales. He joined the Australian Garrison Artillery in 1926 and was an executive-member (1929-30) of the New South Wales Constitutional Association. Employed by Country Broadcasting Services Ltd, he was general manager (1935-38) of 2GZ Orange, a foundation director (1936-38) of Northern Broadcasters Pty Ltd and country vice-president of the Australian Federation of Commercial Broadcasting Stations. In 1938 he was appointed station manager (later deputy general manager) of 2GB Sydney and sales manager for Macquarie Broadcasting Services Pty Ltd. At 2GB he conducted surveys to assist programme planning and to sell air-time to advertisers.

As temporary lieutenant colonel, Anderson commanded the 9th Field Regiment, Australian Field Artillery, from May 1940 until he transferred to the Reserve of Officers in August 1941. He was mobilized and appointed temporary major in May 1942, joined the A.I.F. in July, performed staff duties with II Australian Corps and retired in October 1943.

Next year Anderson organized a large survey to show what 'scientifically-applied methods of measuring the likes and dislikes of the Radio Listening Audience could establish'. After his report, *Radio Research in Australia*, was published in 1944, he resigned from 2GB to establish the Anderson Analysis of Broadcasting, a company he wholly owned until 1958. His main competitor was McNair [q.v.] Survey Pty Ltd. Anderson offered clients a national radio survey (subsequently expanded to cover television and the press) which he ran at least three times a year, based on about five hundred homes. Ratings de-

pended on interviews with housewives who reported on the household's listening behaviour; in 1947 Anderson switched to diaries, supplemented by interviews.

By the early 1960s Anderson had established a smaller market research division, Mecar Pty Ltd, and opened offices in all the mainland capital cities and in New Zealand. By late 1973, when his and McNair's organizations merged, he had over one hundred full-time staff and many part-time interviewers, mostly women. His recreations included motoring, tennis, golf and swimming; in later life he played lawn bowls. He died on 9 February 1974 at St Ives and was cremated; his wife and daughter survived him.

W. A. McNair (ed), *Some Reflections on the First Fifty Years of Market Research in Australia 1928-1978* (Syd, nd); R. R. Walker, *The Magic Spark* (Melb, 1973); *Commercial Broadcasting*, 24 Aug 1944; *Broadcasting and Television*, 10 June 1965; Anderson papers (NL); information from Mr M. Eve, Wahroonga, Dr R. Olsson, St Ives, and Mr K. Sievers, Balmoral, Syd.   MURRAY GOOT

ANDERSON, HARRY ROSS (1917-1961), professor of law, was born on 11 December 1917 at Fremantle, Western Australia, son of William Henry Anderson, civil servant and soldier, and his wife Gladys May, née Steadman, both Australian born. Ross was educated at Perth Modern High School and the University of Western Australia (LL.B., 1938). Winning a Rhodes scholarship in 1938, he attended Exeter College, Oxford, and graduated with first-class honours in jurisprudence (B.A., 1940; M.A., 1945). On his return to Perth, he joined the Australian Military Forces in October 1940 and was commissioned lieutenant in March 1942. He transferred to the Australian Imperial Force on 1 September and was attached to the Australian Intelligence Corps, New Guinea Force, in April 1943. That month he was seconded to the Air Liaison Group. Returning to Australia in March 1944, he spent six months at Tarakan, Borneo, in 1945 and was demobilized in Brisbane early next year.

On 6 February 1946 Anderson married Suzette Daphne Walcott Chase at St Mary's Anglican Church, West Perth. Having been admitted to the Bar on 18 March 1947, he practised in Perth before accepting a research scholarship at the University of Western Australia in 1948. Next year he was appointed senior lecturer in law at the University of Queensland. Promoted chief lecturer (reader) in 1952, he became foundation professor of public law in 1960.

Anderson taught contract, constitutional and administrative law, and public international law. His research in constitutional and administrative law, particularly on section 92 of the Constitution of the Commonwealth of Australia, produced a series of scholarly and thought-provoking articles that appeared in the *Australian Law Journal* in 1953, 1955 and 1959. He also wrote extensively on Commonwealth-State relations, contributing 'The States and Relations with the Commonwealth' to *Essays on the Australian Constitution* (edited by R. Else-Mitchell, Sydney, 1952, 1961) and 'The Constitutional Framework' to *The Government of the Australian States* (edited by S. R. Davis, Sydney, 1960). On sabbatical in England in 1956, Anderson began a large-scale study of judicial control of administrative tribunals and continued this work while he was a visiting fellow (1959) at the Australian National University, Canberra; he published on the subject in the *University of Queensland Law Journal* in 1956 and 1957.

An excellent administrator, Anderson was editor (1950-61) of the university's law journal, secretary of the staff association and a member (1960) of the senate. He was also an active member of the Labor Party and the Labor Lawyers' League. As president of the Queensland Civil Liberties League he had briefly been involved in public controversy in 1953 over his criticism of the State Labor government's printers and newspapers bill, at which time he was criticized in parliament by the attorney-general. Keenly interested in the arts, particularly ballet, and a former interstate hockey player, Anderson was a dynamic, popular and sociable man with a wide range of friends. Survived by his wife and two daughters, he died of cancer on 23 February 1961 at the Repatriation General Hospital, Greenslopes, and was cremated. The Ross Anderson memorial prize in constitutional law is awarded by the university.

PD (Qld), 1953-54, p 578; *Univ Qld Law J*, 4, 1961, p 95; *Univ Qld Gazette*, May 1961; *Courier-Mail*, 19 Nov 1959, 24 Feb 1961; *Age* (Melb), 23 Feb 1961; *West Australian*, 24 Feb 1961; Univ Qld Archives.
                                                    K. W. RYAN

ANDERSON, JAMES OUTRAM (1894-1973), tennis player, was born on 17 September 1894 at Enfield, Sydney, eighth child of James Outram Anderson, clerk, and his wife Patience, née Laycock, both native-born. Educated at Camden Grammar School, in 1912 James was the first interstate player to win the Victorian schoolboys' singles championship. He became New South Wales singles champion in 1914. During World War I Anderson farmed at Forbes and married Maud Irene Whitfield (d. 1955) at St James's Anglican Church, Sydney, on 24 March 1917.

New South Wales champion in 1919, he represented Australasia that year in the Davis Cup Challenge Round and with G. L. Patterson [q.v.11] defeated the British in Sydney. Anderson again represented Australasia in 1922 and Australia in 1923 in the challenge rounds played in New York. Between 1919 and 1925 he played in fifteen Davis Cup ties. His greatest achievement came in 1923 when he beat in five sets the American Wimbledon champion William ('Little Bill') Johnston, previously undefeated in the Davis Cup. As a result, Anderson was ranked number three in the world. He won the Australian men's singles in 1922, 1924 and 1925, and with (Sir) Norman Brookes [q.v.7] the Australian men's doubles in 1924. The only important overseas title that Anderson won was the men's doubles at Wimbledon (with Randolf Lycett) in 1922, although he was twice a semi-finalist in the singles.

Nicknamed 'The Greyhound', Anderson had an extremely hard, flat, shoulder-high, forehand drive. He was celebrated for his mascot, a large toy kangaroo which he brought on court. William Tilden, the American champion of the 1920s, described Anderson as 'tall, ungainly, almost awkward, taciturn, grim, unsmiling, yet interesting and to a great majority of all who see him, fascinating . . . [He] gives the impression of ruthlessness in plan which is so often belied by his charming smile and generous acknowledgment of his opponent's good shots'. Anderson was often seen as the archetypal colonial, tall and angular, with his hair parted down the middle and plastered to his head. Known to tennis enthusiasts as 'J.O.' and as Jim to his friends, he thrilled thousands with his 'sparkling armory of drives, stop, half and full volleys', but had a suspect backhand.

In 1923 the Lawn Tennis Association of Australia refused Anderson any reimbursement for business losses incurred during his five-to-seven-month tours in the three previous years. In 1924 he declined to represent Australia. That year he established J. O. Anderson & Co. Ltd to operate a chain of sports depots, but encountered difficulties and only retained one outlet in Pitt Street. In December 1926 Anderson turned professional and set up as a tennis coach in Sydney. He tried unsuccessfully to regain his amateur status in 1930. The New South Wales Lawn Tennis Association gave him a testimonial in 1940, after he had been seriously ill. On 18 November 1957 he married a widow Mabel Little, née Pearce, at the district registrar's office, Chatswood. Still 'quick-witted and very spry', he moved to The Entrance and continued coaching until the 1960s. Anderson died on 23 December 1973 at Gosford and was cremated. His wife survived him, as did the son and four daughters of his first marriage.

W. T. Tilden, *The Common Sense of Lawn Tennis* (Lond, 1924); P. Metzler, *Great Players of Australian Tennis* (Syd, 1979); G. K. Smith, *The Sweet Spot* (Melb, 1982); A. Voss, *Tilden and Tennis in the Twenties* (NY, 1985); J. Barrett, *100 Wimbledon Championships* (Lond, 1986); *Lawn Tennis and Badminton*, 17, no 1, 1 May 1926, p 7, no 32, 4 Dec 1926, p 891; *SMH*, 19 Nov 1912, 29 Oct, 26 Nov 1930, 5, 6 Jan 1940, 21 Nov 1973; *Argus*, 20, 25 Nov 1912, 2 Nov, 11 Dec 1922, 12 Nov 1923, 30 Jan 1924, 8 Sept 1925, 30 Nov, 1 Dec 1926; *Table Talk*, 18 Feb 1926; *Australian*, 28 Apr 1971.

VIRGINIA O'FARRELL

ANDERSON, ROBERT HENRY (1899-1969), botanist, was born on 12 March 1899 at Cooma, New South Wales, son of native-born parents Rev. William Addison Smyth Anderson, Presbyterian clergyman, and his wife Jane, née Thompson, late Corbett. Educated with his elder brother (Sir) William [q.v.] at Fort Street Boys' High School, Robert attended the University of Sydney (B. Sc. Agr., 1921) and won the Belmore [q.v.3] scholarship (1917). Fair haired, blue eyed and 5 ft 6 ins (167.6 cm) tall, he enlisted in the Australian Imperial Force on 6 June 1918 and embarked for Britain, but was recalled from Cape Town after the Armistice was signed and never again left Australia.

On 4 January 1921 he became a botanical assistant at the National Herbarium of New South Wales, Botanic Gardens, Sydney, under J. H. Maiden [q.v.10]. Anderson married Isabel Ellen Tyler on 10 March 1923 at the Presbyterian Church, Manly. While largely occupied in routine identification and advice to farmers in the 1920s and 1930s, he published research papers on the saltbush family (*Chenopodiaceae*). Given his limited field-experience, his books, *Tree Planting on the Farm* (1931) and *The Trees of New South Wales* (1932), were skilful compilations and were later expanded and updated.

As botanist and curator from 1936, Anderson ran the herbarium, already administratively divorced from the gardens; appointed chief botanist and curator in 1945, he took charge of both institutions which were responsible to separate masters and had rigidly non-transferable funds. Although he was granted the composite title of director and chief botanist in 1960, functional unity was achieved only by his successor.

Anderson struggled with those politicians and public servants who thought that, so long as lawns were mown and farmers' weeds identified, all was well. In the herbarium he built up a group of scientific botanists who produced authoritative publications, but his expectations of a new herbarium building remained unfulfilled. Science engaged him less than management, yet—encouraged by Joyce Vickery [q.v.]—he founded a journal of taxonomic botany, *Contributions from the New South Wales National Herbarium*; by a characteristically benign sleight of hand, he gulled the government printer and accountants into believing that a new *Flora of New South Wales* was part of the *Contributions*.

The gardens, Domain and Centennial Park required constant defence against government incursions. Anderson lost a valiantly-fought battle when the Cahill Expressway (1959) sundered his territory, destroying historic Fig Tree Avenue. Stocky and convivial, with a dry humour, Anderson combined healthy cynicism with essential kindness, fairness and affability; he relished quirkiness and delighted in outwitting departmental bureaucrats. He saw himself as a democratic socialist, but was nonetheless gratified by the redesignation of his institution as the Royal Botanic Gardens after a visit by the Queen Mother in 1958.

Anderson enabled his scientists to travel a little in Australia for collecting, and sometimes abroad, but did not himself seek such opportunities; he remained somewhat parochial and unduly satisfied with his institution. He introduced professional landscape design, appointed a botanical collector and revived exchange programmes: his administration began the Botanic Gardens' recovery from their long decline. Though he spent only 10 per cent of his time on the herbarium, it was on this scientific side that most improvement occurred. His appointments included an uncommonly high proportion of women.

Anderson lectured on forestry at the University of Sydney (1925-66) and served on the council of the Linnean Society of New South Wales (president 1940-41, honorary secretary 1966-69). Elected an honorary fellow (1966) of the Australian and New Zealand Association for the Advancement of Science, he was president of the geranium section of the Royal Horticultural Society of New South Wales; he belonged to the Everglades garden committee of the National Trust of Australia and to Bonnie Doon Golf Club.

His wife's death in 1962 plunged him into depression, but on 3 October 1963 in the registrar-general's office, Sydney, he married his secretary, a divorcee Phyllis Zena May, née Goddard, late Bell. Retiring in March 1964, he was garden editor of the *Australian Women's Weekly* until 1966. Survived by his wife and by the daughter of his first marriage, he died at his Chatswood home on 17 August 1969. His ashes were buried in his beloved Botanic Gardens where the original National Herbarium, now named the Anderson Building, bears a plaque with his likeness.

L. Gilbert, *The Royal Botanic Gardens, Sydney* (Syd, 1986); Linnean Soc NSW, *Procs*, 95, pt 1, 30

Nov 1970, p 3; *Contributions from the N.S.W. National Herbarium*, 4, no 5, 1972, p 245; Roy Botanic Gardens, Syd, *Annual Report*, 1984-85; *SMH*, 5 Mar 1964, 1 Aug 1968, 19 Aug 1969; *Daily Telegraph* (Syd), 11 Mar 1964.

L. A. S. JOHNSON

ANDERSON, SIR WILLIAM HEWSON (1897-1968), businessman and political organizer, was born on 13 March 1897 at Petersham, Sydney, son of native-born parents William Addison Smyth Anderson, student, and his wife Jane, née Thompson, late Corbett. Robert Henry [q.v.] was his brother. Young William grew up in New South Wales at Cooma, Bowenfels, Liverpool and Arncliffe while his father (who had been ordained a Presbyterian minister) moved from parish to parish and was for a time a gaol chaplain. Educated at Fort Street Boys' High School, Anderson enrolled at the University of Sydney in 1914, but gave up his studies to enlist in the Australian Imperial Force in August 1916. He served as a gunner in the 4th Divisional Ammunition Column and then with the 10th Field Artillery Brigade on the Western Front where he was twice wounded in action. The war left him with a slight but permanent deafness, and was a traumatic experience which influenced the rest of his life.

Having been discharged in May 1919, Anderson worked briefly for Queensland Insurance Co. in Sydney and in 1920 joined the Shell Co. of Australia Ltd as an audit clerk. He resumed studies part time at the University of Sydney and graduated with honours (B.Ec., 1920). On 22 April 1922 he married Elizabeth Catherine Shea in the Arncliffe Presbyterian Church; they were to have three children. Sent as chief accountant to Shell's New Zealand company in 1925, he became assistant manager in 1930. Anderson transferred to the Australian head office in 1933 and Melbourne became his permanent home. In 1935 he was promoted chief accountant and in 1950 became assistant general manager. When Shell established an Australian board in 1951, he was appointed a director. In addition to being the chief accounting and financial executive of Shell Australia from 1935 until he retired in 1957, he was a director of several subsidiary companies of the Shell group.

Anderson was one of the most prominent of thousands of people, often ex-servicemen, who became active in public life in the early years of World War II because of dissatisfaction with both the Australian Labor Party and the United Australia Party. He disliked Labor not only for its socialism and pacifist streak, but also because in the years of the Hitler-Stalin pact he judged Labor to be sub-ject to communist influence through the left-wing unions. Yet, he also despaired of the U.A.P. which was internally divided and at odds with the Country Party; furthermore, he thought that the U.A.P. was excessively influenced by big business and almost non-existent at the local branch level.

With some friends, Anderson formed a protest conservative group called the Services and Citizens' Party, one of several 'splinter' bodies of the right which appeared in the early 1940s. It demanded a greater role for ordinary non-Labor citizens, as well as relief for ex-servicemen who had been unemployed or who were economically tied to depressed farms. After the splinter parties won almost 20 per cent of the vote in Victoria at the 1943 Federal elections, Anderson and other representatives of these groups met the U.A.P. leader (Sir) Robert Menzies [q.v.] at Albury in 1944 and agreed to form the Liberal Party.

The Victorian branch of the Liberal Party chose Anderson as its first president (1945-48). He was federal president in 1951-56. In both positions he sought to represent the rank and file of the branches against the parliamentarians. Although he employed occasional bombast against Menzies and other politicians, he formed a friendship with the prime minister with whom he shared much in aspirations and background. Anderson saw his own role as being in the organizational wing and never aspired to a parliamentary career.

A prolific pamphleteer, he articulated a view that was strongly anti-radical and scourged socialists, pacifists, left-leaning churchmen and 'class warfare'. Anderson advocated patriotism, equality of opportunity, social welfare, free enterprise and what would later be known as economic nationalism. He abhorred speculation and sharp business practices, and hoped that manual workers, among whom he grew up, would vote Liberal. Tending to see things in sharp black and white, he had a flair for torrid phrases, as when he attacked the 'red ants' who remained in the public service from the 1941-49 Labor governments.

He also disliked and distrusted the Country Party, and opposed its 1948 proposal to ban the Communist Party of Australia. When the 40-hour week was being discussed, he recommended shorter working hours allied to greater productivity. As a supporter of the move by Premier John Cain and Opposition leader Thomas Hollway [qq.v.] to break the power of the Country Party (derived from the unequal electoral distribution of the 1930s and 1940s), Anderson was propelled in 1952 into a liaison with the State Labor Party. He supported the Catholic-oriented A.L.P. industrial groups and deplored sectarianism during the excitement in 1954 of the Labor Party split. From 1955 the government of (Sir)

Henry Bolte fulfilled many of Anderson's hopes.

While the extreme left portrayed him as a sinister figure—a representative of international big business behind Menzies—Anderson usually took pains to keep his business and political activities separate. Clashes of interest, however, did arise, such as over petrol price control. Some colleagues regarded his outspoken political role as an embarrassment to the company, but his seniors in Shell accepted it. As the Shell executive in charge of personnel after World War II, Anderson put his views favouring the 'plain man' and equal opportunity for all into practice through a staff welfare programme and by ensuring that the company recruited from a wider field than tended to happen at head office before 1939.

When the events required it, Anderson devoted about forty-five minutes in the morning to political affairs; he then cleared his desk and worked for the company for the rest of the day; he generally came home for dinner. His wife and children did not feel that his public life impinged unduly on his time with them. Anderson's highly ordered approach, intense nervous energy, clarity of mind and sheer ability enabled this dense packing of each working day. A staunch Christian conviction, unwavering since his childhood in country manses, was one of his great motivating forces. He was for years an elder of Ewing Memorial Presbyterian Church, East Malvern, and a delegate to the State assembly. Anderson was of a generation which still found no contradiction between a fervent Australian patriotism and a strong sense of Scottishness, including a love of Robert Burns's poetry (his grandfather, a police inspector, had insisted on his grandchildren reading it to him each week).

Wiry and of middle height, bespectacled and plainly dressed, to his critics Anderson appeared moralistic, strict, uncomfortably blunt and a tough political opponent. Others found him a loyal and thoughtful friend, with an attractive, dry sense of humour. Following his retirement, he was a member of the board of the Reserve Bank of Australia from 1959 until his death, federal treasurer (1956-68) of the Liberal Party and president (1960-67) of the (Royal) Dental Hospital of Melbourne which named its new auditorium after him. He belonged to the Athenaeum, the Savage and the Metropolitan Golf clubs. Anderson had been appointed C.B.E. in 1950 and knighted in 1965. Survived by his wife, daughter and two sons, Sir William died on 25 March 1968 in Wellington, while holidaying in New Zealand, and was cremated.

K. West, *Power in the Liberal Party* (Melb, 1966); P. Aimer, *Politics, Power and Persuasion* (Syd, 1974); *Shell Times*, 7, no 2, 1968; *SMH*, 20, 21 Nov 1951, 26 June 1965, 26 Mar 1968; K. B. White, A Political Biography of Thomas Tuke Hollway (M.A. thesis, La Trobe Univ, 1975); information from Lady Anderson, East Malvern, Mrs M. Thompson, Greensborough, and Mr G. W. Ramsden, Toorak, Melb.

ROBERT MURRAY

ANDERSON, WILLIAM HOPTON (1891-1975), air force officer, was born on 30 December 1891 at Kew, Melbourne, third son of Edward Anderson, a surveyor from England, and his Victorian-born wife Florence, née Handfield. Educated at Melbourne Church of England Grammar School, William played football, joined the cadets and was a member of the school's rifle team. He gained first-class honours and an exhibition in Greek and Latin at the 1910 senior public examinations. In December he was given a permanent commission in the Royal Australian (Garrison) Artillery; he served the next four years in Sydney. Transferring to the Australian Naval and Military Expeditionary Force in March 1915, he proceeded to Rabaul, German New Guinea, and took charge of the battery on Matupi Island in Simpson Harbour.

Having taken home leave, Anderson was appointed captain in the Australian Flying Corps, Australian Imperial Force, on 14 January 1916, and embarked for Egypt with No. 1 Squadron. In May he was sent to England for pilot training; service with the Royal Flying Corps followed. He left for France in August 1917 as a flight commander in No. 3 Squadron, A.F.C. (No. 69 Squadron, R.F.C.), a corps reconnaissance unit. On 21 October, when he was spotting for the artillery near Lens, his aircraft was attacked by German scouts. Anderson's 'gallant and skilful' flying enabled his observer to return fire and to keep the enemy at bay until help arrived. Ten days later Anderson piloted one of two R.E.8s which beat off four Albatross scouts. He completed his mission on each occasion. During an artillery-ranging flight near Messines Ridge, Belgium, on 6 December, he engaged an enemy reconnaissance two-seater plane which his observer shot down.

Promoted temporary major in January 1918, Anderson transferred to England in command of No. 7 Training Squadron. He was awarded the Distinguished Flying Cross in June and the Belgian Croix de Guerre next month. In October he returned to No. 3 Squadron as commanding officer, but was hospitalized in January 1919. After his repatriation in May, he was mentioned in dispatches as further recognition of his war service. On the inauguration of the (Royal) Australian Air Force on 31 March 1921, he was appointed squadron leader and the

R.A.A.F.'s third most senior officer. For most of 1921-26 he performed the personnel duties of the second air member of the Air Board and concurrently commanded No. 1 Flying Training School, Point Cook, Victoria, in 1925-26; he had previously been in charge of the school in 1920-21. Promoted wing commander on 23 March 1927 while studying at the Royal Air Force Staff College, Andover, England, he spent the next two years as R.A.A.F. liaison officer at the Air Ministry in London.

Anderson briefly commanded No. 1 Aircraft Depot, Laverton, Victoria, in 1929, before holding a series of appointments to the Air Board as air member for supply (1929-33 and 1936-40), air member for personnel (1933-34, 1940 and 1943-44) and air member for organization and equipment (1941-42). He had attended the Imperial Defence College in England in 1935 and was acting chief of the Air Staff from 9 January to 10 February 1940. Interspersed with his Headquarters appointments were postings as air officer commanding, Central Area (1940-41) and Eastern Area (1942-43), and commandant, R.A.A.F. Staff School, Mount Martha, Victoria (July to November 1943 and from October 1944). His promotions had been steady: group captain in December 1932, air commodore on 1 January 1938 and acting air vice marshal in September 1941. He retired in April 1946 with the honorary rank of air vice marshal.

Despite his seniority, Anderson had never been one of the R.A.A.F.'s forceful figures. Known throughout the service as 'Andy' or 'Mucker', he had a long, sorrowful face which complemented his normally silent and retiring manner. J. E. Hewitt remembered him as 'an admirable man but . . . slow and so immersed in the minutiae of administration that some important policy matters languished . . . one of the nicest persons . . . although courageous he was indecisive and loath to take disciplinary action'. Honorary chairman (1947-71) of the Victorian committee of the Services Canteens Trust Fund, Anderson had been appointed O.B.E. in 1933 and C.B.E. in 1934. He was a member of the Naval and Military Club, Melbourne, and listed his only recreation as tennis. A bachelor, he lived with his unmarried sister Isabelle in Jolimont Terrace, East Melbourne. There he died on 30 December 1975, his birthday. He was buried in Boroondara cemetery, Kew, after a service at Holy Trinity Anglican Church, East Melbourne, where his sister later endowed a stained-glass window in his memory.

F. M. Cutlack, *The Australian Flying Corps* (Syd, 1923); S. S. Mackenzie, *The Australians at Rabaul* (Syd, 1927); G. Odgers, *Air War Against Japan 1943-1945* (Canb, 1957); D. N. Gillison, *Royal Australian Air Force 1939-1942* (Canb, 1962); K. Isaacs, *Military Aircraft of Australia 1909-1918* (Canb, 1971); J. E. Hewitt, *Adversity in Success* (Melb, 1980); W. Perry, *The Naval and Military Club, Melbourne* (Melb, 1981); R. Williams, *These are Facts* (Canb, 1977); C. D. Coulthard-Clark, *The Third Brother* (Syd, 1991); *Age* (Melb), 3 Jan 1976; information from Mr K. M. Bulow, Dandenong, Melb.   C. D. COULTHARD-CLARK

ANDERSON, WILLIAM WALLACE (1888-1975), sculptor, was born 20 January 1888 at Dean, Victoria, twin son and third child of William Anderson, farmer and later member of the Legislative Assembly, and his wife Helen Glover, née Naples, both Victorian born. Sent to Geelong College (1902-03), Wallace studied engineering at nearby Gordon Technical College (1904-05) where he also took modelling-classes at night with J. Tranthim-Fryer. In Melbourne about 1914 he attended night-classes for life-drawing, given by C. D. Richardson [q.v.11] at the Victorian Artists Society, and for drawing at the National Gallery schools, while teaching by day at Sunshine Technical School.

In 1915 Anderson enlisted in the Australian Imperial Force. He was 5 ft 8 ins (172.7 cm) tall, with a fresh complexion, hazel eyes and brown hair. On 6 May 1916 at Scots Church, Melbourne, he married Gladys Ada Andrews with Presbyterian forms, before embarking in July for England. He served in France as a lieutenant in the 23rd Battalion. In April 1918 he was appointed museums officer and sculptor to the A.I.F; he was based in the Australian War Records Section, London, with sculptors William Bowles and Web Gilbert [qq.v.7,9]. Anderson toured battlefields in France, Egypt and Palestine, making models of the landscape and gathering records for use in later works. After the war he attended Chelsea Polytechnic. In 1920 he returned to Melbourne and continued his job, with the Australian War Museum, producing models, dioramas and sculpture in an annexe of the Exhibition Building. From 1930 he engaged in private practice as a sculptor. Moving to Canberra, he worked for the Australian War Memorial in 1944-46. When he returned to Melbourne he taught modelling for a short period at Footscray Technical College, but by 1947 had resumed his own work, though he ceased large-scale sculpture.

Anderson had produced a number of bronze war memorials and memorial portraits for Melbourne and for Victorian country towns. One of the earliest was 'Spirit of Anzac' (1928), situated in Johnstone Park, Geelong. His most famous work is that of Simpson [q.v.9 J. S. Kirkpatrick] and his donkey (1935), which he completed after winning a competition conducted by the Victorian Division of the Australian Red Cross. Anderson's fee was £350; the cast, made by the Chiurazzi Foundry, Naples, Italy, cost £40. The work stands at the Shrine of Remembrance, Melbourne, and has become well known as a symbol of the Anzac tradition.

In 1937 Anderson completed a life-sized, bronze statue of King George V for Geelong. Between 1939 and 1945 he executed a series of nine busts of Australian prime ministers for the Botanic Gardens, Ballarat. One of his last public works, a figure of a soldier in bronze, completed about 1950, stands as the war memorial outside the Box Hill Town Hall.

Having first shown with the Victorian Artists Society in 1915, Anderson exhibited regularly with it from 1921 to 1936, with the Australian Sculptors' Society in 1933, with the Victorian Sculptors' Society in 1949, and with the Australian Academy of Art in 1939 and 1943. He also exhibited at the Bread and Cheese Club (of which he was a member) in 1940 and 1946, and held one-man shows in Melbourne at Tye's Gallery (1953) and the Joshua McClelland Print Room (1967). Predeceased by his wife, Anderson died on 7 October 1975 at Geelong and was cremated. His son and two daughters survived him.

H. W. Malloch, *Fellows All* (Melb, 1943); K. Scarlett, *Australian Sculptors Exhibition Lists* (Melb, 1979), and *Australian Sculptors* (Melb, 1980); *Herald* (Melb), 26 Apr 1933, 3 June 1939, 19 Nov 1949; *Age*, 27 Apr, 1 June 1933, 22 June 1936, 14 July 1953, 10 Oct 1975; *Argus*, 27 Apr 1933, 12 Feb 1935, 22 June 1936, 18 July 1939, 14 July 1953; *Geelong Advertiser*, 11 Oct 1975; W. W. Anderson, Autobiography (held by Mr R. Anderson, Beachmere, Qld, *and* copy in Aust mss collection, SLV); K. Scarlett papers (AMPA).

KEN SCARLETT

ANDREW, MARSHALL (1897-1960), medical practitioner, was born on 6 September 1897 at Willoughby, Sydney, youngest of four children of John Andrew, printer and stationer, and his wife Jessie Davidson, née Colvin, both migrants from Scotland. Educated at Barker College, where he was head prefect, and at the University of Sydney (M.B., Ch.M., 1923), Marshall served as a resident medical officer at Sydney Hospital in 1923-24 before working overseas. He returned to New South Wales and entered general practice. On 16 October 1929 he married Agnes (Nancy) Hood Fenwick at St Philip's Anglican Church, Sydney.

Moving his practice to Picton that year, Andrew became visiting medical officer at the Queen Victoria Sanatorium, Thirlmere, and at the Picton Lakes Village, thereby beginning his lifelong involvement in the treatment of tuberculosis. In 1939 he sold his Picton practice and visited Britain and Scandinavia to study the treatment of the disease. Back in New South Wales later that year, he settled at Leura in the Blue Mountains, and was appointed medical superintendent of the Bodington Red Cross Home and the Queen Victoria Home for Consumptives, Wentworth Falls. At a time of austerity and shortages Andrew demonstrated considerable technical ingenuity in using discarded components to construct necessary but unobtainable equipment, such as tomography apparatus. In 1946 he returned to private practice as a chest specialist.

A bout of viral pneumonia weakened his health and led him in July 1949 to take the position of State director of tuberculosis, with the immediate task of implementing the Commonwealth-State anti-tuberculosis programme. In some quarters his appointment met only grudging support: a commentator in the *Sydney Morning Herald* suggested that, had a larger salary been offered, the State could have obtained an outstanding expert. While that newspaper continued to criticize the New South Wales Labor government's allegedly dilatory record on tuberculosis, it did not directly attack Dr Andrew who was, himself, to be frustrated by public service constraints and delays.

By the time Andrew resigned in January 1960, deaths from tuberculosis in New South Wales had fallen from 769 in 1949 to 224 in 1959, and the number of new cases detected had dropped from 1642 to 1166 over the same period. He gave due emphasis to the detection, treatment and rehabilitation of tuberculosis sufferers, and took particular pride in the increased number of chest clinics (from 8 to 9 in Sydney, and from 2 to 40 in country areas), the elimination of waiting lists for treatment and the additional facilities in public hospitals. The retreat of tuberculosis, however, probably resulted as much from improvements in general nutrition and housing standards, the spread of pasteurization and the efficacy of new drugs as from the formal anti-tuberculosis campaign with its compulsory mass X-rays and special pensions. Nonetheless, Andrew had played an important role in achieving the willing co-operation of private practitioners and public health authorities in the implementation of a major campaign, and was praised for his dexterity in overcoming previously strained relations.

Andrew's interests included photography and contract bridge, but his greatest passion was for golf: he was a champion club player and a dedicated member of the Picton, Leura and Killara clubs. He was also a director of the Queen Victoria Homes for Consumptives and later of the family printing firm, John Andrew & Co. With his wife Nancy he had supported the Blue Mountains Grammar School at

Springwood. Andrew possessed most of the virtues commonly associated with doctors of his era. Dedicated and hard working, with a strong sense of right and wrong, he was generous to friends and patients.

He never fully recovered from Nancy's sudden death in October 1959 which, with his retirement, left him bereft. In mid-1960 he went abroad. He died of myocardial infarction on 25 July at Newport, Wales, and was cremated. His two sons survived him; his estate was sworn for probate at £54 451. The Marshall Andrew unit at Wollongong Hospital is named in his memory.

B. B. Schaffer and D. C. Corbett (eds), *Decisions* (Melb, 1965); F. B. Smith, *The Retreat of Tuberculosis* (Lond, 1988); Director-General of Public Health (NSW), *Annual Report*, 1953-60; *MJA*, 15 July 1961; *Hist Studies*, no 80, Apr 1983; *SMH*, 6, 15 May 1949, 29 Jan, 28 July 1960; information from Mr J. Andrew, Wentworth Falls, NSW, and Dr M. J. A. Andrew, Elanora Heights, Syd.

JAN MCDONALD

ANDREWS, ROLAND STUART (1897-1961), industrial chemist and administrator, was born on 20 September 1897 at Granville, Sydney, eldest son of native-born parents Thomas Joseph Andrews, draper, and his wife Margaret Elizabeth, née Cormack. Roland attended Sydney Technical High School and, after being rejected for military service, studied chemistry at the University of Sydney (B.Sc., 1919). He began work as a shift chemist with Broken Hill Proprietary Co. Ltd at Newcastle. The sheltered and genteel background provided by his Quaker mother had not prepared him for the harsh working conditions then prevailing in heavy industry which were to affect him profoundly: although he had no formal training in management, he proved a successful 'shift boss' in the coke-oven plant, mainly because of his empathy with the workforce.

In 1925 Andrews left B.H.P. and became head chemistry teacher at Sydney Technical College. He took leave to study the treatment of coal in the United States of America. On 28 August 1926 he married Kathleen May Foster Waitt at the Methodist Church, Lindfield, Sydney. Next year he was appointed chief chemist to the Metropolitan Gas Co. in Melbourne, the largest and probably the most conservative gas company in Australia.

The first qualified scientist to be employed by the company, Andrews initially addressed the prevailing issues of gas quality and gas production. He then turned his attention to a problem which had plagued the Victorian industry since its formation in the 1850s: how to make gas from Victorian brown coal and avoid dependence on the unsettled coal industry of the Hunter Valley in New South Wales. In the 1930s Andrews attempted to modify existing black-coal carbonizing plant to gasify brown coal or brown-coal briquettes, but eventually acknowledged its technical impossibility. In the late 1930s and early 1940s, assisted by researchers at the University of Melbourne, he investigated two German processes for the gasification of brown coal before concluding that neither was suitable for use with Victorian brown-coal briquettes.

On the outbreak of World War II Andrews and his team were called upon to conduct war-related research for the Ministry of Munitions and the Director of Explosives Supply. The 1940s provided no respite from strikes and by the end of the war the Metropolitan Gas Co. and the Victorian government were desperate to use the State's brown coal for gas production. With a company engineer, R. J. Bennie, he was sent to England in 1946. To gain entry to Germany, Andrews was temporarily appointed colonel in the British Army. There he contacted Dr F. S. H. Danulat and E. A. Brüggemann who had both been involved in the development of the Lurgi brown-coal gasification process. On his recommendation, in 1947 the two Germans were brought to Australia; in July 1948 they reported that the Lurgi process was suitable for Victorian brown coal.

With the primary objective of building a Lurgi plant at Morwell, the Gas and Fuel Corporation of Victoria was formed in December 1950; Andrews was its chief technical officer. On 1 January 1952 he became chairman and managing director of the corporation. The demands of administering the construction, and of commissioning the technically advanced plant, were considerable. Labour was scarce and relatively unskilled, and the industrial climate turbulent. Andrews, however, had retained his respect for the workforce and the Gas and Fuel Corporation remained virtually free from strikes throughout the ten years of his leadership. Officially opened by the Duke of Edinburgh in November 1956, the Morwell plant cost some £10-12 million; it marked the culmination of more than twenty-five years work by Andrews, and was a tribute to his qualities as scientist and administrator.

A quiet, unassuming Christian, Andrews was an excellent public speaker and a dedicated scientist who contributed extensively to the literature on fuel. In 1948 he had graduated D.Sc. from the University of Melbourne. A member of the Institute of Chemical Engineers and the Institute of Gas Engineers, and a fellow of the Institute of Metals and the Australian Academy of Science, he was appointed C.M.G. in 1957. His hobbies included tennis, stamp-collecting, and bushwalking with an eye to geological specimens. Andrews died of hypertensive coronary disease on 14 October 1961 at his Glen Iris home and was cremated. Two sons survived him, as did his wife who had been foundation president (1955) of the Women's Gas Association.

R. C. Proudley, *Circle of Influence* (Melb, 1987); *Gascor News*, Sept-Oct 1961; *National Gas Bulletin*, Oct 1961; Roy Aust Chemical Inst, *Procs*, Jan 1962; *Herald* (Melb), 24 Dec 1955, 16 Oct 1961; *Age* (Melb) and *Sun News-Pictorial*, 16 Oct 1961; information from Mr B. Andrews, Glen Iris, Melb.

RAY PROUDLEY

ANDRONICUS, JOHN DAMIANOS (1894-1973), coffee merchant, was born on 23 October 1894 at Mylopatamo (Potamós), Kithira, Greece, youngest of eleven children of Damianos Nicholas Andronicus, fisherman, and his wife Vassiliki, née Karidis. The pressure of population on limited resources encouraged migration, as it had done in Greece for centuries. John followed five of his brothers to Australia, reaching Sydney in the *Bremen* on 10 November 1908. He went to school, initially with no knowledge of English, at West Maitland and Tamworth before joining his brothers' business in 1910.

The most prominent of them, Emanuel, had opened a chocolate shop—with coffee as a sideline—in George Street near Circular Quay in 1904. The Andronicus brothers also conducted an enterprising wholesale business with Greek shopkeepers in several country towns. Emanuel prospered. He was Greek consul in Sydney in 1924-30 and helped many Greeks to establish themselves in what he always thought was a land of opportunity. A warm supporter of the Labor Party, he encouraged Greek Australians to vote in State and Federal elections. Meanwhile John was learning the business: he became skilled in tea and coffee blending, and in assisting with sales, especially on the north coast. He, too, prospered, and was naturalized in 1924. On 29 December 1928 he married Kathleen Ellen Gordon at St Sophia's, the Greek Orthodox cathedral in Sydney. They were to have two sons, Charles and George.

In 1936 John bought the firm and next year established Andronicus Bros. He and the indefatigable Kathleen ran the business between them. From Arabia, Africa, India, Brazil and New Guinea, they imported coffee beans which they roasted and ground for both the retail and wholesale trades; in addition, they sold continental foods such as olives, sesame seeds, cheeses and halva, as well as hand-made chocolates. John worked fourteen hours a day, seven days a week; it would be years before he could spend much time on his extensive coin collection, his passion for woodworking, his love of boating, or his penchant for driving fast cars.

The influx of European migrants after 1945 helped to acquaint Australians with foreign tastes and increased the popularity of European foods. The advent of Nescafé instant coffee in 1947 appears to have stimulated demand for real coffee. Soon the Andronicus family was selling their coffee in bulk to grocers' shops and cafés. In the early 1960s Charles and George established their own wholesale company, Andronicus Coffee Pty Ltd. John and Kathleen continued at the George Street shop until 1973 when it was closed to make way for 'development' (the Regent hotel now stands on the site). Three months later, on 15 July 1973, Andronicus died at his Gordon home and was cremated with Anglican rites; his wife and sons survived him.

John had long aspired to build a business that could be taken over and enjoyed by his sons. In this ambition he eminently succeeded. He left a well-established company with an excellent reputation for stability and probity. His sons found no difficulty in obtaining credit to expand until, in 1983, they sold out, like so many successful Australian family businesses in recent decades, to a multinational corporation, in this case the Swiss-owned Nestlé Australia Ltd.

R. Ostrow, *The New Boy Network* (Melb, 1987); K. Dunstan, *The Perfect Cup* (Syd, 1989); *SMH*, 14 Aug 1954, 9 Feb 1960, 11 Feb 1974; naturalization file, A1/1 24/26002 (AA); information from Mr C. Andronicus, Syd, and Mr H. Gilchrist, Canb.

D. W. A. BAKER

ANGAS, SIR JOHN KEITH (1900-1977), pastoralist, was born on 30 January 1900 at Lindsay Park, Angaston, South Australia, fourth child of English-born Charles Howard Angas, sheep-farmer, and his wife Eliza Etty, née Dean, and great-grandson of George Fife Angas [q.v.1]. Keith attended the Collegiate School of St Peter, Adelaide, and Geelong Grammar School, Victoria (1914-18), where he proved a humane house captain and became an honorary member of the junior teaching staff. In 1920 he toured Britain, driving an Armstrong Siddeley chassis, with a soapbox for a seat and no windscreen; he later designed the coachwork and had it custom-built in Adelaide. In 1922 he published *Safari Days*, describing six months in British East Africa during which he shot a lion which had mauled his leader. At St Cuthbert's Anglican Church, Prospect, Adelaide, on 30 April 1924 Angas married Gwynnyth Fay Good. After his father's death in 1928, he inherited Lindsay Park, the family property on which he bred sheep and horses, and ran deer.

Blessed with charm, *élan* and a delightful sense of humour, Angas was six feet (182.9 cm) tall and of impressive build, with brown hair and hazel eyes. In 1939 he enlisted in the Australian Military Forces and was posted to the 13th Field Brigade, Royal Australian Artillery. On 10 February 1942 he transferred to the Australian Imperial Force as a captain and from July was a member of the Australian Army Service Corps, South Australian Lines of Communication Area. His appointment terminated in July 1944.

Angas belonged to many and various organizations: he was president (1947-50) of the Liberal and Country League of South Australia, and was knighted in 1952; he was chairman (1952-62) of the South Australian Institute of Medical and Veterinary Science, the South Australian Jockey Club, the Graziers' Federal Council of Australia (1939-40), Elder Smith [qq.v.4,6] & Co. Ltd, Horwood Bagshaw Ltd and Bagot's Executor Trustee Co. Ltd; he was, as well, a director on the Adelaide board of the Colonial Mutual Life Assurance Society Ltd. A governor of the Anti-Cancer Foundation of South Australia and vice-president of the local branch of the Royal Geographical Society of Australasia, he was a councillor (1938-61) of St Mark's College and in 1961 joined the committee on the future of tertiary education, Australian Universities Commission. While president (1973-75) of the Royal Automobile Association of South Australia, he drove a late-model Holden.

Although he was a respected figurehead, Sir Keith was disposed to defend the *status quo* and was seldom influential on the bodies he served. Philanthropic and generous, he donated over £40 000 to the Royal Agricultural and Horticultural Society of South Australia, of which he was president (1951-59) and treasurer. He belonged to the Adelaide and Melbourne clubs, enjoyed golf and bowls, and at the age of 65 still listed water-skiing as his recreation. Angas also painted landscapes and sculpted the horses' heads for the gateway to the stables at Lindsay Park. In 1965 he sold the property to a syndicate, led by the thoroughbred horse-trainer Colin Hayes, and moved to North Adelaide.

Recognized as one of the last Anglo-Australian gentlemen in South Australia, Sir Keith represented a type which succumbed to the rapid changes of the post-Playford era. Survived by his wife, daughter and son, Angas died on 13 April 1977 at Thorngate and was cremated, as he wished, without 'fuss or funereal pomp'. His portrait by Paul Fitzgerald is held by the family.

S. Nicol, *Bullock Tracks and Bitumen* (Adel, 1978); J. Brown, *Town Life in Pioneer South Australia* (Adel, 1980); C. and M. Kerr, *Royal Show* (Adel, 1983); *South Aust Motor*, 60, no 4, July 1977; Geelong C of E Grammar School, *Corian*, July-Aug 1978; *Australian*, 8 July 1967; *Advertiser* (Adel), 5 June 1952, 20 June 1973, 14 Apr 1977; *The Times*, 3 June 1977; Geelong C of E Grammar School Archives.   R. W. LINN

ANGLES, CYRIL JOSEPH (1906-1962), sporting commentator, was born on 1 October 1906 at Surry Hills, Sydney, second of eleven children of Victor Emmanuel Angles, labourer, and his wife Ethel Josephine, née Smith, both Sydneysiders. His mother averred that Cyril cried until he was eighteen months old. The family shifted to the Kensington district when he was 4 and he was later sent to Marist Brothers' High School, Darlinghurst, where he distinguished himself as a sprinter in 1919. Having ridden his pony at Payten's [q.v.11] paddock, Randwick, he was apprenticed as a jockey to Jack Phoenix, but put on weight and left after two years. By then he belonged to the sub-culture of the turf which flourished around the five courses near his home and he next worked as a clerk for his father, 'Lordy' Angles, who had become a bookie. Through the influence of his brother Fred, a big punter, in 1924 Cyril was employed as a tipster and commission agent by the self-styled 'Mastermind of the Turf' Rufe Naylor [q.v.10] who got him a job in 1931 with radio station 2KY.

Encouraged in his new career by Emil Voigt [q.v.12], Angles broadcast between thirty and fifty-eight races each week. He moved to 2UW by February 1935, forming a popular racing service with his former rival Charles Lawrence [q.v.10], and was involved in the protracted legal struggle between that station and the Victoria Park Racing Club in 1936-38 over the right to call races from outside the track. Before being allowed to broadcast on course, Angles covered events from the laundry of a flat overlooking the Kensington track, from a roost in the branches of a Moreton Bay fig-tree flanking Warwick Farm, from a chair precariously perched upon a table on the back of a lorry that parked next to Rosehill and from a platform atop some rickety scaffolding at Ascot.

The accuracy of his incisive and unhurried descriptions, delivered in a flat, mechanical and slightly abrasive voice, established his reputation and in 1940 he was promoted head of 2UW's sporting department. Rejected as medically unfit for service in World War II, Angles joined 2GB on 1 December 1945 as the highest-paid broadcaster in Australia. He was to return to 2UW by January 1958. During his career he estimated that he had called 30 000 horse, trotting and greyhound races, as well as commenting on a sporting gallimaufry that included boxing, wrestling, athletics, cycling, ice-hockey, football, cricket, swimming and most other codes down to ping-pong. He even appeared in a revue, *They're Racing*, with George Wallace junior [q.v.] at Brisbane's Theatre Royal in May 1949. With his income secure, Angles had stopped betting as early as 1938—you 'can't beat the game'—but frugality was foreign to him. Open hearted, he did not know how to refuse a request and gave his money away, saying 'she'll be apples'. With wavy hair combed carefully back, sharp eyes, arched brows, prominent teeth and a full lower lip, he dressed in a dark suit and tie, and was over-weight, cheerful and loyal 'from go to whoa'.

On 17 November 1928 Angles had married Ivy Janet Manders at St Michael's Anglican Church, Surry Hills. They had met when both of them were aged 16 and been sweethearts ever since. She meant 'the world' to him and was a 'good little brick' who took the bad times with the good. Angles was a devoted husband and the proud father of three daughters, his 'little princesses'. A keen yachtsman, tennis and billiard player, he belonged to City Tattersall's, the Albert and the Professional Musicians' clubs; he owned a much-thumbed copy of Don Athaldo's [q.v.] *Health, Strength & Muscular Power* and his favourite author was Edgar Wallace. For the last seven years of his life Angles fought a battle with cancer, for which he underwent radium treatment and numerous operations. Survived by his wife and daughters, he died of cardiac disease on 29 July 1962 at his East Lindfield home and was buried with Catholic rites in Northern Suburbs cemetery.

Wireless Weekly, 15 Feb 1935, 11 Dec 1936, 29 Jan 1937, 2, 9, 16, 23, 30 Sept 1938; *Parade*, Oct 1964; *SMH*, 30 July 1962; *Sun-Herald*, 24 June, 1 July 1979; Angles papers (ML); information from Mr N. B. Nairn, Lyneham, Canb.

JOHN RITCHIE

ANGWIN, HUGH THOMAS MOFFITT (1888-1949), engineer and public servant, was born on 8 October 1888 at Angaston, South Australia, son of Thomas Britton Angwin, Wesleyan clergyman, and his wife Mary Jane, née Moffitt. Hugh attended South Broken Hill Public School and Prince Alfred College, Adelaide, before studying at the University of Adelaide and the South Australian School of Mines and Industries (B.Sc., 1910; Dip. Electrical Engineering, 1912). In 1911 he joined the Public Works Department as a draftsman and won the Angas [q.v.3] engineering scholarship which enabled him to work in England in 1912. Next year he rejoined his department and converted his degree (B.Eng.). Serious, meticulous, gentle and self-effacing, he was 5 ft 8½ ins (174 cm) tall, with hazel eyes and dark brown hair. Late in 1917 he enlisted in the Australian Imperial Force, but only reached France in October 1918. Before returning home, he inspected river and dock works in England.

Appointed assistant resident engineer, River Murray Works, Angwin was stationed at Blanchetown from 1919 until promoted assistant constructing engineer in Adelaide in 1924. At the Methodist Church, Renmark, on 16 August 1928 he married Edna Turnbull, a 21-year-old Englishwoman. Two years later in Adelaide he became chief engineer to the South Australian Harbors Board. He joined the board as a commissioner in 1935 upon his appointment as engineer-in-chief of the Engineering and Water Supply Department. Plans for the state-aided industrialization of South Australia involved co-operation with Broken Hill Pty Co. Ltd which needed water for a blast furnace at Whyalla. Angwin's project to pipe River Murray water from Morgan to Whyalla and the north was completed in 1944 and praised by Premier (Sir) Thomas Playford as 'one of the most important public works ever undertaken in the State'. That year Angwin was appointed C.M.G.

During World War II his department, though understaffed, handled large projects, including the mining of brown coal at Leigh Creek. Having visited Canada and the United States of America in 1944-45, Angwin reported to the State government in 1946 on the use of low-grade coals in North America. In that year he became chairman of the new Electricity Trust of South Australia; the government was criticized for burdening him with an additional demanding job. Angwin was efficient and impartial: he delegated authority, noted his staff's needs and tactfully eased departmental formality. Among his achievements were the Barossa-Salisbury and Mannum-Adelaide pipelines, the design and construction of sewage-treatment works at Glenelg, major barrages, irrigation drainage plans, the completion of Mount Bold and the design of South Para reservoirs, as well as a contribution to the Metropolitan Floodwaters Scheme.

Chairman (1941-46) of the Adelaide division of the Institution of Engineers, Australia, and deputy-commissioner (1946-49) of the River Murray Commission, Angwin was a councillor of the South Australian School of Mines and Industries, an active Methodist and a Rotarian. In 1947 he had been a member of the royal commission into the State Electricity Commission of Victoria. Angwin died suddenly of coronary thrombosis on 12 September 1949 in Grenfell Street, Adelaide. Parliamentary tributes belatedly acknowledged him as a fine public servant who should not have been overloaded. Survived by his wife and two daughters, he was buried in Centennial Park cemetery; his estate was sworn for probate at £5120. He is commemorated by an annual prize for mechanical engineering at the South Australian Institute of Technology.

D. A. Cumming and G. C. Moxham, *They Built South Australia* (Adel, 1986); M. Hammerton, *Water South Australia* (Adel, 1986); *PD* (SA), 1949, p 652; *Advertiser* (Adel), 1 Jan 1944, 13 Sept 1949; *News* (Adel), 31 Aug 1946; information from Mrs E. Angwin, Glenunga, Adel.

SUZANNE EDGAR

ANNAND, DOUGLAS SHENTON (1903-1976), graphic designer and artist, was born on 22 March 1903 at Toowoomba, Queensland, third child of Frederick William Gadsby Annand, accountant, and his wife Helen Alice, née Robinson, both Queenslanders. Having taken the commercial course at the Central Technical College, Brisbane, in 1920 Douglas joined the English, Scottish & Australian Bank. Five years later he began work as a commercial artist at Reed Press and attended night-classes at Brisbane Central Technical College under L. J. Harvey [q.v.9]. While being taught by F. J. Martyn Roberts, Annand freelanced in 1926: he was commissioned by a Brisbane jewellery firm and prepared wildflower designs for the Royal Worcester Co. Ltd, England. On 18 August 1928 he married Maida Fulcher Morris (d. 1954) at the Ann Street Presbyterian Church, Brisbane; they were to have two sons.

He was employed by Samson Clark & Co. Ltd, an advertising agency, from 1928 and transferred to its Sydney office in 1930; retrenched, he joined Allied Advertising Artists. In 1931 he left to become a freelance artist and designer. Working from his studio in Sydney, he was initially assisted by his sister Helen. At first he concentrated on graphic design, especially for textiles, wrapping papers, labels, magazine covers and advertisements. Between 1935 and 1939 he drew for Sydney Ure Smith's [q.v.11] publications, the *Home, Art in Australia* and the *Australian National Journal*. In 1937 he designed the ceiling for the Australian pavilion at the Paris International Exhibition; he was art director (1938-39) of the Australian exhibition at the New York World's Fair where his murals brought major recognition.

In 1941-44 Annand was a camouflage artist with the Royal Australian Air Force. Stationed for two years in North Queensland, he painted and drew regularly, and exhibited water-colours in Sydney and Melbourne. His linear style often used simple colour washes for dramatic effect. The strongest paintings placed ambiguous perspective and com-

pressed forms in a symbolic relationship, and united them with landscape to form a framing but secondary aspect of the composition. Some of these works revealed the influence of the British artist Paul Nash. After the war Annand became more involved in mural painting and completed commissions for the Peninsular & Oriental Steam Navigation Co., the office of radio station 2UE, the University of Melbourne's new Wilson [q.v.6] Hall and the international terminal at Sydney airport. From the mid-1950s he developed an interest in architectural work, like the large, glass structures he completed in 1966 for the Colonial Sugar Refining Co., Sydney.

Tall and balding, with brown eyes and a trim moustache, Annand was gentle in manner and a discursive talker. His innovative experiments with diverse media led to new approaches and injected vitality into the design arts. In 1932 he had won a competition to design a poster to celebrate the opening of the Sydney Harbour Bridge. Awarded two Australian Commercial and Industrial Artists' Association medals in 1940, he won the Sulman [q.v.12] prize for his murals in 1941, 1947 and 1951. His posters won prizes in 1960 at the Adelaide Festival of the Arts and in 1968 at Milan, Italy. He was a member of the Society of Artists, the Contemporary Art Society, Sydney, and the Society of Industrial Designers, London.

On 12 March 1957 at Wesley Church, Melbourne, Annand had married a divorcee Ann Selwyn, née Moran, late McCrae; he divorced her in 1962. Survived by a son of his first marriage, he died on 14 December 1976 at Wahroonga, Sydney, and was cremated. His work is held in the Australian National Gallery and the Australian War Memorial, Canberra, and in State galleries in Brisbane, Melbourne and Sydney.

S. Ure Smith (ed), *Douglas Annand* (Syd, 1944); J. Campbell, *Australian Watercolour Painters, 1780-1980* (Adel, 1983); R. Searle, *Douglas Annand Watercolours 1935-50*, exhibition cat (Townsville, 1988); *Art and Aust*, 15, no 1, 1977; *Courier-Mail*, 27 May 1970, 6 July 1974; *Australian*, 19 Oct 1974; *Townsville Daily Bulletin*, 19 Dec 1987; *Aust Financial Review*, 21 Sept 1989; D. Annand file (Qld Art Gallery L, Brisb); information from Mr A. M. Annand, St Ives, Syd, and Miss H. Annand, Hamilton, Brisb.

BETTINA MACAULAY

ANNOIS, LEONARD LLOYD (1906-1966), artist, was born on 1 July 1906 at Malvern, Melbourne, son of William Alfred Annois, clerk, and his wife Elsie Miriam, née Lloyd, both Western Australian born. William —whose father had arrived at Fremantle from Portugal in 1864 and set up as a shipchandler—had moved with his wife to Victoria in 1904. Educated at Melbourne High

School, at 17 Len began an engineering career, first with the Melbourne Harbour Trust, next with a civil engineering firm and finally with Malvern City Council. He then became a concrete salesman. On 17 February 1928 at the registrar's office, Collingwood, he married Mavis Martha Nunn who belonged to the Victorian Potters' Group.

Losing his job in the Depression, he attended classes at the National Gallery schools under the directorship of Bernard Hall, with W. B. McInnes [qq.v.9,10] as drawing-master. In 1935 Annois found employment with G. J. Coles [q.v.] & Co. Ltd and in 1946 was appointed manager of the new advertising department. Throughout these years he continued painting and exhibiting. Having been introduced to water-colour and taught by James Flett to admire the art of Blamire Young [q.v.12], he painted historical scenes, but, after studying the English water-colour school, turned to landscape. He built a home in sparsely-inhabited North Balwyn in 1938 and chose as his painting-ground the Yarra Valley, as well as the Pentland Hills which he studied on early excursions to Bacchus Marsh.

In 1942-43 Annois worked as a production illustrator with the Directorate of Armoured Fighting Vehicles and the Commonwealth Aircraft Corporation Pty Ltd. After the war he joined the council of the Victorian Artists Society and engaged in the production of a new magazine, the *Australian Artist*. He was a foundation member of the committee which established the National Gallery Society of Victoria. In 1950 he made the first of several journeys abroad. In Italy he studied frescoes and brought his skills to Melbourne where he executed murals in fresco secco in such buildings as the Pharmacy College of Victoria, Parkville, St John's Church of England, Camberwell, and Melbourne High School.

From 1935 Annois had exhibited widely and regularly at the Victorian Artists Society, the New Melbourne Art Club, the Athenaeum gallery and interstate; he held his first one-man show at Tye's Gallery in Bourke Street in 1941. He was elected associate (1952) and member (1958) of the Royal Society of Painters in Watercolour, and in 1960 became president of the National Gallery Society of Victoria. He won awards for his water-colours throughout Australia, among them the Wynne prize (1961 and 1964).

Discarding the popular sunburnt plains and blue distances seen through gum trees, Annois had a fresh perception of the Australian landscape. Characteristic themes in his work are the open, barren hills around Bacchus Marsh, or the border between city and country as he found it in the Yarra Valley from North Balwyn to Templestowe and Heidelberg. The mixture of open country and native bush, interspersed with European trees surrounding the occasional villas, provided the blend of architecture and scenery which he had admired in the towns of Italy and Greece.

A *bon vivant*, Annois was 6 ft 4 ins (193 cm) tall and weighed seventeen stone (108 kg). He was a gourmet, a cricket fan and a bird-lover. Survived by his wife, son and daughter, he died suddenly at a friend's dinner party at Toorak on 10 July 1966 and was cremated. In 1969 a posthumous exhibition of his water-colours of Central Australia (inspired by a visit made in 1964) was held in Melbourne. Brian Finemore saw in them 'a freedom and breadth of handling, an opulence of colour and a wealth of lyrical intimations' which brought his art to its full flowering. Reviewing the same exhibition, Patrick McCaughey equated Annois's best work with that of the young Fred Williams.

K. Bonython, *Modern Australian Painting and Sculpture* (Adel, 1960); B. Finemore, foreword in *The Central Australian Landscape. Leonard Annois 1906-1966,* exhibition cat (Melb, 1969); *Len Annois A Retrospective Exhibition,* exhibition cat (Melb, 1974); N. C. Manning and A. J. Cobcroft, *Leonard Lloyd Annois* (Melb, 1976); *Len Annois, 1950-1960, Water Colours,* exhibition cat (Melb, 1979); R. Haese, *Rebels and Precursors* (Melb, 1981); A. Sayers, *Drawing in Australia* (Canb, 1989); M. Rich, *Crouch Prize Winners,* exhibition cat (Ballarat, Vic, 1990); *Age* (Melb), 10 Feb 1962, 11 July 1966, 2 Apr 1969, 1 Nov 1972; *Sun News-Pictorial, Herald* (Melb) and *SMH,* 11 July 1966; Annois file (AMPA); Croll papers (LaTL). URSULA HOFF

ANTHONY, HUBERT LAWRENCE (1897-1957), politician and farmer, was born on 12 March 1897 at Warren, New South Wales, son of George Edward Anthony, a native-born labourer, and his Irish wife Honoria Elizabeth, née McNab. Educated at Warren Public School, in September 1911 Larry joined the Postmaster-General's Department as a telegraph messenger. He was employed as a postal assistant at Peak Hill when he enlisted in the Australian Imperial Force on 28 October 1914. Embarking for Egypt in December with No. 2 Signal Troop, he served at Gallipoli from April 1915 until illness caused him to be evacuated to England in August; he returned to Australia in 1916 and was discharged from the A.I.F. on 4 October.

Having worked as a clerk and studied accountancy and economics in Sydney, in 1919 Anthony took up a soldier-settler block near Tweed Heads and was a shire councillor (1919-22). Anticipating that his first crop of bananas would be successful, on 21 June 1921 he married Mary Jessie Stirling (d. 1941) in the Ann Street Presbyterian Church,

Brisbane. The crop became infected with 'bunchy top' and was condemned. Larry and Mary walked off their farm penniless. He borrowed money and tried to grow sugar-cane on another farm, but this attempt also proved a financial disaster. Using savings accumulated from selling land on commission at Burleigh Heads and Surfers Paradise, Anthony returned to banana-growing and was to emerge as one of Australia's largest producers. In 1928 he founded the New South Wales Banana Growers' Federation; he also helped to initiate research which led to the elimination of the 'bunchy top' parasite.

As a Country Party candidate, he won the Federal seat of Richmond at the 1937 general elections and was to hold it until his death. In October 1940 he was appointed minister assisting the treasurer and the minister for commerce in the government of (Sir) Robert Menzies [q.v.]; in June 1941 Anthony became minister for transport. When Labor came to office under John Curtin [q.v.] in October, Anthony joined a group of Opposition members who fought the government with increasing effectiveness and he earned a reputation as a 'rough, rugged, tough fighter, always in debates . . . restless to get into the fight on all subjects at all times'; he was several times suspended from parliament. On 24 April 1946 in the Anglican Church of St John the Baptist, Canberra, he married a 25-year-old widow Lyndall Marion, née Ingram, late Thornton. Following the coalition parties' victory in December 1949, he was appointed postmaster-general. His progress from messenger-boy to minister gave him immense satisfaction.

Championing the supply of automatic telephone-exchange equipment to rural areas, Anthony endeavoured to improve postal and telegraph services through the use of new equipment. In 1951 he took the additional portfolio of civil aviation. The industry developed rapidly during his tenure: Qantas Empire Airways Ltd expanded its overseas services; the foundations of the two-airline policy—by which major domestic trunk routes were reserved for two principal airlines—were laid; and advanced technology came into operation. Anthony's main responsibility, however, was to supervise preliminary work for the advent of television in Australia. While the government was accused of procrastination, Anthony considered that he could learn from other countries' experiences. After a fact-finding mission to Britain and the United States of America in 1952, he introduced the 1953 television bill, the first step in establishing a dual system of public and private television stations. He was responsible for appointing the royal commission on television which reported next year.

Suffering several illnesses from the early 1950s, Anthony relinquished civil aviation in 1954. He was on sick leave in the last three months of that year, but rejected advice to leave the ministry. Disappointed that he had not been able to finalize the introduction of television, he was finally imposed upon to resign in January 1956. His acceptance next month of a directorship with Philips Electrical Industries Pty Ltd provoked criticism. Dark haired and solidly built, he was a blunt, instinctive politician who worked hard and was a popular local member. He loved reading, took a keen interest in the life of Napoleon and in Marxism, believed in the rights and potential of the individual, and was a staunch anti-communist. Anthony was a devoted husband and father. He died of cerebrovascular disease on 12 July 1957 at Murwillumbah and was cremated with Presbyterian forms. His wife and their daughter survived him, as did the daughter and two sons of his first marriage; his son Doug succeeded him as member for Richmond. The family holds a portrait of Larry Anthony by Leslie Moline.

PD (Cwlth), 18 Feb 1953, p 31, 27 Aug 1957, p 3; *Richmond River Herald*, 5 Oct 1937; *SMH*, 28 Oct 1940, 27 June 1941, 19 Dec 1949, 11 May 1951, 24 Nov 1952, 10 May, 29 Sept 1954, 13 July 1957; *Sunday Sun* (Syd), 3 Dec 1944; information from and Anthony's Gallipoli Diary held by Rt Hon D. Anthony, Sunnymeadows, Murwillumbah, NSW.

LLOYD BRODRICK

ANTON, CHARLES WILLIAM (1916-1966), ski-field promoter, was born on 23 November 1916 in Vienna and named Karl Anton, second child of Elieser (Alois) Schwarz, a Jewish timber-merchant who was later baptized, and his wife Stella, née Schwarz. Karl was educated at the Technisches Gewerbemuseum, Vienna, and worked as a clerk for the Sun Insurance Office Ltd in Austria. For his military service in 1937-38 he chose the dragoons, though he was no horseman. Dismissed from the army and forced to leave Austria after the *Anschluss*, he reached Sydney in the *Orford* on 14 December 1938. He changed his name by deed poll on 8 March 1939. Enlisting in the Australian Military Forces on 7 March 1942, he was posted to the 3rd Employment Company (for 'aliens'). Anton was naturalized on 15 February 1944 and transferred to the Australian Imperial Force in July 1945. As a member of the army team, he competed in the Allied Services Ski-Meeting in September at Charlotte Pass before being demobilized in December.

Debonair, 5 ft 4 ins (162.6 cm) tall, with blue-grey eyes and brown hair, Anton had married Betty Estelle Caldwell on 12 March

1942 at St Stephen's Presbyterian Church, Sydney. Full of ideas and a gifted organizer, he tackled situations head on: he often wrote to the *Sydney Morning Herald* and in 1942 defended 'stateless' Europeans. After the war he worked with Edward Lumley & Sons (N.S.W.) Pty Ltd and subsequently set up as an insurance broker within the firm. Divorced in March 1948, he married Margaret Evelyn Foster at the McNeil Memorial Presbyterian Church, Waverley, on 10 July that year; they were to be divorced in August 1960.

Frequenting the Snowy Mountains, Anton realized that more accommodation was needed on the main range to make use of descents on the western faces. In 1950 he founded and presided over the Ski Tourers' Association which, assisted by the Kosciusko State Park Trust, built a skiers' lodge at Lake Albina. He then encouraged his followers to build a second hut (Kunama) and a rope tow, thereby opening the downhill runs between the Chalet Hotel and Lake Albina.

Undaunted when Kunama was destroyed by an avalanche in July 1956, Anton looked to other areas to develop; he was also worried by changing policies of the trust, which later resumed Lake Albina lodge. With his friends, Thyne Reid [q.v.] and the hydrologist Tony Sponar, he explored the south-eastern side of the range in 1956 and found at Friday Flat on the Thredbo River a natural valley with slopes descending to an accessible road. Anton formed a syndicate and in 1957 the State government approved development. A public company, Kosciusko Thredbo Ltd, with Reid as chairman and Anton as a director, was formed to build a 300-bed hotel. In two years Thredbo had fifty-two lodges and the longest chairlift in Australia. At Anton's behest, in 1959 the S.T.A. built Kareela, an Austrian-style hut at the top of the Mount Crackenback chairlift, where he married 25-year-old Jutta Margaret Eva Olivier with Presbyterian forms on 3 October.

Conflict between the trust and Kosciusko Thredbo Ltd loomed when Anton proposed to establish two ski-lifts beyond Thredbo. Frustrated after the takeover of the company by Lend Lease Corporation Ltd in 1961 and by the trust's stonewalling tactics, Anton established lodges at Perisher and Falls Creek as part of his plan for a network in the New South Wales and Victorian ski-fields. To reflect his vision, he unilaterally renamed the S.T.A. the Australian Alpine Club.

While he was never able to overcome his accentuated Arlberg technique, Anton was a keen competitive skier who promoted inter-club racing, introduced summer events and brought the State Ski Championships to Thredbo in 1958. He helped to raise the standard of ski-racing in Australia by supporting instructors from Austria and by urging Aus-

tralian skiers to compete abroad. Survived by his wife, their son and daughter, and by the daughter of his first marriage, he died of meningococcal septicaemia on 17 September 1966 at Cooma and was cremated with Anglican rites. His ashes were interred on Mount Crackenback behind a plaque unveiled by the minister for lands Thomas Lewis on 10 June 1968. Anton Huette at Mount Hotham and Mount Anton are named in his honour.

W. Cross (ed), *Twenty-One Years of the Australian Alpine Club* (priv pub, np, nd); M. Norst, *Austrians and Australia* (Syd, 1988); *Hostel-Yarn*, Jan-Feb, May-June 1961; *SMH*, 1 Sept 1942, 8 Dec 1950, 28 Jan 1952, 13 July 1954, 13 July, 3 Aug 1956, 30 Jan 1957, 19 Sept 1966, 11 June 1968; *Financial Review*, 30 June 1960; naturalization file, A435/1 item 44/4/1110 (AA, Canb); information from Dr E. Lebensaft, Österreichisches Biographisches Lexikon Redaktion, Vienna, Mrs J. Lewis, Darling Point, and Mr and Mrs L. Smith, Church Point, Syd.
　　　　　　　　　　　　　　　　　　KERRY REGAN

APPLEROTH, ADOLPHUS HERBERT FREDERICK NORMAN (1886-1952), jelly manufacturer, was born on 30 December 1886 in West Melbourne, third surviving child of William Appleroth, a Russian-born driver, and his wife Emma, née Audebart, daughter of a Melbourne wine merchant. William had reputedly been a Russo-Finnish sea captain who jumped ship. The family moved to Sydney where Bert began work in 1902 as a messenger-boy at the Lipton's Tea agency, then took a job as a tram conductor. He began experimenting with mixtures of gelatine and sugar in the bath in his parents' home at Paddington, and hawked the jelly crystals that he produced door-to-door, using trams as transport. At St Michael's Anglican Church, Sydney, on 19 February 1910 he married a 19-year-old dressmaker Ferri Marion Wotzasik.

Leaving the tramways in 1917, Appleroth rented premises at 10 shillings a week in which to manufacture his jelly crystals. He marketed some jellies under the name 'De-Luxe'. In 1926 he formed a company, Traders Ltd, and was joined by a partner Albert Francis Lenertz (1891-1943) who became managing director. The business operated from Sussex Street in the city before moving to Alice Street, Newtown, in 1927. Inspired by feats in aviation, that year Appleroth named his product 'Aeroplane Jelly'.

In 1930 Lenertz wrote the words and music of the Aeroplane Jelly song which was to become the longest-running advertising jingle in Australian history. It was first recorded in 1930, sung by Amy Rochelle, an actress who did child imitations. The song was again recorded in 1938, sung by Joy King, a young girl chosen as the result of a competition. Her recording was used for more than fifty years. Lenertz produced and announced radio programmes over Sydney stations 2KY and 2SM, and used the song as the signature tune. Eventually, the jingle was broadcast over commercial radio one hundred times each day:

I like Aeroplane jelly,
Aeroplane jelly for me,
I like it for dinner, I like it for tea,
A little each day is a good recipe . . .

It was the quintessential radio-advertising campaign.

After Lenertz left the firm in 1934, Appleroth chartered a Tiger Moth aeroplane, emblazoned with his product's name, to make deliveries to rural areas. This caper proved particularly popular with children, his jelly's greatest consumers. In 1935 he held a model-aeroplane display in Centennial Park, Sydney, and in the late 1940s sponsored radio broadcasts involving prisoners at Goulburn gaol which were rounded off with an exhortation to buy 'Aeroplane Jelly'. By 1949 Appleroth's factory had an annual turnover of £170 000. His publicity stunts, and the song, made his product a national icon.

Appleroth was a Freemason. He gave money to the Federation of New South Wales Police-Citizens Boys' Clubs and to the Hospital Saturday Fund. In 1950 he bought a racehorse, Typhonic. Appleroth suffered from hypertension and died of a coronary occlusion on 17 July 1952 at his Croydon home; his wife and son survived him. He left an estate valued for probate at £9025 and appointed the formidable Ferri as governing or managing director of several family companies. His portrait is held by Traders Pty Ltd.

A'sian Post, 8 Dec 1949; *SMH*, 18, 19 July 1952; *Weekend Australian*, 10-11 June 1978, 19-20 Jan 1985; A. F. Lenertz papers (ML); information from Traders Pty Ltd, Ryde, Syd.   PAUL BRUNTON

ARCHER, ALISTER (1890-1965), cattleman, was born on 6 June 1890 at Larvik, Norway, son of James George Lewis Archer, a Queensland station-owner of Scottish descent, and his wife Louise Stewart, daughter of Sir Robert Mackenzie [q.v.5]. Educated at Larvik Grammar (1896-1905) and High (1905-08) schools, Alister came to Queensland in 1909 to learn the cattle business and began jackerooing on Torsdale, one of Archer Bros [qq.v.1] Ltd's stations in Central Queensland. In 1910 he helped to drove two hundred head of stud cattle to the Gulf country, to which he later returned as head stockman on Magoura station. Robert Stubbs

Archer [q.v.7], managing director of the family pastoral firm, described his fair-haired and grey-eyed kinsman as 'a smart stockman and drover with his head screwed on the right way', and thought that he would make a first-class station-manager.

When World War I began, Archer was with his parents in Norway, but came back to Queensland and enlisted in the Australian Imperial Force on 23 July 1915 at Rockhampton. He was commissioned in December and transferred from the infantry to the 5th Light Horse Regiment which disembarked at Suez in April 1916. Appointed troop officer, 4th (Anzac) Battalion, Imperial Camel Corps, in November 1916, he learned 'how to handle and ride the brutes . . . none too pleasant at first'. In July 1918 (when the brigade was disbanded) he was posted to the 14th Light Horse Regiment with the rank of captain. He had served in Egypt at the defence of the Suez Canal and in campaigns that led to the fall of Damascus.

Seconded in April 1919 as aide-de-camp to Lieutenant General Sir Harry Chauvel [q.v.7], he led the light horse in the victory march through London in May. After a brief visit to Norway he returned to Australia with Chauvel in September; Archer's appointment terminated in December. On 1 October 1919 at St James's Anglican Church, Sydney, he had married his cousin Joan Marie, daughter of Robert Stubbs Archer.

In 1920 Archer was appointed manager of Gracemere stud-farm, near Rockhampton, and secretary of Archer Bros Ltd. His duties included the preparation and showing of stud beef-cattle at Queensland and Sydney shows. Gracemere Hereford Stud, established in 1862, continued to contribute to the upgrading of northern cattle herds and at the 1925 Brisbane Exhibition was awarded a trophy by the Hereford Herd Book Society of England. Archer became a partner in the firm next year and its managing director in 1932. Argentinian chilled beef had excluded Queensland frozen meat from the British market and the northern beef industry in Australia was at an ebb. Although pure-bred herd bulls sold for less than £5 in 1936, Archer maintained his herds at their high standard and bred 'bulls which we know will stand up to tropical conditions'.

Following the dissolution of the partnership of Archer Bros Ltd, in 1949 the directors approved the sale of Gracemere to Alister and his wife. They carried on the station's tradition of gracious hospitality. A prolific correspondent with a keen sense of humour, he had an encyclopaedic knowledge of the history of Central Queensland; he was proud of his family and preserved the large collection of Archer papers. Survived by his wife, daughter and two sons, Archer died on 10 April 1965 at

Rockhampton and was buried in the private cemetery at Gracemere.

L. McDonald, *Rockhampton* (Brisb, 1981) and *Cattle Country* (Brisb, 1988); *Morning Bulletin*, 20 Apr 1965; A. Archer letters to Norway, 1915-18, general correspondence, 1929-38 (ML) and 1944-53 (held by Mr R. C. M. Archer, Gracemere station, Rockhampton, Qld, who also provided family information); Archer family papers (Rockhampton and District Hist Soc).   LORNA McDONALD

ARCHER, CAROLINE LILLIAN (1922-1978), telephonist and Aboriginal publicist, was born on 22 February 1922 at Cherbourg Aboriginal Reserve, near Murgon, Queensland, daughter of a White father Norman Brown and an Aboriginal mother Lillian Masso, later Fogarty. Caroline was raised under the supervision of the Queensland Department of Native Affairs which segregated people of Aboriginal descent on reserves. Her grandmother had been gaoled and then sent with her family from the Charters Towers region to Cherbourg when she refused to allow its members to be separated and the boys assigned to cattle-stations. As a child, Caroline suffered from malnutrition which left her with a permanent limp and continuing poor health. She was educated at the reserve school to fourth grade, a level considered sufficient for an Aboriginal girl. At 14 she was employed in domestic work by the Kay family of Whetstone station, near Inglewood, who paid her the equivalent of a White worker's wage and encouraged her to further her career.

Caroline moved to Brisbane, working from 1935 to 1949 at the Canberra Hotel and gaining switchboard skills. By the force of her own efforts she was able to gain full citizen's rights by obtaining exemption from the Acts regulating Aborigines: official approval was usually based on an examination of the applicant's conduct and standard of living. In 1950 she became the first Aboriginal trunkline operator employed by the Postmaster-General's Department in Brisbane. On 29 December 1951 at the Baptist City Tabernacle she married Frederick Frank Archer, an English-born aircraftsman and photographer. Forthright and independent, Mrs Archer developed a special interest in increasing an appreciation of Aboriginal culture among both White Australians and younger Aboriginal people. To provide an incentive for the practice of crafts and a training ground in business skills for young Aborigines, she opened an artefact shop at Surfers Paradise: the shop was named Jedda after the heroine in Charles Chauvel's [q.v.7] film of 1955.

Caroline became an early champion of the need to patent Aboriginal arts, crafts and designs to avoid commercial imitations.

An active member of the One People of Australia League—a multi-racial organization founded 'To weld the Coloured and White Citizens of Australia into one People'—Archer was its first Aboriginal executive-officer (1974) and later State president. She took a particular interest in reviving the Miss OPAL Quest and conducted a deportment course for Aboriginal models. An unsuccessful candidate for the National Aboriginal Consultative Committee in 1973, she was consciously 'middle of the road' in her views; she had little regard for radical solutions to racial issues and referred to herself as an 'Australian first and then an Aborigine'. Her close friend and sometime president of OPAL, Senator Neville Bonner, described her as a serene, well-groomed lady, with a 'barely controlled trace of mischief' and the tenacity of a bulldog.

Archer's deep concern for improved race relations led her to work for the Queensland Department of Education and later for the Department of Aboriginal Affairs, Canberra: she addressed schools and other groups on aspects of Aboriginal culture. In 1977 she was awarded the Queen's jubilee medal. Survived by her husband, son and two daughters, she died from injuries sustained in a motorcar accident on 8 December 1978 near Coonabarabran, New South Wales, and was cremated.

J. P. M. Long, *Aboriginal Settlements* (Canb, 1970); C. D. Rowley, *Outcasts in White Australia* (Canb, 1971); H. Radi (ed), *200 Australian Women* (Syd, 1988); *OPAL*, Mar-Apr 1973, p 7; *AIA News*, 4, no 1, Jan-Feb 1978, p 2; *Courier Mail*, 13 Nov 1970, 16 Nov 1973; F. F. Archer, Notes on his wife Caroline (ts in ADB file); N. T. Bonner, Memoir of Caroline Archer, 1991 (ms in ADB file).

B. A. BALLARD

ARCHER, DAVID MARWEDEL (1897-1959), merino studmaster, was born on 21 February 1897 at Gracemere station, near Rockhampton, Queensland, son of Robert Stubbs Archer [q.v.7], grazier, and his Tasmanian-born wife Alice Manon, née Marwedel. David Archer [q.v.1] was his grandfather. Young David was educated at Rockhampton Grammar School, Sydney Church of England Grammar School (Shore) and Hawkesbury Agricultural College.

Brown haired, hazel eyed and 5 ft 9½ ins (176.5 cm) tall, on 4 February 1916 he enlisted in the Australian Imperial Force and embarked in May with the 3rd Mobile Veterinary Section. From England, his unit was directed to France where, on occasion, he performed as a baritone singer and violinist in army concerts. In April 1918 Archer was transferred to the 26th Battery, 7th Field Artillery Brigade, as a bombardier. At the end of the war he had planned to study stock-breeding in England, but his leave was cancelled and he returned to Australia through North America at his father's expense. He was demobilized in Sydney in October 1919. Although he survived France (as his father wrote that year) 'without a scratch', he suffered throughout his life from the effects of mustard gas.

The postwar collapse of the beef-cattle industry led Archer in 1920 to jackerooing on Oondooroo, a sheep-station at Winton, where he became overseer. In 1922 he moved to Strathdarr station, near Longreach; there, on 7 July 1926 he married with Anglican rites Alison Claire, daughter of Angus Nicholson Mackay whom Archer succeeded that year as manager of Strathdarr. During his thirty-five years on the station he was to establish a reputation as one of the best merino studmasters in Queensland. Archer's letters to the press revealed not only his keen mind, but a realistic and forthright attitude, especially in any sheep-breeding controversy. He was prepared to defend his theories about breeding animals to suit the environment and was vindicated by his results. Strathdarr sheep were the major winners in State shows, taking out sixty-three grand championships over eighteen years. In 1951 he judged merinos at the Sydney Sheep Show. He resigned from Strathdarr in 1957 to breed stud sheep at his own property, Honan Downs, Dartmouth.

Archer was also a fine horseman, and a breeder and trainer of the hacks, hunters and stockhorses so essential in his lifetime. A successful exhibitor of horses at Longreach shows, he was an active participant in racing in the central west. He was vice-president (1941-45) of the Queensland Merino Stud Sheepbreeders' Association, its longest serving president (1945-59) and a life member (1951). Chairman of the Longreach branch of the United Graziers' Association, he was a life member and vice-president of the Longreach Pastoral and Agricultural Society. In 1959 he was appointed C.B.E. Archer died of cancer on 10 June 1959 in St Martin's Hospital, Brisbane, and was cremated; his wife, daughter and two sons survived him.

L. McDonald, *Rockhampton* (Brisb, 1981); *Qld Country Life*, 6 Dec 1958; *Longreach Leader*, 29 Aug 1930; Archer family papers (Rockhampton and District Hist Soc); news-cuttings (held by author, West Rockhampton); family information from Mrs C. Williams, Ilfracombe, Qld.

LORNA MCDONALD

ARCHER, MARY ELLINOR LUCY (1893-1979), librarian and scientist, was born on 13 November 1893 at Malvern, Melbourne, daughter of Oakeley Archer, a civil engineer from England, and his Victorian-born wife Lucy Georgina Elizabeth, née Gaunt. Lucy was a sister of Cecil, (Sir) Ernest, (Sir) Guy and Mary Gaunt [qq.v.8], and in 1906-18 was principal of Trinity College Hostel (later Janet Clarke [q.v.3] Hall). Educated at the Church of England Girls' Grammar School, Melbourne, and the University of Melbourne (B.Sc., 1916; M.Sc., 1918), Mary added Ellinor Lucy to her name, but was to be known as Ellinor Archer professionally. After graduating she became a government research scholar in botany and joined the teaching staff of Trinity College.

In November 1918 Archer was appointed secretary and investigator to the special committee on seed improvement of the Advisory Council of Science and Industry (Commonwealth Institute of Science and Industry from 1920). The committee endeavoured to improve crops and published bulletins in 1922-23 (which she probably wrote) on the classification of barleys, oats and wheats. In May 1923 she took charge of the institute's library; following the inauguration (1926) of the Council for Scientific and Industrial Research, her post was reclassified in 1929 as librarian and scientific assistant. She was secretary to the citrus preservation committee, compiled a register of agricultural research, and was effectively head librarian and supervisor of libraries in divisions and experimental stations. Visiting scientific libraries in Britain in 1936, she studied the universal decimal classification and, on her return, encouraged its introduction in C.S.I.R. libraries. Her title was changed to chief librarian in January 1946.

A foundation member (1937) and first female president (1948-49) of the Australian Institute of Librarians, Archer made a lasting contribution to her profession. She had been appointed to the institute's board of certification and examination in 1941. When the A.I.L. was reconstituted as the Library Association of Australia, she served as an active past president (1950-53). Having attained her objectives of including special librarianship in the national examination system for librarians and of establishing the special libraries section within the L.A.A., in 1952 she became the section's first president.

As one of Australia's foremost special librarians with charge of a national library system, Archer travelled frequently. She went to Perth in 1954 to establish a library for the Commonwealth Scientific and Industrial Research Organization's Western Australian regional laboratory and visited a number of special libraries, offering goodwill and advice;

her friendly and informal approach was appreciated. Archer urged inter-library co-operation through the standardization of codes and forms: she published her views in the *Australian Library Journal* and addressed the L.A.A.'s eighth conference (1955) on the subject. She advocated membership of the professional association and promoted the education of librarians.

Although Archer liked to say that she had entered her calling by accident, she became a successful librarian and senior administrator in an organization which had few women in positions of authority. She gathered about her a dedicated staff and regarded it as immaterial that they were predominantly female. Fierce in argument, imaginative in her hopes for her profession and outspoken in her judgements, she maintained that librarianship was as much about people as books, and no occupation for introverts. Archer saw the establishment of an information section within C.S.I.R.O. as a threat to the library service. Beyond the requirements of her work, she read little except detective stories and travelogues. Small and slight, with bright, brown eyes and a sallow complexion, she was intelligent and energetic. She retired on 17 December 1954 and was appointed M.B.E. in 1956.

In addition to further trips abroad, Archer sold books to aid the Save the Children Fund, belonged to the Lyceum Club, was a keen walker and photographer, and painted wildflowers. She died on 3 May 1979 at Toorak, Melbourne, and was cremated; her estate was sworn for probate at $100 086. The L.A.A. instituted the Ellinor Archer award in her honour; it was first bestowed in 1984.

H. Bryan (ed), *ALIAS*, 1 (Syd, 1988); Inst of Science and Industry, *Bulletin*, nos 22-23, 1922, no 26, 1923; Aust Inst of Librarians, *Procs*, 1949, 1956; *Aust Lib J*, 1, no 3, Jan 1952, 2, no 3, July 1953, 4, no 1, Jan 1955, 22, no 10, Nov 1973; *Argus*, 7 Dec 1948; CSIRO records, Canb; information from Ms J. A. Conochie, East Melb, Mr P. H. Dawe, Mont Albert, Ms J. Korn, Jolimont, and Mr J. Simkin, Richmond, Melb.   JEAN P. WHYTE

AREK, PAULUS (1929-1973), teacher, trade unionist and politician, was born on 3 December 1929 at Wanigela in the Northern District of Papua; his father, previously a cook for the Anglican bishop of New Guinea, was a mission schoolteacher. Because of his youth, Paulus avoided forced labour for the occupying Japanese. He received primary education at the local mission school and in 1946 went to the new Sogeri Education Centre, near Port Moresby, for further training.

In 1951 Arek began a seventeen-year association with the Education Department as a teacher at Sogeri; in 1953 he was a delegate to the second South Pacific Conference in Noumea. About this time at Wanigela he married Ethel Breda with Anglican rites. Transferred to Manus Island in 1954, he became headmaster at Popondetta (1956), Iokea (1957) and Daru (1958). Having displeased the authorities, he was exiled to a school five hundred miles (805 km) up the Fly River; after a year he was allowed to return to Popondetta with reduced status. He resigned to contest the seat of Popondetta in the 1964 elections for the new House of Assembly, but finished second in the poll.

For the next four years Arek again served as headmaster of Popondetta Primary School, while playing an active part in local affairs. As founder and president of the Northern District Workers' Association, he negotiated a pay increase for plantation and other workers. He was also founder and president of the Popondetta Workers' Club and vice-president of the Higituru Local Government Council. When elections for the assembly were called in 1968, Arek nominated for the Ijivitari Open electorate and defeated five opponents with an absolute majority.

Although sympathetic to the aims of the Pangu Pati, Arek declared himself an Independent. He met informally with other union leaders in the House to discuss issues affecting workers and was foundation president (1970) of the Federation of Papua New Guinea Workers' Associations. An ardent nationalist, he advocated localization of the public service and decisive planning for self-government and independence.

In 1968 Arek was one of two special representatives to the United Nations General Assembly where he heard an Afro-Arab resolution calling for prompt independence for Papua New Guinea. Impressed by the conviction of the African nationalists, whose countries he visited, Arek nevertheless felt that they had underestimated the difficulties of a rapid transition. Following his motion in the assembly, in October 1969 a select committee on constitutional development was established with representatives from all parties and Arek as chairman. In 1970-71 it held hearings throughout the country. Although he was supported by the Pangu representatives—and by such regions as Bougainville and the Gazelle Peninsula—in his objective of an early transfer of power, Arek was sensitive to the qualms of the conservative committee-members and cautious Highlanders, as well as to the political advantages of compromise. The committee's report, presented to the assembly in March 1971, recommended preparations for self-determination in 1972-76. Its proposals concerning the structure of parliament and the electorates formed the blueprint for self-government (1973) and independence (1975).

Re-elected in 1972, he was appointed minister for information in (Sir) Michael Somare's coalition government. Arek subsequently joined the People's Progress Party, Pangu's coalition partner. His main achievement as minister was to oversee the creation of the National Broadcasting Commission. He died of cancer on 22 November 1973 in the General Hospital, Port Moresby, just eight days before self-government was proclaimed and the N.B.C. inaugurated.

Arek's career as a responsible and diplomatic politician was at odds with his more turbulent personal life. A tall, handsome, well-built man with close-cropped hair and beard, he was no 'pillar of rectitude'. His forceful personality, flamboyance, quick temper and addiction to alcohol combined on several occasions to put him on the wrong side of the law. One colleague recalled him as a charming, likeable and clever rogue. For all that, he was respected—in Chief Minister Somare's words—as 'a true nationalist'. Five thousand people attended the service at St John's Anglican Church which preceded Arek's burial in Port Moresby cemetery. His wife and eight children survived him; one son Hudson became chairman of the P.P.P.

PD (HA PNG), 3, no 18-24, Aug-Nov 1973, p 3186; *Herald* (Melb), 26 Dec 1968, 6 Jan 1969; *SMH*, 27, 30 Dec 1968, 10 Jan, 16 Aug 1969, 18 Nov 1970, 5 Jan, 17 June 1971, 29 Apr, 24 June, 29 Aug 1972, 22 June, 23 Nov 1973; *Canb Times*, 4 Oct 1969; *Sun News-Pictorial*, 8 Oct 1969, 23 May 1970, 23 May, 13 June, 25 May 1973; *Age*, 23 June 1970, 23 Nov 1973; *Australian*, 20 Nov 1970; *Post Courier*, 23, 27 Nov 1973; 'Arek, Goresau Paulus', Dictionary of Contemporary Papua New Guinea Biography drafts (held at UPNG).

DIANE LANGMORE

ARGYLE, JESSIE (1900?-1955), domestic, was born in the East Kimberley region, Western Australia, daughter of an Aboriginal woman and a White cattleman. The child's European name was Gypsy. Under the terms of the Western Australian Aborigines Act (1905)—which gave the legal guardianship of Aboriginal children to a chief protector who was permitted to remove them from their parents—Gypsy and her half-brother were deemed to be orphans and taken from Argyle police station to Wyndham in 1906; the journey of some 150 miles (240 km) by foot took ten days. From Wyndham they were dispatched in the cattle-steamer, *Bullara*, to Fremantle and thence by train to the Swan Native and Half-Caste Mission, Guildford, an Anglican-run reformatory and industrial school. As was common practice, the chil-

dren's names were changed: Gypsy became Jessie Argyle and her brother Thomas Bropho. She was interned there for thirteen years and trained as a domestic servant.

In 1920 Jessie was contracted to work at Bridgetown for her first employers; she held positions as a servant for the next decade. Aboriginal servants remained under the strict control of the Aborigines Department, received low wages for long working hours, and experienced poor living conditions, isolation, curfews and abuse. When she suffered from a recurring bone-disease in her left leg and required hospitalization, the department labelled her a 'malingerer' and in 1924 ordered her to go to the Moore River Native Settlement for twelve months to be 'cured'. She believed that the reason for her removal was her relationship with an Englishman, Edward Alfred Byron Smith, which contravened departmental views on inter-racial contact. Jessie worked in the sewing-room and in the nurses' quarters. Conditions at the institution were notorious and she eventually obtained her release after smuggling a letter to a previous boss. Although monitored by the department and by her employers, from 1925 she continued her liaison with Edward.

On 3 February 1930 Jessie and Edward were married at St Bartholomew's Anglican Church, East Perth, the department having changed its attitude and given permission. The house that the couple rented in Glendower Street, North Perth, became a focal point for the local Aboriginal community. It also provided a haven for domestic servants between jobs, for women visiting their children in institutions, for people seeking contact with relatives, and for those who simply wanted companionship, or to join one of Jessie's marathon card games. Departmental officials were unable to shed their prejudices and harboured suspicions that these gatherings served the purposes of crime and prostitution. During World War II a number of Aboriginal soldiers also stayed at Jessie's place. A large woman of strong character and dignity, Jessie was a lively raconteur, affectionately known as the 'Duchess of Glendower Street', or, more plainly, as 'Mum Smith'.

Suffering from diabetic ulcers, Jessie was admitted to Royal Perth Hospital in 1954. Her left leg was amputated. Friends and relations came to the hospital to give their support, to have a yarn and to play cards with her. Survived by her husband and daughter, she died there on 1 September 1955 of coronary insufficiency associated with septicaemia and was buried in Karrakatta cemetery. One of the real old girls had gone.

West Australian, 3 Sept 1955; Jessie Argyle personal file (WA Dept of Community Services, Perth);

E. Smith diaries *and* photographs (held by author, Inglewood, Perth); personal information.

STEPHEN KINNANE

ARIDA, JOSEPH DOMINIQUE (1863?-1924) and RICHARD DOMINIQUE (1872?-1944), merchants, were born probably at Bcharré, Lebanon (Syria), sons of Dominique Arida and his wife Matilda, née Rafoul. The family was prominent among the Maronite community: another son was to become titular archbishop of Tripoli and patriarch of Antioch, and a nephew titular bishop of Cyprus. Following the Druse massacres in the 1860s and the building of the Suez Canal, the mountain villages of Lebanon declined. Two Arida brothers set up in Argentina whence Joseph (Yusef Lahoud) travelled to Brisbane, probably in 1881 or 1882.

With the collapse of his first business in Queen Street, Joseph lost the capital he had brought to Australia. Having revisited Argentina, he opened a drapery at Charters Towers, followed by a wholesale warehouse in 1886, and sent for his younger brother Richard (Rachid Lahoud) who managed the warehouse when Joseph toured North Queensland in a hawker's caravan.

By 1892 the brothers had established outlets at Hughenden, Winton and Cloncurry. Within a few years they were producing their own 'JDA' brand boots, and trading by mail order and through travelling salesmen. Business was spectacularly successful. By the turn of the century Joseph spent much of his time in Europe and America, buying for the growing chain, while Richard acted as Australian manager. In 1908 J. & R. D. Arida amalgamated with Anthony stores which were mostly located at such mining towns as Selwyn and Normanton, and included a sizeable business in Collinsville.

Richard was a member (1900) of the Charters Towers Traders' Association, the School of Arts committee, the local hospital board of management and (from about 1907) the chamber of commerce. Appointed to the Townsville Harbour Board in 1916, he was also involved in the water and fire-brigade boards, the Towers Pastoral, Agricultural and Mining Association, and a number of sporting bodies. He was a co-guarantor of the Christian Brothers' school at Mount Carmel which helped to make Charters Towers a local educational centre. The Aridas were deeply committed to the labour movement and Richard was a trustee of a branch of the Australian Workers' Union. They saw no contradiction between their status as wealthy businessmen and their support for a movement which they regarded as fundamentally humanitarian and consistent with their involvement in the Catholic Church.

On 13 October 1884 Joseph had married Adma Rahma Antony in Buenos Aires. She travelled with her husband and was only rarely at Charters Towers. When World War I broke out they were at Mount Lebanon, and were interned by the Turks. Joseph bribed his way out of prison and escaped to the mountains; there he became known for his charity during the famine that followed the Turkish blockade. After the war he went to Khartoum where he had invested in real estate in 1904. Survived by his wife, two daughters and two sons, he died in that city on 21 March 1924.

Although he had retired in 1918, Richard remained principal shareholder and governing director of the company. Management fell increasingly to his niece Mrs Wadiha Anthony and to her son Albert Joseph who became manager in 1924. Richard turned to investment in cotton-growing and wool-milling. He became a director of Charters Towers Electric Supply Co. Ltd, North Australian Worsted & Woollen Mills (Charters Towers) Ltd and the Atlas Assurance Co. Ltd. Increasingly, however, his time was spent in study and public affairs. He spoke seven languages, delivered popular lectures on 'political economy', and was accepted as an authority on Egypt and the Middle East. Courteous, charming and engaging, he was 'one of the most respected men in the north'.

Photographs of the young Richard Arida show a short, neat man with generous eyes and a splendid moustache. He was as generous with words as he was with his time and money; the local newspapers delighted in reporting his lengthy and colourful speeches. Both brothers were known for their philanthropy. The Arida house had been a home to Lebanese immigrants who received business training there before setting out on their own. In 1932 Richard was awarded the Lebanese Distinguished Order of Merit for his service to the community in Australia. He died on 7 September 1944 at Charters Towers and was buried in the local cemetery. Richard had never married and the business was bequeathed to his partners the Anthonys who, in effect, had run it for many years.

Queensland and Queenslanders (Brisb, 1936); *Nth Qld Register*, Christmas ed 1894; *Courier-Mail* and *Northern Miner*, 8 Sept 1944; Philips collection (JCUL); press-cuttings collected by Mr R. D. Arida (held by Mr R. Anthony, Charters Towers, Qld).

DIANE MENGHETTI

ARKWOOKERUM, PERET (1924-1978), Aboriginal dancer, was born in 1924 on the west coast of Cape York Peninsula, Queensland, in his mother's country, centred on Hersey Creek; his father's land lay north of

Edward River. Peret's principal totem was possum and his dialect *Kugu-Mu'inh,* one of several in the *Kugu-Nganychara* group. While still a boy, he was a renowned hunter: his peers recalled that, as children, 'we would always follow him; we couldn't go hungry'. As a young man, Arkwookerum achieved the highest ceremonial status and became one of a select coterie known as the Aurukun mission's 'field bosses'. Its members organized ceremonies, instructed the young and provided leadership in all spheres. Though Arkwookerum's knowledge of traditions was encyclopaedic, he was by no means bound by them, and confidently introduced new features into dancing and ceremonial life.

To many, he was the most brilliant dancer in Cape York Peninsula and one of the finest in Australia. His dancing radiated power and commitment, and his performances at Aurukun vitalized his people. Arkwookerum created a series of songs and dances relating to the brolga that were to be accepted in ritual. Somewhat shy and retiring, he remained in his own locality until 1971 when he was taken to visit Cairns. Next year he went to Fiji to dance at the first South Pacific Festival of Arts. He gave public performances in Darwin, at the Aboriginal Arts Board seminar in Canberra in 1973 and on tour with the Queensland Festival of Arts in 1974. His honest explanation was, 'I am dancing for my land'.

His 'country' was his abiding concern. Despite his close kin being split between the Edward River and Aurukun, Arkwookerum had battled for a land claim in the Edward River Aboriginal Reserve for many years. His difficulties were legion, ranging from the issue of legal status, inadequate finance and broken agreements to problems of transport, lack of support from authorities and even instructions to leave the reserve. Peret was intelligent, thoughtful and sceptical by disposition: 'Silly people' was his only comment on European perceptions that he was a terrorizing 'master sorcerer'. In 1977 he travelled to Canberra to talk to officials about his land claims. By the late 1970s, with aid from the Federal government, he was moving steadily towards his objective—an outstation at a coastal site in his mother's country, with permanent drinking water and the possibility of access by aircraft.

An associate member (1977) of the Institute of Aboriginal Studies, Canberra, Arkwookerum appeared in two films, *Dances at Aurukun* (1964), made under the auspices of the institute, and *Lockhart Festival* (1974). He undertook the task of systematically identifying birds from his region and, while in Brisbane in early 1972, explained *Kugu-Mu'inh* kin terminology. Survived by his wife Tallah, two daughters and three sons, he died on 8 August 1978 at South Kendall River outstation. In the post-burial ceremonies, to the sound of one of Peret's brolga songs, the spirit was sent off to an underwater sandbank at the mouth of Christmas Creek. Next day the camp was smoked and his possessions distributed or destroyed.

Aust Inst of Aboriginal Studies Newsletter, no 11, Mar 1979.
                                          JOHN VON STURMER

ARMITAGE, HUGH TRAILL (1881-1963), banker, was born on 17 February 1881 in Colombo, Ceylon (Sri Lanka), son of Charles Cyrus Armitage (d. 1897), merchant, and his wife DORA ELIZABETH (1858-1946), née Robertson. Born on 14 July 1858 at St Clair, Michigan, United States of America, Dora was educated in England; she married Charles on 18 January 1877 in Colombo. When his firm collapsed in 1882, she took their four children to England where she learned to type. With the youngest three children, she rejoined Charles in Sydney in 1887. His Australian venture also failed and Dora supported the family by teaching typing. Her Ladies' Type-writing Association won a special prize at the 1888 Exhibition of Women's Industries in Sydney. Honorary treasurer (1896-97) and secretary (1897-99) of the National Council of Women of New South Wales, she married Walter White Wingrove Cooke in 1902 and spent most of her later life in England.

Educated at St Philip's Grammar School and Fort Street Model School, Hughie began his career with the New South Wales Mortgage Loan & Agency Co. in 1896, but transferred next year to the Bank of New South Wales. On 24 February 1906 in St John's Anglican Church, Darlinghurst, he married Edith Jane Callow (d. 1947); they were to have four children, one of whom died in infancy and another in childhood. Ambitious and hard-working, he did well with the Wales and in 1909 became accountant at its Perth branch. In 1912 (Sir) Denison Miller [q.v.10], with whom Armitage had been associated in Sydney, persuaded him to join the new Commonwealth Bank of Australia. Armitage returned to Sydney as accountant (chief accountant from 1916), though his role was much wider. He was promoted secretary (January 1921), manager of the Sydney office (1924) and chief inspector (December 1925).

Armitage's appointment as deputy-governor on 1 June 1927 was greeted with enthusiasm by the bank's staff who appreciated his fairness, ability and decisiveness. In July he embarked on a seven-month tour: he opened an agency of the bank in New York and visited London. Giving the 1928 presidential address to the New South Wales branch of the Economic Society of Australia and New Zealand, he put forward a view of world finances which he had formed during his trip. Unlike some of his colleagues, Armitage was interested in developing the Commonwealth's role as a central bank. He established a close relationship with the Federal treasurer E. G. Theodore [q.v.12] and helped him to prepare the unsuccessful Central Reserve Bank bill of 1930. With the Depression worsening, Armitage was critical of the Commonwealth Bank's board of directors who in 1931 refused to approve an increase in the note issue to finance government relief works. The board's failure to prevent the Government Savings Bank of New South Wales from suspending payment on 23 April met with his further disfavour. Having investigated that bank's affairs, he found it to be essentially solvent and believed that, had Miller still been Commonwealth Bank governor 'with unfettered powers', the Government Savings Bank would not have closed its doors.

Appointed C.M.G. in 1941, Armitage succeeded Sir Harry Sheehan [q.v.11] as governor on 1 July. Armitage's initial three-year term was to be extended until 31 December 1948. From mid-1944 he assisted the government to draft bills (enacted next year) to reform the Commonwealth Bank and formally constitute it as a central bank. In making permanent the controls which had been imposed due to wartime conditions, he and J. B. Chifley [q.v.] were careful to point out that the 1935-37 royal commission on monetary and banking systems had recommended that the Federal government have ultimate power over monetary policy. The 1945 banking legislation also directed the Commonwealth Bank to compete actively with the commercial banks; Armitage implemented the change with vigour.

In retirement he joined a number of company boards, including that of Allied Investments Ltd, and retained an interest in business affairs. He had served the community over many years through charitable and benevolent bodies. Armitage lived in Sydney for most of his life. As a young man he had been involved in swimming, sailing and rowing, and in later life he continued to surf; his other recreations included golf and motoring, and he enjoyed weekend farming and riding on a small property in the country. On 6 August 1953 at the registrar's office, North Sydney, he married his widowed sister-in-law Margaret Toshack, née Callow, late Paurs. He died on 17 October 1963 at his Cremorne home and was cremated; his wife survived him, as did a son and daughter of his first marriage.

L. F. Giblin, *The Growth of a Central Bank* (Melb, 1951); R. Gollan, *The Commonwealth Bank of Australia* (Canb, 1968); C. B. Schedvin, *Australia and the Great Depression* (Syd, 1970); S. J. Butlin and C. B. Schedvin, *War Economy, 1942-1945* (Canb, 1977); H. C. Coombs, *Trial Balance* (Melb, 1981); S. Baldwin (ed), *Unsung Heroes and Heroines of Australia* (Melb, 1988); *Bank Notes* (Syd), Jan 1921, June 1927, Jan 1928, Sept 1941; personal recollections of Mr H. T. Armitage, Miss F. A. Manton, Miss M. McCourt, Mr W. H. Wilcock and Sir Bede Callaghan (Reserve Bank of Aust Archives, Syd); Reserve Bank of Aust Archives, Syd; Westpac Banking Corp Archives, Syd; information from Mrs H. Wilson, Cronulla, and Mrs J. St Clair, Nth Turramurra, Syd.   M. R. HILL

ARMSTRONG, SIR ALFRED NORMAN (1899-1966), banker, was born on 6 March 1899 at Auburn, Sydney, fourth surviving child of William John Armstrong, plumber, and his wife Sarah, née Gough, both Sydney-siders. Nothing is known of Alfred's schooling. At 15 he joined the Australian Bank of Commerce Ltd and on 25 April 1916 moved to the Commonwealth Bank of Australia. Initially employed in administrative work, he transferred in 1924 to the inspectors' department and in 1935 was promoted sub-inspector. While gaining experience in the bank's London office in 1936, he was briefly attached to the Bank of England. He returned to Sydney in May 1937 and resumed his former duties.

In 1940 he became a special assistant to the chairman of the bank's board of directors, Sir Claude Reading [q.v.11]. Appointed general manager of the industrial finance department on 11 September 1945, 'Jack' Armstrong implemented government policy to finance the development of small manufacturing enterprises. He successfully diverted funds to investment and helped to ease the postwar shortage of capital; his aggressive reduction of interest rates took business from hire-purchase companies. By 1949 the department was not meeting its primary objective of providing a source of long-term loans for small manufacturers, and its activities were reduced. From 1945 Armstrong had been a member of the Federal treasurer's advisory committee on capital issues, originally established to conserve resources for war purposes; in 1950-53 he served on the reconstituted capital issues board. He was also a member (1949-51) of the Commonwealth Bank's advisory council.

Having been promoted assistant-governor (commercial banking) in December 1951, Armstrong was responsible for the general supervision of the four lending departments: general banking, industrial finance, rural credits and the mortgage bank. On the inauguration of the Commonwealth Trading Bank of Australia in June 1953, he was appointed general manager and soon advocated increased private savings to accelerate economic development. He was made deputy managing director and a member of the board when the Commonwealth Banking Corporation was established in 1960. Appointed C.B.E. in 1962, he retired from the bank on 5 March 1965 and was knighted that year.

Sir Alfred's financial and management skills had benefited a range of bodies: he was a member of the Decimal Currency Board (deputy-chairman 1963-66), the Australian Wool Board (deputy-chairman 1964-66) and the Export Development Council (chairman 1965-66); from 1964 he was also a member of the board of the International Wool Secretariat and chairman of the Australian Meat Board selection committee; he was, as well, a long-serving director of the New South Wales division of the National Heart Foundation of Australia. Tall, broad shouldered, with reddish hair, Armstrong was his own man and somewhat a loner, though he could mix well when occasion required. His support of the Commonwealth Bank Bowling Club (New South Wales) earned him the office of patron (1955) and life membership.

On 14 January 1965 in St John's Anglican Church, Darlinghurst, Armstrong married a 64-year-old divorcee Rose, née Neschling, late Lands. Survived by her, he died of coronary vascular disease on 1 July 1966 at Essendon, Melbourne, and was cremated.

S. J. Butlin and C. B. Schedvin, *War Economy 1942-1945* (Canb, 1977); H. C. Coombs, *Trial Balance* (Melb, 1981); R. T. Appleyard and C. B. Schedvin (eds), *Australian Financiers* (Melb, 1988); *Bank Notes* (Syd), Nov 1963, Aug 1966; *Pastoral Review*, 19 July 1966; *SMH*, 12 Sept 1945, 27 Oct 1953, 6 Feb, 6 July 1965, 2 July 1966; *Age* (Melb), 11 June 1953; information from Sir Bede Callaghan, Gordon, Syd.   D. J. ANDERSON

ARMSTRONG, JOHN IGNATIUS (1908-1977), politician, was born on 10 July 1908 at Ultimo, Sydney, the seventh son of a seventh son, to William Armstrong, hotelkeeper, and his wife Ellen, née Hannan, both from Ireland. Educated at St Bede's School, Pyrmont, and Marist Brothers' High School, Darlinghurst, John was lightweight boxing champion of the metropolitan Catholic colleges. He lived and worked in the family hotel (the Butcher's Arms, later the Dunkirk) and joined the labour movement. Teamed with J. A. Beasley [q.v.], in the early 1930s he won a *Labor Daily* debating competition. Elizabeth Healey, a local Labor matriarch, urged Armstrong to stand for the Sydney Municipal Council. In 1934 he was elected an alderman for Phillip Ward, which he was to represent until 1948.

As leader of the shareholders' committee of the troubled Greater Union Theatres Ltd, he helped (Sir) Norman Rydge [q.v.] to become chairman of the company. Armstrong's political ambitions were boosted in 1937 by his inclusion in Labor's 'Four A's' team of Senate candidates, selected partly because their names would be at the top of the ballot paper. In July 1938 he entered Federal parliament. On 25 October 1945 in the Church of the Holy Family, Lindfield, Sydney, he married a 27-year-old secretary Joan Therese Josephine Curran. Appointed minister for munitions in 1946, Armstrong was chosen in March 1948 by Prime Minister J. B. Chifley [q.v.] to take charge of arrangements for the proposed Australian visit of King George VI, but the King's failing health forced the tour to be cancelled. Next month Armstrong accepted the supply and development portfolio. In 1949 the Opposition focussed on his powers as a means of attacking government policy. From 1951 to 1956 he was deputy-leader of the Opposition in the Senate.

In 1952 he had visited South-East Asia, calling on anti-communist leaders in the region. Although he was not a member of B. A. Santamaria's Catholic Social Studies Movement, in the mid-1950s Armstrong's right-wing views and Catholicism led to accusations of his involvement with the industrial groups. Labor's left-wing faction disliked his denunciations of communism and his business connexions: he was chairman of Metropolitan Theatres & Investment Co. Ltd, and a director of Amalgamated Pictures Ltd and other companies. His speeches advocating wage cuts were used against him by forces gathering around Lionel Murphy. The 1960 pre-selection ballot for the next Senate election relegated Armstrong to an unwinnable fourth position on the Labor ticket, and he passed from Federal politics in 1962.

He had never lost interest in local government and announced his intention that year to run against Harry Jensen, the Labor lord mayor of Sydney; the party averted the threat to its unity by making Armstrong chairman of Sydney County Council in 1963. Succeeding Jensen as lord mayor in 1965, Armstrong had his term abbreviated when the government of Premier (Sir) Robert Askin replaced the city council by three commissioners in November 1967. Managerial inefficiency was the nominal reason, the inordinate cost of rebuilding the Domain baths being one instance cited. In reality, the government wanted to take the council out of Labor's hands and did so by contracting its electoral boundaries.

The return to private life enabled Armstrong to pursue business interests and to exercise his talent for helping others. Nicknamed 'the Golden Barman', he had a large clientele seeking his assistance and advice. His wife remarked that he was unable to sit down to a meal without being called to the telephone. His expanding art collection included works by Sir William Dobell [q.v.], Sir Russell Drysdale, (Sir) Sidney Nolan, Clifton Pugh, Fred Williams and Brett Whiteley; John Olsen painted a ceiling of Armstrong's home at Collaroy. In Labor circles Armstrong let it be known that he was interested in the post of Australian high commissioner in London. The appointment was one of the earliest which the Whitlam government made in December 1972. Before Armstrong left Sydney, he provoked controversy by stating that Australia must one day become a republic. His two years in London were distinguished by the patronage he offered to Australian artists, many of whom were making their names in Britain.

An enthusiast for a non-Imperial system of Australian honours, Armstrong was appointed A.C. in 1977. He died of myocardial infarction on 10 March 1977 at Batemans Bay, New South Wales. Accorded a state funeral, he was buried in Northern Suburbs cemetery, Sydney; his wife, son and four daughters survived him.

R. Murray, *The Split* (Melb, 1970); F. A. Larcombe, *The Advancement of Local Government in New South Wales 1906 to the Present* (Syd, 1978); M. R. Matthews, *Pyrmont and Ultimo* (Syd, 1982); *PD* (NSW), 1967-68, pp 1325, 1374, 1455; *Sunday Telegraph* (Syd), 17 Dec 1972; *Daily Telegraph* (Syd), 1 Mar 1975, 12 Mar 1977; *SMH*, 24 Sept 1969, 24 Mar 1973, 22 Feb 1975, 12 Mar 1977; M. Pratt, interview with J. I. Armstrong, 11-12 Nov 1975 (ts, NL).   EDMUND CAMPION

ARMSTRONG, MILLICENT SYLVIA (1888-1973), playwright and farmer, was born on 1 May 1888 at Waverley, Sydney, fourth daughter of William Harvey Armstrong, a merchant from Ireland, and his Tasmanian-born wife Jeanie, née Williams. Millicent was educated at Shirley, Woollahra, matriculated in French and Latin in 1905, followed her sisters Ina Beatrice and Helen Daphne to the University of Sydney (B.A., 1910) and graduated with first-class honours in English. Helen had graduated with firsts in French, English and German in 1902 and was a librarian at the Public Library of New South Wales in 1911-21. Millicent's interest in literature had been revealed when she wrote a story for *Theatre* magazine under the nom de plume, 'Emily Brown'. She left Australia for London in August 1914 with the intention of finding a publisher for her first novel, but was almost immediately involved in war-work, probably in canteens.

From 1916 Millicent was attached as an orderly to a unit of the Scottish Women's Hospitals for Foreign Service and worked from March 1917 at the ancient Abbaye de Royaumont, Asnières-sur-Oise, France. She was sent to the advance hospital at Villers-Cotterets, Aisne, which was taken over by the French military and became Hôpital Auxiliaire d'Armées No. 30. There she first experimented with drama. Written partly in English and partly in French, and solely as entertainment for the wounded, her pantomimes, melodramas and variety shows were performed by staff and some of the casualties, using makeshift props and costumes. In the face of the German advance in May 1918, the hospital was evacuated to Royaumont: Miss Armstrong was awarded the Croix de Guerre for her bravery in rescuing wounded soldiers while under fire.

Returning to Australia after the war, Millicent briefly owned and operated the Amber Tea Rooms at Goulburn. In 1921 she made an application under the Returned Soldiers Settlement Act and was granted title to 1028 acres with a capital value of over £2600 at Gunning on land previously owned by Ina's husband Leo Watson of Wollogorang. Helen acquired an adjoining block. In producing vegetables, flowers, pigs and wool at Clear Hills, Millicent and Helen suffered from the same chronic indebtedness which characterized Australian closer-settlement schemes, despite the size of their holding and family financial support. During her early years in the country Millicent completed at least three one-act plays which were based on her experiences: *Fire* gained third place in the Sydney *Daily Telegraph* competition of 1923; *Drought* was awarded the 1923 Rupert Brooke prize of £25, was performed in London and won a prize in 1934 from the International One-Act Play Theatre; *At Dusk* appeared in 1937 in a collection of Australian one-act plays. Two other plays, *Thomas* and *Penny Dreadful*, both drawing-room dramas, were published with *Drought* in a selection of her work in 1958.

Tall, slim and possessing unfeigned modesty, Miss Armstrong once described her life as being 'too much like that of a great many other people of [her] generation'. After Helen's death in 1939, Millicent became a grazier at Kirkdale, Yarra; by 1953 she was living at Goulburn. She died in a local hospital on 18 November 1973 and was cremated with Anglican rites. Unmarried, she bequeathed Clear Hills to her nephew John Edward Lightfoot.

G. E. Hall and A. Cousins (eds), *Book of Remembrance of the University of Sydney in the War 1914-1918* (Syd, 1939); L. Rees, *A History of Australian Drama*, 1 (Syd, 1978); *Green Room Pictorial*, Mar 1924, p 18; *SMH*, 5 Jan 1924, 19 July, 23 Aug

1934; *Goulburn Evening Post*, 20 Nov 1973; Settlement Purchase Registers, 1919-36, Gunning (NSWA).

KATE BLACKMORE

ARMSTRONG, THOMAS (1885-1955), businessman and politician, was born on 26 December 1885 at Binchester, Durham, England, son of Thomas Armstrong, cabinet-maker, and his illiterate wife Margaret, née Watson. The family migrated next year to New South Wales and settled in the Newcastle district. Tom was educated with his brother and five sisters at Wickham Superior Public School, from which he joined J. & A. Brown [qq.v.3], colliers and shipowners, as a clerk. On 2 December 1908 at Tighes Hill Methodist Church he married Anice Mary Pepper (d. 1948); they were to have three children.

While Armstrong worked his way up, the firm expanded considerably under the direction of John Brown [q.v.7]: it acquired several high-producing mines at south Maitland and integrated operations through its railways, tugboat fleet and engineering works. Armstrong was a member (1914) of the Institute of Incorporated Accountants of New South Wales and an associate (1930) of the Commonwealth Institute of Accountants. He had become general manager of J. & A. Brown by 1929. When John Brown died childless in 1930, he stipulated in his will that Armstrong should continue as general manager and left to him and to Sir Adrian Knox [q.v.9] the residue of his £640 380 estate: Armstrong received an additional legacy of £10 000 and an annual fee of £1000 as executor; he also seemed to inherit Brown's antagonism to trade unions.

From 1931 Armstrong was a director of the new company, J. and A. Brown & Abermain Seaham Collieries Ltd (chairman 1937-54). He was, as well, chairman of South Maitland Railways Pty Ltd and of Intercolonial Investment, Land & Building Co. Ltd, a director of Hexham Engineering Pty Ltd, president of the Newcastle Chamber of Commerce (1936-43) and chairman of the Northern Colliery Proprietors' Association. Having been active in politics for many years, Armstrong was elected in 1935 to the Legislative Council and remained a member until his death; he became northern president of the United Australia Party and later held positions in the Liberal Party. He contributed to debates on the coal industry and, as chairman of the New South Wales Combined Colliery Proprietors' committee, was appointed by Prime Minister Curtin [q.v.] to the Commonwealth Coal Commission. In 1945 Armstrong sat on the Commonwealth commission into the coal-mining industry; predictably, he criticized striking miners.

Despite his business and political life, Armstrong found time for civic and charitable duties. He was an alderman and mayor of Wickham, a leader and lay preacher in his local Methodist Church, deputy chairman of the State government's Housing Improvement Board, founder and president of the Newcastle branch of the Young Men's Christian Association, and vice-president of Toc H and of the Newcastle and District Association for Crippled Children. A Freemason, he was president of the Rotary Club of Newcastle and a governor of Rotary International. Bald and cigar-smoking, he belonged to the Newcastle, New South Wales and Newcastle City Bowling clubs.

Having suffered for nine years from Parkinson's disease and arteriosclerosis, Armstrong died of cerebrovascular disease on 13 June 1955 at his Newcastle home and was cremated. He was survived by his son and a daughter. His estate was sworn for probate at £175 285; he bequeathed £1000 to each of five local organizations.

PD (NSW), 24 Aug 1955, p 11; *Aust Coal, Shipping, Steel and the Harbour*, 1 July 1955, p 49; *SMH*, 4 Apr 1930, 27 Feb 1934, 29 May 1937, 14 Feb, 24 May, 26 Nov, 13 Dec 1941, 7, 10 Jan, 28 Oct 1942, 28 Oct 1943, 9 Jan 1945, 14 June 1955; *Newcastle Morning Herald*, 1, 4 Apr 1930, 4 Jan 1950, 14 June 1955.

DAVID POPE

ARNOTT, ALWYN JAMES (1899-1973), professor of dentistry, was born on 20 December 1899 at Paddington, Sydney, son of George Arnott, a bank clerk from Scotland, and his English-born wife Jane Annie, née Rounsevell. Educated at Fort Street Boys' High School, 'Gil' studied dentistry at the University of Sydney (B.D.Sc., 1922; D.D.Sc., 1929). With two other members of the dental undergraduates' society, in 1921 he set up the university's Dental Research Trust Fund.

On 2 January 1924 he married Adeline Agnes Sitz with Presbyterian forms in her father's house at Toowoomba, Queensland. That year Arnott became superintendent of the United Dental Hospital, Sydney. He played a central part in founding a research scholarship in 1932—funded jointly by the Australian Dental Association (New South Wales branch) and the Walter and Eliza Hall [qq.v.9] Trust—and in establishing a research laboratory at the hospital two years later.

In 1935 Arnott was appointed McCaughey [q.v.5] professor of dentistry at the University of Sydney and was made dean of the faculty. Concerned at the inadequacies of the dental hospital, he went abroad that year with its chairman Sir Harry Moxham to study hospital design and teaching facilities. In 1939 a new, six-storey building was completed in Chalmers Street, Sydney, and the Institute of Dental Research was to be established at this hospital in 1946. Having been elected secretary (1928) of the newly constituted A.D.A. (New South Wales branch), Arnott did much to conciliate vigorous opponents of the amalgamation of the two pre-existing societies. He was president of the State branch of the A.D.A. in 1934 and federal vice-president in 1935-37.

In November 1939 Arnott was transferred from the Reserve of Officers to the Australian Army Medical Corps (Dental Service) with the rank of temporary major. Seconded to the Australian Imperial Force, on 25 June 1941 he embarked for England where he served as a facio-maxillary dentist. Returning to Sydney in April 1942, he was allotted in July to No. 1 facio-maxillary and plastic surgery unit, 113th Australian General Hospital. In March 1944 he was appointed consulting dental surgeon with the rank of lieutenant colonel at Land Headquarters. Working with (Sir) Kenneth Starr [q.v.], he made a distinguished contribution to the treatment of facial war-injuries. He was placed on the reserve in December 1945.

Reverting to his university posts of professor and dean, Arnott incorporated new knowledge and concepts into dental education and practice. Under the Commonwealth Reconstruction Training Scheme, enrolments in first-year dentistry increased from about fifty to three hundred. Arnott arranged further extensions to the dental hospital; he also began planning to double its size and to provide expanded, modern accommodation for the Institute of Dental Research. In 1947 he was the founding chairman of the postgraduate committee in dental service. He supported the proposal to introduce a graduate diploma in public health dentistry and, with his faculty colleagues, convinced the university of the need for a full-time master of dentistry degree. In 1952 he was active in setting up a department of preventive dentistry in the hospital. As a fellow (1952-61) of the university senate, he succeeded in 1955 in gaining three associate chairs for his faculty. In June 1957 the recently completed dental hospital was opened by the premier J. J. Cahill [q.v.].

Eloquent, determined and persuasive, Arnott was the A.D.A.'s representative on the National Health and Medical Research Council; he chaired its dental advisory committee which, in 1952, resolved that fluoride should be added to public water supplies. He was a member (1935-64) of the Dental Board of New South Wales and a foundation councillor of the Royal Australasian College of Dental Surgeons. A recognized authority on oral surgery and pathology, he was a consultant to major hospitals and to the Royal Australian Navy. He also became a fellow of the American College of Dentists (1932) and of the International College of Dentists (1933), and a fellow in dental surgery of the Royal College of Surgeons, England (1948). In 1956 he won the Fairfax Reading prize for his service and contribution to dental science. Appointed C.B.E. in 1964, he retired that year from the university.

Essentially a family man, Arnott enjoyed spending more time with his children and grandchildren. He was a Freemason and belonged to the Australian Jockey Club. A sociable and generous host to his friends, he enjoyed bridge and, when younger, had played tennis and golf. He died on 5 January 1973 at Camperdown, Sydney, and was cremated; his wife, son and two daughters survived him.

R. W. Halliday, *A History of Dentistry in New South Wales 1788 to 1945*, A. O. Watson ed (Syd, 1977); Univ Syd, *Gazette*, June 1951; Aust Dental Assn (NSW Branch), *Newsletter*, 30 Jan 1973; *Aust Dental J*, Feb 1973; *Dental Outlook*, no 37, Mar 1973; *SMH*, 10 Oct 1934, 16 Apr 1940, 30 Dec 1950, 16 Mar 1964, 8 Jan 1973; information from Mrs G. K. Vanderfield, Bellevue Hill, Syd.

N. D. MARTIN

ARNOTT, MARGARET; *see* OPPEN

ARTHUR, HAROLD FRANK MILTON (1908-1972), motorcycle rider and speedway promoter, was born on 12 December 1908 at Lismore, New South Wales, sixth child of native-born parents, John Mathew Arthur, farmer, and his wife Sarah Jane, née Livingstone. The family moved to Crows Nest, Queensland, where Frank was brought up on a dairy-farm. He had already shown ability as a motorcycle racer when sporting entrepreneur A. J. Hunting opened 'the world's first' quarter-mile (0.4 km) speedway in the arena of the Brisbane Exhibition Ground in 1926. Arthur raced there and, with Vic Huxley and Billy Lamont, soon became one of the three top riders in Australia.

Sydney's Speedway Royal opened at the Showground shortly after Brisbane's; others followed quickly, and by 1927 the boom had spread to England. Hunting organized a group of established Australian riders, including Arthur, to race in England in 1928 where Arthur had a successful and lucrative season (top riders won as much as £250 at a single meeting). Returning to Queensland, he married Edna Lyle Collier Irving on 21 December that year at the Ann Street Presbyterian Church, Brisbane.

On subsequent tours of England, while he continued his solo career, Arthur was always accompanied by at least one other Australian rider under contract. The winner of two British championships, he and Huxley dominated international speedway racing until 1932. Arthur was tall and thin, 'almost to the point of gauntness'; diffident, with somewhat stooping shoulders, he could be easily mistaken 'for a curate from a none-too-well-nourished East End parish'. He combined riding skills with business acumen: 'The last man in the world one would have thought to be a speedway rider', he was believed to be the most successful of them all in preserving his winnings.

Following the huge success of the Tests in England—where Arthur had captained four Australian teams (his four-man squad was known as 'Arthur's Tigers')—in 1933 he made an unsuccessful attempt to launch speedway racing in the United States of America. He retired next year. In partnership with Johnny Hoskins and Bert Prior, he formed Empire Speedways Pty Ltd in Sydney and brought a British speedway team to race in the eastern States. To boost the four-wheel version of speedway, which had begun in England in 1932 and reached Australia in 1934, he introduced British midget-car drivers during the 1935-36 season. Mobilized in the Militia on 13 January 1941 and commissioned acting lieutenant next year, he served in Australia as a transport instructor until November 1945.

As a promoter, Arthur shaped Australian speedway's formative years and revived it after World War II when he imported two-wheel and four-wheel speedway stars, and resurrected the motorcycle Tests. His last major contribution to local speedway was his launch of stock-car racing at the Showground during the 1954-55 season. Involved in promoting the Brisbane Exhibition speedway from 1946 until 1969, he commuted from his home in Sydney. Arthur was also a successful racehorse-owner who joined several syndicates and was a prominent member of Tattersall's Club, Brisbane. Survived by his four daughters, he died of a coronary occlusion on 11 September 1972 at Dover Heights, Sydney, and was cremated with Anglican rites.

T. Stenner, *Thrilling the Million* (Lond, 1934); W. J. Shepherd, *Encyclopaedia of Australian Sport* (Syd, 1980); *National Speed Sport*, 12 Aug 1967; *Courier-Mail*, 12 Aug 1972; *Telegraph* (Brisb), 11 Sept 1972, 8 Jan 1982, 18 Mar 1983; *Daily Mirror* (Syd), 19 Oct 1979.
GRAHAM HOWARD

ASHBURN, IDA NANCY (1909-1980), headmistress, was born on 3 August 1909 at Esk, Queensland, daughter of John Mark Ashburn, grazier, and his wife Ida Victoria, née Thorn, both Queenslanders. The fourth of five children, Nancy spent her early years on the family property, Rocklea, near Barcaldine. After the Ashburns moved to Brisbane, she was educated at a small private school at Clayfield and in 1923-27 at Somerville House where, as an outstanding student, she was noted by the co-principals Constance Harker [q.v.9] and Marjorie Jarrett 'for future use'. Having attended Teachers' Training College, Brisbane, on a scholarship, in 1929 she was appointed assistant-teacher at Albert State School, Maryborough. In May 1930 she was transferred to Monto State School from which she resigned at the end of the year to become mistress-in-charge of a new primary school to be established at Clayfield.

Intended to service Somerville House, the school opened modestly in 1931 with six students, but from 1933 pupils were taught to junior secondary level. An energetic and dynamic teacher, Ashburn also undertook all secretarial and administrative tasks in her early days at Clayfield College. During regular Friday afternoon visits by the co-principals, administrative problems and plans were discussed: while Miss Harker gave French conversation lessons, Miss Jarrett inspected the buildings and grounds. In 1934 Ashburn was appointed headmistress. In the meantime she had taken up part-time study, majoring in classics, at the University of Queensland (B.A., 1936). As principal, in 1937 she encouraged the formation of a parents' committee which was one of the first in a Queensland school. A regular communicant at St Mark's Anglican Church, Clayfield, she maintained a good working-relationship with members of the Presbyterian and Methodist Schools Association who governed the college.

During World War II Miss Ashburn trained as a nurse with the State Voluntary Aid Detachment and her home at Clayfield provided hospitality to servicemen (her only brother Colin was killed in action). For twenty years from 1959 she served on the State branch of the Repatriation Department's Soldiers' Children Education Board as an 'active and devoted member'. Although a senior secondary form commenced in 1939, Clayfield College was never large. When she retired in 1964 it had 15 mistresses and an enrolment of 360 (including 45 boarders), and she had been in a position to know her pupils personally. Nicknamed 'Ashie' by the students, she moved around the school with an athletic stride and jingled her keys as a warning system. Her detachment was tempered by a sense of humour and former pupils remembered her firmness and her friendliness. Interviewed in 1963, she had observed:

'In the 1930's the girls were just as keen to do something with their lives and to start on a career as they are now'.

A keen bushwalker and golfer, Ashburn was interested in art and also belonged to the Scribblers' Club of Brisbane. She died on 20 October 1980 at Clayfield and was cremated. A portrait is in the Nancy Ashburn Library, opened at Clayfield College in 1964.

History of Clayfield College 1931-1973 (priv pub, nd, Brisb); *Courier-Mail*, 20 Sept 1963, 21 Oct 1980; Ashburn papers (Nancy Ashburn L, Clayfield College, Clayfield, Brisb); Ashburn, staff card, Hist Unit, Qld Dept of Education, Brisb.

GEOFFREY SWAN

ASHBY, SYLVIA ROSE (1908-1978), market researcher, was born on 4 June 1908 at New Sawley, Derbyshire, England, fourth child of Baptist parents Walter Bertrand Ashby, journeyman bricklayer, and his wife Bertha, née Powell. The family migrated to Melbourne about 1913 and settled at Hawthorn. Educated at Auburn, Hawthorn and Camberwell state schools, in 1923-24 Sylvia attended Zercho's [q.v.12] Business College where her shorthand and typing were reported to be 'very weak indeed' and she was seen to have 'too many outside hobbies'. She was a keen athlete, and excelled in hockey and the javelin. To help with curvature of the spine, she was to exercise regularly at a gymnasium in her middle age.

In the late 1920s Sylvia was employed by J. Walter Thompson Australia Pty Ltd, a recently established branch of the American advertising agency. She enrolled at the University of Melbourne in 1930, but was moved to the firm's Sydney office; she worked in the market research and psychology departments in both Melbourne and Sydney under Rudolph Simmat and W. A. McNair [q.v.] before going abroad in 1933. Although she joined Charles Hobson's advertising agency in London, she spent much time reorganizing his library.

Back in Sydney by 1936, Sylvia set up the Ashby Research Service which she was to promote as the first, 'independent', market-research agency. Initially, business was slow: the ideas were new, budgets were tight, and executives knew little and cared less about market research. For some, she was either too young or 'a woman'. Moreover, she was attractive—slim, 'dark haired and softly spoken', with 'keen, dark eyes'. One of her first commissions was to study the local market for (Sir) Frank Packer's [q.v.] *Australian Women's Weekly* in 1937. It marked the start of a relationship which culminated in Packer's buying her out and subsequently selling the

business back to her for the same price that he had paid for it.

Ashby's clients were diverse and included the National Bank of Australasia which was interested in the use of safe-deposit boxes, the Australian Gas Light Co. which was interested in its workforce as well as its clients, and the Pick-me-up Condiment Co. Ltd which was interested in baked beans. As investigators, she employed mainly married women whom she thought made the best interviewers. At busy times she hired John Stuart Lucy, a journalist from New Zealand, who contributed much to the business. She married him on 4 November 1939 at St Peter's Anglican Church, Watsons Bay.

In 1940 Sylvia was commissioned by Sir Keith Murdoch [q.v.10], director-general of information, to conduct a survey on the war effort, almost certainly the first Australia-wide survey of public opinion. When she turned down a later contract from the Herald and Weekly Times Ltd, Murdoch approached Roy Morgan to conduct the Australian Gallup Poll. Meanwhile Sylvia was sampling New South Wales opinion for the Sydney press and surveying commercial radio audiences. After the war she continued to take polls on referenda and on Federal elections.

Her most important postwar venture, however, was the Ashby Consumer Panel. Launched in 1945 in Sydney and then gradually extended, the panel tried to monitor what householders were buying (brand, type, size, variety, flavour and so on), where they shopped and how much each purchase cost. The panel comprised about three thousand households, each taking part for up to three years. A 'Baby Panel', to monitor purchases made for infants, was also established in 1962. In all her work Sylvia was 'something of a perfectionist' (a less meticulous researcher might have made more money), if she did sometimes succumb to the occupational hazard of blowing her own trumpet.

Busy and ambitious as she was, Sylvia did not neglect her two children. On weekends her time was devoted to them; school holidays were enjoyed together, sometimes at 'the farm', her husband's property at Narrabeen. At home there was always a maid or housekeeper; Susan was sent to Frensham and Richard to Geelong Church of England Grammar School. Sylvia collected antiques, especially on her regular visits overseas; deprived of dolls as a girl, she was to build up an impressive collection of antique ones.

Early in 1974, as her health began to fail, Sylvia sold the business to Beacon Research Co. Pty Ltd. Towards the end of her life she calculated that Ashby's had been involved in no fewer than 3573 pieces of market research. Confined to a wheelchair, she divided her time between her homes at Killara and

Palm Beach. She died of cancer on 9 September 1978 at Palm Beach and was cremated; her husband, daughter and son survived her.

W. A. McNair (ed), *Some Reflections on the First Fifty Years of Market Research in Australia 1928-1978* (Syd, nd); *Better Business*, Oct 1954; *Newspaper News*, 8 July 1960; *SMH*, 13 Apr 1937, 17 Nov 1938; *Sun News-Pictorial*, 13 Oct 1939, 17 Apr 1946, 23 Jan 1948; *Herald* (Melb), 2 July 1946; *Argus*, 22 Dec 1953; Zercho's Business College records (Univ Melb Archives). MURRAY GOOT

ASHKANASY, MAURICE (1901-1971), barrister and Jewish community leader, was born on 3 October 1901 at Mile End Old Town, London, and named Moses, third child of Solomon Ashckinasy, a tailor's cutter from Palestine, and his Russian-born wife Annie, née Cohen. The family came to Australia when Maurice was 9 and settled in Melbourne. Their resources were meagre: Solomon was primarily a traditional Jewish scholar and Annie augmented his income by hawking clothes. Educated at state schools, among them Melbourne High School, Maurice studied law at the University of Melbourne (LL.B., 1923; LL.M., 1924) and was awarded the Hastie exhibition (1919) for psychology, logic and ethics. He was admitted to the Bar in May 1924 and read with (Sir) Robert Menzies [q.v.], with whom he maintained a lifelong friendship. On 29 June 1927 Ashkanasy married Heather Helen Epstein at the East Melbourne Synagogue. He steadily built up a varied practice and took silk in 1940.

On 2 July 1940 Ashkanasy transferred from the Reserve of Officers to the Australian Imperial Force, with the rank of lieutenant. He embarked on 3 February 1941 with the 8th Division for Singapore, served as deputy assistant adjutant-general and legal officer, A.I.F., Malaya, and was promoted major in October. After Singapore fell, on 13 February 1942 he made an adventurous escape with a small group in a lifeboat; they finally reached Fremantle, Western Australia, by way of the Netherlands East Indies. He continued to serve as assistant adjutant-general, with the rank of lieutenant colonel, in III, I and II Corps, and New Guinea Force, and was mentioned in dispatches. In September 1944 he ceased active duty and in February 1945 returned to the reserve with the rank of honorary colonel.

Ashkanasy resumed his career at the Bar and established a reputation as a leader. A generalist, he appeared in a wide range of causes and jurisdictions. His work was thorough, his advocacy powerful and skilful; he was widely (and at times warily) recognized as a strategist whose skills and success

in negotiating settlements were highly satisfactory to his clients. Elected vice-chairman of the Victorian Bar Council in March 1952, he was chairman in 1953-56. He helped to alleviate the shortage of suitable chamber accommodation by supporting the proposal to plan, finance and construct Owen Dixon [q.v.] Chambers as a principal home for the Victorian Bar and played a major role in promoting other projects which contributed significantly to the welfare, prestige and strength of the Bar. Ashkanasy was also chairman of the Victorian and vice-president of the Australian sections of the International Commission of Jurists. An active member of the Australian Labor Party, he stood unsuccessfully for the Federal seat of Balaclava in 1946 and for the Senate in 1958.

Throughout his life Ashkanasy was deeply involved in Jewish community affairs, interests and causes. He saw the Zionist aspiration translated into reality with the establishment of the State of Israel, of which he was a staunch and articulate advocate. Within Australia he promoted at State and national levels effective organizational structures for Jewish community life, in particular those which enabled a Jewish viewpoint to be presented to governments and to the nation. His work assumed increasing importance as the Australian Jewish community grew in size and diversity in the postwar years.

In the early 1920s Ashkanasy had taken a leading part in the foundation of the Judaean League, an umbrella organization for Jewish youth, sporting and cultural groups. His belief that the 'totality of Jewish life' should be expressed through central community organizations (representing a wide variety of institutions, clubs and congregations) was fulfilled in 1947 when, largely under his leadership and guidance, the Victorian Jewish Board of Deputies was established; he was its foundation president. At the national level, the Executive Council of Australian Jewry had been established in 1944; Ashkanasy served as its president five times over the next two decades. He successfully presented Australian claims to postwar German reparations bodies and backed the Melbourne Jewish day-school, Mount Scopus College, where his name is honoured. For long a central figure in most aspects of Jewish communal life in Australia, he gave firm and purposeful—if somewhat dictatorial and at times controversial—leadership to the community. He was appointed C.M.G. in 1961.

Survived by his wife, daughter and two sons, Ashkanasy died of heart disease on 2 April 1971 at his Frankston holiday home and was buried in Springvale cemetery; his estate was sworn for probate at $159 389. William Kaye, the chairman of the Victorian Bar Council, spoke of Ashkanasy's eminence as a

Queen's Counsel and as a leader of the Bar. Special mention was made of his appearances for indigent persons on the brief of the public solicitor and of the way he had encouraged young barristers. A national Jewish award is named in his honour.

K. Anderson, *Fossil in the Sandstone* (Melb, 1986); H. L. Rubinstein, *Chosen, the Jews in Australia* (Syd, 1987); *Aust and NZ Jewish Year Book 1988; Herald* (Melb), 2 Oct 1968; *Age* (Melb), 3 Apr 1971; *Aust Jewish Times*, 8 Apr 1971.

ZELMAN COWEN

ASHLEY, WILLIAM PATRICK (1881-1958), politician, was born on 20 September 1881 at Singorambah, near Hay, New South Wales, son of James Ashley, a native-born overseer, and his Irish wife Julia, née O'Connell. Bill attended primary school at Hay and went to South Africa in May 1902 as a trooper in the 5th Battalion, Australian Commonwealth Horse; the unit saw no action and returned in August. Having set up as a tobacconist at Lithgow, he married Theresa Ellen Maloney on 5 July 1921 in St Mary's Catholic Cathedral, Sydney. Ashley was the local organizer of J. B. Chifley's [q.v.] unsuccessful campaign in 1925 to win the Federal seat of Macquarie for the Labor Party, and later served as an alderman and mayor of Lithgow.

In 1937 he entered the Senate as a member of J. T. Lang's [q.v.9] 'Four A's' team: these candidates had been nominated partly because their surnames would appear at the top of the ballot paper. Closely interested in the welfare of the State's coalminers, Ashley argued in parliament that Prime Minister (Sir) Robert Menzies [q.v.] possessed ample powers to settle a dispute which had led the miners to strike in 1940. When Labor came to office on 7 October next year, Ashley joined John Curtin's [q.v.] government as postmaster-general and minister for information. Sponsoring the Australian broadcasting bill in 1942, Ashley endorsed the existing system by which a national broadcasting service (financed by listeners' licence-fees) competed with commercial radio stations. His administration of the troublesome information portfolio brought him into conflict with the Australian Broadcasting Commission and with the public relations sections of other departments. Acting in concert with J. A. Beasley and H. V. Evatt [qq.v.], he encouraged the A.B.C. to develop an independent news service and issued instructions that coverage be directed towards Australia and the South-West Pacific.

Following Curtin's decision to make A. A. Calwell [q.v.] minister for information, on 21 September 1943 Ashley became vice-president of the Executive Council. On 2 February 1945 he was appointed minister for supply and shipping: *inter alia*, the portfolio entailed responsibility for the matériel requirements of the armed forces, except munitions. After the 1946 election he had the additional duty of leading the government in the Senate. Prime Minister Chifley rearranged the ministry on 6 April 1948, giving Ashley the new Department of Shipping and Fuel: it entailed the supervision of shipping, stevedoring and associated industrial relations, of the production and distribution of coal, as well as of the import and allocation of liquid fuels and petroleum products.

Chifley relied on Ashley to resolve industrial disputes during the reconstruction of the stevedoring and coal industries. Ashley's intervention in mid-1948 averted a coalminers' strike; his efforts, however, in 1949 were less successful. In May he informed union representatives that the Commonwealth government would give financial support to a scheme for long-service leave. In June the miners were incensed to learn that government involvement amounted to nothing more than levying an excise on coal to fund a scheme which would be awarded by the Coal Industry Tribunal and which had the potential to involve industrial discipline. The issue contributed to the ensuing strike, the handling of which cost the government dearly. Ashley had implemented Chifley's policy of buying petrol from British oil companies to assist postwar economic recovery in Britain. When British suppliers could not meet Australia's needs, Ashley introduced the liquid fuel (rationing) bill in 1949. In the election campaign that year he challenged Opposition claims that rationing could have been avoided; despite his crusade, the government was defeated.

Ashley served as leader of the Opposition in the Senate in 1950-51 and remained a senator for the rest of his life. A member of E. J. Ward's [q.v.] left-wing faction, he supported the efforts of Chifley and Evatt in 1950 to shore up Labor's stand against the Communist Party dissolution bill. He favoured an internationalist foreign policy based on support for the United Nations. In the tumultuous years preceding the 1954-55 split in the Labor Party, he allied himself with Evatt against the right wing. Living at Coogee, Sydney, Ashley was a man of simple tastes and regular habits who set store by punctuality and was 'neatness itself in person and dress'. He died on 27 June 1958 in Sydney Hospital and, after a state funeral, was buried in Randwick cemetery; his wife and daughter survived him. Senators on both sides expressed admiration for his tough and combative style in debate and his unfailing sense of humour.

L. F. Crisp, *Ben Chifley* (Melb, 1961); G. C. Bolton, *Dick Boyer* (Canb, 1967); K. S. Inglis, *This is the ABC* (Melb, 1983); J. Hilvert, *Blue Pencil Warriors* (Brisb, 1984); R. Murray, *The Split* (Syd, 1984); T. Sheridan, *Division of Labour* (Melb, 1989); *PD* (Cwlth), 1940, p 365, 1942, p 577, 1949, pp 1808, 1876; *PD* (Cwlth, Senate), 1958, p 4; *SMH*, 28 June 1958; Dedman papers (NL).   DAVID LEE

ASHTON, HAVELOCK RACE (1895-1971), newspaper editor, was born on 19 December 1895 at South Yarra, Melbourne, son of Havelock McBlann Ashton, an artist from England, and his Tasmanian-born wife Hariette Race, née Allison, late Fletcher. Young Ashton was educated at private schools in Melbourne and, after the family moved to Sydney, at St John's Parochial School, Darlinghurst. Early in 1915 he gained a cadetship on the *Sun*, an afternoon broadsheet, and was to work for Sun Newspapers Ltd and its successor, Associated Newspapers Ltd, until 1953.

As 'Frank Harry' Ashton, he enlisted in the Australian Imperial Force on 13 October 1915 and embarked for Egypt in November. By March 1916 he was in France, fighting with the 1st Australian Field Artillery Brigade; he was gassed at Ypres, and promoted corporal in October 1918. Known as 'Frank' in the army and throughout his newspaper career, he rejoined the *Sun* after being discharged on 26 August 1919.

In 1920 Ashton was in London, working with the Sun-Herald Cable Service. He returned to Sydney in 1923 with an English wife, Phyllis Florence, née Clark, whom he had married on 10 June 1922 at the Bexleyheath parish church, Kent; they were to remain childless. From 1928 he was successively cable-editor, chief sub-editor and news-editor of the *Sun* until he succeeded T. C. Dunbabin [q.v.8] in 1934 as editor of the barely profitable and rabidly anti-Labor *Telegraph*, a morning paper. Under the steadier, more placid Ashton, the *Telegraph* gave a balanced view of politics, choosing to play down the 1935 State election campaign in preference to stories on the jubilee celebrations for King George V. Ashton won back many Labor readers. On the paper's sale to Consolidated Press Ltd in 1936, he returned to the *Sun* as associate editor; he became editor in 1942.

His reputation as 'the last of the gentleman editors' had been established while he was with the *Telegraph*. Through Ashton's direction, the *Sun* projected a sense of sober responsibility and public duty in contrast to its tabloid competitor, Ezra Norton's [q.v.] brash *Daily Mirror*, launched in 1941. Although sales of the *Mirror* overtook the *Sun*, Ashton maintained his views that the *Sun* should be a family newspaper, a vehicle of record as well as of entertainment, and that accuracy was as important as meeting a deadline. At staff farewells or presentations, he usually took the opportunity to reinforce this philosophy with a courtesy and integrity that were widely respected. Practising what he preached, he was involved in community affairs, notably as a member of the war orphans' appeal committee of the Legacy Club of Sydney. Such causes could depend on useful paragraphs in the *Sun*, alongside the tearful appeals from small boys whose puppies had strayed. Ashton never failed to raise his hat when he passed the Cenotaph in Martin Place.

Ill health, aggravated by his war service, forced him to take several months leave in 1950 and early retirement late in 1953. In August that year Associated Newspapers had been bought by John Fairfax [qq.v.4,8] & Sons Ltd, but, to the distress of many journalists and readers, Ashton's type of afternoon newspaper had gone for ever. A member of the Australasian Pioneers' and Journalists' clubs, he lived quietly with his wife at Leura in the Blue Mountains. At Phyllis's prompting, they returned to England in 1958. Frank corresponded with former colleagues and clearly missed old friends. Survived by his wife, he died on 6 June 1971 in his home at Newmarket, Suffolk, and was cremated.

R. B. Walker, *The Newspaper Press in New South Wales, 1803-1920* (Syd, 1976) and *Yesterday's News* (Syd, 1980); G. Souter, *Company of Heralds* (Melb, 1981); *Reveille* (Syd), 1 Nov 1933; *Sun* (Syd), 1 Aug 1942, 10 Oct, 22 Dec 1953, 9 June 1971; *Newspaper News*, 2 Oct 1950; Legacy Syd, records; information from Mr J. Macdougall, Lindfield, Mr T. J. Gurr, Turramurra, and Mr J. Ulm, Clifton Gardens, Syd.   STUART INDER

ASHTON, JAMES HAY (1899-1973), grazier, businessman and polo player, was born on 23 September 1899 at Woollahra, Sydney, eldest of four sons of James Ashton [q.v.7], journalist, and his wife Helen, née Willis. From Sydney Preparatory School young Jim attended Sydney Church of England Grammar School (Shore) where he was boxing champion, and an athletics and Rugby Union representative. He briefly worked in a Sydney accountant's office, visited South America with his father, then went to England in 1918 to join the Royal Flying Corps, but the Armistice intervened. Returning home, he jackerooed on Coreena station, near Barcaldine, Queensland. In 1920 James senior bought Markdale, a property at Binda, New South Wales, which was to be owned and worked by his sons, and managed by James.

There James and his brother Robert came under the influence of Colonel Henry Macartney [q.v.10] who had helped to form the

Goulburn Artillery Polo Club as a sporting inducement for young men to join the local mounted field artillery unit. The two Ashtons began playing regularly in 1922. According to Macartney, James was the 'moving spirit' and 'disciplinarian' who persuaded his younger brothers to join the club; from 1926 the Ashtons competed as a team with James captain, Philip No. 1, Geoffrey No. 2 and Robert 'back'. Representing Goulburn in the artillery colours of red and blue, the brothers won the first of their five Countess of Dudley [q.v.8 Dudley] cups in Sydney in 1928: their last was in 1939.

Accompanied by their parents, in 1930 the Ashtons took twenty-five ponies to England. Winning 16 out of 21 matches, including the Whitney Cup, they reached the final of the Champion Cup at Hurlingham, but lost 9-7. The polo-playing King Alphonso XIII of Spain presented a trophy to James senior in recognition of his 'sporting enterprise' and his sons' 'brilliant display' in the final. Now rated a 26-goal team, they were acclaimed as one of the best combinations to visit the United States of America where they impressed with their skill and sportsmanship, won several matches on Long Island and sold their ponies for $US77 600.

From 1932 James acted as attorney and adviser to the New Zealand & Australian Land Co. Ltd (Edinburgh) and in 1932-34 served on the executive of the Graziers' Association of New South Wales. During the Depression he and his brothers bred and trained polo ponies for export, mainly to India. In 1934 Millamolong at Mandurama was acquired; there, through careful management, James developed a commercial Hereford herd, and a high-class merino flock bred first on Burrabogie and then on The Lagoons (Binalong) blood. On 28 February 1935 at St Mark's Anglican Church, Darling Point, Sydney, he married Irene Marie Anderson.

The Ashton brothers again played in England in 1937 where their horsemanship and teamwork proved even more successful. In what they considered to be their best performance, they beat the British Army (6-5) at Aldershot, and, with Robert Skene replacing Philip, won the coveted Champion Cup at Hurlingham. They met expenses by selling their ponies for over £10 000 at Tattersall's in London. At the height of his career James was rated a 7-goal player whose captaincy enabled the brothers to defeat higher-rated teams; as a side, the Ashtons were unbeaten 'off the stick' in Australia in eleven years.

A trustee of the Sir Samuel McCaughey [q.v.5] settlements (from 1936) and bequests (from 1939), Ashton became a director of Pitt, Son & Badgery [qq.v.5,3] Ltd and of the Coreena Pastoral Co. Ltd. During World War II he served on the board of the Common-wealth Bank of Australia; he was also a director of the Mutual Life & Citizens' Assurance Co. Ltd from 1940 (chairman 1963-69), the New South Wales Land & Agency Co. Ltd from 1941 and the Peninsular & Oriental Co. of Australia Pty Ltd (chairman 1960-69).

Ashton was six feet (182.9 cm) tall, spare in build, energetic, disciplined and methodical. He maintained high standards of private and public duty. Somewhat reserved in manner, with an acerbic wit, he took a keen interest in world affairs, finance and sport in general. On retiring from polo, he set up a thoroughbred stud and raced some of his horses, including Belubula, under his own colours. As an ardent free trader, very much involved in rural politics behind the scenes, he opposed the protectionist policies of (Sir) John McEwen [q.v.] and the wool reserve price scheme; his closest friend was James Dunlop McLeod. Survived by his wife, two sons and two daughters, Ashton died on 24 June 1973 at St Luke's Hospital, Darlinghurst, and was cremated. A portrait of him by Paul Fitzgerald is held by Ashton's elder son James William of Millamolong.

Field (Lond), 2 July 1938; *People* (Syd), 6 June 1951; *Pastoral Review*, July 1973; *A'sian Insurance and Banking Record*, 26 July 1973; *SMH*, 8 July 1929, 14, 30 June, 7 July, 11 Aug 1930, 25-27 June 1973; *The Times*, 23, 24, 27, 30 June 1930, 22 May, 17, 18, 21, 24, 28 June 1937; *NY Times*, 29 July, 6, 10, 14, 20 Aug 1930; *Land* (Syd), 14 June 1990; information and news-cuttings from the Ashton family, Syd, and Mandurama, NSW.

G. P. WALSH

ASTON, RONALD LESLIE (1901-1969), engineer and academic, was born on 23 July 1901 at the Salvation Army maternity home, Burwood, Sydney, son of Frances Emma Aston who came from Staffordshire, England. Educated at Newington College (1912-17), Ron won scholarships, was dux of the school and shared the John West [q.v.2] medal. Enrolling in engineering at the University of Sydney (B.Sc., 1921; B.E., 1923), he transferred to science and won the John Coutts scholarship before graduating in civil engineering with first-class honours, the university medal and the Barker [q.v.3] graduate scholarship.

A resident at Trinity College, Cambridge (M.Sc., 1925), he worked in the Cavendish Laboratory under (Sir) Geoffrey Taylor on the effect of boundaries on the deformation of single crystals of aluminium. Aston tutored in mathematics and physics at Trinity College, University of Melbourne, in 1926-29, and qualified for a Ph.D. from Cambridge in 1932 (admitted, 1955) for his work while officer-in-charge of the seismic section of the Imperial Geophysical Experimental Survey in Australia.

Having returned in 1930 to the University of Sydney as lecturer in surveying and civil engineering, Aston was to have contact with many students. They respected 'the Doc' (as he was affectionately known) for his ability and understanding; they also enjoyed the annual camps where he taught them not only surveying skills, but also to appreciate native flora and fauna. Appointed associate-professor of geodesy and surveying in 1956, he had great strength, tenacity and general knowledge.

A founder (1946) of the Association of Professional Engineers, Australia, Aston was vice-president (1954-62) of its State branch and a federal councillor for eighteen years. He was a member (1948) of the National Committee on Geodesy and Geophysics, president (1948-49) of the Royal Society of New South Wales, editor (1948-55) of the *Australian Journal of Science* and a fellow of the Institution of Engineers, Australia. As a hard-working honorary fellow of the Institution of Surveyors, Australia, he advised on establishing the degree-course in surveying at the University of New South Wales in 1958.

Constantly interested in the young, he gave time and substance to many youth organizations, including those of the Methodist Church of Australasia, various orphanages and the Boy Scouts' Association. He adopted an orphan in 1947. Those who knew Ron Aston valued his wisdom, humility and capacity to work for others. On his retirement from the university in 1967, graduates established the annual R. L. Aston prize for the most successful student in fourth-year surveying. He died of a coronary occlusion on 7 September 1969 at Denistone and was cremated. Unmarried, he was survived by his adopted son John.

Aust Surveyor, 22, no 8, 1969; *Professional Engineer*, 23, no 8, 1969, p 10; *SMH*, 8 Mar, 1 Apr 1926, 4 July 1932; personal information.

JOHN CURDIE

ATHALDO, DON (1894-1965), strongman, was born on 26 November 1894 at Condobolin, New South Wales, son of Frederick Horace George Lyons, a carpenter from Queensland, and his native-born wife Elizabeth, née Power, who died of tuberculosis soon afterwards. Named Walter Joseph, he was sickly and could not walk properly until aged 5. He later saw the strongman 'Dr Gordon' at Fitzgerald Bros' Circus, read about ancient Greece and built himself up by taking correspondence courses in physical culture.

Apprenticed to a blacksmith for five years, Lyons followed that trade and won repute as a circus strongman. In 1915-16 he served as a shoeing-smith corporal with the Australian Naval and Military Expeditionary Force at Rabaul, New Britain. Twice in 1916-17 he enlisted in the Australian Imperial Force, only to be twice discharged as medically unfit. Rejoining the A.N. and M.E.F. in November 1917, he returned as a shoeing-smith corporal to Rabaul where, after briefly being discharged in 1919, he served until 1921. On 22 August that year he married Vera Elizabeth Stewart at the Warren Methodist Church, Marrickville. He resumed blacksmithing at Leichhardt, boxed for a time as a light-welterweight and was involved in numerous other sports.

Adopting the name 'Don Athaldo', in the 1920s he published *Health, Strength & Muscular Power*; a sequel, *Meet Don Athaldo*, followed. He made his reputation by spectacular demonstrations of strength and by his flair for showmanship. Probably his most famous feat was pulling a touring car with six passengers more than half-a-mile (805 m) up the hill in William Street, Sydney, to Kings Cross. His recovery from various ailments with 'self-cures' became part of the weakling-to-he-man story that he created for public consumption; his invented past included competitions in Leningrad and Tokyo, and a tally of 486 medals.

Athaldo's income derived from his gymnasium, from public exhibitions and above all from correspondence courses that preached physical fitness. His philosophy combined the idealized man of action with new concerns about health, masculine beauty and virility. Rejecting 'abnormal development' fostered by weight-lifting, he stressed diet, fresh air and 'dynamic tension', but was prepared to give his name to a line of body-building merchandise. 'Athalding', it was claimed, would overcome bad breath, bad habits, cancer, stammering, brain fag, virile weakness and pimples, while developing a pleasing personality and the Oriental secret of calmness.

Although only 5 ft 4 ins (162.6 cm) tall and weighing between 11 and 12 stone (70 and 76 kg), 'The Pocket Atlas' was debonair and dressed with style. When performing, he wore a leopard skin and leather ankle-boots. With a preference for large, red, American, convertible motorcars, he was something of a lady-killer and man about town. He also had an interest in stock-car racing. In January 1941 he understated his age to enlist in the Australian Military Forces as a physical-education instructor and was involved in recruiting. For a time he taught unarmed combat, but developed osteo-arthritis and was discharged medically unfit in 1944. During the war he and Vera separated.

Survived by his wife and two daughters, he died of a coronary occlusion on 24 May 1965 at his Ettalong home and was buried in the Catholic section of Botany cemetery. He had bequeathed his business to his secretary Catherine Thelma Nelson, with whom he had lived for many years, his car to a son-in-law, and £5 per week to his wife.

SMH, 17 May 1941, 20 Oct 1963, 27, 30 May 1965; *Sun* (Syd), 15 May 1974; information from Dallas and Ruth Eggins, Taree, NSW.

RICHARD WHITE

ATKINSON, ELLEN (1894-1965), Aboriginal community leader, was born in August 1894 at Madowla Park, near Echuca, Victoria, fourth daughter of Alexander (Alick) Campbell, a labourer who came from the Baraparapa people near Kerang, and his wife Elizabeth, née Briggs, a descendant of Tasmanian and Port Phillip Aborigines. The Campbells moved across the Murray River to Cumeroogunga, a government reserve in New South Wales, and Ellen remembered a happy childhood in a large, extended family: each of her parents had seven children by a previous marriage and four from their own. Ellen's family suffered intermittently at the hands of governments and bureaucracies: having shifted to New South Wales because of Victorian decisions to evict 'half castes' from Aboriginal settlements and to refuse them relief, they were to return to Victoria when authorities in New South Wales threatened to take their children to institutions for training as servants and labourers.

On 3 May 1911 Ellen married EDWIN ATKINSON (1888-1952) with Anglican rites at Christ Church, Echuca. They lived at Cumeroogunga, a thriving, farming community, and had four children. Eddy worked as a carpenter, handyman and fisherman; in the harvest season they both picked peas, beans and fruit, and camped wherever there was work. In 1913 they were 'converted' by a 'native evangelist' from the Australian Inland Mission. Eddy began to preach, while Ellen assisted by playing the organ at services and by conducting Sunday School. Both of them were unpaid, so they continued to earn their living as they had previously done. In 1922 Eddy took over from his uncle as the local pastor, but remained unpaid. Appointed 'native helper' by the A.I.M. in May 1925, he was promoted 'native missionary' in 1928.

The Depression was particularly hard for Aborigines. The Atkinsons supported William Ferguson, William Cooper and Jack Patten [qq.v.8,11] who led Aboriginal protests against discrimination. Although the Aboriginal community had farmed Cumeroogunga successfully, White settlers used pressure to have the fertile land appropriated and Cumeroogunga was gradually dismantled. In 1939

the remaining inhabitants, including Eddy and Ellen, crossed the Murray River in protest and camped at Barmah, Victoria.

In 1940 the Atkinsons visited Melbourne and found that World War II had brought Aborigines better conditions, work and pay. They then travelled throughout Victoria, holding services in Aboriginal communities. The couple returned to Cumeroogunga in 1941 and lived there contentedly for several years. Evicted after the war, they crossed into Victoria and settled at Mooroopna where Eddy became a salaried pastor for the Victorian Churches of Christ, with Ellen assisting as before. After his death in 1952, he was succeeded by a nephew (Sir) Douglas Nicholls.

Ellen continued to help in the local church. Known widely as 'Aunty Ellen', she was a loving mother and grandmother, a good neighbour, a community leader and 'a real battler'. She died on 30 August 1965 at Mooroopna and was buried in the local cemetery; her two sons and two daughters survived her.

D. Barwick, 'Coranderrk and Cumeroogunga', in T. S. Epstein and D. H. Penny (eds), *Opportunity and Response* (Lond, 1972); I. White, D. Barwick and B. Meehan (eds), *Fighters and Singers* (Syd, 1985); *Australians, 1938* (Syd, 1987); *Pix*, Nov 1941.

ISOBEL WHITE

ATKINSON, RICHARD ASHLEY (1913-1944), air force officer, was born on 21 May 1913 at Emmaville, New South Wales, second child of John Atkinson, a mine manager from England, and his native-born wife Emily Henrietta, née Grant. Educated at The King's School, Parramatta, Dick belonged to the rifle-shooting team and rowed in the first VIII. He enrolled at the Imperial College of Science, Technology and Medicine, University of London (B.Sc.Eng, 1935), joined the Royal Air Force's reserve in 1933 and learned to fly. Atkinson later worked as a mining engineer at Wiluna, Western Australia, Broken Hill, New South Wales, and briefly at Ranong, Siam (Thailand). Mobilized on 31 August 1939, he was posted in October to No. 205 Squadron, R.A.F., a long-range reconnaissance unit based in Singapore.

While patrolling three hundred nautical miles (556 km) north-east of Singapore on Christmas Day 1941, his Catalina flying boat was attacked by a Japanese aircraft and set on fire. Atkinson was forced to put the machine down in the sea. He and his crew, all suffering from burns, spent eight hours in the water before they were sighted from the air and subsequently rescued by a Dutch submarine. For his steadiness and courage throughout the ordeal, Atkinson was awarded the Distinguished Flying Cross. Seconded to the Royal Australian Air Force in March 1942, he became a flight commander next month in No. 11 Squadron; he flew bombing, reconnaissance, supply-dropping and sea-rescue missions in Catalinas. In September he was promoted temporary squadron leader. Posted to command a detachment of No. 11 and No. 20 squadrons at Cairns, Queensland, he took part in night-raids on Rabaul, New Britain, on 8 and 9 October, with his aircraft hazardously laden with incendiary bombs: the operation involved two eighteen-hour flights in a period of forty-two hours. Appointed commanding officer of No. 11 Squadron in January 1943, Atkinson was awarded the Distinguished Service Order for his determination in the face of the enemy.

On 6 March 1943 in St John's Anglican Church, Cairns, he married 20-year-old Joan Patricia Jackson, a stenographer. Promoted acting wing commander in May, he supported the use of Catalinas for aerial minelaying, then in its infancy. Having served at No. 3 Operational Training Unit, Rathmines, New South Wales, from June to October, Atkinson returned with his wife to England. In April 1944 he was posted to Coastal Command's No. 248 Squadron, based at Portreath, and flew Mosquitoes on anti-shipping sorties. Transferring to No. 235 Squadron in August, he commanded this unit from October, after it had moved to Scotland as part of the formidable Banff Strike Wing; his leadership and tactical ability were evident in a number of successful missions. Atkinson was 5 ft 6 ins (167.6 cm) tall, with brown eyes and dark brown hair; quiet and unassuming, he was well liked.

Leading an attack on enemy ships lying in Vilnesfjord, Norway, on 13 December 1944, he had reached the target when anti-aircraft fire severed his Mosquito's starboard wing and his plane crashed into the sea. Atkinson's body was never recovered; his wife and 3-month-old son survived him. A Bar to his D.F.C. was awarded posthumously and his name is inscribed on the Runnymede Memorial, Surrey.

D. N. Gillison, *Royal Australian Air Force 1939-1942* (Canb, 1962); D. Vincent, *Catalina Chronicle* (Adel, 1978); R. C. Nesbit, *The Strike Wings* (Lond, 1984); AWM records; information from Ministry of Defence, Lond, Mr W. A. Atkinson, Southport, Qld, and Mr J. Bellis, Torrens Park, Adel.

DAVID VINCENT

AUNGER, HORACE HOOPER MURRAY (1878-1953), overlander and motor engineer, was born on 28 April 1878 at Narridy, near Clare, South Australia, fifth of nine children of John Aunger, farmer, and his wife Ann Moriah, née Tucker. Educated in Adelaide, Murray served his apprenticeship in the Kilkenny workshops of G. E. Fulton & Co., consulting engineers. He then joined the cycle works established by Vivian Lewis; they later collaborated with Tom O'Grady in building the first petrol-driven motorcar in South Australia. Riding Lewis bicycles, Aunger was the colony's one-mile (1.61 km) champion in 1899 and in 1901 held the Australian record for fifty miles (80.5 km). On 5 October 1904 at the Methodist Church, Bowden, he married Emily Charlotte Pearce (d. 1931).

As co-driver and mechanic, Aunger made two attempts with Henry Hampden Dutton to be the first to cross Australia from south to north by motorcar. They left Adelaide in Dutton's Talbot on 25 November 1907; Darwin lay almost 2100 miles (3380 km) away. Obstacles confronted them on long sections of the route: rivers, treacherous sandhills and boulder-strewn country had to be traversed which no modern motorist would tackle without the advantage of four-wheel drive. Beyond Alice Springs, Northern Territory, the partners met the pioneering cyclist F. E. Birtles [q.v.7]. The pinion in the Talbot's differential collapsed south of Tennant Creek and the vehicle had to be abandoned with the onset of the wet season. Dutton and Aunger returned on horseback to the railhead at Oodnadatta, South Australia, and thence to Adelaide.

It was a reverse, not a defeat. Determined to try again when the rains ended, Dutton bought a larger and more powerful Talbot. With Aunger, he left Adelaide on 30 June 1908. At Alice Springs, Ern Allchurch joined the team. Tennant Creek was reached in thirty days; the stranded car was repaired, driven in convoy to Pine Creek and freighted by train to Darwin. Continuing their journey by car, the trailblazers reached their destination on 20 August. International motoring circles have recognized both expeditions' feats of skill and endurance. The second Talbot is preserved in the Birdwood museum, South Australia.

Speed-record attempts between Australia's capital cities received wide publicity. In 1909 Aunger accompanied Robert Barr Smith in his Napier which set a new time for the Adelaide-Melbourne journey, but they held the record for only a few weeks. Aunger regained it in February 1914, driving a Prince Henry Vauxhall with F. Bearsley; they attained speeds of over 80 miles (128.7 km) per hour on the pipeclay of the Coorong. They next broke the Adelaide-Broken Hill record in the same car. In 1922 Aunger joined another expedition of three cars that travelled from Adelaide to Darwin and back; the party included his brother Cyril, Samuel White [q.v.12] and a local parliamentarian Thomas

McCallum who explored the possibilities for settlement along their route.

Having left Lewis Cycle Works in 1909, Aunger established Murray Aunger Ltd which held franchises for several well-known cars. In 1925 Chief Commissioner W. A. Webb [q.v.12] persuaded him to become motor engineer with the South Australian Railways on an annual salary of £1000. There had been a large increase in the use of motors in the railways and Webb had also commenced bus services to various parts of the State. A number of politicians believed that Aunger (previously an agent for railcars bought by the S.A.R.) had received favoured treatment from Webb. Aunger twice visited Britain and the United States of America for the S.A.R.

In 1930 Webb returned to America. For several years attempts were made in political circles to wreak petty revenge upon Aunger, despite his having played an important part in rehabilitating the State's railway system. He was dismissed in June 1937 for contravening section 37 of the South Australian Railways Commissioner's Act (1936); cabinet rejected his application for two months long service leave. On 6 June 1942 he married a widow Eileen Victoria, née Scott, late Woods, at the Congregational Church, North Adelaide. They moved to Melbourne. Aunger died on 14 September 1953 at Mordialloc and was cremated; his wife survived him, as did the two daughters of his first marriage.

F. Blakeley, *Hard Liberty* (Lond, 1938); T. R. Nicholson, *The Trailblazers* (Lond, 1958); D. Blackwell and D. Lockwood, *Alice on the Line* (Adel, 1965); R. I. Jennings, *W. A. Webb, South Australian Railway Commissioner, 1922-1930* (Adel, 1973); P. Donovan, *Alice Springs* (Alice Springs, NT, 1988); R. Linn, *Nature's Pilgrim* (Adel, 1989); A. Barker, *An Illustrated Treasury of Australian Epic Journeys* (Melb, 1990); G. Davison (ed), *Journeys into History* (Syd, 1990); *Sth Aust Motor*, 2 Mar, 1 July 1914, 1 Jan 1916; *Mail* (Adel), 22 July 1922, 22 Dec 1923; *Chronicle* (Adel), 26 Dec 1925; *News* (Adel), 7 Mar 1938, 21 Sept 1953; *Advertiser* (Adel), 15 Sept 1953; PRG 877 (Mort L).   JOHN PLAYFORD

AXON, SIR ALBERT EDWIN (1898-1974), engineer, businessman and university chancellor, was born on 21 December 1898 at New Farm, Brisbane, only child of Herbert Fisher Axon, a mercer from England, and his Irish-born wife Florence Emily, née Parker. Bert was educated at the Normal State School, Brisbane, and Brisbane Grammar School (1912-16). Outstanding in football, gymnastics and rowing, he was a prefect in his final year and topped the open scholarship examinations for entry to the University of Queensland. He completed first-year engineering, then enlisted in the Australian Im-

perial Force on 11 April 1918; transferring to the Australian Flying Corps in June, he became an air mechanic, but reverted to the infantry in October. World War I ended while he was in a troop-ship in the Indian Ocean; he returned via New Zealand and was discharged in Brisbane in December. In 1919 he resumed his university course and graduated in mechanical and electrical engineering (B.E., 1923; M.E., 1928). Axon next worked in England, Switzerland and the United States of America, studying the design, manufacture and testing of electrical generating and transmission equipment. In 1920 he had elected to spend a year with the City Electric Light Co. Ltd, Brisbane: he was to maintain that this experience, together with his time in workshops overseas, helped him in finding practical solutions to many of his clients' problems.

On his return to Brisbane in 1926, he joined the consulting engineer A. E. Harding Frew and took charge of the firm's electrical and mechanical department. On 5 June that year Axon married Hilda Harris Withecombe in the Congregational Church, Eagle Junction. In 1929 he set up as a consulting electrical and mechanical engineer, advising authorities in Queensland and New South Wales; he later added two assistant-engineers to his staff. He was one of four members of a royal commission in 1936 to inquire into all matters concerning electricity in the State. Their report recommended a move towards public ownership of electricity undertakings through a State Electricity Commission, with generation and distribution being controlled by various area boards. Axon was a part-time member of the commission in 1938-47.

In 1948 he established A. E. Axon & Associates. During the years when towns had separate electricity authorities, the firm handled the design and supervised the installation of power stations and distribution systems. After this work was transferred to the S.E.C., Axon and Associates diversified into the design of electrical installations, lifts, mechanical services, and air-conditioning for hospitals, office buildings and factories; they also evaluated sugar-mills and electrical industries, and in 1937 formed a partnership with (Sir) Walter Bassett [q.v.] in Melbourne to design mechanical services for Queensland.

On 14 February 1942 Axon began full-time duty in the Australian Army Ordnance Corps with the rank of major. In July he transferred to the Australian Imperial Force and in December was appointed a deputy-director, Australian Electrical and Mechanical Engineers, Queensland Lines of Communication Area. Promoted temporary colonel next year, he was released at the request of the Queensland government in September 1944.

Axon had a long association with the University of Queensland. Actively involved with the Men Graduates' Association from 1926, he was a member of the senate in 1935-66 and chairman (1956) of the buildings and grounds committee. He was elected chancellor in 1957 and held that position until ill health forced his retirement in 1966. His nine years in office saw accelerated expansion within the university, considerable expenditure on the development of the St Lucia site and sweeping changes in the methods of administration.

As principal of his firm (which by 1957 had four associates), Axon remained prominent in the business world. Chairman of Queensland Cement & Lime Co. Ltd, he was a delegate to the Cement and Concrete Association of Australia and a member of its council; he was also chairman of the South Brisbane Gas & Light Co. Ltd (later Allgas Ltd), and a director of the Commonwealth Banking Corporation (1959-64), Walkers Ltd and Union Trustee Co. of Australia Ltd. In 1959 he was appointed K.B.E.

Active in the Institution of Engineers, Australia, he had been a committee-member (1929-37) and chairman (1936) of its Brisbane division and a councillor (1937-40). In 1960 Axon was awarded the institution's (Sir) Peter Nicol Russell [q.v.6] medal and was elected an honorary fellow in 1966. He belonged to the Institution of Electrical Engineers, London, the American Society of Mechanical Engineers and the Institute of Electrical and Electronic Engineers of America. The universities of Melbourne and of New England conferred honorary doctorates on him in 1961, as did the University of Queensland in 1972.

Blue eyed and fair haired, Axon was of middle height and robust build. Although he was dogged, honest, unassuming and sympathetic, he did not tolerate fools and 'could be plain spoken when his patience was tried'; in spite of his gregarious nature, he never lost an air of authority, though he was seldom entirely at ease on formal occasions. He was devoted to his mother who had encouraged him in his youth and who participated in some of the chancellor's public functions. Hilda, a graduate of the university, had taught mathematics and sport at Somerville House, Brisbane, before her marriage; she fulfilled the responsibilities of a chancellor's wife graciously, and worked effectively for the Women Graduates Association and Women's College.

During his later years Sir Albert suffered from Parkinson's disease. Survived by his wife, son and daughter, he died on 17 February 1974 in Brisbane and was cremated; his estate was sworn for probate at $233 865. Axon's portrait by John Rigby is held by the University of Queensland.

R. L. Whitmore (ed), *Eminent Queensland Engineers* (Brisb, 1984); M. I. Thomis, *A Place of Light and Learning* (Brisb, 1985) and *A History of the Electricity Supply Industry in Queensland*, 1, 1888-1938 (Brisb, 1987); *Univ Qld Gazette*, May 1959, p 11, vol 61, 1966, p 1; staff files *and* selected documents of family records (Univ Qld Archives).

W. I. GEORGE

B

BADCOE, PETER JOHN (1934-1967), army officer, was born on 11 January 1934 at Malvern, Adelaide, son of Leslie Allen Badcock, public servant, and his wife Gladys Mary Ann May, née Overton. Educated at Adelaide Technical High School, in 1950 Peter entered the South Australian Public Service as a clerk. He enlisted in the Australian Regular Army on 10 June 1950. Graduating from the Officer Cadet School, Portsea, Victoria, on 13 December 1952, he was allocated to the Royal Australian Artillery. Postings to the 14th National Service Training Battalion (1953 and 1955-57) and the 1st Field Regiment (1953-55 and 1957-58) followed. On 26 May 1956 he married 17-year-old Denise Maureen MacMahon in the Methodist Church, Manly, Sydney.

Promoted temporary captain, in December 1958 Badcock was sent to Army Headquarters as a staff officer. In 1961 he changed his surname to Badcoe. While serving in Malaya with the 103rd Field Battery from September 1961 to November 1963, he spent a week (7-14 November 1962) in the Republic of Vietnam (South Vietnam). He saw the conditions under which the South resisted communist insurgency which was led by the Democratic Republic of Vietnam (North Vietnam). Back in Australia, Badcoe returned to the 1st Field Regiment, but in 1965 transferred to the infantry; in June 1966 he was promoted provisional major. He arrived in Saigon on 6 August to join the Australian Army Training Team Vietnam. Short, round and stocky, with horn-rimmed spectacles, Badcoe did not look a hero. He was a quiet, gentle and retiring man, with a dry sense of humour. His wife was his confidante. Badcoe neither drank alcohol nor smoked; bored by boisterous mess activities, he preferred the company of a book on military history. To his colleagues he was an enigma, yet many humoured his boundless enthusiasm in field exercises and his off-duty discourses on martial matters.

Serving in Thua Thien province, in December 1966 Badcoe became operations adviser at provincial headquarters, Hue. On 23 February 1967, during a small operation in the Phu Thu district, he ran across almost 650 yards (594 m) of fire-swept ground to assist a platoon of the South Vietnamese Popular Forces. Taking charge of the unit, Badcoe led it in a frontal attack, averting defeat and inflicting heavy casualties. He collected the corpse of an American adviser and braved further volleys to rescue one who was wounded. Commanding the province's reaction company on 7 March, Badcoe conducted a series of fierce assaults which put to flight a strong People's Liberation Armed Forces (Viet Cong) formation and saved the district headquarters of Quang Dien and its defenders.

On 7 April 1967 he wrote his last letter to his wife: 'It's time I came home. I'm getting bitter and cynical . . . I can see more and more good about the Vietnamese and less and less about the US advisers'. That day he learned that the 1st Division Reaction Company was in difficulty near the hamlet of An Thuan. Knowing that the company would be denied air support unless advisers were present, he drove there by jeep with a United States Army sergeant. On arrival, Badcoe found that the force had fallen back. He took charge and rallied the men in the face of withering fire. Crawling ahead, he made several attempts to silence a machine-gun with grenades. His sergeant at one stage pulled him out of the line of fire. Rising again to throw another grenade, Badcoe was shot and killed.

For his feats of gallantry and leadership, he won the Victoria Cross and the United States Silver Star; the Republic of Vietnam awarded him its National Order, three Crosses for Gallantry and the Armed Forces Honour Medal. Badcoe had been highly respected by his Vietnamese and American comrades-in-arms. Survived by his wife and three daughters, he was buried in the Terendak military cemetery, Malacca, Malaysia. His widow presented his decorations to the Australian War Memorial.

I. McNeill, *The Team* (Canb, 1984); L. Wigmore (ed), *They Dared Mightily*, revised and condensed by J. Williams and A. Staunton (Canb, 1986); *Advertiser* (Adel), 17 Oct 1967; *Mirror* (Syd), 22 Oct 1967; AWM records; Dept of Defence (Army Office), Canb records; information from Mrs D. Clarke, Mount Lawley, Perth.   IAN MCNEILL

BAILE, ALBERT HENRY (1882-1961), bandmaster, was born on 10 August 1882 at Battersea, London, son of Albert Arthur Baile, a house-decorator, and his wife Lucy Jane, née Poole. The family migrated to Queensland in 1887, then followed the gold rush to Western Australia. Arthur moved to Perth in the late 1890s and became a greengrocer. Bert learned to play the clarinet, flute and piccolo under George Campbell, and by 1900 had begun to study brass instruments; as a cornetist, he entered band contests at Ballarat, Victoria. On 23 November 1903 at the Wesley manse, Wright Street, Perth, he married Jessie Elizabeth Preedy. He joined his father's business and about 1910 took over the Beaufort Street shop.

Secretary of the Perth City Band by 1908, Baile won several State championships while bandmaster (1913-20). He also conducted the Perth Operatic and Choral societies (1916-18), played nightly before picture shows with Baile's Premier Band and toured India in 1919 with the flautist Lance Kennedy. Appointed conductor of the Steel Works Band in 1920, he moved to Newcastle, New South Wales, and worked as a clerk; next year he won the B and A grade New South Wales championships. He was a founder (1923) and musical director of the Newcastle Operatic Society.

On a world tour in 1924-25 the Newcastle band won the British Empire and the English championships, and gained third place in the World championship; it also played for three months at the British Empire Exhibition at Wembley. In 1926 Baile was appointed conductor of the Australian Commonwealth Band which toured Britain, North America, South Africa, New Zealand and Australia. During the following five years he made further world tours with the band. Settling in Sydney, he and his wife maintained separate addresses.

In 1931 he was made conductor of the Bondi Beach Concert Band which was taken over by the St John Ambulance Brigade, New South Wales District, in 1938; a district officer in the brigade, Baile became the musical director. Giving his birth date as 1893, he enlisted in the Australian Military Forces on 28 November 1941 and was posted to the 7th Military District (Perth) Headquarters Band as a warrant officer. From November 1942 he served mainly with armoured brigades at home. He conducted the Massed Regimental Bands (as well as Peter Dawson [q.v.8]) in the Sydney Town Hall to launch the Fourth Victory Loan in October 1945. Commissioned lieutenant on 10 November, he was attached to headquarters, Second Army, in connexion with a military survey of bandmasters and bandsmen. His appointment terminated on 5 April 1946.

Baile was undefeated with the St John Ambulance Brigade Band in competitions from 1948 to 1959 and won the Australian A grade championship six times. In addition, the band played during race-meetings at Randwick and at charitable functions. From 1955 he had also conducted the Burwood Band and lifted it from C to A grade in three years. Throughout his career he made thirty-six appearances as conductor in band contests, was awarded twenty-two first placings and was the dominant Australian brass bandsman.

A registered adjudicator for the Australian Band Council and for the Band Association of New South Wales, Baile augmented his income by coaching bands and soloists. He was small, sturdy and clean shaven, neat in appearance, methodical and polite. Survived by his wife, son and daughter, he died on 13 March 1961 at his Bondi Junction home and was cremated with Anglican rites.

A. McL. Sharp (comp), *The Band of St. John Ambulance Brigade, District of N.S.W.* (priv pub, Syd, 1990); *A'sian Bandsman*, 1, no 1, Jan 1955, p 2, 2, no 3, Mar 1956, p 11, 7, no 4, Apr-May 1961, p 13; *West Australian*, 28 Mar 1908, 14 May 1910, 28 Dec 1912, 8 Nov 1913, 21 Feb 1920; *Newcastle Morning Herald*, 29 Sept 1923, 10, 11 Mar, 30 Sept 1924, 25, 27, 28 Apr 1925; *The Times*, 29 Sept 1924, 22 May 1926; *Argus*, 2 July 1925; *SMH*, 15 Oct 1927, 13 Mar 1931.   ALLAN McL. SHARP

BAILEY, ERIC GEORGE (1906-1945), policeman, was born on 14 October 1906 at Tenterfield, New South Wales, ninth child of Arthur Peter Bailey, compositor, and his wife Jane, née Bush, both native-born. Eric worked as a postal assistant before joining the New South Wales Police Force on 16 March 1927. After training, he was transferred to Sydney's No. 4 Division on 14 June, and sent to The Rock in 1928; he then served at Gundagai, Narrandera and other rural stations. Bailey was confirmed an ordinary constable on 16 March 1928. He married Florence May O'Connor at Mount Carmel Catholic Church, Waterloo, on 24 November that year.

Promoted constable 1st class on 23 April 1938, Bailey was next stationed at Moruya on the south coast. In 1940 he arrested a criminal at Batemans Bay and was commended for bravery, cool-headedness and devotion to duty. Learning that a fishing trawler had been attacked by a Japanese submarine off Moruya on 3 August 1942, he and Sergeant Horace Miller set out at night in a pleasure launch in heavy seas to assist with the rescue of the survivors. Bailey was highly commended and awarded six months seniority for conspicuous bravery; he also received a certificate of merit from the Royal Shipwreck Relief and Humane Society of New South Wales.

On 4 January 1945 Bailey was transferred to Blayney, south-west of Bathurst. On a hot summer evening eight days later, while on duty in Adelaide Street, he was informed that a drinker at the Exchange Hotel was displaying a revolver. When Bailey questioned the offender, Cyril Norman, and declared that he would search his room, Norman drew a revolver and shot him. In the ensuing struggle two more shots were fired, but Bailey managed to handcuff Norman and restrain him until Constable Grady arrived. Bailey told

Grady: 'He shot me through the back. Don't let him get away . . . I had a go. I didn't squib it'. Fatally wounded by the first shot, Bailey died hours later on 12 January 1945 in Orange Base Hospital, his wife at his side.

Norman was charged with the murder and that of Maurice Hannigan, a Sydney shop-keeper from whom he had stolen guns and ammunition. Although he was convicted, the death sentence was later commuted to life imprisonment.

Bailey was posthumously awarded the George Cross, instituted in 1940 by King George VI and intended primarily for civilians, which recognized 'acts of the greatest heroism or of the most conspicuous courage in circumstances of extreme danger'. The first Australian policeman to be so honoured, he was also posthumously promoted sergeant 3rd class and awarded the George Lewis trophy in 1945 for the most courageous act by a policeman. Bailey was accorded an official police funeral in Sydney and was buried in the Anglican section of Rookwood cemetery. His daughter and son John, who was to join the New South Wales police at the age of 16, also survived him.

I. Bisset, *The George Cross* (Lond, 1961); L. Wigmore (ed), *They Dared Mightily* (Canb, 1963); *Police News* (Syd), Feb 1945, p 7, Sept 1945, p 9, Oct 1947, p 44; *SMH*, 14, 20 Jan, 8, 22 Feb, 5 Aug 1945, 30 Oct 1946, 11 Sept 1947; *Sun* (Syd), 17 Jan 1979; service records of E. G. Bailey, police registry, NSW Police Dept, Syd.　　CHRISTA LUDLOW

BAILEY, SIR KENNETH HAMILTON (1898-1972), lawyer and public servant, was born on 3 November 1898 at Canterbury, Melbourne, eldest child of Ernest Thomas Bailey, bank clerk, and his wife Alice Gertrude, née Wells, both native-born. From Canterbury State School, Kenneth went to Wesley College where in 1916 he was dux, senior prefect, captain of athletics and gymnastics, and overall sports champion; that year he won the 440-yards event at the combined public schools meeting. He entered Queen's College, University of Melbourne (LL.M., 1933), but interrupted his course when he enlisted in the Australian Imperial Force on 25 January 1918. Arriving in England in July, he served briefly in France with the 105th Howitzer Battery, Australian Field Artillery, and was discharged in Melbourne on 15 May 1919.

Resuming his studies, Bailey was awarded a Rhodes scholarship and won a Blue for athletics. In 1920 he proceeded to Corpus Christi College, Oxford (B.A., 1922; B.C.L., 1923; M.A., 1927) and in 1924 was called to the Bar at Gray's Inn, London. That year he returned to the University of Melbourne as vice-

master of Queen's College and lecturer in history. At the Melbourne Town Hall he delivered the seventh Methodist Laymen's Memorial Lecture in which he argued that the Church should not support war and should defend conscientious objectors. In his college chapel on 12 August 1925 he married a teacher from England EDITHA OLGA YSEULT (1903-1980), daughter of Frank Samuel Donnison.

Appointed professor of jurisprudence in 1927, Bailey became dean of the law school in 1928 and increasingly involved himself in issues of international relations. Two years later he accepted the new chair of public law. Under Bailey and his colleague George Paton, the law school was noted for its conservative, Oxford influence and for the calibre of its two young professors. Bailey lectured in a frugal, concise style, emphasizing legal analysis rather than the dynamic qualities which could be found in the law. As dean, he appeared to students to be a remote figure, given to occasional, personal nonconformity: he was known as 'the green Dean' because he wore a suit of that then unfashionable colour. In the 1930s he was prominent in the Australian Student Christian Movement and changed his allegiance from the Methodist to the Anglican Church.

While on leave in England in 1937, he acted as an adviser to the Australian delegation at the Imperial Conference and was an Australian envoy to the eighteenth session of the League of Nations at Geneva, Switzerland. In January 1943 Bailey moved to Canberra where he became a consultant on constitutional matters and foreign affairs in the Attorney-General's Department. He chaired the 1943-44 committee of inquiry into public-service promotions and in 1944 undertook research for the Constitution alteration (post-war reconstruction) bill.

At the request of H. V. Evatt [q.v.], Bailey was an adviser to the Australian delegation at the United Nations Conference on International Organization, held from 25 April to 26 June 1945 at San Francisco, United States of America. Enjoying Evatt's trust, Bailey had a relatively free hand in the committees which revised the preliminary Statute of the International Court of Justice and prepared the final draft of the Charter of the United Nations. His ability to work long hours with little sleep won the admiration of (Sir) Paul Hasluck. Bailey went to London with the United Nations Preparatory Commission where his capacity to use plain language in official documents attracted favourable comment. Between 1946 and 1969 he was to attend a number of sessions of the General Assembly. In 1958 and 1960 he led Australian missions to the United Nations conferences on the Law of the Sea, held at Geneva. He chaired a committee at both conferences and played a major role in developing the international conventions on the continental shelf and the territorial sea.

In 1946 Bailey had been appointed secretary to the Attorney-General's Department and solicitor-general of the Commonwealth. As a result of his intellectual dominance and the contributions of the talented lawyers he selected to join him, the department established a high standard of legal professionalism. Nevertheless, clients sometimes experienced long delays, due in part to Bailey's increasing workload. He advised Federal governments on the validity of new legislative powers and on how to meet ensuing constitutional challenges. Although usually content to leave argument in court to private barristers, he made substantial and thorough preparations for such cases. Bailey was appointed C.B.E. in 1953 and knighted in 1958; in 1964 he became the first Commonwealth Q.C.

As high commissioner to Canada in 1964-69, Bailey impressed ministers and officials in that country with his erudition in international affairs. In 1966 he was nominated as a judge on the International Court of Justice, but failed to be elected due to a controversial decision by its retiring president Sir Percy Spender who had been nominated in 1958 in preference to Bailey. Back in Australia, he acted as special adviser in international law to the Attorney-General's Department and to the Department of External Affairs. Ill health prevented him from lecturing at the Hague Academy of International Law in 1971. Bailey had been made an honorary fellow of Corpus Christi College in 1947. He was chancellor of the Anglican Diocese of Canberra and Goulburn in 1957-64. Canada's Dalhousie University (1966), the Australian National University (1970) and the University of Melbourne (1972) conferred honorary doctorates of laws on him. The last was presented at a ceremony in Canberra Hospital where he was a patient; he courageously responded with a cryptic address on the necessity for law to contain violence in a world of change.

Sir Kenneth was not a prolific writer, but his articles were stylish and analytical. A small, lithe man, of scholarly countenance and unfailing courtesy, he spoke in mellow tones, and with measured language. While not given to outward displays of emotion, he was highly sensitive and devoted to his family. In his work he was persistent, demanding and frequently of closeted mind. Readily accepting existing social and official hierarchies, he was one of the small band of distinguished senior officers who moulded the character of the postwar public service. Bailey died on 3 May 1972 in Canberra and was cremated; his wife and three sons survived him.

Yseult had been founding president (1943) of the Canberra Nursery Kindergarten Society and president (1946-50) of the Australian Capital Territory branch of the National Council of Women. She was appointed O.B.E. in 1961. Lady Bailey was an accomplished potter.

A. Watt, *Australian Diplomat* (Syd, 1972); P. Hasluck, *Diplomatic Witness* (Melb, 1980); P. G. Edwards, *Prime Ministers and Diplomats* (Melb, 1983); *Current Notes on International Affairs*, 43, May 1972, p 222; *Age* (Melb), 4 May 1972; *Canb Times*, 11 Aug 1980; Bailey papers *and* M. Pratt, Interview with Sir Kenneth Bailey, 1971, ts (NL); personal information.   JACK E. RICHARDSON

BAILEY, VICTOR ALBERT (1895-1964), physicist, was born on 18 December 1895 at Alexandria, Egypt, eldest of four surviving children of William Henry Bailey, a British Army engineer, and his wife Suzana, née Lazarus, an expatriate Romanian linguist. After William's death, Victor was raised by Suzana, chiefly in Egypt, and became fluent in French, Italian and Arabic. From the age of 12 he was educated on scholarships at a French school in Beirut and at King Edward VI School, Southampton, England. He won the latter's chess and sports championships before going up in 1913 to The Queen's College, Oxford (B.A., 1920; D.Phil., 1923). He read mathematics for a year, then switched to engineering. Following the outbreak of war, he was assigned to the Birmingham Small Arms Co. and in June 1918 was drafted into the Signals Corps, Royal Engineers, but poor eyesight kept him in England.

Returning to Oxford, he graduated with first-class honours and worked as a research student and demonstrator in the electrical laboratory under J. S. (later Sir John) Townsend. Bailey immersed himself in studying the conduction of electricity in gases. On completing his doctorate he was appointed associate-professor of physics at the University of Sydney in 1923. The department there was small and lacked a coherent research programme, but Bailey was able to continue investigating the drift and diffusion of electrons, and thus to provide an opportunity for some advanced students to gain experience in research. On 31 August 1934 at the district registrar's office, North Sydney, he married Joyce Hewitt, a 23-year-old pianist from New Zealand.

In 1934 Bailey and D. F. Martyn [q.v.] published an influential analysis of the 'Luxembourg effect', the modulation of a passing radio signal by an intervening powerful source, first noted by an observer in Holland as interference from Radio-Luxembourg on a signal received from Switzerland. The analysis relied heavily on Bailey's familiarity with electron behaviour since it depended on the novel idea that the mean velocity of the electrons in a region of the ionosphere, and hence the ionosphere's absorbing power in that region, could be significantly affected by a powerful radio signal passing through it. The theory quickly won wide acceptance, although Bailey later modified it when he correctly predicted that 'gyro-magnetic' resonance would occur as a result of free electrons at the point of interference of the two waves rotating in the Earth's magnetic field. On this basis, he proposed that radio signals might be used to generate artificial aurorae in the upper atmosphere for experimental purposes!

Bailey had earlier collaborated with the entomologist A. J. Nicholson [q.v.] in developing, in mathematical form, interesting ideas on the balance of interacting populations of host and parasite species; their work generated a series of papers that influenced the field of population statistics. Bailey delighted in mathematical manipulation and also published on such topics as the graphical solution of differential equations and the mental multiplication of large numbers.

Promoted professor (of experimental physics) in 1936, Bailey set up intensive training courses for the Australian armed services in the new, secret techniques of radar during World War II. His heavy workload probably contributed to his persistent heart problems which led him to decline to run the school of physics when Professor O. U. Vonwiller [q.v.12] retired in 1946. Bailey unsuccessfully applied in 1949 for Vonwiller's chair which was not filled until Harry Messel was appointed in 1952. Next year Bailey became research professor.

In the postwar period he extended his investigation of the gyro-interaction phenomenon and of wave propagation in ionized media, steadily including in the analysis more of the many variables involved. Bailey was widely recognized as a leading authority who achieved results in what has come to be known as 'plasma physics'. He was elected a fellow of the Australian Academy of Science in 1955. After retiring from the university in 1960, he enthusiastically advocated the counter-intuitive idea that the Sun carries a net electric charge. This idea led him to make predictions about the interplanetary magnetic field, but the notion has never been widely accepted.

Bailey's tolerance in matters of religion aroused the ire of many bigots. A likeable eccentric who deliberately flouted conventions for which he could see no justification, he inspired students with his ebullient enthusiasm for physics, which gave rise to many stimulating if sometimes wild ideas. *En route*

to take up a visiting professorship at the Catholic University of America, Washington, D.C., he died on 7 December 1964 at Geneva, Switzerland; his wife survived him, as did their two sons and two daughters who all became scientists.

R. W. Home, *Physics in Australia to 1945* (Melb, 1990); *Aust J of Science*, 27, 1964-65, p 227; *Nature* (Lond), 205, 9 Jan 1965, p 128; *Aust Academy of Science Yearbook*, 1967, p 45; *Hist Records of Aust Science*, 7, pt 2, 1988, p 179; *SMH*, 12 June 1949; *The Times*, 24 Dec 1964; Bailey papers *and* Physics Dept files (Univ Syd Archives). R. W. HOME

BAIN, GEORGE KEITH (1888-1961), company manager, was born on 28 February 1888 at Ashfield, Sydney, youngest of six children of Lewis Potter Bain, a broker from Scotland, and his native-born wife Annie, née Learmonth. Lewis had widespread banking connexions and in 1877 established himself as a stock and share broker. Educated at Sydney Grammar School, Keith joined Dalgety [q.v.4] & Co. Ltd. He was an 'expert motor driver', 5 ft 10½ ins (179.1 cm) tall, with blue eyes and dark hair, when he enlisted in the Australian Imperial Force on 25 September 1916. He served in France and Belgium from June 1917 and was promoted lance sergeant with the 5th Divisional Supply Column. In March 1918 he transferred to the 5th Divisional and in October to the 1st Divisional mechanical transport companies; he was confirmed as company quartermaster sergeant in March 1919.

Discharged in Sydney on 7 November, Bain returned to Dalgetys and on 18 January 1922 at St Mark's Anglican Church, Darling Point, married Muriel Australie Carter (d. 1948), a descendant of Conrad Martens [q.v.2]. To the dismay of his conservative father, in 1921 Keith had joined Australian Guarantee Co. Ltd, a private finance company, as secretary at £8 a week. After it was restructured in 1925 as a public company, Australian Guarantee Corporation Ltd, he and Muriel became shareholders. Bain was prominent in the growth of the hire-purchase, finance and motor-vehicle industries by providing finance to purchase motorcars and trucks. His firm had close relations with the Ford Motor Co. of Australia Pty Ltd and with motor dealers such as Larke [q.v.], Neave & Carter Ltd.

Bain took over as general manager of A.G.C. and of Traders Finance Corporation in May 1939. By then the number of cars registered in New South Wales had risen from some 28 000 in 1922 to almost 328 000. The emergence of money-lending groups like A.G.C. made the finance industry more respectable. Bain was a councillor of the Employers' Federation of New South Wales from

1937 and, as its president (1943-44), deplored the effect on wartime production of lawless strikes, especially on the coalfields. On retiring in 1956, he became a director of A.G.C. In the late 1950s the company was restructured, with the Bank of New South Wales (Westpac) as a major shareholder.

Known as 'G.K.' in the motor trade, Bain was regarded as 'a good bloke' who operated by instinct rather than by the book. Tall and jovial, he was the butt of many jokes about his large girth. He valued personal contact with his business associates and staff. A committee-member of the New South Wales Club, he was captain of the Australian Golf Club during the war and won its A.I.F. Cup. From the mid-1920s he lived in Tarrant Avenue, Bellevue Hill, and later had a holiday house at Palm Beach. On 13 November 1954 he married a former army nurse Clerice ('Claire') Marie McMahon at St Canice's Catholic Church, Elizabeth Bay. Survived by her, and by the son of his first marriage, Bain died on 21 February 1961 in St Vincent's Hospital, Darlinghurst, and was cremated with Anglican rites. His portrait by Paul Fitzgerald is held by the family.

Motor Traders Assn J, Apr 1961; *Sun* (Syd), 25 Oct 1944; *SMH*, 26 Oct 1944; news-cutting book (held at Aust Guarantee Corporation, Syd); news-cuttings and information from Mr J. Bain, Point Piper, Syd.   CAROL LISTON

BAKER, ADA WINIFRED WEEKES (1866-1949), teacher of singing, was born on 11 December 1866 at Strawberry Hills, Sydney, ninth child of George Frederick Baker, auctioneer, and his wife Sarah Wilkinson, née Epsley, both English born. At 15 Ada started to teach singing at Wagga Wagga to earn money to take lessons in Sydney. She also raised £50 for the local hospital and £38 in 1886 for the survivors of the shipwrecked *Ly-ee-moon*. On 23 April 1887 she married a clerk Charles Henry Hall (d. 1937) in Sydney with Congregational forms; their daughters Beatrice and Vera were born in 1887 and 1889.

Marriage and motherhood did not prevent Ada Baker from pursuing a career. A 'vivacious' soprano with a 'rich voice', she appeared on Harry Rickards's [q.v.11] vaudeville circuit in 1894-98 and as Zorilda in C. B. Westmacott's [q.v.12] pantomime, *Sinbad the Sailor*, in December 1896; she made commercial cylinder-recordings in 1898 for Allan [q.v.3] & Co., Melbourne music publishers, and toured China and India with a Gilbert and Sullivan opera company. The Halls lived in Perth in 1901-05. Ada taught singing, performed with the Fremantle Orchestral Society, the Perth Musical Union and the

Lyric Club, and played Clairette in Lecocq's comic opera, *La Fille de Madame Angot*.

Although her husband remained in the West, by 1908 Ada was back in Sydney, with a studio in George Street. From about 1911 she lived at Pymble and by 1918 had moved her city studio to Paling's [q.v.5] building, Ash Street. She taught both solo and choral singing, revived Ethel Pedley's [q.v.11] St Cecilia Choir (which raised £1000 for the local branch of the British Red Cross Society during World War I) and supported the Australian Music Teachers' Alliance. Known professionally as 'Madame Ada Baker' by 1921, she showed 'infectious enthusiasm and energy' in staging concerts and over forty light operas and musical comedies—such as *Ma Mie Rosette* (in 1935) and *Les Cloches de Corneville* (in 1939)—for her pupils and to raise money for charity. Many of her young singers enjoyed success at eisteddfods.

Patriotic and generous, in 1927 Ada became a life governor of the Rachel Forster Hospital for Women and Children; between 1927 and 1933 her pupils raised £500 for this institution. In February 1945 she sponsored a 'grandmothers for victory league' to raise money for the Third Victory Loan: one of her five grandsons had been killed while serving with the Royal Air Force. She donated the proceeds of a concert in 1947 to the Food for Britain Appeal.

Ada worked until she was 82; in her later years she taught singing in schools. Past pupils remembered her as 'a legend' and honoured her retirement with a testimonial concert in Sydney Town Hall in 1949. Survived by her daughters, she died that year on 24 July at her Pymble home and was cremated with Anglican rites.

The Grand Tivoli Variety Album No 5 (Syd, 1898); J. Summers, *Music and Musicians* (Perth, 1910); E. Keane, *Music for a Hundred Years* (Syd, 1954); *SMH*, 25 Aug 1895, 25 Dec 1896, 22, 29 Feb 1908, 15 Jan 1910, 5 Aug 1912, 6 Apr 1918, 26 July 1924, 3 Dec 1936, 27 July 1939, 27 Feb 1945; *Aust Musical News and Digest*, 1 Sept 1947, 1 Sept 1949; Tivoli (Syd) programmes, 1894-98, *and* Rachel Forster Hospital, Records (ML); Fremantle Orchestral Soc, Foundation and Early History, *and* Concert reports, *and* Perth Orchestral Soc, Cuttings, *and* Perth Musical Union, Ledger-book, *and* Programmes (BL); information from Mr J. Clarke, St Ives, Mrs J. McCoy, Thornleigh, and Miss E. Todd, Darling Point, Syd.   ANNE O'BRIEN

BAKER, EUPHEMIA ELEANOR (1880-1968), photographer and Bahá'í, was born on 25 March 1880 at Goldsborough, Victoria, eldest of eleven children of Victorian-born parents John Baker, miner, and his wife Margaret, née Smith. In 1886 Effie was sent to live with her grandparents at Ballarat. Her grandfather Henry Evans Baker (d. 1890) imbued in her a lifelong fascination with scientific instruments, an aptitude for creativity and a sense of inquiry. Having attended Mount Pleasant State School and Grenville College, she studied at Ballarat East School of Art and received a grounding in colour and composition from P. M. Carew-Smyth [q.v.7] at the Ballarat Fine Art Gallery's school.

With a quarter-plate camera in Perth in 1898 and in the Ballarat district next year, Effie took photographs which she developed, printed and presented in albums to her parents. She moved to Black Rock, Melbourne, in 1900 to live with her great aunt Euphemia, a headmistress whose independence and professional success impressed her. In 1914 Effie published a booklet of seven of her hand-coloured photographs, *Australian Wild Flowers*, which was reprinted in 1917, 1921 and 1922. In addition, she sold intricate wooden 'Australian toys', made doll's houses for charities and depicted Australian wildflowers in water-colour.

While living at Beaumaris, in 1922 Effie and her friend Ruby Beaver attended 'New Thought' meetings at the centre established in Melbourne by Julia Seton Seers, a Californian medical practitioner. There they heard Hyde Dunn who was touring Australia with his wife Clara to promote the Bahá'í faith that had originated in Persia in the nineteenth century. He emphasized the need for world unity based on racial equality and inter-religious understanding, and advocated equality of the sexes. Effie was captivated and that year became a Bahá'í.

In 1923 she visited Tasmania and Western Australia with the Dunns; next year she went to New Zealand with Martha Root, an internationally-known Bahá'í teacher and Esperantist. Effie was to join four New Zealanders on a pilgrimage to the Bahá'í holy shrines at Haifa, Palestine. She hoped that the sea voyage would cure the lead poisoning she was suffering (caused by many years of licking her paint-brushes). They left Adelaide in January 1925. After the pilgrimage and several weeks in England, Effie accepted the invitation of Shoghi Effendi, guardian of the Bahá'í faith, to remain at Haifa as hostess of a new pilgrim hostel for Western Bahá'ís. She had made firm friends with the women in his family, welcomed the opportunity for practical service to her faith and grasped the opportunity to meet some fascinating people.

Shoghi Effendi appreciated Effie's talents. Early volumes of the Bahá'í yearbook included her photographs of the Bahá'í monument gardens on Mount Carmel. She also made models of landscapes to assist him in planning new sections of the gardens. Her most difficult assignment came late in 1930 when he commissioned her to make a record of locations associated with the origins of the Babí and Bahá'í religions. Speed was essential because towns and buildings were being razed in the Persian government's modernization programme. Moreover, Shoghi Effendi wanted photographs to accompany his translation of *The Dawn-Breakers* (New York, 1932), Nabil Zarandi's epic account of the religions' origins.

At a time when European women expected little protection in the region, Effie travelled by train and car through Iraq to Persia where her brief experience of the 'luxury' of Tehrān hotels contrasted with her journeys by mules across rugged terrain on freezing nights. Often dressed in a black chador, for eight months in 1930-31 she moved between locations, keeping well hidden her No. 1A Kodak and her half-plate clamp camera with triple extension. The lack of photographic supplies and the need to check her work before leaving each place tested her abilities to the full. Without a darkroom or running water, she developed film at night to ensure that she had at least one satisfactory print from the photographs taken at each site. She brought back to Haifa more than a thousand good prints; some 400 have been published.

Returning home to Goldsborough in February 1936, she lived with her elderly mother and from 1945 with her sister Esther, a nurse. In 1963 Effie moved to a small flat at the Bahá'í national headquarters at Paddington, Sydney, again acted as hostess and took care of the archives. Although she shared prints of her photographs and art-works with her friends, she shied from publicity: her achievements were little known beyond her own circle. Cheerful, with ready humour, Effie was fond of children and gave them undeserved gifts and tales of adventure. She died on 2 January 1968 at Waverley and was buried with Bahá'í forms in Mona Vale cemetery. In 1981-82 her work was included in a national exhibition, Australian Women Photographers 1890-1950.

Bahá'í Assembly, *To Follow a Dreamtime* (Syd, 1970); B. Hall and J. Mather, *Australian Women Photographers 1840-1960* (Melb, 1986); *Herald of the South*, 7, Apr 1986.   GRAHAM HASSALL

BAKER, SIR HENRY SEYMOUR (1890-1968), barrister and politician, was born on 1 September 1890 at Liverpool, Lancashire, England, son of Sidney James Baker, Congregational clergyman, and his wife Lydia Charlotte, née Lee. The family emigrated to New Zealand where Henry attended Palmerstōn High School; with his parents, in 1907 he moved to Launceston, Tasmania. Having joined the *Daily Post* in 1908 as a journalist, he worked at Launceston and later in Hobart.

In 1911 he was foundation treasurer of the Tasmania district of the Australian Journalists' Association, formed by local members of the Writers and Artists' Union. He studied law at the University of Tasmania (LL.B., 1913; LL.M., 1915) and was articled with Simmons, Wolfhagen, Simmons & Walch.

On 26 February 1915 Baker enlisted in the Australian Imperial Force and from April 1916 served with the 4th Field Ambulance in Egypt and on the Western Front. After training in England, he was commissioned in August 1917, posted to the 13th Battalion in Belgium and promoted lieutenant in November. During the allied advance through fog and heavy fire near Le Verguier, north of St Quentin, France, on 18 September 1918, although 'suffering intensely' from a leg wound, he located and captured parties of the enemy. For his 'bravery, coolness and resource', he was awarded the Distinguished Service Order; he was also mentioned in dispatches.

Baker returned to Australia in February 1919 and his appointment terminated in May. Admitted to the Tasmanian Bar in December, in 1920 he became a pupil in the Melbourne chambers of (Sir) Owen Dixon [q.v.], with whom he maintained an enduring friendship. On 19 March that year Baker married Effie Millicent Sharp at the Memorial Congregational Church, Hobart. A partner in Griffiths [q.v.9], Crisp & Baker and subsequently in Finlay, Watchorn, Baker & Solomon, as a barrister he had a better grasp of broad principles than of details.

In June 1928 Baker was elected to the House of Assembly as a Nationalist member for Franklin; he was immediately appointed attorney-general and minister for education. A highly conservative member of the establishment and a supporter of State rights, he served in the McPhee and Lee [qq.v.10] ministries, and was leader of the Opposition from 1936 to 1946. He entered the Legislative Council as member for Queenborough in May 1948 and was president of that chamber from June 1959 until his death. A good public speaker whose modesty, rectitude and honesty stamped him as a son of the manse, Baker earned wide respect. He was serious and principled, but rather inflexible in his views; he had difficulty in adjusting to changing values and in establishing personal relationships with those younger than he.

A long-serving member (1928-34 and 1940-63) of the council of the University of Tasmania, he was appointed deputy-chancellor in 1956 and became chancellor after the death in July of Sir John Morris [q.v.]. As deputy-chancellor, Baker had chaired the committee of council which investigated allegations of sexual misconduct made against the professor of philosophy Sydney Sparkes Orr [q.v.]. Otherwise fair-minded, Baker put what he perceived as the interests of the university above a fair inquiry. The charges were upheld and on 16 March Orr was summarily dismissed. Orr countered with legal action against the university and castigated Baker's committee as a Star Chamber. The ensuing court proceedings divided the university and the community for many years; Baker and five colleagues resigned from the council in 1963 when the university offered Orr a financial settlement.

President of the Southern Law Society (1939-41) and the Southern Tasmanian Bar Association (1953-56), Baker was vice-president (1955) of the Tasmanian branch of the International Commission of Jurists and a director of the Australian Mutual Provident Society; he was also a member of the Returned Sailors', Soldiers' and Airmen's Imperial League of Australia, and of the Tasmanian, Hobart Legacy, and Naval and Military clubs. His hobbies were reading, gardening and walking. Appointed C.M.G. in 1946, he was elevated to K.C.M.G. in 1961. He took an active part in a conference of presiding officers of Australian parliaments, held in Canberra in January 1968. Survived by his wife, daughter and three sons, Sir Henry died on 20 July 1968 at Sandy Bay; following a state funeral, he was cremated. Postgraduate fellowships in law and in political science instituted by subscription at the University of Tasmania bear his name and were first awarded in 1971.

W. H. C. Eddy, *Orr* (Brisb, 1961); R. Davis, *Open to Talent* (Hob, 1990); *Weekly Courier* (Launc), 24 Oct 1928; *Mercury* (Hob), 22-24 July 1968, 14 Mar 1969; *Mercury Southside News*, 13 June 1969; *Examiner* (Launc), 22-24 July, 4 Sept 1968, 4 Feb 1969; Univ Tas Archives; Dixon papers (held by Mr J. D. Merralls, Melb); family information.

H. A. FINLAY

BAKER, MABEL JEWELL (1885-1967), headmistress, was born on 30 December 1885 at East Adelaide, third of nine children of William Kendall Baker, carpenter, and his wife Harriett Ann, née Chaston, both South Australian born. At the Advanced School for Girls, Adelaide, where Ellen Benham and Madeline Rees George [qq.v.7,8] taught her, Mabel proved an eager student; she was slender, erect, composed and had a ready sense of humour. Having been a pupil-teacher in 1904-06 at Parkside and Walkerville public schools, she attended the University Training College in 1907-08. Miss Baker next taught for four years at Payneham Public School where inspectors reported that she was hard-working, thorough, cultured and scholarly, though lacking firmness and force, qualities she later acquired. Between 1907 and 1913 she passed nine arts subjects at the University of Adelaide and belonged to the Women Students' Club; with other 'Young Lady Teachers', she had protested in 1907 at the inequity of females being paid lower salaries than their male counterparts.

From 1913 Miss Baker taught history, geography and English at Walford girls' school, Malvern. Promoted senior mistress next year, she took over when Miss Benham died in 1917. As owner-headmistress of Walford House School which then had forty-eight pupils, Miss Baker aimed to balance intellectual, cultural, physical and spiritual development, as well as to instil an ethos of self-discipline, citizenship and service. While fostering the Anglican connexion, she welcomed students of different faiths and denominations; she ran a friendly, if strict, school, and one that was free from snobbishness.

The staff she chose wisely. Brilliant teachers remained for decades, enhancing Walford's academic reputation, but science facilities were scarce and secretarial classes began only in 1941. By 1920 boarders were accommodated in a property that her mother bought at Hyde Park; by 1936 the entire school had moved there. Mabel's sister Amy ('Miss Dob'), her confidante, was a teacher and bursar; another sister Florence ('Miss Flo') had charge of the boarding-house. Impeccably groomed, straight-backed and never hatless, the headmistress daily inspected the school with a benevolent, eagle eye. Walford prospered by careful management, despite her private habit of reducing fees for parents in straitened circumstances.

In 1922 Miss Baker was an original member of the Adelaide Lyceum Club. She was a founding member (1924) and president (1943 and 1954) of the Association of Headmistresses of Girls' Secondary Schools of South Australia, and in 1937 worked for the Adelaide conference of the New Education Fellowship. Next year she inaugurated the Walford Parent-Teacher Association and became a foundation councillor of University Women's (later St Ann's) College, serving until 1961.

Although a royalist and patriot, she tolerated pacifist views in her school during World War II; she sat on the Educational Broadcasts advisory committee (1943-55) and the Soldiers' Children committee (1955-61). Styling herself Miss Jewell Baker, she visited Britain in 1951. She sold her flourishing school (450 pupils) to the Anglican Church when she retired in 1955. Appointed O.B.E. in 1956, she lived with Amy, enjoyed Walford contacts and domesticity, and learned to use a broom. She died on 17 June 1967 at Westbourne Park and was buried in North Road cemetery. A school history (1968), the Baker building and the Mabel Jewell Baker scholarships at Walford Anglican School for Girls commemorate her.

H. Jones and N. Morrison, *Walford A History of the School* (Adel, 1968); *Walford House School Mag*, 1917-55; M. J. Baker, Historical Survey, ts, nd, *and* news-cutting, nd, Walford Old Scholars' Assn archives (held at Walford ASG); Education Dept (SA), Director of Education, correspondence files, 23 Nov 1907, *and* Teachers' Classification Bd, Teachers' History Sheets, 1882-1960 (SAA); St Ann's College Council, Minutes, July 1938-Aug 1961 *and* Assn of Headmistresses of Girls' Secondary Schools of SA, Minutes, 1924-55 (Mort L); Register no 1926, Student records, Univ Adel; information from Miss M. Wait, St Peters, Miss V. Swift, Goodwood, and Mrs J. Prince, Walkerville, Adel.

HELEN JONES

BAKER, SIDNEY JOHN (1912-1976), philologist, was born on 17 October 1912 in Wellington, New Zealand, son of English-born parents Sidney George Baker, journalist, and his wife Lillian Selby, née Whitehead. Educated at Wellington College, he attended Victoria University College in 1930-32, but did not graduate; he was later to evince some rancour when academic critics alleged that his publications lacked scholarly rigour. Jack to his New Zealand friends, Sid to his Australian, he came to Sydney in 1935 and lived at Kings Cross with Ross McGill and Peter Harding. Very much the young intellectual, he was influenced by Sigmund Freud and Friedrich Nietzsche, and admired D. H. Lawrence. Baker worked briefly as a journalist on the *Daily Telegraph* before joining the Bathurst *National Advocate*. On 14 August 1936 he married a typist Eena Dale ('Sally') Young at the district registrar's office, Bathurst; they were to have two daughters: Suzanne born in 1939 and Stephanie five years later.

Having visited London in 1938-39, Baker returned to the land of his birth where he published *New Zealand Slang* (Christchurch, 1941?), but was soon back in Sydney working on the *A.B.C. Weekly*. Twice rejected as unfit for active service, in 1942 he crewed in a trawler engaged by the United States Army Small Ships Division to ferry arms and supplies to New Caledonia. He had received a Commonwealth Literary Fund fellowship and published his *Popular Dictionary of Australian Slang* (Melbourne, 1941) which was to run to three editions by 1943. The book marked the beginning of his devotion to collecting and to interpreting Australian colloquialisms as a manifestation of national character. With his appetite whetted by finding Australian and New Zealand words and phrases which were unfamiliar in London, he fossicked unremittingly and became the tireless correspondent of hundreds of Australians as he compiled his major work, *The Australian Language* (1945). His interpretation of the Australian character was based on his ordering of the thousands of Australianisms that he identified and on what he regarded as the inventiveness of the idiom. A whole stratum of the vocabulary which E. E. Morris [q.v.5] had previously neglected was categorized by Baker as, for example, the language of the soil, the bush, the road or the city. His categories have not been shaken by subsequent, more sober, accounts.

Again a Commonwealth literary fellow in 1950 and 1964, Baker published two supplements to *The Australian Language—Australia Speaks* (1953) and *The Drum* (1959)—before a second, heavily revised edition of *The Australian Language* appeared in 1966. He wrote a host of articles on the subject which were published in the *Encyclopaedia Britannica*, in other popular reference works and in journals such as *American Speech*. His interest was undying, his energy unflagging, his fascination with the vitality and life of Australian English endless.

Meanwhile, he worked on the *A.B.C. Weekly* (1941-42), *Daily Telegraph* (1943-46), *Melbourne Herald* and *Sun News-Pictorial* (1946-47) and the *Sydney Morning Herald* (from 1947); he edited the latter's Saturday book pages in 1953-63. Advisory editor of the *International Journal of Sexology* (Bombay), he published articles on linguistic psychology from 1948 until 1955. Nonetheless, it was Baker's 'magnificent obsession', rather than anything emanating from his journalistic career, his novels, *Time is an Enemy* (New York, 1958) and *The Gig* (1960), or his biography of Matthew Flinders [q.v.1], *My Own Destroyer* (1962), that ensured his honoured place as an Australianist.

His was a private quest that carried its own strains and brought its own rewards. Divorced in 1950, on 16 June at the registrar general's office, Sydney, he married a journalist Noni Grace Irene Rowland; she left him in 1953. Divorcing her in 1957, he married a 27-year-old make-up artist, Barbara Spence Still, on 24 May 1958 in the same registry. He had the reputation of fractiousness and irascibility, and was not an easy person to live with. From about 1942 he suffered from multiple sclerosis which made his remaining life a struggle. A frail figure, bespectacled and bearded, he was increasingly handicapped, though never defeated, and never idle. Survived by his wife, and by the daughters of his first marriage, he died of cancer on 2 February 1976 in Sydney Hospital and was cremated. Allan Ashbolt remarked at his funeral: 'he was always at work—not out of any puritan zeal, but because he knew that creative work was the purpose, the essence, the real joy of existence'.

Aust Author, 8, Apr 1976, p 26; *SMH*, 3 June 1941, 3 Oct 1949, 31 Oct 1964, 3 Feb 1976; Baker papers (ML *and* NL); information from Ms Suzanne Baker, Balmain, Syd; personal information.

W. S. RAMSON

BALDESSIN, GEORGE VICTOR JOSEPH (1939-1978), painter, sculptor and printmaker, was born on 19 May 1939 at San Biagio di Callalta, Italy, son of Venetian-born Luigi Baldessin and his wife Carmella, née Cervi, a naturalized Australian who returned to Victoria that year. The family, separated by war, was re-united on 17 February 1949 when father and son arrived in Melbourne. Living at Carlton, the parents worked in factories while George attended St Brigid's primary school, Fitzroy, and the Christian Brothers' school, St Thomas's, at Clifton Hill. Luigi and George were naturalized in 1954.

Before leaving school, Baldessin became a part-time waiter at the city's Menzies Hotel: what he witnessed there provided the 'Banquet for no Eating' theme which he later exploited in sculptures and etchings. In 1958-61 he studied painting at the Royal Melbourne Technical College, but turned with more enthusiasm to sculpture and printmaking. Fired by descriptions of the latest trends in Europe, Baldessin worked a passage to London in 1962. He attended printmaking classes at the Chelsea School of Art, then journeyed to Spain. Goya's etchings, films by Ingmar Bergman and Luis Bunuel, and Fred Williams's 'Music Hall' prints inspired Baldessin's first etchings of performers and acrobats. Their taut outlines and areas of aquatint introduced the ironically interpreted human figure which remained his favourite subject.

Studying under the sculptor Marino Marini at Milan's Brera Academy of Fine Art, Italy, in 1963, Baldessin was warned against excessive elegance. He returned in July to teach printmaking at the Royal Melbourne Institute of Technology and to prepare his first solo exhibition which was shown at Melbourne's Argus Gallery in 1964. Next year he had the first of many exhibitions at the Rudy Komon Gallery, Sydney. In 1966 he won the Alcorso-Sekers travelling scholarship award for sculpture and went to Japan. Slim, dark and blue eyed, on 26 January 1966 Baldessin had married Alison Patricia Walmsley at the office of the government statist, Melbourne; they were divorced in 1970. He married Shirley Anne ('Tess') Edwards on 10 April 1971 at the Presbyterian Church, Kangaroo Ground. On their St Andrews property, site of his gabled, bluestone studio, they hosted an artists' cricket match on Boxing Day 1972.

At his city studio, established by 1968, Baldessin attracted a following of younger artists. Having invented silver-aluminium foil prints in 1970, he won the 1971 Comalco invitation award for sculpture. Following his 1974 retrospective at the Mornington Peninsula Arts Centre, the Australian National Gallery, Canberra, acquired 279 of his prints and etching plates. In 1966-75 his works were shown in the United States of America, Yugoslavia, Poland, England, South East Asia, New Zealand, India, Japan and at the XIII Bienal de Sao Paulo, Brazil, where he represented Australia with twenty-five silver laminate etchings entitled 'Occasional Images from a City Chamber' and a sculptural installation, 'Occasional Screens with Seating Arrangement'.

From 1975 Baldessin and Tess lived in Paris where George attended the Lacourière printworks, befriended Imants Tillers and became interested in medieval images of Mary Magdalene. Returning to Australia, he explored this interest in the 'Tympan' which he painted with four other artists at the Realities Gallery, Melbourne, in 1977. Baldessin died on 9 August 1978 at Heidelberg from injuries received in a motorcar collision. Survived by his wife and their two sons, he was cremated. A memorial exhibition was held at the National Gallery of Victoria in 1983.

The virtuosity, originality and style of Baldessin's images elicited some criticism. G. R. Lansell accused him of 'mannered artifice', but most agreed with Alan McCulloch who praised the tireless energy which in one decade earned the artist a major reputation as both sculptor and printmaker. Baldessin's work balanced sophisticated refinement with savage compositional distortions, nervous intensity and disturbing ambiguities to describe eternal aspects of the human condition. If enigmas have emerged, they can be attributed—at least in part—to an identity torn between postwar Europe and nascent, multicultural Australia.

C. Mercwether, *Australia: XIII Bienal de Sao Paulo, 1975*, exhibition cat (Sao Paulo, Brazil, 1975); R. Lindsay and M. J. Holloway, *George Baldessin*, exhibition cat (Melb, 1983); *Art and Aust*, 7, no 2, Sept 1969, p 153; *Imprint*, 4, 1975; *Aspect: Art and Literature*, 4, nos 1-2, 1979, p 102; *Art Bulletin of Vic*, 22, 1982; *Herald* (Melb), 16 June 1964; *Australian*, 13 Nov 1965, Weekend edn, 19-20 Aug 1978; *Age* (Melb), 10 July 1967, 23 Oct 1971; *Nation*, 31 Aug 1968; *Bulletin*, 31 May 1969; R. W. Lockwood, George Baldessin Etchings: 1963-1972 (ts, 1973, held by its author).

JENNY ZIMMER

BALDWIN, ALEC HUTCHESON (1891-1971), professor of tropical medicine, was born on 24 December 1891 at Kyneton, Victoria, son of Robert Baldwin, a locally-born grocer, and his wife Annie, née Fraser, a Queenslander. Alec was educated at Kyneton College, Wesley College and the University of Melbourne (M.B., B.S., 1917). Appointed captain in the Australian Army Medical Corps in December 1917, he transferred to the Australian Imperial Force on 21 March 1918. He served on the Western Front with the 5th Field Ambulance from September. Granted leave in May 1919, he took charge of the isolation wards at the Birmingham and Midlands Free Hospital for Children, England. He returned to Melbourne where his A.I.F. appointment terminated on 4 April 1920; he took his diploma of public health that year.

Finding difficulty in obtaining training in established institutions amid the postwar influx of returned medical officers, Baldwin spent eighteen months with the Australian Hookworm Campaign. In 1922 he was awarded a scholarship by the Rockefeller Foundation which enabled him to work at the Johns Hopkins University, United States of America, and at the London School of Hygiene and Tropical Medicine (Dip.T.M. & H., 1923). Returning to Australia, he joined the Commonwealth Department of Health and was posted as relieving officer to its laboratory at Rabaul, in the mandated Territory of New Guinea.

From 1924 Baldwin was acting-director of the Australian Institute of Tropical Medicine at Townsville, Queensland. There, on 5 March 1927 at St Peter's Anglican Church, he married a nurse Beatrix Rebecca Fitzmaurice. When the institute was merged in 1930 with the new School of Public Health and Tropical Medicine in Sydney, he became deputy-director and worked under Professors Harvey Sutton [q.v.12] and (Sir) Edward Ford. Baldwin undertook research into tropical diseases in Australia, the Pacific and South East Asia, published ten articles and attended international conferences.

In 1942, with the rank of temporary wing commander, Baldwin was appointed to the Royal Australian Air Force as director of hygiene and tropical medicine; he was promoted acting group captain on 1 September 1943. His advice on malaria and other tropical diseases was valued by the R.A.A.F., for which he also built hygiene and tropical units, organized training among medical officers and other ranks, and fostered research into scrub typhus and schistosomiasis. In March 1943 he was appointed R.A.A.F. representative to the Combined Advisory Committee on Tropical Medicine, Hygiene and Sanitation which was set up to brief General Douglas MacArthur [q.v.]. On demobilization, Baldwin returned to the School of Public Health and Tropical Medicine and in 1947 became professor of tropical medicine by special arrangement with the Commonwealth Department of Health. He retired in 1956.

Fair haired, blue eyed and 5 ft 7 ins tall (170.2 cm), Baldwin was kindly, modest and approachable. An alert conversationalist with a good fund of stories, he was a member of the University Club, Sydney, and the Navy, Army and Air Force Club, Melbourne, and enjoyed bushwalking, golf and photography. Survived by his wife and son, he died on 29 December 1971 in his home at Epping, Sydney, and was cremated.

A. S. Walker, *Medical Services of the R.A.N. and the R.A.A.F.* (Canb, 1961); Cwlth Dept of Health and Univ Syd, *School of Public Health and Tropical Medicine, 1930-1980* (Syd, 1980); J. A. Young *et al* (eds), *Centenary Book of the University of Sydney Faculty of Medicine* (Syd, 1984); *MJA*, 1974, vol 1, p 769; personal information.

H. O. LANCASTER

BALDWINSON, ARTHUR NORMAN (1908-1969), architect, was born on 26 February 1908 at Kallaroo, near Kalgoorlie, Western Australia, son of native-born parents Horace Stanley Baldwinson, railway employee, and his wife Florence Augusta, née Griese (Grice). Arthur was educated at Quorn Public School, South Australia (1920-21), and the Goldfields High School, Kalgoorlie (1922 and 1925); while living at the Cottesloe household of his uncle, the schoolmaster Charles Grice, who interested him in poetry, literature and art, he went to the High School, Perth (1923-24). He attended the Imperial Jamboree of boy scouts at Wembley, London, in 1924.

A talented sketcher, Baldwinson was encouraged to study architecture and in June 1925 enrolled at the Gordon Institute of Technology, Geelong, Victoria. Having qualified in 1929, he taught there until 1931. He won the William Campbell sketching competition in 1930 and next year was admitted as an associate of the Royal Victorian Institute of Architects. The Depression brought building to a standstill. After saving £42 for the fare, in April 1931 he reached London where he was employed as a casual illustrator and in the office of the Australian-born architect Raymond McGrath. In 1934 Baldwinson travelled through Europe, visiting galleries and modern buildings. That year he worked in London for E. Maxwell Fry, a leading English modernist, who was joined by the architect Walter Gropius, a refugee from the Nazis. Baldwinson became Gropius's assistant in 1935, designing halls of residence at Cambridge and Oxford, and the college at Impington, Cambridgeshire.

In November 1936 Baldwinson agreed to join the Melbourne architects Stephenson [q.v.12] & Meldrum [q.v.] and soon took charge of major projects in the firm's Sydney office. Within one year he returned to Melbourne where, on 18 September 1937 at the government statist's office, he married Elspeth Lee-Lewes; they were to remain childless.

Settling in Sydney in March 1938, Baldwinson won all three categories in a competition organized by the Timber Development Association of Australia: his experience with Gropius had enabled him to design simple houses in the modern style. He entered private practice, first at Manly and then in the city, assisted only by Elspeth as secretary and typist. That year, with John Oldham, he designed 230 houses and recreational and shopping facilities for the Coomaditchy Lagoon project at Port Kembla, only part of which was completed. His domestic work in Sydney produced some influential designs: William Collins's uncompromisingly modern house (1938) at Palm Beach, a rectangular box, clad in Sydney blue-gum weatherboards, on a rock-faced sandstone base, its severity relieved by a strong, diagonal, external staircase; and the Kingsford Smith house (1939) in dense bushland on Pittwater, another timber-framed building, with simple massing and a low-pitched, skillion roof.

In 1939 Baldwinson became a founding member of the Modern Architectural Research Society which was disbanded late in 1943 when most of its members were away on war service. In 1940 the Maritime Services Board engaged him to design major reconstructions of the ferry wharves at Manly and Circular Quay; the clean lines of these cream-painted, timber-clad structures were appropriately 'modern' and 'maritime'.

Appointed principal architect (1940) for the Commonwealth Aircraft Corporation Pty Ltd factory at Lidcombe, he left Sidney Hirst in charge of his practice. Baldwinson was based in Adelaide until early 1942, converting General Motors-Holden's [q.v.9] Ltd's plant at Woodville for aircraft production. Seconded to the Commonwealth Department of Aircraft Production at Fishermens Bend and Essendon, Melbourne, he designed buildings for the production of Lancaster aircraft. From 2 August 1943 until the end of the war he was chief architect of the Beaufort division. In January 1946 Baldwinson produced a series of prefabricated houses for the State government, using the Beaufort facilities at Fishermens Bend; a steel-framed prototype was erected in three weeks in May at the Treasury Gardens. The government ordered five thousand houses, but only twenty-three were built.

From 1946 Baldwinson worked from an office in Sydney. He designed houses (often in bushland settings) in the modern style, mainly for artists and photographers, including a split-level home for Richard Foot and his wife Elaine Haxton at Clareville (1949) and Max Dupain's at Castlecrag (1952). Cleanly planned and crisply detailed, these houses used large areas of glass to take advantage of the views and the sun. Baldwinson designed in 'an unaffected fashion', uninfluenced 'by conventions or tradition'. Unlike many of his contemporaries, he often used natural timber finishes to add a touch of warmth. As happened to Sydney Ancher [q.v.] and Harry Seidler, one of Baldwinson's designs was rejected by local councillors who alleged that it was 'more like an air raid shelter than a home'. His own house at Greenwich (1953) was described by one alderman as 'a fruit box on four walls'.

Beyond his busy practice, Baldwinson was involved with the Royal Australian Institute of Architects as New South Wales correspondent (1948-55) for its journal, *Architecture*; he was an assessor for the (Sir John) Sulman [q.v.12] award (1950) and became a fellow (1951) of the R.A.I.A. From 1953 he was senior lecturer in town and country planning at the University of Sydney. His business partners included Charles Vernon Sylvester-Booth (1953-58), Charles Peters (1956-58) and Geoffrey Twibill (1958-59); the firm designed houses, motor showrooms and factories; their Hotel Belmont won the Sulman medal in 1956. Baldwinson produced a perspective drawing of Jørn Utzon's winning design for the Sydney Opera House which was presented to the public on 30 January 1957.

Late in 1960 Baldwinson closed his office, but continued to teach until 1969. With Elspeth, he went abroad in 1961 and 1966-67. At weekends he visited and photographed old buildings for the State branch of the National Trust of Australia. Survived by his wife, he died of myocardial infarction on 25 August 1969 in Royal North Shore Hospital and was cremated with Anglican rites. The quiet, unassuming modesty which had so endeared Arthur Baldwinson to his friends may help to explain why his achievement was relatively unrecognized in his lifetime.

R. Boyd, *Victorian Modern* (Melb, 1947) and *Australia's Home* (Melb, 1952); *Art and Aust*, 1 Dec 1941, 7, no 3, Dec 1969; *Architecture Aust*, Oct 1950, 59, no 1, Feb 1970, 66, no 1, Feb 1977; *RAIA News*, 6, no 12, Dec 1969; *Architectural Science Review*, 12, no 4, Dec 1969; R. Apperly, Sydney Houses 1914-1939 (M.Arch. thesis, Univ NSW, 1972); G. C. Holman, Arthur Baldwinson, His Houses and Works (B.Arch. thesis, Univ NSW, 1980); *Argus*, 19 Mar, 26 July 1938; *Australian*, 27 Oct 1967.
                            RICHARD E. APPERLY*
                            PETER REYNOLDS

BALMER, JOHN RAEBURN (1910-1944), air force officer, was born on 3 July 1910 at Bendigo, Victoria, son of Sydney Raeburn Balmer, lawyer, and his wife Catherine Haswell, née Macdonald, both Victorian born. Educated at Scotch College and the University of Melbourne, John joined the Royal Australian Air Force as an air cadet on 19 December 1932. He completed two flying courses, was commissioned on 1 April 1933 and transferred to the Permanent Air Force in November. His most important pre-war posting (July 1935-November 1937) was with No. 1 Flying Training School, Point Cook, Victoria, where he won repute as an exacting but imaginative instructor: he once parachuted from a training aircraft, leaving his reluctant but capable pupil to make the landing alone. Keenly interested in long-distance motoring, with another R.A.A.F. officer Balmer drove from Perth to Melbourne in December 1936, taking 65 hours 10 minutes to complete the journey and breaking the record by some 17 hours. In October-November 1938 he and a co-driver cut the round-Australia record from 45 to 23½ days.

From June 1940 Balmer commanded No. 13 Squadron, a general reconnaissance unit based in Darwin; on 1 April 1941 he was promoted temporary wing commander. After a series of short postings, on 18 March 1942 he assumed command of No. 100 Squadron which was equipped with Australian-built Beauforts. He was appointed O.B.E. in June. Balmer's exploits in the South-West Pacific Area established him as a leader. On the night of 25-26 June he took charge of a strike against a Japanese steamer in New Guinea's Huon Gulf. The assault was carried out at low altitude and pressed with great determination, but a later analysis failed to confirm the vessel's sinking. In October he led the squadron's torpedo-bombers from Milne Bay, Papua, on an ambitious 950-nautical-mile-flight (1760 km) to attack enemy ships sheltering off the Shortland Islands, near Bougainville.

Arriving in England in June 1943, he became commanding officer of No. 467 Squadron, R.A.A.F., on 18 August. It was a bad time for the squadron: seven of its twenty-one Lancasters were lost that month. Balmer flew his first operation on the night of 27-28 August in a raid against Nuremberg which cost Bomber Command 4.9 per cent of the attacking force. He led his unit against Hanover on 22-23 September and 18-19 October, and against Berlin on 18-19 November and 15-16 February 1944. His next German target was Frankfurt on 18-19 March. Thereafter, the Royal Air Force concentrated on pre-invasion objectives in occupied France; Balmer took part in four such strikes in March-April. He was awarded the Distinguished Flying Cross in April for his skill, efficiency and devotion to duty; his promotion to temporary group captain was gazetted on 4 May.

'Sam' Balmer was known as a sardonic man who was intolerant of fools and of over-conservative authority; his subordinates regarded him as a 'dynamic' commanding officer. Having logged some 5000 flying-hours, on the night of 11-12 May 1944 he attacked a military camp at Bourg-Léopold (Leopolds-burg), Belgium. His aircraft did not return and his death shook the squadron. Unmarried, Balmer was a Presbyterian. His remains were later interred in the Heverlee war cemetery, near Leuven, Belgium.

J. Herington, *Air War Against Germany and Italy 1939-1943* (Canb, 1954) and *Air Power Over Europe 1944-1945* (Canb, 1963); D. N. Gillison, *Royal Australian Air Force 1939-1942* (Canb, 1962); J. D. Balfe, *War Without Glory* (Melb, 1984); M. Middlebrook and C. Everitt, *The Bomber Command War Diaries* (np, Lond?, 1985); A. Powell, *The Shadow's Edge* (Melb, 1988); C. D. Coulthard-Clark, *The Third Brother* (Syd, 1991); *SMH*, 6 July, 22 Dec 1936, 26 July 1937, 21 Oct, 3 Nov 1938; AWM records.   JOHN McCARTHY

BALSON, RALPH (1890-1964), artist, was born on 13 August 1890 at Bothenhampton, Dorset, England, third of six children of Charles Frederick Balson, journeyman baker, and his wife Martha, née Larcombe. Having attended the local village school, he was apprenticed in 1903 to a plumber and house-painter. In 1913 Ralph migrated to Sydney. Emilie Kathleen Austin came from England to join him and they were married at All Saints Anglican Church, Woollahra, on 7 September 1914. They first lived at Bondi and from about 1920 at Pagewood; he supported his wife and three children by working as a house-painter, but took up art in his spare time.

In the early 1920s he began night-classes at Julian Ashton's [q.v.7] Sydney Art School under Grace Crowley, Anne Dangar [qq.v.], Henry Gibbons and Ashton himself. Balson's early work, mostly small, post-impressionist sketches of his domestic surroundings, was shown in his first one-man exhibition in 1932 at Dorrit Black's [q.v.7] Modern Art Centre where, in the evenings, he also attended a sketch club.

In the 1930s Balson deepened his awareness of modern art through contact with other artists, particularly Crowley. In 1934-37, with such modernists as 'Rah' Fizelle [q.v.8] and Frank Hinder, he sketched in the studio of the Crowley-Fizelle school at 215a George Street. Painting and drawing from the figure, they explored geometric, cubist principles of composition. In 1939 they formed the nucleus of Exhibition 1, a group show of modernist

painting and sculpture at David Jones's [q.v.2] art gallery; among their few patrons were Herbert and Mary Alice Evatt [qq.v.]. After the closure of her school, Crowley invited Balson to share her studio at 227 George Street; he painted there at weekends. They continued to work together, becoming increasingly detached from the stylistic fashions of the Sydney art world.

Balson's exhibition in 1941 at Anthony Hordern & Sons [qq.v.4] Ltd's gallery marked the beginning of his 'Constructive Paintings' —geometric abstractions employing overlapping planes of colour. Later works in this series were shown in an exhibition with the sculptor Robert Klippel at the Macquarie Galleries in 1952. Following his retirement in 1955, Balson painted more prolifically and in a less formalized manner. He divided his time between Sydney and Crowley's country home, High Hill, at Mittagong, where he had a garden studio. In 1953 his work was included in exhibitions in Britain and Italy. The 'Non-Objective Paintings', his major series of the late 1950s, consisted of complex fields of dappled colour. In the 1960s he produced a difficult and critically contentious series of 'Matter Paintings', fluid abstractions in which he literally poured the paint on to his work; a year abroad in 1960 had encouraged this late, spontaneous direction.

Socially, Balson was shy and reticent. Between 1949 and 1959 he taught part time at East Sydney Technical College. Students respected this near-sighted, suburban painter, with his tradesman's clothes, who made no display of ego. For Balson, self-effacement was a philosophical principle. Late in life he wrote about the wider view behind his abstract art: a world which no longer had humanity at its centre, a universe like Einstein's of indeterminacy and change.

Survived by his daughter and two sons, Balson died on 27 August 1964 in Royal Prince Alfred Hospital and was cremated. Despite his humble circumstances, he had achieved a body of work that was among the most advanced modern painting of his generation in Sydney.

R. Free, *Balson Crowley Fizelle Hinder*, exhibition cat (Syd, 1966); B. Adams, 'Metaphors of Scientific Idealism: the Theoretical Background to the Painting of Ralph Balson', in A. Bradley and T. Smith (eds), *Australian Art and Architecture* (Melb, 1980) and *Ralph Balson* exhibition cat (Melb, 1989); *Art and Aust*, 2, no 4, Mar 1965, pp 248, 290; *Aspect*, no 22, Oct 1981, p 4; *Nation*, 31 Aug 1968; *Bulletin*, 19 Sept 1989; *SMH*, 3 Aug 1932, 3 May 1944, 11 Apr 1953, 24 Feb 1962, 6 Sept 1964, 3 Mar 1990.   BRUCE ADAMS

BAND, JOHN MORRELL (1902-1943), naval officer, was born on 22 March 1902 at

South Shields, County of Durham, England, son of John Oliver Band, master mariner, and his wife Margaret, née Morrell. The family moved to London where young John's education at Enfield Grammar School was interrupted by trips to sea with his parents. He followed his father into the Merchant Navy, gaining his first-mate's certificate in 1924. When his venture as part-owner of a trading vessel was curtailed by the Depression, Band went to China and accumulated enough money to settle on a farm at Nyeri, Kenya. There he bred Ayrshire cattle and did safari work. In 1932 at Nanyuki he married Clara Violet Howes.

After his cattle died of disease, Band tried running guns and smuggling potatoes to Ethiopia, but was apprehended. By the late 1930s he was sailing in coastal steamers in the Pacific and had bought land at Woorim on Queensland's Bribie Island. Keen to be in uniform in the event of war, on 1 September 1939 he obtained an appointment as temporary sub-lieutenant in the Royal Australian Naval Reserve. From October that year to July 1940 he served in the armed merchant cruiser, H.M.S. *Moreton Bay*, undergoing an arduous series of patrols in Japanese waters. His subsequent ships included H.M.A.S. *Moresby* and the cruiser, *Hobart*, in which he saw action in May 1942 during the battle of the Coral Sea. On 1 October he was posted to command the naval section of the Combined Training Centre at Toorbul Point, near Brisbane.

The school instructed Australian and American soldiers and sailors in amphibious warfare. Band was in his element, teaching landing operations to his students, and training them to be physically and mentally tough. Over six feet (182.9 cm) tall, well built, part buccaneer and part gentleman, he had a ready, sardonic grin which he used effectively when deriding his juniors. Although a strict disciplinarian, he could be charming and had a fund of stories about his adventures. In January 1943 he was promoted temporary acting lieutenant commander and in July took charge of the mobile base staff organization in Port Moresby. Appointed port director at Buna, Papua, next month, he took initiatives which enabled its facilities to handle shipping twenty-four hours a day.

On 22 September 1943 Band led the beach party accompanying the seaborne assault against Finschhafen, New Guinea. As beachmaster, he was responsible for placing markers and for providing inshore navigational assistance to subsequent waves of landing craft. The first attackers arrived at 4.45 that morning, but—due to an error—found themselves at Siki Cove, south of their objective of Scarlet Beach. Band leapt ashore and called his men to follow. According to one

account, a Japanese shouted, 'Who's there?' Band answered, 'The navy', and was hit by a burst of machine-gun fire. Despite his wounds, he continued to direct operations and saved a group of vessels from beaching in the wrong position. He died next day and was buried in Bomana war cemetery, Port Moresby; his wife and daughter survived him; he was posthumously awarded the United States Navy Cross.

D. Dexter, *The New Guinea Offensives* (Canb, 1961); G. H. Gill, *Royal Australian Navy 1942-1945* (Canb, 1968); AWM records; information from Mrs G. M. Thornton, Eng, and Dept of Transport, Cardiff, Wales.   HUGH JARRETT

BANKS, DONALD OSCAR (1923-1980), composer, was born on 25 October 1923 in South Melbourne, son of Donald Waldemar Banks, musician, and his wife Elsie Catherine Sophia, née Carlson, both Victorian born. Educated at Cambridge College, Albert Park, during the Depression young Don transferred to Middle Park Central School and next to Melbourne Boys' High School. He had begun piano lessons at the age of 5 and learned to play the saxophone, violin and trombone in his youth. From an early age he 'sat in' on his father's dance band, and later played trombone with other bands, including that of Graeme Bell.

On leaving school, Banks was employed as an office-boy for a solicitors' firm and then for a hardware company. In 1941-46 he served in the Australian Military Forces, mainly with the Australian Army Medical Corps in Melbourne. Small and wiry (8 st. 7 lb., 54 kg), he was judged unfit for tropical service. Through the postwar Army Rehabilitation Scheme, he undertook a diploma course at the University Conservatorium of Music in 1947-49: he studied composition with A. E. H. Nickson and Dorian Le Gallienne [qq.v.], and graduated with first-class honours. Banks performed publicly his *Sonatina for Piano* before departing for England in 1950.

In London he studied with Matyas Sieber, won the Edwin Evans memorial prize for composition in 1952, and supported himself by taking jobs as a copyist and as a member of a dance band. After working briefly with Professor Milton Babbitt at Salzburg, Austria, in 1953 Banks won an Italian government scholarship to study with Luigi Dallapiccola at Florence, Italy.

On 5 August 1953 at the register office, Paddington, London, Banks married Valerie Frances Miller, a children's welfare officer. His compositions began to win recognition: that year his *Four Pieces for Orchestra* was performed by the British Broadcasting Corporation, and Schott & Co. commenced publishing his works. In 1954 he won the City of Haifa (Israel) prize for chamber music. Commissions followed from the B.B.C., the Edinburgh, Bromsgrove and Farnham festivals, the Peter Stuyvesant Foundation, the University College, Cardiff, and the English Bach Festival. He won the Sir Arnold Bax Society medal in 1959. A fellow Australian, Barry Tuckwell, gave the first performance of Banks's *Concerto for Horn and Orchestra* with the London Symphony Orchestra in 1966. To support his family, Banks also worked commercially, notably as a composer of scores for Hammer horror films.

His creativity was characterized by the emphasis he gave to the craft and professionalism of being a composer. Banks's personality and training attracted him to serial theory and techniques. He co-operated in developing an early synthesizer, the VCS1, and became interested in electronics as a possible source for new sounds; in a number of works he strove to combine conventional acoustic instruments with new synthetic ones, as in his *Commentary* for piano and tape.

Jazz continued to influence his work. He sought to bring together jazz and art musicians in works such as *Equations I, II* and *III* (1963, 1969, 1972), *Settings from Roget* (1966) which he wrote for Cleo Laine, *Meeting Place* (1970) for jazz ensemble, chamber group and electronics, *Synchronos '72* for jazz ensemble, various instruments, electronics and visual displays, *Take 8* (1973) for jazz ensemble and string quartet, and *Nexus* (1971), one of his best-known works, for jazz ensemble and symphony orchestra.

Proud of his Australian identity, in the early 1950s Banks had founded—with Margaret Sutherland—the Australian Musical Association as 'a platform for Australian performers and to get exposure for Australian composers'. He was also chairman (1967-68) of the Society for the Promotion of New Music, a foundation member of the British Society for Electronic Music and patron of the Jazz Centre Society, London. In 1969-71 he was musical director at Goldsmith College, University of London.

Having attended the Perth Festival in 1970, Banks returned permanently to Australia in 1972 when he took up a creative arts fellowship at the Australian National University, Canberra. Next year he was appointed head of composition studies at the Canberra School of Music where he founded an electronic music studio. He was chairman (1973-74) of the music board of the Australian Council for the Arts and an executive-member of the Composers' Guild of Australia. From 1978 he was head of composition at the New South Wales State Conservatorium of Music.

Small and frail-looking, with glowing eyes, Banks was animated in movement and gesture. He valued 'mateship' and battled to secure composers' rights. His vision for music in Australia included a high level of professionalism for Australian composers, a steering away from self-conscious nationalism and an absorption of world music which he hoped would lead to the emergence of an Australian 'sound'. In 1980 he was appointed A.M. After suffering for eight years from chronic lymphocytic leukaemia, he died of cancer on 5 September 1980 in his home at McMahons Point, Sydney, and was cremated. His wife, two daughters and son survived him.

R. Covell, *Australia's Music* (Melb, 1967); J. Murdoch, *Australia's Contemporary Composers* (Melb, 1972); F. Callaway and D. Tunley (eds), *Australian Composition in the Twentieth Century* (Melb, 1978); *Musical Times*, 93, 1952, 95, 1954, 109, 1968; *Music Review*, 14, 1953, 16, 1955; *Musical Opinion*, 76, 1953, 86, 1962; Roy Musical Assn, *Procs*, 93, 1967; *Hemisphere*, 18, no 4, Apr 1974; *Australian*, 25 Mar 1970, 3 Nov 1973, 19 Apr 1978; H. de Berg, Donald Banks (taped interview, 1972, NL).

LARRY SITSKY

BANNAN, ELIZABETH MARGARET (1909-1977), educationist, was born on 5 June 1909 in North Sydney, eldest daughter of William Patrick Bannan, a detective from Ireland, and his native-born wife Jane Helen, née Anderson. Both parents instilled a strong sense of independence in their daughters, encouraging them to 'speak out' and to 'stand up' as women. Elizabeth and her two sisters went to Fort Street Girls' High School and continued their studies to tertiary level. In 1931 she graduated B.A. from the University of Sydney, with honours in English, education and anthropology. That year she was awarded the Jones medal and the Walter Beavis prize in the graduate course at Teachers' College, Sydney.

After teaching English in government secondary schools, in 1937 Bannan was appointed lecturer at Teachers' College, under the direction of Alexander Mackie [q.v.10]. She was away on an exchange programme in 1939-40 as visiting lecturer at the University of Oregon, United States of America. Back at Teachers' College, Bannan became warden of women students when Elizabeth Skillen [q.v.11] retired in 1943.

Inspired by the progressivism of the 'new pedagogy' and by the impact of the 'communication programme' on the elementary curriculum, Elizabeth returned to the U.S.A. on a Carnegie fellowship in 1949 to explore the teaching of 'reading' from kindergarten to primary level. She addressed these issues in two articles, and in an unpublished report on the merits of the 'individualised reading programme' which she introduced to the college. In 1950 she represented Australia at a general conference of the United Nations Educational, Scientific and Cultural Organization and the International Bureau of Education, Geneva, Switzerland.

Dean of women (from 1957) at Teachers' College, Miss Bannan retained her duties as head of the English department. She was discreet and compassionate, and handled problems with 'sympathy, tact, fairness, flexibility and understanding'. In 1960 and again in 1964 she revisited the U.S.A. to study 'programmed instruction' which she added to the college curriculum in 1965.

Respected by her colleagues and regarded with awe by her students, Elizabeth maintained an aura of elegance and sophistication. She had blue eyes, delicate skin and wore her hair in soft, chestnut waves. Tall, slim and impeccably dressed, the dean of women embodied restrained dynamism. During dinner parties in her home at Double Bay and later at Cremorne, she enjoyed blending intellectual conversation with wine and wit. In more private moments, she turned to the poetry of Robert Browning and Gerard Manley Hopkins.

Her contribution as an educational innovator was formally acknowledged in 1967 when she became the third woman in New South Wales to be admitted as a fellow of the Australian College of Education. In 1974 she was awarded the British Empire medal. Elizabeth continued her work at the college after her retirement in 1973, becoming a member (from 1974) of the first council. She died of a coronary occlusion on 26 July 1977 at her sister's home at Ballina and was cremated. Bannan's portrait by Judy Cassab is held by the University of Sydney.

R. S. Horan, *Fort Street* (Syd, 1989); *NSW Police News*, June 1922, p 11; Teachers' College, Syd, *Council 1974-76*, p 4; *Quidnunc '77*, 1, Aug 1977; *SMH*, 21 May, 6 June 1931, 6 Jan 1965, 13 Aug 1977; *North Shore Times* (Chatswood, Syd), 24 Aug 1977; Univ Syd Archives; information from Mrs K. A. Priddle, Ballina, NSW.

MARIA S. VARVARESSOS

BANNING, ARTHUR ALEXANDER (1921-1965), poet, was born on 27 June 1921 in Royal North Shore Hospital, Sydney, son of Arthur Antoine Banning, a waiter from Belgium who later became a theatre proprietor, and his native-born wife Helma Louise, née Hall, of Scots and Swedish descent. As a result of a difficult birth, the infant suffered from athetoid cerebral palsy, a spastic condition against which he was to struggle all his life. Lex's 'own particular demon', as he called

it in a poem, was involuntary movement of the arms, neck, face and legs which made him grimace and stagger, distorted his speech, but left his intellect and creativity unimpaired.

His father died when Lex was aged 4; thereafter Banning mostly lived at Punchbowl with his mother. Although he attended public schools, and was able to read though not to write, the boy could not sit normally in class. For the most part he was left to educate himself by such means as perusing encyclopaedias. About 1936 he was found employment at Sydney Observatory; during three or four years there he learned to type. Little is known of his life for four years after leaving the observatory, except that all his teeth were extracted.

In 1944 Lex Banning was admitted as an unmatriculated student to the faculty of arts at the University of Sydney. Over the next five years he distinguished himself scholastically, dictating all his exam papers, and became a notable figure on campus and at such downtown coffee lounges as Repin's and Lincoln Inn. Another of his haunts was the Royal George, a hotel frequented by the libertarian 'Push', where Banning drank unsteadily but to good effect. He edited the Arts Society magazine, *Arna*, and in 1949 co-edited the student newspaper, *Honi Soit*. That year he graduated with second-class honours in English and history.

Banning's sardonic appearance—austere lips enclosed by a short, dark beard and moustache, sharp nose, tired, deep-set eyes and a widow's-peak hairline—was well matched by his mocking sense of humour and by his disillusioned poetry which sometimes verged on nihilism. His work, published in *Meanjin*, *Southerly*, the *Sydney Morning Herald* and the *Bulletin*, was collected in three books: *Everyman His Own Hamlet* (1951), *The Instant's Clarity* (1952) and *Apocalypse in Springtime and other Poems* (1956). Although despairing, Banning's verse was, in the judgement of one critic, 'the product of a brilliant mind, agile wit and passionate heart'.

In the early 1950s Banning worked as librarian at the Spastic Centre, Mosman. He went to London and, soon after arriving there, on 27 January 1962 at the register office, Lambeth, married 26-year-old Anne Agatha Ferry, a medical practitioner and friend from Sydney. They returned to Australia in 1964, but separated soon afterwards. Banning again took up residence at his mother's home where, on 2 November 1965, he died of 'poisoning self-administered—no evidence accidentally or otherwise'. He was buried in the Presbyterian section of Rookwood cemetery. In the words of his poem, 'Nursery Rhyme', evoking the crooked man who walked a crooked mile, Banning had 'reached his crooked mile's end' and been 'straightened out by death'.

R. Appleton and A. Galloway (eds), *There was a Crooked Man* (Syd, 1987); S. Baldwin (ed), *Unsung Heroes and Heroines of Australia* (Melb, 1988); *Twentieth Century*, Autumn 1958; *SMH*, 25 Apr 1961, 3 Nov 1965; Banning papers, 1944-65 (ML).

GAVIN SOUTER

BANVARD, YVONNE 'FIFI' (1901-1962), actress, was born on Christmas Day 1901 in Melbourne, daughter of William Horley, an actor from England, and his Victorian-born wife Annie, née Moore. William and his relations toured the world as 'The Flying Banvards'. When her parents separated, Yvonne trouped around America with her mother, a dancing mistress, in the Pollard Lilliputian Opera Company, and at the age of 7 made her début as Fifi in *The Belle of New York*; henceforward she was to be known on and off as 'Fifi'. After touring North America with the Oliver Morosco company and appearing with the Alcazar stock company at San Francisco, she emerged as one of Mack Sennett's bathing girls and performed in moving pictures for three years. With exaggeration, she later claimed to have studied ballet with Anna Pavlova before deciding that 'it was easier to sing a comic song'.

Returning to Victoria, on 19 November 1920 Yvonne married an American actor-producer Edward Ralph de Tisne (d. 1931) at Chelsea with Congregational forms. She joined the Fullers' [qq.v.8] vaudeville circuit and, with her husband, did a song-and-dance act, 'Fifi and her Excess Baggage' (1921). In Melbourne in 1921-22 she appeared in the successful pantomime, *Bluebeard*, as an exotically costumed Fatima with more than a resemblance to Theda Bara. As 'Yvonne Banvard', from September 1922 at the New Theatre Royal, Brisbane, she was the leading lady with the Reynolds-de Tisne Players in over forty productions. The company disbanded in July 1923 when her marriage broke up. Banvard was next engaged by J. C. Williamson [q.v.6] Ltd for a long run of musical comedies and won admirers for her portrayal of the 'vivacious and peppy' Lady Jane in *Rose Marie* (1926-27). On 7 September 1928 at St John's Anglican Church, Toorak, she married a Perth merchant Ernest Cephas Hunter Broadhurst; they were to be divorced in 1936.

In February 1931 Banvard returned to Australia from the U.S.A. to tour with Clem Dawe in 'gay and sparkling' variety shows. As the platinum vamp June East, she appeared with Roy Rene [q.v.11] in the Cinesound film *Strike Me Lucky* (1934); by 1939 she was playing in Brisbane. Based in Sydney in the 1940s, she blossomed as a wireless personality, taking part in the 'Bob Dyer Variety Show', radio comedies and such serials as 'Mrs 'Obbs'. On 22 July 1944 at St John's Anglican Church, Darlinghurst, Sydney, she affirmed that she was a 30-year-old spinster and married 29-year-old Charles Kilburn, a clerk in the Royal Australian Air Force; they were to be divorced in 1950.

In 1948-49 Fifi produced a number of plays, including Eugene O'Neill's *Ah, Wilderness!*, for the Whitehall management at the Minerva Theatre, Kings Cross. She moved to Hobart in 1950 with Gwenyth Friend, a set-designer and sister of the artist Donald Friend. Leasing the Theatre Royal, Yvonne formed a repertory company, Fifi Banvard Productions; despite favourable reviews, the venture was a financial disaster. Back in Sydney in 1952, she resumed work in radio and produced several plays at the Independent Theatre for (Dame) Doris Fitton; in 1958 she supported (Sir) Robert Helpmann in Noel Coward's *Nude with Violin* at the local Theatre Royal. Commended for her 'theatrical ebullience', Fifi made her farewell appearance as Mae Peterson in the musical, *Bye Bye Birdie* (1961). She died of myocardial infarction on 24 June 1962 at St Vincent's Hospital, Darlinghurst, and was cremated; she left her estate to Gwen Friend, with whom she had shared a flat at Double Bay.

A woman of energy and passion, Fifi said that she preferred serious dramatic roles, but it was her flair for comedy and sense of the burlesque that made her popular. In her later years she remembered the theatre as a place of 'glamour, romance and good fellowship', and rued its becoming 'cold hard business'.

H. Porter, *Stars of Australian Stage and Screen* (Adel, 1965); *Qld Soc Mag*, Dec 1922, p 51, Mar 1923, p 37, Nov 1923, p 37; *Argus*, 28 Feb 1927; *Mercury* (Hob), 5, 19 Sept 1950, 3, 17 Oct, 4 July 1952; *SMH*, 12 Mar 1950, 30 July 1953, 24 Aug 1958, 19 Oct, 13 Dec 1961, 26 June 1962; Theatre Royal (Hob), Theatre programmes, 1950-52 (SLT).

ANNE-MARIE GAUDRY

BARACCHI, GUIDO CARLO LUIGI (1887-1975), Marxist scholar and political activist, was born on 11 December 1887 at South Yarra, Melbourne, son of Pietro Baracchi [q.v.7], an astronomer from Italy, and his Victorian-born wife Kate, née Petty. Educated at Melbourne Church of England Grammar School, in 1904-05 Guido studied classics at the University of Melbourne, but did not graduate. In 1913 he visited Europe where he became a guild socialist. Having returned home on the outbreak of World War I, he took a leading part in the anti-war movement. His written and spoken opinions produced a hostile reaction from the university authorities, and from some fellow students who dunked him in the university lake. In 1917 Baracchi helped to found the Victorian Labor College. Encouraged by Lesbia Harford [q.v.9], he joined the International Industrial Workers, successor to the banned Industrial Workers of the World, and edited its journal, *Industrial Solidarity*.

On 17 January 1918 Baracchi married an actress Kathleen Tobin in a civil ceremony in Melbourne. That year he was found guilty of 'making statements likely to prejudice recruiting' and 'attempting to cause disaffection among the civil population'. He was fined, and gaoled for three months for refusing to meet the conditions required by the court. In 1920 he was a foundation member of the Communist Party of Australia and co-edited—with Percy Laidler [q.v.9]—the *Proletarian Review* (from October, the *Proletarian*).

Divorced in 1922, Baracchi went to Europe with a dress designer Harriett Elizabeth 'Neura', née Whiteaway, late Zander, whom he married on 29 March 1923 at the register office, St Giles, London. He belonged to the German communist party in Berlin and edited the English-language edition of the communist journal, *International Press Correspondence*. In 1924 he joined the Communist Party of Great Britain. Back in Melbourne in 1925, he advocated the dissolution of the C.P.A. on the ground that it had too little support to survive: for this action, he was charged with 'right wing deviation' and expelled. Using some of the considerable wealth that he had inherited from his parents, he took his wife on a luxury tour of Asia. In 1926-29 he lectured in economics at the Victorian Labor College.

Confessing that his 1925 proposal had been a mistake, in 1932 Baracchi sought readmission to the Communist Party. He was refused, but was entrusted with some papers to be taken secretly to the Soviet Union. Accompanied by his *de facto* wife, the playwright Betty Roland, in 1933 he reached London and left for a twenty-one day visit to Leningrad and Moscow. The visit became a stay of more than a year during which they both worked, Guido as a translator in the Co-Operative Publishing Society for Foreign Workers and Betty as a journalist on the *Moscow Daily News*.

Returning to Australia with Betty in 1935, Guido regained party membership. They lived together in Melbourne for two years before moving to Sydney where Guido became co-editor of the *Communist Review*. Admirers of Walter Burley Griffin [q.v.9], they bought land and built a house (designed by Griffin's partner Eric Nicholls) at Castlecrag. In 1942 their relationship broke down and on 22 August 1946 at the courthouse,

Manly, Guido married a divorcee Ula, née Gray, late Maddocks, a nurse.

In the meantime Baracchi had changed political direction. From the outset he had denounced World War II as an imperialist war, but for reasons different from those advanced by the C.P.A. leadership which had initially supported the struggle against Nazism. Baracchi was suspended from his party positions and required to answer ten questions about his political beliefs. He did so at great length, citing authorities such as Marx, Engels, Lenin and Trotsky. Approving reference to Trotsky, who was anathema to the Stalinist leadership of the party, was sufficient in itself to guarantee expulsion, which occurred in February 1940. He joined the small but eloquent group of Trotskyists in Sydney, speaking at their public meetings and contributing to their publications.

For the rest of his life Baracchi continued to study and advocate Marxist ideas with a Trotskyist slant. He joined the Australian Labor Party with the aim of influencing its policy in a socialist direction. In his party branch he advocated a more explicit socialist objective, workers' control in industry and, before it became popular, active opposition to Australia's involvement in the war in Vietnam. Following his divorce from his third wife, on 14 July 1962 in the registrar's office, Chatswood, he married another divorcee, the artist Ethel Victoria, late Carson, daughter of Karl Reginald Cramp [q.v.8].

As a wealthy man, Baracchi was an unusual figure in the bohemian artistic, and radical political, circles in which he moved. He was one of very few serious Australian students of the vast literature of Marxism at that time. Although he fancied himself as a poet, he was curiously blind to the fact that all but a fragment of his verse was little better than doggerel. He knew and corresponded with many leading writers, among them Katharine Susannah Prichard and Vance and Nettie Palmer [qq.v.11].

While campaigning for the A.L.P. at Penrith, Baracchi collapsed and died on 13 December 1975; he was buried in Eastern Creek cemetery. Predeceased by his wife, he was survived by a daughter of his first marriage, by Betty Roland's daughter and by the daughter of another woman with whom he had shared a brief liaison.

B. Walker, *Solidarity Forever* (Melb, 1972); B. Roland, *The Eye of the Beholder* (Syd, 1984) and *An Improbable Life* (Syd, 1989) and *Caviar for Breakfast* (Syd, 1989) and *The Devious Being* (Syd, 1990); A. Turner, Independent Working Class Education in Australia 1917-1929 (M.Ed. thesis, Univ Melb, 1981); J. N. Rawling papers (ANUABL); interview with Ms B. Roland, Syd, 14 Mar 1991.

ROBIN GOLLAN

BARANYAY, ISTVAN; *see* BRADLEY, STEPHEN

BARBER, GEORGE CALVERT (1893-1967), theologian and Methodist Church leader, was born on 24 January 1893 at Bendigo, Victoria, son of Henry Bride Barber, Primitive Methodist minister, and his wife Laura Elizabeth, née Pickett, both English born. Four of Calvert's uncles were Methodist ministers in Britain and his mother was a well-known local preacher. Educated at Wesley College, Melbourne, where he won an exhibition in the senior year, he took a job with the Union Bank of Australia and qualified as an accountant. While working in Sydney, he became convinced of his vocation to the ministry.

Enlisting in the Australian Imperial Force on 10 February 1916, Barber served on the Western Front as a stretcher-bearer with the 5th Field Ambulance. After being wounded in the left leg on 2 November 1917, he was hospitalized in England. On 20 November 1918 he sailed for Australia. In 1919 Barber entered Queen's College, University of Melbourne, and graduated (B.A., 1922) with first-class honours in philosophy and the Laurie [q.v.10] prize. Sturdy in build, he was a member of the college football team.

In 1922 Barber began his ministry at Nyah and later served at Toorak, in Hobart and at Geelong. On 24 March 1926 he married Mavis Gertrude Bond in the Methodist Church, Gordon, Sydney. At the University of London he completed a Ph.D. (1938) in comparative religion with a thesis on 'The concept of sin in the great religions of the East'. He entered enthusiastically into the life of the English Methodist Church and subsequently maintained contact with many of its leaders.

Succeeding A. E. Albiston [q.v.7] in 1937 as professor of theology at Queen's College, Melbourne, Barber was to hold the position until his retirement in 1959 and to have a profound influence on men preparing for the Methodist ministry. During this period he held numerous offices in the church and community. He was president of Wesley College's council (1939-58), the Melbourne College of Divinity (1946) and the Victoria and Tasmania Conference of the Methodist Church. As registrar of the Melbourne College of Divinity from 1947, he improved its academic standards and extended its range of operations. In 1951-54 he was president-general of the Methodist Church of Australasia. With Rev. Dr A. H. Wood, he was prominent in the Methodist Church's movement towards union with the Presbyterian and Congregational Churches: because of frequent delays, chiefly over the short-lived proposal for an episcopacy, Barber did not see his hope fulfilled.

His period of leadership coincided with the rapid growth of churches in the 1940s and 1950s. Skilful in debate, he was one of the last, great, church statesmen before the secular 1960s and the age of consensus in all things. Apart from his teaching, Barber's most valuable gift to the church was his leadership and administration; behind that lay a theological understanding which gave depth and substance to his public preaching and shaped the Australian Church in two decisive decades. He was appointed C.B.E. in 1958 and became a fellow of Queen's College.

As a theologian, Barber rejected the liberalism of the early decades of the twentieth century and declared—in the Reformed tradition—the dominance of the word of God. While sharing the insights of such continental thinkers as Karl Barth and Emil Brunner, he modified their theology along British lines. His work made Neo-orthodoxy, as it was called, more acceptable and influential in Australia than its European expression could have been. Because the study of comparative religion suffered serious neglect after the 1930s, Barber's special interest in that area was never fully developed. While chairman (1939-49) of the Australian Student Christian Movement and president (1952-53) of the Australian council of the World Council of Churches, he formed close friendships with theologians from other denominations. He died on 31 July 1967 at Heidelberg and was cremated; his wife, two daughters and son survived him.

Minutes of the Victoria and Tasmania Conference of the Methodist Church of A'sia, 1919-67; *Minutes of the General Conference of the Methodist Church of A'sia*, 1951-54; *Spectator* (Melb), 9 Aug 1967; Barber papers and sermons (held by Rev B. Barber, United Faculty of Theology, Queen's College, Univ Melb).

E. F. OSBORN

BARBER, HORACE NEWTON (1914-1971), botanist and geneticist, was born on 26 May 1914 at Warburton, Cheshire, England, son of Horace Maximilian Barber, printer's traveller, and his wife Mary, née Newton. Educated at the County High School for Boys, Altrincham, and Manchester Grammar School, Newton read the natural science tripos at Emmanuel College, Cambridge (B.A., 1936; M.A., 1944; Sc.D., 1963). Supervised by C. D. Darlington, in 1936-40 Barber carried out research on plant and animal cytology at the John Innes Horticultural Institution, Merton, Surrey, for which he was awarded a Ph.D. by the University of London in 1942. In February 1941 he had joined the irregular army of applied scientists at the

Ministry of Aircraft Production's telecommunications research establishment. He later served as a flight lieutenant with the Royal Air Force Volunteer Reserve in the Mediterranean and South East Asia, and wrote an irreverent account of his wartime adventures in air force jargon for his family.

A lecturer in botany at the University of Sydney from March 1946, Barber married a fellow lecturer Nancy Patricia O'Grady at St Mary's Catholic Cathedral on 20 April that year. In 1947 he was appointed foundation professor of botany at the University of Tasmania and extracted from a surprised administration the basic requirements of 'glasshouses, an experimental garden and a gardener'. Enthusiastic and dedicated, he believed that the 'business of a professor is to teach his students' and did much to encourage high standards of biological instruction. His interest in undergraduates extended to a strong record of overseeing postgraduates, a number of whom went on to contribute as academics and research scientists to genetics and plant breeding.

Barber quickly applied his pre-war interests in cytology and genetics to Australian plants and animals. His curiosity in natural history and his more formal disciplinary interests led to a spread of publication in experimental cytology, taxonomy, physiological and selection genetics (particularly in *Eucalyptus*), in ecology and forestry, and in biogeography, palaeobotany and mycology. He travelled widely in the bush and, with the eye and ear of the trained observer, took every opportunity (both as raconteur and writer) to re-create the atmosphere, mood and even redolence of those journeys.

Dean of science (1951-55), Barber returned to Hobart after a year as a Rockefeller fellow (1953-54) at the California Institute of Technology, United States of America, to be plunged into the controversy over the dismissal of Professor Sydney Orr [q.v.]. In an anomalous position as chairman of the staff association (from 1955) and of the professorial board (1956-59), he served on Miss Kemp's and the vice-chancellor's committees of inquiry. A regular spokesman for the university council, he was elected to the Tasmanian Club.

In 1964 Barber became foundation professor of botany at the University of New South Wales, Sydney. He was noted for the quality, lucid exposition and focussed humour of the television lectures he prepared for first-year students. As chairman (1968-70) of the professorial board, he filled the post with inimitable style and considerable distinction, but his belief in integrated biological sciences was contrary to the convenience of the university. Impatient and frustrated, in 1970 he accepted the foundation chair of biological sciences at the University of Newcastle, but was never to take up the post.

At an imperial height of 6 ft 7 ins (200.7 cm) and with a slight limp (the legacy of a motorcar accident in the United States), Newton Barber was a conspicuous figure wherever he went. He had toured New Guinea in 1963 and, after visiting Africa for the Royal Society, London, assisted the University of Ibadan, Nigeria, in 1967 to develop biological sciences; it was characteristic of the man to report that the standard of English among Nigerian students was better than that of their Australian counterparts. Having contributed papers to an international conference on chromosomes at Oxford in 1970, he revisited Nigeria to study the genetics of tropical plants and to lecture at the University of Ife.

His formal contributions to biological science had been acknowledged by his election as a fellow of the Australian Academy of Science (1958) and of the Royal Society, London (1963), and by his appointment as a trustee of the Australian Museum (1964). Barber's peregrinating and frequently informal contributions to academic discourse and scholarship were widely appreciated by colleagues, among whom he had the reputation of originating more ideas than any other botanist in Australia.

A fiercely principled individual, scientifically rigorous in all he undertook, Barber was a devoted family man and one who took pride in the achievements of the many students and colleagues whose careers he touched. He died of sarcoma on 16 April 1971 at his Epping home and was buried with Anglican rites in the Field of Mars cemetery. His wife and daughter survived him, as did his son Michael, professor of mathematics at the Australian National University.

W. H. C. Eddy, *Orr* (Brisb, 1961); *Univ Tas Gazette*, vols 1-3, 1956-65; *Yearbook of Roy Soc* (Lond), 1964; Univ NSW, *Univ News*, May 1971; *Aust Academy of Science Yearbook*, 1972; *Biog Memoirs of Fellows of Roy Soc* (Lond), 1972; Barber lectures, filmed by closed-circuit TV (NL film collection).

DEREK ANDERSON

BARCLAY, EDMUND PIERS (1898-1961), radio dramatist and writer, claimed to have been born on 2 May 1898 at Dinapore, India, son of Major Edmund Compston-Buckleigh, from Middlesex, England. Young Edmund maintained that he was educated at Stonyhurst, joined the Middlesex Regiment on 11 August 1914, and won the Military Cross and Croix de Guerre while serving with the Royal Flying Corps: if he did these things, it was not under the names Barclay or Compston-Buckleigh. He further asserted that, following the war, he worked as a journalist in Fleet Street, London, until sacked for costing his employers £2000 in a libel suit; he then reputedly ran his own short-lived, weekly newspaper.

Arriving in Australia in August 1926, Barclay was determined to demonstrate that 'he was the world's greatest novelist'. Meanwhile, he worked as a journalist, wrote film scripts (including that for Ken Hall's *The Silence of Dean Maitland*, 1934), short stories, plays, newspaper articles and verse, and sank to 'that abomination of desolation, writing advertising'. On 17 December 1933 he was employed by the Australian Broadcasting Commission as a dramatist. A golden age of radio drama began under the aegis of (Sir) Charles Moses and W. J. Cleary [q.v.8]. The first radio play Barclay wrote was 'An Antarctic Epic', for which he received five guineas.

Much of his work, especially for schools, involved dramatizing history and literature. 'Spoiled Darlings', a model colonial romance, and 'Murder in the Silo', an effective psychological thriller set in the Depression, were often repeated on the A.B.C. Barclay's use of dialogue and sound effects gave his radio plays a distinctive Australian flavour. He eventually published two novels from his radio serials, based on stories of his father's experiences in India, *Khyber* (1936) and *Shanghai* (1937). Barclay's epic family saga, 'As Ye Sow', written in 1938 for the Australian sesquicentenary, established his reputation. It was heard every Monday night for nine months by thousands of listeners. *Neath Southern Skies*, a pageant commissioned by the Department of Education, was performed by a thousand secondary school students at Sydney Town Hall in March 1938.

Despite his enormous output, Barclay wrote very little for the stage. In 1934 he collaborated with Varney Monk [q.v.10] as composer and Helene Barclay as lyricist to write *The Cedar Tree*, a musical romance produced by Frank Thring [q.v.12] in Melbourne. Barclay's talent for adaptation, with his sure ear for dialogue and sound patterning, turned such classics as *Les Miserables, The Idiot* and *The Fortunes of Richard Mahony* into radio masterpieces. He also collaborated closely with Joy Hollyer on many dramas.

Tall and thin, with lank, ginger hair, Teddy Barclay had great energy, a careless charm and a cynical edge to his nature; although affable, he often annoyed his colleagues. He had a reputation as a womanizer and as a big drinker, and often disappeared for days on end. From one incident involving a dispute over pay, Leslie Rees emerged with a bloodied nose and Barclay was eventually forced to apologize. His relationship with his wife Helene, who wrote some plays for the

A.B.C., was desperately unhappy. Although tempestuous, he made a major contribution to the establishment of radio drama in Australia and was described by Rees in *Hold Fast to Dreams* (1982) as 'something of a minor genius'. Survived by his daughter and son, Barclay died of a coronary occlusion on 26 August 1961 at Gosford and was buried in Point Clare cemetery with Catholic rites.

A. W. Thomas, *Broadcast and be Damned* (Melb, 1980); C. Semmler, *The ABC—Aunt Sally and Sacred Cow* (Melb, 1981); K. S. Inglis, *This is the ABC* (Melb, 1983); *Listener-In*, 29 Dec 1934; *Radio Pictorial of Aust*, 1 Dec 1935; *Wireless Weekly*, 15 Jan 1937, 20 Mar 1938, 3 Jan 1940; *ABC Weekly*, 22 Mar 1947; *SMH*, 3 Jan 1940, 28 Aug 1961; SP368/1 box 2, SP613/1 box 21, SP1011/2 box 9, SP1558/2 box 63 (AA, Syd); ABC Radio Archives (Syd).

MARION CONSANDINE

BARCLAY, NATHANIEL (1894-1962), soldier settler and politician, was born on 1 October 1894 at Adavoile, Armagh, Ireland, son of Jonathan Barclay, farmer, and his wife Alice, née Turner. Nat attended the local school until he was 14, then left his family's small, mixed farm to live in Newry where he was apprenticed to a grocer. Emigrating with a brother in 1914 to join their eldest brother in Melbourne, Nat enlisted in the Australian Imperial Force on 29 December and served with the 5th Battalion at Gallipoli from May 1915. Invalided to Australia in February 1916, he recovered and from December fought in France with the 59th Battalion. He was promoted sergeant in May 1917. Wounded in his right shoulder in September, he was subsequently awarded the Distinguished Conduct Medal for 'carrying important messages through heavy fire'. He returned to Australia in 1918 and was discharged on 14 March.

Having been employed as a labourer in Melbourne, Barclay travelled to the Mallee in 1920 to work in contract gangs clearing land for the Red Cliffs soldier-settlement scheme. In July 1922 he was granted a conditional purchase-lease for allotment No. 448, a property of sixteen acres (6.5 ha) on the Red Cliffs estate: he planted grape-vines on thirteen acres and citrus fruit on one. On 6 December 1924 at St John's Anglican Church, Healesville, Barclay married London-born Daisy Florence Heritage; they were to remain childless. He served as an instructor with the Australian Military Forces in 1940-42. A resourceful woman, Daisy managed the block during his absences. Although not especially productive, their property became a showpiece. In 1954 Queen Elizabeth II and Prince Philip inspected it, to the delight of the Barclays who were fervent royalists.

In 1945 Barclay had gained Country Party endorsement for the Legislative Assembly seat of Mildura after the sitting member A. G. Allnutt [q.v.] was expelled from the party. Barclay was defeated, but narrowly won the seat from Labor in 1947, retained it in 1950, before losing it in 1952. He was again returned to parliament for Mildura in 1955—ironically benefiting from the Cain [q.v.] government's 'two-for-one' electoral redistribution which brought the Country Party strongholds of Ouyen and Robinvale into an expanded Mildura electorate—and held the seat in 1958 and 1961. Barclay took his place on a number of parliamentary bodies, among them the State Development Committee (1950-52 and 1958-62). In 1961 he attended a parliamentary conference in London, visited his birthplace and revisited battlefields in France.

Barclay's electoral campaigns reflected his political concerns. While not averse to raising the communist spectre, his policy speeches and election advertising were overwhelmingly parochial, as were his relatively infrequent and brief parliamentary contributions on such issues as freight costs, transport, education, health and housing in his electorate. He was interested in the administration of soldier-settlement schemes, in which he was well versed through his activities on the Soldier Settlement Classification Committee in 1946-47. As president (1938-41 and 1944-46) of the large Red Cliffs subbranch of the Returned Sailors' and Soldiers' Imperial League of Australia (Returned Sailors', Soldiers' and Airmen's I.L.A. from 1940), he worked for the rehabilitation of local ex-servicemen.

Solidly built, 5 ft 9 ins (175.3 cm) tall, with blue eyes beaming in a broad, smiling face, Barclay was a consummate local member. He won repute as an effective lobbyist by drawing upon a disarming personality, a wealth of influential contacts and a stubborn tenacity. The Sunday evening train to Melbourne was often delayed at Ouyen station while Barclay listened to constituents from the southern part of his electorate. President (1958-59) of the Mildura Shire Council, he was involved in Legacy, sat on the board of the Knox Memorial Presbyterian Church at Red Cliffs, and was a Freemason and a Knight Templar. Survived by his wife, Barclay died of a coronary occlusion on 11 September 1962 in the Freemasons' Hospital, East Melbourne, and was buried in Red Cliffs cemetery. In 1964 the Red Cliffs public gardens were renamed 'Barclay Square'.

M. Lake, *The Limits of Hope* (Melb, 1987); *PD* (Vic), 11 Sept 1962, p 51; *Sunraysia Daily*, 12-14 Sept 1962; Crown Lands and Survey files, correspondence no 2341/12 (PRO, Vic); information from Mr R. W. Barclay and other family members, contacted via Ms D. Barclay, Kew, Melb.

ARDEL SHAMSULLAH

BARCLAY-HARVEY, SIR CHARLES MALCOLM (1890-1969), landowner and governor, was born on 2 March 1890 at Kensington, London, son of James Charles Barclay-Harvey, gentleman, and his wife Ellen Marianne, née Hills. Educated at Eton and Christ Church, Oxford, Malcolm was commissioned in the 7th Battalion of the Gordon Highlanders, Territorial Force, on 1 August 1909. On 7 February 1912 in the parish church of St Margaret, Westminster, he married Margaret Joan Heywood (d. 1935); they were to have one daughter. After being invalided out of the army in 1915, he was attached to the British Ministry of Munitions in World War I.

As the Conservative member for Kincardineshire and West Aberdeenshire, Scotland, in 1923-29, he sat in the House of Commons. In 1924 he had succeeded his father as laird of Dinnet, inheriting a 14 000-acre (5666 ha) estate in Aberdeenshire, and in 1924-29 was parliamentary private secretary to the secretary of state for Scotland. Barclay-Harvey regained his parliamentary seat in 1931 and again held the private secretaryship in 1932-36. He was knighted in 1936. On 23 March 1938 in the crypt chapel of St Stephen, Westminster, he married a widow Lady Muriel Felicia Vere Liddell-Grainger, daughter of the 12th Earl of Lindsey and grand-daughter of J. C. Cox [q.v.3] of Sydney.

Upon being appointed governor of South Australia in March 1939, Sir Malcolm resigned from the House of Commons and was appointed K.C.M.G. With his wife and two stepchildren, he arrived in Adelaide and took office on 12 August, just before the outbreak of World War II. He worked tirelessly for the war effort and travelled throughout the rural areas; his formidable and energetic wife founded the Lady Muriel Nurses' Club for servicewomen and visited every Red Cross branch in the State. Whenever possible the vice-regal couple lived at their summer residence, Marble Hill, in the Adelaide Hills, where they restored the beautiful gardens. Barclay-Harvey installed a model railway there and in 1943 the South Australian Railways named the first of its new 4-8-4 locomotives after him. On medical advice, he retired on 26 April 1944. During his term he had been honorary colonel of the 4th Battalion of the Gordon Highlanders; he had also invested profitably in Australian stocks and shares.

Returning to his beloved Scottish estate, which became renowned for its land management, Barclay-Harvey was appointed deputy-lieutenant for Aberdeenshire in 1945 and served as a member (1945-55) of the Aberdeenshire County Council. He was grand master mason (1949-53) of the Freemasons Scottish Constitution and in 1964 was made prior for Scotland of the Order of St John. He enjoyed shooting and fishing and anything to do with railways: he wrote *A History of the Great North of Scotland Railway* (London, 1940) which ran to three editions. A courteous, friendly man who believed that public duty went with privilege, Barclay-Harvey died in London on 17 November 1969; his wife survived him, as did the daughter of his first marriage.

O. S. Nock, *Railways of Australia* (Lond, 1971); C. Thornton-Kemsley, *Through Winds and Tides* (Montrose, Scotland, 1974); *Greater Than Their Knowing* (Adel, 1986); *National Trust of SA Newsletter*, no 83, June 1977; *Evening Standard* (Lond), 1 Mar 1939; *The Times*, 18 Nov 1969; *Advertiser* (Adel), 19 Nov 1969; information from Mr D. I. Liddell-Grainger, Ayton Castle, Berwickshire, Scotland.   JOHN PLAYFORD

BARDON, RICHARD (1886-1969), Presbyterian clergyman, was born on 4 July 1886 at Randwick, Sydney, only child of Richard Bardon (d. 1886), a civil service clerk from Ireland, and his Victorian-born wife Elizabeth, née Harding. Raised by his mother at Ipswich, Queensland, Richard attended Ipswich Grammar School in 1900-02.

He taught for six years in state primary schools, before studying at the University of Sydney (B.A., 1912). Close contact during his youth with the Presbyterian clergyman Peter Robertson attracted Bardon to the ministry; he was later to describe Robertson as 'caring for the widow and the orphan in the day of trouble—and for many days afterwards'. In 1912 Bardon entered the Presbyterian Theological Hall within Emmanuel College, University of Queensland. On 21 January 1913 he married a schoolteacher Elsie Mary Florence Watson (d. 1966) at the Park Church, Glenelg Street, South Brisbane; they were to have four children.

Following his student pastorate at Bald Hills, Bardon was ordained in late 1914 and settled in the parish of Killarney. There he developed a distinctive ministry characterized by 'a deep insight into human problems and a strong pastoral sense'. In 1920 he responded to a call to Mackay where he and his family were to stay until 1944. Over almost a quarter of a century he traversed an area that spread from Proserpine to Sarina, sharing and leading in the pioneering work of church and society. In the same manner as they had assisted the Mackay community to recover from the losses of World War I and the cyclone damage of 1918, the Bardons responded during the Depression to the needs of the unemployed in practical and sensitive ways. He held affection for country folk, helped the disadvantaged, and showed concern for single mothers and for the mentally ill. Outside his pastoral responsibilities, he contributed to the local newspaper and radio, and captained the town's cricket team.

Bardon lectured to theological students in 1918, 1929 and 1950-52, and was acting-principal (1929) of Emmanuel College and chairman (1949-51) of its council. In 1933 he was elected moderator of the Presbyterian Church of Queensland and was clerk of its assembly in 1944-57; he was also moderator-general (1951-54) of the Presbyterian Church of Australia and, with other church leaders and prominent jurists, was a signatory to the 1951 'Call to the People' which aimed to promote moral values in society. Having served in the Brisbane parishes of Wilston (1944-48) and Kalinga, he retired in 1952 and was appointed O.B.E. in 1954. He had edited (1945-50) *The Presbyterian Outlook*, completed *The Centenary History of the Presbyterian Church of Queensland* (1949) and was to write a perceptive biography, *James Gibson MA, DD* (1955): his clear style was strengthened by discerning comment and enlivened by wit.

Devoted to reaching and serving ordinary men and women, Bardon confronted them, and the Church, with the hopes and demands of the kingdom of God. His ministry reflected his search for truth and relevance, and his belief in 'the strength of kindness'. Survived by his daughter and two of his sons, he died on 6 August 1969 in Brisbane and was cremated.

Aust Presbyterian Life, 30 Aug 1969; *Courier-Mail*, 8 Aug 1969; Presbyterian Church of Qld Archives, Fortitude Valley, Brisb; information from and family papers held by Mr P. Bardon, Indooroopilly, Brisb.   IAN GILLMAN

BARDSLEY, DORIS (1895-1968), nurse, was born on 9 April 1895 at Gorton, Lancashire, England, daughter of Joseph William Bardsley, tea merchant, and his wife Arabella, née Whincup. Doris was educated at Lister Drive School, Liverpool. Shortly before World War I the family came to Brisbane and settled at Coorparoo. Trained at the Diamantina Hospital for Chronic Diseases, South Brisbane, Doris registered as a general nurse on 10 February 1920, gained her midwifery certificate at (Royal) Women's Hospital, Melbourne, and was matron (1922-23) at St Denis's Hospital, Toowoomba, Queensland. In October 1923 she joined the staff of the Maternal and Child Welfare service and subsequently completed the course in child welfare established at Diamantina Hospital by Ellen Barron [q.v.7].

After a year in charge of the Maternal and Child Welfare Training Centre, Fortitude Valley, on 9 April 1925 Bardsley was appointed sister-in-charge of Queensland Government Baby Clinics. Under the directorship of Dr A. J. Turner [q.v.12], the network of clinics expanded greatly during Bardsley's twelve-year term. During the 1920s she was a delegate to the National Council of Women of Queensland which supported the expansion of child-welfare services and mothercraft education; she was also a member of the technical sub-committee of the Mothercraft Association. In October 1937 Bardsley became acting-superintendent of infant-welfare nurses and, on Barron's retirement, was appointed superintendent in August 1939. Alert, attractive, informed and formidable, Bardsley helped with the development of residential homes for mothers and babies with feeding problems, introduced a correspondence service which offered ante-natal advice, and initiated mothercraft courses in secondary schools. In 1942 she secured the agreement of the registrar-general to notify the baby-clinic service of all births in country areas.

A councillor (1926-57) of the Queensland branch of the Australasian Trained Nurses' Association (later the Royal Australian Nursing Federation), Bardsley was State president in 1949-53 and national president in 1951-56. Besides making several study tours, she represented Australian nurses at overseas conferences, among them the congress of the International Council of Nurses in London (1937), Brazil (1953) and Turkey (1955). She served on the board of directors of the I.C.N. from 1951, on the grand council and on the education committee. Bardsley pursued her interest in the teaching of nurses through her membership of the Queensland Nurses' and Masseurs' Registration Board (1933-55), and the National Health and Medical Research Council's committee on nursing. Committed to the development of postgraduate education, she was a foundation member (1948), vice-president and president (1952-53) of the College of Nursing, Australia, and was elected a fellow in 1962.

From 1953 to 1961 Bardsley had been adviser-in-nursing to Queensland's Department of Health and Home Affairs. In addition, she served at State and national levels on the Florence Nightingale Memorial Committee of Australia which selected nurses to travel abroad and qualify as tutor-sisters. Miss Bardsley retired to Sydney in 1961. She died on 21 January 1968 at Mosman and was cremated with Anglican rites.

A Biographical Record of Queensland Women (Brisb, 1939); R. Patrick, *A History of Health and Medicine in Queensland 1824-1960* (Brisb, 1987); *PP*(Qld), 1927, 1, pp 1179, 1181; *Qld Health*, 1, no 4, June 1963, pp 21, 26; *Aust Nurses J*, 66, no 2, Feb 1968, p 34; *Courier-Mail*, 27 Jan 1968.

HELEN GREGORY

BARGE, ANTHONY JAMES (1928-1980), police officer and educationist, was born on 7 January 1928 at Lambeth, London, son of Arthur Basil Barge, chauffeur, and his wife Hilda Marion Jessie, née Haines. Placed in an orphanage when his parents separated, Tony sailed for New South Wales as a child migrant and arrived at the Fairbridge [q.v.8] Farm, Molong, on 1 June 1938. He attended its public school until he was 14, then completed a three-year farm-training course. Having worked as a dairyhand for eighteen months, he decided that he was unsuited to life on the land and went to Sydney where he was employed as a porter and tram conductor.

On 3 August 1948 Barge joined the New South Wales Police Force and was posted to Darlinghurst station. He married Verna Marea Tidmarsh on 9 September 1949 at St Patrick's Catholic Church, Kogarah. In 1949-52 he performed traffic duties, then served successively in the public safety bureau, the scientific investigation bureau and the vice squad. Transferred to the criminal investigation branch in 1956, he was promoted detective senior constable on 3 August 1960. Next year he moved to the Police Training Centre, Redfern, as an instructor.

A voracious reader, Barge steadily improved his qualifications: in the early 1950s he had studied at Sydney Technical College; he completed the basic in-service training course for technical teachers in 1963 and gained his Leaving certificate next year. He was promoted sergeant 3rd class in September 1965 and made director of detective training in 1968. His work on the initial detectives' course, which he presented that year, earned him a commendation from Commissioner N. T. W. Allan [q.v.]. In 1970 Barge undertook a world tour of police training establishments; on his return, he put forward a comprehensive proposal to improve the instruction and promotion of officers. He completed a diploma in criminology at the University of Sydney in 1971.

Barge resigned on 4 February 1973 to become senior technical adviser in the Commonwealth Department of Customs and Excise. His efficiency in advancing training and operational procedures led in 1974 to his promotion to assistant-director, in which post he was responsible for forming the Coastal Air-Sea Operations Support Group. Transferring to the Commonwealth Police Force in

October, Barge was appointed principal, Australian Police College, Manly, with the rank of superintendent 1st class. He revised the drugs course, but his greatest contribution was in furthering the education of commissioned officers. An inspiring teacher, he impressed students with his enthusiasm, imbued them with his ideals and introduced them to new concepts, especially in management science.

Awarded the Queen's Police Medal for Distinguished Service (1976), he was reassigned in early 1977 as officer-in-charge, New South Wales District, and promoted chief superintendent. Barge was six feet (182.9 cm) tall and broad in build, with grey eyes and brown, receding hair; he was a gregarious man who enjoyed golf. Ill health forced him to retire in June 1978. He died of a cerebellar tumour on 12 May 1980 at Kogarah and, after a police funeral, was cremated. His wife, daughter and three sons survived him.

Aust Federal Police, *Platypus*, 2, no 3, July 1980; service records of A. J. Barge, NSW Police Dept, Syd, *and* Aust Federal Police, Canb; information from Fairbridge Foundation, Syd, Mr A. R. Bunt, Aranda, Canb, Mr R. Lendrum, Forestville, Mr O. Taylor, Frenchs Forest, and Mrs V. Barge, Beverley Park, Syd.   BRUCE SWANTON

BARKER, GEORGE HERBERT (1880-1965), bookseller and naturalist, was born on 21 January 1880 at Hunters Hill, Sydney, son of native-born parents George Robert Barker, a hospital messenger, and his wife Catherine, née McNeil. Educated at Fort Street Model School, in 1897 young George began work at Angus and Robertson's [qq.v.7,11] bookshop where he became friendly with James Tyrrell [q.v.12] who was to encourage him to set up as a bookseller. In 1907 Barker sailed with his father to Brisbane. They rented space in the Australian Hotel Building in Albert Street for thirty shillings a week and began business with several cases of second-hand books on extended credit from Tyrrell. On 26 April 1911 Barker married Florence Wilhelmina Elphick at All Saints Anglican Church, Tumut, New South Wales; they were to have six children.

Expanding trade necessitated successive relocations of Barker's Book Store to premises in Adelaide Street and finally in Edward Street. A new section dealing with technical books was added and a lending library introduced. The bookshop became pre-eminent in Brisbane, catering particularly to students. A foundation member (1924) and sometime president of the Queensland Booksellers' Association, Barker was also instrumental in forming the Australian Booksellers' Association; as its president (1949-51), he led a group of Australian booksellers to Britain to negotiate trading terms.

While still at school, Barker had belonged to the Australian Flora Society; he became its treasurer and curator of its herbarium. After arriving in Brisbane, he joined the Queensland Naturalists' Club, of which he was a councillor (from 1910) and president (1920-21, 1935-36 and 1947-48). An enthusiastic camper, he was the club's honorary excursions secretary, as well as treasurer and librarian. 'G.H.B.' donated many natural history books to the Q.N.C.'s library and freely lent even the most expensive books from his personal collection. The study of birds was one of his major interests and his bookshop became a focal point for ornithology in Queensland. He was a member of the Royal Australasian Ornithologists' Union for nearly half a century, and secretary (1922-56), treasurer and president (1940-41) of its Queensland branch. Noted for his fluent expression, he contributed papers to the *Emu* and to the *Queensland Naturalist*, including two in collaboration with H. G. Barnard [q.v.].

A member of the Royal Society of Queensland and of the Astronomical Society, Barker was foundation treasurer (1930-46) of the Queensland National Parks Association. Perhaps his greatest passion was for ground orchids: he loved searching for them and was an office-bearer of the Queensland Orchid Society. He was president of the Young Men's Christian Association, Brisbane, a warden at St Alban's Anglican Church, Wilston, and also involved with the Boy Scouts' Association. Leaving the management of his bookshop to his only son, Barker retired in 1954. He died on 25 June 1965 at Windsor and was cremated; his son and three daughters survived him. George Barker Pty Ltd was taken over by Angus & Robertson Ltd in 1973.

H. M. Whittell, *The Literature of Australian Birds* (Perth, 1954); Aust Booksellers Assn, *The Early Australian Booksellers* (Adel, 1980); *Emu* (Melb), 65, pt 4, Mar 1966, p 314; *Qld Naturalist*, 18, nos 1-2, June 1966, p 1; information from Mr G. E. E. Barker, Chermside West, Brisb.

M. E. ZERNER

BARKER, HAROLD JAMES (1913-1969), air force officer, was born on 29 November 1913 at Gayndah, Queensland, third child of James Frederick Barker, crown lands ranger, and his wife Mary Christina, née Barth, both Queenslanders. Having served in the South African War and World War I, James remained in the Australian Military Forces as a Militia officer and retired in 1931 as an honorary lieutenant colonel. Harold was educated at South State and at the Christian Brothers' Sacred Heart Boys' High schools, Bundaberg.

He worked in a local menswear store and soldiered part time (1931-34 and 1939-41) in the 47th Battalion of the Militia, attaining the rank of sergeant. Accepted for aircrew training, he enlisted in the Citizen Air Force of the Royal Australian Air Force on 2 March 1941; he gave his religion as Anglican and listed his recreations as sailing, surfing and hockey. Of middle height and slim build, he had blue eyes, a dark complexion and brown hair.

In September 'Tib' Barker was sent to Canada for observer training. Drawn to him by his bearing, self-possession and air of genial authority, his forty-two fellow trainees unanimously voted him course leader, a decision they were never to regret. He was commissioned on 4 April 1942 and in June navigated a Hudson aircraft to England where he began operational training with the Royal Air Force's Bomber Command. In November he joined No. 467 Squadron, R.A.A.F., as a Lancaster navigator. Between February and July 1943 he completed twenty-five operations, attacking targets in Germany and Italy. His skill and determination enabled his crew to obtain excellent night-photographs of heavily defended enemy territory. For the initiative, keenness and courage he displayed throughout this tour, he was awarded the Distinguished Flying Cross on 13 August.

After training in two-seater Mosquito aircraft, Barker was posted on 11 February 1944 to No. 139 (Jamaica) Squadron, R.A.F. This squadron was a unit of Pathfinder Force, an elite group which improved the accuracy of night-attacks by locating and illuminating targets for the main formation of bombers. Initially, he and his pilot flew sorties over Europe as target-markers, a task that required the most precise navigation. Promoted acting squadron leader on 7 August 1944, Barker subsequently crewed with a pilot whose role was master-bomber; they directed attacks on a wide range of enemy targets. Barker's proficiency during sixty-five Mosquito operations—including fifteen over Berlin—together with his enthusiasm and devotion to duty led to the award of a Bar to his D.F.C. Returning to Australia in June 1945, he was demobilized in October. On 19 January 1946 in St Andrew's Anglican Church, Lutwyche, Brisbane, he married a hairdresser Edna McMillen Christie; they lived at Collaroy, Sydney.

In 1946-54 Barker flew with Qantas Empire Airways Ltd, navigating Lancastrians, Short 525 (Hythe) flying boats, Constellations and Douglas DC4s. He resigned to become proprietor of Dee Why Footwear in Sydney, but rejoined Qantas in 1965 and was later a recruitment officer in the airline's cadet-pilot scheme. While playing golf at Long Reef, Barker suffered a coronary occlusion and died on 1 March 1969 at Mona Vale District Hospital. Survived by his wife, son and two daughters, he was cremated.

J. Herington, *Air War Against Germany and Italy 1939-1943* (Canb, 1954) and *Air Power over Europe 1944-1945* (Canb, 1963); AWM records; information from Mrs K. Nass, North Balgowlah, Syd, and Mr K. Hansen, Hobart, Tas; personal information.   DON CHARLWOOD

BARKER, JAMES (1900-1972), Aboriginal station-hand, was born on 28 July 1900 at Cunnamulla, Queensland, son of William Barker, a German-born pastoral worker originally named Bocher, and his wife Margaret (d. 1922), née Ellis, a Murawari woman. His parents separated when Jimmie was 5. Brought up by his mother among his relations on Milroy station by the Culgoa River, New South Wales, he spoke Murawari and learned the traditions of his people; he also developed a keen interest in the engineering technology used on grazing properties.

Following publicity about the Aborigines Protection Board's new powers to remove children from their families, in 1912 Margaret shifted with her children to Brewarrina 'mission', a station administered by the A.P.B. where a restricted primary syllabus was taught in the segregated public school. Appalled by the repressive discipline and by the denigration of Aboriginal culture, they left for the unsupervised camp near Brewarrina. The local public school was also segregated and the family reluctantly returned to the mission. By 1915 Jimmie had taught himself to read. He was 'apprenticed' by the A.P.B. and worked on a sheep-station where he slept in a chaff room and was physically abused.

In 1922 Barker returned as a handyman to Brewarrina station in order to be near his mother. There, on 17 December 1924, he married Evelyn Isobel Wighton (d. 1941) with Anglican rites. A central figure in his community, he negotiated between Aborigines and bureaucrats, and attempted to shield his fellow residents from excesses of managerial power. Jimmie opposed the A.P.B.'s concentration of some five hundred Aborigines on the station in housing barely adequate for one hundred. He refused to take part in the enforced relocation of the Wangkumarra people from Tibooburra to Brewarrina in 1938.

Barker openly supported William Ferguson [q.v.8], Herbert Groves [q.v.] and Pearl Gibbs in their campaign to abolish the A.P.B. He described the conditions on Brewarrina station, thereby providing much of the information revealed in 1937 to the Legislative Assembly's select committee on the administration of the A.P.B. Jimmie took his six surviving children to live on the banks of the Barwon River outside Brewarrina in 1942. He worked as a handyman at the town's hospital. Obliged by illness to retire in 1963, he staked an opal claim at Lightning Ridge and mined for some years before returning to Brewarrina.

In 1968 Barker passed on his knowledge of the Murawari language to the Australian Institute of Aboriginal Studies. He soon grew interested in recording his life and the history of his community. In so doing, he celebrated the Murawari culture of his childhood and recalled the support, as well as the problems, of Aboriginal community life. At the same time, he relentlessly detailed the oppressions and discriminations of rural racism. Survived by three sons and two daughters, he died on 7 July 1972 at Brewarrina and was buried in the Old Mission cemetery. His tapes, edited by Janet Mathews, were published as *The Two Worlds of Jimmie Barker* in 1977.

PP (NSW), 1938-39-40, 7, p 597; Aborigines Protection and Welfare Bds, Minute-books, 1900-39, 1940-48 (NSWA); information from Mr R. Barker, Brewarrina, NSW, and the late Ms P. Gibbs, Mr H. Hardy and Mr J. Barker (tapes held by author).   HEATHER GOODALL

BARKMAN, FRANCES (1885-1946), teacher and Jewish welfare worker, was born in March 1885 at Kiev, Russia, daughter of Joseph Barkman, a teacher of Hebrew, and his wife Anna. With her parents, Frances migrated to Melbourne in 1891 and was educated at the Rathdowne Street State School and the Melbourne Training College. While teaching in the Victorian Education Department, she graduated (Dip.Ed., 1909; B.A., 1915) from the University of Melbourne.

From an early age Barkman developed cultural interests which she later demonstrated by convening the dramatic circle of the Lyceum Club; as a young teacher in suburban state schools and then at the Continuation School, Melbourne (1911-36), she was energetic in organizing dramatic performances. Her major academic area was French, in which subject she was appointed an examiner at the university public examinations. For her 'outstanding interest and promulgation of French literature, art and teaching', she received two awards in the 1930s from the government of France. Throughout her career she was a leading member of the Alliance Française in Victoria.

To help alleviate the distress of Jews who had fled from the Nazis, the Australian Jewish Welfare Society was established in Sydney in 1936. A Victorian branch was founded in Melbourne soon after. Barkman served as the branch's honorary secretary and arranged for local assistance to new arrivals in Victoria. She influenced the activities of the women's auxiliary and saw to it that representatives from the society met incoming ships with refugees on board. At her initiative, in 1939 a home was set up for thirty-two refugee children. This home, the Balwyn estate, Larino, became the permanent location of the relief-service offered to juveniles by the Melbourne Australian Jewish Welfare and Relief Society. When Larino was sold in 1965, two new Frances Barkman Houses were established to commemorate the founder.

During World War II Barkman had become an inaugural member of the Free French Movement in Australia and was a leading advocate of its cause throughout the German occupation of France. From 1942 she taught at MacRobertson [q.v.11 Robertson] Girls' High School where she took charge of war relief organization, 'bullying' her students into raising money for the patriotic fund and 'doling out skein after skein of khaki wool' for them to knit their quota of balaclavas. Following the liberation of France in 1944, she began moves to obtain French educational materials for Australian schools and was keenly supported by the French government.

After years of selfless work at the expense of her health, Frances Barkman died of cancer on 28 September 1946 at St Vincent's Hospital, Fitzroy, and was buried with Jewish rites in Fawkner cemetery. Most of her family had been massacred in Kiev during the 1905 pogroms; her will named the University of Melbourne and the Australian Jewish Welfare Society as her chief beneficiaries, and provided educational bursaries for students in the Jewish Refugee Children's Home.

A. Inglis, *Amirah* (Melb, 1983); MacRobertson Girls' High Schol, *Pallas*, 1946, p 6; Aust Jewish Welfare and Relief Soc, *Welfare*, July 1985, p 6; information from Jewish Museum of Aust, Melb.

PAUL R. BARTROP

BARNARD, HENRY GREENSILL (1869-1966), zoologist, naturalist and grazier, was born on 11 April 1869 at Crescent Lagoon, Rockhampton district, Queensland, fourth of seven children of GEORGE BARNARD (1831?-1894), pound keeper and grazier, and his wife Maria Trafalgar (d. 1874), née Bourne, both from England. In 1873 the family moved west to Coomooboolaroo, an unstocked station of some 170 square miles (440 km²) near Duaringa.

George built his collection of insect and bird eggs into one of the best in the southern hemisphere; in regard to insects, he specialized in moths, butterflies and beetles. He corresponded extensively with experts in

Australia, England, France, India, Chile and Finland, and supplied A. J. North with notes for his *Descriptive Catalogue of the Nests and Eggs of Birds found breeding in Australia and Tasmania* (Sydney, 1889). Maria Barnard was a talented artist who drew and painted specimens while the colours were still fresh. By 1891 the collection had grown so large that George built a private museum at the station. Following George's death the collection was acquired by (Baron) Rothschild's private museum at Tring, England, now part of the British Museum (Natural History).

Many naturalists and zoologists visited Coomooboolaroo. The Norwegian Carl Lumholtz, a guest in 1883, had described the remarkable abilities of George's sons in *Among Cannibals* (London, 1889). The boys were trained in collection and preservation from an early age; they were also tutored in Aboriginal lore by Blacks who lived on the property; and they excelled at mimicking bird calls. Lumholtz was astonished at their skill on excursions where they went barefoot, unworried by any type of ground. To collect certain insects, they climbed the highest trees by cutting toe-holes with tomahawks. They were able to run and catch flying beetles in their hands. Lumholtz was further impressed by their dexterity with guns, by the quality of their observations and by the extent of their knowledge, much of it derived from expeditions, such as the one they had made seventy miles (112.7 km) south to Fairfield station in 1882.

When Henry Barnard was 19, his father gave him permission to accompany Archie Meston [q.v.5] on a government-sponsored expedition to explore the Bellenden Ker Range. The party made important geographical and biological discoveries, and found a male golden bowerbird (*Prionodura newtoniana*). Meston named Barnard's Spur in Harry's honour. Harry was to alternate collecting trips with his usual station-work at Coomooboolaroo and his later management of Rio cattle-station in the Central district. In 1894 he accompanied the family's English friend A. S. Meek (then collecting for Rothschild) on an expedition to Cooktown, and to the Trobriand, Woodlark and Egham islands off mainland New Guinea. Two years later Harry collected at Cape York for (Sir) Charles Ryan, William Snowball and W. H. D. Le Souef [qq.v.11,12,10].

On 22 November 1899, at Mount Perry, Harry married a governess Alice Maud Mary Elworthy with Presbyterian forms; they were to have eight children. He collected again at Cape York in 1899 for H. L. White [q.v.12], and his contributions figure prominently in White's bird collection now in the Museum of Victoria, Melbourne. A member (from 1901) of the Royal Australasian Ornithologists'

Union, Henry wrote numerous papers on birds. Having retired from Bimbi, his property near Duaringa, he lived at Rockhampton and then in Brisbane. Survived by three sons and three daughters, he died on 7 October 1966 in South Brisbane and was cremated.

His elder brother CHARLES ASHMALL BARNARD (1867-1942) was a founding member and president (1922-23) of the R.A.O.U. He wrote little, but a paper (with notes by Henry) on the birds of Coomooboolaroo, presented to the 23rd congress of the R.A.O.U. at Rockhampton in 1924, was an outstanding contribution to ornithology. Covering a period of fifty years, it allowed him to detail and speculate on changes in the composition of the bird fauna. In 1937 Charles and Harry collected a rare specimen of the northern hairy-nosed wombat (*Lasiorhinus krefftii*) from Epping Forest station, 75 miles (120.7 km) west of Clermont. A 'gentleman in his outlook and mode of life', Charles was retiring and shunned publicity. He was a councillor of Duaringa Shire for fifty years and sometime president. When he died, his collection of bird-skins—acquired initially by G. M. Mathews [q.v.10]—passed to the American Museum of Natural History, New York.

Another brother WILFRED BOURNE BARNARD (1870-1940) accompanied Meek in 1890 on his first collecting trip into the ranges near Coomooboolaroo, but arthritis obliged him to leave Meek alone for some time. Although he went with Meek and Harry to Cooktown and New Guinea in 1894, rheumatism and fever forced him to return to Queensland from Woodlark Island. Meek bought Wilfred's collection for some £500. Wilfred managed an outstation in the Peak Downs region and did not resume collecting until the 1920s. Chiefly interested in moths and butterflies, he collected from Cape York, the south and west of Queensland, northern New South Wales, Western Australia and Tasmania. After Wilfred's death, A. J. Turner [q.v.12] described new species in the collection which was bequeathed to the Council for Scientific and Industrial Research, and then donated to the Queensland Museum.

Two other members of the Barnard family were active naturalists. A sister Mabel Theodore (Hobbler) specialized in lepidoptera; she also wrote notes on beetles, contributed to the journal of the Queensland Naturalists' Club and was a councillor of the Nature-Lovers' League. Her half-brother Ernest (by George's second marriage—to Sarah Ann Wilkinson) was interested in ornithology and published several notes on birds.

A. S. Meek, *A Naturalist in Cannibal Land* (Lond, 1913); A. Musgrave, *Bibliography of Aus-*

tralian Entomology 1775-1930 (Syd, 1932); H. M. Whittell, *The Literature of Australian Birds* (Perth, 1954); L. McDonald, *Rockhampton* (Brisb, 1981); N. Chaffer, *In Quest of Bowerbirds* (Adel, 1984); *Entomologist* (Lond), 27, 1894, p 228; *Qld Naturalist*, 5, 1922, p 48, 18, 1967, p 74; *Emu* (Melb), vol 22, 1923, plates 62, 64, vol 24, 1925, plates 27, 44, p 252, vol 42, 1942, p 128, vol 66, 1967, p 391; *Memoirs of the Qld Museum*, 11, 1939, p 283, 12, 1941, p 40, 24, 1986, pp 57, 185.

GLEN INGRAM

BARNARD, HERBERT CLAUDE (1890-1957), politician, was born on 16 October 1890 at Mole Creek, near Deloraine, Tasmania, son of Ernest Walter Barnard, wheelwright, and his wife Charlotte, née Tipper. Educated at Invermay State School, Claude left at the age of 14 to work in a nursery. In 1909 at Launceston he was employed as an engine cleaner in the Tasmanian Government Railways; he later became a fireman, then an engine driver. Raised as a Methodist, on 6 March 1912 in the Baptist Tabernacle, Deloraine, he married a blacksmith's daughter, Martha Melva McKenzie; they lived in Hampden Street, East Launceston, had three sons and a daughter, and Barnard attended the local Baptist chapel.

One of the founders (1920) and State secretary of the Australian Federated Union of Locomotive Enginemen, he was also president of the Launceston Trades Hall Council. As secretary of the Bass division concil of the Australian Labor Party, in the 1931 Federal elections Barnard was unable to find a candidate to stand against J. A. Guy [q.v.] who had defected to the United Australia Party with Joseph Lyons [q.v.10]. Barnard drafted himself, but lost. Two years later he became State president of the A.L.P. In 1934 he won Bass by a narrow margin and entered the House of Representatives. Obliged to spend six months at a time in Canberra for parliamentary sittings, he lived with his wife in the Kurrajong Hotel, but remained devoted to his children who reciprocated the affection.

On 3 July 1941 Barnard was appointed to, and in November became chairman of, the joint parliamentary committee on social security. Between 1941 and 1946 the committee tabled nine reports which raised broad principles of social welfare and made recommendations on such matters as unemployment benefits, state housing, national schemes for health and hospital services, maternal and child welfare, old-age, invalid and widows' pensions, planning for postwar reconstruction, and the consolidation of related legislation. The committee was not the sole source of ideas about the future scope of social services, but many of its proposals were incorporated in the extensive legislative pro-

grammes undertaken by the governments of John Curtin and J. B. Chifley [qq.v.]. Although Barnard resigned as chairman in 1944, he remained a committee-member until 1946 and contributed much to the foundations of the Australian welfare state.

In May 1944 he had attended the International Labour Organization conference at Philadelphia, United States of America, where he was chiefly concerned with social security issues. Appointed minister for repatriation in November 1946, he had personal knowledge of the predicament of returned servicemen and war widows: during World War II two of his sons had been wounded; a third was killed in action, leaving a wife and child. Barnard's tenure in what he later called the 'suicide portfolio' was not easy. Incensed at what it perceived as inaction on pension increases, the Returned Sailors', Soldiers' and Airmen's Imperial League of Australia accused him of weakness and incapacity. It was further claimed that Barnard was insensitive to the plight of war widows. His conflicts with the war pensions entitlement appeal tribunals provided additional ammunition for the Opposition in parliament. He lost his seat in the 1949 general elections.

A right-wing member of the A.L.P., Barnard came from the traditional trade-union base of his party. His radical view of social justice sprang from his religious convictions; he was not a doctrinaire socialist and took more interest in parochial and personal issues than in ideology. He showed concern for his constituents, carrying a notebook to record the grievances of those he met at public meetings or on regular tours of his electorate. Anomalies in the payment of welfare benefits and in the provision of services to particular localities were rectified as a result of his work as a local member. Among the institutions which benefited from his commitment to social and charitable activities was the Launceston Girls' Home, whose board of management he chaired in 1954-56. Courteous and solicitous, he visited the wards of the Launceston General Hospital on Sunday afternoons. Barnard's loyalty to his party and constituency were rewarded by his election to the Tasmanian House of Assembly in 1950 as a member for Bass, an electorate he was to represent until his death.

A tall man, with a fresh complexion, round face and bald head, Barnard was a teetotaller and an inveterate cigar-smoker. Tasmanians esteemed him for his industry and integrity, and regarded him as a man of the people who was as welcome in the Launceston Working Men's Club as he was in the Memorial Baptist Church, Wellington Street. Survived by his wife and two sons, Barnard died of cancer on 6 December 1957 in Launceston Public Hospital; following a state funeral, he was cremated. His widow was made a life member (1967) of the Labor Party; his son Lance became Federal member for Bass in 1954 and deputy prime minister (1972-75).

T. H. Kewley, *Social Security in Australia, 1900-72* (Syd, 1973); *Age* (Melb), 30 Nov 1942; *SMH*, 13 May 1944, 25 Feb, 18 Dec 1949; *Herald* (Melb), 17 July 1947; *Sun News-Pictorial*, 25 Oct 1948; *Argus*, 29 Oct 1948; *Examiner* (Launc), 7 Dec 1957; information from Hon L. Barnard, Newstead, Launc, Tas.   R. J. K. CHAPMAN

BARNES, JOHN FRANCIS (1904-1952) and LEWIS GABRIEL (1907-1983), publicans and politicians, were born on 4 October 1904 and 13 January 1907 at Gympie, Queensland, second and fourth sons of Queensland-born parents George Daniel Barnes, licensed victualler, and his wife Bridget Maria, née Gorey, late Moore. After their parents separated, the children were raised by their father and educated at Christian Brothers' High School, Gympie. Frank was a commercial traveller in wine and spirits, before becoming licensee of the Commercial Hotel, Bundaberg, in 1937. A failed police prosecution for selling liquor after hours was to launch him on an extraordinary political career. Passionately convinced of widespread police and political corruption, he initiated numerous, successful prosecutions for breaches of the liquor laws that earned him the sobriquet 'the Bundaberg Bombshell'. An 'able bush-lawyer', he lost only one of thirty-one applications to the Supreme Court of Queensland.

In 1941, as an Independent 'Andrew Fisher [q.v.8] Laborite', Barnes won the Legislative Assembly seat of Bundaberg from the Australian Labor Party. In his maiden speech on 2 September he declared himself opposed to the Forgan Smith [q.v.11] government, opined that 'the most important question in life is sex', described the liquor issue as 'filthy and disgraceful', denounced Jewish financial domination and revealed his sympathy for Social Credit economics—although he always claimed to be a follower of the policies of his friend King O'Malley [q.v.11]. This speech marked the beginning of a 'nine years war with parliament' during which Barnes was suspended from the House eight times.

A robust public speaker, given to extravagant language, he was placid and kindly in his personal relations. Always sartorially splendid in a white suit and pith helmet, he was a political showman, never above stage-managing incidents to attract publicity. Humour was part of his political style: when rebuked by chairman of committees Sam Brassington in October 1943 for not apologizing to the House 'in a decent and manly way',

Barnes knelt on the floor, clasped his hands, and intoned, 'I humbly withdraw the statement'. He was suspended for two weeks.

In late 1942 he had claimed that the mysteriously missing Marjorie Norval (former social secretary to Mrs Forgan Smith) had been 'shanghaied to California'. When he refused to reveal his source to the police, the government amended the Coroner's Act (1930) to make it an offence to withhold such information. After Barnes declined to name his source a second time, the coroner jailed him. In court on 1 June 1943 Barnes impenitently named his informants as 'Detective Smith' and 'Citizen Jones', but later conceded that he had been duped. On 20 January 1943 Frank had married a munition worker Everleen Dorothy Buchanan at the general registry office, Brisbane.

His litigiousness was a persistent irritant to the government. Having ruled that suspension from parliament precluded Barnes from occupying a room at the country members' lodge, the Speaker directed the police to evict him. In May 1946 Barnes, in the Full Court of Queensland, won his case for assault against a policeman on the grounds that the lodge was no part of Parliament House. He was less fortunate that year when the government legislated to garnish his salary to retrieve a £30 fine, imposed for a breach of parliamentary privilege. While often scandalizing his colleagues, Barnes managed to retain his Bundaberg seat until defeated by Labor's E. J. Walsh [q.v.] in April 1950.

Frank had been joined in the assembly by his brother Lewis who, as a 'King O'Malley Laborite', won a by-election for Cairns in October 1942. Like Frank, Lou was a commercial traveller for a brewery before becoming manager of the Queen's Hotel, Maryborough. On 21 April 1934 he married 33-year-old Muriel Eileen Burke at St Mary's Catholic Church, Beaudesert.

It was as a farmer from Beaudesert that Lou won his northern coastal seat, following a two-week campaign in which he was assisted by Frank. One effect of his surprising victory was the government's amendment of the Electoral Act (1892) to replace contingent with plurality voting. Less flamboyant and controversial than Frank, Lou lost Cairns to Labor in May 1947. He then established a menswear store at Southport and served (1949-52) on the South Coast City Council, from which he resigned in protest at the cost of a mobile library.

Lou was six feet (182.9 cm) tall, studious in appearance and prematurely bald, while Frank was a little shorter, with olive skin and a mop of dark, curly hair. Both were skilful amateur conjurers and each was an accomplished sportsman: Lou shone at lawn bowls and Frank at game fishing. Towards the end of Frank's life they had a serious falling out over Lou's return to the Catholic faith, which both had rejected in their youth. Frank was reduced to straitened financial circumstances. After suffering from chronic renal disease for several years, he died of coronary embolism on 12 May 1952 at Bundaberg and was buried in the local cemetery with Anglican rites; his wife, daughter and infant son survived him. Lou died on 2 June 1983 at Southport and was buried in Musgrave cemetery with the forms of the Jehovah's Witnesses; his wife and two sons survived him.

C. Lack (ed), *Three Decades of Queensland Political History, 1929-1960* (Brisb, 1962); I. Moles, *A Majority of One* (Brisb, 1979); *PD* (Qld), 2 Sept 1941, p 149, 14 Oct 1943, p 918, 19 Aug 1952, p 9; *Sunday Mail* (Brisb), 8 Nov 1942; *Truth* (Brisb), 17 July 1943; *South Coast Bulletin*, 1 June 1949, 7 May 1952; *Bundaberg Daily News* and *Courier-Mail*, 13 May 1952; family information.   B. J. COSTAR

BARNES, SIDNEY GEORGE (1916-1973), cricketer, was born on 5 June 1916 at Annandale, Sydney, third and posthumous son of Alfred Percival Barnes, grazier, by his wife Hilda May, née Jeffrey, both native-born. Having attended Stanmore Public School, Sid undertook advanced training as a mechanical fitter. He played first-grade cricket for Petersham from 1934 and competed against such established Test players as W. J. O'Reilly, showing scant respect for their achievements and brash confidence in his own ability.

After one full season for New South Wales, in 1938 Barnes was the youngest player chosen to tour England in the Australian team led by (Sir) Donald Bradman. Despite missing half the matches because of injury, Barnes managed to score 720 runs (average 42.35) and to play in the fifth Test. In 1940-41 he scored six successive centuries. He enlisted in the Australian Imperial Force on 13 May 1942; after dislocating his shoulder, he was discharged on 1 September for service in a reserved occupation. On 11 June that year he had married a schoolteacher Alison Margaret Edward at St Augustine's Anglican Church, Stanmore. Except for coaching tours in the country with Jack Chegwyn, he played little cricket for three years, but scored centuries in five successive matches for New South Wales in 1945-46.

In December 1946 Barnes and Bradman set an Australian Test record of 405 for the fifth wicket in the Sydney Test against W. R. Hammond's touring English team: each of them scored 234, which was to remain Barnes's highest Test score. As an opener with Arthur Morris, Barnes changed his batting style from free-flowing strokes to 'dogged and defiant' stonewalling, and be-

came a complete back-foot player, with square strokes both sides of the wicket. He was also a competent leg-break bowler, a substitute wicket-keeper and 'a glorious and versatile fieldsman'. On his second tour of England in 1948, Barnes was outstanding: he amassed 1354 runs, averaged 56.41 in all matches and 82.25 in Tests, and scored 141 at Lord's. Competitive and audacious, 'Suicide Sid' was much criticized for fielding at point or short leg, just five yards (4.6 m) from the batsman: at Old Trafford, Manchester, he received a full-blooded stroke in the ribs that sent him to hospital for ten days.

Barnes had become known as a stormy petrel with a penchant for antagonizing administrators and for humorous displays of disaffection. When an Australian appeal was turned down during the 1948 tour, Barnes gathered up a stray dog and presented it to the umpire with the comment: 'Now all you want is a white stick'. Moreover, he had been the only player to take his wife to Britain and had returned with a home movie of the tour and shown it around Australia for charity.

Irked by this sort of behaviour, the authorities reacted savagely: in 1951-52 the selectors chose Barnes for the third Test against the West Indies, but were overruled by the Australian Board of Control for International Cricket on grounds other than his ability. The matter became a *cause célèbre* after Barnes sued the writer of a letter to the editor of the *Daily Mirror* (24 April 1952) for damages. At the court hearing, the board's secretary was obliged to produce the minutes of all relevant meetings. The case was settled and in the public eye the board was seen to have acted on such trivial incidents as when Barnes jumped a turnstile at the Melbourne Cricket Ground against an attendant's wishes.

During the 1952-53 season he was passed over for Test selection against the touring South Africans. Named twelfth man for New South Wales in a match against South Australia, Barnes appeared at the drinks interval dressed in a grey suit, complete with red carnation, and carrying a tray with scented spray, a portable radio and cigars. He caused further controversy by criticizing the behaviour of A. L. Hassett's Australian team in England in his book, *Eyes on the Ashes* (London, 1953), and by his autobiography, *It isn't Cricket* (Sydney, 1953). His cricket career was over: he had scored 8333 first-class runs at an average of 54.11, while in 13 Tests he amassed 1072 runs at 63.06.

He published *The Ashes Ablaze* (London, 1955) and turned to full-time writing, especially for the *Daily Telegraph*: his attitude and style were critical of players and officials whenever possible. Barnes rarely forgave a slight or forgot a good turn. Stocky, with blue eyes and powerful wrists, he had a passion for physical fitness, and was an enthusiastic big-game fisherman and golfer. He died on 16 December 1973 at his Collaroy home from barbiturate and bromide poisoning, self-administered; the coroner was unable to determine intent. Survived by his wife, daughter and two sons, Barnes was cremated.

J. Pollard, *Australian Cricket* (Syd, 1982); P. Derriman, *True to the Blue* (Syd, 1985); *People* (Syd), 15 Mar 1950; *Aust Cricket*, Feb 1974, p 26; *Wisden Cricketers' Almanack*, 1974; *Age* (Melb), and *The Times*, 17 Dec 1973; *SMH*, 20 Mar 1945, 18 Dec 1946, 23 Aug 1952, 6 Nov 1953, 17 Dec 1973, 8 May 1974; *Daily Mirror* (Syd), 27 June 1983.   BRIAN STODDART

BARNETT, EMILY CAROLINE (1860-1944), explorer, was born on 1 November 1860 in a ship in the Bay of Bengal, India, daughter of Captain George Cayley Robinson, Royal Artillery officer, and his wife Mary Harriet, née Woodward. Following Caroline's birth, Robinson took his family to England. They lived at Weston-super-Mare, Somerset, where Caroline was educated, and migrated to Australia in 1876. She gave her place of residence as her uncle's home at Goodna, Queensland, when she married Irish-born Harry Alington Creaghe, a station-manager, on 7 December 1881 in St Paul's Anglican Church, Ipswich; they were to have three sons, the first of whom died in infancy.

In December 1882 the Creaghes left Sydney by steamer to join Ernest Favenc [q.v.4] and his wife on Thursday Island. Favenc planned to explore a region in the Northern Territory bounded by the Nicholson River, Powells Creek and the Macarthur (McArthur) River. The two women were to be part of the expedition. Travelling by sea, the party landed at Normanton on 17 January 1883. There Elizabeth Favenc became ill and her husband escorted her to Sydney, while Caroline accompanied Harry and four other men on a two hundred-mile (321.9 km) ride south-west to Carl Creek station which they reached at the end of the month; one man died of sunstroke *en route*. Ten weeks later they retraced their steps as far as Gregory Downs station where Favenc and Lindsay Crawford were waiting. On 14 April the explorers set out westwards.

Battling thirst and flies, with food supplies dwindling, they were frequently exhausted and occasionally in fear of attack by Aborigines, but reached the telegraph station at Powells Creek on 14 May. After a few days rest Harry and Caroline, now pregnant, drove the weaker horses north to Katherine telegraph station. Favenc and Crawford pushed east to inspect the country near the Mac-

arthur River. Accompanied by Alfred and Augusta Giles of Springvale station, the Creaghes made a leisurely journey to Port Darwin and left for Sydney by sea on 22 August. From 1 January 1883 Caroline had kept a diary of her adventures which contained descriptions of topography and vegetation, observations of frontier life and comments on the relations between Whites and Aborigines.

The Creaghes returned to the land in Queensland where Harry was accidentally killed in 1886. On 10 December 1889 in St Paul's Church, Rockhampton, Caroline married English-born Joseph Jupp Smallman Barnett (d. 1922); they were to have six children. Joseph was the manager of nearby Apis Creek and Marlborough stations. Intending to visit her sister, in 1899 Caroline sailed for New Zealand with five of her children and a nurse as the only passengers in the *Perthshire*. Disabled by a broken propeller-shaft on 28 April, the ship drifted perilously in the Tasman Sea for seven weeks until she was taken in tow and returned to Sydney: Caroline recounted the experience to a press interviewer with characteristic equanimity. She and Joseph lived at Marlborough for some twenty years, before shifting to Rockhampton —where Caroline ran a guest house—and finally moving to Sydney in 1920. Two of her sons, one of whom died of wounds in France, served in the Australian Imperial Force in World War I. Survived by a son of her first marriage, and by three sons and two daughters of her second, she died on 11 November 1944 in Royal North Shore Hospital, Sydney, and was cremated.

C. Frost, *The Last Explorer, the Life and Work of Ernest Favenc* (Townsville, 1983); W. Maff, *Katherine's No Lady* (Katherine, 1986); D. Carment, R. Maynard and A. Powell (eds), *Northern Territory Dictionary of Biography*, 1 (Darwin, 1990); *PP*(SA), 1883-84 (181); *SMH*, 20 June 1899, 13, 14, 20 May 1976; E. C. Creaghe Diary (ML); Alfred Giles Diary (Mort L); information from Mr E. R. Barnett, Newport, Syd.   WINSOME J. M. MAFF

BARRENGER, HENRY AYLWIN (1900-1976), public servant, was born on 31 May 1900 at Prahran, Melbourne, son of Thomas William Charles Barrenger, jeweller, and his wife Anne, née Aylwin, both Victorian born. Educated at Hawksburn State School, in 1915 Harry joined the Postmaster-General's Department as a messenger. Two years later he was appointed clerk in the Department of Home and Territories. On 23 February 1924 at All Saints Church, St Kilda, he married Lily Adelaide Danson with Anglican rites; they moved to Canberra in 1927 with the first relocated Federal public servants and their families.

Advancing steadily within the Department of the Interior, Barrenger was involved in the administration of the Northern Territory and made frequent visits there. His responsibilities included Aboriginal welfare policy and he served as secretary to the initial conference of Commonwealth and State Aboriginal authorities, held in Canberra on 21 to 23 April 1937. Among other duties in the 1930s, he acted as secretary to the Commonwealth Literary Fund and to the oil advisory committee. In 1938 he became an associate member of the Commonwealth Institute of Accountants. He was promoted chief clerk in Interior's central administration branch in 1945 and assistant-secretary next year. As first assistant-secretary from 1948, he oversaw the substantial expansion occasioned by the transfer of most of the remaining government departments to Canberra. Barrenger acted as secretary of the department. On one such occasion in January 1949 there was controversy over the enforced removal to Adelaide and Alice Springs of Aboriginal children who had been evacuated to Penrith, New South Wales, in World War II; he dismissed protests against the move, arguing that the children had to obey the orders of their legal guardian, the Northern Territory director of native affairs.

In 1954 Barrenger became a nominated member of the Australian Capital Territory Advisory Council. Although the council exercised no power and had only limited influence on parliamentary ministers, he insisted that community concerns voiced at its meetings be taken seriously by the Department of the Interior. A member of the Police Arbitral Tribunal and of the Commonwealth Stores Supply and Tender Board, he was a director and an active chairman (1965-72) of Commonwealth Brickworks (Canberra) Ltd. Aboriginal bark-painters at the Maningrida settlement in the Northern Territory benefited from his efforts to establish a forest reserve to provide a future source of bark. Respected for his hard work and integrity, Barrenger was never ruffled and had an 'unfailing sense of humour'. He related well to others, and was noted for his sympathy and compassion. Accessible to and supportive of his staff, he improved morale in his department and stood up to the permanent head William McLaren [q.v.] when necessary. Barrenger was appointed O.B.E. in 1964; he retired from the public service and the advisory council in 1965.

He was active in the Barton Tennis, Canberra Bowling and Manuka Cricket clubs, and also interested in films and philately. Predeceased by his wife, Barrenger died on 26 August 1976 at Woden Valley Hospital and was buried in Canberra cemetery with Baptist forms; his daughter and son survived him.

Aboriginal Welfare. Initial Conference of Commonwealth and State Aboriginal Authorities (Canb, 1937); E. Sparke, *Canberra 1954-1980* (Canb, 1988); *SMH*, 26 Jan 1949; *Australian* (Canb edn), 15 Apr 1965; *Canb Times*, 15 Apr 1965, 1 Sept 1976; *Canb Courier*, 22 Apr 1965; ACT Advisory Council, Minutes, 12 Apr 1965 (NL).

IAN CARNELL

BARRETT, JAMES NOEL (1903-1958), agriculturist and grazier, was born on Christmas Day 1903 at Prahran, Melbourne, second son of (Sir) James Barrett [q.v.7] and his English wife Marian, née Rennick, late Pirani. Noel was educated at Melbourne Church of England Grammar School and Trinity College, University of Melbourne (B.Agr.Sc., 1925). In 1927 he bought Yera (1820 acres, 737 ha) at Edgeroi, near Narrabri, New South Wales. On 19 June 1929 at St Albans Anglican Church, Quirindi, he married Nancy Morphett Mair of nearby Colly Creek station; they were to have six children.

Highly energetic and innovative, Barrett devoted his life to the betterment of agriculture and became one of the State's most progressive farmers. Alone or with others, he pioneered wheat-growing on the north-western slopes of New South Wales, contract harvesting of pasture seed (especially curly Mitchell grass), use of pneumatic tyres on farm machinery, bulk handling of wheat, growing and harvesting of linseed and sunflower oilseed, and, in 1947, aerial spraying with insecticides. He adapted and designed new farm equipment, including a system for delivering wheat from his auto-header to motor trucks and bulk railway-waggons. Yera was developed into a highly-mechanized model property: in 1939 it had 1100 acres (445 ha) under wheat and 600 (243 ha) under lucerne, and carried 580 sheep and 120 cattle.

Unremitting in his efforts to improve farming practices, Barrett gave radio broadcasts and contributed numerous letters and articles to the press on subjects such as pasture improvement, soil erosion and fodder conservation. In 1942-45 he was agricultural adviser on farm mechanization and machinery pools to the Federal minister for commerce and agriculture William Scully [q.v.]. After the war Barrett served on the general council of the Wheat and Woolgrowers' Association of New South Wales and, with C. D. Renshaw, was a State delegate to the Australian Wool and Meat Producers' Federation. In 1946 Barrett strongly opposed the Federal government's wheat stabilization plan.

In 1949 he purchased Maida Vale, a run-down 1760-acre (712 ha) property at Ebor, west of Dorrigo; in 1954 he related the story of its rehabilitation in a series of articles in the *Pastoral Review*. Barrett was a driving spirit behind the Hernani Dog Proof Association in 1953-56 and hoped that this co-operative of landowners from the district near Maida Vale would set a pattern for others in erecting dingo fences. In the late 1950s he planned to irrigate the whole of Yera which, on completion, would represent an investment of £200 000 and make his property 'one of the best and safest in Australia'. These plans were unrealized, but one of his last ventures on Yera was to set up a merino stud founded on Rossmore (Burren Junction) blood.

Tall, with a slightly gangling walk, Barrett was widely admired for his sincerity, thoroughness and ingenuity. He had a good— if unusual—sense of humour and was a delightful travelling companion; like his father, he was also an able and forceful communicator. Overwork and worry, however, undermined his health and affected his hitherto sound judgement. On 6 July 1958 he drove his truck into the Clarence River at Grafton and drowned; the coroner returned a verdict of suicide. Survived by his wife, two daughters and three of his sons, Barrett was cremated; his estate was sworn for probate at £72 817.

Pastoral Review, May, July, Aug 1939, May 1942, May-Oct 1954, Nov 1955, Feb, July 1956, Jan 1957, Aug 1958; *SMH*, 29 Dec 1927, 8, 27 July 1937, 29 May, 5 June, 13, 18, 19 July, 4 Aug 1939, 29 Jan, 5, 18 Sept 1941, 14 Jan, 14 Sept 1943, 6 Feb, 8 May 1945, 4 Feb 1946, 28 May, 1 July 1955; *Land* (Syd), 10 July 1958; information from Mr C. D. Renshaw, Binnaway, and Mr M. J. Kealey, Gosford, NSW.　　　　　G. P. WALSH

BARRY, SIR JOHN VINCENT WILLIAM (1903-1969), judge and criminologist, was born on 13 June 1903 at Albury, New South Wales, eldest child of Australian-born parents William Edward Barry, a house-painter of Irish descent, and his wife Sarah Lena Jeanette, née Keene. Educated at a local convent school, at St Patrick's College, Goulburn, and at the University of Melbourne, in 1921 John was articled to Luke Murphy and two years later qualified as a lawyer through the articled clerks' course. In this period he was involved in a murder trial which resulted in the accused being hanged. Barry became and remained an opponent of capital punishment.

Admitted to the Victorian Bar on 3 May 1926, he read with (Sir) Eugene Gorman [q.v.] who claimed to have learned more from Barry, with his 'high intelligence and precocious maturity', than Barry, twelve years younger, learned from him. Handsome and imposing, Barry progressed rapidly as a barrister. He proved himself versatile, initially developing an extensive jury practice, and later an appellate and High Court practice.

On 16 August 1930 at the district registrar's office, Mosman, Sydney, he married Ethel May Prior (d. 1943). He was a foundation vice-president (1935) of the Australian Council for Civil Liberties (president 1946) and foundation secretary of the Medico-Legal Society of Victoria (president 1948-49). While a member of the governing body of the Victorian Bar, he spearheaded measures aimed at curbing the discourtesy of Justice (Sir) James Macfarlan [q.v.10]. Barry joined the Australian Labor Party in 1939, stood unsuccessfully for the Federal seat of Balaclava in 1943 and was a member of the Victorian central executive in 1945-47. A member of the Australian Journalists' Association from 1943, he was elected chairman of its ethics committee. He was, as well, a member of the Overseas Telecommunications Commission in 1946-47.

At the Bar, Barry's progress was not diminished either by his willingness to represent unpopular causes, or by his political activism. Appointed K.C. in 1942, he was counsel assisting (Sir) Charles Lowe [q.v.] in the commission of inquiry into the Japanese air-raid (19 February) on Darwin. Next year he represented the Federal Labor politician Eddie Ward [q.v.] before the royal commission into the 'Brisbane Line'; in 1944 he was appointed commissioner to investigate the suspension of civil government in Papua. Arthur Calwell [q.v.] pressed hard in Federal cabinet to have Barry appointed to a vacancy on the High Court in 1946, but the attorney-general Dr H. V. Evatt preferred to woo the Catholic vote by appointing Sir William Webb [qq.v.] from Queensland.

On 14 January 1947 Barry was appointed to the Supreme Court of Victoria. Next year, he presided over *R.* v. *Jenkins, ex parte Morison*, which was to become famous as the 'Whose Baby' case, a bitterly-contested custody fight over a child who had been accidentally swapped in hospital. To Barry's displeasure, his decision to direct that the child be returned to its natural parents was reversed on appeal, with the ultimate outcome resting on the decision of Webb. On 28 July 1951 at the office of the government statist, Melbourne, Barry married 34-year-old Nancy Lorraine Hudson, a dress designer.

In his early years on the court Justice Barry was the one progressive element on an extremely conservative bench, but he soon showed that he was able to handle with ease any type of case. Many of his decisions broke new ground, particularly in the field of criminal law. During his later years on the court he sat almost exclusively in the matrimonial jurisdiction where he paved the way for no-fault divorce. It was said that he could find adultery proved on the evidence of an amorous glance. While it was unusual for a man of such distinguished intellect to choose to specialize in divorce, it suited the chief justice to have a judge who volunteered to do the work and who could do it so expeditiously. It also suited Barry to have more time for his interest in criminology. He continued to participate in appellate work.

After his appointment as a judge, Barry gave up most of his political activities, but he took on a great deal of extra-judicial work, concentrating on his writing and on the field of criminology where he was a crusader. Foundation chairman of the board of studies in the department of criminology at the University of Melbourne from 1951, and of the Victorian Parole Board from 1957, he remained deeply involved in the work of both until his death. He had advocated the introduction of the parole system as a means of conditioning the public to accept an alternative to imprisonment, and the lead that he set in parole was substantially copied elsewhere in Australia. He had a greater influence on Australian penological theory and practice than any contemporary.

In 1955 and 1960 Barry led two Australian delegations to United Nations congresses on the prevention of crime and on the treatment of offenders, the first at Geneva and the second in London. In 1960 he was appointed chairman of the section of the United Nations Congress that examined short-term imprisonment. So valued were his contributions to criminology in the Victorian and Australian contexts that Barry's memory would be perpetuated by having a lecture (University of Melbourne) and a library (Institute of Criminology, Canberra) named after him.

A prolific writer, he claimed that he did not find writing easy. His book, *Alexander Maconochie* [q.v.2] *of Norfolk Island* (1958), was an outstanding contribution in the spheres of criminology and Australian history. It substantially corrected previous misapprehensions as to the significance of Maconochie and led the University of Melbourne to confer a doctorate of laws (1969) upon Barry. His study (1964) of John Price [q.v.2], the inspector-general of penal establishments in Victoria who was murdered by convicts in 1857, has a special value in its analysis of cruelty and the abuse of power.

Barry was the co-author of texts on Australian criminal law and on the ethics of advocacy; he also contributed to the *Australian Dictionary of Biography*. He wrote journal articles on many subjects, although aspects of crime and punishment remained the primary focus of most. The first of his substantial articles in the *Australian Law Journal* had appeared in 1931. Lectures which he was unable to deliver in 1968 were published posthumously as *The Courts and Criminal Punishments* (1969). He admitted that many problems confounded him: he was baffled that some people acted criminally and others did not, concerned that some people might have been born with less capacity than others for pity or honesty, and determined that ignorance of such matters should be lessened. His writings evidenced his strong conviction that hanging, flogging and like punishments brutalized society, and were ineffective.

If the volume of Barry's learned writing was enormous, the number of letters that he wrote was prodigious. He corresponded regularly with the British reformer, Baroness Wootton of Abinger, who wrote: 'As everyone who knows him must agree, he is one of the most learned, stimulating, vital and kindly men that anyone could ever wish to meet. That he should also be a judge is a constant delight and astonishment to those whose judicial stereotypes are derived from the United Kingdom'.

Although he was a highly intelligent and industrious man, ready to be innovative and to adopt a more scientific approach to the law, Barry was also a person of great complexity, exemplified by many apparent contradictions, the most notable being his handling of his fellow men and women. He was a willing and courteous helper to many, whether judges seeking a second opinion, or academics with thorny curriculum or departmental problems, or prisoners wanting to be paroled. But to others who faced him on the bench, he was discourteous in the extreme, conducting his court in such an interventionist and autocratic way as to create widespread resentment. He could upbraid practitioners with acerbity, particularly for using words inappropriately. A similar approach had to be made to him about his behaviour on the bench to that which he himself had made to Macfarlan. In court he had difficulty in accepting that the high standards which he set for himself could not always reasonably be met by others. In 1959 he wrote of the sad decline since 1945 in the punctilious observance of the rules of court.

He was a perceptive critic, but his capacity for probing and sceptical analysis was not always appreciated. His disposition to stimulate others to action by persistently irritating them was also resented. Another of his annoying idiosyncrasies was his perfectionist attitude to his writing, which made him bristle at editors' suggestions of the slightest change.

Critical of others who accepted knighthoods, Barry was able to rationalize his own acceptance of the honour in 1961 as being the necessary consequence of 'having followed precedent'. He rejected dogmatic religion because of his refusal to accept anything he found to be irrational, yet he carried a St Christopher medal. His thousands of letters revealed his reasoned analysis of numerous problems, but little of his deeper feelings. Described by more than one commentator as being a felicitous user of words, he was almost inarticulate on the subject of his own relationships. He had strong ties to his mother and was greatly influenced by her, and was happily married twice, but his perception of the role of women was conservative.

Late in life Sir John graduated from the University of Melbourne (LL.B., 1963). In 1966-69 he was the senior puisne judge of the Supreme Court. Barry died of cancer on 8 November 1969 at Armadale, Melbourne. A rationalist and sceptic for most of his life, he was cremated without a service. His wife and their daughter survived him, as did the son and daughter of his first marriage.

Chief Justice Sir Henry Winneke said of Barry in his tribute delivered in court on 11 November 1969: 'Wide learning, subtlety and alertness of mind, constant industry and great courage he possessed in ample measure. These fine qualities combined with a deep compassion for those in adversity or distress to produce a character which earned him the everlasting affection of his friends and the admiration and respect of his profession'.

B. Wootton, *In a World I Never Made* (Lond, 1967); A. A. Calwell, *Be Just and Fear Not* (Melb, 1972); N. Morris and M. Perlman, *Law and Crime, Essays in Honour of Sir John Barry* (NY, 1972); *Victorian Reports*, 1969; *Univ Tas Law Review*, 1970; Barry papers (NL).   BERNARD TEAGUE

BARRY, KEITH LEWIS (1896-1965), medical practitioner, musician and journalist, was born on 11 September 1896 at Parramatta, New South Wales, son of native-born parents Alfred Barry, musician, and his wife Ruth Ann, née Meads. Alfred was a teacher and organist who inculcated in his young son a love and appreciation of music. Keith attended Hayfield and Sydney Grammar schools. At the University of Sydney he enrolled in medicine, held the Busby musical scholarship and was a committee-member of the glee club. Having been refused enlistment in Australia, Barry sailed for England in 1916. Commissioned in the Dorset Regiment on 30 May 1917, he served on the North-West Frontier in India, and with the Royal Flying Corps in India and Egypt. He was promoted lieutenant in November 1918, sent on special duties to Ireland and demobilized in 1919.

Back in Sydney, Barry entered Wesley College and graduated from the university (M.B., Ch.M., 1924). After studying in England, he became a doctor at the Newcastle coalfields, New South Wales, and in 1927 bought a busy practice at Dee Why. Intensely active and versatile, he presided over the university musical society, organized and conducted a local choral society, became organist of the Mosman Presbyterian Church and music critic for the Sydney *Daily Telegraph*, and began writing anonymously a weekly column, 'The Diary of a Doctor Who Tells', which was to be syndicated throughout Australia for thirty years.

On 19 February 1929 Barry married Gladys Ada Price at St Stephen's Presbyterian Church, Sydney. Late in 1930 he was found to have contracted pulmonary tuberculosis and was immediately sent to a sanatorium in the Blue Mountains. Barry stoically accepted the apparent end of his medical and musical activities, but continued his 'Diary' and wrote *Music and the Listener* (1933). Against all expectations he recovered from his illness by 1934. As a ship's doctor, he worked his passage to Britain where, in addition to gaining further medical experience in various hospitals, he studied developments in radio in England and Germany. He regularly broadcast for the British Broadcasting Corporation.

On his return to Sydney, Barry resumed as music critic for the *Daily Telegraph*, and wrote and broadcast for the Australian Broadcasting Commission. He was invited to become its part-time programme adviser and in October 1936 was appointed controller of programmes (assistant general manager — programmes from 1958); he fostered the growth of the A.B.C.'s music, concert and spoken-word broadcasting. Level-headed and diplomatic in many early crises over broadcasting policy, Barry impressed his colleagues with his affability, sense of humour and indefatigable nature. He made frequent overseas visits for the A.B.C. and represented Australia at meetings of the United Nations Educational, Scientific and Cultural Organization and of the International Music Council. He was a federal vice-president of the Arts Council of Australia.

Although he no longer practised, Barry managed to keep abreast of medical developments, as reflected in his weekly 'Diary' and in his work from 1948 as State and later federal president of the National Tuberculosis and Chest Association. He also helped to organize tuberculosis conferences in Sydney in 1955 and 1960 which were opened by Sydney Symphony Orchestra concerts in the university's Great Hall. Throughout his life he remained a member of the State branch of the British Medical Association, the postgraduate committee in medicine at the University of Sydney and the Australian College of General Practitioners.

Of shortish stature and inclined to rotundity with age, Barry nevertheless possessed remarkable agility as a sportsman: he was a low-handicap golfer and, as an A-grade tennis player, regularly defeated younger colleagues to win the annual A.B.C. tennis championship. He belonged to the New South Wales Lawn Tennis Association, and to the University, Journalists' and Leura Golf clubs. Having retired from the A.B.C. in 1960, he continued energetically and enthusiastically his music and cultural activities, launching the first Sydney Northside Arts Festival in 1963 and journeying abroad several times. He died of coronary vascular disease on 14 January 1965 at his Wollstonecraft home and was cremated with Anglican rites. His wife and son Graham, who became a leading medical practitioner in the Bahamas, survived him.

G. E. Hall and A. Cousins (eds), *Book of Remembrance of the University of Sydney in the War 1914-1918* (Syd, 1939); *Home*, 1 Oct 1933; ABC, *Radio-Active*, Mar 1949, Oct 1960, Jan 1965; NSW National Tuberculosis and Chest Assn, *Report*, June 1965, p 9; *MJA*, 21 Aug 1965; *Bulletin*, 17 Mar 1927, 23 Nov 1960; *SMH*, 16 Jan 1965; ABC Archives, Syd.   CLEMENT SEMMLER

BARRY, WILLIAM PETER (1899-1972), trade union official and politician, was born on 30 June 1899 at Northcote, Melbourne, fifth child of William Barry, miner, and his wife Susan Agatha, née Robinson, both native-born. William senior was a founder of the Quarrymen's Union and an organizer of the Municipal Employees' Union. Educated at St Brigid's School, North Fitzroy, and St George's School, Carlton, young Bill became a foundry worker at the Newport railway workshops. At 17 he joined the British Australasian Tobacco Co. Pty Ltd where his duties included tobacco-tasting; for the rest of his life he was an inveterate pipe-smoker. On 16 August 1924 at St Mary's Catholic Church, West Melbourne, he married a machinist Mary Moodie.

An aggressive debater and prominent member of the Carlton branch of the Australian Labor Party, Barry was secretary of the Tobacco Workers' Union in 1924-31. Having won a surprise pre-selection victory over William Slater [q.v.], in July 1932 he was returned at a Legislative Assembly by-election for Labor's blue-ribbon seat of Carlton. 'Something of a favourite' of John Wren [q.v.12], Barry led the right-wing faction and was secretary of the parliamentary Labor Party in 1938-55. Minister of transport in the four-day Cain [q.v.] government of September 1943, he held the portfolios of health, housing and forests under Cain in 1945-47 and was again minister of health in Cain's cabinet in 1952-55.

Bill was a genial man with a flair for pub-

licity, but his use of invective often embarrassed his colleagues: he labelled (Sir) Archie Michaelis [q.v.] a 'refo'; he said of (Sir) Wilfrid Kent Hughes [q.v.] that 'a few years in the Jap camps did not do him much good'; he accused Melbourne city councillors of 'racketeering'; he forced Cecil McVilly [q.v.10] to resign as chairman of the Hospitals and Charities Commission and branded him a 'Sawdust Caesar'. Barry never lacked ambition. He contested the deputy-leadership after the death of Herbert Cremean [q.v.] in 1945 and hoped to displace Cain as leader. Barry's wife Mary, 'a woman of notably independent and outspoken mind', served on the central executive of the Victorian branch of the party in 1950-55 and was secretary (1947-55) of the women's central organizing committee.

The Barrys had little to do with the industrial groups, but were staunch anti-communists. In the split of 1955—an event which Barry tried to avert—both were expelled from the Labor Party. Barry became joint-leader (with Patrick Coleman) of the Anti-Communist Labor Party (later the Democratic Labor Party). When Barry led his breakaway group across the floor in April 1955—in support of the no confidence motion which brought down the Cain government—thirty pieces of silver were thrown at his feet. In the ensuing election the contest for Carlton was 'the bitterest and most violent of the campaign'. Barry received dead rats in the mail. Defeated by Labor's Denis Lovegrove [q.v.], as a D.L.P. candidate Barry unsuccessfully contested Fitzroy in 1961 and Greensborough in 1967.

A member (1939-55) of the Melbourne City Council, Barry had been its representative on the Melbourne and Metropolitan Board of Works (1945-55) and on the Olympic Organising Committee (1952-55); he was also a trustee (1946-55) of the Exhibition Building. Kate White's biography of John Cain has referred to allegations that Barry was corrupt when minister for housing, but there is no evidence of personal wealth. After losing his seat, he ran a milk bar and later a licensed grocery. In his last years he lived in an East Brunswick hotel. Survived by his wife, three sons and four daughters, he died on 21 December 1972 at Fitzroy and was buried in Melbourne general cemetery.

R. Murray, *The Split* (Melb, 1972); K. White, *John Cain and Victorian Labor, 1917-1957* (Syd, 1982); *Herald* (Melb), 30 June 1953, 21 Dec 1972; information from Mr W. P. Barry, Rosanna, Melb.
                                                            GEOFF BROWNE

BARTON, EDWARD GUSTAVUS CAMPBELL (1857-1942), electrical engineer, was born on 11 December 1857, at Toorak, Melbourne, son of George Elliott Barton, a barrister from Ireland, and his Scottish wife Jane Crichton, née Campbell. Edward attended school at Dunedin, New Zealand, received engineering training in Scotland and studied in Germany at Karlsruhe Polytechnische Schule in 1875-79. Gaining further experience in Scotland, in 1882 he superintended the first commercial electric-lighting system in Britain at Godalming, Surrey. He returned to New Zealand and became a consultant there, and in Australia, for the next three years. During this period he erected electrical plant for the Phoenix Gold Mines at Gympie, Queensland, and worked for the Australasian Electric Light, Power & Storage Co. Engaged in 1886 to complete lighting installations in the parliamentary buildings and the government printing office in Brisbane, he was appointed government electrician. He was retained as an adviser after he resigned in 1888 to form a partnership with C. F. White.

By mid-1888 Barton, White & Co., manufacturers of electrical equipment, were ready to supply electric light to the public from a small, direct-current generator driven by a steam-engine. Their first customer was the General Post Office in Brisbane, but progress was slow in the face of conservatism and competition from gas. Barton married Mary Allen Sutton on 13 September 1893 at the general registry offices, Brisbane. In 1896 the company went into liquidation, and was then reformed as the Brisbane Electric Supply Co. Ltd, of which Barton was manager. Its first power station, in Edison Lane, off Creek Street, was superseded within eleven years by a new building in Ann Street, where in 1901 Barton installed the first steam turbine in Queensland. The firm became the City Electric Light Co. Ltd in 1904: Barton was general manager and a director before resigning to become a consultant. In 1908 he was elected to the Legislative Assembly as a member for Brisbane North, but did not seek re-election the following year.

Closely interested in technical education, Barton had lectured (part time) on electricity in 1889 and in electrical engineering and physics until 1904 at the Brisbane Technical College; he was president (1905) of its council. In 1901 he had proclaimed his enthusiasm for the establishment of a local university in his inaugural address to the Queensland Institute of Engineers; in 1910 he was appointed to the first senate of the University of Queensland and chaired the buildings and grounds committee.

Though Barton's venture in Barton, White & Co. had been opposed by his parents who doubted his business ability and mistrusted his partner, Barton showed vision and versatility in successfully pioneering the State's electricity-supply industry. He was noted for cultivating a comprehensive knowledge which he was always willing to share with his staff. Unpretentious, active and keenly interested in sport, he was also aware of social problems and served as president (1910-15) of the Brisbane Institute of Social Service.

The variety of technical papers which Barton contributed to learned societies reflected a range of interests that included wireless telegraphy. His views on electric railways were advanced: in a lecture to the Queensland Electrical Association in 1901 he had argued the advantages of alternating current over direct current and outlined its possible application to south-east Queensland. A councillor (1892) of the Queensland Institute of Mechanical Engineers, he was president of the Queensland Electrical Association (1899-1900) and of the Queensland Institute of Engineers (1901-02). In Queensland from 1907 to 1915 he represented the Institution of Electrical Engineers, London, of which he was a member. A founding associate member of the Institution of Engineers, Australia, he became a member in 1921. He was a fellow of the Royal Meteorological Society (1909) and the Royal Geographical Society, London (1914).

In 1915 Barton went to England to work for the British Ministry of Munitions. Possibly because of his fluency in French, German and Italian, he later joined an information department of the Admiralty. About 1918 he developed an interest in the British Decimal Association whose members regarded him as a lecturer of 'unexcelled interest and charm'; he was the association's chairman in 1938-42. Barton made Europe his home after World War I, but visited Australia several times in the 1920s. Survived by his son, he died on 14 June 1942 at Watford, Hertfordshire, England, and was cremated.

R. L. Whitmore (ed), *Eminent Queensland Engineers* (Brisb, 1984), and for bibliog; S. A. Prentice, 'Edward Barton, Pioneer Electrical Engineer', *Memoirs of the Qld Museum*, 27, pt 1, Sept 1988; W. I. George and S. A. Prentice, Some References to Early Professional Engineering Societies in Queensland (1890-1919), 1989, *and* S. A. Prentice, Contributions by E. G. C. Barton to Technical Education in Queensland, 1990 (tss, Fryer L).

S. A. PRENTICE

BARUNGA, ALBERT (1910?-1977), Aboriginal community leader, was born probably in 1910 at Kunmunya, near Derby, Western Australia. His father Arai and mother Maudie Kaiimbinya belonged to the Worora tribe, into which Albert was initiated. The family lived as hunter-gatherers. During

World War I Arai was accused of murder, arrested and taken away in chains; the charge was found to be false and he was released from prison; he died in 1919. To avoid adoption by his uncle 'Big Charlie', Albert joined Willie Reid, a part-Aboriginal pearler and fisherman, from whom he learned sailing skills and a knowledge of coastal waters. The association ended when Barunga was taken to the Kunmunya Presbyterian Mission.

Because he was too old to attend school, he was taught to ride horses and handle cattle. Following the arrival in 1927 of Rev. J. R. B. Love [q.v.10], Barunga formed a close association with the new missioner and helped to translate the Gospel of St Mark into the Worora language. Albert showed aptitude for learning and became fluent in English. In 1929 he assisted (Sir) Charles Kingsford Smith [q.v.9] who had been forced to land the *Southern Cross* on the flats of the Glenelg River estuary. Barunga guided Australian naval vessels on coastal patrols in 1942 and also worked for the Americans in wartime.

After 1945 Kunmunya mission fell into decline. In 1951 the three tribes who lived there decided to move to Wotjulum, near the Cockatoo Island iron-ore mine. Finding this site unsuitable, they shifted five years later to Mowanjum in the vicinity of Derby. Barunga's intended wife Cudiana died shortly after giving birth to their child. On 30 December 1956 he married her sister Barbara Pugjawola at the Presbyterian Mission Church, Mowanjum. With Alan Mungulu, Albert endeavoured to keep the three tribal groups together, and worked to revive and maintain their traditions. 'Whatever he did, he seemed to do well, whether it was riding a horse, spearing a fish, growing tomatoes, sailing a lugger, or telling a story.'

While visiting New Zealand on an adult-education tour in the late 1960s, Barunga was impressed by the evident strength of Maori culture which contrasted with the extensive loss of Aboriginal heritage. In late 1969 he became an enthusiastic member of the Aboriginal Theatre Foundation, established that year to revive traditional dances and crafts; he was later president of its West Kimberley branch. A leading councillor at Mowanjum, he was also active on a range of other State and Federal committees, and emerged as a spokesman for tribal Australia. In 1972 he delivered a paper, 'Sacred Sites and their Protection', to a national seminar organized in Canberra by the Australian Institute of Aboriginal Studies. Housed in the capital by an anthropologist Professor Derek Freeman, he lobbied ministers for Aboriginal Affairs and advocated 'friendship and harmony between black and white'. He once remarked: 'if everybody asked and talked things over then we could all work together, and live happy together in the world'—words which exemplified the gentle and intelligent temperament for which he was widely esteemed.

Barunga died of a cerebral embolus on 30 August 1977 at Derby and was buried in the local cemetery with the forms of the Uniting Church. His daughter and seven sons survived him.

M. McKenzie, *The Road to Mowanjum* (Syd, 1969); *Visions of Mowanjum* (Adel, 1980); *Identity*, Oct 1971, p 17; *Overland*, no 101, 1985, p 85; The Worora, Albert Barunga and the Rev J. R. B. Love: edited conversation between D. Freeman and Mrs M. Love, Adel, 1972 (ms Aust Inst of Aboriginal Studies, Canb); Dept of Aboriginal Affairs (WA) file on A. Barunga.   WARWICK DIX

BASSER, SIR ADOLPH (1887-1964), optician, jeweller and philanthropist, was born on 26 June 1887 at Kraców, Austria-Hungary (Poland), son of Jewish parents (Leo) Wolf Basser, a stall-owner, and his second wife Lea, née Glaser. Named Abraham, he left school at 15, continued his education with private tutors and was trained in optometry in Berlin. Styling himself Adolph, he migrated to New South Wales in 1908 and joined his half-brother Isadore at Lithgow. Basser became a travelling salesman, peddling spectacles to settlers in isolated areas. He was subsequently to explain his success: 'I didn't watch the clock, I worked very hard. But I am not a worrier'.

By 1910 he was practising as an optician in Challis House, Sydney, with another half-brother Solomon (d. 1918). On 18 December 1912 Adolph married Miriam Nelson with Jewish rites at her father's Darlinghurst home. Naturalized next year, he was 5 ft 8 ins (172.7 cm) tall and stockily built, with black hair and brown eyes. After an informer had accused him of being an 'enemy subject', Basser was cleared by military intelligence in 1916. Late that year he moved with his wife to Darling Point. Both dabbled in real estate; Miriam had owned land since 1910 in Clarence Street. About 1916 he transferred his business there. By 1921 he had established Deller & Basser Ltd, manufacturing jewellers, in the same street and was also to register under the Opticians Amendment Act of 1931.

Basser formed a proprietary company to buy out one of his major customers, the large Sydney manufacturing jewellers, Saunders Ltd, in December 1928. He kept his office in its three-storeyed, corner building in Railway Square. As managing director, he expanded the business rapidly. During the Depression he bought the stock of other jewellers, held a sale and made a handsome profit. In 1931 he acquired a rival firm, William Farmer & Co.

Ltd, and opened branch stores, designed to display 'the finest jewellery and gifts', on the corners of Liverpool and Pitt streets in 1933 and King and Pitt streets in 1935. The business flourished after World War II and in December 1948 Saunders Ltd was registered as a public company. Its Wollongong branch was opened by the premier J. J. Cahill [q.v.] in April 1957. The company merged with Angus & Coote (Holdings) Ltd in 1960 and Basser became a director.

From 1916, when his horse had won at the Kensington pony track and he had collected £200, Basser's great love was racing. In the decade following World War II he spent lavishly at yearling sales and bought more than forty horses. He paid 2600 guineas for the yearling which he later raced as Delta. Trained by Maurice McCarten and ridden by Neville Sellwood [qq.v.], Delta won £48 169 in prize-money and twenty-two races, including the Victoria Derby (1949), the Victoria Racing Club St Leger (1950), and in 1951 the Australian Jockey Club Metropolitan and the Melbourne Cup. Basser reputedly won £50 000 in bets on Delta in the cup, and divided the £10 000 prize between McCarten and Sellwood. A careful punter, Basser stuck mainly to his own horses, such as Empire Link (winner of the Queen Elizabeth Stakes in 1953) and Indian Empire (for which he paid 4000 guineas, the top price at the Melbourne yearling sales that year).

Keenly interested in scientific and medical research, in 1950 Basser gave £50 000 to the Royal Australasian College of Physicians. He endowed the Adolph Basser Trust with £100 000 in 1953 and next year gave £50 000 to the University of Sydney to build its first computer; he later doubled both gifts. Appointed C.B.E. in 1955, he was awarded an honorary doctorate of science by the University of Sydney the same year. A string of large donations followed, chiefly to hospitals, and to medical, scientific and educational bodies, including £25 000 each to St Vincent's Hospital, the National Heart Foundation and Mount Scopus College, Melbourne, £40 000 to found Basser College, University of New South Wales, and £20 000 to Beth Rivkah Girls' College, Melbourne.

As well as his more spectacular benefactions, Basser helped many individuals and small projects, and supported Jewish, Christian and non-denominational causes, among them the Sir Moses Montefiore Jewish Home, the Children's Medical Research Foundation, the Sydney Opera House and the Federation of New South Wales Police-Citizens Boys' Clubs (of which he was made a life governor in 1957). He also provided a fountain for Chifley Square, Sydney, and a £100 prize for the best contribution to *Quadrant*. Each year from 1952 he bought a £1000 Legacy badge which

he had made into cufflinks. When he went south for the Melbourne Cup he contributed annually to the Lord Mayor's Fund for Metropolitan Hospitals and Charities.

Quiet, well-dressed and bespectacled, Basser was a modest figure at the many ceremonies that marked his benefactions. 'It gives me happiness to give away money', he said in 1960, in his marked Polish accent, on donating £25 000 to establish a library at the Australian Academy of Science, Canberra. A 'sprightly man', noted for his 'gentle manner' and the 'twinkle in his eye', Basser enjoyed an occasional game of golf or bowls, and 'was partial to a drop of Scotch'. He belonged to Tattersall's, the Australian Jockey and Manly Golf clubs, and to the Royal Automobile Club of Australia. Every two years he took a sea cruise to unwind and also to meet his scattered relations.

Knighted in 1962, Basser suffered a stroke that year and retired from public life. He died on 20 October 1964 at his Edgecliff home and was cremated with Methodist forms; his wife and son survived him. Basser's estate was sworn for probate at £610 416; he left his racing trophies to his godson John Sellwood and made bequests to his relations in Australia, New York, London, Berlin and Israel. Sir Adolph's portrait is held by Basser College.

C. H. Bertie, *Days of Moment in Australia, 1788-1938* (Syd, 1937); D. Barrie, *The Australian Bloodhorse* (Syd, 1956); B. Ahern, *A Century of Winners* (Brisb, 1988); *SMH*, 7 Nov 1951, 2 July 1953, 13 Feb 1954, 6, 15 May, 15 Dec 1955, 18 Feb 1956, 4, 28 Apr, 27 Aug, 20 Sept 1957, 5 Feb, 4 Sept 1958, 22 June, 2 July 1959, 2 Feb, 12 Mar 1960, 2 June 1962, 2 Sept 1963, 21 Oct 1964; *Bulletin*, 9 Oct 1957; *Sun News-Pictorial*, 2 June 1962; *Herald* (Melb), 21 Oct 1964; *Syd Jewish News*, 23 Oct 1964; *Sun-Herald*, 8 Sept 1985; Naturalization file, A1 25/20670 (AA, Canb); Intelligence file, ST 1233/1, item N 3084 (AA, Syd).   ANDREW LEMON
MARTHA RUTLEDGE

BASSETT, FLORA MARJORIE, 'MARNIE' (1889-1980), historian, was born on 30 June 1889 at the University of Melbourne, daughter of (Sir) David Orme Masson [q.v.10], professor of chemistry, and his wife Mary, née Struthers. (Sir) James Irvine Orme Masson [q.v.10] was her brother. Marnie spent 'delicious childhood years' on Melbourne's campus, fishing for yabbies in the university lake, accompanied by Professor (Sir) Walter Baldwin Spencer's [q.v.12] children, and bicycling on the curving drive around the System Garden. With her only sister Elsie, she was taught at home by governesses; for twelve weeks at the age of 17 Marnie was enrolled at the Church of England Girls' Grammar School. After taking shorthand and typing lessons, she became her father's secretary, helping him in 1914 to organize the Melbourne conference of the British Association for the Advancement of Science. There she met eminent scientists, among them her future brother-in-law, the anthropologist Bronislaw Malinowski.

Marnie's family background and three extensive trips to Europe in her girlhood fostered her love of history, literature and music. Although her mother did not favour degree courses for girls, in her early twenties Marnie attended history lectures given by Professor (Sir) Ernest Scott [q.v.11]. Encouraged by him, she studied a parcel of neglected papers and, in an article in the *University Review* in June 1913, concluded that the true founder of the university had been Hugh Childers [q.v.3]. While her conclusion has now been refuted, her article was remarkable for its initiative and perception, and indicated an unusual historical aptitude. At Scott's request, in 1915 she gave five lectures to history students on French colonial policy and was awarded a government research scholarship that year.

Before she could complete her research, Marnie became absorbed in war-work as secretary to Professor Richard Berry [q.v.7] who had been appointed part-time registrar of the 5th Australian General Hospital. When (Sir) David Rivett [q.v.11] succeeded him, she continued her secretarial duties, transferring with Rivett to the 11th A.G.H., Caulfield. In 1916 she sailed for England: her ship *Arabia* was torpedoed in the eastern Mediterranean and she escaped in a lifeboat before being rescued. In London she worked with (Sir) Henry Barraclough [q.v.7], honorary lieutenant-colonel in charge of Australian munitions workers in England and France. She wrote lively letters home to her father, trenchantly defending democracy against his increasing pessimism. Having returned to Melbourne, she met (Sir) Walter Bassett [q.v.], a senior lecturer in engineering; they were married on 25 January 1923 at her father's university home by Rev. Dr Edward Sugden [q.v.12] of Queen's College.

Marnie was an unaffectedly domestic person, devoted to her husband and family; she refused to employ a nanny for her three children. She was equally devoted to her friends, especially the females, many of whom were intellectuals. She had been one of the earliest members of the Catalysts, a women's discussion group founded in Melbourne in 1910, and the papers she read to that society are among her most vigorous and evocative writings. Such pursuits kept her mind active during her child-rearing years.

On the eve of World War II, with her children growing up, Marnie again began to write. *The Governor's Lady* (1940), a study of Anna Josepha, the wife of Philip Gidley King [qq.v.2], made Marnie a pioneer in the then neglected field of women's history. Her most celebrated book, *The Hentys* (1954), is a classic in Australian history, combining diligent research, intelligent handling of historical evidence, and a prose style that is clear and harmonious. She also published two works on voyages of discovery, *Realms and Islands* (1962) and *Behind the Picture* (1966), and a vivid volume called *Letters from New Guinea, 1921* (1969) which described her travels when aged 32. In her ninety-first year she was engaged on a life of Henry Gisborne [q.v.1] which was published posthumously with one of her Catalyst papers as *Henry Fyshe Gisborne and 'Once Upon a Time . . .'* (1985). When writing several of her books she attended weekly seminars at the university and was a great encourager of young historians.

Lady Bassett's achievement was recognized by honorary D.Litt. degrees from Monash University (1968) and the University of Melbourne (1974); she also became a foundation fellow (1969) of the Australian Academy of the Humanities. These honours were a particular source of pleasure to one who had never enrolled at a university. Survived by her daughter and a son, Marnie Bassett died on 3 February 1980 at her Armadale home and was cremated.

G. Blainey, *A Centenary History of the University of Melbourne* (Melb, 1957); J. M. Gillison, *A History of the Lyceum Club* (Melb, 1975); L. M. Weickhardt, *Masson of Melbourne* (Melb, 1989); *Univ Melb Gazette*, June 1980; *Age*, 23 Feb 1980; M. Bassett papers (LaTL *and* Univ Melb Archives); personal information.   ANN BLAINEY

BASSETT, SIR WALTER ERIC (1892-1978), engineer, was born on 19 December 1892 at Hawthorn, Melbourne, son of Walter Bassett, salesman, and his wife Caroline, née Loxton, both English born. Young Bassett was educated at Wesley College and at the University of Melbourne (B.E., 1916; M.Mech.E., 1927). Commissioned in the Australian Imperial Force on 30 September 1915 and posted to the 5th Field Company, Engineers, he embarked on 23 November 1915 for Egypt and served on the Western Front. On the night of 4/5 August 1916 at Pozières, France, he won the Military Cross for constructing machine-gun emplacements in captured trenches and for digging a communication trench while under heavy fire. He transferred as lieutenant to the Australian Flying Corps on 19 April 1917 and served with No. 40 Squadron. Wounded in action on 1 June, he was evacuated to England and declared permanently unfit for service. After his appointment terminated on 28 January 1918, he studied aeronautics. He returned to Melbourne with a seriously damaged hip which necessitated the use of one or two walking-sticks for the rest of his life.

On 25 January 1923 Bassett married with Methodist forms Flora Marjorie 'Marnie' [q.v. Bassett] at the university residence of her father Sir David Masson [q.v.10]. Bassett had joined the staff of the university's engineering school in 1919: he lectured in mechanical engineering and aerodynamics, and organized the building of the first wind tunnel in Australia. Enjoying the right of private practice and a growing reputation as an engineer, he was consulted by an increasing number of architects about projects which required the heating and ventilation of such buildings as St Paul's Cathedral chapter house, Frankston Orthopaedic Hospital, and the Melbourne and Williamstown town halls.

In 1928 Bassett began a full-time consulting engineering practice, W. E. Bassett & Partners. During the Depression his office designed and supervised the construction of steam, heating, hot-water and ventilation services in St Vincent's, the Austin, Epworth and Mercy hospitals, Melbourne, and in the Wangaratta hospital, as well as in office buildings and stores for G. J. Coles [q.v.] throughout Australia, and in many smaller city buildings. Among his early designs was the full air-conditioning of the Bank of New South Wales's new headquarters in Melbourne, using a 50-ton R carbon dioxide machine. Later, the first centrifugal machines to be used in Australia were the Bassett-designed installations in Parliament House, Adelaide, and in the head office of the *Courier-Mail*, Brisbane. He completed industrial commissions for Australian Paper Manufacturers Ltd and Ford Motor Co. Ltd, and at MacRobertson's [q.v.11 Robertson] Pty Ltd where a 650-psi (4.4 megapascals) boiler was installed. By 1939 the practice had opened offices in New South Wales.

During World War II Bassett was chairman of the Army Mechanisation Board and a member of the Commonwealth Advisory Committee for Aeronautics. His practice was involved in work for the Department of Aircraft Production, the Allied Works Council, various munition buildings and the new military hospitals located in each State. For the Royal Australian Air Force, he designed and installed six low-pressure chambers to enable personnel to be trained for high-altitude operations. He was commissioned by Commonwealth Serum Laboratories to assist with the installation of a bottle-fermentation plant for penicillin production.

The decade 1945-55 marked a period of postwar recovery. Bassett's office was responsible for building services in country hospitals and in numerous factories that sprang up or were relocated in the outer suburbs. He also provided large, high-pressure, hot-water boilers for General Motors-Holden's [q.v.9] Ltd and the bagasse incinerator boilers for the Queensland sugar industry.

His practice had employed a staff of two in 1928; by his retirement in 1971, the staff numbered two hundred and fifty, located in nine offices, with three associate companies overseas. Bassett retained control of 'things technical and things business', but, to ensure the continuity of a professional organization, he allowed junior engineers with ability to progress to senior level and partnership, regardless of their 'parents or finance'. Thus the firm prospered through the post-1955 boom years. Bassett remained an active consultant until his death.

A member of the engineering faculty of the University of Melbourne until 1957, Bassett won its Kernot [q.v.5] medal in 1948. He contributed to the establishment of a degree course in aeronautical engineering in Sydney and to the establishment of the Aeronautical Research Laboratories at Fishermans Bend, Melbourne. In 1958 he joined the interim council of Monash University: through its building committee, he had much to do with the original planning; he was to be a member of its first council and its engineering faculty until 1973; the main lecture theatre in the engineering school bears his name. Bassett was awarded honorary doctorates of engineering (Monash University, 1970) and of laws (University of Melbourne, 1974).

Knighted in 1959, Bassett was active in professional and community affairs. A foundation member and president (1942) of the Institution of Engineers, Australia, he had received its (Sir) Peter Nicol Russell [q.v.6] medal for 1958. He was an honorary member of the Australasian Institute of Mining and Metallurgy (from 1973) and a member of the Gas and Fuel Corporation of Victoria Ltd (1951-75). His company directorships included Mount Lyell Mining & Railway Co. Ltd (president 1969-74), Renison Ltd (chairman 1958-68), the Colonial Mutual Life Assurance Society Ltd and several fertilizer companies. Sir Walter was a trustee and sometime chairman of the Museum of Applied Science in Melbourne, and an honorary consultant and member of the finance committee of the radio telescope at Parkes, New South Wales. In 1963 he was elected president of the Melbourne Club. He was also foundation president of the Copper Producers' Association of Australia.

Bassett was a forceful and decisive character who found it hard to tolerate foolishness, but was forgiving of ignorance. The uninformed he set out to educate, lucidly and patiently. He had an uncanny knack of grasping the salient problems and of solving them at the outset. A formidably competent person, he succeeded in his work, and in his recreations which included sailing, fishing, golf and woodwork. His life, perhaps more than that of most men, was a joint affair. In the Bassett home he and Marnie created an environment of singular quality—warm and hospitable, stimulating and interesting. He died on 8 March 1978 at Toorak and was cremated. His wife, daughter and a son survived him; his elder son was drowned in World War II. J. Carington Smith's [q.v.] portrait of Sir Walter is held by the University of Melbourne.

A. E. Tweddell (comp), *W. E. Bassett and Partners* (priv pub, Melb, nd); R. Proudley, *Circle of Influence* (Melb, 1987); Inst of Engineers, Aust, *J,* Jan 1959; *Univ Melb Gazette,* July 1970, June 1978; *The Times,* 21 Mar 1978; Univ Melb Archives.

J. S. HARDY

BASTOW, STEWART HENRY (1908-1964), chemist and administrator, was born on 22 February 1908 at Folkestone, Kent, England, second son of Arthur Henry Bastow, engineer, and his wife Muriel Amy, née Bazeley. Arthur's father Henry Robert Bastow had trained as an architect (with the author Thomas Hardy) at Dorchester in the 1850s before migrating to Tasmania. Educated at The Hutchins School, Hobart, Stewart had a strict upbringing. He attended the University of Tasmania (B.Sc., 1929) and undertook research in electrochemistry for A. L. McAulay [q.v.10]. Of imposing physique, Bastow rowed for the university and was Australian royal tennis champion in 1929.

L. F. Giblin [q.v.8]—a man whom Bastow was long to admire—advised him to enter King's College, Cambridge (Ph.D., 1932). At the university's physical chemistry laboratory, he studied surface chemistry under (Sir) Eric Rideal and was awarded an 1851 Exhibition senior studentship; with F. P. Bowden [q.v.], Bastow investigated the physical properties of solid and liquid surfaces. He was captain of the university's real tennis team and won a half-Blue; one of his friends was C. P. (Baron) Snow. From 1934 Bastow gained industrial research experience in England. On 20 August 1937 in St Mary Magdalene's parish church, Littleton, Middlesex, he married Perle ('Pam') Camden.

Having joined the Anglo-Iranian Oil Co. Ltd that year as senior chemist, in 1938 Bastow established a laboratory at Masjid-i-Sulaiman, Iran, to examine 'drilling-mud' problems in the oilfields. He returned to England following the outbreak of World War II. Commissioned in the Royal Engineers in December 1940, he was promoted temporary

major on 9 July 1943. As officer commanding No. 806 Smoke Company, he had the task of laying smokescreens to cover assaults during the allied advance across North-West Europe in 1944-45. He was awarded the Distinguished Service Order (1945).

In April 1945 he secured a release from military service to take up the post of officer-in-charge of the Council for Scientific and Industrial Research's lubricants and bearings (tribophysics) section at the University of Melbourne. Bastow's leadership and wisdom enabled him to transform a wartime programme of research and development to one geared to peacetime needs, despite problems of staff shortages and unsuitable accommodation. He planned a new laboratory, and established groups to work on metal physics, chemical reaction kinetics and the properties of clay suspensions. In early 1947 Bastow visited the Territory of Papua-New Guinea where he advised the Australian Petroleum Co. Pty Ltd on drilling-fluids. Next year C.S.I.R.'s tribophysics section was raised to divisional status.

Interested in languages, in 1948 Bastow completed a course in Russian at the University of Melbourne and translated a Russian monograph which was published as *Hardness Reducers in Drilling* (1948). In May 1949 he was appointed a full-time member of the executive of the Commonwealth Scientific and Industrial Research Organization, a position he was to hold until his death; from January 1957 to June 1959 he was chief executive officer. Responsible for land research and regional survey, he championed C.S.I.R.O.'s efforts to develop the resources of northern Australia. He was also involved in harnessing his country's limited water supplies: having participated in a joint Commonwealth-States conference in 1959 on underground water, he was appointed in 1960 to the Australian Academy of Science's standing committee on hydrology.

Bastow travelled frequently throughout Australia, promoting the research achievements of C.S.I.R.O., expounding the benefits that science could bring to the community and advocating the application of scientific research to industry. His modesty and charm made him a popular visitor at C.S.I.R.O.'s laboratories and outlying field-stations, while he was much sought as a speaker by a range of organizations. An unpretentious man, he became impatient with pompous people and used searching questions to bring them down to earth. He was sympathetic, ready to assist juniors, and 'made it his business to get to know personally as many members of the staff as possible and kept a diary in which he recorded the details of their background and work'. Vice-president (1962) of the Royal Australian Chemical Institute, he was a member (from 1963) of the council of Monash University.

Survived by his wife, daughter and four sons, Bastow died of cardiac disease on 23 January 1964 in Melbourne and was cremated after a secular service. A laboratory at C.S.I.R.O.'s division of materials science and technology, Clayton, was named after him.

Roy Aust Chemical Inst, *Procs*, Feb 1964, p 65; *Aust Physicist*, Apr 1964, p 6; *Coresearch*, Feb 1964, p 1; King's College Cambridge, *Annual Report of Council*, Nov 1964, p 20; CSIRO Archives (Canb); records and archives, CSIRO Division of Materials Science and Technology (Clayton, Melb); family letters and papers held by, and information from, Mrs P. Bastow, Kew, and Dr T. J. Bastow, Hawthorn, Melb.   J. A. SPINK

BASTYAN, SIR EDRIC MONTAGUE (1903-1980), army officer and governor, was born on 5 April 1903 at Seaforth, Lancashire, England, eldest son of Lieutenant Samuel James Bastyan, Royal Field Artillery, and his wife Maude Mary, née Dare. Educated at West Buckland School and the Royal Military College, Sandhurst, Edric was commissioned in 1923, sent to India, Malta and Palestine, and trained as a staff officer. On 11 January 1934 he married Marjorie Dorothy Bowle at the parish church, Wivenhoe, Essex, England. He served in North Africa and Italy during World War II, became a staff officer in the Eighth Army in 1943, and was appointed O.B.E. (1942), C.B.E. (1943) and C.B. (1944). His work in 1945 as major general in charge of administration, Allied Land Forces, South East Asia, was praised by W. J. (Viscount) Slim [q.v.]. In Germany with the British Army of the Rhine in 1946-48, Bastyan was head of logistics during the Berlin airlift. Senior staff appointments in Britain followed. In 1957 he was promoted lieutenant general, appointed K.B.E. and posted as Commander of British Forces, Hong Kong, where he was also a member of the Executive and Legislative councils until 1960.

A divorcee, Bastyan had married Victoria Eugenie Helen Bett on 21 October 1944 in Rome. She had performed intelligence duties for the British in Italy, Gibraltar and the Middle East (1939-44), and been mentioned in dispatches. On retiring from the army in 1960, Bastyan accepted the governorship of South Australia and arrived in Adelaide on 4 April 1961. A dapper man with a high forehead and a well-groomed moustache, he was a fluent speaker, with a quick wit and a zest for meeting people; he loved sport and was to become the best known and most popular of the State's governors. He was appointed knight of grace of the Order of St John (1961), K.C.M.G. (1962) and K.C.V.O. (1963). Lady

Bastyan, also an excellent speaker, was fluent in six languages; she supported hospitals, loyal societies and immigrant organizations.

In the 1962 State elections the premier Sir Thomas Playford lost his majority in the House of Assembly, the result being Labor 19 seats, Liberal 18 and Independents 2. Labor's leader F. H. Walsh [q.v.] waited upon the governor, claiming that with 54 per cent of the votes he had a mandate to form a ministry. Bastyan maintained that, as neither party had won a majority of seats, it should be left to the assembly to resolve the crisis when parliament met. Next year the Playford government bought a vice-regal holiday home at Victor Harbor—which Bastyan named Anookanilla (meaning 'thank you')—and gave the governor an overdue salary increase. Playford regarded Bastyan as the 'most intelligent' governor he had met. When Labor won office in 1965, Walsh, too, found Bastyan conscientious and helpful. Ignoring party policy that only Australians should hold gubernatorial office, Walsh extended Bastyan's term by two years. The governor even charmed Walsh's successor Don Dunstan. Though given to scorning imported governors as 'satraps', Dunstan publicly praised Bastyan and extended his term to 1 June 1968. From April to June 1967, during Baron Casey's [q.v.] absence, Bastyan had been administrator of the Commonwealth.

Labor lost two seats in the South Australian election of March 1968. An Independent, Tom Stott [q.v.], held the balance of power and promptly announced that he would support the Liberals. The Opposition leader Steele Hall wanted to form a ministry, but Dunstan, with 52 per cent of the votes, advised Bastyan to let the assembly determine his government's fate. By orchestrating massive public protest against the electoral system in the ensuing six weeks, Dunstan undermined the incoming Hall government. The governor would have been denounced for partisanship if he had interfered in the crisis by insisting on Dunstan's resignation. Labor was defeated on the floor of the House. Bastyan admonished Premier Hall to brook no resistance from his party to electoral reform.

On 14 February 1968 it was announced that Bastyan had been appointed governor of Tasmania. Immigrants from twenty-two countries gave a farewell ball before he left Adelaide in June. Having visited Britain, he arrived in Hobart on 2 December. Although he and his wife were to succeed in Tasmania, they did not enjoy their time there as much: Hobartians seemed more informal and less punctual, and Sir Edric had developed emphysema. The 1969 elections gave Tasmania a hung parliament, with the Centre Party's Kevin Lyons holding the balance of power.

When the Liberal leader W. A. Bethune showed the governor a written agreement that he and Lyons had made, Bastyan commissioned them to form a coalition government in March. After Lyons defected from the ministry in March 1972, on Bethune's advice Bastyan dissolved the assembly.

On 30 November 1973 Bastyan relinquished office. He retired with his wife to North Adelaide. A competent artist, he sold many drawings and paintings for charity, and held a solo exhibition at Hahndorf in 1974. Survived by his wife and son, he died on 6 October 1980 in North Adelaide; following a state funeral at St Peter's Anglican Cathedral, he was cremated. The principal building of the State Library of South Australia, and a power station and dam in Tasmania were named after him.

W. Slim, *Defeat into Victory* (Lond, 1956); N. Blewett and D. Jaensch, *Playford to Dunstan* (Melb, 1971); D. Dunstan, *Felicia* (Melb, 1981); *PP* (Tas), (16), 1972; *Adel Law Review*, 2, no 3, 1969, p 303; Bastyan papers (held by Mr D. I. G. Bastyan, Sandy Bay, Hob); information from Messrs R. S. Hall, Canb, R. M. Hague, Gilberton, D. A. Dunstan, Norwood, Adel, and E. E. O'Farrell, Oyster Cove, Tas.

P. A. HOWELL

BATESON, CHARLES HENRY (1903-1974), journalist and historian, was born on 4 August 1903 in Wellington, New Zealand, son of Charles Bateson, a company manager from England, and Welsh-born Alice Lowe, née Rossiter. Educated at Hurworth school, Taranaki, Henry compiled the *New Zealand Lawn Tennis Annual* in 1920. He arrived in Australia in 1922 and married a journalist Coy Catherine Foster-Lynam (d. 1962) at St Peter's Anglican Church, East Sydney, on 27 August 1923. Having joined the staff of Ezra Norton's [q.v.] newspaper, the *Truth*, Bateson won repute as a leader-writer and as a talented administrator; at various times he edited and managed the Melbourne *Truth*.

During World War II Bateson was publicity officer for the Department of the Interior until appointed principal information officer on 30 December 1940. Later, as a war correspondent, he met two pilots on leave in London, V. P. Brennan [q.v.] and Ray Hesselyn, and collaborated with them in writing *Spitfires over Malta* (London and Sydney, 1943). In 1944 he published *First into Italy* (London), an account of the Allied invasion.

Greatly interested 'in the maritime history of Australia and the Pacific, both sail and steam', Bateson regretted having started research 'over late' in life, but even so accomplished much. In *The Convict Ships 1787-1868* (Glasgow, 1959) he sought first to stir the readers' imagination by 'sketching the

story of the quest for the great southern continent', then to contrast the adventurous spirit of those who participated with the 'drab motives' of the officials involved in dispatching the first fleet. He viewed the convicts as the real pioneers of Australia. The book was well researched and remains the standard work of its kind. Equally interesting was *Gold Fleet for California* (1963), his study of the men and ships that sailed from Australia and New Zealand for America in 1849. His life of Patrick Logan [q.v.2] was published in 1966.

After News Ltd took control of Norton's publications in 1960, Bateson became editorial manager in New South Wales of its subsidiary, Mirror Newspapers Ltd; as a senior executive he organized the launching of the *Australian* newspaper. On 28 November 1964 he married a travel agent Ann Graham at the registrar-general's office, Sydney. He was a member of the Royal Australian Historical Society, and between 1958 and 1966 edited the *Log*, the journal of what was to become the Nautical Association of Australia. Known as 'Hank', he belonged to the Journalists' and New Zealand clubs in Sydney. Following his retirement in January 1966, he published *The War with Japan* (1968).

Bateson also contributed several brief monographs to an Oxford University Press series on early Australia. He contemplated writing eight volumes on Australian shipwrecks and published one in 1972 dealing with the period 1622-1850; *Dire Strait*, a history of Bass Strait, appeared in 1973. His history of Burns, Philp [qq.v.7,11] & Co. Ltd remained uncompleted when he died suddenly of coronary vascular disease on 5 July 1974 at his Vaucluse home. He was cremated; his wife survived him, as did the daughter of his first marriage. The Mitchell [q.v.5] Library was bequeathed 1300 of Bateson's books, together with 125 boxes, 5 cartons and 1 parcel of his papers, which provide further indication of his industry and knowledge.

SMH, 30 Dec 1940; *Australian* and *Daily Mirror* (Syd), 9 July 1974; Bateson's collection of books *and* correspondence *and* shipping records (ML).

B. H. FLETCHER

BATT, WILLIAM PERCY (1879-1947) and HARRY CYRIL LESLIE (1885-1947), yachtsmen, were born on 3 December 1879 and 10 May 1885 in Hobart, sons of Tasmanian-born parents Henry Batt, carpenter, and his wife Ellen, née Rose. Percy, nicknamed 'Skipper' by his mother, was fascinated by the activity of the slipways below their Battery Point home and amused himself by fashioning boats from slivers of wood. Educated at Battery Point Model School and Macquarie

Street State School, he had his first taste of competitive sailing with the Derwent Model Yacht Club where the serious production and racing of model boats awakened his interest in hull and rig design.

Percy joined his father in the building trade, then served apprenticeships to a tin-smith and a cooper. By the 1907-08 season he was an accomplished helmsman and won four Derwent Dinghy Sailing Club races in the 15-foot 'boxie', *Lalla Berri*. From 1911 he was a master cooper, working from Salamanca Place. On 16 October 1916 he married Myrtle Agnes Bisdee with Anglican rites at the Church of St James the Apostle, New Town. Eight days later he enlisted in the Australian Imperial Force. Embarking for England on 11 May 1917, Skipper served briefly in France with the 1st Field Artillery Brigade; he returned to Tasmania where he was discharged in September 1919.

Harry shared his brother's passion for sailing. He, too, had raced model yachts before his first appearance in the Hobart Regatta of 1905. As helmsman of the 'boxie', *Lahloo*, he won at the New Norfolk Regatta and was Derwent Dinghy Sailing Club champion (1905-10). After working for a watchmaker and jeweller, he became an ironmonger's assistant. On 17 August 1911 he married a 19-year-old bookbinder Emily Eden Jones at St George's Anglican Church, Hobart; they were to have two sons and three daughters. Harry graduated to class-yachts in 1912 when he and Skipper purchased *Weene*; in 1914 he won the Ocean Race and a first-class event at the Hobart Regatta.

In 1924 Skipper was commissioned to design the Royal Yacht Club of Tasmania's challenger for the Forster [q.v.8] cup. Presented in 1922 to stimulate interstate competition between one-design, 21-foot, restricted class yachts, the cup was one of Australia's premier yachting trophies. The *Tassie*'s keel was laid on 18 December and construction completed in four weeks. Described as a 'rough Huon Pine yacht' and given little chance against the opposition, on 7 February 1925 she won an intense tacking duel to take the first heat by 50 seconds; the five man crew, with Skipper as helmsman and Harry as for'ard hand, increased that margin in the two remaining heats.

Having again won in Perth (1926) and Adelaide (1927), Skipper was defeated in 1928 by a yacht of his design, *Tassie Too*, sailed by his brother Harry. A third yacht designed by Skipper, *Tassie III*, was launched late in 1929 and, with Harry as helmsman, won in Hobart in 1931. As helmsmen, Percy and Harry Batt dominated the competition until 1938. Skipper's yachts won the Forster cup seventeen times, the Albert [q.v.7] cup seven times, and were victorious in the as-sociated Mosman and Griffith cups. Five ft 6½ ins (168.9 cm) tall, with fair hair and blue eyes, Percy closely resembled his brother; they behaved like twins and each seemed to be able to read the other's mind. Both men thoroughly understood the theory of hull and rig design, had the uncanny knack of sensing wind shift and were highly respected by their crews.

Following his retirement from active competition in the late 1930s, Percy spent his time encouraging young sailors, and designing and building boats for his family and friends. Survived by his wife and daughter, he died of heart disease on 7 April 1947 at his Battery Point home and was buried in Cornelian Bay cemetery. The Royal Yacht Club of Tasmania named a trophy in his memory.

Harry Batt served as rear commodore (1925-28, 1932-33 and 1940-41) and vice-commodore (1934-37, 1942 and 1944) of the club; he continued to race *Weene* and won the Commodore's Trophy (1947). He died of coronary vascular disease on 4 December 1947 at Battery Point and was also buried in Cornelian Bay cemetery; his wife and five children survived him. His son Neall became a distinguished helmsman and winner of the Stonehaven [q.v.12] and Forster cups. The names of the Batt brothers are commemorated in the Tasmanian Sporting Hall of Fame.

E. H. Webster, *A Hundred Years of Yachting* (Hob, 1936); Roy Yacht Club of Tas, *Sailing On* (Hob, 1980); G. Norman, *Yachting and the Royal Prince Alfred Yacht Club* (Syd, 1988); *Mercury* (Hob), 7, 9 Feb 1925, 10 Apr, 5 Dec 1947; Batt family records (held by Miss J. Batt and Mrs R. Balfe, Battery Point, Hob).   JEFFERY BOYES

BATTARBEE, REGINALD ERNEST ('REX') (1893-1973), artist, was born on 16 December 1893 at Warrnambool, Victoria, fifth child of George Edward Battarbee, a bacon-curer from England, and his Irish wife Mary Miller, née Wilson. Educated at the local state school and at Warrnambool Academy, Reginald worked in his father's business, then turned to mixed farming. On 28 January 1916 he enlisted in the Australian Imperial Force and in March 1917 joined the 58th Battalion in France. During the fighting at Bullecourt on 12 May he was shot through the chest, face and both arms. He was invalided to Australia in November and hospitalized until late 1920; his left arm remained crippled. Unable to resume farmwork, in 1921-23 'Rex' Battarbee studied commercial art in Melbourne, but developed a preference for the outdoor life of a landscape painter.

In 1928 he and fellow commercial artist

John Gardner saved money to buy a T-model Ford which had been converted to a caravan: they set out on a fifteen-month trip, painting in Victoria, New South Wales and Queensland. Two years later they travelled to western New South Wales and the Flinders Ranges in South Australia. Their work appeared in successful exhibitions in Melbourne and Sydney. On an expedition to South and Central Australia in 1932, they showed their paintings at the Hermannsburg Lutheran mission, on the Finke River, west of Alice Springs in the Northern Territory. Returning to the Centre in 1934 to paint the Macdonnell and James ranges, Battarbee and Gardner again displayed their work at Hermannsburg —this time for the benefit of the Aborigines. The representation of places familiar to the local Aranda (Arunta) people had great impact; among the viewers was Albert Namatjira [q.v.], then known simply as Albert, who asked for materials in order to do his own painting.

Rex's and Jack's brightly coloured landscapes attracted notice in Melbourne art circles, and they became prolific exhibitors and writers about inland Australia; in 1934 Battarbee won a Victorian centenary art prize for water-colour. He undertook his third visit to Central Australia in 1936 and found Albert. still waiting for him at the mission. With the permission of the superintendent Pastor Friedrich Albrecht, Battarbee employed Albert as cameleer during excursions, each of one month, to Palm Valley and the Macdonnell Ranges. Battarbee taught Albert basic water-colour painting, and was astonished and inspired by his pupil's aptitude; he included three of Albert's works in his 1937 Royal South Australian Society of Arts showing in Adelaide and next year arranged a solo exhibition for Namatjira at the Fine Art Society Gallery, Melbourne.

About 1940 Battarbee moved permanently to Central Australia. He conducted classes for an expanding group of Aboriginal artists and arranged further exhibitions of Namatjira's paintings in the southern capitals. As the Hermannsburg school of water-colourists developed, Battarbee became its promoter and helped to regulate the supply and distribution of its works to art markets; he was a member (from 1943) and chairman (1951-56) of the Aranda Arts Council and a member of the two advisory committees also formed to protect the artists' interests. During World War II the authorities considered closing Hermannsburg on the ground that its German staff constituted a security risk. A compromise was reached, however, and in 1942 Battarbee was appointed a protector of Aborigines and Commonwealth government officer overseeing the mission. There, on 7 October 1950, he married with Lutheran forms 30-year-old Ada

Bernice Loone, a Baptist lay missionary; Albrecht conducted the service.

The Battarbees lived at Alice Springs and opened an Aboriginal art gallery, Tmaramara, in their home. Rex continued to paint and exhibit. In 1964-66 Bernice ran the Battarbee Centralian Arts gallery, Adelaide, while her husband was briefly a patient in the Repatriation General Hospital, Daw Park. Returning to Alice Springs, Battarbee was appointed O.B.E. in 1971 for his services to art and Aborigines. He had been attracted to Central Australia by the variety and luminosity of colours to be found in the region. Although he believed that he had a sound sense of colour and that his best paintings would be remembered, he also expressed the view that his discovery of Namatjira would outlive the memory of his own art. Battarbee was a fellow (1937) of the Royal South Australian Society of Arts; he wrote *Modern Australian Aboriginal Art* (Sydney, 1951) and— with his wife— *Modern Aboriginal Paintings* (Adelaide, 1971).

Of middle height, lean, dark complexioned and softly spoken, Battarbee listed his recreations as music, walking, athletics and gardening, as well as studying nature and the Australian Aborigines. Survived by his son and daughter, he died on 2 September 1973 in the Old Timers' Home, Alice Springs, and was buried with Methodist forms in the town's cemetery. His work is represented in the Art Gallery of South Australia and the National Gallery of Victoria.

T. G. H. Strehlow, *Rex Battarbee* (Syd, 1956); J. D. Batty, *Namatjira* (Syd, 1963); K. Dowdy, *A Vagabond and His Easel* (Warrnambool, Vic, 1984); J. Hardy, R. and V. Megaw (eds), *Heritage of Namatjira* (Melb, 1991); *People* (Syd), 21 Nov 1951; *Sun News-Pictorial*, 16 July 1942; *Herald* (Melb), 3 Sept 1955; *SMH*, 4 Sept 1973; T. G. Strehlow, Interview with Battarbee, 1 Nov 1960 (H. de Berg tapes, ts, NL).   JANE HARDY

BATTYE, MARGARET (1909-1949), lawyer, was born on 9 August 1909 at Subiaco, Perth, only child of Charles Battye, librarian, and his wife Nellie May, née Robertson, both Victorian born; J. S. Battye [q.v.7] was her uncle. Educated at Perth Modern School, Margaret graduated from the University of Western Australia (LL.B., 1931; B.A., 1933) and was admitted to the Bar in 1933. She established a practice in Perth in partnership with Mary Hartrey who had also graduated in law that year. In June, dressed in a jumper, brown serge skirt and matching hat, Battye reputedly became the first woman to represent a client in a Western Australian court of law. She won the case. Battye earned favourable comment for the manner in which she had conducted her brief, and was congratulated by the presiding magistrate and opposing lawyer. From 1936 she practised on her own as a barrister and solicitor, and from 1939 worked for the Council for Civil Liberties.

In 1934 she had joined the Western Australian branch of the Australian Federation of University Women (president 1937) which planned to establish a university women's college. Appointed to the proposed college's fund-raising committee in 1938, she acted as its solicitor and was a member of its executive in 1942. Negotiations proceeded to take over the lend-lease quarters, used by American officers during World War II, which were situated close to the university. Agreement was reached in 1945 and Battye was appointed to the Women's College council next year. She was responsible for drawing up the original constitution under which the Women's University College (later the University Women's College and from 1960 St Catherine's College) functioned with little alteration for many years. As president (1947-48) of the Western Australian branch of the A.F.U.W., she hosted their conference in Perth.

A keen supporter of and honorary legal adviser to the Women's Service Guilds, Battye also exercised a guiding influence in organizing the Perth-based Business and Professional Women's Club which was founded in 1946; she was its first president and later a vice-president of the federal body. She belonged, as well, to the Karrakatta and Soroptomists' clubs, and was president of both in 1949. In addition, she chaired a national committee for the United Nations' commission into the status of women and acted as honorary solicitor to the Western Australian section of the Fellowship of Australian Writers.

Battye had been a member of the original working committee of the Liberal Party of Australia's Western Australian division; she represented the division at the first federal council meeting in Sydney in 1945 and was given responsibility for the foundation of the State women's committee; she was a State delegate to the party's federal conference in Canberra in 1946.

Described as 'a big person in every way, physically, intellectually and in personality', Battye was vital, friendly, witty and fun loving, but extremely serious about subjects close to her heart. She died of thyrotoxicosis on 16 November 1949 at Subiaco and was buried in the Presbyterian section of Karrakatta cemetery. A plaque on the library wall in St Catherine's College commemorates her.

M. V. Woods and W. W. Bisset, *The First Fifty Years of the Activities of the Western Australian Association of University Women* (Perth, 1973); N. Stewart, *St Catherine's College* (Perth, 1978) and *As*

I Remember Them (Perth, 1987); *Civil Liberty*, 2, no 4, Jan 1939, 3, no 3, Feb 1941; *Milady*, July 1949; *Daily News*, 22 June 1933; *West Australian*, 17, 18 Nov 1949; Records, Fellowship of Aust Writers, WA section *and* St Catherine's College *and* WA Assn of University Women (WAA); Liberal Party of Aust (WA division), Minutes of Emergency Cte, Jan 1945-Apr 1949 (Liberal Party Office, Perth); information from Sir P. Hasluck, Perth, and Miss M. F. F. Lukis, Nedlands, Perth.

M. MEDCALF

BAUDINET, DORA ISABEL (1883-1945), nurse, was born on 19 April 1883 at Coongulmerang, near Bairnsdale, Victoria, third child of Tasmanian-born parents, Edmund Chaulk Baudinet, grazier, and his wife Helen Jane, née McKay. Edmund had died eight days earlier after being paralysed in an accident. Assisted by her brothers-in-law, Helen returned to Hobart where her children attended the Friends' High School. Dora left school in 1898 and was employed as an assistant-teacher before entering Hobart General Hospital as a student-nurse. Having obtained her certificate in 1910, she nursed privately, worked as a hospital sister and transferred to St Margaret's, Launceston, where she became acting-matron.

On 15 June 1915 Baudinet was appointed to the Australian Army Nursing Service and posted to the 1st Australian General Hospital. She embarked in the *Wandella* two days later and served as a staff nurse in Egypt, France and England. Dora returned to Melbourne in the *Benalla* and her appointment terminated in Tasmania on 12 November 1917. She nursed at Roseneath and at the Repatriation Hospital, Hobart, and on 24 January 1923 took a post with the Education Department as school nurse for the Hobart area. A seriousminded and compassionate woman, she devoted herself to the welfare of children. She never married.

While visiting New Zealand in 1937, Baudinet was impressed by the convalescent holiday homes that she saw there. Next year, with others concerned for child welfare, she formed the Sunshine Association of Tasmania. It aimed to build a holiday house by the sea where isolated or underprivileged children might enjoy improved nutrition, medical and dental treatment, and healthy fun in homely surroundings. The association found a suitable site at Howrah, and quickly gained government encouragement and promises of financial aid. Dora worked as fund-raising secretary and donated 10.5 acres (4.2 ha) of the beachfront estate. Plans for the home were prepared by 1943, but building was delayed by wartime restrictions and shortages.

An active member of the Returned Army Sisters' Association (president 1945) and secretary of the Army Sisters' Memorial Home at Lindisfarne, Baudinet belonged to the Davey Street Congregational Church and supported its youth movement. She was also a foundation member of the Nurses' Club, a member of the Royal Society of Tasmania and vice-president of The Friends' School Old Scholars' Association.

Retiring from the Education Department in 1944, Baudinet died of cancer on 19 December 1945 in Royal Hobart Hospital and was cremated. The bulk of her estate, sworn for probate in Victoria and Tasmania at £7473, was bequeathed to the renamed Tasmanian Sunshine Association; its Dora Baudinet home was opened on 11 August 1951. With the backing of the State government and the Tasmanian Teachers Federation, and through the fund-raising efforts of school pupils and service clubs, holidays were provided for thousands of children. Although rising costs forced the sale of the home in 1985, the association continues to sponsor underprivileged children.

A. Downie, *Our First Hundred Years* (Hob, 1975); M. Baudinette, *The Baudinette Story* (Warrnambool, Vic, 1990); Nurses Club and Nurses Bureau (Hob), Minutes, 1922-45 (held by Aust Nursing Federation, Hob); Application for employment as teacher, ED 2/26/2356, *and* Appointment as school nurse in Hobart, ED 13/211, p 336, *and* Correspondence, Sec of Dir of Education, ED 10/37/0196 (TA).   A. RAND

BAUME, FREDERICK EHRENFRIED (ERIC) (1900-1967), journalist, author and broadcaster, was born on 29 May 1900 at Auckland, New Zealand, eldest of four sons of Dunedin-born Frederick Ehrenfried Baume (d. 1910), barrister, member of parliament and compulsive gambler, and his wife Rosetta Lulah, née Leavy, a schoolteacher from San Francisco, United States of America. His parents, both unorthodox Jews, had German ancestry. Eric (as he was always known) enjoyed a privileged childhood, although his quick-tempered father often beat him. He was educated at King's College (1910-11), Auckland Grammar School (1913-14) and Waitaki Boys' High School, Oamaru (1915). On leaving school, he served as a bandsman with the Garrison Artillery, Territorial Force, for three years.

Matriculating at Auckland University College in 1917, Baume briefly studied law, then joined the *New Zealand Herald* (edited by William Lane [q.v.9]) as a proof-reader before becoming a cub reporter. He began writing verse and drawing cartoons which were published in New Zealand and Australia. In 1919-20 he was sub-editor of the *Waipa Post* and in 1921 moved to the *Dominion*, Wellington, for

which he wrote editorials. On 17 December that year Baume married Mary Caroline Jack in the Methodist Church, Whangarei. The choice of church had been Mary's; Eric rarely attended the synagogue and at times was accused of being anti-Semitic. They were to have three children.

Having worked for the Christchurch *Sun*, Baume became editor of the *Timaru Herald* in 1922. Invited to join the *Daily Guardian*, owned by (Joynton) Smith's [q.v.11] Newspapers Ltd, he sailed for Sydney in June 1923. One of Smith's Newspapers founders, Robert Clyde Packer [q.v.11], became Baume's mentor and successively promoted him chief sub-editor, news editor and night editor.

Next year his wife joined him. In 1925 Mary developed rheumatoid arthritis: Baume maintained that her illness kept the family in debt, but he was addicted to gambling and often lost his entire salary on payday. He played slot machines, two-up, poker, roulette and *chemin de fer*, and bet on the races; later in life he stuffed his wallet with Sydney Opera House lottery tickets. A lieutenant in the 4th Battalion, Australian Military Forces, in 1926-30, Baume became known to naval intelligence as a 'strong supporter' of the New Guard.

When the *Daily Guardian* was sold to Sir Hugh Denison's [q.v.8] Associated Newspapers Ltd in 1930, Baume became managing editor of the *Referee*. In 1931 Packer moved to Associated Newspapers and recruited Baume as editor of its *Sunday Sun and Guardian*. Eric was energetic and full of ideas. Although Baume described himself as Packer's 'devoted servant', Packer subsequently believed that Eric betrayed him in boardroom intrigues. In 1935 Baume was appointed assistant editor-in-chief, with responsibility for the *Sunday Sun*, *Telegraph* and *Woman* magazine. The task proved too much for him and he reverted to being editor of the *Sunday Sun*.

In the 1930s the Baumes lived in a large house at Gordon. There they entertained politicians and artistes such as Gladys Moncrieff [q.v.10] and Colonel de Basil's Ballets Russes de Monte Carlo. The roulette wheel was always spinning. From 1932 Baume wrote thirteen books, mostly novels like *Half-Caste* (1933). He had begun wireless broadcasting in the early 1930s with a programme called 'Pros and Cons'; from 1936 he ran 'The 2GB News Review'. In 1937 he visited America and in Mexico met Leon Trotsky whom he interviewed for a series of syndicated articles.

Returning to Sydney in 1938, Baume resumed his editorship of the *Sunday Sun* and his radio work with 2GB. That year one of his news commentaries, critical of Germany, led to complaints from the German consul-general and to Baume's consequent removal from the air. He was urged to enter politics by Ethel Elizabeth Falkiner, widow of the wealthy grazier F. B. S. Falkiner [q.v.8]. She befriended Eric and Mary, giving them jewellery and £20 000; despite her later request, the money was not returned. Baume sued *Smith's Weekly* for revealing the incident in 1941, but did not proceed with the writ.

In August 1939 Ezra Norton [q.v.] had appointed him European correspondent for Truth and Sportsman Ltd which from 1941 included the new *Daily Mirror*. Leaving his family in Sydney, Baume established the office in London, in rooms at the Savoy Hotel. He lived in an adjacent suite where he entertained many celebrities; his bed had black, silk sheets. In England he became friendly with the Countess of Oxford, widow of prime minister Herbert Asquith, and with Lady Margaret Stewart, daughter of Lord Londonderry. Baume was reputedly the first to report Germany's intended invasion of Russia. He travelled on the Continent during the war and indulged his passion for uniforms. Caught in the bloody battle at Arnhem, the Netherlands, he described his nine days under continuous barrage in *Five Graves at Nijmegen* (1945). An imposing figure in evening dress or in uniform (with which he sometimes wore a digger's slouch hat), he was six feet (182.9 cm) tall, with black hair, dark eyes and a strong, straight nose.

Late in 1949 Baume was recalled to Australia; having seen a photograph of him wearing spats, Norton had roared: 'get him back here, he's been duchessed'. Baume became deputy editor-in-chief of the Truth and the Sportsman group, but was dismissed in 1952. During this time Eric developed an ulcer and a nervous tic in his left eye. He grew a large moustache. Next year he returned to radio with four 2GB programmes. In late 1956 he joined the new television station, ATN-7, as its news-commentator. There he was nicknamed 'Eric Boom' from his habit of bumping into the sound boom when he leapt from his studio chair to deliver the punch line of his live show, 'This I Believe'. His by-line also appeared in the *Sun* newspaper column, 'Face the Facts', which was largely ghosted by his nephew Michael Baume.

A natural showman and actor, Eric became a television celebrity. He was tempted back to newspapers in 1958 after Norton asked him to return as editorial director. When Norton sold Truth and Sportsman later that year, Baume was stripped of his authority and paid out of his contract. He resumed work on 2GB and contributed freelance commentaries for the press and television. From January 1964 on ATN-7 he compered a new television panel show, 'Beauty and the Beast', in which he and four women answered viewers' letters. On air, Baume was deliberately beastly to his fellow panellists, a tactic which made the programme even more popular. He liked to say of most people at this time, 'they love me yet they hate me'. In 1966 he was replaced—his performance had slipped due to ill health and to his own boredom with the programme. He told his biographer Arthur Manning that he was a serious writer and commentator, not a court jester.

Because of his medical bills and gambling habit (he continued to lose large sums at the Journalists' and Imperial Service clubs), Baume was forced to continue working beyond normal retirement age. He was a fellow of the Royal Geographical Society, London, and in 1966 was appointed O.B.E. Survived by his wife, son and two daughters, he died of cardiac and renal disease on 24 April 1967 at his apartment at Kirribilli; following a non-denominational service, he was cremated. His debts exceeded his assets by more than $4000.

A. Manning, *Larger Than Life* (Syd, 1967); P. Baume, *Baume—Further Record* (priv pub, Gordon, NSW, 1980); R. B. Walker, *Yesterday's News* (Syd, 1980); *Woman's Day*, 31 Oct 1966; *Nation* (Syd), 25 July 1964, 6 May 1967; *Bulletin*, 6 May 1967; Intelligence report, MP 1049/9 file 1887/2/35 (AA); Baume papers (held by Senator M. Baume, Parliament House, Canb).   VALERIE LAWSON

BAZLEY, ARTHUR WILLIAM (1896-1972), military historian and public servant, was born on 4 August 1896 at South Yarra, Melbourne, eldest child of Arthur Edwin Bazley, coach-builder, and his wife Georgina Victoria, née Gibson, both native-born. Educated at South Yarra State School, young Arthur was employed as a clerk on the *Argus* newspaper. He served three years in the senior cadets and three months with the artillery, and claimed to be 19 when he enlisted on 5 October 1914 in the Australian Imperial Force. Although formally designated batman to the war correspondent C. E. W. Bean [q.v.7], he assisted him as clerk and typist.

Embarking from Melbourne that month, 'Baz' served at Gallipoli and helped Bean to edit *The Anzac Book* (London, 1916). They worked together on the Western Front from April 1916 to June 1917; Bazley was then transferred to the War Records Section at A.I.F. Headquarters, London, and made several visits to France in 1918. He was promoted staff sergeant in November. Next year pneumonic influenza forced him to withdraw from Bean's mission to Gallipoli, but he rejoined the group in Cairo, returned to Australia in May and was discharged from the A.I.F. in August. He was awarded the Meritorious Service Medal. On 1 October 1919 at

Christ Church, South Yarra, he married with Anglican rites Annie Celia Chalk (d. 1941), a Londoner.

Bean and his staff had begun to compile *The Official History of Australia in the War of 1914-1918* (Sydney, 1921-42). In late 1919 they arrived at Tuggeranong homestead in the Federal Capital Territory where they were based until moving to Victoria Barracks, Sydney, in 1925. Bazley was librarian and did Bean's devilling; he left the team in 1939. From 1930 to 1940 he contributed his 'Celebrities of the A.I.F.' column to the journal, *Reveille*: distinguished by their accuracy, fairness and sense of proportion, his articles provide a rich source of biographical material. He was to maintain his talent for writing through his work on unit histories and as editor (1950-67) of *Stand-To*; he became a life member of the Returned Sailors', Soldiers' and Airmen's Imperial League of Australia in 1954.

In 1940 Bazley had been appointed chief clerk and librarian of the Australian War Memorial, Canberra, which opened the following year. As its acting director (1942-46), he helped to select war artists, to organize the production and screening of the documentary film, *Sons of the Anzacs* (1944), and to arrange an Australia-wide exhibition of war paintings and photographs. He was a member (1942-60) of the War (Commonwealth) Archives Committee. Joining the Department of Immigration in 1946, he was given the task of examining whether enemy subjects who had been interned during the war should be deported or allowed to remain. In 1948-51 he was secretary to the Commonwealth Immigration Advisory Council. From 1951 he chaired the Temple Society Trust Fund Advisory Committee which investigated claims made by immigrants who had owned property in Palestine before the establishment of the Israeli state in 1948. Between 1956 and 1961, the year of his retirement, he worked to reunite people from Eastern Europe with their families in Australia.

Warm towards his fellows, Bazley helped and advised many; to those who sought his aid, he gave much and asked for nothing. He continued his association with the A.W.M.'s records collection and gave valuable assistance to the Australian Dictionary of Biography. Some 5 ft 11 ins (180.3 cm) tall, with brown hair, grey-blue eyes and a fair complexion, he had married Mary, née McPhee, late Scott, on 16 April 1949 in the Fullerton [q.v.4] Memorial Church, Sydney. Survived by his wife, and by the son and two daughters of his first marriage, he died on 31 July 1972 in Canberra Hospital and was cremated with Presbyterian forms.

C. E. W. Bean, *Gallipoli Mission* (Canb, 1952); D. McCarthy, *Gallipoli to the Somme* (Lond, 1983);

Stand-To (Canb), 6, no 7, Feb-Aug 1959; *Canb News*, 16 Nov 1970; *Canb Times*, 2 Aug 1972.

A. J. SWEETING

BEAK, WILLIAM (1878-1966), grazier and studmaster, was born on 15 January 1878 at Mount Hedlow, near Rockhampton, Queensland, sixth child of Henry Beak (d. 1908), a farmer from England, and his Irish wife Essie, née Matchett. Following primary schooling at Mount Hedlow, William learned cattle husbandry from his father, a pioneer settler who in 1905 founded a pastoral company, Henry Beak & Sons, when he had acquired several Central Queensland cattle stations after a disastrous drought. In 1904 William had managed one of them, May Downs, Clermont. At Calioran homestead, South Yaamba, on 6 March 1913 he married Flora McKenzie, daughter of another pioneering family, with the forms of the John Knox Presbyterian Church.

William's interest in the genetics of breeding began in 1913 when he bought two 'freak', hornless Hereford bulls with the aim of producing polled progeny. In 1919 the company was the first to import polled Hereford cattle from the United States of America. One of these bulls, Polled Gemnation, was mated with progeny from the 'freak' hornless bulls to establish the breed. Beak was instrumental in forming the Australian Poll Hereford Breeders' Association in 1922 (later the Australian Poll Hereford Society) at Rockhampton; he became its patron in 1932. He was to be elected a life member of the American Polled Hereford Association in recognition of his work with the breed in Australia. The family firm had been dissolved in 1929. Next year eight carcases which Beak selected from polled steers were deemed to be the world's best by the meat market at Smithfield, London.

Stud cattle-breeding and carcase-judging fascinated Beak. He published *The Key to Divine Designs and their Guidance for the Improvement of Beef Quality* (Rockhampton, 1956). This booklet described his discovery of 'the wonderful power of telegony', a controversial theory in cattle-breeding. A second pamphlet, *Passing on more Discoveries by a Layman* (Rockhampton, 1957), included his findings on the control of sex in animal-breeding; it also described how to judge internal features of fat steers by tapping them with the fingers and listening to the sounds. He had demonstrated this unusual technique at the 1932 Royal National Agricultural and Industrial Association's show in Brisbane and its effectiveness was confirmed by the result of a subsequent carcase assessment in London.

Following his father, Beak had sat on the Livingstone Shire Council in 1904-05; he was a councillor of Broadsound shire in 1911-19. He returned to one of the company's coastal properties and again served on the Livingstone Shire Council in 1919-27 and 1933-36 (chairman 1921-27). A public-spirited man, he was, as well, chairman of the Rockhampton Harbour Board (1924-26) and of the Central Queensland Racing Association (from 1924), and a member of the local hospital board. Survived by his four daughters, Beak died on 5 June 1966 at Rockhampton and was buried in North Rockhampton cemetery with Anglican rites. Later that month it was announced that he had been appointed M.B.E. for services to the beef cattle industry.

L. McDonald, *Rockhampton* (Brisb, 1981) and *Cattle Country* (Brisb, 1988); *Australasian*, 14 May 1939; *Morning Bulletin*, 21 July 1908, 7, 11 June 1966; information from Mrs B. Westphal, Sorrento, WA.
LORNA McDONALD

BEAN, SIR EDGAR LAYTON (1893-1977), parliamentary draftsman, was born on 15 October 1893 at Moonee Ponds, Melbourne, son of George Alfred Bean, accountant, and his wife Amelia Florence, née Davey, both Victorian born. Educated at Scotch College, Perth (1906-10), Ted enrolled at the University of Adelaide (B.A., 1913) where he had a brilliant career: he won the Barr Smith [q.v.11] prize for Greek (1911) and a David Murray [q.v.5] scholarship (1913). Having obtained through the university a free passage to travel to England, in 1914 he entered Merton College, Oxford, to read classics (B.A., 1919; M.A., 1922). World War I interrupted his studies: he enlisted in the British Army in August 1915, served in France with the Royal Field Artillery and was wounded in action.

After the war Bean returned to Adelaide. In 1920 he joined the Crown Solicitor's Department as a clerk and began a degree in law at his old university (LL.B., 1922); he was admitted to the South Australian Bar on 21 April 1923. From 1922 he had been an associate of Justice Poole [q.v.11] of the Supreme Court of South Australia. On 8 April 1926 at Chalmers Congregational Church, Adelaide, Bean married Constance Mary Greenlees. Appointed that year as the State's parliamentary draftsman, he was to hold the post until 1959 and to frame some 1500 bills.

Although he was reputedly South Australia's finest parliamentary draftsman and possibly the best in the country, his greatest achievement was in editing, with J. P. Cartledge [q.v.], the nine volumes of *The Public General Acts of South Australia, 1837-1936* (1937-40). Bean was appointed C.M.G. in 1937. In addition to being a member of the South Australian Government Superannua-

tion Fund Board (1928-62) and of the State Public Service Board (1942-51), he chaired the local government commission (1930-34), the Insurance Premiums Committee, the education inquiry committee (1942-49) and the Teachers' Salaries Board (1946-64); he was also a director of Southern Television Corporation Ltd (1960-70) and of News Ltd. A member of the board (1960-71) of the Minda Home for Weak-Minded Children, he had become involved when his eldest son John went to live there.

On 25 March 1942 Bean was mobilized in the Australian Military Forces; promoted lieutenant in July, he served in the 3rd Battalion of the Volunteer Defence Corps before resigning in November 1944. He was knighted in 1955. Few people knew him intimately. Shy, well organized and neatly dressed, he was regarded as a 'workaholic'. Gilbert Seaman thought that Bean had the best and the clearest brain of all of his colleagues: 'he was not a harsh realist . . . he had the personal touch'. As (Sir) Thomas Playford's unofficial 'right-hand man', Bean exercised an extraordinary influence on the premier and was one of the few who were with Playford throughout his political career. They talked issues over and went fishing together; because Playford was largely self-educated, their friendship resembled that of pupil and teacher, with Playford the pupil.

Bean liked reading and walking. He belonged to the Pickwick, the Adelaide, and the Naval, Military and Air Force clubs, and joined the Eucalypts, an exclusive club of twelve members whose objectives were to promote truth, good fellowship, brotherly love and wisdom. The group met monthly in one another's homes for a ceremonious pipe and coffee, and to hear and discuss papers about literature, history or philosophy. Those read by Bean show his liberal ideals. Survived by his wife and two sons, Sir Edgar died at Leabrook on 28 July 1977 and was cremated.

W. Crocker, *Sir Thomas Playford* (Melb, 1983); S. Cockburn, *Playford* (Adel, 1991); *Register* (Adel), 23 Nov 1915; *Advertiser* (Adel), 11 May 1937, 1 Jan 1955, 2 Aug 1977; information from Dr M. Bean, Adel, Mr A. G. S. Bean, Perth, and Mr G. Seaman, Adel.
PATRICIA SUMERLING

BEASLEY, FRANK REGINALD (1897-1976), professor of law, was born on 25 August 1897 at Summertown, Oxfordshire, England, son of Benjamin Joseph Beasley, telegraphist, and his wife Fanny Ellen, née Radbone. Educated at Magdalen College School, Oxford, Frank was sent for reasons of health in 1914 to join relations in Western Australia. On 10 May 1915 he enlisted in the Australian

Imperial Force and served with the 11th Battalion at Gallipoli and in France; he was promoted lieutenant on 21 November 1916. Granted leave in 1919, he studied with the Council of Legal Education, London, and at Wadham College, Oxford, where he graduated (B.A., 1920) with honours in jurisprudence. He returned to Australia and was demobilized in October 1920.

Enrolling in law at the University of Sydney, Beasley graduated with first-class honours (LL.B., 1924) and was admitted to the New South Wales Bar. He worked for the directors of Farmer [q.v.4] & Co., lectured in international relations for the university's adult education programme, became a university examiner in political science and jurisprudence, and joined the Round Table movement and the Grotius Society. From seventeen applicants who included (Sir) Kenneth Bailey [q.v.], in 1927 Beasley was appointed foundation professor of law at the University of Western Australia. On 10 October that year he married Helen Grace Moore (d. 1952) at St Matthew's Anglican Church, Manly, Sydney.

In establishing the faculty of law, Beasley succeeded in attracting and holding the support of Perth's practising lawyers, to some extent by employing leading members of the profession as part-time lecturers. His own speciality was constitutional law. While his students recognized the quality of his teaching, they tended to contrast the Olympian formality of his classes with less rigid requirements elsewhere. Widely appreciated for his encouragement of university sporting bodies, Beasley was president of the University Boat Club and coached its VIII to victory in the 1930 intervarsity competition.

He frequently spoke on radio about international affairs: his public discussions aroused controversy during the 1930s and sometimes provoked criticism from members of State parliament. Six feet (182.9 cm) tall, with blue eyes and brown hair, Beasley was by nature efficient and direct, if at times impatient and even domineering. He came to play a significant role on the small but influential professorial board. As its chairman in 1939, he was appointed acting vice-chancellor on the death of H. E. Whitfeld [q.v.12]. Beasley's early introduction of significant reforms in the administration enhanced his role, but created friction with some senior members of the senate and led him to resign from the post on 25 July 1940.

Called up for full-time duty with the Militia in October 1941, Captain Beasley was seconded on 27 July 1942 as deputy assistant adjutant-general at 4th Divisional headquarters, Western Australia. In this post he revealed his characteristic administrative efficiency and emphatic initiative. Having trans-

ferred to the A.I.F., he was promoted temporary major in September, but lack of opportunity for active service prompted his return in 1943 to the university where tuition in law had been suspended. From the consequential revival in 1944 of the law faculty's activities until he retired from the university in 1963, Beasley undertook the normal intramural duties of a senior professor, was president (1952-54) of the staff association and continued his involvement in adult education. Despite early postwar difficulties in the relationship between the faculty and the Barristers' Board, he secured a satisfactory range of full-time teaching staff. Juniors feared and relished his dry, acerbic wit. In 1948 he founded the university's *Annual Law Review*. He married a 25-year-old secretary Ann Poynton on 1 May 1956 at the registrar's office, Perth.

In 1963 the Beasleys moved to Melbourne where Frank became a consultant on the establishment of Monash University's law school. There he held office as a special lecturer and library adviser until late 1970, interspersed with eighteen months as visiting professor at the University of Singapore and six months at the Australian National University, Canberra. Beasley was awarded honorary doctorates of laws from the universities of Melbourne (1956) and Western Australia (1974). Survived by his wife and their daughter, and by the son and daughter of his first marriage, he died on 3 June 1976 at Armadale, Melbourne, and was cremated. The University of Western Australia's law library bears his name and his bust stands at its entrance.

F. Alexander, *Campus at Crawley* (Melb, 1963); B. de Garis, *Campus in the Community* (Perth, 1988); *Gazette of Univ WA*, 14, no 1, Mar 1964, p 6; Univ WA, *Univ News*, 7, no 4, June 1976, 8, no 8, Oct 1977; *Aust Law J*, 50, Sept 1976; *SMH*, 26 Sept 1927; *West Australian*, 9 June 1976.

FRED ALEXANDER

BEASLEY, JOHN ALBERT (1895-1949), trade unionist and politician, was born on 9 November 1895 at Werribee, Victoria, son of native-born John Beasley, a blacksmith who later turned to farming, and his wife Catherine, née Hogan, from County Tipperary, Ireland. Educated at St Andrew's Catholic Primary School, Werribee, young Jack worked on his father's farm, then dug holes for electricity poles in the country and Tasmania. In 1916 he was in Adelaide constructing outdoor installations, and continued to learn the electrical trade at Port Augusta; next year at Moonta he advised the town council on equipment purchases.

Completing his training at Broken Hill, Beasley went to Sydney in 1918, worked at the Commonwealth Naval Dockyard, Cockatoo Island, and became a shop steward for the New South Wales branch of the Electrical Trades Union of Australia. In 1920 he was employed by the electricity department of Sydney Municipal Council and represented his union as a delegate to the Labor Council of New South Wales. He was president of the council (1922-28) and of the E.T.U. (1924-30). By 1925 he was an electrical installation inspector and in December 1926 supervisor of appliance sales in the electricity department.

Beasley's intellectual grasp of the vital social role of unionism complemented his experience, and ensured that he was foremost among young labour movement leaders in the 1920s. He was fascinated by oral accounts of the work of the Labor Council since 1871: he revelled in reading the plethora of pamphlets on the importance of the 'working class' in Western history and the heady promises of Lenin's 1917 revolution. These ideas clashed with the day-to-day work of the council. So, as Beasley mastered the complexities of industrial relations in Australia, and probed for a policy of reform within contemporary economic and social structures, he was excited and disturbed by the prospect of the 'workers' paradise' that was believed to follow the overthrow of existing society.

His dilemma was intensified by his membership of the Australian Labor Party which sought reform through a programme modified by electoral demands. In the early 1920s, charmed by the garrulous utopianism of J. S. Garden [q.v.8], secretary of the Labor Council, Beasley sought solutions in visionary revelations. Aware of the Labor Party's ban on membership of other parties, he did not join the Communist Party of Australia, though Garden was one of its founders in October 1920 and leader of the 'Trades Hall Reds'. At the All-Australian Trade Union Congress in Melbourne in June 1921, Beasley was impressed by the influence of Garden and A. C. Willis [q.v.12] on the formulation of a socialist objective for the labour movement, but was perplexed when the A.L.P. diluted the aspiration in Brisbane in October.

Because of his activity in union affairs, Beasley was able to postpone a decision of where his true loyalties lay. But he remained close to Garden and was elected with him to the New South Wales Labor Party executive in June 1923. Garden's expulsion from the party in November confirmed Labor's ban on links with the Communist Party. At the 1924 party conference Beasley's plea for Garden's readmission was turned down; his failure prompted him to question his youthful ideals, though his liberalism led him to argue that

unions should remain free to employ communists.

In May-June 1926 Beasley was an Australian representative at the eighth and ninth sessions of the International Labour Conference, held at Geneva, Switzerland. He returned on 17 September, appalled at the excesses of Italian fascism and disconcerted by the realities of Russian communism. His new insights quickened his rejection of extremism. At Mary Immaculate Church, Manly, on 5 February 1927 he married Alma Matilda Creighton. He consolidated his political base in the West Sydney Federal electorate and won the seat at the general election on 17 November 1928.

Beasley had been in the cockpit of Labor factionalism since 1923. Small, dark and dapper, he liked cricket, billiards, cards and the pictures. Although his latent strength of will and purpose had matured by 1928, it had not diminished his friendliness and popularity, which were unaffected by his being a non-smoker and teetotaller. He was a fluent speaker, logical, quick-fire and tireless, responsive to the mood of Labor audiences indoors and in the open. He deserved the gold medal awarded to him by the Labor Council.

As he drifted from Garden, Beasley drew near to J. T. Lang [q.v.9], the dominating head of the New South Wales Labor Party. With Lang's blessing, he retained West Sydney at the elections on 12 October 1929 and became an honorary minister in J. H. Scullin's [q.v.11] government, assisting him in the industry portfolio which had previously been part of the attorney-general's responsibilities. He quickly gained Scullin's confidence.

Beasley's wide-ranging plans to dissolve the chaos surrounding the control of Federal industrial relations were soon nullified by the Depression. The government was trapped in spiralling financial constraints which Lang (New South Wales premier, 1930-32) chose to ignore. The ensuing, deep division between Lang and Scullin, and his treasurer E. G. Theodore [q.v.12], forced Beasley finally to support the artful 'Lang Plan' against Theodore's more circumspect solutions for the Depression. In the snarl of internecine strife Beasley lost his cabinet post on 3 March 1931.

In parliament he headed seven Lang dissidents and became leader of the Federal 'Lang Labor Party' on 27 March when the New South Wales branch was expelled from the A.L.P. The conflict intensified and Lang conspired with Beasley and his followers to bring down the Scullin government on 25 November. The sobriquet 'Stabber Jack' that Beasley acquired could have been more justly added to Lang's opprobrious titles. In 1931-35 Beasley helped Lang in his impossible mission to take over the A.L.P. The Federal Lang faction variously survived the elections of 1931 and 1934, highlighted by a swing against Beasley of 23 per cent in 1931 which failed to unseat him. Lang lost State elections in 1932 and 1935. These defeats, together with the unity hopes of John Curtin [q.v.], who became leader of the Federal Labor Party on 1 October 1935, resulted in the return of the 'Langites' to the A.L.P. in February 1936. Beasley could now look forward in relative tranquillity to the probability of fruitful ministerial achievement.

But he was still entangled with Lang who, from 1936, was being assailed by Laborites growing in number and power. Beasley served on Labor's Federal executive, where his defence of Lang was unavailing, and was New South Wales director of the 1937 Federal election campaign, again lost by Labor. The infiltration of the party by communists enabled Lang to cling to the State leadership and aroused Beasley to vigorous and perceptive criticism of the C.P.A.'s Stalinist doctrines. Yet, as a delegate at the 1939 Federal triennial conference, he could not prevent a directive for a special unity conference to decide his patron's position. Lang was replaced by (Sir) William McKell on 5 September, two days after World War II began.

The Stalinists had not been dislodged. They exploited confusion at the 1940 State conference, allowing Lang to form a new group, the Australian Labor Party (Non-Communist), with Beasley as its Federal leader from 2 May. Curtin said that they had again stabbed Labor in the back; but he 'dished' the Stalinists decisively in August, and consolidated rising electoral support for the Labor Party. Adjusting with discernment to Labor's resurgence at a time of grave national danger, Beasley persuaded the Lang breakaways to rejoin the A.L.P. in February 1941. At last he was his own man, a seasoned politician of great potential, determined to put past animosities behind him.

In October 1940 Beasley had joined the Advisory War Council established by Prime Minister (Sir) Robert Menzies [q.v.]. From this vantage-ground he observed the disintegration of the Menzies and (Sir) Arthur Fadden [q.v.] conservative governments, and took a vital role in the events that preceded the formation of Curtin's government on 7 October 1941. Beasley joined the War Cabinet as minister for supply and development (supply and shipping from 17 October 1942). The pressures of the post increased immeasurably when Japan entered the war in December 1941. Chairman of the Allied Supply and of the Australian Food councils, and a member of the production executive of cabinet, he became Curtin's indispensable lieutenant, not only in the immense work of organizing Australia's war effort, but also in mobilizing the labour movement's united support. Beasley's unrivalled knowledge of the complexities of trade union and Labor Party internal politics was invaluable. In late 1942 and early 1943, against traditional objections, he facilitated Curtin's successful attempt to extend the area of compulsory military service: he was bitterly attacked by Lang for his actions.

Despite his massive workload, Beasley found time to reflect on his department's achievements and published three articles in the Melbourne *Age* in March 1944. That year, *inter alia*, the department had to arrange production of 88 million garments, 31 million pairs of socks and stockings for civilians, and up to 26 million uniforms for Australian, British and American troops. Overall, in 1940-43, it placed contracts valued at £373 million; in 1944 an estimated 20 000 contracts worth £60 million would be arranged. Among the other items produced were 'hundreds of thousands of machetes' for jungle warfare, and 'hunting knives used for stabbing a Japanese or killing an animal for food'. Beasley was proud of his department's accounting system which was 'close to' perfect. Scientific resources were being tapped, and future plans included an aluminium-ingot industry at a cost of £3 million.

He had suffered from hypertension from about 1935. His incessant administrative duties brought on a breakdown early in 1944. During H. V. Evatt's [q.v.] trips abroad, Beasley had acted as attorney-general and minister for external affairs. To relieve him, Curtin persuaded Beasley to head the Australian delegation to the twenty-sixth session of the International Labour Conference at Philadelphia, United States of America, in April 1944. His health deteriorated, however, and he resigned his ministry on 2 February 1945 to become vice-president of the Executive Council. He recovered and served as acting-minister for defence until Curtin's death on 5 July. In F. M. Forde's government, from 6 July Beasley held the defence portfolio, as well as the vice-presidency of the Executive Council. He continued as minister for defence in J. B. Chifley's [q.v.] government from 13 July. But Beasley's health remained delicate and, having been appointed to the Privy Council on 1 January 1946, he became resident minister in London. He resigned from parliament on 15 August and that day was appointed high commissioner.

Beasley had been an exemplar of 'the Labor man', who, with minimal formal education, had been able to build on diligence and great native intelligence. He had thrived on spacious experience, based on unremitting trade union and party action, supplemented by sufficient reading of progressive social and political theory. His Catholicism and marriage had tempered the zeal that might have led him into the blind alley of extremism. Increasing insight had finally helped him to escape from his gullible deference to older and wayward men, and to make an outstanding contribution to the nation's war organization.

By 1946 the turbulence of Beasley's career —together with his illness—precluded any further advancement in the A.L.P. But his past did not prevent him from being a successful high commissioner who moved easily in several levels of British society. His accumulated knowledge of torrid meetings proved beneficial in August at the Paris Peace Conference. He was applauded when he told Andrei Vyshinsky that Australia would not be abused for speaking its mind and that Russian intimidation would not be tolerated: 'We had the right to speak of Europe. Our dead of two wars earned us that right'.

In 1947 Beasley was admitted freeman of the City of London and honorary freeman of the Worshipful Company of Butchers. Visiting Sydney, he died suddenly of hypertensive cerebrovascular disease on 2 September 1949 at St Vincent's Hospital. After a requiem Mass at St Mary's Cathedral he was buried in Frenchs Forest cemetery; he was survived by his wife, two sons and two daughters; his estate was sworn for probate at £33 274.

On 7 September Lang pre-empted Chifley in reporting Beasley's death to parliament. 'In the turbulence of politics', he said, 'Mr Beasley was called upon to make many critical decisions . . . and the final judgment about what is right and what is wrong must be left to history to determine'.

L. F. Crisp, *Ben Chifley* (Melb, 1961); A. A. Calwell, *Be Just and Fear Not* (Melb, 1972); J. Robertson, *J. H. Scullin* (Perth, 1974); L. F. Fitzhardinge, *The Little Digger* (Syd, 1979); B. Nairn, *The 'Big Fella'* (Melb, 1986); R. McMullin, *The Light on the Hill* (Melb, 1991); *Cavalcade*, July 1942; *Daily Telegraph* (Syd), 10 Apr 1926; *Aust Worker*, 4 Dec 1929; *Smith's Weekly* (Syd), 17 Oct 1930; *Sun* (Syd), 22 Oct 1930; *Age* (Melb), 21-23 Mar 1944; *Argus*, 29 Aug 1946; *SMH*, 3 Sept 1949; *The Times* (Lond), 3 Sept 1949; Labor Council of NSW records, 1920-29 (ML).   BEDE NAIRN

BEATTIE, WILLIAM ANDERSON (1902-1980), agricultural consultant, was born on 4 July 1902 at Avondale, Auckland, New Zealand, son of Melbourne-born Robert Martin Beattie, medical practitioner, and his wife Jane Bowie, née Anderson, a New Zealander. Educated at Auckland Grammar School, Bill attended Auckland University College (B.A., 1923; LL.B, 1924). He proceeded to Trinity Hall, Cambridge (B.A., 1947; M.A., 1949), where he gained a first-class pass in the law

tripos in 1925. Back home, he practised as a barrister and solicitor in Auckland and at Dargaville before becoming a farmer at Tangiteroria in the mid-1930s. Beattie campaigned to improve the breeding and marketing of pigs, and was a member of the National Pig Industry Council. He played Rugby Union, was a long-distance runner and won prizes for marksmanship.

Having come to Australia on business in December 1939, Beattie understated his age when enlisting in the Australian Imperial Force on 23 October 1941. Posted to the 4th (2nd/4th) Independent Company, he served in the Northern Territory for six months and on Timor from September 1942 to January 1943: he averred that however bad Northern Territory beef might be, it was preferable to Timor water buffalo. On 11 September Beattie transferred to the Royal Australian Air Force and was commissioned two months later. In 1944-45 he performed intelligence duties in Australia, the Solomons, New Guinea, the Moluccas and the Philippines. His appointment terminated on 8 November 1945.

'An extremely able man with a very logical mind, considerable adaptability and a capacity for good honest work', on 13 May 1946 in Melbourne Beattie was engaged as a senior research officer by the Council for Scientific and Industrial Research to undertake a comprehensive survey of the Australian beef cattle industry. He travelled throughout the country in a utility truck. Although sorely tempted, he once helped to ferry beer across Coopers Creek, South Australia, on a hot day without opening a bottle. His reports, presented in 1952-53, stressed the need for improved breeding and pastures, and for new railways to bring stock to market in better condition. He advanced these ideas in the press and at a meeting with Federal parliamentarians in June 1952. Two years later he published a successful textbook, *Beef Cattle Breeding and Management* (Melbourne).

Having left the Commonwealth Scientific and Industrial Research Organization in 1952, Beattie joined the Australian Estates Co. Ltd as assistant general manager; he divided his time between the head office in Melbourne and cattle properties in North Queensland. From 1955 to 1958 he participated in a United Nations Food and Agriculture Organization project to foster primary production in South American countries. He held directorships in Wright, Stephenson & Co. Ltd and other companies, and established his own stock and farm management consultancy in Melbourne. Beattie was Victorian president (1964-68) of the Royal Society for the Prevention of Cruelty to Animals and served on the council of the Institute of Public Affairs from 1964 (chairman 1975-77). He wrote extensively on the economic development of Australia and the Third World. Unpretentious and unassuming, he was liked and respected by his associates.

On 5 January 1927 Beattie had married Annie Isabel McLean in the Presbyterian Church, Whangarei, New Zealand. They were divorced in 1942. His second wife was Lillian Grace, née Holder, with whom he lived at St Kilda and Caulfield, Melbourne. On 8 September 1956 he married Kathleen Mary (Kay) Tucker-Smith in the United States of America. There were no children of his marriages. Survived by his wife, he died on 14 July 1980 at Ringwood, Melbourne, and was cremated.

IPA Review, July-Sept 1980; *Country Life*, 10 July 1947; *Age* (Melb), 20 Sept 1962; *Herald* (Melb), 5 Sept 1964; CSIRO Archives, Canb.

H. J. W. STOKES

BEATTY, WILLIAM ALFRED (1902-1972), writer and broadcaster, was born on 27 November 1902 at Paddington, Sydney, only son of James Joseph Beatty, waiter, and his wife Margaret, née Brazil, both Dublin born. On leaving Christian Brothers' College, Waverley, Bill worked as a clerk, gave piano lessons and recitals, and travelled in the Far East and the United States of America. Deeply impressed by the Americans' pride in their history, he determined to arouse in Australians a greater interest in their own past.

In 1936 Beatty joined the fledgling, Catholic-owned radio station 2SM as announcer and pianist. His programme, 'Cuckoo Court', featured his first broadcasts on Australiana which provided the basis for his illustrated 'Believe Bill Beatty' items in the *Wireless Weekly* (1939-41) and *A.B.C. Weekly* (1941-43). In June 1941 he was appointed to the Australian Broadcasting Commission as a script and continuity writer. In addition, he wrote and broadcast a weekly, 15-minute, dramatized talk, 'Australoddities', a programme of local curiosities and amazing facts, which was to run for over four hundred sessions. Beatty also presented Australiana items on the 'Children's Session' in 1941-44. His programme fitted the patriotism of the war years and their aftermath when the A.B.C. came under pressure to include more Australian material. 'Australoddities' continued on air as a small, but popular, item.

Beatty roamed widely, collecting material for his programme and writings; correspondence with his listeners and readers provided much information. His first publication, *This Australia, Strange and Amazing Facts*, by 'Believe Bill Beatty', appeared in 1941 and was read over the British Broadcasting Corporation network in 1946. He followed it with *Amazing Australia* (1943) and *Australia, the Amazing* (1944). In 1946 he declined a lecture tour in the United States because he was unable to afford the fare. When 'Australoddities' moved to another A.B.C. network in 1950, its audience dropped and the programme ended in December 1951.

From 1952 until 1960 Beatty worked as a clerical assistant in the Commonwealth Department of Trade and Customs in Sydney to enable him to continue to support his sister and her children. Meantime, he pursued his main interest—Australian folklore. Fourteen of his books were published between 1950 and 1970, among them *Unique to Australia* (1952), *Come A-Waltzing Matilda* (1954) and *A Treasury of Australian Folk Tales and Traditions* (1960). He combined his knowledge of Australian history with his journeys to produce several travel guides, including *The White Roof of Australia* (London, 1958) and *Around Australia with Bill Beatty* (Melbourne, 1966).

His writings presented bits of history, anecdotes, firsts, bests, oldests and other miscellaneous information, and made entertaining reading. He was an early popularizer and chronicler of Australian traditions who recalled his life's work as 'a relentless but rewarding pursuit' to rescue and preserve nearly-forgotten tales. A slim, handsome man, with glasses and a pencil-thin moustache, Beatty never married, and lived with his sister and her family at Newport. He died there of ischaemic heart disease on 13 April 1972 and was buried in the local cemetery with Catholic rites.

Wireless Weekly, 19 Apr, 28 June 1941; *Age* (Melb), 25 June 1960; H. de Berg tapes, Bill Beatty (NL); Scriptwriters, NSW, biog files: Bill Beatty (ABC Document Archives, Syd); William Beatty, Aust programme material, Australoddities, correspondence and scripts, 1938-48, SP 300/1, box 2, Series B, SP 341/1, box 64, SP 368/1, boxes 2 and 6, SP 1011/2, box 11, SP 1297/2, box 14, Series C (AA).

JAN BRAZIER

BEAVIS, LESLIE ELLIS (1895-1975), army officer, was born on 25 January 1895 at Bathurst, New South Wales, son of Horace Colin Dean Beavis, photographer, and his wife Emma Weston, née Bailey, both native-born. Educated at Bathurst District School, Les was a member of the New South Wales contingent of school cadets sent to England in 1911 for the coronation of King George V. In March 1913 Beavis entered the Royal Military College, Duntroon, Federal Capital Territory; his course was abridged because of the outbreak of war and he topped his graduation class in June 1915. Appointed lieutenant in the Australian Imperial Force, he sailed for the Middle East in November with the 5th Field Artillery Brigade.

After service in Egypt, Beavis reached the Western Front in April 1916. His qualities were soon recognized: in July he was given command of the 12th Battery, 4th F.A.B., and promoted captain. In 1917 he spent six months undertaking staff training at Cambridge, England, and in the field at 2nd Division headquarters, France. Transferring to the 14th F.A.B. in September, he took command of the 53rd Battery and was promoted major. In the fighting east of Ypres, Belgium, his unit experienced sustained gas-attacks. Beavis remained at his post and assisted other batteries which had lost many of their officers until the effects of gas forced him to be evacuated to England on 4 November. For his actions, he was awarded the Distinguished Service Order. On 21 April 1918 near Vaux-sur-Somme, France, he witnessed the last moments in the air of the German flying ace Manfred von Richthofen, the 'Red Baron'. In the ensuing dispute over who shot von Richthofen down, Beavis was to remain adamant that his Lewis-gunners were responsible, an opinion which appears to be supported by the evidence.

Twice mentioned in dispatches, after the war Beavis remained in England to attend ordnance and advanced artillery courses at Woolwich. On 12 August 1919 in All Souls parish church, Hampstead, he married Ethel May Blumer, a Sydneysider. Following a short attachment to the Australian High Commission in London, he came home in 1922. He performed regimental and staff duties in several postings, then returned to England in 1928 as a student at the Staff College, Camberley. His experience was broadened by two years with the directorate of operations and intelligence, Imperial General Staff, and by a further posting to the high commissioner's office. Back in Australia, in April 1936 Beavis was appointed chairman of the Defence Resources Board, an organization established to advise the government on mobilizing industry for war; it was widely assumed that conflict in the Far East could occur by 1939.

With knowledge of the operations of a similar body in Britain to guide him, Beavis argued for the development of the manufacturing and technological capabilities of private industry before hostilities began, and, to that end, urged that work orders be placed with firms. He was aware that Britain's initial reliance on government munitions production in World War I had resulted in near disaster. Beavis's conclusions appeared in the board's report, a document notable for its command of the issues and for the practical solutions it offered. In contrast, A. E. Leighton [q.v.10], the controller-general of munitions supply, held

that scarce funds should be spent on government factories in the first instance. To the probable detriment of Australia's early war effort, Leighton's view prevailed, the board was disbanded and in April 1937 Beavis resumed army duties.

Promoted colonel on 2 November 1939, he transferred to the A.I.F. in April 1940 and embarked for the Middle East next month. He rapidly assumed increasingly senior supply positions on the staff of Lieutenant General Sir Thomas Blamey [q.v.] and on 17 December was promoted temporary brigadier and made director of ordnance services. In this demanding post Beavis was expected to supply the A.I.F. with the best equipment available, on time and within budgetary constraints. Changes in operational circumstances and the competing claims of the British forces added to his difficulties. Beavis's negotiating ability, perseverance, strength of personality and occasionally fiery temper ensured his success. He was appointed C.B.E. in 1942.

Returning with the A.I.F. to Australia, on 6 April Beavis was promoted temporary major general and appointed master-general of the ordnance, in which post he was the senior officer responsible for the logistic support of the army at home and abroad. Through his equipment, design, inspection and maintenance divisions, he co-ordinated the efforts of government and private producers with the needs of the army's supply service and operational formations. Beavis was at the pinnacle of his military career and his tasks demanded all his administrative and technical skills. Instead of easing his burden, the approach of peace placed new obstacles in his way: as some of the sense of urgency was lost from the war effort, he began to experience an increase in bureaucratic pettiness and obstructionism. In December 1946 he was seconded to the Department of Defence and appointed chairman of the new weapons and equipment development committee. He served on a number of other bodies that were charged with formulating and implementing policy on research and development, production-planning and supply. Held in high regard in international military and industrial circles, he was appointed C.B. in 1952. His rank had been made substantive in 1948; he retired from the army on 26 January 1952.

From 1952 to 1954 Beavis held the position of Australian high commissioner to Pakistan. He was honorary colonel of the Royal Australian Army Ordnance Corps in 1954-60. In retirement he took an interest in the affairs of the Citizen Military Forces and the Returned Sailors', Soldiers' and Airmen's Imperial League of Australia. Fair haired and 5 ft 11 ins (180.3 cm) tall, he was companionable and modest. His recreations were golf and tennis. Survived by his son and daughter, Beavis died on 27 September 1975 in the Repatriation General Hospital, Heidelberg, Melbourne; following a military funeral, he was cremated.

P. Hasluck, *The Government and the People 1939-1941* (Canb, 1952); G. Long, *To Benghazi* (Canb, 1952) and *The Final Campaigns* (Canb, 1963); D. P. Mellor, *The Role of Science and Industry* (Canb, 1958); J. D. Tilbrook, *To the Warrior His Arms* (Canb, 1989); D. M. Titler, *The Day the Red Baron Died* (NY, 1970); *Army J*, no 322, Mar 1976, p 16; AWM records.   JOHN D. TILBROOK

BECHER, OTTO HUMPHREY (1908-1977), naval officer, was born on 13 September 1908 at Harvey, Western Australia, son of Francis Joseph Becher, orchardist, and his wife Antonia Amalie, née Vetter, both native-born. Entering the Royal Australian Naval College, Jervis Bay, Federal Capital Territory, in 1922, Humphrey had a good scholastic record, and won colours for hockey and tennis. In 1926 he served in H.M.A.S. *Adelaide* and H.M.A.S. *Brisbane* as a midshipman, then travelled to Britain for further sea-training and professional courses with the Royal Navy.

Returning to Australia in 1930, Lieutenant Becher went to sea in the R.A.N.'s heavy cruisers *Australia* and *Canberra* before electing to specialize; in 1932-34 he was based in England where he took the long course at the R.N.'s gunnery school, H.M.S. *Excellent*. On 7 January 1935 in St Michael's Anglican Church, Vaucluse, Sydney, he married Valerie Chisholm Baird; they were to have three sons. Following postings to H.M.A.S. *Cerberus*, Westernport, Victoria, and to H.M.A. ships *Canberra* and *Stuart*, Becher was promoted lieutenant commander on 16 June 1938 and again sailed for Britain. At the outbreak of World War II he was squadron gunnery officer in the cruiser H.M.S. *Devonshire*. In May 1940 the ship supported the withdrawal of troops from the Namsos region of Norway: for his performance during the operation Becher was awarded the Distinguished Service Cross. Joining H.M.A.S. *Napier* in November 1940, he saw action in the Mediterranean.

On 26 April 1942 he returned to *Cerberus* as officer-in-charge of the gunnery school. He was posted in command of the destroyer, *Quickmatch*, on 3 March 1944. Pressing home a successful attack on the Japanese naval base at Sabang, off Sumatra, on 25 July, Becher showed such coolness, skilful ship-handling and courage in the face of enemy batteries that he was awarded a Bar to his D.S.C.; he was mentioned in dispatches for his service in *Quickmatch*, and was promoted commander on 31 December. From 1945 to 1948 he performed staff duties at Navy Office, Melbourne, then went back to sea to commission the new aircraft-carrier, *Sydney*. His posting in command of the Sydney shore-establishment, H.M.A.S. *Watson*, was cut short on 28 July 1950 when he hurriedly relieved Captain (Vice Admiral Sir) Alan McNicoll as commanding officer of another destroyer, *Warramunga*, about to sail for Korea.

Throughout a busy deployment, Becher confronted numerous operational problems which included poorly-charted waters, severe weather conditions, and complex control arrangements involving senior commanders from Britain and the United States of America. On 5-6 December 1950 *Warramunga* took part in the hazardous evacuation of Chinnamp'o. Her accurate bombardment of Haeju in August 1951 received special praise. Becher had been promoted captain on 31 December 1950; he was awarded the Distinguished Service Order and appointed to the Legion of Merit (U.S.A.) for his exploits in Korea. In the period from late 1951 to 1962 he occupied senior staff posts in Navy Office, Melbourne and Canberra, among them appointments as deputy-chief of Naval Staff (1952-54 and 1959-62); he attended the Imperial Defence College, London (1956), and commanded the aircraft-carriers, *Vengeance* (1954-55) and *Melbourne* (1957-58). Having acted in the rank for twelve months, he was promoted rear admiral on 7 January 1960. He was appointed C.B.E. in 1961, and was head, Australian Joint Services Staff, London, in 1962-63.

In January 1964 Becher succeeded McNicoll as flag officer commanding H.M. Australian Fleet. Next month H.M.A. ships *Melbourne* and *Voyager* collided off the southern coast of New South Wales. The incident was to make Becher a controversial figure. He discussed the evidence he would give (to the royal commission inquiring into the loss of *Voyager*) with *Melbourne*'s commanding officer, Captain R. J. Robertson, D.S.C., R.A.N., which gave rise to speculation of collusion. For all that, Becher's subsequent contention that *Melbourne* should have challenged *Voyager*'s final movements may have helped to influence the royal commissioner Sir John Spicer [q.v.] to blame Robertson unduly for the disaster. In 1965 Becher became flag officer in charge, East Australia Area; he retired on 6 March 1966. As director-general of recruiting for the armed forces in 1966-69, he opposed conscription, believing that it lowered professional standards.

Popular, personable and an accomplished ship's captain with vast operational experience, as a naval officer Becher displayed dash and occasional flamboyance. In his retirement he refrained from public comment on naval matters, and was chairman of the Council of the Institute of Marine Sciences, University of New South Wales. He enjoyed golf and tennis. Survived by his wife and sons, Becher died of myocardial infarction on 15 June 1977 in Sydney Hospital and was cremated.

F. B. Eldridge, *A History of the Royal Australian Naval College* (Melb, 1949); G. H. Gill, *Royal Australian Navy 1939-1942* (Canb, 1957) and *1942-1945* (Canb, 1968); H. Hickling, *One Minute of Time* (Syd, 1965); R. O'Neill, *Australia in the Korean War*, 2 (Canb, 1985); *Age*(Melb), 29 Nov 1944; *SMH*, 16 Feb 1955, 18, 19 Mar 1964, 15 June 1977.   TOM FRAME

BECKER, SIR JACK ELLERTON (1904-1979), entrepreneur, was born on 4 October 1904 at North Unley, Adelaide, only son of Percy Harold Becker, clerk, and his wife Mabel Martha, née Gully. Jack attended public schools and was apprenticed to a jewellery manufacturer. Capitalizing on the craze for popular music, he taught himself to play the banjo and other instruments. From the age of 16 in his spare time he gave lessons so profitably that he was able to visit the United States of America.

From 1926 Becker worked as a salesman at Allans [q.v.3] Ltd's music shop in Adelaide. On 1 November 1928 at St Augustine's Anglican Church, Unley, he married a fellow employee Gladys Sarah Duggan. He promoted the formation of fife bands in fifty-three schools, selling them instruments made to his design. The English music firm, Boosey & Hawkes Ltd, gave him their South Australian agency. In 1932 he quit Allans and founded the Adelaide Drum and Fife Band, comprising the top two hundred schoolboy players. It performed several week-long seasons in Adelaide's largest theatres, gave wireless broadcasts, and toured Melbourne and Sydney in 1936-37; some parents resented having to pay for the expensive uniforms that Becker ordered.

In 1932 he had named his studio the Adelaide College of Music. For part-time teachers, he engaged soloists from leading dance bands and from the Adelaide Symphony Orchestra. He formed huge banjo, saxophone and other ensembles, including 'the world's largest' boys' military band. As the conductor, he stood, massive and broad-shouldered, resplendent in a scarlet uniform with gold aglet, brass buttons and white gloves. Avowedly to raise money for patriotic and other causes, but also to publicize his college, Becker established the Music League of South Australia which mounted *On Parade*, an annual extravaganza involving one thousand players. The first production, in December 1939, set the pattern: seats for all nine performances sold in advance, and, after Becker claimed most of the proceeds to cover expenses, there was a modest surplus for charity.

The sale of Adelaide College in 1942 gave Becker his first fortune. His earlier diversification into pastoralism had failed, and wartime controls limited his profits when he sold the twenty-four blocks he had bought at Torrens Park in 1941. Thenceforward he speculated primarily in rural land which was ripe for closer settlement or suburban subdivision. Learning the results of David S. Riceman's work on mineral deficiencies in the soil at Robe, in 1943 Becker bought 7000 acres (2833 ha) of the well-watered but barren Ninety Mile Desert (Coonalpyn Downs) in that region and invited Riceman to conduct experiments there. Riceman found that the addition of traces of copper and zinc had significant effects. Becker sold the land for forty times his purchase price. The commissioner of taxation demanded a cut, but the High Court of Australia held that the land had not been bought for profit-making by resale.

More gainful speculations followed near Adelaide, with Becker's solicitor and accountant devising complex tax-avoidance schemes. Becker's most dramatic coup was facilitated by Premier Playford's tardiness in giving the South Australian Housing Trust adequate funds to buy land for the satellite city of Elizabeth. In 1957, shortly after Becker had bought 1266 acres (512 ha) there for £149 000, the trust was finally empowered to begin to acquire it. Becker haggled and received £853 000. Despite admitting that he had known the land was likely to be designated as urban, he persuaded the High Court that his purchase had been for pastoral purposes; the taxation commissioner's demand for £350 000 was dismissed with costs.

In 1960-61 the Australian Academy of Science was in financial difficulties. Its president Sir John Eccles secured Prime Minister (Sir) Robert Menzies's [q.v.] agreement to recommend Becker for a knighthood—if he came to the rescue. Following long negotiations, the tycoon contracted to give £200 000 over ten years. This arrangement settled the academy's debts and created an invaluable endowment fund. Having severed connexions with their only child because she had married a naval stoker against their wishes, the Beckers also undertook to make the academy their principal and residuary legatee. Becker was appointed a fellow (1961) of the academy and knighted in 1962, and the academy's Canberra headquarters was named Becker House. The Commonwealth Scientific and Industrial Research Organization's scientists and Sir Mark Oliphant were appalled, but Eccles had brooked no opposition. There was much chaff about Sir Ellerton's honours being obtained on hire purchase; wits asked if the laurels could be repossessed because his instalments were often in arrears.

In 1971 the Beckers retired to Pembroke, Bermuda, where they built a villa with grounds containing an artificial waterfall and a garden gnome. Sir Ellerton died there on 9 May 1979 and was buried on the island. His daughter, an impoverished, invalid pensioner, received nothing. Lady Becker died on 3 January 1985. Since then the academy has received a further $3 million from the estate. A perfectionist and 'a great hater', obsessional in his quest for wealth, status, *objets d'art* and luxurious living, Becker had retained few friends. His one 'generous' action was a tax-deductible purchase of privilege.

S. Cockburn and D. Ellyard, *Oliphant* (Adel, 1981); A. D. McCredie (ed), *From Colonel Light into the Footlights* (Adel, 1988); K. Preiss and P. Oborn, *The Torrens Park Estate* (Adel, 1991); *Aust Women's Weekly*, 31 Dec 1975; *Hist Records of Aust Science*, 5, 1982, and for bibliog; *Advertiser* (Adel), 16 Aug 1972; *Herald* (Melb), 9 Sept 1975, 21, 23, 24 Nov 1981; *Sunday Mail* (Adel), 13 May 1979; Music League of SA pamphlet collection (Mort L).

P. A. HOWELL

BECKER, JOHANNES HEINRICH (1898-1961), medical practitioner and Nazi, was born on 27 September 1898 at Schmalkalden, Thuringia, Germany, son of Heinrich Thomas Becker, art teacher, and his wife Frieda Johanne Luise, née Hornäffer. In World War I Johannes joined the German Army. Wounded twice, in 1917 he fought at Verdun, France, and at Ypres, Belgium, and was awarded the Iron Cross. He was a corporal by the time of the Armistice. Fair haired and blue eyed, he bore scars on his forehead, hand and arm. Becker studied medicine at the University of Marburg, graduated in 1924 and spent a year as a ship's doctor before migrating to South Australia in 1927.

Having practised at Tanunda in the Barossa Valley, Becker applied for naturalization in 1930, but lacked the necessary five-years residence to qualify. On 22 August 1932 at St Stephan's Lutheran Church, Adelaide, he married Mona Gertrude Price; they were to have two children. Because of his German credentials he was never registered as a medical practitioner in Australia, yet he worked as a doctor until 1939, which involved him in a continuing struggle with the local branch of the British Medical Association. He was backed by his patients and by the premier (Sir) Richard Layton Butler [q.v.7]. During the dispute Becker won two libel cases, as well as the admiration of many German-

Australians. While often considered charming and diplomatic, he could also be intolerant, imperious and forthright in expressing his extreme views. He had visited Germany in 1933-34.

In the 1930s Becker attracted the attention of the public, and of Australia's security services, through his association with Hitler's National Socialist German Workers' Party (*Nationalsozialistische Deutsche Arbeiterpartei*). He joined the N.S.D.A.P. (Nazi Party) on 1 March 1932 and next year was appointed state trustee (*Landesvertrauensmann*) for Australia; he later became state leader (*Landeskreisleiter*) for the South Pacific and head of the Tanunda branch. In 1936 he was allegedly approached by the State secretary of the Australian Labor Party who asked him to stand for the South Australian parliament.

Becker supported the radical wing of the N.S.D.A.P. and his relations with South Australia's German-Australian elite were cool. His wartime experiences had turned him against the Fatherland's traditional ruling class and his aversion extended to men like Dr Rudolf Asmis, the German consul-general in Sydney, with whom he clashed over methods of bonding German-Australians to the Nazi cause. Becker's approach—through propaganda, in fostering 'Friends of the New Germany' and by confronting opponents—failed to impress the authorities in Berlin. He was removed as state leader late in 1936.

Following the outbreak of World War II, Becker was interned at Tatura, Victoria, and at Loveday, South Australia. His role in Nazi organizations in both camps was a limited one. Paroled in 1946, he made headlines in November 1947 when he was discovered as a stowaway on a ship lying off Watsons Bay, Sydney, bound for Panama. Next month he was deported to West Germany where his exoneration by a 'denazification' tribunal in December 1948 was assisted by the disappearance of a dossier on his Australian activities. Despite repeated appeals, he was never allowed to re-enter Australia. In 1953 Becker's marriage was dissolved in the Supreme Court of South Australia. Survived by his son and daughter, he died on 21 February 1961 at Bremen, West Germany.

J. Perkins, 'Dr Asmis and the "Rescue of Deutschtum" in Australia in the 1930s', *JRAHS*, 73, no 4, 1988, p 296, and 'The Swastika Down Under: Nazi Activities in Australia, 1933-39', *J of Contemporary Hist*, 25, no 1, 1991, p 111; AP308/1, SA15163 (AA, Adel), *and* A4391/1 51/11/6691, A472, W31449 (AA, Canb), *and* SP1714/1, N41719 (AA, Syd).   JOHN PERKINS

BEDFORD, RUTH MARJORY (1882-1963), writer, was born on 2 August 1882 at

Petersham, Sydney, second daughter of native-born parents Alfred Percival Bedford, clerk, and his wife Agnes Victoria who was the seventeenth child of Sir Alfred Stephen [q.v.6]. Percy and Agnes were first cousins. With her sisters Sylvia and Alfreda, Ruth was educated at home and grew up in a family that was clannish and prominent in Sydney society. In 1892 she wrote to her mother that she would try to be 'more clever and good', a promise honoured next year with the publication of *Rhymes by Ruth* (revised and reprinted 1896).

She swam regularly with one of her 'closest and dearest friends' Dorothea Mackellar [q.v.10], and the two of them enjoyed play-acting characters they had invented. Ruth's *Sydney at Sunset and other Verses* appeared in 1911. After the death of her mother and a broken engagement, she went abroad in 1912, toured the Continent, shared a flat in London with Dorothea and returned in 1913. They co-authored two light and racy novels, *The Little Blue Devil* (London, 1912) and *Two's Company* (London, 1914), based on their 'play people'.

As a 'children's poet' Bedford published several collections of verse, including *Rosy-cheeks and Goldenhead* (London, 1913) and *Hundreds and Thousands* (1934). At 40, she claimed that she was still able to write with her 'own thoughts of the times of ten or eleven'. One London literary agent rejected her work as 'very slight and almost too innocuous', but the Brisbane *Courier-Mail* approvingly remarked that she had 'not been caught in the stream of so-called modernism'. Throughout her long career as a full-time writer Bedford stuck to simple subjects and published seven collections, among them *The Learner and other Verses* (1937) and *Who's Who in Rhyme and Without Reason* (1948). Her poems appeared in anthologies and in the *Sydney Morning Herald* for thirty years. She also wrote plays: *Postman's Knock* was commended at the Australian Play Society's 1932 competition and several were accepted by the Australian Broadcasting Commission.

Photographs taken from adolescence to old age show her strong, rectangular face, dominated by dark eyes and prominent teeth. In 1923 Bedford told *Aussie* magazine that 'children come first in her affections, and then people, books, the stage, surfing, pictures and travel'. A cousin described her as 'sprightly' and forthright. Most of Ruth's life was spent at Edgecliff and Woollahra with her sisters and members of Sydney's literary world. As its secretary, she represented the Sydney P.E.N. Club at a convention in Buenos Aires in 1936; she also belonged to the Women's Pioneer Society of Australasia.

Her last work, *Think of Stephen* (1954), was also her most acclaimed. Sponsored by the Commonwealth Literary Fund, it was a warm chronicle of the domestic and social life of her mother's family, for which Ruth drew on her grandmother's diaries and letters. Professor Kathleen Fitzpatrick, among others, reviewed it favourably, and the book prompted a letter of praise (and an invitation to lunch) from Patrick White. Slowly worn down by illness, Bedford died on 24 July 1963 at Paddington and was cremated with Anglican rites.

J. Brunsdon (ed), *I Love a Sunburnt Country: the Diaries of Dorothea Mackellar* (Syd, 1990); *Aussie*, Apr 1923, p 43; *BP Mag*, 1 Sept 1936, p 15; *SMH*, 29 Apr 1932, 11 June, 7 Dec 1936, 24 May, 14 Nov 1953, 26 July 1963; H. de Berg, Ruth Bedford (taped interview, 15 Sept 1961, NL); Stephen papers (ML).   JANE CONNORS

BEDNALL, COLIN BLORE (1913-1976), journalist and media manager, was born on 13 January 1913 at Balaklava, South Australia, son of Adelaide-born parents Edward Blore Bednall, bank manager, and his wife Naomi Caroline Gertrude, née Ferry. The family was Anglican. Colin was educated at Pulteney Grammar School and the Collegiate School of St Peter, Adelaide. On his father's death during the Depression, Colin left school and followed his elder brother into journalism on the *Adelaide News* where he soon came to the attention of the proprietor (Sir) Keith Murdoch [q.v.10]. After working as a reporter on the Melbourne *Sun* and *Herald* in 1932-37, Bednall was special correspondent in Darwin in 1937-38: he made a name by reporting Japanese intrusions in northern waters and by exposing the *Larrakia* fiasco. In Darwin he met Hilda Marion, daughter of the administrator of the Northern Territory, Aubrey Abbott [q.v.], and married her on 4 February 1939 at St Anthony of Padua's Catholic Church, Radlett, Hertfordshire, England.

Murdoch had encouraged Bednall to go abroad for experience and in 1938 arranged a job for him with Australian Associated Press in London. As aviation correspondent (1942-44) for the *Daily Mail*, he became well known to the British public: he flew as a qualified gunner in allied bombing raids over Germany and graphically described his experiences in the press. He was briefed by top Royal Air Force sources, and his articles contributed to the pre-eminence of the air war in British strategic planning and in the public mind. Bednall was one of a group of notable Australian war correspondents in the European theatre which included Alan Moorehead and Chester Wilmot [q.v.]. In 1945 Bednall served briefly as a war correspondent attached to Lord Louis (Earl) Mountbatten's command on the Indian subcontinent; at the end of the war he was appointed O.B.E. for his services to the allied cause. Although Lord Rothermere had made him assistant editor of the *Daily Mail* in 1944, Bednall was persuaded by Murdoch to accept managing editorship of Queensland Newspapers Pty Ltd whose main outlet was the *Courier-Mail*. After Murdoch's death, in 1954 Bednall became managing editor of the Melbourne *Argus*.

In 1953 he had been appointed to the royal commission on television. When GTV-9 (one of Melbourne's first two commercial television stations) was formed in 1956 by a consortium led by Sir Arthur Warner [q.v.], Bednall was the station's first managing director; Sir Frank Packer [q.v.] bought GTV-9 in 1960. Despite competition from the Herald and Weekly Times Pty Ltd which controlled HSV-7, Channel 9 soon led the ratings, largely due to Bednall's astuteness in promoting Australian content and fostering a number of television personalities, among them Graham Kennedy who described Bednall as the most important influence in his life. At GTV-9 Bednall assisted Prime Minister (Sir) Robert Menzies [q.v.] in using television for election campaigns.

In newspapers and in television Bednall usually managed to satisfy his employers by running profitable enterprises; at the same time, he assisted journalists and performers to develop their talents. To a marked extent this dual achievement stemmed from the force of his personality: he had strong views, new ideas and a sense of what the public wanted, and he was prepared to back his judgements. Proprietors sometimes considered him extravagant in the way he backed his shows; it was over a financial disagreement of this nature that he left GTV-9 in 1965.

Unlike many strong-minded people, Bednall had the ability to listen to and encourage the views of others. He was a large, gregarious man of considerable personal charm who combined informality with courtesy. While involved in the higher echelons of the media, and in the worlds of politics and business, he mixed with all sections of society and with both sides of politics. From his background as a journalist, he developed wide-ranging interests: he published a booklet, *Dingoes* (1967), acquired a collection of Australian paintings and wrote an extensive (unpublished) autobiography.

In 1965 Bednall was appointed to the United Nations Educational, Scientific and Cultural Organization's committee on space communications which was based in Paris. Next year he tried to organize an Australian mining industry council. From 1966 to 1969 he managed a new English-Chinese television station, run by an international consortium in Hong Kong; the poverty he saw there dramatically altered his political views. On his return to Australia, he became active in Labor politics (then highly unusual for a member of the Melbourne Club) and stood unsuccessfully against (Sir) Phillip Lynch for the Victorian seat of Flinders in the Federal elections of 1972 and 1974. Bednall was a part-time media consultant to Prime Minister Gough Whitlam in 1973-75; he subsequently accepted various consultancies and wrote a media column for the *Age*. He died suddenly of hypertensive coronary vascular disease on 26 April 1976 at his Portsea home and was buried in Sorrento cemetery; his wife, son and two daughters survived him. To commemorate him, the Australian television industry instituted an annual Colin Bednall award for outstanding services to the medium.

S. Hall, *Supertoy* (Melb, 1976); K. Dunstan, *No Brains At All* (Melb, 1990); *TV Times*, 20 July 1966; *Age*, 9 July 1965, 27 Apr 1976; *Nation*, 8 Jan 1966; *Sun News-Pictorial*, 30 July 1970; *National Times*, 29 May-3 June 1972; Bednall papers (NL); information from Mrs M. Bednall, Nth Fitzroy, Melb, and Mr R. Kinnear, Berwick, Vic.

PATRICK MORGAN

BEESTON, DORIS ANNE (1897-1940), kindergarten teacher, was born on 22 September 1897 at Hindmarsh, Adelaide, daughter of John Spencer Beeston, clerk, and his wife Anne Japp, née Boath. Educated at Hindmarsh and Adelaide high schools, Dorrie attended Adelaide Kindergarten Training College (1915-17). There she studied the Montessori methods introduced by Lillian de Lissa [q.v.8] and gained a diploma with first-class honours. In 1918-21 she was directress of the Franklin Street Free Kindergarten Training Centre for Students, in Adelaide's poor West End, where she expanded social work among parents and 'old scholars'. Tall, calm and earnest, with her dark hair severely pulled back, Miss Beeston 'had a presence'.

A Congregationalist, in 1922-23 she directed the Montessori Kindergarten of the Mathison Congregational Church at Croydon, Sydney, before returning to Adelaide and taking charge of the Bowden Free Kindergarten in 1924. In June, Beeston became the first paid general secretary of the South Australian Kindergarten Union. She influenced educational goals, nurtured malnourished, ill-clad children during the Depression, and inspired other people to work with her. Using her 'clear business head and organizing ability', she steadily expanded the union and embarked on fund-raising campaigns with her friend Jean Bonython [q.v.].

Beeston had been secretary (1924-27) of the local Dalcroze Society. In 1935 she investigated nursery schools in Victoria, began similar programmes in Adelaide and was appointed to the foundation South Australian Board of Social Study and Training. She was a member of the National Council of Women's child welfare and housing committees. Next year she organized a national kindergarten conference in Adelaide, joined the Women's Centenary Council of South Australia and helped to stage the pageant, *Heritage*.

In 1937 Beeston won the Catherine Helen Spence [q.v.6] scholarship which enabled her to go abroad to study child welfare, including parent education. From March 1939 she visited nursery schools and kindergartens in Britain and France, and attended lectures by specialists on early childhood. When World War II began she helped to evacuate young children from London to Kent. In 1940 she began a course under de Lissa at Gipsy Hill College, Brighton, and accepted the wardenship of its emergency nursery school. Having volunteered to serve Britain's Children's Overseas Reception Board, she was appointed an escort.

On 1 August Beeston sailed from Liverpool for Australia with 477 child evacuees in the *Batory*. During the dangerous, ten-week voyage she supervised sixteen boys, aged 7 to 14, and reached Adelaide on 15 October. Recalled for duty within two weeks, she left Sydney for England in the *Rangitane*, but was killed on 26 November 1940 when a German raider shelled the vessel in the Pacific Ocean.

After news of her death reached Adelaide, a memorial service was held in St Peter's Anglican Cathedral on 13 January 1941. Through a public appeal, the Kindergarten Union raised money for the Doris Beeston memorial building which was opened in July 1941 at the Kindergarten Training College, North Adelaide.

H. Jones (ed), *Jubilee History of the Kindergarten Union of South Australia 1905-1955* (Adel, 1975); *Advertiser*(Adel), 16 Oct, 5 Dec 1940, 14 Jan 1941; Kindergarten Union of SA, Executive and Organizing Cte, Minutes, 30 June 1924, 15 Oct 1935, 11 Feb 1936, *and* SA Education Dept correspondence files (SRSA); C. H. Spence Scholarship Advisory Cte, Minutes, 23 Oct 1940, 2 Nov 1945 [sic] (SA Education Dept, Adel); information from Mrs J. Turnbull and Ms G. Palmer, Grange, and Mrs L. Retalic, Hazelwood Park, Adel.   HELEN JONES

BEET, WILLIAM IRONSIDE ASHLEY (1878-1957), medical practitioner, was born on 9 December 1878 at Sheepwash, Devon, England, second of six children of Joseph Frederick Beet, schoolmaster, and his wife Lucelle Selina, née Ashley. In 1886 the family migrated to Queensland. There they successively lived at Clermont, in the Copperfield district and at Townsville West. Ashley was educated at Townsville Grammar School and raised in a strict Methodist home where family pride was important. Intelligent, inquiring and with an inventive mind, he was an avid reader and a talented violinist. He matriculated in 1894 and two years later travelled to England to study medicine. Having been a student and assistant medical officer at London Hospital, in 1901 he qualified as a licentiate of the Royal College of Physicians and was admitted to the Royal College of Surgeons. He then spent a year as medical officer at the West Ham Infirmary before returning to Queensland in December 1902.

In 1903 Beet was appointed medical officer to the eight-bed hospital at Beaudesert, on a salary of £145 a year and with the right to private practice. A table from the matron's room served as his first operating bench. In 1911 he sailed for England as ship's doctor in the *Fifeshire*. The vessel was wrecked off Cape Guardafui, Somaliland, and the passengers were forced to take to open boats before being rescued, and brought to Aden and thence to England. During the voyage Beet met Lola McCamley whom he married on 3 April 1912 at St Philip's parish church, Kensington, London. After completing the R.C.S. diploma in public health, in August he brought his wife to Beaudesert.

Transport was so difficult that the doctor travelled to the patient. Beet's grey horse often had to be rested at homesteads, or a fresh mount saddled to enable him to complete the journey: 'nothing was too much bother for him', regardless of the blackest night, winter frosts or driving rain. On one occasion he rode 70 miles (112.7 km) in a day. As transport modernized, Dr Beet progressed to a pony-trap, a springless motorbike, a tramway tricycle and finally to a motorcar. Nonetheless, he remained indelibly imprinted in popular memory as a brown-haired, bespectacled man, tearing around the countryside on a motorbike.

The community loved him, and countless babies—White and Aboriginal—were named after him. Stockily built, with a hesitant expression, he was friendly, if a little shy. Small talk never interested him. He had energy and stamina, and enjoyed rifle-shooting, cricket, tennis, golf, bowls and fishing. In a rural community he frequently had also to act as the veterinarian. When he retired in June 1947, the locals turned out *en masse* at the showground to farewell him.

Aged 69, Beet moved to Southport, but ten years later returned to Beaudesert where he spent his last months in the district to which he had given forty-two years of his life. He died there on 27 April 1957 and was cremated; his wife and two daughters survived him.

S. Baldwin (ed), *Unsung Heroes and Heroines of Australia* (Melb, 1988); *Beaudesert Times*, 4 July 1947; Beaudesert Hist Soc files; P. Morrison, William Ashley Beet (ts, 1966, held by Beaudesert Hist Soc).
                                          AILSA ROLLEY

BEGG, KENNETH GOWAN (1901-1975), businessman, was born on 22 October 1901 at Prahran, Melbourne, son of Arthur Begg, contractor, and his wife Caroline Mary, née Gowan, both Victorian born. Educated at Melbourne Church of England Grammar School in 1915-20, Kenneth showed no particular scholastic promise, but became a prefect, represented the school in athletics, football and rowing, stroked the first VIII and was captain of boats. Once he had gained experience with several mercantile firms and studied commercial subjects at night, he worked in Sydney for Henry York, a general merchant and agent for German dyestuffs, before going to New Zealand in 1926 to manage York's business there. On 12 December 1928 at All Saints Anglican Church, Woollahra, Sydney, Begg married Helen Raine.

Having bought shares to acquire 80 per cent of the capital, in 1931 Begg became sole owner of York's expanded company, Dyes & Chemicals (N.Z.) Ltd. These transactions had taken place in the Depression when Begg had confidence and his employers none. After World War II had severed links with German companies, in 1940 Begg negotiated the sale of his business to Imperial Chemical Industries of Australia and New Zealand Ltd which appointed him managing director of I.C.I. (N.Z.) Ltd. In 1942 he moved to Melbourne to manage the chemical division of I.C.I.A.N.Z.; he became commercial director (1946), commercial managing director (1948) and chairman and managing director (1953).

Begg made a smooth transition from agency work to head the complex, manufacturing organization in which petrochemicals were a rapidly-growing component. The transfer and adaptation of technology from the I.C.I. parent and from other sources demanded research and development skills of high order. Laboratories which were opened in 1956 produced several innovations that had international success, such as the flame ionization detector (1957) used in gas chromatography. When corporate growth required new headquarters, the firm moved in 1958 from the central business district to an eighteen-storey tower in East Melbourne: in 1990 I.C.I. House became the first, modern, high-rise block to be added to Victoria's historic buildings register.

Tall and dignified, Begg was highly regarded throughout the company for being approachable and humane; he was, at the same time, a very private and self-effacing man who shunned publicity. He served as a trustee (1958-64) of the National Gallery of Victoria, was a member of the Australian Atomic Energy Commission, the advisory council of the Department of Supply, the board of management of Alfred Hospital and the council of the Victorian Artists Society, and belonged to the Melbourne and Australian clubs. Retiring to Portsea in 1963, he played golf, went fishing and cultivated carnations commercially. He died on 2 March 1975 at Portsea and was cremated; his wife, daughter and two sons survived him.

ICIANZ, *Circle*, Summer 1950, 19 July 1963; *A'sian Insurance and Banking Record*, 25 May 1953, p 206; *Herald* (Melb), 5 May 1953; *Age*, 6 May 1953, 5 Mar 1975, 22 Mar 1990; G. Blainey, Unpublished history of I.C.I.A.N.Z. (1959, Company Archives, Melb); information from Mr A. M. G. Begg, Portsea, Vic, Sir Archibald Glenn, Toorak, Melb, and Mrs N. James, Patterson Lakes, Vic.
                                    L. W. WEICKHARDT

BEGGS, ARTHUR RICARDO (1906-1978), pastoralist and sheep-breeder, was born on 4 October 1906 at Hopkins Hill station, Chatsworth, Victoria, eldest son of Robert Gottlieb Beggs [q.v.7], grazier, and his wife Amy, née Ricardo. Arthur was educated at Geelong Church of England Grammar School (1918-25) where he won colours in football, rowing and athletics, and became a prefect. He began his career as a pastoralist on his father's property, Buln Gherin, at Beaufort. In 1928 he and his brother Ralph bought another family property, Niawanda, from their stepbrother Robert Balcombe Beggs. On 23 April 1930, at the Hamilton Presbyterian Church, Arthur married Elsie Helen Shaw.

From his family he inherited a pride in sheep-breeding. He was to prove himself a grazier of courage and imagination, and to make Buln Gherin—which he purchased from the family trust in 1945—a model property. Primarily interested in the merino breed, he was a member and chairman of both the Victorian and Australian stud merino breeders' associations. Yet he did not overlook the importance of other breeds: he was also president of the Australian Sheepbreeders' and of the Australian Superfine Woolgrowers' associations. Recognizing the importance of being involved in policy-making if initiatives relating to rural industries were to be fulfilled, Beggs served as vice-president of the Graziers' Association of Victoria and of the Australian Woolgrowers' and Graziers'

Council. He was, as well, a member of the Australian Wool Board in 1964-72 and of its wool advisory research committee.

Fascinated by science, Beggs had served in 1928 as field-officer on a project established at Buln Gherin by the Council for Scientific and Industrial Research to investigate the nutritional value of pastures. A staunch advocate of the re-opening of the school of veterinary science at the University of Melbourne, he was a member of the faculty in 1962-78. He belonged to the Australian Pastoral Research Trust, and was president of the Melbourne College of Textiles and of the Melbourne Wool School's advisory council. Receptive to new ideas, he supported the establishment of the Marcus Oldham Agricultural (later Farm Management) College, Geelong, and was its chairman (1962-76): the computer and seminar centre was to be named after him in March 1990.

Beggs was appointed C.B.E. in 1957. Gentle, courteous and unassuming, he was a respected leader in the Anglican Church, a member of synod, a lay canon (from 1953) and a councillor of the diocese of Ballarat (1956-72). He was a director of the Australasian Temperance & General Mutual Life Assurance Society (T. & G. Mutual Life Society Ltd) from 1959. Despite his commitments in many fields, he had found time for his own community. The Ballarat Agricultural and Pastoral Society was placed on a sound footing under his leadership after World War II. He was a founder and life member of the Ripon Rural Fire Brigade and a member (1932-64) of the board of management of the Ripon Peace Memorial Hospital (president, 1939-64). Survived by his wife, son and two daughters, he died on 8 April 1978 at Beaufort and was cremated with Anglican rites.

H. Anderson, *The Flowers of the Field* (Melb, 1969); J. O. Randall, *Teamwork* (Melb, 1976); I. Wynd, *Success Through Endeavour* (Geelong, 1987); Geelong C of E Grammar School, *Corian*, July-Aug 1978; *Riponshire Advocate*, 28 Apr 1978; information from Beaufort Hist Soc, Vic.

MARJORIE WAITE

BEHAN, SIR HAROLD GARFIELD (1901-1979), grazier and local government leader, was born on 22 February 1901 at Rockhampton, Queensland, son of Thomas Behan, a surveyor from Ireland, and his native-born wife Mary Beatrice, née Landy. Brought up on Garfield station, Jericho, he bore permanent scars from being severely burnt at the age of 12. He was educated at Nudgee College, Brisbane, and Brisbane Grammar School. When his father retired from the Jericho Shire Council in 1922, its members appointed 'Paddy' (as Harold was generally known) to

the vacancy. In 1926 the Behans moved to Bilbah Downs, a property in the neighbouring shire of Isisford. Within weeks Paddy became a local councillor and continued to belong to the Isisford Shire Council (except for a short interval in 1936) for fifty-three years; in 1951-79 he was its chairman. He was also a member (1926-79) of the Blackall hospitals board. On 25 June 1928 Behan had married a nurse Frances Kathleen Hockings at Corpus Christi Catholic Church, Nundah; widowed not long after, he married another nurse Phyllis Ethel Estelle Turner on 8 June 1935 in the sacristy of St Patrick's Church, Blackall.

A delegate to the annual conference of the Local Government Association of Queensland, in the mid-1930s Behan played an important role in forming the Western Queensland Local Government Association. Following Phyllis's death, he married a 26-year-old nurse Kathleen Bridget Costello at St Mary's Church, Ipswich, on 16 September 1942. That year, he joined the executive committee of the L.G.A.Q.; in 1948 he was elected junior vice-president and in 1949 senior vice-president. One of the more prominent personalities at its conferences, he enjoyed widespread respect and popularity. He was a born raconteur, blessed with an encyclopaedic memory, and had a seemingly inexhaustible supply of yarns and anecdotes with which he entertained fellow delegates, often at the Gresham Hotel where he stayed during his frequent trips to Brisbane. In May 1952 he was elected unopposed to the presidency which he held for twenty years.

In 1948 Behan had promoted the establishment of the Australian Council of Local Government Associations (later the Australian Local Government Association) to represent their interests at the national level; he was a State representative on this body until 1973 and was thrice president. With (Sir) Allan Sewell, Behan investigated local government in Darwin: on their recommendation, it received the status of a city in 1959. He also advised on the establishment of local government in the Territory of Papua and New Guinea.

Meantime, as a grazier Behan had been active in pastoral circles and constantly involved with the wool industry. He was a member of the executive and president (1962-68) of the Central and Northern Graziers' Association. Combined with his role in the L.G.A.Q., his position as a councillor (from 1944) of the United Graziers' Association of Queensland strengthened his efforts to secure State legislation for the control of animal and vegetable pests on rural lands. When the Queensland government set up a co-ordinating board in 1944, Behan was the local government representative and remained on it until 1975. As a member (1964) of the Australian Wool Industry Conference, he was the graziers' representative on the Queensland Employers' Federation from 1965. Appointed M.B.E. (1958) and C.M.G. (1967), he was knighted in 1977 'for distinguished service to local government and primary industry'.

Survived by his wife, their son and two daughters, by the son and daughter of his first marriage and by the daughter of his second, Sir Harold died on 7 August 1979 in Brisbane and was buried in Pinaroo lawn cemetery, Aspley. His detailed knowledge and understanding of rural problems, coupled with his negotiating ability, stamina and willingness to go anywhere to discharge the responsibilities of office, made him a legend in Queensland local government circles.

D. Jounquay, *The Isisford Story* (Isisford, Qld, 1975); R. Kerr, *Freedom of Contract* (Brisb, 1990); Local Govt Assn of Qld, *Annual Conference Procs*, 1942, 1944, 1948, 1949, 1952, 1972; *Locgov Digest*, 6, no 5, Aug-Sept 1972, p 2; *Notable Queenslanders 1975*; D. Tucker, A History of Local Government in Queensland (ms held by author, Dept of Govt, Univ Qld) *and* taped interview with Mr J. C. H. Gill, Oct 1987 (held by author).

DOUG TUCKER

BEHREND, FELIX ADALBERT (1911-1962), mathematician, was born on 23 April 1911 at Charlottenburg, Berlin, eldest of four children of Felix Wilhelm Behrend, schoolteacher, and his wife Maria Sophie, née Zöllner; although Lutheran, the family had Jewish ancestry. Educated at the Herderschule from 1917, young Felix graduated with distinction in 1929 and spent the next four years studying mathematics, physics and philosophy at the University of Berlin (Ph.D., 1933).

Leaving Nazi Germany for England, Behrend went to the University of Cambridge where he worked for eighteen months with the number theorists Harold Davenport and G. H. Hardy. In June 1935 he was employed by a life-insurance company at Zurich and in October was sent to its branch in Prague. He had decided to settle there when the political events of 1938-39 made his appointment as *Privatdozent* at the Charles University of Prague (Sc.D., 1938) impossible, obliging him to return to Switzerland and then to England.

Arrested as an 'enemy alien' in 1940, Behrend was transported to Australia on the *Dunera* and interned at Hay and at Orange, New South Wales, and at Tatura, Victoria. Until the end of 1941 he continued to instruct his fellow internees in a scientific programme that covered late-secondary and early-tertiary mathematics, physics, chemistry and medicine. He taught ordinary differential equations, elementary and advanced vector analysis, projective and differential geometry, complex analysis, and differential and integral calculus.

Acting on advice from the Royal Society, London, the British Home Office authorized Behrend's release from internment. In 1942 he was appointed tutor in the mathematics department of the University of Melbourne. On 26 May 1945 in the chapel of Queen's College he married with Methodist forms Daisy Helen Pirnitzer, a Hungarian-born teacher of dancing. He was naturalized that year. Promoted lecturer (1943), senior lecturer (1948) and associate professor (1954), he published sixteen of his twenty-five mathematical papers while in Australia. He worked on the distribution of prime numbers, using Lejeune Dirichlet's series, and on analysis, geometry (the ellipses bounding a given convex set within and without), algebraic equations, the foundations of mathematics and axiomatics. Most of his papers were short, only one exceeding twenty pages. He introduced modern general topology to the university and was an outstanding teacher. Modest, with a dry sense of humour and a warm nature, he had personal and professional integrity; he examined students' work with clear eyes after setting questions that were penetrating but fair.

Influenced when young by the writing of Thomas Mann, Behrend wrote essays and short stories in German and in English. His children's book, *Ulysses' Father* (1962), was published posthumously. He loved classical music and had sung bass in the Melbourne Philharmonic Society choir. Survived by his wife and two daughters, he died of a cerebral tumour on 27 May 1962 in Epworth Hospital, Richmond, and was cremated. In 1963 the Behrend memorial lecture in mathematics was established at the University of Melbourne with funds provided by his widow.

B. Patkin, *The Dunera Internees* (Syd, 1979); C. Pearl, *The Dunera Scandal* (Syd, 1983); P. Bartrop, *The Dunera Affair* (Melb, 1990); *Aust Mathematical Soc J*, 4, 1964, p 264; Behrend papers (Univ Melb Archives).

J. J. CROSS

BELISARIO, JOHN COLQUHOUN (1900-1976), dermatologist, was born on 30 April 1900 at Double Bay, Sydney, only child of Guy Alexander Fernandez Belisario, solicitor, and his wife Isobel Colquhoun, née Fraser, both Sydneysiders; John Belisario [q.v.3] was John's grandfather. Educated at The King's School, Parramatta, and the University of Sydney (M.B., Ch.M., 1926; D.D.M., 1947;

M.D., 1950), he served as a resident medical officer at Royal Prince Alfred Hospital in 1926-28. While pursuing postgraduate dermatological studies in Europe, he met American-born Freda Adele ('Peggy') Sauber whom he married on 10 November 1930 at All Saints Anglican Church, Woollahra, Sydney.

His principal base as a dermatologist and clinical teacher was R.P.A.H. where he was an honorary assistant physician (1932-44), honorary physician (1944-60) and honorary consulting physician (1960-76) for diseases of the skin; he was also a member (1955-76) of its board of directors. Concurrently Belisario held appointments at five other Sydney hospitals and conducted a busy private practice at 143 Macquarie Street. In every aspect of his work his energy and enthusiasm were prodigious. A prolific contributor to journals and meetings, he became internationally known. His clinical interests covered the whole range of dermatology, but his book, *Cancer of the Skin* (1959), established his reputation in that field, and most of his subsequent publications dealt with various types of skin cancer.

Having been a Militia officer from 1927, Belisario was appointed lieutenant colonel in the Australian Imperial Force on 1 July 1940 and commanded the 2nd/3rd Casualty Clearing Station in Greece. For his bravery, efficiency and leadership during the German invasion of April 1941 and the allied evacuation under fire from the mainland and thence from Crete, he was to be appointed O.B.E. on 30 December. Promoted temporary colonel in August 1941, he had charge of the 2nd/5th Australian General Hospital in the Middle East until January 1942 and from January 1943 to May 1944 in Port Moresby where he built it into a large, efficient hospital which gave first-class service during the campaign to drive the Japanese from Papua New Guinea. His appointment was terminated in August 1944.

From December 1941 Belisario had also been consultant dermatologist to the A.I.F., an important post because of the frequency of disabling skin diseases among troops in the deserts and, later, in the jungles. He was elevated to C.B.E. in 1945 and received the Efficiency Decoration in 1946. Belisario engendered a spirit of camaraderie in each of the units he commanded. For many years after the war his Macquarie Street consulting rooms were a meeting-place for old comrades on Anzac Day.

Throughout his life Belisario strove to promote dermatology as an academic discipline. At the University of Sydney he was lecturer (1945-61) in diseases of the skin, and the instigator and first supervisor (1946-56) of a training course leading to the diploma of dermatological medicine. Although he did not

succeed in his ultimate objective of persuading the university to found a chair of dermatology, the position was created after his death: the first incumbent established his office in the John Belisario Institute of Dermatology which had been created at R.P.A.H. in 1959 on Belisario's initiative. Foundation president of the Dermatological Association of Australia in 1949 and of its successor, the Australasian College of Dermatologists, in 1966, Belisario was elected a fellow (1959) of the Royal Australasian College of Physicians and was appointed C.M.G. in 1968.

Belisario was 5 ft 11 ins (180.3 cm) tall and imposing, with a cheerful disposition and a seemingly perpetual smile. His enthusiasm for all he undertook and his generosity in helping others mitigated his apparent fondness of publicity. He regularly attended St Mark's Anglican Church, Darling Point, and belonged to the Union, Royal Sydney Golf and American National clubs, but his family and dermatology were his life. The sudden death of his wife in 1974 devastated him and much of his old drive left him. Survived by his two daughters, he died on 3 August 1976 in the Sacred Heart Hospice, Darlinghurst, and was cremated. A portrait by Vaire Lubus is held by the Australasian College of Dermatologists.

A. S. Walker, *Clinical Problems of War* (Canb, 1952) and *Middle East and Far East* (Canb, 1953), and *The Island Campaigns* (Canb, 1957); I. Brodziak (ed), *Proudly We Served* (Syd, 1988); *Aust J of Dermatology*, 17, 1976, p 127; Belisario file (Roy A'sian College of Physicians Archives, Syd); Belisario papers (NL); information from Miss D. Belisario, Woollahra, and Mrs B. Grose, Bellevue Hill, Syd.

                G. L. McDONALD

BELL, ARTHUR FRANK (1899-1958), agricultural scientist and public servant, was born on 9 November 1899 in South Brisbane, fifth child of Queensland-born parents Frank Bell, produce buyer, and his wife Ellen Louisa, née Hopkins. Educated at Ipswich Grammar School, in 1916 Arthur joined the Queensland Department of Agriculture and Stock as a junior assistant. On 19 December 1917 he enlisted in the Australian Imperial Force and served as a gunner on the Western Front in late 1918. In England he attended the Manchester College of Technology in 1919, before returning to Brisbane and being discharged in December. Bell rejoined the department, studied part time at the University of Queensland (B.Sc., 1925) and won a sugar research travelling scholarship in 1924. After graduating from the University of California (M.Sc., 1926), he obtained a diploma of membership (1927) of the Imperial College, University of London.

In 1928 Bell was appointed plant pathologist to the Bureau of Sugar Experiment Stations, Brisbane. On 15 January 1929 he married a schoolteacher Rose Isobel Bartholomew at All Saints Anglican Church, Duaringa; they were to remain childless. While attending the triennial conference (1932) of the International Society of Sugar Cane Technologists at Puerto Rico, Bell learned of and later reported on the success of the giant American toad (*Bufo marinus*) in reducing populations of cane beetles—then the scourge of the Queensland sugar industry. In 1935 a colony of these toads was brought to Queensland from Hawaii, where they had been introduced from South America. That year Bell convened the State's first annual conference of cane-pest and disease-control boards. Having been acting-director of the bureau from 1943, he was appointed its director two years later. Following a review which he had helped to carry out in 1944, the Department of Agriculture and Stock was radically reorganized. In 1947 Bell became the first qualified scientist to be appointed under-secretary of this department.

A large, robust man, with an orderly view of the world and the interest of industry at heart, he was ambitious and always busy, yet approachable and good natured. Bell was a member of the Council for Scientific and Industrial Research (Commonwealth Scientific and Industrial Research Organization from 1949), and chairman (1948-55) of its Queensland committee. Active in professional bodies, he was general secretary (1932-35) of the International Society of Sugar Cane Technologists and president (1941-46) of the local body in Queensland; federal president (1948) and a fellow (1958) of the Australian Institute of Agricultural Science, he was awarded the A.I.A.S. medal in 1954 and the Farrer [q.v.8] medal in 1956. Bell broadcast and lectured widely; his published papers included *A Key to the Field Identification of Sugar Cane Diseases* (1929). He was a member of several committees of inquiry and had a recognized capacity for reducing complex problems to understandable terms.

Survived by his wife, Bell died of a coronary occlusion on 14 May 1958 at his desk in Brisbane and was cremated with Presbyterian forms. The A. F. Bell memorial medal for agricultural science at the University of Queensland has been awarded annually since 1959 by the State branch of the A.I.A.S.

Queensland Bureau of Sugar Experiment Stations, *Fifty Years of Scientific Progress* (Brisb, 1950); P. J. Skerman et al, *Guiding Queensland Agriculture, 1887-1987* (Brisb, 1988); *Qld Agr J*, 65, 1947, p 43; *J of Aust Inst of Agr Science*, 14, 1948, p 93, 20, 1954, p 61; *Aust Sugar J*, 45, 1954, p 485; *Aust J of Science*, 21, Aug-Sept 1958, p 40; *North Qld Register*, 21 Nov 1931; *Queenslander*, 9 Jan 1936, pp 15, 19; *Qld Times*, 13 June 1947.

PETER L. LLOYD

BELL, COLIN BASIL PETER (1902-1976), grazier, was born on 22 May 1902 at Canning Downs, near Warwick, Queensland, second child of Colin Basil Peter Bell, station-manager, and his wife Sibyl Frances, née Needham, both native-born; he was a great-grandson of Thomas Bell who had acquired Jimbour station, near Dalby, in 1844, and a grandson of Sir Joshua Bell [q.v.3]. Educated at The Southport School and Sydney Church of England Grammar School (Shore), young Colin began his working life in the time-honoured tradition of pastoralists' sons as a jackeroo, at Portland Downs, Queensland, in 1921. Having been employed as an overseer (1923-28) on Evesham station, between Longreach and Winton, he spent two years in England at an uncle's stud and training stable. Back in Queensland, on 4 March 1930 Bell married Hilda Walsh in St Alban's Anglican Chapel, The Southport School. Uncharacteristically, the young couple began their married life on a dairy farm near Boonah, but soon acquired Dandaraga, a sheep-station near Ilfracombe, and subsequently added Rocklea in the same district.

His rise to power within two of the State's most important and established interest groups—the United Graziers' Association of Queensland and the Queensland Employers' Federation—began with his active involvement in the Central and Northern Graziers' Association, one of a number of largely autonomous district bodies whose delegates constituted the U.G.A. As C.N.G.A. president (1953-58), Bell played a prominent role in the successful resolution, in favour of the employers, of the 1956 shearers' strike. Moving to Brisbane, he became president (1959-71) of the U.G.A. He developed an enviable reputation as a highly effective lobbyist on behalf of the interests he represented: some saw the 1960s as the golden era of the association, despite severe droughts which hit sheep-owners hard. Under Bell's leadership, the U.G.A. strongly supported Sir William Gunn's reserve-price scheme for wool which was introduced in 1970. The association assisted members to obtain freehold of their land, and monitored the consequences of containerization on beef exports and the effects of land development under the brigalow scheme.

Bell was also president of the Queensland Employers' Federation for a record fifteen years from 1958. In this capacity, combined with his role in the U.G.A., he became the acknowledged spokesman on industrial relations for all Queensland employers and carried authority with State governments. A member of the federal Graziers' Council and of the Australian Woolgrowers' Council, he was chairman of the United Graziers' Co-operative Shearing Co. Ltd and of the State board of the Co-operative Insurance Co. He was, as well, a director of the *Queensland Country Life* newspaper and a foundation member of the State Rural Reconstruction Board. In 1968 he was appointed C.B.E.

For relaxation, Bell bred, trained and trialled sheepdogs, with much success. Tall and in later life heavily built, he 'could be over-bearing, autocratic, rude and fearfully aggressive at times', but charming, kind and considerate at others. One of his most remarkable abilities was 'to converse easily with graziers on any issue and usually persuade them to a consensus view'. Survived by his wife, daughter and two sons, he died on 17 August 1976 in Brisbane and was cremated.

R. Kerr, *Freedom of Contract* (Brisb, 1990); *Qld Country Life*, 5 June, 6 Nov 1958, 5 Mar, 2 July 1959, 19 Aug 1976; *Qld Newsletter*, 19 Aug 1976; *Courier-Mail*, 2 July 1959, 13 May 1971, 18 Aug 1976; *SMH*, 3 July 1959, 8 June 1968.

MARGARET BRIDSON CRIBB

BELL, DAVID (1902-1973), businessman, was born on 9 February 1902 at Langbank, Renfrewshire, Scotland, eldest son of William John Bell, ploughman, and his wife Agnes, née Heggie. William migrated to Western Australia, leaving his wife, five sons and daughter in Scotland until he could become established. For three years he worked as a farm labourer in the York district where his family joined him in 1911. David attended the local school and at the age of 14 went to work in the cartage business at Guildford which his father bought for £100 and which comprised two horses and two drays. The Bells moved to Guildford in 1917; on leaving school, William's sons Robert and Alexander joined the family firm.

At St Hilda's Anglican Church, North Perth, on 7 March 1936 David married Eleanor Vera Moss, a shop-assistant. Next year the brothers endeavoured to persuade their father to modernize and expand the business. They wanted to hire trucks and an excavator, but William was loath to deviate from horse power (which he continued to use until his death in 1952). David, Robert and Alexander set up as Bell Bros in 1937. During World War II their company provided essential services by upgrading airfields in various parts of the State. From 1945 the brothers shifted the emphasis of their activities back to cartage and in 1949 obtained proprietary limited

status for their company. Dave was appointed chairman and managing director.

As the firm grew rapidly, especially in its trucking operations, Bell Bros Pty Ltd purchased sixty-three acres (25.5 ha) on the outskirts of Guildford. A major employer in the region, a justice of the peace and a councillor of five years standing, in December 1954 Dave was elected mayor of the Guildford Town Council. He held office for almost five years until the council was subsumed into the Swan shire, a move which he had advocated.

By 1959 Bell Bros dominated transport and heavy haulage in Western Australia, including the cartage of raw materials from the Fremantle docks. Experience in this field led to Bell's five-year appointment (from 1 October 1960) on the Australian Coastal Shipping Commission. He was also a longstanding member and sometime president of the Swan District Rotary Club, a faithful supporter of the Swan District Football Club, an organizer of the 1962 Commonwealth Games in Perth, and president (1962) of the Western Australian Institute and Industrial School for the Blind. The year 1965 marked a milestone in his life: he was appointed O.B.E. and his company went public, becoming incorporated as Bell Bros Holdings Ltd on 21 May with the issue of 1.5 million shares at five shillings premium, and 8 per cent debentures. Listed on the Sydney, Melbourne and Perth stock exchanges on 25 June, the shares provided the company with the necessary capital to take advantage of the boom years that followed.

Having basically grown by expansion, the company then began a series of takeovers in related areas, its first acquisition being Swan Quarries Pty Ltd which it converted to Bellcrete. Bell Bros Holdings hired out its equipment on a larger scale, moved into road-making and mining ventures in the north of the State, and acquired aircraft. Significant restructuring occurred during the late 1960s. Major areas of activity were given independent divisional status (namely, contracting, quarrying, concrete and special products), but were responsible to a central holding company, of which Bell remained managing director and chairman until his death. In 1970, when he was appointed to the Commonwealth Transport Advisory Committee, his companies employed over 2600 people and constituted one of the largest firms in Western Australia. Expanding off-shore in 1971, Bell Bros Holdings took over the Canadian firm SPIR-L-OK Industries Ltd (a culvert manufacturer) and merged its operations with the special products division.

Known for being as tough as nails, Dave also had an enviable reputation for fairness. His personal philosophy was very much 'do unto others as you would have them do unto you' and compromise rather than conflict was his byword. One of his longtime employees summed him up as 'a hard man but a good bloke'. Bell died on 29 November 1973 at Subiaco and was cremated; he was survived by his wife, two daughters, and son Graham who had joined the company in 1954. A portrait of David Bell hangs in the Guildford Library.

Bell Bros Holdings Pty Ltd, *Prospectus*, no 1, 9 July 1965; *Swan Express*, 8, 22 Dec 1954; *SMH*, 17 Sept 1960; *West Australian*, 17 Sept 1960, 12 June 1965, 30 Nov 1973; W. L. Bremmell, The History of Bell Bros Holdings Ltd (Perth, 1970, ts BL); Perth Stock Exchange Archives, file no 25, box 18, 10 May-1 July 1965 (BL) interview with Mr G. Bell, Belmont, Perth, 4 June 1991 (tape held by author, Dept of Economic Hist, Univ WA).

PAMELA STATHAM

BELL, GEORGE (1882-1970), surgeon, was born on 10 July 1882 at Warrambine, near Shelford, Victoria, eldest of seven children and only son of Lewis Bell, a sheep-farmer from Scotland, and his native-born wife Mary Ann, née Armstrong. The Bells were pastoralists mainly in the Hay-Booligal area of New South Wales. George attended Scots College, Sydney, where in 1900 he was dux, school captain and played in the first XI and Rugby XV. Graduating from the University of Sydney (M.B., 1906; Ch.M., 1910), he held junior and senior residencies at Sydney Hospital in 1906-07. Bell entered general practice in 1908, sharing his uncle's rooms in College Street, and in 1910 was appointed relieving assistant honorary surgeon at Sydney Hospital.

Commissioned captain in the Australian Army Medical Corps, Australian Imperial Force, on 25 April 1916, he was sent to the 3rd Australian General Hospital, Brighton, England, as surgical assistant to (Sir) Henry Newland [q.v.11]; at Newland's recommendation, Bell was posted to the 3rd Australian Casualty Clearing Station on the Western Front in April 1917. He displayed excellent surgical technique and dedication in dealing with the large number of casualties during the offensives on the Somme in April and May, and his long hours of working without a break became legendary. In August the hospital was moved to the Ypres salient where Bell again performed outstandingly. With A. W. Holmes à Court [q.v.9], he carried out one of the earliest direct blood transfusions. During the Ypres offensive, the A.C.C.S. was shelled and had to be moved to the rear. Early in 1918 Bell was appointed surgical specialist to the 1st A.C.C.S. as a temporary major.

For his achievements, he was mentioned in dispatches and appointed O.B.E. in 1919.

Returning to Sydney in June, Bell resumed practice in College Street. He was visiting surgeon to the Prince of Wales Hospital, Randwick, in 1919-47, and to Sydney Hospital in 1921-42; thereafter he was consulting surgeon to each hospital. Bell was a foundation fellow (1927), councillor (1938-50) and president (1949-51) of the Royal Australasian College of Surgeons. He was, as well, surgical consultant to the Royal Australian Navy from 1929, and an honorary surgeon commander (1941-47) and captain (1947-69) in the reserve. Deputy-chairman (1941-42) of the New South Wales Medical Coordination Committee, he was its executive officer (1942-46).

Bell was active in the British Medical Association: State president (1931-32) and treasurer (1934-55), he was also treasurer (1935-44) and vice-chairman (1939-44) of the federal council. In 1941 he was sued for negligence by Mrs Stella Hocking following her thyroidectomy; in 1947, after six trials and some £70 000 in legal fees, the Privy Council upheld the award of £800 to Mrs Hocking. Honorary treasurer and president (1964) of the postgraduate committee in medicine at the University of Sydney and founding honorary treasurer (1946-69) of the Australian Postgraduate Federation in Medicine, Bell was elected an honorary fellow of the Royal College of Surgeons, England, in 1958 and elevated to C.B.E. in 1967.

Possessing an intense love of the outback and a simple, strong, quiet faith, Bell regularly attended St Stephen's Presbyterian Church, Sydney. There, one Sunday, he had met Rev. John Flynn [q.v.8] and been inspired by his endeavours. In 1935 Bell was a convener of a public meeting to develop the Australian Aerial Medical Services (Royal Flying Doctor Service from 1954) and in 1937 helped to establish its Broken Hill base. President (1937-38 and 1953-54) of the New South Wales section and federal president (1938-40 and 1959-61), he was to be associated with the service until 1969. He also had a long association with the New South Wales Bush Nursing Association of which he was president in 1953-59.

At St Stephen's Church on 11 October 1945 Bell married Elena Adèle Quinn, whose love and support were so important to him. He was a big man, six feet (182.9 cm) tall and weighing fifteen stone (95.3 kg), but surprisingly deft. A member (from 1921) and chairman (1954-69) of Scots College council, he was a board-member of Sydney Hospital, and could be seen in all weather on the course at Royal Sydney Golf Club. Survived by his wife, Bell died at his Rose Bay home on 22 August 1970 and was cremated.

Scots College Old Boys' Union, *Lang Syne*, 16, no 3, Sept 1969, p 4; *MJA*, 30 Mar 1970; *SMH*, 19, 26 Dec 1947, 10 June 1967, 1 Sept 1970.

W. D. REFSHAUGE

BELL, HECTOR HERCULES (1876-1964), contractor and tramways administrator, was born on 1 December 1876 at Richmond, Melbourne, seventh child of Frank Richborough Herbert Bell, railway guard (later inspector of railways), and his wife Emily, née Roberts. Having been 'educated privately', Hector ran away from home at the age of 14 rather than follow his father's footsteps into the Victorian Railways. After three difficult years as a bush itinerant, he returned home and became a blacksmith. He then tried his hand at contracting, but had no luck. In Melbourne on 1 June 1895 he married Emma Watson (d. 1945) with Presbyterian forms. They went to Perth where for two years he worked on the construction of the causeway bridge over the Swan River.

Back again at Richmond, he battled to establish himself in turn as a confectioner, wood merchant and contractor. Emma kept the pot boiling by running a second-hand clothing shop, above which they lived. An impressive and tough operator, in 1911 Bell was elected to the Richmond City Council. For the next twenty-six years he applied himself to civic affairs as leader of the Labor group and chairman of the public works committee. Rewarding opportunities came with his appointment as Richmond's member on the Melbourne and Metropolitan Board of Works and as a founding member (1915) of the Hawthorn Tramways Trust, of which he rose to be deputy-chairman. As his municipal career flourished, so did his contracting business, and in 1924 he moved with his wife and three children to a handsome home at Hawthorn. These were unsavoury years for Richmond council: as the Australian Labor Party took control of local politics, faction fights and family feuds occupied much of the councillors' time and energy.

Although he kept his distance from the wildest elements in the party, as Labor leader Bell was implicated in some electoral irregularities. An Anglican, who later claimed not to have tasted 'strong drink' until he was 45, he still incurred the wrath of local Protestant critics. Having suffered a savage attack by Rev. George Lamble [q.v.9] from the pulpit of St Stephen's Church in May 1921, Bell declared himself 'ashamed to be an Anglican' and withdrew his youngest daughter from the Sunday School.

In July 1935 Bell was elected deputy-chairman of the Melbourne and Metropolitan Tramways Board, to which he had been appointed in 1919 by the Lawson [q.v.10] Nationalist government. In 1936 he succeeded Alexander Cameron [q.v.7] as chairman, on a salary of £1750—a sum that was to remain unchanged until he retired in 1949. He was appointed C.B.E. in 1950.

As chairman of the M.M.T.B., Bell gave distinguished service to the people of Melbourne. Within a year the board had posted its first surplus since 1927. The remaining conversions of cable to electric trams were completed, efficiency improved, fares went down and profits up. Bell worked tirelessly during the war as petrol rationing cut the use of private motorcars. Night services were extended to move shiftworkers around the city. The 1936 surplus had been £1410; by 1942 it had multiplied a thousandfold. Sadly for Melbourne's postwar reconstruction, those windfall profits were required under the Melbourne and Metropolitan Tramways Act to be distributed to participating municipal councils. With peace came declining patronage, shortages of labour and materials, and union militancy. Bell had always 'talked tough' with communists in the 1930s; in 1948 he accused Clarrie O'Shea, State secretary of the Australian Tramway and Omnibus Employees' Association, and his followers (whom Bell believed comprised only 25 per cent of the workers) of 'always holding a pistol at our heads'. In retrospect, however, union officials were to remember Bell more fondly than his successor Robert Risson.

Bell's achievements as a transport boss were tarnished a little by his 'old Richmond habits'. His speech was salty; certain contractors were favoured for the board's tenders; at public expense, a large air-raid shelter was added to his house as a conference-room for board-members; and his retirement was marred by his none-too-subtle attempts to have his son promoted to a senior position for which he had little qualification. John Wren [q.v.12] esteemed Bell enough to venture into land speculation with him on Melbourne's western fringe. When he died at his Hawthorn home on 12 November 1964 Bell left a realty of £21 080 and a personalty of £22 809, each being a one-third part of a family trust. Survived by his son and two daughters, he was buried in Boroondara cemetery, Kew.

J. McCalman, *Struggletown* (Melb, 1984); Melb and Metropolitan Tramways Bd, *Annual Reports*, 1936-42, 1947; *Leader* (Melb), 3 Aug 1901; *Richmond Guardian*, 28 May 1921, 6 Sept 1924, 28 Aug 1926, 3 Mar 1934; *Richmond Weekly*, 12 July 1929; *Richmond Chronicle*, 1 Sept 1933; *Sun News-Pictorial*, 7 May 1945; *Argus*, 19 Jan 1945, 8 Jan 1948; *Herald* (Melb), 4 Oct 1947, 28 Sept 1949, 31 Oct 1951; information from Mr N. Maddock, East Bentleigh, Melb; personal information.

JANET McCALMAN

BELL, JOHN RENISON (1889-1973) and MARY TESTON LUIS (1903-1979), air force officers, were husband and wife. John was born on 25 May 1889 at Scottsdale, Tasmania, son of George Renison Bell, mining agent, and his wife Phoebe, née Cox. Educated at the Friends' High School, Hobart, he worked as a clerk and accountant in solicitors' offices at Devonport and Launceston. On 8 January 1915 he enlisted in the Australian Imperial Force. After training as a signaller, he embarked for Egypt with reinforcements for the 12th Battalion; because he gave first-aid to fellow soldiers in the troop-ship, he was nicknamed 'Doc'.

Having seen action at Gallipoli soon after the first landings, he was evacuated to England on 20 August with enteric fever. Bell transferred to the Australian Flying Corps in April 1917. Commissioned as an observer in June, he proceeded to France two months later with No. 3 Squadron, A.F.C. (No. 69 Squadron, Royal Flying Corps). On 6 December, while artillery-ranging over Messines Ridge, Belgium, he shot down a German reconnaissance aircraft. In January 1918 he went to England and qualified as a pilot, rejoining his squadron in September. He was mentioned in dispatches and his appointment terminated in Hobart in July 1919. Bell was 5 ft 6 ins (167.6 cm) tall, with brown eyes and a slim build; quiet, courteous, but self-assured, he had a striking command of words.

Mary was born on 3 December 1903 at Launceston, Tasmania, daughter of Rowland Walker Luis Fernandes, a clerk from England, and his native-born wife Emma Dagmar, née Mahony, great-granddaughter of Jonathan Griffiths [q.v.1]. Her parents separated in 1906. Educated at Broadland House Church of England Girls' Grammar School, Launceston, and St Margaret's School, Devonport, at 14 she took a job with a Devonport solicitor to supplement her mother's income. Mary was a serious-looking and ambitious girl, scarcely five feet (152.4 cm) tall and interested in flying. She met John in 1919. Obtaining a commission in the Royal Australian Air Force on 30 August 1921, he served at Point Cook, Victoria, and at R.A.A.F. Headquarters, Melbourne. He married Mary on 19 March 1923 in St Andrew's Anglican Church, Brighton. In 1925 the Bells sailed for England. John attended the Royal Air Force Staff College, Andover, before carrying out liaison duties with the R.A.F. Mary learned to fly and gained a British private pilot's licence in April 1927.

Returning to Melbourne in February 1928, John was promoted squadron leader; next month Mary secured an Australian private pilot's licence. John resigned from the air force on 8 September 1929 to join the Shell Co. of Australia Ltd; he was to become its chief aviation officer in New South Wales. Mary qualified in December 1930 to hold a ground engineer's licence. By 1939 the Bells were living in Brisbane where John was Queensland manager of Airlines of Australia Ltd. As the threat of war grew, Mary (known as 'Paddy') assumed the leadership of some forty women undertaking instruction in aircraft maintenance at Archerfield aerodrome and formed the Women's Air Training Corps on 17 July 1939. Elected commander, she organized the voluntary corps on semimilitary lines. John was mobilized in September and posted to the directorate of organization and staff duties at R.A.A.F. Headquarters, Melbourne. Next year he was promoted acting group captain and made director of organization.

In February 1940, as commandant, Mary established W.A.T.C. headquarters in Melbourne; she instituted branches in other States and pressed for the formation of a women's air force auxiliary. Air Chief Marshal Sir Charles Burnett [q.v.] asked the Bells to draw up a preliminary plan for the employment of airwomen. Shortages of male ground-staff eventually led to the establishment of the Women's Auxiliary Australian Air Force in February 1941. That month Mary was appointed staff officer (W.A.A.A.F. administration), with the rank of acting flight officer. Considered to be a 'socialite' and to lack managerial experience, she was overlooked for the post of director and resigned from the W.A.A.A.F. on 5 June. She rejoined the service in October 1942, worked in several directorates and resumed civilian life on 11 April 1945.

John had been appointed O.B.E. in 1943. He held acting air commodore's rank when he left the air force in October 1945. The Bells farmed in Victoria and later in Tasmania until 1968. John died on 22 August 1973 in Hobart and was buried in Mersey Vale Memorial Park cemetery, Spreyton; Mary died on 6 February 1979 at Ulverstone and was buried beside him; their daughter survived them.

H. N. Wrigley, *The Battle Below* (Syd, 1935); S. Mann, *The Girls Were Up There Too* (Canb, 1986); J. Thomson, *The WAAAF in Wartime Australia* (Melb, 1991); *SMH*, 15 Apr 1937, 4 June 1941, 1 Jan 1943; *Mercury* (Hob), 24 Aug 1973; J. R. Bell papers (held by Mr J. S. Bell, Devonport, Tas); J. R. and M. T. Bell papers (held by Mrs J. Lambert, St Helens, Tas).   JOYCE THOMSON

BELLEW, HELEN; *see* KIRSOVA

BELZ, MAURICE HENRY (1897-1975), mathematical statistician, was born on 1 February 1897 at Auburn, Sydney, eleventh child of John William Belz, a carpenter from Germany, and his Australian-born wife Elizabeth Esther, née Saunders. Educated at Sydney Boys' High School and the University of Sydney, Maurice studied arts and engineering before graduating (B.Sc., 1918) with the John Coutts scholarship and the university medal in mathematics. In 1920 he received a Barker [q.v.1] graduate travelling scholarship and proceeded to Gonville and Caius College, Cambridge (M.Sc., 1922). He worked at the Cavendish Laboratory under Sir Ernest (Lord) Rutherford.

In 1923 Belz took up a lectureship in mathematics at the University of Melbourne. He married a medical practitioner Florence Marjorie Hughes on 19 May 1928 at St Mary's Anglican Church, Caulfield. That year he was promoted senior lecturer and in 1929 introduced a course in the theory of statistics. Awarded a Rockefeller Foundation fellowship in 1932, he left next year to undertake research at the London School of Economics and the University of Oslo into the application of mathematics to economics. At Professor (Sir) Douglas Copland's [q.v.] invitation, in 1937 he began teaching mathematical economics in the faculty of commerce at Melbourne and published with Professor J. H. Michell [q.v.10] *The Elements of Mathematical Analysis* (London). When the university, at Belz's instigation, formed the first autonomous department of statistics in Australia in 1948, he became its head, first as an associate-professor of mathematical statistics and in 1955-63 as professor. In 1947 he had been a Carnegie fellow at Harvard University and the University of North Carolina, United States of America; he also attended the founding meeting of the Biometric Society and became a charter member of its first council; in 1952-53 he was a research associate at Princeton University.

Many of the initial generation of Australia's professional statisticians were either trained or taught in Belz's department. He established a course for graduates from science and industry, and encouraged university researchers and industrial organizations to seek statistical assistance from departmental staff. During visits to Britain (1961, 1964 and 1970-72) he worked both as a consultant and as a lecturer to executives in British Petroleum Co. Ltd in London, and prepared *Statistical Methods for the Process Industries* (London, 1973) for publication.

A council-member (1935-47) of the University of Melbourne, Belz was sub-dean (1942-44) of the arts faculty. He represented the university on the National Standards Association's committee on statistical quality control, was vice-president (1924-61) of the Mathematical Association of Victoria and published *Notes on Statistics for Matriculation General Mathematics* (1948). Elected a member (1948) of the International Statistical Institute, he was made an honorary life member of the Statistical Society of Australia (1970) and of the Australian Society for Operations Research.

Belz was president (1944-70) of the French-Australian Association of Victoria and was appointed to the Légion d'honneur in 1954. Fond of the theatre, he was foundation president (1939) of the graduate drama club, the Tin Alley Players. He also loved gardening at his Hawthorn home, where he and his wife were warm and generous hosts. Belz died on 28 March 1975 at Parkville and was cremated with Presbyterian forms. His wife survived him; they had no children. A bronze plaque by Andor Meszaros is attached to the Maurice H. Belz prizes board at the University of Melbourne.

Univ Melb Gazette, July 1947, Mar 1948, Spring 1990; *Aust J of Statistics*, 12, no 1, 1970, p 64, 17, no 1, 1975, p 56; Mathematical Assn of Vic, *Vinculum*, Maurice Belz memorial issue, 1976; Univ Melb Archives; information from honorary secretaries of Aust Soc for Operations Research, Parkville, Melb, *and* Statistical Soc of Aust, Syd.

BETTY LABY

BENDRODT, JAMES CHARLES (1891-1973), roller-skater and restaurateur, was born on 26 June 1891 at Victoria, British Columbia, Canada, son of James Peter Bendrodt, a Danish sea-captain, and his wife Emily Caroline Delphina, née Swanson. Having attended school at Vancouver, Jimmy worked his passage to Sydney as a stoker, arriving by 1910 with only £5. Dark, lithe and muscular, he claimed to have been a lumberjack and to hold Canadian roller-skating titles.

With his partner George Irving, Bendrodt prospered as a trick-skater in Sydney and on country tours. Appointed manager of the new Imperial Roller Rink, Hyde Park, he soon secured the lease and fostered an exclusive and decorous image that was to characterize all his enterprises. Early in 1914 he reopened the building as the 'Imperial Salon De Luxe' to cater for American dance crazes. On 16 August Bendrodt enlisted in the Australian Naval and Military Expeditionary Force and three days later sailed for Rabaul in the *Berrima*. He returned to Sydney in January 1915 in charge of prisoners of war. To his lasting regret, he did not see action during the operations in German New Guinea or while serving with the Canadian Expeditionary Force in 1918.

Meantime, he had played bit parts with J. C. Williamson [q.v.6] Ltd which convinced him that he was 'a lousy actor' but 'a terrific showman'. Back in Sydney in 1919, Bendrodt taught dancing (until 1939) at Macdonnell House, 321 Pitt Street, and in 1923 established J. C. Bendrodt & Co. In the face of government and union obstacles, he imported foreign entertainers, including 'colored' minstrels for the opening of the Palais Royal dance hall that year. Wealthy entrepreneurs backed his enterprises: Ezra Norton [q.v.] was to contribute to the Trocadero nightclub and cabaret which opened in 1936.

The purchase of a mare for £100 in 1923 had inspired Bendrodt to take up racing and breeding. Although labelled 'a mug trainer' who was to cosset imported bloodstock on a 140-acre (56.7 ha) stud farm by the Nepean River, Bendrodt earned the respect of the jockey Bill Cook for his methods. Confronted with the Depression, Bendrodt saved the beleaguered Palais Royal in July 1931 by encouraging his employees to gamble their last wages on his unknown horse, Firecracker, which won at Menangle. A big plunge in 1937 on his filly, Gay Romance, helped him to finance Prince's Restaurant in Martin Place in 1938; with 'soft lights, sweet music' and good food, it rivalled Romano's [q.v.11].

Quick to anticipate fashion, in December 1937 Bendrodt formed a company to transform the Palais Royal into the opulent Ice Skating Palais which featured Canadian figure-skating and ice-hockey stars. Employees remembered him as a hard boss, willing to reward initiative or bend the law. He was tried in August 1939 for minor fraud over payments to employees, fined in 1951 for understating taxable income in the early 1940s, and forced to admit to a royal commission in 1952 that Prince's regularly ignored State liquor regulations. Lavish entertainments at the restaurant were criticized in wartime, though Bendrodt claimed that American troops had benefited.

On 5 August 1939 Bendrodt had married his dancing partner Frances Nellie ('Peggy') Dawes at Hunters Hill with Congregational forms. In later life he was noted for his imported suits, red carnation buttonhole, jewelled cigarette-case and manicured hands, as well as for his collections of Meissen porcelain and Bohemian crystal. Yet, he also relished his reputation for toughness which was heightened by an enduring Canadian drawl and by a penchant for 'bouncing' drunks. His boldness and opportunism were again exhibited in 1956 when he opened the Caprice, a lavish, 'floating' restaurant at Rose Bay, which became a Mecca for celebrities.

Childless himself, Bendrodt was not afraid to parade a heartfelt love of animals. He made an emotional radio appeal in World War II to halt the killing of pet dogs when meat was rationed. Abandoning the turf in the early

1950s because it involved 'too much distress', he campaigned against cruelty to animals. His vivid, personal tales were broadcast and appeared in American magazines. At the urging of his 'literary godfather' Frank Clune [q.v.], he published three popular collections, *A Man, a Dog, Two Horses* (1946), *Nine O'Clock* (1949) and *Irish Lad* (1966). Bendrodt retired in 1967, looking at 72 'like a younger and happier Somerset Maugham', and lived quietly at Darling Point. Survived by his wife, he died on 17 February 1973 in St Vincent's Hospital, Darlinghurst, and was cremated with Anglican rites.

Theatre Mag, 1 June 1912, 1 May 1914; *People* (Syd), 25 Apr 1950; *SMH*, 14 May 1910, 1, 18, 19, 30 Aug 1939, 13 Sept 1945, 30 May 1946, 12 Apr 1950, 16 Mar 1951, 21 Feb, 27 Aug 1952, 1 Sept 1953, 30 Oct 1956, 4 July 1966, 18, 22 Feb 1973; *Sun-Herald*, 23 Dec 1984; F. P. Clune collection (NL); Customs and Excise Office, NSW, Series A1 item 23/2723 (AA, Syd).   IAIN MCCALMAN

BENHAM, EDWARD WARNER (1872-1948), lawyer and academic, was born on 20 January 1872 at Norwood, Adelaide, second child of Richard Somersal Benham, a librarian from England, and his wife Margaret, née Haynes. Educated at the Collegiate School of St Peter (1882-87) and the University of Adelaide (LL.B., 1891), Edward was articled to J. R. Anderson in 1892 and admitted to the Bar on 12 July 1895. He specialized in civil cases, particularly property, became managing clerk in 1897 with Anderson & Castle and later entered partnership with R. A. C. Castle. With A. J. McLachlan, Benham worked on a revised South Australian *Magistrates' Guide* (1906) which comprised 589 detailed, comprehensive pages of legal procedure, schedules and forms, ranging from 'Abduction' to 'Yards' (cleansing thereof).

While continuing to practise in the city, from 1910 Benham lectured at the university. After turning off his hearing-aid, he dictated rather dull, uninspiring lectures, with little explanation or discussion. A hard examiner, he seemed reserved, remote and a very private person to his students, but they recognized his high ideals, his professionalism and his mastery of the law of property, and—beyond his earshot—called him Teddy. He also taught private international law in 1923-26 and, from 1928, the law of Equity. Having applied for the chair in 1919, he withdrew from the field one month later. He was troubled by continuing sickness and next year travelled to New Zealand. On 21 June 1924 at St Cuthbert's Anglican Church, Prospect, he married 37-year-old Violet Margaret, daughter of H. C. E. Muecke [q.v.10]; they were to remain childless. In 1935 they visited England and Scotland where he observed the teaching of law. After acting as dean of the faculty at the University of Adelaide in 1937 during Professor A. L. Campbell's [q.v.] absence, Benham retired next year.

Among the literary and debating societies to which he belonged were the St John's Young Men's Society (affiliated with the South Australian Literary Societies' Union), the exclusive Pickwick Club, the Adelaide branch of the English-Speaking Union (president 1934-37) and the Eucalypts Society (president 1938). Benham's initial speech (1912) to the last-mentioned body was on optimism and pessimism in the works of Sir Walter Scott and Thomas Hardy; in succeeding years he favoured European literary and political topics. Richard Benham had been the State's first public librarian and in 1932 his son was a member of the committee that established the Friends of the Public Library of South Australia (vice-president 1942-48).

Following a long and painful illness, Edward Benham died on 21 June 1948 at his Thorngate home and was cremated. After his widow's death in 1969, the details of his will were made public. The bulk of their estate (approximately $200 000) was left to the University of Adelaide which endowed two annual prizes, for theses in English literature and English political history, and used the major part of the bequest to buy books in those subjects and in law. $20 000 was spent on a bronze sculpture by Henry Moore, 'Reclining Connected Forms' (1969), for the university's grounds.

R. R. Chivers, *The Benham Family in Australia* (Adel, 1970); A, C Castles, et al (eds) for Faculty of Law, Univ Adel, *Law on North Terrace* (Adel, 1983); *Advertiser* (Adel), 18 Nov 1938, 23 June 1948; papers of Eucalypts Soc, Friends of the Public L of SA *and* Literary Societies' Union (Mort L); registry correspondence (Univ Adel Archives).

MARGARET J. JENNINGS

BENJAFIELD, DAVID GILBERT (1919-1980), professor of law, was born on 5 June 1919 at Killara, Sydney, younger son and fourth child of Vivian Benjafield, surgeon, and his wife Muriel Brooke, née Lovett, both Tasmanian born. David was educated at Sydney Grammar School on a scholarship, but at the age of 15 was stricken by poliomyelitis which left him paralysed from the waist down and confined to a wheelchair. He matriculated by correspondence.

Prevented from becoming a medical practitioner by his permanent physical incapacity, Benjafield followed his elder brother into the law. In 1941 he entered the University of Sydney (LL.B., 1945); he won numerous prizes, graduated with first-class honours and

the university medal, and was admitted to the Bar on 19 February 1945. A member of University Chambers—which included (Justice) Paul Toose and (Sir) Maurice Byers—Benjafield specialized in writing opinions and soon gained a reputation for work of high quality. Although his court appearances were limited by his immobility, he was one of the junior counsel led by H. V. Evatt [q.v.] who appeared in 1948 for the Commonwealth in the Bank Nationalization case.

A tutor of the university's external students, especially ex-servicemen, Benjafield was appointed lecturer in law in 1948. On 10 January that year at St Mary's Catholic Cathedral, Sydney, he married a stenographer Shirley Patricia Murphy. Accompanied by her, he went to England in 1950 and entered Lincoln College, Oxford (D.Phil., 1952), on a scholarship. There his interest was stimulated in administrative law, then virtually unknown in Australia.

Promoted full-time senior lecturer on his return home, Benjafield mainly taught constitutional law, the law of real property and, later, administrative law. An excellent teacher with a quick analytical mind, he was popular with both students and staff. He was quiet, friendly, patient and considerate, and had an endearing sense of humour. Appointed associate-professor (1956) and professor of law (1959), in 1962 he produced with Professor W. G. Friedmann the second edition of *Principles of Australian Administrative Law* (the only authoritative text on the subject); with a former student (Professor) Harry Whitmore, he published further editions in 1966 and 1971. Benjafield, Toose and Ray Watson compiled *Australian Divorce Law and Practice* (1968), another standard textbook.

An original member (1966) of the New South Wales Law Reform Commission, Benjafield studied the existing English rules of Supreme Court procedure and adapted them, where appropriate, to local conditions. Like other commissioners, he stressed the need for simplicity, clarity and uniformity in the court's jurisdictions. The Supreme Court Act (1970) reflects ideas that Benjafield had subscribed to since his student days. In 1972-73 he served a further term on the commission. Influenced by work done in Canada, he was convinced of the need for a system of appeals from administrative decisions, but considered that the commission's draft legislation was too narrow. He argued that administrative actions impinged on virtually all individual acts and that bureaucrats should be required to account for their decisions. At the same time, he jealously protected the sovereignty of parliament and the authority of legislation. His recommendation to establish an ombudsman was translated into legislation in 1974, but many of the changes suggested in the commission's 1973 report remained to be implemented.

As dean of law (1968, 1975-77) and a fellow (from 1968) of the university senate, in the 1970s Benjafield guided the development of the Law School and its introduction of doctoral studies. He was a member of the St Ives Pistol Club, and enjoyed chess and reading detective stories. From 1962 he had served on the council of management of the Paraplegic and Quadriplegic Association of New South Wales. In June 1979 he was appointed C.B.E. Survived by his wife and two sons, he died of cancer on 26 April 1980 in Royal North Shore Hospital and was cremated. His portrait by Noel Thurgate is held by the University of Sydney.

J. and J. Mackinolty (eds), *A Century Downtown* (Syd, 1991); *Aust Law J*, 54, June 1980, p 378; *SMH*, 26 Aug 1965, 28 Apr 1980; Faculty of Law, Univ Syd, Minutes of Meetings, 1965-80; information from Mrs S. P. Benjafield, Roseville, and Prof W. L. Morison, Northbridge, Syd; personal information.   BOHDAN BILINSKY

BENNETT, AGNES JESSIE (1880-1969), community worker, was born on 22 February 1880 at California Gully, near Eaglehawk, Victoria, fourth child of George Dixon, a goldminer from England, and his Scottish-born wife Jessie, née Watson. In 1890, aged 38, George died of tuberculosis and Jessie took over as mine-manager. The family's savings were lost when she deposited crushings from the mine in a bank that was never to reopen. Agnes attended school, cared for her younger sisters and nursed her mother until 1902 when Jessie also died of tuberculosis.

Following a married sister to the Western Australian goldfields, Agnes arrived at Kalgoorlie in August 1906. There she became a piano teacher. On 26 February 1908 she married with Presbyterian forms Thomas Henry Bennett (d. 1932), a cordial manufacturer from Adelaide; their only child was stillborn. Agnes subsequently devoted herself to helping another sister rear her six children.

Mrs Bennett became involved in community work, particularly in raising funds for Kalgoorlie's horse-drawn ambulance (obtained in 1910) and its first motor ambulance (bought in 1921). She accompanied local doctors on trips to the 'woodline' to treat sick or injured men, first at Kurrawang and later at Lakewood. Between 1925 and 1930 she passed first-aid and home-nursing courses run by Mrs K. Elliott for the St John Ambulance Association. When a home nursing division was established at Kalgoorlie in June 1934, Bennett superintended its fifteen members. For two years meetings were held at Dugan Street, and money was collected to buy splints and bandages.

With the outbreak of World War II, she obtained approval from the Kalgoorlie Municipal Council to use a shop in Hannan Street as a practice and class-instruction room, and furnished the air-raid dressing-station there with seven beds. The numbers attending her classes increased and in May 1940 Bennett received permission to form a Voluntary Aid Detachment, of which she was appointed commandant. In addition to teaching first aid and home nursing, she supervised route marches and parades, helped at the hospitals and organized Christmas parties for servicemen's families. She relinquished her V.A.D. post in 1943 to concentrate on her work for the St John Ambulance Association. Between 21 August 1941 and 30 July 1943 she had also served on the council of the Kalgoorlie branch of the National Aerial Medical Service of Australia (Flying Doctor Service).

Before and after the war, Bennett's duties with the ambulance association included attendance at public and sporting functions where first-aid treatment was often needed, demonstrating home nursing, decorating halls and arranging dinners for functions, attending church and Anzac Day parades, and organizing local and State competitions and examinations. Fund-raising was a constant challenge. She was appointed serving sister (1946) and officer sister (1960) in the Order of St John. When Kalgoorlie's new sub-centre was opened on 10 September 1950, a room was named after her. Because of failing eyesight, she was relieved as superintendent in 1953, but served on the reserve list for another decade. From 1948 she had, as well, instructed No. 2 Company of the Girl Guides' Association of Western Australia.

Gentle, compassionate and dignified, with a slight stature that belied her strength of character, 'Addie' was often in pain from ailments that plagued her until the end of her life. She died on 25 July 1969 at Kalgoorlie and was buried in the local cemetery.

Kalgoorlie Miner, 11 Sept 1950, 8 Jan 1960, 28, 30 July 1969; *Daily News* (Perth), 30 July 1969; St John Ambulance Assn records, Perth; family papers and scrap-book (held by Mrs B. Baker, Palmyra, Perth).   PHYL GARRICK

BENNETT, EMILY (1871-1941), feminist and political organizer, was born on 29 January 1871 at Camperdown, Sydney, eighth daughter and ninth child of Irish-born parents Denis McNamarra, soap boiler, and his wife Mary Elizabeth, née Green. On 11 April 1894 at her mother's Camperdown home Emily married with Catholic rites Francis Andrew Bennett, a widower with three young children, who lived at Cootamundra. Their only son was born next year. The family moved to Singleton where Frank set up as an auctioneer and served as mayor (1902, 1903 and 1907), town clerk (1908-12) and secretary of the Northern Agricultural Association. After he drowned in a dam in September 1913, Emily returned to Sydney.

Active in the cause of women before and during World War I, in 1921-23 Emily Bennett was organizing secretary of the Women's Reform League of New South Wales which was led by Laura Luffman [q.v.10]. Supporting the Progressive Party in State politics and believing that 'Woman has come into her own', Bennett made strenuous efforts to rally 'one hundred thousand women' to the movement and represented the league on numerous allied organizations in Sydney, among them the National Council of Women, the New Settlers' League of Australia and the League of Nations Union.

A loyal supporter of Bessie Rischbieth [q.v.11], Bennett helped to secure the Australian Federation of Women Voters in the early 1920s. She was a member of its delegation to the International Woman Suffrage Alliance's ninth congress, held in Rome in May 1923. It was a thrilling experience. She shook hands with Mussolini, and the delegation was entertained by the British ambassador and received by the Pope. Bennett served on a committee (chaired by the suffragist Chrystal Macmillan) which examined the loss of British nationality by women who married foreigners. She then spent some happy months in London and had her faith in Empire-wide feminism and in extra-parliamentary organization confirmed. With Henrietta Frederica Bennett, who had joined the Theosophical Society in Australasia in Perth in 1915 and later come to Sydney, she was to watch over the federation's interests in New South Wales.

Admired for her skills and extensive knowledge of the women's movement, Emily Bennett worked hard behind the scenes to establish the United Associations (of Women) in December 1929; she was a founding vice-president and honorary organizing secretary in 1930. Next year, when the U.A. decided to endorse women candidates in the coming elections, she was appointed campaign director. She advocated reforms to the laws affecting marriage, divorce and child custody. In 1932 Jessie Street [q.v.] declared her 'the best feminist I know'.

Practically without income due to a bank crash, Bennett appealed to Rischbieth: a feminist benefit was held at Farmer [q.v.4] & Co. Ltd's store in June 1932. Appointed industrial organizer in July for the Australian Women's Guild of Empire, founded by Adela Pankhurst Walsh [q.v.12], Bennett was to promote the causes of Empire and anti-communism until the guild's demise in 1939. She had been appointed a justice of the peace and had joined the Women Justices' Association of New South Wales in 1933; she also joined the Theosophical Society in 1935 and was attached to the Radio Lodge.

Despite serious illnesses in 1919 and 1928, Emily Bennett continued to live strenuously and in her last years often spoke in the Domain. She participated in the A.F.W.V.'s 1938 conference in Sydney, but by late 1939 was unable to attend its State committee meetings. Survived by her son, she died of complications from a fractured arm on 10 May 1941 at Manly District Hospital and was cremated with Anglican rites. In a photograph of the 1923 delegation she stands directly behind Rischbieth, tall, angular, intense.

Woman's Voice, 1916-23; *Empire Gazette*, 1932-39; *SMH*, 25 Aug 1921, 10 Mar 1923, 3 July 1931, 24 June 1932; Rischbieth papers *and* AFWV records (NL); AWGE papers (Univ Wollongong Archives); information from Theosophical Soc, Syd.

J. I. ROE

BENNETT, HENRY GORDON (1887-1962), army officer and businessman, was born on 16 April 1887 at Balwyn, Melbourne, second child of George Jesse Bennett, a schoolmaster from Cape Town, and his native-born wife Harriet, née Bentley. Alfred Edward Bennett [q.v.7] was Gordon's younger brother. Educated at Balwyn State School and Hawthorn College, Gordon was employed by the Australian Mutual Provident Society as an actuarial clerk. On 14 August 1908 he was commissioned in the Citizen Military Forces and posted to the 5th Infantry Regiment. He was promoted major in 1912.

Transferring to the Australian Imperial Force on 19 August 1914, Bennett embarked for Egypt in October as second-in-command of the 6th Battalion. In the Gallipoli landings of 25 April 1915 he was one of the leaders of the advance to Pine Ridge. Wounded that afternoon while directing fire at Turkish positions, he was evacuated to a hospital ship, but absented himself to return to the front. He gained a reputation for leadership and courage under fire—and for his seeming immunity to serious injury—particularly in the 2nd Brigade's assault against Krithia on 8 May. Next day he was promoted temporary lieutenant colonel and assumed command of the 6th Battalion. Overlooked for this advancement some months earlier, he had responded with bitterness, a facet of his character which was to become more pronounced. Bennett was appointed C.M.G. (1915) and twice mentioned in dispatches for his deeds at Gallipoli.

During operations in France, from April 1916 he alternated as battalion and acting brigade commander. On 18 November that year at the Scottish National Church, Chelsea, London, he married Bessie Agnes Buchanan whom he had met in Melbourne. Aged 29, he was promoted temporary brigadier and given the 3rd Brigade on 3 December. His reputation as an exceptional frontline commander grew as a result of his performances at Bullecourt, France (April to May 1917), the Menin Road (September) and Passchendaele (October), Belgium, and again in France at the Hindenburg line from September to November 1918. In contrast, his prickly temperament and tendency to act without orders from divisional headquarters provoked Major General (Sir) William Glasgow [q.v.9] to observe: 'Bennett is a pest!' C. E. W. Bean [q.v.7] was to recall Bennett's jealousy, criticism of superiors and quarrels with other officers. For his service on the Western Front, Bennett was awarded the Montenegrin Order of Danilo (1917) and the Distinguished Service Order (1919); he was appointed C.B. in 1918 and six times mentioned in dispatches.

After returning briefly to Melbourne, where his A.I.F. appointment terminated on 31 August 1919, he moved to Sydney. There he worked as a clothing manufacturer and a public accountant. In 1922 he was appointed chairman of the State Repatriation Board and in October 1928 became one of the three commissioners administering the City of Sydney. Bennett was prominent in the All for Australia League from 1931 and was a member of the Defence of Australia League. He presided over the Chamber of Manufactures of New South Wales (1931-33), the Associated Chambers of Manufactures of Australia (1933-34) and other professional organizations.

Bennett retained his passion for the army. In 1921-26 he had commanded the 9th Infantry Brigade. He was promoted major general on 1 August 1930 while in command (1926-32) of the 2nd Division. Along with some other citizen-officers in Australia's essentially part-time army, he resented the influence of the handful of regular (Staff Corps) officers. His distaste of permanent-service officers, stemming from earlier experience, increased during two decades of peace. In late 1937 he published a series of newspaper articles on defence policy which criticized regular officers and which led to his being censured by the Military Board.

On the outbreak of World War II Bennett was junior only to Sir Brudenell White [q.v.12] and Glasgow, and was in no doubt that, if an Australian expeditionary force were raised, he would be its commander. He was therefore furious when Major General Sir Thomas Blamey [q.v.] (an ex-regular officer with whom he had clashed) was appointed to head the 6th Division and later the A.I.F. The decision to pass over Bennett was not a matter of revenge on the part of politicians and senior Staff Corps officers, as he and his supporters alleged; his military qualities were generally acknowledged. Because of his temperament, he was considered unsuitable for a semi-diplomatic command, and one that involved subordination to British generals. Bennett was as scathing of British officers as he was of Australian regulars.

Worse was to come. On the formation of the A.I.F.'s 7th, 8th and 9th divisions, command in each instance went to others. Bennett languished in Eastern Command until August 1940 when White's sudden death occasioned the appointment of Major General (Sir) Vernon Sturdee [q.v.] as chief of the General Staff. Sturdee nominated Bennett to succeed him as commander of the 8th Division on 24 September. The humiliation of the first year of the war combined with his ambition to spur Bennett to make up lost ground, particularly against Blamey. In February 1941 Bennett flew to Malaya and established his headquarters. He was to be joined by only two of his brigades, the third being detached for service elsewhere. His relationships with his senior officers were unhappy and some of them attempted at one stage to have him recalled on medical grounds. Bennett's dislike of regular officers was unabated and was felt within his command, but his most antagonistic relationship was with Brigadier H. B. Taylor [q.v.], a former C.M.F. officer. Bennett's dealings with British senior officers, especially with the general officer commanding, Malaya, Lieutenant General A. E. Percival, were similarly devoid of harmony.

Japanese troops landed in Malaya on 8 December and soon pushed British and Indian forces southward. Given command of Westforce on 9 January 1942, Bennett was made responsible for the defence of north-west Johore. He was confident that his Indian and Australian formations would halt the enemy advance, but his dispositions were fundamentally unsound: despite a successful Australian ambush at Gemas on 14 January, he fared no better than the British commanders whom he had derided. By the end of the month the defenders had withdrawn to Singapore. The Japanese assault on 8 February carried all before it. Again, Bennett's conduct of operations was questionable and Percival noted that his interest in the campaign seemed to wane towards the end. Surrender negotiations began on 15 February. That night Bennett handed over command of the 8th

Division to Brigadier C. A. Callaghan [q.v.] and left Singapore by sampan. He arrived in Melbourne on 2 March.

The response in Australia to Bennett's escape was mixed. His action was applauded by those who thought that he had valuable lessons to impart on methods of fighting the Japanese. Others, including many senior officers, denounced him for deserting his troops who became prisoners of war. Although Bennett was promoted temporary lieutenant general on 7 April and made commander of III Corps in Perth, Blamey ensured that he would never again have command in the field. Bennett unavailingly petitioned politicians for help. Bitterly disappointed, he transferred to the Reserve of Officers on 9 May 1944. Immediately, he was again at loggerheads with military authorities over his account of the Malayan campaign, *Why Singapore Fell* (Sydney), which was largely an apologia. Although Blamey tried to prevent the book's publication, it came out later that year.

On the release of prisoners of war in 1945, a letter from Percival which accused Bennett of unlawfully vacating his command was passed to Blamey. A military investigation found that Bennett had relinquished his command without permission. The reaction of his defenders, many of whom had served with him in World War I or in the 8th Division, was vociferous and the government commissioned (Sir) George Ligertwood [q.v.] to inquire into the matter. The commissioner's findings failed to provide Bennett with the vindication he sought. While never questioning Bennett's personal courage, Ligertwood concluded that his action had been unjustified.

Bennett's stated reason for leaving Singapore was that he had learned how to defeat the Japanese (but had been let down by British and Indian troops) and he was obliged to communicate his knowledge to military authorities. Yet, he had proved no more proficient than other commanders in Malaya and his tactics were outdated. Just as important to him was his wish to lead the Australian army, a consuming aspiration which had been sharpened by not being given an early command. His prejudice against regular officers and his ambition clouded his professional judgement at the most important point in his career. When his most cherished goals were in tatters, he convinced himself that blame for his failure lay with others.

After the war Bennett became an orchardist at Glenorie, near Sydney, until 1955. He continued his interest in military matters and wrote articles on many topics, among them the virtues of a citizen army. Survived by his wife and daughter, he died on 1 August 1962 at Dural and was cremated with Anglican rites. His portrait by James Quinn [q.v.

11] is held by the Australian War Memorial, Canberra.

L. Wigmore, *The Japanese Thrust* (Canb, 1957); F. Legg, *The Gordon Bennett Story* (Syd, 1965); A. B. Lodge, *The Fall of General Gordon Bennett* (Syd, 1986); Percival papers (Imperial War Museum, Lond); Bennett papers (ML); AWM records.

A. B. LODGE

BENNETT, NORMAN LOUIS (1899-1974), sugar technologist, was born on 3 March 1899 at Irvinebank, Queensland, son of Frederick Bennett, a native-born schoolteacher, and his Irish-born wife Hannah, née Desmond. Educated at Brisbane Grammar School, Norman won a scholarship to the University of Queensland (B.Sc., 1921). After graduating, he spent a year at the South Johnstone sugar-mill before returning to the university (B.Sc.App., 1923). Bennett won a government travelling scholarship in 1924 to study sugar technology. He visited major sugar-producing centres, including Java and Cuba, and worked in a modern engineering plant in Scotland; he also completed a postgraduate course at Louisiana State University (M.Sc., 1926) in the United States of America. On his return, he was the first mill technologist to be appointed to the Bureau of Sugar Experiment Stations, Brisbane. In the Catholic presbytery, Emerald, on 28 December 1928 he married a nurse Myrtle Ivy Daniels.

Finding Bennett's style abrasive, the bureau's director H. T. Easterby transferred him to Mackay to establish a sugar-mill technology division. As a mill adviser, Bennett found that incompatible methods made the comparison and analysis of results impossible. To improve efficiency, he implemented a 'mutual control scheme', involving uniform methods and the sharing of production data. Having attended a conference of the International Society of Sugar Cane Technologists in Cuba, in 1929 Bennett organized a meeting at Mackay which formed the Queensland Society of Sugar Cane Technologists; he was its foundation secretary. A. S. Hamilton, chairman of the Racecourse Co-operative Sugar Mill, appointed Bennett manager upon his leaving the bureau in 1932. Bennett remedied the mill's ailing finances within a four-year target. He was permitted by the board to buy (at a discount) shares previously issued to farmers in lieu of dividends and to benefit from their redemption. Though he selected able rather than highly qualified staff, he persistently interfered in their work, causing unrest and resentment. Bennett resigned in 1947, but many blamed Hamilton for engineering his departure.

For several years Bennett was a rather

unsuccessful storekeeper at Kin Kin until he was appointed chief chemist of the run-down Invicta sugar-mill at Giru in 1954. As its successful manager, he secured its future by ensuring that cane grown on one-time tobacco farms was assigned to the mill in 1964, and celebrated this victory by blowing the mill's whistle incessantly. In 1960 he had also become director of the Haughton Sugar Co.

Somewhat eccentric, Bennett slept with the lights on and developed unusual hobbies when his work lacked sufficient challenge. The presidency of the Q.S.S.C.T., of which he was an honorary life member (1934), escaped him because he refused to serve first as vice-president. Denied entry to the city club, Bennett and Hamilton had defiantly established the Mackay Suburban Bowling Club, but allegedly fell out when Bennett opposed his own father's promotion to A grade. In 1964 Bennett retired to Bowraville, New South Wales, to raise cattle. Survived by his son and three daughters, he died on 8 April 1974 at Macksville and was cremated.

Discussions of the 1979 Conference of the Australian Society of Sugar Cane Technologists (Mackay, Qld, 1979); J. Kerr, *A Century of Sugar: Racecourse Sugar Mill* (Mackay, 1988); *PP* (Qld), Qld Bureau of Sugar Experiment Stations, Reports, 1924-32; *Aust Sugar Year Book*, 1, 1940-41, p 109; *Aust Sugar J*, Apr 1974, p 69.   JOHN D. KERR

BENNETTS, HAROLD WILLIAM (1898-1970), veterinary scientist, was born on 18 July 1898 at Carlton, Melbourne, son of William Rawling Bennetts, iron merchant, and his wife Sarah Jane, née Clark, both Victorian born. From his father, Harold acquired a love of music and nature, and, from boyhood, showed interest in animal anatomy. Educated at Wesley College, he studied veterinary science at the University of Melbourne. In January 1918 he enlisted in the Australian Imperial Force and trained as a gunner; he was discharged in April 'for family reasons'.

Having graduated (B.V.Sc., 1919; M.V.Sc., 1920; D.V.Sc., 1931), in 1921-22 Bennetts worked for the Commonwealth Department of Health as bacteriologist in charge of the emergency laboratory at Cairns, Queensland, during an outbreak of bubonic plague and subsequently as a microbiologist in Townsville. Returning to Melbourne in 1923, he was appointed to the university as a lecturer and demonstrator in veterinary pathology and bacteriology under Professor H. A. Woodruff [q.v.12]. Bennetts was 6 ft 3¾ ins (192.4 cm) tall, gaunt in appearance, with a fresh complexion, blue eyes and fair hair. He married

Jean Muir Sinclair with Presbyterian forms on 28 January 1924 at the Park Church, South Brisbane; they were to have three children.

The crucial decision of his career was made in 1925 when he accepted the recently-created position of veterinary pathologist with the Western Australian Department of Agriculture. In 1928-35 he was seconded, part time, to the Council for Scientific and Industrial Research in order to use its better facilities and to have contact with leaders in his field. Much of Bennetts's work, however, was carried out in professional isolation and with inadequate resources. His first 'laboratory' in Perth consisted of two small cubicles in the basement of the department with a floor space of some 240 sq. ft (22.3 m^2). To the 'chagrin and malaise' of staff and citizens, animals were housed and post-mortems conducted in a small lane between the department and Government House.

Despite these obstacles, Bennetts achieved world recognition for his monographs and for his contributions to controlling major diseases in livestock. His work on enterotoxaemia and enzootic ataxia proved invaluable to sheep-raisers. He introduced two new concepts into veterinary pathology: those of diseases due to the absorption of bacterial toxins from the bowel and diseases due to a deficiency of essential trace elements. With his colleagues, he extended knowledge of copper deficiency in ruminants and also identified naturally occurring oestrogens in pasture as the cause of clover disease or ovine infertility.

In 1947 an animal health and nutrition laboratory was completed at Hollywood; Bennetts was its principal until 1959, except for eighteen months in 1952-53 when he was hospitalized with tuberculosis. He published the results of his researches in over one hundred papers in scientific journals. His collaborative work with C. A. Gardner [q.v.], on the effects of toxic plants on livestock, culminated in their book, *The Toxic Plants of Western Australia* (1956). Late in his career Bennetts worked on lupinosis in sheep. His resignation from the department in December 1959, four years before his stipulated retirement, was seen as a great loss to veterinary science. In 1960-66 he was employed as a technical consultant by William Cooper & Nephews (Australia) Pty Ltd.

Dr Bennetts belonged to the Weld Club and enjoyed gardening and swimming. He had been appointed C.B.E. in 1948. The Royal Society of Western Australia, of which he was president (1934-35), awarded him the Kelvin medal in 1955 and he received the Australian Veterinary Association's Gilruth [q.v.9] prize in 1957. An honorary member (1950) of the Royal Society of Medicine, London, and a fellow (1946) of the Australian and New Zealand Association for the Advancement of Science, he was, as well, a fellow (1954) of the Australian Veterinary Association and a corresponding member (1957) of the Académie Vétérinaire, France. Bennetts died on 28 August 1970 at Shenton Park, Perth, and was cremated with Anglican rites. He was survived by his wife, daughter and a son.

Roy Soc of WA, *J*, 40, 1956-57, p 1; *Aust Veterinary J*, 33, no 9, Sept 1957, p 241; *Wesfarmers News*, 2 June 1960, p 36; H. W. Bennetts, Veterinary Research in Western Australia, ms, Perth, nd, *and* M. R. Gardner, Obituary: Harold William Bennetts, C.B.E., D.V.Sc., ms, Perth, 1970 (held by L, Dept of Agr, Perth). 　　JILL E. MAUGHAN

BENNETTS, RICHARD JOHN (1925-1978), journalist and intelligence officer, was born on 3 January 1925 at North Fitzroy, Melbourne, elder son of native-born Richard Bray Bennetts (d. 1938), an employee in the boot trade, and his wife Dorothea, née Foster, from England. Educated at Northcote High School, John left at 15 to be the breadwinner for his mother and younger brother. He joined the Melbourne *Herald* as a cadet reporter, but in January 1943 enlisted in the Citizen Military Forces.

Transferring to the Australian Imperial Force on 13 April, Bennetts held posts in Australia, mainly with the Armoured Corps, until his arrival in April 1945 at Advanced Land Headquarters on Morotai Island. He was detached to the Allied Intelligence Bureau from July and served in Borneo. In December he went to New Guinea where he edited the army newspaper, *Guinea Gold*. Discharged on 13 September 1946 with the rank of staff sergeant, he resumed his cadetship at the *Herald*. In 1947 he won the Montague Grover [q.v.9] prize and, on qualifying as a journalist next year, was transferred to the parliamentary press gallery in Canberra. Having visited Britain and Europe on a Viscount Kemsley travelling scholarship, he returned to Australia in 1950 and began part-time studies at the Canberra University College (B.A., 1956). He married Margaret Jeanette Feakes on 22 September 1951 at Scots Church, Melbourne.

In 1954 Bennetts joined News Ltd as chief of the Canberra bureau and political correspondent for the Adelaide *News*. Awarded a J. William Fulbright travel grant in 1957, he lectured on journalism at Michigan State University, United States of America. Next year he completed a diploma in journalism at the University of Melbourne. Back in Canberra, he was active in the Australian Journalists' Association. In March 1960 he was appointed head of the Melbourne *Age*'s office in the press gallery. In addition, he subsequently became national-affairs commentator for the Australian Broadcasting Commission, local correspondent for Associated Press, Reuter and Agence France-Presse, president (1966) of the press gallery, and a part-time lecturer in political science (1965-67) at the Australian National University where he began a master of arts degree. In brief interludes he also acted as copy-editor at the *Age*'s head office (a job he had filled at the *Herald*) and accompanied leading politicians on their trips abroad.

Sent to Singapore in 1967 to be the *Age*'s South East Asia correspondent, Bennetts toured the region and saw combat zones in the Republic of Vietnam (South Vietnam) and Laos. In 1968 he was appointed senior lecturer in political science at the School of General Studies, A.N.U. From January 1970 he worked as political correspondent for the *Canberra Times*, but later that year accepted an analyst's post in the Joint Intelligence Organization, Department of Defence. As the co-ordinator of current intelligence, he collated material for the daily digest given to the prime minister and other high-ranking officials. He was in Port Moresby in 1974-75 as Australian defence representative, before reverting to his former post in Canberra. Appointed J.I.O. attaché, Washington, in 1976, he exchanged information and liaised with American intelligence agencies. On his return home, in 1977 he was made head of current intelligence in the new Office of National Assessments.

As a journalist, Bennetts had been a sound reporter who largely excluded his attitudes from his commentaries. From the mid-1960s there have been allegations that he was the Australian Security Intelligence Organization's 'man' in the Federal parliament's press gallery. Although made explicit after his death, the claims were veiled during Bennetts's lifetime and he denied them vehemently. Discussion with former officers indicates that he had no formal links with security and intelligence organizations in his years as a journalist and casts doubt on his being an informant. In January 1974 the *Australian Financial Review* reported that, as an intelligence officer, Bennetts was suspected in Labor circles 'of being associated with newspaper stories damaging to the Government', but not a skerrick of evidence was advanced.

When the suggestions first gained currency Bennetts was older than most of his peers in the press gallery which seethed with intrigues and suspicions at the best of times; he was politically more conservative and had little sympathy for the Vietnam protest movement. The roots of the unproven claims may lie in mutual antipathy between an old and a new generation. Bennetts was a keen bush-walker, trout-fisherman, skier, swimmer and carpenter (who built his own holiday home). He died of subarachnoid haemorrhage on 3 July 1978 at Cooma, New South Wales, and was cremated. His wife, son and two daughters survived him.

Age (Melb), 22 Apr 1968; *SMH*, 22 May 1968, 4 July 1978; *Aust Financial Review*, 2 Jan 1974; *Canb Times*, 4 July 1978, 17 Feb 1991; *National Times*, 13 Oct 1979; information from *Canb Times* and Office of National Assessments, Canb; family information.   JACK WATERFORD

BENSON, SIR CLARENCE IRVING (1897-1980), Methodist clergyman and journalist, was born on 1 December 1897 at Hull, Yorkshire, England, son of Walter Benson, ship foreman, and his second wife Mary, née Mear, a staunch Methodist and Sunday School teacher. Educated at local schools and at Hull Technical College, he developed an interest in literature and history. In 1916 he enrolled at Cliff College, Sheffield, an evangelical training institute for lay missionaries, and in May departed for Australia. He arrived in Melbourne 'as a stranger in a strange land'.

The Victorian Methodist Home Missionary Society appointed him to Cavendish, near Hamilton, where the young man's preaching soon attracted attention. He kept notebooks which documented the careful preparation of his sermons. His conversational style of preaching and well-modulated voice complemented his tall and commanding—if rather austere—presence. In 1918 Benson was accepted as a probationer for the Methodist ministry and appointed to Toorak, Melbourne. There he became a protégé of Rev. W. H. Fitchett [q.v.8] whom Benson described as being 'like a father to him' and who encouraged him to write. In 1923 Benson began to contribute a weekly column, 'Church and People', to the *Herald*. Appearing every Saturday until 1979, it made him widely known beyond the Methodist denomination.

On 14 April 1919 at the Methodist Church, Toorak, Benson had married Agnes Lyell. Ordained in April 1922, he ministered at the Albion Street Church, Brunswick, until recruited in 1926 to Central Methodist Mission at Wesley Church. Occupying the pulpit of Melbourne's most important Methodist church enabled Benson to build a large congregation, especially for his Sunday-evening book sermons and winter lecture series. He was appointed superintendent minister in 1933, a position he held until his retirement in 1967. During these years he became Melbourne's best-known and most controversial minister through the forthright comments he

made on public issues in radio broadcasts, such as his 'Questions and Answers' programme (1938-44) on 3LO, in his *Herald* articles and at the mission's Pleasant Sunday Afternoon gatherings.

Under Benson's direction the P.S.A. became a national institution. He chose a range of speakers and issues, but the overall thrust reflected his belief in spiritual renewal rather than in an interventionist state as the way forward in the postwar period. Its platform was used to promote moral rearmament in the 1940s and anti-communism in the Cold War years. The most frequent speakers were (Sir) Robert Menzies and R. G. (Baron) Casey [qq.v.], whom Benson counted among his friends. Broadcasts of the P.S.A., at first on 3LO and then on 3DB, had by the 1950s an Australia-wide audience, attracted by well-known orators, musical soloists and Benson's opening comments on current issues. He also used the programme to plead for donations to the mission's work.

An enthusiastic Anglophile and patriot, Benson gave broadcasts and published articles which reflected his admiration of (Sir) Winston Churchill, the royal family and the British Empire, while Anzac Day and the main battles of World War II were given special attention. He perceived a moral crisis in the 1950s, and often focussed on liquor and gambling, together with the growing consumer society, as contributing factors. Benson's writing style was more suited to journalism than to books: his sermons and articles were compiled rather than written, and drew on his personal library as well as an extensively-indexed collection of newspaper and magazine cuttings. His published monographs included *A Century of Victorian Methodism* (1935), *The Eight Points of the Oxford Group* (1936), and *The Man with the Donkey* (1965) which presented a selective, heroic interpretation of the Australian legend of Simpson [q.v.9 J. S. Kirkpatrick].

Possessing a large personal library, Benson was an avid collector who bought and sold books, manuscripts and autographs. In the public sphere, he was trustee (1942-46) of the Public Library, museums and National Gallery of Victoria (vice-chairman 1945), chairman (1940-66) of trustees of the Public Library of Victoria and deputy-chairman (from 1966) of its successor, the Library Council of Victoria. He was also president (1938-49) of the Library Association of Victoria and chairman (1947-56) of the Free Library Service Board. Having himself substituted the reading of books for his lack of formal education, he regarded libraries as 'a practical demonstration of democracy's faith in universal education as a life-long process'. The main exhibition area of the State Library of Victoria, opened in 1967, was named Irving

Benson Hall, though by this time Benson and the council had been criticized for the management of the library, and for its failure to expand and attract resources.

Although he had been elected president of the Victoria and Tasmania Conference of the Methodist Church of Australasia in 1943, Benson used his image and his fund-raising ability to distance himself from the conference. Many of his public statements were in opposition to Church resolutions, and his links with the commercial and political elite of Melbourne—reflected in his membership of the Melbourne and Savage clubs—were regarded with ambivalence. Benson had his supporters and admirers within the Church, but he did not actively participate in denominational committees or in decision making. Late in his career at the mission, he disagreed bitterly with the conference when it voted to support later closing-hours for hotels, and clashed with it over the appointment of his successor. At Benson's farewell, a former minister of the mission observed that, like all great men, Benson had not escaped criticism and that 'probably the criticism from within the Church has been greater than from outside'.

Benson had an international reputation as preacher and journalist. In 1939 the University of Toronto, Canada, awarded him an honorary D.D. He was appointed C.B.E. in 1960 and knighted in 1963. In stature and personality he was a dominating figure whose conservative views on church and society were shared by many Australians, yet his reserved and often supercilious manner prevented him from being a popular Church leader. After twenty-three years as a widower, Sir Irving married Marjorie Ruth Featonby on 30 December 1967 at Wesley Church. He died on 6 December 1980 and was buried in Brighton cemetery; his wife survived him, as did the three daughters of his first marriage.

Age (Melb), 8 Dec 1980; Irving Benson collection (LaTL); Wesley Church Mission records (Wesley Church Mission, Melb).

RENATE HOWE

BERGMAN, GEORGE FRANCIS JACK (1900-1979), soldier and historian, was born on 8 April 1900 at Lissa, Posen, Germany (Leszno, Poland), elder son of Jewish parents Ludwig Bergmann (d. 1932), a German clothing manufacturer, and his French wife Hedwig, née Krayn (d. 1940). Jack to his family, Franz to his student friends, he was educated at the Royal Comenius Gymnasium, called up for national service in 1917 and joined the Freikorps Lepper to defend Lissa during the Polish revolution. He attended the univer-

sities of Berlin, Breslau (Wroclaw), Heidelberg and Munich (Ec.D., 1922), and worked part time in an attorney's office until completing his legal studies. Called to the Bar of the High Court on 7 December 1929, he practised as a solicitor at Munich.

After Adolf Hitler seized power in 1933, Bergmann fled to Paris in August and managed an estate for two years. On 2 July 1935 he married Hilde Baum at the mairie du 19e Arrondissement. He worked as a freelance journalist and gained a certificate in mechanical engineering at the École Professionelle Diderot. An intrepid mountaineer and skier, he had belonged to the Alpenveiren and now joined the Swiss Alpine Club.

From 7 December 1939 Bergmann served with the Foreign Legion in North Africa until, on 10 October 1940, he was interned at Colomb-Bechar, Algeria, by the Vichy government. Liberated in February 1943, he enlisted on 13 April in the British Army and in May transferred to the Royal Electrical and Mechanical Engineers as a fitter. That year he gave evidence to a French military tribunal against officers in charge of Hadjerat-M-Guil, the 'Algerian torture camp' where he had been disciplined.

Meanwhile he learned through the New York branch of his old student club, the Jewish Fraternity of the Kartell Convent, that his wife had fled to Argentina, divorced him (invalidly) in Mexico and remarried; his brother Walter was in La Paz, Bolivia. Sergeant Bergmann confessed to being 'a little tired and embittered by the thought that I can see no promotion and that all my superior officers could all be my sons'. He went on to serve in Italy, and was attached to British intelligence as an interpreter in Austria. On 9 July 1947 he reached Melbourne in the *Tamaroa* and was discharged in Sydney; he Anglicized his name by deed poll on 26 August.

Cut off from intellectual work, his degrees unrecognized, Bergman tried selling dresses and in April 1948 bought a delicatessen shop in Oxford Street that failed. He joined the Commonwealth Public Service as a post office technician in February 1949 and was naturalized on 10 June. Having been granted a divorce in France in 1948, at the Temple Emanuel, Woollahra, on 22 January 1950 he married a widow Émilie Raik, née Gerstl, a laundry manageress from Prague. The marriage was to prove a disappointment: she did not share his interests, especially in bushwalking, and he was irritated by her perpetual card-playing. He joined the B'nai B'rith (1953), the Youth Hostels Association (1956) and the Liberal Party (1959); he was appointed a justice of the peace on 29 July 1957. Advancement in the public service proved difficult and he was increasingly frustrated by 'his silly routine job'.

Undertaking original research 'in the spirit of an explorer', Bergman uncovered the remarkable stories of Esther Johnston [q.v.2] and of many other early Jewish settlers. His biography of Gustav Weindorfer [q.v.12] was published in Austria in 1954 and an English version in Hobart in 1959. A member (1953) and vice-president (1954) of the Blue Mountains Historical Society, in April 1956 Bergman believed himself the first 'new-Australian' to be elected to the Royal Australian Historical Society. From 1958 he was a committee-member (vice-president 1968-79) and mainstay of the Australian Jewish Historical Society, contributing almost forty articles to its journal. Bergman wrote short histories of several Jewish institutions, lectured widely and published in the *Australian Encyclopaedia, New Citizen, Die Alpen, Der Bersteiger, Sydney Jewish News* and *Australian Jewish Times*. He was delighted to be invited to contribute to the *Australian Dictionary of Biography* and was sometimes consulted by Professor Douglas Pike [q.v.].

Having retired from the public service in 1965, Bergman made a world tour and lectured on Australian Jewry in the United States of America, Britain, Germany and Israel. Back 'home', as 'George Klaffe' he penetrated extreme right-wing organizations and set up extensive files on anti-Semitic and neo-Nazi activities in Australia for the New South Wales Jewish Board of Deputies. With Rabbi John Levi and a grant from the Memorial Foundation for Jewish Culture, New York, he produced his major work, *Australian Genesis: Jewish Convicts and Settlers, 1788-1850* (Adelaide, 1974).

Small and birdlike, with sparse, brown hair and blue eyes, George Bergman had great 'courage and physical toughness'. He also possessed 'a profound love and understanding' of painting, music, literature and the theatre. A perfectionist, he was intolerant of those who did not meet his own high standards and inevitably quarrelled with many people. He remained an avid traveller, and bequeathed the Roman and Egyptian antiquities he had collected to the Nicholson [q.v.5] Museum. Survived by his wife and stepdaughter, he died on 21 October 1979 at Vila, New Hebrides, and was buried in the Jewish war section of Rookwood cemetery, Sydney, in a grave designated 'Sergeant R.E.M.E. Army Number BNA/13809597'.

Aust Liberal, Jan 1960, p 12; Aust Jewish Hist Soc, *J*, 8, 1979, p 397; *SMH*, 8 May 1961; *Aust Jewish Times*, 25 Oct 1979; Naturalization files, A446/1 item 61/508, A439/1 item 51/11/6256 (AA); Bergman diaries *and* papers (ML *and* Wiener L, Lond, *and* Leo Baeck Inst, NY); information from Mrs E. Bitel, Mosman, Syd.

MARTHA RUTLEDGE

BERRICK, NORMAN DAVID (1905-1970), metallurgist, was born on 28 December 1905 at West Maitland, New South Wales, second son of Jewish parents George Edward Berrick, an accountant from Melbourne, and his wife Amy Florence, née Friedman, a Sydneysider. George became a well-known wine and spirits merchant at Newcastle.

Joining the Broken Hill Proprietary Co. Ltd in 1920, Norman attended Newcastle Technical College at night and in 1926 obtained a diploma in metallurgy. On 5 November 1932 he married a kindergarten teacher Ré Miriam Heymanson (d. 1932) at the Synagogue, Toorak Road, Melbourne. Employed from 1934 by the Shell Co. of Australia Ltd, in 1936 he developed from his own research a rod, 'Cobalide One', claimed as the first hard-facing alloy using chromium carbide for its strength. He married a nurse Dorothy Fern Bennett on 9 June 1939 at the Presbyterian Church, Mosman, Sydney, and from 1941 worked for the Ministry of Munitions.

Moving to Sydney by 1945, Berrick registered his company, Cobalide (Industrial) Pty Ltd, and began manufacturing next year; a site at Alexandria was acquired for an office and factory in 1951. The company produced specialized alloys in the form of welding electrodes and rods for hard-facing metals under the names of Cobalide and Cobalarc. By strengthening the surfaces that received heavy wear on earth-moving equipment, drill bits and valves, the process saved costly replacements. The firm also produced casting, wires and powders, as well as technical handbooks for its customers, and introduced electrodes with larger diameters and moisture-proof flux coatings. Berrick's brother, Alan, was involved as commercial manager.

As managing director, Norman displayed innovation, energy and personal involvement in overseas markets and research. He was a member of a trade mission to the Far East in 1954 and received a gold medal in 1956 for a paper presented to the South African Institute of Welding; he combined lectures and factory visits during his numerous trips. In 1963 the Commonwealth government presented the company with an award for outstanding export achievement. By then the largest manufacturer of hard-facings in the southern hemisphere, the firm exported three-fifths of its products for use in thirty countries, ranging from bridge-building in Scotland to tin-dredging in Malaysia, while also making Australia self-sufficient in these materials. British Oxygen Co. Ltd, an overseas distributor which held a controlling interest in the company, sold it in 1967 to a subsidiary, Commonwealth Industrial Gases Ltd. Berrick resigned next year due to ill health.

Of middle height and medium build, carefully groomed and a pipe-smoker, he had a good voice and enjoyed singing, like other members of his family. Civic-minded, in 1966 he anonymously donated over $14 000 for a bus turn-around at the Hunters Hill wharf, near his home. Berrick died of pneumonia on 8 March 1970 at Mosman and was cremated. His wife, their two daughters and their son survived him.

Cwlth Industrial Gases Ltd, *Comwelder*, no 66, Apr-May 1970; *Argus*, 17 Nov 1932; *SMH*, 24 Jan 1957, 29 Mar 1967; *Newcastle Morning Herald*, 14 Mar 1970; cuttings and papers held by Mrs A. Cameron and family, Northbridge, Syd.

L. E. FREDMAN

BERRY, DAME ALICE MIRIAM (1900-1978), Country Women's Association leader, was born on 28 April 1900 in Sydney, eldest daughter of Charles Roy McKenzie, a native-born mining engineer, and his wife Matilda, née Abram, from New Zealand. Alice was educated at a one-teacher school at Cobar, where her father was the gold-mine manager, and at Waverley Superior Public School, Sydney. Following business-college training, she was employed as a secretary to a real-estate agent at Wentworthville. On 11 June 1921 she married Henry Berry at St Stephen's Presbyterian Church, Sydney. Henry had successively been a woolclasser, grazier and merchant; he enlisted in the Australian Imperial Force in March 1916 and served in the 1st Light Horse Regiment in the Middle East.

After the birth of two daughters, the family moved to a sheep-property near Tumut and lived there until 1927. When it was apparent that the health of one of their daughters would benefit from a warmer climate, the Berrys went to Queensland and took up land opened for closer settlement in the Mount Abundance district, near Roma. Alice gained first hand experience of the problems which beset women in rural areas: lack of facilities, bad roads, poor communications, fitful mail and inadequate medical care. At the time that she became a founding member and secretary of the Mount Abundance branch of the Country Women's Association of Queensland in 1928, the locality had no township. She quickly came to appreciate how the C.W.A. could bridge isolation, and find ways of improving life for women and children.

As adept at outdoor work on their sheep-station, Sheria, as in 'all the things that housewives feel they ought to do', she was capable of swimming her horse across a swollen creek to attend C.W.A. meetings. In 1932 the family moved to Woolabra—a 42 000-acre (16 997 ha) property in the Charleville district—where she continued to juggle domestic and C.W.A. responsibilities. Her initiative in getting a stationhand's wife to hospital, when a flooded creek blocked the way, was to be long remembered throughout the region: the sick woman was ferried in an old, tin bath, propelled by men swimming at either end of the tub, to the ambulance on the opposite bank. Mrs Berry worked tirelessly for those projects dear to countrywomen—education, mothers' hostels, the aerial medical service and access to seaside cottages. Involved in other organizations, during World War II she worked for the Red Cross Society and the Australian Comforts Fund; she was also a commissioner of the Girl Guides' Association.

Henry Berry's indifferent health brought a return to Brisbane in 1945, but Alice maintained her ties with the country as the C.W.A.'s councillor for the Western Division of Queensland. In 1948 she was appointed State international officer. That year, after Henry's death, she took on the management of Woolabra. Deputy-president (1951-52) of the State C.W.A., she was its president in 1953. Having led the Queensland delegation to the conference of the Associated Country Women of the World in Copenhagen in 1950, she did so again, to Toronto, Canada. There, in 1953, she was the first Australian to be elected president of the A.C.W.W. Re-elected unopposed in 1956, she served its six million members in twenty-seven countries for a further three years. During her term of office she twice toured the world to visit member nations. She returned to Queensland and was president (1961, 1962) of its C.W.A.

Very tall, dark haired, dark eyed and vivacious, a fluent speaker with a rich, deep voice, Alice Berry became a well-known spokeswoman. Her conviction that women 'in any country and of any race are much the same' derived from her breadth of vision, and from her interest in internationalism and world peace. Within the C.W.A. she was admired for her practical accomplishments and experience, and for strong leadership that was combined with humour and warmth. She was appointed O.B.E. in 1954 and in 1960 elevated to Dame Commander of that order. In 1962 she was elected national president of the C.W.A. Retiring from office in 1963, she worked on the State association's archives for ten years. In 1971 she was made a member of honour of the A.C.W.W.

Survived by her daughters, Dame Alice died on 18 September 1978 at Royal Brisbane Hospital and was cremated.

Qld Countrywoman, 1947-53, 1960-65, 1970-72; *SA Country Woman*, 1969; *Courier-Mail*, 10 May 1952, 21 Aug 1953, 1 Jan, 17 May 1960; Alice Berry, OL files; cuttings collection (QCWA

Archives, Brisb); information from Mrs B. Draper, Cherrybrook, Qld.   HELEN TAYLOR

BERTLES, ZOE EMMA (1880-1975), librarian, was born on 8 May 1880 at West Maitland, New South Wales, fifth child and youngest daughter of Samuel Bertles, a builder from England, and his native-born wife Emma Cecilia, née Evans. Educated at West Maitland Girls' High School, Zoe ran a small private school at Quirindi until 1912. She then enrolled at the University of Sydney (B.A., B.Ec., 1916), supporting herself by part-time teaching.

Probably encouraged by Nita Kibble [q.v.9], in April 1915 Bertles was appointed library-assistant at the Public Library of New South Wales. Her high qualifications were quickly recognized and her ability was exploited; from 1917 she also worked after hours as research officer for the Premier's Department. Reclassified as cataloguer in 1919, she was described by the principal librarian W. H. Ifould [q.v.9] as one of his two ablest. That year she topped the higher grades examinations for library staff.

In August 1920 Bertles was promoted ahead of more senior colleagues to take charge of the country circulation department. She showed initiative and organizing ability in this section which, for the next twenty-five years, provided almost the only public and school library service beyond Sydney. In cramped quarters in the Mitchell [q.v.5] wing, and later in a custom-built extension, Bertles and her staff responded to the growing demand for good books; they developed a service which drew acclaim from its users, support from country politicians, wistful glances from interstate and considerable overseas interest. In 1935 the Munn-Pitt [q.v.11] report on libraries found that these country services had 'amply proved their worth'.

Although she lacked the knowledge of Australiana of Ida Leeson [q.v.10], Bertles was a serious contender for the position of Mitchell librarian in 1932. She continued to draw quiet satisfaction from her work. Addressing the first conference of the Australian Institute of Librarians in 1938, she reported that use of the country service had more than trebled since she had taken charge. In 1942 she was promoted to the new position of chief cataloguer and in July 1944 became senior technical officer of the Library Board of New South Wales. She retired in 1946.

An active member of the Professional Officers' Association of New South Wales, Bertles had represented her fellow officers in salary negotiations with the Public Service Board. She was a foundation member of the Business and Professional Women's Club of Sydney. Energetic and generous with her own time, she assisted the libraries of the Boys' Brigade and the Young Men's Christian Association, catalogued for the Great Synagogue in Sydney and organized Rabbi Brasch's private library.

Miss Bertles was small and slightly built, with piercing, brown eyes and a fine sense of humour. She retained the 'gentle, almost prim, manner of the good schoolmistress', but was 'easy to work with, never temperamental nor bad-tempered, never showing likes or dislikes, always helpful, compassionate, and understanding'. Zoe lived at Mosman. She died there on 27 February 1975 and was cremated.

Aust Lib J, 24, no 7, Aug 1975, p 328; Bertles papers (ML); SLNSW archives and confidential papers (SLNSW); information from Miss J. F. Arnot, Double Bay, Miss M. Dobbie, Lane Cove, Mrs M. Hancock, Eastwood, and Miss W. Radford, Chatswood, Syd, and Mr and Mrs J. Read, Banora Point, NSW.

DAVID J. JONES

BEST, GODFREY JACOB MARSHALL (1894-1970), insurance manager, was born on 20 August 1894 at Leytonstone, Essex, England, son of Samuel Best, a germ-malt factor, and his wife Rachel, née Britten. Educated at Essex County High School, in 1911 Godfrey joined the London office of the Prudential Assurance Co. Ltd as a junior clerk. He served in France with the London Rifle Brigade before being commissioned in May 1915 in the London Regiment (Royal Fusiliers); he was later attached to the King's African Rifles and was promoted lieutenant in July 1917. On 24 November that year he married Hylda Lilian Andrews at the parish church, Basingstoke, Hampshire. He was employed by the Ministry of Labour until August 1919.

Returning to the Prudential, by 1924 Best had become a fellow of the Chartered Insurance Institute. Next year he tutored candidates for the institute's examinations and lectured for the London County Council. In 1930 he was transferred to Sydney as assistant-manager of the company's Australia and New Zealand branch; he was to become manager in 1938. A staunch supporter of Britain and the Empire, in 1931 Best endorsed the Prudential's lead in encouraging large insurance companies and investment houses to defend the pound sterling by transferring £100 million of foreign investments to the Bank of England in exchange for British government sterling securities. He explained that the company 'is not merely a commercial concern, but rather a national institution willing and eager for public service'.

In December 1939 Best pleaded for greater co-operation with the United States of America and suggested that Australia should form a Pacific peace pact with Canada, New Zealand, the U.S.A. and, eventually, Japan. He deplored the short-sightedness of vested interests in Australia which had 'torpedoed' a trade agreement with the Americans. In July 1940 he warned Sydneysiders that they could not afford to be complacent about their security; by December, as chairman of the National Emergency Services citizens' committee, he organized mock air-raids over the city. As a councillor of the Australian-American Co-operation Movement, in 1943 Best advocated even closer ties with the Americans so that Australia could play a significant part in postwar negotiations. He urged the Big Brother Movement to prepare for increased immigration after the war and supported the Food for Britain Appeal. Best met the challenge of World War II by expanding Prudential's business threefold. Having visited England in 1946, he retired in 1948 and moved from Vaucluse to Longueville.

Best was chairman (1955-68) of Sebels (Australia) Ltd, and a director of Hanimex Corporation Ltd and the Acme Bedstead Co. Ltd. A lifelong member of the Boy Scouts' Association (which he had joined in 1909), he was chairman (from 1943) of the State executive and in 1954 became chairman of the federal council. In 1958 he was appointed M.B.E. Resourceful, reliable and confident of the future, he belonged to the Australian, Imperial Service and Elanora Country clubs, and to the Legacy Club of Sydney; he enjoyed tennis, golf, swimming and trout-fishing. Survived by his wife and daughter, he died on 4 March 1970 in hospital at Wahroonga and was cremated with Presbyterian forms.

A. C. Gray, *Life Insurance in Australia* (Melb, 1977); *A'sian Insurance and Banking Record*, 21 Apr 1948; *SMH*, 2 Sept 1931, 23 July 1938, 8 Dec 1939, 12 July, 4, 11, 12 Dec 1940, 26 Aug, 23 Sept, 15 Oct 1943, 25 Apr 1946, 11 Sept 1948, 1 Oct 1949, 12 June, 9, 11 Aug 1958, 10 Mar 1970.

L. M. HEATH

BEST, SIR JOHN VICTOR HALL (1894-1972), dentist, was born on 22 December 1894 at Neuchâtel, Switzerland, son of Rev. John Henry Hall Best, the English chaplain, and his wife Laura Louisa, née Kountze. After serving from 1903 at St James's Cathedral, Townsville, Queensland, John senior moved his family to Sydney in 1905, first to All Saints, Woollahra, and in 1907 to Lane Cove. Educated at public schools, young Jack was coached for the matriculation examinations by Florence Oakes. Best studied dentistry at the University of Sydney (B.D.S., 1916),

graduated with first-class honours and practised at Mount Gambier, South Australia, in 1917-21. He went to the United States of America in 1921 and entered Harvard University (D.M.D., 1922) where he formed a chain of enduring friendships and became a life member of Delta Sigma Delta fraternity.

Returning to Sydney, Best established a practice in Macquarie Street and joined the Australian Club. On 19 December 1927 at St Mark's Anglican Church, Darling Point, he married Marion Esdaile Burkitt. She was to become an interior designer and to enhance his surgery with antique furniture and with the brilliant colours which were her trademark. John and Marion were keen golfers who belonged to Royal Sydney Golf and Elanora Country clubs; they won several trophies in the 1930s.

A gifted administrator, Hall Best (as he was by now generally known) was honorary secretary (1925-27) of the Society of Dental Science, a founder in 1928 of the Australian Dental Association, a council-member (1928-54) and president (1935-37) of its New South Wales branch, federal president (1940-44 and 1950-54) of the A.D.A. and a member (1937-51) of the Dental Board of New South Wales. He published extensively in Australian and American journals. While interested in improved techniques in most branches of dentistry, he gave special attention to dentures.

A member (from 1940) of the Central Medical Co-ordination Committee, in December 1942 Hall Best volunteered for the Australian Imperial Force and served as a consulting dental surgeon with the rank of lieutenant colonel. As chairman of the central dental advisory committee within the Directorate of Manpower, in 1943-44 he was confronted with a serious shortage of dentists, and had to allocate personnel to balance the demands of the armed services and the needs of civilians. He transferred to the Reserve of Officers in April 1944.

When Hall Best was appointed president of the 12th Australian Dental Congress, to be held in Sydney in August 1950, he immediately went to Europe and the U.S.A. to investigate the latest methods of visual education. He arranged the televising of a dental operation for the congress and invited specialists of international standing to address its members. By introducing Dr Basil Bibby to government leaders and public health authorities, he increased their understanding of the importance of adding fluoride to drinking water. Hall Best persuaded interstate dentists to agree to publish one journal instead of three and in 1955-72 chaired the board of the *Australian Dental Journal*; its first issue appeared in February 1956.

He did much to raise the status of the

Australian dental profession at home and abroad. Awarded the R. Fairfax Reading memorial prize (1955) by the Dental Alumni Society of the University of Sydney, he was knighted in 1956. Hall Best was a fellow of the American College of Dentists (1938), the Australian College of Dental Surgeons (1969) and of the Royal College of Surgeons, England (1949). He wore a pale-blue dental jacket when his colleagues still wore white.

Sir John grew orchids in his garden at Queen Street, Woollahra, and acquired land at Collaroy for his plants. He was president (1957-60) of the Orchid Society of New South Wales, and a founder and first president (1961-64) of the Australian Orchid Council. Well dressed and dapper, intelligent and witty, he enjoyed reading biographies and history. He was also interested in the architecture of English parish churches and in High Church liturgy and ceremonial. A warden for many years, he regularly worshipped at Christ Church St Laurence. He died on 27 February 1972 at his Woollahra home and was cremated; his wife, son and daughter survived him.

R. W. Halliday, *A History of Dentistry in New South Wales, 1788 to 1945*, A. O. Watson ed (Syd, 1977); Dental Alumni Soc of Univ Syd, *Apollonia*, v 2, no 3, Dec 1955, p 15; *Aust Dental J*, v 1, no 1, Feb 1956, p 66, v 17, no 2, Apr 1972, pp 147, 150, v 21, no 1, Feb 1976, p 1; Aust Dental Assn (NSW Branch), *Newsletter*, Apr 1972, p 3; *Aust Orchid Review*, June 1972, p 85; *SMH*, 21 Aug 1937, 16 Aug 1950, 18 Dec 1952, 2 Jan 1956, 12 Apr 1972; information from Mrs D. Broughton, Woollahra, Syd.   A. O. WATSON

BEST, KATHLEEN ANNIE LOUISE (1910-1957), nurse and army officer, was born on 28 August 1910 at Summer Hill, Sydney, second child of Rupert Dudley Best, commission agent, and his wife Emily Edith, née Stevenson, both native-born. Educated at Bondi Public and Cleveland Street Intermediate High schools, Kath completed nursing training at Western Suburbs Hospital and midwifery at the Women's Hospital, Crown Street. She became a staff nurse at Wyong Hospital, acting-matron at the Rachel Forster Hospital for Women and Children, Sydney, and deputy-matron of the Masonic Hospital, Ashfield. On 30 May 1940 she was appointed to the Australian Army Nursing Service, Australian Imperial Force, and posted as matron of the 2nd/5th Australian General Hospital.

Embarking for the Middle East in October, she impressed a member of her staff as 'a young, enthusiastic nurse, and a perfectionist' who ruled with a firm hand, but 'was always very fair'. In December the hospital opened at Rehovot, Palestine, and on 10 April 1941 moved to Greece where the Anzac

Corps was encountering a German assault. Medical personnel had to contend with constant air-raids. By 25 April almost all the nurses and physiotherapists from the 2nd/5th A.G.H. had been evacuated to Crete. Best and a party of thirty-nine nurses were chosen from volunteers to remain and care for the wounded, but, later that day, were ordered to leave. They endured a hazardous voyage to Crete. For her courage and efficiency throughout the evacuation, Best was awarded the Royal Red Cross (1942).

Back in Palestine, she reorganized the hospital. For some time she had charge of a nurses' staging camp at Suez, Egypt; enclosed by a high, barbed-wire fence and with only one gate, it was popularly known as 'Katie's Birdcage'. In August 1941 she went with the 2nd/5th A.G.H. to Eritrea, Ethiopia. She returned to Australia in March 1942 and her A.I.F. appointment terminated on 13 June. Next month in Melbourne she was made controller of full-time voluntary aid detachments (Australian Army Medical Women's Service from September). Relinquishing the post in February 1943, she was promoted lieutenant colonel and posted as assistant adjutant-general (women's services). In September 1944 she transferred to the Reserve of Officers and accepted the assistant-directorship of women's re-establishment and training, Department of Postwar Reconstruction: her responsibilities included helping servicewomen and female war-workers adjust to peacetime conditions. On 12 February 1951 'K.B.' was recalled from the reserve and appointed founding director, Australian Women's Army Corps (Women's Royal Australian Army Corps). She was promoted honorary colonel on 17 September 1952 and appointed O.B.E. in 1956.

Five ft 5 ins (165.1 cm) tall, with blue eyes and a fair complexion, Best was committed to her duties and an inspiring leader; yet she was also modest about her achievements and had a lively sense of humour. She died of melanomatosis on 15 November 1957 in Epworth Hospital, Richmond; after a military funeral at Toorak Presbyterian Church, she was buried in Fawkner cemetery. Her portraits by Nora Heyson and Geoffrey Mainwaring are held by the Australian War Memorial, Canberra.

I. Brodziak (ed), *Proudly We Served* (Syd, 1988); *Aust Women's Digest*, Oct 1944; *SMH*, 2 Jan, 1 May, 3, 4 July, 21 Sept 1942, 9, 28 Jan, 12 Feb, 15 Mar 1943, 16 Aug, 18 Sept, 18 Nov 1944, 2 Aug 1945, 27 Jan, 15 Feb, 22 Apr 1951, 1 Feb 1953, 2 Jan, 28 Oct 1956, 21 July, 16 Nov 1957, 7 Nov 1959; *Herald* (Melb), 2 July 1942, 18 Aug 1944, 27 Jan 1951, 16, 23 Nov 1957; AWM records; information from Mrs G. Ellis, Clovelly, Syd, Lieut-Colonel G. Cardwell, Lieut-Colonel P. Shaw and Major A. Norris, Dept of Defence, Canb.

MERRILYN LINCOLN

BEVERIDGE, ADA (1875-1964), Country Women's Association leader, was born on 15 February 1875 at Townsville, Queensland, third child of Frederick Joshua Wathen Beardmore, commission agent, and his wife Emily Anne, née Commins, both from New South Wales. Educated at Sydney Girls' High School (on a scholarship) and the University of Sydney (B.A., 1896), Ada graduated with first-class honours in English and became a schoolteacher. On 20 January 1904 at St James's Anglican Church, Croydon, she married a grazier James William Caldwell Beveridge. She settled into country life at the family property, Tenandra Park, Gundagai, and later moved to Billabong station near Junee.

After raising two sons (born in 1906 and 1908), Mrs Beveridge began to devote considerable time to organizations that aimed to improve the welfare of women. With her connexion Jessie Sawyer [q.v.], she joined the Country Women's Association of New South Wales soon after its establishment in 1922 and founded a branch at Junee in 1926. An international vice-president (1937-40) of the Pan-Pacific Women's Association when Georgina Sweet [q.v.12] was president, Ada attended its conferences in Honolulu (1934) and at Vancouver, Canada (1937). She was an executive-member of the New South Wales Bush Nursing Association (1938-49), the Australian Aerial Medical Services and the regional committee of the Young Women's Christian Association.

Having been a vice-president of the C.W.A. until 1937, Mrs Beveridge was State president in 1938 40. Despite a serious motorcar accident in 1939 and a bout of pneumonia next year, she pursued her presidential tasks with energy, visiting branches throughout New South Wales and travelling 14 720 miles (23 689 km) in six months. She attended interstate conferences, commuted between the C.W.A.'s office in Sydney and her country home, and represented the association's interests at local, State and national levels.

Her presidency coincided with the outbreak of World War II. As a committee-member of the Women's Voluntary Services, Mrs Beveridge toured the countryside, mobilizing country women to support the war effort. From 1939 she represented the C.W.A. on the executive of the Lord Mayor's Patriotic and War Fund, and was a foundation director and executive chairman (1940-42) of the Women's Australian National Services; she also helped to establish the Women's Voluntary National Register and the women's land section (Australian Women's Land Army). Ada lent Billabong station for their training camps and subsequently to accommodate evacuees. She was appointed M.B.E. in 1941.

When she stood as an Independent candidate for the Senate in 1943, Beveridge was obliged by the C.W.A.'s apolitical stance to 'lay aside' her former activities. Unsuccessful in the elections, she resumed leadership of the association at a local level and continued to be an active member of the branch which she had established in 1939 at Nangus, her nearest village. She was a delegate to the Associated Country Women of the World conferences in Amsterdam (1947) and Copenhagen (1951). An intrepid traveller who had flown over Alaska in 1937, she enjoyed gardening and reading, and belonged to the Lyceum, Women's and the Queen's clubs, as well as the Royal Empire Society. Following her husband's death in 1959, Ada moved to Roseville, Sydney. Survived by her sons, she died there on 20 January 1964 and was cremated.

H. Townsend, *Serving the Country* (Syd, 1988); Pan-Pacific Women's Assn, *Procs of 4th Conference, Vancouver, Canada*, 1937; *Aust Women's Weekly*, 14 Aug 1943; *SMH*, 16 Apr 1932, 11 Sept 1934, 27 Sept 1937, 26 July, 17 Oct 1938, 4 Mar 1939, 8 July 1940, 12 June, 17 July 1941, 4 Feb 1942, 24 July 1943; *Gundagai Independent*, 10 July 1943; Country Women's Assn of NSW, Annual Reports, 1939-40 (Syd), and Minutes, Junee Branch, 1926 (Junee, NSW), and Nangus Branch, 1939 (Nangus, NSW); information from Prof W. A. Beveridge, Wentworth Falls, NSW.   JULIE GORRELL

BEVERIDGE, DOROTHY CHRISTINA (1894-1978), public servant, was born on 21 November 1894 at Paddington, Sydney, eldest child of English-born Robert Christopher Beveridge (d. 1905), accountant, and his wife Matilda, née MacConaghy, a Sydneysider. Dorothy was educated at Sydney Girls' High School where in 1910 she passed the junior public examination. Having trained at the Metropolitan Business College, in 1911 she was employed by the Public Service Association of New South Wales. Next year she joined the State public service as a typist at the Department of Public Works, with an annual salary of £95. Although the Labor premier W. A. Holman [q.v.9] had that year announced a commitment to 'equal pay for equal work', the policy implemented by the Public Service Board limited wages, promotion prospects and tenure for women by appointing them to jobs 'of more or less mechanical nature'.

In 1915 Beveridge gained reclassification as a shorthand-typist with a salary loading of £50 per annum; in 1919 she was appointed to a clerical position, only recently opened to women, in the new Department of Local Government, on a salary of £225. That year, with other women activists, she formed the women's clerical sub-section of the P.S.A., of which she was secretary (1923-29) and president (1929-31, 1932-39 and 1940-45).

A major figure in the P.S.A. campaign for implementation of equal pay for equal work for women clerical officers under the Industrial Arbitration (Amendment) Act (1926), Beveridge continued to campaign with her colleagues for the broad issue and to press specific cases before the Public Service Board. She put a case for improved rates of pay for temporary shorthand-typists, but had only limited success. Although handicapped by the reduction of public service salaries during the Depression, she collected evidence for the P.S.A.'s basic-wage committee and helped to co-ordinate the work of women's representatives on its other committees.

In October 1937 women denounced as 'hollow mockery' the Industrial Arbitration (Amendment) Act which raised the basic public service salary of males to £3 16s. 0d. per week, but in practice reduced that of female clerks by two shillings to £2 1s. 0d. Members of the women's clerical sub-section of the P.S.A. compiled dossiers on claims for discontinuation of the percentage formula in favour of setting a female rate based on the needs of an adult woman. They provided additional evidence to that being amassed by Muriel Heagney [q.v.9] for the Council of Action for Equal Pay.

An 'indefatigable' stalwart, Beveridge was a member of the P.S.A. council, and of its management and arbitration committees. She inspired many other working women to become involved in the postwar phase of the campaign. In 1948 she ceased her active role in the P.S.A. Awarded a Queen Elizabeth II coronation medal in 1953, she retired in 1958 from the Department of Local Government where she had remained a clerk and long-time secretary of the building regulation advisory committee. Unmarried, she lived with her mother (d. 1951) in a flat at Cremorne. In 1961 Dorothy visited Rhodesia with the Business and Professional Women's Club of Sydney; that year she was appointed M.B.E. A devout Presbyterian, she took an interest in the ordination of women and the revision of the hymn-book, and was superintendent of the Mosman Kirk's Sunday School. She died on 24 November 1978 at Mosman and was cremated.

D. Deacon, *Managing Gender* (Melb, 1989); *Red Tape*, Dec 1929, June 1930, May 1932, Mar 1940, Feb 1945.
LOUISE CHAPPELL
LENORE COLTHEART

BEVERIDGE, JESSIE; see SAWYER, JESSIE

BIAGGINI, ERNEST GORDON (1889-1978), educationist, was born on 10 March 1889 at Stoke Newington, London, son of Charles Edward Biaggini, a clerk of Italian descent, and his wife Eveline Harriett, née Thompson. The family was Protestant. Gordon suffered infantile paralysis which left physical and mental scars. He attended Stamford Hill Collegiate and Wood Green Higher Grade schools, but his boyhood promise was frustrated by his family's financial difficulties and he became a clerk with a corset manufacturer. In 1912 he won an exhibition at night-school to attend the London School of Economics, but overwork led to a breakdown.

Hoping to improve his health, Biaggini embarked in the *Berrima* for Australia. He was stranded without money in Melbourne in 1915 and eventually took a job as a book-keeper in outback Queensland; he then taught at several schools in New South Wales before accepting an appointment in 1917 as a master at Brisbane Grammar School. On 9 December 1919 he married an Irish Catholic, Mary Cuttler; although they regularly attended Mass, he was never converted to her faith. They remained childless.

Having graduated (B.A., 1924) from the University of Queensland and won a (John) Archibald [q.v.7] scholarship, in 1925 Biaggini joined the tutorial classes department of the University of Adelaide: he organized courses at Renmark (where he lived in a wooden shack) and later at other country towns and in Adelaide. In 1932-56 he was the tutor in charge of Workers' Educational Association classes in Adelaide and studied at the local university (M.A., 1932; D.Litt., 1944). He had returned to the L.S.E. in 1933, but was unable to remain long enough to complete his Ph.D. In England he met F. R. Leavis who wrote the foreword to Biaggini's pioneering work of practical criticism, *English in Australia* (Melbourne, 1933), and the preface to his *The Reading and Writing of English* (London, 1936), a school text which influenced many South Australians. He edited a series of W.E.A. pamphlets, wrote *A New World for Education* (Adelaide, 1944) and published his memoirs, *You Can't Say That* (Adelaide, 1970).

Gordon Biaggini was a remarkable teacher. Tall and handsome, with a good voice and considerable charm, he awakened and stimulated the minds and critical faculties of the many men and women who attended and re-attended his classes. He alerted students to the tenets of good taste and to the slipperiness of language, upholding honesty and clarity while attacking sentimentality and humbug. He battled to maintain traditional standards of excellence in English, yet was progressive in focussing on word connotations and denotations.

Although the organization was poorly funded, and Biaggini so underpaid that he was compelled to do much hackwork, he made the W.E.A. a force in South Australia. A shy, tactless, pessimistic man, he suffered bitterly, believing himself always denied the advancement he deserved and resenting those above him whom he believed—with reason—to be his inferiors. He was beloved by his wife and gained the respect, admiration and affection of his students and most of those with whom he worked in adult education. After his wife's death in 1968, he was cared for by Leonore Isabel Riordan whom he married on 9 January 1974 in the registrar's office, Adelaide. Survived by her, he died on 1 December 1978 at Hartley Hospital, Brighton, and was buried in Brighton North cemetery.

Aust J of Adult Education, 4, no 2, Dec 1964, p 42, 11, no 1, Apr 1971, p 63; *Issue*, 4, no 8, Nov 1969, p 11; *Meanjin Q*, 47, no 4, Summer 1988, p 723; *Advertiser* (Adel), 17 Oct 1970, 5, 9 Dec 1978; L. Arnold, ABC radio interview with E. G. Biaggini, 1969 (held in J. D. Somerville Oral Hist collection, Mort L).   BARBARA WALL

BIDDLECOMBE, JANET (1866-1954), pastoralist and philanthropist, was born on 24 April 1866 in Melbourne, seventh daughter and youngest of eight children of George Russell [q.v.2], pastoralist, and his wife Euphemia Carstairs (d. 1867), both Scottish born. She was educated privately by Mrs Pfund, a schoolmistress at St Kilda. Motherless from infancy, Janet was a close companion to her father and, as his last unmarried daughter remaining at Golf Hill, Shelford, Victoria, developed an interest in the property. After her father's death in 1888, she grew concerned at her brother Philip's (d. 1898) inadequate management of Golf Hill. With his agreement, she assumed control of the encumbered estate and for several years struggled to restore its former prosperity.

On 7 July 1900 at Scots Church, Melbourne, Janet married John Biddlecombe, an English naval officer; they were to remain childless. After service in South Africa, he retired from the Royal Navy and worked as a jackeroo before taking over management of Golf Hill. Together, the Biddlecombes built up a Hereford stud (registered in 1906) until it became one of the leading herds in Australia. From 1924 they won prizes almost annually at the Sydney and Melbourne royal shows. Following John's death in 1929, Janet maintained the herd's pre-eminence: in 1947 her cattle gained every group prize in the Hereford section at the Sydney Royal Show. Under her direction, from a flock of some 25 000, Golf Hill also produced some of the best comeback wool in the Geelong region. A shrewd but self-effacing woman, she encouraged sound management by her knowledge and lack of interference.

Janet Biddlecombe maintained a tradition of secret philanthropy begun before her husband's death. They had financed the construction of six masters' houses at Geelong Church of England Grammar School; the school named a road after them. Mrs Biddlecombe continued to befriend the school, offering hospitality to its headmaster (Sir) James Darling, and, with the Bell family, providing a music school. She supported Shelford Presbyterian Church—built on Golf Hill land—and the Geelong branch of the Australian Red Cross Society, and sponsored the publication of a narrative of her father's life and of the papers of the Clyde Co.

In October 1953 Mrs Biddlecombe decided to sell her world-famous cattle, many of which, including Marshall Lass, Winifred, Corisanda, Marinda, Best Girl, Harmony, Cora and Oyster Girl, were descended from the elite studs of Herefordshire, England. She hoped that the herd's dispersal would improve the Hereford breed throughout the country. The auction obtained record Australian and British Commonwealth prices, and proceeds of the sale—about £125 000—went to charity.

Until the last few weeks of her life Mrs Biddlecombe retained a lively interest in the running of the property, which still carried 14 000 sheep. She died on 15 February 1954 at Golf Hill and was cremated with Presbyterian forms. Her estate, sworn for probate at £554 585, established a Golf Hill bequest for the Bethany Babies' Home, Geelong, the Victorian Association of Braille Writers and the Victorian Society for Crippled Children. Many other institutions then learned the identity of their long-time, anonymous benefactor: the Red Cross named an ex-servicemen's convalescent home after her and the Royal Flying Doctor Service of Australia commemorated her at its base at Derby, Western Australia. A portrait of Janet Biddlecombe by Watt Webb is held by the La Trobe Library, Melbourne.

J. R. Darling, *Richly Rewarding* (Melb, 1978); W. Bate, *Light-Blue Down Under* (Melb, 1990); *Pastoral Review*, 16 May 1929, 16 Mar 1954; *SMH*, 12 Apr 1938, 11 Aug 1954; *Herald* (Melb), 29 July 1953, 16 Feb 1954; *Argus*, 30 Oct 1953, 16 Feb 1954; *Geelong Advertiser*, 16 Feb 1954, 26 Feb 1955.   DIANE LANGMORE

BIGGS, FREDERICK (c.1875-1961), Aboriginal bushworker and singer, was born in a lambing camp near Ivanhoe, New South Wales, son of a White stockman and an Aboriginal woman called Polly. He was raised in the traditional territory of the Ngiyambaa (or Wangaaybuwan) Aborigines in the hinterland of the Lachlan and Darling rivers where the country is arid, although after rain the creeks and swamps teem with birdlife. Pastoralists had occupied the region, but their stations—such as Willandra and Trida—were vast and sparsely settled, allowing the Aboriginal inhabitants to carry on a modified version of their old life.

From his mother, Fred inherited the bandicoot totem; he inherited his surname from his Aboriginal 'father' Moses Biggs who took him through the *burba* initiation ceremony when Fred was aged about 14. As a young man, Biggs worked at different jobs in the pastoral industry and at one time drove the mail-cart around the various stations. He married a Ngiyambaa woman Nancy Parkes who was his 'right meat'; they were to have seven children.

About 1919 a drought and the subdivision of the big stations compelled the Ngiyambaa to converge on Carowra Tank where missionaries provided intermittent instruction. In 1926 the Aborigines Protection Board took control of the community. Due to a shortage of water, the Ngiyambaa were moved in 1934 to Menindee on the Darling River which was also occupied by the Baagandji and other Aboriginal groups. In 1949 the Ngiyambaa were relocated at Murrin Bridge, near Lake Cargelligo, far away from their own country.

After his initiation Biggs had taken part in the ritual life of his people up to the last *burba*, held in 1914; he declared that he was 'very very sorry that it was all finished'. In the early 1920s an attempt to revive the *burba* failed because of an epidemic that killed several of the senior men. Fred retained his commitment to Ngiyambaa lore and passed on parts of his knowledge to researchers. Late in life he was to express a hope that the traditions might be taught in schools. In 1943 he and his kinsman Jack King provided Ronald Berndt with information on the 'Clever Men' or *shamans*; from 1957 Biggs informed anthropologists about the intricacies of the kinship system. He also dictated myths and recorded songs. Some of this material was later published in Roland Robinson's *Aboriginal Myths and Legends* (Melbourne, 1966). The song which Biggs had composed about a White boy who was lost in the bush is included in the cassette, *Songs of Aboriginal Australia*.

Biggs was a small, wiry man; an accident had made him blind in one eye. In his eighties he remained remarkably spry and active, and went out in his sulky to get wood from which to make artefacts for sale. He told his stories with zest, relishing their moments of ribald comedy. Still possessing a strong voice, he seized opportunities to record his songs. He died on 14 March 1961 at Lake Cargelligo and was buried in Murrin Bridge cemetery; his four daughters and two of his sons survived him.

S. Wild (ed), *Songs of Aboriginal Australia* (cassette, Canb, nd); T. Donaldson, *Ngiyambaa* (Cambridge, 1980); *Oceania*, 17, no 4, 1947-48, p 327, 18, no 1, 1948-49, p 60, 29, no 3, 1958-59, p 200.   JEREMY BECKETT

BINDI, DAISY (1904?-1962), Aboriginal activist, was born about 1904 on a cattle-station near Jigalong Aboriginal Reserve, Western Australia, daughter of Aboriginal parents who were called 'Jimmy' and 'Milly'. Daisy's Aboriginal name was Mumaring. As a child, she worked on Ethel Creek station, learned household skills and appears to have received no formal education. She later became an accomplished horsewoman. Living and working with the Nyangumarda people on a number of pastoral stations, she both saw and suffered indignities inflicted by the police who regularly raided Aboriginal camps and shot dogs on which the community depended to hunt kangaroos. From her husband she acquired the name Bindi; no other evidence has been found of their union.

Aware of the unfairness of working for no regular pay, in 1945 Daisy responded to the call made by Don McLeod at Marble Bar. He was an elected spokesman for the Aborigines and, with Dooley Bin Bin and Clancy McKenna, urged Aborigines who worked on large sheep and cattle stations to strike for better conditions. A fluent and lively speaker, Daisy organized a meeting to convey the message. She demanded and received wages from her White employer at Roy Hill station and used the money to hire a truck with which to collect local workers when the strike began on 1 May 1946.

Although the employers sought assistance from the police and the Native Welfare Department to prevent the strike, five hundred men, women and children walked off the stations south of Nullagine and made their way to Port Hedland. At Nullagine, Daisy talked her way through a police confrontation where she claimed that she had never heard of McLeod, and, with eighty-six others, made her way via Marble Bar to Canning Camp on the Shaw River.

A 'tall, spare woman', with 'long, sensitive fingers', in the late 1950s Daisy suffered from diabetes, but lived in relative comfort at the Pindan Pty Ltd co-operative settlement, Port Hedland, one of the early Aboriginal ventures of its kind in Western Australia and a product of the strike. The residents worked in the mining industry and received equal pay.

Having had a leg amputated after an accident in the bush, in October 1959 Daisy visited Perth to be fitted with an artificial limb. There she successfully lobbied parliamentarians for a school at the Pindan co-operative. She also visited and spoke at meetings of the Western Australian branch of the Union of Australian Women which supported Aboriginal rights.

In 1960 the co-operative split into some who wished to continue with McLeod and others who thought that his struggles against mining interests were counterproductive to the Aboriginal cause. Daisy joined those who left the McLeod camp. Little else is known of her. Katharine Susannah Prichard [q.v.11] wrote an article about her in 1959 and in 1966 Kath Walker was to make her the eponymous heroine of a poem. Daisy Bindi died of uraemia on 23 December 1962 at the Native Hospital, Port Hedland, and was buried in the local cemetery.

C. D. Rowley, *The Remote Aborigines* (Canb, 1971); R. M. and C. H. Berndt (eds), *Aborigines of the West* (Perth, 1979); K. S. Prichard, *Straight Left*, R. Throssell ed (Syd, 1982); M. Bosworth, 'Daisy Bindi', in H. Radi (ed), *200 Australian Women* (Syd, 1988); UAW, *Our Women*, Mar-May 1960; *Aboriginal News*, 1, no 12, Apr 1975, p 10; *Daily News* (Perth), 3 Sept 1959; letter from Mr D. McLeod to author, 22 June 1991 (held in ADB file).   MICHAL BOSWORTH

BINI, ELZIO LUCIANO (1926-1979), teacher and Italian community leader, was born on 5 August 1926 at Salcano, Gorizia, Italy (Solkan, Slovenia), son of Ernesto Bini, railway worker, and his wife Lucia, née Traiber. Educated at Udine and at Gorizia, Elzio matriculated in classical languages and science. He enrolled at the University of Venice, but his course was interrupted by World War II: by 1945 he had become a liberation fighter with the Osoppo brigade in Carnia. In 1947 he studied at the Biblioteca Nationale Braidense, Milan.

Under the aegis of the International Refugee Organization, Bini arrived in Melbourne on 26 April 1950 and soon moved to Hobart. From November he worked for Cadbury Fry Pascall Australia Ltd in its milk-condensing section. Awarded a studentship in 1951 by the Education Department, he attended the University of Tasmania (B.A., 1956) while employed as a shiftworker at the Electrolytic Zinc Co. of Australasia Ltd. From February 1954 he was an assistant-teacher and librarian at Burnie High School; next year he was engaged as resident master to teach French and Latin at The Hutchins School. Naturalized in 1956, he visited Italy three years later. On 30 March 1959 at Verona he married Nerea Angela Buccino. The couple established a travel agency in Collins Street, Hobart.

Reported to have declined a career in the Italian diplomatic service, Bini assisted Claudio Alcorso and succeeded him in 1963 as honorary vice-consul for Tasmania. Despite his heavy consular and business commitments, Bini taught part time at Hobart Technical (1964, 1966), Hobart Matriculation (1965-71) and Elizabeth Matriculation (1967-71) colleges, and at the Sacred Heart School (1979). Committed to multiculturalism and ethnic welfare, he pressed for Italian language classes at secondary and tertiary levels, and for the extension of English lessons for new immigrants.

Five ft 5 ins (165.1 cm) tall, with dark hair and brown eyes, Bini was a gentle man with immense energy. He was widely respected for his accessibility and helpfulness. Closely involved in the cultural life of the Italian community, he was a founding member of Hobart's Australian Italian Club (1955), Juventus Soccer Club (1956) and Dante Alighieri Society (1956); he was appointed to the Order of the Star of Italian Solidarity in 1967. With his brother, he edited an anthology of modern Italian literature, *Dolci Inizi* (1968). In 1976 Bini was co-ordinator of the Tasmanian relief appeal for victims of the earthquake in north-eastern Italy. That year he was appointed A.M.

While finalizing travel documents for Giuseppe Mampieri, Bini was fatally shot on 31 May 1979 at Hillborough Road, South Hobart; his presumed murderer Mampieri died the same day from self-inflicted gunshot wounds. Survived by his wife, two sons and three daughters, Bini was buried in Cornelian Bay cemetery after a requiem Mass conducted by the Catholic archbishop of Hobart.

M. di Benedetto, *The Australian Italian Club, Twenty Fifth Anniversary* (Hob, 1980); *Mercury* (Hob), 1 Feb 1967, 12 June 1976, 1, 5 June 1979, *Giornale di Gorizia* (Italy), 3 June 1979; E. Bini file, Education Dept (Tas), Hob; records, Univ Tas; information from Mr L. Bini, East Ivanhoe, Melb, Mr C. Alcorso, Berriedale, and Mrs N. Bini-Maluta, Taroona, Hob.   DINO OTTAVI

BINNEY, SIR THOMAS HUGH (1883-1953), naval officer and governor, was born on 9 December 1883 at Douglas, Isle of Man, eldest son of Thomas Godfrey Binney, gentleman, and his wife Susan Lockhart, née Hobson. Intent on a career in the Royal Navy, at the age of 13 Hugh joined the training ship, H.M.S. *Britannia*, Dartmouth, as a cadet. For most of the years from 1899 to 1914 he served at sea. He saw action as gunnery officer of the *Queen Elizabeth* during the

Dardanelles campaign; he was promoted commander in 1916 and awarded the Distinguished Service Order in 1919. Binney performed duties aboard the *Hawkins* on the China Station and became captain in 1922; he commanded the *Nelson* (1928-30) and the *Hood* (1932-33), and in 1931-32 was officer-in-charge of the Tactical School at Portsmouth, England. As rear admiral (1934), he commanded the 1st Battle Squadron, Mediterranean Fleet, from 1936. At the outbreak of World War II he was in charge of the Imperial Defence College, London. From 1939 he was flag officer (ashore), Orkneys and Shetlands, Scotland. Having been appointed C.B. in 1935, he was elevated to K.C.B. in 1940. Promoted admiral in 1942, he served as flag officer-in-charge, Cardiff, and retired in mid-1945. At the parish church of St Martin-in-the-Fields, London, on 31 October 1942 he had married Elizabeth Bride Blair-Imrie; they were to remain childless.

On 24 December 1945 Binney succeeded Sir Ernest Clark [q.v.8] as governor of Tasmania. Although he was later described as an uncontroversial governor whose decisions were accepted 'without question', Binney's term coincided with a period of political turmoil. The Legislative Council twice rejected supply in 1948, forcing the Cosgrove [q.v.] government to an early election. Cosgrove again asked Binney to dissolve the parliament in 1950 when his minority government faced 'legislative impotence' after the resignation of the Speaker W. G. Wedd (an Independent) in protest at the appointment of Thomas D'Alton [q.v.] as agent-general. The dissolution was granted only after Binney 'satisfied himself that no alternative Government was possible'. His term of office was extended in 1950 and he was appointed K.C.M.G. in 1951.

The Binneys were unostentatious residents of Government House and made a determined effort to fit into the life of the Tasmanian community: they travelled extensively, and tirelessly attended a host of public functions. A keen sailor, Sir Hugh regularly raced with the Royal Yacht Club of Tasmania and won the Derwent Sailing Squadron pennant (1951). Lady Binney was active in the Girl Guides' Association and the Australian Red Cross Society. She represented Tasmania on the executive of the Country Women of the World Association, supported many charitable organizations and was a frequent visitor at Clarendon Children's Home. A tubby man who sometimes wore an incongruous bowler-hat, Binney had a modest and friendly demeanour which enhanced his gubernatorial role. He cherished the British Empire as 'an empire of ideals, rather than of territories'. Having retired on 8 May 1951, he returned to England. Following surgery for cholecystitis, he died of pulmonary embolism on 8 January 1953 at Colchester; his wife survived him.

W. A. Townsley, *The Government of Tasmania* (Brisb, 1976); *Who Was Who*, 1951-1960; *The Times*, 2 Nov 1942, 10 Jan 1953; *Mercury* (Hob), 6 Nov, 26 Dec 1945, 6 Jan, 3, 5, 6, 8 May 1951; *Age* (Melb), 16 May 1951.   SCOTT BENNETT

BINNIE, WILLIAM MORE (1874-1954), mine-manager and company director, was born on 3 July 1874 at Menteith, Perthshire, Scotland, son of 16-year-old Margaret Jane More, a farmer's daughter. After his mother married coalminer Archibald Binnie in 1878, William took his stepfather's surname. Educated at Bathgate Academy, West Lothian, in 1889 William came to Queensland with his family in the *Jumna*. He learned coalmining skills while prospecting with Archibald on the West Moreton field, won prizes at Ipswich Technical College and in 1906 gained a mine-manager's certificate (first class). On 7 July that year he married Scottish-born Agnes Tait at Ipswich with Presbyterian forms; they settled at East Ipswich and were to have three children.

H. G. Noble employed Binnie to manage the Denham Colliery at Swanbank where coal quality and production gradually improved. In 1908 Binnie became secretary of the West Moreton Colliery Owners' Association and moved to W. R. Black's [q.v.7] Blackheath Colliery as manager; due to his abrasiveness with unionists and his employment of day-labourers on jobs previously done by miners, he was less successful there. Appointed manager of Noble's Wattle Creek Colliery in 1909, he supervised its expansion into the company's premier operation, Noblevale No. 1. He left in 1912 for a holiday in Scotland. On his return, he spent a year in North Queensland: he discovered the 'Bowen Seam' (which led to the opening of the Collinsville coalfield) and named a local hill 'Binnie's Knob'. Back at Ipswich in 1915, Binnie was reappointed manager of Noblevale No. 1 and four years later became Noble's mine superintendent.

He branched out independently in 1922, opening the old Aberdare Colliery, a small pit at Blackstone. In partnership with the Hart brothers, in 1927 Binnie worked the Aberdare seam. He was at his best in running small-scale, short-term underground ventures and in 1938 formed United Collieries Pty Ltd which operated in the Ipswich and Rosewood region. A board-member of several colliery companies and managing director of Maranoa Collieries Ltd, he was chairman of the West Moreton District Coal

Board before it was taken over by Queensland Coal Board. Binnie expanded his business interests into sawmilling, pottery and the production of fertilisers. Energetic, technically efficient, blunt but humorous, he had a tough, driving nature which made him one of the most successful entrepreneurs in the Ipswich area. He was particularly noted for the keen business sense that enabled him to operate marginal coalmines profitably.

Binnie retired to Indooroopilly with shareholding interests in Aberdare collieries, Bowen Consolidated Coal Mines Ltd, Tannymorel Coal Mining Co. Ltd, Dinmore Pottery Ltd, General Fertilisers Ltd, Queensland Machinery Co. Ltd and Mathers Pty Ltd. Survived by his wife, daughter and a son, he died on 5 April 1954 at Indooroopilly and was buried in Toowong cemetery.

R. L. Whitmore, *Coal in Queensland*, 2 (Brisb, 1991); *Qld Government Mining J*, 9, 1908, pp 5, 376, 10, 1909, p 543, 11, 1910, pp 142, 170, 55, 1954, p 453; *Brisb Courier*, 29 May 1908, p 3; *Qld Times*, 22 Apr 1919, 13 May 1925; Z1965 IMM/123 *and* A/44280 (QA).   RUTH S. KERR
RAYMOND L. WHITMORE

BIRCHELL, MICHAEL JAMES (1945–1967), panel-beater and soldier, was born on 2 June 1945 at Marrickville, Sydney, only child of native-born parents James William Birchell, shop-assistant, and his wife Alice Catherine, née Taylor. James had served in the Australian Imperial Force in World War II; after his discharge in August 1945, the family settled at Coonabarabran. Educated locally, Mick competed for his high school in swimming, captained its Rugby League team and gained his Intermediate certificate. In 1962 he moved with his parents to Tamworth where he worked for a firm of panel-beaters and studied welding at night at the technical college. Birchell continued playing Rugby League as full back for Tamworth City juniors; solidly built and 5 ft 9 ins (175.3 cm) tall, he earned a reputation for being a tough but fair opponent. His other interests were parties and girls.

In 1965 the Federal government began inducting, by ballot, 20-year-old single males for two-year engagements in the Regular Army Supplement: the conscripts could be required to serve overseas. In April the government announced that combat troops would be sent to the Republic of Vietnam (South Vietnam). When news of his call-up arrived, Birchell informed his parents that he would 'make the best of it'. He enlisted on 30 June 1965 and was posted in September to the 6th Battalion, Royal Australian Regiment, based in Brisbane. In January 1966 it was confirmed that his battalion was to proceed to Vietnam. Birchell's mother and father came to Brisbane to watch their son march off to war on 21 May. Arriving in Saigon in June, Birchell was sent to the 1st Australian Task Force base at Nui Dat, Phuoc Tuy province. Apart from an occasional major operation, 6th R.A.R.'s principal duties were to protect the camp perimeter and to undertake long-range patrols. A member of No. 5 Platoon in 'B' Company, Birchell prided himself on never missing a patrol.

On 17 February 1967 the battalion was ordered into positions near Lang Phuoc Hai to block the withdrawal of an enemy force. Instead of a party of retreating troops, it encountered a unit of the People's Liberation Armed Forces (Viet Cong) which was well armed, dug-in and hidden by dense scrub. 'B' Company arrived in helicopters and began an attack, but met sustained resistance. As No. 5 Platoon continued forward, three undetected machine-guns opened fire on its right flank, halting the assault and inflicting heavy casualties. Removing the wounded became urgent. Birchell was instructed to provide cover with his machine-gun. Despite the enemy's intense fire, he ran to take up his post, but was seen to fall. It was later found that he had been hit by two rounds and killed outright. Of the 28 men in No. 5 Platoon that day, 14 were either killed or wounded. A total of 187 national servicemen from Australia lost their lives to enemy action in the Vietnam War.

Following a military funeral with Anglican rites, Birchell was buried in West Tamworth lawn cemetery. A number of his comrades were to name their sons Mick in his honour.

I. M. Williams, *Vietnam* (Syd, 1967); P. King, *Australia's Vietnam* (Syd, 1983); F. Frost, *Australia's War in Vietnam* (Syd, 1987); *Northern Daily Leader*, 20 Feb 1967; information from Mr J. W. Birchell, Tamworth, NSW, and Mr J. P. O'Halloran, Hamersley, Perth.   JOHN KNOTT

BIRD, MARGARET HENRIETTA (1888–1963), bookseller, was born on 22 November 1888 at Beechworth, Victoria, daughter of James William Ingram, bookseller, and his wife Catherine, née Woodside, both Victorian born. Margaret's father was the son of James Ingram, a Scot who had opened a bookshop at Beechworth in 1855 and subsequently developed a large business in north-eastern Victoria. James admitted his son to partnership in 1887, trading as James Ingram & Son. In 1898 they sold out and James William established premises specializing in educational books at 227 Little Collins Street, Melbourne. He continued to trade as James Ingram & Son until his retirement in 1913.

A boarder at Oberwyl girls' school, St Kilda, Margaret matriculated and became governess to a grazier's family at Moulamein, New South Wales. On 28 January 1922 at Hawthorn she married with Presbyterian forms William Ellis Bird, a teacher turned accountant who had served in the Australian Imperial Force. In 1918 he had opened a second-hand bookshop at 427 Little Collins Street, but moved to 280 Russell Street next year. Scholarly and idealistic, with somewhat utopian ideas, he edited a booklet, *Zapataland* (1919), about a communist State in Mexico. Working together in the shop, the Birds catered for booklovers, students and bohemians. They established a group, known as the 'Heretics', to discuss the works of G. K. Chesterton, and frequently invited chosen customers to dine with them. In 1925 they moved their burgeoning business to 21 Bourke Street.

When William died in 1927 from injuries received in a street accident, Margaret continued to trade as Ellis Bird's Bookshop. She built up a substantial personal connexion and, after Cole's Book Arcade closed in 1929, hers was said to be the most popular bookshop in the city. Customers roamed freely between tables stacked in relaxed order with second-hand books and Mrs Bird never interfered, although she was capable of giving advice on a wide range of subjects. She continued the tradition of offering hospitality to radical intellectuals, literary people and booklovers; among those she entertained in her large, upstairs room were the artist Harold Herbert, the critic Jimmy MacDonald [qq.v.9,10], and the writers Vance and Nettie Palmer, Bernard O'Dowd and Marie Pitt [qq.v.11].

Tall and slim, with high cheekbones and 'silver hair curving back in a bun', Mrs Bird wore low-waisted, full-sleeved dresses befitting 'the old-fashioned dignity of her calling'. Friends thought she had turned conservative when she became a Catholic after her husband's death. Regarded by some as stern, she was taken to court by a man whom she had hit with a book. In 1955, after she had lost £15 000 in an unfortunate investment, the Bourke Street property was sold and the purchaser occupied part of it, leaving Margaret in the cramped, smaller portion. Having retired in 1959, she lived with her sisters at Hawthorn. She died on 1 February 1963 at Coburg and was buried in Burwood cemetery with Catholic rites.

Aust Booksellers Assn, *The Early Australian Booksellers* (Adel, 1980); J. Sendy, *Melbourne's Radical Bookshops* (Melb, 1983); *Herald* (Melb), 1 Feb 1963, 5 Jan 1979; *Age* (Melb), 2, 9 Feb 1963; *Nation* (Syd), 23 Feb 1963; personal information.

J. P. HOLROYD

BIRDSEYE, SYLVIA JESSIE CATHERINE (1902-1962), bus driver, was born on 26 January 1902 near Port Augusta, South Australia, daughter of Charles De Witt Merrill, stationhand, and his wife Elizabeth Ann, née Kirwan. The Merrills led an itinerant existence and often lived in hessian huts. Sylvia's friends, the Birdseye family of Port Augusta, went to Adelaide where Alfred Birdseye bought the horse-and-coach business of John Hill [q.v.4] & Co. Ltd that ran the route from the capital to Mannum. He converted it to the State's first, motorized, country bus service. In 1921 Sylvia went to work for him and joined his daughter Gladys in driving the tray-top Buick and the Studebaker sedans; two years later they gained their commercial licences.

An attractive, slight woman, with wavy, auburn hair, on 23 October 1923 Sylvia married Alfred's son, Sydney Alick Birdseye (d. 1954), at Flinders Street Presbyterian Church, Adelaide. He was responsible for repairing the firm's vehicles. The fleet included a red Reo charabanc (with canvas side-flaps), modified by a lengthened wheel base and extra seats; freight went on top, on the running-board and on the front mudguards. While taking a spell, Sylvia slept strapped to the luggage under a tarpaulin on the roof. She gave everything she had to her job: though jocular, she was tart to shearers suffering hangovers and to passengers late for the bus. For work, she wore overalls or jodhpurs, a cap and jacket: all were covered in dust and stained with grease. She learned to fit bearings and piston rings, to grind valves and to fix a gearbox. With Gladys, Sylvia changed a wheel in four minutes; on her own, she replaced an axle in twenty minutes. Her two children, born in 1926 and 1927, accompanied her on the buses.

The company extended its operations in 1928 to Port Augusta and Port Lincoln, across gravel roads with few bridges over the creeks; for townships like Cleve, Kimba and far-west Ceduna, it provided a lifeline. The firm bought a gleaming Straight-Eight Nash and Sylvia became a director. She bet heavily at the races, but helped many with food parcels during the Depression. In 1938 she waded through a swollen creek, fixed a block and tackle to the far bank, and winched her bus and sixteen other vehicles to safety. A flood in 1946 was the only hazard which prevented her from running to time—by eight days: with twenty-five passengers, the coach was bogged south of Whyalla; aeroplanes dropped rations and Mrs Birdseye forged an alternative route through scrub, spinifex and sand.

After Gladys retired in 1960, Sylvia continued to drive. Operating from premises in Hindmarsh Square that combined office, home and depot, she also began to use lorries. Her schedule included the 250-mile (402.3 km) northern newspaper run (five nights a week), an 845-mile (1360 km) return trip to Port Lincoln (each weekend), as well as vehicle maintenance. She was nicknamed 'Grandmother Queen of the Open Road' and 'The Little Atom'. While preparing to drive to Port Lincoln, Mrs Birdseye died of a cerebral haemorrhage on 9 August 1962 at Woodville and was buried in Centennial Park cemetery; her daughter and son survived her. She is commemorated by a cairn and drinking fountain near the Iron Knob turn-off on the Lincoln Highway. Her daughter Sylvia inherited Birdseye Bus Service and retained an interest in it until 1983; she, too, was as familiar with a spark plug as a lipstick.

S. Nicol, *Bullock Tracks and Bitumen* (Adel, 1978); L. Spriggs (ed), *Cleve on the Yadnarie Plains* (Cleve, SA, 1979); H. Radi, *200 Australian Women* (Syd, 1988); *People*, 4 Dec 1968; *News* (Adel), 18 Aug 1959; *Advertiser* (Adel), 10 Aug 1962, 23 Aug, 2 Sept 1965, 3 June 1973; *SMH*, 6 Sept 1966, supp; E. Harry, 'Mrs Sylvia Birdseye' (radio talk on 5CL, 31 Oct 1971, ts held in Mort L); information from Mrs P. Butler, Elizabeth East, Mrs B. Tickle, Belair, and Mrs S. Dyer, Tusmore, Adel.

SUZANNE EDGAR

BIRTWISTLE, IVOR TREHARNE (1892-1976), journalist, was born on 8 April 1892 at Beaumaris, Melbourne, son of James Birtwistle, architect, and his wife Emily, née Davies, both Victorian born. The family moved to Perth where Ivor attended Claremont State School. In 1908 he was employed as a fileroom-boy by the *Western Mail* and apparently remained with that weekly until 1912 when his involvement with the Presbyterian Church led to his editing the *Presbyterian*. In 1913 he became an ordinand in the Church's Home Mission; following some months at Beverley, he resigned to join the literary staff of the Melbourne *Age*.

Only 5 ft 3 ins (160 cm) tall, with hazel eyes and dark-brown hair, on 13 February 1915 Birtwistle enlisted in the Australian Imperial Force and served with the 22nd Battalion on Gallipoli, in Egypt and at the Somme (France) where he was severely shell-shocked on 28 July 1916. After he was discharged in Melbourne on 22 June 1917, an aunt gave him money to travel to the Solomon Islands to recuperate. There he visited the Methodist mission at Kokeqolo, New Georgia. Returning to Melbourne in 1918, he was appointed publicity officer for the national committee of the Young Men's Christian Association, which he had joined in Perth in 1912. During 1919-20 he was vice-chairman of the Repatriation Board of Victoria and in 1920 promoted the Peace Loan campaign. He went to Perth

that year to work on the *West Australian* under (Sir) Alfred Langler [q.v.9]. As its police and, subsequently, political reporter, Birtwistle emerged as a familiar figure: with his bowler-hat and cane, he was dapper, precise and well mannered.

Appointed editor of the *Western Mail* in 1924, Birtwistle married Kathleen Winifred Broadley with Presbyterian forms on 21 November 1925 at Ross Memorial Church, West Perth. As editor (1924-39), he continued the emphasis which his predecessor Alfred Carson [q.v.7] had given to matters of community interest. Birtwistle encouraged readers to contribute personal recollections to sections of the paper entitled 'Dolly Pot' and 'A Digger's Diary', while 'Virgilia' provided a focus for women from rural areas. He also made the *Mail* a vehicle for comprehensive news coverage, especially after 1927 when C. P. Smith [q.v.11] succeeded Langler as managing editor of West Australian Newspapers Ltd and introduced a less conservative policy. In 1930-40 Birtwistle was director of studies in technical journalism at the University of Western Australia. Seconded as deputy-director of the State's Department of Information in 1939-40, he rejoined the *West Australian* in 1941 as night sub-editor until the end of the war when he was appointed chief day-editor of 'Life and Letters'. In early 1950 he became inaugural counsellor of cadet journalists and, from 1952, was also literary editor, positions he held until his retirement in 1957.

President (1929-37 and 1946-47) of the Western Australian Surf Lifesaving Association, Birtwistle managed its State team in 1947. Having been a publicity officer for the Western Australian Boy Scouts' Association, he was president of the State executive in 1938-50. He was, as well, a vice-president and director of the Western Australian Y.M.C.A., and an active member of the Returned Service's League of Australia and of the Gallipoli Legion of Anzacs of Western Australia. At Cottesloe, where he lived, he was involved in local government. In 1952 he was appointed O.B.E.

Birtwistle had been a founding member (1926) of the (Royal) Western Australian Historical Society and its honorary secretary (1926-28); he succeeded E. O. G. Shann [q.v.11] as chairman in 1928, and was president in 1952-57 and 1960-64. From the beginning, Birtwistle's discretion and tact were invaluable in reconciling the diverging views of the early settlers' descendants on the committee. The society's push for the establishment of the National Trust of Australia (Western Australia) succeeded in 1959: Birtwistle was an inaugural member and councillor, and helped in the trust's assessments of buildings.

In the early 1960s he moved to his cottage at Roleystone. A member of the Armadale-Kelmscott Shire Council in 1964-69, he fostered research into the district's past as president of the local historical society and encouraged school children to participate by writing essays. His influence led the council to provide a site for History House at Armadale and to treble the amount donated by the public. The $30 000 building was opened two months before Birtwistle's death; he was the first curator of the museum's archives. Survived by his wife, son and daughter, Birtwistle died on 15 June 1976 at Roleystone and was cremated with Anglican rites.

E. Jaggard, *A Challenge Answered* (Perth, 1979); *Artlook*, 2, Aug 1976, p 13; *RWAHS Newsletter*, July 1976, p 2; *RWAHSJ*, 8, pt 1, Dec 1977, p 7; *West Australian*, 16 June 1976; *Comment News*, 28 June 1976; I. T. Birtwistle, Personal Reminiscences as a File Room Boy of West Australian Newspapers, nd, ts, *and* Minutes of General Assembly of Presbyterian Church of WA, 1912, 1913, *and* Minutes of YMCA (Perth), 1920, 1939-65, *and* Boy Scouts' Assn (Perth) press releases (BL); RWAHS records, Nedlands, Perth and BL; History House, Armadale, WA, records.   ANNE PORTER

BISCHOF, FRANCIS ERICH (1904-1979), police commissioner, was born on 12 October 1904 at Gowrie Junction, near Toowoomba, Queensland, fourth child of August Bischof, dairy-farmer, and his wife Sophia Carolina, née Riethmuller, both native-born. One of a family of nine, Frank helped to milk the cows each morning before walking to the Wilsonton primary school. After attending Toowoomba Grammar School, he worked in a cheese factory until he joined the Queensland Police Force as a constable in 1925. He married a dental assistant Dorothy May Alice Gledhill on 22 February 1930 at St Mary's Anglican Church, Alderley, Brisbane.

A detective constable stationed from 1933 at the Criminal Investigation Branch, Brisbane, Bischof became a sergeant in 1939. Promoted inspector in 1949, he spent six months studying police methods and organization in Britain (including Scotland Yard) and Europe. In 1950 he was chosen to investigate the Bulimba elections fraud. Over these years 'the Big Fella'—6 ft 2 ins (188 cm) tall and 16 stone (101.6 kg) in weight—developed a reputation as a crime-buster, securing thirty-two convictions in thirty-three murder investigations. One notorious case related to the murder of a taxi driver at Southport: Bischof's interrogation trapped the suspect Arthur Halliday into admitting guilt. In 1955 Bischof was appointed officer-in-charge of the C.I.B.

When (Sir) Francis Nicklin's [q.v.] Country-Liberal government named Bischof, a Free-mason, as commissioner of police in January 1958, the appointment was criticized by the Opposition as political patronage. Labor argued that at least two other inspectors were more suitable. To some, Bischof's promotion marked the ascendancy of a Masonic cabal over the 'Green Mafia' (police of Irish-Catholic descent) who had dominated the force under Labor. Responding to the controversy, in the 1960 election campaign Nicklin spoke of setting up a three-member commission to administer the police, a proposal which failed to gain cabinet support.

The commissioner was convinced that his first tasks were to boost police morale and to improve their reputation in the community. In August 1958 he 'shook up' the force by transfers and new appointments. A Crime Prevention Bureau and a Public Relations Bureau were established, as well as a pipe-band. Bischof counselled his staff: 'If you're news on the front page you don't have much to worry about. It's when they start putting your wrongdoings on the back page that we'll all start to panic'.

Bischof appeared frequently at public functions throughout the countryside, encouraging various initiatives whereby the community could support and co-operate with police activities. He became well known for his interest in the welfare of children, particularly through the expansion of youth clubs. Foundation chairman of the Queensland Police-Citizens Youth Welfare Association, in 1959 he was named Queensland's first 'Father of the Year', though he was childless. He often conducted counselling sessions for young lawbreakers on Saturday mornings in his office and in 1963 arranged for the formation of the Juvenile Aid Bureau under a senior constable (Sir) Terence Lewis who was to become commissioner. That year Bischof was appointed M.V.O.; in 1965 he was awarded the police medal.

For all that, a constant barrage of political criticism accompanied Bischof's efforts. Allegations and suggestions of corruption, abuse of power or negligence on the part of individual police officers were insistently raised in parliament by C. J. Bennett, E. J. Walsh [q.v.] and Tom Aikens. Disquiet also arose over police zeal in controlling street demonstrations. In October 1963 Bennett's allegations that Bischof and other police frequented, encouraged and condoned a call-girl service in a Brisbane hotel led to a royal commission (1963-64) into the police force and the National Hotel. In the face of unreliable and restricted evidence, Justice (Sir) Harry Gibbs of the Supreme Court of Queensland did not find that a call-girl service operated or had police sanction. He did find irregularities, however, in the enforcement of the licensing laws in that 'the hotel was let off due to friendship between it and the force'. The limited terms of reference did not require the commission to consider the policing of prostitution, or to examine corruption in relation to members of the licensing branch and the consorting squad. Gibbs's inquiry might have been frustrated by a cover-up: in 1971 one of the witnesses Shirley Brifman [q.v.] admitted to perjury in her evidence, but her death cut short any attempt at further investigation.

During Bischof's commissionership a network of corruption—particularly identified with the licensing branch and the consorting squad—was becoming entrenched. It led to the protection of vice figures, among them starting-price bookmakers who continued to flourish despite restrictive legislation, and prostitutes who began operating from hotels after the Nicklin government had closed the brothels. The existence and extent of the network became public only when G. E. Fitzgerald's commission of inquiry into possible illegal activities and associated police misconduct (1987-1989) began gathering evidence. This commission revealed that 'certain police were said to enjoy Bischof's favour, and to be his "bag-men"', and that they collected protection payoffs. As Fitzgerald observed, 'in some respects police corruption had acquired a quaint quasi-legitimacy by the Bischof era'.

With only 240 days until his retirement, Bischof took leave somewhat suddenly on 13 February 1969. Suffering from hypertension, he spent three periods in hospital before being boarded out of the force on medical grounds. The reasons for his retirement became apparent when Sir Thomas Hiley (State treasurer 1957-65) published his account of 'The case of the corrupt Commissioner' in the Brisbane *Courier-Mail* on 18 September 1982 and exposed Bischof's weakness as an 'inveterate punter'. Some country bookmakers had complained to Hiley of a police protection racket, with proceeds flowing through to Brisbane; aided by betting sheets, Hiley established the extent of Bischof's habit; he then confronted Bischof who capitulated. It was later stated that during his last three years in office Bischof had received treatment for psychotic depression. In December 1974 he was charged with stealing, but the Crown filed a no-true bill. Bischof's interests included bowling, and he was sometime patron of the Queensland Amateur Water Polo Association. Survived by his wife, he died on 28 August 1979 in South Brisbane and was cremated.

P. James, *In Place of Justice* (Deception Bay, Qld, 1974); G. E. Fitzgerald, *Commission of Inquiry into Possible Illegal Activities and Associated Police Misconduct* (Brisb, 1989); *Courier-Mail*, 5 June 1967, 18 Sept 1982; *Sunday Mail* (Brisb), 9 Feb 1969; *Sunday Sun* (Brisb), 24 Oct 1976, 2 Sept 1979; Police Dept (Qld) records (Brisb), *and* personnel file AF 8912 (QA).

W. ROSS JOHNSTON

BISHOP, LIONEL ALBERT JACK (JOHN) (1903-1964), musician and festival director, was born on 26 October 1903 at Aldinga, South Australia, second of six children of Henry Bishop, saddler, and his wife Harriett Fortescue, née Field. His education began at Aldinga Public School, under John Bourke, a gifted man who encouraged his pupils to look beyond the district's farming jobs. Singing was learned by the tonic sol-fa system and, although no instrumental music was taught, there were eagerly-awaited, annual school concerts. Henry's shop adjoined the village post office; in about 1908 the postmaster's daughter Eleanor Giles began Jack's piano lessons, being paid with bowls of eggs. He won prizes locally and in 1915 came third in the under-12 piano section at the Ballarat (Victoria) South Street competitions; the adjudicator A. E. Floyd [q.v.8], who later called the adult Bishop 'the little wizard', commented, 'A very artistic performance . . . I feel sure playing will develop greatly'.

In January 1917 Jack entered Adelaide High School and also became a scholarship pupil of William Silver, a leading Adelaide pianist and teacher, with whom he later went to live. Although he had not matriculated, in 1919 Bishop won the Alexander Clark memorial scholarship and began studying at the Elder [q.v.4] Conservatorium of Music at the University of Adelaide. He travelled with Silver in 1921 to England, Europe and the United States of America. In 1922, after completing his third year of study, he won the Elder overseas scholarship, which provided for a three-year course at the Royal College of Music, London; funds for his fare and a piano were raised by two benefit concerts, at one of which he appeared with several conservatorium staff.

Among his six hundred fellow students were Constant Lambert, (Sir) Michael Tippett and Stanford Robinson; his teachers were Herbert Howells (composition), Herbert Fryer (piano, first study), and (Sir) Adrian Boult and (Sir) Malcolm Sargent (conducting, second study). The staff also included Gustav Holst, Ralph Vaughan Williams, Gordon Jacob and John Ireland in composition, and (Dame) Myra Hess and Kathleen Long in piano. It was an exciting time in English music. Bishop was considered 'a brilliant pianist' and 'a gifted conductor' who had 'the ability to attack the subject of Music in many directions and to do it with marked success'. He left in July 1926, without graduating, to begin his professional career with choir and orchestral conducting, lecture recitals in schools and, in 1927, two broadcasts for the British Broadcasting Corporation.

Through Silver's relations, Bishop had met Margaret Eleanor Harvey whom he married on 28 December 1927 at the parish church, Little Eaton, Derbyshire. In January 1928 they sailed for New Zealand where he had been appointed conductor of the Royal Wellington Choral Union. He made his debut on 2 June with Mendelssohn's *Elijah*, giving a fine performance with 'a graphic reading of the score'. For six years Bishop profoundly affected musical life in New Zealand. In 1930 he established the Wellington Philharmonic Orchestra (Jan Kubelik, Benno Moiseiwitsch, Isador Goodman and Peter Dawson [q.v.8] appeared with it) and organized his first, full-scale festival, Music Week, in which he was soloist in Beethoven's 'Emperor' concerto. He formed a chamber group, gave lessons, recitals and wireless talks, and directed a Haydn bicentenary festival in 1932 and a Brahms centenary festival in 1933. He founded the Juvenile Concert League, introduced orchestral concerts for children and was music master (1928-31) at Scots College; in addition, he adjudicated, lectured for the Workers' Educational Association and was vice-president of the Music Teachers' Association.

Known as John from the 1930s, he was formally to adopt that name in 1960. In December 1933 Bishop resigned to teach at the University of Melbourne's Conservatorium of Music under Professor (Sir) Bernard Heinze, who aptly termed him a 'practical idealist'. The pay was small. He took private pupils, gave recitals, broadcast, examined, and travelled to every capital city as an adjudicator and a conductor; he became an examiner (1936) for and a member of the Australian Music Examinations Board. Bishop lived with his family at Mont Albert, but his city studio in Post Office Lane became his musical centre. He formed the Oriana Choir and the Chamber Music Guild, and contacted British composers, among them Benjamin (Lord) Britten, for their latest works.

Disappointed at not being accepted as a regular conductor of Australian Broadcasting Commission orchestras, but with acknowledged 'flair for administration and organization', extraordinary energy, enthusiasm and interest in youth, in 1937 Bishop was appointed director of music at Scotch College, Hawthorn. He transformed the school's musical life. Every student, from Grade 4 up, had to be in a house choir and had to play an instrument for at least one year. Distinguished musicians played alongside the boys in recitals, festivals were organized, house chamber groups were formed, a school music

captain was appointed: music was raised to the same status as sport.

Bishop's influence widened. In 1940 he became founding president of the Victorian School Music Association. He sat on the music panel of the Council for the Encouragement of Music and the Arts, and on the A.B.C.'s advisory committee for youth and educational broadcasts. In 1943 he began discussions with Ruth Alexander, music mistress at Melbourne Church of England Girls' Grammar School, which led to the establishment of the National Music Camp for orchestral students, at Point Lonsdale, in 1948. This, in turn, led to the formation of the Australian Youth Orchestra which, under Bishop, gave its first performance in the Sydney Town Hall on 9 March 1957. The *Sydney Morning Herald* critic wrote that the orchestra 'proved resoundingly its right to be taken seriously'.

Having applied unsuccessfully in 1938 for the chair of music at the University of Cape Town, South Africa, and in 1945 for the directorship of the New South Wales State Conservatorium of Music, in 1948 Bishop returned to Adelaide to succeed E. H. Davies [q.v.8] as Elder professor of music and director of the Elder Conservatorium. His lack of academic qualifications caused initial hostility, but his charm, tact, and superb abilities soon won over the detractors. He revitalized a tired department, introduced new courses, established an honours degree, built up a music library and engaged excellent staff. As a Carnegie travelling fellow, in 1952-53 he made a thirteen-month tour of Britain and America to investigate music education. He formed the Elder String Quartet as a permanent ensemble (1959) and laid foundations for the University of Adelaide Wind Quintet (1965). In 1960 Bishop began to devise a new degree course which included musicology and electronic music, and made the first appointments for these subjects in Australia. Regular staff and student recitals were held; there were festivals of Australian, Czechoslovakian, contemporary and other music; the University Music Society, a university choir and a madrigal club were formed.

Extra-curricular concerns crowded his well-organized life. By 1963 he was chairman of the A.M.E.B., a member of the Adult Education Board and of the United Nations Educational Scientific and Cultural Organization's (Australian) committee for music, president of the Adelaide Film Festival and federal president of the Arts Council of Australia, while continuing as director of the National Music Camp Association and the A.Y.O. Bishop's honours included his appointment as O.B.E. (1953), a fellowship of the Royal College of Music (1957), the Dvorak medal (1959), and honorary doctorates of music awarded by the universities of Melbourne (1963) and Adelaide (1964).

After visiting the International Festival of Music and Drama in Edinburgh in 1952, Bishop had been fired with the idea of a similar festival for Adelaide. 'I love festivals', he remarked, 'because they give us cause to rejoice'. Following discussions in 1958 with Sir Lloyd Dumas [q.v.], a committee was formed, £15 000 was guaranteed and Bishop became the first artistic director of the Adelaide Festival of Arts. He was also on three of its special committees and conducted four concerts with the A.Y.O. during the first festival in 1960. He continued as artistic director for the 1962 and 1964 festivals, planning ahead while running the conservatorium.

From about 1961, Bishop's health had caused concern—rheumatic fever as a child had probably affected his heart; by 1963 he had to rest daily on his office sofa and during the 1964 festival was confined to bed with laryngitis. But he maintained his demanding schedule. In October-November he was in Paris with the Australian delegation at the general conference of U.N.E.S.C.O. and then spent a fortnight visiting institutions in Germany before travelling to England. He died suddenly of hypertensive cardiovascular disease on 14 December 1964 in the foyer of Australia House, London, and was cremated; his wife, son and daughter survived him. Margaret died in 1966, three weeks after attending an Adelaide Festival of Arts performance of Berlioz's *Requiem Mass* in his memory. 'A few people, like yourself', she had written to Ruth Alexander, 'knew . . . how deeply we lived in unison'.

Bishop's contribution to Australian music was immense. Under his dynamic direction, Adelaide's conservatorium became the finest in the country. His driving artistic force had initiated significant, national cultural movements. A small, elegant man, with an artistic shock of white hair, piercing but kindly blue eyes and a sense of humour, he could wield a mailed fist in velvet. He gave the arts, especially music, prominence in Adelaide in the 1950s, and was a leader in society, as well as at the university. He astounded businessmen with his commercial astuteness, and delighted students by his informality and understanding.

'Prof', as he was known, aroused love and loyalty. 'He owed more to one woman's intelligence, patience and love than to any other source of support.' To his close-knit family, he was a devoted father and husband, and their home reflected shared tastes in art, music and gardening. Income from the *Advertiser*'s gift of £5000 is used by the university to commission a musical work in his honour for the Adelaide festival. A bronze bust of Bishop by John Dowie and a portrait by Wladislaw Dukiewicz are held in the Adelaide Festival Centre board-room which bears his name; another bust by Valerie Hicks stands in the foyer of the university's Elder Hall.

W. G. K. Duncan and R. A. Leonard, *The University of Adelaide, 1874-1974* (Adel, 1973); D. Whitelock, *Festival!* (Adel, 1980); A. Hewlett, *Cause to Rejoice* (Adel, 1983); C. Symons, *John Bishop, a Life of Music* (Melb, 1989); *News* (Adel), 14 Aug 1954; *SMH*, 11 Mar 1957; *Advertiser* (Adel), 16 Dec 1964; family papers (held by Mr and Mrs J. L. Porter, Burnside, Adel).

ALAN BRISSENDEN

BLACK, ARNOLD BARHAM (1889-1964), mining engineer, was born on 12 September 1889 at Norwood, Adelaide, son of John McConnell Black [q.v.7], botanist and journalist, and his wife Alice, née Denford. Arnold was a cousin of the artist Dorrit Black [q.v.7]. Educated at the Collegiate School of St Peter, he gained associate diplomas (in metallurgy, 1910, and mining, 1913) from the School of Mines and Industries, and in 1911 joined Broken Hill Associated Smelters at Port Pirie. Next year he moved to Broken Hill, New South Wales, and in 1914 transferred to Broken Hill South Ltd. Already active in the Old Collegians' Association, on 9 September that year Black married Dulcie Kate Goss in the school chapel; they were to have a son and two daughters.

He published his first paper—on mine dam tailings—in 1925. After observing hydraulic stowage in 1934 at the Mount Lyell Mining & Railway Co. Ltd in Tasmania, in 1938 he and Frank Thomas began to pump tailings mixed with water into the mined-out portions of the underground workings; he also used pneumatic means to blow tailings into cavities, but both methods encountered difficulties. An enthusiastic member of the Australasian Institute of Mining and Metallurgy, Black was to publish technical papers (supported by his competent photography) in its *Proceedings* between 1941 and 1946; he documented the progress and the ultimate success of his research which resulted in much safer and more economic mining at the South Mine by 1941. His hydraulic stowage process was later to be introduced in other Broken Hill and Australasian mines. Becoming underground manager in 1942, Black was noted for the care and respect that he showed for the workers; he was also particularly helpful to students who trained in the mines. In 1953, with R. Pittman Hooper, he wrote an important paper on mining methods in use in 'Australia and adjacent territories'.

Pondering on the possible origin of the vast

Broken Hill ore body, Black was among the first to propose that the minerals had been deposited at the time of the formation of the original, sedimentary layers, an idea that was later taken up enthusiastically by many geologists. Although never a committee-member of the Barrier Field Naturalists' Club (formed in 1920), he acted as lanternist for its lectures for over thirty years and photographed interesting features in the region; he was elected an honorary life member in December 1954. He spent much of his free time exploring the evidence of Aboriginal occupation, and recording sites; in 1945 he published a paper on this work with Charles Fenner [q.v.8]. Black also produced elegant pieces of furniture from the readily available 'fracture' boxes, while trees from the seeds he gathered and planted are still flourishing on the South Mine leases.

A member of the Volunteer Defence Corps in 1942-45, Black was acting-manager of the mine for several months in 1951. At the age of 65, he apparently hoped to become manager of the South Mine on Thomas's retirement, but Black's assistant Arthur Lewis was offered the position. Black retired on 31 December 1954 and was presented with a handsome chair by the underground workers—a rare acknowledgement by the 'daily paid' miners to a 'boss'. Lewis resigned in sympathy with him. Both moved to Adelaide.

About 1953 Black had been asked to advise on the development of uranium mining at Radium Hill, South Australia, a controversial operation promoted by the State and Federal governments. He continued in this consultancy for some years, and also advised South Australian Barytes Ltd. He was a member of the South Australian Board of Examiners for mine managers, Royal Society of South Australia (1956), Royal Geographical Society of Australasia (South Australian branch) and the Anthropological Society of South Australia. A man with firm ideas and the ability to express them, Black was 'remembered for his surpassing understanding of and affection for human beings as individuals'. Survived by his wife and daughters, he died on 29 August 1964 at his St Georges home and was cremated; his estate was sworn for probate at £57 972.

G. Blainey, *The Rise of Broken Hill* (Melb, 1968); D. A. Cumming and G. C. Moxham, *They Built South Australia* (Adel, 1986); H. King, *The Rocks Speak* (Melb, 1989); *Advertiser* (Adel), 31 Aug 1964; W. Hodder, History of the South Mine, 1965, ms, *and* Minutes, Barrier Field Naturalists' Club mss (Charles Rasp L, Broken Hill, NSW); family papers (held by Mrs S. Clissold, Seacliff, Adel).

D. F. BRANAGAN

BLACK, EDWARD WILLIAM (1902-1971), musician, was born on 5 December 1902 at Northam, Western Australia, eldest of four children of William Henry Black, railway employee, and his wife Augusta, née Niedermeyer, both Melbourne born. Educated in Northam and at Perth Modern School, Eddie was taught music by his mother and from 1920 studied piano, violin and composition at the Elder [q.v.4] Conservatorium of Music, Adelaide (Mus.B., 1924). In 1927 he went to London where he completed three diplomas at the Royal College of Music. He was a member of the London Stock Exchange Dramatic and Operatic Society's orchestra and music master at St Peter's College, Lewisham.

On his return to Perth in 1932, Black settled into a busy schedule. He toured the eastern States for the Australian Broadcasting Commission, performed as an accompanist, taught piano and violin, gave radio broadcasts and conducted the Metropolitan Orchestral Society in Perth. On 29 September 1934 he married a former student Bessie Sultana Bockelberg in the West Leederville Methodist Church; they were to have three sons. A winner of several State and national competitions for composers, among them an A.B.C. contest in 1934, he wrote unashamedly conservative and romantic compositions: while some were larger works for violin, piano and string quartet, most were piano pieces, with occasional songs. For eight years he also played the viola with the Perth Symphony Orchestra.

During World War II Black served with the Australian Army Education Corps as teacher, soloist and accompanist. His 'wonderful sense of fun, brisk speech and warm personality' made him 'an ideal lecturer'. As president of the Western Australian Music Teachers' Association for some twenty years between 1945 and 1971, he launched its *Bulletin*, re-established its musical festival, inaugurated country festivals through the Adult Education Board, introduced annual lectures for music teachers and effected an affiliation with the Guild of Young Artists and the Religious Teachers' Association of Music and Speech. His vigorous leadership transformed the W.A.M.T.A.

Black was unfailingly courteous to teachers and gentle to pupils, but maintained rigorous standards as a marker. He conducted the University of Western Australia Choral Society and in 1952-61 lectured (part time) in music at the university. An examiner for the local branch of the Australian Music Examinations Board for over thirty years, he was appointed federal examiner in practical music in 1965. He was a delegate to national conferences and committees, and an adjudicator for the Mobil Quest and the Darwin festival. A short man with hazel eyes and a warm smile, Black was a strong-minded perfectionist who preferred to work alone. Rex Hobcroft considered him a natural and highly gifted musician who opened up 'large musical tracts' in Australia. In 1971 Black was appointed M.B.E. and elected federal director of studies on the A.M.E.B. Survived by his wife and sons, he died of hypertensive cardiovascular disease on 26 November 1971 at his Claremont home and was cremated with Anglican rites.

The Edward Black memorial fund finances projects to stimulate music teaching, and the Edward Black memorial prize for open piano solo is presented annually at the W.A.M.T.A.'s musical festival.

R. Jamieson, *What Harmony is This?* (Perth, 1986); *Edward Black Memorial Concert*, 27 May 1972, programme (Perth, 1972); *Canon*, 12, no 1, Aug 1958, p 421; *Aust J of Music Education*, 10, Apr 1972, p 57; *Aust Composer*, June 1972, p 38; *West Australian*, 1 Jan, 29 Nov 1971, 21 June 1975; Univ WA Archives; information from and papers held by Mr D. Black, Rossmoyne, Perth.

RONDA JAMIESON

BLACKALL, RUBY CONSTANCE ETHEL (1880-1951), charity organizer, was born on 7 May 1880 at Gympie, Queensland, fourth of six children of English-born parents Edwin Thomas, banker, and his wife Emmeline Sarah Jane, née Brett. Moving to New South Wales by 1903, Ruby trained as a nurse at (Royal) Newcastle Hospital and received her certificate in June 1905. At St Andrew's Anglican Church, Waratah, on 5 June 1907 she married Thomas Blackall, a dentist and pharmacist who had served in the Boer War from 1899 and joined his father's city dental practice upon his return from South Africa. His family was well known around Newcastle and the Lake Macquarie district where Blackalls Park is named after them.

In June 1916 their daughter Lynette was born deaf, which was to be the catalyst for Ruby's dedicated charity work. Thomas was an alderman (1925-41) on Newcastle Municipal Council and in December 1929 was elected mayor. In February 1930 he and his wife convened a public meeting in the town hall to form a Newcastle branch of the Adult Deaf and Dumb Society of New South Wales. Mrs Blackall was appointed president of the women's auxiliary and her husband, as mayor, was patron of the committee. In March that year rooms for the society were opened. She worked tirelessly at fund-raising, and at social and related activities. Building started on permanent premises for the society in 1935 and Blackall House, named in Ruby's honour, was opened next year by Sir Frederick Stewart [q.v.12]. In her speech at the function Mrs

Blackall acknowledged that she and her husband knew the tragedy of deafness in their own lives. By this time she was the branch's honorary secretary and later served as secretary-superintendant until 1951. She oversaw many of the society's developments. In 1950, after much fund-raising, a holiday and rest home for the deaf at Lake Macquarie was begun; she marched around the building site with gusto, but did not live to see the home opened.

Despite her personal grief, Ruby Blackall possessed great energy, and was an accomplished public speaker and administrator. She was associated with other charitable causes: as mayoress, with Thomas's assistance she had formed a Sunshine Club for needy children and she helped to establish a Newcastle branch of the New South Wales Society for Crippled Children. Photographs of her reveal a determined, capable woman, with small, round glasses and bobbed hair. Thomas died in 1941. Next year Lynette married William Frederick Harvey who died in 1946. Predeceased by two sons and survived by her daughter, Ruby Blackall died on 23 August 1951 in Royal Prince Alfred Hospital, Sydney; after a service at Christ Church Cathedral, Newcastle, she was cremated.

Newcastle Morning Herald, 24 Oct 1899, 24 Dec 1929, 14 Feb, 8, 10 Mar 1930, 22 Aug 1936, 10 Dec 1941, 24 Aug 1951; Newcastle Branch, Deaf Soc of NSW, History of the Branch (ms, copy held at ADB, Canb); Newcastle City L files; information from Mrs M. Forrester, Kingsgrove, Syd.

EMMA GRAHAME

BLACKBURN, DORIS AMELIA (1889-1970), politician, peace campaigner and civil rights activist, was born on 18 September 1889 at Hawthorn, Melbourne, daughter of Lebbeus Hordern, estate agent, and his wife Louisa Dewson, née Smith, both Victorian born. Encouraged by several of her teachers at the progressive school, Hessle College, Camberwell, Doris began her political career in the Women's Political Association and in 1913 acted as campaign secretary for Vida Goldstein [q.v.9]. Doris's driving impulses were compassion for the underprivileged and concern for social justice in general rather than for women's rights alone. On 10 December 1914 in Melbourne she was married by Frederick Sinclaire [q.v.11] to Maurice McCrae Blackburn [q.v.7]. Impressed by his principled and intellectual approach to politics, she shared with Maurice a marriage that was as much a political as a personal partnership. He drew her into the labour movement and together they campaigned vigorously against conscription in 1916-17.

While her children were young, Mrs Blackburn was content to play a supporting role, but found time to be president (1928-30) of the Women's International League for Peace and Freedom and to work for the Woman's Christian Temperance Union. She also took up informally the study of psychology and modern educational theories. Believing that 'a child when born was the expression of a good idea and when given the opportunity for self expression would grow into a good citizen', she became involved in such groups as the free kindergarten movement, the Victorian Playgrounds Association, and the Citizens' Education Fellowship whose monthly magazine she edited in the 1920s.

The experience of the Depression heightened Blackburn's sense of urgency about the need for reform, but it was the growing threat of war that brought her back into full-time public activity. Her opposition to war sprang initially from a conviction that it wasted human and material resources and undermined the freedoms it was supposed to defend, but by the late 1930s she came to see fascism as an even greater threat. She transferred her energies from the pacifist W.I.L.P.F. to lead the women's commission of the International Peace Campaign which aimed to strengthen support for the League of Nations and the idea of collective security. Clashing with the Australian Labor Party, she resigned her membership of that organization in 1938. Characteristically, she stressed education as the best means to avert armed conflict, but, once World War II began, directed her attention to defending civil liberties and to pressing for a negotiated settlement.

Supported by a radical breakaway group of the A.L.P., in 1946 Blackburn won the Federal seat of Bourke, formerly held (1934-43) by her husband who had died in 1944. Although she was isolated on the crossbenches, she quickly established her credibility as an Independent Labor member and as an intelligent, vocal politician with a coherent programme centred on women's rights, family support, child care, education, housing welfare, civil rights, and opposition to the testing and use of guided missiles. Unimpressed by broad theoretical solutions, she was generally content with 'chipping away' at the worst aspects of problems and with remaining in personal contact with her constituents.

In 1949 Blackburn was defeated for the new seat of Wills and again in 1951. She then placed at the service of voluntary organizations the skills she had acquired in parliament, which included the ability to design practical measures to implement policy decisions. Blackburn continued her peace advocacy in the W.C.T.U., and in W.I.L.P.F. for which she travelled to Europe in 1952. Through the

Council for Civil Liberties (president 1948), the Howard League for Penal Reform, the Women's Prison Council and the Save the Children Fund, she pursued her concern for social justice; she also promoted pre-school education. Her attention was drawn to the plight of Aborigines when she visited the Woomera Rocket Range in South Australia, and in the 1950s she co-founded the Aborigine Advancement League and the Federal Council for Aboriginal Advancement.

Slender and shortish, Blackburn was a forceful woman with a flair for organization who responded purposefully to the wrongs, injustices and wasted lives she saw around her. She valued individual effort and devoted herself to arousing in the public—and in women in particular—a keen sense of the need for and the possibility of reform. Survived by her two sons and one of her two daughters, she died on 12 December 1970 at Coburg, Melbourne, and was buried in Box Hill cemetery with Presbyterian forms.

M. Lake and F. Kelly (eds), *Double Time, Women in Victoria, 150 Years* (Melb, 1985); M. Geddes, *A Great Idea* (priv pub, Melb, 1987); M. and D. Blackburn papers (LaTL).   CAROLYN RASMUSSEN

BLADIN, FRANCIS MASSON (1898-1978), air force officer, was born on 26 August 1898 at Korumburra, Victoria, son of Frederick William Bladin, engineering contractor, and his wife Ellen, née Douglas, both Victorian born. Educated at Melbourne High School, Francis attempted to enlist in the Australian Imperial Force, but his parents refused their consent. In February 1917 he entered the Royal Military College, Duntroon, Federal Capital Territory; having graduated in December 1920, he went to England for a sixteen-month attachment to the British Army. Meanwhile, the Royal Australian Air Force was seeking applications from naval and army officers to undertake flying training. Seconded to the R.A.A.F. and made flying officer on 30 January 1923, Bladin completed the course that year at No. 1 Flying Training School, Point Cook, Victoria. Postings to the school's staff followed. On 20 December 1927 at Jeir station, near Yass, New South Wales, he married Patricia Mary Magennis.

In 1929 he was sent to England and attended the Royal Air Force Staff College, Andover. Returning to Australia, he commanded several units in Victoria in 1931-39. He had been promoted wing commander on 12 March 1937 and was one of the small coterie of R.A.A.F. officers who, by age and experience, were ready to assume the responsibilities of higher rank in war. From March 1940 to August 1941 Bladin was director of operations and intelligence at R.A.A.F. Headquarters, Melbourne. He was granted the acting rank of air commodore in September 1941. Briefly air officer commanding, Southern Area, and assistant chief of the Air Staff, on 25 March 1942 he became A.O.C., North-Western Area, with headquarters near Darwin. Allied reverses and the recent experience of Japanese bombing raids on Darwin and Broome had reduced morale; an invasion of northern Australia seemed imminent.

Counter-attacking with his meagre force of Hudson bombers from No. 2 and No. 13 squadrons, Bladin reorganized his command and began to rectify deficiencies in equipment, communications and training. On 20 June he led a flight of five bombers in a strike against Kendari aerodrome, Celebes, Netherlands East Indies, destroying three enemy fighters on the ground and causing widespread damage. While returning to base, his aircraft drove off nine attacking fighters without loss to their own numbers. For his part in the action he was awarded the United States of America's Silver Star. He was appointed C.B.E. in 1943. Bladin's forces were steadily augmented: by April he controlled five bomber and four fighter squadrons, with personnel from Australia, the U.S.A., Britain and the N.E.I. In a theatre where the war was being fought mainly in the air, his principal task was to defend the flank of the concentrated allied forces to the east. The last Japanese raid in strength over the Darwin region took place on 6 July. Acting Air Vice Marshal A. T. Cole [q.v.] relieved Bladin on the 21st and reported that the command was 'well organized, keen and in good shape'.

In August 1943 Bladin was posted to Britain and appointed senior air staff officer of the R.A.F.'s No. 38 Group which had been formed to plan and co-ordinate British airborne operations in the projected Allied invasion of Europe. Flying to France on D-Day (6 June 1944) to drop glider-borne troops, he returned to the Continent three days later for service with the invading forces. He was repatriated in October, having been mentioned in dispatches for his work in Britain. His appointment that month as deputy chief of the Air Staff, R.A.A.F., gave him respite from the rigours of operational duties, but negotiations were well advanced for him to assume command of No. 238 Group, R.A.F., when the war ended in August 1945. From January 1946 to June 1947 he was chief of staff at the headquarters of the British Commonwealth Occupation Force, Kure, Japan; he had become acting air vice marshal on 1 March 1946.

During his next appointment as A.O.C., Eastern Area, Sydney, on 1 October 1948 Bladin was promoted substantive air vice marshal, three weeks before he took office as air member for personnel in Canberra. He was appointed C.B. in 1950 and retired in October 1953. Tall, strongly built and deliberate in his actions, Bladin was a thoughtful man who weighed decisions carefully. There was little that was harsh about him, yet he had an inner toughness, could be firm when necessary and was respected. Loyal, courteous and gentlemanly, with a slow but ready smile, he was fond of his pipe and abstemious in his drinking habits. Golf was his favourite recreation. Even in his younger air force days he possessed an aura of responsibility, a characteristic which almost from the start earned him the nicknames of 'Dad' and 'Pop' —usually the former—by which he was known throughout the service. There was no self-seeking strain or thrusting ambition in his nature; he did not become a controversial figure and was seldom in the public eye until after his retirement. Australia and the R.A.A.F. could have done with more of his kind.

Although kept busy on his property, Adastra, near Yass, Bladin found time to be a spokesman for and national treasurer (1951-54 and 1956-69) of the Returned Sailors', Soldiers' and Airmen's Imperial League of Australia (Returned Services League from 1965). He recorded his religious affiliation as Presbyterian in 1917, married with Catholic rites in 1927 and in 1963 became secretary of the national committee which collected funds for building the multi-denominational Anzac Memorial Chapel of St Paul, Duntroon. His wife was involved in community service and assisted needy families of former air force personnel. Predeceased by her, and survived by their son and two daughters, Bladin died on 2 February 1978 at Box Hill, Melbourne; after an air force funeral at the Church of Our Lady of Good Counsel, Deepdene, he was buried in Springvale cemetery. His portrait (1956) by (Sir) William Dargie is in the Australian War Memorial, Canberra.

G. Odgers, *Air War Against Japan 1943-1945* (Canb, 1957); D. N. Gillison, *Royal Australian Air Force 1939-1942* (Canb, 1962); J. Herington, *Air Power Over Europe 1944-45* (Canb, 1963); *People* (Syd), 24 Feb 1954; F. M. Bladin, Autobiographical Memoir (1953, ts, AWM); AWM records; Bladin family papers (held by Mrs J. Crock, Kew, Melb).

R. N. DALKIN

BLAIR, HAROLD (1924-1976), singer and Aboriginal activist, was born probably on 13 September 1924 at Cherbourg Aboriginal Reserve, near Murgon, Queensland, son of Esther Quinn. She gave him the surname Blair in gratitude to the family who had 'adopted' her. Six months after his birth, he and his teenage mother were transferred to the Purga Mission near Ipswich; when Harold was aged 2, Esther was sent away to take a post as a domestic servant. Harold remained at Purga under the care of the Salvation Army mission staff until he was almost 16: he worked on the dairy farm and received a limited education, designed to enable him to gain employment as a farm labourer. He entertained visitors by mimicking Richard Crooks and John McCormack whose records he frequently played on an old, wind-up gramophone.

Under the wartime manpower regulations, Blair was dispatched in 1942 to the cane-fields in the Childers area where his robust physique and affable personality made him a popular worker. He sang on the canefields and in local concerts. When Marjorie Lawrence [q.v.10] visited Brisbane on a concert tour in 1944, Blair was granted an audition and encouraged to take his singing more seriously. In March 1945 he sang on radio in 'Australia's Amateur Hour' and gained a record number of votes. With the help of friends, he sought enrolment at the conservatorium in Sydney and at the university conservatorium in Melbourne, but was rejected because of his limited education. Finally accepted by the Melbourne (Melba [q.v.10]) Conservatorium of Music, Albert Street, East Melbourne, Blair worked hard to improve his education, learn foreign languages and master the fundamentals of music. In 1949 he gained a diploma of music.

On 30 July 1949 Blair married a fellow student Dorothy Gladys Eden at Camberwell with the forms of the Churches of Christ. Because she was White, their union provoked racist comment. Encouraged by Todd Duncan, the Black American baritone, Blair left for the United States of America to study singing; they could not afford a fare for Dorothy. In New York he took part-time work as assistant-choirmaster and also cleaned offices to earn an income. The Australian Society of New York organized a benefit concert at which he performed on 18 March 1951 in the New York Town Hall.

That year Blair appeared as a guest artist for the Australian Broadcasting Commission's jubilee tour of Australia. He was well received by his audiences, but reviewers were frequently critical. Winter chills and the strain of constant performance had wrought havoc with his vocal chords. Some listeners wondered whether his studies in the United States of America had spoiled his tenor voice: Margaret Sutherland said that he 'went away singing like John McCormack', but returned 'without a middle register'.

Reluctant to be again separated from his young wife, Blair decided to continue part-time study in Melbourne and accepted a job in a large department store. In 1956 he began teaching part-time at the Albert Street conservatorium (renamed the Melba [q.v.10] Memorial Conservatorium). He spent 1959 in Europe, singing and attending Moral Rearmament conferences. Back in Melbourne, he became the proprietor of a service station in 1962 and later of a milk bar, and then worked briefly as the superintendent of an Aboriginal mission station in South Australia. In 1967 he was appointed music teacher in the Victorian Education Department; his work with the choirs at Sunshine and Ringwood technical schools received acclaim. Meanwhile, he continued to sing. Praised in 1962 for his lead in a popular burlesque of *Uncle Tom's Cabin* in Melbourne and as Mundit in the Aboriginal opera, *Dalgerie*, at the Sydney Opera House in 1973, he made numerous concert appearances.

Interested in politics as a vehicle by which to foster the cause of Aborigines, in 1964 Blair had stood unsuccessfully as Labor candidate for the Victorian Legislative Assembly seat of Mentone. His interests increasingly centred on Aboriginal advancement. Following a visit by a team of marching girls from the Cherbourg reserve to Melbourne's 1962 Moomba festival, he had begun the Aboriginal Children's Holiday Project, which was to provide vacations in Melbourne for three thousand children from Queensland mission stations. Expanding interstate, its outstanding achievement was largely due to Blair's drive and enthusiasm. The Miss Junior Victoria quest, initiated by the scheme, gave financial assistance to many Aboriginal projects, including the Institute for Aboriginal Development at Alice Springs, Northern Territory.

A member (1957-59) of the Aborigines' Welfare Board in Victoria, Blair also became involved in the Aboriginal Advancement League, the Federal Council for the Advancement of Aborigines and Torres Strait Islanders, and the Commonwealth Aboriginal Arts Board. In January 1976 he was appointed A.O. He died of myocardial infarction on 21 May 1976 in East Melbourne and was cremated. His wife, daughter and son survived him.

100 Famous Australian Lives (Syd, 1969); K. Harrison, *Dark Man, White World* (Melb, 1975); Aborigines' Friends Assn, *Annual Reports*; *People* (Syd), 4 July 1951; *Bulletin*, 3 July 1965; *Courier-Mail* and *Canb Times*, 22 May 1976; *SMH*, 22 May, 19 June 1976; information from Mrs D. Blair, Melb, and Miss N. Blair, Syd.

ALAN T. DUNCAN

BLAKE, FLORENCE TURNER (BLAKE) (1873-1959), artist and benefactor, was born on 26 October 1873 at Armidale, New South Wales, sixth surviving child of William Albert Braylesford Greaves, a surveyor from England, and his native-born wife Anne, née Mackenzie. William later owned Newbold station on the Clarence River and a family home, Braylesford, at Bondi, Sydney. Florence sold puppies from her pet pug to pay for her first art lessons. One of Julian Ashton's [q.v.7] earliest students, she exhibited her oil painting, 'Panel, Roses', in September 1896 with the Society of Artists, Sydney. Tom Roberts and Henry Fullwood [qq.v.11,8] had visited the Greaves family at Newbold in 1894; Roberts's 'Portrait of Florence' (painted about 1898) depicted the profile of a winsome, stylish, young woman with a mass of fine, curly, dark hair. He also painted a portrait of her mother.

On 30 April 1902 at St Luke's Anglican Church, Concord, Sydney, Florence married William Edward Kugelmann Mofflin of William Mofflin & Co., wool and skin merchants; they were to remain childless. Although some of her works bear her married name, she divorced her husband in 1915. She later used her Christian name 'Blake' (after an ancestor) as her surname.

Florence is best known for her watercolour paintings on silk fans, especially 'Frivolers' (1916) and 'Garden of Dreams' (1920), both purchased by the National Art Gallery of New South Wales, and 'The Silver Moon', bought by the National Gallery of South Australia in 1918: these subjects reflected her love of fantasy and soft colours. Charles Conder's [q.v.3] fan paintings influenced her style as they did that of her contemporary Thea Proctor [q.v.11].

From 1925 to 1929 Florence lived in Europe, studying under Professor Henry Tonks at the Slade School of Fine Art, University College, London. The Impressionist painter Lucien Pissarro, who noticed her copying in the Tate gallery, gave her one of his landscapes, which influenced the subject and style of her painting, 'Le Brusc, South of France'. Back in Sydney, she reputedly treasured her studios more than her homes and lent paintings from her collection to the National Art Gallery of New South Wales. She had many friends connected with that institution, among them G. V. F. Mann [q.v.10] whose portrait she painted, (Sir) James McGregor, and B. J. Waterhouse [q.v.12] who designed her house, Menlo, at Bellevue Hill. Having exhibited a few pictures in the early 1930s, she began to suffer incipient blindness in 1939.

Florence Blake died at Ryde on 8 April 1959 and was cremated. She left almost the whole of her estate, valued for probate at £54 214, to the Art Gallery of New South Wales, by far the largest bequest it had then

received. The money was particularly welcome at a time when 'statutory grants were barely sufficient for local purchases'. The income from the Florence Turner Blake bequest has been used to purchase works in a variety of media, including an etching by Picasso, a tapestry by John Olsen and Donald Friend's Sri Lanka notebook.

H. Topliss, *Tom Roberts, 1856-1931*, 2 vols (Melb, 1985); Art Gallery of NSW, *Acquisitions*, 1959, pp 5, 7; Trustees of National Art Gallery of NSW, *Annual Report*, 1965 *and* Minutes of Mthly Meetings, 1958-67 (held at Art Gallery of NSW); *Daily Telegraph* (Syd), 13 Aug 1959; Society of Artists (NSW), Exhibition cats, 1896-1933, *and* biog file (Art Gallery of NSW); Blake papers (ML).　　　　　　　　　　　　　　JILL WATERHOUSE

BLAKE, RICHARD CHARLES (1903-1967), egg marketer, was born on 5 July 1903 at Newtown, Sydney, son of Richard Daniel Blake, a carpenter from London, and his native-born wife Laura Louisa Amelia, née Amos. Migrating at an early age with his parents to New Zealand, Richard was educated at Auckland Grammar School and Seddon Memorial Technical College. After returning to New South Wales, he initially had a varied career. In 1926 he was a delegate on the central council of the Workers' Educational Association and completed a university extension course in economics. About 1927 Blake established a small business at Marrickville and on 24 March 1928 married a ledger-keeper Lilias Isabel Stuart Topp at the local Presbyterian church. By 1931 he was a senior partner in T. Norman & Co., commercial agents in Sydney, and represented the firm in the Parkes area. Politics also attracted him. Advocating 'abolition of pre-selection and party politics, extension of Federal Government powers and abolition of State Governments and Governors', in February he unsuccessfully contested the Federal by-election for Parkes as the Economic Reform candidate.

By 1934 Blake was a poultry farmer at Cronulla, Sydney, and in 1937 was elected to the Egg Marketing Board as a representative of the producers. As its chairman (1940-43), he edited the periodical, *Poultry Farmer*, and wrote *Modern Marketing as practised by the Egg Marketing Board of N.S.W.* (1940), a modest but significant contribution to the reconstruction of Australian primary industries. In the 1943 election of board members he was defeated because of his 'dictatorial attitude' and his failure to protect the interests of producers, particularly over the disastrous cold-storage project. He was a representative for eleven years from 1937 on the Australian Oversea Transport Association.

During World War II the Commonwealth government appointed Blake assistant-controller of egg supplies in 1943 and a member of the Egg Industry Advisory Board. With his extensive experience in marketing, he joined the Australian Egg Board when it was established in 1948 and in October became its superintendent of exports. In 1953-55 he was based in London as the board's official agent. Back in Australia in 1955, he served as Commonwealth representative and chairman of the Australian Egg Board until 1967.

Held 'in high regard by his associates', Blake was zealous in his commitment to the poultry industry, but was able to spend some time with his family, tending the garden at his home in Burns Road, Lane Cove, and playing lawn bowls. He was a governor of the Poultry Husbandry Research Foundation at the University of Sydney from 1961, chairman of the First International Egg Marketing Conference in 1962, deputy-chairman of the Twelfth World's Poultry Congress in Sydney that year and president (1962-66) of the World's Poultry Science Association. In 1963 he was appointed O.B.E. Blake died of hypertensive cerebrovascular disease on 28 February 1967 in a private hospital at Hunters Hill and was cremated. His wife and daughter survived him.

Egg Marketing Bd of NSW, *A Decade of Egg Marketing in N.S.W.* (Syd, 1961); Aust Egg Bd, *Annual Reports*, 1948-58; *SMH*, 16 Jan, 2 Feb 1931, 15 Sept, 21, 25 Oct 1943, 7 Oct 1958, 8, 16 Aug 1962, 8 June 1963, 31 Aug 1964 supp, 21 Feb 1967.   PAUL ASHTON

BLAMEY, SIR THOMAS ALBERT (1884-1951), army officer and commissioner of police, was born on 24 January 1884 at Lake Albert, near Wagga Wagga, New South Wales, eighth child of Richard Henwood Blamey, butcher, and his native-born wife Margaret Louisa, née Murray. Born in Cornwall, England, Richard had come to Australia in 1862 at the age of 16. Having worked as a cattleman in Queensland, he moved to the Wagga Wagga district where he took up a small property, and also found jobs as a contract drover and as an overseer of shearing-sheds.

Educated at Wagga Wagga Superior Public School, Thomas was employed from 1899 as a local pupil-teacher and participated enthusiastically in the school cadets. In July 1903 he became an assistant-teacher at Fremantle Boys' School, Western Australia. There he continued to develop his leadership skills, particularly in the cadets. He attended Claremont Methodist Church, organized church activities and preached occasional sermons. By early 1906 he had been offered the post of probationary minister at Carnarvon, but, before accepting, saw an advertisement inviting applications for commissions in the Commonwealth Cadet Forces. In an Australia-wide military examination Blamey was placed third; he was appointed lieutenant on the Administrative and Instructional Staff in November, and posted to Melbourne.

Throughout the next five years he applied himself to his work with the cadets and endeavoured to improve his military knowledge. On 8 September 1909 he married 34-year-old Minnie Caroline Millard with Anglican rites in her parents' home, Hylands, at Toorak. They were to have two sons: Charles, known as 'Dolf' (b. 1910), died in an aeroplane crash in 1932 while serving with the Royal Australian Air Force; Thomas (b. 1914) became a solicitor and served in the Australian Imperial Force in World War II. In 1910 their father had transferred to the Australian Military Forces and was promoted captain.

Following a competitive examination, in 1912 Blamey began the course at the Staff College, Quetta, India, indicating his resolve to make a success of his career. Initially unaccompanied by his family, he lived in the mess for a year. Late in 1913 he graduated with a B pass. In his report the commandant claimed that Blamey 'came here uneducated (in a military sense) but all his work during his first year was characterised by a very genuine determination to overcome this defect. By the end of the first year he had succeeded beyond all expectation'. The commandant also noted: 'If he is not gifted with a large amount of tact he is not, in any way, conspicuously devoid of that very necessary quality'. When Blamey was sent to England in May 1914 for further experience, his family sailed home to Melbourne.

On the outbreak of World War I Major Blamey served briefly at the War Office in London before joining the 1st Australian Division in Egypt as general staff officer, 3rd grade (intelligence). He landed at Gallipoli on 25 April 1915, with Major General (Sir) William Bridges and Colonel (Sir) Brudenell White [qq.v.7,12], and next month led a small patrol behind enemy lines in a daring effort to locate Turkish guns. In July Blamey was promoted temporary lieutenant colonel and went back to Egypt to help form the 2nd Division; he returned to Gallipoli in September and was appointed the division's assistant-adjutant and quartermaster general.

In the early months of 1916 the A.I.F. began moving to France. By July, when the 1st Division was in action on the Somme, Blamey had succeeded White as chief of staff. After short periods in command of a battalion and a brigade (in which he saw no action), Blamey continued as G.S.O.1, 1st Division, until June 1918. He was then promoted temporary brigadier and made chief of staff of the Australian Corps under Lieutenant General Sir John Monash [q.v.10].

Working in close partnership with his commander, Blamey helped to plan the successful battle at Hamel in July, the offensive beginning on 8 August and the subsequent breaking of the Hindenburg line. Blamey was not the driving force behind the corps' achievements —with a commander of Monash's calibre that was not possible. Nor was he was a mere clerk, responding to Monash's directions. With strong views on the conduct of operations, he was not afraid to express his opinions to Monash and—on his commander's behalf —kept a firm grip on activities throughout the corps. Blamey bore wide responsibility and gained a deep understanding of all facets of contemporary warfare. The demanding Monash thought that Blamey 'possessed a mind cultured far above the average, widely informed, alert and prehensile. He had an infinite capacity for taking pains'. General (Baron) Birdwood [q.v.7], the commander of the A.I.F., described him as 'an exceedingly able little man, though by no means a pleasing personality'. Blamey was awarded the Distinguished Service Order (1917) and the French Croix de Guerre (1919); he was appointed C.M.G. (1918) and C.B. (1919), and was mentioned in dispatches seven times.

Returning to Melbourne in October 1919, he was posted as director of military operations at Army Headquarters. Next year he became deputy chief of the General Staff. In 1922 he was sent to the high commissioner's office in London as colonel, General Staff, and Australian representative on the Imperial General Staff. By March 1925 he was back in Australia as second chief of the General Staff. His military career seemed assured, but his rapid rise had engendered considerable jealousy. The Australian army was still largely a citizen force and there were young militia brigadiers who, unlike Blamey, had commanded troops in battle. Furthermore, his fellow regular officers, such as Sir Harry Chauvel, J. G. Legge, V. C. M. Sellheim, (Sir) Julius Bruche, W. A. Coxen, C. H. Foott, C. H. Brand and T. H. Dodds [qq.v.7,10,11,7,8,8, 7,8], were senior to him, and some of them made it clear to the minister for defence that they would 'resent most strongly being passed over' if Blamey were to be promoted.

In 1925 (Sir) Stanley Argyle [q.v.7], the Victorian chief secretary, offered Blamey the post of chief commissioner of police, at an annual salary of £1500. He decided to leave the regular army. Transferring to the Militia on 1 September, he took office that day. Lingering dissension over the 1923 strike by officers of the Police Force of Victoria and community tension during the Depression were to make his tenure difficult. His administration began, however, with controversy of a more personal nature. On 21 October police raided a brothel and found a man with Blamey's police badge. Blamey privately maintained that he had lent his key ring, including the badge, to a friend, but refused to name him. Publicly, he claimed that the badge had been stolen.

The Labor government of Premier E. J. Hogan [q.v.9], which took office in 1929, saw Blamey as a member of the conservative establishment. It has been recently suggested that, while chief commissioner, Blamey was head of the 'White Army', a right-wing, secret army prepared to defend the state if there were an attempt at a communist or Catholic takeover. Although the evidence of Blamey's leadership is circumstantial, by training and instinct he was an autocrat; he considered himself to be the supreme commander of the police force and acted accordingly. The force's official historian observed that 'Blamey's style of dealing with public protest was confrontationalist, readily violent, and generally ruthless'. While he did much to improve the standard of the police, he broke their union. On the recommendation of Argyle's United Australia Party government, he was knighted in 1935, but on 9 July 1936 (Sir) Albert Dunstan's [q.v.8] Country Party administration forced him to resign for issuing an untrue statement in an attempt to protect the reputation of one of his senior police officers.

Blamey's life was at its nadir. His wife had died in 1935. In 1937 he relinquished command of the 3rd (Militia) Division, which he had held for six years as a major general, and went on the Unattached List, his career apparently over. Nevertheless, he retained the support of such men as (Sir) Robert Menzies, R. G. (Baron) Casey and (Sir) Frederick Shedden [qq.v.]. From early 1938 Blamey supplemented his income by making radio broadcasts on international affairs. At Shedden's suggestion, that year Blamey was appointed chairman of the Commonwealth government's Manpower Committee and controller-general of recruiting. Shedden later explained: 'The aim was twofold. His military experience and organizing ability would be most valuable to the Committee, and he would be brought back into the Defence Organization as the most probable Army Commander in the event of war'. On 5 April 1939 Blamey married a 35-year-old artist Olga Ora Farnsworth at St John's Anglican Church, Toorak.

War was declared in September and on 13 October Blamey was promoted lieutenant general and appointed to command the 6th Division, the first raised for the new A.I.F. In early 1940 the government decided to raise another division. Blamey received the resulting corps command, as well as a charter spelling out his responsibilities as commander of the A.I.F. His advancements reflected his quickness of mind and force of personality more than a scarcity of other suitable officers. In Gavin Long's [q.v.] view, he 'had a mind which comprehended the largest military and politico-military problems with singular clarity, and by experience and temperament was well-equipped to cope with the special difficulties which face the commander of a national contingent which is part of a coalition army in a foreign theatre of war'.

Yet, Blamey was out of touch with recent developments in military technology and his immediate background had prepared him for high command rather than for commanding a corps or division on the battlefield. His strengths and weaknesses were revealed in the Middle East. As commander of the A.I.F. (gazetted December 1940), he fought long and hard to maintain its integrity against the designs of the British commanders-in-chief, General (Earl) Wavell and General Sir Claude Auchinleck. Blamey's performance was uneven. His most obvious error was his failure to inform the Australian government early enough that he had strong doubts about the wisdom of the Greek campaign. Learning this lesson well, he never again failed to let the government know his views. He commanded the Australian Corps (briefly renamed the Anzac Corps, as it included the New Zealand division) in April 1941 during its skilful withdrawal down the Greek peninsula and its evacuation from beaches previously reconnoitred by him in expectation of such an eventuality.

His chief of staff Brigadier (Sir) Sydney Rowell [q.v.] has claimed that at the height of the withdrawal Blamey was 'physically and mentally broken'. The allegation has had some corroboration, but has been fervently denied by a number of senior officers, and Blamey's aide-de-camp recalled that in Greece he never saw him 'fearful or abnormally troubled'. Whatever the truth regarding his performance in the field—and Wavell was favourably impressed—Blamey angered his senior staff when he chose his son to fill the one remaining seat on the aircraft carrying him out of Greece.

On 23 April 1941 Blamey was appointed deputy commander-in-chief, British Forces in the Middle East. He was reluctant to give up the corps command and continued to make his presence felt. In June he intervened in the Syrian campaign to alter the strategy of General (Baron) Wilson whom he believed was exercising insufficient control. Seeking to reassemble the A.I.F. as one formation, Blamey successfully demanded that the tiring 9th

Division be relieved at Tobruk in August-October. On 24 September he was promoted general.

He never had the classical physique of a commander in the field. Sporting a grey-white moustache, he was rotund and only 5 ft 6½ ins (168.9 cm) tall, but both Wavell and Auchinleck had quickly learned not to underestimate his determination or energy. Next year Wavell described Blamey as: 'Probably the best soldier we had in the Middle East. Not an easy man to deal with but a very satisfactory man to deal with'. Auchinleck was less complimentary; he found Blamey likeable, but held that 'he wasn't a general I should have chosen to command an operation'.

Although Blamey enhanced his reputation in the Middle East, he failed to win the unanimous support of a small and influential group of senior A.I.F. officers. There were many tensions in the force's upper echelons where ambitious, and sometimes disaffected, regular and militia officers vied for commands. Perhaps Blamey could never have kept them all contented. It was not his style to curry favour with subordinates, but he seems occasionally to have provoked antipathy towards himself rather than to have tried to dissipate it. His relations with soldiers were also strained. Rarely able to inspire their complete loyalty and trust, he enjoyed life to the full in a manner which they understood but did not expect to find in their commanders.

By the end of 1941 (Sir) Winston Churchill, the British prime minister, was close to asking the Australian government to recall Blamey, mainly because of his stand on Tobruk. The start of hostilities in the Far East rendered the request unnecessary and in March 1942 Blamey arrived in Melbourne to take up his new appointment as commander-in-chief of the Australian Military Forces. The task he faced was immense and complicated, overshadowing that presented to any previous Australian military leader. In early 1942 the country seemed in danger of attack by the more powerful Japanese, and Blamey had to prepare for his country's defence with the forces then available. Although the Australian army appeared numerically large, it was predominantly composed of partly-trained militiamen. He was to be responsible for training, administering and expanding the army to some twelve divisions and their associated support establishments.

The American General Douglas MacArthur [q.v.] had been appointed supreme commander of the South-West Pacific Area with authority over all Australian, American and Dutch forces in the region. Blamey became commander of the Allied Land Forces and was responsible to MacArthur for both the land defence of Australia and the offensive operations planned by MacArthur. When John Curtin [q.v.] established the Prime Minister's War Conference—consisting usually of himself and MacArthur—as the senior body for the high direction of the war, MacArthur became the government's principal strategic adviser. Shedden acted as secretary and liaised between the prime minister and supreme commander. Blamey resented his exclusion from strategic policy making. In response to his threat to resign, he was told that he would retain his direct access to the prime minister on matters of broad military policy.

Blamey's role as Allied Land Forces commander was to cause him the most problems. MacArthur intended to carry out the function himself and to conduct operations by means of task forces under his immediate control. After the Japanese landed on the north coast of Papua in July 1942, additional Australian troops were rushed north and placed under the command of Lieutenant General Rowell. The Japanese were defeated at Milne Bay in September, but there was disquiet at MacArthur's headquarters (which had moved to Brisbane) about the concurrent Australian withdrawal along the Kokoda Track. Faced with a possible defeat, MacArthur persuaded Curtin to send Blamey to Port Moresby to take personal command—in effect to become the task force commander.

Rowell saw Blamey's arrival on 23 September as a reflection on his ability. He had lost respect for Blamey in Greece, and had neither the forbearance nor goodwill to make the arrangement work. For his part, Blamey was fighting for his professional life. MacArthur had the ear of the prime minister and there were Australian senior officers who either coveted Blamey's position or felt that he had damaged their careers by the favouritism he had shown to others. Blamey could not afford to show weakness and on 28 September relieved Rowell of his command. There was probably no alternative, but Blamey's decision polarized feeling among senior Australian officers. About this time MacArthur privately considered Blamey to be a 'sensual, slothful and doubtful character but a tough commander likely to shine like a power-light in an emergency. The best of the local bunch'.

Next month Blamey removed Major General Arthur Allen [q.v.] who had been commanding the 7th Division on its counteroffensive along the Kokoda Track. Blamey thought that he was not in a sufficiently strong position to resist the constant demands for a faster advance from MacArthur who was still in Brisbane. In November Blamey addressed troops of the 21st Brigade —who had been hammered by superior Japanese forces on the Kokoda Track—and

seemed to accuse them of having run like rabbits. Whether his words were misunderstood or not, the soldiers were indignant.

The Australians and later the Americans drove the Japanese back to a beach-head on the north coast of Papua where they were vanquished by late January 1943. While the victory was costly, both in battle casualties and in sickness, Blamey partially reestablished his standing with MacArthur. American reversals had even given him an opportunity to tell MacArthur that he preferred Australian troops to Americans, for at least he knew that the Australians would fight. MacArthur, nevertheless, had already decided to use the task force arrangement to ensure that Americans would never again serve under Australian command. Retaining Blamey as formal Allied Land Forces commander, in February he established a separate task force for United States formations, the deployment of which was to be beyond Blamey's control. In Long's words, the new organization was achieved 'by stealth and by the employment of subterfuges that were undignified, and at times absurd'.

There is no evidence that Blamey was worried by MacArthur's machinations at this stage. Rather, he was more concerned with preparing for the coming offensives of 1943. For much of the year either Lieutenant General Sir Edmund Herring or Lieutenant General Sir Iven Mackay [q.v.] commanded New Guinea Force, but Blamey bore the final responsibility for planning and execution, and MacArthur insisted that Blamey was the task force commander. Major operations included the advance towards Salamaua (May to August), the seizing of Lae in September, the subsequent advance up the Markham and Ramu valleys, the landing at Finschhafen (September) and the fighting at Sattelberg in November. An impressive orchestration of land, sea and air forces which brought quick victories for relatively slight losses, the 1943 campaigns were a justification of Blamey's training policies and an indication of the high level of expertise that had been developed in the Australian army.

By early 1944 the strategic situation had changed markedly and it was clear that henceforward the Americans would provide the bulk of land forces in the South-West Pacific theatre. Blamey realized that MacArthur planned to give the Australian army a minor role for at least the next year. In April he accompanied Curtin on his visits to the United States and Britain. In London Blamey was attracted by a British proposal for a joint British and Australian force to advance north from Darwin into the Netherlands East Indies. The proposal was vigorously opposed by MacArthur and did not come to pass. Curtin and Shedden supported MacArthur, and Blamey found himself increasingly at odds with the Australian government.

At the outset Blamey had established a good working relationship with Curtin and later claimed that he had 'no need to worry about rear armour'. He continued to hold Curtin in high regard, but in late 1944 clashed with the prime minister and Shedden over manpower issues. Discontent over Blamey's administration of the army was a further source of friction. In a large citizen army, thrown together by a democracy in a war for survival, inequities, inefficiency and tensions were inevitable. Despite his prodigious capacity for work, Blamey had taken too many tasks upon himself. Yet, he refused to relinquish his administrative duties, his operational responsibilities, or his nominal command of Allied Land Forces. In his view, he needed to retain his authority to safeguard Australia's interests against the Americans, and he believed that he was the only Australian commander who could do so effectively.

In early 1945 Blamey was criticized in Federal parliament for maintaining too many generals, for side-tracking potential rivals, for conducting unnecessary operations in New Guinea and on Bougainville, and for providing insufficient administrative support to the forces therein engaged. Many of these claims were without foundation. For example, the Bougainville campaign was approved by the government and administrative support was provided. Moreover, problems over the size of the army related to its future use, and Blamey found himself making decisions without any clear strategic directive from the politicians. For all that, he was open to charges of favouritism over some of his appointments.

The issues concerning the operations of I Australian Corps in Borneo underlined Blamey's difficulties. MacArthur planned that I Corps would report directly to his headquarters, thus by-passing Blamey. When Blamey objected, he was permitted to place a senior liaison officer at MacArthur's headquarters in Manila. Troops of the 9th Australian Division captured Tarakan in May-June 1945, and Labuan and Brunei in June. MacArthur's directive that the 7th Division seize Balikpapan in July had been questioned by Blamey who persuaded the acting prime minister J. B. Chifley [q.v.] to suggest that the idea be abandoned. MacArthur replied that the plan had to proceed because it had been ordered by the United States Joint Chiefs of Staff. He did not add that the joint chiefs had given their approval only after he had told them that not to do so would 'produce grave repercussions with the Australian government and people'. Curtin remained loyal to MacArthur and agreed to the operation in

which 229 Australians died and 634 were wounded. Japan did not surrender one minute earlier as a result of the action.

Blamey's disputes with the government and MacArthur should not overshadow the importance of his contribution to Australia in World War II. While he had little opportunity to display his ability as a field commander in the Pacific, he quickly grasped the nature of the war: the need to use sea and air resources, the debilitating effects of climate and terrain, the necessity for thorough training and fitness, and for frequent reliefs for commanders and soldiers, the importance of logistics and the value of accurate intelligence. He did not immerse himself in detail, preferring to leave it to his first-rate chief of staff Lieutenant General (Sir) Frank Berryman, but he had a clear and at times astonishing grasp of detail. Apart from his miscalculation over the use of Bren-gun carriers at Buna, Papua, in December 1942, Blamey did not waste Australian lives. And he always protected Australian interests. Brigadier (Sir) Kenneth Wills, controller of the Allied Intelligence Bureau, commented: 'Few people realize how much of the credit of the successful Australian operations, both in the Middle East and in New Guinea, was due to the Chief's personal control and planning'.

In 1942 Blamey had made it clear that he would resign as commander-in-chief at the war's end. Having attended the surrender ceremony in Tokyo in September 1945 as the Australian representative, he offered to resign that month. For a time the government chose to retain him, informing him in early November that the complexity of the problems confronting the army made it desirable for him to remain in office. In mid-November the minister for the army suddenly advised Blamey that he was to be relieved on 1 December. This peremptory dismissal of the government's top military adviser—without accompanying recognition or reward—showed the depth of feeling against him in some quarters of the Labor Party. He had been appointed K.C.B. (1941) and G.B.E. (1943), and was awarded the Greek Military Cross (1941), the United States' Distinguished Service Cross (1943) and the Netherlands' Grand Cross of the Order of Oranje-Nassau (1946).

Blamey's critics have assigned personal motives to his actions. To them, he was a self-seeking, devious manipulator who struggled ruthlessly to retain his powerful position and to bolster his ego. In contrast, his supporters have called him Australia's greatest general. To them, he was a wise and forceful administrator who fought relentlessly to maintain Australian independence in military matters and who had a genuine concern for the welfare of his troops. A credible evaluation of

Blamey's character lies somewhere between these two views, probably closer to the second. In retrospect it is hard to think of another Australian general with the prestige, force of personality and understanding of politics who could have filled his role.

He had serious flaws in his character, but, as Curtin said, 'when Blamey was appointed the Government was seeking a military leader not a Sunday School teacher'. Unwilling to admit his own faults and unremitting in the pursuit of personal enemies, Blamey was blunt and, on occasions, tactless. Perhaps the stories of his womanizing and drinking grew with the telling, but he never seemed to understand that a public figure cannot expect to keep his private life to himself. Possibly his greatest failing was that he did not appreciate the importance of public relations. Conversely, there was a sensitive side to Blamey's nature which few saw and he had interests beyond military and public affairs, such as his involvement in the early discussions to found the Australian National University.

Retiring to Melbourne, he devoted himself to business affairs, to writing and to promoting the welfare of ex-service personnel. In the late 1940s he became involved in 'The Association': similar to the earlier 'White Army', it was established to counter a possible communist coup. After Menzies came to power, on 8 June 1950 Blamey was promoted field marshal. A few days later he fell gravely ill. On 16 September, in hospital, he received his field marshal's baton from the governor-general. Survived by his wife and by his son Thomas, Blamey died of hypertensive cerebral haemorrhage on 27 May 1951 at the Repatriation General Hospital, Heidelberg, and was cremated. Crowds estimated at 250 000 lined the streets of Melbourne at his state funeral. His estate was sworn for probate at £27 899.

A portrait of Blamey by (Sir) Ivor Hele is held by the Australian War Memorial, Canberra. Portraits by (Sir) William Dargie are in the rooms of the Commercial Travellers' Association of Victoria, and the Naval and Military Club, Melbourne. A statue by Raymond Ewers stands in Kings Domain, Melbourne, adjacent to the Shrine of Remembrance. The main Department of Defence buildings in Canberra are grouped around Sir Thomas Blamey Square where a bas-relief likeness of him was unveiled in 1984.

P. Hasluck, *The Government and the People 1939-1941* (Canb, 1952) and *1942-1945* (Canb, 1970); G. Long, *To Benghazi* (Canb, 1952) and *Greece, Crete and Syria* (Canb, 1953) and *The Final Campaigns* (Canb, 1963); J. Hetherington, *Blamey, Controversial Soldier* (Canb, 1973); S. F. Rowell, *Full Circle* (Melb, 1974); D. M. Horner, *Crisis of Command* (Canb, 1978) and *High Command* (Canb,

1982); N. D. Carlyon, *I Remember Blamey* (Melb, 1980); R. Haldane, *The People's Force* (Melb, 1986); M. Cathcart, *Defending the National Tuckshop* (Melb, 1988); J. Hetherington, Blamey, Field-Marshal Sir Thomas Albert (ts, held by ADB, Canb); D. H. Dwyer, Interlude with Blamey (ts, 1970, copy held by author, Deakin, ACT); Blamey papers (AWM); Dept of Defence files *and* Shedden papers (AA).

D. M. HORNER

BLANCHARD, JULIAN RALPH (1892-1980), Presbyterian minister, was born on 27 September 1892 at Broadwater, New South Wales, second son of native-born parents George Alfred Blanchard, headmaster, and his wife Elizabeth, née Dempsey. In 1902 George died, leaving Elizabeth with three sons. She moved to Sydney where Ralph was educated at Fort Street Model School and gained a bursary to the University of Sydney (B.A., 1913). After training for the ministry at St Andrew's College, he was ordained on 12 July 1917 and inducted into the Presbyterian Church of Australia's suburban parish of Ryde-Meadowbank. On 25 January 1919 he married a schoolteacher Doris Rachel Raysmith at St Stephen's Church, Sydney.

Having been appointed in 1919 to Ross Memorial Church, West Perth, in 1922 Blanchard was elected moderator of the General Assembly of the Presbyterian Church of Western Australia. He became well known for his concern with the relations between church and state, and for his engagement in social issues. Prepared to cross swords with politicians over gambling laws, he denounced wine saloons as snakepits dealing in poison and death, which prompted a suit for slander: rather than apologizing, he contested the case and lost; the plaintiff received nominal damages. While principal of Presbyterian Theological Hall, Perth, Blanchard lectured there in church history and also taught at the nearby Kindergarten Teachers' Training College.

Leaving for New Zealand in 1926, he served at St John's Church, Wellington, and was on the boards of Scots and Queen Margaret colleges. Blanchard moved to Adelaide as incumbent of Scots Church in September 1939. He was moderator of the South Australian assembly for two terms in 1942-43 and moderator-general of the Australian assembly in 1948-51. With other religious leaders, he organized public meetings in Adelaide during World War II and in its aftermath, and issued manifestos containing Christian ideals for postwar development and social justice. He feared that 'humanity hangs precariously on the edge of an unspeakably terrible abyss'. Strongly ecumenical in outlook, Blanchard included Anglican and Catholic bishops among his friends. In 1949 he attended a conference of Asian churches in Bangkok and in 1950 visited the United Church of South India. He was appointed C.B.E. in 1957.

Following his retirement next year, he travelled abroad, received an honorary degree (D.D., 1958) from the University of Edinburgh and relieved at parishes in Edinburgh, London and Amsterdam, as well as at Jaffa, Israel. Returning to Australia in 1965, he settled in North Melbourne where he joined a local history association. Blanchard had been an army and school chaplain, and was also involved in the Young Men's Christian Association and the Australian Student Christian Movement. He enjoyed cricket, singing and poetry, particularly the work of John Shaw Neilson [q.v.10]. Blanchard's published pamphlets were mostly for youth conferences whose members once sang to him: 'If you want to keep your flock, keep your eye upon the clock'. Well groomed, bespectacled and slightly pompous, though not without humour, he was an eloquent speaker—learned, forceful and challenging. Survived by his wife, son and two daughters, he died on 30 July 1980 at Parkville and was cremated.

Presbyterian, 1 Sept 1921, 1 June 1922; *Presbyterian Banner*, Aug, Nov 1939; *Nth Melb News*, Aug-Sept, Oct-Nov 1980, Sept-Oct 1982; *West Australian*, 1-3 Sept 1921; *Advertiser* (Adel), 20 Feb 1950; Presbyterian Church Archives (Mort L); information from Mrs M. Fox, Ringwood, Melb.

J. H. LOVE

BLAND, FRANCIS ARMAND (1882-1967), public servant, academic and politician, was born on 24 August 1882 at Macdonaldtown, Sydney, eldest of six children of Charles Edward Bland, a native-born shunter, and his wife Eva Emily, née Strehz, a New Zealander. Armand attended Greigs Flat Public School while his father was farming at Pambula. On the family's return to Sydney, he completed his schooling at Peakhurst and at Kogarah Superior public schools. Having passed the junior public examination in 1897, he began work as a clerk with Bosch [q.v.7], Barthel & Co. Two years later he joined N. F. Giblin, an official assignee, and in 1901 passed the public service examination. On 1 February he was appointed to the taxation department in the State Treasury. Moving to the Public Service Board in 1903, he was assistant to R. F. Irvine [q.v.9] who fostered his lifelong interest in education and in an emerging field of study—public administration. Bland was clerk to the Local Government Clerks' and Auditors' Examining Committee and from 1914 secretary to the Board of Examiners.

At All Souls Anglican Church, Leichhardt, on 19 December 1908 Bland married Eliza-beth Bates Jacobs; they were to have one son before she died in 1910. On 7 September 1912 he married Lillian Victoria Orr (d. 1951) at St Philip's Anglican Church, Sydney. The family grew by three sons and two daughters, although Lillian's eldest son lived only one day. To rectify his lack of formal education, Bland studied at night. After matriculating, he embarked upon arts, law and economics at the University of Sydney (B.A., 1909; LL.B., 1912; M.A., 1914) where in 1910 he shared Professor Pitt Cobbett's [q.v.8] prize for political science. The law was now open to the bright young man: he was admitted to the Bar on 31 July 1913 and had the opportunity to read with an Equity barrister (Sir) Frederick Jordan [q.v.9], later chief justice. (Sir) George Beeby [q.v.7], minister for justice, sought Bland's services as a legal officer in his department, but the board refused to release him because Irvine had claimed Bland as his 'private secretary'.

Irvine's appointment in 1914 as professor of economics at the university did not sever the link between patron and protégé. Bland accepted with alacrity an invitation from Meredith Atkinson [q.v.7] to become a part-time tutorial-class lecturer at Helensburgh and Wollongong; from 1915 Bland also lectured part time on public administration, under Irvine. In 1916, 'with confident recklessness', he took leave to study at the London School of Economics under Professor Graham Wallas. To support his family, Bland relied on savings and fees from the tutorials he gave at Oxford, Liverpool and Leeds which brought him into contact with the leaders of the Workers' Educational Association in England.

Back in Sydney, in 1918 Bland was appointed assistant-director of tutorial classes at the university under G. V. Portus [q.v.11] who relied on his administrative, financial and political skills to consolidate the status of the department of tutorial classes and its close relationships with the W.E.A. Although Bland's activities in adult education were soon overshadowed by his contributions to public administration, he continued to take tutorial classes for thirty years. Editing *Australian Highway* from 1919 to 1935, chairing the joint committee for tutorial classes, and, according to Portus, being 'the life and soul of the party—at sing-songs, games, swimming and dressing-up' at summer schools, indicated his diverse contributions to the cause of adult education.

Bland continued to teach two half-courses at the university, public administration (lecturer from 1930) and municipal administration. Lacking textbooks in the field of Australian government, let alone public administration, he filled the gap himself. A set of notes for students allowed free rein to his inimitable lecturing style—a 250 words a minute 'outpouring of frankly biased comment on current affairs', 'delivered with clarity, fire and passion and conviction'. From course handouts, he produced his books: *Shadows and Realities of Government* (1923), *Budget Control* (1931), *Planning the Modern State* (1934) and *Government in Australia* (1939).

A much-needed fillip came when he was visiting professor of government (1929-30) at Washington Square College of Arts and Science, New York University: in 1930 a three-year diploma course in public administration, designed for unmatriculated public servants, was introduced in Sydney. The content of the course—economics, public administration, modern political institutions and prescribed arts subjects—reflected Bland's belief that universities 'should aim to provide well-educated candidates rather than technically trained officials'. His view set him apart from his main protagonist Professor (Sir) Douglas Copland [q.v.] at the University of Melbourne who advocated a heavy concentration of financial and economic subjects. Former diploma students recalled how a seemingly innocent question about that day's editorial in the *Daily Telegraph* would set Bland fulminating for at least thirty minutes. The 'Prof' was friendly and generous to students—too generous, his colleagues felt, when he bent the by-laws outrageously in their favour.

Rarely drawing a clear line between scholarship and partisanship, in 1932 he launched an 'S.O.S.' campaign to highlight the sacking of senior public servants by J. T. Lang [q.v.9] and what he saw as the introduction of 'a spoils system', whereupon Lang used financial threats to pressure the university senate to silence Bland. Unrepentant, Bland informed the vice-chancellor Sir Mungo Mac-Callum [q.v.10] that he had no intention of writing or speaking as F. A. Bland of Strathfield—people only listened to him because of his position at the university. His polemics paid off: in 1935 Premier (Sir) Bertram Stevens [q.v.12] secured an increased parliamentary vote for the university to establish a chair in public administration, to which Bland was appointed. He was later to claim, with some justification, that the story of his long association with Stevens was 'mainly written in the countless [unofficial] memoranda that I wrote for him on almost every subject'.

Most of Bland's more scholarly works had been completed before he accepted the chair. An executive-member of the Sydney University Settlement, he sat on the Board of Social Studies and the Bursary Endowment Board, and in 1944-64 served as a fellow of the senate, elected by the graduates. Beyond the university, in 1935 he helped to 'profession-alize' the public service by establishing the State regional group of the Institute of Public Administration, with the support of Geoffrey Remington [q.v.]. From 1937 Bland (helped by T. H. Kewley) was foundation editor of *Public Administration* until 1947.

Associated with local government since 1906, Bland had eventually become chairman of the Local Government Clerks' and Auditors' Examination Committee. 'In season and out of season' he addressed the annual conferences of various local government bodies, trying to infuse 'some life and strength' into the 'puny frame' of Australia's anaemic third tier of government. He was also the (unacknowledged) author of the Local Government Association's *A Charter for Greater Local Government* (1945), and one of his special interests during his visit to England in 1936-37 was developments in local government. An ardent States-righter, he fought the 1944 and 1946 referenda in his native-land.

Many voluntary organizations benefited from Bland's enthusiasm. He was vice-president of the Constitutional Association of New South Wales, foundation chairman of the Constitutional League of New South Wales (1947) and of the Taxation Institute of Australia, an active member of the Australian Institute of Political Science and the Institute of Pacific Relations, as well as a founder of the Sydney group of Round Table and the Royal Institute of International Affairs (Chatham House). His other London connexions centred on the Round Table and on the Royal Institute of Public Administration, of which he was the Australian council-member.

A devoted High-Churchman, Bland was for many years a lay reader and a member (secretary 1921-27) of the Synod of the Diocese of Sydney and of the Provincial Synod. Possibly to seek harmony after the discord of synod battles, he began to train choirs. He was a council-member of The King's School, Parramatta, and of Moore Theological College.

After retiring from his chair in 1947 and visiting Britain where he took an interest in Commonwealth affairs, Bland turned his considerable energies to partisan politics. Unsuccessful in a bid for pre-selection as a Liberal candidate for the Senate, in 1951 he was elected to the House of Representatives as the Liberal member for Warringah. Many expected that he would prove a mere backbench ornament, but Bland put his polemics about the proper role of parliament into practice. In his maiden speech he criticized the Menzies [q.v.] government for allowing increasing power in the hands of the executive. By re-establishing the joint committee of public accounts, he mocked the traditional wisdom that parliamentary committees were rendered ineffectual by the strong party system. As the J.C.P.A.'s indefatigable chairman, he presided over the drafting of a number of 'memorable' reports that embarrassed ministers and senior public servants alike. One of Bland's academic successors claimed that it was among 'the most effective committees that has ever existed in an Australian parliament'. In 1958 Bland was appointed C.M.G. Three years later he failed to gain re-endorsement and retired from parliament.

Bland's influence on public life, particularly between the wars, was considerable. He averaged fifty addresses a year and wrote numerous newspaper articles. A generation of New South Wales senior public servants bore the stamp of his thinking, and non-Labor politicians, especially during the Stevens administration, were receptive to his advice. His prolific writings have been criticized for their contradictions, but, as a zealous reformer, he was more concerned with the practical issues of government than with elegant, theoretical frameworks. Essentially a nineteenth-century liberal who had flirted with Fabianism, Bland once described himself as 'an uncompromising opponent of the extension of centralized authority' and 'an incorrigible Federalist'. He argued vehemently for an educated, efficient and independent public service, devoted to the public interest.

Although references to his works are rare, Bland's preoccupations are still debated intensely—preoccupations such as accountability, politicization and the career service, open government, administrative tribunals, public enterprise and the statutory corporation, and problems of implementation. His insistence on the separation of politics from administration, long out of fashion, has recently been embraced enthusiastically by the managerial school. Unfortunately, Bland's proselytizing style often distracted from the substance of his argument.

'Even in his domestic life he broke records, outliving three wives and marrying a fourth', wrote one of his obituarists. On 3 July 1954 he married his widowed cousin Ida Mary Warby, née Bland, at St Luke's Anglican Church, Mosman; she died on 11 March 1960. On 12 December that year the resilient Bland, aged 78, married his secretary Gertrude Rollins at St Canice's Catholic Church, Elizabeth Bay. One wag among his academic colleagues observed, only half in jest, that 'Blandee was now probably looking for a new house near a school'.

Having defied for more than a quarter of a century the predictions of his doctors that his heart condition would not stand his gargantuan workload, Bland died of pneumonia on 9 April 1967 in St John of God Hospital, Burwood, after falling and breaking three ribs at his home. A memorial service was held at St Anne's Anglican Church, Strathfield, the suburb in which he had lived for most of his life. His body was bequeathed to the faculty of medicine, University of Sydney. He was survived by his wife, the son (Sir Henry) of his first marriage, and by a son and two daughters of his second. Portraits of Bland by Dora Toovey are held by the University of Sydney and Parliament House, Canberra; the former depicts a recently retired Bland in academic dress with a mischievous twinkle in his eyes, as though about to begin a lecture with his characteristic, 'Well, peoples'.

B. and H. Carey, *Educating the Guardians* (Syd, 1985); L. Foster, *High Hopes* (Melb, 1986); *Public Administration*, 7, 1948, 26, 1967; *IRAS*, 41, 1975; *Aust J of Public Administration*, 48, 1989; *SMH*, 7 Mar 1935, 9 May 1945, 22 Nov 1947, 25 Aug 1950, 1 Jan 1958, 9 June 1961, 10 Apr 1967; Bland papers (Univ Syd Archives).

ROSS CURNOW

BLESING, ALBERT PERCY (1879-1949), farmer and politician, was born on 9 September 1879 at Hamilton, near Kapunda, South Australia, one of eight children of Ernst Gotthilf Blesing, farmer, and his English-born wife Elizabeth, née Flower. Ernst's parents had migrated from the German States in 1841. When Percy was 6, the family moved to Laura where he attended the public school; at 12 he began full-time work as a farmhand. In 1893 his family took up Glenholme, a 1400-acre (567 ha) block at Bangor, nine miles (14.5 km) north-west of Wirrabara in the lower Flinders Ranges, and transformed it into a thriving mixed farm. Percy, however, spent years away, shearing in South Australia, New South Wales and New Zealand. He was dark haired, tall and robust, and sported a bushy moustache as a young man. On 4 July 1911 in the Methodist Church, Wellington Square, North Adelaide, he married Eliza Muriel Annie Glasson; they were to have five children. With his brother Victor, Percy took over Glenholme in 1912 and was sole owner from 1920.

A founding member (1917) of the Country Party Association, Blesing became a representative for the seat of Northern in the Legislative Council in 1924 and moved to suburban Prospect. After the rout of the non-Labor parties in the 1930 State polls, he and his House of Assembly colleague Archie Cameron [q.v.] took their party's rump into the Emergency Committee which helped in defeating the Scullin [q.v.11] government in the 1931 Federal elections. Between May and June 1932 they negotiated the formation of the Liberal and Country League in South Australia. When (Sir) Richard Layton Butler [q.v.7] led the L.C.L. to victory in April 1933

Blesing was appointed minister of agriculture and of local government.

His experience in farming, on the board of the South Australian Voluntary Wheat Pools Ltd and on the advisory committee to the board of the State Bank of South Australia made Blesing a stubborn advocate for his constituents. During his record term as minister of agriculture (1933-44) he fought for rural rehabilitation, agricultural education and the expansion of the Port Lincoln freezing works. As minister of local government (1933-38), he supervised a five-year road improvement programme; as minister of afforestation (1938-44), he promoted the extensive planting of *pinus radiata* in the State's south-east.

Yet, Blesing was out of his depth. Even the *Country News*, of which he was a director, acknowledged his inexperience of 'big business' and his tendency in parliament to 'skim the surface of the subject', leaving departmental officials 'to fill in the details'. Administration did not interest him. Failing to appreciate the role of cabinet, he burdened it with inappropriate concerns. In the Legislative Council he was outshone and out-manoeuvred by urbane, educated lawyers, businessmen and pastoralists. Premier (Sir) Thomas Playford disapproved of his minister's activities at Tattersall's Club and was irritated by his gaffes. After Blesing refused to resign his portfolio, in May 1944 Playford submitted the resignation of the entire cabinet and appointed a new one; Blesing was replaced by (Sir) George Jenkins [q.v.9].

Blesing was devastated. Although he sometimes voted against Playford, he was re-elected in 1947. He continued to play bowls and golf. Next year he was made a director of the South Australian Farmers' Co-operative Union Ltd. Following a gall-bladder operation, he died on 2 March 1949 in the Memorial Hospital, North Adelaide; he was accorded a state funeral and was buried at Wirrabara. His wife, two sons and two daughters survived him.

H. Sizer, *Yet Still They Live* (Adel, 1974); *PD* (SA), 1 Aug 1944, p 71, 2 Aug 1949, pp 87, 94, 156; SA Government, *Gazette Extraordinary*, 15 May 1944; *Country News* (Adel), 21 May, 4 June 1932, 4 Feb, 29 Apr, 6 May 1933, 21 Dec 1935; *Advertiser* (Adel), 16 May 1944, 3, 4 Mar 1949; E. A. Herbert, A History of the Country Party in South Australia (B.A. Hons thesis, Univ Adel, 1959); R. F. I. Smith, The Butler Government in South Australia, 1933-1938 (M.A. thesis, Univ Adel, 1964).

JENNY TILBY STOCK

BLIGH, ROSEMARY BEATRICE (1916-1973), gardener, was born on 27 September 1916 at Edgecliff, Sydney, third of five children of native-born parents James Henry Forbes Gordon, grazier of Werriwa, Bungendore, and his wife Gladys Noel Lydia, née Bowker. Raised in the country, Bea was educated at Ascham, Sydney, and Frensham, Mittagong, and later learned to type. On 1 March 1941 at St Philip's Anglican Church, Bungendore, she married Francis Leonard Bligh, grazier of Pejar Park, near Goulburn; he served as a flying officer with the Royal Australian Air Force, leaving his bride to run the property.

At Pejar Park, Bea found a small, bluestone cottage, and a few flowering shrubs and pine trees. Inspired by the wild and romantic garden at Manar, her grandfather's home near Braidwood, and encouraged by Winifred West [q.v.12] who provided numerous plants, she began to make a garden. She had to contend with many difficulties: rock and impervious, clay soil, bitter winters and fierce summers, and the country hazards of grasshoppers and marauding sheep, cows and horses.

After World War II the house was extended to accommodate her four children. Slight in build, with a cloud of dark hair, Mrs Bligh played tennis and was a member of Royal Sydney Golf Club; she also belonged to the Ski Club of Australia and later the Ramshead hut at Thredbo. She did most of the work in the garden, with occasional help from station-hands. Resourceful at finding plants, she carried home quince seedlings on the pommel of her saddle and once brought back an alpine fern while skiing from the summit of Mount Ramshead. After years of experiment and the ruthless elimination of mistakes, Pejar Park won first prize in the homestead section of the *Sydney Morning Herald* garden competition in 1965. A garden of surprises, its main features were shady trees, smooth, weed-free lawns, raised beds filled with hardy perennials, a long, white wall with espaliered apples and pears, a wistaria-covered pergola, a separate vegetable garden and a willow-shaded pool used to water stock on the far side. She bought wrought-iron gates with the prize-money. In succeeding years the garden was awarded second, third and fourth prizes.

As a result of requests for advice from friends and strangers, Beatrice wrote *Down to Earth* (1968) in which she described the Pejar garden, her mistakes and the short cuts she had discovered; in addition, she provided a calendar of plants that flourish on the Southern Tablelands. On several occasions she opened the garden to raise money for charity. She lectured to garden groups and joined the garden committee of the State branch of the National Trust of Australia.

An overseas fellow of the Royal Horticultural Society, London, she visited numerous gardens on trips abroad and also studied those in dry regions of India, Iran, Africa, Greece and Spain. She was fascinated by the history of gardening and wrote *Cherish the Earth* (1973), a carefully-researched and illuminating account of gardening in Australia. The book was a tribute to her courage: completed a week before she died of cancer on 18 January 1973 in hospital at Goulburn, it was published posthumously. Beatrice's husband, two daughters and twin sons survived her.

C. F. Simpson et al (eds), *Ascham Remembered 1886-1986* (Syd, 1986); *Belle*, May-June 1986, p 163; *SMH*, 19 Nov 1965, 30 Aug 1973; *Canb Times*, 7 July 1970; family information.

MARTHA RUTLEDGE

BLOMFIELD, ISLA STUART (1865-1959), nurse, sanitary inspector and health visitor, was born on 9 July 1865 near Mudgee, New South Wales, eldest of eight children of native-born parents Henry Wilson Blomfield, grazier, and his wife Margaret, daughter of James Cox [q.v.1]. Isla was raised in the Anglican faith. She was well educated and probably had a governess. After six months work at the Coast Hospital, Little Bay, she began nursing on 21 January 1896 at (Royal) Prince Alfred Hospital where Matron Susan McGahey noted that she was 'ever mindful of the patients' comfort'. On qualifying, Blomfield left in November 1899 for a 'long holiday'.

Having obtained an obstetrics certificate from Queen Charlotte's Lying-in Hospital, London, in 1901 she toured hospitals in the United States of America. Following further nursing at R.P.A.H., Blomfield spent three years in China and gained experience in treating infectious diseases. In 1909 she travelled by train across Siberia, visited Berlin and represented the Australasian Trained Nurses' Association at the International Council of Nurses' congress in London.

Back in Sydney, Blomfield qualified as a health inspector, with certificates from the Royal Sanitary Institute, London, and the East Sydney Technical College. Active for a decade on the A.T.N.A. council, she advocated the foundation of a college of nursing. Her frequent articles in the *Australasian Nurses' Journal* urged her colleagues to be more professional and assertive, provided advice on nursing cholera and dysentery patients, and promoted smallpox vaccination; they also expressed her demand for greater government intervention, as well as conveying her feminist and humanitarian ideals.

Nurse-in-charge (1910-11) of the Alice Rawson School for Mothers, in 1911 Blomfield was appointed nurse inspector by the Sydney Municipal Council's health committee. Under the supervision of W. G. Armstrong [q.v.7], she continued to 'educate' new mothers: as part of the campaign to reduce infant mortality, she visited over 1400 mothers a year until the government Baby Health centres took over in 1915. Continuing as sanitary inspector with special concern for women's health and tubercular patients, she maintained her neonatal interests. At the 1917 Infant and Child Welfare Conference she recommended subsidized milk as a means of improving maternal nourishment. From 1918 she was an executive-member of the Royal Society for the Welfare of Mothers and Babies, established by the Holman [q.v.9] government to oversee infant welfare.

Blomfield actively promoted her public health interests through membership of the Playgrounds Association, the Health Society of New South Wales (later Health Association of Australia), the standing committee on public health of the National Council of Women, the Board of Social Study and Training, the Professional Women Workers' Association and the Women's Club. With her mother (d. 1927), she lived at the Astor, Macquarie Street. She retired in 1930.

Dr Armstrong judged that Isla's 'tact, natural charm and sympathy' had overcome much of the hostility of mothers to official interference. She registered as a general nurse in 1930, visited Britain twice more and, at the age of 79, took up sculpture. Blomfield died, unmarried, on 16 August 1959 at her Potts Point flat and was cremated with Christian Science forms.

K. O'Connor (comp), *Our Babies, the State's Best Asset* (Syd, 1989); *A'sian Nurses J*, 15 Dec 1911, p 410, 15 Aug 1912, p 258, 15 Aug 1914, p 254, 15 Dec 1915, p 409, 15 Sept 1916, p 304, 15 Nov 1916, p 367, 15 Dec 1916, p 398, 16 Apr 1917, p 137, 15 July 1921, p 234, 16 June 1930, p 166; NSW Dept of Public Health, *Report of Director-General of Public Health*, 1913-15, 1923-26; *SMH*, 28 Feb 1930, 3 Nov 1955; M. A. Foley, The Women's Movement in New South Wales and Victoria, 1918-1938 (Ph.D. thesis, Univ Syd, 1985); V. Cowden, 'Mothers, as a rule, do not know . . .' Mothercraft Campaigns in the Inner Suburbs of Sydney 1904-1914 (B.A. Hons thesis, Univ NSW, 1980); Roy Prince Alfred Hospital, Record of service, nursing staff, 1890-1897 (RPAH Graduate Nurses Assn Museum, Syd); family information.

JUDITH GODDEN
MEREDITH FOLEY

BLUMENTHAL, STANLEY JOSEPH (1893-1972), trade unionist, was born on 23 August 1893 at Waverley, Sydney, second son of Gustavus Adolphus de Blumenthal, a 'professor of phrenology' from Germany, and his native-born wife Evelyne, née Bignell. Attesting that he was a produce merchant, on 11 August 1914 Stanley enlisted in the Australian Naval and Military Expeditionary Force, and took part in the capture of German

New Guinea. His engagement expired on 4 March 1915. Exactly one month later he joined the Australian Imperial Force. Five ft 4 ins (162.6 cm) tall, with brown eyes and a dark complexion, Blumenthal served at Gallipoli from August to December; he saw action in Egypt and Palestine in 1916-18 with the 12th Light Horse Regiment and the 4th Machine-Gun Squadron; he was discharged in Sydney on 28 October 1919.

Moving to the Federal Capital Territory, he took a job as a park ranger and performed much of his labour on horseback with the help of a blue heeler. Blumenthal married Amy Irene Botterill on 11 June 1927 at St Stephen's Presbyterian Church, Sydney. He was one of the first Rugby League referees in the Canberra district. An office bearer in the local branch of the Australian Workers' Union, in 1937 he was elected treasurer of the Australian Capital Territory Trades and Labour Council. Next year he became secretary. As a result of a dare over a lunchtime drink, on 23 June 1941 he joined the Citizen Military Forces, and was employed on garrison and instructional duties in Australia. After nearly a year of inappropriate treatment which exacerbated his arthritis, he was discharged medically unfit on 11 May 1943.

Back in Canberra, Blumenthal was employed as a clerk at the Kingston bus depot and resumed his part-time post with the T.L.C. Under his stewardship, the labour movement grew rapidly as he oversaw the unionization of building workers involved in the city's many construction projects. He was an energetic advocate for the service staff at Parliament House. In 1946 Blumenthal played an important role in the controversy surrounding the dismissal of Ernest Fields who had been valet to the governor-general's chief of staff, Brigadier Derek Schreiber. Having left his post in acrimonious circumstances, Fields worked at the Hotel Kingston, but was soon discharged, allegedly at Schreiber's instigation. Prime Minister J. B. Chifley [q.v.] intervened and a public inquiry was announced, but, before it began, Blumenthal was able to negotiate Fields's reinstatement without loss of pay.

Blumenthal held mixed attitudes to postwar immigration. In 1947 he warned prospective migrants from the United States of America that Australian labour standards were higher than those in their own country. At A. A. Calwell's [q.v.] request, he went to Perth where he met British migrants and explained Australian trade union principles and work ethics to them. He was sometime president and a life member of the Australian Capital Territory branch of the Labor Party. Survived by his son, Blumenthal died on 1 August 1972 in Canberra and was buried in Canberra cemetery with Catholic rites. One legacy of his union activity is the Territory's annual picnic on trades and labour day.

SMH, 18, 19, 25 Jan 1946, 9 Sept 1947; *Canb Times*, 3 Aug 1972; Trades and Labour Council (ACT), Minute-book (ANUABL); information from Mr M. Blumenthal, Griffith, Canb.

GEORGE MORGAN

BOAKE, CAPEL; *see* KERR

BOAS, HAROLD (1883-1980), architect, town planner and Jewish community leader, was born on 27 September 1883 in Adelaide, third son of ten children of Abraham Tobias Boas [q.v.7] and his wife Elizabeth, née Solomon. Harold was educated at Whinham and Prince Alfred colleges, Adelaide. Indentured in 1899-1904 to the architect Edward Davies, he studied at the South Australian School of Mines and Industries and became a member of the South Australian Institute of Architects. Boas moved to Perth in June 1905 and transferred to the Western Australian institute; he was subsequently to become a fellow of the Royal Australian Institute of Architects. Having joined the firm of M. F. Cavanagh & Austin Bastow, he worked with different architects before settling with Oldham, Boas, Ednie-Brown & Partners. At the Brisbane Street Synagogue, Perth, Boas married Sadie ('Sarah') Cohen on 29 March 1911.

During World War I, although a Jew, he was involved in the Australian Young Men's Christian Association's dealings with the Australian Imperial Force. In London in 1917 Boas sent cards to soldiers and to their next of kin, visited the wounded in hospital and arranged gifts and loans. He published *The Australian Y.M.C.A. with the Jewish Soldier of the Australian Imperial Force* (London, 1919) and compiled the illustrated *Australian Jewry Book of Honour, the Great War, 1914-1918* (Perth, 1923).

With his partners, Boas had designed the King's (open-air) picture theatre in Perth (1905), a warehouse for Sands & McDougall [qq.v.6,10] Ltd and the Nedlands Park Hotel (1907); he was also to design premises for radio station 6WF (1924), aircraft hangers in the 1920s, bulk-storage wheat silos during the 1930s, the Emu Brewery in Mounts Bay Road, the Adelphi Hotel, the Gledden Building, various churches and private homes.

In 1914-16, 1926-42 and 1944 Boas represented South Ward on the Perth City Council. A member (from 1914) of the Town Planning Association of Western Australia and chairman (1928-30) of the State government's Metropolitan Town Planning Commission, he also belonged to the British and

American town planning institutes. He chaired (1930-33, 1938-42) the City of Perth's town planning committee, and was foundation president (1931) of the Town Planning Institute of Western Australia and an inaugural member of the State division of the Town Planning Institute of Australia.

He had helped to inaugurate the Young Liberal League of Western Australia (1911) and founded the popular, anti-socialist Argonauts Civic and Political Club (1925); with Nationalist political affiliations, he was influential in the Western Australian Consultative Council. In 1932 Boas stood unsuccessfully for the Legislative Council as an antisecessionist. After working for the Federal government in Melbourne during World War II, he returned to Perth where he was briefly responsible for the disposal of wartime buildings and plant. In May 1947 he founded the anti-Zionist journal, *Australian Jewish Outlook*. He was president of the Western Australian branch of the United Nations Association and represented Australia and the Council of Australian Jewry at the U.N. conference in Bangkok in 1950. Vice-president (1952) of the Liberal Jewish Group, he was a founder (1954) and life member of Temple David.

Boas lived in Mount Street in the house which he had designed in 1925. He worked professionally and was active in public affairs until late in life. Predeceased by his wife and survived by their two daughters, he died at Subiaco on 17 September 1980 and was cremated.

J. S. Battye (ed), *Cyclopedia of Western Australia*, 1 (Adel, 1912); D. Mossenson, *Hebrew, Israelite, Jew* (Perth, 1990); *Architecture in Aust*, 56, no 1, Feb 1967, p 116; *Labour Hist*, no 18, May 1970, p 32; *Aust Jewish Hist Soc, J*, 9, pt 1, June 1981, p 71; *Politics* (Syd), 12, no 1, May 1977, p 124; *Maccabean*, 26 Sept 1980, 28 Sept 1983; *West Australian*, 1 Apr 1976, 18, 19 Sept 1980; M. Pitt-Morison, Immigrant Architects in Western Australia, 1885-1905, ts, *and* H. Boas, Autobiography: Bricks and Mortar, 1971, mf and ts (BL); Boas papers (Jewish Hist Soc, Perth, *and* BL).   MAX POOLE

BOASE, LEONARD CHARLES (1888-1975) and **ALLAN JOSEPH** (1894-1964), army officers, were born on 5 July 1888 and 19 February 1894 at Gympie, Queensland, second and fourth sons of Charles Boase, journalist, and his wife Harriett Jane, née Hughes, both from England. Educated at Maryborough Grammar School, Leonard was an inspector with the Northern Assurance Co. Ltd, Brisbane, when he enlisted in the Australian Imperial Force on 3 January 1916. Posted to reinforcements for the 52nd Battalion, he was briefly stationed in Egypt before moving to England in June. He joined his battalion on the Western Front in September, but returned to England in November for officer-training.

Commissioned on 28 March 1917, Leonard went back to his unit next month. On 8 June at Messines, Belgium, he led a bombing party against a company of Germans, capturing some and forcing the remainder into the open. Two days later he held an isolated position until his ammunition was expended: meantime, he kept the enemy engaged and enabled supporting troops to operate more freely. For these actions, he was awarded the Military Cross. At Dernancourt, France, on 5 April 1918 Lieutenant Boase's platoon defended a tactically important section of the line. Under his leadership, the men withstood repeated assaults until only two or three survived. Although wounded, Boase made a final effort to hold his ground, dashing among the foe and throwing bombs until he was overpowered. His comrades thought that he had been killed in the action, but he recovered as a prisoner of war. He was awarded the Distinguished Service Order; evidence suggests that he was recommended for the Victoria Cross.

Back in Brisbane, on 31 May 1919 in St Mark's Anglican Church, Albion, Leonard married Ada May Hockings. He was 5 ft 6 ins (167.6 cm) tall, with blue eyes and fair hair. Having resumed work in insurance and become a foundation member (1928) of the Legacy Club of Brisbane, he retired in 1950 and lived quietly, first at Southport, then at Buderim. Survived by his wife and daughter, he died on 6 August 1975 at Nambour and was cremated; his son Peter had been killed over France in 1943 while serving with the Royal Australian Air Force.

Allan Boase was educated at Brisbane Grammar School where he was champion gymnast in 1909-10. Entering the Royal Military College, Duntroon, Federal Capital Territory, he graduated in August 1914 and was posted to the 9th Battalion, A.I.F. In September he embarked for Egypt. After landing at Gallipoli on 25 April 1915, he and his platoon were part of the advanced party which reached Lone Pine. They withdrew under fire and dug in at 'Daisy Patch' next day. Boase was wounded and evacuated; his boat capsized and he narrowly escaped drowning. He rejoined his unit in September. Arriving on the Western Front in June 1916, he was promoted major in the 12th Battalion on 1 December and later performed staff duties. He was repatriated in January 1918.

Sent to the 5th Military District, Perth, in May 1921 Allan transferred to the 13th Mixed Brigade. On 30 August 1922 in St Andrew's Presbyterian Church, Perth, he married Williamina Boyd Norman. Next year he went to England to attend the Staff College, Camberley. From 1926 he served in a succession of staff positions in Perth and Melbourne, and in 1937-39 was an exchange officer in India. Promoted colonel on 2 November 1939, he became commandant, Command and Staff School, Sydney. In April 1940 he was seconded to the A.I.F. as assistant-adjutant and quartermaster general, 7th Division, and in October embarked for the Middle East. When headquarters, A.I.F. Base Area, was formed at Gaza in November, he was placed in charge as temporary brigadier with responsibility for local administration and the handling of convoys. He was to be appointed C.B.E. (1942).

In August 1941 he took command of the 16th Brigade. Following the decision to reinforce the garrison in Colombo, in March 1942 Allan was promoted temporary major general and made general officer commanding, A.I.F., Ceylon. Returning to Australia, in September he became major general, General Staff, First Army, with headquarters at Toowoomba, Queensland. Twelve months later he was in New Guinea as commander of the 11th Division. His headquarters was moved to North Queensland in July 1944; he was appointed general officer commanding, Western Command, Perth, in April 1945. Postings followed as Australian army (1946-48) and defence (1948-49) representative in London. On 12 March 1949 he was promoted temporary lieutenant general and given charge of Southern Command, Melbourne; he remained there until his retirement on 20 February 1951.

Dark complexioned and 5 ft 7 ins (170.2 cm) tall, Allan enjoyed gardening and golf. He died of a coronary occlusion on 1 January 1964 at East St Kilda and was cremated. His wife and daughter survived him, as did his son Neil who became a commodore in the Royal Australian Navy. Allan's brothers Francis and Colin had also served in World War I; Colin was killed at Gallipoli.

C. E. W. Bean, The Story of Anzac, 1 (Syd, 1921) and The A.I.F. in France, 1916, 3 (Syd, 1929), 1918, 5 (Syd, 1937); G. Long, To Benghazi (Canb, 1952) and Greece, Crete and Syria (Canb, 1953); D. McCarthy, South-West Pacific Area—First Year (Canb, 1959); D. Dexter, The New Guinea Offensives (Canb, 1961); K. Willey, The First Hundred Years (Melb, 1968); Brisb Grammar School Mag, June 1950; AWM records; information from Mrs J. Lethbridge, Toowoomba, Qld, and Cdre N. A. Boase, Double Bay, Syd.   GEORGE DICKER

BODENWIESER, GERTRUD (1890-1959), dancer, choreographer and teacher, was born on 3 February 1890 in Vienna, younger daughter of Johann Theodor Bondi, auction-broker, and his wife Maria, née Tandler. Taught at home by governesses, from an early age Gertrud showed a talent for dancing. In c.1905-10 she was trained in classical ballet by Carl Godlewski, but soon recognized that this art form had 'become a mere exhibition of virtuosity'.

Proponents of the New Dance, such as Isadora Duncan and Ruth St Denis, had already appeared in Vienna. From 1910 Gertrud began to develop her own style, aiming to motivate 'the most primordial powers of human sensibilities'. She was influenced by cultural and spiritual renewals occurring in Vienna at the turn of the century, and by pioneers of the New Dance, including François Delsarte, Rudolf von Laban and Emile Jacques Dalcroze. By 1917 she had adopted the surname 'Bodenwieser'. She made her first appearance on 5 May 1919 at the Wiener Konzerthaus with six numbers; the novelty of her style was recognized and praised by critics.

Convinced that the New Dance required thorough training, Bodenwieser soon provided instruction at her private school (1919-20) and at the Neues Wiener Konservatorium. On 27 June 1920 in Vienna she married with Jewish rites Friedrich Jacques Rosenthal, a theatre director; they were to remain childless. Between 1920 and 1938 Gertrud taught on a contract basis at the Akademie für Musik und Darstellende Kunst. She incorporated Dalcroze's system into the foundations for her curriculum at the academy and in 1922 appeared with a group of pupils. She was appointed professor in 1928.

From an early stage she had co-operated with the Sprechtheater (living theatre). With her husband's assistance, the 'Bodenwieser-Gruppe' appeared in the 1923 production of Ferdinand Raimund's Der Verschwender at the Deutsches Volkstheater, a production in which the dance was considered to have equal merit with the spoken word, music, costumes and design. In 'Klabund's' Der Kreidekreis her dancers functioned as a mimic choir as well as stagehands. Bodenwieser collaborated with Max Reinhardt in the 1927 production of Das Mirakel; she subsequently taught (1932-34) gymnastics and the dance at Reinhardt's 'seminary'.

Numerous tours from 1926 onward provided her ensemble with essential funds; two of her groups often performed simultaneously in different countries. Of great significance in Bodenwieser's work was Dämon Maschine (1923)—part two of the dance-drama Gewalten des Lebens—which portrays the transformation of a group of people into a machine. She usually danced the role of the Dämon herself (until retiring from the stage in 1934); this item formed part of almost every programme of her guest performances and in 1931 was awarded a first prize at Florence, Italy. Bodenwieser regarded the 1934 tour of Japan as also providing an opportunity to publicize Austria: the *Wiener Walzer* (*Viennese Waltz*) was invariably performed at the end of each programme.

In her non-abstract dance-dramas, such as *Wer will Frau Wahrheit herbergen?* (1930) and *Die Masken Luzifers* (1936), in which Lucifer personifies intrigue, terror and hatred, Bodenwieser analysed the disintegration of humane values in an era of political totalitarianism. The message of these dance-dramas was prophetic, not only in relation to the impending calamity for the world, but also for the Rosenthals. Following the Nazis' invasion, she and her husband were forced to flee from Austria in May 1938. Gertrud joined some of her dancers in Bogota, Colombia; Jacques went to France, was apprehended by the Gestapo, interned and died in the concentration camp at Auschwitz, Poland, after 31 August 1942.

On her arrival in Sydney on 23 August 1939, Madam Bodenwieser was met by her main group which had just completed a tour in Australia. Continuing to display amazing energy and creative productivity, she gave recitals, opened a studio and prepared a tour of the Australian capital cities for 1940. Although utterly unaccustomed to her style of dancing, audiences and critics reacted with enthusiasm. During the war she arranged frequent performances for the war effort and for charity.

Gravitating to Kings Cross, she became a familiar figure, dressed always in black, and absorbed in her thoughts and dreams. Her inability to discover the fate of her husband frustrated her efforts to become naturalized until 1950, when he was pronounced dead by a court in Vienna. In her Pitt Street studio she created and rehearsed works for her recitals and tours, entertained visitors and trained her dancers. She conducted a wide range of classes, from creative dance movement for young children to mime and movement for professional actors (attended by Peter Finch [q.v.] and Leonard Teale). Bodenwieser also taught at well-known schools, Hopewood House and Abbotsleigh, and for the Young Women's Christian Association; in addition, she ran classes for the Workers' Educational Association, the National Fitness Council and the Australian College of Physical Education.

Always rather fastidious, with beautiful, dark hair and eyes, she seemed small beside her Australian dancers. In manner she was somewhat self-deprecating, but, beneath the grace and charm, she was utterly determined, even ruthless, in pursuit of her artistic aims. Bodenwieser choreographed group dances, solo dances, dance-dramas and comedies, as well as dances for operettas, plays and musical comedies. Her new major dance works, *Cain and Abel* (1941), *O World* (1945), *The Life of the Insects* (1949) and *Errand into the Maze* (1954), continued to express the gamut of human experience.

From 1940 to 1954 the Bodenwieser Ballet toured Australian cities and country centres. The ensemble was chosen to make the first use of the Arts Council of Australia's mobile theatre unit to bring cultural entertainments to remote areas. She took her company on tours to New Zealand (1947 and 1949-50), South Africa (1950), Rhodesia (1950) and India (1952).

Her dancers took part in the film, *Spotlight on the Australian Ballet* (1948), and two of her comedy ballets were televised (1958) by the Australian Broadcasting Commission. Gertrud Bodenwieser died of a coronary occlusion on 10 November 1959 at her Potts Point flat and was cremated. She explained her artistic origins in her posthumous book, *The New Dance* (1970). Her significance has been acknowledged in the establishment of the Bodenwieser Dance Centre and the Gertrud Bodenwieser Archives in Sydney.

F. J. Rosenthal in *Österreichisches Biographisches Lexikon, 1815-1950* (Vienna, 1988); P. Stefan (ed), *Tanz in dieser Zeit* (Vienna, NY, 1926); R. Lämmel, *Der Moderne Tanz* (Berlin, 1928); J. Mayerhöfer (ed), *Tanz 20. Jahrhundert in Wien* (Vienna, 1979); E. H. Pask, *Ballet in Australia* (Melb, 1982); H. Koegler and H. Günther, *Reclams Ballettlexikon* (Stuttgart, 1984); O. Schneider, *Tanz-Lexikon* (Vienna, 1985); *Kunstnachrichten* (Vienna), 1937, special issue no 1, p 33; *Aust Dance*, June 1971, p 20; *SMH*, 12 Nov 1959; G. Renner, *Gertrud Bodenwieser* (D.Phil. thesis, Univ Vienna, 1981); naturalization file, A435/1 item 50/4/5033 (AA); programmes, press-cuttings and documents (Gertrud Bodenwieser Archives, Vaucluse, Syd).

H. REITTERER
MARIE CUCKSON

BOELKE, GRACE FAIRLEY (1870-1948), medical practitioner, was born on 4 July 1870 at South Kingston, Sydney, second of four children of Thomas Charles Robinson, a clerk from Tasmania, and his Sydney-born wife Eliza Agnes, née Butler. Grace passed her junior public examination while attending St Vincent's College, Darlinghurst, and was tutored privately for matricuiation. At the University of Sydney (M.B., Ch.M., 1893) she was awarded the MacCormick [q.v.10] prize for surgery in her third year, was ranked first in the midwifery examination in her finals and was one of the first two women to graduate in medicine. University testimonials referred to her 'zeal, energy and enthusiasm'.

Grace was nominated for a position at the Hospital for Sick Children. Despite excellent references, her application was rejected: the objection was 'not against [Dr Robinson] as an individual but against the female doctor in the abstract'. She was appointed resident medical officer at the Benevolent Asylum, Pitt Street. Five ft 5 ins (165.1 cm) tall, with dark hair and striking, blue eyes, Grace was 'of noted beauty'. On 5 May 1894 at her parents' Double Bay home she married with Lutheran forms Paul Wilhelm Rudolph Boelke, a German-born, fellow medical graduate; they were to live at Manly.

In 1909 Grace became assistant medical inspecting officer with the Department of Public Instruction. After she had held the position for six years, the State branch of the British Medical Association questioned the suitability of her appointment in 1915. She resigned her post and her membership of the B.M.A. The anti-German feeling shown towards her took no account of her activity in 1903 as a member of the women's branch of the British Empire League in Australia.

In 1912 Grace had formed the Professional Women's Association, dedicated to improving social conditions for women and children. She was convenor (1913-26) of the standing committee on health for the National Council of Women of New South Wales, a founding member (1921) of the State branch of the League of Nations Union and vice-president of the Town Planning Association. In 1923-26, as medical director of Berlei [q.v. Burley] Ltd, she had responsibility for the health and welfare of nearly six hundred female employees and for collaborating with designers on the 'correct anatomical lines of their garments'.

Following her husband's death in 1923, Grace had travelled abroad, inquiring into the state of health of women and children, and investigating circumstances in the workplace. In later life she suffered from asthma and moved to Leura in the Blue Mountains. Dr Boelke died on 17 February 1948 at Manly and was cremated with Anglican rites. Childless, she left most of her estate (sworn for probate at £31 429) to the library of the Royal Society of Medicine, London, for the endowment of medical research.

U. Bygott and K. Cable, *Pioneer Women Graduates of the University of Sydney 1881-1921* (Syd, 1985); National Council of Women, *Biennial Reports*, 1913-18; *JRAHS*, 61, pt 4, Dec 1975; *SMH*, 11, 24 Oct 1919, 24 Sept, 17 Oct 1921, 15 Oct 1924, 3 Oct 1925, 11, 23, 25 Mar, 17 Apr 1926; Boelke papers (Univ Syd Archives); information from Sr G. Campbell, Darlinghurst, and Miss B. Heagney, Hist of Medicine L, Roy A'sian College of Physicians, Syd.　　　　　　　LYN BRIGNELL

BOGLE, GILBERT STANLEY (1924-1963), physicist, was born on 5 January 1924 at Wanganui, New Zealand, fourth child of Archibald Hugh Bogle, licensed surveyor, and his wife Bertha Isabel Langley, née Reeve, both New Zealanders. Educated at Wanganui Collegiate School, in 1942 Gilbert entered Victoria University College, Wellington (M.Sc., 1946), to read physics. Although Bogle was eligible for war service in 1945, Professor D. C. H. Florance persuaded the manpower authorities to allow him to remain at university where he was directed to work as an assistant in the laboratory and to extend his honours course over two years.

A talented musician and linguist who was active in student affairs, Bogle went to England in 1947 as a Rhodes scholar and entered Oriel College, Oxford (B.A. Hons, 1949; D.Phil., 1952). Under A. H. Cooke of New College, he worked for two years at the Clarendon laboratory on paramagnetic resonance experiments at very low temperatures and published the results in a series of jointly-authored articles in the *Proceedings of the Physical Society* (London, 1951-55). Bogle's mentors noted that, 'for an experimenter', he had 'an unusually good grasp of the theoretical side'. Nicholas Kurti commended the quality of his research and the speed with which he completed his doctoral thesis which was used by students for several years as 'a kind of textbook'.

On 11 September 1950 at the parish church, Great Dunmow, Essex, Bogle married Vivienne Mary Rich, a schoolteacher and fellow graduate of Victoria University College; they were to have four children, one of whom was born after Gilbert's death. From July 1952 Bogle lectured in physics at the University of Otago, New Zealand, where he established what Florance described as quite a 'Bogle school of low temperature research'. His achievements in research and teaching brought him a senior lectureship in September 1955, but he was outgrowing Otago. 'I think that he is to some extent wasting his abilities there', wrote Cooke. Bogle had applied for a position as senior research officer in the Commonwealth Scientific and Industrial Research Organization's division of physics at the National Standards Laboratory, Sydney. His referees' support was warm and unequivocal: Kurti remembered him as 'a real live wire if ever there was one'.

Appointed for three years from 5 September 1956, Bogle began work with the cryogenics group. By October 1957 he had been given an 'indefinite appointment'. G. H. Briggs, chief of the division, found the new recruit 'noteworthy for his mental powers, his breadth of knowledge, his capacity for original ideas, his drive and enthusiasm, his range of experimental techniques and his outstanding ability as a lecturer'. Believing Bogle to be 'too good a man to tie down to work which did not offer him much scope for his special abilities', Briggs encouraged him to resume his research on paramagnetic resonance.

In recommending Bogle for accelerated advancement, Briggs drew attention to the link between his work and the recent development of maser (microwave amplification by stimulated emission of radiation) technology. Bogle's theoretical and practical contribution to the production of a 21-cm maser amplifier for use in radio astronomy earned him high praise from Briggs's successor R. G. Giovanelli who, in 1960, successfully urged his reclassification as principal research officer. By 1962 Bogle was regarded by his chief as 'the most brilliant member of the staff'. Meanwhile, Bogle had been offered a two-year appointment in 'quantum electronics' at the Bell Telephone Research Laboratories, New Jersey, United States of America. C.S.I.R.O. granted him leave of absence.

On 21 December 1962, shortly before Bogle and his family were due to leave for the U.S.A., he met MARGARET OLIVE CHANDLER, née Morphett (1934-1963), at a Christmas party. Born on 2 April 1934 at Wentworthville, New South Wales, Margaret became a nurse and, on 24 December 1957 at St Stephen's Presbyterian Church, Sydney, married Geoffrey Arnold Chandler, a scientific photographer employed by C.S.I.R.O. Five years later, a housebound mother of two, she was immediately attracted to the engaging 'Gib' Bogle. Encouraged by her husband, she needed little persuading to accept Bogle's offer of a lift home from a New Year's Eve party at Chatswood, to which Bogle had ensured the Chandlers were invited. Some time between 4.45 a.m. and 6.00 a.m. on 1 January 1963 Bogle and Margaret Chandler died in bushland on the eastern bank of the Lane Cove River, near Fullers Bridge, Chatswood.

The discovery of the bodies some 40 feet (12 m) apart—both half-naked, but Bogle's discreetly draped with folded clothing and a piece of carpet, and Chandler's in greater disarray, covered by cardboard cartons—created a mystery that remains unsolved. Baffled police, forensic scientists and the coroner J. J. Loomes were unable to determine what had caused their deaths. While poison seemed the most likely cause, no toxic substance was detected. Was it murder, suicide or accident? Revelations of previous and concurrent infidelities by Bogle and the Chandlers, as well as the libertarianism of the Sydney 'Push' with which Geoffrey Chandler was associated, made the coronial inquiry and police investigations a media circus.

Chandler challenged popular assumptions of his guilt in a candid book, *So You Think I Did It* (Melbourne, 1969), but the police were more suspicious of Margaret Fowler, a scientifically-trained librarian. A jealous Fowler,

for three years Bogle's lover, was a suspect against whom no evidence could be produced. She in turn apparently related the deaths in some way to chemical-warfare research. Both Fowler and Geoffrey Chandler later gave credence to never-substantiated allegations by Catherine Dalton, widow of G. C. J. Dalton [q.v.], that her friend Bogle was assassinated when he was about to disclose Australian Atomic Energy Commission security leaks and American espionage improprieties in Australia. After Peter Wright (a former officer of Britain's M.I.5) claimed that an alleged Soviet spy Sir Roger Hollis had recommended Bogle to the Australian Security Intelligence Organization, Chandler speculated that Bogle had been 'eliminated' as a Soviet agent.

Although discarded in the mid-1960s—along with theories of poisonous gas, dry ice, weed-killer, aphrodisiac and shellfish toxin—the favoured explanation by the late 1980s was death by an accidental overdose (self-administered or unwitting) of lysergic acid diethylamide (L.S.D.); the hallucinogen (supposed to have been produced clandestinely in a C.S.I.R.O. laboratory) would have been untraceable at the time. Bogle's burial in Northern Suburbs cemetery on 13 March 1963, Chandler's cremation two days later and the failure to preserve tissue samples from either body left their deaths a tantalizing enigma.

C. R. Dalton, *Without Hardware* (Canb, 1970); S. Gardiner, *The Commissioner Allan Story* (Syd, 1973); A. Sharpe, *Crimes that Shocked Australia* (Syd, 1982, 1987); A. Atkinson (ed), *Famous Court Cases* (Syd, 1987); B. Toohey and M. Wilkinson, *The Book of Leaks* (Syd, 1987); *SMH*, Jan-June 1963, 22 May 1989; *Daily Mirror* (Syd), 27 Mar 1981; *Sun-Herald* (Syd), 28 May 1989; CSIRO Archives (Canb).   CAMERON HAZLEHURST

BOLAND, HAROLD (1891-1956), shearer and trade unionist, was born on 21 October 1891 at Long Angle, near Grenfell, New South Wales, sixth child of Thomas Charles Edmund Boland, farmer, and his wife Elizabeth, née Tout, both native-born. Having no formal education worth mentioning, except in the 'school of hard knocks', Harry was variously a shearer, wool-presser, sawmiller, tree-feller, fencer and miner in the Bogan River district. He joined the Australian Workers' Union in 1905. Employed as a clerk in Sydney, Boland married a dressmaker Amy Forrest (d. 1954) on 13 April 1914 in the Church of Our Lady of Mount Carmel, Waterloo. In 1920 he became an organizer for the A.W.U., travelling mostly by bicycle between Nyngan and Peak Hill, and along the Cobar-Wilcannia and Bourke tracks.

In search of work in 1923, he went to Queensland where he was employed as a shearer. He was successively the A.W.U.'s Western District organizer (from 1924), district secretary at Longreach, organizer for the Southern District at Gympie and Far Northern District secretary (from 1941) at Cairns. In 1947 he was elected Queensland president and headed the 'largest branch of the largest union in Australia'. Through his involvement in the State branch of the A.W.U., he had developed a close friendship with Clarrie Fallon [q.v.] and became its secretary in 1950. That year he was elected president of the State branch of the Australian Labor Party and joined the federal executive. He was also chairman of the union's newspaper, the *Worker*. Heavily built and physically powerful, Boland had a 'quaint streak of humour' that often left his associates wondering whether or not he was serious. A devout Catholic, he was a member of the Holy Name Society.

In March 1955 Boland was one of six Queensland delegates to the A.L.P. federal conference in Hobart where, following a dispute over the composition of the delegation from Victoria, seventeen delegates from four States agreed to boycott the conference. Five Queensland delegates, including Premier Vince Gair and the State treasurer E. J. Walsh [qq.v.] joined the boycott, leaving Boland as the sole Queenslander to take part in the deliberations. The conference resolved to withdraw official A.L.P. support for the controversial industrial groups (set up in the 1940s by the A.L.P. to fight communist influence in trade unions) of which Boland had long been suspicious.

The Queensland A.W.U. president R. J. Bukowski [q.v.] led the attack against the industrial groups in Queensland, though Boland suspected him of having previously used them to promote his position in the union. When Gair and the other boycotters returned from Hobart, they faced Bukowski's open criticism. Boland remained on cordial terms with Gair, despite having rejected his approaches in Hobart, and played a lesser role in the ensuing controversy. As one of Labor's 'old hands' who was deeply loyal to the party, he was not prepared to canvass its difficulties in public. The subsequent shift in power—when the A.W.U. transferred its support from the parliamentarians to the industrial wing in the Queensland central executive—created the conditions for the official 'split' in the Queensland branch of the A.L.P. in 1957. Some had believed that the conciliatory and experienced Boland might have been able to avoid such a result.

Late in 1955 an industrial dispute that was to last nearly a year erupted in the shearing industry over a cut in the shearing rate. Again called to the forefront, Boland made regular appearances in the State Industrial Court.

Before the dispute was resolved, he died of a coronary occlusion on 25 July 1956 at his Tingalpa home and was buried in Hemmant cemetery. His daughter and two sons survived him.

N. Mackerras and A. O'Shannessy, *A Gathering of Bolands* (priv pub, np, nd); D. J. Murphy et al (eds), *Labor in Power* (Brisb, 1980); R. Fitzgerald, *A History of Queensland from 1915 to the early 1980s* (Brisb, 1984); *Worker* (Brisb), 28 Feb, 14, 21, 28 Mar 1955, 30 July 1956; *Courier-Mail*, 16 Mar 1955, 26 July 1956; J. Moran, Interview with Mrs D. Vowles (copy in H. Boland file, OL).

JOHN MICHAEL MORAN

BOLLIGER, ADOLPH (1897-1962), biochemist, was born on 8 October 1897 at Zürich, Switzerland, eldest son of Adolf Bolliger, master baker, and his wife Thekla Eugenie, née Ackermann. Educated at Baden and at Zürich Gymnasium, young Bolliger matriculated at the University of Zürich in 1917. His studies there were interrupted by military service with the Swiss Army and by a semester at the University of Geneva (1918); in 1919 he entered the University of Basle (Ph.D., 1922). On 1 August 1922 at the registry office, Zürich, he married Clara Coradi. After working in the chemical and dye industry at Konstanz, Germany, in 1923 Bolliger migrated to the United States of America. As a biochemist, he specialized in cardiovascular disease at Henry Ford Hospital, Detroit. In 1926 the American Medical Association awarded him and two colleagues silver and gold medals for their research.

A meeting with the Australian surgeon Gordon Craig [q.v.8] led Bolliger to accept a proposed post at Royal Prince Alfred Hospital. He arrived in Sydney with his wife and two sons in July 1928. Two years later he was appointed director of the Gordon Craig Research Laboratories at the University of Sydney. He had a wide-ranging interest in medical and biological subjects which left him open to some criticism on the ground of superficiality. Individually and jointly he published over 170 papers and short communications, including studies in analytical and organic chemistry, biochemistry, anatomy, physiology and experimental pathology. Bolliger was naturalized in 1935. Divorced in Switzerland, he married a laboratory technician Dorothy May Dark on 16 October 1937 at the district registrar's office, North Sydney; they were to have three sons.

From 1938 Bolliger turned his attention to various aspects of the life of marsupials. His work on hormone-produced changes in the sex organs and their accessories of the possum, *Trichosurus vulpecula*, was significant. In 1955 he was appointed reader and two years later the university conferred on him a D.Sc. for his chemical studies of integuments and his observations on marsupials. Active in a range of scholarly societies, Bolliger contributed papers at scientific meetings in Australia and abroad. He was a member (from 1933), a councillor and president (1945-46) of the Royal Society of New South Wales, presided over section N of the Australian and New Zealand Association for the Advancement of Science meeting in Perth in 1947, and was a founding member (1958) of the Australian Mammal Society. Awarded the (E. H.) Rennie and the Henry G. Smith [qq.v.11] medals respectively in 1936 and 1947 by the (Royal) Australian Chemical Institute, he also received the local Royal Society's medal for 1961.

Bolliger had a charming personality, but his hearty manner tended to overwhelm some people. His main recreations were hiking and skiing, and he belonged to the Swiss Club of New South Wales. After Dorothy's death in June 1961, he married a 28-year-old secretary Jocelyn Anne Elliot on 28 September 1962 at the Evangelical Lutheran Church, Goulburn Street, Sydney. Survived by his wife and by his five sons, he died of a cerebral haemorrhage on 22 October 1962 in Sydney Hospital and was cremated with Anglican rites.

Roy Soc of NSW, *J and Procs*, 96, 1962-63, p 171, 97, 1963-64, p 126; *Aust J of Science*, 26, no 2, 1963, p 42; *MJA*, 27 Apr 1963, p 635; Univ Syd Union, *Union Recorder*, 26 Sept 1963, p 227; Roy Soc of NSW Archives (Syd); Naturalization file, A440/1 item 51/12/1922 [34/10485] (AA).

R. BHATHAL

BONIWELL, MARTIN CHARLES (1883-1967), public servant, was born on 25 February 1883 at Surbiton, Surrey, England, son of Charles Edmund Boniwell, builder's foreman, and his wife Martha Ann, née Bewers. The family migrated to Hobart where Charles established himself as a builder. Educated at The Hutchins School, in May 1899 Martin entered the Tasmanian Public Service as a clerk. He studied part time at the University of Tasmania (LL.B., 1911) and became a prominent oarsman. In May 1912 he transferred to the Commonwealth Attorney-General's Department, Melbourne. On 19 September that year he married Ruby Mary Okines with Anglican rites at All Saints Church, Hobart.

Designated chief clerk and legal-assistant in 1921, Boniwell was admitted in 1924 as a barrister and solicitor of the Supreme Court of Tasmania and of the High Court of Australia. In 1926 he went to Geneva as adviser to the Australian delegation to the seventh session of the League of Nations. Moved with his department to Canberra in 1927, he was promoted assistant-secretary and assistant parliamentary draftsman in February 1932. A shortage of qualified officers ensured that his skills in the wording of legislation were much in demand. Seconded to the Treasury for two weeks in 1934, he drafted amendments to the Income Tax Assessment Act necessitated by the recommendations of the 1933-34 royal commission on taxation. He was appointed C.B.E. in 1936.

During the absence of (Sir) George Knowles [q.v.9] at the 1937 Imperial Conference, Boniwell acted as Commonwealth solicitor-general. He formulated the Empire Air Service (England to Australia) Act (1938) which ratified agreements between the British and Australian governments and their respective national carriers for the provision of a flying-boat service. Following criticism over the disastrous crash of the airliner *Kyeema* at Mount Dandenong, Victoria, on 25 October 1938, Boniwell was chosen in December to be a member of the departmental committee which investigated civil aviation administration, criticized existing shortcomings and proposed organizational arrangements for the new Department of Civil Aviation.

In February 1939 he succeeded J. C. Westhoven as public service arbitrator and returned to Melbourne to take up the post. Boniwell's appointment was opposed by the staff associations and his early determinations confirmed their members' fears that he would 'lean towards the official side' in making remuneration awards. The National Security (Economic Organization) Regulations circumscribed his powers during World War II, but he continued to anger the associations in peacetime by behaving more like a judge than an arbitrator. Insisting on his independence, he refused routinely to endorse agreements which they had made with the public service commissioner. Boniwell was relieved in 1946 and transferred to Canberra as acting parliamentary draftsman. Confirmed in the position in 1948, he retired next year.

Boniwell's recreations included golf and gardening. He died on 6 January 1967 at Caulfield, Melbourne, and was cremated; his wife and four daughters survived him.

G. E. Caiden, *Career Service* (Melb, 1965); H. E. Renfree, *History of the Crown Solicitor's Office* (Canb, 1970); J. Gunn, *The Defeat of Distance* (Brisb, 1985); *SMH*, 23 June 1936, 11 Mar, 2 Apr 1937, 10, 30 Dec 1938, 9 Feb 1939; ANGAM CP 162, Summary note, *and* CP 402/1, *and* A 432 (AA, Canb) *and* MP 1353/3 (AA, Melb).

CAMERON HAZLEHURST
MARGOT KERLEY

BONNEY, EDMUND GARNET (1883-1959), journalist and public servant, was born on 24 November 1883 at Paddington, Sydney, son of William Henry Bonney, a draftsman from New York, and his wife Annie Maria, née Cooper, a Sydneysider. William died in Edmund's early childhood and Annie remarried. Educated at a public school at Newcastle, Edmund moved with his family to Wyalong, then Coonamble, engaging in a variety of bush jobs; he later went to sea. He was employed as a compositor at Dunedin, New Zealand, when he married 18-year-old Elizabeth Julia Johnson on 9 July 1907 in the local registrar's office; they were to have two children before being divorced in 1928.

Taking up journalism at Grafton, New South Wales, at the age of 26, Bonney worked for the *Sydney Morning Herald* then moved to Melbourne about 1917 to join the *Argus*. He was general president of the Australian Journalists' Association in 1920-21, news editor of the *Sun News-Pictorial* in 1922-24 and became chief of staff on the Melbourne *Herald* in 1926. On 13 February 1928 in the Collins Street registry office he married Minnie Hester. From 1932 he was editor-in-chief of the Adelaide *News* and *Mail*. Having spent a holiday motoring across the United States of America, in 1938 he returned to the *Argus* as editor. Appointed chief publicity censor for the Commonwealth in April 1941, he immediately took a tough and uncompromising line in implementing War Cabinet policy: not only was material detrimental to military security proscribed; any news or comment which the enemy might use to damage the morale of Australians or their allies was also prohibited. Bonney transferred to Canberra in December.

Following a review of its functions, in October 1943 he was made director-general of the expanded Department of Information. The decision next month—to make W. Macmahon Ball (controller of the Australian Broadcasting Commission's shortwave department) responsible to Bonney—led to a bitter confrontation and to Macmahon Ball's resignation. Encouraged by Arthur Calwell [q.v.], the minister for information, Bonney persisted in censoring the publication of any material which could create an unfavourable impression of Australia abroad. Sections of the press argued that he was being unduly severe and that he was restricting commentary for political purposes. Conflict with the Newspaper Proprietors' Association came to a head when Bonney's department suppressed (Sir) Frank Packer's [q.v.] Sydney *Sunday Telegraph* of 16 April 1944 for appearing with blank spaces that indicated where censorship had occurred. On 17 April all the Sydney dailies carried the story and were seized. That day the High Court of Australia issued an injunction against the Commonwealth government; by 19 May a code of censorship principles had been accepted by the contending parties.

Loyal to his political masters, Bonney was a superb administrator who attracted similar loyalty from his staff. It was to his credit that, as peace approached, his department was able to take on a new role and advertise Australia in foreign countries. The publicity aimed to attract migrants, tourists and trade, and to promote the nation's contribution to the war effort in order to support Australia's claims in postwar settlements. In 1948-51 Bonney was director of the Australian News and Information Bureau in New York; from 1952 he was the British Travel Association's special representative in Australia. A tall, well-built man, with a 'thatch of iron-grey hair' in middle age, he had twinkling, blue eyes and smoked a straight-stemmed pipe. Survived by his wife, and by the daughter of his first marriage, he died on 27 February 1959 at Avalon, Sydney, and was cremated with Anglican rites.

P. Hasluck, *The Government and the People 1942-1945* (Canb, 1970); J. Hilvert, *Blue Pencil Warriors* (Brisb, 1984); *People* (Syd), 6 May 1953; *Newspaper News*, 6 Mar 1959; *Advertiser*, 28 Feb 1959.

JOHN HILVERT

BONYTHON, CONSTANCE JEAN (1891-1977), charity worker, was born on 7 November 1891 in Adelaide, elder daughter of Charles Herbert Warren, merchant, and his wife Alice Maria, née Downer. A fun-loving girl, Jean enjoyed an affectionate and carefree childhood at Elgin, College Park, but in nearby Hackney she and her sister 'Bobbie' saw hardship and they raised money to buy Christmas toys for poor children. Educated at Dryburgh House School, Payneham, and Geelong Church of England Girls' Grammar School, Victoria, in 1910 Jean attended the University of Adelaide where she enjoyed 'the social side'.

At her début in 1911, she met the widower (Sir) John Lavington Bonython [q.v.7] whom she married on 11 December 1912 in St John's Anglican Church, Halifax Street, thereby becoming 'the Baby Mayoress' of Adelaide (her husband was mayor in 1911-13 and lord mayor in 1927-30). In addition, at 21 Jean became stepmother to three children and mistress of Carhayes, Wakefield Street. By 1920 she had borne (Sir) Lavington two sons and a daughter, and found time to write her *Verses* (1922). The Bonythons also owned Eurilla, their holiday house in the hills, and St Corantyn where they entertained in town: in 1928 Jean organized in one week three mayoral balls and a garden party with 6500 guests at Victoria Park racecourse. She was the 'hostess of the year'.

The Depression proved 'the most strenuous and nerve-wracking period' of her life. In her efforts to help the 'many people afflicted', she shopped for the Lord Mayor's Unemployment Relief Fund, spoke on radio and wrote to South Australian women's guilds for assistance. The response was generous. In 1930 the Unemployed Sales Depot opened in Stephens Place, Adelaide, where craftwork made by unemployed ex-servicemen was sold; Jean helped at the depot on Monday mornings for sixteen years and each week arranged a floral display in the window. Her husband was knighted in 1935.

Renowned for her leadership and hard work, she was a member of some twenty-five committees and made her greatest contributions to those concerned with women and children. She had joined the Halifax Street Free (later Keith Sheridan) Kindergarten in 1913 (president 1925-71) and the committee of the South Australian Kindergarten Union in 1924 (chairman 1933-52). When the Lady Gowrie [q.v.9] Child Centre opened in 1940, Lady Bonython was its chairman and remained so until 1971. She was a founding delegate to the Australian Association for Pre-School Development and, on retiring in 1952, became life vice-president. That year the Jean Bonython Kindergarten at Belair was named after her. Having joined the committee of the School for Mothers' Institute and Baby Health Centre (later Mothers' and Babies' Health Association) in 1925, she was its president (1953-65) and patroness (1974): in the former capacity, she often visited country centres and received débutantes at balls. Lady Bonython was appointed O.B.E. in 1954. Adelaide's Torrens House Mothercraft Hospital named its Jean Bonython Wing in 1966.

One of the two women on the centenary celebrations committee in 1936, Jean gave Adelaide its first floral carpet, the forerunner of annual Flower Days. A patron of young artists, she was a life member of the Royal South Australian Society of Arts. In 1939 the Australian Broadcasting Commission formed the Adelaide Symphony Orchestra and she was president (1939-64) of its ladies' committee (later the South Australian Symphony Orchestra subscribers' committee). Among the other causes she espoused were those of the Royal Society for the Prevention of Cruelty to Animals, the Royal District and Bush Nursing Society of South Australia, and the Queen Victoria Maternity Hospital. At a meeting of the latter's ladies committee, she said, 'I do wish we were called "women" . . . The term "ladies" has come down so sadly'.

Her husband died in 1960. With her sense of design, her passion for flowers, her collec-

tion of Staffordshire figures and her cats, Lady Bonython created harmonious surroundings. Her personal wealth was not great, but she was rich in kindness. Tall, elegant and beautifully dressed, she was both confident and intelligent, although in public speaking she made many gaffes. She was known as 'one of the good things of Adelaide'. A stroke in 1970 brought seven, dragging years of pain, relieved by dictating her reminiscences. Her son Warren edited and published them as *I'm No Lady* (1981). Survived by her three children, Jean Bonython died at Stirling on 11 June 1977 and was cremated.

Kindergarten Union of SA, *Annual Report*, 1913-71; Mothers and Babies Health Assn of SA, *Annual Report*, 1925-77; *Advertiser* (Adel), 16 June 1933; information from Mr C. W. Bonython, Magill, Mrs M. Ellicott, Nth Glenelg, Miss H. Artlett, Hackney, and Miss B. Davis, St Georges, Adel.

JOYCE GIBBERD

BOOTH, ANGELA ELIZABETH JOSEPHINE (1869-1954), eugenicist, was born on 27 October 1869 at Liverpool, Lancashire, England, and registered as Elizabeth, daughter of Thomas Plover, labourer, and his illiterate wife Eliza, née Hall. Despite her humble origins, Elizabeth claimed to have been educated at Liverpool and 'on the Continent'. In 1896 she migrated to Australia and on 7 January 1897, styling herself Angela Elizabeth Josephine, married a medical practitioner and divorcee JAMES BOOTH (1861-1944) at St Andrew's Anglican Cathedral, Sydney.

In 1901 the Booths moved to Broken Hill where they took a keen interest in community affairs: James served as a non-Labor alderman (1909-16), founded the local art gallery and co-founded the Broken Hill Nursing Society. Angela was concerned with the role that women might take to improve social and political conditions: she joined the Women's Political Association and the Liberal Education Society, and addressed audiences on the need for women to participate in public life.

Shortly before World War I the Booths settled in North Melbourne where Angela involved herself in the middle-class, activist community. Resigning from the W.P.A. in 1915 in protest against its pacifist stance, she supported conscription and saw the war as morally correct. Like many others, however, she was alarmed at the spread of venereal diseases and wanted to rebuild a stable and healthy postwar society.

In her writing and lecturing Booth held that the wise management of sexuality was essential. A dedicated eugenicist, she called for the eradication of venereal diseases, the elimination of prostitution and the planned birth of healthy, wanted children. During World War I she had founded the Association to Combat the Social Evil and delivered an address on prostitution to a large Workers' Educational Association conference in Sydney. Optimistic that the 'sex problem' could be remedied by social reform, she maintained that women were forced into prostitution through economic necessity and that prostitution was encouraged by a double standard of morality. Booth's solution was threefold. Women must receive equal pay; they must become active in government; and the public must be educated in 'racial responsibility': sexual restraint and planned parenthood would lead to a better society.

While her husband was president of the Australian Literature Society (1927) and of the Playlovers' Club (1929), Angela was politically active as a conservative. President of the North Melbourne branch of the National Federation and a leading member of both the Australian Women's National League and the Women's Citizen Movement, she enjoyed the support of such groups as the Housewives' Association. She was councillor (1926-33) for the Warrandyte riding of the Doncaster and Templestowe shire where the Booths owned a property, Nilga. In 1927 she was appointed a justice of the peace. Later that year she unsuccessfully sought Nationalist endorsement for State parliament and in 1929 failed to win the Legislative Assembly seat of Brighton as an Independent Nationalist. In her campaigns she urged women to vote together, believing that the concerns uniting them were more important than party politics.

The Depression seriously damaged Angela's faith in liberal reform. Rather than criticizing the capitalist system, she grew convinced that the alleged proliferation of 'mental defectives' in society was the greatest single cause of unemployment and crime. From the late 1920s the Booths argued that legislation should be enacted to provide for 'the sterilisation of the unfit'. As chairman of the North Melbourne Children's Court, James introduced psychological testing of delinquents. He warned that 'Moron breeds Moron'. The Booths met like-minded reformers through the Racial Hygiene Association of New South Wales.

In 1936 James and Angela became founding members of the Eugenics Society of Victoria, a body which included prominent citizens dedicated to the promotion of selective breeding. In its early years Angela served as the society's vice-president. With its president W. E. Agar [q.v.7], she was one of the group's major proponents of sterilization, which she presented as an altruistic operation to spare the unfit from the burden of parent-

hood and to protect society from racial degeneration. In 1938 the Eugenics Society published her lecture, *Voluntary Sterilization for Human Betterment*, a policy for which it unsuccessfully lobbied the Victorian government next year.

Following James's death in 1944, Angela remained on Nilga. Age and distance curbed her activities. She returned to Melbourne about 1950 to live at Toorak and later at Sandringham where she died on 5 September 1954 and was cremated. A stepdaughter survived her.

M. Lake and F. Kelly (eds), *Double Time, Women in Victoria, 150 Years* (Melb, 1985); *Housewife* (Melb), 5 Dec 1929; *Woman Voter*, 8 July 1915; *Herald* (Melb), 27 Aug 1926, 4 May 1929, 3 Sept 1931; *Age* (Melb), 7 Aug 1944, 10 Sept 1954; *Argus*, 7 May 1921, 28 Aug 1926, 14 Nov 1929, 10 Apr 1934.
GRANT MCBURNIE

BOOTH, SIR CHARLES SYLVESTER (1897-1970), businessman, was born on 23 February 1897 at Halifax, Yorkshire, England, son of John Thomas Booth, schoolmaster, and his wife Ada, née Wilson. Educated at King Edward's School, Birmingham, Charles enlisted in the British Army in World War I and was commissioned in the Royal Engineers Special Reserve. He was attached to the Australian Corps in France with the local rank of major and was mentioned in dispatches. After the war he served a deferred apprenticeship in mechanical engineering with Armstrong Whitworth & Co. Ltd at Newcastle-upon-Tyne.

In 1923 Booth came to Australia as secretary and accountant to a contracting company set up by Armstrong Whitworth & Co. Ltd. In 1929 he was appointed Australian representative of Walmsley Chas. & Co., later Walmsley (Bury) Ltd, a member of the Armstrong Whitworth group and one of the leading British pulp-and-paper engineering firms. He married Ellen Myra Grant, a trained nurse, on 22 September 1939 at the Toorak Presbyterian Church, Melbourne. They lived quietly, with shared interests in photography, gardening and collecting paintings; they were to remain childless.

One of two businessmen outside the firm who joined the postwar planning committee of Australian Paper Manufacturers Ltd in 1942, Booth was made a director two years later. He left Walmsley in 1946 to become assistant managing director of A.P.M. and worked to Sir Herbert Gepp [q.v.8] whose restless, turbulent spirit was propelling the company to adopt new techniques, establish new mills and acquire additional forests. Succeeding Gepp in 1948, Booth steered A.P.M. through a period in which it faced financial crisis from its over-ambitious expansion programme, challenges to its monopoly, and the hostility of those who opposed its entry into the field of container-making. Although he had received no formal training in management, he established an effective company structure, secured new banking arrangements and made peace with the firm's customers. The trade unions found him approachable. Convinced of the importance of management training for executives, he was a member of the University of Melbourne Summer School of Business Administration from its inception in 1954. He succeeded Essington Lewis [q.v.10] in 1959 as chairman of the Australian Administrative Staff College, Mount Eliza, and held that office for ten years.

A devout Presbyterian, Booth had supported 'A Call to the People of Australia', the national movement promoted in 1951 by the lieutenant-governor of Victoria, Sir Edmund Herring, which aimed to boost moral and spiritual values in postwar Australia. Booth was also a trustee of the Toorak Presbyterian (later Uniting) Church and a member of its board of management.

When he retired as managing director in 1959 and became chairman of A.P.M., the company was securely established as the country's leading pulp-and-paper maker. Under his direction it had pioneered the use of native eucalypts for papermaking and become the largest private forester in Australia. In 1959 Booth accepted an invitation from the secretary-general to be a member of the United Nations' committee on industrialization. At the request of the Commonwealth government, he represented Australia at a conference at Cambridge, England, on administrative organization for economic development which was arranged by the Royal Institute of Public Administration.

Having retired as chairman in 1966, Booth remained on the A.P.M. board until his death. Stockily built and 5 ft 9 ins (175.3) tall, he moved at a leisurely and deliberate pace. With blue eyes framed by gold-rimmed spectacles, his pale face was seldom animated. Although not a gregarious person, he was comfortable among his peers. He enjoyed his membership of the Savage Club, and later joined the Melbourne and other interstate clubs. There was an old-fashioned formality in his office relationships: no Christian names except for one or two of his closest colleagues; strict punctuality for all meetings; and the secretarial staff knew that he would not tolerate split infinitives, or allow papers to be perforated with multiple pin-holes. While some found him unduly fastidious, none questioned his competence or his achievements.

Booth was chairman of the Victorian committee of the Industrial Fund for the Advancement of Scientific Education in Schools and of the Melbourne board of the Bankers' and Traders' Insurance Co. Ltd. He was a member of the State committee of the Winston Churchill Memorial Fellowships, the University of Melbourne appointments board, the council of the Institute of Public Affairs and the Victorian Overseas Foundation Association. Appointed to the Order of the White Rose of Finland in 1960 and C.B.E. in 1964, he was knighted in 1969. Sir Charles died at his Toorak home on 27 June 1970 and was cremated; his wife survived him. His estate was sworn for probate at $178 764. In 1973 his fine collection of Australian art was sold by the auctioneers, Christie.

S. Sayers, *Ned Herring* (Melb, 1980); E. K. Sinclair, *The Spreading Tree* (Syd, 1990); *IPA Review*, 24, July-Sept 1970; APM Ltd Archives, Melb; information from Rev D. Hodges, Toorak Uniting Church, Melb, and Sir G. Allard, Kooyong, Melb.

E. K. SINCLAIR

BOOTH, EDGAR HAROLD (1893-1963), soldier, university lecturer and administrator, was born on 12 February 1893 at Petersham, Sydney, second son of John Booth, a bank clerk from Scotland, and his English-born wife Maud Theresa, née Martyn. Edgar received a good education at Chatswood Public and Fort Street Model schools under A. J. Kilgour [q.v.9], but always resented the fact that his brothers and sister were taught in Britain or at private schools in Sydney. In 1911-13 he studied engineering at the University of Sydney (B.Sc., 1914; D.Sc., 1936) and in March 1915 was appointed an acting-lecturer and demonstrator in physics. He joined the Sydney University Scouts and was commissioned in the Citizen Military Forces in August.

Transferring to the Australian Imperial Force in June 1916, Booth sailed for England with artillery reinforcements on 14 September and saw action in France and Belgium. Promoted lieutenant in March 1917, he commanded a heavy trench mortar battery of the 5th Division. He was awarded the Military Cross for his actions on 6 September: while bombarding a strong position in the Ypres sector, he came under continuous shellfire and was wounded; although forced to move his post, he performed his tasks exactly to schedule. He wrote the unit diary which contains a graphic account of the action.

Returning to Sydney in April 1919, Booth resumed lecturing at the university and became well known for his imaginative and effective teaching. He was proud of his war service and much of his subsequent career had a military flavour. After a persistent courtship he married 19-year-old Jessie Annie ('Kitty') Wilcox of Darling Point at

St Mark's Anglican Church on 9 April 1924: the groom was in uniform.

Booth's work as president (1923-25) and as a director in the 1920s of the Sydney University Union showed him to be an energetic and able administrator; he was also president (1928-32) of the Science Teachers' Association of New South Wales. He wrote a successful textbook on physics, co-authored another with Phyllis Nicol [q.v.] and published a number of articles. His major research on geophysical exploration stemmed from his association with the Imperial Geophysical Experimental Survey in 1929-31. Awarded his doctorate in 1936, he was president (1936-37) of the Royal Society of New South Wales. In 1937 (Sir) Robert Wallace [q.v.12] chose him to initiate the New England University College at Armidale.

As warden Booth was responsible for all aspects of student and academic administration, and for the close and sometimes difficult relations with the University of Sydney. He proved tireless in promoting the college and identified himself with its future as an independent university. Booth created a distinct atmosphere on campus by insisting that students eat all meals at Booloominbah (even when most of the undergraduates had to be accommodated in the town) and ensured that they learned the arts of formal dining. Strict but friendly, he took seriously his role *in loco parentis*. His major triumph was to marshal politicians, public servants and local citizens to prevent the army from taking over the college in 1942 for a field-hospital.

Booth annoyed many at the University of Sydney by persistently pushing for autonomy and in early 1945 was embroiled in a nasty dispute over the wording of minutes of a meeting. Soon after the incident he announced his resignation. He probably used his Armidale contacts, especially J. P. Abbott [q.v.], to secure an appointment as chairman of the International Wool Secretariat and representative of the Australian Wool Board in London. Booth promoted the use of wool by leading fashion designers and was vice-president of the Clothing Institute in Britain. He liked London, though not its weather, and was back in Sydney by 1949, at something of a loose end.

He served terms on the Standards Association of Australia and on the Australian National Research Council, and belonged to the Australian and University clubs, Sydney, and the Junior Carlton Club, London. The University of New England conferred a doctorate of science on him in 1955. Booth was 5 ft 10½ ins (179.1 cm) tall and solidly built. He liked good food and wine, possessed a ready sense of humour which could incline to the Rabelaisian, but had an authoritarian style and at times lacked tact. Survived by his wife,

son and daughter, he died of cancer on 18 December 1963 at his Vaucluse home and was cremated. His organizing abilities, energy and desire for recognition had done much to ensure the survival of the Armidale college. Norman Carter's [q.v.7] portrait of Booth is held by the University of New England.

B. Mitchell, *House on the Hill* (Armidale, NSW, 1988); *UNE Union Record*, Mar 1964; Roy Soc NSW, *J and Procs*, 97, July 1965, p 222; B. Mitchell, 'One Man's War', Armidale and District Hist Soc, *J and Procs*, 31, Apr 1988; War diary, 5th Aust Field Artillery Brigade (AWM); UNE Archives.

BRUCE MITCHELL

BOOTH, JOSEPH JOHN (1886-1965), Anglican archbishop, was born on 26 May 1886 at Middlesbrough, Yorkshire, the posthumous and only child of Joseph Booth, pawnbroker, by his wife, Mary Elizabeth, née Barker. Leaving Bell School, Middlesbrough, at the age of 13 (when his mother died), he worked as a farm labourer and then as traveller for a grocery firm. At 15, when he was confirmed in the Anglican Church, Booth was also attending services in a Methodist chapel: there he found friendship and eventually a vocation to the ministry. Lacking formal schooling and family connexions, he emigrated to Australia where he anticipated that his 'gumption and grit', together with his independent spirit, would be better appreciated.

He arrived in Melbourne in 1910, settled in Footscray and encountered a different situation from the one he had left: whereas the Methodist Church was unwelcoming, in the vigorous Anglican parish of St John's he found cordiality and spiritual nourishment. Booth resolved to seek Anglican orders. To support himself until he could begin training, he initially worked in the grocery firm of Moran & Cato [q.v.7] Pty Ltd and later as a millhand in the Colonial Ammunition Co. Ltd. In 1913 he entered Ridley College and next year became a licentiate in theology. Made deacon in 1914 and ordained priest on 21 December 1915, he served his curacy at St Stephen's, Richmond.

On 19 September 1916 Booth was appointed chaplain in the Australian Imperial Force; reaching France, he was posted in January 1917 to the 2nd Infantry Brigade and attached to the 8th Battalion on the Western Front. The letters which he sent to his fiancée from the troop-ship and the battlefields give a frank account of life in the trenches during some of the worst fighting of the war and show the writer going about his duties with complete commitment to the needs of the troops. For his courage during the fighting in

France at Lagnicourt and Quéant in April, he was awarded the Military Cross. His nineteen months in the trenches showed Booth that he had special gifts for working with men and that he could earn the respect and affection of soldiers of all ranks; the experience removed any remaining regrets which he harboured about the circumstances of his upbringing.

When his appointment terminated in January 1919, Booth became vicar at St Paul's, Fairfield, Melbourne. On 30 April at St Columb's Anglican Church, Hawthorn, he married Beryl Gertrude Bradshaw. He studied at the University of Melbourne (B.A., 1922) and, from 1924, while vicar at St Paul's, Geelong, worked towards an M.A., but was excluded from the examination as he had not attended the required number of lectures. His love of reading and history survived this rebuff, though his respect for academics did not.

The 'most prominent of the younger school of clergymen around Melbourne', Booth remained at Geelong until 1932. By then the Anglican Church in Victoria was suffering hardship: the parishes felt the effects of the Depression; St Paul's Cathedral faced the decreasing value of its endowments; and the Melbourne diocese was embarrassed with financial responsibility for several Church schools. After he had conducted a successful campaign to raise money to complete the cathedral spires, Booth was moved to Melbourne as organizing secretary of the Home Mission Fund. In 1934 he became Melbourne's first coadjutor bishop, with the title of bishop of Geelong; at the same time, he held the archdeaconries of Dandenong, Melbourne and Geelong.

Booth and Archbishop Head [q.v.9] made an excellent team. Head's scholarly interests and administrative skills were complemented by Booth's local knowledge and practical insights; a bond of mutual affection reinforced their mutual respect. When Head died in December 1941, Booth was on a tour of duty (September 1941 to January 1942) as senior chaplain at A.I.F. Headquarters in the Middle East. He returned with all speed to administer the diocese and in April 1942 was enthroned as archbishop.

Remembered more for his character and personality than for any intellectual or visionary leadership, Booth had—according to his coadjutor bishop John McKie—the qualities of a Yorkshireman: toughness, directness, honesty, integrity and, above all, a sense of reality. With a fine voice, Booth was a persuasive speaker and popular preacher. A good mixer, confident and totally without 'side', he possessed natural authority. His management of synod, sometimes by direct and terse intervention, became legendary. All his gifts were dedicated to his diocese. He was barely concerned with anything outside it—certainly not with the constitutional debates that preoccupied the Anglican Church during his episcopate. At the vital general synods of 1950 and 1955 he did not speak, leaving McKie to carry the Melbourne case. Although Booth attended the Evanston Assembly of the World Council of Churches in the United States of America and the Anglican Church Congress at Minnesota in 1954, he showed little interest in the growing ecumenical movement or in the affairs of the worldwide Anglican Communion. His strong pastoral sense was evident in his care for his clergy, in the establishment (largely with state funds) of homes for the elderly and in the setting up of the Melbourne Diocesan Centre to promote the ministry in industrial suburbs.

From 1952, when his diabetes was diagnosed, Booth began to slow down, but his work did not suffer. Having identified the new generation of leaders (two of whom subsequently became archbishops) and given them scope to exercise their gifts, he retired in 1956, leaving the diocese in good heart and ready to respond to the initiatives of his successor Archbishop (Sir) Frank Woods. Booth had received a D.D. (Lambeth) in 1943 and been appointed C.M.G. in 1954. He died on 31 October 1965 in East Melbourne and was cremated; his wife and two of their three daughters survived him. A portrait by James Quinn [q.v.11] hangs in the chapter-house of St Paul's Cathedral.

A. de Q. Robin, *Making Many Rich* (Melb, 1978); J. McKie, *Four Archbishops* (Melb, 1983); Booth letters, 1916-19 (LaTL); information from Bishops R. Dann, Canterbury, Melb, and J. A. Grant, Melb.   K. A. R. HORN

BOROVANSKY, EDOUARD (1902-1959), ballet director, was born on 24 February 1902 at Prerov, Moravia (Czechoslovakia), seventh child of Frantisek Skrecek, railway clerk, and his wife Arnosta. He was christened Eduard Josef. A plain but by no means impoverished village life kept him in touch with folk-dance, and with Czech and German music. The Church, which he was later to abandon, provided Catholic doctrine, ritual and art. On leaving school, he worked as an accountant before being called up for military service in the Slovakian air force.

At 19, a more or less untaught baritone, Skrecek joined the chorus of the Olomouc Opera Company but, thanks to his early gymnastic training, transferred to the *corps de ballet* almost at once. In a time of growing nationalism, a stage career among local singers and dancers could satisfy idealism, as well as providing a modest income. In September 1923 he successfully auditioned for the Prague National Theatre, focus of many Czech aspirations, and thereafter worked his way through chorus parts and crowd scenes, a handsome masculine presence, if not a highly accomplished technician. After watching Anna Pavlova's performances in Prague, in 1928 he gained a place in her corps and changed his name to Borowanski. His career as a dancer of character roles was securely launched, and internationalism began to replace his earlier sense of where his talents and ambitions should lead.

His first appearance with the Pavlova Ballet was in Hamburg, Germany; seasons in Britain, South America and Asia followed. As principal dance-mime with the company, he toured Australia in 1929, and was delighted by the enthusiasm and friendliness of audiences. The Pavlova Ballet, however, existed only for the sake of the ballerina herself, and, on her death a year later, the company disappeared. With his companion—the Russian-born XENIA NICOLAEVA Krüger, née Smirnoff (1903-1985), whose Bolshoi-based training was far more thorough than his own—Edouard Borovansky, as he was now known, pieced out a living in Paris, then Prague and Berlin, mostly by teaching children in makeshift studios. He was to marry Xenia, a divorcee, on 14 October 1933 at the register office, Westminster, London.

Not until 1932 was he fully employed again, in Colonel de Basil's Ballet Russe de Monte Carlo. Among his roles with this famous, intrigue-ridden roadshow were the Strong Man in *Le Beau Danube,* Polkan in *Le Coq d'Or* and the Shopkeeper of *La Boutique Fantasque.* He also rehearsed and shepherded supernumeraries in ballets requiring crowds, and, as a much-travelled performer in his thirties, held considerable authority among the dancers themselves. All this was good preparation for a directorial career, and, after the company (now renamed The Royal Covent Garden Russian Ballet) visited Australia in 1938, Borovansky and his wife decided to remain. Czechoslovakia had been taken over by Hitler; within months Europe would be at war. Whatever future there might be for ballet in the antipodes, there was no immediate prospect of turning back.

Above a shop selling devotional artefacts, shaken by the rattling trams of Elizabeth Street, the Borovanskys established their Melbourne Academy of Russian Ballet where 'Classical and Character Dancing, Mime and Make Up' were to be taught. Instruction was basically Xenia's field, Boro himself acting rather as producer and entrepreneur. From the start, he plunged himself into the realities of the local scene. He might present himself as a cosmopolitan, a man of the European theatre, but holding aloof was hardly his style. His studio was hired in conjunction with

Eunice Weston, a respected teacher of dance: the first Borovansky students appeared under the aegis of existing schools, or as contributors to National Health Week in 1939, or to the *Spectacular Historical Pageant Representing the Growth of the British Empire* (1940). But by December 1940 the Borovansky Australian Ballet Company was able to fill the small Comedy Theatre with a programme of new and old ballets, and a troupe of dancers headed by Laurel Martyn.

Queensland-born Martyn had shone in small roles with the Vic-Wells Ballet, London, before returning to Australia. A dramatic dancer of unusual range, she was also one of the most intelligent women Borovansky ever employed; it was a sign of his own intelligence that he provided opportunities for Martyn's creativity to flourish. Even before his first, two-night season at the Comedy, he had encouraged the formation of the Melbourne Ballet Club where new choreography could be seen. Under its auspices, on a stage inside the Borovansky studio, Martyn's *Sigrid* began its long-lasting Australian career (over six hundred performances). Another outstanding young dancer, Dorothy Stevenson, choreographed *Sea Legend,* with Australian music, decor and costumes, while, working with designer William Constable, Martyn produced a powerful expressionist piece, *En Saga,* on the theme of women and war. The Ballet Club had become a centre for artists and audiences alike.

Only with difficulty, though, could this experimental impetus carry over into the professional company Borovansky was destined to run. In July 1942 he presented a five-night season at the shabbily grandiose Princess Theatre. The programme, mixing classics with lightweight, new creations, filled the house, and proved to the management of J. C. Williamson [q.v.6] Theatres Ltd that ballet was potentially big business. On this basis, 'the Firm' allied itself to Borovansky, so that he gained access to its theatres throughout Australia, but took on the burden of its commercial imperatives. In an age before government subsidies and subscription audiences, a professional company could survive only in this way. The Sydney-based Kirsova [q.v.] Ballet (1941-44), having refused the embrace of commerce, died of its own uncompromisingness, despite an Australia-wide following. Nonetheless, the standardizing effect of commercial management was always evident in Borovansky's repertoire and style of production. Large, colourful, familiar works were what 'the Firm' preferred, and Borovansky was developing a performance style of bold statement and dry, brisk muscularity to carry them off.

Naturalized in 1944, Boro became a colourful identity in Melbourne. Outlandish and volatile, with an earthy sense of humour—'just a bloody peasant', he insisted self-mockingly—he was notorious for his despotic treatment of his dancers. By the end of the year his forty-strong company had toured the mainland capitals, Tasmania and New Zealand with a repertoire that included *Giselle, Swan Lake* (Act II), *Les Sylphides, En Saga, Capriccio Italien,* (Sir) Frederick Ashton's *Façade,* and a symphonic fantasy, *Vltava,* patriotically Czech in music, theme and imagery. The titles themselves are some indication of how little Australian content was thought to signify. In 1945 the company again toured Australia, with an astonishing, eight-month season in Melbourne where the tried favourites of pre-war 'Russian ballet', *Le Carnaval, Scheherazade* and *Le Beau Danube,* appeared together with a new work by Borovansky himself, *Terra Australis.*

At the end of the season Martyn left the company to create (out of the Ballet Club) what would become the long-surviving Victorian Ballet Guild; her choice of the small, experimental group over the glamorously professional stage brought into focus the dilemma Borovansky faced. He had built a strong, commercially attractive operation on the basis of the school run by his wife and a keen sense of what the public would pay to see. His dancers included Martin Rubinstein, Leon Kellaway, Peggy Sager and the even younger Kathleen Gorham. From his own studio came Vassilie Trunoff and tiny, brilliantly talented Edna Busse. Yet, as artistic director, he was in effect an employee of J. C. Williamson Theatres, whose own policies largely dictated what he could do. During the next eighteen months, in between seasons of *Coppelia* and other favourites, the Borovansky Ballet (as it was now called) became the dance-chorus for two operettas and toured New Zealand a second time—only to be disbanded early in 1948. The company could hardly have done more to promote the success of 'the Firm', but, despite all Boro's efforts, J.C.W.'s financial backing was withdrawn. It must have been the more galling to watch Ballet Rambert and the National Theatre Ballet captivating the very audiences his own endeavours had built up.

Despite the Australian public's appetite for ballet in the postwar years, Borovansky never managed to gain for his dancers the continuity of employment their professional development required. Time and again, a successful season would be followed by months of dispersal in which they would have to make a living for themselves. It was dismayingly unlike the conditions under which the great European companies grew. Part of the trouble was the timidity and greed of the entrepreneurs; part, the audience expectation that ballet should be exotic and on the biggest scale. Even had Boro wished to diversify his enterprise, he would have had to create a new, more specialized public of the kind that the Victorian Ballet Guild was establishing for itself.

Instead, he waited, irascibly, until in 1951 —sponsored by the Education in Music and Dramatic Arts Society, in conjunction with 'the Firm'—he was able to assemble a new company, the Borovansky Jubilee Ballet, which presented his most ambitious production yet: a full-sized *Petrouchka.* By the end of 1952 he had surpassed even that, with a complete *Sleeping Princess,* while highlights of later seasons included Massine's *Symphonie Fantastique* (1954), John Cranko's *Pineapple Poll* (1954) and David Lichine's full-length *Nutcracker* (1955). Gathered and dismissed and reassembled, the Borovansky Ballet proved it could tackle almost anything within its chosen range of entertainment style, and the guest appearances of Margot Fonteyn and other artists of the Royal Ballet in the 1957 season seemed a recognition of the company's international standing.

To the last, its repertoire was solidly conservative—*Swan Lakes* and *Graduation Balls* interspersed with original, would-be crowd-pleasers—but its dancers had an energy and individualism that carried them beyond the pallid limits of establishment art. Perhaps by the end of the 1950s the company was simply repeating a formula upon which it had already relied too long, yet the confidence and technique of its members had never been so consistently strong.

At the start of a Sydney season, Borovansky died of a coronary occlusion on 18 December 1959 at Randwick and was buried with Anglican rites in Box Hill cemetery, Melbourne. His wife survived him; they had no children. Boro's death left behind some of the finest dancers he had presented in the nineteen interrupted years of his company's career, including Garth Welch, Robert Pomie, Jeffrey Kovel, Estella Nova and Rosemary Mildner; his company not only became the basis of a permanent national ballet, but nourished the origins of smaller, scattered groups, and a lively interest in dance Australia-wide.

Boro's achievement would not have been possible without the gifts of his wife. While his interest was in stage-performance, Xenia schooled and formed the dancers of his corps in early years, then, as the company developed, soloists and principals who came through the academy under her direction. The Borovansky Ballet never shut itself off from other dance styles. The 19-year-old Marilyn Jones, arriving from quite outside the organization, was made a ballerina overnight in his last *Sleeping Princess.* Indeed, the personal qualities—even, at times, the deficiencies—of particular dancers were warmly greeted by audiences who came to see them again and again. The company was both an intensely personal creation, where one man did almost everything, and a national ballet, eager to draw on whatever talent it could employ. In becoming, proudly, 'a din-kum bloody Aussie', Borovansky had found a place both for his keen sense of national identity and for the international experience of the dance world in which he had played his memorable part.

F. Salter, *Borovansky* (Syd, 1980); E. H. Pask, *Ballet in Australia* (Melb, 1982); Borovansky papers (NL).   ROBIN GROVE

BORRIE, EDWIN FULLARTON (1894-1968), civil engineer and town planner, was born on 17 April 1894 at Brunswick, Melbourne, son of New Zealand-born parents James Borrie, grocer, and his wife Katherine Isabella, née Fullarton. The family later moved to Kew. Educated at local schools and at Scotch College, Edwin graduated from the University of Melbourne with first-class honours in civil engineering (B.C.E., 1915; M.C.E., 1927).

During World War I Borrie was one of ten young Australians nominated for commissions in the British Army's Royal Engineers. He embarked on 29 December 1915 and served with the 229th Field Company for two years in France. In March 1916 he was commissioned and in September 1917 promoted temporary lieutenant. He was wounded in April 1918 and awarded the Military Cross in June. Having been appointed to the staff of the assistant-director of works in Egypt, Borrie was demobilized on 15 July 1919. He married Hilda Lilian Richards on 15 November at Hawthorn Presbyterian Church, Melbourne. After working briefly with a private firm which made concrete houses, he joined the Tasmanian Hydro Electric Department to assist with the design and construction of the Great Lake Dam. Subsequently, he was employed by the State Electricity Commission of Victoria at Yallourn.

In 1924 the Melbourne and Metropolitan Board of Works chose Borrie as its first engineer of main drains. As chief engineer of sewerage (1929-50), he managed Melbourne's ever-extending system and supervised the design of a sewage treatment plant at Braeside for the south-eastern suburbs. In 1935 he was invited to prepare a report on the sewerage system at Auckland, New Zealand, and in 1937 toured Britain, Europe and North America to study sewerage practices.

Seconded to the Allied Works Council from 1941 to 1944 as director of engineering, Borrie travelled throughout Australia and was involved in projects vital to the war effort. On returning to the Board of Works, he gave his attention to extending the sewerage system and to planning for growth. Two important reports were prepared: *The Future Population of Melbourne* (1944) and *The Future Urban Boundaries of Melbourne and the Distribution of Population Therein* (1948).

In 1950 Borrie successfully applied for the new position of chief planner in the Board of Works. His interest in town planning had long been developing: during his 1937 trip to the United States of America he had been particularly interested in Los Angeles which, he thought, shared similar conditions and planning challenges with those of Melbourne. He co-ordinated a team, which included an architect, an economist, a surveyor and a sociologist, to map, survey and prepare a master plan as a guide for the development of the city. Although he took a course in statistics to extend his skills, he considered 'common sense and judgement' to be the main qualifications for a good town planner. Aware of the need to convince Melburnians of the advantages of his plan, Borrie often spent his evenings at public meetings, explaining and promoting it.

The plan, published in 1954, sought to rationalize the development of Melbourne through land-use zoning and by reserving land for such future public purposes as roads, parks and schools. It was well received and widely acclaimed. In 1955 Borrie was awarded the (Sir James) Barrett [q.v.7] medal by the Town and Country Planning Association of Victoria. That year the Board of Works was granted a continuing planning role and Borrie's position as chief planner was made permanent. He continued to refine the plan until 1959 when he retired.

Six feet (182.9 cm) tall, fair haired, with a small moustache, Borrie was a stern but fair taskmaster who worked extremely hard. He enjoyed sport, gardening, and reading detective stories when it rained. President (1947) of the Melbourne division of the Institution of Engineers, Australia, he was also active in the work of Legacy. On retirement, he moved to Mount Eliza, but, finding that his advice as a planner was still valued, he set up as a consultant. In February 1961 he was appointed to prepare a plan for the Melbourne City Council. Completed by 1964, it provided for a new civic centre, for a town hall and plaza, and for open spaces around the city. The council did not act on it. Survived by his wife and son, Borrie died on 27 August 1968 at Kew and was cremated.

T. Dingle and C. Rasmussen, *Vital Connections* (Melb, 1991); *MMBW Officers J*, June 1950, p 25,

July 1959, p 17; *Aust Builder*, Sept 1950, pp 473, 518; *Herald* (Melb), 12 Dec 1964; information from Melb and Metropolitan Bd of Works.

CAROLYN RASMUSSEN
TONY DINGLE

BOSTOCK, WILLIAM DOWLING (1892-1968), sailor, soldier, airman, grazier and politician, was born on 5 February 1892 at Surry Hills, Sydney, third child of William Masefield Bostock, a clerk from England, and his Spanish-born wife Mary, née Dowling. Educated at The School, Mount Victoria, in June 1911 young William went to sea as a wireless operator. On 23 November 1914 he enlisted in the Australian Imperial Force and was posted to the 2nd Signal Troop (Engineers). Having sailed for Egypt in December, he landed at Gallipoli on 25 April 1915, but was evacuated in August with dysentery.

In Egypt in April 1916 Bostock transferred as a sergeant to the Signal Squadron, Anzac Mounted Division. Discharged from the A.I.F. on 17 February 1917, he was commissioned next day in the Royal Flying Corps Special Reserve. He went to England to train as a pilot and in August joined No. 48 Squadron in France. Invalided to England in March 1918, he later transferred to the Royal Air Force. For his service on the Western Front he was awarded the Belgian Croix de Guerre (1918). On 6 March 1919 he married his Australian fiancée Gwendolen Meade Norton (d. 1947) at St Peter's parish church, Southampton. Retiring from the R.A.F. on 22 October, he returned home and resumed his civilian career.

On 14 September 1921 Bostock was appointed flying officer in the newly-formed Royal Australian Air Force and posted to No. 1 Flying Training School, Point Cook, Victoria. He was in England in 1926-28, attending the R.A.F. Staff College, Andover; while there, he was promoted squadron leader. After a further posting to Point Cook, in December 1929 he became director of training at R.A.A.F. Headquarters, Melbourne. Moving to New South Wales in November 1931 to command No. 3 Squadron at Richmond, he was also station commander from 1933. Next year he was promoted wing commander and in 1935 was appointed O.B.E. In 1936 he went to England on exchange with the R.A.F. Back in Melbourne in 1938, he took over as director of operations and intelligence; promotion to group captain followed in September. One year later, on the eve of war in Europe, he was appointed deputy chief of the Air Staff.

As Air Chief Marshal Sir Charles Burnett's [q.v.] 'right-hand man', Bostock gained rapid advancement to temporary air commodore (June 1940) and substantive air vice marshal (1 October 1941); he was to be appointed C.B. in January 1942. Burnett's tour was due to expire and it was clear that he wanted Bostock to succeed him as chief of the Air Staff. On 8 December 1941 the Japanese entered the war. After victories in Malaya, the Philippines, the Netherlands East Indies and New Guinea, they bombed Darwin. The Allies formed South-West Pacific Area Command under General Douglas MacArthur [q.v.] from the United States of America. Australian combat forces in the region were transferred to the command on 17 April 1942.

Following an acrimonious dispute between Burnett and the minister for air A. S. Drakeford [q.v.], Prime Minister John Curtin [q.v.] agreed that the commander, Allied Air Forces, would have operational control of R.A.A.F. units, while responsibility for their administration would remain with the chief of the Air Staff and the Air Board. As a consequence, command of the R.A.A.F. would be divided between two headquarters. Relishing the opportunity for operational duties, on 2 May 1942 Bostock became chief of staff to the Allied Air Forces commander, Lieutenant General George H. Brett, an American. Three days later Air Commodore (Sir) George Jones was promoted air vice marshal and appointed chief of the Air Staff.

At his headquarters, which moved to Brisbane in July, Brett headed an integrated staff of Australian and American officers, and exercised operational control through the existing R.A.A.F. network of area commands. Increased activity made this arrangement cumbersome and confusing to both partners. Major General George C. Kenny, who was sent from the U.S.A. to replace Brett in August, found operational procedures 'chaotic'. It was agreed that Kenny would have two subordinate commands: the U.S. Fifth Air Force and R.A.A.F. Command. In September Kenny appointed Bostock air officer commanding, R.A.A.F. Command, responsible for the defence of Australia (other than the north-east) and for operations against Japanese bases in the Netherlands East Indies. In an attempt to end the divided command of the R.A.A.F., a complex round of negotiations ensued. Jones and Drakeford wanted the chief of the Air Staff to have overall authority. Supported by Kenny and MacArthur, Bostock argued that responsibility for the administration of units under his operational control should be transferred to him. Curtin mediated, but could not resolve the impasse.

Dual control presented Bostock with numerous problems. Jones refused to delegate his authority over support functions needed for the conduct of operations. Disputes arose between R.A.A.F. Headquarters and

R.A.A.F. Command headquarters in regard to appointments of officers, requirements for operational training, construction of airfields and camp sites, and the supply of ammunition, fuel, replacement aircraft and reserves of bombs. Units received conflicting orders while the vitriolic correspondence between Bostock and Jones continued. In March 1943 Bostock advised Kenny that 'under the existing conditions . . . I am unable to ensure the development of the maximum fighting efficiency of my command'. The matter was again referred to Curtin, but, because he was unwilling to alienate either Drakeford or MacArthur, no changes were made.

From late 1942 the Allies had begun to repulse the Japanese. R.A.A.F. Command's principal roles were then to protect the sea lanes to New Guinea and to maintain the offensive against the Netherlands East Indies. Exhibiting 'exceptional tactical ability', Bostock directed attacks by Australian—and sometimes by Dutch and American—forces which destroyed aerodromes, shipping, oilstocks and harbour facilities as far afield as Java and New Britain, and gradually helped to gain supremacy in the air over the Netherlands East Indies. For his work to November 1944, he was awarded the American Medal of Freedom with Silver Palm.

In March 1945 Kenny gave Bostock responsibility for air-support of the projected invasion of Borneo by I Australian Corps. Bostock immediately established an advanced headquarters at Morotai, from which he controlled the R.A.A.F.'s First Tactical Air Force, the American Fifth and Thirteenth air forces, and a force of heavy bombers in Darwin and Western Australia. The Borneo landings were planned in three phases: the first against Tarakan on 1 May, the second against Labuan and Brunei on 10 June, and the third against Balikpapan on 1 July. Formidable defences, including well-placed gun sites and concrete blockhouses, had been constructed at each site. With skilful timing and handling, Bostock directed a sustained assault which so reduced the fortifications that the invading troops only suffered light casualties. He participated in the landings at Labuan and Balikpapan, and went forward to inspect the ground while fighting was still in progress. MacArthur described the Labuan-Brunei air campaign as 'flawless' and Bostock was awarded the Distinguished Service Order.

With the cessation of hostilities, Kenny invited Bostock to represent the R.A.A.F. at the formal surrender of the Japanese in Tokyo Bay on 2 September. 'An able officer of driving temperament', Bostock was regarded by contemporaries as having one of 'the Air Force's best brains'. Kenny recalled that, on first meeting him, he 'looked gruff and tough . . . but he impressed me as being honest and I believed that, if he would work for me at all, he would be loyal to me'. Bostock proved the prediction to be accurate, although, under the 'mischievous' dual-control arrangement, it was a wonder that he had been able to perform as effectively as he did. With several other senior officers, on 19 April 1946 he was compulsorily retired, six years before his prescribed age.

Bostock bought a grazing property at Molyullah, near Benalla, Victoria. As special aviation correspondent to the Melbourne *Herald*, in June 1946 he wrote the 'RAAF's Unhappy Story', a series of articles attacking the government and the Air Board over the divided-command issue. He contributed regularly to the *Herald* on air force and defence subjects throughout the late 1940s and the 1950s. Standing as a Liberal, in 1949 he was elected to the House of Representatives as the member for Indi. An active back-bencher and a member of the joint committee on foreign affairs, he often spoke on defence matters and was not afraid to criticize the Menzies [q.v.] government. He was defeated in the 1958 elections.

In February 1946 he had been appointed to the board of management of the Australian War Memorial, Canberra. Bostock married a 33-year-old clerk Nanette Mary O'Keefe on 1 June 1951 at St Peter's Catholic Church, Toorak, Melbourne. He died on 28 April 1968 at Benalla; after an air force funeral at St Paul's Anglican Cathedral, Melbourne, he was cremated. His wife and their three sons survived him, as did the two daughters of his first marriage.

G. Odgers, *Air War Against Japan 1943-1945* (Canb, 1957); D. Gillison, *Royal Australian Air Force 1939-1942* (Canb, 1962); R. Williams, *These are Facts* (Canb, 1977); J. E. Hewitt, *Adversity in Success* (Melb, 1980); C. D. Coulthard-Clark, *The Third Brother* (Syd, 1991); *PD* (Cwlth), 30 Apr 1968, p 946; Bostock papers (AWM).

A. D. GARRISSON

BOSWELL, ROBERT WILLIAM McGREGOR (1911-1976), scientist and public servant, was born on 30 September 1911 at North Carlton, Melbourne, only son of Robert Boswell, driver, and his wife Belinda, née Hoey, both Victorian born. Educated at University High School, young Boswell joined the Victorian Department of Public Instruction as a teacher and studied part time at the University of Melbourne (B.Sc., 1933; M.Sc., 1935); he gained a Blue for lacrosse and became a research scholar. Under the guidance of Professor T. H. Laby [q.v.9], Boswell and three colleagues used radio direction-finding to trace the movements of thunderstorms associated with cold fronts crossing southern Australia. For his work he was awarded a Fred Knight scholarship. From February 1935 he continued his investigations on behalf of the radio research board of the Council for Scientific and Industrial Research.

Entering the Postmaster-General's Department in May 1936, Boswell was granted leave in October to take up his scholarship in Britain. There he was employed by Siemens Brothers & Co. Ltd. In July 1937 he represented England at lacrosse. During his journey home, on 10 April 1938 in Colombo he married Mavis Collins; she had sailed from Australia to meet him. Back in Melbourne, he designed and tested telecommunications equipment. Commissioned engineer lieutenant in the Royal Australian Naval Volunteer Reserve on 14 April 1943, he served at Navy Office and briefly at sea; his duties involved the installation of radar in R.A.N. ships. His appointment terminated in January 1946. That year he transferred to the south-east regional office of the Department of Civil Aviation as a senior airways engineer.

In April 1948 he moved to Salisbury, South Australia, where he became a principal scientific officer at the Long Range Weapons Establishment. One of his initial responsibilities was to design an electronic timing system for the Woomera Range. Set up jointly by the British and Australian governments to test guided weapons, the range lacked any means of co-ordinating records made by separate instruments during a firing. Boswell developed a central timing unit which proved so successful that more were made and exported to Britain. After one year he was placed in charge of the range and pioneered a rigorous method of project planning. He was promoted superintending scientist in 1951 and deputy-controller, trials and instrumentation, in 1955; next year he was appointed O.B.E. As controller (director), Weapons Research Establishment, from 1 December 1958, he became known as 'Mr Rocket Range'. Boswell ran the facility during its busiest and most fruitful period, dominating the organization and inspiring his staff to find solutions to new technical problems.

Raised to the post of secretary, Department of National Development, in January 1965, he moved to Canberra. Among other duties, he chaired the Snowy Mountains Council. In 1969 he went to London as deputy high commissioner. He returned to be chairman of the Australian Atomic Energy Commission (based at Lucas Heights, Sydney) and took up the post in April 1972. Under his stewardship the commission acquired responsibility for the exploitation of uranium, in addition to its functions as a research and regulatory body, and as a producer of isotopes. Boswell was a member of the science and industry forum of the Australian Academy of Science and of the council of Canberra College of Advanced Education (from 1972). He sat on the Federal government's committee of inquiry on museums and national collections, and urged the college to provide courses for conservators of cultural and ethnic materials. President (1974) of the general conference of the International Atomic Energy Agency, he became a government-appointed director of Mary Kathleen Uranium Ltd in 1975.

Bill was tall and husky, with dark hair, bushy eyebrows and a rugged face. Comfortable in positions of authority and confident in his knowledge, he commanded respect. His style was epitomized in his rendering of Horatio Nelson's aphorism: 'no captain can do wrong if he places his ship alongside that of an enemy'. Boswell was also a good mixer who enjoyed social activities and appreciated classical music. He died of myocardial infarction on 17 February 1976 at Lucas Heights and was cremated; his wife, son and daughter survived him.

S. S. Richardson, *Parity of Esteem* (Canb, 1979); P. Morton, *Fire Across the Desert* (Canb, 1989); *Search* (Syd), 6, no 9, Sept 1975; *Atomic Energy in Australia*, 19, no 2, Apr 1976; *SMH*, 15 July 1963, 9 Nov 1964, 20 Mar 1972, 21 Jan 1975; *Canb Times*, 13 Nov 1964, 19 Feb 1976; information from Mrs M. Boswell, Forrest, Canb; personal information.   T. F. C. LAWRENCE

BOSWORTH, RICHARD CHARLES LESLIE (1907-1964), chemist and academic, was born on 17 January 1907 at Westbourne Park, Adelaide, son of Richard Leslie Eugene Bosworth, surveyor, and his wife Isabella Bissett, née Watson. Educated at Scotch College where he was twice dux, in 1925 Richard enrolled at the University of Adelaide (B.Sc., 1928; B.Sc. Hons, 1930; M.Sc., 1931; D.Sc., 1938); in 1930 he was awarded a David Murray [q.v.5] research scholarship. On 12 August 1933 he married Thelma Hilda Emma Boon at St Augustine's Anglican Church, Unley; they were to have three children. That year he won an 1851 Exhibition scholarship and entered Trinity College, Cambridge (Ph.D., 1935): he worked under Professor (Sir) Eric Rideal and in 1936 won the senior Rouse Ball studentship and the 1851 Exhibition senior studentship.

Returning to Australia in 1938, Bosworth was appointed research chemist to the Colonial Sugar Refining Co. Ltd in Sydney. During World War II he worked on the production of drugs, particularly vitamin C, for the armed forces. In 1948 he became manager of C.S.R.'s research department, a position he held until 1957 when he joined the New South

Wales University of Technology (later University of New South Wales) as associate-professor and head of the physical chemistry department.

A world authority on heat transfer and transport processes in applied chemistry, he contributed papers to the second and third volumes of *Principles of Sugar Technology* (Amsterdam, 1959, 1963), edited by Pieter Honig. Bosworth published seventy-nine papers (eleven jointly) and three books: *Physics in Chemical Industry* (London, 1950), *Heat Transfer Phenomena* (Sydney and New York, 1952) and *Transport Processes in Applied Chemistry* (Sydney and London, 1956). He co-authored, with P. D. Lark and B. R. Craven, *The Handling of Chemical Data* (London, 1968).

Advocating the importance of basic science in industry, Bosworth argued that more physicists should be employed in the chemical field and urged that greater attention should be given in university courses to 'the consolidation of familiar physical principles with a view to the fitting of students for industrial posts'. In 1961 he was a visiting professor at the University of Canterbury, New Zealand, and guest lecturer at the New Zealand Chemical Society, Auckland; next year he was awarded a visiting professorship to the University of Illinois, United States of America, but illness prevented his going there.

Bosworth was president of the Royal Society of New South Wales (1951-52), of the State branch of the British Society of Rheology and of the University of New South Wales Chemical Society (1958). He had been awarded the H. G. Smith [q.v.11] medal by the Royal Australian Chemical Institute in 1952 and the medal of the Royal Society of New South Wales in 1958. A shy man, whose research was his main interest, he was also a skilled photographer whose cinematographic films have been donated to the National Film and Sound Archive, Canberra. Survived by his wife, son and a daughter, he died of athero-sclerotic heart disease on 24 March 1964 in Sydney and was cremated. His estate was sworn for probate at £25 548.

Roy Aust Chemical Inst, *Procs*, 31, no 4, Apr 1964, p 128; *Chronicle* (Adel), 13 July 1933; *SMH*, 5 Apr 1958, 17 Feb 1959; Roy Soc of NSW Archives, Syd; Bosworth papers (Univ NSW L Archives); information from Prof R. and Ms M. Bosworth, Como, Perth.   R. BHATHAL

BOURKE, JOSEPH ORMOND ALOYSIUS (1908-1965), public servant and university administrator, was born on 14 November 1908 at Glebe, Sydney, second child of Joseph Ormond Aloysius Bourke, a lecturer at Sydney Training College for Teachers, and his wife Winifred Francis Xavier, née Maher, both native-born. His parents were teachers and young Joe grew up in an intellectually stimulating atmosphere. After her husband's sudden death on 24 November 1912, Winifred resumed teaching and Joe attended schools in various parts of the State. He rebelled against his paternal grandmother's strict Catholicism. One influence upon his drive and ambition was the wish to demonstrate that his abilities matched those of his father.

Studying at North Sydney Boys' High School, in 1924 Bourke passed the Leaving certificate with first-class honours in English and was placed fifth in the State in that subject. In March 1925 he joined the public service as a clerk in the licences reduction board, Department of Attorney General and Justice, and enrolled as an evening student at the University of Sydney (B.A., 1929) where he was influenced by Professor John Anderson [q.v.7]. Bourke became a committed socialist and joined the Australian Labor Party in 1927. As a founder of the university's Labor club and president (1928-29) of the evening students' association, he made his mark as a debater. He married Lily Aileen Cowled on 22 December 1934 at the Methodist Church, Junee; they were to remain childless.

In 1936 Bourke was appointed acting-secretary of the correspondence courses in the teaching division of the technical education branch of the Department of Public Instruction. From mid-1942 he was executive officer, transport and communications, on the State War Effort Co-Ordination Committee and next year was seconded to the Commonwealth Department of Supply and Shipping where he served as superintendent of personnel. In October 1945 he was made registrar of Sydney Technical College.

For at least thirty years Bourke lectured and examined in university extension courses, Workers' Educational Association classes and public service training programmes. He was widely known, particularly before World War II, as a speaker at labour rallies. Tall, dark and shockheaded, he had 'an urbane manner', but was a 'firebrand when roused'; he 'spoke rather slowly, relying on the deep organ-like notes of his powerful voice for effect'. Among his friends he numbered many political figures, though he was closest to those of the left, especially C. E. Martin [q.v.]. Bourke had divorced Lily in 1944 and on 28 August 1948 married a 27-year-old telephonist Eva Mary Naughton with Presbyterian forms at Fullerton [q.v.4] Memorial Church, Sydney.

From August 1947 to September 1951 he was an inspector with the Public Service Board, before becoming assistant-director of the Department of Technical Education.

Bourke worked closely with W. C. Wurth [q.v.] towards the foundation in 1949 of the New South Wales University of Technology (University of New South Wales, 1959); he also came into contact with the university's vice-chancellor (Sir) Philip Baxter. Bourke resigned on 6 April 1954 to become the first bursar of the new university.

As bursar, his influence was pervasive. He pressed vigorously for the establishment of a faculty of arts, was closely involved in the introduction of administrative and managerial studies, and played an important part in the creation of a medical school and in building a university union; in addition, he supported improved library services and the development of residential colleges. Baxter and Bourke gradually forged a very close working relationship and, with the registrar Godfrey McCauley, made up a strong management team. In addition to being a member of many university and hospital boards, Bourke was vice-president of the Old Tote Theatre Club.

In attempting to lay down administrative procedures to cope with the pressures arising from rapid growth, Bourke drew heavily on public service practices. By so doing, he aroused considerable controversy and criticism, particularly from academic staff who resented what they saw as excessive regulation. Few regarded him with indifference, which possibly reflected the complexities of his character. He was a romantic, a lover of art, music and literature, but one who could be pragmatic, even ruthless, in resolving difficulties; he was a traditionalist, yet also a visionary who encouraged the university to strike out in new directions; he was loyal, though not silent about the faults of those he supported.

Survived by his wife, son and daughter, Bourke died of lymphosarcoma on 11 November 1965 at Little Bay; following a requiem Mass at St Anthony's Catholic Church, Clovelly, he was buried in his father's grave in Waverley cemetery. A fountain at the University of New South Wales commemorates him.

Red Tape, 25 Feb 1937; *Technology*, Dec 1965; *SMH*, 12 Nov 1965; NSW Public Service employee record cards (NSWA); Baxter *and* Bourke papers (Univ NSW Archives); information from Mrs E. Bourke, Chatswood, Syd.

KENNETH W. KNIGHT

BOWDEN, FRANK PHILIP (1903-1968), physicist and physical chemist, was born on 2 May 1903 in Hobart, sixth of seven children of Frank Prosser Bowden, telegraph manager, and his wife Grace Elizabeth, née Hill, both Tasmanian born. Educated at The Hutchins School and the University of Tasmania

(B.Sc., 1925; M.Sc., 1927), Philip did his postgraduate research in electrochemistry under A. L. McAulay [q.v.10]. Awarded an 1851 Exhibition scholarship, in 1927 he entered Gonville and Caius College, Cambridge; he undertook further studies in electrochemistry with (Sir) Eric Rideal and obtained a Ph.D. in 1929.

At St Michael's parish church, Pimlico, London, on 12 December 1931 Bowden married Hobart-born Margot Hutchison. In the 1930s at Cambridge he turned his scientific interests to friction and lubrication. A series of brilliant experiments led him to develop a theory of friction that was to provide the foundation and stimulus of much of his later work, and bring him an international reputation. He realized that the area of real contact between two solid surfaces is small: consequently, when a force is applied normal to the surfaces, the local regions of contact deform, leading to strong adhesion; sliding causes high temperatures at the contacts (hot spots).

Following a lecture tour of the United States of America in 1939, Bowden was visiting Australia when World War II began. He offered his services to the Council for Scientific and Industrial Research, and in November became officer-in-charge of its new section of lubricants and bearings which was to be established at the University of Melbourne. Bowden's team successfully combined fundamental studies with applied research useful to the war effort. They developed flame-throwing fuels, portable equipment for measuring the muzzle velocity of projectiles, and casting techniques for the production of bearings for aircraft-engines; in addition, they evaluated special lubricants for machine tools and aircraft. Bowden also showed the importance of hot spots in initiating explosion, chiefly in nitroglycerine; apart from its scientific interest, his work had implications for the safe handling of explosives.

In 1945 Bowden returned to Cambridge and next year was appointed reader. With financial assistance from the Ministry of Supply, he acquired equipment and built up a group dedicated to research on solid explosives, friction and lubrication. His experiments on the initiation of explosion led him to conclude that the reaction develops from a hot spot that must be capable of producing more energy by further chemical decomposition than is dissipated by processes such as thermal conduction. He carried out important work on the friction of non-metallic solids, including snow and ice. Other significant lines of inquiry included the nature of friction at high speeds, the effects of gases on the adhesion of initially clean surfaces, the structure and properties of absorbed boundary layers, and, in the late 1950s, the deformation and fracture of solids, particularly at very high strain rates. Bowden's fundamental investigations had practical applications. He forged links with several companies, set up a research establishment for Tube Investments Ltd and became a director (1958) of English Electric Co. Ltd. His advice was also sought by government: he was chairman (1955-62) of the executive committee of the National Physical Laboratory.

Bowden's group was made a sub-department of the Cavendish Laboratory in 1957. With David Tabor, he published *The Friction and Lubrication of Solids*, Part I (Oxford, 1950) and Part II (1964); *Initiation and Growth of Explosion in Liquids and Solids* (Cambridge, 1952) and *Fast Reactions in Solids* (London, 1958) were both co-authored with A. D. Yoffe. Bowden had received a D.Sc. from the University of Tasmania (1931) and an Sc.D. from Cambridge (1938); he was elected a fellow of the Royal Society in 1948, made C.B.E. in 1956 and appointed to a personal chair in 1967. He had little stomach for theoretical analysis, favouring a direct experimental approach 'characterized by simplicity and elegance'.

His scientific integrity, enthusiasm, and concern for the personal and professional well-being of his staff earned Bowden respect, loyalty and affection. He enjoyed a happy family life. A 'lightly-built man with fine features', he had a complex character. Shy and reserved, gentle, charming and courtly, he was also tough and ambitious, and a shrewd judge of men and affairs. In his *Strangers and Brothers* series of novels, C. P. (Baron) Snow, a close friend from student days at Cambridge, 'drew on Bowden as the prototype of [Francis] Getliffe, the gifted, wise and sensitive scientist'. Survived by his wife, daughter and three sons, Bowden died of lung cancer on 3 September 1968 at Cambridge. His death cut short a still active scientific career.

D. P. Mellor, *The Role of Science and Industry* (Canb, 1958); *DNB*, 1961-70; C. B. Schedvin, *Shaping Science and Industry* (Syd, 1987); T. Bowden, *The Way My Father Tells It* (Syd, 1989); *New Scientist*, 7, no 183, 19 May 1960, p 1266; *Biog Memoirs of Fellows of Roy Soc* (Lond), 15, 1969, p 1; *Chemistry in Aust*, 56, no 5, May 1989, p 157; *The Times*, 4, 10, 13, 16 Sept 1968; CSIRO Archives, Canb.   ALEX C. McLAREN
J. A. SPINK

BOWDEN, GEORGE JAMES (1888-1962), farmer, soldier and politician, was born on 17 March 1888 at Moyhu, Victoria, son of William Henry Bowden, farmer, and his wife Catherine Christina, née McCalman, both native-born. George was educated at state schools at Whitfield and Benalla, and later worked as a commission agent in Melbourne. Enlisting in the Australian Imperial Force on 6 March 1915, he served with the 24th Battalion and was promoted captain on 16 January 1918. He was wounded at Gallipoli, and gassed and wounded on the Western Front. For his daring reconnaissance before the battle for Mont St Quentin, France, in September 1918, he was awarded the Military Cross.

On demobilization in July 1919, Bowden commenced farming at Koo-wee-rup, West Gippsland. He joined the United Country Party in 1923 and was a member (1928-38, president 1930-31) of the Cranbourne Shire Council. As a Country Party candidate, he unsuccessfully contested the Legislative Assembly seat of Mornington in 1935 and 1937. He became prominent in Country Party affairs in a period when the party dominated Victorian politics and experienced dramatic internal dissension. The expulsion of (Sir) John McEwen [q.v.] for joining the Lyons-Page [qq.v.10,11] Federal coalition government in 1937 precipitated a splinter Liberal Country Party and created a serious rift between the Victorian branch and the Federal Country Party. Simultaneously, Premier (Sir) Albert Dunstan [q.v.8] was engaged in a bitter dispute with party power-broker Albert Hocking [q.v.] over the executive's attempts to direct the State parliamentary party.

A Hocking supporter and a vigorous opponent of the Liberal Country Party, Bowden served as vice-president of the U.C.P. in 1938-39 and president in 1940. He was re-elected president in 1941 and 1942, and, though opposed by three candidates, narrowly won the final ballot for president in 1943. Victorian Country Party unity and harmonious relations with the Federal organization were restored that year, but Bowden played a relatively minor role in the negotiations because of his military commitments. Having been mobilized in October 1939, he was appointed temporary lieutenant colonel on 13 March 1942 and commanded the 9th Garrison Battalion, Australian Military Forces, from that month until October 1943. He was transferred to the Reserve of Officers in December.

Gippsland was a Liberal Country Party stronghold, with the House of Representatives seat being held by a long-time McEwen supporter, Thomas Paterson [q.v.11], whom Bowden had unsuccessfully challenged at the 1940 election. With the party split mended, Paterson retired from parliament and campaigned for Bowden in Gippsland in 1943. Bowden just managed to overcome the Labor landslide to win the seat on preferences; his military record did not prevent his being heavily out-polled by the Labor candidate

W. T. G. Williams in the servicemen's vote.
Holding Gippsland until his retirement in December 1961, Bowden re-established it as a
safe Country Party seat. His parliamentary
career was solid rather than spectacular: he
never attained cabinet rank, but was chairman of committees in 1959-61. Gough
Whitlam stated that he 'kept a good committee' and recalled that Bowden's impartiality waned only once when, carried away by
a colleague's rhetoric, he interjected from the
chair: 'Hear, hear!' Bowden quickly regained
his composure and rebuked himself by calling:
'Order!'

Noted for his keen sense of humour, he was
well liked by his parliamentary colleagues. Six
feet (182.9 cm) tall and erect, he retained his
soldierly bearing and was always in demand as
an Anzac Day speaker. Bowden never married. When his health deteriorated due to his
war wounds, his sister cared for him at his
Murrumbeena home. He died on 8 June 1962
at the Repatriation General Hospital, Heidelberg, and was buried in Cheltenham cemetery; his estate was sworn for probate at
£23 542.

C. E. W. Bean, *The Australian Imperial Force in
France During the Allied Offensive, 1918* (Brisb,
1983); *PD* (Cwlth), 7 Aug 1962, p 8; *Vic Country
Party Annual Conference Report*, 1940, 1943;
Countryman (Melb), 12 Apr, 20 Sept 1940, 23 July,
13, 27 Aug 1943, 21 June 1962; *Age* (Melb), 9 Mar
1961, 9 June 1962.   B. J. COSTAR

BOWDEN, VIVIAN GORDON (1884-
1942), trade commissioner and diplomat, was
born on 28 May 1884 at Stanmore, Sydney,
second son of Vivian Rothwell Bowden, a
native-born storekeeper, and his wife Mary
Ann (Marian) Harrison, née Cazaly, from
England. Vivian senior founded the merchant
house of Bowden Bros & Co. Ltd. Educated at
Sydney Church of England Grammar School
(Shore) and in England at Bedford Grammar
School, Gordon went to Europe to study the
silk industry, worked as a silk inspector at
Canton, China, and in 1908 joined a branch of
the family firm in Japan.

Back in England, Bowden was commissioned in the British Army Service Corps
on 4 February 1915; for his work in France he
was mentioned in dispatches. In January 1917
he transferred to the Royal Engineers. On 3
July that year he married Dorothy Dennis at
the Chapel Royal, Savoy, London. He served
on the Western Front and was promoted temporary major in May 1918. Demobilized on 21
March 1919, he returned to the East and in
1921 became managing director of A. Cameron & Co. (China) Ltd, Shanghai. Bowden
was prominent in the affairs of the expatriate
community and kept on friendly terms with
the locals. In 1935 he was made Australian
government trade commissioner in China,
one of the first in the new service. 'Cultured,
practical' and effective, he was appointed
C.B.E. in 1941. As 'Vivian Gordon', he had
published two novels, *The Skipper* and *Rumfy*
(London, 1929, 1930), which were serialized
in *Blackwood's Magazine*.

In 1941 the Australian government closed
its Shanghai office and appointed Bowden
official representative in Singapore. He began
duty in September, reporting to the minister
for external affairs H. V. Evatt [q.v.] and his
department. The Japanese invaded Malaya on
8 December. A member of the Far Eastern
War Council from that month, Bowden observed the enemy's rapid advance, recognized early that defences—particularly air
power—were inadequate, and assisted the
government to challenge British 'official optimism' that Malaya could be held. On 23
December he cabled that, without reinforcements of 'large numbers of the latest fighter
aircraft', Singapore would fall. Prime Minister John Curtin [q.v.] immediately expressed
concern to his counterpart (Sir) Winston
Churchill; a 'handful of Hurricanes' arrived in
January 1942.

Realizing that capitulation was imminent,
on 9 February Bowden asked the department
for permission to leave the island. He was told
that he should stay: 'Otherwise we shall be
deprived of independent information and
effect on morale would be bad'. If necessary,
he was to seek diplomatic immunity and await
a possible future exchange of officials with
Japan. By 14 February (the day before the
British surrendered) there was no point in
remaining. He transmitted his last message,
advising the department that he and his staff
intended to depart. They sailed next morning
in a motor launch, the *Mary Rose*.

On 17 February 1942 Japanese patrol
boats intercepted the vessel and escorted her
to Banka Island, Netherlands East Indies. The
prisoners were held in a cinema-hall at Mun-
tok where Bowden informed his captors in
their own language of his diplomatic status
and remonstrated with guards who attempted
to remove his personal possessions. Soldiers
beat him and took him outside. A local resident saw 'an elderly white-haired gentleman'
forced to dig a shallow grave and stand at its
edge before being shot. Bowden was survived
by his wife, two daughters and son Ivor who
was Australian ambassador to Iran (1974-78)
and Pakistan (1984-87).

L. Wigmore, *The Japanese Thrust* (Canb, 1957);
W. J. Hudson and H. J. W. Stokes (eds), *Documents
on Australian Foreign Policy 1937-49*, 5, 6 (Canb,
1982, 1983); W. J. Hudson and W. Way (eds), *Documents on Australian Foreign Policy 1937-49*, 8
(Canb, 1989); A. R. Taysom, History of the Aus-

tralian Trade Commissioner Service, 3 (Canb, 1983, ts, NL); A1066, item H45/580/6/4 (AA); information from Mr I. G. Bowden, Deakin, Canb.

DARRYL BENNET

BOWE, ETHEL JESSIE (1906-1961), army matron-in-chief, was born on 27 May 1906 at Maldon, Victoria, fifth of eleven children of Abraham James Bowe, bricklayer, and his wife Edith Jane, née Dorman, both Victorian born. The family lived in a stone cottage built by Jessie's paternal grandfather. She attended Maldon State School, worked in the local hospital and trained as a nurse at Melbourne Hospital in 1927-30. Having completed midwifery at Queen Victoria Hospital, she joined the Australian Army Nursing Service Reserve in 1931 and returned to the Melbourne next year; she was a tutor-sister at Perth Hospital in 1935-38 and at the Melbourne in 1939.

Appointed sister in the A.A.N.S. on 19 December 1939, Bowe was called up in March 1940 for service with the Australian Imperial Force. Two months later she sailed for the Middle East in charge of thirty-two nurses from the 2nd/2nd Australian General Hospital. Diverted to England, they were attached to the 2nd/3rd A.G.H. at Godalming, Surrey, during the Battle of Britain. Bowe finally reached Egypt in December and began work with the 2nd/2nd A.G.H. at Kantara. From April to June 1941, as temporary matron, she helped to establish the 2nd/11th A.G.H. at Alexandria, amidst a rush of casualties from the Western Desert, Greece and Crete. She became matron of the 2nd/2nd A.G.H. in September. Back in Australia in March 1942, she took three months leave, then rejoined her unit at Watten, Queensland. For her resourceful and capable administration of the hospital, she was awarded the Associate Royal Red Cross (1944). In March 1943, with the rank of major, she transferred to Melbourne as assistant to the matron-in-chief. Promoted temporary lieutenant colonel and appointed principal matron, Advanced Land Headquarters, in February 1945, Bowe was based on Morotai Island from April to November; she was to be awarded (1948) the United States of America's Bronze Star medal for her services.

In early 1946 she became matron of the 115th Military (Repatriation General) Hospital, Heidelberg, Melbourne, and from March 1947 held the additional post of principal matron, Southern Command. Bowe sailed for Europe in November with a group of German and Italian internees and prisoners of war. Her A.A.N.S. appointment terminated on her arrival in England in January 1948. Following several months of advanced training, she went to Austria as chief nurse for the Inter-national Refugee Organization; in 1950 she came home to Victoria to be matron at the Austin Hospital, Heidelberg. 'Bowie', as she was widely known, rejoined the Australian Military Forces in June 1951. Appointed matron-in-chief and granted the rank of honorary colonel on 17 September 1952, she administered the Royal Australian Army Nursing Corps with determination, putting 'the service on a footing unequalled in the Commonwealth'. She was awarded a Florence Nightingale medal (1953) and the Royal Red Cross (1955), and in 1957 was appointed honorary nursing sister to Queen Elizabeth II. Active in professional organizations, Bowe gave the eighth annual oration for the New South Wales College of Nursing in 1960; she was appointed O.B.E. that year.

Miss Bowe, who was five feet (152.4 cm) tall, with blue eyes, light brown hair, elfin features and considerable charm, impressed her colleagues as being 'every inch a lady'. Having suffered from cancer for six years, she died on 13 October 1961 in the Repatriation General Hospital, Heidelberg; following an Anglican service with full military honours at Christ Church, South Yarra, she was cremated.

A. S. Walker, *Medical Services of the R.A.N. and R.A.A.F.* (Canb, 1961); *The New South Wales College of Nursing Annual Orations, 1953-1976* (Syd, 1977); G. Blackman and J. Larkin, *Australia's First Notable Town, Maldon* (Syd, 1978); E. W. Gault and A. Lucas, *A Century of Compassion* (Melb, 1982); P. Adam-Smith, *Australian Women at War* (Melb, 1984); R. Goodman, *Our War Nurses* (Brisb, 1988); Aust Army Nursing Service *and* Roy Aust Army Nursing Corps records (Dept of Defence, Canb); AWM records; information from Mr S. L. Bowe, Maldon, Vic, Brig P. M. McCarthy, Chatswood, Syd, and Mrs C. Hewins, Melb.   JAN BASSETT

BOWER, HELEN ROSALIE (1923-1980), community arts director, was born on 28 January 1923 at Coonabarabran, New South Wales, second daughter of English-born parents Edward Lionel Stephenson, farmer, and his wife Minnie, née Tidswell. Educated at home on her family's property, Eulin, and at Ravenswood Methodist Ladies' College, Gordon, Sydney, Ros attended the University of Sydney (B.A., 1947) where she won the Henry Lawson [q.v.10] prize for poetry. She worked concurrently as a cadet reporter on the *Sun* newspaper. On 28 December 1946 she married a Melbourne barrister Wallace Frederick Warne at St Stephen's Presbyterian Church, Sydney; they were to be divorced in 1956.

Moving to Melbourne, she performed journalistic services for the Australian Red Cross Society and in 1948 transferred to the *Argus*. In 1955 she was a freelance journalist in London before returning to Melbourne to join the *Woman's Day*. On 1 December 1956 in the office of the government statist, Queen Street, she married Herbert Michael Bower, a medical practitioner. For much of the period 1957-68 she produced HSV-7's television panel show, 'Tell the Truth', and was also employed as a scriptwriter. Her *Women in Australian Society* (1970)—published under her maiden name—documented patterns of women's employment, and contributed to debate on issues such as equal pay and equality of opportunity.

In 1969 the Australian Council for the Arts appointed Bower as a consultant. She drafted papers on education and the arts, on local government involvement, and on programmes to widen access and participation in artistic activities. In the early 1970s she helped to form the community arts and regional development committee of the Australia Council. In 1978 the committee became the community arts board. The new body was given the same policy and financial autonomy as the council's six other boards, and in May Bower became first director of the community arts board. Travelling each week to Sydney, she was responsible for providing support to arts centres, workshops and festivals, to specialist organizations, and to people in disadvantaged and remote regions. In September-October 1979 she visited Britain, France and Sweden to study approaches to community arts in those countries.

Bower was an attractive woman whose vitality and energy enhanced her presence. She was highly articulate, forthright in her views and incisive in her assessments. Her greatest attributes were her vision and her knowledge of how to convert ideas into tangible results. With a passionate faith in cultural democracy, she championed artists and others to help Australians to explore new ways of seeing themselves through the arts. She enjoyed a warm and intellectually rich private life. Ill health occasioned her retirement in December 1979. A volume of her poetry, *Flower and Thorn*, was published in 1980. Bower died of cancer on 19 May 1980 at South Yarra and was cremated; her husband and two sons—one from each of her marriages—survived her. The Australia Council's Ros Bower memorial award commemorates her.

Community Arts Bd, Aust Council, *Caper* (Syd), 10 May 1981; *Sun News-Pictorial*, 10 Sept 1964; *SMH*, 11 May 1978; *Age* (Melb), 10 June 1980; information from Dr H. Bower, South Yarra, Melb; personal information.   ANDREA HULL

BOWHAY, CLAUDE (1907-1970), sheepbreeder, was born on 21 June 1907 at Cumnock, New South Wales, son of George Henry Bowhay (d. 1937), hotelkeeper, and his wife Anne, née McCormack. Educated at St Stanislaus' College, Bathurst, Claude later managed his father's merino stud, Buckinbah, at Yeoval. At St Joseph's Catholic Church, Orange, on 21 July 1938 he married a bookkeeper Clarice Elizabeth Kell.

The Bowhays aimed to breed big-framed sheep whose wool would have bulk, density and a soft handle. In the mid-1930s they brought Uardry and Haddon Rig infusions into what had been basically Wanganella blood. A Buckinbah ewe took the grand championship in 1936 at the Sydney Sheep Show; by 1940 the stud's group entries had thrice been runners-up in the Stonehaven [q.v.12] Cup. After the sale of George Bowhay's land in 1945, Claude removed the family stud to St George, Queensland, and renamed the new property Buckinbah. On its first entry in the Queensland State Sheep Show in 1960, Buckinbah showed the supreme champion ram. From that year to 1967 (with the exception of 1966) the stud won the prize for aggregate points. At the Sydney Sheep Show in 1964 a Buckinbah ewe was the first Queensland merino to win a grand championship and the stud was ranked second in the Stonehaven Cup. Bowhay judged at shows throughout Australasia, frequently in Sydney, and in 1968 at Palermo, Argentina.

By 1970 Buckinbah was selling more rams than any other Queensland stud and Bowhay's wide, commercial, wool-growing experience gave him great influence in the industry. A councillor from 1940 to 1946 of the New South Wales Sheepbreeders' Association, in 1962 he was invited to rejoin the council in an unprecedented tribute to an interstate 'expatriate'. He was a councillor (from 1946) and president (1959-62) of the Queensland Merino Stud Sheepbreeders' Association, and president (1965) of the Australian Association of Stud Merino Breeders. As a United Graziers' Association councillor, he represented the Central Graziers' Association of Queensland and was a member (as one of the three delegates from the Australian Woolgrowers and Graziers' Council) of the Australian Wool Industry Conference. In 1969 he was appointed C.M.G.

Like his father, Claude Bowhay had been active in local government. In 1942-45 he served on Amaroo Shire Council, New South Wales. From 1951 he was a councillor of Balonne shire, Queensland. During his chairmanship (1954-70) of the shire (which carried some 10 per cent of Queensland's sheep) became one of the most prosperous in the State. Its electricity scheme was among the largest administered by a local council, and, in Bowhay's term, water supplies were expanded, towns sewered, facilities improved and St George was linked to a bitumen highway. Jovial and weatherbeaten, with dark, merry eyes under bushy brows, Bowhay was characterized by intelligence, conscientiousness, patience and a genial charm.

Survived by his wife, son and three daughters, he died of cancer on 15 October 1970 at Chermside Hospital, Brisbane, and was buried in St George cemetery.

G. O. Armstrong, *In Mitchell's Footsteps* (Brisb, 1968); G. Simpson and W. C. Skelsey (comp), *The Queensland Merino Stud Sheepbreeders' Association 50th Anniversary Souvenir Book 1983* (Toowoomba, Qld, 1983); C. Massy, *The Australian Merino* (Melb, 1990); *Pastoral Review*, 14 June 1935, 11 June 1940, 18 Sept 1961, 18 Nov 1970; *Balonne Beacon*, 21 Oct 1970.   S. J. ROUTH

BOWMAKER, ALFRED ERNEST (1895-1968), soldier and rice-farmer, was born on 11 September 1895 at Glebe, Sydney, third son of native-born parents William Henry Bowmaker, fruiterer, and his wife Frances Jane, née Upton. Educated at Leichhardt Public School, Alf served in the cadets for four years and worked as a drapery salesman. Having been a staff sergeant-major (1915-16) in the Permanent Military Forces, on 15 February 1917 he enlisted in the Australian Imperial Force. He was posted in December as a sergeant to the 33rd Infantry Battalion on the Western Front. In April 1918 he was badly gassed; after months in hospital in France and England, he was discharged in Sydney on 23 March 1919.

Briefly employed in the public service, in 1921 Bowmaker took up a block near Leeton under the Returned Soldiers Settlement Act (1916). With his father's help, he built a house mainly from bush timber and cleared his block. On 15 February 1922 he married Irene Clara Goldie at the Methodist Church, Haberfield, Sydney. She arrived at the farm in the middle of a heatwave and cooked their first meals in a kerosene tin. Bowmaker's block, like much of the Murrumbidgee Irrigation Area and most Australian closer settlement schemes, was too small to be viable. He supplemented his disability pension from the Department of Repatriation by working on the roads. When farm sizes were increased in the late 1920s, Bowmaker joined others in successful experiments with rice-farming. A founder in 1930 of the Ricegrowers' Association of Australia (president 1931 and 1952-64), he was also a member (1931-43) of the Rice Marketing Board.

The physical strain of the pioneering years affected his health; in 1936 he moved into Leeton and employed a share-farmer. Bowmaker became prominent in many community organizations, including the soldiers' and music clubs, the parent's and citizens' association, the Methodist Church and the Far West Children's Health Scheme. In 1940-45 he was captain and company commander of the Leeton unit of the Volunteer Defence Corps. As the rice industry rapidly expanded in the late 1940s, Bowmaker's involvement increased. With the assistance of others, he established the Ricegrowers' Co-operative Mills Ltd at Leeton in 1950, despite opposition in Sydney to 'Hill Billy farmers tampering with high finance'. The mill prospered from the outset, marketing its product as 'Sun White Rice' and initiating exports as the industry boomed in the 1950s and 1960s. Bowmaker remained a prominent figure and served on several government committees involved with the industry. In 1965 he was appointed M.B.E.

Lean and of middle height, with fair hair, grey eyes and spectacles, Bowmaker was a devout Methodist who often attended church twice on Sundays to fulfil his lay responsibilities. He dressed modestly. Capable of displaying both austerity and kindness, he had a reputation for humour in his public speeches and possessed a fine singing voice. Survived by his wife and two daughters, he died suddenly on 5 September 1968 near Leeton and was buried in the local cemetery. His book, *A Brief History of Leeton*, was published posthumously that year.

M. Maguire, *Living Memories* (priv pub, Leeton, NSW, 1984); *Ricemill News*, 6, no 1, Sept 1968; *Murrumbidgee Irrigator*, 11 Jan 1966; G. Bickford, funeral oration, Methodist Church, Leeton, 1968, is held by Miss E. Bowmaker, Leeton, NSW, who also provided information.   F. J. ROSS

BOYD, DOUGLAS THORNLEY (1896-1964), grazier and wool industry leader, was born on 19 October 1896 at Prahran, Melbourne, son of William Boyd, grazier, and his wife Edith Teresa, née Thornley, both Victorian born. Douglas spent his early years at Tarrone, his father's property near Koroit, where he was tutored privately before being sent to Geelong College. He subsequently managed Tarrone and later Barooga, William's station across the Murray River from Cobram. On 27 January 1920 at Christ Church, St Kilda, Douglas married Eina Alice Florence Pennicott with Anglican rites. When Barooga was sold for subdivision he bought Woorooma East, near Deniliquin, New South Wales. In 1933 he purchased Chatsworth Park, Tabilk, Victoria, which became the family home.

Active in running his properties, Boyd demanded hard, efficient work from his men. When asked in a Riverina hotel what his boss was like, a station-hand replied: 'He's a tough bugger but fair'. Boyd enjoyed tennis and played polo with Riverina teams: the row of cups in his home testified to his prowess. He belonged to the Australian Club, both in Melbourne and Sydney. Tireless in the interests of the grazing industry, he was president (1936-37) of the Graziers' Federal Council, vice-chairman (1942-54) of the Australian Woolgrowers' and Graziers' Council, and vice-president (1937-40) of the Graziers' Association of the Riverina.

An inspiring leader of the industry, Boyd was a member of the Australian Wool Board from its inception in 1936. On returning from a trip to Europe in 1937, he reported to the board's chairman (Sir) Dalziel Kelly [q.v.9]: 'To my mind the representation of our industry in London is long overdue. Today and in the future the primary producer will have to organise and take an active part in finding markets for his produce'. Promotional activities were developed and expanded considerably during Boyd's chairmanship (1943-53) and he fought successfully for uniform labelling of textiles.

In 1937 he had attended the conference of Australian, New Zealand and South African woolgrowers which met in Melbourne and led to the establishment of the International Wool Secretariat. A member of the Central Wool Committee in 1939-45, Boyd chaired the International Wool Publicity and Research Executive in 1940-48 and the Wool Bureau Inc., New York, in 1949-50 and 1951-52.

Although he was essentially shy and reserved, and was sometimes mistakenly seen as aloof, Boyd became a polished speaker who used his commanding voice to great effect. He gave his services generously and set high standards, both for himself and for the staff of the organizations with which he was associated. In 1951 he was appointed C.M.G. Divorced on 12 March 1951, three days later he married Marjory Mary Purbrick, née Tate Sutherland, also a divorcee, at the government statist's office, Melbourne.

Despite his vision and contribution to the industry, Boyd became the victim of wool politics and resigned on 30 June 1953, the day before the Australian Wool Board changed its name to the Australian Wool Bureau. He retired from public life and devoted himself to the management of his properties. In 1959 he sold Woorooma East and bought a small property, Deloraine, near Wallan, Victoria. Survived by his wife, and by the four daughters of his first marriage, he died of a coronary occlusion on 10 May 1964 at Deloraine and was cremated with Anglican rites. His estate was sworn for probate at £275 636.

J. O. Randell, *Teamwork* (Melb, 1976); Aust Wool Bd, *Annual Report*, 1964; *Pastoral Review*, June 1964; *SMH*, 15 Jan 1937, 30 Aug 1943, 19 Dec 1944, 11 June 1948, 12 May, 10 June 1950, 1 Jan, 21 June 1951, 1 July 1953; G. MacKinnon, *History of the Australian Wool Board and* personal records (held by Miss G. MacKinnon, South Yarra, Melb).
MARJORIE WAITE

BOYD, EILEEN ALBERTA (1890-1975), singer, was born on 13 December 1890 in Sydney, fourth child of Albert Boyd, a hotelkeeper from Victoria, and his Sydney-born wife Margaret, née Shalvey. Eileen was taught elocution by Harry Leston and dancing by Tom Donnelly. Billed as 'The Baby Baritone, Clog Dancer and Whistler', in 1900 she toured New Zealand with Dix's Gaiety Company. In May next year she appeared in Brisbane before joining J. C. Williamson's [q.v.6] Royal Comic Opera Company and later performing with Harry Rickards's [q.v.11] vaudeville circuit. In Sydney she attended St Vincent's College, Potts Point; on tour she had a tutor.

Pictured in 1904 as a sweet-faced girl with modest, downcast eyes, Eileen grew to only 4 ft 10 ins (147.3 cm), but had a voice of remarkable purity and power. She studied with Signor Steffani who took her to Paris in 1910. In London she sang at National Sunday League concerts in 1913. Compared favourably with (Dame) Clara Butt, Miss Boyd was described as 'a rare contralto' with a vivacious manner. After training with Sir Henry Wood, she sang under the conductors Sir Edward Elgar, (Sir) Hamilton Harty and (Sir) Edward German.

During World War I Eileen reputedly arranged and performed in at least 350 concerts. From 1914 she recorded songs, some martial in character, for Jumbo records. On 1 May 1915 at the register office, Brentford, Middlesex, she married a 42-year-old master mariner Hugh Ernest Roberts; he died on 24 October, leaving her with a son and a 13-year-old stepdaughter. Eileen twice toured Britain (1915 and 1917) with Peter Dawson [q.v.8] and Mark Hamburg; with Clara Butt, she sang Elgar's *The Dream of Gerontius* before King George V and Queen Mary in 1917.

A remunerative contract from Hugh McIntosh [q.v.10] brought her to Sydney later that year, with both children. Disappointed at finding only revue parts, she worked in music-hall and made three Asian tours. On 6 September 1920 at the Congregational parsonage, Richmond, Melbourne, she married a widower Horace Gordon Lane; they were to have one son. Back in Sydney, Eileen's 'domestic arrangements' obliged her to decline invitations to join Melba's [q.v.10] opera company and to audition at the Metropolitan Opera House, New York. Although she turned to teaching, she took part in the Australian Broadcasting Co.'s first transmission to England in 1927 and resumed recording with the Columbia Graphophone Co. Ltd. Her most successful record (*My Dear Soul* and an Australian song, *I passed by your Window*) remained on sale for twenty years. A concert was held in her honour in 1935 and next year she appeared as soloist with the Royal Philharmonic Society of Sydney. She toured New Zealand (1936 and 1937), and for the Australian Broadcasting Commission (1937), but the microphone cast doubts on the quality of her voice and she found it increasingly difficult to obtain engagements.

Impoverished after her husband's death in 1941, Eileen worked in the Commonwealth Department of Labour and National Service and in the Commonwealth Employment Service for fourteen years. Generous and spirited, she continued to sing at fund-raising concerts for charitable organizations (raising almost £8000 for the Anzac House appeal in 1957) even after she retired to Hammondville homes in 1966. Survived by her two sons, she died there on 14 September 1975 and was cremated.

A'sian Stage Annual, 1904; *Achievement*, 1967; *Otago Witness*, 24 Oct 1900, 15 May 1901; *Brisb Courier*, 6 May 1901; *The Times*, 13 Feb 1913; *T&CJ*, 15 Dec 1915; *SMH*, 6 Mar 1935, 19 Sept 1936, 6 Mar 1937, 16 Sept 1939, 15 Oct 1958; Boyd file, ABC Archives (Syd); P. Burgis, discographer, Imperial Concert Agency (Lond), publicity material (annotated by Boyd, pc held by author, Glebe, Syd); information from Mrs R. E. McDonald, Warrnambool, Vic, and Mrs O. C. Sharpe, Hammondville, Syd; family information.

ROSEMARY BROOMHAM

BOYD, MARTIN à BECKETT (1893-1972), author, was born on 10 June 1893 at Lucerne, Switzerland, fourth son of Arthur Merric Boyd [q.v.7] and his wife Emma Minnie, née à Beckett. His parents, both painters, were then touring Europe, accompanied by their elder children, Gilbert, William Merric and Penleigh [qq.v.7]. Travelling with them was Emma Minnie's mother, Emma à Beckett, matriarch of the family, whose private fortune (the legacy of her ex-convict father John Mills, founder of the Melbourne Brewery) supported the Boyds. In March 1890 Emma's husband W. A. C. à Beckett [q.v.3] had bought Penleigh House, Wiltshire, from a cousin: they intended to divide their time between the Grange—their home at Harkaway, outside Melbourne—and the Wiltshire property.

In Melbourne's financial crash of 1892-93 the à Becketts' income was halved; Penleigh House was sold; and the Boyds, returning to Melbourne with Emma à Beckett in December 1893, were to live on a much smaller allowance. Martin Boyd's idealization of

Europe may have stemmed from a sense of deprivation; the stories told to him in his childhood powerfully evoked a myth of past glories. The family suffered a deeper loss in January 1896 when 9-year-old Gilbert was killed in a riding accident at the Grange. Martin and his brothers nevertheless had a happy and secure childhood, living first at Sandringham, on Port Phillip Bay, and later (1906-13) at Tralee, a dairy farm at Yarra Glen which the Boyds bought with the hope of establishing Merric on the land. A fifth child, Helen, was born in 1903.

In 1906 Martin became a weekly boarder at Trinity Grammar School, Kew, where the headmaster George Merrick Long [q.v.10] gave this small Anglican establishment an unusually informal, non-authoritarian atmosphere. Boyd did respectably in academic work; he edited the school magazine, the *Mitre*; he developed a love of English poetry; and, through Long's example, he began to consider a future as a clergyman. Hitherto his main religious influence had been his mother's strict fundamentalism, while his own temperament inclined him to Anglo-Catholicism. Canon Long, neither a High-nor a Low-Churchman, seemed to offer an acceptable compromise between the two extremes.

In 1912 Boyd enrolled as a theological student at St John's College, St Kilda; he soon became bored and restless, missing social life and finding no spiritual or aesthetic sustenance. Like his elder brothers Merric and Penleigh, Martin had no sense of urgency about earning a living. Accepting, however, his mother's suggestion that he might try architecture, he was articled in 1913 to the Melbourne firm of Purchas & Teague. Boyd liked the work well enough and showed promise, especially in domestic architecture, but he had no professional ambition. He wrote a play and some poems, and went to as many parties as possible. It was the pleasant, easy social life of pre-1914 Melbourne that he missed when the outbreak of war changed the direction of his life.

Boyd was reluctant to enlist. His instincts, he later said, were pacifist; yet, in a family with close loyalties to Britain, it was only a matter of time before he would feel the pressure to volunteer. After Gallipoli, when several of his friends were killed, he made up his mind. He chose not to join the Australian Imperial Force, but to sail for Europe to seek a commission in a British regiment; if he were to be killed, he would at least have seen England. In August 1915 he left Melbourne in the *Miltiades*. Having completed an officers' training course, in the summer of 1916 he was posted to the Royal East Kent Regiment, known as the 'Buffs'.

By good fortune Boyd's experience of the

trenches was delayed until early 1917. As he waited, he explored the English countryside and visited Penleigh House. He stayed in country houses, discovered the London theatre and went to a great many dances. Adaptable, amusing and sociable, he made himself at home in English life. Although less striking in appearance than his elder brothers, he was considered handsome: he was tall and well built, with a clear complexion and fine, grey-blue eyes.

While spending his leaves at the London house of his mother's sister Ethel and her husband Charles Chomley [q.v.7], editor of the *British-Australasian*, Boyd often helped his uncle and cousins with cutting and pasting copy on the dining-room table and occasionally writing a paragraph or a review. It was a useful, if amateurish, introduction to a writer's life, though it is possible that Boyd would never have become a serious writer if he had not been sent to fight in France in 1917. His first autobiography, *A Single Flame* (1939), written when another world war was imminent, describes the impact of the trenches on a sheltered, sensitive young man. Brought up to believe that a life of absolute virtue was 'not only possible but usual', he was confronted for the first time with suffering and violence, not in any abstract way but in his own nature. Killing was evil—and he himself was capable of killing. He was a competent officer, he had plenty of physical courage and he enjoyed the comradeship of the regiment.

In September 1917 Boyd applied for a transfer to the Royal Flying Corps. There the casualty rate was even higher than in the infantry, but flying avoided the immediate horror of fighting hand to hand. He went as observer on bombing raids over Belgium in early 1918 before returning to England to train as a pilot. Boyd chose the single-seater fighter plane, the Sopwith Camel, because he did not want to risk the life of an observer. The Armistice came as he was awaiting orders to return to France. In his poems (*Verses*, privately published c.1919, and *Retrospect*, 1920) Boyd's incipient pacifism is less apparent than his idealization of the doomed youth of his generation.

After his demobilization in May 1919, Boyd sailed for Melbourne in the troop-ship, *Prinz Hubertus*. It was a disappointing homecoming. Because his war experience had been with the British rather than the A.I.F., he had little shared experience with other returned men, and he was said to have become 'too English'. His parents were living in Murrumbeena, where Merric had established a pottery. Martin did not want to be drawn into this enterprise, nor did he want to resume his training as an architect. His closest friends at this time were his second cousins Mim and

Nancy Weigall; and there is reason to believe that he was in love with Nancy. If so, it was not a whole-hearted courtship: what Boyd wanted most was to go back to England, which he did in May 1921, with his parents' reluctant consent and an allowance of £100 a year.

In London again, Boyd wrote for the *British-Australasian*, but after two years he had accomplished little; and London social life had ceased to charm him. In August 1923 he was spending a few weeks retreat at Batcombe, Dorset, with a new order of Anglican Franciscan friars, when he had news from Melbourne that his brother Penleigh had been killed in a motorcar crash. Desolate at the loss, Martin decided to join the monastic community in its mission to derelicts. The spiritual renewal and 'disinterested love' he had hoped to find at Batcombe seemed to lose itself in squabbles between the 'High' and 'Protestant' elements; after a brief period as a novice (in which he appointed himself as cook), Boyd left the order.

The experience gave him material for his first novel, *Love Gods*, published in 1925 and favourably reviewed. His next work, *Brangane* (1926), drew on the eccentric London career of the Australian writer Barbara Baynton [q.v.7], then by her third marriage the Baroness Headley. *The Montforts* (1928) which, like its predecessors, was published under the pseudonym 'Martin Mills', was based on the history of the à Beckett family in Australia; some thinly-veiled portraits caused offence in Melbourne. It won the Australian Literature Society's first gold medal in 1929.

In 1925-38 Boyd lived mainly in Sussex, in rented, seaside cottages; he wrote in winter and travelled in Europe in summer. His novels of this period, *Scandal of Spring* (1934), *The Lemon Farm* (1936), *The Picnic* (1937) and *Night of the Party* (1938), deft social comedies with serious undertones, show his grasp of English life and manners. In *A Single Flame*, written during the Munich crisis, he debated the morality of war, and concluded that appeasement of Hitler was futile as well as dishonourable. The semi-allegorical *Nuns in Jeopardy* (1940) explored good and evil in human nature in a desert-island setting. *Lucinda Brayford* (1946) brought together all the preoccupations of Boyd's earlier work. With its Australian-born heroine, it moved from pre-1914 Melbourne to England in the 1940s. Written in Cambridge where Boyd made his home for the war years, it reflected the renewal of his religious faith and the clarification of his ideas about war. When British bombs fell on civilian targets in Germany, Boyd denounced church and state for what he saw as crimes against humanity.

Lucinda Brayford had high praise from

critics in Britain and sold well; it was translated into Swedish and Danish, and, as a Literary Guild choice in the United States of America, added welcome dollars to Boyd's small bank balance. He already had his own cottage, Plumstead, Little Eversden, outside Cambridge, bought when his share of his mother's estate came to him following his father's death in 1940.

With his first major literary success, Boyd felt ready to go back to Australia. In June 1948 he sold Plumstead, and made plans to restore and live in his à Beckett grandfather's home, the Grange. A great deal of energy and money transformed the neglected, old house into an elegant, neo-Georgian setting for Boyd's eighteenth-century furniture. He commissioned his nephew Arthur Boyd to paint frescoes in the dining room; this ambitious work was lost when the house was demolished in the late 1960s.

Living at the Grange proved lonely and disappointing; there was little left of the life Boyd remembered, and, as in 1919, he was seen as 'too English'. *Lucinda Brayford* was ignored in a literary climate which devalued expatriate writing and Boyd found his reputation obscured by the rising stars of his nephews, Arthur and Robin Boyd [q.v.]. The one great gain, however, was the new perspective on his past: it provided a new subject which he took back with him to England in 1951. The Langton series of novels—*The Cardboard Crown* (1952), *A Difficult Young Man* (1955), *Outbreak of Love* (1957) and *When Blackbirds Sing* (1962)—had its initial impulse in Boyd's discovery of his à Beckett grandmother's diaries at the Grange. Having failed to make the past live again at the Grange, Boyd made enduring art from that failure. The first three novels won high praise in Britain and the U.S.A.; in spite of their Anglo-Australian themes and settings, they were scarcely noticed by Australian reviewers.

Lonely and restless again in England, Boyd went to Rome in 1957 and lived for the rest of his life in a series of *pensiones* and apartments, on a diminishing income. The last Langton novel was a critical failure, as was the Roman comedy, *The Tea-Time of Love* (1969). In 1965 he published a second autobiography, *Day of My Delight*. Although his wit, charm and generosity had won him many friends in England, Boyd became isolated in Rome. His main resource was the 'English Centre' of the Church of San Silvestro where, as he often complained, he met too many priests and 'R.C. ladies'. Boyd's faith in youth, especially the anti-Vietnam War protesters of the late 1960s, was his mainstay against depression in this period. He defended them in *Why They Walk Out* (1970), a personal statement of belief, published at his own expense.

In Rome Boyd's affections were centred on an Italian youth Luciano Trombini, for whom he played a quasi-paternal role until Trombini married and moved to Milan in 1964. No record of any closer or more lasting attachment appears in Boyd's life, and, although the question of his homosexuality is often raised, it has never been demonstrated that any one of a series of sentimental friendships with young men amounted to an affair. The only sexual relationship for which there is persuasive evidence involved a woman of his own age during his Sussex years. Those who knew Boyd best stress his 'correctness', his reticence and a fastidious temperament which would not easily adapt to casual sex, nor, perhaps, to any full emotional commitment. It may be questioned whether anyone was allowed to know his deepest feelings.

His family and friends were unprepared for his reception into the Catholic Church which took place a few days before he died of cancer on 3 June 1972 in the Hospital of the Blue Nuns, Rome. His niece Mary Perceval and Arthur Boyd who, with his brothers Guy and David, had helped Martin Boyd financially during his last illness, attended his burial in Rome's Protestant English cemetery, after a service in which the Anglican vicar joined the Catholic priest in prayer. Boyd had lived just long enough to see his major works reprinted and his literary stature recognized in Australia; and, to his astonishment and ironic amusement, he was awarded a Commonwealth Literary Fund pension—for life—as he awaited his death.

B. Niall, *Martin Boyd* (Melb, 1988), *and* for bibliog; Martin Boyd papers *and* Emma à Beckett diaries (NL).　　　　　　　　　BRENDA NIALL

BOYD, ROBIN GERARD PENLEIGH (1919-1971), architect and critic, was born on 3 January 1919 at Armadale, Melbourne, younger son of Theodore Penleigh Boyd [q.v.7], artist, and his wife Edith Susan Gerard, daughter of J. G. Anderson [q.v.3]. The couple had a daughter Pamela who died in infancy. Their elder son John à Beckett Penleigh ('Pat') was to become a distinguished pilot. Edith, a miniaturist and water-colourist, had been the auburn-haired model for several paintings by E. Phillips Fox [q.v.8]. Martin Boyd [q.v.] was Robin's uncle.

Until he was 3, Robin lived in a Picturesque house, The Robins, at Warrandyte, designed and built in 1913 by his father. In 1922 he made the first of many journeys abroad, accompanying the family to Europe where his father arranged to bring an exhibition of modern art to Australia. Within days of his return, Penleigh was killed in a motorcar accident in 1923. Edith moved to one of the city's earliest apartment blocks at Toorak and in 1927 bought a brick bungalow at East Malvern, from which Robin walked to the Lloyd Street central school and then (1930-35) to Malvern Grammar.

Leaving school, Boyd studied at night at the Melbourne Technical College and the Melbourne University Architectural Atelier, while working during the day in the office of A. & K. Henderson where he was articled for three years to Kingsley Henderson [q.v.9]. The job in the Bank Place office was inimical to Boyd's growing Modernist ideas and he threw himself into the formation of the Victorian Architectural Students' Society. With his three-generation background in aesthetic affairs and his striking appearance, fair hair, clear, blue eyes and light colouring, he was at 19 a charismatic leader in V.A.S.S. affairs. Boyd founded its monthly newsfold, *Smudges*, which soon became the voice of the re-awakening profession. He wrote every editorial and in each issue singled out buildings for either a 'blot' or a 'bouquet'. When he designated an apartment building in South Yarra a 'blot', its architects threatened legal action. To avoid heavy damages he published a retraction, but, by using Gothic typeface, still managed to convey his opinion of the building.

Having completed his articles, he worked in several offices, quit the atelier over a design decision by the director Leighton Irwin [q.v.9] and obtained the post of sole assistant to (Sir) Roy Grounds. On 27 December 1941 at Scots Church, Melbourne, Boyd married Dorothea Patricia Madder. They had known each other from childhood: Patricia's mother was the sister of William Merric Boyd's [q.v.7] wife who was the mother of Robin's cousin Arthur. Despite the wartime housing shortage, the young couple managed to lease a flat in Grounds's noted Clendon (the subject of a 'bouquet' on its completion in 1939) at Armadale.

Enlisting in the Citizen Military Forces on 21 November 1939, Boyd was mobilized on 11 November 1941 and posted to the survey directorate, headquarters, Southern Command, Melbourne. In July 1942 he joined No. 3 Field Survey Company in Queensland and was confirmed sergeant in October. Embarking for Port Moresby in March 1943, next month he transferred to the Australian Imperial Force. He remained in Papua until April 1944 when, taking leave, he saw his 14-month-old daughter for the first time. From March 1945 he served at Bendigo, Victoria, with the Land Headquarters Cartographic Company. He was discharged in September with the rank of acting warrant officer, class 2.

Throughout his army service Boyd maintained his involvement with architecture. The preparation of military maps meant that drafting facilities were readily available, and with his colleagues—notably Kevin Pethebridge and Francis Bell (Kingsley Henderson's nephew)—he entered competitions and prepared designs for houses. He also contributed to army publications and constantly debated the future form of the Australian home. His first partnership, Associated Architects—Boyd Pethebridge & Bell, produced a significant house at Kew and a factory at Hawthorn.

In 1946 Boyd left the partnership to become director of the Small Homes Service, set up by the Royal Victorian Institute of Architects in conjunction with the *Age*. The service aimed at promoting rational house-design and to this goal he was to bring his talents in design and in communication. He prepared for publication the illustrations of members' submissions; he drew up standard specifications and rationalized working drawings so that they were acceptable to owner-builders; and he produced a weekly article for the *Age* on all aspects of design as it affected the house. The service opened in July 1947. Within a short time Robin Boyd had become a household name.

In 1947 the Boyds moved into a new house which they had built at Camberwell. In the same year Robin passed the registration examination, was made an associate of the R.V.I.A., and won the Robert [q.v.9] and Ada Haddon travelling scholarship, which took him to England and Europe in 1950. He continued to run the Small Homes Service until December 1953, while at the same time writing and lecturing part time at the university. As a lecturer he was impressive, preparing his material carefully and delivering it in a clear, incisive voice. The majority of the commissions in his growing practice were for houses and from this period came some of his most creative work. He prepared all drawings himself, working in his distinctive, left-handed style. In 1953 he designed Australia's first project home, the Peninsula house, and next year produced a standardized window-wall for Stegbar Ltd: he later described this work as 'brief-case practice'. After completing his last article for the *Age*, he immediately began to write weekly pieces for the *Herald*. During these busy years Boyd continued to take an active role in public and professional affairs. He published *Victorian Modern* (1947), *Australia's Home* (1952) and *The Australian Ugliness* (1960). The last two books, which discussed architecture in terms of the total environment, were to be regarded as classics.

In July 1953 Frederick Romberg, Boyd and Grounds formed a partnership. Located in a terrace house in Albert Street, East Melbourne, their office flourished from its inception. The long-awaited postwar boom had arrived. Their commissions ranged from flats to factories, and from schools to churches. Houses continued to form a significant part of the practice, which was uncommon in a major office. Although the three partners were prominent as individuals, the firm maintained design unity. Some buildings revealed the hand of one or other of the architects, but in general the firm developed a corporate style, combining the philosophies of the trio and representing the advanced thinking of that era. Their work was a distinctive Australian form of the International Style, then called Contemporary.

Boyd's focus remained domestic. In all, about one hundred houses were built from his designs. Because of his fascination with the flexibility offered by frame construction, many of his earlier houses (Gillison, Darbyshire, Myer and Richardson) have been reclad, extensively altered or destroyed. In contrast, the Clempson house at Kew has been restored and its 1959 furniture reinstalled. Of his subsequent, more substantial work, the Featherston-Currey house, Ivanhoe, the Baker house, Bacchus Marsh, and the house he built for himself at South Yarra (1959) best illustrate Boyd's wide, analytical approach. To him, each building presented a challenge, to be solved from the ground up. He had a consistent approach to design problems, but the solutions were always different. His Domain Park apartments, South Yarra, Menzies [q.v.] College at La Trobe University, McCaughey Court at Ormond [q.v.5] College, University of Melbourne, and the Tower Hill Museum at Warrnambool showed his willingness to embrace unconventional plan-forms and construction methods. Among his other buildings were the John Batman and President motor inns, Melbourne, the Black Dolphin Motel at Merimbula, New South Wales, and the zoology building, Australian National University, and Churchill House, Canberra.

While spending 1956-57 as Fulbright scholar and visiting professor at the Massachusetts Institute of Technology, Boyd travelled around the United States of America and his admiration for the country and the people was fostered. He was particularly influenced by Walter Gropius, professor of architecture, Harvard University. At the same time, however, Boyd chastised Australians for their mindless emulation of America, in 1957 coining the term 'Austerica': the belief that 'everything desirable, exciting, luxurious and enviable in the 20th century is American'. In 1958 he became a fellow of the Royal Australian Institute of Architects.

Boyd's life was profoundly affected when Grounds accepted on 18 December 1959 a commission to design the Victorian Cultural (Arts) Centre. Although the partnership had been included in the appointment, Grounds preferred to proceed on his own. Romberg & Boyd was founded in 1962 and the firm produced notable work during the straitened early 1960s. Romberg accepted the chair of architecture at the University of Newcastle in 1965, but remained in the partnership. Boyd, already a national figure, was by then widely recognized internationally. He travelled frequently, to Europe, the U.S.A., South East Asia and Japan. In 1962 he published *Kenzo Tange* and *The Walls Around Us*; in 1963 *The New Architecture*; in 1965, probably his most important work of architectural theory, *The Puzzle of Architecture*. These were followed by *The Book of Melbourne and Canberra* (Adelaide, 1966), *New Directions in Japanese Architecture* (New York, 1968) and (with Mark Strizic) *Living in Australia* (Sydney, 1970).

A trustee (1965) of the National Gallery of Victoria and a member (1968) of the National Capital Planning Authority, in 1967 Boyd delivered the Boyer [q.v.] lectures (published as *Artificial Australia*) for the Australian Broadcasting Commission. That year he was awarded an honorary doctorate of letters from the University of New England. He designed the Australian Expo exhibits at Montreal, Canada (1967), and Osaka, Japan (1970), and wrote the scripts for the broadcast commentaries. Having previously written for the *Australian* in 1964-65, he published regular articles in the Sunday edition from 1970. He was an honorary fellow of the American Institute of Architects and a fellow of the Royal Society of Arts.

In 1969 Boyd was awarded the gold medal of the R.A.I.A.; he became an honorary fellow in 1970. As president-elect of the Victorian chapter, he revamped its journal, *Architect*, and made it a critical force. He also instigated the Melbourne Papers (a series of lectures by visitors). Boyd supervised every detail of any publication in which he was involved, choosing every typeface and often producing illustrations.

In January 1971 he was appointed C.B.E. That year he was invited to be one of five judges of an international competition for a new building to provide office accommodation for members of the British parliament. He returned home in September and died of subacute bacterial endocarditis on 16 October 1971 in Royal Melbourne Hospital. After a private service in the chapel of Ormond College, he was cremated. His wife, son and two daughters survived him; his estate was sworn for probate at $13 958.

Shocked by his early death, the R.A.I.A. arranged a public tribute to its popular Victorian president in the garden of its headquarters, Robert Russell [q.v.2] House (Boyd had suggested the name), during which excerpts from his writings were read. In 1973 Boyd was posthumously named recipient of the American Institute of Architects' architecture critics' medal. In 1989 the Royal Melbourne Institute of Technology held a symposium on his work.

When he died, Boyd was Australia's best-known architect, esteemed both for his writings and his buildings. Although he declared that he was essentially a 'practising architect', his greatest contribution was as a critic of and an advocate for the profession—a social commentator, publicist and polemicist, and an arbiter of taste and standards, who challenged Australian complacency and apathy about its architecture and environment. According to the architect Sir James Richards, he was 'a persistently civilizing influence on Australian life'. Many of Boyd's books remain in print; his last work, the *Great Great Australian Dream* (Sydney, 1972) summed up the pretensions of his profession and the frustrations of his generation. He had become an authority on architecture, but his abiding interest was the design of buildings, many of which, especially his houses, are the subject of increasing interest and continuing study.

Despite his sometimes acerbic social comment, Boyd was a sociable man of unfailing good manners, kindness and charm. He never lost his engaging modesty. That quality and an all-pervasive sense of humour distinguished him even more than his capacity for work and his pursuit of excellence.

J. Hetherington, *Uncommon Men* (Melb, 1965); *Robin Boyd: the Architect as Critic*, exhibition cat (Melb, 1989), and for bibliog; P. Dobrez and P. Herbst, *The Art of the Boyds* (Syd, 1990); *Architect* (Melb), 3, no 17, 1971; *Architecture in Aust*, 62, no 2, Apr 1973; *Transition*, Nov-Dec 1981; *Age* (Melb), 12 Nov 1969, 18 Oct 1971; *The Times*, 23 Oct 1972; C. Hamann, Three Leaders of Melbourne Architecture 1926-1971 (Ph.D. thesis, Monash Univ, 1978); Grounds, Romberg and Boyd archive (Monash Univ).   NEIL CLEREHAN

BOYD, WALTER HUBERT (1900-1970), solicitor, was born on 26 June 1900 at Ahoghill, County Antrim, Ireland, son of William Boyd, farmer, and his wife Eliza Jane, née McClelland. Walter was educated at Ballymena Academy where he developed a lifelong love of Rugby Union football. During World War I he served with the British Army and met R. L. H. Peterson, a solicitor for whom Boyd's elder brother Lowry worked at Longreach, Queensland. After the Armistice, Boyd matriculated and studied medicine for a year at the Queen's University of Belfast. Peterson, with whom he had kept in touch, persuaded him to migrate in 1922 and enter into articles of clerkship with him. Boyd was

admitted as a solicitor on 3 May 1927. He married Thelma Lilea Forrest on 18 December 1929 at St Andrew's Presbyterian Church, Brisbane.

In 1931 he was admitted to partnership by Peterson who subsequently entered into partnership with J. K. Cannan in Brisbane, leaving Boyd to carry on their practice in the Central West. He became a partner in the Brisbane firm in 1946. A councillor (1949-69) of the Queensland Law Society, he was vice-president in 1952-54, president in 1954-56 and served on sub-committees which examined complaints, ethics and legislation. His enthusiasm inspired others, and his sense of humour and sincerity ensured his popularity. While a member of the society's public relations and social committees—which were particularly suited to his warm and outgoing personality—he was especially keen to advance the interests of younger members of the profession. Considering that the formality of the admission ceremony was rather starchy, he persuaded the council to entertain newly-admitted solicitors at lunch, thus introducing them to the society's management and affairs.

During the time he had been based at Longreach and in the Central West, Boyd played Rugby League football and cricket; when he moved to Brisbane he was able to resume his interest in Rugby Union, as an administrator. For many years he was president of the Great Public Schools Rugby Club. He chaired the Queensland Rugby Union's management committee in 1958-62 and, as president (1965-70) of the Q.R.U., helped to secure Ballymore Park, Brisbane, as its permanent home. Boyd was a Rotarian and a Freemason. In 1965 he was appointed O.B.E. On 29 January 1970 he retired from the Queensland Law Society Council, but was immediately appointed to its statutory committee, the judicial body which dealt with all forms of professional misconduct.

Survived by his wife, daughter and two sons, Boyd died of a coronary occlusion on 10 May 1970 at St Lucia and was cremated with Presbyterian forms.

Law Inst J, Mar, July 1970; *Proctor*, Oct 1989; *Courier Mail*, 11 May 1970; Qld Law Soc Archives *and* Qld Rugby Union Archives, Brisb; information from Mr H. E. Peterson, Toowong, Brisb.

J. C. H. GILL

BOYER, SIR RICHARD JAMES FILDES (1891-1961), grazier, publicist and broadcasting chief, was born on 24 August 1891 at Taree, New South Wales, third and youngest son of Frederick Cartwright Boyer, a Wesleyan minister, and his wife Marianne, née Pearson, both English born. Educated at

Wolaroi Grammar School, Orange, Newington College and the University of Sydney (B.A., 1913; M.A. Hons, 1915), Richard entered the Methodist ministry. In 1914-15 he was a probationer on the new Canberra circuit, preaching at the Cotter Dam to navvies who allowed him ten minutes from their two-up on Sunday mornings.

Hoping for an appointment as a chaplain in the Australian Imperial Force, in March 1915 he became a Young Men's Christian Association camp secretary at Alderley, Brisbane. The appointment did not eventuate and he enlisted on 24 April. Boyer sailed to Egypt with the 26th Battalion and reached Gallipoli in September; he was evacuated next month with enteric fever and repatriated in January 1916. Having obtained a commission in the A.I.F. on 22 January 1917, he joined the 1st Battalion on the Western Front in July. He was gassed in September near Passchendaele, Belgium, and again invalided to Australia where his appointment terminated on 13 October 1919. Too shaken and cynical to return to the ministry, he went jackerooing near Morven, Queensland. In 1920 he took up 38 652 acres (15 642 ha) in the district and named his property Durella. On 22 May that year at Eastwood, Sydney, he married with Methodist forms Eleanor Muriel Underwood who had nursed him during the war.

After an initial struggle, the Boyers succeeded through good management and a timely shift from cattle to sheep. Their achievement earned the respect of fellow pastoralists. Boyer became president of the Warrego Graziers' Association in 1934 and, following a visit to Europe in 1935, increased his involvement in the affairs of the wool industry. He opposed the Commonwealth government's trade diversion policy in 1936, pamphleteered ably for the 'No' case during the 1937 marketing referendum and urged the lowering of tariffs to stimulate exports of primary produce. President of the United Graziers' Association of Queensland (1941-44) and of the Graziers' Federal Council of Australia (1942), he co-operated with the Federal Labor government on marketing and industrial relations matters, gained tax concessions for pastoral improvements and sat on the Australian Meat Industry Commission. He championed the ill-fated Queensland Dried Meats Co-operative Association, formed in 1945 with the aim of establishing an abattoir and freezing works at Winton.

Placing Durella in the hands of a manager, Boyer had moved to Brisbane in 1937 and to Sydney in 1940, seeking opportunities for public service. His interest in foreign affairs grew after he attended the 1938 British Commonwealth Relations Conference at Lapstone, New South Wales, and made a second European tour in 1939. He avoided domestic politics and in 1940 refused Country Party nomination for the Queensland seat of Maranoa in the House of Representatives. That year he was appointed honorary director of the American division of the Department of Information; in 1942 and 1945 he went abroad for conferences of the Institute of Pacific Relations. President (1946-49) of the Commonwealth council of the Australian Institute of International Affairs, he launched the journal, *Australian Outlook*. In the 1940s and 1950s Boyer devoted his formidable energies to the Australian national committee of the United Nations Appeal for Children, to Sydney Rotary Club's international service committee and to the Good Neighbour movement.

In 1940 he had been appointed a member of the Australian Broadcasting Commission and on 1 April 1945 became chairman. Amendments to the Broadcasting Act in 1948 added two public servants to the commission's membership, but Boyer resisted further encroachments on its autonomy by persuading J. B. Chifley [q.v.] to maintain its unfettered discretion over political broadcasts. Boyer's 'part-time' job occupied most of his working hours. His relationship with the general manager (Sir) Charles Moses has been summarized as 'never intimate and never had a showdown'. As chairman, Boyer had a style that resembled 'a brotherly pow-wow' and his idealism struck some as ingenuous; yet, he was a shrewd and patient tactician whose judgement was trusted.

As the introduction of television approached, the A.B.C. was given responsibility in 1954 for the national service. Boyer fought off a proposal to replace the serving commissioners with three full-time 'experts' and presided over the inauguration of ABN-2 on 5 November 1956. Appointed K.B.E. that year, he declined the post of high commissioner to Canada. Although he suffered the first of a series of coronary attacks in 1957, he agreed to chair the committee of inquiry into public service recruitment: its 1959 report recommended improved selection procedures, including permanency for married women. The A.B.C. was troubled by staff unrest over pay, conditions and autonomy, but that year Boyer encouraged plans for the programme, 'University of the Air', and initiated the annual lectures that were to bear his name.

Wary of political interference, in 1945 he had secured from John Curtin [q.v.] a public statement recognizing the A.B.C.'s 'special independence of judgement and action'. Politicians, however, continued their meddling and critics claimed that the A.B.C.'s independence would last only if unexercised. Boyer drew on considerable reserves of tact in dealing with governments. His liberalism favoured a hearing for all significant viewpoints; politicians—Labor or otherwise—preferred a consensus which offended nobody. In May 1961 (Sir) Robert Menzies' [q.v.] cabinet quashed a planned A.B.C. documentary (to be scripted by Rohan Rivett [q.v.]) on relations between the United States of America and Canada. Gravely ill, Sir Richard contemplated resigning in protest. He died of coronary thrombosis on 5 June 1961 at his Wahroonga home and was cremated with Presbyterian forms. His retirement had been scheduled for 30 June.

A man of 'long, spare country frame', Boyer had spoken of himself as a 'bushie', but subscribed all his life to the *Hibbert Journal.* He was a humorous raconteur who reminded his colleague Sir John Medley [q.v.] of Falstaff's memorable picture: 'O, you shall see him laugh until his face be like a wet cloak ill laid up'. Happy in his family life, Boyer was survived by his wife, daughter and son Richard who was a director (1983-86) of the Australian Broadcasting Corporation.

G. C. Bolton, *Dick Boyer* (Canb, 1967); K. S. Inglis, *This is the ABC* (Melb, 1983); R. S. Kerr, *Freedom of Contract* (Brisb, 1990); Sir Richard Boyer papers (NL).   G. C. BOLTON

BOYLE, JOHN (1904-1979), surveyor and public servant, was born on 14 March 1904 at Marrickville, Sydney, seventh child of John Boyle, quarryman, and his wife Annie (Joanna), née Sweeney, both native-born. Educated at Christian Brothers' High School, Lewisham, young John studied arts as an evening student at the University of Sydney. In 1926-27 he was a cadet draftsman in the New South Wales Department of the Attorney-General and of Justice, and on 29 August 1933 became a registered surveyor. He married a schoolteacher and fellow debating enthusiast Philomena Margaret Flynn on 26 October 1935 at St Brigid's Catholic Church, Marrickville.

During the Depression Boyle worked for A. F. Hall & Co., civil engineers and surveyors of Newcastle. Frequently unemployed, he sailed alone to Papua in 1937 and for almost twelve months surveyed the Fly River region. On his return to New South Wales, he undertook contract jobs for local councils. In 1942 he joined the Commonwealth Public Service and moved to Canberra. Initial engagements in defence projects took him to Maralinga, South Australia, and to Kalgoorlie, Western Australia. He travelled to Norfolk Island in 1945 where he surveyed the island's aerodrome. Back in Canberra, he was promoted senior surveyor (1950) and chief surveyor (1952), and ap-

pointed Commonwealth surveyor-general in March 1964.

Intent on innovation, Boyle shed extraneous official tasks in order to implement efficiencies in the Australian Survey Office, which had been expanding from the early 1950s to meet the demands of construction, mining and space-exploration projects. He introduced one of the public service's first electronic computers and acquired advanced surveying equipment, including distance-measuring instruments. At an international conference in Portugal and on tours of Britain and the United States of America, he examined the latest photogrammetric devices and techniques. Dedicated and determined, he asserted his authority, but, in confronting issues and challenging bureaucratic controls, he came into conflict with members of the Public Service Board.

A keen Labor supporter, Boyle was loyal to his professional colleagues. He established and was foundation president (1964) of the Commonwealth Professional Surveyors' Association, and also advocated the introduction of university degrees in surveying. Chairman of the Surveyors' Board of the Australian Capital Territory, he was a member (1964-69) of the National Mapping Council of Australia. From 1960 he had belonged to the Canberra division of the Institution of Surveyors, Australia. Sturdy in build, he had a steady, confident gaze.

Late in Boyle's term of office his authoritarianism and inability to accept advice put him at odds with his staff who allowed his retirement to pass without ceremony. He spent his final years quietly and enjoyed bowls, gardening and watching football. Survived by his wife and two sons, he died on 21 August 1979 in Royal Canberra Hospital and was buried in Canberra cemetery.

Canb Times, 15 Mar 1969, 3 Sept 1979; information from Mrs P. M. Boyle, Merrylands, Syd, Mr K. Wellspring, Aust Surveying and Land Information Group, and Mr R. Wenholz, Registrar, Surveyors Bd of the ACT, both at Cameron Offices, Belconnen, Canb.   HELEN BOXALL

BRADFORD, LESLIE (1878-1943), metallurgist, was born on 9 March 1878 in Delhi, India, youngest of seven children of George Augustus Bradford, customs collector, and his wife Amelia Caroline, née Moore. Les attended Bishop Cotton School, Simla, until the family migrated to Adelaide in 1892. Next year he entered the School of Mines and Industries where in 1896 he obtained associate diplomas in mining and metallurgy. Having moved to Broken Hill, New South Wales, in 1897, two years later he joined the

Broken Hill Proprietary Co. Ltd as an assayer at its smelter at Port Pirie, South Australia, but soon repaired to Broken Hill as metallurgist. On 26 April 1902 at All Souls Church, St Peters, Adelaide, he married Mabel Ellen Müller.

Working under G. D. Delprat [q.v.8] and with A. D. Carmichael, in 1902 Bradford invented an improved desulphurization process for treating ores and about 1912 perfected the flotation process of separating silver-lead and zinc. Writing in the early 1960s, W. S. Robinson [q.v.11] declared that no other metallurgical development in the last fifty years had 'added so much to the wealth of the world'. In 1915 Bradford was transferred to the company's Newcastle steelworks. He was to regard his innovative work on the open hearth there as the most difficult he had performed. An entrepreneur, able to perceive and exploit opportunities, Bradford resigned in 1920 to establish the Bradford Kendall foundry in Sydney to produce alloy steel casting. He and his partner had raised the necessary capital by punting on the racehorse, Jack Findlay, which had four straight wins (1919-20). After Bradford Kendall Ltd was registered as a public company in 1922, B.H.P. attracted Bradford back as production superintendent; he became manager of the steelworks in 1924. Sydney Technical College awarded him an honorary fellowship in 1927 for his original research in the steel industry.

Appointed general manager of B.H.P. in Melbourne under Essington Lewis [q.v.10] in 1935, Bradford became chief executive officer in 1938. He had remained an active director of Bradford Kendall Pty Ltd, by then a major foundry, and in 1940 set up Bradford Insulation Ltd to manufacture rock-wool from steelworks' slag. He was also a director of Australian Iron and Steel Ltd, Lysaght Bros & Co. Ltd, Bullivants' Australian Co. Pty Ltd and Titan Nail & Wire Pty Ltd. President (1926) of the Australasian Institute of Mining and Metallurgy, in 1937 he was awarded its medal for his work on flotation and in steelmaking. He was a member of the American Institute of Mining and Metallurgical Engineers, and of the Iron and Steel Institute, London.

Described as 'gently spoken, sensitive and withdrawn', Bradford was 'enthusiastic and intense', with sympathetic brown eyes and a dark, brushy moustache. By 1935, however, the moustache had gone, with most of his hair. A 'keen collector of paintings, he loved the theatre and a game of bridge', and showed a keen appreciation of motorcars. He was president (1930-34) of the Newcastle Club and belonged to the Union Club, Sydney, and the Australian and Athenaeum clubs in Melbourne.

Survived by his wife, three sons and twin daughters, Bradford died of coronary vascular disease on 20 June 1943 at his Toorak home and was cremated. A laboratory in the South Australian Institute of Technology is named after him in tribute to his 'outstanding work in the realm of mining and metallurgy'. His portrait by (Sir) William Dargie is held by the University of Melbourne.

W. S. Robinson, *If I Remember Rightly*, G. Blainey ed (Melb, 1967); G. Blainey, *The Steel Master* (Melb, 1971); J. Burns (ed) for A'sian Mineral Heritage Trust, *Leslie Bradford Golden Jubilee Oration* (Melb, 1987); *Critic* (Adel), 5 Apr 1902; A'sian Inst of Mining and Metallurgy records (Melb); Univ Melb Archives.　　D. F. FAIRWEATHER

BRADLEY, CLAUDIA PORTIA BURTON- (1909-1967), orthopaedist, was born on 28 November 1909 at Richmond, New South Wales, only daughter of native-born parents Alan Godfrey Burton Bradley, farmer, and his wife Ruby Malvina, née Drayton. Alan was the youngest child of Henry Burton Bradley [q.v.3]. At 11 Claudia was diagnosed as having diabetes. She spent a year in the Coast Hospital, Little Bay, becoming one of the first diabetics in the world to receive insulin; for the rest of her life she was to inject herself daily with insulin. She attended Cleveland Street Intermediate High School, matriculated in 1928 and—styling herself Burton-Bradley—enrolled as an evening student in pharmacy and in arts at the University of Sydney (B.A., 1940; M.B., B.S., 1943). Apprenticed to a pharmacist in King Street, she qualified in 1930 and was pharmacist at Western Suburbs Hospital (1933-38). She had 'always wanted to study medicine' and supported herself while completing her degrees.

A 'tallish, slender young woman of kindly disposition and conspicuous clarity of mind and diction', Dr Burton-Bradley was a resident medical officer at Royal North Shore Hospital in 1944, then a senior resident at the Rachel Forster Hospital for Women and Children. She also conducted clinics with the New South Wales Society for Crippled Children where she met Audrie and Neil McLeod, founders of the Spastic Centre of New South Wales. Claudia was appointed its first medical director in January 1945. Next year she also became honorary clinical assistant in physiotherapy at Royal North Shore Hospital and in 1947 honorary assistant orthopaedic surgeon to the Rachel Forster Hospital. She lived with her family at Five Dock until she married a 48-year-old widower Joel Austen Phillips on 20 July 1945 at the Court House, Manly. He was a retired company director; they lived together at Mosman with his two daughters. Claudia continued to use her own name professionally.

Pioneering cerebral palsy research in Australia, she wrote three major articles based on her observation of children at the Spastic Centre: 'Infantile Cerebral Palsy' and 'The Spastic Child' (*Medical Journal of Australia*, March 1949, June 1957), and 'Clinical Features of Children Suffering from Neurological Sequelae of Rh Iso-Sensitization' (*Australasian Annals of Medicine*, August 1956). She kept in touch with international specialists and in 1951 spent three months in the United States of America where she worked with W. M. Phelps at Baltimore. In like manner, she often invited overseas visitors to Mosman. Her treatment included surgery and bracing, as well as a team approach to habilitation that involved physiotherapists, speech therapists and occupational therapists. Burton-Bradley's medical reports for the Spastic Centre stressed the potential of cerebral-palsy sufferers to lead useful and independent lives, and she encouraged bright children to go on to university. She began one paper, delivered to the State branch of the British Medical Association in 1956, with a plea for the 'maintenance of dignity in relation to these children as fellow beings'.

A 'private sort of person' who had a 'commanding' stature, Burton-Bradley was active in the Australian Orthopaedic and the Australian Paediatric associations; she was, as well, an honorary fellow of the Australian College of Speech Therapists and honorary consultant to the World Federation of Occupational Therapists. With Mrs Audrie McLeod, she formed the Australian Cerebral Palsy Association in 1952—Claudia chaired its medical and educational committee. She was later made an honorary member of the American Academy for Cerebral Palsy and chair of its programme committee. In addition, she sat on the editorial board of *Excerpta Medica*.

All this Burton-Bradley achieved despite a diabetic condition which worsened as she reached middle age. She retired as director of the Spastic Centre in 1962, but continued as its director of research and development for two years. A member of the Diabetic Association of New South Wales, she was sometime acting-president. Paradoxically, her poor health was her stimulus: she felt that the timely discovery of insulin had extended her life and she determined to do something worth while with it; but she also feared that her life would be short which made her energetically committed to her work. A world expert in her field, Claudia Burton-Bradley was appointed M.B.E. in 1966. Survived by her husband and stepdaughters, she died of a coronary occlusion on 5 October 1967 at her Cremorne home and was cremated with Anglican rites.

The Spastic Centre Story (Syd, 1948); Aust Cerebral Palsy Assn Incorporated, *Proceedings of the Sixth Medical and Educational Conference* (Syd, 1961); *MJA*, 30 Mar 1968; *Woman's Day*, 30 July 1951; *Aust Paediatric J*, 4, no 3, Sept 1968; Rachel Forster Hospital for Women and Children, *Annual Report*, 1968; information from Sir Burton Burton-Bradley, Port Moresby, Papua New Guinea, Miss B. Le Gay Brereton, Wamberal, NSW, Dr R. Dewey, Spastic Centre of NSW, Allambie Heights, and Mrs A. McLeod, Seaforth, Syd.

ANNE O'BRIEN

BRADLEY, EILEEN BURTON (1911-1976) and JOAN BURTON (1916-1982), bush regenerators, were born on 14 August 1911 and 2 September 1916 at Neutral Bay, Sydney, third and fourth daughters of native-born parents John Houghton Bradley, dentist, and his wife Caroline Mary, née Drummond. Both sisters attended Wenona School. Graduating from the University of Sydney (B.Sc., 1938), Joan was employed as an industrial chemist. Eileen helped at home and also worked for a dentist. After World War II they bicycled around England, Wales and Scotland, taking particular pleasure in woodlands and forests. They later ran a small decorating business from their Mosman home, where their widowed mother joined them. All three were keen gardeners. Joan was also a skilled carpenter and a black-and-white photographer.

Systematic observers of the natural environment, the sisters studied the habits of three families of the Superb Fairy-wren, *Malurus cyaneus*, which frequented their garden and nearby Ashton Park. They used colour-coded rings to identify individual birds. Their 'Notes on the Behaviour and Plumage of Colour-ringed Blue Wrens' appeared in *Emu* (1958). When numbers fell dramatically in 1966, Joan alerted the press that minute doses of organochlorines over long periods caused sterility in small birds.

Eileen and Joan walked regularly in Ashton Park and on Chowder Head. Observing that attempts to control weeds by slashing and clearing resulted in rampant regrowth, they formulated an alternative strategy. The sisters hand-weeded where they walked, doing less than an hour a day and being careful to replace the bush litter which—they believed —contained the seedbank for new growth. They waited for the bush to regenerate. In *Weeds and their Control* (1967) and in Joan's *Bush Regeneration* (1971) they developed the three principles of the Bradley method of bush regeneration: work outward from less infested to more seriously infested areas;

minimize disturbance, and replace topsoil and litter; allow regeneration to set the pace of the work. Selected hand-tools were the only implements permitted. The Bradleys opposed the use of chemicals and criticized the controlled-burning programme begun in 1971 by the State's Forestry Commission. From 1962 the sisters had kept records of their work. Following an experimental burn in Ashton Park in 1966, they noticed the introduction of weeds and began to watch regrowth after other controlled burning. By 1973 they proclaimed that regular 'cool fires' did more damage to bushland than the wildfires which it was intended to control. In contrast, intense fire stimulates regrowth.

By 1975 bush regeneration was gaining public support and the value of their work was becoming acknowledged. That year the restoration and landscaping of bushland in suburban North Sydney was funded as a National Estate project. Next year money was available to the State branch of the National Trust of Australia for an experiment in weed-control at Ludovic Blackwood Memorial Sanctuary, Beecroft. The trust adopted the Bradley method, employing Joan to supervise the work and to develop its training programme.

The sisters had been supported in their work by the Mosman Parklands and Ashton Park Association, formed in 1964 to oppose a projected car-park for Taronga zoo within Ashton Park. Members of the association joined the Bradleys as volunteer weeders. As their method became more widely known, similar organizations of volunteers formed and local government authorities began to employ bush-regeneration teams. The sisters did not seek to re-create pristine bushland, but waited to see what returned. Sometimes there was no regeneration. Retention of natural litter inhibits germination of some species. The Bradley principles have been modified in practice as knowledge of conditions for germination accumulates: the prescription of small hand-tools has gone and the limitations on regeneration in seriously degraded bushland are better understood. A science has been refined since the Bradleys established its bases.

Eileen died of myocardial infarction on 24 February 1976 in Sydney Hospital, Joan of the same illness on 18 May 1982 at Clifton Gardens; both were cremated. Joan's notes for a revised edition of *Bush Regeneration* were used for *Bringing back the Bush: the Bradley Method of Bush Regeneration* (1988), edited by Joan Larking, Audrey Lenning and Jean Walker.

Wenonian, 1948; National Trust of Aust (NSW), *Bulletin*, 1976-77; *Mosman Daily*, 6 July 1966, 8 Nov 1967, 24 Oct 1970, 9 June 1972, 25 May 1982, 20 Sept 1985; *SMH*, 1 June 1972, 2 Feb 1973, 16 Aug 1980, 21 May 1982; E. Bradley, Control Burning and Wildfire (1972, ms, held in Mosman Municipal L); information from Ms E. Elenius, Syd.   HEATHER RADI

BRADLEY, STEPHEN LESLIE (1926-1968), kidnapper and murderer, was born on 15 March 1926 in Budapest and named István, son of József Baranyay, architect, and his wife Klara (Clarisse), née Kramer. A divorcee since 1948, István arrived in Melbourne in the *Skaugum* on 28 March 1950. He found jobs as a life-insurance salesman, male nurse and as an electroplater at a poker-machine factory. On 1 March 1952 he married Eva Maria Laidlaw (who had changed her name by deed poll from Laszlo) at the Presbyterian Church, Gardiner. They had one daughter before Eva was killed in a car accident on 26 February 1955. István changed his name by deed poll to Stephen Leslie Bradley in August 1956.

In November 1957 Bradley was charged with false pretences in Sydney, but the charge was allowed to lapse. In the registrar general's office on 8 December 1958 he married Magda Wittman, née Klein, a Hungarian divorcee with two children, who owned a boarding house at Katoomba. In 1959 the guest house burnt down, but he failed to make any money on the insurance settlement. He reputedly lived beyond his means. Short, stocky, dark haired and balding, he dressed well and liked to drive big cars. Prison authorities subsequently described him as tense, insecure and intelligent, with a sociable and engaging personality, but also deemed him a hopeless liar, a confidence man and an opportunist who was desperate to make money quickly. Frustrated at his circumstances, he brought his family to Sydney, determined 'to do something big'. In June 1960, after the report that Bazil Henry Parker Thorne, of Bondi, had won first prize in the Sydney Opera House lottery, Bradley hatched his plan to kidnap the Thornes' only son, 8-year-old Graeme.

On 7 July 1960 Graeme failed to arrive at school and the boy's disappearance was reported to police. Later that day Bradley rang the Thornes, demanding a £25 000 ransom; he rang off without finalizing arrangements during a second call that night. The incident was immediately reported in the media and became Australia's most sensational kidnapping case. On 16 August two boys found the body of Graeme Thorne in the bush near Seaforth. Forensic tests established that he had been bashed and strangled soon after the kidnapping. An extensive police investigation resulted in scientific and eyewitness evidence which linked Bradley to the crime. Meantime,

Bradley had sailed for England with his family. On 10 October he was arrested in Colombo. He was extradited on 18 November, convicted of murder on 29 March 1961 and sentenced to life imprisonment, a sentence that was upheld on appeal.

In June 1961 Bradley was transferred to Goulburn gaol where he was employed as a hospital orderly. Professing innocence, he claimed that he had confessed to the crime through fear lest his family be harmed. He seemed oblivious of the pain suffered by the Thornes. Bradley died of a coronary occlusion on 6 October 1968 while playing in the gaol tennis competition, and was buried in the Catholic section of Goulburn cemetery. His daughter survived him.

SMH and *Sun* (Syd), July 1960-June 1961; *Herald* (Melb), 7 May 1961, 7 Oct 1968; *Age* (Melb), 5 Aug 1971; case report, NSW Police Dept, Syd; case file NSW Prisons Dept, Syd.

STEPHEN GARTON

BRAIN, SIR HUGH GERNER (1890-1976), businessman and public benefactor, was born on 3 December 1890 at Prahran, Melbourne, second son of native-born parents William Joseph Brain, builder, and his wife Florence, née Payne. Self-described as 'a pretty feeble kid' who suffered from marasmus, Hugh did not attend Armadale State School until aged 8. In 1905 he won a scholarship to University High School, a coeducational private school run by Otto Krome [q.v.9].

During a school excursion to the Fitzroy gasworks, a platform collapsed, plunging Brain and other students onto coke beneath. His skull was fractured. Advised to take the next two years quietly, he abandoned his ambition to study law. He sat the State public service examinations in 1906 and gained employment in the office of the public service commissioner. His memoirs wryly tell of his first task. Summoned to the office of Commissioner Charles Topp [q.v.6], he was told, 'Good morning, kindly empty my chamber'. He taught himself the Script method of shorthand, a skill which brought quick transfer to a shorthand and typist's place in the Premier's Office where he worked closely with Premiers Bent, Murray and Watt [qq.v. 3,10,12]. In 1913 horizons widened through his job with the Commonwealth government's interstate commission, Department of Trade and Customs.

A member of the Malvern Rifle Club, Brain was initially rejected as a volunteer for the Australian Imperial Force on physical grounds: he was only 5 ft 5½ ins (166.4 cm) tall and slightly built. He eventually enlisted

on 13 July 1915 and embarked for the Middle East in November. Posted to I Anzac Corps headquarters in March 1916, he rose to warrant officer while serving on the Western Front and was awarded the Meritorious Service Medal (1917). In August 1917 he was commissioned and transferred to A.I.F. Headquarters, London, as deputy assistant adjutant-general. Promoted captain in August 1918, he returned to Melbourne in June next year for duty with the business board of administration, Department of Defence. He was appointed M.B.E. (1918) and O.B.E. (1919), and placed on the Reserve of Officers on 30 September 1919.

After the war Brain took George Swinburne's [q.v.12] advice, left the public service and joined Edward H. Shackell & Co.: the firm administered secretarial and shareholding matters for the Baillieu-engendered Collins House group of companies, based on the Broken Hill silver, lead and zinc resources, and governed from Collins Street. Shackell was the brother-in-law of W. L. Baillieu [q.v.7]. With Aubrey Bulte, recruited from the Public Works Department, Brain worked as secretary to the Electrolytic Zinc Co. of Australasia Ltd, Metal Manufactures Ltd, Amalgamated Zinc (de Bavay's [q.v.8]) Ltd, Minerals Separation Ltd and Hampden Cloncurry Copper Mines Ltd. On 3 June 1920 at St Mary's Anglican Church, Caulfield, he had married Monica Eva Futcher.

In 1929 Brain, Bulte, Victor Bolderman, Ellis Davies [q.v.] and Marsden Blackwell purchased shares in Edward H. Shackell & Co. On Edward's death in 1932, the group assumed control, with Edward's brother Harold as governing director. The company was renamed Secretariat Pty Ltd. At its peak, Secretariat administered the affairs of forty-seven firms, including over thirty gold-mining companies. The goldminers were dispensed with in the late 1930s as the company concentrated on the manufacturing firms, Electrolytic Zinc, Associated Pulp & Paper Mills Ltd, Metal Manufactures and its subsidiaries, Austral Bronze Co. Pty Ltd, Cable Makers Australia Pty Ltd and Austral Standard Cables Pty Ltd.

During World War II Brain's business talents were put to public use. He was deputy-director of hirings, Army Headquarters, Melbourne, honorary assistant-secretary, business matters, Department of Defence, and business member (1941-42 and 1944-46) of the Naval Board; he was also a member of the Naval Charter Rates Board, of the committee establishing war-damage insurance regulations and of the paper industry wartime advisory council. In addition, he performed part-time staff duties with the Volunteer Defence Corps in 1943-46.

Secretary of Gold Mines of Australia Ltd,

Western Mining Corporation Ltd and Western New South Wales Electric Power Pty Ltd, Brain was a director of Austral Bronze and Cable Makers of Australia, and joint managing director of Metal Manufactures. In 1956-68 he was chairman of the Australasian Temperance & General Mutual Life Assurance Society. By 1960 Bulte, Davies and Blackwell had died. The shares of Secretariat were sold jointly to E.Z., A.P.P.M. and W.M.C. Brain retired from the company that year and established a consultancy in Lonsdale Street.

Named Victorian Father of the Year in 1959, Brain gave his £500 award to Melbourne Legacy, an organization with which he was actively associated from 1930 (president 1935). He sat on the Baillieu Education Trust from its foundation in 1935 (chairman 1941-52), and for some thirty years was a member of the Soldiers' Children's Education Board and the advisory board to the Council for Christian Education in Schools. Although not a graduate, he chaired the University of Melbourne's appointments board for twelve years and was a board-member of the summer school of business administration for fourteen; he was, as well, a councillor of Ormond [q.v.5] College, a trustee of St Hilda's College and a fund-raiser for International House. For over thirty years he was a member of the Schools' Board and its successor, the Victorian Universities and Schools Examination Board, and chairman of its finance committee.

Among his other public positions, Brain was a trustee of the Cairnmillar Institute, a member of the advisory board of the Melbourne Young Women's Christian Association, chairman of the appeal committee of the Melbourne Lord Mayor's Fund for Hospitals and Charities, a member of committees of the Presbyterian Church of Victoria and chairman of the Anzac Fellowship of Women. He had been a special constable during the 1923 police strike and a member of a large, anti-subversion group in Melbourne during J. T. Lang's [q.v.9] turbulent premiership of New South Wales. In 1951 he was associated with Sir Edmund Herring in 'A Call to the People of Australia'. Brain was for many years a member of the finance committee of the Liberal Party, Victorian branch. In 1963 he was appointed foundation president of the Victorian Institute of Licensed Shorthand Writers. For forty-five years he was honorary secretary of Premises Ltd, the company which backed the Athenaeum Club, of which he was made an honorary life member. He was also 'moneyer' for nearly twenty years of the Beefsteak Club.

Brain was an energetic, talented and highly valued servant, rather than a leader. With a sound sense of humour, he was fond of practical jokes. As a hobby, he wrote limericks about hundreds of Legacy members. His honours, including life membership of the Australasian Institute of Mining and Metallurgy, culminated in a knighthood in 1972. Sir Hugh died on 31 December 1976 at Heidelberg and was cremated with Presbyterian forms; his wife, son and two daughters survived him.

Melb Legacy, *Bulletin*, 18 Jan 1977; Brain papers, Univ Melb Archives.   FRANK STRAHAN

BRAIN, LESTER JOSEPH (1903-1980), aviator and aviation administrator, was born on 27 February 1903 at Forbes, New South Wales, second son of Austin Lionel Bennett Brain, a mine-manager from England, and his native-born wife Katie Mary, née Murray. After topping his class in mathematics at Sydney Grammar School, in 1919 Lester joined the Commercial Banking Co. of Sydney Ltd. He was one of five civilian applicants accepted by the Royal Australian Air Force for the twelve-month course in flying-training which began in January 1923 at Point Cook, Victoria. Passing out at the head of his group, Brain was commissioned in the air force reserve. In April 1924 he moved to Queensland to become a pilot with Queensland and Northern Territory Aerial Services Ltd.

On 7 February 1925 he made the first scheduled QANTAS flight from Cloncurry to Camooweal. Later that year he flew (Sir) Fergus McMaster [q.v.10] and his brother Francis on a one-week tour intended to establish Francis as a political candidate. In 1925-26 Brain helped the American L. J. Stark prospect by air for a gold-reef in the Tanami Desert, Northern Territory. Brain's familiarity with the northern terrain made him the logical choice to conduct a search for the hapless aviators Keith Anderson and Robert Hitchcock whose aircraft, the *Kookaburra*, went missing in April 1929 while they were endeavouring to rescue (Sir) Charles Kingsford Smith and Charles Ulm [qq.v.9,12]. For locating the *Kookaburra* near Wave Hill and for subsequently finding two British flyers who had crashed on the Arnhem Land coast, he was awarded the Air Force Cross that year. (Sir) Hudson Fysh [q.v.8] reported to QANTAS's board that the publicity Brain had gained for himself and his company 'could probably not have been bought for any money'.

In recognition of his skills and maturity, in March 1927 Brain had been appointed chief instructor at the airline's Brisbane Flying School and QANTAS's local branch manager. 'My job was Manager, Pilot, Flying Instructor, Sales Manager, Secretary and Typist all rolled into one', he recalled. On 8 July 1930 he married Constance Pauline Brownhill at Holy Innocents' Catholic Church, Croydon, Sydney. When QANTAS transferred its headquarters to Brisbane that year, Brain, by now chief pilot, was put in charge of sales, demonstrations, agency tours and taxi trips. Although no longer employed as a regular pilot on domestic routes, he delivered the company's first D.H.86 airliner from Britain in 1934 (by which time he had logged 6694 flying hours), and took the controls for inaugural mail and flying-boat services.

Promoted flight superintendent (1934) and flying operations manager (1938), Brain continued to fly scheduled services to Singapore and Karachi. As early as 1935, however, he had told Edgar Johnston, controller-general of civil aviation, that he was willing to take a drop in his gross annual income (over £1000) for a position in the 'administration and executive side of aviation'. In February 1936 he expressed interest in becoming Johnston's deputy and in early 1939 was an unsuccessful candidate for the post of director-general of civil aviation.

Brain had been appointed flying officer on 1 March 1935 in the Citizen Air Force Reserve. He was to rise to temporary wing commander (1944) and to supervise the support which Qantas Empire Airways Ltd provided to the allied war effort. A key figure in organizing Q.E.A.'s ferry service that brought eighteen Catalina flying boats from San Diego, United States of America, to Australia in 1941, he piloted the first plane delivered; his direct flight across the South Pacific was the third ever completed. In early 1942 Brain had charge of ground-staff at Broome, Western Australia, an important staging point and refuelling base for aircraft which evacuated refugees from the Netherlands East Indies. During the Japanese air-raid on 3 March, he rowed out to rescue survivors from flying boats in the harbour. His action was commended by King George VI.

In spite of its reservations about Brain's limited financial experience, in late 1945 Q.E.A.'s board made him assistant general manager. With Fysh only eight years older, he saw no prospect of further promotion. When the Australian National Airlines Commission advertised a salary of £2250 a year for an operations manager of the new Trans-Australia Airlines, Q.E.A. could not make a competitive offer to retain its most valuable operational executive. T.A.A.'s chairman (Sir) Arthur Coles was sufficiently impressed with Brain to appoint him general manager in June 1946; his salary was to start at £3000 per annum, with possible increments increasing the sum to £5000.

Given a right of veto over the choice of his top three executives and control over all other appointments, Brain began work in Melbourne with twenty-one staff. Within four months the fledgling airline was organized into eight departments, employing one thousand people throughout the country and equipped to begin scheduled passenger services. In partnership with Coles, who handled political issues, Brain proved to be an exceptionally creative administrator.

Overcoming resistance from government departments that were reluctant to yield staff, offices, buildings and hangars, Coles and Brain provided a formidable, price-cutting challenge to T.A.A.'s principal competitor, Australian National Airways Pty Ltd. Favourable financial treatment and arrangements for the acquisition of aircraft fuelled accusations that T.A.A. was the tool of a socialist bureaucracy. But the morale of the young, mostly ex-service, staff was sustained by forthright leadership and shrewd public relations. The two-airlines policy instigated by the Menzies [q.v.] government finally legitimated Brain's successful business, while guaranteeing the survival of one major private operator.

Uncomfortable with a more interventionist chairman G. P. N. Watt, who resisted the general manager's expected salary increases, Brain resigned in March 1955. After five years in Sydney as managing director (1955-60) of de Havilland Aircraft Pty Ltd, suppliers of Vampire trainers to the R.A.A.F., he accepted a directorship and consultancy with East-West Airlines Ltd. Brain was appointed A.O. in 1979. A playing member of Royal Sydney Golf Club, he also belonged to the Australian Club; the Athenaeum Club, Melbourne—with which he had enjoyed reciprocal rights—declined to have him as a member, allegedly because he was a leader of a government business enterprise. Survived by his wife, two sons and two daughters, Brain died on 30 June 1980 in Sydney and was cremated.

S. Brogden, *The History of Australian Aviation* (Melb, 1960); D. Gillison, *Royal Australian Air Force 1939-1942* (Canb, 1962); H. Fysh, *Qantas at War* (Syd, 1968); I. Sabey, *Challenge in the Skies* (Melb, 1979); D. Smith and P. Davis, *Kookaburra* (Syd, 1980); J. Gunn, *The Defeat of Distance* (Brisb, 1985) and *Challenging Horizons* (Brisb, 1987); N. M. Parnell and T. Boughton, *Flypast* (Canb, 1988); *Courier-Mail*, 2 July 1980; Eric White & Associates, Wings Across Australia, ts, 1965 (Aust Airlines, Public Affairs records, Melb); Aust Airlines, personnel records (Melb).

CAMERON HAZLEHURST

BRAKE, JOHN (1890-1970), agriculturist, sportsman and soldier, was born on 11 November 1890 at Horsham, Victoria, fifth of seven children of native-born parents James Hugh Brake (1853-1915), storekeeper and later politician, and his wife Barbara Stevenson, née McDougall. John was educated at Princes Hill State School, Hawthorn College and the University of Melbourne (B.Agr.Sc., 1916). His sporting record was brilliant: the champion schoolboy athlete of Victoria (1908) and a triple Blue in athletics, football and rifle-shooting at university, he was to be Australian pole-vault (Australasian record) and high and long jump title-holder, and an outstanding Australian Rules ruckman for Melbourne and Victoria. He was 6 ft 1 in. (185.4 cm) tall.

In March 1915 Brake joined the Department of Agriculture as an officer supervising field tests and research, largely at Werribee. On 12 November he enlisted in the Australian Imperial Force. Commissioned on 1 April 1916, he served on the Western Front in the 8th Field Artillery Brigade from January 1917, eventually as adjutant. On 21 April 1918 he saw Baron von Richthofen shot down and it was later claimed that he was one of the Australians who lifted the body from the red triplane. Brake's appointment terminated in Australia on 21 December 1919. At Scots Church, Melbourne, on 19 July 1921 he married Grace Glendinning Taylor.

After running a mixed farm at Yering, in May 1924 Brake rejoined the Department of Agriculture as senior field officer. In 1926 he was appointed senior inspector and in 1934 agricultural superintendent. As a reservist, he was mobilized in September 1940 with the rank of captain (major from November) in the Royal Australian Artillery, but throughout 1941 he commanded the Melbourne University Rifles. On 9 March 1942 he was released to the department to work on food production.

In Brake's period as superintendent his division 'fostered improved cultivation methods, the use of superphosphate, subterranean clover seeding, pasture topdressing, fodder conservation, ley farming, the development of irrigated pastures, the recognition of the importance of potash and the determination of trace element deficiencies of Victorian pasture lands'. He was a member of committees investigating Mallee sand drift (1933), the tobacco industry (1934) and soil erosion (1937); the last led to sustained advice to farmers on 'retaining a dense vegetative cover'. Brake chaired the Farms Competition Association for twenty years, was Victorian representative on the Australian Barley Board, a departmental member of the Pasture Improvement League from 1931 and deputy-chairman from 1935 of the Victorian Wheat Advisory Committee. He directed a staff of more than two hundred, including about seventy graduates, was responsible for five State research farms, wrote prolifically for the *Journal of Agriculture, Victoria*, and often

broadcast to farmers. An enthusiastic educator, he used such means as the Better Farming Train and the department's mobile extension unit. On his retirement in November 1955, colleagues spoke warmly of the loyalty and affection 'J.B.' commanded.

Brake was president (1938) of the Victorian branch of the Australian Institute of Agricultural Science, a Presbyterian elder, a Rotarian, and a member of convocation (1933-47) and council (1947-55) of the university. For over twenty years he chaired the Victorian Football League's tribunal and in 1949-55 was chairman of the commissioners who reviewed club boundaries. Brake retired to Guildford. He died at Castlemaine on 16 May 1970. Survived by his wife and two sons, he was buried in Box Hill cemetery.

Dept of Agr (Vic), *Thirty Years of Agricultural Production with John Brake* (Melb, 1956); P. J. Carisella and J. W. Ryan, *Who Killed the Red Baron?* (Lond, 1969); *J of Agr* (Vic), Apr 1940, Jan 1956; *Argus*, 5 May 1924, 1 Feb 1934; family information.   GEOFFREY SERLE

BRAND, SIR DAVID (1912-1979), storekeeper and premier, was born on 1 August 1912 at Dongara, Western Australia, eldest of four children of Albert John Brand, a native-born farmer, and his wife Hilda, whose father Samuel Mitchell had represented Geraldton (1884-85) in the Western Australian Legislative Council and Murchison (1897-1901) in the Legislative Assembly. Shortly after his birth, David's parents went farming at Northampton and then at Mullewa from 1924. Educated locally, David was obliged by his family's circumstances to leave school at 14 to help on the farm. At Mullewa he became secretary of the local branch of the Primary Producers' Association, the parent organization of the Country Party, of which his father was a member.

In 1935 Brand moved to the goldfields and worked at the Golden Horseshoe Mine, successively as a truck driver, treatment-hand, filter specialist and shift boss. During these years he was active in the Methodist church and as a scoutmaster. Five feet 10 ins (177.8 cm) tall, with grey eyes and dark hair, he enlisted in the Australian Imperial Force on 23 November 1939; posted to the 2nd/11th Battalion, he embarked for the Middle East on 20 April 1940. He fought in North Africa, was promoted corporal and was sent to Greece where he was wounded on 24 April 1941. After being hospitalized, he returned to Fremantle in August for further treatment and was discharged medically unfit from the A.I.F. in April 1942. Mobilized in September, he served as an instructor with the 7th

Battalion, Volunteer Defence Corps, in the Geraldton area and was promoted warrant officer in January 1943. He married Doris Elspeth McNeill on 20 March 1944 at the Mingenew Methodist Church. Following his discharge from the Australian Military Forces in January 1945, he took over the general store at Dongara.

When the Legislative Assembly seat of Greenough was declared vacant after the war —its Labor incumbent John Verdun Newton had been reported missing in action in a bombing raid over Germany in January 1944 —Brand became the first candidate in Australia to be endorsed by the newly-formed Liberal Party. With the aid of Country Party preferences, he won the by-election in October 1945 from Newton's brother by 308 votes. The Liberal-Country Party coalition came to power in April 1947 under (Sir) Ross McLarty [q.v.] and Brand was appointed government whip. In October 1949 he entered the cabinet as honorary minister for housing, forests and local government. From April 1950 he was minister for works, water supply and housing. He worked closely with the director of works (Sir) Russell Dumas [q.v.] to secure the 1952 agreement with the Anglo-Iranian Oil Co. for the establishment of a refinery at the new Kwinana industrial area; in later life Brand described the achievement as the greatest of his career. His youthful enthusiasm and practical common sense assisted in this development and in attracting investment capital for other secondary industry projects, including a steel rolling mill and a cement factory.

After the coalition's defeat in 1953, Brand became deputy-leader of the Opposition and, on McLarty's retirement, its leader from 1 March 1957. The coalition regained office in 1959 and Brand was sworn in on 2 April as premier, treasurer and minister for tourists —posts he held until 3 March 1971. His eleven years, eleven months and one day as premier exceeded by more than a year Sir John Forrest's [q.v.8] record.

Brand presided over one of the most exciting periods of development in Western Australia's history. In 1960 the Commonwealth government lifted its embargo on the export of iron ore, enabling exploitation of large deposits in the Pilbara and the development of a major export industry. Agreement was also reached with Western Aluminium and Alwest Pty Ltd for the mining of bauxite in the Darling Range and for its processing at Kwinana and Bunbury respectively, and with Western Mining Corporation Ltd for building a nickel refinery; furthermore, a titanium oxide plant was established at Bunbury. Funds were secured from the Commonwealth for the main Ord River dam in the Kimberley region, for the east-west, standard-gauge railway link

and for beef roads in the north. Oil and gas deposits were discovered in commercial quantities. The State's population rose rapidly to over one million and, after 1968, Western Australia no longer sought assistance from the Commonwealth Grants Commission. In June 1969 the premier was appointed K.C.M.G.

Having experienced four successive election victories, in the early 1970s the government ran into problems with rising land prices, housing shortages and the impact of wheat quotas in the farming districts. Brand was deeply wounded when parliament refused to allow the demolition of the archway from the Pensioner Barracks which had been built during the colonial period. His government's insistence (in the Weebo stones episode) that quarrying should be allowed on what was regarded as an Aboriginal sacred site increased the resentment of environmental groups. Even then, Labor won the 1971 election by only one seat. Sir David had collapsed while speaking at a public function in his last year in office and stepped down as leader of the Opposition in June 1972. Suffering poor health, he retired as the member for Greenough on 21 August 1975. He died of hypertensive cardiovascular disease on 15 April 1979 at Carnamah and, after a state funeral, was cremated; his wife, daughter and two sons survived him.

Brand was a man of the people. While he was more a doer than a thinker, he had vision and believed in the virtues of individual effort. He showed concern for handicapped children as patron of the Spastic Welfare Association and was president (from 1973) of the State branch of the Boy Scouts' Association. A quiet but effective political leader, he was willing to learn from capable public servants like Dumas and had the capacity to manage the *prima donnas* in his cabinets. His partnership with his aggressive and dynamic deputy (Sir) Charles Court proved exceptionally successful: both of them saw economic development as fundamental to securing social ends. Brand also succeeded in maintaining cordial relations with his Country Party partners. Above all, he had the fortune to govern in what was generally a period of prosperity.

L. Hunt (ed), *Westralian Portraits* (Perth, 1979); G. S. Reid and M. R. Oliver, *The Premiers of Western Australia 1890-1982* (Perth, 1982); *PD* (WA), 1 May 1979, p 1453; *Elders Weekly*, 19 Apr 1979; Spastic Welfare Assn of WA, *Centreline*, Winter 1979; *West Australian*, 1 Oct 1949, 23 Mar 1959, 19 Mar 1960, 15, 19 May, 14 June 1969, 8 Feb 1970, 12 May, 3, 6, 7 June 1972, 21, 22 Aug 1975, 22 June 1977, 16, 19 Apr 1979; *Weekend News*, 19 Feb 1966, 22 Feb 1969 supp, 3 June 1972; *Independent* (Perth), 9 Nov 1969; *Sunday Times* (Perth), 6 Apr 1969, 8 Feb 1970; *Daily News* (Perth), 25 Feb 1980.   DAVID BLACK

BRAND, WALTER LEVI (1893-1964), Jewish welfare worker, was born on 3 June 1893 at Hackney, London, son of David Brand, a horse-hair merchant, and his wife Rose, née Harris. Educated at the Haberdashers' Aske's Hampstead School (1905-08), Walter visited Australia in 1911. During World War I he enlisted and served in the Royal Army Medical Corps on the Western Front. Migrating to Sydney in 1920, Brand worked as a manager in his uncle's fur and hide business. On 14 September 1921 at the city's Great Synagogue he married Vera Rosetta Davis; they were to remain childless. With the onset of the Depression, his business collapsed. Vera, a fashion designer, opened a successful shop in Elizabeth Street while he hawked vacuum cleaners.

A council-member (1922-46) of the Sir Moses Montefiore Jewish Home, in 1940-64 Brand was general secretary of the Australian Jewish Welfare Society, serving under three presidents, Sir Samuel Cohen, Saul Symonds [qq.v.8,12] and Sydney Einfeld. Brand was involved with the administration and upkeep of Jewish migrant hostels in which he maintained that rules were necessary 'to govern the activities of the inmates'. Mutual Enterprises Pty Ltd had been established in 1939 to provide interest-free loans to newcomers and he ran the company until 1947. Despite health problems, he dedicated himself to his welfare work. He often met refugees at their ships' first Australian port of call, but, hampered by his officious manner and his lack of Yiddish or any other European language, he found it difficult to reassure the newcomers.

Retaining a scrupulously apolitical stance, Brand dealt effectively with government authorities in Canberra. In World War II he helped to persuade the authorities to change the status of refugees from 'enemy aliens' to 'refugee aliens'. His contribution to Jewish welfare aroused controversy because Brand was seen by his clientele as being insensitive to their needs. He came into conflict with the Association of Refugees (later Association of New Citizens) over conditions in internment camps, and warned the secretary of the Department of the Interior in 1942 and Australian intelligence in 1945 against the association's campaign on behalf of internees. In the long term, Brand's inadequacy in handling the new arrivals created a sense of bitterness and resentment among many of them. His role became more administrative in the late 1950s when sub-committees were created to represent different national groups. In 1956-57 he travelled with Einfeld to Europe, Morocco and the United States of America.

Brand regularly attended annual citizenship conventions in Canberra and was an executive-member of the State branch of the New Settlers' League of Australia (later the Good Neighbour Council of New South Wales). He was active in the Sydney Jewish Aid Society, the New South Wales Association of Jewish Ex-Servicemen and Women, and the New South Wales Jewish War Memorial (president 1949-52). In addition, he was secretary of the Australian Federation of Jewish Welfare Societies and a member of the New South Wales Board of Jewish Deputies. He supported schemes to bring out orphaned children who had survived the Holocaust and sponsored three, among them William Markovicz. Survived by his wife, Brand died of a cerebral haemorrhage on 31 March 1964 at Surfers Paradise, Queensland, and was buried in Rookwood cemetery, Sydney.

A. Andgel, *Fifty Years of Caring* (Syd, 1988); N. Keesing, *Presidents of the New South Wales Jewish War Memorial* (Syd, 1988); *Young Men's Hebrew Assn News*, 13 Nov 1947; *SMH*, 3 Apr 1964; S. D. Rutland, The History of Australian Jewry, 1945-1960 (Ph.D. thesis, Univ Syd, 1990); Minutes and correspondence, Aust Jewish Welfare Soc Archives, Syd; Dept of the Interior, A433/1, 46/2/1220 (AA); information from Mr W. Marr (Markovicz), Bellevue Hill, Syd.

SUZANNE D. RUTLAND

BRAND, SIR WILLIAM ALFRED (1888-1979), cane-grower and politician, was born on 22 August 1888 at Childers, Queensland, son of William Brand, a farmer from England, and his native-born wife Isabella, née Cocking. Having attended Apple Tree Creek State School, Alfred farmed the family cane-holdings at Huxley. On 22 May 1913 at Childers he married Myrtle Maud Kingston with Methodist forms.

In October 1920 Brand was elected to the Legislative Assembly for the seat of Burrum; after a redistribution, from June 1932 he represented Isis. A vigorous debater, he was renowned as a staunch, 'sonorous-voiced' advocate for primary industries, especially sugar. His effectiveness was limited by his spending all but three years (1929-32) of his State political career in Opposition. One of eighteen original members of the parliamentary Country Party, he was the leading spirit among four party members (including E. H. C. Clayton, W. A. Deacon and H. F. Walker) who declined to join the short-lived merger with the United Australia Party that formed the Country-National Party in April 1941. In the assembly the four sat apart from the shaky coalition until it collapsed. A reconciliation involving the parliamentary members, the Queensland Country Party and its Western Division saw the emergence of the Australian Country Party (Queensland), of which Brand was deputy parliamentary leader from 1944 until 1947. He retired from the assembly in April 1950, but in 1954 was persuaded to contest the Federal seat of Wide Bay (against the former prime minister Frank Forde) which Brand won and retained until he retired from parliament in December 1958.

Outside politics, his energies as a successful cane-grower were devoted to the sugar industry. A director (from 1939) of the Isis Central Sugar Mill Co. Ltd, he became chairman in 1940 and held this position for twenty-five years. For long an active member of the Australian Sugar Producers' Association, he was a vice-president in 1940 and its president from 1943. In his 1944 presidential address he described the sugar industry as 'maligned, misunderstood and misrepresented'. At the time of his accession the industry was at an ebb, its production having fallen to a sixteen-year low due to manpower shortages in wartime. Despite his political affiliations, in sugar matters Brand's competence was respected by his Labor opponents. In 1950 the urgent representations of the A.S.P.A. executive persuaded the ailing Labor premier E. M. Hanlon [q.v.] to travel to Britain—for the second time in little over a year—to negotiate a favourable sugar agreement. As A.S.P.A. leader, Brand presided over the postwar recovery and growth of the industry: Australian sugar production rose from half a million tons in 1943 to two million tons in 1964, the year of his retirement. Appointed C.B.E. in 1958, he was knighted in 1965.

Survived by his wife, son and two of his three daughters, Sir Alfred died on 26 October 1979 at Childers and was buried in Apple Tree Creek cemetery with Anglican rites.

C. Lack (comp), *Three Decades of Queensland Political History, 1929-1960* (Brisb, 1962); U. Ellis, *A History of the Australian Country Party* (Melb, 1963); *PD* (Qld), 31 Oct 1979, p 1541; *Aust Sugar Year Book*, 1944-45, 1952; *Aust Sugar J*, Nov 1979, p 351.
                                            BRIAN F. STEVENSON

BREEN, HAROLD PATRICK (1893-1966), public servant, was born on 30 April 1893 at Richmond, Melbourne, son of Patrick Breen, fellmonger, and his wife Catherine, née McSweeney, both Victorian born. Educated at St Patrick's College, East Melbourne, on 23 December 1910 Harold entered the Commonwealth Public Service as a clerk in the ordnance branch of the Department of Defence. He studied accountancy at night-school and in 1917-21 was secretary of the department's district contract board.

While with the munitions supply board, in 1926 Breen began a major survey of the capability of commercial industry to produce military equipment. Before completing the task, he transferred to the Council for Scientific and Industrial Research, becoming an assistant-secretary. In 1940 he was made assistant-secretary in the Department of Supply and Development, and next year moved to the Department of Munitions where he administered the stores and transport branch. Shifting to the Department of Postwar Reconstruction, he was director of the secondary industries division from 1945 and of industrial development from 1947. He was appointed secretary, Department of Supply and Development, in August 1949. On the establishment of the Department of Defence Production in May 1951, he became its first permanent head. Breen was appointed C.B.E. in 1953 and retired in 1957.

Believing in his country's capacity for self-reliance, particularly in defence, Breen contributed to that goal through his work. He was an early advocate of the need for Australia to recognize its relationship to Asia. Although he made no secret of his Labor sympathies, and his admiration for John Curtin and J. B. Chifley [qq.v.], he ranked Howard Beale, a Liberal, among his favourite ministers. Beale in turn considered him to be 'upright', 'conscientious, scholarly, articulate and intelligent, and a good if somewhat wintry administrator'. Breen could be fiery when others failed to meet his ideals. A tallish, handsome man, with hazel eyes and dark, curly hair, he was a keen sports follower and a bushwalker.

His personal life was marred by tragedy. On 18 March 1916 he had married Agnes Rose O'Sullivan in St Joseph's Catholic Church, Collingwood; she died of tuberculosis in 1923, leaving him with three daughters. He married Rosa Marguerita Maree Carrodus on 1 March 1930 in St John's Church, East Melbourne. In 1934 Rosa died in childbirth and the baby also died. Ten years later Breen's eldest daughter died of tuberculosis. On 20 May 1957 in St Gabriel's Church, Reservoir, he married a 48-year-old public servant Constance Jessie Gillespie.

Breen wrote an unpublished autobiography, 'The Years After'. A devout Catholic, he bequeathed money to the Society for the Propagation of the Faith. He died of diffuse interstitial pulmonary fibrosis on 6 July 1966 at Malvern and was buried in St Kilda cemetery; his wife survived him, as did two daughters of his first marriage.

D. P. Mellor, *The Role of Science and Industry* (Canb, 1958); H. Beale, *This Inch of Time* (Melb, 1977); S. J. Butlin and C. B. Schedvin, *War Economy 1942-1945* (Canb, 1977); *Age* (Melb), 7 July 1966; information from Mrs S. Opray, East Malvern, Melb.
                                            DAVID BLAAZER

BRENNAN, VIRGIL PAUL (1920-1943), air force officer, was born on 6 March 1920 at Warwick, Queensland, fifth child of Edgar

James Brennan, solicitor, and his wife Katherine, née O'Sullivan, both Queenslanders. Educated at Christian Brothers' School, Warwick, Downlands College, Toowoomba, and Brisbane State High School, Paul became a law clerk in Brisbane and studied part time at the University of Queensland. After enlisting in the Citizen Air Force of the Royal Australian Air Force on 8 November 1940, he trained as a pilot in Australia and Canada. 'Digger' Brennan arrived in Britain in August 1941. Following operational training, he served briefly in the Royal Air Force's No. 64 Squadron. He was promoted temporary flight sergeant on 4 January 1942 and next month was sent to the Mediterranean.

Posted to No. 249 Squadron, on 7 March Brennan piloted one of fifteen Spitfires which flew from the aircraft-carrier, H.M.S. *Eagle*, to Malta. In mid-March the Germans began a major air assault on the island. Brennan and his comrades intercepted the waves of attacking bombers and their protective fighter screens: they had to contend with fatigue and inadequate rations while battling the enemy's superior forces. Proving himself a determined and courageous pilot, as well as an excellent shot, Brennan won his first victory ten days after his arrival when he destroyed a Messerschmitt 109. Further successes followed: on 20 April he shot down another Me-109; later in the day he dispatched a Junkers 88. Wounded in the left arm on 12 May, he was commissioned and awarded the Distinguished Flying Medal that month. By the time he left Malta in July, he had survived twenty-two combats, and been credited with the destruction of at least ten enemy aircraft and with damaging several more; a Distinguished Service Cross was added to his previous award for gallantry.

On his return to England, Brennan and Pilot Officer Ray Hesselyn, a New Zealander from No. 249 Squadron, collaborated with the journalist Henry Bateson [q.v] in recording their experiences in *Spitfires over Malta* (London and Sydney, 1943). Granted the rank of acting flight lieutenant and posted as an instructor to No. 52 Operational Training Unit, Brennan was subsequently repatriated on 17 April 1943. Slightly built and 5 ft 9½ ins (176.5 cm) tall, he had dark hair and brown eyes. Although there was aggression in his manner, he had an easy-going nature, an engaging sense of humour and was loyal to his friends; his flair for oratory made him a forceful debater. On 1 May he joined No. 79 Squadron, R.A.A.F. His commanding officer observed that he was strained and tired, and that he seemed to be marshalling his reserves for the unit's forthcoming deployment to Goodenough Island, off Papua. For all that, Brennan shared his operational experience with other pilots.

During their journey north, on 13 June 1943 the squadron's Spitfires reached Garbutt airfield, Townsville, Queensland. Brennan landed his aircraft in the stream of fighters, but the plane which should have landed behind him overran Brennan's machine and collided with it. Brennan died of his injuries on the way to hospital. He was buried with Catholic rites in Townsville war cemetery.

J. C. Waters, *Valiant Youth* (Syd, 1945); J. Herington, *Air War Against Germany and Italy 1939-1943* (Canb, 1954); L. McAulay, *Against All Odds* (Syd, 1989); AWM records.　　DAVID WILSON

BRETT, JAMES FAIRLIE (1884-1966), timber merchant and industrialist, was born on 19 May 1884 at Maryborough, Queensland, second of six children of English-born Horatio Alma Brett, auctioneer, and his wife Marion, née Fairlie, from Scotland. Following Horatio's death in 1895, the family lived with the Fairlies. Jimmie was educated at Maryborough State School and at 14 joined his uncle's local timber firm, James Fairlie & Co. Having learned the trade and been the company's travelling salesman, about 1905 he joined a log-dealer Abe Boldery in what was to be a thirty-year association. They cleared farmland at Kingaroy where settlement was spreading rapidly: bullock-teams hauling logs to the railhead turned the main street into a deep-rutted, red-dirt track. From 1908 the partners worked out of a small sawmill at Blackbutt, south of Nanango.

For a brief time Brett also managed timber companies at Blackbutt before establishing his own business there in 1914. In the previous year he had bought Martello—a house with great verandahs overlooking the Brisbane River—where he installed the women of his close-knit family. He himself lived at Blackbutt where he was a councillor (1914-20) and chairman (1922-24) of Nanango shire. In 1918 he joined his brother Bertie and two others in B. C. Brett & Co. Operating from Windsor and supported by a Victorian government contract, this venture in 1921 became Brisbane Sawmills Pty Ltd. Two years later the complementary hardware business of Brett & Co. Pty Ltd was opened in Brisbane.

Short, lean, dark and dynamic, James began the pattern of constant travel, supervision, organization and negotiation that would hold together an expanding group of firms. When facilities in Brisbane became necessary, he acquired and reclaimed riverside land at Hamilton on which to build the wharf and vast warehouses that became a city landmark. Bretts' Wharves & Stevedoring Co. Ltd (incorporated in November 1928) handled general cargo, as well as huge quantities of timber for export.

As an enthusiastic promoter and deputy-chairman (1928-31) of the Primary Producers Bank of Australia Ltd, Brett made strenuous but unsuccessful efforts to solve its Depression-induced problems. He was credited with never having sacked any of his own employees during this period. Though he avoided political affiliations (and was known to have deliberately misdirected his donations to rival parties to emphasize his impartiality), Brett was outspoken about government responsibility for the economy—while predictably opposing state-run sawmills. After Premier Forgan Smith [q.v.11] ultimately agreed to relinquish state mills at Imbil, Nanango and Yarraman, Brett formed the joint-venture Yarraman Pine Pty Ltd, of which he was founding chairman from 1932 until 1966. In 1934 Blackbutt and Yarraman's first agricultural show was held on fifteen acres (6 ha) donated by Brett and Boldery who gave the show society five cottages and provided another for the local branch of the Country Women's Association.

Keen to promote organizations for ensuring price stability and the regulation of marketing, from 1933 Brett was deputy-chairman of the Pine Exports Association. That year his Brisbane Sawmills began to manufacture plywood. Dubbed 'Mr Plywood' (rather inappropriately, considering his bluntness and fierce independence), he was a driving figure in founding both the State and the Australian Plywood Boards, and was the latter's first chairman (1939-65). As foundation chairman (1943-62) of the Queensland Sawmillers' Association, he presided over the meeting which resolved on the amalgamation to establish the Queensland Timber Board. On the opening of a new timber frontier in New Guinea, a Brett enterprise was established there in 1942, but it remained moribund during World War II. Headquarters in the three-storeyed Bretts Building in Brisbane, where the group's interests were centralized after 1947, were refurbished in the finest timbers, making it a showpiece for the industry.

Wharves and half a dozen new mills were acquired between 1944 and 1949, and a distributing agency was opened in Sydney. A pre-war millionaire, and one of Queensland's most influential industrialists, Brett was chairman of all companies in the family group, and director of wool, gold, oil and several cement companies. While recognizing a responsibility to live well, he remained largely indifferent to his personal comfort. Timber remained his first, and last, love. By no means averse to the company of women, he never married, and on occasion earnestly recommended this policy to others. Brett died on 31 March 1966 in Brisbane and was cremated with Presbyterian forms; his estate was sworn for probate at $1 578 503.

Industrial Aust and Mining Standard, 29 Mar 1928, p 319; Qld Chamber of Manufactures, *Yearbook*, 1972, p 17; *Courier-Mail*, 24 Aug 1967; information from Mr W. J. Brett and Mrs J. B. Nutting, Brisb.

MARGARET STEVEN

BRETT, PETER (1918-1975), professor of jurisprudence, was born on 4 September 1918 at Stoke Newington, London, and named Isidore Peter, third child of Jewish parents Alfred Bretzfelder, builder, and his wife Raie, née Prince. Educated at a private preparatory school and at St Paul's School, Hammersmith, at 16 he was articled to Ernest Bevir & Son, solicitors. He graduated with first-class honours from the University of London (LL.B., 1939). Having changed his name by deed poll to Peter Brett, on 30 September 1939 he married Doris Theresa Moses at the register office, Paddington; they were later divorced. Brett served with the British Expeditionary Force in Europe (1940) and in the West African Force (1941-43); as temporary captain, Royal Fusiliers, he was again in Europe between 1944 and 1946. From that year until 1951 he was a legal assistant in the Office of the Treasury Solicitor, London. Meantime, on 18 August 1949 at St Basil's Anglican Church, Artarmon, Sydney, he married Margaret Hingst Stobo, an Australian nurse whom he had met in London.

In 1951 Brett was appointed senior lecturer in law at the University of Western Australia (LL.M., 1954). Between 1952 and 1954 he published several articles in which he revealed his characteristic clarity, pungency and creativity, as well as a critical judgement which did not always genuflect to legal authority. Appointed senior lecturer at the University of Melbourne in 1955, Brett became reader in 1961, the first Hearn [q.v.4] professor of law in 1963 and professor of jurisprudence in 1964. He was Ezra Ripley Thayer teaching fellow (1958-59) at Harvard University (doctorate of juridical science, 1960) in the United States of America, and a visiting professor at the University of Texas (1959 and 1967), and at both the University of Colorado and York University, Toronto, Canada (1973).

Short in stature, Brett had tight, greying curls and a mobile face, dominated by flashing eyes which were magnified by thick spectacles. He was a fluent and sometimes eloquent speaker, and a stimulating, though occasionally disconcerting, teacher. His chief interests were criminal law, evidence, administrative law and legal philosophy, and he taught and wrote extensively in these subjects. He was generous in sharing ideas, and encouraged his colleagues and students to undertake interdisciplinary research.

In his writing Brett re-examined the philosophical and psychological bases of the law—particularly the criminal law—in the light of modern learning, and undertook a searching reappraisal of the aims of the law and its relation to moral values. His major books were *An Inquiry into Criminal Guilt* (Sydney, 1963) and *An Essay on Contemporary Jurisprudence* (Sydney, 1975). A keen sense of injustice led him to challenge the outcomes of three murder trials: the Tait case (1962) in Victoria, the Beamish case (1966) in Western Australia and the Ratten case (1972-73) in Victoria.

As president of the Federation of Australian Universities Staff Associations, Brett secured the settlement of its long-standing dispute with the University of Tasmania (which had followed the dismissal of Professor Sydney Sparkes Orr [q.v.]), and maintained a commitment to academic freedom and autonomy through his service on F.A.U.S.A.'s committees. He also chaired the academic sub-committee of the professorial board, University of Melbourne. Brett enjoyed music, literature and the theatre. In his later years he expressed no formal religious beliefs, but as a Freemason played a prominent part in the United Grand Lodge of Victoria. He died of a coronary occlusion on 9 May 1975 at his Ivanhoe home and was cremated with Masonic forms; his wife, their three sons and adopted daughter survived him.

L. Waller, *Summons* (Melb, 1975); *Aust Law J*, 49, May 1975; *Vestes*, 18, no 2, Nov 1975; *The Times*, 13 May 1975; information from Mrs W. Aikman, Point Lonsdale, Vic; personal information.   LOUIS WALLER

BREWSTER, SARAH AGNES ANGUS (1874-1957), headmistress and naturalist, was born on 29 April 1874 at Belmore Barracks, Sydney, tenth child of William Brewster, an armourer from Scotland, and his English-born wife Sarah, née Morton. In 1890, aged 15, Agnes was appointed a probationary pupil-teacher at Castlereagh Street Infants' School (her appointment was confirmed in November) and in 1892 moved to Crown Street Public School. After passing the relevant examinations, she was promoted to a class 1 teacher in 1893 and in December 1894 gained a full scholarship to Hurlstone Training College. From 1896 she held appointments at public schools at Woollahra, Randwick, Fort Street, and East and West Maitland.

In 1911 Miss Brewster accepted the post of demonstrator in nature study and elementary science at Sydney Technical College; for her original work, she was one of the first two women to be made a college fellow (1921). Appointed science mistress in 1912 at Sydney Girls' High School, from 1920 she was also *ex officio* deputy-headmistress. In 1928-30 she held similar positions at North Sydney Girls' High School and, after a short term as principal of Newcastle Girls' High School, in January 1931 became founding principal of Hornsby Girls' High School. She stocked the library, filled bare corridors with pictures and had avenues planted with shrubs; under her guidance the barren grounds were turned into an oval, and tennis and basketball courts; she also imparted her love of nature to many of her students before she retired from teaching on 31 January 1938.

A dedicated student of botany and geology, Brewster had been a prominent member of the Linnean and Field Naturalists' societies of New South Wales, the Sydney University Botanical Society (vice-president), the Secondary School Science Society, the State branch of the Australian Forest League and the Wild Life Preservation Society of Australia. She presented many papers to these bodies, including one to the Linnean Society in 1915. With Constance Le Patrier, she published *Botany for Australian Students* (1916); Agnes, her sister Mabel and Naomi Crouch wrote *Life Stories of Australian Insects* (1920, revised 1946); her *Botany for Australian Secondary Schools* appeared in 1929.

In retirement she devoted time to natural history at an old farmhouse at Clarence in the Blue Mountains where she had family and friends as guests. She later lived at St Leonards. Agnes was proud of the Brewster name and of the heraldic motto on the family coat of arms—*verite soyez ma garde*—granted by Queen Elizabeth I in 1561. She died on 29 December 1957 in Royal North Shore Hospital and was cremated with Congregational forms. Her career in education, especially at Hornsby, was widely acknowledged by students and colleagues who remembered her dignity, presence, scholarship, integrity and unfailing courtesy. In 1965 the library at Hornsby Girls' High School was dedicated to her memory.

M. Metzke, *The History of Hornsby Girls' High School, 1930-1990* (Syd, 1990); Hornsby Girls' High School, *Torch*, 1937, 1958; *SMH*, 3 Jan 1958, 30 Dec 1989; Miles Franklin papers (ML); information from Enid Saunders (née Brewster), Killara, Syd, and Margaret Brewster, Canb.

R. ELSE-MITCHELL

BRIDGEFORD, SIR WILLIAM (1894-1971), army officer, was born on 28 July 1894 at Smeaton, Victoria, second child of George Bridgeford, baker, and his wife Christina Gordon, née Calder, both Scottish born. Educated at Ballarat High School, in March 1913 William entered the Royal Military College, Duntroon, Federal Capital Territory. He graduated on 28 June 1915 and was commissioned in the Permanent Military Forces. Next month he was appointed lieutenant in the Australian Imperial Force and posted to the 29th Battalion. He embarked for Egypt in November. Promoted captain on 12 March 1916 and transferred to the 8th Machine-gun Company that day, he sailed for France in mid-June.

His company fought as a component of the 5th Division in the disastrous battle of Fromelles in July. When a number of his junior officers became casualties, Bridgeford reorganized three sections under noncommissioned officers, arranged for ammunition supplies and kept the guns in action. For his efforts, he was awarded the Military Cross. From April 1917 to February 1918 he trained in staff duties at 8th Brigade and 5th Division headquarters. Rejoining his unit (later designated the 5th Machine-gun Battalion), he was gassed in April and evacuated to England. He returned to the front in August and was promoted temporary major on 23 September. After brief employment as a staff officer, he was repatriated in March 1919.

In keeping with reductions to the military establishment, Bridgeford resumed his substantive rank of lieutenant, but was granted the rank of honorary major in the P.M.F. On 22 November 1922 he married a divorcee Phyllis Wallinea, née Frederico (d. 1971) in Scots Church, Melbourne. Having held a succession of posts as brigade major from 1919, he was a company commander (1925-26) at R.M.C., Duntroon, and attended the Staff College at Quetta, India, in 1926-27. Back in Australia, he carried out staff and instructional duties before going to London in 1938 to take the course at the Imperial Defence College. At the outbreak of war he was a temporary lieutenant colonel, acting as military liaison officer in the Australian high commissioner's office. 'An able and widely-experienced soldier', in June 1940 he was promoted temporary brigadier and selected to command the A.I.F.'s 25th Brigade, then being formed in England. In November he became deputy-adjutant and quartermaster-general on the headquarters of I Corps in the Middle East. For his administration of the corps and his efforts to keep units supplied during the Greek campaign, he was appointed C.B.E. (1941) and awarded the Greek Military Cross.

Travelling home via the Netherlands East Indies in early 1942, Bridgeford was pro-

moted temporary major general and made D.A. and Q.M.G., First Army, on 6 April. He commanded the 3rd Armoured Division from April 1943. As D.A. and Q.M.G., New Guinea Force, between August 1943 and April 1944 he contributed to the successful operations which culminated in the occupation of Madang; he was appointed C.B. (1945). On 1 July 1944 he assumed command of the 3rd Infantry Division and led it during the fighting on Bougainville in 1944-45. He was four times mentioned in dispatches for his service in World War II. Returning to Australia, in January 1946 he was appointed quartermaster-general and third member of the Military Board at Army Headquarters, Melbourne. On 1 October 1948 his promotion to substantive major general was gazetted. In July-August 1950 he took a team of officers from the three services to Malaya to obtain information on the campaign against communist insurgents and to advise on jungle-fighting techniques. Bridgeford's report convinced the Australian government that it could offer little support to the British, especially given the decision (made in July) to send servicemen to Korea.

Promoted temporary lieutenant general in February 1951, he had charge of Eastern Command until November when he departed for Tokyo to become commander-in-chief of the British Commonwealth forces in Japan and Korea. Occupying units were being withdrawn from Japan, but Bridgeford's Korean responsibilities were to embroil him in controversies with the governments of other Commonwealth countries. In May 1952 he allowed British and Canadian soldiers to be deployed as guards alongside those from the United States of America whose treatment of prisoners of war had received unfavourable publicity. Complaining of Bridgeford's alleged lack of consultation over a measure which had political implications, the Canadian government pressed for his removal; the Australian and British authorities endorsed his decision. Later that year the British government raised questions about his post as part of its successful attempt to place its own senior representative at United Nations Command Headquarters. Bridgeford was appointed to the Legion of Merit (U.S.A.) on his return to Australia in February 1953. He retired as honorary lieutenant general on 14 March.

In May 1953 he was made chief executive-officer for the forthcoming Olympic Games, to be held in Melbourne, and was subsequently appointed K.B.E. (1956). Six ft 1 in. (185.4 cm) tall, with blue eyes and a fresh complexion, 'Big Bill' was a bluff, genial man who enjoyed shooting and golf. He was active in the affairs of the Returned Sailors', Soldiers' and Airmen's Imperial League of Australia and had been honorary federal treasurer in 1954-56. In his retirement in Melbourne and at Warra, Queensland, he was a director of several companies, including Goulburn-Murray Television Ltd. Sir William died on 21 September 1971 at Kenmore, Brisbane. After a military funeral, he was cremated with Presbyterian forms. His son and stepdaughter survived him.

C. E. W. Bean, *The A.I.F. in France*, 1916 (Syd, 1929); G. Long, *To Benghazi* and *The Final Campaigns* (Canb, 1952, 1963); R. O'Neill, *Australia in the Korean War 1950-53*, 1-2 (Canb, 1981, 1985); J. Grey, *The Commonwealth Armies and the Korean War* (Manchester, Eng, 1988); *Sun News-Pictorial*, 14 Apr 1953, 28 Feb 1957; *Courier-Mail*, 23 Sept 1971; AWM records.　　　　　　JEFFREY GREY

BRIFMAN, SHIRLEY MARGARET (1935-1972), prostitute, was born on 7 December 1935 at Atherton, Queensland, thirteenth child of native-born parents James Emerson, labourer, and his wife, Beatrice, née Currey. Shirley took a job as a barmaid. On 13 June 1957 at the courthouse, Cairns, she married Szama Brifman, a 42-year-old, Polish-born hotel-proprietor. The marriage was to endure, despite her career as a prostitute which probably began in a North Queensland hotel. As 'Marge Chapple', Brifman was working in 1958 in one of Brisbane's half-century-old brothels. Next year Frank Bischof [q.v.], the recently appointed commissioner of police, unilaterally closed the 'houses': the Department of Health was thereby relieved of regulatory responsibility, but opportunities for corruption were extended. A personal favourite of some police officers preferred by Bischof, Brifman was well placed to continue working out of hotels. Dark haired, slim and petite, she was 5 ft 1 in. (154.9 cm) tall; she had a lively personality, spoke with a slightly nasal tone, laughed easily, and could be garrulous.

In 1963 Brifman moved to Sydney. That year she was a star witness at the Queensland royal commission into the police and the National Hotel. Schooled in her evidence by police (according to her own account), she denied that she had ever been a prostitute, and accused the chief witness to police misconduct at the hotel of having 'done an abortion on me'. Although her testimony was almost wholly false, she succeeded in impairing the inquiry. Her later confession was to cast doubt on the evidence of a number of other witnesses. Until 1968 she worked in Sydney from the lounge of the Rex Hotel, King's Cross. She subsequently opened brothels at Potts Point and Elizabeth Bay (controlling up to fifteen 'girls' and claiming that she earned $5000 a week in 1969) under police protection, purchased by both cash and

favours. In June 1971 Brifman and her husband were charged with offences related to prostitution. Her arrest, despite protection papers, apparently induced her to appear on national television to make allegations of police corruption. She then fled to Queensland.

As one of the few criminal sources on the era of police-controlled organized crime, Brifman has considerable historical significance. From July to October 1971 she was interviewed by senior police from New South Wales and Queensland. In her recorded responses to 320 questions, she named over fifty police from both States, the majority in connexion with specific crimes or corruption. Her allegations involved prominent policemen, but the Crown's case against the only officer to face criminal charges collapsed when she was found dead of barbiturate intoxication on 4 March 1972 in her flat at Clayfield, Brisbane. She was due to face a procuring charge on 17 March in Sydney and to give evidence of perjury against a detective senior sergeant on 22 March in Brisbane. Her death was treated as suicide and, at the request of the Queensland police, no coroner's inquest was held. Brifman was buried in Atherton cemetery with Presbyterian forms; her husband, son and three daughters survived her.

In March 1978 in the South Australian House of Assembly the attorney-general Peter Duncan tabled a 64-page document containing Brifman's responses to the New South Wales police interviews in 1971.

P. James, *In Place of Justice* (Deception Bay, Qld, 1974); A. W. McCoy, *Drug Traffic* (Syd, 1980); R. Fitzgerald, *A History of Queensland from 1915 to the early 1980s* (Brisb, 1984); D. Hickie, *The Prince and the Premier* (Syd, 1985); E. Whitton, *Can of Worms*, 2 (Syd, 1987); P. Dickie, *The Road to Fitzgerald* (Brisb, 1988); (G. E. Fitzgerald) *Commission of Inquiry into Possible Illegal Activities and Associated Police Misconduct* (Brisb, 1989); Roy Com into Allegations Made Against Members of the Police Force in Relation to the National Hotel, 1963-64, Report and Transcripts of Evidence (roneoed copy, Parliament House, Brisb); Queensland Police, Records of interview with S. M. Brifman, 28 Sept-26 Oct 1971 (copy held by author, Nth Quay, Brisb).　　　　　　PHIL DICKIE

BRIGGS, ERNEST (1905-1967), poet, broadcaster and critic, was born on 24 January 1905 in Sydney, son of Charles James Briggs, a bootmaker from Victoria, and his Queensland-born wife Jessie, née Waters. After his mother's death in 1908, Ernest was raised by his father. A small, frail child with a speech impediment (eventually cured through therapy), he spent much time on lonely bush ramblings; from his father, he gained a love of ballads and song, and of family and colonial history. Ernest was a fifth-generation Australian, descended from Thomas Rowley [q.v.2]. Educated at Kogarah Public School, he became a radio broadcaster and moved to Queensland in 1931 to join station 4BK, Brisbane. He was subsequently a general announcer, continuity manager, programme director, feature writer and publicity officer. Mobilized in the Militia on 6 February 1942, Briggs served as a clerk at New Guinea Force headquarters before being discharged medically unfit on 14 December in Brisbane.

While he read William Blake and John Millington Synge, many of his ideas were inspired by W. B. Yeats and by the 'Celtic Twilight' movement. Briggs's discovery of the works of Yeats, with whom he had previously corresponded, and on whom he later lectured and wrote, transformed his life. He published his first volume of poetry, *The Merciless Beauty*, in 1943: in it, he reflected his early personal and mystical experiences which were to lead to his subsequent interest in theosophy, spiritualism and the religions of the East. His brief term in New Guinea resulted in the powerful, concentrated emotionalism of *The Death of the Hare* (1949); its title was derived from Yeats.

Briggs reverted to his childhood experiences when writing the meditative lyrics in *The Secret Listener* (1949) and published a third volume of poetry, *The Timeless Flowers*, in 1952. For his sequences on Yeats, *The High Ascent and Other Poems* (1953), he was admitted to the Poetry Society of America. In 1961 and again in 1962 he was awarded the literature diploma of the Leonardo da Vinci Academy, Rome, for his contributions to international culture and understanding.

As a music critic, Briggs wrote reviews for the Brisbane *Courier-Mail*, the *Sunday Mail* and the music journal, *Canon*. He made a notable collection of historical recordings, specializing in vocal art and poetry. Towards the end of his life, in his anxiety for recognition, he experimented unsuccessfully with writing novels and plays, and undertook editing, biography and autobiography. His corpus extends to over forty works in manuscript or limited private editions, some of which have been set to music. Represented in several anthologies, he also contributed to the literary journals, *Meanjin* and *Aspect*.

Of medium build, with small hands, a high forehead and frizzy, ginger hair, Briggs had a light baritone voice. Despite a shy, otherworldly outlook, he impressed many people and was known for his spontaneous generosity. Briggs remained a bachelor. He died of myocardial infarction on 21 June 1967 in Brisbane and was cremated with Methodist forms.

C. H. Hadgraft, *Queensland and Its Writers* (Brisb, 1959); *Literary Review. Australia Number*, Winter, 1963-64; *Bulletin*, 1 Mar 1944; *Daily Mercury*, 25 Mar 1944; *Telegraph* (Brisb), 21 June 1967; *Courier-Mail*, 22 June 1967; E. Briggs, Blow Away the Morning Dew (autobiog, ms, OL); Briggs papers (Fryer L, Univ Qld, *and* OL, *and* Syracuse Univ L, NY; information from Mr C. Goode, St Lucia, Brisb; personal information.

JOHN P. SIMPSON

BRILL, WILLIAM LLOYD (1916-1964), air force officer, was born on 17 May 1916 at Ganmain, New South Wales, fourth child of Victorian-born parents Edward Henry Brill, farmer, and his wife Bertha, née Logan. Educated at Yanco Agricultural High School, William took up wheat-farming at Grong Grong in partnership with his brothers. He served two years in the Militia before enlisting in the Citizen Air Force, Royal Australian Air Force, on 11 November 1940. After training in Australia and Canada, he was commissioned on 28 July 1941 and arrived in England next month.

In January 1942 he joined No. 460 Squadron, R.A.A.F., attached to the Royal Air Force's Bomber Command; the squadron operated Wellingtons and Brill was posted as an aircraft captain. On the night of 29-30 May he flew through squally weather on a strike against factories at Gennevilliers, Paris. Anti-aircraft fire damaged his aeroplane's hydraulic system and put the rear turret out of action. Undeterred, he inspected his target from only 1500 feet (457.2 m), pressed home the attack and hit his objective. Bad weather made the home journey hazardous, but he succeeded in landing safely without flaps and with one wheel disabled. He was awarded the Distinguished Flying Cross in June for his courage and determination.

After thirty-one sorties, Brill was seconded to the R.A.F. in November 1942 for instructional duties. His second operational tour began on 1 January 1944 with his posting as a flight commander in No. 463 Squadron, R.A.A.F. Four weeks later, during a night-raid over Berlin, incendiary bombs dropped by an aircraft above fell onto Brill's Lancaster, starting fires in the fuselage and a wing, impairing rudder controls and rendering the compass unserviceable. On later missions his aircraft sustained damage from shrapnel and bullets, yet he invariably managed to return to base. For his leadership, skill and gallantry, he was awarded the Distinguished Service Order in May. That month Acting Wing Commander Brill took command of No. 467 Squadron, R.A.A.F. In July, while bombing St Leu d'Esserent, France, his successful efforts in driving off three German nightfighters won him a Bar to his D.F.C. Having completed fifty-eight sorties, he came back to Australia in January 1945. On 29 January 1945 he married a teacher Ilma Margaret Kitto at the Methodist Church, Ganmain.

Transferring to the Permanent Air Force in September 1948, Brill was to command four different R.A.A.F. bases between that year and 1964. As wing commander, he was staff officer to the chief of the Air Staff in 1952-54 and director of personnel services in 1956-59; as group captain, he was D.P.S. in 1960-63. Imperturbable in nature and exceptionally fair-minded in outlook, he was 5 ft 9½ ins (176.5 cm) tall, with blue eyes. Brill endeavoured to make service life congenial, particularly for the airmen, and recognized—more than many of his peers—that aircrew and aircraft are useless without efficient and contented ground-staff. Dedicated to community service, he was a Freemason and was appointed in 1962 Boy Scouts' commissioner in charge of Canberra area development. He died of myocardial infarction on 12 October 1964 at Campbell and was buried in Canberra cemetery with Anglican rites; his wife, daughter and two sons survived him.

J. Herington, *Air War Against Germany and Italy 1939-1943* (Canb, 1954) and *Air Power Over Europe 1944-1945* (Canb, 1963); *SMH*, 24 Feb 1962; *Canb Times*, 13 Oct 1964; records (AWM).

BRIAN EATON*

BRISBANE, DAVID WILLIAM (1888-1960), engineer, and SIR HUGH LANCELOT (1893-1966), businessman, were born on 20 January 1888 and 16 March 1893 at Fitzroy, Melbourne, second and third sons of Victorian-born parents Hugh Brisbane, ironmonger, and his wife Charlotte, née Fithie. The family moved to Western Australia in 1894.

Lance was educated at Fremantle Boys' School and Perth Technical School. In 1909 he began an apprenticeship as a draughtsman with the Perth branch of the building materials manufacturer, Wunderlich [q.v.12] Ltd, and rose rapidly through the ranks. On 2 August 1915 he enlisted in the Australian Imperial Force. He served in Australian and British units in the Middle East, was mentioned in dispatches and awarded the Egyptian Order of the Nile. Promoted temporary major in February 1919, he returned to Australia where his A.I.F. appointment terminated on 14 October. Lance rejoined Wunderlich and in 1920 managed the company's clay-roofing tile plant in East Perth; moved into marketing next year, he eventually became State sales manager. Five feet 11 ins (180.3 cm) tall, with blue eyes and fair hair, he married Frances Leonard Hoyle on 21 September 1921 at St Mary's Anglican Church, West Perth.

In 1927 the business entrepreneur Reginald Long bought a controlling interest in Westralian Potteries Ltd and in 1929 recruited Brisbane as general manager. Although Lance was not a major shareholder, the firm's name was changed to H. L. Brisbane & Co. Ltd. Despite the Depression, he managed to expand the company until it challenged Wunderlich as market leader. In 1938 Wunderlich agreed to merge its Western Australian operation with H. L. Brisbane & Co., in return for an undertaking that Lance would not attempt to expand his business interstate. H. L. Brisbane & Wunderlich Ltd became the State's largest clay-tile producer, securing a virtual monopoly in the industry.

Over the next twenty-eight years Lance built the company into a large and diversified manufacturing enterprise, moving into stainless-steel products, clay sewer-pipes, porcelain, refractory bricks, aluminium fabrication, building cladding and plastics. An industrialist of the old school, with a thoroughgoing knowledge of all aspects of the business, he placed great importance on the loyalty and enthusiasm of his employees; his paternalistic management and manner of handling industrial relations had been largely responsible for his firm's survival through the Depression. Most of his company's postwar success resulted from capital investment in new products and processes rather than from acquiring other firms.

Believing that a strong manufacturing sector was essential to Western Australia's economic future, Lance enthusiastically promoted industrial development. As chairman during World War II of the local board of area management, Commonwealth Department of Munitions, he was sometimes criticized for placing his State's interests ahead of a coordinated national war effort. Knighted in 1961, Brisbane was appointed that year by the Brand [q.v.] government to its Industries Advisory Committee, a body composed of leading businessmen. He also served on such charitable institutions as the National Heart Foundation of Australia and the Princess Margaret Hospital for Children. Politically conservative but pragmatic, Brisbane was a friend of Labor's A. R. G. Hawke and the Liberal (Sir) Charles Court; both of the major political parties encouraged his business ventures and supported his vision for the State's progress. Survived by his wife and two daughters, Sir Lance Brisbane died on 4 February 1966 in Bethesda Hospital, Claremont, and was cremated; his estate was sworn for probate in Western Australia at $178 442.

David was educated at Scotch College and Perth Technical School. In 1908 he joined the State Department of Public Works as an engineering cadet and by 1912 was an assistant-engineer. He married Myra Gladys Richardson on 10 December 1913 at the Katanning Baptist Church. Having accepted a position in 1919 as divisional engineer for the Federated Malay States railways, in 1923 he was made managing director of Fogden, Brisbane & Co., Singapore, consulting engineers, a firm which was to execute a range of major public works throughout Asia and the Middle East for the British Admiralty, War Office and Air Ministry.

Returning to Perth in early 1942 following the Japanese attack on Singapore, on 28 July David became a skipper (sub lieutenant) in the Royal Australian Naval Auxiliary Patrol.

During World War II he was appointed managing director of the Midland Railway Co. of Western Australia Ltd, the State's last privately-owned railway. He also worked with (Sir) Russell Dumas [q.v.] on the establishment of the Anglo-Iranian oil refinery at Kwinana, chaired the board of West Australian Newspapers Ltd and was appointed C.B.E. in 1958. Survived by his wife, son and three daughters, David Brisbane died in Royal Perth Hospital on 2 August 1960 and was cremated with Presbyterian forms; his estate was sworn for probate in Western Australia at £68 416.

V. Colless, *Men of Western Australia* (Perth, 1937); B. Moore, *From the Ground Up* (Perth, 1987); *West Australian*, 3 Aug 1960, 5 Feb 1966.

BRYCE MOORE

BROADBENT, HARRY FRANK (JIM) (1910-1958), aviator, was born on 25 March 1910 at Chiswick, London, son of Joseph Gibbs, a music-hall vocalist known as 'Frank Harwood', and his wife Madge Adelaide (d. 1928), daughter of Harry Rickards [q.v.11]. Educated at Wychwood College, Bournemouth, Harry was brought to Australia after his parents' divorce. In 1923 his mother married John Allan Broadbent, of Windella station, Narrandera; henceforward her son preferred to be known as 'Jim Broadbent'.

Inspired by the 1928 flights of Bert Hinkler and (Sir) Charles Kingsford Smith [qq.v.9], he joined the New South Wales section of the Australian Aero Club, and received a private pilot's licence on 20 November 1929. Next year he went to England, but was frustrated in his attempt to break Kingsford Smith's England-Australia record. Back in Australia, Broadbent bought an Avro Avian in 1931. On 12 August he flew solo from Brisbane to Sydney, Melbourne and Adelaide, linking the cities for the first time by air in one day. Within a month he set a round-Australia record by flying 7475 miles (12 030 km) in 7 days, 8 hours, 25 minutes. On 31 December

that year he married Beryl Elizabeth Bower at St Jude's Anglican Church, Randwick.

After winning the annual New South Wales Aerial Derby on 14 May 1932, Broadbent purchased a three-seat Puss Moth monoplane. He obtained a commercial licence and started an air taxi service, but all Puss Moths were grounded, pending accident investigations. He acquired and trained racehorses until the ban was lifted. Having won the Victorian Aerial Derby on 18 March 1933, he reactivated his air taxi service.

On 17-20 May 1935 Broadbent flew 7140 miles (11 490 km) around Australia in his new Puss Moth in the astonishing time of 3 days, 9 hours, 54 minutes (a record that remains unbroken). Leaving Darwin on 10 October, his aircraft was damaged near Basra, Iraq, and he continued to England by Imperial Airways Ltd. A simultaneous take-off from Croydon was made on 2 November by Broadbent and C. J. Melrose [q.v.10] in Percival [q.v.11] Gulls. Broadbent reached Darwin on 9 November, reducing 'Smithy's' 1933 England-Australia solo record to 6 days, 21 hours, 19 minutes, and was awarded the Oswald Watt [q.v.12] gold medal for 1935.

Next year Broadbent joined Butler [q.v.] Air Transport Co. and flew the Charleville-Cootamundra section of the England-Australia airmail route. Meanwhile, a friendly rivalry had developed between him and the New Zealand aviatrix Jean Batten. She broke his 1935 England-Australia record in October 1936, but he regained it by lowering the time to 6 days, 8 hours, 25 minutes (27 April-3 May 1937) in his Leopard Moth, *Windella*. On 18-24 October Batten cut his record to 5 days, 18 hours, 15 minutes. Broadbent had to abandon two attempts to break her record. Determinedly, he then flew a Vega Gull out of Darwin on 18 April 1938 and landed in England on the 22nd: his time was 5 days, 4 hours, 21 minutes. His achievement was the last of the pre-World War II record flights on the England-Australia-England routes and his time remains a record for its class.

In 1938-39 Broadbent piloted flying boats between Sydney and Singapore for Qantas Empire Airways Ltd. He served with Royal Air Force Ferry Command, conveying aircraft from Canada and the United States of America to Britain and Australia (1941-43), and flew Lockheed Electras for the allied Directorate of Air Transport (1943-44).

Having divorced his wife in July 1948, Broadbent married 24-year-old Meris Chilcott Rudder at St John's Presbyterian Church, Wahroonga, on 27 January 1950. He took her to England in 1952 and flew Bristol freighters with Silver City Airways. In November 1954 he began piloting Short Solent flying boats for Aquila Airways Ltd from Southampton to Lisbon, Madeira and Las

Palmas. From 29 September 1958 he was attached as an instructor to the Portuguese airline, Artop. On 9 November that year Broadbent reported that he was making an emergency landing in a Martin Mariner flying boat in the Atlantic, west of Portugal. No trace of the aircraft, crew or passengers was ever found. His wife, and the two daughters of his first marriage, survived him.

Jim Broadbent was essentially shy and kept to himself. He had endeavoured to avoid publicity. The Australian aviatrix Nancy Bird recalled that he read detective stories on his long flights and was always anxious to get back into the air to find out 'who dunnit' (he called his English home, The Case is Altered). Nancy and Jean Batten regarded Jim as 'the best sportsman they had ever met'. The meticulously prepared strip-maps which he used for his record-breaking flights are held by the National Library of Australia.

N. Bird, *Born to Fly* (Syd, 1961); J. Batten, *Alone in the Sky* (Auckland, NZ, 1979); N. M. Parnell and T. Boughton, *Flypast* (Canb, 1988); *Aircraft* (Melb), 1929-39; *Flight* (Lond), 1930-39; *SMH*, 8 Aug 1931, 21 May 1935, 14 Oct, 4, 5 May 1937, 18, 19 Mar, 25 Apr, 6 May 1938, 11 July 1941, 11 Nov 1958; information from Mrs G. Sykes, Kirribilli, and Mrs N. Bird Walton, St Ives, Syd.

KEITH ISAACS

BROADBY, REGINALD ROSLYN (1904-1956), trade union leader, was born on 25 June 1904 at Queenstown, Tasmania, son of Reginald Saunders Broadby, a native-born bootmaker, and his wife Ruby Olive, née Ward. Reg was educated at Queenstown State School and from childhood absorbed the staunch though moderate trade-union traditions of the isolated, vulnerable mining towns of the rugged Tasmanian west coast. He moved to Melbourne in 1925 and on 5 December at the Catholic Church of Saints Peter and Paul, South Melbourne, married Ellen Enright, a dressmaker from Queenstown.

After working as a clerk and commercial traveller, Broadby joined the Melbourne and Metropolitan Tramways Board as a conductor in 1926. Forced into part-time work by the Depression, he became active in union affairs, originally through involvement in the Tramways Athletic and Social Club. By the late 1930s he was taking the moderate position against Clarrie O'Shea, the communist secretary of the Australian Tramways and Motor Omnibus Employees' Association. O'Shea led the militant Victorian branch while Broadby became a leader of the moderate national organization of the union, holding the positions of general secretary (1944-48) and arbitration advocate; he was also State

president (1944-46). Broadby was, as well, president of the Melbourne Trades Hall Council in 1944-45 and of the Victorian branch of the Australian Labor Party in 1949-50.

As the Cold War reached into nearly every section of the union movement, the Communist Party of Australia operated a well-organized and disciplined faction which won control of the left wing of the union movement. The fine balance between left and right was shown by the margin of only one vote in 1948 when the interstate executive of the Australian Council of Trade Unions chose Broadby ahead of the communist candidate for the new position of assistant-secretary. In 1949 he was elected secretary, succeeding Albert Monk [q.v.] who became president.

At first Broadby was an influential supporter of 'the (Catholic) Movement' (later National Civic Council) and the A.L.P. industrial groups, which together combated the communist advance in the unions. He had been foundation secretary (1946) of the A.L.P. industrial groups committee which was appointed by the (State) central executive of the party. By the early 1950s, however, Broadby, Monk and a number of other senior Labor men had turned against the anti-communist force and formed a 'centre' faction, believing that the anti-communist 'groupers' were becoming too aggressive and disruptive, and beginning to resemble their opponents. Broadby complained about Labor 'getting rid of one intolerance only to replace it with another'. He was further alarmed by rising sectarian suspicions and tensions. Like his allies, he wanted to create an ideological wedge and balance of power to unify and develop the A.C.T.U.

This faction, with Broadby among its leaders, supported the 'anti-grouper' side in the Labor split of 1955 and he returned to the Victorian central executive of the A.L.P. After years of being attacked by the left, his moderating position earned him bitter opposition from some former friends. His personal ease was not helped by being a Protestant with a Catholic wife and family.

Slight in build, industrious and methodical, Broadby was regarded as a sensible, conciliatory secretary who helped to establish the foundations of Monk's twenty-year presidency of the A.C.T.U. Broadby was distressed by the fanaticism and hostility of the era, but held to the belief that the divisions within the unions were manageable. A popular spokesman for the unions, he gave press interviews, addressed community groups and attended international conferences.

In 1955 the Cain [q.v.] Labor government appointed Broadby a (part-time) commissioner of the State Savings Bank of Victoria. He died of asthma complicated by bronchiectasis on 14 July 1956 at Williamstown. Former tramways colleagues lined the street when his mile-long funeral procession passed Essendon depot on its way to Fawkner cemetery where he was buried with Presbyterian forms. His wife, son and two daughters survived him.

R. Murray, *The Split* (Melb, 1970); J. Hagan, *The History of the A.C.T.U.* (Melb, 1981); K. White, *John Cain and Victorian Labor 1917-1957* (Syd, 1982).
                                        ROBERT MURRAY

BRODIE, SIR ISRAEL (1895-1979), rabbi, was born on 10 May 1895 at Newcastle-upon-Tyne, England, second son of Aaron Brode, drapery traveller, and his wife Jane, née Magid, immigrants from Kovno (Kaunas), Lithuania. The product of a pious home, with scholars and rabbis among his ancestors, Israel attended Rutherford College of Technology, Newcastle; intent on a rabbinical career, in 1912 he enrolled at both University College and Jews' College, London (B.A., 1915). Having graduated with first-class honours in Hebrew, Aramaic and Syriac, he proceeded in 1916 to Balliol College, Oxford (B.Litt., 1921). His studies were interrupted by service as a British Army chaplain in France in 1917-19.

After congregational and welfare work in London's East End, in 1923 Brodie succeeded Joseph Abrahams [q.v.7] as rabbi to the Melbourne Hebrew congregation (whose synagogue was then situated in Bourke Street, but from 1930 in Toorak Road, South Yarra) and as head (1923-37) of the Victorian Beth Din, the Jewish religious court. In 1926 he published the first of several editions of *English Prayers and Readings*. He continued an involvement with adult education: his series of lectures on Judaism and Christianity, delivered in 1932, were appreciated by followers of both faiths.

His impact extended beyond Melbourne. Brodie made several interstate visits and pressed for solidarity among the scattered Jewish communities of Australia. Welcoming the increase in Eastern European Jewish immigrants to Victoria during the 1920s, he chided congregants who viewed the influx as a threat to their own standing in the general community. He led efforts to assist the social and economic integration of these newcomers —who were to spearhead a reinvigorated Melbourne Jewish community—and championed their cause in the *Australian Jewish Herald*.

Brodie lacked the squeamishness towards the Zionist movement evinced during the interwar period by many Australian Jews who feared that the spectre of 'dual loyalties' might call into question their vaunted devotion to the British Crown and Empire. He believed that Zionism was not only just itself, but also a necessary adjunct to Judaism and a stimulus to Jewish consciousness. In 1927 he became foundation president of the Zionist Federation of Australia (of which Sir John Monash [q.v.10] was honorary president) and served in that capacity until 1937 when he relinquished his pulpit and returned to England.

During World War II Brodie served as an army chaplain in France and was one of the last evacuees from Dunkirk. He subsequently became a chaplain in the Royal Air Force in the Middle East and in 1944 was made senior Jewish chaplain to the British forces. Appointed principal of Jews' College in 1946, on 30 June at the Great Synagogue, London, he married a Warsaw-born schoolteacher, Fanny Levine; they were to remain childless. Energetic and effective as a rabbi, gifted with ability and intellect, he found that his deep-seated Zionism had assumed a particular relevance in the light of the Holocaust. In 1948 he succeeded Dr Joseph Herman Hertz as chief rabbi of the British Commonwealth. Determined to consolidate his authority among the antipodean congregations and to boost their morale, Brodie made several visits to Australia, notably in 1952 and 1962. He retired in 1965 and was knighted in 1969.

Short in stature, dark, somewhat rotund, with a neat goatee and a mellifluous voice, Sir Israel was a man of dignity and sincerity whose tenure of office and solid body of published scholarship were distinguished. Survived by his wife, he died on 13 February 1979 at Lambeth, London.

A. Wynn, *The Fortunes of Samuel Wynn* (Melb, 1968); N. Rosenthal, *Look Back with Pride* (Melb, 1971); *DNB*, 1971-1980; B. Patkin, *Heritage and Tradition* (Melb, 1972); H. L. and W. D. Rubinstein, *The Jews in Australia* (Melb, 1991); *Jewish Chronicle* (Lond), 16 Feb 1979; *Daily Telegraph* (Lond), 14 Feb 1979; *Aust Jewish Times*, 22 Feb 1979; *Aust Jewish Herald*, 23 Feb 1979; Melb Hebrew Congregation records (Synagogue Archives).
                                HILARY L. RUBINSTEIN

BRODNEY, MARIA MAY (1894-1973), labour activist, was born on 13 April 1894 at Malvern, Melbourne, daughter of John Francis, labourer, and his wife Julia, née Roonan, both Irish Fenians who migrated separately to Australia in 1888. Educated at Catholic and state schools, in 1910 May took a job as an apprentice underwear-machinist with Craig Williamson Pty Ltd. She rejected Catholicism in her teens and began a lifelong campaign against social and economic inequality.

May was initially attracted to the socialist-feminism of Vida Goldstein [q.v.9] and the

Women's Political Association. With others from the W.P.A., in 1914 she founded the Women's Industrial and Social Union. Frustrated by its lack of success, she turned in 1915 to the craft-based Federated Clothing Trades' Union, hoping to organize women workers in the shirtmaking, whitework and dressmaking sections of the clothing trades. She rapidly rose to positions of responsibility on the union executive and represented fellow workers on the Underclothing Board, the Court of Industrial Appeals and the Trades Hall Council.

In 1916-17 May was involved in the anticonscription campaigns, primarily as secretary of the Militant Propogandists of the Labor Movement. Her association with radical, left-wing politics continued after the war. Inspired by the Bolshevik victory in Russia, she was a foundation member (1920) of the Melbourne branch of the Communist Party of Australia.

On 12 March 1924 May married ALFRED TENNYSON ('BOB') BRODNEY (1896-1984) at the registry office, Collins Street, Melbourne; although Jewish, he was an atheist. Born on 3 May 1896 in Melbourne, son of Maurice Brodzky [q.v.7], journalist, and his wife Florence, née Leon, Bob had travelled widely with his family in childhood and spent years in the United States of America to avoid conscription during World War I. Returning to Australia in 1918, he anglicized his surname, moved from Brisbane to Sydney and joined the Australian Socialist Party; in October 1920 he helped to found the C.P.A. He moved to Melbourne in 1923 and next year, with May, assisted in re-establishing the defunct Melbourne branch. Disillusioned with the party's increasingly doctrinaire stance and tactics, they resigned their membership in 1925.

Throughout the 1920s May contributed her earnings and domestic labour to support her husband, father and two brothers, all of whom were in and out of work. Employed as a clerk with Maurice Blackburn [q.v.7] & Co., Bob studied law at the University of Melbourne (LL.B., 1939). After graduating, he began a long career in labour litigation, and became a senior partner in Blackburn's firm and later a solicitor to the Australian Council of Trade Unions.

May continued as a clothing-industry delegate until 1929. Thereafter, she was increasingly involved in the Victorian Labor College, of which she was a founding member, trustee (1923) and secretary (1937-56); she also set up and ran its bookstall at Flinders Street railway station. During the Depression she was a representative on the Shop Assistants' Wages Board, and was active in campaigns to support striking timberworkers, unemployed women and girls, and those con-

victed in the Greek Club bombing case of 1929. She returned to industry in World War II, first in the clothing trades and next in the metal trades. In both cases, as in her ongoing work in the V.L.C., she was active in combating communist influence.

A small woman, with heavy brows and intense eyes, Mrs Brodney was widely known for her quick temper, sharp wit and outspoken views. Following Hitler's non-aggression pact with Stalin in August 1939 and the C.P.A.'s refusal to support the war effort, she joined the Labor Party in 1940. Vilified as a Trotskyist by the C.P.A., she remained an independent Marxist. She died, childless, on 21 August 1973 at Mount Evelyn, Victoria, and was cremated. Bob Brodney died on 17 May 1984 at Elsternwick, Melbourne.

B. L. Ellem, *In Women's Hands?* (Syd, 1989); Aust Soc for the Study of Labour Hist (Melb branch), *Recorder*, 66, Oct 1973; *Labour Hist*, 40, May 1981, p 95; A. T. and M. M. Brodney papers *and* S. Merrifield collection (LaTL).

RAELENE FRANCES

BRODRIBB, NOEL KENRIC STEVENS (1885-1965), public servant, was born on 27 December 1885 at Kew, Melbourne, son of Thomas Brodribb [q.v.3], assistant inspector-general of schools, and his Victorian-born wife Emily Jane, née Stevens. Educated at Kew High School and the Working Men's College, Melbourne, where he studied assaying, Noel showed an early interest in explosives and weaponry. On 4 October 1909 he was appointed chemist at the Commonwealth Government Cordite Factory, Maribyrnong. He held a provisional commission for three months in 1909-10 in the Corps of Engineers, Australian Military Forces. Assistant manager from 1912 at the Maribyrnong factory, in February 1917 he became manager with a salary of £800. On 9 June 1914 at St Philip's Anglican Church, Sydney, he had married Kathleen Elsie Allan.

After the government decided in 1918 to centralize the manufacture of arms, ammunition and cordite at Tuggeranong, Federal Capital Territory, Brodribb was gazetted chief chemical engineer, Australian Arsenal, but the project was soon abandoned and he remained in Melbourne. Appointed O.B.E. in 1920, he acted as controller-general of munitions supply during A. E. Leighton's [q.v.10] absences in 1923 and 1933. Brodribb went to Britain in 1936-37 'to study new technical practices and to develop personal contacts with key scientists and engineers'. On his return he was made controller-general, in charge of an organization which he had done much to sustain and which was expanding in anticipation of war.

In 1938 he was seconded to become inspector-general of works and supplies; he was also a member of the Council of Defence. When he resumed his post on 17 June 1939 he was an experienced manager and engineer; practical-minded, he concentrated on technical detail and on the job in hand. He worked hard, appearing confident to one observer, though another sometimes found him jumpy and nervous. Punctilious and patriotic, Brodribb was a familiar figure at the Naval and Military Club, Melbourne. With the appointment of Essington Lewis [q.v.10] as director-general of munitions in June 1940, Brodribb served as his deputy and took charge of the government component of armaments production. Australian manufacturing, both public and private, geared up for its greatest challenge. From June 1939 to June 1943 government factories increased from 4 to 48, their workforce from 5055 to 55 954 and the value of their production from £1 326 172 to £38 million: they were able to supply the armed forces with a vast range of high-quality munitions. For his services Brodribb had been elevated to C.B.E. in 1941. Chairman of the Australian Shipbuilding Board from 1943, he sat on other bodies which endeavoured to improve production and to foster technological development.

Brodribb reverted to his permanent appointment in 1945 and retired on 26 December 1950. As chairman (1953-61) of the Australian Aluminium Production Commission, he saw the Bell Bay plant open in Tasmania in 1955. He was a director of Mount Lyell Mining & Railway Co. Ltd and Clyde Industries Ltd, and a fellow (1924) of the Institute of Chemistry, London. Of middle height, strongly built and neat in appearance, he played golf and was fond of bridge. Brodribb died on 27 January 1965 at Hawthorn, Melbourne, and was cremated; his son survived him.

D. P. Mellor, *The Role of Science and Industry* (Canb, 1958); *SMH*, 16 Oct 1920, 23 Dec 1935, 20 Dec 1939, 12 June 1941, 26 Oct 1943, 30 May 1945, 8 Feb 1955; A. T. Ross, The Arming of Australia: the Politics and Administration of Australia's Self Containment Strategy for Munitions Supply 1901-1945 (Ph.D. thesis, ADFA, 1986); J. L. Knight, Explosives in Australia (ms held by Mrs F. Knight, Blackburn, Melb); information from Dr L. A. Brodribb and Sir A. Glenn, Melb.

DARRYL BENNET

BRONNER, RUDOLPH (1890-1960), radio administrator, was born on 27 September 1890 at Lyndoch, South Australia, son of Charles Bronner, a schoolteacher from Switzerland, and his wife Marian, née Schmidhauser. Educated at the Collegiate School of St Peter and at the University of Adelaide (B.A., 1912; M.A., 1926), Rudi graduated with honours in philosophy. His application for a Rhodes scholarship was unsuccessful: legend has it that he was beaten by the toss of a coin. In 1914 he sailed on a free passage to England where he entered Balliol College, Oxford, and read philosophy and social sciences. One of his friends was Aldous Huxley.

On 7 April 1917 at St Botolph's parish church, Cambridge, Bronner married a fellow South Australian Pauline Berkeley Bartels. He was commissioned in the London Rifle Brigade on 26 April and served on the Western Front (where he was wounded) until World War I ended. Returning to Adelaide, he tutored for the Workers' Educational Association of Australia. In 1921 he moved to the University of Melbourne as assistant-director of tutorial classes and a member of the university's extension board; he was later a part-time lecturer in sociology. Between 1928 and 1934 he lectured in English at the University of Freiburg, Germany, achieving fluency in that country's language and developing an enduring love of its literature.

Back in South Australia, in September 1935 Bronner was appointed to the staff of the Australian Broadcasting Commission as assistant-controller of talks (federal controller from November) and shifted to Sydney. When a separate department of school broadcasts was established in 1937, he became its controller (director of youth education from 1945).

Bronner performed brilliantly in developing an educational and school-broadcasting system that was to be one of the brightest jewels in the A.B.C.'s crown. Slightly built, but wiry—as a young man he had played lacrosse and was lightweight boxing champion of his battalion—he was fair haired and handsome, with a perpetually quizzical expression. He was modest and unassuming, and, while intolerant of cant and humbug, had a rare understanding of human foibles. Precise in speech, with only a trace of an Oxford accent, he was witty and companionable, and inspired the devotion of his staff and the respect of his colleagues. Bronner recognized the difficulties he faced in persuading the educationally independent States to agree to a system of national radio broadcasts, but, by his charm of manner, tact and diplomacy, wooed their directors of education to join the federal advisory committee for school broadcasts, which planned annual programmes. The outcome was such internationally admired productions as 'Kindergarten of the Air' and the current-affairs series, 'The World We Live In'.

As one of the few intellectuals in the A.B.C.'s early hierarchy, Bronner had wide-ranging influence. His originality of mind and shrewd judgement helped to shape procedures and policies that were cardinal to the organization's emergence as a recognized and valued national institution. He retired in 1955. After suffering one stroke in August 1959, he died of another on 17 January 1960 at Weroona Private Hospital, Wahroonga, and was cremated; his wife survived him, as did their daughter Elizabeth, an early aviatrix. The A.B.C.'s general manager (Sir) Charles Moses wrote: 'We have had no one else like Rudi Bronner in the ABC. I don't think we ever will. He was a rare man'.

K. S. Inglis, *This is the ABC* (Melb, 1983); C. Semmler, *Pictures on the Margin* (Brisb, 1991); *Radio Active*, 14 Aug 1950, 14 Oct 1955, Feb 1960; ABC staff file, SP 413/1, item Rudolph Bronner (AA, Syd).
　　　　　　　　　　　　　　CLEMENT SEMMLER

BROOKER, WILLIAM EDWARD (1891-1948), premier and fitter-and-turner, was born on 4 January 1891 at Hendon, Middlesex, England, son of Henry Brooker, journeyman instrument-maker, and his wife Sarah Ann, née Knowles. Edward was educated at Enfield School, London. He worked for his father and as a clerk for the Asiatic Petroleum Corporation before managing Henry's business. A member of the Territorial Force, Brooker served from August 1914 with the Royal Army Medical Corps on Gallipoli, at Salonika and in Palestine. He was training as an observer pilot when demobilized in April 1919 with the rank of sergeant. At St Andrew's parish church, Bethnal Green, London, on 13 September 1919 he married Lydia Grace Minnie Wilson.

Postwar difficulties persuaded Brooker, then employed as a mechanical engineer, to take a free, ex-serviceman's passage to Australia. Arriving in Melbourne with his wife and infant son in the *Orsova* on 31 August 1921, he moved to Tasmania and was briefly employed as a labourer on a farm at St Marys. From 27 October he was a pipe-fitter at Cadbury Fry Pascall Australia Ltd, Hobart.

A member of the Amalgamated Engineering Union, Brooker joined the Australian Labor Party and in May 1931 was an unsuccessful candidate for the State seat of Franklin. Next year, attracted by the ameliorative possibilities of Major C. H. Douglas's economic ideas, he was founding president of the Hobart branch of the Douglas Credit Association. Campaigning on a platform which included social credit policies, Brooker was returned to the House of Assembly in June 1934 as a Labor member for Franklin, an electorate he was to represent until his death. The Ogilvie [q.v.11] Labor government (1934-39) held office with the support of an Independent G. S. Carruthers [q.v.7] who was another Douglasite.

A 'vigorous and able debater' with a 'high degree of administrative ability', Brooker served as government whip (1936-39). In Robert Cosgrove's [q.v.] cabinet (1939-47) he was minister for transport (1939-42), chief secretary (1939-43) and minister for tourism (1942-43); in November 1943 he was given the portfolio of lands and works, and that of postwar reconstruction. Meanwhile his party support steadily increased. Elected to the State executive of the A.L.P. in 1935, he was Tasmanian delegate to federal conferences (1936 and 1940) and to the federal executive (1941-48). He was the party's State president (1943) and treasurer (1946-48), and twice topped the Franklin poll (1941 and 1946).

In December 1947 Cosgrove was indicted for bribery and conspiracy. Pending a decision on the charges, on the 18th Brooker became premier. Following Cosgrove's acquittal, Brooker resigned the premiership on 24 February 1948 and was appointed treasurer and minister for transport. An avid reader, a keen musician and a dabbler in poetry, he was a justice of the peace, vice-president of the Glenorchy branch of the Returned Sailors', Soldiers' and Airmen's Imperial League of Australia, a member of the Hobart Public Hospitals Board and belonged to Legacy. Survived by his wife, three sons and two daughters, Brooker died suddenly of acute pulmonary oedema on 18 June 1948 at his Montrose home and was buried in Cornelian Bay cemetery. Hobart's northern outlet, the Brooker Highway, commemorates him.

R. P. Davis, *Eighty Years' Labor* (Hob, 1983), *and* 'Social Credit and the Tasmanian Labor Movement', *PTHRA*, 25, no 4 (1978); *Mercury* (Hob), 19, 21 June 1948; Social Welfare Dept, M1/201 (TA); information from Mr E. Brooker, Hob, and Miss E. Brooker, Midway Point, Tas.
　　　　　　　　　　　　　　　　　R. P. DAVIS

BROOKES, DAME MABEL BALCOMBE (1890-1975), society and charity leader, was born on 15 June 1890 at Raveloe, South Yarra, Melbourne, only child of Harry Emmerton, a solicitor from England, and his Victorian-born wife Alice Mabel Maude, née Balcombe. Mabel was a grand-daughter of Alexander Balcombe [q.v.3]. Brought up in the comfort and confidence of moneyed Melbourne, she nevertheless remembered her childhood as lonely. Withdrawn from kindergarten because her mother thought that Mabel was developing a bad accent, she did not attend school thereafter and was taught by her bookish father and a succession of governesses—an education interrupted by a breakdown in health and a year spent at The Briars, the family property at Mornington. There she developed a romantic fascination with Australia's colonial history, and with St Helena and the exiled Napoleon.

When a young man told her mother that at 14 Mabel was 'dull, plain and reads too much', 'Father gave up the idea of an academic career for me and built a ballroom instead'. Short, with a large nose, but too lively to be plain, she was articulate, inquisitive and very strong-willed. She relished society—especially in Edwardian London, where her parents took her to be presented at court—but never felt constrained by its prejudices. At 18 she unexpectedly became engaged to (Sir) Norman Brookes [q.v.7], almost thirteen years her senior and recently famous as the first non-Briton to win Wimbledon. He was dour, she ebullient; both were competitive, ambitious, and determined. They were married, with some splendour, in St Paul's Anglican Cathedral, Melbourne, on 19 April 1911.

In 1914 Mabel and a baby daughter accompanied Norman to Cannes, France, where serious tennis was part of the aristocratic Riviera season, the social intricacies of which Mabel had to master. Norman won the singles and doubles at Wimbledon, and the doors of the well-bred and wealthy were opened to the couple in Britain and in the United States of America, where Norman and Tony Wilding regained the Davis Cup (which Mabel used as a rose bowl until it was consigned to a bank). In August war suddenly ended the idyll; Wilding went to Europe, to enlist and in 1915 to die, and the Brookeses returned to Melbourne.

Norman was appointed commissioner for the Australian branch of the British Red Cross in Cairo. Mabel joined him in 1915 and helped to set up a rest home for nurses. In May 1917 he transferred to Mesopotamia and she came back to Melbourne where she relieved the tedium of wartime motherhood by writing three sentimental novels, *Broken Idols* (1917), *On the Knees of the Gods* (1918) and *Old Desires* (1922). The *Bulletin*'s report that 'Norman Brookes' brilliant wife . . . has the inventive faculty of a born fictionist' was mistaken.

After the Armistice, the family settled at Kurneh (a large house opposite Raveloe) and acquired Cliff House at Mount Eliza. Norman resumed his previous employment at Australian Paper Mills Co. Ltd, becoming chairman in 1921. Mabel showed more interest than he did in life on the family's Queensland cattle-stations of which he was part-owner. They spent some months abroad, every year or so, on a busy social round, initially with tennis at its centre. Encounters with the famous were later described with relish in Mabel's *Crowded Galleries* (1956).

Like other young matrons of her class, Mabel was sought as a supporter of good causes and proved to have a genius for leadership in committees of management. Having served on the committee of the (Royal) Children's Hospital in 1918, she went on to become president of the Children's Frankston Orthopaedic Hospital, the Anglican Babies Home at Frankston and the Society for the Prevention of Cruelty to Children. She was also an original member of the Girl Guides' Association's executive committee (and a divisional officer), foundation president of the Institute of Almoners and of the Animal Welfare League, a member of the Australian Red Cross Society's federal executive and president of the Ladies Swimming Association (though her own sport in youth had been skating).

Mabel Brookes's greatest contribution was as president (1923-70) of the Queen Victoria Hospital, staffed by women for women. Under her leadership three new wings, one named after her, were added in ten years, and the committee accepted Sir William McPherson's [q.v.10] offer to set up the Jessie McPherson Community Hospital, opened in 1931. Mabel brilliantly represented its needs to governments and benefactors.

Important in this success was her talent for organizing grand social functions. The Brookeses' entertaining was lavish; in 1933, when their eldest daughter Cynthia married Lord Mayor (Sir) Harold Gengoult Smith, in St Paul's Cathedral, 1500 guests attended the reception at the Melbourne Town Hall and 40 000 spectators blocked the streets. The second daughter's wedding was almost as grand, prompting a harassed policeman to hope that the youngest of the three would elope.

War ended such spectacles. Kurneh became a Red Cross convalescent home, and the Brookeses moved to nearby Elm Tree House where they entertained large numbers of Australian and American officers, among them Lyndon Baines Johnson. Mabel appeared in uniform herself, as commandant of the Australian Women's Air Training Corps, and in plainer garb when she signed on as a shiftworker at the Maribyrnong munitions factory. Other war-work included establishing Air Force House and organizing, at the request of the minister for the army, an annexe for servicewomen at the Queen Victoria Hospital.

Claiming a 'tremendous prejudice against women in public life', Mabel Brookes twice stood for parliament—in 1943 for the Federal seat of Flinders as a Women for Canberra candidate, and in 1952 for the State seat of Toorak for the Electoral Reform League. A vigorous campaigner, she attracted few votes but much public attention. She described herself as a liberal conservative, her platforms including free education from kindergarten to university, a health service to reduce infant mortality, reform of mental hospitals, and housing for the poor. She was a formidable lobbyist: her dramatic confrontation with Prime Minister Chifley [q.v.] over bank nationalization was described by Dame Enid Lyons, and Mabel formed a particularly close relationship with John Cain [q.v.] and (Sir) Henry Bolte.

After World War II Mabel's leadership in society was undisputed. She was appointed C.B.E. in 1933 and D.B.E. in 1955, for services to hospitals and charity. Her name, and her photograph—usually in a boldly floral dress under a plain coat, big-bosomed and commanding—were constantly before the public. With style and panache, she entertained an extraordinary range of visitors to Melbourne, frequently at the request of State or Federal governments, and had special pleasure in welcoming President Johnson to her home, an occasion marked by a political demonstration.

Mabel continued to write indefatigably, *St Helena Story* appearing in 1960 and *Riders of Time* in 1967. She wrote of her substantial collections of furniture and *objets d'art*, of books and especially Australiana, and of relics of Napoleon. Her gesture in purchasing the freehold of the pavilion which Napoleon had occupied on her great-grandfather's estate on St Helena, and presenting it to the French nation, won her appointment as chevalier de la Légion d'honneur in 1960. She became president of the Book Collectors' Society, the Heraldry Society and the women's committee of the National Trust of Victoria. She also wrote of her interest in the supernatural: she claimed to have seen ghosts and believed in reincarnation.

When Norman died in 1968, Mabel sold much of her collections of books and furniture (but not her Napoleonic relics which she left to the National Trust for display at The Briars), and resigned most of her posts, including presidency of the Queen Victoria Hospital, by then a teaching hospital of Monash University which conferred on her an honorary LL.D. in 1967. A travelling scholarship for opera singers was named in her honour.

Dame Mabel published *Memoirs* in 1974. She died on 30 April 1975 at South Yarra. Sir Robert Menzies [q.v.] paid tribute to her as 'one of the most remarkable women of our time', possessed of 'a beautiful organising mind'. Survived by two daughters, she was buried in St Kilda cemetery. Her estate was sworn for probate at $308 653. Portraits by Sir William Dargie and Clifton Pugh are held by the family.

G. H. Swinburne, *The Queen Victoria Memorial Hospital* (Melb, 1951); E. M. Lyons, *Among the* *Carrion Crows* (Adel, 1972); *Woman's World*, 1 Feb 1933, p 40; *Sun News-Pictorial*, 10, 28 Nov 1952, 9 June 1955; *Herald* (Melb), 15 Nov 1952, 16 Nov 1954, 9 June 1955, 30 Apr 1975; *Age* (Melb), 27 Nov 1952, 9 June 1955, 23 Feb 1968, 1 May 1975; *Australian*, 5 Feb 1973, 1 May 1975; family papers and press-cuttings (held by Mr N. Gengoult-Smith, Melb).

J. R. POYNTER

BROOKS, SIR REGINALD ALEXANDER DALLAS (1896-1966), governor, was born on 22 August 1896 at Cambridge, Cambridgeshire, England, only son of Dallas George Brooks, a theological graduate and later a chaplain in the Royal Navy, and his wife Violet Ruth, née Shepherd. Educated at Dover College, where he distinguished himself at sport, young Brooks was commissioned in the Royal Marines on 22 August 1914. He was severely wounded at Gallipoli, mentioned in dispatches and awarded the French Croix de Guerre. Invalided home, he served in the Grand Fleet from 1916 and specialized as an artillery officer. For his 'very fine' direction of the howitzer on the exposed quarter-deck of H.M.S. *Vindictive* at the assault on Zeebrugge, Belgium, on 23 April 1918, he was awarded the Distinguished Service Order. Promoted brevet major (7 May 1918), he was again mentioned in dispatches. In the 1920s he captained the Combined Services' cricket and hockey teams, and also played golf and hockey for the navy. On 3 December 1924 at St Paul's Church, Knightsbridge, he married his cousin Muriel Violet Turner Laing.

Graduating from the R.N. Staff College in 1934, during World War II Brooks served as deputy director-general (military) of the Foreign Office's political warfare executive. (Sir) Noel Coward described him as 'large and good-looking and impeccably dressed . . . a typical Royal Marine officer, which means that he was efficient, sentimental and had perfect manners'. In January 1945 Brooks returned to corps duty as major general, General Staff. He was appointed C.M.G. in 1943, C.B. in 1946 and, that year, commandant general, Royal Marines, with the rank of lieutenant general. Promoted general and appointed K.C.B. in 1948, he left the marines in May 1949.

Following the retirement in February 1949 of Sir Winston Dugan [q.v.], governor of Victoria, Sir Dallas was chosen as his successor. His Gallipoli experience and his sporting prowess ensured a warm reception from press and public. The Australian Labor Party had wanted an Australian, but the premier T. T. Hollway [q.v.] preferred an Englishman who would have no ties with State politics and who would preserve the link between the throne and the people of Victoria. The appointment was not announced until the premier had steered a bill through parliament, raising the governor's salary to £6000, with an annual grant of £4000 for expenses, and the government began to renovate the dilapidated, damp and underfurnished Government House.

Brooks came in October 1949 to a State which was suffering postwar shortages and unrest, and which had endured twenty-five years of minority government and political instability. He had his political blooding in June 1950 when the minority Hollway government was defeated in a no-confidence motion by a union of the Country Party under (Sir) John McDonald and the Labor Party, led by John Cain [qq.v.]. Brooks commissioned McDonald to form a ministry which, supported by Labor, lasted until October 1952. When an alliance of Labor and Hollway's breakaway Liberals rejected supply in the Legislative Council, Brooks refused McDonald's request for a dissolution and commissioned Hollway to form a ministry which lasted less than two days. On 31 October Brooks recommissioned McDonald, then granted him a dissolution. Labor won at the polls in December. In 1953 Cain extended Brooks's term to 1956.

With his height, commanding figure and splendid dress-uniform, Brooks looked every inch a viceroy, but a genial and approachable manner removed any hint of reserve. Possibly on the instructions of King George VI, he opened the gates of Government House to the people of Victoria and carried out his duties in ways suited to a changing society. An honorary member of the Victorian Operative Bricklayers' Society and No. 1 ticket-holder of the Richmond Football Club, he regularly appeared at the Christmas party of the Shop Assistants' Union and became the first governor to attend a meeting of the Trades Hall Council. The advent of (Sir) Henry Bolte's Liberal government in 1955 saw Brooks embark upon a new role as advocate for a developing industrial economy. In 1956 Bolte offered him a third term of office.

Promoted K.C.M.G. (1952), K.C.V.O. (1954) and G.C.M.G. (1963), Brooks thrice served as administrator of the Commonwealth. In 1961 he suffered a heart attack. He retired as Victoria's longest-serving governor, and one of its most popular, in April 1963. After revisiting England, he returned to Melbourne and built a house at Frankston. He died there of a coronary occlusion on 22 March 1966 and was cremated; his wife and daughter survived him.

N. Coward, *Future Indefinite* (Lond, 1954); S. Sayers, *Ned Herring* (Melb, 1980); *Globe and Laurel*, Apr 1966; *SMH*, 18 Apr 1962; *The Times*, 22 Mar 1966; *Age* (Melb), 23 Mar 1966; *Herald* (Melb), 27 Mar 1966.   P. H. DE SERVILLE

BROPHY, JAMES (1889-1969), public servant and community leader, was born on 26 September 1889 in South Melbourne, eldest child of Richard Brophy, labourer, and his wife Catherine, née Mackey, both from Ireland. Having been educated at St Patrick's Jesuit College, Melbourne, in 1906-07 Jim attended Carmelite College, Terenure, near Dublin, but decided against the priestly vocation and returned to Victoria. He gained first place in the July 1908 Commonwealth Public Service clerical examination and on 5 October joined the Department of Home Affairs. In 1912 he was admitted as a licentiate of the Incorporate Institute of Accountants, Victoria. Promoted and transferred to Sydney that year, by 1919 he was accountant in the Sub-Treasury, Queensland. On 14 January 1922 at St Brigid's Catholic Church, Red Hill, Brisbane, he married 20-year-old Elizabeth Constance Ridley (d. 1965). They moved to Melbourne in 1927 and to Canberra in 1930.

Allotted a government-owned house, the Brophys quickly settled into life in the 'bush capital'. Tradesmen found a welcome cup of tea in Connie's kitchen and Jim became a stalwart of the local Catholic community. He enrolled his children at St Christopher's School, Manuka, joined the Knights of the Southern Cross, served on all manner of committees and was a consummate fund-raiser: as 'Bingo Master', he was 'as thorough with the threepences' as with 'the millions of pounds in the Treasury'. A keen chorister and Australian Rules football supporter, he was drawn into Canberra's embryonic sporting and cultural organizations by his ten children. In 1938 he was a foundation member of the Canberra Eisteddfod Society (chairman of committees 1940-42). Next year he joined the Canberra Amateur Swimming Club (president 1946-67) and the Australian Capital Territory Hockey Association (president 1945-64). He simplified rules, rewrote constitutions, organized finances, coached and examined referees, and promoted country sport.

Meantime, Brophy's career flourished. He privately managed the household accounts of The Lodge for J. B. Chifley [q.v.] and by 1949 was a first assistant-secretary in the Treasury. Of middle height, almost blind in one eye, with a shock of white hair and a face that 'conveyed gravity and dignity', he was widely respected, but could be stubborn. On 22 May 1951 his 'earnest' prayers were answered when he was appointed auditor-general for the Commonwealth; leaving nothing to chance, he had also pressed his claims with the prime minister. Brophy insisted on the independence of the audit office and refused to certify the accounts of agencies which did not meet his exacting standards. He urged the government to expand and clarify his powers, and took pride in the early submission of his annual reports. His term was extended to 25 September 1955 by an Act of parliament.

Brophy had been appointed knight of the Papal Order of St Gregory the Great in 1950 and I.S.O. in 1954. In retirement he redoubled his community work. A member of the Canberra Community Hospital board, he was deputy-coroner in 1958-64. He was also president (1953-69) of the Australian National Eisteddfod Society, and vice-president of the New South Wales Amateur Swimming (1951-68) and Hockey (1960-68) associations. In 1960 he officiated at the Olympic Games. Survived by four sons and six daughters, he died on 24 May 1969 in Canberra Hospital and was buried in Canberra cemetery.

A. J. McGilvray, *The Hallowed High Adventure* (Syd, 1973); *SMH*, 25 Sept 1952, 12 Nov 1953, 16 Apr 1955, 31 Aug 1958; *Canb Times*, 3 Oct 1968, 26 May 1969; Canb and District Amateur Swimming Club papers (NL); family papers (held by Mr R. Brophy, Narrabundah, Canb); Treasury correspondence files, Series A571/1-23/662, 23/32500, 24/6578 and Treasury personnel file, A1939/1, S.286 (AA).   HILARY KENT

BROSE, HENRY HERMAN LEOPOLD ADOLPH (1890-1965), scientist, was born on 15 September 1890 in Adelaide, younger son of Johann Ernst Adolph Bröse, tobacconist and hairdresser, and his wife Wilhelmine Catharina Johanna, née Gerdau, immigrants from Germany. Educated (1899-1907) at Prince Alfred College, in 1908 Henry won a pianoforte scholarship to the Elder [q.v.4] Conservatorium of Music, but accepted a bursary to the University of Adelaide. He was awarded a Blue in athletics and graduated (B.Sc., 1910) without completing the honours programme in mathematics. In 1911-12 he taught French at his old school and, on his third attempt, won a Rhodes scholarship in 1913.

At Christ Church, Oxford, Brose studied mathematics. He spent Christmas 1913 with relations in Germany and was impressed by what he saw. Returning there in the summer of 1914, he was arrested at Hamburg and interned next year at Ruhleben, outside Berlin. The camp's harsh conditions gradually improved, intellectual and entertainment programmes were developed, and Brose gave several series of mathematics lectures. Asked about theories of the ether and Albert Einstein's theory of relativity, he obtained two new German books by Erwin Freundlich and Moritz Schlick which he translated into English. In poor health, he was released in 1917 into the custody of the Saxon consul at Hamburg as a tutor to his children.

Back at Oxford, Brose was granted B.A. and M.A. degrees (1919) in consideration of the recent wartime conditions. Supervised by Professor F. A. Lindemann (later Viscount Cherwell), he began a D.Phil. on 'a critical history of the theory of relativity'. When relativistic mechanics proved too difficult, Brose began making spectroscopic measurements of the reflecting power of metal surfaces for ultraviolet light, before transferring to work under J. S. Townsend on electricity in gases. He completed a thesis (D.Phil., 1925) on the motion of electrons in oxygen. In 1920 the books that Brose had translated at Ruhleben were published by Cambridge and Oxford universities respectively. From that year until 1933 he translated sixteen German physics texts, written by such authors as Hermann Weyl, Arnold Sommerfeld, Max Born and Max Planck, that were vital to English-speaking scientists.

In 1926 Brose taught physics for the academic year at the University of Sydney. On this visit he met an Adelaide friend Jean Halliday Robertson, an actress who was touring Australia, and married her on 14 May 1927 at the register office, St Marylebone, London. By then he had become reader in atomic physics at University College, Nottingham. Cultured and personable, he was generally popular with students, although less so with some of his colleagues. In 1931 he was awarded a D.Sc. by the University of Adelaide and became foundation Lancashire-Spencer professor of physics at Nottingham.

Brose translated new German theoretical texts and experimented with the passage of electrons through gases; he gave public lectures and radio broadcasts on physics; he published papers on an optical pulse-beat recorder and on fingerprint detection; and he studied the application of physics to the problems of cancer. In addition, he arranged visits to his laboratories by learned societies and invited Professor (Sir) Lawrence Bragg, son of his Adelaide teacher Sir William Bragg [qq.v.7], to lecture at Nottingham; he fostered English-German relations, and spoke of Germany's place in science and in technical education; and he continued to play music. In 1930 and 1931 Einstein lectured at Nottingham and Oxford: he spoke German, Brose acted as interpreter and his verbatim translations appeared in the *New York Times*. Brose also assisted a clergyman's wife to write popular science books, but was named as co-respondent in her divorce, and costs and damages were awarded against him. There was considerable publicity and in 1935 he resigned his chair.

Often separated by their careers, that year the Broses were reunited in Sydney where he was appointed by the New South Wales Cancer Research Committee as a physicist and research worker at the university's medical school. He explored 'the relation between the phosphorus content of the blood and the cancerous condition of the individual', and developed assays of improved sensitivity which—with Dr E. B. Jones—he tested in patients. Later, he published papers on the medical use of X-rays. The committee disbanded in April 1938. In July Brose wrote to the vice-chancellor and to the media, blaming the cancer programme's failure on the committee, particularly Professors Henry Priestley and Oscar Vonwiller [qq.v.11,12]. Whatever the value of Brose's work—which has still to be assessed—several angry people remained in the university. He travelled in Germany and the United States of America before practising in Sydney as a pathologist and biochemist. Brose offered cancer diagnosis and treatment by William Koch's and Norman Baker's discredited methods; some found his assistance of benefit, others thought him a quack. He subsequently became Australian agent for Bioglan Laboratories Ltd, England.

Because Brose had publicly defended several German initiatives, after the outbreak of World War II police investigated his activities. In September 1940 he was arrested and interned. Next month Justice (Sir Colin) Davidson [q.v.8] chaired a committee that examined Brose's appeal. Following an extensive hearing, no evidence was found that Brose had committed 'a positive act against the British Commonwealth'. Nonetheless, due to some very critical statements, including those of three professors from the University of Sydney and Dr Jones's wife, it was held that Brose was a person, 'of marked energy and mental capacity and is in need of money . . . he could undoubtedly be of great potential danger to this country'. His internment continued, at Orange, New South Wales, and then at Tatura, Victoria.

Brose's wife and supporters lodged many unsuccessful appeals; he often felt close to 'becoming desperate or even mental'. Late in 1943 he was released under severe restrictions to work as an agricultural labourer at Terrigal, New South Wales. The restrictions were revoked in June 1945, but surveillance continued. During his internment Jean had worked part time as an actress, and their family and friends had maintained the Bioglan agency. Having resumed his business, in 1948 Brose publicly supported John Braund's extravagant claims to cure cancer by injections.

Survived by his wife and son, Brose died on 24 February 1965 at Kirribilli, Sydney, and was cremated with German Evangelical Lutheran forms. Talented and versatile, ambitious and forthright, he was too often naive or foolish. His translations are his enduring memorial.

D. Sladen (ed), *In Ruhleben* (Lond, 1917); H. M. Moran, *Viewless Winds* (Lond, 1939); R. W. Home (ed), *Australian Science in the Making* (Cambridge, 1988) *and* for publications; R. W. Home, *Physics in Australia to 1945* (Melb, 1990); J. D. Ketchum, *Ruhleben* (Toronto, Canada, 1965); Brose papers (held by author, La Trobe Univ); Univ Syd Archives; S.A367/1 item C/68717, S.A472/1 item W1968 (AA, Canb).
                                                    JOHN JENKIN

BROUGHTON, EDWARD RENATA (MUHUNGA) (1884-1955), soldier, was born on 6 September 1884 at Ngapuke, Hawkes Bay, New Zealand, son of William Muhunga Broughton, sheep-farmer, and his wife Atiria, née Hauwaho, both New Zealand born. Educated to matriculation level at Wanganui Collegiate School, Edward followed his father onto the land. In February 1902 he overstated his age in order to serve in South Africa with the 9th Contingent, New Zealand Mounted Rifles. Back home, he was discharged in August. Broughton married Imimaima Waikari. He worked as a licensed land agent and native agent, and in 1909 was secretary to the chief judge of the Native Land Court.

On 4 January 1915, when Broughton enlisted in the New Zealand Expeditionary Force, he registered under the additional name Muhunga, made no reference to having previously been an Anglican, and was recorded as being 5 ft 9 ins (175.3 cm) tall and 13 st. 5 lb. (84.8 kg) in weight. He reached Gallipoli in June and was commissioned on 15 November. Proceeding to France in December 1916, he saw action with the Maori (Pioneer) Battalion, was promoted captain (1917) and was mentioned in dispatches. His service ended in New Zealand on 4 May 1919. In the early 1920s he moved to Australia and lived in Melbourne. Attesting that he was a retired bookmaker and a Catholic, and giving 1900 as the year of his birth, he enlisted in the Australian Imperial Force on 10 June 1940. Three months later he was discharged, appointed temporary captain in the Militia and posted to the 3rd Garrison Battalion, from which he was seconded to the Recruit Reception Depot. Transferring to the Army Camp Service in October 1942, he was allotted to the 8th Employment Company.

The company consisted of refugees from Nazi persecution, most of them transported from Britain in H.M.T. *Dunera*; all had volunteered for army service and joined from internment camps. Apart from the detachments based in New South Wales at Albury and Tocumwal, the unit was stationed in Melbourne where it provided labour on the docks, in warehouses and at railway yards. While 'Tip' Broughton was reticent about himself, he was devoted to the men he commanded. Intelligent, well read and gifted with a sense of humour, he learned German phrases, spoke to his charges in two languages, knew many of them by their first names, respected Jewish custom and did much to restore their confidence as free men. Comprising volunteers between 18 and 60 years of age, and including some veterans from World War I, they constituted a unique entity in the Australian forces. Captain Broughton was a humane leader who enjoyed their affection and respect.

Broughton's appointment terminated on 24 May 1944. He lived briefly in Darwin before retiring to Melbourne. Survived by his son, he died of hypertensive coronary vascular disease on 9 May 1955 at Middle Park, Melbourne, and was buried in Fawkner cemetery. One of his men, Erwin Frenkel, wrote Broughton's obituary in the *Australian Jewish News*; a bust of Broughton is in the Jewish Museum of Australia, Melbourne.

C. Pearl, *The Dunera Scandal* (Syd, 1983); *Aust J of Politics and Hist*, 31, no 1, 1985, p 78; *Aust Jewish News*, 13 May 1955; information from NZ Dept of Defence, Wellington, NZ.   KLAUS LOEWALD

BROWN, ALFRED JOHN (1893-1976), architect and town planner, and DORIS JOCELYN (1898-1971), landscape gardener, were husband and wife. Alfred was born on 8 October 1893 at Auckland, New Zealand, son of Daniel Chadwick Brown, an English-born schoolteacher, and his wife Annie Smith, née Henderson, a New Zealander. Educated at Auckland Grammar School, Alfred was articled in 1908-12 to a local architect. He worked in Sydney as a draughtsman for Kent, Budden & Greenwell, architects, while attending Sydney Technical College for two years, then for Mason & Wales, Dunedin. Enlisting in the New Zealand Expeditionary Force on 19 October 1915, Brown served with the 3rd Field Company, New Zealand Engineers; he was wounded in France in May 1917 and invalided to England. In August he was sent on a course at the Architectural Association School, London, and discharged from the army as medically unfit in June 1918. An associate (1919) of the Royal Institute of British Architects, he was appointed assistant-architect to Louis de Soissons at Welwyn Garden City, Hertfordshire.

At the parish church, Hornchurch, Essex, on 12 June 1920 Brown married Doris Jocelyn Giles; they had been engaged since 1915. Jocelyn was born on 13 August 1898 at Toowong, Brisbane, eldest child of Sydney Reynolds Giles, an accountant from England, and his native-born wife Georgina Munro, née Hull. Brought up near Warwick, Jocelyn moved with the family to Sydney by 1909. She was educated at Summer Hill and attended classes at the Royal Art Society of New South Wales. Trained as a draughtsman, she was apprenticed to Jones & Jardine, commercial artists.

Alfred Brown adopted the current English town-planning ideologies exemplified at Welwyn Garden City, a model 'New Town' initiated by (Sir) Ebenezer Howard: with medium- to low-density suburban enclaves separated by minor roads, it had a modest industrial base; the housing was unpretentious, with Arts and Crafts overtones. Awarded the Soane medallion in 1922, Alfred travelled with Jocelyn in France and Italy. From January 1924 they were based at Auckland where she worked as a commercial artist; her clients included Arthur Yates & Co. Ltd, seed merchants.

Moving to Sydney with her husband and two sons in the midst of the Depression in 1930, Jocelyn worked for John Sands [q.v.6] Ltd. Alfred found architecture unrewarding. In 1931-37 he was Vernon [q.v.12] memorial lecturer in town planning at the University of Sydney and also lectured for the University Extension Board. He was president (1933-34) of the Town Planning Association of New South Wales and founding chairman (1934-36) of the breakaway Town and Country Planning Institute (later Royal Australian Planning Institute). Serving on various government planning committees, he wrote letters to and articles for the *Sydney Morning Herald* on topics ranging from church vestments to metropolitan sprawl. In 1940-45 he was employed by the Commonwealth government (to devise camouflage) and by the Department of Labour and National Service.

Brown expounded his ideas in *Town and Country Planning* (Melbourne, 1951, revised 1969), written with H. M. Sherrard. It influenced town planning in Australia and became the standard text for Denis Winston's course at the University of Sydney. Predictably, the book drew attention to English ideas and endorsed the 'garden city' concept; while it cited English and overseas examples, it paid scant regard to the Australian urban experience.

Influenced by her years at Welwyn, Jocelyn made gardens for herself in Sydney at Comely, Woollahra (1930-35), Fountains, Killara (1937-41), and Greenwood, St Ives (1941-45). She began to receive commissions as she became more widely known through her articles (December 1939 to September 1942) in the *Home*. These were based on her practical experience, embellished by her drawings of flowers, and supplemented with plans and diagrams. She admired and emulated the ideas of the English gardener Gertrude Jekyll, an exponent of the Arts and Crafts movement. Jekyll saw the house and garden as a single composition, and was inspired by the cottage garden rather than by the grander landscapes of the eighteenth century or the exotic collections of the nineteenth.

Adapting this style to Australian conditions, Jocelyn structured her gardens around carefully chosen features built near the house—paving, steps, walls, a lily-pond or birdbath—and gave them a sense of coherent design by her use of contained vistas. The formal elements close to the house were combined with lawns, hedges and rockeries, and enhanced by larger vertical elements provided by trees farther away. Her gardens were planned to complement the Neo-Georgian domestic architecture championed in the 1930s by John Moore, Hardy Wilson, Leslie Wilkinson [qq.v.10,12] and by her husband: he designed Fountains where she laid out her first ambitious garden.

Becoming a skilled plantswoman, Jocelyn created garden 'pictures', with foliage and flowers in carefully structured settings. She employed subtle combinations of colours in her mixed borders and carefully detailed the plant varieties in her articles in the *Home*. Delighting in a lavish display of blooms, she especially liked silver-foliaged plants and traditional favourites—roses, campanulas, poppies, delphiniums, irises, daffodils and lilies— as did the English Edwardian gardeners upon whom she drew. Unlike Edna Walling [q.v.], Jocelyn used Australian native plants sparingly, preferring eucalypts only as backdrops. The combination of ordered, flowery walks and native forest in the background is a particularly happy one at her best-preserved suburban garden, Greenwood. Her two most notable country gardens are at St Aubins, Scone (1940), and Coolabah, Young (1956).

Prominent in the Society of Arts and Crafts of New South Wales, Jocelyn was a member of the Business and Professional Women's Club, and lectured in landscape design at the University of Sydney. In 1952 she was elected a fellow of the Institute of Landscape Architects, England. A large, good-humoured, friendly woman, with brown, curly hair, she was generous with her advice and her gifts of plants. The Browns fulfilled a dream by moving in 1945 to The Hermitage, an old house between Camden and The Oaks, but in 1950 settled at Appin where they built a house and created a garden, Appin Water. From 1950 to 1970 Alfred practised at Wollongong. Both played chess and enjoyed painting in oils and water-colours; Jocelyn exhibited with the Art Society, Auckland, and the Society of Artists, Sydney. She was skilled in 'the gentle art of flower arrangement' and contributed a chapter to (Dame) Helen Blaxland's *Collected Flower Pieces* (1948). Jocelyn died on 3 October 1971 at Camden and was buried in Appin cemetery. On 12 September 1972, at Campbelltown, Alfred married a widowed nurse Alison Paterson, née Norris; they soon separated. Survived by her, and by a son of his first marriage, he died on 21 October 1976 at Wollongong and was buried beside Jocelyn at Appin.

Principal Women of the Empire, 1 (Lond, 1940); H. Proudfoot, *Gardens in Bloom* (Syd, 1989); *Art and Aust*, 25, no 4, 1988; Roy Aust Planning Inst, *J*, 15, no 2, May 1977, p 48; *SMH*, 28 July 1933, 10 Aug, 26 Sept 1934, 19 Oct 1971; B. Stockton, The Gardens of Jocelyn Brown (B.Arch. Hons thesis, Dept of Landscape Architecture, Univ NSW, 1978); A. J. Brown, Curriculum Vitae (copy held by ADB) *and* ms Notes on the Gardens of Jocelyn Brown (ML).   HELEN PROUDFOOT

BROWN, ARNOLD (1894-1960), army officer, was born on 22 July 1894 at Hunters Hill, Sydney, twelfth child of James Brown, representative and agent, and his wife Clara, née Marshall, both English born. Educated at Sydney Grammar School, Scots College and Bathurst Experiment Farm, Arnold worked as a jackeroo at Condobolin and as an overseer on a sheep-station at Cobar. In 1914 he went to Western Australia with the intention of buying land, but on 5 March 1915 in Perth enlisted in the Australian Imperial Force. He was 6 ft 1½ ins (186.7 cm) tall and weighed 12 st. 10 lb. (80.7 kg). Posted to the 28th Battalion and promoted sergeant, he left Australia in June and served at Gallipoli from September to December. He was commissioned on 12 February 1916 in Egypt.

Next month the battalion moved to France. For his efforts in patrolling and consolidating the front line at Pozières in July-August, Brown was awarded the Military Cross. Promotion to captain followed in September. While leading a bayonet charge at Flers on 16 November, he was shot through the neck. Evacuated to England, he rejoined his unit in January 1917 and was promoted temporary major in April. During the second battle of Bullecourt, on 3-4 May he organized and conducted bombing raids on enemy trenches, for which he was awarded the Distinguished Service Order. Wounded in September, he was again hospitalized in England and was mentioned in dispatches. By February 1918 he was back in action, on occasions in temporary command of the battalion. He returned to Australia in April 1919 and his A.I.F. appointment terminated on 30 July.

At the Pitt Street Congregational Church, Sydney, on 6 January 1920 Brown married Freda Mary Thompson. That year, as a soldier-settler, he took up Bective station near Coonabarabran. In 1926 he sold this holding and bought Mow Rock, a wheat and wool-growing property in the same district. Active in public affairs, in the early 1930s he was vice-president of the Coonabarabran sub-branch of the Returned Sailors' and Soldiers' Imperial League of Australia, president of the town's branch of the Sane Democracy League and a 'zone' commander of the New Guard. Brown unsuccessfully contested the seat of Gwydir as a Country Party candidate at the 1931 Federal election. He leased Mow Rock in 1935 and became a partner in a stock and station agency. In 1938 he was a foundation member of the National Defence League of Australia (president of its central council 1947).

Joining the A.I.F. on 1 May 1940, Brown was posted to the 2nd/1st Pioneer Battalion and sailed for the Middle East. He assumed command in December and was promoted lieutenant colonel on 9 March 1941 in Libya. From April to September the battalion operated as infantry in the defence of Tobruk. Brown was mentioned in dispatches and appointed O.B.E. (1942) for his services in Cyrenaica. Repatriated in March 1942, he commanded the 36th Battalion in Papua (May to September) before returning to his old unit in New Guinea. He was in hospital for most of the five months to March 1943, left the pioneers in June, and subsequently held command and administrative positions in New Guinea, Melbourne, Queensland and Singapore. In early 1946 he presided over military courts in Darwin which tried Japanese war criminals. The apparent leniency of some punishments caused a public outcry, but he defended the sentences passed. His A.I.F. appointment terminated on 29 August.

Brown farmed near Windsor, New South Wales, until deteriorating health forced him off the land. In 1949 he became director of the Immigration Holding Centre, Scheyville. Classified in 1958 as totally and permanently incapacitated due to war service, he died of ischaemic heart disease on 6 March 1960 at Batemans Bay and was buried in the local cemetery with Anglican rites. His wife, two daughters and one of his two sons survived him. Both his sons had served in the A.I.F., one being killed in action.

H. B. Collett, *The 28th* (Perth, 1922); C. E. W. Bean, *The A.I.F. in France*, 1916-18 (Syd, 1929, 1933, 1942); H. K. Kahan, *The 28th Battalion AIF* (Perth, 1969); B. Maughan, *Tobruk and El Alamein* (Canb, 1966); S. and L. Brigg, *The 36th Australian Infantry Battalion* (Syd, 1967); G. Osborn (ed), *The Pioneers* (Syd, 1988); *Reveille* (Syd), Nov 1932, June 1960; *SMH*, 11 Apr 1917, 2, 8, 15 Dec 1931, 17 Mar 1932, 15 Nov 1938, 26 Feb, 18, 19 Mar 1946; *Dubbo Liberal*, 10, 12 Dec 1931; Records AWM *and* Dept of Veterans' Affairs, Canb; infor-

mation from Mr L. Brown, Nambucca Heads, NSW.

J. B. HOPLEY

BROWN, GORDON (1885-1967), politician, was born on 11 February 1885 at Chesterfield, Derby, England, son of William Brown, a shoe salesman and Primitive Methodist, and his wife Jane, née Woodcock. Educated at Clay Cross Grammar School, Gordon grew up in modest, happy circumstances. He was apprenticed as an engineer's pattern-maker, joined the Social Democratic Federation and became 'steeped in Marxian theory'. A restless disposition led him through a range of jobs, from piano salesman to coalminer. Anxious to understand the lives of the 'submerged tenth', he left full-time employment to move through the workhouses: his radicalism was fuelled by experiencing the 'fearful conditions' of the itinerant poor. Brown sailed to Canada where he was imprisoned for street agitation, then came back briefly to Britain before migrating to Australia in 1912.

Although he took part in public meetings in Sydney, he grew dissatisfied with 'the reiteration of generalities' in socialist oratory. Yet, he continued his activities on moving to Queensland in 1913 and spent further terms in gaol. On 21 December 1914 in St Andrew's Presbyterian Church, Brisbane, Brown married Beatrice Agnes Hinchsliff. In 1918 he found work with a time-payment firm. Finally convinced of the necessity for more organized industrial politics, he joined the Shop Assistants' Union and the Labor Party. From 1925 to 1927 he was vice-president of the Trades and Labour Council of Queensland. He was elected to the Senate in 1931.

Throughout the 1930s Brown spoke often on the issue of economic protection. Arguing against Empire trade preferences, he maintained that Australia's secondary industries should be assisted to attain 'self-reliance and independence'. In his speeches, as well as his keen interjections, he called for thorough economic management and equity in welfare provision, rather than for more radical reforms. His preference for a 'lighter vein' in serious proceedings led to his suspension from the House. Deputy-leader (1935-38) of the Opposition in the Senate, he was chairman of committees from 1941 until 1943 when he became president of the Senate. While Brown refused to wear the wig and robes of office, he was proud to be the custodian of the chamber's privileges and authority.

Believing in the constructive role of propaganda and in the need to educate the young, he took a close interest in the morale campaigns of World War II and in the Workers' Educational Association, and criticized ex-

273

cessive censorship then and later. He emphasized the skills of oratory and counselled colleagues on the art of delivery. Brown was renowned for the 'stories' he told in Yorkshire brogue, regardless of the company. Following a serious illness and his replacement as president in 1951, his contributions in the Senate tended to be incisive—sometimes teasing—questions, rather than extended speeches. He later published his autobiography, *My Descent from Soapbox to Senate* (Brisbane, 1953).

Brown was over six feet (182.9 cm) tall, 'strong in t' arm' and an optimist by nature. Throughout his life he applied principle and conscience to public issues. He retired in 1965. Survived by his wife, son and two daughters, he died on 12 January 1967 in Brisbane and, after a state funeral at St Philip's Anglican Church, Annerley, was cremated.

PD (Cwlth), vol 137, 1932, p 2859, vol 152, 1936, p 2360, vol 164, 1940, p 241, vol 168, 1941, p 599, vol 169, 1941, p 358, (Senate), vol 11, 1957, pp 237, 836; *People* (Syd), 17 Jan 1951, p 8; *Courier-Mail*, 13 Jan 1967; *Sun* (Syd), 14 July 1977.

NICHOLAS BROWN

BROWN, HORACE PLESSAY (1916-1971), statistician and economist, was born on 7 December 1916 in Melbourne, second child of Clifton Plessay Brown, Anglican clergyman, and his wife Emma Nodin, née Wilcox, both native-born. Educated at Caulfield Grammar School (dux 1933) and at Trinity College, University of Melbourne, Horrie graduated with first-class honours in his economics subjects (B.A., 1938). While still an undergraduate, he was part-time research assistant to Professor L. F. Giblin [q.v.8] who taught him to regard statistical data—painstakingly collected and tabulated—as the proper raw material upon which to base economic theory. In 1938 Brown spent a term as an economics lecturer at the University of Western Australia before returning to Melbourne in October to take a post with the Commonwealth Grants Commission.

On 27 March 1941 in Canberra he joined the research section of the Treasury's bureau of census and statistics. Secretary to the Commonwealth committee on uniform taxation, he was associated with the advisory committee on financial and economic policy, and later with the investment and employment committee which was chaired by J. B. Chifley [q.v.] who became a close friend. Brown assisted with the introduction of 'pay-as-you-earn' income taxation, and was largely responsible for drawing up the pioneering national income and expenditure papers of 1944-45 to 1948-49. With D. V. Youngman,

he developed sampling techniques for the bureau's series, *Quarterly Business Survey*, begun in 1947. Promoted director of research that year, Brown was 'an outstanding but almost invisible member of the *maquis* which worked to exchange information and to influence policy, regardless of Departmental demarcations or ministerial pre-opinions'.

On 7 September 1946 he had married a fellow economist Helen Margaret McCulloch in St John's Anglican Church, Sorrento, Victoria. Frustrated in his work, he accepted a readership in economic statistics at the research school of social sciences, Australian National University. On his departure from the bureau he provided (Sir) Stanley Carver [q.v.] with a list of its general deficiencies and specific items which required attention, and nominated sixty 'neglected categories of statistics'. Brown was elected to the International Statistical Institute in 1952. Although a key adviser to the Federal Labor Opposition, he did not join the party until shortly before his death. He volunteered his services as an expert witness on behalf of the Australian Council of Trade Unions in the basic wage case of 1952-53: 'his evidence . . . amounted to the most thorough-going review of the Australian economy yet undertaken'. Having helped to prepare A.C.T.U. submissions in support of a 40-hour week, he again appeared before the Commonwealth Conciliation and Arbitration Commission in the 1970 national wage case. While at the A.N.U., he helped students, colleagues and others with his encyclopaedic knowledge, and published papers on social accounting, income distribution measurement and retail price indexation.

Never a doctrinaire economist, Brown was a pragmatist whose statistical expertise enabled him to use precise indicators as the basis for policy-making. His work was distinguished by its 'unusual blend of creativeness and scepticism'. He was an accomplished woodcraftsman and loved fishing. Survived by his wife, daughter and son, he died of coronary vascular disease on 30 January 1971 in Canberra and was cremated. A library at the R.S.S.S., A.N.U., is named after him.

C. Forster and C. Hazlehurst, *Australian Statisticians and the Development of Official Statistics* (Canb, 1988); *Economic Record*, 47, Mar 1971, p 115; *Canb Times* and *Financial Review*, 2 Feb 1971; Brown papers (held by Mrs H. Brown, Turner, Canb).

MARGOT KERLEY

BROWN, LOUISA ALICE (1875-1959), factory inspector, was born on 22 July 1875 in Adelaide, daughter of Henry Thomas Brown, carpenter, and his wife Catherine, née Toohill. After leaving school, Louisa worked as a clerk; she was later employed as a factory forewoman with responsibility for 'staffs of girls' that ranged from 30 to more than 60 in number. Moving to Sydney with her sister, in 1914 she was appointed an inspector responsible to the State minister for labour and industry.

On 15 December 1915 Brown became an inspector of factories and shops, an industrial inspector and an inspector (under the Early Closing Acts) in the New South Wales Department of Labour and Industry. Her duties involved overseeing some of the largest factories in Sydney and every trade that employed women. She persistently negotiated with employers for improved conditions for female workers and encouraged them to provide additional benefits for their employees, such as dining-rooms and free medical and dental advice. Brown's reports also revealed her compassion for those families who found it necessary to send young girls and boys to work during the Depression. Rather than disallowing all girls under 14 from working, Louisa considered each application on its merit and—although 'reluctant to recommend such applications'—found that 'some scenes of poverty I witnessed seemed to justify it'. On other occasions she approached government departments to provide assistance.

Politically active outside her work, Brown had been secretary (1923-24) of the National Council of Women of New South Wales, vice-president (1929) of the Waverley women's branch of the National Association of New South Wales and a committee-member of the National Women's Club. On 1 June 1930 she was appointed senior woman inspector of factories and shops, a position previously held by Belle Golding [q.v.9], under whom she had worked. Brown retired in 1940. During World War II she took a job as an office assistant in the Department of Labour and Industry; her services were terminated on 31 July 1946.

Like other women who had long public service careers when the marriage bar was in force, Brown remained single. She continued to live with her sister at Waverley. Louisa died on 21 June 1959 at the War Memorial Hospital, Waverley, and was cremated with Anglican rites.

D. Deacon, *Managing Gender* (Melb, 1989); Dept of Labour and Industry, Report on the Working of the Factories and Shops Act, 1912, during the years 1917, 1918, 1926, *PP* (NSW), 1918, 1919, 1927.   LOUISE CHAPPELL

BROWN, MAURICE (1917-1980), administrator, was born on 19 August 1917 in Hobart, second son of Rev. Jeffrey Brown, a Congregational minister, and his wife Eliza-beth Maud, née Duffield. Educated at Melbourne High School and the University of Melbourne (LL.B., 1937), Maurice was admitted as a barrister and solicitor on 1 March 1939. At the Independent Church, Kew, on 7 September 1940 he married a schoolteacher Margaret Agatha Stuckey.

In 1939 Brown had joined the administrative staff of the University of Melbourne; he worked under the registrar J. F. Foster [q.v.], from whom he learned the craft, and with whom he developed a lifelong friendship. Brown rose to be deputy-registrar and academic secretary before moving in 1950 to the new Australian National University, Canberra, as assistant-registrar. In 1954 he was appointed registrar of the University of Malaya, Singapore, but resigned after three years rather than face the growing hostility to foreigners.

Among those whom Brown consulted about his future was Sir Douglas Copland [q.v.], principal of the Australian Administrative Staff College, who invited Brown to join him as registrar when the college opened in 1957 at Mount Eliza, Victoria. Brown also participated in the course-work as a syndicate leader, and through his classes in writing and speaking which he published as *Getting Across* (1971).

In 1964 he succeeded Sir Ragnar Garrett [q.v.] as the college's principal. Six feet (182.9 cm) tall, good looking and a fashionable dresser, Brown was enthusiastic and jovial, an amusing conversationalist, a bon viveur and a convivial host who delighted in the opportunity to get to know the future business leaders of Australia. In his leisure time he was an apiarist and hobby farmer. He resigned from the college in 1971 and, with his wife, fulfilled an abiding ambition to motor overland to Britain; he recorded this adventure in *A Plague of Peacocks* (1972).

On his return Brown practised as a private consultant, using to advantage the contacts he had made in his years at the college. Having resumed his association with the University of Melbourne in 1967 as a member of council, he was deputy-chancellor (1973-78) and executive-member (1974-75) of the Australian Universities' Commission's committee on the open university. He also chaired the Victorian government's committee of inquiry into child care.

Brown's most challenging task came as chairman (1978) of the Victorian Public Service Board, on which he had served as government nominee from 1975. The (Sir Henry) Bland committee of inquiry into the Victorian Public Service (1974-75) had criticized the board for its insensitivity to the needs of the service and for its acceptance of the *status quo*. Brown brought to the office of chairman qualities uncommon among his predecessors:

experience in management, imagination, flexibility and a genial persuasiveness. The implementation of the Bland recommendations had just begun when Brown died of a subarachnoid haemorrhage on 13 February 1980 while visiting Wellington, New Zealand. Survived by his wife, daughter and three sons, he was cremated.

Bd of Inquiry into the Vic Public Service, Reports, *PP* (Vic), 1974-76, 7 (9), p 181, (34), p 371, (47), p 429; *Univ Melb Gazette*, Mar 1980, p 15; Vic Public Bd, *Annual Reports*, 1978-80; *Age* (Melb), 22 Feb 1980; private papers (held by Mrs M. Brown, Kew, Melb); personal information.

OWEN PARNABY

BROWN, MORVEN SYDNEY (1914-1965), professor of sociology, was born on 31 May 1914 at Wagga Wagga, New South Wales, son of Sydney Morell Brown, labourer and later policeman, and his wife Marjorie Rose, née Graham, both native-born. Morven was educated at Parramatta High School and the University of Sydney (B.A., 1934; Dip.Ed., 1935; M.A., 1943). While teaching at Yanco Agricultural (1936-38), Manly Intermediate (1939-41) and Canterbury Boys' (1943) high schools, he took university courses in anthropology and studied for his M.A. in education. In 1944 he was appointed temporary lecturer in child welfare and in 1947 became a lecturer at Teachers' College, Sydney. On 31 December 1938 he had married a milliner Jean McDonald at the Presbyterian Church, Auburn.

Awarded Carnegie (1948-49) and Leon Research (1949) fellowships, Brown read at the Institute of Education, University of London (Ph.D., 1950). His thesis was a sociological study of a grammar school in a working-class area of London. Appointed senior lecturer in education at the University of Sydney in 1951, he had charge of a course on child growth and development. In 1955 he became director of the university's department of social work.

Brown moved to the New South Wales University of Technology in 1958 as professor of sociology and head of the school of humanities and social sciences. Following the recommendation of Sir Keith Murray in his report on Australian universities, the reconstituted (1959) University of New South Wales established a faculty of arts. Brown became dean in 1960 and developed Australia's first department of sociology. The teaching began with several service courses for scientists and engineers; as his department expanded, a systematic sequence of courses in the discipline was provided. Brown also initiated a diploma in social work as a precursor to the school of social work (established in 1968).

A skilled debater in his undergraduate days and a talented amateur actor, Brown was a member of the boards of the National Institute of Dramatic Art and of the Old Tote Theatre Company. He was an excellent impromptu speaker. His students found his lectures the more piquant because of his occasional absent-mindedness in unwittingly repeating them. With a strong, practical interest in social welfare, he chaired the Good Neighbour Council of New South Wales; a member of the Commonwealth government's Immigration Advisory Council, he was interested in the welfare of immigrants and in the sociology of the Australian family.

Brown published little: two articles in the *Forum of Education* in 1954-55 were pioneering reports on the relationship of intelligence, school performance and father's occupational group to the holding power of selective high schools in Sydney. His later writing touched on the immigration programme, feminism, social disadvantage, and the role of the humanities and social science in general education. Foundation president (1963) of the Sociological Association of Australia and New Zealand, he belonged to the Rotary Club of Sydney and enjoyed playing tennis and squash. He died of subarachnoid haemorrhage on 9 October 1965 at St Vincent's Hospital, Darlinghurst, and was cremated; his wife, daughter and son survived him.

Univ NSW, *Alumni Papers*, 1, no 3, Oct 1984, p 4; *SMH*, 14 July 1956, 11 Oct 1965; *Daily Telegraph* (Syd), 11 Oct 1965; teachers' records, Dept of Education (NSW) Archives, Syd; Brown papers (Univ Syd Archives *and* Univ NSW Archives); family and personal information.

W. F. CONNELL

BROWNBILL, FANNY EILEEN (1890-1948), politician, was born on 28 April 1890 at Modewarre, Victoria, seventh child of James Alford, a native-born labourer, and his English-born wife Ann, née Abbot. Educated at state schools in the Moriac district, Fanny grew up in impoverished circumstances. In 1913 she became housekeeper to WILLIAM BROWNBILL (1864-1938), a master baker and widower with four children. Born on 19 January 1864 at Newtown, Victoria, William was a Geelong city councillor in 1896-1936 (mayor, 1913-14). On 24 January 1920 at Newtown, Fanny married William with the forms of the Churches of Christ. That year he entered the Legislative Assembly as the Labor member for Geelong; he held the seat until 1932 and from 1935 until his death on 29 April 1938.

At the by-election which followed William's death, Fanny was Labor's candidate. Several days before the election R. G. (Baron) Casey [q.v.] stated that a woman could not stand up to the 'rough and tumble of Parliamentary life' and that the subdued atmosphere of the Senate would be more suitable than the House. Fanny replied, 'I am perfectly confident that my sex can do most things just as well as men'. She defeated the United Australia Party candidate by nearly three thousand votes and was the first woman to win a parliamentary seat for her party in Victoria. Re-elected in 1940, she was unopposed in 1943 and 1945, and easily defeated her Liberal opponent in 1947.

Her remarkable electoral popularity reflected the lengths she took to meet the needs of her constituents. Mrs Brownbill was particularly concerned with child and youth welfare. School curricula also interested her and she was president (1947-48) of Matthew Flinders Girls' School. She was a dedicated member of the Geelong Ladies' Benevolent Society and in the depressed 1930s was the only female member of the public assistance committee. In 1935 she was appointed to the managing committee of Glastonbury, the Protestant orphanage at Geelong. During World War II she took a leading role in the local branches of the Australian Red Cross Society and the Australian Comforts Fund, and in 1945 helped to establish Grace McKellar House, a home for elderly people. Wherever possible, she pressed women's right to employment, and their claims to serve on juries and as justices of the peace.

Tall (5 ft 8 ins; 172.7 cm) and slender, Fanny was unassuming and tolerant in manner, but determined and effective. She was as much social worker as parliamentarian. Once a week she visited the poorer homes in her electorate on foot (she did not drive). On weekends she baked and delivered roast dinners for up to thirty needy people. She was an active member of the Churches of Christ. Survived by her daughter and son, Fanny died of heart disease on 10 October 1948 at Geelong and was buried in the nearby Western cemetery. Of her parliamentary career, she had said: 'I cannot claim to have had any specific bill introduced but it is not necessary to have legislation brought down to make your presence felt'.

PD (Vic), 19 Oct 1948, p 2966; Sun News-Pictorial, 7, 14 May, 6 June 1938, 29 June 1944, 13 June 1947, 11 Oct 1948; Argus, 12 June 1947, 11 Oct 1948; Age, 11 Oct 1948; information from Mr J. Brownbill, Mrs D. Drayton, Mr S. McAdam, Geelong, Vic, Mr R. Brownbill, Sandringham, Mrs J. Hawken, Keysborough, Melb, Mr and Mrs Beecroft, Moriac, Vic.   JOANNE W. THOMAS

BROWNE, SIR DENIS JOHN WOLKO (1892-1967), paediatric surgeon, was born on 28 April 1892 at Toorak, Melbourne, second son of native-born parents Sylvester John Browne (d. 1915), gentleman, and his wife Anne Catherine, daughter of Sir William Stawell [q.v.6]. Denis was a nephew of T. A. Browne, better known as 'Rolf Boldrewood', and of (Sir) Richard Stawell [qq.v.3,12]. Sylvester was involved in mining at Broken Hill; after severe losses, he left his family in Melbourne and went in 1892 to Coolgardie, Western Australia, where he remade his fortune.

In 1901 the family moved to Minembah, a station in the Hunter River valley near Singleton, New South Wales. Denis was educated privately in Melbourne and at Minembah before he boarded (1905-10) at The King's School, Parramatta. Awarded a Burton [q.v.1] exhibition to St Paul's College, University of Sydney (M.B., 1914), he won Blues for shooting and tennis; he also excelled at billiards, golf and horsemanship (breaking horses to augment his finances). Denis was 6 ft 3 ins (190.5 cm) tall, with brown hair and green eyes; extra long at birth, he had been given the Aboriginal name 'Wolko', meaning 'big man'. Called 'splinter Browne' as a student, in later life he was to be affectionately known as 'D.B.'

On 26 March 1915 he was appointed captain in the Australian Army Medical Corps, Australian Imperial Force. From September he was regimental medical officer with the 13th Light Horse Regiment at Gallipoli. Evacuated in November with typhoid fever, he was invalided to Australia. In August 1916 Browne arrived in France and next month was posted to the 12th Field Ambulance; he was promoted major in April 1917 and served on the Western Front until July 1918. That month he joined the 3rd Australian Auxiliary Hospital, Dartford, England. His exceptional surgical ability was noted and he was granted leave in 1919 to gain experience under the orthopaedic surgeon Sir Robert Jones at the Royal Southern Hospital, Liverpool. Browne resigned his A.I.F. commission on 28 December, then worked in the Middlesex and London hospitals.

A fellow (1922) of the Royal College of Surgeons, England, Browne soon became resident medical superintendent at The Hospital for Sick Children, Great Ormond Street, London. At the Catholic Cathedral, Ashley Place, on 21 April 1927 he married an Australian novelist Helen de Guerry Simpson [q.v.11]; she shared with him a love of riding, acting, history and politics, and introduced him to literary circles. Helen died in 1940, leaving a daughter Clemence.

Consultant surgeon at Great Ormond Street from 1928, Browne was noted for his skill, his original thinking and for his many contributions to surgical literature. He devised a simple, sound technique for the repair of cleft palate and hare-lip, advocated 'controlled movement' in treating talipes and congenital dislocation of the hip, and clarified diagnosis of undescended testes and of imperforate anus. In addition, he was a pioneer of neonatal surgery who advocated the need for special skills in managing and nursing children. Fascinated by technique, he designed instruments for operating on babies and young children, and splints that allowed controlled movement. His tremendous technical skill sometimes distracted attention from his more important achievements.

On 10 December 1945 at the registry office, Chelsea, Browne married Lady Moyra Blanche Madeleine Ponsonby, 24-year-old daughter of the 9th Earl of Bessborough. A trained nurse, she was to become vice-president (1970-85) of the Royal College of Nursing and superintendent-in-chief, St John Ambulance Brigade.

As his experience and stature rapidly grew in and beyond Britain, Browne developed a worldwide reputation which attracted many young surgeons from the British Isles and from overseas to study in his clinic at Great Ormond Street. He travelled widely, lecturing and operating, he received honorary memberships of a multitude of professional societies and he held Hunter professorships four times (1947, 1949-51). His contributions spanned the surgery of childhood, both in practical methods of treatment and in the causes of congenital abnormalities. Typically, he read a paper to the Royal Society of Medicine on Byron's lameness, 'based on a careful study of the appliance the poet wore'.

Browne was an imposing figure, always well dressed, and appeared somewhat haughty, but he was compassionate with children. Maddened 'by any suffering or disfigurement that he thought remediable', he was forthright and rather intolerant of those who did not share his views and aspirations, especially on the rapidly evolving specialty of paediatric surgery after World War II. His strong leadership—supported by like-minded younger colleagues whom he had trained—resulted in the establishment of the British Association of Paediatric Surgeons, of which he was foundation president in 1953-57. The association flourished and became a major forum for disseminating new ideas and for teaching surgery of the foetus, new born babies and children. The Denis Browne medal, the highest award of the association, was struck in his honour.

In 1957 Browne was awarded the Royal College of Surgeons' Dawson Williams prize and the American Academy of Pediatrics' William E. Ladd memorial medal. He retired from The Hospital for Sick Children that year, but continued to practise in Harley Street. In 1961 he was appointed K.C.V.O. by Queen Elizabeth II and to the Légion d'honneur by the French government. He visited and lectured in Australia in 1965; the Royal Australasian College of Surgeons elected him an honorary fellow, the highest honour the college could bestow. In January 1967 he succeeded as president of the International College of Surgeons.

Among his other appointments, Browne was a member (1952-56) of the British Broadcasting Corporation's general advisory council and chairman of the medical group of the Royal Photographic Society of Great Britain. He belonged to the Garrick Club. Unusually widely read, with a rather cynical sense of humour, he loved the country and shot regularly (with guns he had modified, just as he had played tennis with a circular racquet). Sir Denis died on 9 January 1967 at his home in Wilton Street, Westminster. Survived by his wife, and their son and daughter, and by the daughter of his first marriage, he was buried with Anglican rites at Stansted Park, Rowlands Castle, Hampshire, after a service in the Bessboroughs' private chapel. An obituarist in *The Times* wrote:

Whichever of his various talents he was exploiting—playing tennis at Wimbledon, lecturing students at home or pundits abroad, coping with a baby's cleft lip or club foot—he gave everything he had, with towering energy.

H. H. Nixon, et al, *Selected Writings of Sir Denis Browne* (Farnborough, Eng, 1983) and for publications; P. P. Rickham (ed), *Progress in Pediatric Surgery* (Heidelberg, Germany, 1986); *British Medical J*, 21 Jan 1967, p 178, 25 Feb 1967, p 508; *Advertiser* (Adel), 5 May 1965; *The Times*, 10, 27 Jan 1967; B. K. Rank, Citation on presentation of Sir Denis Browne for Honorary Fellowship of the Royal Australasian College of Surgeons, 17 May 1965 (ts, RACS Archives, Syd).

F. DOUGLAS STEPHENS

BROWNE, GEORGE STEPHENSON (1890-1970), professor of education, was born on 8 May 1890 at Malvern, Melbourne, son of George Browne, an ironmonger from England, and his Victorian-born wife Lydia Mary, née Purcell. Educated at Armadale State School and Melbourne Continuation School, in 1907 he became a junior teacher in the Department of Education. He entered Melbourne Teachers College in 1910, gained his Trained Teachers Certificate in 1911 and studied part time at the University of Melbourne (B.A., Dip.Ed., 1913). Appointed temporary head teacher at Kamarooka in 1912, he held the same post at Charlton Higher Elementary School (1912-14) and was second master (1915-16) at Horsham High School. On 18 April 1916 Browne enlisted in the

Australian Imperial Force. He was 5 ft 7½ ins (171.5 cm) tall, with a fair complexion, grey eyes and light-brown hair. He embarked on 27 May for England where he was commissioned. Proceeding to France in March 1917, he served with the 10th Medium Trench Mortar Battery and in August won the Military Cross: in charge of two Stokes Mortar teams, 'although his guns were several times blown out of position, he succeeded in replacing them in action'.

Wounded in November 1917, Browne was invalided home and his appointment terminated in May 1918. He returned to England in October to study at Balliol College, Oxford (B.A., 1922), and impressed the master A. L. Smith as being 'open to new ideas . . . a man of much force of character as well as great personal attraction'. Browne also completed a diploma of education at the University of London in 1919. Next year he was appointed master of method (secondary) at the Melbourne Teachers College, but the appointment was deferred to enable him to take the vice-principalship of Lancaster Teachers' Training College and an Oxford travelling scholarship which gave him five months to observe educational practices in Germany and the United States of America.

Returning to Melbourne Teachers College in 1922, Browne married Rosalind Haig Malcolm (d. 1938) on 15 February 1923 at St John's Anglican Church, East Malvern. That year he was appointed vice-principal of the college. He brought great drive for reforming the methods of teaching and the curricula used in Australian primary schools. His first enthusiasm was for the Dalton plan of individualized teaching which he had seen successfully carried out in England and the U.S.A. In the mid-1920s he favoured in a somewhat eclectic way the Project Method that developed in the U.S.A. from John Dewey's educational philosophy. Browne edited *Education in Australia* (London, 1927), a substantial volume written by leading educators from all States.

In 1931 he spent a semester as a visiting professor at the University of California; then, under a grant from the Carnegie Corporation of New York, he studied various practices of curriculum revision in the U.S.A. and England. Browne's book, *The Case for Curriculum Revision* (1932), based on his research, was his most influential piece of writing. It persuasively summed up the activity movement which was expanding overseas, and argued the case for an injection into Australian primary schools of 'an up-to-date and dynamic curriculum, better school equipment, more experimental work, freedom from external examinations, and the enlistment of the scholars' enthusiasm in activities and constructive work'. In those words,

Browne adumbrated the programme of educational change which he was to advocate for the rest of his career. He chaired a departmental curriculum revision committee in 1932-34 which produced and tried out new courses for all primary school subjects, but in practice much of the proposed reform was watered down and adjusted to established routines. Browne's zeal, however, was undiminished. He continued for the next three decades to argue the case for progressive education.

In 1933 Browne was appointed to the joint position of professor of education at the University of Melbourne and principal of Melbourne Teachers College. Henceforth his main concerns were with the university and with the education of secondary schoolteachers. Eventually, in 1939, the dual position was split; Browne relinquished the position of college principal and became full-time professor of education.

During the 1930s Browne's main administrative task was to organize and advance the new structure of the university's graduate courses and qualifications in education. In 1936 a bachelor's degree in education was established as a two-year postgraduate course, while the master's degree (established in 1926) became a pure research course. Browne and his part-time staff were thus responsible for producing in an Australian university, for the first time, graduate courses in education beyond the level of the requirements of teacher-training. For the next fifteen years his school led the field.

Browne's central interest as professor of education was in the production of good, progressively-minded teachers for secondary schools. His lectures were well-organized examples of excellent teaching technique. In them he emphasized the need for innovation. Enthused by the international New Education Fellowship Conference which was held in Australia in 1937, he was president of the Educational Reform Association (1939) and of the Victorian Institute of Education Research (1936-56); he was also a member of the Australian Council for Educational Research (1938-44). He admired the Tasmanian Area Schools of the 1930s, and the moves towards educational decentralization which were tentatively begun in the 1940s and 1950s in New South Wales and Queensland. With an abiding interest in comparative education, he collaborated with the American J. F. Cramer in writing *Contemporary Education: a Comparative Study of National Systems* (New York, 1956).

Beyond the university, Browne was involved in school broadcasting and conducted a popular current affairs session on radio. After his retirement in 1956, he ran a television programme on GTV-9, 'Professor Browne's

Study', which continued for ten years. He was a member of the Melbourne, Naval and Military, and Legacy clubs. Survived by his daughter, Browne died on 23 May 1970 at Camberwell and was cremated. His portrait (1970) by Nornie Gude is in the Institute of Education, University of Melbourne.

Education Dept (Vic), *Vision and Realisation*, L. J. Blake ed (Melb, 1973); D. Garden, *The Melbourne Teacher Training Colleges* (Melb, 1982); C. Turney (ed), *Pioneers of Australian Education*, 3 (Syd, 1983); Univ Melb, *Gazette*, Apr 1957, July 1970, *and* Archives, *and* Registrar's Office records; personal information.   W. F. CONNELL

BROWNE, JOSEPH ALEXANDER (1876-1946), lawyer and politician, was born on 25 February 1876 at Darlows Creek, near Adelong, New South Wales, second son of Edward Brown, a native-born farmer, and his wife Eliza Jane, née Hodge, who was born at sea *en route* to Australia from England. Joseph was educated at Grenfell Superior Public and Fort Street Training schools, and taught at Wombat, Grenfell, Willoughby and Penrith in 1893-1903.

Having formed a friendship with W. A. Holman [q.v.9] at Grenfell, Browne joined the Labor party in 1897. Next year he helped Holman to win the Legislative Assembly seat of Grenfell and enrolled in law at the University of Sydney (LL.B., 1904). An evening student from 1899, he was a clerk in the Department of the Attorney-General and Justice in 1903-04. He was prominent among the young Labor men who sought to qualify in law; in addition to Holman, he coached W. M. Hughes and D. R. Hall [qq.v.9]. Browne was admitted to the Bar on 6 May 1904 and read in chambers with (Sir) George Rich [q.v.11]; his first brief came from (Sir) George Beeby [q.v.7] in 1904. Concentrating on Equity cases and specializing in company law, by 1910 Browne was a leading junior. On 7 January 1909 he had married Laura Hannah Amos at the Methodist manse, Brunswick, Melbourne; they were to remain childless.

Although he left the Labor Party in 1904, Browne retained links with his many political friends. In March 1912, at Holman's persuasion, he was among eleven men nominated to the Legislative Council. He espoused the council's traditional role as an independent house of review, and criticized Holman's scheme to extend the duration of the Legislative Assembly after the premier formed a National government in 1916.

Browne was not a Catholic, but in 1924 he led the Legislative Council in perceiving the dangers to a liberal-democratic society of T. J. Ley's [q.v.10] proposed amendments to the 1899 Marriage Act which sought to nullify the 1908 *ne temere* papal decree. He derided those 'who can see but one little aspect of religion, and no matter what happens, they think the Pope is behind it'. In 1925 he crowned his attack on sectarianism by successfully amending the legalisation. When J. T. Lang tied with P. F. Loughlin [qq.v.9,10] in September 1926 in a caucus ballot for leadership, Browne's opinion that, as Lang had not been defeated, he remained leader, helped Lang to stay as premier. In 1931 Browne actively opposed Lang's attempts to make the council a party-political House.

He had a successful legal career and assisted the royal commissioner J. L. Campbell [q.v.7] in his 1919 inquiry into the coal industry. Made a K.C. in March 1926, Browne was appointed president of the Industrial Commission of New South Wales on 16 June 1932. He criticized the complexities of the Factories and Shops Amendment Act, 1936, and that year spent much time travelling on the buses as part of his examination of the working conditions of transport employees. Because of ill health he resigned from the commission on 2 July 1942. Survived by his wife, he died on 13 November 1946 and was buried with Anglican rites in Rookwood cemetery.

H. V. Evatt, *Australian Labour Leader* (Syd, 1942); B. Nairn, *The 'Big Fella'* (Melb, 1986); *SMH*, 30 Mar 1912, 3 Dec 1931, 17 June 1932, 3 July 1942; Teachers' records (Dept of Education Archives, Syd).   BEDE NAIRN

BROWNE, WILLIAM ROWAN (1884-1975), geologist and teacher, was born on 11 December 1884 at Lislea, County Londonderry, Ireland, and baptized in the Church of Ireland, sixth of eight children of James Browne and his wife Henrietta, née Rowan, National School teachers. Educated from 1897 at Coleraine Academical Institution, in October 1903 William entered Trinity College, Dublin, but soon withdrew, suffering from tuberculosis. He was advised to take a long sea-voyage and left for Australia in February 1904.

Reaching Sydney, Browne recovered after five months in a Blue Mountains sanatorium, then worked as a tutor at Inverell and on Wollogorang, near Goulburn. He gained classical and mathematical scholarships at the 1906 matriculation examinations, but, persuaded by the attractions of geology, enrolled in science at the University of Sydney (B.Sc., 1911; D.Sc., 1922). He never regretted the decision, even when Professor (Sir) Edgeworth David [q.v.8] went to Antarctica in 1908, leaving the department temporarily under W. G. Woolnough [q.v.12]. Browne graduated with first-class honours in mathematics and geology, and the university medal in geology.

Following a year at the Adelaide observatory, in 1911 Browne was appointed demonstrator in geology at the University of Sydney. Apart from six months in 1912 at the University of Adelaide standing in for (Sir) Douglas Mawson [q.v.10], Browne's academic career was fixed in Sydney. He became assistant-lecturer in geology (1913) and lecturer (1916). On 1 June 1915 at the Presbyterian Church, Neutral Bay, he had married Olga Marian Pauss (d. 1948), daughter of the consul for Norway; they were to have two daughters.

Browne gained his doctorate with the university medal in 1922 for work in igneous and metamorphic petrology, based on field-studies at Broken Hill, and was promoted assistant-professor next year. Petrology commanded much of his attention until the early 1930s, although it increasingly shared place with more Davidian aspects of science—stratigraphy, orogenesis and physiography. He became widely known as a versatile geologist with a flair for synthesis.

In March 1934 David informed Browne that he was to take over and finish *The Geology of the Commonwealth of Australia*. Five months later David was dead, leaving Browne honoured but daunted. In science, as distinct from academic office, he became David's successor; no mere disciple, he had a mind of his own and used it. In November 1935, after purchasing an unseen manuscript from David's estate, the New South Wales government commissioned Browne to bring the work to publication. What had been bought, however, turned out to consist of bundles of rough notes; of some chapters there was practically nothing. Relieved of academic duty for several years, Browne began gathering detail afresh and making his own ordered refinement within David's framework. Writing progressed slowly, slower still when he had to resume teaching in 1940 (his title was then changed to reader), but by 1946 the London publishers held copy to match the title David had promised them some twenty years previously. Printed copies appeared in July 1950. Those aware of the long gestation were not deceived by the title-pages of the three volumes: David's name had a right to be there—but as inspirer rather than as author. Browne had crafted, in the name of his mentor, a landmark in the literature of Australian geology.

The practical challenges of engineering geology began to engage Browne's interest in 1943 when the Metropolitan Water, Sewerage and Drainage Board invited him to investigate the provisional site for a storage reservoir on the Warragamba River. Once

the place was shown to be geologically unpromising, Browne identified a better site. In 1946 the board adopted his recommendation; its president T. H. Upton [q.v.] remarked that the geological advice had already saved £2 million in construction costs. Browne continued as geological adviser until the dam was completed in 1960. Among other notable engineering works for which he contributed site studies was the Gladesville Bridge, Sydney.

Quaternary geology and the conservation of nature dominated Browne's later years. He had been the senior member of a party of scientists and geographers detailed early in 1946 to make a reconnaissance survey of the Kosciusko State Park. He withdrew from the university in December 1949 to begin an extraordinarily active and fruitful retirement. On 16 February 1950 at St Nicholas's Anglican Church, Coogee, he married IDA ALISON Brown.

She had been born on 16 August 1900 at Paddington, Sydney, daughter of William George Brown, an insurance clerk from New Zealand, and his wife Alison, née Logan, a Sydneysider. Educated at Fort Street Girls' High School and the University of Sydney (B.Sc., 1922; D.Sc., 1932), Ida graduated with first-class honours and the university medal in geology. Having briefly held a science research scholarship, she demonstrated in geology at the university until 1927. That year she was awarded a Linnean Macleay [q.v.5] fellowship which enabled her to develop geological investigation of the South Coast, a study in which she combined field-mapping with laboratory work in petrology. She travelled extensively abroad, attending scientific congresses and research institutes.

Ida returned to demonstrating at the university early in 1934 and next year succeeded W. S. Dun [q.v.8] as assistant-lecturer in palaeontology, once she had hurriedly acquired new expertise. Promoted lecturer (1940), in 1941 she published a notable paper on fossiliferous Silurian and Devonian sequences of the Yass district. She had successfully negotiated the shift from hard-rock to soft-rock geology, both in her research and teaching. More distinctly palaeontological papers on Palaeozoic invertebrates (especially brachiopods) followed, as did studies in palaeontological stratigraphy. Ida became a senior lecturer in 1945, but resigned in August 1950.

The Brownes worked from home, making joint forays to their respective field-areas. Every summer from 1951 to 1955 William led parties of biologists and geologists to Kosciusko. He and Ida continued their field-work privately until 1965. While some of his interpretations of glacial history at Kosciusko may now be controverted, the importance of his careful and sustained research is unquestioned. He saw not only the landforms, but also the flora and fauna as under threat from human agencies. His David memorial lecture of 1952, in which he advocated restricted use of the high country, drew fierce criticism, particularly from grazing interests. The proclamation in 1962 of a 'primitive area' for conservation—although far smaller than Browne thought appropriate—owed much to his unflinching efforts as a publicist.

The couple supported local societies and frequently published in their journals. The Royal and the Linnean societies of New South Wales each claimed William as a member for over sixty years. He was a councillor of the Linnean Society for almost fifty years and its president (1928-29, 1944-45); Ida was a member from 1924, a councillor (1941-50) and president (1945-46). William was president of the Royal Society (1932-33): he received the (W. B.) Clarke [q.v.3] medal (1942), the society's own medal (1956) and had a volume of its *Journal and Proceedings* dedicated to him (1966). A member of the same society from 1935, Ida was a vice-president (1942-50), honorary editorial secretary (1950-53) and president (1953-54). Both belonged to the Australian National Research Council and to the Australian and New Zealand Association for the Advancement of Science; William was president of Section C (geology) at its Hobart congress in 1949 and Mueller [q.v.5] medallist (1960). A fellow (1954) of the Australian Academy of Science, he was a councillor in 1957-60. He was also a founder (1927) of the Geographical Society of New South Wales (president 1929-30, 1948-49) and in 1952 of the Geological Society of Australia (president, 1955-56); the latter society now awards the W. R. Browne medal as its highest honour. Ida, too, had a long association with that society.

Careful, disciplined, with a seemingly unfailing memory, Browne was a rare scholar and stylist. A master of uncluttered argument, he communicated his thought without flamboyance, but with a humour the more memorable for its solemn delivery. He shone in the field, as observer and kindly instructor, and never complained when his spare, wiry frame underwent punishing exercise. Survived by his wife, and by the daughters of his first marriage, he died on 1 September 1975 at Darlinghurst and was cremated. His final publication had appeared six months earlier.

Ida's last years were blighted by a slow, paralysing illness which required the attention of nurses and the constant care of her husband. She died on 21 October 1976 at Edgecliff and was cremated. Reserved and dignified, at times unbending but helpful withal, Ida had made for herself a career in science, then not easy for a woman. Strength of character, intellect and a capacity for meticulous attention to detail served her well.

Aust Geographer, 13, 1976, p 237; Linnean Soc NSW, *Procs*, 102, 1977, p 76; Roy Soc NSW, *J*, 110, 1977, p 75; *Records of the Aust Academy of Science*, 4, 1979, p 65, and for list of publications; personal information. T. G. VALLANCE

BROWNELL, RAYMOND JAMES (1894-1974), air force officer, was born on 17 May 1894 at New Town, Hobart, son of William Percival Brownell, draper, and his wife Julie Ann James, née Scott. Raymond was educated at Leslie House School, Hobart, and Scotch College, Melbourne, where he proved an accomplished sportsman. He was apprenticed with a firm of public accountants and auditors in Hobart. In 1912 he joined the Australian Field Artillery, Australian Military Forces. With his father's grudging consent, on 12 September 1914 he enlisted in the Australian Imperial Force; his height of 5 ft 4½ ins (163.8 cm) almost led to his rejection.

Posted to the 9th Battery of the 3rd Field Artillery Brigade, Brownell sailed for Egypt in November. He witnessed the landings at Gallipoli on 25 April 1915; instead of disembarking with his unit, he was sent to Alexandria where the army made use of his accountancy experience. In July he rejoined his battery, and was among the last troops to be withdrawn from Gallipoli on the night of 19-20 December. Promoted provisional sergeant in February 1916, he arrived in France next month. On 21-22 July at Pozières he maintained communications between the firing-line and the battery while under intense shell-fire; he was awarded the Military Medal.

Deciding that flying would be an improvement on life in the trenches, Brownell was selected for the Royal Flying Corps. He repaired to England for training and, while there, played Australian Rules football. Commissioned on 17 March 1917, he was posted to No. 45 Squadron. He began operational flying on the Western Front in September. The squadron was transferred to Italy in December, and in February 1918 Brownell was promoted temporary captain and made flight commander. During a three-month period he brought down six enemy aeroplanes. For his deeds he was awarded the Military Cross.

In April 1918 he left No. 45 Squadron and embarked for Hobart on compassionate leave to visit his mother who was seriously ill. During the return journey to Britain in

September, he almost died of pneumonic influenza. He accepted a commission in the Royal Air Force, but, when his mother's health again deteriorated, he resigned and was home in Tasmania by September 1919. Having worked as a sub-accountant for a firm of merchants in Melbourne and as a clerk with the Hobart City Council, on 13 September 1921 he was appointed flying officer in the Royal Australian Air Force and posted to Point Cook, Victoria. On 26 August 1925 he married Rhyllis Jean Birchall at St Andrew's Presbyterian Church, Hobart. In 1926-28 Brownell had charge of No. 1 Squadron and in 1928-34 was director of personal services at R.A.A.F. Headquarters, Melbourne. He went to England in 1934 for exchange service with the R.A.F. and was promoted wing commander on 1 April 1936.

Early in 1938 Brownell took command of the R.A.A.F. base at Pearce, Western Australia; he enjoyed the autonomy and the opportunities for flying which his new post offered. Additional units were placed under his supervision and he was promoted temporary group captain in December 1939. Ordered to Singapore in August 1940, he established R.A.A.F. headquarters, Sembawang, toured the Malay peninsula, and played tennis and cricket. A year later he was recalled to Australia, promoted acting air commodore and made air officer commanding, No. 1 Training Group, Melbourne. In charge of some thirty establishments in southern Australia, he piloted his tours of inspection whenever possible. On 1 January 1943 he returned to Pearce as A.O.C., Western Area: his responsibilities included training and directing long-range bombing operations. He was appointed C.B.E. in January 1945. Next July he proceeded to Morotai Island, Netherlands East Indies, to become A.O.C., No. 11 Group, and was present at the Japanese surrenders in Manila and Tokyo, and on Morotai.

Already nominated for early retirement, on 24 March 1947 Brownell was placed on the retired list on medical grounds. He secured a partnership in the stockbroking firm of S. G. Brearley & Co., Perth. From 1951 to 1967 he was chairman of the associated sporting committee of the National Fitness Council of Western Australia. Despite his almost apologetic manner, 'Brownie' was firm and used his authority when necessary. He possessed marked powers of observation, quick reactions, judgement and determination; his zest for life, concern for others and warm smile endeared him to many. Survived by his wife and two daughters, Brownell died on 12 April 1974 at Subiaco; following an air force funeral, he was cremated. His autobiography, *From Khaki to Blue,* was published posthumously.

G. Odgers, *Air War Against Japan 1943-1945* (Canb, 1957); D. Gillison, *Royal Australian Air Force 1939-1942* (Canb, 1962); R. J. Brownell, *From Khaki to Blue,* C. Coulthard-Clark ed (Canb, 1978); *West Australian,* 8 Sept 1936, 17 Jan 1938, 6 Feb 1939, 1 Jan, 2 July 1945, 10 Apr 1946, 15 Apr 1974; AWM records.   LEIGH EDMONDS

BRUNTON, CHRISTINE DOROTHY (1890-1977), actress, was born on 11 October 1890 in Melbourne, third child of John Brunton (d. 1909), an artist from Scotland, and his second wife Cecily Christina, née Neilsen, an English-born actress. Dorothy was educated at Alford House, Sydney, and from 1905 at Presbyterian Ladies' College, Melbourne. Brought up in theatrical circles (her father became a scene-painter for Bland Holt [q.v.4]), she first appeared on stage in Holt's production of *The White Heather* on 22 April 1908 at the Theatre Royal, Adelaide, and toured with the company next year. In Sydney she studied singing (from 1910) with Madame Grace Miller Ward, wife of Hugh Ward [q.v.12], then joined J. C. Williamson's [q.v.6] New Comic Opera Company in September 1911. Miss Brunton made the most of any chances, whether playing small parts or understudying. The *Bulletin* drama critic repeatedly pressed her claims to leading roles. As Jolan in *Gypsy Love* (1914) she was described as 'the merriest and most mischievous little creature possible'.

In Sydney and Melbourne during World War I Brunton starred, almost without a break, in musical comedies—such as *High Jinks* (1915) and *The Girl in the Taxi* (1915) —and enlivened them with her charm, humour, 'zest and sparkle'. In addition to singing and dancing, she was an accomplished actress, especially as a soubrette. Her most famous role was Letty in *So Long, Letty* (1915-16); its marching song was adopted by servicemen who carried their golden-haired 'Diggers' Delight' shoulder-high to her cab each night.

After visiting the United States of America from September 1917, Brunton sailed for London. On 28 August 1918 she made her début as Fan Tan in *Shanghai* at Drury Lane. She was 'literally worshipped by Australians . . . they cheered, they coo-eed, they whistled with ear-splitting shrillness and joyous abandon'; the male star was not pleased. In December she took over the lead in *Soldier Boy* at the Apollo Theatre and in 1919-20 appeared in *The Bantam, V.C.* and *Baby Bunting.* Her cosy flat in Regent Street was known as 'The Diggers Rest'; there Dot entertained soldiers 'ranging in rank from privates to generals'. She was tender hearted and generous; her dresser Lillian Banks averred that no one 'knows of her charitable work or what she gives away'.

Critics welcomed Brunton's return to Sydney in October 1920 in *Yes, Uncle!* and *Baby Bunting* (1920-21). She also appeared in two comedies with Alfred Frith before leaving for Los Angeles to visit her brother. Back home, in 1924 she joined Hugh J. Ward Theatres Pty Ltd for a string of musical plays. In 1926 she acted with Guy Bates Post in a drama, *The Climax*; they toured South Africa, then took the play to London where it failed at the Little Theatre in 1927. Next year Dorothy toured as Fleurette in *The White Camellia* with Harry Welchman; she played the same part at Daly's, London, in 1929, but suffered from serious chest trouble. In Sydney again, she appeared as Betsy Burke in *Dearest Enemy* in 1931 and starred in revivals of pre-war musical comedies. She refused to take part in a radio version of *Dearest Enemy* in May 1933 because the Australian Broadcasting Commission had suppressed 'every little swear word'. As Kitty Hamble and Bella Tout in *Road House* she 'roused the audience to shouts of laughter'. Her only films, *Seven Keys to Baldpate* (1916) and *Clara Gibbings* (1934), were failures.

On 15 August 1931 at Wesley Church, Melbourne, Dorothy married with Methodist forms Ben Dawson (d. 1948), a merchant and a divorcee; they lived in London from about 1935. Dorothy was badly injured by German bombing in 1944; some four years later she was diagnosed as suffering from Parkinson's disease. Returning to Sydney in 1949, she later visited Sweden in search of a cure and gained some relief. A forgotten 'darling of the theatre', Brunton lived quietly with a companion at Bellevue Hill, and took pleasure in reading and classical music. She died on 5 June 1977 at the Sacred Heart Hospice, Darlinghurst, and was cremated.

Who's Who in the Theatre (Lond, 1947); *SMH*, 23 July, 2 Aug 1909, 3, 4 Feb 1911, 14 Jan, 22 May 1918, 18 July 1919, 20 Feb 1924, 11 June 1928, 4 Feb 1931, 16 May, 4 Sept 1933, 22 Feb 1934; *Bulletin*, 1 Feb, 16 May 1912, 24 Dec 1914, 30 Dec 1920; *Argus*, 7 Sept 1914, 24 Apr 1916, 2 June 1924; *Australasian*, 3 Apr, 10 July 1915, 29 Apr, 9 Sept 1916, 17, 31 Mar 1917; *The Times*, 29 Aug 1918, 13 Jan, 3, 17 July, 26 Sept 1919; *Punch* (Melb), 24 Apr 1919; *Sun-Herald*, 5 Mar 1972.

MARTHA RUTLEDGE

BRYAN, EDITH (1872-1963), teacher of the deaf, was born on 29 June 1872 at Derby, Derbyshire, England, eldest of six children of William Lloyd, master tailor, and his wife Mary, née Johnson. Educated at the local council school, in 1887-91 Edith served as a pupil-teacher at the Royal Institute for the Deaf and Dumb, Derby. Having obtained a diploma (1892) from the College of Teachers of the Deaf, London, she taught in Ireland at the Dublin Institute for the Deaf, then at the Jews' School for the Deaf, London, before returning to Derby in 1893. By 1895 she had arrived in South Australia where, on 29 June at St James's Church, West Adelaide, she married Cecil Charles Bryan, another teacher from the Derby institute, who was appointed senior teacher at the Blind, Deaf and Dumb Institution, Brighton. Following her husband's death in January 1897, Edith took a private teaching post at Portrush, Antrim, Ireland, then returned to England in 1899 to teach at the Deaf School, Bristol.

Appointed head teacher of the school section of the Queensland Blind, Deaf and Dumb Institution, Brisbane, she arrived there on 12 November 1901. When the Queensland government assumed responsibility in 1918 for what had previously been a charitable organization, Mrs Bryan became an employee of the state. Because of the increase in numbers resulting from the compulsory clauses of the Blind, Deaf and Dumb Instruction Act of 1924, it was deemed appropriate that a man should take over the school in 1926; Edith retained charge of the deaf section of the school until she retired in 1937.

Bryan had been trained in the oral tradition of teaching the deaf. Children entering the school were taught orally until their aptitude could be ascertained; they were then placed in either an oral or a sign-language group. She had been deeply influenced by the work of Thomas Arnold and used his textbooks in training pupil-teachers. Familiar with the 1889 recommendations of the royal commission on the condition of the blind, the deaf and the dumb in the United Kingdom, she was an advocate for change in Queensland: she supported early compulsory education for the blind and the deaf, and recommended appropriate teacher-training. According to some of the pupil-teachers she had trained, Mrs Bryan was a quietly assertive woman, with natural dignity. The deaf community, for whom she continued to work after her retirement, had great faith in her integrity and competence. Her proficiency in sign language was frequently enlisted in interpreting.

An active member of the Queensland Adult Deaf and Dumb Mission which she had helped to establish in 1902, she chaired a parent support-group which she had also promoted. The mission named the Edith Bryan Hostel in her honour. At its opening in 1950 she was described as 'one of the world's foremost workers for the deaf'. She died on 29 March 1963 at Ascot and was cremated with the forms of the Baptist Church of which she had been a lifelong member.

Qld Deaf and Dumb News, 1937-39; Qld Adult Deaf and Dumb Mission, Minutes, 1902-63 (held by Qld Deaf Soc Inc, Newmarket, Brisb); Qld Special Education Archives (Special Services Resource Centre L, Annerley, Brisb); Bryan staff card, History Unit, Dept of Education (Qld), Brisb; Qld Inst for the Blind, Deaf and Dumb records (QA).

GEOFFREY SWAN

BRYAN, SYDNEY JAMES (1883-1957), trade unionist, was born on 17 March 1883 at Ultimo, Sydney, son of James Newport Bryan, brewer, and his wife Margaret, née O'Brien, both native-born. Educated locally, Syd completed an apprenticeship as an electrical mechanic and joined the government railway workshops. He was a member of the State branch of the Electrical Trades Union from 1903 and attended the conference of the Political Labor League in January 1910 as an E.T.U. delegate. On 3 May 1907 he had married Ellen Beatrice Richardson at St Barnabas's Anglican Church, Sydney.

After his trade career was curtailed in October 1912 when his right hand was mutilated in an electrical accident, Bryan became State organizer for the E.T.U. In mid-1915 he formed a Queensland branch of the union; next year he travelled thousands of miles to nurture its affairs and membership. Moving to Queensland permanently, he was State secretary of the union from March 1918 until November 1944 and its federal president in 1920-24 and 1928-44. He played a prime role in 1926 in establishing a branch of the E.T.U. in Western Australia. He had also been a Brisbane City Council alderman (1924-25).

An able and conscientious advocate, in 1919 Bryan had succeeded in his efforts to have a 44-hour week implemented in his industry in Queensland and had convinced Justice T. W. McCawley [q.v.10] that 'apprentices only, and not other juniors' should be engaged in electrical work. In 1923, as a result of Bryan's lobbying, legislation for an improved system of licensing electrical workers was enacted and he became a foundation member of the newly created Electrical Workers' Board. From that year he attended Labor conventions, usually representing the E.T.U., but occasionally one of the three other organizations of which he was also secretary: the Federated Miscellaneous Workers' Union, the Queensland Theatrical and Amusements Employees' Association, and the Federated Jewellers, Watchmakers and Allied Trades' Union. He was president of the Queensland Trades and Labor Council in 1929-37. As the representative of a union under the mantle of the T.L.C. rather than that of the Australian Workers' Union, he was frequently outmanoeuvred by the combined forces of Premier Forgan Smith [q.v.11] and

Clarrie Fallon [q.v.], the president of the State executive of the Australian Labor Party and secretary of the Queensland branch of the A.W.U. Nonetheless, at Forgan Smith's instigation, Bryan and Fallon travelled to Canberra in 1942 to protest, unavailingly, to the Labor government over the introduction of uniform income tax.

As Labor became seemingly entrenched in government in Queensland, Bryan became more conservative. A member (1932-47) of the Queensland central executive of the A.L.P., he was party secretary in 1940-52. The executive remained neutral during the strikes of 1946 and 1948, often ignoring representations from their own constituents. Bryan turned his attention to obtaining a party broadcasting licence (granted in 1947) and raised £35 000 in debentures to finance radio station 4KQ. He gradually shed his many responsibilities, but retained until 1955 his secretaryship of the jewellers and watchmakers union. Survived by his wife, two sons and three daughters, he died on 25 July 1957 in South Brisbane and was cremated with Methodist forms. The S. J. Bryan bursary fund was established for the children of E.T.U. members.

A. Dawson, *Points and Politics*, D. Murphy ed (Brisb, 1977); D. J. Murphy et al (eds), *Labor in Power* (Brisb, 1980); Aust Labor Party (Qld) records (OL).

BRIAN F. STEVENSON

BRYANT, BERYL ANNEAR (1893-1973), actress and producer, was born on 9 January 1893 in New York, daughter of George Edwin Bryant (d. 1943), actor, and his wife Elizabeth Anne, sister of Harold Desbrowe Annear [q.v.7]. George had moved to America after a dispute with J. C. Williamson [q.v.6], but was invited back to Melbourne in 1906 to direct *The Squaw Man*. Beryl attended the Church of England Girls' Grammar School.

She acted in Pathé Frères' film, *For a Woman's Sake* (1911), and in *Road to Ruin*, *The Crisis* and *The Reprieve* for Lincoln-Cass Films in 1913. Her first appearance for J. C. Williamson Ltd was in Melbourne in 1917 in *Outcast*. At her parents' South Yarra home on 22 April 1921 she married a manufacturer Albert Edward Mayor (d. 1941) with Anglican rites. They lived in Sydney where their three children were born. In 1923 she joined the New London Dramatic Company; her performance as Blackie in *The Faithful Heart* was praised for 'its gripping poignancy and naturalness'. She toured for Hugh J. Ward [q.v.12] in 1924, starring in *The Man in Dress Clothes*.

In difficult financial circumstances in 1931, Bryant began teaching elocution. That year she took over Carrie Tennant's Community

Playhouse, Forbes Street, which re-opened as Bryant's Playhouse. Her father quit his retirement to help. She ran the tiny theatre as a practice ground for students and as a social venue for theatre enthusiasts, and thought that the small stage lent itself 'to unusual and experimental plays'. Bryant directed and acted. She did seasons of Shaw, Barrie, Shakespeare and Chekhov, and plays by Molière, Zola, Pinero, Maeterlinck, Strindberg and Ibsen. *Peer Gynt* was staged in the garden of her Vaucluse home.

Miss Bryant, as she was known professionally, was a vigorous promoter of theatre. She was a member of the Sydney Players' Club, the New South Wales division of the British Drama League and the Playwrights' Advisory Board, and was an organizer of Drama Week. To encourage local talent, she held one-act play competitions, offering local writers the opportunity to have their work performed: 'it is futile to wait until playwrights become marvellous men before accepting their plays; they should be given workshops where plays and actors may be tested by trial and error in actual performance'.

Charles Chauvel [q.v.7] valued the training she gave his actors; Leslie Rees praised her choice of plays as 'almost recklessly courageous'. A younger generation benefited from her enterprise. Bryant's Playhouse staged the first public performances (1935) of Patrick White's *Bread and Butter Women* and *The School for Friends*; his mother Ruth gave financial backing to the playhouse and became a valued friend of its proprietor.

The Playhouse moved to Phillip Street in 1942 and closed in 1946. Beryl had joined Moral Re-Armament about 1935 and from 1946—although in poor health—took part in its stage productions in Europe, the United States of America, the Philippines, Vietnam, Burma and India. From 1956 she lived in Melbourne. Survived by her daughter and two sons, she died on 31 May 1973 at South Caulfield and was buried beside her husband in South Head cemetery, Sydney.

Syd Players' Club, *Play*, 1935; *Aust Theatre News Mthly*, 1939; *SMH*, 24 Mar 1934, 13 Oct 1938, 16 Nov 1940, 4 Apr 1942, 6, 13 June 1973; *Age* (Melb), 1 Mar 1943; Tildesley papers (ML); theatre programmes (ML *and* Syd Opera House L); information from Ms A. Mayor, Adel, Mr C. B. Mayor, Melb, and Ms P. White, Syd.

HEATHER RADI

BUCHANAN, GORDON HENRY; *see* ALDEN

BUCHANAN, HERBERT JAMES (1902-1965), naval officer, was born on 10 March 1902 at Fitzroy, Melbourne, son of Herbert James Buchanan, a pastry-cook from Gippsland, and his English-born wife Emily Jane, née Wood. Educated at Scotch College, Melbourne, young Buchanan was a 1916 entrant at the Royal Australian Naval College, Jervis Bay, Federal Capital Territory. Graduating in 1919, he went to Britain next year to take sea-training and professional courses with the Royal Navy. In 1924 he returned to Australia, but after two years was back in England where he completed the Long and the Advanced gunnery courses. Home again, he was promoted lieutenant commander in February 1932 while in charge of the gunnery school at H.M.A.S. *Cerberus*, Westernport, Victoria. On 21 March that year he married Florence Knarhoi Ellis with Anglican rites at Christ Church, South Yarra.

During the next six years Buchanan was at sea. Promoted commander on 30 June 1938, he attended the R.N. Staff College at Greenwich, England, in 1939. He was executive officer of the British cruiser *Diomede* when World War II broke out. In February 1940 he assumed command of the destroyer H.M.S. *Valentine*. Operating off the coasts of Belgium and the Netherlands in support of Dutch and French forces, the ship was damaged by bombs on 15 May. Buchanan beached the stricken vessel and conveyed the wounded to safety; for his actions he was awarded the Distinguished Service Order. Sent to Dunkirk, France, later that month, he oversaw the evacuation of allied soldiers and was mentioned in dispatches.

As assistant-director of plans (1941-43) at Navy Office, Melbourne, Buchanan was involved in the development of Garden Island Dockyard, Sydney, and in equipping R.A.N. ships with radar. In May 1943 he took command of H.M.A.S. *Norman*, attached to the British Eastern Fleet. Promoted acting captain on 2 November 1944, he was transferred to *Napier* as senior officer of the 7th Destroyer Flotilla. He proposed innovations in gunnery and radar, and endeavoured to ensure that his ships received adequate logistic backup. *Napier* supported sea-borne assaults in Burma, then accompanied allied forces to Japan. There, on 30 August 1945, Buchanan led a naval landing-battalion in the occupation of Yokosuka; he was mentioned in dispatches for his service in *Napier*.

In October he was posted as deputy-chief of Naval Staff to Navy Office where he played a key role in postwar planning, particularly for a carrier force. Buchanan next commanded the cruisers *Shropshire* (1946-47) and *Australia* (1947-48). He completed the course at the Imperial Defence College, London, in 1949. While commodore superintendent of training at H.M.A.S. *Cerberus* in 1950-52, he enlisted community support in Melbourne to found the

White Ensign Club for sailors. In 1953 he captained the aircraft carrier, H.M.A.S. *Sydney*, at the coronation naval review in England and was appointed C.B.E. That year he was promoted commodore, first class, and joined the Naval Board as chief of naval personnel. At a time of budgetary restraint, his attempts to improve pay and allowances achieved little. Buchanan's interest in officer-training saw better results, with more emphasis on the recruiting of older entrants and the initiation of plans to return the R.A.N. College to Jervis Bay.

His forthright, determined and sometimes abrasive approach could provoke unnecessary conflict, and his relations with the minister for the navy (Sir) William McMahon were strained. The politically acute chief of Naval Staff, Vice Admiral Sir John Collins, came to believe that Buchanan's obduracy was not helping the navy's cause. The qualities which had helped to make him an excellent seagoing leader were not suited to staff work. In February 1955 Buchanan was made acting rear admiral and flag officer in charge, East Australia Area. Despite professional and social success in Sydney, he retired on 9 March 1957 as a substantive captain and honorary rear admiral.

Remaining in Sydney, Buchanan became managing director of Bell's Asbestos & Engineering (Australia) Pty Ltd and a board-member of other companies; he was president (from 1957) of the executive committee of the Australian Outward Bound Memorial Foundation. He had a happy family life and enjoyed sailing as a recreation. Survived by his wife and two sons, he died of cancer on 15 March 1965 at Point Piper and was cremated.

F. B. Eldridge, *A History of the Royal Australian Naval College* (Melb, 1949); S. W. Roskill, *The War at Sea 1939-1945*, 1 (Lond, 1954); G. H. Gill, *Royal Australian Navy 1942-1945* (Canb, 1968); M. A. Payne and L. J. Lind, *N Class* (Syd, 1972); R. Hyslop, *Aye Aye, Minister* (Canb, 1990); *SMH*, 15, 16 May 1947, 21 Aug, 26 Nov 1951, 18 Jan 1955, 14 Oct 1959, 17, 29 Nov 1960, 1 Sept 1961, 17 Aug 1963, 16 Mar 1965; *Sun* (Syd), 12 Apr 1983; J. B. Foley papers (copies held by author, Mosman, Syd); information from Mrs F. K. Buchanan, Watsons Bay, Mrs H. B. Farncomb, Rose Bay, Lieut Cmdr J. Buchanan, Vaucluse, Syd, and Mr R. Hyslop, Yarralumla, Canb.   J. V. P. GOLDRICK

BUCKINGHAM, ASHLEY JAMES (1898-1962), retailer, was born on 11 April 1898 at Petersham, Sydney, third of four sons and seventh child of William Buckingham, a draper from England, and his Scottish-born wife Hannah Jane, née Gellatly. William had opened his drapery in 1878; after several moves he re-established it in Riley Street by 1895 and occupied the corner of Riley and Oxford streets by 1904. A leading Baptist layman, in 1905 he addressed the Baptist World Congress in London on 'Ethics in Business' which—for him—meant honesty and self-control, and required the three Gs— 'Grit, Go and Gumption'; he also advocated profit-sharing with employees.

Educated at The Kings School, Parramatta, in 1915 Ashley joined his father's business. He enlisted in the Australian Imperial Force on 11 November 1918, the last day of World War I. At St James's Anglican Church, Sydney, on 18 June 1925 he married Doreen Blanche Watson.

In 1928, when his brother William (1893-1967) succeeded their father as chairman of Buckingham's Ltd (registered as a public company on 16 September 1920), three of the brothers were active in the firm. Buckingham's had been one of the earliest retailers in Sydney to introduce an easy credit system which encouraged spending among the respectable working classes of nearby suburbs who were relatively unaccustomed to shopping for anything but necessities. Its policy became a model for other retailers. 'Mr Ashley', as he was known to employees, took responsibility for Buckingham's Ashleys stores (the first was opened in the Imperial Arcade in 1936, followed by others at Wollongong and Katoomba). Next year he launched Curzons in Pitt Street (another was later established in Brisbane), smart but inexpensive fashion stores where working girls learned about style from salesgirls who were prettier and more fashionably dressed versions of themselves.

Of the brothers in the business, Ashley was the most gregarious and publicly active. Representing Gipps Ward on Sydney Municipal Council in 1941-44, he chaired its improvements and town-planning committee. He favoured city development to maximize access and attraction to retail facilities. A council-member of the Retail Traders' Association of New South Wales from 1940, Buckingham was vice-president (from 1947) and president (1948-51); he also presided over the Australian Council of Retailers in 1950-51. He admired American modernity and visited the United States in 1946. On his return, he argued that Australia was ready for an expansion of consumerism—if government lifted restrictions on the import of American capital. He lobbied Federal and State governments to end rationing and price controls that had been imposed during World War II.

Among his other business interests, he was director of Bussell Bros Ltd from 1946, chairman of its successor, Grocery and General Merchants Ltd, and a director of Nile Textiles

Ltd. Joint managing director of Buckingham's by 1948, Ashley expanded the business after taking over as managing director in 1955. In 1957-58 he amalgamated the Ashleys' and Buckingham's chains, and financed new stores by selling the firm's Queensland interests. A member of the American National, New South Wales, Australian Jockey and Australian Golf clubs, Buckingham preferred to live in flats, although he later acquired a holiday home at Newport which allowed him to go fishing as well as to play golf. He was only 5 ft 3½ ins (161.3 cm) tall, with grey eyes and brown hair; in published photographs late in life he appears to resemble a Pontiac potato. Survived by his daughter and son, Ashley died of cerebral thrombosis on 10 January 1962 at his Potts Point home and was cremated; his estate was sworn for probate at £50 599. The family sold Buckingham's in 1967.

Retail Traders' Assn of NSW, *J*, Jan 1962; *SMH*, 26 Nov 1926, 14 Oct 1941, 6 Mar 1944, 16 Dec 1948, 20 Jan 1950, 11, 13 Jan 1962.

BEVERLEY KINGSTON

BUCKLAND, EDWIN (1871-1959), shire councillor, was born on 14 June 1871 at White Hills, Victoria, son of James Smith Buckland, a butcher from England, and his Adelaide-born wife Elizabeth, née Smith. The family left Sandhurst in 1880 and bought Kington Vineyard in the neighbouring district of Goornong. On 15 December 1897 Edwin married Julia Henrietta Oberin at St George's Anglican Church, Goornong.

Having invested in the gold-mines at Fosterville in 1896, Edwin worked for ten years as engine driver for Stewarts United Gold Mining Co., of which he and his father were part-owners. In 1906 he returned to the family farm and four years later was elected to the Huntly Shire Council. He served as a councillor for the next forty-nine years and was reputed to have missed only two meetings; he was president on seven occasions, the first in 1914, the last in 1959.

As councillor, Buckland took a keen interest in local issues; he was active in securing the provision of water for the town of Goornong and in erecting several local bridges. More important to him was the provision of reliable water for the farmers of the Huntly and surrounding districts. He attended the first meeting (1904) convened to call for the damming of Lake Eppalock, acted as the secretary of the Coliban investigation committee and gave evidence to government inquiries into the project, but was to die before he saw the completion of his dream.

Aware of the need for local councils to act in concert, from 1914 Buckland was a member of the Municipal Association of Victoria (president 1946) and of the Northern Municipal Association which he served as president for twenty-two years. He was, as well, a foundation and life member of the Victorian Decentralisation League, president of the Bendigo Agricultural Society and belonged to the Victorian Country Fire Authority (president 1954). Involved in many other community organizations, he was also a justice of the peace for more than thirty years and a sworn valuator for at least twenty-two. For his services to the Huntly council, he was appointed M.B.E. in 1950.

Ted Buckland was said to be 'the best known personality in Bendigo and the North'. Although his ideas were not always shared, the *Elmore Standard* reported that everyone admired 'the enthusiasm which he infused into everything which he considered would be for the advantage of his district'. A Freemason of long standing, he was master of the Campaspe Lodge at Elmore. He died on 31 May 1959 at White Hills and was buried in Bendigo cemetery. Predeceased by his wife, he was survived by five daughters and three sons.

Shire of Huntly Anniversary Book (Elmore, Vic, 1941); M. Shaw, *Our Goodly Heritage* (Bendigo, Vic, 1966); *Annals of Bendigo*, 7, 1988; *Age* (Melb) and *Bendigo Advertiser*, 1 June 1959; *Elmore Standard*, 4 June 1959.

CHARLES FAHEY

BUCKLAND, WILLIAM LIONEL (1899-1964), businessman and philanthropist, was born on 11 December 1899 at Mansfield, Victoria, son of Frederick John Buckland, a stock and station agent from England, and his Victorian-born wife Maria, née Meader; he was a nephew of (Sir) Thomas Buckland [q.v.7]. Educated at Mansfield Agricultural School, Bill was employed as a junior clerk by the Bank of New South Wales in Melbourne. In 1919 he opened a bicycle shop at Armadale, sold it for a small profit a year later and sailed for San Francisco, United States of America, where he found work with a motor-accessory firm. Aged 21, he returned to Melbourne with goods valued at £200 which formed the basis of the chain of Buckland wholesale motor-accessory and spare-parts companies. Working a ninety-hour week for many years, by the early 1950s he owned twenty-five companies which included service stations, insurance and finance organizations, and large pastoral properties in most States.

In 1952 Buckland sold his thirteen Southern Cross service stations to Ampol Petroleum Ltd for shares in Ampol Exploration, a deal which netted him more than £500 000 by 1953. He sold most of his motor interests in 1957 to Siddons Industries Ltd for a directorship of that firm and shares worth £663 000; he distributed thousands of these shares to his past employees. In 1960 he sold 11 000 square miles (28 490 km^2) of property, including the world-renowned Victoria River Downs cattle-station, Northern Territory, to L. J. Hooker [q.v.] Investment Corporation Ltd for £5 million. He gave his only newspaper interview after the Hooker transaction. To Buckland, work was to be turned into assets and assets into money: in 1953 he had bought Windlesham Moor, a mansion in England, with the thwarted intention of starting a merchant bank and world insurance company.

Opinions about Buckland were deeply divided. With a brilliant financial mind, he was meticulous, competitive and arrogant. At times, he skated close to the business edge. Because he liked to be in control, he preferred private to public companies. Yet, many people found him shy and amicable. He inspired loyalty from employees, gave donations to charities throughout his life and was intense in his patriotism.

A close person who was difficult to know, Buckland was naive about the cost of everyday living. While never discussing business at home, he allowed his preoccupations with control and parsimony to carry over into the private sphere. He had married Enid Maud Mellington Darby on 13 April 1921 in the district registrar's office, Waverley, Sydney. The early financial struggle and his nature contributed to an unhappy home life. He gave little time to his family, but was aware of and upset by their image of him. Marred by arguments about money, the union ended in divorce in 1947. His marriage to 29-year-old Patricia Adams on 16 July 1951 at John Knox Presbyterian Church, Gardenvale, Melbourne, saw him more content.

Survived by his wife, and by the son and daughter of his first marriage, Buckland died of a coronary occlusion on 22 November 1964 at his Toorak mansion and was cremated. His Victorian estate, sworn for probate at £924 537, was part of a gross estate of £4 829 644. The family contested his will in three highly-publicized court cases and in 1967 he was posthumously named for tax evasion (in 1947-49 and 1957-59). The bulk of his estate was dedicated to setting up a charitable trust, the William Buckland Foundation. Its income was to be divided equally between public benevolent institutions in Victoria and scientific or educational applicants. The foundation, administered by the Trustees, Executors & Agency Co. Ltd, has made annual distributions since December 1966.

D. Corbett, *Politics and the Airlines* (Lond, 1965); S. Brogden, *Australia's Two-Airline Policy* (Melb, 1968); K. A. J. Buckland, *'Few Gods—Some Heroes—Many Warriors'* (priv pub, np, 1977); J. Siddons, *Spanner in the Works* (Melb, 1990); *Vic Law Reports*, 1966; *Aust Financial Review*, 5 May 1960; *Herald* (Melb), 25, 26 Nov 1964, 1 Mar 1965; *Age* (Melb), 26, 28 Nov 1964, 9, 10, 11, 27 Nov 1965, 5-7, 9 Apr, 19 May 1966, 22-23, 26 Sept 1967; information from Mr J. Buckland, Mansfield, Mr W. Buckland, Mount Eliza, Vic, Mrs P. Lyons, Point Piper, Syd, Sir J. Balderstone, Mont Albert, Melb, and from other informants.

CAROLE HARRIS

BUCKMASTER, ERNEST (1897-1968), artist, was born on 3 July 1897 at Hawthorn, Melbourne, eldest son of Harry Amos Buckmaster, a straw-hat manufacturer from England, and his Victorian-born wife Letitia Martha, née Chandler. A puny lad, Ernest was taken by his grandparents to help on their mixed farm at Box Hill until he was 14. He attended the local state school where he enjoyed nothing more than drawing, in which his precocious talent was recognized from the age of 4.

In 1913 he was apprenticed to James Beament, a signwriter and amateur artist. After Buckmaster was rejected for military service, Beament encouraged him to join the Victorian Artists Society and to enrol at the National Gallery Art School where in 1918-24 he received his only formal art training, from Bernard Hall and W. B. McInnes [qq.v.9,10]. Although critical of his unorthodox techniques, both were pleased with his work. Between 1919 and 1924 he sold nineteen of the paintings he exhibited with the V.A.S. and won most of the prizes available at the school.

Apart from 1931, he exhibited with V.A.S. every year from 1919 until 1943. At Buckmaster's first two solo exhibitions in 1926, Hall made purchases for the Felton [q.v.4] bequest. Buckmaster's first Sydney exhibition in 1927 at the Macquarie Galleries, managed by Basil Burdett [q.v.7] and John Young [q.v.], led to portrait commissions. In 1928 he exhibited with Janet Cumbrae Stewart [q.v.8] and the Australian Art Association. Commissioned by the Commonwealth Historic Memorials Committee, he also completed a posthumous portrait of Adam Lindsay Gordon [q.v.4] that year.

A councillor (1929-30) of the V.A.S., in 1930 Buckmaster was helped by a patron to travel abroad. In 1932 his portrait of Sir William Irvine [q.v.9], the lieutenant-governor of Victoria, won the Archibald [q.v.3] prize. Next year he held solo exhibitions in Adelaide, Sydney and Melbourne, and his portrait of Alice Bale [q.v.7] was included in the Australian Art Association's last exhibition. He also exhibited with the Twenty Melbourne Painters (1933-62) and the Australian Academy of Art (1938-46), of which he was a foundation member.

On 12 February 1936 Buckmaster married Dorothy Laura Cook at the Methodist Ladies' College, Kew. That year he painted a commissioned portrait of the lieutenant-governor of Western Australia, Sir James Mitchell [q.v.10]. In Perth Buckmaster completed eleven portraits in three months, and still held his customary, annual exhibition in Melbourne. Divorced on 15 February 1939, seven days later he married Florence Botting at the Presbyterian manse, South Melbourne.

In 1941 Buckmaster won the National Gallery of Victoria's subject picture prize. A successful exhibition in 1944 at David Jones's [q.v.2] art gallery, Sydney, resulted in a commission from Dominion Breweries to paint landscapes for hotels in New Zealand. On 24 August 1945 he was appointed an official war artist, commissioned to paint the Japanese surrender in Singapore. He arrived two days late for the ceremony, but completed twenty-five pictures for the Australian War Memorial. In 1951 his book, *The Art of Ernest Buckmaster*, was published by Lothian [q.v.10]. He won the Albury (Regional Art Centre) prize in 1950 and 1963.

Buckmaster never deviated from his convictions or from his chosen techniques. While scorning modernism, he was respected for his integrity and for his well-argued opinions. After a heart attack in 1959, he began writing notes on his theories and methods, and expressed his concerns in letters to the press. In 1964 he resumed annual exhibitions. Survived by his wife, and by their three sons and two daughters, he died on 18 October 1968 at his Warrandyte home and was buried in Lilydale cemetery. The Art Gallery of New South Wales holds Buckmaster's self-portrait.

Australasian, 11 Nov 1933; VAS, Minute-books (LaTL); Public L, Museums and National Gallery of Vic, Annual Reports, 1919-24, and AMPA artists files and indexes (SLV); family papers (held by Mr N. Buckmaster, Melb).   JOYCE MCGRATH

BUILDER, GEOFFREY (1906-1960), physicist and radio engineer, was born on 21 June 1906 at Cue, Western Australia, eldest child of native-born parents Alfred Ernest Builder, a managing agent for a rural supply company, and his wife Grace, née Clark. The family later moved to Geraldton. Geoffrey was educated in Perth at the Church of England Grammar School, Guildford. On passing the Leaving certificate in 1922, he was apprenticed as a fitter at the railway workshops

and studied at night at Perth Technical School. In 1925 he enrolled at the University of Western Australia (B.Sc., 1928); he majored in mathematics and rowed in the winning crew at the intervarsity regatta in 1927.

While tutoring at the university in 1928, Builder studied advanced physics and completed the course externally after moving to the Carnegie Institution of Washington's magnetic observatory at Watheroo. His chief responsibility was to maintain the observatory's radio link with Washington, but he also investigated atmospheric potential gradients on which he published his first papers. In 1930 he passed the M.Sc. preliminary course at the University of Western Australia as an external student and was then accepted by (Sir) Edward Appleton in his laboratory at King's College, University of London (Ph.D., 1933; D.Sc., 1956).

Taking up research on the physics of radio propagation and the ionosphere, Builder specialized in instrumentation. It seems that it was he who persuaded Appleton of the advantages for investigating the ionosphere of the pulse-echo method (developed at the Carnegie Institution) over Appleton's own frequency-change method. Builder also designed the apparatus for the British expedition in 1932-33 to Tromsö, Norway, to investigate ionospheric conditions at high latitudes for the International Polar Year.

He returned to Australia in 1933 to a position in Sydney with the Radio Research Board where his work again dealt mainly with instrumentation. Next year he became director of the research laboratories at Amalgamated Wireless (Australasia) Ltd. Builder recruited excellent staff and built his institution into the country's premier industrial research establishment. During World War II the A.W.A. laboratories contributed significantly to Australia's radio and radar capabilities.

In contrast to the gentleness that later characterized his behaviour, Builder was at that time an abrasive administrator. In November 1940 A.W.A. replaced him as director of the laboratories and gave him a roving commission to strengthen Australia's international radio links. A temporary major in the Australian Military Forces in February-August 1942, he advised on radar before being appointed acting general manager of Airzone Ltd, a wartime supplier of electronic equipment to the Department of Defence. Subsequently, with two colleagues from Airzone, he set up private companies to manufacture electrical equipment, specializing in constant voltage transformers.

In 1947 Builder joined the University of Sydney as a temporary lecturer in physics; in 1950 he was appointed senior lecturer. An enterprising and sympathetic teacher, he developed ideas on the foundations of relativity theory that continue to provoke discussion. He was a fellow of the Institute of Physics, London, and of the American and Australian institutions of Radio Engineers. At St Peter's Anglican Church, Ballarat, Victoria, on 25 May 1936 he had married Margaret Bettie Mitchell, a laboratory technician from Perth. His recreations included gardening at their home at Burwood, Sydney, carpentry and tennis. Builder died of a coronary occlusion on 17 June 1960 at Croydon and was cremated; his wife, son and three daughters survived him.

R. W. Home, *Physics in Australia to 1945* (Melb, 1990); *Listener In*, 8 Dec 1934; *Aust J of Science*, 23, Nov 1960, p 155; Univ Syd, *Gazette*, Nov 1960, p 297; AWA Pty Ltd papers (ML); Physics Dept files (Univ Syd Archives).   R. W. HOME

BUKOWSKI, ROCHUS JOSEPH JOHN (1901-1960), trade unionist, was born on 7 August 1901 at Mount Morgan, Queensland, second child of Joseph Aloysius Bukowski, a tailor born at sea, and his wife Elizabeth, née McInnes, from Brisbane. The child of a father who was proud of his Polish background, Roch was raised as a Catholic. Growing quickly to a massive size, he became renowned as a school bully at Christian Brothers' College, Rockhampton, where one of his victims was the physically smaller V. C. Gair [q.v.]. Bukowski also attended Nudgee College, Brisbane. After leaving school, he worked as a labourer in a variety of rural and mining jobs, and briefly prospected in New Guinea. On 9 September 1921 he married a 27-year-old nurse and widow Grace Lily Dumbrell, née Evans, at St Joseph's Catholic Cathedral, Rockhampton.

While employed as a canecutter at South Johnstone in the early 1930s, Bukowski came to the attention of Australian Workers' Union organizers. Aspiring A.W.U. leaders and Australian Labor Party politicians needed the support of union bosses like Clarrie Fallon [q.v.] if their careers were to progress. By the 1920s the Queensland A.W.U. leadership had been effectively insulated from formal challenge by rules which required candidates for official positions to be endorsed by the executive. The size of the union within the Queensland labour movement and its strength in rural areas ensured its dominant role in the ruling A.L.P. The main threat to this monopoly lay in communist-inspired attempts to foment unofficial strikes and to form breakaway unions. Large and ruthless, Bukowski was useful as an enforcer in the violent and bitter industrial relations of the time.

In this role he rose to prominence in 1934-35 when the A.W.U., the Queensland government and the Colonial Sugar Refining Co. combined to suppress communist-led, canecutter strikes against unhealthy work practices. Bukowski earned the nickname 'Midnight Joe' for his alleged, intimidatory, nocturnal visits to strike leaders. Although he had ceased to be an active churchgoer and had little time for clerics, the passionate anti-communism of the Polish Catholic Church remained a lifelong influence and helped to advance his career in the A.W.U. He was appointed a full-time A.W.U. organizer at Ayr in 1935, then at Mackay (1939-40) and Townsville (1940). A widower, on 12 May 1938 Bukowski married Ailsa Barbara McGrath at the Sacred Heart Church, Ayr; they were to be divorced in 1945.

In 1941 Joe was elected central district secretary of the A.W.U. and appointed one of its delegates to the Queensland Labor-in-Politics Convention. Next year he became southern district secretary, based in Brisbane. There, on 3 September 1946, he married Alma Elizabeth Williams at the Salvation Army Temple. The 1950 Labor-in-Politics Convention appointed him secretary of its industrial groups committee. In 1951 he advanced to A.W.U. State president, editor of the *Worker* and heir apparent to A.W.U. secretary Harry Boland [q.v.]. Bukowski's involvement with the industrial groups brought him into contact with B. A. Santamaria's Catholic Social Studies Movement. The ancient enmity between Bukowski and Gair had continued to fester, and, after Gair's elevation to premier on 17 January 1952, relations between the parliamentary Labor Party and the A.W.U. soured. 'The Movement's' support for Gair was one factor that turned Bukowski against it, and against the industrial groups which he had helped to create. In 1954 H. V. Evatt's [q.v.] denunciation of the groups was enthusiastically endorsed by Bukowski in the *Worker* and was followed by impassioned attacks on 'the Movement's' supporters at A.W.U. conventions in 1955.

The political struggle was mirrored industrially by Gair's support for employers' moves to cut the A.W.U. shearing award rate, which led to a prolonged, official, pastoral strike in 1956. Seeking support for the strike and for his confrontation with Gair, Bukowski drew close to the left-wing Queensland Trades and Labor Council, led by (Sir) John Egerton, from which the A.W.U. had remained aloof for decades. When Boland died in July 1956, Bukowski was appointed secretary of the State branch of the A.W.U. and also president of the Queensland central executive of the A.L.P. He immediately reaffiliated the A.W.U. with the T.L.C. This unlikely axis had the strength in the A.L.P. to direct government policy, an advantage pressed incessantly by Bukowski who was reported as saying that the rule book was unnecessary when you had the numbers.

Matters came to a head in early 1957 when the Queensland central executive pressed Gair to comply with the 1956 convention's direction to introduce three weeks annual leave for public servants. When Gair repeatedly refused, Bukowski and Egerton organized the numbers on the executive to expel him from the A.L.P. on 24 April 1957. They thereby split the parliamentary Labor Party, occasioning the government's defeat on 12 June.

After Gair's removal, the now feared and hated Bukowski soon fell out with his allies in the T.L.C. Motions critical of A.W.U. behaviour within the party were passed during 1958. Finally, on 18 December, he was suspended as president for his allegedly drunken and intimidatory behaviour towards Brisbane Labor alderman Jean Howie at the executive's Christmas party held the previous week. In a characteristically impetuous response, he disaffiliated the A.W.U. from the T.L.C. and the A.L.P. on 23 February 1959. The following month his A.L.P. membership renewal was rejected by the Oxley branch of the party. Subsequent negotiations made it clear that any reaffiliation of the union with the A.L.P. would be contingent on Bukowski's removal. Embittered and lonely, he died of a coronary occlusion on 20 January 1960 at his Annerley home and was buried with Catholic rites in Lutwyche cemetery. He was survived by his wife, their daughter and two sons, by a daughter of his first marriage and by two sons of his second.

R. Murray, *The Split* (Melb, 1970); D. J. Murphy et al (eds), *Labor in Power* (Brisb, 1980); D. J. Murphy (ed), *The Big Strikes* (Brisb, 1983); R. Fitzgerald and H. Thornton, *Labor in Queensland* (Brisb, 1989); W. Swan, Factionalism—The Case of Queensland Labor 1959-1966 (B.A. Hons thesis, Univ Qld, 1975); Aust Labor Party, Qld Labor-in-Politics Conventions *and* Qld Central Executive, Minutes, 1941-58 (OL); Aust Workers Union, State Conventions, Minutes, 1954-59; information from Mr E. Bacon, Enoggera, and Mr M. Cross, Ashgrove, Brisb.   HAROLD THORNTON

BULCOCK, FRANK WILLIAM (1892-1973), politician and administrator, was born on 6 June 1892 at Mount Arapiles, near Horsham, Victoria, third child of Thomas Bulcock, carpenter, and his wife Eliza, née Grove, both English born. Educated at the local state school, Frank studied agricultural and veterinary science at Sydney Technical College, then won a Department of Agriculture bursary to Wagga Wagga Experiment Farm where he topped the class in 1913.

Next year he went to Queensland and became an active member of the Western Queensland branch of the Australian Workers' Union, assisting in the preparation of an award claim for pastoral workers. On Christmas Day 1917 he married a schoolteacher Florence Violet Edwards with Presbyterian forms at Beecroft, Sydney.

At a by-election on 20 December 1919 Bulcock won the Queensland Legislative Assembly seat of Barcoo for Labor. From 17 June 1932 until 15 December 1942 he was secretary for agriculture and stock—the first incumbent in Queensland to have had an academic and practical background in agriculture and veterinary science (in 1940 he became a registered veterinary surgeon). Making his mark in parliament as a capable speaker, tenacious debater and industrious worker, he once tabled over 150 regulations in a single day, and piloted 72 bills through the House in his career as minister.

Bulcock helped to establish a chair in veterinary science at the University of Queensland, the Tropical Research Station at South Johnstone, North Queensland, and the Milk Board. He promoted tropical grasses and legumes, accelerated research on the tick problem, improved the operations of marketing boards, introduced legislation to stabilize the dairying industry and re-organized the Agricultural Bank. Recognizing the importance of scientific contributions to the development of agriculture and horticulture, he made provision for a departmental biometrician to support the statistical analysis of field experiments. He was president (1932-42) of the Queensland Council of Agriculture and a founding member (1933-42) of the Commonwealth Agricultural Council.

In December 1942 Bulcock resigned from parliament and took up the appointment of Commonwealth director-general of agriculture. Under Prime Minister Curtin [q.v.] he organized the wartime planning of essential agricultural production (including machinery, fertilizers and vegetable seeds), as well as the associated organization of labour. He represented Australia abroad at food and agricultural conferences, and confirmed his capacity as a technical expert, administrator and negotiator. Following his resignation in 1952, the Federal government seconded him next year to the Scarce Commodities Committee, Washington, United States of America, with responsibility for fertilizers, phosphate rock and sulphur.

As agricultural counsellor (1952-59) to the Australian high commissioner in London, Bulcock acted as liaison officer between the Australian and British governments' departments of agriculture. During this period he led the Australian delegation to five sessions of the United Nations Food and Agriculture

Organization. He was a member (1952-59) of the Australian Agricultural Council and a life member (1943) of the Royal Agricultural Society, London; in 1956 he was awarded the medal of the Royal Society of Arts, London, for a paper on Australian pastoral industries.

Retiring to Queensland, Bulcock campaigned in elections for the Labor Party and corresponded with governments on a range of issues. A long public life 'had not blunted his integrity, his moral earnestness or his kindness'. He was cultured, deeply read and adept at quoting passages from Shakespeare, and had 'lost neither the desire nor the ability to communicate with the ordinary man'. Survived by his wife, daughter and an adopted daughter, Bulcock died on 19 January 1973 at his Mount Nebo home and was cremated.

C. Lack (comp), *Three Decades of Queensland Political History, 1929-1960* (Brisb, 1962); P. Murphy, *A Memorable Family Reunion* (Brisb, 1973); P. J. Skerman et al, *Guiding Queensland Agriculture, 1887-1987* (Brisb, 1988); *Courier-Mail*, 22, 24 Jan 1973.
                                                    DENISE K. CONROY

BULL, LIONEL BATLEY (1889-1978), veterinary scientist and administrator, was born on 27 April 1889 at Hawthorn, Melbourne, second of four children of Thomas William Bull, a herbalist from England, and his Victorian-born wife Kate Marina, née Harris. The family enjoyed a leisurely and comfortable life on their property at Ormond. Educated at University High School, Lionel was a student at W. T. Kendall's [q.v.9] Melbourne Veterinary College when that institution was absorbed by the University of Melbourne in 1908. Bull became a licentiate in veterinary science in 1911 and next year graduated B.V.Sc. In September 1912 he accepted an appointment as first assistant to (Sir) Trent de Crespigny [q.v.7], director of the laboratory of bacteriology and pathology at Adelaide Hospital. On 17 November 1913 Bull married Beatrice Johannah Reay at the Methodist manse, Pirie Street, Adelaide.

Responsible for most of the laboratory's bacteriological work, he encouraged veterinary colleagues to submit material and promptly initiated research, both in human and animal bacteriology and in infectious diseases. In 1917 Bull identified the pathogenic yeast *Torula histolytica* in a fatal case of Torula meningitis; clinical pathologists still use his Indian-ink method of demonstrating the presence of the organism in the patient's cerebrospinal fluid. The University of Melbourne awarded him a D.V.Sc. in 1919 and in 1925 he was made director of his laboratory. In 1929 he isolated, named and described the causal organism of 'lumpy wool' in sheep and

in 1935 set up an investigation into bovine mastitis. His most significant work in bacteriology dated from about 1930: he studied the natural history of caseous lymphadenitis of sheep and showed that wounding the animals during shearing was the main cause of the condition. At the University of Adelaide in 1930-33 he lectured on bacteriology to medical and dental students.

On 13 January 1934 Bull was appointed deputy-chief of the Council for Scientific and Industrial Research's division of animal health and immediately went on a tour of veterinary establishments in Britain, Europe and the United States of America. Returning to Australia, in July 1935 he succeeded J. A. Gilruth [q.v.9] as chief of the division. Bull set up a new laboratory at the Veterinary Research Institute, University of Melbourne. Next year his organization absorbed C.S.I.R.'s division of animal nutrition and was renamed the division of animal health and nutrition. Almost from the outset, there was friction between Bull and H. R. Marston [q.v.], officer-in-charge of the Adelaide Nutrition Laboratory. Marston wanted to concentrate on fundamental research; Bull required him to relate his work to problems in the field. The antagonism continued until 1944, culminating in the creation of a division of biochemistry and general nutrition under Marston; Bull's truncated domain was then titled animal health and production.

Over the next ten years Bull established sections to investigate animal breeding and genetics, as well as animal physiology, and studied ecto- and endo-parasites of cattle in tropical Australia. In 1937 he had conducted field-trials to determine whether the myxoma virus could be used to control the rabbit plague in Australia. Forced by quarantine authorities to make his observations in unsuitable environments, away from mosquito-breeding sites, he concluded in 1944 that the virus was ineffective. His findings embroiled him in a public controversy with Dame Jean Macnamara [q.v.10]. From 1938 he had chaired a co-operative investigation into the origins in sheep of 'yellows'—haemolytic jaundice with intense anaemia. Bull's vigorous leadership and authority engendered confidence among the members of his team who made fundamental advances in understanding the complex interactions of minerals in the nutrition of sheep. They concluded that 'yellows' resulted from three main types of chronic copper poisoning.

During his career Bull published eighty-eight scientific works, including papers on enterotoxaemia of sheep, 'swell head' of rams and botulism in horses. He retired as chief on 30 June 1954, but continued to work as a senior research fellow with the Commonwealth Scientific and Industrial Research Organization. Concentrating on hepatoxic pyrrolizidine alkaloids affecting livestock, with C. C. J. Culvenor and A. T. Dick he published *The Pyrrolizidine Alkaloids* (No. 9 in the series, 'Frontiers of Biology') (Amsterdam, 1968). The book stressed the importance of such alkaloids among plant poisons in Australia, as well as summarizing recent knowledge of their chemistry, toxicology and pathogenesis, and the pathology produced by them. Bull finally left C.S.I.R.O. in 1968.

He had been made an honorary member of the comparative medicine section of the Royal Society of Medicine, London, in 1945, and an honorary associate of the Royal College of Veterinary Surgeons in 1949. That year he was elected a fellow of the Australian Veterinary Association. Bull was appointed C.B.E. in 1952. A fellow (1954) of the Australian Academy of Science, he served as councillor (1959-61) and vice-president (1960-61). In 1955 the Australian and New Zealand Association for the Advancement of Science awarded him the Mueller [q.v.5] medal and he received the Gilruth prize from the Australian Veterinary Association. Awarded an honorary LL.D. by the University of Melbourne in 1967, he also won the A.N.Z.A.A.S. medal that year. He was elected a foundation fellow of the Australian College of Veterinary Scientists in 1971.

Bull was fiercely proud of the veterinary profession. He appreciated the need for it to be seen and heard in relation to Australia's livestock industries. Yet, he was essentially a scientist, with a keen, critical faculty. Early in his career he had developed confidence in his ability to plan investigations. Although he assumed the role of leader when working with others, he was ready to acknowledge the contributions of his colleagues and his competitors. He worked hard and expected his associates to do likewise. While willing to listen to differing opinions and to weigh them against his own, he made the final decision in matters for which he was accountable and accepted full responsibility. On occasions he could be intimidating to his juniors. No one took liberties with him in conversation; few called him by his Christian name; for most of his life he addressed his associates by their surnames. A good lecturer, he readily participated in scientific discussions, and eschewed cant and hypocrisy. He had a fine mind and an artist's perception of beauty in nature. Bull left a mark on many facets of veterinary science, particularly the health and production aspects of animal industries.

He and his wife belonged to the Musica Viva Society and frequently attended its performances. After studying art as a young man, he returned to painting in retirement and joined the Victorian Artists Society. His work was successfully exhibited and sold; he presented paintings to the Wallaby Club, of which he was a member, and to the Australian Academy of Science. Tennis was another of his recreations. Survived by his son and daughter, Bull died on 5 May 1978 at Fitzroy; his body was given to the anatomy department at the University of Melbourne. Murray Griffin's portrait of Bull is in the Parkville laboratory of C.S.I.R.O.'s division of animal health.

Hist Records of Aust Science, 5, no 4, Dec 1983, p 51, *and* for list of publications; *Age* (Melb), 29 June 1954; *Herald* (Melb), 2 July 1954; CSIRO Archives, Canb.   ERIC L. FRENCH

BULLEN, ALFRED PERCIVAL (1896-1974) and LILIAN ETHEL (1894-1965), circus proprietors, were husband and wife. Perce was born on 8 February 1896 at Kiama, New South Wales, son of Alfred Weston Bullen, a native-born newspaper proprietor, and his wife Alice, née Thomas, from New Zealand. Ambitious to drive a Rolls-Royce motorcar and to own a first-class circus, Perce soon tired of working as a cub reporter on the *Kiama Independent*. With his savings, he bought a pony to give rides to local children, and a few pairs of roller-skates for hire. He began a vagabond life, travelling around country shows with a performing sheep and pony.

On 7 August 1917 at Holy Trinity Church, Dawes Point, Sydney, Bullen married a vaudeville dancer Lilian Ethel Croan with Anglican rites. She had been born on 8 May 1894 at Botany—daughter of George Croan, labourer, and his wife Emily Eleanor, née Wythes—and went on the stage as a child. Beginning with a merry-go-round, Perce, Lil and his brother Albert improvised a travelling circus-carnival. They soon bought an elephant, then added a shooting gallery, performing horses, monkeys and dogs, and a small sideshow where Perce, billed as 'Captain Alfredo', introduced his lone, performing lion.

By 1922 the Bullens had made enough money to organize their own circus. They travelled over dirt roads from one country town to the next in bumpy, horse-drawn wagons. Perce acquired an Alpha electric-lighting plant and sometimes 'amalgamated' with another small circus, such as Lloyd's. Their three sons Stafford, Kenneth and Gregory were born between 1925 and 1930; following the custom of travelling circus people, Perce and Lil adopted children (Mavis and Jules) to complete their family.

In the early 1930s Bullen Bros Circus travelled mostly in Queensland with a show that included its own brass band and a menagerie.

Perce, the ringmaster, also juggled and trained the 'big cats'. Lilian played the cornet, juggled, worked monkeys, dogs and horses, and, with three young girls, appeared in a dancing troupe, 'The Four Marzellas'. When she retired from the ring she took over the administration and worked hard to ensure her family's success. A 'colourful and forceful' personality, if somewhat temperamental, she proudly flaunted her diamond rings and was known as 'Tiger Lil'. In the mid-1930s the show drifted to Western Australia where the Bullens settled for a time before returning to Queensland. With the introduction of fuel-rationing during World War II, they laid up their circus at Yeppoon, outside Rockhampton, only to find thousands of American servicemen camped nearby. In canvas sidewalls only, Bullen and his young family entertained the troops, several times a day. Stafford walked the tightwire. Business became so profitable that Mrs Bullen had more girls working for her than she had with the circus on the road.

The family built one of Australia's most exciting circuses of the postwar era. Its extensive menagerie included thirteen elephants. In the late 1940s Perce worked four lions, two tigers, two leopards, two Himalayan bears and a collie dog—'all in the same cage'. He treated the animals well and was never attacked by any. His white Rolls-Royce led the procession of long, brightly-decorated caravans from town to town. When he presented—as a special attraction—a Bentley used by Queen Elizabeth II during the 1954 royal visit, his publicity stunt occasioned a public outcry. By 1955 the two-ringed circus had twenty-six acts of international class, its own mobile power plant, three diesel lighting plants, a schoolteacher, fifty-six vehicles and caravans, and eighty permanent staff who called Bullen 'Pop'. Bullen's Circus was a family affair: the boys and their wives took leading parts, and conducted their wild-animal and trapeze acts with zest and polish.

Since 1933 new assets had been acquired from the profits and put in Lilian's name. Her personality permeated the organization, whether she charmed local officials, or volubly reprimanded errant circus-hands. In 1957 Bullen's Circus Pty Ltd was registered in Queensland, with Lilian as governing director. Although the circus was a joint enterprise, differences of opinion between its members occasionally reached the courts and made headlines. 'Tiger Lil' died of cancer on 4 January 1965 in King George V hospital, Camperdown, and was buried in Rookwood cemetery; she left over $170 000 to the Cancer Council of New South Wales.

Perce rose early each morning to paint or decorate several caravans by mid-afternoon, all the while impeccably attired in his suit and tie. He wore a diamond tie-pin and a diamond ring that never left his hand, and had gold-capped teeth. Loving nothing more than to lead a parade of his circus, he sat in top-hat and tails astride his favourite horse. At St Nicholas of Myra's Catholic Church, Penrith, on 3 January 1969 Bullen married a widow Daisy Ruth Wood, née Usher. Faced with the increasing popularity of television, Bullen's Circus gave its final performance on 25 May that year at Parramatta. His sons established lion safari-parks; Perce happily retired to the family estate at Wallacia. Survived by his wife and by the children of his first marriage, he died on 11 August 1974 at Penrith and was buried in Eastern Creek cemetery.

G. Greaves, *The Circus Comes to Town* (Syd, 1980); *Outdoor Showman*, Dec 1955; *Sun News-Pictorial*, 5 Apr 1961, 11 May, 24 July, 19 Nov 1963, 16 June 1966; *SMH*, 10, 11 Apr 1963, 12 Aug 1974; *Sunday Telegraph* (Syd), 18 Aug 1974; family information from Dr E. Aldin, Tregear, NSW, Mrs R. Goss, Brisb, Mr M. King, Glebe, Syd, and Mr G. Greaves, Charlestown, NSW.

MARK VALENTINE ST LEON

BULLEN, KEITH EDWARD (1906–1976), seismologist and professor of applied mathematics, was born on 29 June 1906 at Auckland, New Zealand, eldest son of George Sherrar Bullen, a New Zealand-born linotype operator and later journalist, and his wife Maud Hannah, née Burfoot, from England. Keith was educated at Bayfield School, Auckland Grammar School (1919-22) and Auckland University College (B.A., N.Z., 1926; M.A., 1928; B.Sc., 1930). He taught at A.G.S. (1926-27) and lectured in mathematics at his former college (1928-31 and 1934-40).

In England in 1931 he entered St John's College, Cambridge (Sc.D., 1946), and soon decided to become a research student. Assigned to (Sir) Harold Jeffreys for supervision, he collaborated with him in constructing earthquake travel-time tables of greater accuracy than those that were then available. The work first appeared in 1935 and was republished in 1940 after its authors took into account the ellipticities of the different layers within the Earth. In 1932 Bullen had visited Europe and the Soviet Union (where he was arrested and tried as a spy for taking photographs in an unmarked military area, but was released). With permission to work away from Cambridge, next year he gave a special course of lectures at the University College of Hull. Back at Auckland, on 15 May 1935 he married Florence Mary Pressley at St David's Presbyterian Church.

Senior lecturer (from 1940) at the University of Melbourne, in 1946 Bullen accepted the chair of applied mathematics at the University of Sydney. He published *An Introduction to the Theory of Seismology* (Cambridge, 1947; 3rd edition 1963), *Seismology* (New York, 1954) and a text for first-year students, *An Introduction to the Theory of Mechanics* (1949; 8th edition 1971). In 1947 his and Jeffreys's findings had become the official tables of the International Association of Seismology and Physics of the Interior of the Earth. All Bullen's calculations were done on a manual Odhner desk-calculator: similar calculators were used in his department for research and teaching until electronic computers became available. Much of his later work was devoted to substantiating the theory of the Earth's solid inner core. Confirmatory evidence eventually came with the recording of free oscillations of the Earth following the earthquake in Chile in May 1960.

Bullen strongly supported the international scientific effort in seismology—the mathematical study of earthquakes and earthquake waves, and their paths through the Earth's interior. In his 1955 address as president (1954-57) of the International Association of Seismology, he proposed that the known times of nuclear explosions be published so that the resulting earthquake waves could be studied with greater precision. The idea was scientifically sound and seismic observatories now routinely record nuclear explosions. However, the proposal was then misunderstood by some and interpreted to suggest that nuclear bombs should be exploded at definite times for seismic purposes, which was certainly not his intention. Bullen was also vice-president of the International Council of Scientific Unions' committee on Antarctic research (1958) and of the International Union of Geodesy and Geophysics (1963-67), chairman (1971-75) of the international committee for the Standard Earth Model and a member (1973-76) of the governing council of the International Institute of Seismology and Earthquake Engineering, Tokyo.

His lectures showed his concern for the proper application of relevant mathematics to scientific problems, particularly in the Earth sciences; in addition, he stressed the need for clear exposition and good use of English. Bullen was always courteous, but his disagreement with T. G. Room, professor of pure mathematics at the University of Sydney, was widely known. The basis of their disagreement was Bullen's view that applied mathematics was a separate discipline to be studied for its own sake; Room held that pure and applied mathematics were inseparable, and should be taught together.

In 1968 Bullen was elected to the Pontifical Academy of Science, Rome. The iniative for his appointment came from his support for all seismological observatories, including those operated by the Jesuits. Despite his Anglican upbringing, he always preferred an agnostic point of view in his scientific work. Throughout his professional career he would not accept one theory over another until a crucial scientific test could be devised to settle the matter. When the geological controversy over continental drift arose, it was unfashionable to accept Alfred Wegener's theory; Bullen's view, that continental drift should not be rejected out of hand, was unpopular because one was expected to be either a 'drifter' or 'non-drifter'. His stand was vindicated as compelling evidence for the validity of continental drift became available, notably from rock magnetism.

Loaded with scientific honours in Australia and overseas, Bullen had been elected a fellow of the Royal Astronomical Society (1933), the Royal Society, London (1949), the Australian Academy of Science (1954) and the American Geophysical Union (1962). Among his many prizes and awards were the Bicentennial medal of Columbia University, New York (1955), the William Bowie medal of the American Geophysical Union (1961), the Day medal of the Geological Society of America (1963), the research medal of the Royal Society of Victoria (1966) and the gold medal of the Royal Astronomical Society (1974). He was an honorary fellow of the Geological Society of America (1963), the Geological Society of London (1967), the Royal societies of New Zealand (1963) and of New South Wales (1974), a foreign member of the American Academy of Arts and Sciences, Boston (1960), and a foreign associate of the National Academy of Sciences, Washington (1961). He was awarded honorary D.Sc. degrees by the universities of Auckland in 1963 and Sydney in 1975, and was guest lecturer at many universities and institutions at home and abroad. After he retired in 1971, he taught at the Seismological Institute in Tokyo and the University of British Columbia, Canada.

Bullen enjoyed travel and visited seismic observatories in out-of-the-way places to encourage the staff in their scientific work, and to ensure that they understood and appreciated the need for accuracy in interpreting seismic records, particularly in the timing of seismic onsets. He usually took the opportunity to add to his magnificent collection of coins. Physically, he was about 5 ft 6 ins (167.6 cm) tall and in his later years was conscious of his weight. Troubled by deafness from 1934, he managed quite well with a hearing-aid. He retired in 1971 and published *The Earth's Density* (London, 1975). Survived by his wife, son and daughter, he died of myocardial infarction on 23 September 1976 at Auckland and was cremated.

McGraw-Hill Modern Men of Science (NY, 1966); *Biog Memoirs of Fellows of the Roy Soc*, 23, 1977, p 19; *SMH*, 22 Dec 1945, 19 Mar 1949, 10 June 1956, 25 Mar 1960, 20 June 1961, 8 Mar 1966, 20 Jan 1972, 5 Oct 1976; Faculty of Science and K. E. Bullen papers (Univ Syd Archives).

DENIS E. WINCH

BUNNING, WALTER RALSTON (1912-1977), architect, town planner and writer, was born on 19 May 1912 in South Brisbane, twin son of George Edward Bunning, an English-born pastoralist, and his wife Edwina Mary Huey, née Edkins, a Queenslander. Raised with five siblings at Braeside station, Walter went to the Slade School, Warwick. He studied art for a year at East Sydney Technical College, then worked in the offices of Carlyle Greenwell (Sibyl Morrison's [q.v.10] husband) and Stephenson [q.v.12] & Meldrum [q.v.] while attending Sydney Technical College at night. Bunning helped to produce the architecture students' news-sheet, won the Kemp medal on qualifying in 1933 and became an associate of the college in 1936. Awarded a travelling scholarship by the Board of Architects of New South Wales, in 1937-39 he studied town planning at the Regent Street Polytechnic, London, travelled in Europe, and was employed by architects in London, Dublin and New York.

An associate (1938) of the Royal Institute of British Architects, Bunning returned to Sydney and helped to form the short-lived Modern Architectural Research Society. He was elected an associate (1939) of the Royal Australian Institute of Architects (councillor 1939-42 and fellow 1951). In 1940-42 he was chief draftsman with H. Ruskin Rowe. During World War II Bunnning worked as a specialist in camouflage, served as executive officer (1943-45) on the Commonwealth Housing Commission and wrote much of its influential 1944 report. On 13 April that year at the district registrar's office, Paddington, he married a divorcee Audrey Gillian Carington-Walters, née Edkins; they were to remain childless. In 1945 he was appointed town planner under a Commonwealth scheme to redevelop the munitions plant at St Marys as factories.

A tireless writer of articles on the future of housing and town planning, Bunning believed that buildings should be designed to suit the Australian environment. He elaborated his view in *Homes in the Sun* (1945). According to Robin Boyd [q.v.], the book established Bunning as 'the best known architectural publicist in the country'. In 1945 Bunning established a practice in Sydney and twelve months later took C. A. Madden into partnership. Kevin Smith and Noel Potter joined Bunning & Mad-

den in 1960, and Arthur Robb did so in 1969. The firm designed many public buildings in Sydney and Canberra, and won the competition (1949) for Anzac House, Martin Place, Sydney. Opened in 1957 in College Street, Anzac House was one of Australia's first curtain-wall buildings and won the Royal Institute of British Architects' bronze medal (1958). The firm was awarded the Sir John Sulman [q.v.12] medal for Liner House, Bridge Street, in 1962. Bunning & Madden gained many government and university commissions, including Bruce Hall, Australian National University (1961), and International House, University of Sydney (1967), but learned in 1957 that it had failed in its bid to design the Sydney Opera House. Bunning became a staunch critic of Jørn Utzon and of the opera house's spiralling cost, claiming in 1966 that it would be a second-rate building 'from a functional point of view'.

Forthright in his criticisms, Bunning accused State governments of being too timid in town planning, and called for tougher controls over land and housing design. Like Boyd, he despised the detritus of suburban Australia and attacked the spread of television aerials, advertising hoardings and the destruction of trees. He abhorred the dull products of the State housing commissions, but approved 'the spontaneous outburst of gay homes' at seaside resorts. One of Bunning's most highly regarded buildings was his own split-level house in Ryrie Street, Mosman (1952), overlooking Quakers Hat Bay. The National Library of Australia (1968, design approved 1964), said to have been inspired by the Parthenon after his visit to Greece, remains Bunning's best-known building. As principal architect, he interested himself in all aspects of construction and furnishings, including the design of art works, and in 1965 visited France to arrange for the weaving of tapestries to hang in its foyer.

Bunning's most important contribution to postwar Australia was to stress that well-designed housing and town planning were inextricably linked. A large, calm, lumbering man, he spent much of his life working for government committees and professional boards for little or no payment. Chairman (1945-64) of the Town and Country Planning Advisory Committee, he chaired or served on inquiries into Paddington (1968), which recommended be declared a historical area, into the location of an Olympic Games complex (1972-73) and into the environment of the Myall Lakes (1974). As a founding member (1970-77) of the Sydney Cove Redevelopment Authority, he bore some responsibility for plans to build high-rise hotels and office blocks in the Rocks: this scheme was effectively modified by the 'Green Bans' campaign.

Fond of opera and ballet, Bunning also enjoyed playing the violin, painting, writing, tennis and golf. He lived at Bellevue Hill and at Mosman before moving to Potts Point, and belonged to the All Nations Club, Royal Sydney Yacht Squadron, Australian Golf Club, the Wine and Food Society, and the Commonwealth Club, Canberra. Among other positions, he was a member (from 1948) of the Arts Council of Australia, a trustee (1958) of the Art Gallery of New South Wales (president 1974-77), a fellow (1954) of the (Royal) Australian Planning Institute, a councillor (1971) of the University of New South Wales and a trustee of the Museum of Applied Arts and Sciences. He was appointed C.M.G. in 1975. Survived by his wife, he died of a cerebral tumour on 13 October 1977 at Eastern Suburbs Hospital and was cremated.

R. Boyd, *Australia's Home* (Melb, 1952); J. Yeomans, *The other Taj Mahal* (Lond, 1968); Bunning & Madden, *The Work of Bunning and Madden* (priv print, Syd, 1970); J. M. Freeland, *Architecture in Australia* (Syd, 1972); J. Taylor, *Australian Architecture since 1960* (Canb, 1990); *Architecture in Aust*, 66, Jan 1978, p 33; *Roy Aust Planning Inst J*, 16, Feb 1978, p 20; *SMH*, 28 Apr 1937, 31 Aug, 21 Dec 1948, 28 June 1953, 23, 26 Apr 1957, 15 May 1958, 28 Apr 1959, 12 May, 12 Dec 1962, 18 June 1964, 11 Mar 1966, 15 Oct 1977; H. de Berg, Walter Bunning (taped interview, 1971, NL); Bunning papers (NL); information from Mr J. Fisher, Cammeray, Syd.   PETER SPEARRITT

BURBIDGE, NANCY TYSON (1912-1977), botanist and conservationist, was born on 5 August 1912 at Cleckheaton, Yorkshire, England, only daughter of William Burbidge, clergyman, and his wife Mary Eleanor, née Simmonds. Appointed to the Anglican parish at Katanning, Western Australia, William brought his family to Australia in 1913. Eleanor opened a primary school at the rectory and in 1922 founded the Katanning (Kobeelya) Church of England Girls' School. Nancy was educated there, and at Bunbury High School and the University of Western Australia (B.Sc., 1937; M.Sc., 1945; D.Sc., 1961).

Awarded a prize by a group of shipping companies of a free passage to England, Burbidge spent eighteen months in 1939-40 at the Herbarium, Royal Botanic Gardens, Kew, during which she revised the Australian species of the genus *Enneapogon*. She returned to Perth and for the next three years studied the ecology and taxonomy of Western Australian plants. In 1943 she became assistant-agronomist at the Waite [q.v.6] Agricultural Research Institute, Adelaide, where she worked on regenerating native pasture in arid and semi-arid regions of South Australia. Appointed systematic botanist in the Council for Scientific and Industrial Research's division of plant industry, Canberra, she commenced duty on 11 October 1946. Her initial task was to provide an identification service, but she was soon organizing and expanding the division's plant collection and her position was changed to curator, Herbarium Australiense. As secretary (1948-52) of the systematic botany committee of the Australian and New Zealand Association for the Advancement of Science, she edited *Australasian Herbarium News* until her secondment in 1953 to be Australian botanical liaison officer at the Kew herbarium, London. There, she photographed and indexed type specimens of Australian plants before resuming her Canberra post in 1954.

The results of Burbidge's work were seen in a stream of journal articles, among them 'The Phytogeography of the Australian Region' which appeared in the *Australian Journal of Botany* in June 1960: this important monograph contributed to the award of her D.Sc. She published *The Plants of the Australian Capital Territory* (Canberra, 1963, with Max Gray); a *Dictionary of Australian Plant Genera* (Sydney, 1963); *Australian Grasses*, in three volumes (Sydney, 1966, 1968 and 1970); *Flora of the Australian Capital Territory* (Canberra, 1970, again with Max Gray); and she prepared the compilation *Plant Taxonomic Literature in Australian Libraries* (edited by A. McCusker, Sydney, 1978). Burbidge's *The Wattles of the Australian Capital Territory* (Canberra, 1961) and *The Gum Trees of the Australian Capital Territory* (Canberra, 1963) were intended for the general reader. She illustrated many of her publications with her own drawings. A competent administrator as well as a talented botanist, in 1967 she was promoted senior principal research scientist, Commonwealth Scientific and Industrial Research Organization. From July 1973 to March 1977 she directed the Flora of Australia project which was sponsored by the Australian Academy of Science.

Burbidge had been a founding member (1960) of the National Parks Association of the A.C.T. Her work as its secretary, committee member (for eleven years), president (for two terms) and leader of numerous weekend walks helped the N.P.A. to become the Territory's main conservation body. The series of drawings accompanying her 'Eyes or No Eyes' column in the *NPA Bulletin* were a charming feature of that periodical. Prominent in efforts to create protected areas, she lobbied for the establishment of the Tidbinbilla Fauna Reserve and the recreational area at Gibraltar Falls. She led the campaign which was eventually to result in the delineation of

Namadgi National Park. Burbidge's love of the bush was reflected in her encouragement of the publication, *Mountains Slopes and Plains*(Canberra, 1975), a composite work by N.P.A. members.

She was a long-time member of the Australian Federation of University Women and president (1959-61) of its Canberra association. As president (1957-58) and international secretary (1961-68) of the Pan-Pacific and South East Asia Women's Association, Burbidge supported a range of causes, including scholarships for Aboriginal women and moves to establish a women's hall of residence at the University of Papua New Guinea. The Royal Society of New South Wales awarded her the 1971 (W. B.) Clarke [q.v.3] medal for her achievements in taxonomic botany and ecology. Active in the Royal Society of Canberra, she was one of the initiators of the Australian Systematic Botany Society and in 1973 established the Committee of Heads of Australian Herbaria to co-ordinate projects and procedures. She was appointed A.M. in 1976.

As a student, Miss Burbidge had been conscientious and dedicated to the subject that was to be her life's work. In maturity she balanced a puckish sense of humour with a capacity for sudden anger over 'anything she considered to be unjust or shabby'. She died of carcinomatosis on 4 March 1977 in Woden Valley Hospital and was buried in Canberra cemetery. Her love of nature and her contribution to Australian botany are commemorated by an altar-frontal, showing banksias and honey-eaters, in St Michael's Anglican Church, Mount Pleasant, Perth, and by the Nancy T. Burbidge Memorial, an amphitheatre in the National Botanic Gardens, Canberra.

D. Popham (ed), *Reflections* (Perth, 1978); N. Stewart, *As I Remember Them* (Perth, 1987); Aust Federation of Univ Women (Syd), *Newsletter*, no 62, May 1977; *Brunonia*, 1, no 1, 24 Feb 1978; National Parks Assn of the ACT Inc, *NPA Bulletin*, 17, no 3, Mar 1980; *Canb Times*, 5, 9 Mar 1977, 10 Sept 1980; CSIRO Archives, Canb; information from Rev E. H. Burbidge, Mount Pleasant, Dr A. Burbidge, Wanneroo, Perth, and Mr M. Gray, Canb, ACT; personal information.

GEORGE M. CHIPPENDALE

BURGE, FRANK (1894-1958), Rugby League footballer and council cleaner, was born on 14 August 1894 at Darlington, Sydney, sixth of eight surviving children of native-born parents Peter Burg, carrier, and his wife Emily Rosina, née Pickering. Educated at Darlington Public School, Frank played for the South Sydney Football Club with his siblings Peter (1884-1956) and Albert ('Son') (1888-1943) who were to become Rugby internationals. The brothers later joined Glebe. At 14 Frank entered second grade as centre. One Saturday he played an extra game, as a winger, and became the youngest to appear in a first-grade match in either Rugby code. A forward in Glebe's first-grade Rugby League side in 1911, he reputedly missed selection in the Kangaroo team to tour Britain because the selectors thought him too young to take on the tough English forwards.

In 1912 Burge made the State side: he scored three tries in a match against Queensland and toured New Zealand. A member of State teams against Queensland in 1913-15, 1919-21 and 1926, he played in all three Tests against England in 1914. Next year he tried to enlist in the Australian Imperial Force, but was rejected due to a speech impediment. He represented Australia against New Zealand in 1919 and reached his peak on the 1921 Kangaroo tour of England, scoring 33 tries in 23 games. One of the code's greatest scoring forwards and an accurate goal-kicker, he had an uncanny power to anticipate passes and, being 'big and powerful and very fast', was able to streak 'with bull-like resolution to the white line'. His pet move was to dash from the scrum and take a reverse pass from the half-back before the opposition could stop him.

Known as 'Chunky' or 'Mr Elegance', Frank was a fitness fanatic who went for long training-runs, occasionally with (Sir) William McKell. Between 1911 and 1922 Burge played 149 games for Glebe, and returned in July 1923 for his 150th match and a testimonial, a guaranteed minimum of £100. He coached (1923-25) at Grenfell before turning out in third grade for Glebe in 1926. That year he was appointed captain of New South Wales in the hope of restoring the State to football supremacy. He played his last season in 1927, as captain-coach of St George.

In the 1930s Burge coached St George, Newtown, Canterbury, Western Suburbs and North Sydney; he developed many notable players, but never a team that won a first-grade premiership. A labourer for most of his life, after World War II he worked as a Sydney County Council cleaner, and sometimes as a commentator and correspondent. On 9 June 1948 he married 51-year-old Millie Gladys Dyson at the district registrar's office, Rockdale. A life member of the New South Wales Rugby League, in 1950 Burge was the third league player to be elected to honorary membership of the Sydney Cricket Ground. He collapsed after watching a North Sydney-Newtown match and died of heart disease on 5 July 1958 at Marrickville. Survived by his wife, he was cremated with Anglican rites.

G. Greenwood (ed), *Australian Rugby League's Greatest Players* (Syd, 1978); G. Lester, *The Story of Australian Rugby League* (Syd, 1988); *Redcap, Qld Rugby League Annual*, 1927; *SMH*, 21 Sept 1950, 7 July 1958; *Sun-Herald*, 6 July 1958; information from Mr M. Solling, Glebe, Syd.

KRISTINE CORCORAN

BURGMANN, ERNEST HENRY (1885-1967), Anglican bishop and social critic, was born on 9 May 1885 at Lansdowne, near Taree, New South Wales, third child of Henry Burgman(n), bushman, and his wife Mary Ann Philomena, née Flick, both native-born. The son of a German-immigrant cooper, Henry worked a small selection in the district's heavily timbered country. Ernest remembered an adventurous childhood within a close and secure family atmosphere. He was educated at Koppin Yarratt Public School (to 1898) and for a year at Cleveland Street Superior Public School, Sydney.

The Church of England offered Burgmann a way out of the narrow world of timber-getting and dairying. His Christian faith developed in an untroubled fashion, nurtured by his parents and by the muscular example of pioneer Anglican clergy. Studying part time and cutting logs for a living, he gained his licentiate (1907) from the Australian College of Theology. In 1908 he went back to school at Taree to matriculate and next year entered St Paul's College, University of Sydney (B.A., 1912; M.A., 1914). He was ordained priest on 18 October 1912. A short stay in London in 1914-15 as curate at South Wimbledon confronted him with conflicting attitudes towards war and brought him into contact with schools of Anglican theology that ranged from tractarianism to modernism. Burgmann returned to a rectorship at Wyong on the central coast of New South Wales. On 8 February 1916 in the Church of St Peter, Neutral Bay, Sydney, he married 20-year-old Edna Carey Crowhurst whom he had prepared for confirmation.

After twelve months as travelling secretary for the Australian Board of Missions, in 1918 Burgmann was appointed warden of St John's College, Armidale. He soon established a reputation as an inspiring director of ordinands, a witty teacher and a wide-ranging thinker. G. V. Portus [q.v.11] secured Burgmann's services for the Workers' Educational Association where he became a successful instructor in psychology and social issues. Largely at his instigation, St John's was transferred to Morpeth, near Newcastle. There, from 1925, he filled a niche as a social activist. During the Depression he supported the unemployed and the evicted, and wrote for newspapers and magazines on the Church's

responsibility for the welfare of the nation. He tried to rouse Anglicans to ally themselves with the working class in a peaceful effort to transform the capitalist system and to be in a position to mediate in the event of revolution.

With Roy Lee, his vice-warden at St John's, Burgmann endeavoured to sharpen pastoral training by imbuing priests with a sense of national vision and by adding an intellectual edge to their capacities. He was a major and continuing influence on a generation of clergymen who passed through the college. Burgmann, Lee and A. P. Elkin [q.v.] founded the *Morpeth Review*, a quarterly designed for those 'on the borderland of institutional religion'; it featured articles by prominent commentators on economics, anthropology, religion and current affairs. Described as 'one of the most interesting might-have-beens' in Australian periodical literature, the *Review* ceased in 1934 when Burgmann was called to be bishop of Goulburn (Canberra and Goulburn from 1950). He was consecrated in Christ Church Cathedral, Newcastle, on 1 May and enthroned in St Saviour's Cathedral, Goulburn, three days later.

Burgmann's appointment surprised many, himself included, and quickly became part of the growing mythology that he was a prophetic figure who was destined to be at the centre of religious and secular life. Although incorporating the fledgling national capital, Goulburn was a conservative country diocese. Burgmann was obliged to spend most of his time in rehabilitating it from the effects of the Depression. Yet, he refused to abdicate the role of social and church critic. He maintained his interest in working-class struggles and took up rural issues, such as soil erosion and hydro-electric power. His monthly letters to the diocesan paper, *Southern Churchman*, became national news. Energetically improving his 'team', he promoted university and continuing education for the clergy, and sought well-trained men and women for posts in the diocese: his episcopal colleagues accused him of 'sheep-stealing'.

World War II catapulted Burgmann into new prominence as president of the Australia-Soviet Friendship League. He was criticized by conservatives for his support of the Russian alliance and for his endorsement of the Federal Labor government's reconstruction strategies. Though he never joined a political party, his heart and head were always with Labor. He admired John Curtin and J. B. Chifley [qq.v.], and forged a mutually respectful friendship with H. V. Evatt [q.v.] who appointed him to the Australian delegation at the 1948 United Nations Assembly in Paris. Burgmann was active in the campaign against (Sir) Robert Menzies' [q.v.] attempt in 1951 to ban the Communist Party of Australia. In

1956 Burgmann was again dogged by controversy when he and the Catholic bishop Eris O'Brien [q.v.] accepted the Commonwealth's offer to subsidize interest payments on loans raised to erect church schools in Canberra.

Burgmann's great obsession was the building of a collegiate library in Canberra—founded on the lines of that in Westminster Abbey, London—to stimulate advanced theological research by postgraduates. He aimed to provide a setting wherein a distinctive Australian theology might develop. St Mark's Anglican Memorial Library opened in 1957, but insufficient funds prevented it from developing beyond a useful addition to the Church's scholarly resources. Burgmann's own theology and churchmanship were in the broad tradition of Anglicanism, although his emphasis on the church as a goad of the state in the pursuit of social justice remained a minority view. Admitting to being comfortable within the boundaries set by the London symposium on liberal Catholicism (*Essays Catholic and Critical*, 1926), he was a sacramentalist who acknowledged the power of God in creation, while also being committed to the pursuit of a truth 'no longer fenced on any side'. He steered a middle way for his varied clergy and lay adherents, and provided refuge for some who had experienced religious intolerance.

From about the age of 30 Burgmann wrote prolifically, mainly essays and booklets on social reform, together with interpretations of scripture which were informed by imaginative historical insight. His scholarship was broad rather than deep, and was conveyed in sharp, intelligible prose. A gifted story-teller, he regretted that he did not have time to develop his academic leanings. In 1944 he published his autobiographical tract, *The Education of an Australian* (Sydney), which celebrated his bush upbringing and explored his drive for learning. Burgmann retired in 1960. Awarded an honorary Th.D. by the Australian College of Theology, he was appointed C.M.G. in 1961. For three years as warden he nursed St Mark's until compelled by ill health to stop. He died on 14 March 1967 in Canberra and was cremated; his wife, two sons and three daughters survived him. Burgmann's many admirers tenaciously cling to the legend of the 'bushman bishop'.

R. T. Wyatt, *The History of the Diocese of Goulburn* (Syd, 1937); A. P. Elkin, *The Diocese of Newcastle* (Syd, 1955); *St Mark's Review* (Canb), no 50, Nov 1967; *Colloquium*, 9, no 1, Oct 1976, p 36, no 2, May 1977, p 7; P. J. Hempenstall, '"This Turbulent Priest": E. H. Burgmann During the Great Depression', *Aust J of Politics and Hist*, 27, no 3, 1981, p 330; Burgmann papers (NL).

PETER HEMPENSTALL

BURHOP, ERIC HENRY STONELEY (1911-1980), physicist, was born on 31 January 1911 in Hobart, third child of Henry Augustus Burhop and his wife Bertha, née Head, both Salvation Army officers. His parents' evangelistic duties resulted in the family moving frequently during Eric's early years. He attended Ballarat and Melbourne high schools, and won a scholarship to the University of Melbourne (B.Sc., 1931; B.A., 1932; M.Sc., 1933). After completing his undergraduate degrees with first-class honours, he undertook a master's degree in natural philosophy. His thesis involved a critical survey of the new, quantum mechanical theory of the production of band spectra from diatomic molecules, together with a difficult but successful experimental study of the probability of ionizing atoms and generating X-rays by electron impact. Burhop was awarded an 1851 Exhibition scholarship and went to the University of Cambridge to work in the Cavendish Laboratory under Lord Rutherford.

At Cambridge the investigation of the atomic nucleus was entering a new era. In 1932 one of two new, fundamental particles discovered in that year, the neutron, had been found by researchers at the Cavendish and the first artificial nuclear disintegration had also been carried out there. Burhop was assigned an experimental project on deuteron-deuteron disintegrations that linked closely with research that Rutherford himself had been doing in collaboration with the Australian (Sir) Mark Oliphant who became Burhop's supervisor. At the same time and place, Burhop also collaborated with another Melbourne graduate (Sir) Harrie Massey in extending the approach to quantum theory developed by the Cambridge theorist P. A. M. Dirac to analyse the inner-shell ionization of atoms. This research linked in with Burhop's previous work on X-rays and also led him to consider the related phenomenon of radiationless emission of electrons, the so-called Auger effect, on which he subsequently became a leading authority.

Actively involved in the intense, left-wing political discussions that were then a feature of Cambridge life, Burhop thereafter devoted considerable time to promoting socialist ideals, being particularly concerned with the role and responsibility of the scientist in society. The Australian security service was to open a file on him; in 1948 his application for the chair of physics at the University of Adelaide was rejected, allegedly on account of his political views; and in 1951 British authorities briefly impounded his passport before backing down in the face of the ensuing publicity.

In 1936 Burhop had returned to Melbourne. On 23 December that year at Thornbury he married Winifred Ida Stevens with Salvation Army forms. He took up a lectureship at the University of Melbourne where Professor T. H. Laby [q.v.9] was anxious to see work in nuclear physics introduced into his department. Using apparatus he had brought with him from England, Burhop established Australia's first research programme in this area. The early fruits of his work were incorporated into his Cambridge Ph.D. (1938), completed in Melbourne under Laby's supervision. In mid-1939 Burhop successfully commissioned a 300-kev accelerator producing a homogeneous neutron beam that was intended to underpin future work by his group. He also continued, by correspondence, his collaboration with Massey on the theory of ionization of atoms. In addition to contributing lectures on modern physics to the department's undergraduate teaching programme, he offered special courses on quantum mechanics for postgraduates.

With the outbreak of World War II Burhop worked on the production of optical munitions for the Australian armed services. In 1942 he transferred to the Radiophysics Laboratory in Sydney where he joined a group investigating the production of resonant cavity magnetrons. He later returned with (Sir) Leslie Martin to the University of Melbourne and helped Oliphant, who was visiting Australia, to set up a pilot plant to produce magnetrons and klystrons for use in Australian-made radar equipment. In May 1944 Burhop went to the United States of America to join the Manhattan Project for the development of the atomic bomb. He joined the British group led by Massey, and worked at Berkeley, California, and Oak Ridge, Tennessee, on the separation of uranium isotopes by electromagnetic means. With David Bohm and others, he carried out theoretical analyses of the atomic collision processes involved.

After the war, Burhop became lecturer in mathematics in Massey's department at University College, London. He was promoted to reader in 1949. When Massey transferred to the department of physics, Burhop went with him. He was professor of physics by conferment of title in 1960-78.

In his postwar research Burhop further extended his work on atomic collisions, co-authoring with Massey the well-known treatise, *Electronic and Ionic Impact Phenomena* (1952). He devoted most of his energy, however, to investigating the nucleus and the subnuclear realm. In 1957, with C. F. Powell and G. P. S. Occhialini, he established the long-running European K-meson collaboration, which used large nuclear-emulsion stacks to study the interactions with nuclei of K-mesons produced by high-energy accelerators. He was involved in several other large-scale, international collaborations. At the European Centre for Nuclear Research (C.E.R.N.), near Geneva, Switzerland, he served as secretary (1962-63) of a committee to advise on future European accelerator developments and drafted its highly influential Amaldi Report. In a collaboration at C.E.R.N. in 1973, his University College bubble-chamber group discovered the so-called neutral currents in weak interactions, an important step towards the subsequent unified theory of weak and electromagnetic forces. In 1975-76 Burhop led two major experiments, one at Fermilab in the U.S.A., the other at C.E.R.N., using a combination of emulsion with spark chamber or bubble chamber to detect short-lived, charmed particles produced in neutrino interactions in the emulsion. The results were important theoretically and the technique was widely imitated.

A foundation member (1939) of the Australian Association of Scientific Workers, Burhop was concerned to see that the vast, new power that had been unleashed in 1945 was not misused. He helped to establish the British Atomic Scientists Association and was in demand as a public speaker on the subject of atomic energy. In the mid-1950s he played an important role in the negotiations between Frédéric Joliot-Curie and Bertrand Russell, which led to the founding of the Pugwash conferences, held in Nova Scotia, Canada. He was elected a fellow (1963) of the Royal Society, London, and was its Rutherford memorial lecturer in 1979. A founder (1969) of the British Society for Social Responsibility in Science and president (1971-80) of the World Federation of Scientific Workers, he was awarded the Joliot-Curie medal of the World Peace Council in 1966, the Lenin International Prize for Peace in 1972, and Bulgaria's Order of Cyril and Methodius in 1973.

Tall and well made, with a strong sense of compassion, Burhop was good at dealing with people, and at organization and administration. He was a prodigiously hard worker, but also a devoted family man. Survived by his wife, daughter and two sons, he died of empyema complicating stomach cancer on 22 January 1980 at Camden, London.

Aust Left Review, Mar 1980, p 47; *Biog Memoirs of Fellows of Roy Soc*, 27, 1981, p 131; *The Times*, 24 Jan 1980; H. de Berg, Eric Burhop (taped interview, 1970, NL); Burhop ASIO file, A6119, item XR1/50 (AA); Burhop appointments file (Univ College, Lond).   R. W. HOME

BURKE, ERIC KEAST (1896-1974), photographer and journalist, was born on 16 January 1896 at Christchurch, New Zealand, only child of Walter Ernest Burke, clerk, and his wife Amy Eliza Mary, née Thompson, both New Zealanders. The family moved to Sydney in March 1904. Keast was educated at Sydney Church of England Grammar School (Shore) and enrolled at the University of Sydney (B.Ec., 1922). After a year in the Signal Corps, Australian Military Forces, on 19 February 1917 he enlisted in the Australian Imperial Force. Embarking for the Middle East in December, he served as a sapper with the Anzac Wireless Squadron, Mesopotamian Expeditionary Force. The unit operated at Baghdad, and in the field in Persia and on the Kurdistan frontier until November 1919. Burke gained an abiding interest in architecture and archeology. He enjoyed the 'grand fellowship' of army life and was to edit the unit history, 'the memory book of our great adventure', *With Horse and Morse in Mesopotamia* (1927).

Returning to Sydney, Burke was discharged on 28 January 1920. He became associate-editor under his father of the *Australasian Photo-Review*, published by Kodak (Australasia) Ltd. At the Shore chapel on 23 November 1925 he married Iris Lily Daniell. In 1932 he published *Achievement*, a photographic study of the Sydney Harbour Bridge, 'our challenge to Cheops'. Burke exhibited his work in Australia, Europe, London and the United States of America, and was elected an associate of the Royal Photographic Society of Great Britain in 1938 for a portfolio of male figure studies. That year he was appointed Australian chairman of Kodak International salons of photography. During World War II he served as a captain in the Volunteer Defence Corps, worked in intelligence and acted as a 'nightspotter'. He edited *APR* from 1946 until the journal folded in 1956 and was subsequently employed as Kodak's advertising manager.

Recognizing the significance of photography to Australian history, in 1943 Burke had published a series of articles on early photographers, among them W. S. Jevons, J. W. Lindt and C. H. Kerry [qq.v.4,5,9]. Iris became his valued research assistant. In 1953 he found Otto Holtermann's [q.v.4] collection of Beaufoy Merlin's and Charles Bayliss's glass plates, 'neatly stored in fitted cedar boxes' in 'a small suburban backyard shed', a discovery he emotionally compared with that of Tutenkhamon's tomb. The negatives disclosed 'every detail of the lives of our goldfields pioneers'; Burke reprinted a selection in *APR* that year and later published an expanded study, *Gold and Silver* (1973). He lectured on the collection, prepared exhibitions and presented a television series, 'Peeps into the Past with Keast Burke', for the Australian Broadcasting Commission. As consultant in photography to the National Library of Australia, Canberra, he ensured the preservation of historic photographs.

Following his retirement in 1960, Burke was editor and art director of *Australian Popular Photography* in 1961-69, a contributor to the *Australian Dictionary of Biography* and a frequent judge of photographic competitions. He was a man of enormous enthusiasms, with interests as diverse as bushwalking, native flora and fauna, genetics, maps and map-making, amateur radio, architecture and engineering. A member of the Book Collectors' Society of Australia, in 1963 he founded the short-lived Australian Documentary Facsimile Society. Survived by his wife, daughter and three sons, he died on 31 March 1974 in Concord Repatriation General Hospital and was cremated. Collections of his work are held in major Australian galleries and libraries.

Aust Photographer, May 1974, p 20; *Aust Author*, July 1974; *Biblionews*, Mar 1984, p 4; *SMH*, 3 Apr 1974; Keast Burke papers (NL); information from and family papers held by Mrs I. Burke, Syd, and Mrs S. Pigott, Perth.   KIMBERLEY WEBBER

BURKE, JAMES WALLACE (1930-1979), cricketer and stockbroker, was born on 12 June 1930 at Mosman, Sydney, second son of Frank James Burke, motor engineer, and his wife Madge, née Easton, both English born. Madge was a notable club golfer who passed on her skill and love for the game to Jim. He made his mark as a cricketer at Sydney Grammar School (1945-47) and with the Manly club's senior XI when he was only 15.

A right-hand batsman, Burke first played for New South Wales against Western Australia in December 1948, making 76 not out. He was selected for Australia in 1951 for the fourth Test against England at Adelaide and scored 101 not out in the second innings. Dropped after only one Test against the West Indies in their 1951-52 tour of Australia, he worked as a stockbroker's clerk and married Barbara Phyllis Hogbin on 1 May 1952 at St Andrew's Anglican Church, Wahroonga. Omitted from the State side in 1954, Burke adopted a stodgy batting style that annoyed spectators, but got him back into the Test team in 1954-55 after a season in England in the Lancashire Cricket League.

He was chosen for the 1956 tour of England where his dour batting gained him top position in both the tour and Test averages, and inclusion as one of Wisden's 'Five Cricketers of the Year'. By now a fixture in the Australian side, Burke made the then slowest Test century ever recorded by an Australian, 161 against India at Bombay in October 1956, the first hundred taking 368 minutes. At Cape Town on 1 January 1958 in extreme heat he completed 189 in 578 minutes. He broke a rib on this tour and retired, aged 28, after moderate performances against Peter May's England team of 1958-59.

Burke had played 24 Tests (14 against England) and scored 1280 runs at 34.59, including three centuries; in first-class cricket he made 7563 runs at 45, with twenty-one centuries and a top score of 220. His suspiciously flicked off-breaks brought him 8 Test and 101 first-class wickets, both at 29. He took 59 catches. No great stylist, especially once his batting became so determinedly costive, he nevertheless helped Australian cricket through the depressed mid-1950s to its revival against May's side. A touch under six feet (182.9 cm) tall and slimly built, he wore his cap slightly askew (somewhat like his backlift); his presence at the wicket, particularly overseas, gave Australian batting an assurance sadly lacking at other times.

His value, again particularly on tour, was enhanced by his off-field talents as a boogie-woogie pianist, humorist, singer and mimic. After retiring from cricket he became a businessman and a part-time Australian Broadcasting Commission cricket commentator. Divorced in August 1967, he married 26-year-old Judith Anne Cameron on 4 September at the registrar general's office, Sydney. Burke managed the Sydney office of the Melbourne stockbroking firm, Vinton, Smith, Dougall & Co., and was elected to the Stock Exchange of Melbourne in 1976. Depressed by marital problems, by ill health and by the loss of some $153 000 in a 'disastrous gamble on the gold futures market', he shot himself in the heart on 2 February 1979 in the grounds of St Patrick's College, Manly. Following an inquest, he was cremated. His wife survived him, as did the two daughters and two sons of his first marriage.

J. Pollard, *Australian Cricket* (Syd, 1982); D. Frith, *By His Own Hand* (Syd, 1991); *Wisden Cricketers' Almanack*, 1957, 1980; *People* (Syd), 21 Mar 1958; *Sun* (Syd), 12 Oct 1959, 13 June 1979; *Herald* (Melb), 3 Feb, 12 June 1979; *Age* (Melb), 5 Feb 1979; *National Times*, 17 Feb 1979; *Daily Mirror* (Syd), 24 Aug 1979.   W. F. MANDLE

BURKE, PHYLLIS LE CAPPELAINE (1900-1969), social reformer and housing commissioner, was born on 27 January 1900 at Maldon, Essex, England, daughter of John Le Cappelaine Taylor, innkeeper, and his wife Bridget Emily, née Dooley. Phyllis came with the family to Sydney as an infant and was educated at Monte Sant' Angelo convent, North Sydney. She enrolled at the University of Sydney (B.Ec., 1922) and became a schoolteacher. On 31 July 1922 she married a mercer John Murray Burke at St Patrick's Catholic Church, Sydney; she bore him four sons and five daughters between 1924 and 1943.

Mrs Burke undertook extensive political and commercial surveys on market conditions for various firms. In the early 1940s she was an active member of the Legion of Catholic Women and in 1942 was appointed by the Commonwealth government as woman organizer for the War Savings Campaign in New South Wales. Concerned at the dangers to young women from the influx of servicemen during World War II, she campaigned for the eradication of venereal diseases. Like many feminists of the time, she put a deal of energy into the cause of the fledgling United Nations, running the local publicity for its relief and rehabilitation appeal in 1946 and its appeal for children in 1947.

An excellent public relations officer who had a personable manner, tenacity, efficiency and wide social contacts, she also worked for the Australian Red Cross Society, the Smith Family, the New South Wales Society for Crippled Children and the Royal Blind Society. She was active in educated women's circles in Sydney, among them the National Council of Women of New South Wales. Although she was not a member of the United Associations of Women led by Jessie Street [q.v.]—she was wary of Street's support for the Soviet Union—Burke attended their lunchtime meetings and wrote on housing issues for the *Australian Women's Digest*.

Deeply religious, she supported an independent and politically-aware role for women. Despite Archbishop (Cardinal Sir) Norman Gilroy's [q.v.] disapproval, in 1943 Burke formed the Altair group of educated lay Catholic women which included Mary Tenison Woods [q.v.12] and Jean Daly. While calling for government support for larger families, she argued that motherhood and public service were not incompatible. The members of Altair formed a Sydney branch of the St Joan Social and Political Alliance in October 1946; Burke was a committee-member. She promoted the employment of women by government bodies and was appointed to the Housing Commission of New South Wales in 1945. Respected by her colleagues, she stressed the 'feminine viewpoint on the home', and used her influence to sponsor the introduction of modern design and layout in public housing in an attempt to reduce the burden of housework. She retired in 1965; the commission named a block of flats at Artarmon after her in 1968.

Considering herself to be a professional, Burke retained membership of the Economics Society of Australia and New Zealand, and of the Sydney University Women Graduates' Association; from 1954 she was a member of the Australian Broadcasting Commission's advisory committee on women's sessions. She belonged to the Business and Professional Women's Club of Sydney, the Soroptimist, and the Stage and Society clubs, and enjoyed reading, swimming and amateur theatricals. An impressive figure, Phyllis Burke was assertive, direct and confident of her abilities. Survived by her husband and nine children, she died on 20 August 1969 in the Prince of Wales Hospital, Randwick, and was buried in Waverley cemetery.

S. Kennedy, *Faith and Feminism* (Syd, 1985); H. Carey, *Truly Feminine, Truly Catholic* (Syd, 1987); *SMH*, 14 Aug 1942, 9 Feb 1965, 10 Aug 1968; *Sun* (Syd), 15 Feb 1945; Dept of Housing (NSW) Archives.   CAROLYN ALLPORT

BURKE, THOMAS PATRICK (1910-1973), politician, was born on 28 August 1910 at Berkshire Valley, near Moora, Western Australia, and registered as Frederick Thomas, third son of Peter Francis Burke, farmer, and his wife Catherine Mary, née Kelly, both native-born. Tom was to change his given names by licence to Thomas Patrick in 1963. Educated by correspondence and at Miling State School, from 1929 he lived with his parents in Perth where he worked for his father as a cartage contractor, delivering fruit and vegetables to the metropolitan markets. He found time to study accountancy at City Commercial College, achieving excellent results, and to follow a family tradition of labour politics. In 1937 he contested the Federal seat of Perth and later became a prominent Australian Labor Party organizer. On 4 January 1941, as Patrick Thomas, he married a dressmaker Madeline Muirson Orr at St Joseph's Catholic Church, Subiaco.

Enlisting in the Royal Australian Air Force on 16 January 1943, Burke served with the ground staff at Kalgoorlie. On 11 October he transferred to the Reserve, after winning Perth in the August elections for the House of Representatives. Regarded as a rising young man, he dreamed of serving as Federal treasurer in a government led by his State colleague Kim Beazley, but had not attained cabinet rank when Labor went into opposition in 1949. Despite his almost filial regard for J. B. Chifley [q.v.], Burke persuaded the Western Australian executive to support the 1950 Communist Party dissolution bill. To Chifley's chagrin, the resultant majority in the federal executive instructed caucus to let the bill through.

Burke's strong anti-communism also led him to oppose H. V. Evatt [q.v.] as party leader. In August 1954 he stood against Evatt. Defeated by 68 votes to 20, in October Burke tried unsuccessfully to initiate another ballot. At the federal conference in Hobart in March 1955 he was one of the Western Australian delegates who defied the State executive's instructions to take a pro-Evatt stand; F. E. Chamberlain, State secretary and federal president of the A.L.P., remembered Burke's personal abuse and 'venomous hatred'. With Beazley and others, Burke was banned for three years from representing his State at federal conferences. Contrary to expectations, he did not join the breakaway Anti-Communist (Democratic) Labor Party. At the 1955 election he lost his seat to a Liberal, (Sir) Frederick Chaney.

For continuing to criticize Evatt, in 1957 Burke was expelled from the A.L.P. Despite Chamberlain's opposition, he regained his membership in 1964 and unavailingly sought pre-selection for his former seat in 1965 and 1968. In Burke's later years his energies went into promoting his sons' careers in State politics. Terry, the eldest, was to be member for Perth (1968-87); the second son Brian won Balcatta at a by-election in 1973 and was premier in 1983-88.

Although a vehement controversialist, Tom had considerable charm and was devoted to his family. He was a staunch Catholic whose political career foundered on his attempt to reconcile his religious beliefs with his Labor loyalties. A heavy smoker, he died of myocardial infarction on 17 January 1973 in Perth and was buried in Karrakatta cemetery. His wife, three sons and two daughters survived him.

L. F. Crisp, *Ben Chifley* (Melb, 1961); K. Tennant, *Evatt* (Syd, 1970); J. Hamilton, *Burkie* (Perth, 1988); B. Peachey, *The Burkes of Western Australia* (Perth, 1992); *West Australian*, 23 Oct 1957, 18 Jan 1973.   G. C. BOLTON

BURKE-GAFFNEY, THOMAS NOEL (1893-1958), Jesuit priest, seismologist and astronomer, was born on 26 December 1893 at 9 Rathdown Terrace, Dublin, fourth son of Thomas Burke Gaffney, valuer, and his wife Jenny, née O'Donnell. Educated in 1901-12 at Belvedere College, Dublin, Noel entered the Jesuit novitiate at Tullabeg on 17 February 1913. He attended science lectures at the National University of Ireland in 1915-16 and in 1917-19 studied philosophy at Jersey, Channel Islands, and at Milltown Park, Dublin. After teaching at St Francis Xavier's College, Melbourne, in 1921, and at St Ignatius' College, Riverview, Sydney, in 1922-23, he returned to Ireland to complete his theology studies at Milltown Park where he was ordained priest on 31 July 1926.

In September 1928 he returned to Riverview where he taught science until becoming assistant-director of Riverview College

Observatory in 1946 (director from 1952). Although Burke-Gaffney was a dedicated and unorthodox teacher of physics who used ingenious devices like his 'gaffoscope' to illustrate degaussing, he was a poor disciplinarian in the classroom, 'too gentle for the boys of Riverview'. Nevertheless, he was loved by his pupils and famed for his little zoo of native animals—his 'gafferoos' as he called them—which delighted a loyal and devoted following of country boys. He possessed 'an uncanny ability to tame wild creatures', and instilled into his boys the importance and nobility of the natural sciences.

A keen and devoted scientist, Burke-Gaffney published papers on the seismicity of Australia, on the detection of S waves in the Earth's inner core and on special phases from New Zealand earthquakes. His most notable contribution was four papers written with Professor K. E. Bullen [q.v.] on the seismic aspects of nuclear explosions, studies which attracted worldwide attention. Burke-Gaffney was the first to discover that nuclear explosions detonated at or near ground level showed up on seismographs. A council-member (1954-58) and vice-president (1957-58) of the Royal Society of New South Wales, he unstintingly helped many young seismologists and did valuable work as secretary-convenor of the sub-committee on seismology of the Australian national committee for the International Geophysical Year (1957-58).

Father Burke-Gaffney also carried out extensive work on variable stars. A man of great faith, he found it hard to understand how an astronomer could ever be an atheist: 'Astronomy', he said, 'constantly impresses you with the majesty of the Almighty, and the regularity of its laws presupposes the Lawgiver'.

Slightly built and somewhat self-effacing, Burke-Gaffney lived quietly and austerely. Few outside his college friends and scientific colleagues got to know him well, but those who did found him 'a charming and liberal-minded man, graced with a gentle dignity and a delightful humour'. Revered as an outstanding community member, he was truly—*vir Deo deditus et veritati* (a man dedicated to God and to the truth). He died of Hodgkin's disease on 14 September 1958 in Lewisham hospital and was buried in Gore Hill cemetery.

E. Lea-Scarlett, *Riverview* (Syd, 1989); St Ignatius College, Riverview (Syd), *Our Alma Mater*, 1952, 1957, 1958; *Nature* (Lond), 15 Nov 1958, p 1343; *Aust J of Science*, 21, 1958, p 133; Roy Astronomical Soc, *Mthly Notice*, 119, 1959, p 344; Roy Soc NSW, *J*, 93, 1959, p 86; *Belvederian* (Dublin), 1959; *SMH*, 16 Oct 1948, 9 Sept, 4 Oct 1952, 25 Apr 1953, 4 Mar 1954, 8 June, 3 July, 19 Sept 1957, 15 Sept 1958; information from Mr E. Lea-Scarlett, Riverview College, Syd, and Fr S. Redmond, SJ, Dublin.   G. P. WALSH

BURKITT, ARTHUR NEVILLE ST GEORGE HANDCOCK (1891-1959), professor of anatomy, was born on 25 March 1891 at Goulburn, New South Wales, son of Irish-born William Arthur Handcock Burkitt, medical practitioner and pastoralist, and his wife Edith Kathleen Rose, née Ussher, from England. Educated at King's College, Goulburn, Arthur was influenced by his reading of natural history and by his experience of the bush. He enrolled in science and next in medicine at the University of Sydney (B.Sc., M.B., 1916), graduating with first-class honours in both.

Following a residency at Royal Prince Alfred Hospital in 1917, Burkitt was attracted to an academic career and accepted a part-time post as demonstrator in anatomy at the university. On 12 June 1918 at St James's Anglican Church, Sydney, he married a nurse Emily Hordern. Appointed surgeon lieutenant in the Royal Australian Navy on 1 July, he served at sea on the Australia Station. His appointment terminated on 1 October 1919 and he returned to the anatomy department as lecturer and demonstrator. In 1924 he studied at University College, London, on a Rockefeller grant; back in Sydney, he was promoted associate-professor next year. Following the death of his mentor J. I. Hunter [q.v.9], Burkitt became Challis [q.v.3] professor of anatomy in January 1926; he was to hold the post for almost thirty years. In 1930-31 and 1938 he studied the comparative anatomy of the brain at the Netherlands Central Institute for Brain Research, Amsterdam.

Burkitt's tenure of the chair was remembered by all who knew him with affection, often tinged with regret. The affection arose from Burkitt's personal qualities—his courtliness of manner, gentleness of character and diffidence—and from his professional enthusiasms—his love of books and scholarship, and his willingness to help others. It also stemmed from his private enthusiasms—for racing-cars (he owned five at one stage, among them the Bugatti in which W. B. Thompson [q.v.12] won the 1930 Australian Grand Prix, with Burkitt as riding mechanic), for private cars (he owned a large Daimler and a 6.7 hp Fiat) and for his yacht which he moored in Middle Harbour and made available to the R.A.N. in 1941-44.

The regret stemmed from Burkitt's inability to meet his early high promise in research. After a determined start, his scholarship was constrained by his shyness, as well as by the stringencies of the Depression and World War II which no professor could prevent from eroding the infrastructure of his department. It was further constrained by the flood of returned servicemen whose numbers stretched the weakened universities beyond reasonable limit, and then by Parkinson's disease which grew on him in the 1940s, was diagnosed in 1950 and forced him to resign in April 1955. Nevertheless, he published nineteen scholarly papers on neuroanatomy and human anthropology.

From the mid-1930s Burkitt had facilitated the scholarship of colleagues and students by building major collections of neuroanatomical material and scientific literature, and by personal encouragement. He arranged the appointment of J. L. Shellshear [q.v.] as research professor of anatomy (1937-48). Shellshear's work brought distinction to the department and his collection formed the nucleus in 1959 of a museum of comparative anatomy and physical anthropology. Burkitt used his own financial resources to bring together and make available a major collection of European scientific literature which provided the basis of the Burkitt Library in the faculty of medicine. He was fluent in several languages and assisted students by translating for them.

Survived by his wife and two sons, Burkitt died of cerebral vascular disease on 14 December 1959 at Mosman and was cremated. His estate was sworn for probate at £116 453. A sheep-station, Spring Ponds, near Bungonia, New South Wales, which he had inherited from his father, was bequeathed to his sons.

G. E. Hall and A. Cousins (eds), *Book of Remembrance of the University of Sydney in the War 1914-1918*(Syd, 1939); J. A. Young et al (eds), *Centenary Book of the University of Sydney Faculty of Medicine* (Syd, 1948); Univ Syd, *Gazette*, Apr 1960; *MJA*, 9 Apr 1960; *SMH*, 16 July 1924, 4 Nov 1925; *Argus*, 14 Dec 1938; *Herald*(Melb), 9 June 1960; Univ Syd Senate, Minutes, 10 June 1918, 2 Nov 1925, 6 Dec 1954, 16 Dec 1959 (Univ Syd Archives).

JONATHAN STONE

BURLEY, FRANK ARTHUR (1881-1957) and **FREDERICK RICHARD** (1885-1954), corset manufacturers, were born on 29 June 1881 at Richmond, Melbourne, and 29 May 1885 at Hamilton, Victoria, third and fifth children of London-born parents Joseph Walter Burley (d. 1891), fishmonger and commission agent, and his wife Isabel, née Gibson. Both grew up at Ballarat where their two aunts made and sold corsets; as boys, they often helped to scrape the whalebone used for stays. Educated at Urquhart Street State School, Arthur began his career in a grocery, worked in stores in New South Wales, then joined the Mutual Store Ltd, Melbourne. On 20 October 1908 he married Mabel Jane Makeig (d. 1950) with Presbyterian forms at Mosman, Sydney.

Fred attended state schools, began work in a paint store at 13 and in 1900 entered the Ballarat warehouse of Melbourne softgoods merchants, Brooks, McGlashan & McHarg. He studied at night-school and business college, and rose to be departmental manager in 1908. On 21 December that year at the registrar's office, Collingwood, he married a schoolteacher Mabel Jane Mobberley. In 1909 he was sent to the firm's new branch in Sydney where he became warehouse manager.

With capital lent by relations, in 1910 Fred bought a controlling interest in E. Gover & Co., a small, 'made-to-order' corset firm in Market Street. When Arthur joined him in 1912 they formed Unique Corsets Ltd. Next year Fred embarked on the first of many visits to study the corsetry business in Europe and the United States of America. Despite wartime shortages, the company's staff increased from 12 to 60 by 1917. That year Arthur coined the Frenchified tradename, 'Berlei', for a popular new product; in 1919 the firm formally became Berlei Ltd and was registered as a public company in October 1920. With the purchase of W. Zander & Co. that year, Berlei's staff grew to 280 and new machinery was installed for large-scale manufacturing. The firm had three times moved to larger premises before the Burleys bought land in Regent Street and in January 1922 opened Berlei House, seven storeys of offices and workrooms 'constructed on the daylight principle', with display theatre, elegant salesrooms, a library and a roof-top 'playground' for employees.

All stays and lacings at first, Berlei's products grew more varied as their female designers sought new ideas and fabrics overseas. In the *Berlei Review*, founded in 1922 as a trade journal, the brothers warned the willowy 'flapper' against lasting damage to 'muscles and vital organs', or 'excessive figure development in the middle years', and urged her to 'corset for the future'. The means to do so— the dainty 'Berlette' brassiere, light-weight 'Corselette' and wrap-on 'Dance Girdle'— were promoted in elaborate musical revues that toured the capital cities, advertising the entire Berlei range: 'Youth Triumphant' (1924), 'Radiant Woman—At Beauty's Shrine' (1926) and 'Lady Be Beautiful' (1929).

Branch offices were opened in Melbourne (1921), Brisbane (1923), Adelaide (1929) and Perth (1929), and a factory in Melbourne (1927). In 1923 Berlei took over a major competitor, Australian Corsets Ltd, and used its stocks to equip Berlei (New Zealand) Ltd at Auckland. Founding president that year of the 'Australian-Made' Preference League, Fred promoted its 'Great White Train'. Much of the Burleys' success stemmed from their commitment to produce garments of quality and perfect fit, and to render excellent service to customers. They held annual conventions for sales representatives, advised retailers on window display and ran regular training schools for corset-fitters. Insisting on a scientific approach, they employed a physician Dr Grace Boelke [q.v.] to ensure that Berlei garments were 'anatomically correct'.

In 1926 Fred enlisted physiologists at the University of Sydney to assist in an anthropometrical survey of Australian women: the aim was to identify basic figure types, so that ready-made corsets might be designed to fit as if made-to-order. Professor Henry Chapman [q.v.7] led the project. Some seven thousand women were measured in fine detail and the data revealed five fundamental types— big abdomen, heavy bust, big hips, sway back and average proportions. Berlei garments could now be designed and coded accordingly. Using an ingenious device, the Berlei Type Indicator, any corsetiere could compute in a trice the size to suit a client's measurements. Thirty years later the indicator was still a reliable guide to correct fittings.

In 1929 Fred founded Berlei (U.K.) Ltd, with offices in Regent Street, London, and a factory at Slough, Buckinghamshire. The Depression turned a costly venture into an 'uphill fight'. In 1933 Fred, governing director of the Berlei 'triad', took control and settled with his family in England, leaving Arthur as managing director of the Sydney firm. In Australia, Berlei responded to the slump with positive measures. The corset industry fared better than many, not least because feminine curves were back in fashion, moulded by the 'sensation of 1933'— two-way stretch elastic.

In Britain, where the best corsets had been French or American imports, Berlei had to train its own staff, but by 1935 its products were being sold in Paris and praised in *Vogue*. Wartime restrictions slashed Berlei's output and imposed 'utility' standards on the remainder. The factory at Slough was kept busy with government orders, ranging from butchers' aprons to bras and girdles for the women's services. When the government took over the workshops, production continued in the office block, albeit with a much-depleted staff, run from the Burley residence at nearby Denham. Fred joined the Home Guard.

In Australia, the war diminished Berlei's output: many skilled female machinists left to marry, imported materials grew scarce and by early 1942 most of the male staff had enlisted, including Arthur's son Edmund. The firm saw its foremost role as maintaining supplies of popular lines 'so that figure control and comfort may help our women to play their part'. As World War II progressed, Berlei made countless items for the armed services,

from khaki shorts to anti-flash masks. In 1947 Fred returned to Sydney; he and Arthur gradually withdrew from active management of the company. By 1950, with supply again matching demand, Berlei's annual sales in Australia alone exceeded £1 million.

Throughout their long partnership the brothers had complemented each other. Fred, a 'man of vision', dynamic and imaginative, took the lead with bold innovations. By contrast, Arthur was quiet and unassuming, 'accomplished in finance and organisation', the good manager, beloved of his staff, who supplied a prudent 'brake and guide' for Fred's initiative. Both were very tall; but where Fred was strong featured and bright of eye, Arthur had gentler looks and a reflective air.

Yet the two had much in common, in particular a commitment to community service. Arthur was treasurer of the Young Men's Christian Association and in 1934 presided over the Australian Institute of Industrial Psychology. Besides supporting many other worthy causes, both were Rotarians; Fred was Australian district governor (1931-32) for Rotary International and president (1941) of the London branch. Rotary's ideal of co-operative industrial relations governed all their dealings with staff. Their employees, who knew them as 'Mr Fred' and 'Mr Arthur', enjoyed a staff provident fund and a profit-sharing scheme. Personnel management was the province of Mr Arthur. An executive-member of the State branch from 1924, he served as Australasian president (1938-42) of the Australasian Institute of Secretaries and in 1947 became first president of the Australian division of the Chartered Institute of Secretaries, London.

The brothers enjoyed golf and motoring. Arthur was a member of the Australian Golf and Ashfield Bowling clubs; in London Fred belonged to the Royal Automobile Club and in Sydney to that of New South Wales. Fred Burley died of septicaemia on 26 May 1954 at Wahroonga and, after a Congregational service, was cremated; his wife, son, three daughters and adopted son survived him; his estate was sworn for probate at £51 914. Following his brother's death, Arthur became the firm's chairman of directors. Survived by two sons and two daughters, he died on 4 May 1957 at Grose Vale and was buried with Anglican rites in Rookwood cemetery. John Berrie's portrait (1949) of Fred hangs in the Berlei boardroom.

Souvenir of the 'Australian Made' Preference League and the Great White Exhibition Train (Syd, 1926); *Berlei Review*, 1922-42, Sept-Oct 1948, July-Sept 1950, Winter 1954, Spring 1957; *Newspaper News*, 1 Nov 1929, p 9; *Secretary* (Syd), July 1957, p 106; *SMH*, 20 Apr, 17 May 1934, 1 Feb

1945, 16 Aug 1947, 27 May 1954, 6 May 1957, 16 Oct 1982; Berlei Ltd papers (Museum of Applied Arts and Sciences, Powerhouse, Syd).

ANTHEA HYSLOP

BURNE, SIR LEWIS CHARLES (1898-1978), master builder and employer representative, was born on 14 January 1898 at Leederville, Perth, third child of William Charles Edgar Burne (d. 1945), a contractor from Victoria, and his English-born wife Sarah Ellen, née Prior. After nine years in Western Australia, William returned to Victoria with his family. In 1907 he established the building firm which in 1925 became W. C. Burne & Sons Pty Ltd. He served three terms as president of the Master Builders' Association of Melbourne.

Lewis was educated at Christian Brothers' School, Perth, and Xavier College, Melbourne (1907-14), where he performed better athletically (particularly in running) than academically. After Lewis had unsuccessfully attempted the junior public examination, William sent him to learn carpentry and joinery with Bowen & Pomeroy in North Melbourne. On 11 June 1918 he enlisted in the Australian Imperial Force and was attached to the Australian Flying Corps, at Laverton, with the rank of 2nd class mechanic. Discharged on 24 December, he joined his father's firm. On 22 February 1922 at the Church of Our Lady of Victories, Camberwell, he married Florence (Florrie) Mary Stafford.

W. C. Burne & Sons specialized in hospital construction, working to designs by such architects as (Sir) Arthur Stephenson [q.v.12], Ellison Harvie and J. S. Gawler [q.v.]. The firm built St Vincent's, the Mercy, the Prince Henry (first section), the Melbourne, the Women's, part of the Queen Victoria, the Heidelberg Repatriation, and the Eye and Ear hospitals in Melbourne, and several in the country, as well as undertaking other major projects, among them the Corpus Christi Seminary, Glen Waverley. From 1953 Burne was sole managing director of the family firms which included Burne Brothers (Builders), and their hire and building-supplies subsidiaries.

Like his father, Lewis Burne developed an active interest in industrial relations. His presidency (1941-44) of the Master Builders' Association of Victoria began a period during which he was to hold offices at State, federal and international levels: employer representative (1945-61) on the Commonwealth Reconstruction Training Scheme, president (1947) of the Master Builders' Federation of Australia, committee-member (1941-48) of the Building Industry Congress, foundation member and fellow (1951) of the Australian Institute of Builders, executive-member of

the Victorian Employers' Federation from 1943 (president 1948-50 and 1953-61), and president (1957-58) of the Australian Council of Employers' Federations. He was a frequent employer delegate to the International Labour Organization from 1950, and a member of its Asian advisory committee (1951-66) and of its governing body (1957-66).

Throughout these various facets of his public life, Burne exhibited a consistent set of attitudes and values: a belief in well-regulated free enterprise and freedom of association, and in co-operation between employers and employees; a dislike of governments as inherently socialistic and bureaucratic; and an anti-communism natural to a staunch Catholic in the Cold War years.

In his work with the M.B.A., Burne was concerned with the problems of shortages of materials in wartime and the demand for post-war construction. He supported the claims of private contractors and incentives against the inertia of the public sector and its day-labour system. His major contribution was—with Ellison Harvie of Stephenson & Turner—to finalize in 1953 the rise and fall agreement for building contracts to be adopted by the M.B.A. and the Royal Victorian Institute of Architects.

Soon after assuming the presidency of the V.E.F. in 1948, Burne criticized the increasing leftist tendencies of the Chifley [q.v.] Federal government, but was confident that a responsible employer body could prevail, particularly if it worked and consulted with union leaders. It was partly through such consultation that a large number of initiatives were taken by the V.E.F. during the 1950s. These included a campaign for staggered working hours, an overseas scheme for prizes for top local apprentices, the employment of physically and mentally handicapped people, the Over-Fifties Association, the Secretaries' Club, a scheme to train industrial relations officers, a council to review workers' compensation, a push for decimal currency, and sponsorship of the Develop Victoria Council and the Premier Town contest. In addition, there were internal V.E.F. initiatives, such as the creation of an insurance research division, staff superannuation and investment companies, and the agreement to develop the Princes Bridge Station area and to construct the Princes Gate buildings, part of which would become the new V.E.F. headquarters.

Although he was at or near the helm throughout these initiatives, Burne would later condemn some of them as unwise or too expensive. His last years with the V.E.F. were marred by a bitter feud with the long-time secretary, recriminations against other associates and a battle with a younger leadership group which culminated in 1970 when

Burne and two other 'old-guard' ex-presidents were replaced on the executive. Nevertheless, he continued to chair (1955-73) the V.E.F.-owned Federation Insurance Ltd and in 1973 was elected the V.E.F.'s first life member.

Sceptical of the 'twaddle' from government representatives at the I.L.O., Burne also thought that the organization was 'misused for sordid opportunism', notably Soviet communist propaganda. He saw the role of Catholics and other anti-communists—especially after the admission of the Soviet Union as a voting member of I.L.O. in 1954—in terms set out in Albert Le Roy's *The Dignity of Labor* (Maryland, U.S.A., 1957). Le Roy had linked the proposition in the I.L.O.'s Declaration of Philadelphia (1944)—that 'Labor is not a commodity'—with *Rerum Novarum* (1891) and, by inference, with *Quadragesimo Anno* (1931), encyclicals which were fundamental to Burne's beliefs. Communist States posed a threat to the tripartite composition of the I.L.O., and more so to Burne's own group, in that their 'employer' representatives were perceived as being government spokesmen. The lack of freedom of trade unions in these countries was another recurrent concern. In Europe Burne found opportunities to pursue personal, business and semi-political goals; he had a papal audience, met leading building contractors and obtained information about Catholic Action from local priests.

Appointed C.B.E. in 1955, Burne was knighted in 1959. He belonged to the Victoria Golf, the Victoria Racing and the Melbourne Cricket clubs. Survived by his wife, two sons and two daughters, Sir Lewis died on 22 February 1978 at Hawthorn and was buried in Melbourne general cemetery. His estate was sworn for probate at $382 411. Shirley Bourne's portrait of Burne is held by the V.E.F.

S. Thomas, *Challenge* (Melb, 1985); *Building and Construction* (Melb), 13, 20 Mar 1945; *Aust Builder* (Melb), Apr 1950, Mar 1978; *Age* biog file (LaTL); W. C. Burne & Sons Pty Ltd collection *and* Building Industry Congress collection *and* Burne family papers (Univ Melb Archives).

MARK RICHMOND

BURNELL, JOHN GURNER (1885-1967), engineer, was born on 21 January 1885 at Paddington, Sydney, eldest son of native-born parents Hubert Gray Burnell, bank manager, and his wife Emeline Kate, née Wills. His father's death when John was only 10 left a lasting impression, thrusting early responsibilities on him and creating a strong bond with his mother whom he admired throughout his life for her capability and strength of char-

acter. Educated at The Kings School, Parramatta, and the University of Sydney (B.E., 1907), he completed one year of an arts course in 1903 before transferring to mechanical engineering. During his course Burnell gained practical experience at the New South Wales railway workshops and at the Pyrmont plant of the Colonial Sugar Refining Co.

After graduating with first-class honours, in 1908 he was appointed to the new State Rivers and Water Supply Commission of Victoria under Elwood Mead [q.v.10] and by 1911 was chief mechanical engineer. Burnell travelled extensively throughout northern Victoria, supervising the installation and testing of steam-driven pumping plants which provided water for irrigation, stock and domestic use. He came into close contact with the engineering firm, Thompson [q.v.12] & Co. (Castlemaine) Pty Ltd, one of the commission's major contractors.

Commissioned in the Australian Imperial Force on 29 September 1915, Burnell was posted to the 5th Field Company, Engineers. He was then 5 ft 7½ ins (171.5 cm) tall and 10 st. 7 lb. (66.7 kg). Embarking for Egypt on 23 November 1915, he served in France from March 1916 and was awarded the Military Cross for carrying out a dangerous reconnaissance on 13 September at Pozières. He was wounded at Bullecourt on 8 May 1917, convalesced in England and returned to France where he was promoted captain in November. In May 1918 he became staff officer to the chief engineer Brigadier Foott [q.v.8]. Awarded the French Croix de Guerre in November, he performed administrative duties next year in London and took leave to study water supply. On 28 June 1919 at St Paul's Church, Knightsbridge, he married Adèle Dewez (d. 1950); they were to have a son and daughter. His appointment terminated in Australia on 13 February 1920 and he resumed his job in Melbourne.

In 1922 Burnell resigned from the commission to become assistant-manager with Thompson & Co. When the company was reconstructed as Thompsons Engineering & Pipe Co. Ltd in 1925, he was appointed to the board as technical director and promoted to general manager. Responsible for the day-to-day running of the firm's Castlemaine works, he played a major part in building the company into Australia's leading manufacturer of high-efficiency pumps. In 1928 he oversaw the introduction of a standard range of general service pumps and in 1932-33 designed special, centrifugal pumps for treating juices containing cane fibres in Queensland sugar-mills. Having investigated the theory and design of large, axial flow-pumps, in 1939 he persuaded the board to install an hydraulic laboratory with the capacity to measure flows of up to 30 000 gallons

(113 562 litres) per minute and to handle pumping loads of 15 000 horsepower. By 1940 pumping equipment had become Thompsons' major product, representing 40 per cent of the Castlemaine works' output.

During World War II Burnell supervised the manufacture of artillery and tank guns, marine engines, circulating pumps, and other heavy forging and foundry work. After the war he guided the firm through a further period of expansion in which major contracts were obtained to supply condensing and feed-water plant for new, electric power stations across eastern Australia. The Castlemaine works were extensively re-equipped with modern machine-tools and a fabrication shop was built which almost doubled the workshop space.

Throughout his years with Thompsons, Burnell was approached by those outside the firm who valued his expertise. In 1928 he had commenced work on the Australian pump test code, on which he published a paper in the *Journal of the Institution of Engineers* in October 1929. This work subsequently became the basis of an equivalent British standard. He was also engaged to report on pumping and water supply to the irrigation settlements of Mildura, Merbein and Red Cliffs for the Federal Development and Migration Commission. Even major competitors came to him to seek advice on pump-design problems.

Burnell firmly believed in the importance of basic research to engineering design and manufacturing. While at Castlemaine, he conducted many experimental investigations into practical problems and patented design improvements for feedwater heater and de-aerators (1934) and steam desuperheaters (1939). His published research also revealed an involvement in the design of power station feedwater and condensing plant. Other fields in which he was concerned included steam-air ejectors, water jet pumps, water-hammer and cavitation. In 1938 Burnell visited engineering works in England, Sweden, Germany, France and the United States of America where he negotiated Australian manufacturing licenses with several companies. He made a second business trip abroad in 1956.

Actively interested in the welfare of Thompsons' employees, Burnell maintained the firm's almost unblemished industrial record and the policy of paying above-award wages to its best employees. During the Depression he retained its most highly-skilled tradesmen and draftsmen by initiating projects such as the manufacture of steamrollers, even though there was little prospect of the work being profitable.

Convinced of the importance of technical education, Burnell was chairman of the Castlemaine Technical School advisory council and a member (1944-55) of the council of

the University of Melbourne. He retained his early interest in the arts and was a proficient cabinet-maker. President of the Castlemaine Art Gallery (1942-56) and a trustee of the National Gallery of Victoria (1950-56), he acquired an extensive collection of etchings which he bequeathed to Monash University.

In 1946 Burnell had been awarded the Kernot [q.v.5] medal for distinguished engineering achievement in the design and testing of pumps and welded pressure-vessels. In 1951 the Institution of Engineers awarded him the (Sir) Peter Nicol Russell [q.v.6] medal and in 1956 the University of Melbourne conferred on him an honorary doctorate of engineering. On 26 July that year he married a widow Danina Pharazyn, née Truelove, at St John's Church, Napier, New Zealand. He retired as general manager and director of Thompsons in January 1957 and moved to Napier. Survived by his wife, he died on 11 October 1967 at Westminster, London.

The Thompsons-Byron Jackson Centennial (Castlemaine, Vic, 1975); Monash Univ, *Etching and Collecting* (Melb, 1985); Inst of Engineers, Aust, *J*, 24, Jan-Feb 1952, p 32; *Univ Melb Gazette*, Nov 1956; *Herald* (Melb), 11 Mar 1950, 26 Nov 1951; *Castlemaine Mail*, 5 Feb 1957, 17 Oct 1967; R. Burnell (comp), Notes on the Career of John Gurner Burnell (ms, July 1975, copy held by Univ Melb Archives); Thompsons Engineering & Pipe Co, Directors' minute-books, 1925-49 (Univ Melb Archives).
                                    M. S. CHURCHWARD

BURNETT, SIR CHARLES STUART (1882-1945), air force officer, was born on 3 April 1882 at Browns Valley, Minnesota, United States of America, second of four sons of John Alexander Burnett of Kemnay, Aberdeenshire, Scotland, and his wife Charlotte Susan, née Forbes Gordon. Educated in England at Bedford Grammar School, at 17 Charles added a year to his age and joined the Imperial Yeomanry so that he could serve in the South African War. He took his discharge in order to be commissioned (2 October 1901) in the Highland Light Infantry. While seconded to the West African Frontier Force in 1904-06, he fought in Northern Nigeria, was wounded and was twice mentioned in dispatches. In 1909 he resigned his commission and sought his fortune as a part-owner of a shop in Portuguese Guinea. Burnett entered government service in 1911 as assistant-resident at Ilorin, Nigeria.

Rejoining the army on the outbreak of World War I, he qualified as a pilot in November 1914 and in December was appointed to the Royal Flying Corps. On 30 November that year at the register office, St Martin, London, he had married a divorcee Sybil Maud Pack-Beresford, née Bell. A flight commander with No. 17 Squadron in the Middle East in 1915, he had his own squadron in France from 1916. He was promoted temporary lieutenant colonel in October 1917 and given command of the Palestine Brigade's No. 5 Wing. For his part in the campaign that led to the capture of Jerusalem in December, Burnett was awarded the Distinguished Service Order. Appointed C.B.E. in 1919 and four times mentioned in dispatches for his war service, he accepted a permanent commission in the Royal Air Force.

In 1920 Burnett commanded R.A.F. operations in Iraq; following postings in Britain (1921-29), he went back to Iraq for two years as air chief staff officer, in the rank of air commodore. Returning to England, in January 1931 he was appointed director of operations and intelligence, and deputy-chief of the Air Staff. He was promoted air vice marshal in July. Next year he became air officer commanding, British Forces in Iraq; he was wounded while suppressing tribal incursions near Kuwait. Repatriated in 1935, he took charge of Inland Area which was reorganized as Training Command in 1936. Burnett was promoted air marshal and on 10 July made commander-in-chief. For three years he bore a heavy burden as the R.A.F. expanded to meet the growing threat posed by the German *Luftwaffe*. He had been appointed C.B. in 1927 and in 1936 was elevated to K.C.B. In 1939 he was posted as inspector general, R.A.F., and was a member of the British military mission to the Soviet Union in August.

Soon after hostilities began, the government of (Sir) Robert Menzies [q.v.] decided to seek British officers to head the armed services, fearing that Australian officers lacked vital experience. In December 1939 Burnett was selected to be chief of the Air Staff, and the acting occupant of the post Air Vice Marshal S. J. Goble [q.v.9] resigned forthwith. The appointment was more of a snub to Air Vice Marshal (Sir) Richard Williams [q.v.12], who had commanded the second and larger wing of the Palestine Brigade alongside Burnett in 1918, and who had been the senior officer of the R.A.A.F. since its foundation. Arriving in February 1940 for an initial twelve-month term, Burnett knew little of Australian conditions and faced resentment by those who believed that the government's preference for British officers was ill-founded. He was to hold the rank of air chief marshal while in office.

Burnett's principal tasks were to continue the expansion of the R.A.A.F. and to enhance its capacity to contribute aircrew (through the Empire Air Training Scheme) to the R.A.F. This arrangement was controversial in that some Australians—particularly R.A.A.F. officers proud of the record of the country's squadrons in World War I—contended that Australia's national identity would be lost in the British-directed effort and that Australians would receive far fewer senior appointments than their fair share. While Burnett was aware of these undercurrents, he believed that a centralized Empire air force was essential to defeat the *Luftwaffe* and pressed ahead to create a vast structure that aimed in 1940 to have 50 000 recruits trained or under instruction by March 1943. He also worked hard, although less successfully, to build up the numbers of aircraft available to the R.A.A.F. In addition, he devoted considerable energy to the protection of Australian sea lanes and the forward basing of R.A.A.F. units. Furthermore, he intervened strongly to support the formation of the Women's Auxiliary Australian Air Force.

His critics argued that Burnett's devotion to the E.A.T.S. undercut Australia's capacity to protect itself against attack by Japan, but his firmness, directness and ability to recognize merit in an opposing argument were to enable him to survive two years and three months in office. From October 1941 he had to work with Labor's minister for air A. S. Drakeford [q.v.]. Their relationship was not a happy one. Difficulties came to a head early in 1942 when Burnett proposed far-reaching administrative changes, including the abolition of the Air Board. He was replaced in May when the Japanese threat to the South Pacific was growing. Despite the problems he had faced, he was able to look back with satisfaction on the expansion of the R.A.A.F. from a strength of 3489 immediately before the war to 79 074 in May 1942, of whom some 42 per cent were E.A.T.S. personnel. It was a formidable record.

Described as 'a man of strong, decisive mind, with a gift of saying in a few words exactly what he thinks', Burnett had prodigious physical and mental energy. He despised vacillation and scorned the 'selfish place-hunter'. Transferred to the Retired List on his return to England, he was recalled to full-time duty as commandant, Central Command, Air Training Corps, in 1943. Sir Charles was a keen sportsman and a crack marksman. He continued to serve despite ill health. Survived by his wife and four daughters, he died of coronary thrombosis on 9 April 1945 in the R.A.F. hospital, Halton, Buckinghamshire. His daughter Sybil had been an acting squadron officer in the W.A.A.A.F. in 1941-42 and his brother Sir Robert became an admiral (1946) in the Royal Navy.

DNB, 1941-50; F. M. Cutlack, *The Australian Flying Corps* (Syd, 1923); D. Gillison, *Royal Australian Air Force 1939-1942* (Canb, 1962); R. Williams, *These are Facts*(Canb, 1977); G. Jones, *From Private to Air Marshal*(Melb, 1988); *Roy Aero Club Year Book*, 1915-16; *The Times*, 1 Aug 1939, 1 Mar 1940, 11 Apr, 9 May 1942, 11 Apr, 1 May 1945; *Argus*, 6 Jan 1940; *Herald* (Melb), 6 Jan 1940, 19 May 1941; information from the secretary, Old Bedfordians Club, Bedford, Eng; family information.   ROBERT O'NEILL

BURNS, JAMES (1881-1969), businessman, was born on 30 December 1881 at Point Piper, Sydney, eldest of five surviving children of (Sir) James Burns [q.v.7], a Scottish-born merchant, and his second wife Mary Heron, née Morris, from Victoria. Given an austere Presbyterian upbringing, Jimmy attended The King's School, Parramatta, and in 1898 entered his father's firm, Burns, Philp [q.v.11] & Co. Ltd. He spent 1902 in the London office, was assistant-manager (1904) of the Geraldton branch in Western Australia, joined the company's fleet of small steamships based in the New Hebrides, then returned to head office in Bridge Street, Sydney.

Six ft 1 in. (185.4 cm) tall, with brown eyes and dark hair, on 27 March 1913 Burns married Vida Emily Mills at St Mark's Anglican Church, Darling Point; they were to have four children. He was commissioned in the Australian Imperial Force on 24 April 1916. After training in England, he was promoted lieutenant in September 1917 and next month was attached to the 14th Light Trench Mortar Battery in France. He was commended for 'coolness and skill under heavy fire' on 29 July 1918. Wounded in action on 25 August, he recuperated in England and returned to the front in November. He worked in Burns Philp's London office before coming home to Sydney where his A.I.F. appointment terminated on 11 September 1919. His youngest brother Robert had been killed in France in 1916 and his brother John was to die in 1921 as a result of war service in the Mesopotamian desert.

Appointed a director of Burns Philp in 1919, James took over as chairman and managing director on his father's death in 1923. In addition, he became chairman or a director of other companies with which his father had been associated, among them Burns, Philp (South Sea) Co. Ltd, the Queensland Insurance Co. Ltd, Bankers & Traders Insurance Co. Ltd, Bellambi Coal Co. Ltd, Choiseul Plantations Ltd and the Solomon Islands Development Co. Ltd. Apart from the times he travelled abroad, he was also a director of the Bank of New South Wales in 1923-32.

Although less forceful than his father, Burns was a hard negotiator and kept a sharp eye on the operations of his companies which constituted an extensive Australian mercantile, shipping, insurance and copra-producing network. Burns Philp was a powerful force in the South Pacific. The status of Burns and several senior company executives as ex-servicemen enabled the firm to purchase important plantations in New Guinea that were previously German-owned. He opposed attempts by German business interests to move back into New Guinea. In 1934, on being invited to become associated with the London-based Anglo-German Trade Association, he flatly refused, and added: 'I think it would be better for you to get representatives who did not participate actively in the late War'.

Proud of his father's achievements, Burns believed that he should simply do the job, honourably and intelligently, that fortune had provided for him. In the 1930s he developed a chain of some forty retail stores known as 'Penneys', entered the trustee business (Burns, Philp Trustee Co. Ltd was registered in 1938) and later acquired holdings in 'old established country retail businesses', including Mates [q.v.5 Mate] Ltd and Charles Rogers [q.v.6] & Sons Pty Ltd.

Although conservative-minded, modest and cheerful, Burns was regarded by the administration in Papua-New Guinea as a commercial pirate who sought to use political influence to gain monopolies. He preferred independent, Australian insurance companies to their huge, English-based competitors; the QBE Insurance Group Ltd is a monument to his endeavour. Less involved in business affairs after World War II, he continued to attend the Sydney office several days a week, travelling by train from his property at Bowral, until age and illness eventually induced him to retire as chairman and managing director in 1967.

In Sydney, Burns stayed at the Australian Club; he belonged, as well, to Royal Sydney Golf and the Union clubs, and enjoyed trout-fishing at Thredbo with his friends Tom Rutledge [q.v.11] and (Sir) Edward Knox. He served on the board of the Burnside Presbyterian Orphan Homes for over forty years and made generous gifts to that institution. Predeceased by his wife, Burns died on 5 August 1969 at Bowral and was cremated; his estate was sworn for probate at $1 045 194. He was survived by a daughter and by his son David who succeeded him as chairman of Burns Philp.

K. Buckley and K. Klugman, *The History of Burns Philp* (Syd, 1981) and *The Australian Presence in the Pacific* (Syd, 1983); *Sunday Mirror* (Syd), 11 Feb 1962; *Sun-Herald*, 6 Jan 1963; *SMH*, 7 Aug 1969; K. Buckley, QBE: A Century of Australian Insurance (ms held by author, Univ Syd); Burns Philp papers (ANUABL); information from Mr J. D. O. Burns, Syd.   KEN BUCKLEY

BURNS, MICHAEL ELDRIGE SAMUEL;
see BYRNE, SAMUEL

BURROWS, FREDERICK ALEXANDER
(1897-1973), army officer and businessman,
was born on 10 November 1897 at Wah-
gunyah, Victoria, second child of Frederick
Burrows, labourer, and his wife Hester, née
Nugent, both Victorian born. Educated at
Cobar and Corowa public schools, New South
Wales, young Burrows added one year to his
age and described himself as a 'grocer's
assistant' when he enlisted in the Australian
Imperial Force on 28 April 1915. He embarked for Egypt in July and served briefly on
Gallipoli with the 7th Battalion.

In March 1916 Burrows reached France
where he was wounded at Pozières in July and
promoted sergeant in October. At Lihons on
11 August 1918 he led a bombing party which
cleared an enemy trench; for his action he was
awarded the Military Medal. That month he
was again wounded, evacuated to England
and commissioned. He returned to Australia
in May 1919 as a lieutenant and his A.I.F.
appointment terminated on 6 July. Employed
by Cooper Engineering Co. Pty Ltd in Melbourne, Burrows joined the Militia in 1921
and was posted to the 14th Battalion. On
23 March 1922 at St George's Presbyterian
Church, East St Kilda, he married Isabel
Christina Mathieson (d. 1963). After his firm
sent him to Sydney in 1934 as sales-manager,
he transferred to the 36th Battalion; he
was promoted lieutenant colonel and made
commanding officer in August 1938.

Appointed to the A.I.F. on 26 April 1940,
Burrows was given command of the 2nd/13th
Battalion and arrived in the Middle East in
November. Thickset, with 'rather pugilistic
features', tall, erect and alert, he exuded 'a
powerful air of authority and confidence'. His
resonant voice earned him the nickname, 'the
Bull'. At Er Regima, Libya, in April 1941 he
checked the advance of a superior German
force and extricated his battered battalion. In
the withdrawal to Tobruk and throughout its
defence he was an aggressive commander.
During the Sidi Rezegh battles his night-
attack on Ed Duda on 30 November was an
outstanding success. A serious head-wound
next day caused him to be invalided home.
Mentioned in dispatches, Burrows was
awarded the Distinguished Service Order and
the Polish Krzyz Walecznych (Cross of Valour). He had made an indelible impression on
his troops. Their admiration was epitomized
by one soldier who composed a song, *Bull
Burrows' Bomb-Happy Boys*, and later wrote of
him:

For we all know a man when we see one,
And we know that you've well earned
your rest.

Promoted temporary brigadier in May
1942, Burrows commanded the 1st Infantry
Brigade in New South Wales. His wound prevented him from returning to the field and he
was placed on the Retired List on 28 July
1945. He resumed his civilian job and in 1946
opened an Adelaide branch of Cooper's (subsequently Sunbeam Corporation Ltd) which
prospered under his management. Burrows
was a member (1952-55) of the Repatriation
Board for South Australia. He retired in 1959,
devoted himself to the interests of ex-
servicemen, and enjoyed golf, bowls, gardening and philately. On 27 November 1964 at
the Methodist Church, Tusmore, he married
a widow Thelma Villis, née Matthew, late
Cox. He died on 23 May 1973 in the Repatriation General Hospital, Daw Park, and was
cremated; his wife survived him, as did the
son and daughter of his first marriage.

G. H. Fearnside (ed), *Bayonets Abroad* (Syd,
1953); B. Maughan, *Tobruk and El Alamein* (Canb,
1966); AWM records; information from Mrs Y.
Crompton, Marryatville, Adel, Mr F. B. Burrows,
Beaumaris, Melb, and Mr K. J. Hall, Mosman,
Syd.
                                                  A. J. HILL

BURSTON, SIR SAMUEL ROY (1888-
1960), physician and army officer, was born
on 21 March 1888 in Melbourne, fourth child
of James Burston [q.v.7], maltster, and his
wife Marianne, née McBean, both Victorian
born. The family lived at Windarra, a bluestone house in Flinders Street, then at
Carrical, in Mason Street, Hawthorn, from
where Roy rode a pony to Melbourne Church
of England Grammar School. In 1900-05 he
was a bugler in the Victorian and Australian
military forces, but a heart murmur, detected
in his childhood, precluded a full-time army
career. Graduating from the University of
Melbourne (M.B., B.S., 1910), he became a
resident medical officer in the Adelaide Children's Hospital. In 1911-12 Burston was
based in the Northern Territory as a medical
inspector of Aborigines and on his return
practised privately at Mile End. He married
Helen Elizabeth Culross (d. 1959) on 16 April
1913 in St Michael's Anglican Church,
Mitcham.

In October 1912 Burston had been appointed captain, (Royal Australian) Army
Medical Corps. He transferred to the Australian Imperial Force on 26 March 1915 and
embarked for Egypt in June. As a major in the
7th Field Ambulance, he served at Gallipoli
from September until November when he was

evacuated to England with enteric fever. After brief periods in Egypt and England, he was posted to the 11th Field Ambulance and moved to France in November 1916. Burston was awarded the Distinguished Service Order for his supervision of an advanced dressing-station during the battle of Messines, Belgium, in June 1917. Later that month he was promoted temporary lieutenant colonel and made senior medical officer, Australian General Base Depot, Le Havre, France; command of the 1st Australian Convalescent Depot from April 1918 added to his responsibilities. Promoted temporary colonel in November, he took charge of the 3rd Australian General Hospital before assuming in April 1919 the assistant-directorship of medical services for A.I.F. depots in Britain. He was mentioned in dispatches and appointed C.B.E. that year.

Burston's A.I.F. appointment terminated in Adelaide on 7 March 1920. Resuming his civilian practice, he maintained his association with the A.M.F. as deputy-director of medical services, 4th Military District. In 1928 he won the bronze medal of the Royal Humane Society of Australasia for a surf rescue at Victor Harbour. A member of the Royal College of Physicians, Edinburgh (fellow 1937), and an honorary physician at (Royal) Adelaide Hospital from 1933 (honorary consultant physician 1947), he was a foundation fellow of the Royal Australasian College of Physicians in 1938. His military and medical reputations ensured his appointment on 13 October 1939 as assistant-director of medical services, 6th Division, A.I.F. He embarked for the Middle East in April 1940.

On the staff of Lieutenant General Sir Thomas Blamey [q.v.], Burston was successively deputy-director (April) of medical services, I Australian Corps, and director (November) of the A.I.F.'s medical services in the Middle East. He was promoted major general on 16 February 1941. Frequently seen at the front, he anticipated difficulties and took corrective action. Blamey relied on him, and in July used his report on the health of Australian troops in the Tobruk garrison as grounds for the early relief of the 9th Division. For his services in the Middle East, Burston was appointed C.B. (1942).

Back in Australia, by May 1942 he was director-general of medical services at Land Headquarters, Melbourne, and chairman of the central medical co-ordination committee. His handling of the battle against malaria in the South-West Pacific Area was his greatest achievement. Ably supported by Brigadier (Sir) Neil Fairley [q.v.], he ensured that measures originally proposed by Colonel (Sir) Edward Ford were thoroughly implemented. In March 1943 Burston adopted Fairley's

suggestion and established the combined advisory committee on tropical medicine, hygiene and sanitation. Burston's appeal to Blamey led to the establishment of the L.H.Q. Medical Research Unit at Cairns, Queensland, 'one of the most important steps of the war taken in Australia in relation to malaria'.

Burston's personality and experience contributed to his success as medical head of the army, as did his ability to select and direct the activities of outstanding subordinates. While his advisers (especially his friend Fairley) were often technically superior to him, Burston was their natural leader and they knew it. He was *persona grata* to senior members of the A.I.F. Because he could be trusted to keep a confidence, he was asked to be an intermediary in personal conflicts: the prime example had been Blamey's request that he should intercede with Lieutenant General (Sir) Sydney Rowell [q.v.] whom Blamey relieved of command in September 1942. A large and impressive figure, with blue eyes and a fair complexion, Burston looked very much the soldier; his sandy hair earned him the nickname 'Ginger'. He was 'a man of the world, fond of parties, good food and wine', and played tennis and golf. While he liked the trappings of office, he was charming and approachable, and had a particularly happy family life.

Relinquishing his appointment in January 1948, Burston retired to Melbourne. In 1944 he had been appointed a knight of the Order of St John (chief commissioner in 1945-57 and receiver-general of the Priory in Australia from 1957), and in 1945 became honorary physician to King George VI and a fellow of the Royal College of Physicians, London. He was appointed K.B.E. in 1952. The office of honorary colonel (1952-57) of the R.A.A.M.C. was the distinction that probably pleased him most. Sir Samuel had long been interested in horses: a modest punter and owner, he was chairman (1952-60) of the Moonee Valley Racing Club. He was active in the Australian Red Cross Society and other service organizations, and a director of several companies, including David Syme [q.v.6] & Co. Ltd. Survived by his daughter and two sons, Burston died on 21 August 1960 at South Yarra; after a military funeral, he was cremated. Among his portraits, one by (Sir) William Dargie is in the family's possession; another, by (Sir) Ivor Hele, is held by the Australian War Memorial, Canberra.

A. S. Walker, *Clinical Problems of the War* and *Middle East and Far East* and *The Island Campaigns* (Canb, 1952, 1953, 1957); G. L. McDonald (ed), *Roll of the RACP*, 1 (Syd, 1988); *MJA*, 4 Feb 1961; AWM records; information from Sir Samuel Burston, Casterton, Vic.   BRIAN CLEREHAN

BURSTON, WINIFRED CHARLOTTE
HILLIER CROSSE (1889-1976), pianist, was
born on 3 April 1889 at Gaythorn Albion,
near Caboolture, Queensland, fourth child of
English-born parents Thomas Burston, clerk,
and his wife Mary, née Gibson. Raised in
Brisbane and taught by her mother (an accomplished pianist who was still broadcasting
in her nineties), in 1908 Winifred went to
Berlin. She studied under the pianist Theodore Bohlmann at the Stern'sches Konservatorium der Musik, Berlin, and gained its
diploma. Following Bohlmann to the United
States of America, she made public appearances and taught at the Cincinnati Conserva-
tory. She returned to Berlin in 1911 to study
with the Italian pianist and composer Fer-
ruccio Busoni, and his disciple, the Dutch
pianist Egon Petri. Having spent a summer
with the Falzfeins, a noble family who lived
near Kiev, Ukraine, in October 1913 she gave
a recital at the Aeolian Hall, London.

Returning to Queensland in 1914, Burston
taught piano in Brisbane and in 1919 was
appointed to the New South Wales State Conservatorium of Music, Sydney. She encouraged the performance of new works from
Europe and gave Australian premières of
such pieces as Busoni's *Indian Fantasy*
(1914), Bax's *Quintet for Oboe and Strings*
(1923), Delius's *Piano Concerto* and some of
Liszt's later compositions. From Busoni and
Petri she received (and passed on) a grand
European tradition, a particular orchestral
approach to the piano and a liberal attitude
to the art of transcription, soon to become
unfashionable.

Visiting Europe in 1931, Burston discovered and championed Emmanuel Moore's
double-keyboard piano; she purchased and
brought back to Australia a rare example of
this instrument in 1932. She was sufficiently
flexible to overhaul her technique and play
works on the new piano. In the 1930s she was
president of the Sydney centre of the British
and International Music Society, the first
woman council-member of the Musical Association of New South Wales (1936, vice-
president 1939) and of the Associated Music
Clubs of Australia, and president of the
musicians' section of the United Associations
(of Women).

From the 1930s Burston gave many recitals for the Australian Broadcasting Commission. When she returned to Brisbane for
annual holidays she was immediately 'snared'
by local A.B.C. stations to give a series of
piano recitals. In July 1939 she began conducting the Wednesday morning 'Women's
Session' for the A.B.C. in Sydney: her programme usually began with a short talk, then
she played selected records 'of all types—
vocal, instrumental, solo choir, band', and
each week featured a particular composer

or artist. In her late seventies she gave a
series of piano recitals for A.B.C. television,
introducing them herself.

As a pianist, Burston favoured the late
Romantic repertoire and music of the early
twentieth century, and loved Busoni's tran-
scriptions of Bach. Her performance was
marked by a very fluid technique and rhyth-
mic freedom, typical of early twentieth-
century pianism. She had little patience for
preciousness in interpretation and favoured a
broad, robust approach which was concerned
with architecture and design, and avoided
fiddly detail.

Burston had a capacity for renewal and an
enthusiasm for fresh ideas. Quite late in life
she discovered the new, Dutch school of composition and made a special study of this repertoire, once again giving first performances.
She promoted piano music by Australian composers and developed an especially warm
relationship with Roy Agnew [q.v.7], whose
works she performed and whose music she
taught to her pupils.

As a person and a teacher, Burston was
strong and direct, sometimes to the point of
bluntness, and was outspoken when she perceived injustices and anomalies in Australian
educational systems. She was attached to the
Sydney conservatorium until she retired in
1964; she also travelled interstate as an
examiner for the Australian Music Examinations Board until shortly before her death,
visiting many institutions, among them the
Canberra School of Music. Students tended to
remain in touch with her for years after they
graduated from her studio, and were eventually allowed to call her 'Winifred', rather than
'Miss Burston'; out of her hearing, they affectionately referred to her as 'Winnie'. Her
pupils included Geoffrey Parsons, Alan Jenkins, Rainer von Zastrow, Richard Meale and
Larry Sitsky. She died on 24 June 1976 at her
Edgecliff home and was cremated. A fund was
established to endow a scholarship in her
memory at the Canberra School of Music.

Aust Musical News, 1 Sept 1927, p 33; *SMH*, 2
Dec 1916, 17 Aug 1927, 14 Mar 1931, 28 June
1934, 6 July 1976; *Sun* (Syd), 3 Dec 1916; *Canb
Times*, 12 Oct 1977; W. Burston file (ABC Archives, Syd); personal information.

LARRY SITSKY

BURT, WALTER OSWALD (1893-1969),
solicitor and company director, was born on
8 September 1893 at Warrnambool, Victoria,
eldest child of Horace Percy Burt, tailor, and
his wife, Mary Jane, née McSweeney, both
Victorian born. Oswald was dux of the local
state school in 1907 and of the high school in
1910. Having been articled to Arthur Phillips
in Melbourne, on 2 May 1918 Burt was

admitted as a barrister and solicitor of the Supreme Court of Victoria. He had married Esther French on 18 August 1917 at the Presbyterian Church, Koroit.

From 1923 Burt practised as a solicitor in Collins Street, Melbourne, in partnership with George and Rupert Frederick Bullen (Bullen & Burt from 1926). Burt became an authority on mining law and a leading company lawyer; he had considerable success during the 1930s in reconstructing insolvent companies. He was to introduce to Victoria the factoring of debts and the 'ownership' of flats through different classes of shares. When R. F. Bullen withdrew from the partnership in 1942 Burt continued to practise with other partners as Oswald Burt & Co. until 1959; he then served as a consultant to the firm until his death. A merger in 1979 established Middletons Oswald Burt.

Having accepted an invitation in 1934 from F. Oswald Barnett [q.v.7], Burt joined a group of forty people who studied the problems of slum-housing in Melbourne and examined possible solutions. In conjunction with the Labor Party's slum abolition committee, the group persuaded (Sir) Albert Dunstan's [q.v.8] government to set up a Housing Investigation and Slum Abolition Board in 1936. Both Barnett and Burt were appointed to it. The board's report (much of it written by Burt) led to the Housing Act, 1937, which established the Victorian Housing Commission, and to the Slum Reclamation and Housing Act, 1938, which Burt largely drafted.

Appointed a part-time member of the Housing Commission, Burt drew up the Housing (Standard of Habitation) Regulations of 1938. With Barnett, he wrote *Housing the Australian Nation* (1942); with Barnett and F. Heath, *We Must Go On: a study in planned reconstruction and housing* (1944). Barnett later claimed that the government of T. T. Hollway [q.v.] considered them 'too socially minded, too pink in fact'. Burt and Barnett announced in February 1948 that they would not be available for reappointment to the commission. By this time Burt and other members of the commission were somewhat disillusioned by the social problems that had emerged when tenants were moved from slums to new estates.

Admitted as a barrister in New South Wales in October 1948, Burt was called to the Bar at the Inner Temple, London, in November 1951. He became a director of numerous companies, among them City Mutual Life Assurance Ltd, Davies Coop & Co. Ltd, National Trustees, Executors & Agency Co. of Australasia Ltd, Kelly & Lewis Ltd, Factors Ltd and White Crow Ltd; he was sometime chairman of Davies Coop, White Crow and Factors Ltd.

A founder in 1956 of the National Trust of Australia (Victoria) and in 1965 of the Australian Council of National Trusts, Burt drafted the constitution of each of these bodies. With Sir Daryl Lindsay [q.v.10], he persuaded the Federal treasurer Sir Arthur Fadden [q.v.] to have the Income Tax Assessment Act amended in 1957 to allow tax deductibility of gifts to the National Trust. For about thirty-five years Burt had pursued an interest in the fine arts, forming an important collection of Australian Impressionist paintings: Jack Manton was to buy twenty-four of them from Burt's estate which were subsequently purchased by the National Gallery of Victoria.

'Ossie' Burt died on 11 April 1969 in East Melbourne and was cremated. His wife survived him. Their only child Alan, a flying officer with the Royal Australian Air Force, had been killed in action on 31 January 1942. Middletons hold a portrait of W. O. Burt by (Sir) William Dargie and the National Trust of Australia (Victoria) has a drawing of him by Alan Moore.

E. W. Russell, *The Slum Abolition Movement in Victoria 1933-37* (Melb, 1972); P. McCaughey and J. Manton, *Australian Painters of the Heidelberg School* (Melb, 1979); R. Howe (ed), *New Houses for Old* (Melb, 1988); Council of Trustees of National Gallery of Vic, *Art Bulletin of Vic*, no 21, 1981; *Argus*, 26 June 1925; F. O. Barnett, I remember (ts, 1964-65, L of Housing Division, Dept of Planning and Housing, Melb); R. L. Eilenberg, Oswald Burt & Co (ts, May 1985) *and* copy of letter from W. O. Burt to Matthews Pty Ltd (funeral directors), 22 Mar 1968 (both documents held by Mr L. W. Quinn, of Middletons, solicitors, Melb).

PETER BALMFORD

BURTON-BRADLEY, CLAUDIA PORTIA; see BRADLEY, CLAUDIA

BURTON-BRADLEY, EILEEN; *see* BRADLEY, EILEEN

BUSHBY, CHARLES HAROLD (1887-1975), cricket administrator and lawyer, was born on 3 December 1887 at Carrick, Tasmania, son of George Frederick Burton Bushby, stock-dealer, and his wife Victoria Ann Elizabeth, née Robertson. Educated at Longford Grammar School and at Scotch College, Launceston, in 1911 Harold passed his final examinations at the University of Tasmania (LL.B., 1913), winning the James Backhouse Walker [q.v.6] prize. Articled to

M. J. Clarke, he was admitted to the Bar on 21 August 1912 and practised at Launceston and Scottsdale. At Devonport on 6 October 1915 he married with Methodist forms Edith Mary Orme, an English-born nurse; their two sons were to enter the law and join the family firm. Bushby was president (1952-54) of the Northern Law Society and a vice-president (1954-55) of the Law Council of Australia.

Although he was not a particularly skilful player—four games for the North of Tasmania against the South represented the pinnacle of his playing career—Bushby had a strong attachment to cricket. In 1911 he had been appointed to the management-committee of the Northern Tasmanian Cricket Association; he served as secretary and treasurer before becoming chairman in 1924, a position he was to hold for almost fifty years. Elected to the Executive Cricket Council of Tasmania in 1915, he represented the State on the Australian Board of Control for International Cricket from 1919 to 1969. He chaired the board (1919 and 1925-26) and visited England in 1926.

Having been the second choice of both the Victorian and New South Wales delegates to the board, Bushby was somewhat fortuitously selected as manager of the Australian cricket team to tour England in 1934. An imposing figure, over six feet (182.9 cm) tall, he could act with firmness when the occasion demanded it. While not always popular with team members—his ban on the consumption of alcohol in the dressing-room was immediately and deliberately defied—he was a resourceful and dedicated administrator who was respected rather than revered. After the controversial 'bodyline' series in 1932-33, his diplomacy did much to ensure the success of what was in part an ameliorative mission; regaining the Ashes was a bonus. Contacts made and friendships established during the tour encouraged Bushby to return to England to watch Test matches and attend law conferences. He represented Australia at four Imperial Cricket Conferences, and was appointed O.B.E. in 1958 and made an honorary life member of the Marylebone Cricket Club in 1971.

Involving himself in community affairs at Launceston, Bushby was a long-serving administrator of the Presbyterian Church, president of its home for the aged and a director of Scotch College. He was a foundation member of the Liberal Party in Tasmania and served on its federal executive in 1945-50. Survived by his sons and two daughters, he died on 3 October 1975 at Launceston and was buried in Carr Villa cemetery. A stand at the Northern Tasmanian Cricket Association Ground, Launceston, commemorates him.

R. Williams, *A Century of Northern Tasmanian*

Cricket (Launc, 1986); Scotch College, Launc, *Caledonian*, 1975; W. J. O'Reilly, *Bill O'Reilly—A Cricketing Life* (Syd, 1990); *Examiner* (Launc), 9 Mar 1934; *Mercury* (Hob), 12 June 1958, 11 Oct 1975; family papers (held by Mr M. H. Bushby, Launc).   RIC FINLAY

BUTLER, ATHOL PATRICK (1902-1961), sheepdog handler and grazier, was born on 27 April 1902 at Box Hill, Bingara, New South Wales, seventh child of native-born parents Thomas Butler, farmer and grazier, and his wife Isabella Catherine, née Read. Athol attended school at nearby Pallal station, then worked on Box Hill until 1925 when he bought a 4000-acre (1619 ha) property, Kanimbla, thirty miles (48.3 km) northeast of Moree. He played district cricket and tennis at Crooble and Milguy, before starting to train sheepdogs. On 11 October 1930 he married 18-year-old Mary (Mollie) Alice Borland (d. 1987) at the Church of Mary the Immaculate, Waverley, Sydney.

His first dogs were Border Collies, but it was with Kelpies that Butler became identified. In 1946 he entered a large, black-and-tan Kelpie called Johnny (1942-1959) in the National Sheep Dog Trials at Manuka Oval, Canberra. Johnny won the Duke of Gloucester's sash and the first of five annual championships (1946-48 and 1951-52), a feat unequalled by any postwar sheepdog. In his final trial in Canberra in 1952 Johnny required 98 points to win his fifth title: he put up the perfect 100. Governor-General Sir William McKell wrote to congratulate Butler 'on such a really remarkable achievement. We were all most happy to meet you and Johnny and to see a master at his best'. That year Movietone News filmed Johnny working at the Marist Brothers' Agricultural College, Campbelltown, New South Wales.

After winning the novice trial at the Sydney Sheep Show in May 1953 with a red Kelpie, Kanimbla Betty, Butler took her and another Kelpie to the 1954 Queensland championship trials at Goondiwindi where he won the maiden with Woombi Zinc and the open with Betty; in the finals they were the only dogs to pen their sheep. Unlike some competitors, Butler kept his dogs in superlative condition.

He conducted a small, registered stud and had a good demand for his dogs. Believing in the importance of temperament in sheepdogs, he bred for himself in the early days and tried to reproduce Johnny's compliancy, but, in attempting to breed Kelpies more amenable to handling, he produced some dogs that were too soft for the average stockman. Johnny, bought as a pup, was a splendid trial dog, though less good at working sheep in the paddock. Butler's breed, however, improved markedly after he acquired Porter's Don.

Although he was extremely courteous and a good conversationalist, he was a very quiet man with no bluster. A good judge of sheep as well as dogs, Butler was able to see two moves ahead and controlled his dogs by a series of whistles so that they appeared to have the sheep on a string. He was a perfectionist. Nobody else worked Kelpies quite as he did; only Frank Scanlon rivalled his mastery. The style of work which Butler introduced provided the inspiration for young handlers. He retired from working dogs in the mid-1950s. Survived by his wife and three sons, he died of pneumonia on 21 November 1961 at Moree and was buried in the local cemetery with Catholic rites.

A. D. Parsons, *The Working Kelpie* (Melb, 1986), *Training the Working Kelpie* (Melb, 1990) and *The Australian Kelpie* (Melb, 1992); *Canb Times,* 1 Oct 1945, 7 Oct 1946, 6 Oct 1947, 11 Oct 1948, 14, 16 Apr 1951, 14 Mar 1952; *Land* (Syd), 29 May 1953; information from Mr B. Butler, Bateau Bay, NSW, and Mr G. Westcott, Canb.   A. D. PARSONS

BUTLER, CECIL ARTHUR (1902-1980), aviator, was born on 8 June 1902 at Sparkhill, Warwickshire, England, son of Arthur Harry Butler, commercial clerk, and his wife Ann Rebecca, née Seabridge. The family migrated to New South Wales about 1910 and settled at Lithgow. Suffering from dyslexia, Arthur was educated by his mother until he was 9 and subsequently went to Cooerwull Academy, Bowenfels, and Lithgow District Public School. In 1917 he was apprenticed as a tool, jig and gauge maker at the local Small Arms Factory, transferring in 1921 to the Australian Aircraft & Engineering Co. Ltd at Mascot, Sydney. He attended Sydney Technical College at night, obtained his ground engineer's licence in 1923, and worked for the Larkin [q.v.9]-Sopwith Air Craft Supply Co. Pty Ltd and Larkin's Australian Aerial Services Ltd as a ground engineer at Hay. Having gained his pilot's licence in 1927, Butler went 'barnstorming'.

Ambitious to design and construct his own aircraft, in 1930 he completed and tested a small, all-metal, high-winged monoplane. Later that year he piloted a tiny Comper Swift from England to Australia in the record time of 9 days, 1¾ hours. On 30 March 1932 at St Ambrose's Anglican Church, Gilgandra, New South Wales, he married Doris Elaine Garling. With financial support from P. S. Garling (his wife's uncle), in 1934 Butler successfully tendered against stiff competition from established airlines for the Charleville (Queensland) - Cootamundra (New South Wales) section of the England-Australia air-

mail route; he fulfilled the terms of the contract for four years, using D.H. 84 Dragon aircraft.

When the airmail contract expired, Butler Air Transport Co. carried on as a civil airline, serving centres in New South Wales and Queensland. During World War II Butler continued to operate some routes and also made aircraft parts for the government. He refused to accrue large profits from war-effort work and charged only to recover costs.

After the war he registered Butler Air Transport Pty Ltd as a public company. He built up the largest and most successful airline operating in New South Wales, using in turn three Douglas DC-3s, Avro Ansons, D.H. 114 Herons and three Airspeed Ambassadors. Combining determination and efficiency with the ideal of involving the company in the communities it served, Butler encouraged his employees to become shareholders in the firm: in 1947 they owned 51 per cent.

Butler stubbornly resisted efforts by the Commonwealth government to nationalize the airlines, but the implementation of the two-airline policy restrained B.A.T.'s development and was the root cause of his exit from the industry. In the early 1950s, through costly litigation, he averted a takeover by Australian National Airways Pty Ltd; while his purchase in 1955 of two Vickers Viscounts gave him access to Melbourne, it brought him into conflict with other operators. In 1957 Ansett Transport Industries Ltd—by acquiring A.N.A.—had a substantial parcel of B.A.T. shares and bought more from Butler's employees. Butler was effectively forced out of aviation in a bitter shareholding battle in 1958 when (Sir) Reginald Ansett gained control of B.A.T. Following several skirmishes in the courts, the battle ended. Defeated but unbowed, Butler disdained the proffered managing directorship and severed all connexion with the company.

He planned to start afresh with French Caravelle jets, but the Department of Civil Aviation rejected his request to import the aircraft in 1959 on the grounds that airports lacked adequate runways. In addition, there were doubts about his financial viability. Butler fought a dogged, rearguard action to re-enter the industry. It was to no avail. Instead of retiring to lick his wounds, he chaired the New South Wales Ambulance Transport Service Board and, with another famous aviator Nancy Bird Walton, raised funds for an air-ambulance service. In 1958 he was appointed O.B.E.

Some 5 ft 4 ins (162.6 cm) tall, Butler was broad shouldered, with an impish face and a twinkle in his eyes. Essentially quiet and goodnatured, if at times impatient and impulsive, he could keep an audience spellbound for hours with his tales of early Australian aviation. He belonged to the Royal Aero Club of New South Wales, Pymble Golf Club and the Institution of Engineers, Australia; he also liked to play chess. In 1968 Butler suffered a stroke. Although partially paralysed, he taught himself to type and in 1971 published a history of Australian civil aviation, *Flying Start*. He then started to paint—mainly aircraft. In 1975 his picture, 'An Auspicious Occasion', was accepted for the Wynne competition. Survived by his wife and daughter, he died on 13 April 1980 at Wahroonga and was cremated.

Civil Aviation Branch, Dept of Defence, *Report on Civil Aviation in Australia and New Guinea* (Melb, 1933); G. R. Copley, *Australians in the Air* (Adel, 1976); B. Carroll, *Australian Aviators* (Syd, 1980); D. Eyre, *The Illustrated Encyclopedia of Aircraft in Australia and New Zealand* (Syd, 1983); S. Brimson, *Flying the Royal Mail* (Syd, 1984); N. M. Parnell and T. Boughton, *Flypast* (Canb, 1988); *Aircraft*, Mar 1947, p 17; *People* (Syd), 30 Nov 1955; *Aeroplane Mthly*, Oct 1986, p 532; *SMH*, 1, 6 Jan, 23, 30 Mar 1958, 14 Feb, 26 Apr 1975, 14 Apr 1980; C. A. Butler, Autobiography, Butler papers, held by and information from Mrs C. A. Butler, Turramurra, NSW; Oral History transcript: Arthur Butler (nd, NL); Dept of Civil Aviation files; information from Mr B. Abell, Cessnock, NSW, and Mrs N. Walton, St Ives, Syd.

SYLVIA MARCHANT

BUTLER, HILDRED MARY (1906-1975), microbiologist, was born on 9 October 1906 at Elsternwick, Melbourne, daughter of Victorian-born parents Archie Butler, farmer, and his wife Rose Josephine, née Hancock. Hildred was educated at Lauriston Girls' School and the University of Melbourne (B.Sc., 1928; D.Sc., 1946). In 1928 she became bacteriologist to the Baker [q.v.7] Medical Research Institute, under the directorship of W. J. Penfold [q.v.11].

At that time severe—often fatal—infections were common in women during and after childbirth, or following abortion. From 1931 Butler examined material from patients at the (Royal) Women's Hospital, Melbourne, and demonstrated the importance of anaerobic streptococci. By 1937 she had determined that severe infections were due to that group of organisms, together with haemolytic streptococci, *Staphylococcus pyogenes* and *Clostridium welchii*. The 'childbed fever' (puerperal sepsis) of old had been most commonly due to Group A haemolytic streptococcus. In her ten years at the Baker Institute she published eight papers and a monograph, *Blood Cultures and their Significance* (1937).

Transferring to the (Royal) Women's Hospital in 1938 as bacteriologist, Butler cooperated with the clinician A. M. 'Bung' Hill [q.v.] and established a twenty-four-hour, seven-day-week bacteriological service. She proved that infectiousness was linked only with Group A haemolytic streptococci and *Staphylococcus pyogenes*, and had the Victorian midwives' regulations modified accordingly in 1941. As infection with Group A streptococci and *Clostridium welchii* could kill more rapidly than these organisms could grow in culture, she developed an original method of assessing microscopically the stained smears from vaginal and cervical discharges, enabling treatment to start immediately. Hill estimated that, throughout her thirty-three years at the (Royal) Women's Hospital, Butler investigated almost 250 000 women with infections during childbirth and some 64 000 who had aborted. Her findings were recorded in twenty-one papers, published in Australia and overseas. She was treasurer (1940-56) of the Victorian Society of Pathology and Experimental Medicine, and president (1958 and 1964-65) of the Association of Hospital Scientists, Victoria.

Of medium height, trimly built, generally well dressed and carefully coiffured, Hildred wore elegant spectacles behind which her eyes might sparkle or glare. If the latter, she would draw herself up, straighten her dress, hesitate (because of a controlled stammer) and then issue a devastating remark. She was not medically qualified, but her clinical knowledge was respected by the senior medical staff. The juniors probably never regarded her as anything other than a 'proper doctor' and she dealt with them with peremptory authority. Her autocratic attitude was also seen in the laboratory where she had a bell-press under her desk to summon her staff. For all that, they admired and loved her.

Hildred Butler retired in 1971. Despite undergoing numerous operations for cancer, she continued to work, studying the part played by unusual forms of bacteria in causing persistent urinary tract infection. She died on 8 April 1975 in the Royal Women's Hospital and was cremated with Anglican rites. Her portrait by Alan Martin is held by the hospital.

F. Fenner (ed), *History of Microbiology in Australia* (Canb, 1990); *MJA*, 2, 1975, p 844; *Aust and NZ J of Obstetrics and Gynaecology*, 22, 1982, p 11; *Age* (Melb), 16 Apr 1975.   H. D. ATTWOOD

BUTLIN, SYDNEY JAMES CHRISTOPHER LYON (1910-1977), economist and historian, was born on 20 October 1910 at Eastwood, Sydney, second of six children of native-born parents Thomas Lyon Butlin, orchardist and later a railway porter, and his wife Sara Mary, née Chantler. The Butlins lived at Singleton from about 1916;

Syd attended the local public school and, after the family moved, East Maitland Boys' High School (1923-27); he displayed literary and linguistic gifts, and was dux.

In 1926 Thomas was killed by a hit-and-run driver, leaving his dependants penniless. Mary and her daughters were forced to take in washing; Syd became head of the household at the age of 16 and learned frugality and resourcefulness, traits that were to remain with him throughout his life. He was awarded a public exhibition in 1928 and enrolled in economics at the University of Sydney (B.Ec., 1932). Contemporaries included (Sir) John Crawford, (Sir) John Phillips, (Sir) Ivan Dougherty, Mary Willmott Debenham (later Lady Phillips) and his own future wife Dorothy Jean Conen. Professor R. C. Mills [q.v.10] encouraged scholarly excellence and avoided the public policy debate more characteristic of economists at the University of Melbourne. A sound training in economics and economic history was provided by such distinguished teachers as (Sir) Robert Madgwick [q.v.]. Butlin thrived in the freedom of university life. He combined prodigious reading in English literature with economics, and graduated with first-class honours in economics and the university medal.

Awarded several travelling scholarships, Butlin entered Trinity College, Cambridge (B.A., 1934; M. A., 1939), at a time of growing intellectual turmoil surrounding the Keynesian revolution in economic theory. Unlike many of his contemporaries, he was not an uncritical convert: he was a Keynesian in spirit, but was also attracted to the ideas of the monetary theorist (Sir) Dennis Robertson. Returning to Sydney in 1934, Butlin worked as a research officer in the government statistician's office until appointed assistant-lecturer in economics at the university next year. At St Stephen's Presbyterian Church, Sydney, on 9 May 1936 he married Jean who was by then a schoolteacher. He was promoted lecturer in 1939.

Life for a young academic in the late 1930s was intense and challenging. Butlin lectured both day and evening on a wide range of subjects; he contributed regularly to the press and to public inquiries. Public finance was the subject of his early scholarly publications. In 1936 he was invited to lecture on money and banking. The subject was of intense contemporary interest with the royal commission into monetary and banking systems in progress. Characteristically, Butlin sought a historical introduction to the subject. When none could be found, he spent all his spare time over the next decade in writing his own. The outcome was *Foundations of the Australian Monetary System 1788-1851* (Melbourne, 1953), a monograph of rare distinction: rigorous in the use of evidence and theory, comprehensive and imaginative in scope, bold and elegant in structure. On the strength of the book, Cambridge awarded him a doctorate of letters in 1954.

Like many of his contemporaries, Butlin had spent part of World War II in public service. He was director of the economic division in the Department of War Organization of Industry from late 1941 to 1943 in Melbourne. On the principle that the official war historians should have first-hand experience of their subject, he was later commissioned to write the two economic volumes in the official series, 'Australia in the War of 1939-1945', under the editorship of Gavin Long [q.v.]. Again, the task involved great organizing skill and command of a vast amount of data. *War Economy 1939-1942* appeared in 1955; publication of *War Economy 1942-1945* (with C. B. Schedvin) was delayed until 1977 because of the pressure of university teaching and administration.

For most of the period from 1946, when he succeeded Mills in the chair of economics, Butlin was dean of the faculty of economics. With the help of an indefatigable administrative assistant, Joyce Fisher, he presided over the faculty and the department almost single-handed. His staff struggled with heavy teaching loads and inadequate accommodation in the early postwar years. While he was an excellent administrator, his style was of the elite Cambridge and Sydney of the 1930s, and he was less comfortable with the emerging mass institutions of the 1960s. He did not enjoy teaching large classes and his presentation was poor; he was at his best with small groups of outstanding students. Often resisting the creation of new departments and chairs, he found himself somewhat isolated from a number of his senior colleagues. In 1961 he published *Australia and New Zealand Bank* (London), an important history of the major Anglo-Australian banking group. He continued to work within a literary framework and to practise as an economic historian, preferences that did not sit easily with the growing formalist and mathematical trends of the discipline. Wisely he accepted a personal chair at the Australian National University, Canberra, in 1971. He spent his final years preparing an official history of central banking in Australia after 1945 and on a sequel to *Foundations*: his daughter Judith has since published his incomplete texts, the latter as *The Australian Monetary System, 1851-1914* (Sydney, 1986).

An influential figure at the University of Sydney in the 1950s and 1960s, he was a confidant of the vice-chancellor (Sir) Stephen Roberts [q.v]. Butlin was a member of the senate (1963-67), chairman of the appointments board (1954-55, 1958-61) and of the

Social Science Research Council of Australia (1958-62), president of the Economic Society of Australia and New Zealand (1953-54), a member of the Round Table group, and a founder and deputy chairman (1962-77) of Sydney University Press. As a chairman, he allowed committees free rein and then pulled the discussion together in a few, crisp sentences.

Quiet, shy and deeply private, Butlin was also able to draw on immense personal and intellectual reserves. He was a gifted conversationalist and raconteur, an inveterate tea-drinker and chain-smoker, as well as a courteous and kindly man who delighted in the achievements of his family. His complex and occasionally tense relationship with his younger brother Noel, another distinguished economic historian, masked feelings of deep, mutual respect. Survived by his wife, son and daughter, Syd Butlin died of a ruptured abdominal aortic aneurysm on 14 December 1977 in Royal North Shore Hospital, Sydney, and was cremated.

Aust Economic Hist Review, 18, Sept 1978, p 99, and 31, Sept 1991, p 3; *Economic Record*, no 145, Apr 1979, p 143; family information.

C. B. SCHEDVIN

BUTT, CHARLES SINCLAIR (1900-1973), businessman, was born on 28 July 1900 at Warrnambool, Victoria, son of Charles Herbert Stewart Butt, bank teller, and his wife Kathleen Mary, née Finlay, both Victorian born. Educated at Inglewood High School and Melbourne Church of England Grammar School, young Charles subsequently qualified as an accountant. On 21 June 1927 at St John's Anglican Church, Toorak, he married Cicely Ethel Mary Lloyd. Having been initially employed by the Alma Woolscouring Co. at Kensington, he worked for the Rapson Tyre Co. in Tasmania in 1928-32. When it failed, he transferred to the Dunlop-Perdriau [q.v.11] Rubber Co. Ltd in Melbourne. By 1934 Butt was chief accountant at Dunlop. On the advice of (Sir) Ivan Holyman [q.v.], he joined (Sir) Frank Beaurepaire [q.v.7] and in August became general manager of the new Olympic Tyre & Rubber Co. Pty Ltd.

Quiet and methodical, Butt applied his financial and business knowledge to building a sound firm. His professional and managerial skills, with Beaurepaire's organizational qualities, were significant in forming the basis of Olympic's success. Both men fostered a familial relationship with their staff at Footscray and strengthened these bonds by their involvement in local affairs. During World War II, with sources of natural rubber from Asia and New Guinea under Japanese control, the Commonwealth government appointed Butt honorary controller of tyres and rubber. He went abroad with (Sir) Robert Blackwood, Dunlop's technical manager, to study synthetic replacements for natural rubber, and was also sent to New Zealand to advise on control of tyres.

Butt returned to Olympic in 1946 with an enhanced understanding of the problems of supply and an industry-wide reputation for fairness. In 1949 he became vice-chairman of Olympic General Products Pty Ltd, a subsidiary formed to market ancillary manufactures of the tyre and cable companies. Called upon to advise the Commonwealth government in 1950-51 about the production of rubber from Malayan plantations in view of potential terrorist actions in the region, he visited that country, Indonesia and Ceylon. In 1954 he was made managing director of the Olympic Tyre & Rubber Co. When Beaurepaire died in 1956, Butt became chairman of the holding company, Olympic Consolidated Industries Ltd; Ian Beaurepaire, Sir Frank's son, was vice-chairman and succeeded Butt in 1959.

In 1961-67 Butt was chairman of the Commonwealth Serum Laboratories. He remained a director of the various Olympic companies and served on the boards of other firms, including James Chocolates Pty Ltd, Guthrie & Co. (Aust.) Pty Ltd and R. W. Crabtree & Sons (A'sia) Pty Ltd. A member of the Royal Melbourne and the Peninsula Country golf clubs, he also belonged to the Athenaeum Club, Melbourne, and the Commonwealth Club, Canberra. He was appointed C.M.G. in 1962. Survived by his two daughters, Butt died at Shenton Park, Perth, on 21 February 1973 and was cremated with Presbyterian forms. His portrait by (Sir) William Dargie hangs in the foyer of the Olympic Tyre & Rubber Co. offices at Footscray.

G. Lomas, *The Will to Win* (Melb, 1960); *Age* (Melb), *Herald* (Melb) and *Sun News-Pictorial*, 21 Feb 1973; information from Mr I. F. Beaurepaire, Mount Eliza, Vic, and Miss E. Butt, Balwyn, Melb.   D. H. KEMP

BUTTON, PERCY ARCHIBALD (1892-1954), acrobat and itinerant, was born on 22 August 1892 at Marylebone Workhouse, London, son of Sarah Jane Button, kitchenmaid. Percy never knew his parents, but lived with a grandmother on the Isle of Wight until the age of 18, working as a fitter's assistant after leaving school. The story that he was injured while employed in an English circus cannot be proved, but in those years he learned the skills of an acrobat. Emigrating to Western Australia in 1910, he worked at odd jobs as a farmhand and in Perth. On 1 May 1917 Button enlisted in the Australian Imperial Force. He was 5 ft 4 ins (162.6 cm) tall, with blue eyes and brown hair. Sent to England with reinforcements for the 44th Battalion, he was invalided home and discharged on 10 October 1918 without having seen action.

He took to a vagrant life in Perth, sometimes earning a living by selling newspapers and collecting bottles, but soon becoming the city's best-known street entertainer. 'Percy Buttons' attracted bystanders through his clever tumbling, somersaults and the tricks he performed with handcuffs. His battered, upturned hat received many small coins, and he estimated that he averaged ten shillings a day by his street performances. On his best day, at a Royal Agricultural Show, he earned nearly £4, not far short of the weekly basic wage. Frequently arrested for vagrancy— often so that the police could find him warm lodging and a bath—he was nevertheless respected as scrupulously honest: he handed over many valuable articles he had found to the authorities.

Although Button liked a large gin squash now and then, he was no drunkard. He was a keen but unsuccessful speculator in lotteries, and, when he had money, often yielded to the lure of the local Chinese gaming-houses. A stooped, nuggety figure with a ragged moustache, known to some as 'Percy the Unwashed', he was turned away from many hotels and business premises, but dined regularly at a respectable restaurant—always on fried eggs. When a newspaper published a front-page picture of a 'well-known Perth character', scrubbed up in top hat, white tie and tails, few recognized 'Percy Buttons'.

Neither the 1930s Depression nor World War II made much difference to Button's style of living, but, as age slowed his acrobatic prowess, he added the mouth-organ to his repertoire and uncertainly mastered one tune, *The Chestnut Tree*. Attacked by a lout who kicked him in the stomach, Button was also crippled by a hernia; a series of heavily wet, postwar winters further impaired his health. By 1951 his condition had so deteriorated that arrangements were made for his admission to the Old Men's Home at Dalkeith. He died of coronary thrombosis on 5 March 1954 at Claremont Mental Hospital and was buried in Karrakatta cemetery with Catholic rites. The Repatriation Department paid for his funeral.

People (Syd), 8 Nov 1950; *Sunday Times* (Perth), 7, 14 Mar 1954; E. E. Ranford, Oldtimers Who Also Played Their Part (ms, BL).   G. C. BOLTON

BUTTROSE, ALFRED WILLIAM (1912-1978), army officer and businessman, was born on 18 November 1912 at Glenelg,

Adelaide, son of William Frederick Buttrose, clerk, and his wife Priscilla Marion, née Hawkes. Educated at Glenelg Public School and Thebarton Technical High School, in 1928 Alfred joined Elder, Smith [qq.v.4,6] & Co. Ltd and rapidly advanced in the wool department. He enlisted in the Citizen Military Forces, rose to sergeant in the 27th Battalion and in March 1933 was commissioned lieutenant. On 14 December 1935 he married Rhona Marion Barrett at St Cuthbert's Anglican Church, Prospect.

Appointed captain (13 October 1939) in the Australian Imperial Force, Buttrose was posted to the 2nd/10th Battalion which arrived in England in June 1940. He transferred to the 2nd/33rd Battalion and was promoted major in July. The battalion was sent to North Africa and in May 1941 to Syria. Next month, while commanding 'C' Company, Buttrose conducted successful engagements against the Vichy-French in the Merdjayoun sector. He was mentioned in dispatches for his service in the Middle East. The battalion returned to Australia to prepare for operations in Papua and New Guinea; in April 1942 Buttrose was promoted temporary lieutenant colonel and placed in command. Because of his comparative youth, his troops referred to him as 'Alfie the Boy Wonder' and—when his disciplinary measures were not appreciated —as 'The Boy Bastard'. He would win their confidence in battle.

From September to December 1942 the 2nd/33rd helped to push the Japanese back from Imita Ridge, Papua, to Gona on the north coast. In appalling conditions Buttrose deployed his unit with skill and aggression, playing a large part in defeating the enemy at Templeton's Crossing (October), Gorari village (November) and Gona (December). For his deeds, he was awarded the Distinguished Service Order. Reduced in strength from some 550 to 178 men, the battalion was withdrawn to Australia early in 1943. Buttrose was relieved that year due to a long bout of sickness. On recovering, he performed training duties until July 1944 when he took command of the 2nd/5th Battalion.

By January 1945 his battalion was in action in the Torricelli Mountains, south-east of Aitape, New Guinea. Buttrose's troops penetrated the Japanese defences in the Perembil area, and destroyed their forces at Balif, Bulamita and Luwaite. In June the 2nd/5th carried out a vigorous offensive south of Wewak, outflanking and crushing the defenders at Yamil, Ulupu and Ilipem. For his planning and leadership, he won a Bar to his D.S.O. and was again mentioned in dispatches. He relinquished his command in November and transferred to the Reserve of Officers on 8 December.

Resuming work with Elders, Buttrose managed the skin department in Adelaide before moving to Perth in 1948 to be staff superintendent. In May 1950 he rejoined the C.M.F. as temporary brigadier in charge of headquarters group, Western Command. Having commanded (1953-56) the 13th Infantry Brigade, he was to be placed on the Retired List in 1968 as a brigadier. Meanwhile, business took him to Brisbane where he became the company's manager for Queensland in 1958, but he returned to Perth three years later as general manager for Western Australia. The acquisition of the rival pastoral house, Goldsbrough Mort [qq.v.4,5] & Co. Ltd, in 1962 gave him authority over one of the State's largest commercial organizations.

In his military and business careers Buttrose was an imaginative, enterprising and decisive leader. Phlegmatic and ever 'the commanding officer' to subordinates, he expected them to do their best and to give allegiance, but he was compassionate, scrupulously fair and repaid loyalty with his own. He had a tremendous capacity for work and 'never, throughout his life, failed to perform a duty to the satisfaction of his seniors'. Stocky in build, with a broad, fresh face, shining, blue eyes and light-brown hair, he was chairman (1969-78) of the Perth Diocesan Trustees, president (1972-78) of the Meath Ministering League Anglican Homes and a lay canon (1973-78) of St George's Cathedral. The Western Australian government appointed him a member of the Post-Secondary Education Commission in 1976. He was active in many community service bodies, among them Perth Legacy and Rotary.

Survived by his wife, daughter and three sons, Buttrose died of coronary vascular disease on 26 December 1978 at Crawley and was cremated. An offer of appointment as O.B.E. arrived after his death.

W. Crooks, *The Footsoldiers* (Syd, 1971); S. Trigellis-Smith, *All the King's Enemies* (Melb, 1988); 2nd/33rd Battalion Assn, *Mud and Blood*, July 1953, July-Sept 1975, Jan-Mar 1979; *Elders Weekly*, 70, no 2844, 11 May 1978; *Elders (WA) Staff News*, 22, no 19, 11 May 1978; *Countryman* (Perth), 11 May 1978; information from and family papers held by Mrs R. Buttrose, Crawley, Perth; information from Mr M. N. B. Grace, Nedlands, Perth.   KEITH D. HOWARD

BUTTS, LEONARD WILLIAM HENRY (1904-1975), solicitor and businessman, was born on 1 December 1904 at Northfleet, Kent, England, only child of Leonard John Butts, chalk quarry labourer, and his wife Ada Florence, née Johnson. The family migrated to Queensland. Leonard was educated at Wynnum High School and Rockhampton Grammar School. On 16 February 1920 he joined the public service in Brisbane and in August was appointed to the Titles and Stamp Duties Office, Rockhampton; he studied accountancy at night and obtained legal qualifications. He then worked as an articled clerk with Grant & Stumm, a local firm of solicitors. Admitted as a solicitor on 9 December 1929, Butts joined Morris, Fletcher & Cross and became a partner in 1932. At St John's Anglican Cathedral, Brisbane, on 9 December 1933 he married a public servant Helen Margaret Letherland.

Mobilized in June 1940 as a legal services officer at headquarters, First Australian Army, with the rank of captain, Butts was posted to Northern Command operational headquarters in January 1942 and in May was promoted temporary lieutenant colonel. On 20 July he transferred to the Australian Imperial Force and in October 1943 was appointed chief legal officer, I Australian Corps. From May 1944 to July 1945 he served in New Guinea and Bougainville, and was twice mentioned in dispatches. When Butts relinquished his appointment in September 1945, Lieutenant General (Sir) Vernon Sturdee [q.v.] commended his 'integrity, fairness and wholehearted co-operation'. Butts was appointed O.B.E. in 1947.

After the war he returned to Morris, Fletcher & Cross. Butts was a councillor (1946-60) and president (1950-52) of the Queensland Law Society, and sat on a number of its committees, including a statutory committee that investigated allegations of misconduct in 1967-68. Vice-president (1951-54) and president (1954-56) of the Law Council of Australia, he was also an honorary solicitor for many organizations. He was, as well, a director of several prominent firms, among them Elder Smith Goldsbrough Mort [qq.v.4,6,4,5] Ltd, and chairman of the Queensland board of Colonial Mutual Life Pty Ltd; he had played a major role in the formation of the Brisbane Development Association and chaired its inaugural meeting in 1957.

Community minded, Butts was a trustee of the Queensland Anti-Cancer Fund, a director (1959-72) of the Queensland division of the National Heart Foundation of Australia and a councillor (1953) of the St John Ambulance Association; he was appointed a knight of grace of the Order of St John in 1974. In addition, he was a member of the board of the Queensland Theatre Company and of the governing committee of the Australian Elizabethan Theatre Trust. In 1964 he was elevated to C.B.E. Influential, liberal in outlook and gifted with a sense of humour, Butts was respected for his tact, humane judgement and common sense. He retired in 1969, but remained with Morris, Fletcher & Cross as a consultant.

In his retirement Butts was a founding

member (1971) of the interim council of Griffith University, Brisbane, deputy-chairman (1971-75) of its first council and its first deputy-chancellor (from July 1975). A keen sportsman, he was president of the Ithaca and St Lucia bowling clubs, and an inaugural member of the Ashgrove Golf Club. He died on 6 October 1975 in Brisbane and was cremated with Presbyterian forms; his wife, son and three daughters survived him.

Notable Men of Queensland (Brisb, 1950); *Sunday Mail* (Brisb), 11 Aug 1974; *Courier Mail*, 29 May, 1 June 1957, 13 June 1964, 8 Oct 1975, 16 Jan 1976; records of Law Soc of Qld, Brisb; information from Mrs H. Butts, Indooroopilly, Brisb.

M. W. D. WHITE

BYLES, MARIE BEUZEVILLE (1900-1979), solicitor and conservationist, was born on 8 April 1900 at Ashton-upon-Mersey, Cheshire, England, only daughter and eldest child of Cyril Beuzeville Byles, a railway-signal engineer, and his wife Ida Margaret, née Unwin. In March 1912 the family reached Sydney in the *Anchises*. Marie's parents were Unitarians, Fabian socialists and pacifists. Cyril became signals engineer to the New South Wales railways; Ida was a suffragette, a proponent of dress reform, a temperance advocate and a vegetarian. Marie recalled that her mother disliked housework and warned her against economic dependency.

Educated at Presbyterian Ladies' colleges at Croydon and Pymble, Marie was head prefect and dux at Pymble. She graduated from the University of Sydney (B.A., 1921; LL.B., 1924), winning the Rose Scott [q.v.11] prize in private international law. Articled to J. Stuart Thom, Byles was admitted as solicitor on 6 June 1924 and worked as managing clerk for Henry Davis & Co. until 1927. She studied economics at night and wrote about the inherent instability and injustices in capitalism.

As a student, Byles had earned pocket-money by journalism. She wrote on political issues, legal subjects, bushwalking and mountaineering. Her sense of justice drew her to feminism and her admission as the first female solicitor in the State was welcomed by the women's movement which had campaigned vigorously for woman's right to practise law. Briefed by the National Council of Women of New South Wales and other women's organizations, Byles wrote several pamphlets on woman's legal disabilities for the United Associations (of Women) and was included in numerous delegations to ministers —State and Federal—that sought redress. In particular, she argued the case for equal guardianship, and for a married woman's rights to retain her nationality and to have separate domicile. She was also active in the equal-pay campaign.

Byles was an important publicist for the women's movement, writing frequently in newspapers and magazines on discriminatory provisions in the law and discriminatory practices in the courts. As legal correspondent (1927-36) for the *Australian Woman's Mirror*, she drew attention to recent cases where women had experienced disabilities, and revealed how magistrates and judges interpreted the law to make woman's behaviour the issue on trial. She wrote on other matters (tenancy law, making a will, copyright in frocks), but the main thrust of her journalism was to advise women of their rights and of those denied them. In 'Who owns the housekeeping?' she informed them that the money they received from their husbands was, according to law, held in trust to spend for the husband. 'The moral', she added, 'is that legally there is no reward to you for frugality, and that you may as well spend all you can!'

She briefed women barristers when they were available and in 1926 twice briefed Sibyl Morrison [q.v.10] on the one day. From 1929 Byles ran her own practice at Eastwood, successfully enough to employ staff (her preference was for married women) and to become a master solicitor. The work was mainly conveyancing and probate, with some matrimonial matters. Byles disliked litigation. She claimed that she became expert in clawing back from a deceased estate, and avoiding payment of duties on, property that had rightly belonged to the wife.

Walking holidays were part of Marie's childhood. She built a tiny house, Ahimsa, on a sandstone ridge in open forest at Cheltenham where she lived austerely, growing her own vegetables and sleeping on the balcony. Although only 5 ft 2 ins (157.5 cm) tall and not physically robust, she had great endurance. She loved the grandeur of mountains, climbed Mount Cook in 1928, went twice again to New Zealand and wrote of her unconventional experiences in *By Cargo Boat & Mountain* (London, 1931). In 1938 she attempted to scale Mount Sanseto in southern China, but was prevented by bad weather from reaching its summit. Stopped from climbing by a foot injury which never properly healed, she remained an enthusiastic bushwalker. She was elected a fellow (1939) of the Royal Geographical Society, London.

Executive office in the Sydney Bush Walkers brought her into the Federation of Bushwalking Clubs, of which she was honorary secretary (1943-47). She was the first editor of and a regular contributor to the *Bushwalker*: it appeared annually in 1937-48. The federation established information and search services, campaigned for new national parks and legislation to protect native flora and fauna, and endeavoured to conserve 'primitive' areas. In 1947, when she resigned from the federation, she concluded her letter: 'Finally, Mr Secretary, please don't let your wife waste her valuable time writing a reply in flowery style to this letter. I detest such stuff'. With bushwalking friends, she had helped to secure the reservation in 1932 of 650 acres (263 ha) of bushland as Bouddi Natural (National) Park on Pittwater and long served as a trustee. It pleased her that the trust met on the beach. She had retained her connexion with the United Associations of Women, but her other interests left her little free time. She needed rest in 1947.

All her life she opposed the taking of life. She had lectured for the League of Nations Union before World War II and during the war protested against the incitement of hatred of the Japanese. Travelling in 1938 through Burma and Tibet, she had encountered Buddhism and on her return began reading the *Bhagavad Gita*. She resumed worship at her local Unitarian church where a change of ministers left her dissatisfied. She began experimenting with solitude. Each year she spent a week alone on Mount Kosciusko. She began meditation and was an original member (1951) of the Buddhist Society of New South Wales.

After her mother's death in 1953, Marie went first to Rangoon, then to the holy Buddhist sites in northern India and Nepal; for a time she lived as a hermit on the lower Himalayas; she journeyed to Gandhi's ashram and visited Ceylon. It was a healing experience. 'Accept suffering and suffering disappears', was the message she took from Buddhism. In *Footprints of Gautama the Buddha* (1957) and *The Lotus and the Spinning Wheel* (1963) she expounded the teaching of the Buddha: in the former, she disputed the privileged position of the monk as against the nun in contemporary practice; in the latter she set the teachings of Gandhi alongside Buddha's and saw both as necessary in the modern world. Her experiences in meditation centres in Burma and later in Japan led her to write *Journey into Burmese Silence* (1962) and *Paths to Inner Calm* (1965).

Marie built an ashram which became a centre for a small group of adherents to Buddhist teachings. She suffered persistent ill health and severe pain in her foot. Her spiritual diary of her latter years is a record of a continuing struggle to control pain. She spent long periods in meditation. In 1966 an unknown assailant battered her about the head as she slept alone at Ahimsa. Marie spent several months in hospital and never completely recovered. She retired in 1970.

Marie Byles died on 21 November 1979 at her Cheltenham home. She had left sworn testimony of her wish to be allowed to die naturally and requested the Cremation Society of Australia to collect her body. She asked that a friend, preferably a woman, read designated texts at her memorial service. Her ashes were scattered at Ahimsa which she left to the State branch of the National Trust of Australia.

P. Croucher, *Buddhism in Australia 1848-1988* (Syd, 1989); *New Outlook* (Syd), 17 Nov 1923; *Woman's World*, 1 Mar 1932; *Sun-Herald*, 23 Apr 1972; *SMH*, 29 Apr 1972, 14 Nov 1974, 24 Nov 1979, 8 July 1985; Byles papers *and* United Assns (of Women) records (ML); Jessie Street papers (NL).   HEATHER RADI

BYRNE, ETHEL (1895-1957), physician and pathologist, was born on 28 August 1895 at Cookardinia, New South Wales, ninth child of James Byrne, schoolteacher, and his wife Margaret, née Crennan, both native-born. Encouraged by her father to further her education, Ethel attended West Maitland Girls' High School and won an exhibition to the University of Sydney (M.B., Ch.M., 1919). Her appointment as junior resident medical officer at Newcastle Hospital began a close association with that institution which lasted for the rest of her life. She was the only resident medical officer there during the influenza epidemic of 1919 which was followed by an outbreak of tuberculosis next year.

Appointed resident pathologist in April 1920, Byrne resigned in 1928. For almost twenty years she was a consulting pathologist to the hospital, while conducting a successful private practice at Newcastle. She also supervised pathology services at Cessnock, Kurri and Maitland hospitals. Epidemics of diphtheria (1929) and of infantile paralysis and diphtheria (1931-34) placed heavy demands on Byrne and on Dr Ruby Beveridge who had succeeded her as resident pathologist. An annual report praised their 'valuable and zealous work'. During this time Byrne also directed the anti-tuberculosis dispensary in King Street which was maintained by the Department of Health; she continued as director when the chest clinic was transferred to Newcastle Hospital.

In 1943 Byrne was elected a member of the Royal Australasian College of Physicians. Four years later she was appointed staff physician and tuberculosis officer to Newcastle Hospital. She was the sole physician at the chest unit which opened in 1947 at Rankin Park, and was responsible for the establishment of Byrne House (named in her honour) which provided accommodation and rehabilitation for male tuberculosis patients. Sponsored by the Hospitals Commission, in 1955-56 she visited Canada, the United

States of America, Britain and Europe to study recent developments in the treatment of tuberculosis.

A short, slim woman, with a gentle and charming personality, Dr Byrne endeared herself to staff and patients. She died, unmarried, on 5 November 1957 at Royal Newcastle Hospital and was cremated with Anglican rites. A colleague wrote: 'Ethel Byrne's life was completely spent in unselfish service to others. Her recognition of her professional responsibilities, her devotion to family and friends, her help to those in need formed the pattern of her daily life'.

G. L. McDonald (ed), *Roll of the Royal Australasian College of Physicians*, 1, 1938-1975 (Syd, 1988); Newcastle Hospital, *Annual Report*, 1918-57; *MJA*, 1 Mar 1958; *Newcastle Morning Herald*, 6 Nov 1957; information from Dr R. M. Mills, Newcastle, NSW.   MARGARET HENRY

BYRNE, SAMUEL MICHAEL (1883-1978), miner and artist, was born on 10 July 1883 at Humbug Scrub, near Gawler, South Australia, and named Michael Eldrige Samuel, son of James Burns (d. 1890), a blacksmith from Ireland, and his Australian-born wife Elizabeth, née Pope. In 1885 the family moved to Thackaringa, New South Wales, and later to nearby Broken Hill. Following his mother's death in 1892, Sam was brought up by his aunt Emily Tapsell. He attended Broken Hill Superior Public School until 1898, then began work in the Broken Hill Proprietary Co. Ltd's mine. On 20 December 1910 as Samuel Michael Byrne he married with Anglican rites his cousin Florence Pope who came from a South Australian farming family; he registered his change of name in 1941. For fifty-one years he worked as a miner, both as an underground labourer and surface engine driver, until he retired in 1949.

Starting to paint in the early 1950s, Sam was partly guided by May Harding, an art teacher at Broken Hill Technical College. He won prizes at local art shows and was encouraged by the Melbourne painter Leonard French who introduced him to a number of gallery-owners. Sam Byrne exhibited to critical acclaim at the Rudy Komon Art Gallery, Sydney, in 1963 and 1968, with 'Pro' Hart at the Australian Sculpture Centre, Canberra, in 1968, and later with the (Kym) Bonython Art Gallery, Adelaide.

Essentially self-taught, Byrne used a miniaturist technique, disregarding perspective and most academic painting conventions. Although he produced some water-colours, he preferred oils or synthetic enamels on masonite, and sometimes sprinkled silver-lead ore on his pictures to make them sparkle. His work revealed his socialist leanings, particularly in his narrative depictions of the Broken Hill strikes of 1892, 1909 and 1919-20. A prolific artist who frequently produced numerous versions of the same theme, he mainly painted scenes of Broken Hill, full of exact details of mining methods, rabbit plagues and pub life.

His distinct 'primitive' or 'naive' style of painting, with its bright palette and graphic articulation, is usually discussed in the context of the Australian bush painters Henri Bastin and 'Pro' Hart. Some of Byrne's better-known works include 'The Silver City' (1960), Broken Hill Civic Art Gallery; 'Tar and Feathering, 1892 Strike' (1964), Mildura Arts Centre; 'Turks Fire on Picnic Train, Jan 1st 1915' (1964) and 'Waltzing Matilda' (1962). His work was included in the survey exhibition of Australian naive painters at the Benalla Art Gallery in 1976.

Upright and slim, with a wide grin, Byrne loved music and dressed in a pin-striped suit when he visited Sydney. He painted in a rusty, tin shed behind his home and, as if to illustrate his boast 'I'm as old as the city myself', produced from memory a faithful visual chronicle of Broken Hill. Some of his paintings bring to mind parallels with S. T. Gill [q.v.1] and the English artist W. S. Lowry. After he turned 80, Byrne suffered increasingly from glaucoma and arthritis, and the quantity and quality of his output declined. Survived by three of his four sons, he died on 24 February 1978 at Broken Hill and was buried in the local cemetery. A small retrospective of his paintings was held at the Gallery Art Naive, South Yarra, Melbourne, in 1979; his work is held in the Australian National Gallery, Canberra, most State collections and in private collections in Australia, Europe and North America.

A. M. Banfield, *The Innocent Eye*, exhibition cat (Benalla, Vic, 1976); F. Lumbers, *The Art of Pro Hart* (Adel, 1977); G. Lehmann, *Australian Primitive Painters* (Brisb, 1977); B. McCullough, *Australian Naive Painters* (Melb, 1977); R. Moore, *Sam Byrne, Folk Painter of the Silver City* (Melb, 1985); *Art and Aust*, 2, no 1, May 1964, p 10; *SMH*, 24 July 1963, 8 June 1966, 24 Oct 1972; *Age* (Melb), 21 May 1977.   SASHA GRISHIN

BYRNES, ROBERT STEEL (1899-1979), Presbyterian administrator and writer, was born on 6 June 1899 at Goldsborough, near Dunolly, Victoria, youngest of eight children of Patrick James Byrnes, goldminer, and his wife Agnes, née Cairns, both native-born. Educated at Melbourne High School, Robert worked for the Melbourne City Council. He enlisted in the Australian Imperial Force on 28 October 1918, but was demobilized on 24 December. Subsequently appointed an organizing and travelling secretary of the Presbyterian Church of Victoria, he was engaged in youth work for two years. On 3 August 1922 at Northcote he married a teacher Janet Mafeking Perkins. That year they moved to Sydney where he was employed by the Presbyterian Church of New South Wales and graduated from the University of Sydney (B.A., 1932) with the Wilfrid E. Johnson prize in economics.

On 5 August 1940 Byrnes was attached (with officer status) to the A.I.F. as a representative of the Young Men's Christian Association; he embarked for the Middle East with the 7th Division in October. Posted to the 2nd/1st Battalion, he remained with the unit during its service in Egypt and Syria—except when in the Western Desert (October 1941) with the 9th Division—and was made senior representative of the Y.M.C.A. in Egypt. He returned with the battalion to Australia in August 1942 and his appointment terminated in September.

Next month Byrnes became general secretary of the Presbyterian Church of Queensland and treasurer of its assembly. He initiated several developmental projects, including cottage homes for the elderly. A councillor of Emmanuel College, University of Queensland, and of the Presbyterian and Methodist Schools' Association, he was a board-member of Scots College, Warwick, and of the Presbyterian Girls' colleges at Warwick and Toowoomba. He was also president (1952-57) of the Queensland Y.M.C.A., and governor of St Andrew's War Memorial Hospital, Brisbane, and of the Freemasons Homes for the Aged.

Scholarly and courteous, Byrnes was charming and erudite. He wrote *Serving the Church* (1948, 1958) and *The Kirk in Queensland* (1951), and edited (1963-65) the religious journal, *Outlook*. In 1954 he published *Endeavour and Other Poems*. A member (1954) and deputy-chairman (1957) of the Queensland Literature Board of Review, he was co-editor of *The Queensland Centenary Anthology* (1959). State (1952-57) and federal (1960, 1962) president of the Fellowship of Australian Writers, in 1961 he visited the Soviet Union. A volume of his collected poems, *The Light of Setting Suns*, was published posthumously in 1980.

Byrnes was appointed M.B.E. in 1964 and next year retired as the Church's general secretary. Proud of his British heritage and its customs, he was deeply interested in contemporary affairs. He had a shrewd appreciation of personalities, a wide circle of acquaintances and friends, and was a Freemason. Survived by his wife, daughter and three sons, he died on 16 November 1979 in St Andrew's Nursing Home, Brisbane, and was cremated.

Presbyterian Outlook (Brisb), Aug 1965, p 15; Presbyterian Church of Qld, *Assembly Minutes*, 1942, pp 5, 76, 1965, p 55; Univ Qld, *Alumni News*, Mar 1980; *Bulletin*, 15 June 1960; *Courier-Mail*, 1 Jan 1964; R. S. Byrnes file, Presbyterian Church of Qld Archives, Fortitude Valley, Brisb; information from Mr I. S. McF. Byrnes, Coorparoo, and Mr L. J. Davis, Stafford, Brisb; personal information.

J. S. D. MELLICK

BYRNES, SIR THOMAS PERCY FRANCIS (1893-1973), farmer and politician, was born on 28 January 1893 at Eidsvold, Queensland, son of Victorian-born parents, Thomas Byrnes, miner, and his wife, Annie Louisa, née James. Thomas had brought cattle to Queensland and remained to prospect for gold. The family returned to Victoria in 1897 and farmed at Gippsland and then at Nyah West. Educated at Murrabit and Koondrook state schools, in 1907 Percy won a scholarship to Wesley College, Melbourne. He captained the school shooting-team and in 1912 entered Queen's College, University of Melbourne, on a further scholarship; he began an agricultural science course, but left at the end of the year to work in the State Rivers and Water Supply Department. Having declined a teaching post at Wesley in 1915, he enlisted in the Australian Imperial Force on 24 January 1916 and served on the Western Front with the 3rd Pioneer Battalion.

Suffering from tuberculosis, Byrnes returned home and was discharged on 26 December 1917. He was advised that a rural climate would assist his recuperation and moved to the family farm at Nyah where, on 5 June 1918, he married Dorothy Elizabeth Gretchen Judd with Presbyterian forms. After selling the property in 1920, he ran a general store for twelve months before taking up a 35-acre (14.2 ha) block at Woorinen. He concentrated on producing dried fruit and was soon a recognized expert, writing for the *Bulletin* under the pseudonym, 'Grapevine'. Made a director of the Woorinen Cooperative Packing Co. in 1922, he later served on the advisory board of the Council for Scientific and Industrial Research farm at Merbein.

Concern for the welfare of soldier settlers drew Byrnes into politics. He was elected to the Swan Hill Shire Council in 1935 (president 1939-40). At the 1937 and 1940 State elections he contested Swan Hill as an endorsed Country Party candidate, but the seat was easily retained by Frank Old [q.v.11]. On the death of Henry Pye, Byrnes was chosen in 1942 as Country Party candidate for the Legislative Council province of North Western which he won uncontested and held until his retirement in 1969.

Appointed minister without portfolio in the Hollway-McDonald [qq.v.] coalition government on 20 November 1947, Byrnes introduced legislation providing for reconstruction of land in the Mallee. He became leader of the Country Party in the Legislative Council in 1949, held the public works and lands portfolios in the McDonald governments of 1950-52 and was government leader in the Upper House. As minister, Byrnes was committed to Victoria's economic development and regularly criticized the financial policies of the Menzies-Fadden [qq.v.] Federal coalition for retarding the State's growth.

With the election of a majority Liberal government in 1955, Byrnes retained leadership of the Country Party in the council where his party held the balance of power until 1970. Astute in his dealings with Labor and Liberal leaders, he advanced Country Party interests, while winning the respect and affection of his parliamentary colleagues by his good humour and hard work. In 1964 the Country and Labor parties combined to threaten (Sir) Henry Bolte's budget bills in the council: Byrnes was involved in the often tense negotiations with the government which led the premier to make major concessions to the Country Party. When the budget came before the council in October, Byrnes announced—to Labor's chagrin—that his party had decided to grant it free passage.

Knighted in 1964, Sir Percy resigned from parliament in September 1969. He died at Swan Hill on 5 March 1973; accorded a state funeral, he was buried with Presbyterian and Masonic forms in the local cemetery; his wife survived him, as did their son and two of their three daughters. Streets at Swan Hill and Woorinen are named after him.

PD (LC Vic), 30 June 1942, p 13, 20 Nov 1951, p 28, 6 Mar 1973, p 3701; *Countryman* (Melb), 24 Sept 1937, 1 Mar 1940, 24 Apr 1942, 28 Feb 1963; *Sunraysia Daily*, 2 Jan 1964; *Age* (Melb), 9 Sept 1969, 6 Mar 1973; *Swan Hill Guardian*, 5, 8 Mar 1973; family information.   B. J. COSTAR

C

'CADDIE'; *see* EDMONDS, CATHERINE

CADE, JOHN FREDERICK JOSEPH (1912-1980), medical scientist, was born on 18 January 1912 at Horsham, Victoria, son of David Duncan Cade, medical practitioner, and his wife Ellen, née Edwards, both Victorian born. David commanded the 3rd Field Ambulance, Australian Imperial Force, during World War I and was awarded the Distinguished Service Order. In 1932 he became medical superintendent at Sunbury Mental Hospital.

Educated at Scotch College and the University of Melbourne (M.B., B.S., 1934; M.D., 1938), John was a resident medical officer at St Vincent's Hospital in 1935 and at the Royal Children's Hospital in 1936. That year he joined the mental hygiene branch of the Department of the Chief Secretary and was appointed medical officer at Mont Park Mental Hospital. At St Patrick's Catholic Cathedral, Melbourne, on 1 November 1937 he married Estana Evelyn Jean Charles, a double-certificated nurse; they were to have four sons and a daughter.

Having served in the Militia from 1935, Cade was appointed captain, Australian Army Medical Corps, A.I.F., on 1 July 1940 and posted to the 2nd/9th Field Ambulance. He arrived in Singapore in February 1941 and was promoted major in September. From February 1942 to September 1945 he suffered the privations of a prisoner of war in Changi camp.

Demobilized on 2 January 1946, Cade returned to the mental hygiene branch, now in the Department of Health, becoming medical superintendent and psychiatrist at the Repatriation Mental Hospital, Bundoora. Suspecting that some excessive toxin in the urine of manic patients was a product of metabolic disorder, he experimented on guinea-pigs with a disused hospital kitchen as his laboratory. He found that the animals became extremely lethargic and were protected from the toxicity of injected urea when lithium carbonate was given simultaneously. Taking lithium himself with no ill effect, he then used it to treat ten patients with chronic or recurrent mania, on whom he found it to have a pronounced calming effect. Cade's remarkably successful results were detailed in his paper, 'Lithium salts in the treatment of psychotic excitement', published in the *Medical Journal of Australia* (1949). He subsequently found that lithium was also of some value in assisting depressives. His discovery of the efficacy of a cheap, naturally occurring and widely available element in dealing with manic-depressive disorders provided an alternative to the existing therapies of shock treatment or prolonged hospitalization.

In 1952 Cade was appointed psychiatrist superintendent and dean of the clinical school at Royal Park Psychiatric Hospital. Two years later, at the request of the Mental Hygiene Authority which was planning to remodel Royal Park, he visited Britain for six months to inspect psychiatric institutions. On his return, he introduced modern facilities and replaced the rather authoritarian approach to patient care with a more personal and informal style that included group therapy. Concerned at the number of alcohol-related cases, he supported voluntary admission to aid early detection and later proposed the use of large doses of thiamin in the treatment of alcoholism.

Active in professional organizations, Cade was a foundation fellow (1963), State chairman (1963-80) and national president (1969-70) of the (Royal) Australian and New Zealand College of Psychiatrists, and a member (1970-80) of the Medical Board of Victoria. In 1977 he retired from his hospital appointments.

Although the use of lithium revolutionized the treatment of manic-depressive disorders from the 1960s, it was not until 1970 that Cade gained international recognition for his work. That year he received the psychiatric award of the Taylor Manor Hospital, Maryland, United States of America, and was made a distinguished fellow of the American Psychiatric Association. In 1974 he shared the second international award of the Kittay Scientific Foundation in New York with the Danish professor Mogens Schou, whose large clinical trials had validated Cade's research. Appointed A.O. in 1976, Cade was guest of honour that year at an international lithium conference held at New York University's school of medicine.

An 'honourable, upright Christian gentleman', Cade had a mordant sense of humour and an unassuming, rather withdrawn manner. He was modest about his discovery: in his book, *Mending the Mind* (1979), he discussed the use of lithium treatment without mentioning his own part in it. Survived by his wife and sons, he died of cancer on 16 November 1980 at Fitzroy and was buried in Yan Yean cemetery. A portrait by Max Middleton is held by the family.

Recognition of Cade's pioneering work

continued after his death. In 1980 the first John Cade memorial lecture was delivered by Professor Schou at the congress in Jerusalem of the Collegian International Psychopharmacologium (of which Cade had been made an honorary member earlier that year). The John Cade award was inaugurated in 1982 by the Victorian branch of the R.A.N.Z.C.P. and in 1983 the faculty of medicine at the University of Melbourne established the John Cade memorial prize. In 1985 the American National Institute of Mental Health estimated that Cade's discovery of the efficacy of lithium in the treatment of manic depression had saved the world at least $US 17.5 billion in medical costs.

S. Baldwin (ed), *Unsung Heroes and Heroines of Australia* (Melb, 1988); S. Blackall (ed), *The People Who Made Australia Great* (Syd, 1988); *MJA*, 1, 1981, p 489; *Pharmacopsychiatry*, 14, 1981, p 148; *Sun News-Pictorial*, 6 Jan 1954, 16 July 1969, 22 Jan 1977, 19 Nov 1980; *Age* (Melb), 20 Aug 1954, 24 Apr 1974, 22 Jan 1977, 16 Mar 1985, 24 Sept 1987; information from Mrs E. E. J. Cade, Toorak, Melb.   WALLACE IRONSIDE

CADE, WILLIAM RICHARD (1883-1957), musician, was born on 30 June 1883 in Adelaide, son of William Cade, coach-painter, and his wife Esther, née Perkins. Educated at Pulteney Street School and the Elder [q.v.4] Conservatorium of Music (1899-1909) where his violin teacher was Hermann Heinicke [q.v.9], in 1904 Bill won the (Sir) George Brookman [q.v.7] prize for the best performance on a stringed instrument. He excelled as a soloist (violin and viola), played in chamber-music ensembles and orchestras, and gave private lessons. In 1910 he studied at the Conservatorium Der Musik von Max Pohl in Berlin and next year was leader of the Quinlan Opera Company's orchestra in England. Returning home, on 1 May 1912 Cade married a New Zealander Gladys Irene Muriel Odell at Holy Trinity Anglican Church, Adelaide. From that year until 1928 he was associated with J. C. Williamson [q.v.6] Ltd and, in the meantime, conducted for the original (and from 1913 for the new) Wondergraph Picture Theatres. Appointed musical director of the Theatre Royal in 1916, he discreetly introduced music of more substance, even movements from symphonies, and performed violin solos from the pit. In 1928 Hoyts opened a new cinema, the Regent Theatre; Cade became musical director of its seventeen-piece orchestra after resigning as leader of the South Australian Orchestra, a post he had held since 1920. Moving to Melbourne in 1929, he conducted over seven thousand performances as musical director of the Regent and Plaza theatres' orchestras; he succeeded

Joseph Slapoffski [q.v.11] as conductor of the Victorian Professional Symphony Orchestra's eighty players.

Back in Adelaide, in 1935 Cade joined the Australian Broadcasting Commission for which he formed a broadcasting orchestra. The Adelaide Symphony Orchestra and the Celebrity Orchestral Concerts were inaugurated next year, with him as resident conductor. Cade was a sympathetic and popular conductor who blended self-confidence and modesty. Good-looking, with expressive eyes and slicked-back hair, he made a ritual of each concert entrance: a brisk walk on, a step to the podium, a bow, arms outstretched to the applauding audience. He appeared with visiting artists, prepared the augmented Adelaide Symphony Orchestra for conductors from interstate and abroad (once confiding that he felt his own lack of a European name), and fulfilled engagements in capital cities throughout Australia. In 1929 he had formed the Adelaide Wireless Chorus (later Adelaide Singers). He also directed studio broadcasts of operas and musical comedies, conducted the Adelaide Light Orchestra, organized the Students Training Orchestra and Schools' Orchestral concerts, and made recordings.

Following his retirement in 1948, Cade was appointed an honorary life member (1949) of the Musicians' Union of Australia. He continued with the A.B.C. as a presentation officer until 1955 and for relaxation enjoyed motoring, golf and gardening. Survived by his wife and three daughters, he died on 4 August 1957 at his Erindale home and was cremated. James Glennon said that there were no 'dynamic sforzandoes' in Cade's life, 'only a consistent crescendo in a fruitful career'.

Advertiser (Adel), 5 Sept 1913, 23 June 1928; J. Glennon, *Personalities Remembered* (radio talk, 5CL, 7 Nov 1971, Mort L); Performing Arts Collection, Adel Festival Centre Trust; Presscuttings, Document Archives, ABC, Syd; information from Mr and Mrs A. C. Shuttleworth, Heathpool, Adel.   JOYCE GIBBERD

CAHILL, JOHN JOSEPH (1891-1959), railway fitter, trade unionist and premier, was born on 21 January 1891 at Redfern, Sydney, son of Irish-born parents Thomas Cahill, labourer, and his wife Ellen, née Glynn. The family was part of the tightly-knit community of railway workers that had grown up around the Eveleigh railway workshops. Educated at St Brigid's convent school, Marrickville, and Patrician Brothers' School, Redfern, on 2 July 1907 Joe was apprenticed as a fitter at Eveleigh. He joined the Workers' Educational Association, regularly attended lectures and developed his public-speaking skills in debating societies.

A branch officer of the Amalgamated Society of Engineers (Amalgamated Engineering Union from 1920), Cahill went as a delegate to union conferences. He was dismissed from his job on 14 August 1917 for his part in a railway strike and his personal file was annotated 'agitator'. There followed a lean period in which Cahill found it difficult to obtain regular employment. At one stage he was involved in an insurance scheme, collecting money from employees who were offered the chance to enter a weekly draw for a pair of shoes. Prominent in the early 1920s in an unsuccessful revolt by a group of activists against the A.E.U.'s governing body, he was banned from holding office in the union until mid-1925. In May 1922 he was re-employed by the railways. At St Brigid's Church, Marrickville, on 11 November that year he married Esmey Mary Kelly; they were to have a long and happy family life.

Defeated as the official Labor Party candidate for Dulwich Hill at the March 1917 elections, Cahill was elected to the Legislative Assembly for St George in May 1925 (Arncliffe from 1930). He spoke frequently in the House, mainly on railway and constituency matters. Rumours—made public by the *Labor Daily*—proliferated late in 1925 and through 1926 of attempts to bribe four Labor members to cross the floor and bring down J. T. Lang's [q.v.9] first government. Cahill was named and, although the charges were totally discredited, he suffered most of the four. The experience soured his relations with Lang and he voted for P. F. Loughlin [q.v.10] in his leadership challenge to the premier in September 1926.

Nevertheless, Cahill was one of the few of Lang's back-bench opponents to retain pre-selection. Lang was returned to office in October 1930 and caucus elected Cahill government whip. He became a staunch defender of Lang's policies and the 'Big Fella' was later to pay a fulsome tribute to his performance as whip. Defeated in the anti-Lang landslide in June 1932, Cahill was forced to obtain work; he was a shop-inspector for the Fashion Centre Shoe Store until re-elected for Arncliffe in May 1935 (Cooks River from 1941).

When Labor won government in May 1941 under (Sir) William McKell, Cahill became secretary for public works and in June 1944 was also given the local government portfolio. Proving more than equal to his demanding duties, he set up the State Dockyard at Newcastle and the State Brickworks; he also supervised the establishment of the Electricity Authority (which brought electricity to much of rural New South Wales) and the Cumberland County Council. Cahill took a personal interest in this pioneering town-planning scheme and carried through major local-government amalgamations in the late 1940s. While he was minister in charge of energy supply, generating capacity doubled in the postwar years and by the early 1950s 'blackouts' had been eliminated. On 21 September 1949 he became deputy-premier.

Elected party leader and commissioned as premier on 2 April 1952 in succession to the ailing James McGirr [q.v.], Cahill proved to be a gifted politician and a capable administrator, renowned for his ability to work hard and to withstand the pressures of office. His combination of toughness and political acumen was to make him a formidable leader. Discipline was restored to cabinet: Cahill insisted that ministers kept in command of their portfolios and, when necessary, took action to ensure that they did. He relied on Wallace Wurth [q.v.], the powerful chairman of the Public Service Board, as a source of information on what his ministers were doing and as a means of controlling them. In cabinet Cahill tended to scrutinize matters more for their political than their administrative implications. He was an acknowledged master of the difficult art of handling caucus.

An easy mixer, Cahill retained good relations with his colleagues and regularly attended functions in their electorates. In addition, he made himself accessible to backbenchers through the parliamentary dining- and billiards-rooms. By a mixture of bullying and cajoling, the premier usually managed to get his way in caucus. Although generally popular, he was close to few; R. R. Downing was a trusted confidant and adviser. Cahill devoted attention to ensuring that there were no major conflicts between the government and the extra-parliamentary party. He ran brisk and businesslike meetings with the party officers every week (on the day before the State executive met), thereby ensuring that they were fully briefed on the government's activities. Moreover, his government was at the forefront in important industrial reforms, such as improvements in leave and workers' compensation.

During his term of office Cahill carefully coaxed the business community. The government's emphasis on promoting development made for a certain commonality of interest. As one who greatly enjoyed the ceremonial aspects of the premiership, he mixed frequently with business and community leaders at official functions. In parliament he was an aggressive performer, consistently able to outclass and outmanoeuvre the Opposition. Under Cahill the New South Wales Labor style was tough, competent and conservative, with a marked preference for behind-the-scenes manipulation and back-room deals. He won a landslide victory in the February 1953 elections.

Cahill's premiership was dominated by conflict with the Menzies [q.v.] government, by allegations of official corruption and by internal strife within the Australian Labor Party. Wily at exploiting the Federal conservatives' real and alleged failings, he was also convinced, with some justification, that the whole basis of Commonwealth-State financial relations was inequitable, specifically in terms of what New South Wales received from the Federal government through the Loan Council and tax reimbursement grants.

Allegations of scandal and impropriety involved the notoriously corrupt, Labor-controlled Sydney City Council and the police. Two ministers (J. G. Arthur and A. Landa) had charges against them investigated by royal commissions in 1953 and 1958 respectively. In general, the government's attitude that such allegations were politically-inspired attacks, best dealt with by obfuscation and concealment, seems to have been misguided and counter-productive.

By far the greatest test of Cahill's political skills was the need after 1954 to minimize the damage caused by the Labor 'split'. Although he and the majority of government members had no ideological quarrel with the industrial groups formed to counter communist influence in trade unions, they became increasingly disenchanted with the abrasive style of extremists among the 'groupers'. Memories of the chaotic Lang period and the long, cold years in Opposition strengthened the resolve of many Labor parliamentarians to prevent a major party split in New South Wales that would destroy the government.

Cahill's strategy involved presenting a united, non-aligned parliamentary party as a secure rallying point for Labor moderates from every faction. Using all his political skills, he was able to preserve the support of the majority of caucus and to avoid any open breach in the parliamentary party. He and Downing began talks with moderates on the federal executive to try to achieve a compromise that would leave the State party machine in the hands of the more reasonable pro- and anti-'grouper' elements who wanted to keep Labor in power in New South Wales. Cahill made it clear that he was prepared to see some of the die-hard 'groupers' purged to achieve this end. Negotiations with Cardinal (Sir) Norman Gilroy [q.v.] and the Catholic hierarchy in Sydney ensured that the 'groupers' received no encouragement to split from the Labor Party. Although the outcome was at times far from certain, after much intricate and onerous parleying Cahill very largely achieved what he had set out to do. In March 1956 Labor won the State elections and in June the government and the moderates on the federal executive agreed to a modest restructuring of the New South Wales branch of the A.L.P. In return, only the most intransigent 'groupers' were to be purged and control of the party was left to a coterie from the centre that formed around the party officers.

In his final years in office Cahill grew increasingly in public stature: he received honorary doctorates from the universities of Sydney (LL.D., 1952) and New England (D.Litt., 1956), and from the New South Wales University of Technology (D.Sc., 1956); and he visited Britain (1953) and North America (1958). He triumphed in the March 1959 elections when Labor, against all odds, narrowly clung to power. In June Cahill became the longest continuously-serving New South Wales premier. His personal integrity, his determination to do what he believed to be right for the State and his qualities of leadership had won him a measure of respect from even his staunchest opponents. A 'small, thickset man' with 'a broad Irish smile', he had few recreations other than work, but liked an occasional bet, enjoyed a good cigar and had a regular, early-morning swim. He was a trustee and president (1952-59) of Royal National Park.

The premier died of myocardial infarction on 22 October 1959 at Sydney Hospital and was buried in Rookwood cemetery; his wife, three sons and two daughters survived him. Cahill had been motivated and sustained by dedication to his family, devout Catholicism and a determination to improve the lot of the ordinary Australian through the labour movement.

J. T. Lang, *The Turbulent Years* (Syd, 1970); T. Sheridan, *Mindful Militants* (Cambridge, 1975); B. Nairn, *The 'Big Fella'* (Melb, 1986); *PD* (NSW), 29 Oct 1959, p 1573; *Newsday*, 5, 1959; *Labor Daily* (Syd), 7 Sept 1932, 24 May 1935; *Sun* (Syd), 2 Apr 1952, 20 Oct 1959; *Daily Mirror* (Syd), 2 Apr 1952, 22 Oct 1959; *Daily Telegraph* (Syd) and *SMH*, 23 Oct 1959; *Sunday Telegraph* (Syd), 25 Oct 1959; D. Clune, The Labor Government in N.S.W. 1941-1965: a study in longevity in government (Ph.D. thesis, Dept of Government, Univ Syd, 1990) *and* for bibliog; Railway service personal history card: John Joseph Cahill (NSWA); Cahill papers (ML); information from Mr R. R. Downing, Goulburn, NSW, Justice J. J. Cahill, Messrs P. D. Hills, R. B. Nott, J. A. Mulvihill and P. Gallagher, Syd.

DAVID CLUNE

CAHILL, THOMAS VINCENT (1913-1978), Catholic archbishop, was born on 22 February 1913 at Bendigo, Victoria, fourth child of native-born parents Patrick Cahill, coal merchant, and his wife Elizabeth Magdalen, née Cavagna. Educated at St Kilian's School and Marist Brothers' College, Bendigo, in November 1929 Thomas left for Rome where he studied at the Pontifical

Urban University of Propaganda Fide (Ph.D., 1931; D.Th., 1936). He was granted dispensation from lack of canonical age and ordained priest on 21 September 1935.

Back in Australia from late 1936, he assisted at the parish of Sacred Heart Cathedral, Bendigo, until November 1939 when he became secretary to Archbishop John Panico at the Apostolic Delegation, North Sydney. Cahill was appointed privy chamberlain in 1940. His fluency in Latin, Italian and French enabled him to assist in the delegation's branch of the prisoner-of-war information bureau. For this work he was awarded the Papal Cross *Pro Ecclesia et Pontifice*.

In April 1948 Cahill returned as chancellor to his native diocese of Sandhurst, Bendigo. On 11 November he was appointed bishop of Cairns, Queensland. Consecrated on 9 February 1949 at the cathedral, Bendigo, he was enthroned at Cairns on 27 March. Under the entire care of the Augustinian Order, the diocese was an administrative anomaly in the Australian Church. Cahill negotiated with the Augustinians and agreed that they could retain three parishes in perpetuity, introduced secular clergy to minister to the other parishes, recruited seminarians from Brisbane and borrowed clergy from other dioceses. He visited Rome in 1950 and 1960, began the building of a cathedral and developed Calvary Hospital at Cairns, and promoted parish and school projects.

Attending all sessions of Vatican Council II (1962-65), Cahill served on conciliar and post-conciliar commissions which entailed regular journeys to Rome. In Australia, he was secretary to the bishops' committee for liturgy and a member (1960) of the national liturgical commission; he was, as well, second secretary (1964-68) and first secretary (1968-76) to the Australian episcopal conference. In these roles he had a profound influence on local Catholicism. Soon after his consecration, he had successfully proposed changes in Church statutes to allow marriages involving a non-Catholic partner to be solemnized 'before the altar'.

Elevated to the Archdiocese of Canberra and Goulburn on 13 April 1967, Cahill was installed as archbishop on 9 August in the cathedral of St Peter and St Paul, Goulburn. His commitments increased as he familiarized himself with his widespread archdiocese and extended his involvement in the national and international Church. In Canberra, with financial acumen, he initiated the extension (1973) of St Christopher's Co-Cathedral, Manuka, and the construction of Calvary Hospital, Bruce; he also endeavoured to cope with the expansion of the parish system and Catholic education, brought about by the Australian Capital Territory's rapid growth in

population; in addition, he instituted a local permanent secretariat for the Australian episcopal conference. In Rome, he was a member of the commission for religious (1962-67), the sacred congregation for religious (1968-73) and the secretariat for non-believers (1966-73), and sat on the executive of the world synod of bishops, representing Australia in 1967, 1971 and 1974.

Deliberately unobtrusive in public life, Cahill dealt with such issues as state aid to education, abortion, contraception, and the Vietnam War. Only when he reprimanded four priests who dissented from certain aspects of the Papal encyclical, *Humanae Vitae* (1968), did he draw a prolonged public reaction. He preferred personal to political action: through courtesy, conviction and conciliation, he resolved many concerns by direct negotiation with government and community leaders.

His influence as secretary to the episcopal conference reached beyond formulating statements on public issues to the structuring of agendas and the work of committees; one bishop remarked that the conference would need a computer to replace his extraordinary sharpness of mind and memory. Cahill played a major role in the Australian Church's liturgical renewal and in the transition from Latin to English liturgy. The new English language *Sunday Missal* (Sydney, 1971) was published under his authority. His knowledge of canon law and of the Roman Congregation, Propaganda Fide, facilitated the transfer of the Australian Church in 1976 from mission status to general church law.

Cahill was a shy man, ill at ease in casual meetings with the laity, but ready to seek counsel from competent advisers in finance, education, architecture and politics. He was much more at home with his clergy, including younger priests, and was intensely interested in the welfare of men and women in religious orders in his jurisdiction. His compassion for his clergy extended to those who left the ministry in the troubled years after Vatican II.

Quick to grasp the essence of documents or debate, Cahill had a wide knowledge of historical, political and administrative matters. He showed little interest in cultural or artistic subjects, apart from the occasional enjoyment of classical music, and was totally uninterested in sport. In contrast, he was absorbed in ecclesiastical concerns, in a manner which has been styled *Romanità*, and was thoroughly conversant with and supportive of Vatican policies. Although not a reformer by nature or priestly formation, he proved to be wise and adaptable in his governance, and dedicated to implementing the renewal envisaged by Vatican II. His Roman studentship and later experience at the Apostolic Delegation influenced his mode of administration. Contemporaries may have unfairly judged him to be an unspectacular conservative because of his patent churchmanship, but his contributions to national and ecclesiastical life were basic and enduring. He was appointed C.B.E. in 1972.

An intense regime of overwork, irregular diet, lack of rest and excessive travelling took its toll during his years in Canberra. Cahill put on weight and suffered heart ailments. He died of coronary atherosclerosis on 16 April 1978 at St Vincent's Hospital, Sydney, and was buried in the crypt of St Christopher's Cathedral, Canberra.

J. N. Molony, *The Roman Mould of the Australian Catholic Church* (Melb, 1969); M. A. Endicott, *The Augustinians in Far North Queensland 1883-1941* (Syd, 1988); *Canb Times,* 17 Apr 1978; Archives of Aust Bishops' Conference, Secretariat, Braddon, Canb, *and* Diocese of Cairns, Bishop's House, Cairns, Nth Qld, *and* Archdiocese of Canb and Goulburn, Archbishop's House, Canb, *and* Sacred Congregation Propaganda Fide, Rome.

BRIAN MAHER

CAIN, JOHN (1882-1957), premier, was born on 19 January 1882 at Greendale, Victoria, eldest child of Patrick Cane, a farmer from County Clare, Ireland, and his Victorian-born wife Julia, née Brennan. Following a fit of depression, in April 1890 Patrick drowned in the Lerderderg River 'apparently self-committed, while of unsound mind'. The tragedy of his father's death, when John was only 8, may explain some aspects of his subsequent life, including his secrecy about his childhood and age. Despite his reticence, his stocky, strong frame, 'map of Ireland' face, leathery voice and determinedly 'plain man' style all indicated his origins as the son of an Irish-Australian hill farmer.

After Patrick's death John lived with relations and later with his remarried mother. Educated to primary level in the Bacchus Marsh district, he left school and home at about 13, and was employed for several years by farmers in the Goulburn Valley where he earned a reputation as an exceptionally good worker but an argumentative political rebel. About 1907 Cain moved to Northcote, Melbourne. He hawked fruit and rabbits, took a job as a theatre spruiker and about 1911 opened a fruit shop in High Street.

By 1910 he was active in the Victorian Socialist Party where John Curtin [q.v.] was a friend and colleague. Through the V.S.P. Cain adopted what was to become his lifelong habit of addressing all colleagues, friend and foe alike, as 'brother'. By 1914 he had joined the Australian Labor Party and stood unsuccessfully that year for Labor pre-selection for a State parliamentary seat. He sold his shop and

moved into positions that helped to prepare him for a political career, among them organizer for the Theatrical Employees' and for the Clothing Trades' unions. He was vocal in the anti-conscription campaigns of World War I and won election to Northcote City Council as a Labor candidate in 1915. In that election he attracted the support of Patrick John Kennelly, then aged only 15, who was to remain a close friend and political ally.

In 1917 Cain entered the Legislative Assembly as member for the seat of Jika Jika, which encompassed Northcote. He was to represent the district continuously until his death. With its three competing parties, all internally divided, the State parliament offered a challenge in political intricacy which was very different to the warm, rhetorical ways of the V.S.P. Cain had initially been dedicated to a vision of social change that favoured the underprivileged, but, once he was elected, events showed him how difficult this vision was to put into practice, even during the rare periods when Labor held office. On 20 February 1926 at the Brunswick Street Methodist Church, Fitzroy, he married Dorothea Vera Marie Grindrod, a milliner who owned five hat shops and employed fifty workers.

Cain was appointed minister without portfolio in the Prendergast [q.v.11] government (July-November 1924) and in the Hogan [q.v.9] government (1927-28). In his 1929-32 cabinet Hogan elevated him to minister of railways, minister in charge of electrical undertakings and vice-president of the Board of Land and Works, thus giving him responsibility for some of the biggest employers among government utilities at a time of severe economic depression. It was a miserable awakening for one who had previously tended to see nationalization of industry as a cure for social ills.

Although Cain called his portfolio 'the suicide club' and had to retrench railway workers or reduce their working hours (with proportionate pay cuts), the astute and tactful way in which he handled matters increased his standing. Railway revenue was falling at a time of severe budgetary stress and he appeared to grasp the political necessity for doing what had to be done, while also appreciating that the protesting unions had their own worried electorate to satisfy. Unlike Hogan's faction, Cain and the majority of Labor's parliamentarians followed the party's State conference policy of opposition to the 1931 Premiers' Plan. He had earlier supported the plan, but by 1932 the bulk of Labor union and rank-and-file opinion had turned against deflationary policies, and Labor was set to collide with that section of the Country Party which had kept it in office. There was no advantage for an ambitious, young Labor parliamentarian in prolonging the political life of Hogan's ministry by a few more months when the unions and rank and file were withdrawing their support.

The successful no-confidence motion against a divided Labor government precipitated an election in May 1932. The A.L.P. lost fourteen seats. Labor's debacle, however, was Cain's triumph: the depleted parliamentary party chose him as deputy-leader. Five years later it elected him leader when Hogan's successor Thomas Tunnecliffe [q.v.12] retired. By 1937 Cain, who was aged 55 (though claiming to be 50), had moved far from the 'red ragger' of his youth. He was a skilled parliamentarian, with a reputation as an administrator, who had mastered many gruelling lessons in survival. He made the principal objective of his leadership the achievement of a majority Labor government, as opposed to the previous situation where Labor ministries had survived only with Country Party support. Since 1935 the reverse had applied—the Dunstan [q.v.8] Country Party ministry had governed with Labor support. This alliance, forged under Tunnecliffe's leadership, was to last under Cain until 1943.

Despite its many troubles, Labor had been the most united of the three parties before the 1930s. Once the inevitable divisions of wage-cutting and retrenchment were behind it, new problems appeared with the rise of the Communist Party of Australia as a force in the unions and the emergence of a distinctively Catholic element in the labour movement. With Kennelly as his right-hand man in the organizational wing, Cain based his leadership on fostering a stream of opinion which could command the centre. The divisions, nevertheless, became exacerbated. Disciplined, Stalinist communists, deeply hostile to Labor, won power in the unions; the cohesive, secretive Catholic Social Studies Movement and the A.L.P.-endorsed Industrial Groups arose in the 1940s to counter them.

Cain first became premier on 14 September 1943, but the ministry lasted only four days until Dunstan cemented a coalition with the United Australia Party. After Labor had gained four seats from the Country Party in an election called because of splits between the Country Party and Liberals (as the U.A.P. was now known), on 21 November 1945 Cain again became premier. He was 'of medium height, cleanshaven, always dressed in quiet grey or navy blue double-breasted suits, a grey felt hat and black shoes, square jawed and square shouldered'. His trademark was his stubby pipe. Unassuming in manner, he enjoyed being seen as an average citizen. He lived in the same Northcote villa throughout his political career, pottered in the garden at weekends, watched cricket and football matches (without any declared allegiance), and enjoyed occasional visits to the cinema.

His government survived precariously with the support of Independents. Its legislation included measures that gave independent pay tribunals to public servants, teachers and police, long service leave to railway workers and more liberal conditions for workers' compensation; a Land Conservation Authority was also established and the Soldier Settlement Commission's powers were extended. It was a better, longer-lived government than might have been expected, but it fell when the Opposition blocked supply in the Legislative Council on 2 October 1947 in protest against the Federal Labor government's proposal to nationalize the banks. Labor was defeated at the State elections on 8 November, with the loss of five seats.

In 1950-52 Labor again supported a minority Country Party government. From 1940 Cain had been fostering closer political and personal relations with the Liberal leader T. T. Hollway [q.v.] to achieve an agreement on redistributing seats to check the power of the Country Party. The basis of this alliance was mutual despair at the ability of the Country Party to manipulate parliament through its balance of power. The politics were of Byzantine intricacy and Cain became almost obsessive in wheeling and dealing with a variety of interests. Yet, his strategy resulted in adult suffrage for Legislative Council elections, introduced by (Sir) John McDonald's [q.v.] Country Party government in 1952 as the price for Labor support.

The unpopularity of the minority Country Party government in the community, together with division in Liberal ranks about vote-weighting and over Hollway's performance, brought Cain victory at the election of 6 December 1952. He took office on 17 December, with a majority in both Houses, and succeeded in redistributing seats—the crowning legislative achievement of his career. Another coup was the relocation of Tattersall's [q.v.3 G. Adams] lotteries from Hobart to Melbourne in 1953-54. But major difficulties threatened his government. A faction aligned with 'the Movement' and the Industrial Groups had become aggressive in both the parliamentary party and the organizational wing, conflict broke out with the Trades Hall, Cain's increasing inflexibility caused concern, and there was no obvious successor. While these tensions had only a little to do with the main questions of State government, they exacerbated the crisis when the Federal Labor leader Dr H. V. Evatt [q.v.] denounced 'the Movement' and 'groupers' in October 1954, thereby touching off the great Labor Party split of 1955-57. In April 1955 a 'new' State central executive— chosen by a federally-dominated, special

State conference—expelled eighteen Victorian parliamentarians for attending a meeting of the rival faction; in retaliation, those expelled crossed the floor and the third Cain government fell on 19 April. The incoming premier (Sir) Henry Bolte, whose Liberal Party won the elections next month, became the beneficiary of Cain's parliamentary reform.

With no heir on his depleted benches, Cain stayed on as leader of the Opposition. These final years were a bitter harvest. The far left, working closely with the C.P.A. in the unions, had won fifteen years' control of the Victorian A.L.P. Contemptuous of the whole parliamentary process, it wrecked efforts to repair the damage of the split and treated Cain with little respect. He joined the central executive, but despaired at the defeats and rebuffs he suffered, and was stung by the ensuing political embarrassment. Visiting Queensland, he died of a cerebral haemorrhage on 4 August 1957 at Townsville. He had been raised a Catholic, but lapsed in his youth and shared the agnostic views common among socialists; he later softened somewhat in his attitude to religion. Accorded a state funeral, he was buried in Preston cemetery with Anglican rites. His wife, daughter and son John, who was to serve as Victorian premier in 1982-90, survived him.

For all his Labor rhetoric, especially when young, Cain senior was a fairly conservative administrator, ever aware of the limitations of the government purse and of public patience with experimentation. He was adept at making the best of what limited opportunities Labor had in Victoria and at sticking to his strategy of parliamentary reform.

R. Murray, *The Split* (Syd, 1970); K. White, *John Cain and Victorian Labor 1917-1957* (Syd, 1982), and for bibliog.　　　　　　　　KATE WHITE
　　　　　　　　　　　　　　　ROBERT MURRAY

CALLAGHAN, CECIL ARTHUR (1890-1967), army officer and merchant, was born on 31 July 1890 in Sydney, son of Robert Samuel Callaghan, merchant, and his wife Alice Emily, née Whitehead, both Melbourne born. Cecil was educated at Sydney Grammar School before joining his father's firm which imported boots and shoes. Six feet (182.9 cm) tall and well built, he enlisted as a citizen-soldier in the Australian Field Artillery in 1910 and was commissioned next year. On 18 August 1914 he transferred to the Australian Imperial Force and two months later embarked for the Middle East as a captain in the 1st Field Artillery Brigade.

After training in Egypt, he took part in the landing at Gallipoli on 25 April 1915. During operations on 12 July he moved forward with the infantry and, from captured trenches, established telephone communication with his battery; while continuing to advance under heavy fire, he sent back valuable reports. He was awarded the Distinguished Service Order. In October he went to Egypt for three weeks to organize the 5th Howitzer Battery and in December participated in the evacuation from the Gallipoli peninsula. Having transferred to the 5th Divisional Artillery in Egypt, he was promoted major and made acting commander of the 25th Howitzer Battery in March 1916.

Moving to France in June, Callaghan was posted next month to the 13th F.A.B. as a battery commander. On the Somme and in the Ypres sector (Belgium), his unit performed outstandingly in 1917, despite suffering more casualties than other batteries in the division. In March 1918 he was promoted temporary lieutenant colonel and placed in command of the 4th F.A.B., 2nd Divisional Artillery. After serving in June as a liaison officer with French troops at Villers-Bretonneux, in the final advances (August to November) he 'commanded his brigade with marked success'. Appointed C.M.G. and to the French Légion d'honneur in 1919, Callaghan was mentioned in dispatches four times. He sailed for Australia in July and his A.I.F. appointment terminated on 22 January 1920.

Resuming his civilian occupation and his Militia service, Callaghan had charge of the 3rd (1920-21) and the 7th (1921-26) Field Artillery brigades. On 1 May 1926 he was promoted temporary colonel and given command of the 2nd Divisional Artillery; for five years his divisional commander was Major General H. G. Bennett [q.v.]. A substantive colonel from 1929, Callaghan commanded the 8th Infantry Brigade in 1934-38. He was made brigadier, Royal Australian Artillery, Eastern Command, in November 1939. On 1 July 1940 he was selected to be commander, Royal Australian Artillery, in the A.I.F.'s 8th Division; in September Bennett again became his immediate superior. Callaghan visited Malaya in June next year to investigate command problems in the division and arrived in Singapore in August to assume his duties.

In November-December 1941 he administered the division while Bennett acquainted himself with A.I.F. operations in the Middle East. The Japanese landed at Kota Bharu, Malaya, on 8 December. To meet a possible threat to Endau, Callaghan altered the disposition of Australian units. On his return, Bennett strongly disapproved of the changes and ordered the resumption of the previous positions. Throughout the fighting in Malaya, Callaghan's regiments gave fine support to the infantry. Nonetheless, the overall situation deteriorated so rapidly that on 15 February 1942 Lieutenant General A. E.

Percival, the British general officer commanding, Malaya, decided to surrender in Singapore; a cease-fire was set for 8.30 p.m. About two minutes after that time, Bennett called on Callaghan, who was weak from a recent attack of malaria, informed him of his determination to escape and handed over the division to him. Callaghan did not approve of Bennett's action.

Next day, when Bennett's disappearance came to Percival's attention, he formally appointed Callaghan commander of the A.I.F. in Malaya and promoted him temporary major general. Callaghan did all he could to raise morale and to ameliorate the appalling conditions which his men endured in Changi prisoner-of-war camp. Despite the 'starvation diet', he managed to set aside a three-day supply of rations as a reserve for the soldiers. He also insisted that discipline be maintained, whether in regard to smart turnouts or to punctilious saluting. Percival said of him: 'A more loyal or courageous man I never met . . . he bore uncomplainingly his own sufferings'.

In August Callaghan and other senior officers were moved by sea to Formosa (Taiwan). There, in Karenko camp, he was beaten by the Japanese, and suffered from dysentery and malaria; his weight dropped from 13 st. 6 lb. (85.3 kg) to 8 st. 5 lb. (53.1 kg). Having been shifted to Tamasata camp in April 1943 and to Shirakawa camp in June, he was flown to Japan in October 1944 and then to Manchuria. He was freed by the Russians in August 1945.

Callaghan travelled to Morotai where he met the commander-in-chief, General Sir Thomas Blamey [q.v.], to whom he delivered a letter from Percival which stated that Bennett had relinquished his command without permission. At a military court of inquiry into Bennett's conduct, held in Australia in October 1945, Callaghan claimed that he had not immediately informed Percival of Bennett's departure because he had 'felt ashamed'. Next year Callaghan reported to Prime Minister J. B. Chifley [q.v.] on allegations that Australian prisoners of war had been harshly treated by their own officers. Callaghan explained that officers had been obliged to act against individual offenders to prevent the Japanese from punishing prisoners *en masse*. On 27 January 1947, although sick in hospital, he commented on Bennett's and Percival's reports on the operations in Malaya; he supported Percival and found fault with Bennett's account.

Mentioned in dispatches and appointed C.B. (1946) for his leadership and devotion to duty while a prisoner of war, Callaghan was promoted major general in 1947 (with effect from 1 September 1942) and placed on the Retired List on 10 April. He was active in the Returned Sailors', Soldiers' and Airmen's Imperial League of Australia, and a founder of the Ku-ring-gai sub-branch. Callaghan was particular about dress and his involvement in the footwear industry earned him the nickname, 'Boots'. He had a very good memory and retained his strong faith in Christianity. After a long illness, he died, unmarried, on 1 January 1967 at Gordon and was cremated with Methodist forms. The 8th Division Association honoured him with a memorial service.

C. E. W. Bean, *The Story of Anzac*, 1, 2 (Syd, 1921, 1924), and *The A.I.F. in France*, 1916-18 (Syd, 1929, 1933, 1937, 1942); H. G. Bennett, *Why Singapore Fell* (Syd, 1944); A. E. Percival, *The War in Malaya* (Lond, 1949); L. Wigmore, *The Japanese Thrust* (Canb, 1957); A. B. Lodge, *The Fall of General Gordon Bennett* (Syd, 1986), and for bibliog; *Reveille* (Syd), Feb, Mar 1967; *SMH*, 9 Aug 1946; *Methodist* (Syd), 4 Mar 1967; AWM records; information from Miss I. Callaghan, Turramurra, and Dr C. R. B. Richards, Balgowlah Heights, Syd.

R. SUTTON

CALLAGHAN, EMMA JANE (1884-1979), Aboriginal nurse and midwife, was born on 28 February 1884 at La Perouse Aborigines' Reserve, Sydney, the younger of twins of William Foot, fisherman, and Kathleen Sims of the Dharawal tribe. One of Kathleen's fourteen children, Emma regarded John Foster as her father. At the age of 4 she injured her head and was tended by Retta Dixon [q.v. Long] who was to found the Aborigines' Inland Mission of Australia. Although Emma left school after third grade, she wanted to be a nurse. About 1903 Dixon took her to visit the Dunggutti people at the Nulla Nulla Aborigines' Reserve, Bellbrook.

Unlike her mother, Emma had fair skin, blue eyes and red hair. She believed that she had a mission among her people. Returning to Bellbrook about 1905, she attended Sunday services and learned to play the organ; she also helped older Aboriginal women when they assisted in childbirth, earning their trust and respect. From that time she registered Aboriginal births. In addition, she regularly searched the camps and humpies for sick people, crossing flooded creeks and riding through the bush to tend her patients: Aborigines were not admitted to Kempsey hospital until an annexe was built in the 1930s. Emma held religious services for the Dungguttis in the open air under trees or in the small, crudely-built, tin church on the reserve. With the police as witnesses, she buried the dead.

On 20 September 1909 at Nulla Nulla Aborigines' Reserve Emma married with the forms of the Australian Aborigines' Mission Athol Callaghan, a 22-year-old labourer and a

Dunggutti of mixed descent; they were to have eleven children. A competent needle-woman, she made her own hats, as well as clothes for herself, the family and the community (even wedding dresses and ball gowns). During the childhood of her eldest son Harry, she began to learn the intricacies of the tribal language and translated Bible stories into Dunggutti.

About 1928 Mrs Callaghan moved to Armidale to be closer to medical facilities for her husband who was suffering from tuberculosis. Finding that Aborigines were living in appalling conditions on the fringes of the town, she lobbied the mayor and the Anglican bishop until her family obtained a house. Her home soon became an impromptu hospital; she practised as midwife to her people and nursed them without charge. Dr Ellen Kent Hughes [q.v.] visited the Callaghans' home to see patients and any local Aboriginal family in need of treatment. Highly respected among the White community, Emma encountered no personal prejudice.

At Athol's request, the family returned to La Perouse after seven years at Armidale. Through the Homes for Unemployed Trust, in 1939 Emma bought a block of land near the mission, and a timber-and-fibro house was built to plans provided by her friend Kent Hughes. The house became a meeting-place where Sunday School was held, people were married, and children were born and baptized; on Wednesday nights a minister held church services. Emma ran the nearby 'sick bay' and was affectionately known throughout the reserve as 'Lady'.

She worked for the Aborigines' Protection Board, battled for the dole for Aborigines and spoke out for civil rights. Athol died in 1942. At the district registrar's office, Redfern, on 18 October 1945 Emma married a widower Henry James Cook, a Royal Navy veteran who worked as a commissionaire. Following his death in 1964, she became active in the War Widows' Guild and in October that year was presented to Princess Marina, the dowager Duchess of Kent. Survived by five daughters of her first marriage, Emma died on 31 December 1979 at Randwick and was buried with Presbyterian forms in Botany cemetery. In 1985 her home was preserved by the State government.

La Perouse, the Place, the People, and the Sea (Syd, 1987); *Aust Women's Weekly*, 24 Apr 1968; *SMH*, 27 Nov 1985; information from Mr Ray Kelly, Snr, Kempsey, and Mr Reuben Kelly, Uralla, NSW, and Mrs I. Williams, Syd.   SHAY ANN KELLY

CALLANAN, ELLEN (1880-1947), religious Sister and educator, was born on 10 February 1880 at Ardfield, County Cork, Ireland, eldest of ten children of Thomas Callanan, farmer, and his wife Mary, née Lawton. Known as Eileen, she was educated at Ardfield Primary School, and in Dublin at Loreto College and University College.

She came to Australia in 1900 to enter the novitiate of the Institute of the Blessed Virgin Mary at Ballarat, Victoria, and was professed on 22 December 1903. While taking novitiate and post-novitiate courses in teacher-training, Callanan taught matriculation (under supervision) in 1903 and 1905, before enrolling at the University of Melbourne (Dip.Ed., 1908). She completed a B.A. in 1915. Meantime, she had joined the staff of the Central Catholic Training College, Albert Park, where she was later vice-principal. A founder (1912) of the Loreto Free Kindergarten, she co-authored a children's page for the *Advocate*, commenced a school paper, *Children's World*, and planned a series of history readers, one of which was published before her death.

As foundation principal (1918-43) of St Mary's Hall (the Catholic residence for women at the university), Mother Patrick, as she had become, maintained a passion for her homeland. She kept up a lively correspondence with Hilaire Belloc and attended lunchtime debates at the university, during which she did not hesitate to stand and interject. When the United States Army established Camp Pell opposite St Mary's in 1942, Mother Patrick opened the hall to the 4th General Hospital's personnel. She also assisted refugees from Nazism. Under her leadership, students participated in university debates on international and domestic issues, thereby lessening the relative isolation of their hall which was situated in The Avenue, one mile (1.6 km) off campus. Convinced that women should have a broad education, she introduced her students to the writers of the Gaelic renaissance, to art, music and fencing, and to a wide variety of visitors, among them Walter Burley and Marion Griffin [qq.v.9], and Vance and Nettie Palmer [qq.v.11] whom she invited to speak on the Spanish Civil War.

Mother Patrick ensured that religion was integral to daily life. She directed students to contemporary Catholic writers and, on certain evenings, read with feeling from the Gospel of St John which she loved. Her Catholicism was unhampered by subservience. Even when Archbishop Mannix [q.v.10]—whom she deeply admired—arrived unexpectedly, she would sometimes, on seeing his car pull up outside the hall, excuse herself. Deeply offended by anti-Catholic sentiment, she had been careful to exclude Professor William Osborne [q.v.11], who had erred in this regard, from her garden party to honour Cardinal Cerretti in 1928.

Tall, elegant and dignified, with an almost imperceptible limp, Mother Patrick was an unconventional nun who enjoyed a cup of tea with students in the Union canteen. She possessed an independence of mind and of heart which enabled her to engage in political, social and religious life in ways which were then unusual for a Sister in a semi-enclosed Order. Mother Patrick died of hypertensive cerebrovascular disease on 21 July 1947 at St Vincent's Hospital, Fitzroy, and was buried in Boroondara cemetery.

M. Oliver, *All for All* (Syd, 1945); *Loreto Mag,* 1947; Univ Melb, *St Mary's College,* 12, 1978; *Advocate* (Melb), 1 Jan 1916; R. Williams, Our Privilege is Now. A History of St Mary's Hall, University of Melbourne, 1918-1968 (M.Ed. thesis, Monash Univ, 1987); Loreto Archives, Ballarat, Vic, *and* Rathfarnham, Ireland; information from Mrs L. Quinlan, Gembrook, Vic.

ROSEMARY WILLIAMS

CALLAWAY, ARTHUR HENRY (1906-1941), accountant and naval officer, was born on 3 April 1906 at Woollahra, Sydney, son of Arthur Henry Callaway, vocalist, and his wife Cecilia Frances, née Thomson, both Sydneysiders. Educated at Bondi Superior Public School, by 1923 young Arthur was a clerk with Rosenfeld & Co. Pty Ltd, merchants. He joined the Royal Australian Naval Reserve on 1 July 1924 as a midshipman and in April 1928 transferred to the Volunteer Reserve with the rank of lieutenant. His recreations were yachting and rowing; in 1931-33 he was honorary treasurer of the Sydney Rowing Club. An associate-member of the Federal Institute of Accountants, from the early 1930s Callaway practised in the city. In 1932 he became a director and manager of Hygienic Feather Mills Pty Ltd, featherpurifiers of Botany. On 23 November 1935 in St Michael's Anglican Church, Vaucluse, he married Thelma May Rowe.

Having specialized in anti-submarine warfare, Callaway was promoted lieutenant commander on 23 June 1939. He was mobilized in September and served in H.M.A.S. *Yarra* until March 1940. Lent to the Royal Navy, in November he sailed for England. In June 1941 he assumed command of H.M. Trawler, *Lady Shirley,* which operated from Gibraltar; of 477 tons gross, she and similar vessels had been requisitioned for patrol duties. Tall, blue eyed and bearded, Callaway was a quiet, reflective and purposeful man who trained his crew thoroughly and ran a happy ship. On 4 October *Lady Shirley* was searching for a merchantman lying damaged 400 nautical miles (741 km) west of the Canary Islands. At 8.40 a.m. the trawler altered course to investigate a sighting, soon confirmed to be

the conning tower of a German U-boat. The submarine dived to periscope depth.

As *Lady Shirley* closed with her quarry, Callaway dropped a pattern of depth charges and was surprised to see the submarine, U 111, surface in his wake. He immediately turned his ship to bring the four-inch (101.6 mm) gun to bear and, if necessary, to ram the U-boat. Callaway directed operations in a fierce exchange. When a cannon-shell killed *Lady Shirley*'s gunlayer, an officer swiftly took his post; the ship's two Hotchkiss-gunners were wounded, but were able to continue firing. U 111's 105-mm main armament could not be brought into the battle. With their commanding officer slain, the crew scuttled the battered submarine and surrendered. The engagement was over in nineteen minutes. *Lady Shirley*'s adversary had been twice her size, and the forty-four prisoners taken to Gibraltar outnumbered the trawler's complement. For his part in the action, Callaway was awarded the Distinguished Service Order.

Between 3 and 4 a.m. on 11 December 1941, while on patrol in the Straits of Gibraltar, *Lady Shirley* disappeared with all hands. It was later concluded from German records that she had been torpedoed and sunk by a U-boat (U 374) at 35°15'N, 5°26'W. Callaway was survived by his wife and daughter, and by his son Ian who became a commodore in the R.A.N.

A. C. Hampshire, *Lilliput Fleet* (Lond, 1957); P. Lund and H. Ludlam, *Trawlers Go To War* (Lond, 1971); *SMH,* 10, 11 Oct, 20 Dec 1941; information from Naval Hist Branch, Ministry of Defence, Lond, Cdre I. A. Callaway, Deakin, Canb, and Capt S. Darling, Maroubra, Syd.   DARRYL BENNET

CALLINAN, JAMES CLIFFORD (1905-1972), electrical engineer, was born on 14 November 1905 at Bairnsdale, Victoria, fourth child of James Callinan, contractor, and his wife Mary Jane, née Johansen, both native-born. Educated at Essendon High and Caulfield Technical schools, on 26 May 1924 Cliff joined the State Electricity Commission of Victoria; he initially worked in the field, building transmission lines. At St Ambrose's Catholic Church, Brunswick, on 23 February 1935 he married a manageress Sarah (Sadie) Alice O'Brien. From that year until 1947 he was assistant-superintendent of the electrical branch at Yallourn power station. After a year at head office in Melbourne, he returned to Yallourn as electrical superintendent, in charge of operational switching, load regulation and power distribution.

In 1951 Callinan moved to Sydney and subsequently to Cooma as chief electrical engineer for the Snowy Mountains Hydro-electric Authority. Responsible for the design, procurement, installation, testing and commissioning of generating stations and power-transmission facilities, he headed a multinational staff of professionals: some of them were brilliant, some mediocre, and some 'prima donnas'. He welded together a team which made its mark in a predominantly civil-engineering organization, and which enabled the authority to achieve objectives on time and within budget.

From 1954 the electricity commissions of New South Wales and Victoria took responsibility for the transmission of energy outside the proclaimed 'Snowy Mountains Area' and members of Callinan's staff were transferred accordingly. A re-organization in the S.M.H.E.A. placed mechanical plant—including turbines, hydraulic gates and valves, and station cranes and lifts—under his supervision and his title was changed to chief engineer, electrical and mechanical. In 1955 the Snowy Mountains scheme's first power station entered service at Guthega, New South Wales, and Callinan became involved in its operation—a function outside the authority's terms of reference. Following intense negotiations between the Commonwealth and State governments, the Snowy Mountains Council was established in 1959 'to direct the operation and maintenance' of completed works. The authority nominated an operations engineer to be the council's chief executive: Callinan was chosen to fill the additional post.

Despite his gruff manner and his interrogative style, Callinan was humane in outlook and had a lively sense of humour. As a manager, he was a shrewd tactician and a good judge of people; he extracted maximum effort from his subordinates, whose loyalty he both expected and rewarded. He wrote in a fine hand and made full use of his command of language when preparing large contracts. On visits to manufacturers abroad, he adopted a forthright approach which earned respect and gained results. A lonely man who sought company and craved an audience, he loved meetings, especially those he chaired. After he retired on 10 May 1966, these needs remained unsatisfied and his health, which was never robust, deteriorated.

Accepting the job of sheriff's officer at the Cooma Court House, Callinan also promoted the welfare of prisoners at the local gaol. His decency and integrity were reflected in his efforts to rehabilitate former inmates and place them in the workforce; because of his discretion, this work was little known. A well-trained tenor, he had performed with his wife in an amateur musical society; his love of music was later restricted to listening to records and singing in church. The Callinans moved to Melbourne so that Sadie could be nearer to her sisters. Shortly after their arrival, Cliff died of a ruptured abdominal aneurysm on 13 November 1972 at Box Hill and was buried in Springvale cemetery. His wife and son survived him.

Sixteenth Annual Report of the Snowy Mountains Hydro-electric Authority, *PP* (Cwlth), 1964-66, 14; Snowy Mountains Council, *Annual Report*, 1959, 1960, 1966; information from State Electricity Com of Vic, Melb; information from Mr H. H. G. Valks, Holt, Canb, and Mr K. W. Montague, Cooma, NSW; personal information.

C. R. AMPT

CALVERT, FRANCES ELIZABETH; *see* ALLAN

CALWELL, ARTHUR AUGUSTUS (1896-1973), politician, was born on 28 August 1896 in West Melbourne, eldest of seven children of Arthur Albert Calwell, a police constable who was to rise to the rank of superintendent, and his wife Margaret Ann, née McLoughlin, both Victorian born. Arthur's paternal grandfather Davis Calwell was an American, whose Ulster Protestant father had served in the Pennsylvania General Assembly. Davis came to Victoria in 1853 and married a diminutive Welshwoman Elizabeth Lewis who became, in Arthur's phrase, 'the matriarch of the tribe'. His mother, who died when he was 16, was the daughter of an Irishman Michael McLoughlin, who is thought to have deserted ship in Melbourne in 1847. Calwell recorded: 'I grew up in [the] crowded inner [city] area, with its cottages built on fourteen-feet frontages and even less, and with evidence of human misery visible to all'. Aged 6, he suffered a near fatal attack of diphtheria, to which he attributed the high-pitched huskiness of his mature voice.

Raised in the Catholic faith of his mother and Irish maternal grandmother, Arthur attended Christian Brothers' College, North Melbourne, matriculated and entered the Victorian Public Service on 28 March 1913 as a clerk in the Department of Agriculture. In 1923 he was to move to the Treasury. He defied regulations against open involvement in politics, at 19 becoming secretary of the Melbourne branch of the Australian Labor Party.

When the British Empire went to war in August 1914, Calwell, a second lieutenant in the senior cadets, applied for a commission in the Australian Imperial Force. Rejected because of his age, in 1915-21 he served as a lieutenant in the Militia. By 1916 he was a critic of the war and an ardent advocate of a 'No' vote in the conscription referendum which split the Labor Party that year. His activities as secretary of the Young Ireland Society after the 1916 Easter Rising brought him under the surveillance of security authorities. Honorary secretary (from 1917) of the State Service Clerical Association, he was foundation president (1925) of the restructured Australian Public Service Association (Victorian branch). Between 1926 and 1949 he held a range of elective positions in the State branch of the A.L.P.: he was a member of its central executive, its president (1930-31) and a Victorian delegate to the party's federal executive (from 1930).

Calwell's great authority in the Victorian party enabled him to persuade the parliamentary leader, the veteran Thomas Tunnecliffe [q.v.12], to join the leader of the Country Party (Sir) Albert Dunstan [q.v.8] in bringing down the conservative government of Sir Stanley Argyle [q.v.7] in March 1935. Through an arrangement unique in Australian politics, Dunstan formed a Country Party government with Labor support. Among important legislation which Labor secured in return, Calwell took a keen personal interest in the reform of the Melbourne City Council, on which he served as an alderman (1939) and councillor (until 1945).

He had married Margaret Mary Murphy (d. 1922) on 10 September 1921 at St Monica's Catholic Church, Essendon. On 29 August 1932 in St Patrick's Cathedral, Melbourne, he married Elizabeth Marren, social editor of the Catholic weekly newspaper, the *Tribune*, and an Irishwoman of sharp wit and strong will. In 1933 they launched the *Irish Review* as the official organ of the Victorian Irish Association. Hindered as a player by his poor eyesight, Calwell presided over the North Melbourne Football Club in 1928-34.

After the Depression he devoted an increasing amount of his time to the electoral affairs of the Federal constituency of Melbourne, held (since 1904) by the octogenarian William Maloney [q.v.10]. Although Calwell had set his sights on Melbourne as early as 1926, he made no attempt to persuade the 'Little Doctor' to stand aside and did not seek pre-selection elsewhere. Throughout the 1930s he marshalled Victorian Labor against the rebel New South Wales Labor Party and its fiery leader J. T. Lang [q.v.9]. Calwell's collaboration with the federal parliamentary leader John Curtin [q.v.] culminated in the unity conference of August 1939 which broke Lang's power in New South Wales. Maloney died in August 1940. Prime Minister (Sir) Robert Menzies [q.v.] had called Federal elections for 21 September. The Victorian executive endorsed Calwell for Melbourne; he won the seat and was to hold it until his retirement.

With the Menzies government now dependent on the support of two Victorian Independents, Calwell allied himself with a group in the federal Labor caucus, led by H. V. Evatt [q.v.], which urged Curtin to force an election. Curtin preferred to wait and Labor took power in October 1941. Omitted from the first Curtin ministry, Calwell felt free to criticize the budgets of 1941 and 1942 for failing to implement Labor's social programme. He vigorously opposed the wartime internment of Italian immigrants without trial. To the intense irritation of Evatt, the attorney-general, he campaigned for the release of members of the Australia-First Movement, whose continued detention after the outbreak of war in the Pacific struck him as unjust and absurd. 'Unfortunately', he wrote to a constituent in 1942, 'I am not persona grata at the moment with most ministers because I demand that they shall carry out the policy of the Party, regardless of consequences'.

Calwell's disaffection reached its peak when Curtin sought in November 1942 to modify Labor's policy against conscription for military service overseas. 'As a youth, I was an anti-conscriptionist in the 1916 and 1917 campaigns', Calwell told the House of Representatives, 'and I am as much an anti-conscriptionist in 1942'. A special federal conference on 4 January 1943 supported Curtin 24 to 12. In the subsequent caucus debate on 24 March Curtin called Calwell 'the hero of 100 sham fights'. Calwell retorted: 'The way you're going, you'll finish up on the other side, leading a National Government'. Curtin left the meeting and wrote to caucus demanding that the party either 'dissociate itself from the accusation or appoint another leader'. Calwell apologized.

Following the government's landslide election victory on 21 August 1943, Calwell won the last place in the new ministry. Curtin gave him the portfolio of information. Calwell brought to this post an ingrained distrust of the press, sharpened by his capacity for splendid invective and his delight in provocation—'stirring the possum' as he put it. He gave his opinion of the Australian press in parliament in November 1941: 'It is owned for the most part by financial crooks and is edited for the most part by mental harlots'. Mounting antagonism between Calwell and the newspaper proprietors came to a climax on 16 April 1944 with the seizure of copies of the Sydney *Sunday Telegraph* for flouting censorship rules. Next morning the Sydney dailies published a common statement challenging the powers of the censors. Calwell endorsed action by Commonwealth peace officers to confiscate all copies of the offending editions. The High Court of Australia granted an injunction against the suppression. It was at this time that Australian newspaper cartoonists began to caricature Calwell as a cockatoo, seizing on the most obvious aspects of a physiognomy which he himself wryly conceded had 'a kind of rugged grandeur'.

When J. B. Chifley [q.v.] became prime minister in July 1945 he appointed Calwell Australia's first minister for immigration. He was ideally suited for the post and had lobbied eagerly for it. No minister in Chifley's cabinet was so well placed to overcome labour's traditional resistance to large-scale immigration. Calwell shared and boldly articulated the prejudices both of the labour movement and the wider Australian community. More effectively than others could have done in the 1940s, he was able to expand Australia's traditional immigration base beyond the British Isles to include eastern and southern Europe, and to promote aggressive recruitment as the means of preserving a 'White Australia'. Calwell and (Sir) Tasman Heyes [q.v.], his personal choice to head the new department, formed an outstandingly creative partnership.

War-devastated Europe and war-exhausted Britain provided an abundant source of potential immigrants, but their selection and transportation presented intractable problems. Calwell toured Britain and Europe in 1947 to inspect Australian migration offices, visit refugee camps, speed up selection procedures and organize shipping. He enlisted the co-operation of leaders of the Australian Jewish community to arrange passages for survivors of the Holocaust. Of the ships chartered for Jewish refugees, he later frankly stated: 'We had to insist that half the accommodation in these wretched vessels must be sold to non-Jewish people. It would have created a great wave of anti-Semitism and would have been electorally disastrous for the Labor Party had we not made this decision'. Basing his programme firmly on the concept of assimilation, Calwell coined the term 'New Australian' for immigrants, particularly 'displaced persons' from the Baltic states and Eastern Europe. Britain, however, remained the source of about 50 per cent of intending settlers, whose numbers rose from some 30 000 in 1947 to approximately 170 000 in 1949. While he achieved broad support for his policy, crucially from the unions, Calwell's handling of individual cases occasioned recurrent controversy, invariably involving his strict interpretation of the White Australia policy.

In 1948 Chifley placed Calwell in charge of an electoral redistribution to meet the growth and regional changes in population. Calwell produced a radical plan to increase the number of members in the House of Representatives by two-thirds and to have the Senate elected by proportional representation. He was convinced that his redistribution would advantage Labor, and, perhaps more than any of his colleagues, was stunned by the sweep-

ing electoral victory which returned Menzies to office on 10 December 1949.

In the turmoil of the events of 1949 few noticed that, for the first time since 1926, Calwell had failed to win a place on the Victorian central executive. It was an early sign of the rising strength of a younger generation of Catholics, zealous to eliminate communist influence in the Labor Party and the unions. Calwell's dumping was partly a retaliation against a speech he had made at the 1948 State Labor conference criticizing the 'anti-communist obsession' of 'the Movement', a militant group of Catholics led by a publicist of genius B. A. Santamaria. Calwell's eclipse in Victoria was evident when the executive, now controlled by the anti-communist industrial groups, led moves which forced Labor's Federal parliamentarians to pass Menzies' legislation proscribing the Communist Party of Australia. With Chifley's death in June 1951, Calwell was elected deputy-leader under Evatt, defeating three candidates, among them E. J. Ward [q.v.], his old ally against Curtin; he beat the strongest opponent Percy Clarey [q.v.] in the third ballot, 45 to 36.

Although Calwell had criticized Evatt for accepting a brief from a communist-led union in a successful challenge before the High Court against the Communist Party Dissolution Act (1950), he firmly supported Evatt's brilliant campaign for a 'No' vote in the subsequent referendum on 22 September 1951. In the aftermath of a harshly deflationary budget in 1952, and with strong Labor performances in by-elections and State polls, the Evatt-Calwell team entered the 1954 Federal election campaign with high hopes. Calwell's redistribution of 1948 played some part in Labor's failure, by four seats, to win a House of Representatives majority on 29 May 1954, despite a national vote of 50.03 per cent. Evatt's frustration was to have devastating consequences.

Six weeks before the elections, with Evatt absent from Canberra, Menzies had summoned Calwell to his office, minutes before he told the House that Vladimir Petrov, the third secretary of the Soviet embassy, had requested political asylum. After members of Evatt's personal staff were named at the subsequent royal commission on espionage, Calwell was unable to dissuade Evatt from appearing on their behalf at commission hearings in Sydney. Attempts within the A.L.P. to replace Evatt with Calwell were side-tracked by Evatt's fateful press statement of 5 October, alleging that some Labor members, directed from outside the party, had sabotaged the A.L.P.'s 1954 election campaign.

Evatt's charge produced an avalanche of recrimination which split the Labor Party. After a ferocious caucus debate on 20 October, Calwell was one of the minority of 28 (against 52) who voted for a spill of all leadership positions. Evatt thereafter succeeded in making loyalty to himself the test of loyalty to the party. In 1955 the split in the A.L.P., deepest in Victoria, was given its formal shape by the proceedings of the federal conference in Hobart in March and by the formation of the Anti-Communist (Democratic) Labor Party. For Calwell, the most tragic personal consequence of the split was the breach it made in his relations with the man he most loved and admired, the Catholic archbishop of Melbourne, Daniel Mannix [q.v.10].

Despite massive defeats at the Federal elections in December 1955 and November 1958, Evatt retained the leadership until February 1960, when Calwell persuaded the New South Wales Labor government to appoint Evatt chief justice of the State's Supreme Court. On 7 March, by 42 votes to 30 over R. T. Pollard, caucus awarded Calwell the leadership prize for which he had waited so long. In the election for his deputy, Calwell voted for Ward, but welcomed the unexpected win by the 43-year-old Sydney barrister E. G. Whitlam. Despite the disparity in age, background and outlook, Calwell and Whitlam were able to create an effective partnership; Whitlam's fresh style and energy neatly complemented Calwell's earthier robustness.

By November 1961 a credit squeeze by Federal treasurer Harold Holt [q.v.] had produced more than 100 000 unemployed. In his policy speech for the elections next month Calwell proposed a budget deficit of £100 million 'to restore full employment within twelve months'. Menzies routinely denounced this plan as 'wildly inflationary', but was more alarmed by the unprecedented decision of the *Sydney Morning Herald* to switch its powerful support to Labor. On 9 December the A.L.P. gained 15 additional seats, concentrated in Queensland and New South Wales. The final tally gave the coalition parties 62 seats in the House of Representatives to Labor's 60. Calwell's spectacular achievement silenced those on Labor's left wing who had resented his campaign pledge to abandon the party's sacred cow of bank nationalization.

A wider spectrum of Labor members was appalled in January 1962 by Calwell's overexcited response to Indonesia's move to incorporate West New Guinea. He accused President Sukarno of sabre-rattling, 'reminiscent of Hitler's performances at the time of Munich, and just as menacing'. Menzies gleefully seized the opportunity to turn the 'sabre-rattling' charge against Calwell himself. Calwell's newly-won prestige and the Labor Party's new-found sense of initiative were irreparably damaged. Menzies quickly

regained his ascendancy and the A.L.P. federal executive reasserted the authority over the parliamentary party which it had exercised since the split.

Both these developments converged in crisis for Calwell in 1963 when the Labor Party agonized over the government's decision to allow the United States of America to build a naval communications station at Exmouth, Western Australia. In March Calwell and Whitlam were photographed outside the Hotel Kingston, Canberra, waiting to learn the decision of the thirty-six delegates to a special federal conference. This incident provided the source for Menzies' immensely damaging description of the Labor Party's policy-making processes as being controlled from outside by '36 faceless men'. As if to prove the point, the federal secretary F. E. Chamberlain persuaded the federal executive in October to demand that the New South Wales Labor government abandon a budget proposal to provide means-tested assistance to parents with children in private secondary schools. Although Calwell had earlier advised the premier R. J. Heffron [q.v.] that the proposal did not conflict with Labor policy, the executive's intervention revived the ancient and virulent dispute, essentially sectarian in character, about state aid to non-government schools.

Calwell published *Labor's Role in Modern Society* (Melbourne, 1963) as a manifesto. In spite of the party's open brawling and a general economic recovery, he mounted a strong and confident campaign for the elections which Menzies called in 1963, a year ahead of time. But in the weekend (23-24 November) before polling day, Calwell was struck by a series of savage blows. The pre-election opinion poll revealed a decisive reduction in support for Labor. The *Sydney Morning Herald* finally turned against him with a venomous personal attack. On Sunday at St Francis Xavier Cathedral, Geraldton, Western Australia, he heard a sermon on the sinfulness of voting Labor. That evening in Perth he was wrongly informed that Menzies had coupled Labor policies and the assassination, two days earlier, of the United States' president John F. Kennedy. In rage and frustration, Calwell issued a press statement claiming that Menzies had tried to 'smear the Labor Party over President Kennedy's coffin'. On 30 November Menzies regained ten of the seats Calwell had won in 1961.

Relations between Calwell and Whitlam began to deteriorate sharply. In a calculated indiscretion, Whitlam sorely offended Calwell by contrasting the age and vigour of the competing party leaders, should Menzies retire before the elections due in 1966 and be replaced by Holt. During his last electoral contest with Menzies, the 1964 Senate poll,

Calwell was able to return to one of the grand themes of his career: his passionate opposition to conscription. Against the advice of the Military Board, the government announced in November plans for a compulsory call-up of 20-year-old men to be chosen by ballot. Calwell's denunciation failed to find a response in the electorate, which on 5 December gave Labor candidates only 44.7 per cent of the national vote.

On the eve of the Senate campaign, the Vietnam War began to take shape as the dominant issue in Australian politics. In August 1964 the Gulf of Tonkin incident, in which it was claimed that forces of the Democratic Republic of Vietnam (North Vietnam) had fired on American vessels in international waters, exposed the dilemma that was to dog the Labor Party throughout the war: how to condemn the United States' intervention without condemning Australia's ally, the United States. Calwell personified Labor's dilemma and expressed it memorably in an emotion-laden speech at a parliamentary reception for President Lyndon Johnson in October 1966 in which he ended a philippic against the war by reciting the final sentences of the Gettysburg Address.

In April 1965 Menzies had announced the dispatch of an Australian battalion to the Republic of Vietnam (South Vietnam) to help to stop the 'downward thrust by Communist China between the Indian and Pacific Oceans'. Calwell's reply on 4 May proved prophetic as to the war's course and outcome: the U.S.A. faced humiliation in what was essentially a civil war. He asked: 'As the war drags on, who is to say that [Australia's commitment of 800 regular troops] will not rise to 8000, and that these will not be drawn from our voteless, conscripted 20 year olds?' It was only when Menzies' successor Holt included conscripts in the expanding Australian contingent in 1966 that Calwell's deepest emotions became fully engaged in opposition to Australia's involvement.

On the night of 21 June 1966, after addressing a rowdy meeting at Mosman Town Hall, Sydney, Calwell became the victim of an assassination attempt. A 19-year-old factory worker Peter Raymond Kocan discharged a sawn-off rifle immediately after Calwell entered his car, wounding him in the jaw. Described by his defence psychiatrist as a 'borderline schizophrenic', Kocan was sentenced to life imprisonment. In 1968 Calwell wrote to him: 'If there is anything I can do to help you in future in the matter of the mitigation of your sentence . . . I will do it'. Kocan was released in 1976.

Labor's campaign for the 1966 Federal elections fell apart under the strains of Vietnam and tensions over the leadership. Friction between Calwell and Whitlam had intensified since March when Calwell narrowly failed to procure Whitlam's expulsion and Whitlam was unable to orchestrate a spill of leadership positions. Calwell attributed Labor's loss of nine seats on 26 November to 'the disunity in our own ranks on questions of personality and policy during the lifetime of the 25th Parliament'. He refused to call a caucus meeting until 8 February 1967. Whitlam was then elected his successor.

In his last, embittered years, increasingly troubled by osteoarthritis and diabetes, Calwell only once assumed the role of Labor's elder statesman. In August 1967 he strongly opposed a move by Labor senators to join with the D.L.P. in the Senate to reject a budget proposal for increased postal charges. He prophesied that, if the A.L.P. thus helped to raise the pretensions and ambitions of the Senate, then the day would come when the Senate would be used to destroy a Labor government. Appointed to the Privy Council in 1967, he remained in parliament until the 1972 elections in which Labor won office after twenty-three years in opposition.

He published his autobiography, *Be Just and Fear Not* (Melbourne, 1972), a moving, often bitter, account of his turbulent relationship with the two institutions he most loved, his party and his Church. Of his co-religionists who had criticized his acceptance of a Papal knighthood in 1964, Calwell wrote: 'I am afraid that an inordinately large number of my fellow Catholics are fear-stricken, communist-hating, money-making, social-climbing, status-seeking, brainwashed, ghetto-minded people to whom the Pope is too venturesome, and not sufficiently prudent in his dealings with the non-Catholic world on the one hand and the communist one-sixth of the world on the other'. Survived by his wife and their daughter Mary Elizabeth who sustained him with unflinching devotion to the end, he died on 8 July 1973 in East Melbourne. He was buried in Melbourne general cemetery beside his son Arthur Andrew, whose death of leukaemia at the age of 11 in 1948 dealt Calwell the one wound, of a hard-fought life, which never healed.

R. Murray, *The Split* (Melb, 1970); P. Weller (ed), *Caucus Minutes 1901-1949* (Melb, 1975); G. Freudenberg, *A Certain Grandeur* (Melb, 1977); L. Ross, *John Curtin* (Melb, 1977); C. Kiernan, *Calwell* (Melb, 1978); E. Kunz, *Displaced Persons* (Syd, 1988); Calwell papers (NL).

GRAHAM FREUDENBERG

CAMERON, ALLAN GORDON (1909-1960), bank officer and soldier, was born on 16 May 1909 at Fitzroy, Melbourne, son of Lochiel Frederick Arthur Gordon Cameron, a native-born banker, and his English-born wife

Kate Inez Maud, née Bagnall. Educated at Scotch College, Hawthorn, Allan joined the Commercial Bank of Australia Ltd and about 1926 enlisted in the Militia. He rose through the ranks in the 46th Infantry Battalion and was commissioned lieutenant on 15 October 1929, but resigned two years later. On 3 November 1934 he married 19-year-old Margaret Whatnough Stewart at the Presbyterian Church, South Yarra.

Brown haired, muscular, of middle height and compact build, Cameron rejoined the Militia in 1939. On 1 July 1940 he transferred to the Australian Imperial Force as a captain and was posted to the 2nd/22nd Battalion, which became part of the garrison defending Rabaul, New Britain. He was second-in-command of 'C' Company, stationed at Vunakanau airfield, when the Japanese invasion force reached Rabaul on 23 January 1942. Overwhelmed, the Australians withdrew to the south and west. Liaising between four groups retreating westward, in mid-February Cameron sent a message to headquarters in Port Moresby in which he described the engagement at Rabaul and sought instructions. Having been given permission to escape if he considered guerrilla warfare impossible, he and a dozen soldiers sailed a pinnace to Salamaua, New Guinea, arriving on 3 March. The Japanese landed five days later. His party demolished the airfield, fired the petrol dump and shot an enemy soldier at point-blank range before departing for Port Moresby.

Promoted in May, Cameron was appointed brigade major of the 30th Brigade. On 4 August at Deniki he took command of Maroubra Force which was confronting the Japanese advance across the Owen Stanley Range. First in attack, then in defence, this 'ruthless and able soldier' held his small force together for twelve days in the face of increasing enemy pressure. He was awarded the Distinguished Service Order (1943). On being relieved, he performed liaison duties. Cameron was promoted temporary lieutenant colonel on 28 August 1942 and given charge of the 53rd Battalion on 2 September. A week later he assumed command of the 3rd Battalion, then occupying defensive positions at Ioribaiwa, the farthermost point of the Japanese thrust towards Port Moresby. He led the battalion in the Australian drive over the mountains and in the bitter fighting around Gona in November and December, winning a Bar to his D.S.O.

In North Queensland from March 1943 Cameron had charge of the composite 3rd-22nd Battalion. On 5 July he took command of the 2nd/2nd Battalion. Ordered to New Guinea, the unit participated in the ten-month Aitape-Wewak campaign which culminated in the surrender of the Japanese Eighteenth

Army in August 1945; Cameron was mentioned in dispatches. Between December 1945 and October 1946 he successively commanded the 26th Battalion, and the 2nd and 3rd New Guinea battalions on New Britain. Transferring to the Retired List (25 January 1947), he managed a plantation on the island for two years. In 1950 he moved to Victoria and worked a grazing property on the Mornington Peninsula. Next year he took up a 441-acre (178.5 ha) soldier-settlement block on Phillip Island where he ran sheep and cattle.

Cameron was prominent in the Returned Sailors', Soldiers' and Airmen's Imperial League of Australia; he was also a shire councillor (from 1958), a justice of the peace, an elder of the Presbyterian Church and a Freemason. After suffering from hypertensive coronary vascular disease for some years, he died of a cerebral haemorrhage on 8 June 1960 at Cowes and was buried in the local cemetery. His wife, daughter and three sons survived him.

L. Wigmore, *The Japanese Thrust* (Canb, 1957); R. Paull, *Retreat from Kokoda* (Melb, 1958); D. McCarthy, *South-West Pacific Area—First Year* (Canb, 1959); G. Long, *The Final Campaigns* (Canb, 1963); V. Austin (comp), *To Kokoda and Beyond* (Melb, 1988); AWM records.

A. J. SWEETING

CAMERON, ARCHIE GALBRAITH (1895-1956), farmer and politician, was born on 22 March 1895 at Happy Valley, South Australia, son of John Cameron, labourer, and his wife Mary Ann, née McDonald. Educated at Nairne Public School until the age of 12, Archie was employed to clear scrub before working on his father's farm near Loxton. He enlisted in the Australian Imperial Force on 17 April 1916, fought on the Western Front and rose to temporary regimental quartermaster sergeant. Arriving home in July 1919, he was discharged on 7 September.

That year Cameron took up land at Noora as a soldier settler. He served (1920-24 and 1926-27) on the Loxton District Council, read widely in literature and history, and learned to speak fluent German. Received into the Catholic Church from a strict Presbyterian background, he was to become close friends with Dr Matthew Beovich, the archbishop of Adelaide. On 15 April 1925 at St Joseph's Church, Brighton, Cameron married 22-year-old office-worker Margaret Eileen Walsh; they were to have a son and daughter. In 1942 the family moved to a dairy-farm near Oakbank in the Adelaide hills.

Having unsuccessfully stood for the House of Assembly as a Country Party candidate for Wooroora in 1924, Cameron won the seat in

1927 and held it until 1934. As his party's parliamentary leader (1928-32), he played an important role in forming the South Australian Emergency Committee, which brought together the major, local, non-Labor groups from which the Liberal and Country League emerged in 1932. The principal figure in the Emergency Committee (Sir) Grenfell Price [q.v.] wrote that Cameron had 'remarkable abilities and grave faults . . . He was an excellent speaker, and most forceful, but he was unreliable . . . I soon learnt to be careful with Cameron'.

Under the terms of the amalgamation, Cameron was guaranteed endorsement by the L.C.L. for a safe seat in the House of Representatives. In 1934 he was elected to Federal parliament as the member for Barker, a seat he was to retain until his death. He had persuaded his friend and old army comrade (Sir) Thomas Playford to contest Murray (successfully) for the L.C.L. at the 1933 State election.

Cameron chose to sit in parliament as a representative of the Federal Country Party, as he was entitled to do under the rules of the L.C.L. He immediately became the focus of public attention by making an affirmation instead of swearing the oath of allegiance. Soon after, he attempted to have J. S. Garden [q.v.8] expelled from the House on the grounds of his previous communist affiliations. Cameron's obvious talents were recognized by his appointment on 29 November 1937 as an assistant-minister in J. A. Lyons's [q.v.10] cabinet. While acting-minister for commerce in 1938, Cameron became the first minister to be named and suspended from Federal parliament, for calling the Victorian Independent Alexander Wilson [q.v.] a 'clean-skin' (meaning 'unbranded') and refusing to withdraw the remark when called upon by the Speaker.

On 7 November 1938 Cameron was promoted to postmaster-general. His conflict with the broadcasting industry culminated next month when he temporarily revoked radio 2KY's licence because he objected to views expressed by one of the station's news commentators. Cameron is alleged to have told the chairman of the Australian Broadcasting Commission, W. J. Cleary [q.v.8]: 'Forget your charter, I don't believe in boards or commissions—I believe in ministerial control'. (Sir) Robert Menzies' [q.v.] first ministry, installed in April 1939, consisted only of United Australia Party members and Cameron returned to the back-benches.

Following Sir Earle Page's [q.v.11] retirement in September as Federal Country Party leader, a deeply divided party unexpectedly elected Cameron as his successor. With the coalition restored, Cameron was appointed deputy-prime minister, minister for com-

merce and minister for the navy on 14 March 1940. In circumstances as dramatic as those of his election, he lost the Country Party leadership in October, and left the party and the ministry. Throughout the rest of the decade he was to sit with the U.A.P. and subsequently the Liberal Party, becoming a biting critic of the Labor governments of John Curtin and J. B. Chifley [qq.v.]. By 1943 Price thought that Cameron had 'improved immensely', though 'all his old recklessness remained'. He also noted that Cameron 'was one of the few who could reduce Eddie Ward [q.v.] to impotence'.

A temporary major (commissioned 1927) in the Militia, Cameron was mobilized in November 1940 and subsequently worked in the Directorate of Military Intelligence at Army Headquarters, Melbourne. His uniform comprised a World War I Highland beret, World War II battledress and the elastic-sided boots he habitually wore. He combined his military and parliamentary duties, and added to his burden 'the management of the parliamentary concerns of A. M. Blain', the member for the Northern Territory who was a prisoner of war. Cameron's relations with General Sir Thomas Blamey [q.v.] were punctuated by bitter and stormy disputes over the conduct of the war. On 5 May 1944 Cameron was transferred to the Reserve of Officers. After his death it was disclosed that the work he had done on the Japanese order of battle had been of the 'greatest possible value' to army intelligence. Characteristically, he had never talked about it.

With the return of the Liberal and Country parties to office in 1949, Menzies nominated him as Speaker of the House of Representatives. Cameron's fiery independence as minister or backbencher could have easily destabilized the new government. On his election in 1950 he wore the traditional wig and robes of office discarded by his Labor predecessor J. S. Rosevear [q.v.]. Cameron objected to using H. V. Evatt's [q.v.] High Court of Australia wig, which had been presented to parliament, but none other was available, and he contented himself with the statement: 'It will be the first time there has been any clear, straight thinking under this wig'. Cameron's relations with the governor-general, the former Labor premier of New South Wales, (Sir) William McKell, were strained due to personal comments made by McKell ten years earlier. Cameron informed the House in March that, while 'he would fully and courteously discharge all official duties' with McKell, in other matters he would have 'nothing whatever to do with him'.

A firm disciplinarian, Cameron caused an immediate stir by imposing a rigid ban on betting in Parliament House and by forbidding card-playing or any other game of chance. He unavailingly summoned Labor's Gil Duthie to his rooms to be rebuked, but was more successful in implementing his views on propriety in other areas. The print of the racehorse, Phar Lap, which graced the wall of the barber's salon, was ordered to be removed. Cameron also insisted that everyone should be properly dressed in the lobbies, but did not invariably apply his rules to himself: on a hot day he frequently 'received visitors dressed only in shorts and a singlet', his bare feet upon his desk. The cleaning staff resented his weekend habit of walking around the lobbies so attired, fearing that visitors might mistake him for a cleaner and 'damage their prestige'.

Cameron was a tempestuous character, one of the most colourful individualists ever to sit in Federal parliament. Stories are still told about him. He neither smoked nor drank. Holding strong Jacobite views, during a visit to London he charmed the Queen Mother by telling her that 'when there is a Prince named Charles and a Princess named Anne a Cameron may visit Buckingham Palace in perfect safety'. Although a man of stern exterior, he performed many personal kindnesses to members on both sides of politics. As a member of parliament, he was a well-informed and fluent debater, always extremely forceful in expression. As a minister, he was at times irascible, but he was hard working and determined, and a good administrator. As Speaker, he was certainly autocratic and at times eccentric, yet Labor's Clyde Cameron summed him up as 'easily the best Speaker in living memory'. Archie's integrity was never held in doubt, even by his severest critic.

In August 1955 Cameron suffered attacks of influenza which affected his lungs and heart, both weakened by gas in World War I. He died of myocardial infarction on 9 August 1956 in Royal Prince Alfred Hospital, Sydney; accorded a state funeral in Adelaide, he was buried in Mount Barker cemetery. His wife and son survived him. (Sir) Ivor Hele's portrait of Cameron was hung in Parliament House, Canberra, a place which was more placid after his departure.

P. Hasluck, *The Government and the People 1939-1941* (Canb, 1952) and *1942-1945* (Canb, 1970); E. Page, *Truant Surgeon*, A. Mozley ed (Syd, 1963); A. Fadden, *They called me Artie* (Brisb, 1969); E. M. Lyons, *Among the Carrion Crows* (Adel, 1972); P. Spender, *Politics and a Man* (Syd, 1972); J. Hetherington, *Blamey, Controversial Soldier* (Canb, 1973); A. Thomas, *Broadcast and Be Damned* (Melb, 1980); C. Kerr, *Archie* (Melb, 1983); G. Duthie, *I Had 50,000 Bosses* (Syd, 1984); G. Souter, *Acts of Parliament* (Melb, 1988); C. Cameron, *The Cameron Diaries* (Syd, 1990); *Aust Country Party*, 1 Sept 1935; *People* (Syd), 6 Dec 1950; *Herald* (Melb), 9 Aug 1956, 5 Jan 1959; *Advertiser* (Adel) and *Argus*, 10 Aug 1956; *Bulletin*, 15 Aug 1956, 12 Sept 1978; information from Mr R. Cameron, Adel.   JOHN PLAYFORD

CAMERON, DONALD ALASTAIR (1900-1974), politician and medical practitioner, was born on 17 March 1900 at Ipswich, Queensland, son of John Alexander Cameron, a native-born medical practitioner, and his wife Eliza, née Taylor, from Ireland. One of four sons of Donald Cameron [q.v.3], John was president (1912) of the Queensland branch of the British Medical Association. Young Don was educated at Ipswich Grammar School and at the University of Sydney (B.A., 1921; M.B., 1927; B.S., 1931); a resident of St Paul's College, he became senior student, rowed in the first VIII and capped 1926 with a memorable speech at a college dinner.

From 1927 Cameron was a resident medical officer at Royal Prince Alfred and the Coast (Prince Henry) hospitals in Sydney. On 9 August 1933 at his college chapel he married with Anglican rites a nurse Rhoda Florence McLean. Following a short trip abroad, the couple went to live at Ipswich where he joined his father's private practice and also acted as honorary medical officer at Ipswich General Hospital. He was to be chieftain of the Ipswich Caledonian Society and Burns Club, and chairman (1948-56) of trustees of his old school.

Having been appointed captain in the Militia in 1936, Cameron transferred to the Australian Imperial Force on 21 May 1940 as major, Australian Army Medical Corps. From December that year to March 1942 he served in the Middle East with the 2nd/2nd Casualty Clearing Station and the 2nd/9th Australian General Hospital. Promoted lieutenant colonel, he commanded the 2nd/1st Field Ambulance in Papua (September 1942 to March 1943) and during the Aitape-Wewak campaign in New Guinea in early 1945. He was mentioned in dispatches and appointed O.B.E. (1946). After service on New Britain from July, he transferred to the Reserve of Officers on 5 December 1945 as honorary colonel. In 1948-49 he was president of Queensland's Moreton district of the Returned Sailors', Soldiers' and Airmen's Imperial League of Australia.

At the 1949 general elections Cameron won the Federal seat of Oxley. He was a member of the Liberal Party's committee on federal policy, the council of the Australian National University (1951-56) and the parliamentary joint committee on foreign affairs (1952-55). Groomed by Sir Earle Page [q.v.11] to succeed him as minister for health, Cameron took over the portfolio on 11 January 1956. He led the Australian delegation to the tenth session of the World Health Assembly at Geneva in 1957 and was elected vice-president. In 1960-61 he was minister in charge of the Commonwealth Scientific and Industrial Research Organization. He was 5 ft 8½ ins (174 cm) tall, slight in build and dapper in appearance. Taciturn, 'calm, dignified and imperturbable', he was noted for his integrity; Cameron's flashes of dry humour ensured his popularity in parliament.

His devotion to federal responsibilities may have contributed to his defeat by William Hayden at the 1961 elections. Cameron subsequently worked for his former department as Commonwealth medical officer at the General Post Office, Sydney, until his appointment in 1962 as high commissioner to New Zealand. Returning to Brisbane in 1965, he established a general practice at Nundah. A member (1929) and fellow (1971) of the British (Australian) Medical Association, he was president (1969) of its Queensland branch. In 1958 he had been an instigator of the preventive medicine committee of the Royal Australian College of General Practitioners. He served on the council and Queensland executive of the Medical Benefits Fund of Australia Ltd. With Rhoda, he was prominent in launching the State's 'Meals on Wheels' service. He belonged to the Australasian Pioneers' (Sydney) and the Queensland clubs. Survived by his wife, daughter and son, Cameron died on 5 January 1974 at Chermside and was cremated.

H. S. Paterson, *The Ordinary Doctor* (Brisb, 1990); St Paul's College, Univ Syd, *Pauline*, Nov 1927, p 12; *Newsbulletin of Qld Branch of Aust Medical Assn*, 13, no 3, Mar 1974; *MJA*, 22 June 1974, p 1011; *Qld Times*, 8, 11, 23 Dec 1961, 7 Jan 1974; *Courier-Mail*, 7 Jan 1974; *Canb Times*, 8 Jan 1974.
                                    JENNIFER HARRISON

CAMERON, SIR GORDON ROY (1899-1966), pathologist, was born on 30 June 1899 at Echuca, Victoria, son of George Cameron, a Methodist minister from South Australia, and his English-born wife Emily, née Pascoe. Roy was educated at Mitiamo, Lancefield and Dunkeld state schools, Kyneton High School and the University of Melbourne (M.B., B.S., 1922). Before completing a year's residency at the Melbourne Hospital, he was appointed in 1923 Stewart lecturer in pathology at the university and resident medical tutor at Queen's College. Inspired by Professor Sir Harry Allen [q.v.7] towards pathology, prodded by Dr R. H. Strong towards experiment, and assisted by senior technician William Dickinson (who supplied a makeshift animal-house and a colony of guinea-pigs), Cameron pioneered experimental pathology with prize-winning studies of the pancreas.

In early 1925 he succeeded (Sir) Macfar-

lane Burnet as first assistant to C. H. Kellaway [q.v.9] and deputy-director of the Walter and Eliza Hall [qq.v.9] Institute; Cameron specialized in islet regeneration after partial pancreatectomy. From late 1927 he worked for a year under Ludwig Aschoff at Freiburg-im-Breisgau, Germany, and next under A. E. Boycott, professor of morbid anatomy at University College Hospital Medical School, London (D.Sc., 1929). There he chose to remain, despite poor health and previous firm intentions to return to Melbourne. A bachelor, he lived with Boycott's laboratory assistant Fred Crews and his wife, who devoted their lives to him.

At U.C.H.M.S. Cameron was Graham scholar in pathology in 1928-30, Beit fellow for medical research in 1930-33 and—after a term as pathologist at Queen Mary's Hospital —reader in pathology from 1934 to 1937 when he succeeded Boycott in the chair. From 1929 Cameron had pursued extensive, fundamental research on liver diseases and pulmonary oedema. Although a scientific liberal, he was a technical conservative, highly resistant to appeals for expensive modern equipment, yet his laboratory drew aspiring experimental pathologists from all over the world, among them Australians such as G. S. Christie and D. L. Wilhelm [qq.v.]. Assistant-editor (1932-55) of the *Journal of Pathology and Bacteriology*, Cameron sought at least one paper from his department for every issue.

In 1939-45 he was seconded to the Chemical Defence Experimental Station at Porton, Wiltshire, to work with the physiologist Sir Joseph Barcroft on the effects of war gases; evenings were spent in 'deep reading' for *Pathology of the Cell* (London, 1952). Considerable government service followed with the Chemical Defence Board (1945-46), the Agricultural Research Council (1947-56) and the Medical Research Council (1952-56). He had returned to his chair at the University of London in 1945; next year he also became director of the Graham department, U.C.H.M.S. Cameron retired from both positions in 1964.

A meticulous scholar who published 145 scientific papers, he was erudite in the literature of pathology and of Renaissance Italy, in addition to being a mathematician and a pianist. Cameron was of medium build and fit when young; he grew ponderous in body and manner, but retained a keen delight in human absurdity. Bored by politics, he was a benevolent conservative who was firmly attached to the British Empire. He was knighted in 1957. A fellow (1946) of the Royal Society, he was one of its Royal medallists in 1960. Sir Roy took great pride in being foundation president (1962) of the (Royal) College of Pathologists which has a bust of him by R. B. Claughton. Restricted by illness from 1956, Cameron made his only return visit to Australia in 1962 to accept an honorary LL.D. from the University of Melbourne. He died of ischaemic heart disease on 7 October 1966 at Finchley, London.

DNB, 1961-70; Dept of Pathology, Univ Melb, *The Melbourne School of Pathology* (Melb, 1962); F. M. Burnet, *Changing Patterns* (Melb, 1968) and *Walter and Eliza Hall Institute 1915-1965* (Melb, 1971); K. F. Russell, *The Melbourne Medical School 1862-1962* (Melb, 1977); *British Medical J*, 15 Oct 1966; *MJA*, 28 Jan 1967; *Biog Memoirs of Fellows of Roy Soc* (Lond), 14, 1968.   PATRICIA MORISON

CAMERON, KEITH ADDISON (1902-1967), mining engineer and company director, was born on 8 September 1902 at Prahran, Melbourne, son of Victorian-born parents David Cameron, draper, and his wife Louise, née Addison. Educated at Wesley College and the University of Melbourne (B.M.E., 1928), Keith was employed as surveyor and assistant mining engineer (1927-28) at Mount Lyell, Tasmania, and in 1928-30 worked in Canada and Alaska before joining Mount Isa Mines Ltd, Queensland. On 14 March 1932 he married an American, Florence Mary Gibbs, at the Presbyterian Church, Malvern, Melbourne. He returned to Tasmania that year as assistant to the mine superintendent and oversaw the smaller Comstock mine for the Mount Lyell Mining & Railway Co. Ltd.

In August 1933 he joined Gold Mines of Australia Ltd, formed by W. S. Robinson [q.v.11] to initiate large-scale gold exploration and mining. Next year Cameron was appointed field superintendent of the subsidiary, Bendigo Mines Ltd. He explored ore bodies at Bendigo mainly by shaft sinking and driving, but the low fixed-price of gold and the high cost of the operation caused the project to be abandoned in 1937. Taken on by Western Mining Corporation Ltd as general superintendent, Cameron explored the Mount Charlotte ore body in Western Australia (which ultimately came into production in the 1960s) and devised the costing system which was effectively used by that company for many years. In July 1942 he transferred to North Broken Hill Ltd as assistant-superintendent at its Broken Hill mine, becoming manager in July 1945.

In December 1946 Prime Minister Chifley [q.v.] and Premier (Sir) William McKell appointed Cameron inaugural chairman of the Joint Coal Board: 'other mining men had shied away from a task that was bound to prove thankless, even heartbreaking'. The coal industry was in turmoil with low productivity, antiquated mining methods and constant industrial problems. Although his experience had been essentially in 'hardrock' mining, Cameron aimed to improve the living and working conditions of the miners, and to produce coal 'in such quantity and of such quality as will satisfy national requirements'. He set in train many changes to the industry—particularly the elimination of pneumoconiosis, improved safety and rescue standards, mechanization and open-cut mining—but was involved in battles with the unions and the owners, and the press was often critical of his approach to problems. Thirty years later, however, a former colleague commented that Cameron 'must be given the most credit for the resuscitation of the very sick coal industry, not only in New South Wales but in Australia. He made great progress in the face of often passive and at times active resistance from many coal owners, employers and employees'.

In mid-1950 Cameron resigned to become managing director (until 1955) of Mount Morgan Ltd. He worked with J. M. Newman [q.v.] and Genister Shiel in reorganizing the company and remained a director until his death. In 1955 he was one of a group of mining entrepreneurs and financiers who formed Commonwealth Mining Investments (Australia) Ltd to invest in resource companies listed on the stock exchange and to sponsor new companies in metals, beach sands and oil. The success of this finance house led to its acquisition in 1961 by the London-based Consolidated Gold Fields of South Africa Ltd. Always a strong individualist, Cameron could not see a suitable place for himself in the new international structure, so resigned as managing director and accepted the chairmanship of Mount Morgan Ltd, where his skill in negotiations opened up important contracts with Japan.

Throughout his working life Cameron had contributed to such professional bodies as the Australasian Institute of Mining and Metallurgy, Broken Hill Mining Managers' Association, Australian Mining Industry Council, Australian Mineral Industries Research Association Ltd, Gold Producers' Association Ltd and the Queensland Chamber of Mines. His work gave him little time for recreation, but in his earlier years he played golf and he continued to enjoy tennis. Still actively engaged as chairman of Mount Morgan and a director of at least eight mining companies, Cameron died suddenly of a coronary occlusion on 5 August 1967 at his Killara home, Sydney, and was cremated. His wife and two daughters survived him. On his death A. J. Keast [q.v.] wrote that Cameron 'always represented everything that is honest, straightforward, constructive, immensely friendly and very human'. Through the marriage of his daughter Susan to Dr Tony O'Reilly, the family endowed the Keith Cameron chair of

Australian history at University College, Dublin.

SMH, 18 Dec 1946, 15 Mar 1947; *Age* (Melb) and *Aust Financial Review*, 8 Aug 1967; family papers (held by Mrs S. Shuter, Mornington, Vic).

D. F. BRANAGAN

CAMM, PHILIP JOHN (1892-1964), engineer and jam manufacturer, was born on 27 July 1892 in South Melbourne, fourth of five children of DANIEL THOMAS CAMM (c.1864-1941), labourer, and his native-born wife Annie Maria, née Bacchus. Born in Devon, England, Daniel had come to South Australia in 1879 and served with the South Australian Naval Force. He was discharged in 1888 and moved with his family to Melbourne where he found work on the wharves.

In 1894 Daniel bought land at Monbulk in the Dandenong Ranges. There, from 1896, he started to grow berry fruit while his four sons attended the local state school. Using his natural talents as an engineer, he first invented a 'devil' to assist in stump-pulling on the family block and later installed an intricate irrigation system for his plants. Transport of the delicate fruit was difficult on the rough hill-tracks. In 1897 Camm joined other locals to form the Monbulk Co-operative Fruitgrowers' Association and to establish a jam factory near the railway station at Upper Ferntree Gully, then the nearest terminus of Melbourne's suburban railway network. The factory was destroyed by fire in 1909.

With the assistance of his three eldest sons, Camm improved a pulping technique which enabled fruit to be moved more cheaply to the city for processing into jam. Encouraged by this success, in 1909 the family erected a small pulping factory on their property. Increased business, based on locally-grown fruit, required a new and larger plant next year. A bumper crop of local plums in 1913 almost spelt disaster for local growers when prices fell. Daniel, however, bought the entire crop and began to manufacture jam.

In 1912-24 Philip attended night-classes at the Working Men's College, Melbourne, where he studied mechanics and steam-boiler operation. He became the factory's mechanical engineer and developed much of the plant's machinery. In 1914 his brother Robert, who had responsibility for marketing and purchase, enlisted for war service; he died at Passchendaele on 4 October 1917. In his absence, Philip assumed control of the factory.

On 30 August 1913 Philip had married Elsie Veronica Marr at Abbotsford with Methodist forms. After Daniel died on 3 June 1941, Philip took over as managing director of D. Camm & Sons Pty Ltd. The firm thrived and during World War II won large orders with the British Ministry of Food. From this time the company's export trade grew quickly and on trips abroad the Camms saw their jam in England, Europe, North America and Japan. In 1946 Philip moved to Hobart where he set up a Tasmanian branch of the firm, which in 1948 changed its name to Camm's Jams Pty Ltd. It became Monbulk Preserves Pty Ltd in 1957 and on 15 May was registered as a public company. Philip was its chairman until 1960 when he was succeeded by his eldest son. Survived by his wife, daughter and three sons, Philip Camm died on 21 December 1964 at Taroona, Hobart, and was cremated.

Monbulk Preserves Ltd ended as a Camm family business when the whole concern was purchased by the Shepparton Preserving Co. which sold it to Cottee's General Foods Ltd in December 1989. The subsequent economic recession affected operating costs and the old factory at Monbulk closed its doors in May 1991.

H. Coulson, *Story of the Dandenongs, 1838-1958* (Melb, 1959) and The Camms of Monbulk (ms, 1964, held by Ms B. McAllister, The Patch, Vic); A. Winzenried, *The Hills of Home* (Melb, 1988); *Age* (Melb), 4 June 1941, 22 Dec 1964; *Ferntree Gully News*, 6 June 1941; *Free Press* (Belgrave, Melb), 30 Dec 1964, 8 May, 2, 9 Oct 1991; family documents (held by Ms B. McAllister).

ARTHUR WINZENRIED

CAMPBELL, ALAN WALTER (1880-1972), businessman, was born on 27 June 1880 at Apple Tree Gully, near Inverell, New South Wales, sixth of eleven children of John Campbell, a native-born station overseer, and his wife Mary Georgina, née McIntyre, from Scotland. The family moved to Bullerawa station in the Narrabri district where Alan was privately educated, mainly by Scottish tutors. He joined the Sydney woolbrokers, John Bridge & Co. Ltd, in 1895 and rose to be company secretary. In 1906-07 Campbell toured properties in Queensland to determine whether the firm could obtain sufficient woolclips to warrant expansion interstate: a branch was subsequently established in Brisbane. At the age of 28 he was elected a director. On 26 June 1909 he married Millicent Beatrice Cutter at St John's Anglican Church, North Sydney. In 1910 Campbell was appointed sub-manager of the company's Brisbane branch. He enlisted in the Australian Imperial Force on 3 January 1917, served in the Middle East in the Imperial Camel Brigade and the 1st Light Horse Regiment, and returned to Australia in March 1919.

Finalizing 'one of the most unusual business agreements' filed in the State, in 1920

Campbell formed the Queensland Primary Producers' Co-operative Association Ltd (later Primac) which took over the local business of John Bridge & Co. for £75 000 in paid-up shares. The new firm began operations in May, with Campbell as its general manager; he joined the board as managing director in August 1922. Under his guidance, 'Primaries' surmounted its initial uncertainties, the Depression, strong competition and World War II: its ability to attract support ensured that it ultimately became Queensland's largest primary industry co-operative. An early supporter and a trustee of the Australian Country Party, Campbell was particularly active in attempts to safeguard protection for rural industries.

He was closely connected with the formation of Queensland and Northern Territory Aerial Services Ltd, and provided business advice during the discussions which led to its registration in November 1920. Having acted as QANTAS's temporary secretary in Brisbane, Campbell joined its advisory board. At the board meeting on 23 February 1933 he moved the resolution to associate QANTAS with Imperial Airways Ltd in order to provide regular flights to and from Britain.

During World War II Campbell was foundation president (1941-43) of the Australian-American Association; he was also chairman (1941-46) of the Queensland State Wool Committee and later of the Australian Growers' Wool Marketing Committee. A specialist on marketing who advocated a reserve-price scheme within the auction system, he published a *Statement on 'Post J.O.' Wool Marketing* (1950) and *Controlled Wool Marketing* (1963). He kept abreast of rural problems, and was a dedicated supporter of free enterprise and of the co-operative movement. Appointed O.B.E. (1962) and C.M.G. (1967), he retired in September 1968 at the age of 88, but remained a director of 'Primaries' which then had assets of $18 million.

Survived by his son and daughter, Campbell died on 6 December 1972 at Clayfield, Brisbane and was cremated. His Queensland estate was sworn for probate at $144 774.

Qld Country Life, 26 Sept 1968, 28 May 1970; Qld Primary Producers' Co-Operative Assn Ltd, *Circular*, no 52, 18 Dec 1972; *Courier-Mail*, 26 Sept 1968.　　A. L. LOUGHEED

CAMPBELL, ALEXANDER PETRIE (1881-1963), Congregational minister, was born on 4 June 1881 at Redfern, Sydney, second son of English-born Rev. George Campbell and his wife Mary Adam, née Petrie, from Scotland. Ordained at Dundee, Scotland, George had come to Sydney where he served

the Congregational churches at Redfern and Burwood. Alexander was educated at Newington College and the University of Sydney (B.A., 1904), and continued his studies in theology at Camden College, Glebe.

Ordained in 1905 in his father's church at Burwood, Alexander began his first pastorate at Hunter's Hill Congregational Church. On 25 August 1909 at his father's church he married Margaret Elizabeth, daughter of O. C. Beale [q.v.7]. Campbell was called in 1911 to the Killara church where he remained for twenty-seven years during which a growing and influential congregation prospered under his preaching and pastoral care. In 1919 he was chairman of the Congregational Union of New South Wales. He retained a strong interest in theological education as secretary (1920-21) and president (1937-55) of Camden College where he tutored in Greek and taught pastoral theology.

While serving as chairman (1937-39) of the Congregational Union of Australia and New Zealand, in 1938 Campbell became pastor at Burwood. He served there until 1944 when he was called to be moderator of the Congregational Union of New South Wales; previously appointed chairman of its advisory board, he was to serve in this capacity for thirty years. In 1944 the union elected him chairman of the 'Forward Movement'. As moderator, he was a confidant of ministers and the laity.

A deep concern for social justice impelled Campbell to minister to the wider community. He was president (1929) of the Rotary Club of Sydney and vice-president of the New South Wales Society for Crippled Children which was founded by Rotary during his presidential term. Like his father, he served as president (1932 and 1946-63) of the Sydney City Mission. Campbell House at Surry Hills, the mission's centre for homeless and alcoholic men, was to be opened in 1973 and named in his memory. On retiring as moderator in 1951, he edited the New South Wales *Congregationalist*. He wrote *The Great Hill-Climb* (1930) and *A Word for the Road* (1953). In addition to his literary talents, he had a pleasant voice that made him a much-appreciated speaker on radio. Ecumenically, he was widely respected as the architect of Australian proposals for intercommunion.

Campbell was esteemed for his 'austerity tempered with compassion', his concern for others and his 'distaste for party strife', as well as for his discretion, honour and serenity. Congregationalists in New South Wales revered him as an inspiring preacher, a wise administrator and a beloved pastor. In 1962 he was appointed O.B.E. Survived by his wife, daughter and three sons, he died on 13 December 1963 at Wahroonga and was cremated.

J. Garrett and L. W. Farr, *Camden College* (Syd, 1964); J. Owen, *The Heart of the City* (Syd, 1987); *Scottish A'sian*, 5 Nov 1919; *Congregationalist* (Syd), Jan 1964; Congregational Union of NSW, *Year Book*, 1965; *SMH*, 22 Oct 1919, 9 Oct 1937, 2 July 1938, 3 Dec 1963. GEOFFREY BARNES

CAMPBELL, ARCHIBALD STEWART (1898-1978), electrical engineer, was born on 1 May 1898 at Cardiff, New South Wales, second child of James Campbell, a coalminer from Scotland, and his native-born wife Elizabeth Jane, née Jones. Educated at Newcastle High School, Arch passed the Intermediate certificate in 1914 and was apprenticed to an electrical fitter with the Newcastle Electric Supply Council Authority. He undertook the inaugural diploma course in electrical engineering at Newcastle Technical College and in 1924 gained an associateship of Sydney Technical College, with the prize for the best pass in engineering. (In 1940 he was to attend N.T.C.'s first course in industrial management.)

From 1919 Campbell worked as an electrical fitter, rising to leading hand two years later. In 1922 Newcastle Municipal Council sent him for four months experience in the electric supply department of Sydney Municipal Council. At the Methodist Church, Merewether, on 24 May 1924 Arch married Cynthia Margaret Roberts, whose mother was a Campbell; they were to have a son and four daughters. He was promoted test-room foreman (1925) and assistant powerhouse superintendent (1927). In 1929-37 Campbell taught electrical trades part time at N.T.C.; in 1942-57 he was an 'active and valuable' member of the Newcastle Technical Education District Council. Having been admitted to the Institution of Electrical Engineers, London, by thesis in 1940, he was chairman (1941-43) of the Newcastle division of the Institution of Engineers, Australia, and presented four technical papers to the division.

During World War II Campbell had been an educational officer with the Air Training Corps, an authorized assessor of claims under the National Security (War Damage to Property) Regulations and a member (1941-46) of the Newcastle Scientific Manpower (Engineering) Advisory Committee. His creativity and inventiveness were particularly evident when N.E.S.C.A. manufactured electrical machinery for the Royal Australian Navy.

In 1952 Campbell was appointed electrical engineer and manager of N.E.S.C.A. which became largely self-contained as a result of his policy of training electrical cadets and apprentices. He set high standards and paid meticulous attention to detail. In 1956 he went abroad for eight months to report on developments in the electricity industry in Britain, Europe and North America. On the formation of Shortland County Council in 1957, he was made its chief electrical engineer. Campbell rewrote technical reports until they were intelligible to aldermen. He was a skilful negotiator, with a sound business sense, who put N.E.S.C.A. on a firm financial footing. Praised for his fairness and ability to enthuse his staff, he was affectionate and gentle, generous with his time and money, and had a wry sense of humour. A devout Methodist, he was a senior circuit steward and a Sunday-School teacher. He belonged to the Rotary Club of Newcastle and to the Newcastle Business Men's Club (president 1960).

Survived by his wife and two daughters, Campbell died on 10 June 1978 at Merewether and was cremated. In 1933 he had written, 'I have always endeavoured to do my best: no man can do more, but no man should do less'.

Inst of Engineers, Aust, *J*, 13, 1941, 14, 1942; Shortland County Council, Newcastle, *Annual Report*, 1957; Business Men's Club, Newcastle, *Vision*, 2, no 2, 1961, 6, no 1, 1965; *Newcastle Morning Herald*, 12 Mar 1952, 9 Mar 1955, 29 May, 22 Aug 1957, 8 June 1959, 3, 30 Apr 1964, 14 June 1978; *Newcastle Sun*, 28 Aug 1957; information from, and family papers held by Mrs Jane Scott, Newcastle, NSW. MARGARET HENRY

CAMPBELL, ARTHUR LANG (1889-1949), professor of law, was born on 27 May 1889 at Bowral, New South Wales, son of John Lang Campbell, a hotelkeeper from Scotland, and his native-born wife Elizabeth, née Wood; James Lang Campbell [q.v.7] was Arthur's uncle. Educated locally and at Sydney Boys' High School, in 1906 Arthur entered the University of Sydney (B.A., 1909) where he graduated with first-class honours and won university medals for mathematics, French and German. From 1909 he studied mechanical and electrical engineering (B.E., 1913), again topping the first-class honours students; he was sometime president of the undergraduates' association and lectured in mathematics in 1912. After passing the barristers' admission board's examinations, he was admitted to the Bar on 11 May 1914.

For nineteen months from April 1914 Campbell was associate to Justice (Sir) George Rich [q.v.11] of the High Court of Australia before being appointed tutor (vice-principal, 1915-17 and 1919-25) at St Andrew's College at the university. In addition to French and German, he spoke Slavonic languages and from 1915 served as an interpreter, as well as a censor of mail and intelligence, until the end of World War I. He had the rank of honorary captain in the

Australian Military Forces from 1918 to 1920. Appointed M.B.E. that year, he began practising at the Bar and published the annotated *N.S.W. Companies Acts 1899-1918* (1920). In 1922 he travelled to Europe and acted as Rich's secretary at the Assembly of the League of Nations at Geneva. Returning home, Campbell was an examiner and temporary lecturer (1924-25) in procedure in the law school of his old university, an examiner in German at the Royal Military College, Federal Capital Territory, and a reporter for the *New South Wales State Reports.*

Although he had no university degree in law, in September 1925 Campbell was appointed Bonython [q.v.7] professor of law at the University of Adelaide. He joined the local League of Nations Union and spoke at its Regal Café lunches; he also became a Freemason, belonged to the Round Table group, joined the Adelaide Club in 1929 and was one of the coterie who read the manuscript of (Sir) Keith Hancock's *Australia* (London, 1930). While conscientious, Campbell did not prove an outstanding lecturer, but he did enjoy tremendous rapport with his students. President of the university union and of the sports association, he set up a fencing club and played hockey for the university—no mean feat for 'this genial tub of a man' who weighed twenty-two stone (140 kg). He was a member of Scotch College council. In 1936 he published a pamphlet, *Public Administration and Constitutional Law.* The professor was a consummate bridge player, with almost total recall of scores and hands; he loved ballet; his cuisine and his Chinese cook were famous in Adelaide, and he judged wine shows.

In World War II Campbell acted as a broadcasting and film censor in South Australia (1939-41) and New South Wales (1941-45). With J. W. Wainwright [q.v.12], he was a member of the 1945 royal commission on the Adelaide Electric Supply Co. He died of a coronary occlusion on the night of 19/20 March 1949 at his Walkerville home and was cremated. Having spent nearly twenty-five years teaching the importance of making a will, he died without writing one. His two sisters shared his estate which was sworn for probate at £14 280.

A. Castles et al (eds), for Faculty of Law, Univ Adel, *Law on North Terrace* (Adel, 1983); Grand Lodge of SA Archives, Adel; Univ Adel Archives; information from Mrs E. A. Campbell, Brooklyn Park, Adel; personal information.

HOWARD ZELLING

CAMPBELL, COLIN WALLACE (1921-1977), corrective services director, was born on 10 August 1921 in Perth, son of John Alexander Campbell, clerk, and his wife Nellie Frances, née Dowell, both South Australian born. Colin attended Perth Modern School (1934-38) on a scholarship before joining the public service. Having served in the Militia from 1940, he enlisted in the Australian Imperial Force on 23 April 1941 and was posted to the 1st Armoured Division. On 7 August 1943 at Christ Church, Claremont, he married with Anglican rites Norma Lucy North, a private in the Australian Women's Army Service. Campbell was promoted sergeant in September 1943, but declined officer-training. He arrived in New Guinea in October 1944, took part in the Wewak campaign with the 8th Brigade Signals Section and was discharged in Australia on 18 December 1945.

Back in Perth, Campbell rejoined the public service as a probation officer with the Child Welfare Department and was encouraged by the director J. A. McCall [q.v.] to study part time at the University of Western Australia (B.A., 1963) where he majored in psychology. His work in child welfare took place amid community concern over perceived increases in juvenile crime and delinquency. In May 1960 Riverbank was opened as an institution for male juvenile offenders and Campbell became its first superintendent. The newly-recruited staff were given special technical-education training to emphasize Riverbank's rehabilitation aims over its custodial role.

Although it had been standard practice for the superintendent of Fremantle Prison to be given the post, in 1966 Campbell was appointed comptroller general, Department of Prisons. He began as an outsider, briefed to reform a system which he regarded as fifty years out-of-date. His administrative staff at head office was small in number and uniformed staff received minimal training, but his department had charge of six prisons, dominated in size and ethos by the convict-built maximum security prison at Fremantle with more than 450 inmates. A probation and parole board had recently been established and a new prison was under construction at Albany.

In his first annual report Campbell recorded the setting up of an assessment centre at Fremantle Prison with a reorganized committee to classify the inmates, the establishment of an officers' training school and the purchase of land on which to build a new women's prison. Between 1966 and 1977 he implemented changes to make staff more 'professional' and to reintegrate prisoners into the community; his reforms gave expression to his concepts of re-education and rehabilitation, and brought Western Australian prisons into line with contemporary correctional practice elsewhere. Stemming from his international study tour and from his humanitarianism, his innovations also included a residential Officer Training School, an examination-based promotional system for uniformed officers, the employment of psychologists, social workers, teachers and welfare officers to undertake research and treatment, a psychiatric services branch and a scheme of work-release for prisoners. In 1971 his title was restyled director and his department was renamed the Department of Corrections.

A pragmatic, down-to-earth and highly personal administrator, Campbell worked with his members of staff as he found them, earning their support by his loyalty and approachability. He made many decisions and advised his superintendents over a beer while he chain-smoked. Six ft 2 ins (188 cm) tall, physically commanding and gregarious, he had energy and magnetism; he played cricket and hockey, and, as he travelled around the State, combined prison business with the plethora of responsibilities (such as fire-brigade inspection) that came under his jurisdiction. Campbell died of coronary artery disease on 28 September 1977 at his Darlington home and was cremated; his wife and three sons survived him. The remand centre at the Metropolitan Prison Complex, planned during his time as director, bears his name. A portrait by Norman Aisbett is held by Campbell's widow.

J. E. Thomas and A. Stewart, *Imprisonment in Western Australia* (Perth, 1978); Dept of Prisons/Corrections, Annual Reports, 1967-78, *V&P*(WA); Roy Com upon various allegations of assaults on or brutality to prisoners in Fremantle Prison, *V&P* (WA), 1972, 5; *Weekend Mag*(Perth), 11 Nov 1967; *West Australian*, 29, 30 Sept, 1 Oct 1977; Child Welfare Dept (WA), Annual Report, 1945-66 (BL); information from Mr D. Budiselic, Safety Bay, and Mrs N. Campbell, Darlington, Perth.

MARGARET STEADMAN

CAMPBELL, DAVID ALEXANDER STEWART (1898-1970), wool-buyer and editor, was born on 29 July 1898 in North Sydney, eldest son of Gerald Ross Campbell [q.v.7], barrister, and his first wife Mary Fraser, née Stewart (d. 1902). By 1903 the family moved to Moss Vale. David was taught by a governess until he went to Tudor House preparatory school. In 1912-16 he boarded at Scots College, Sydney; proving himself to be a better athlete than a scholar, he failed his Intermediate certificate and the entrance examination for the Royal Military College, Duntroon, Federal Capital Territory. Late in 1916 he enrolled in a three-month wool-classing course at Sydney Technical College, then worked as a jackeroo on a grazing property.

On 4 February 1918 Campbell enlisted in the Australian Imperial Force. Five ft 11 ins (180.3 cm) tall, with brown eyes and hair, he served as a gunner in Egypt and, after the Armistice, in France with the 6th Field Artillery Brigade. In England, he was granted leave to study at Bradford Technical College and gain experience in woolclassing with the nearby firm, (Sir) James Hill & Sons. Back in Sydney, he was discharged on 16 November 1919. In the early 1920s he worked in Melbourne where he learned the wool trade. From 1922 (until retiring in 1963) he was a wool-buyer for the Bradford topmaker, Cooper, Triffitt & Co. Ltd, through its Victorian subsidiary, Sims, Cooper & Co. (Aust.) Pty Ltd.

Shortly after returning home, he became engaged to a nurse Evelyn Grace Elizabeth, daughter of George Edward Rennie [q.v.11]. They were married on 30 December 1924 at St Mark's Anglican Church, Darling Point, Sydney; they lived at Double Bay before moving in turn to Rose Bay, Wahroonga and Pymble. Campbell was a member of the University Club (in 1921 he had attended extension lectures in Japanese at the University of Sydney and was later to enrol as an evening student in economics), the Royal Automobile Club of Australia and the Royal Sydney Golf Club. To his earlier interests, tennis and cricket (he rarely missed a Test match), he added golf.

During World War II Campbell was controlling wool appraiser in New South Wales for the United Kingdom Wool Purchase Arrangement and a member of the Technical Advisory Committee (Wool). From 1949 he was Cooper Triffitt's senior wool-buyer in Australia, and a director of Sims, Cooper, W. Jackson & Co. Pty Ltd and of the Sydney Exchange Co. He served the wool industry in wider capacities: as chairman of the New South Wales and Queensland Woolbuyers' Association (nineteen occasions between 1938 and 1962), of the Australian Council of Wool Buyers (1952-55, 1957-59) and of the Federal Exporters Oversea Transport Committee (Australia to Europe Shippers' Association) (1958-70), and also as a member (1963-70) of the Australian Wool Board. In addition, Campbell was a member of the New South Wales Technical Education Advisory Council (1949-70) and of the University Extension Board (1953-70), an adviser to the Department of Education on wool and textiles, and an examiner in woolclassing. He provided an annual award for the best-classed clip.

Widely read in economics and politics, he took a keen interest in public affairs. With a close friend (Sir) Norman Cowper, he had belonged to the secretive Old Guard and was dedicated to the overthrow of J. T. Lang [q.v.9]. From the 1920s Campbell wrote frequent letters to the *Sydney Morning Herald* and in 1938 staunchly defended appeasement. In 1946, although an indifferent public speaker, he campaigned for (Sir) Ivan Dougherty (Liberal) against the incumbent 'firebrand' of East Sydney, E. J. Ward [q.v.].

A foundation director (1932-60) of the Australian Institute of Political Science, Campbell regularly contributed (1931-34) to the *Australian Quarterly* and was its editor from 1935 until 1959. Cowper described the journal as a continuing 'monument' to Campbell's 'industry, enterprise and wide-ranging interest in political and social questions'. A regular traveller to Britain, Campbell was a council-member (from 1938) and president (1949) of the State branch of the Australian Institute of International Affairs, and was president (1955-57) of its Commonwealth council; he was, as well, a fellow of the Royal Colonial Institute (Royal Empire [Commonwealth] Society) and chairman (1966-70) of the Sydney group of Round Table. On 1 September 1970, while driving his motorcar at Willoughby, Campbell died of myocardial ischaemia. Survived by his wife and two daughters, he was cremated; his estate was sworn for probate at $123 183.

J. Barrett, *Falling In* (Syd, 1979); H. King, *At Mid-Century* (Syd, 1982); L. Foster, *High Hopes* (Melb, 1986); A. Moore, *The Secret Army and the Premier* (Syd, 1989); *Aust Q*, 42, no 4, Dec 1970, p 2; *Pastoral Review*, 17 Sept 1970, p 769; Scots College Old Boys' Union, *Lang Syne*, Dec 1970, p 3; information from Maj-Gen I. Campbell, Potts Point, Dr M. Newlinds, Duffys Forest, Mrs S. Simpson, Gordon, Syd.   MURRAY GOOT

CAMPBELL, DAVID WATT IAN (1915-1979), poet, was born on 16 July 1915 at Ellerslie station, near Adelong, New South Wales, third child of native-born parents Alfred Campbell, grazier and medical practitioner, and his wife Edith Madge, née Watt. Madge was descended from James Blackman [q.v.1]. Her son was registered as David Watt Ian, but baptized with Presbyterian forms David Alfred in 1916. He was educated at home, at a preparatory school and (from 1930) at The King's School, Parramatta, where he held the J. D. Futter memorial scholarship in 1933-34. An outstanding sportsman, he twice won the Buckland Cup for boxing, and was captain of the school, of the Rugby XV and the rowing VIII. By his own apocryphal account, all he did at school was play football: 'They left my mind completely alone . . . I was lucky'. Yet he wrote some poetry, despite his allegation that it was held to be 'very sissy stuff'.

With the support of his headmaster C. T. Parkinson [q.v.11], in 1935 Campbell entered Jesus College, Cambridge (B.A., 1937). While he continued his Rugby career, won a Blue and played in two Test matches for England, he clearly devoted himself to learning in a way he seems not to have done at school. Encouraged by his tutor E. M. W. Tillyard, he changed from the history to the English tripos, and under his influence read widely in literature. The experience of encountering the tradition of English poetry (and its classical antecedents), together with his early knowledge of Australian verse, is reflected in the three poems he published in 1937 in the college magazine, *Chanticlere*, and the *Cambridge Review*. It was at Cambridge, too, that he learned to fly as a member (1936-37) of the local air squadron.

Returning to Australia in 1938, Campbell joined the Royal Australian Air Force on 6 November 1939 as a cadet. On 20 January 1940 at St John's Anglican Church, Toorak, Melbourne, he married Bonnie Edith Lawrence; they were to have two sons and a daughter before being divorced in 1973. Having qualified as a pilot at Point Cook, he was commissioned on 17 February 1940. He served in Australia and completed several courses before being sent to Port Moresby in December 1941 as station navigation officer. On 6 February 1942 he piloted a Hudson on a photographic reconnaissance flight over Rabaul, New Britain. A Japanese fighter attacked the aircraft, causing extensive damage and wounding three of the crew. Although Campbell's left wrist was shattered and part of his little finger severed, he managed to bring the Hudson some 500 miles (805 km) home to base and was awarded the Distinguished Flying Cross.

Back in Australia, he was promoted temporary squadron leader in April 1943 and commanded No. 1 Squadron from December. Next year he led the unit (February to July) and No. 2 Squadron (July to November) on bombing operations from Darwin. Promoted temporary wing commander on 1 July, he was awarded a Bar to his D.F.C. for 'exceptional energy and leadership'. Campbell's appointment terminated on 3 October 1945. The poem, 'Men in Green', and the stories, 'Zero at Rabaul' and 'Tumult in the Clouds', reflect his wartime exploits.

Douglas Stewart, editor of the *Bulletin*'s 'Red Page', recalled that 'a series of lyrics of remarkable quality' began arriving at the magazine's office in 1942 and that Campbell's ambitions were 'to get back on the land as soon as the war was over, and not to be a poet, if a poet means a long-haired gentleman living in a garret with a geranium'. Stewart, who by 1944 had published six of Campbell's poems, also recorded that when David appeared in the office he had 'a dial Frith described as a mixture of George Carpenter and Jack Hulbert'.

Realizing his ambition to return to the land, in 1946 Campbell settled on a family property, Wells station, near Canberra. From this time his poetry became more closely attuned to the realities of the countryside. His daily life as a grazier, his acute observations of the natural world and his deep understanding of European poetry gave him a distinctive poetic voice, learned but not didactic, harmonious but not bland, vigorous but finely tuned. These early poems, most of which first appeared in the *Bulletin*, were published in *Speak With the Sun* (London, 1949). This volume was followed by *The Miracle of Mullion Hill* (1956) and by *Evening Under Lamplight* (1959), a collection of short stories.

In 1961 Campbell moved to Palerang, near Bungendore, New South Wales. He continued to publish regularly in the *Bulletin*, but also began to appear in journals—in particular *Australian Letters*—and to be published abroad. His sequence of poems, 'Cocky's Calendar', in *Australian Letters* in March 1961, marked a new phase in his writing. The longest poem he had so far attempted was the title poem in *The Miracle of Mullion Hill*, but he now showed an interest in developing themes more substantial than a short lyric could hold by bringing poems together in a sequence or set. The volume, *Poems* (1962), collected some of the work from the late 1950s. His output was relatively small from mid-1962 until the end of 1969. He edited the 1966 edition of *Australian Poetry*, and in 1968 published *Selected Poems 1942-1968* for which he received the Grace Leven prize. In that year, too, he moved from Palerang to The Run at Queanbeyan.

The publication of *The Branch of Dodona and Other Poems* in 1970 opened a decade of extraordinary productivity. It also announced a degree of complexity and obliquity in his thinking which had not been so conspicuous in the early work. The Vietnam War provoked reflections on violence and the brotherhood of man; the seasonal activities of the land continued to preoccupy him; and an underlying sense of personal dislocation and anxiety was disguised in myth, dream and fantasy. That year he edited an anthology, *Modern Australian Poetry* (Melbourne), and won the Henry Lawson [q.v.10] Australian Arts award. Between 1973 and 1979 five volumes of his poetry and two volumes of selected poems were published. With Rosemary Dobson, Campbell produced two books of translations in verse of a selection from Russian poets (1975 and 1979), and with the painter Keith Looby, *The History of Australia* (Melbourne, 1976). A selection of short stories, *Flame and Shadow* (Brisbane, 1976), also appeared. He became well known for his public readings and for his support of young poets.

On 18 February 1974 Campbell married Judith Anne Jones, née Dale, at the registrar general's office, Sydney. From May to September 1975 they travelled in England and Europe—his first trip abroad since his Cambridge days. The group of poems, 'Mottoes on Sundials', some of which appeared in *Words with a Black Orpington* (1978), are a precise record of their travels.

David Campbell was a gregarious man who enjoyed company and conversation. Tall and fair and craggy, he was physically large and large minded. To Manning Clark, 'his very presence encouraged everyone in the room to give of their best'. Campbell counted among his close friends Stewart, Clark, Dobson, Patrick White, A. D. Hope and many others, especially those who lived and worked in and around Canberra. He was keenly interested in painting, and many of his poems begin with a painting or painter. A member of the Hawks Club, Cambridge, and Royal Sydney Golf Club, he played polo with more enthusiasm than skill and later took to potting. He shared with Stewart a love of fishing. Throughout his life he was remarkably consistent in his interests and in his view of the world. He loved the land, and valued its history as part of his own, through his family's early and continuous connection with farming. Intuitively grasping the symmetry of natural forms, he acknowledged the force of a creative intelligence. He was serious but not solemn, and his wit was genial and without malice. He had a great passion for life, and was courageous in confronting death. Survived by his wife and the sons of his first marriage, Campbell died of cancer on 29 July 1979 in Royal Canberra Hospital, having proof-read his last volume of poetry, *The Man in the Honeysuckle*, published posthumously that year. His estate was sworn for probate at $192 611. The National Library of Australia, Canberra, holds his self-portrait.

G. Odgers, *Air War Against Japan 1943-1945* (Canb, 1957); D. Gillison, *Royal Australian Air Force 1939-1942* (Canb, 1962); M. Clark, *David Campbell 1915-1979. Words Spoken at his Funeral* (Canb, 1979); H. Heseltine (ed), *A Tribute to David Campbell* (Syd, 1987); *Aust Book Review*, Oct 1979, p 21; *Age* and *SMH*, 4 Aug 1979; *Australian*, 4-5 Aug 1979; Campbell papers (NL); The King's School (Parramatta) archives.   LEONIE KRAMER

CAMPBELL, SIR HAROLD ALFRED MAURICE (1892-1959), journalist, was born on 25 October 1892 at Longwarry, Victoria, fourth son of native-born parents Frederick Joseph Campbell, labourer, and his wife Elizabeth, née Cook (d. 1896). Frederick farmed at South Gippsland until 1895 when he moved his family to Western Australia where he managed timber-mills. Educated at Bunbury, Harold left school at 14 to become a proof-reader's assistant on the local newspaper; he later worked as a reporter with the *Daily News* in Perth.

On 28 February 1916 Campbell enlisted in the Australian Imperial Force and was posted to the Australian Army Medical Corps. Arriving in England in March, he was sent to France next month. There he served with the 13th Field Ambulance. He was awarded the Military Medal for his courage on 24-25 April 1918 when, although wounded, he continued to carry stretchers through shell and machine-gun fire at Cachy, near Villers-Bretonneux. Returning to Australia as a temporary sergeant in July 1919, he was discharged on 27 October.

He resumed work with the *Daily News* and formed a lasting friendship with John Curtin [q.v.], then editor of the *Westralian Worker*. Moving to Melbourne, he joined the *Herald* before crossing in October 1920 to the *Age* where he established his reputation as the Federal political writer. 'Ham' Campbell, as he was always known, was also a keen theatregoer who wrote graceful, well-balanced reviews. He briefly farmed an orchard at an outer suburb in his spare time. On 31 December 1921 at St Kilda he married Queenie Emma May Davy with Presbyterian forms.

In 1926 Campbell was appointed a leader-writer when George Cockerill [q.v.8] departed abruptly for Sydney shortly before the death of the editor G. F. H. Schuler [q.v.11]. L. V. Biggs [q.v.7] succeeded Schuler and the editorship passed to Campbell in February 1939. By then Campbell was chief leader-writer, well seasoned in the generally liberal traditions of the *Age*. He was the fourth editor in his own right since the appointment in 1872 of A. L. Windsor [q.v.6], whose predecessors were editor-writers entirely subservient to the paper's owner-editors, notably Ebenezer and David Syme [qq.v.6].

The *Age* was adopting new approaches to meet the needs of a modern readership and to match its competitors. Publishing news on the front page in place of classified advertisements marked the realization that the paper had to accept technical and editorial freshening to survive. World War II delayed further changes that Campbell and his younger staff wished to make. Plans for essential expansion of plant and departmental reorganization were well advanced when the war ended, but the establishment of a capital fund was hampered because the rights of the beneficiaries were the chief concern of the trust established by David Syme to preserve the *Age*. Nevertheless, an order from the Supreme Court of Victoria cleared the way to forming a public company, David Syme & Co. Ltd, in

June 1948. Campbell was elected a director and deputy-chairman under Oswald Syme; he was also a trustee of the Syme trust.

The reputation earned by the *Age* under Campbell's editorship and his standing as a journalist were acknowledged in 1945 with his appointment by Prime Minister Curtin to the Australian delegation to the conference at San Francisco, United States of America, which drafted the charter of the United Nations. He attended the U.N. General Assembly in New York in 1949 as one of three non-official advisers to the Australian delegation to discuss freedom of information. Appointed C.M.G. in 1953, he was knighted in 1957 for his services to journalism.

Campbell was a temperate editor, self-effacing, famously courteous and insistent always that he was simply 'a working journalist'. He preferred anonymous journalism, condemning the bylined, investigative style as 'muck raking'. He was a director of Australian Associated Press and, as its chairman from 1953 to 1955, was the Australian director of Reuters Ltd; he was also a director of General Television Corporation (GTV-9). Although a councillor of the Victorian Society for Crippled Children and a trustee from 1944 of the Public Library of Victoria (vice-chairman 1946), he was by choice an observer of affairs, not a participant. He belonged to the Melbourne and the Savage clubs where he was regarded as 'somewhat retiring'. After his wife died on 3 August 1949, he centred his interest on the *Age*, on reading and on his grandchildren. He died of a coronary occlusion on 31 July 1959 in East Melbourne and was cremated; his daughter and two sons survived him.

D. M. Dow, *Melbourne Savages* (Melb, 1947); *Age*, 16 Oct 1954, centenary supp, and 1 Aug 1959; *The Times*, 1 Aug 1959; H. Mishael, Lend Me Your Ears (ms, LaTL); Campbell family papers (held by Mrs P. de Wolf, Malvern, Melb); Syme family papers (LaTL).   STUART SAYERS

CAMPBELL, PERSIA GWENDOLINE CRAWFORD (1898-1974), economist, was born on 15 March 1898 at Nerrigundah, New South Wales, elder child of native-born schoolteachers Rodolfe Archibald Clarence Campbell (d. 1905) and his second wife Beatrice Harriet, née Hunt. Persia was educated at Fort Street Girls' High School and the University of Sydney (B.A., 1918; M.A., 1920); in both degrees she obtained first-class honours in history. She then attended the London School of Economics (M.Sc. Econ., 1922) on a scholarship. Her monograph, *Chinese Coolie Immigration* (1923), published in the Studies in Economic and Political Science series, investigated the abuse of indentured-labour regulations and concluded that the system 'benefits money rather than mankind'.

After studying social economy at Bryn Mawr College, Pennsylvania, United States of America, in 1922-23, Campbell returned to Sydney where she worked as assistant-editor for the *Australian Encyclopaedia* and lectured for the Workers' Educational Association. In March 1927 she was appointed assistant research officer in the Industrial Commission of New South Wales and in July next year transferred to the Bureau of Statistics. Interested in Fabian socialism and feminism, she was soon prominent in progressive intellectual circles due to her energy, ability and dedication. She espoused the educational and professional advancement of women and international co-operation, addressed the National Council of Women of New South Wales and judged its peace essay competition, and became a stalwart of women graduates' organizations and of the Pan Pacific (and South East Asian) Women's Association (formed 1928). When the Institute of Pacific Relations was established 'to study conditions of the Pacific people with a view to the improvement of their mutual relationships', she joined the New South Wales branch, and, with R. C. Mills and G. V. Portus [qq.v.10,11], co-edited its first publication, *Studies in Australian Affairs* (1928). She likened the use of psychiatric screening of immigrants to espionage and forcefully demolished A. H. Martin's [q.v.] grounds for the alleged racial inferiority of Southern Europeans.

In 1930 Campbell accepted a two-year Rockefeller fellowship to study agricultural policy in the U.S.A. On 15 October 1931 at the 1st Presbyterian Church, New York, she married Edward Rice junior (d. 1939), a widower with three children; she bore him a daughter and son, and in 1936 took American nationality. The family lived at Flushing, New York. As world agricultural prices fell, Campbell studied America's response. In *American Agricultural Policy* (London, 1933), she examined the evolution of Federal Farm Board policies; through her journal articles, she analysed America's pursuit of international wheat quotas; and she explored the escalation of restrictive policies in her doctoral dissertation for Columbia University (Ph.D., 1940), *Consumer Representation in the New Deal* (1940). The last-mentioned study showed how producers and government had collaborated to stabilize prices and overlooked or over-ridden consumers' interests. She advocated 'that everyone shall be able to secure each day his daily "bread", of good quality, and at decreasing cost, under conditions promotive of human worth'.

Increasingly focussing her work—at practical and theoretical levels—on the consumer, Campbell presented statistical data to the Pan Pacific Women's Conference (Honolulu, 1934) to show the many hours which women spent in purchasing and management. The economic impact of their decisions, the importance of informed choice, of consumer education and of legislation to protect consumers were her dominant concerns. She was a long-serving director of the Consumers Union of United States, the publisher of *Consumer Reports*.

In 1940 Campbell joined the faculty of economics at Queens College, City University of New York. She was described as the head of the college's consumer council and as chairman of social studies, New York branch of the American Association of University Women, in 1942 when she was appointed director of consumer services by the Civilian Defense Volunteer Office, New York. She envisaged a wide-ranging approach to consumer education, through publications, through courses adapted from those she taught at Queens, and through the use of volunteers to monitor goods and prices. Campbell resigned in 1943, giving as her reason the introduction of summer semesters at Queens, but later wrote of the obstruction she had encountered. Her terse comment on the reluctance of some officials to recruit housewives reflected the importance she placed on women's role as consumers. She was later to urge women to acquaint themselves with standards and use their purchasing power to create a demand for labelled goods. Taking a broad view, she included such subjects as housing, medical care and life insurance, in addition to the government's role in the economy, in her massive textbook, *The Consumer Interest* (1949).

In 1948, 1949 and again in 1951 Campbell was adviser on consumer affairs to American delegations to Food and Agriculture Organization conferences of the United Nations. She had long advocated the creation of a department of consumer affairs, capable of providing services to consumers, in the same way that the Department of Agriculture gave research and marketing advice to farmers. In January 1955 Governor Averell Harriman of New York State appointed her to his cabinet as consumer counsel. Although she had limited success with protection legislation (securing little more than a prohibition on 'bait' advertising and an Act that covered general instalment buying), by publicizing consumer issues on radio and by meeting business groups she was able to secure promises of self-regulation and some change in business practices.

At Queens, Campbell chaired (1960-65) the economics department. She published a biography in 1960 of Mary Williamson Harriman, whom she had met while investigating the consumer advisory board of the National Recovery Administration. As chairman of the American branch of the Pan Pacific and South East Asian Women's Association, Persia attended their conferences in Tokyo (1958) and Canberra (1961). The recently formed Australian Consumers Association thanked her for the 'assistance and hospitality unstintingly given [it] by [the] Consumers Union of United States'. She also helped to form the International Organization of Consumers Unions (1960), of which the American and Australian associations were constituent members.

Following the election promises of J. F. Kennedy, in 1961 Campbell drafted the proposal to establish a consumer counsel with a staff of lawyers and economists representing consumer interests in proceedings before regulatory agencies and formulating broad economic policies. In addition, she suggested that consumer advisory committees should be set up in federal departments. The proposals foundered. She was appointed to the Consumers Advisory Council which lacked both executive power and staff. It endorsed the truth-in-packaging and truth-in-lending bills, then before Congress, as being 'in line with the historic exercise of Government responsibility to provide a framework within which the American economy can operate rationally, in terms of honest competition and intelligent consumer choice'. Both bills were obstructed. In denouncing the denial of consumer rights on the ground of race, the council reflected her continued opposition to racial discrimination. A Democrat, Campbell served on President L. B. Johnson's committee on consumer interests and he appointed her to the national advisory committee to the president's representative on international trade negotiations. In 1968 she sat on Mayor Lindsay's Consumer Affairs Advisory Council, though her interests were shifting increasingly to the Third World.

A delegate to the United Nations Educational, Scientific and Cultural Organization conference on adult education (Montreal, 1960), Campbell was keen to develop radio and television programmes for low-income earners. She had faith in consumer organization effecting higher living standards in developing countries. To her Australian audience in 1961 she said, 'if the wage-earner has to pay unduly high prices for consumer products, he is virtually handing back to the manufacturer a proportion of his weekly wage-packet'. After retiring from Queens in 1965 and taking an honorary appointment at the University of North Carolina in 1966, Campbell travelled widely outside America. She chaired the international aid committee of the International Organization of Consumers Unions and represented it before special agencies of the United Nations. In 1966-70 she was a columnist on United Nations economic and social programmes for the *International Development Review*. A delegate to the United Nations Conference on the Human Environment (Stockholm, 1972), she was party to the recommendation that the United Nations establish a permanent organization for environmental action which was implemented that year.

Persia Campbell was a member of the American Economic Association. Survived by her children and stepchildren, she died on 2 March 1974 at Booth Memorial Hospital, Flushing. A fellow director of the Consumers Union of United States recalled the discipline she had brought to meetings and her insistence on the union's place in a larger consumer movement.

Notable American Women (Cambridge, Massachusetts, 1980); H. Radi (ed), *200 Australian Women* (Syd, 1988); *Public Administration Review*, 4, 1944; Aust Consumers' Assn, *Choice*, Feb 1961; Consumers Union of US (NY), *Consumer Reports*, 1959-74; US Congress, *Congressional Record*, 24 Mar, 2 May 1961, 15 Apr, 29 Aug 1962, 26 June 1963; International Office of Consumers Unions (The Hague), *International Consumer*, Spring 1974; *New York Times*, 22 Feb, 30 Apr 1942, 2 May, 13 July 1943, 3 Mar 1953, 24 Dec 1954, 20 Jan 1955, 10 Oct, 13 Dec 1957, 9 Jan 1958, 19 July 1962, 14 Aug 1964, 27 Oct 1968, 3 Mar 1974; *SMH*, 17 Jan 1972.
                                                  SUSAN HOGAN
                                                  HEATHER RADI

CAMPBELL, ROBERT RICHMOND (1902-1972), artist and gallery administrator, was born on 18 July 1902 in Edinburgh, eldest son of Alfred Richmond Campbell, commercial traveller, and his wife Isabella Jane, née Thompson. Educated locally at George Watson's College and at Wallasey Grammar School, Cheshire, England, in 1916 Bob migrated with the family to Brisbane where he worked as a commercial artist. Determined to become a painter, he moved to Melbourne and from 1922 to 1940 lived mainly from his art.

The financial success of his first exhibition, at Sedon Galleries in 1928, enabled him to travel to Europe with Rupert Bunny [q.v.7]. Campbell lived in Paris and London, and sketched his way through France, Spain, England and Scotland. Influenced by the work of Camille Pissaro, Claude Monet, J. M. W. Turner, Peter de Wint and Wilson Steer, he had the ability to capture atmospheric effects of light. During the Depression, however, he had to paint cheap portraits to make ends meet and he returned to Australia in 1932.

On 13 June 1933 Campbell married Jean Elizabeth, daughter of J. H. Young [q.v.], in a secular ceremony at her parents' home at Waverton, Sydney. An assistant in her father's Macquarie Galleries, she later became an art historian and critic. The young couple lived in Sydney and on islands off the Great Barrier Reef, Queensland. Campbell conveyed the shimmering effects of tropical light by using delicate, high-key colours and a restrained palette; his broad washes, luminous effects and decisive lines displayed the controlled simplicity of Oriental art. By the 1950s he was widely regarded as a leading Australian water-colourist.

Having taught part time in Sydney, in 1941 Campbell moved to Tasmania to head the department of art at Launceston Technical College where he abolished the practice of live models posing 'nude' in swimming costumes. Appointed curator of the Art Gallery of Western Australia in 1947, he was president of the Perth Society of Artists. In 1949 he became the first director of the Queensland National Art Gallery: he raised it from the 'worst and dirtiest in Australia to the top ranks', and in 1951 organized a travelling exhibition, the 1951 Queensland Jubilee Art Train.

As director (1951-67) of the National Gallery of South Australia, he promoted art in Australia and Australian art in the world. (Sir) Ivor Hele's portrait (held by the Queensland Art Gallery), which won the Archibald [q.v.3] prize in 1955, showed Campbell as a reflective, private person, with bushy eyebrows, receding hairline, bow-tie and breast-pocket handkerchief. He was courteous and personable, strongly built and of middle height, with expressive, blue eyes, a resonant voice and a passion for art that inspired others.

With grants from the Carnegie Corporation of New York (1956) and from the South Australian government, Campbell visited the United States of America, Britain and Europe. Under his direction the N.G.S.A. was extended by a wing that set new standards in art museum display, workshop and office facilities; the gallery's board was enlarged and staff doubled; the Australian holdings were consolidated and improved, while collections of eighteenth- and nineteenth-century British water-colours and of Aboriginal art were initiated. Educational services increased, and Campbell gave many of the lectures, broadcasts and painting demonstrations. He was also responsible for numerous exhibitions, particularly as visual arts director (1960-68) of the Adelaide Festival of Arts. The gallery attracted valuable bequests and established the M. Vizard-Wholohan prizes. Attendances soared. Campbell was, as well, a council-member of the South Australian School of Arts, and a member of the Royal South Australian Society of Arts and of the Australian Water-Colour Institute.

From 1952 to 1972 Campbell served on the Commonwealth Art Advisory Board which met in Canberra and built up the Australian collection for an Australian national gallery. On the board's behalf, he organized the large exhibition, Australian Painting —Colonial, Impressionist, Contemporary, which was shown at the National Gallery of Canada and in 1962 at the Tate gallery, London. That year he published *The Paintings of Tom Roberts*. An adviser to the Federal government's Historic Memorials Committee, in 1965 he sat on the committee of inquiry into the proposed national gallery. He was appointed O.B.E. in 1958 and C.M.G. in 1967. Next year he took an exhibition of Australian art to India.

Survived by his wife, son and three daughters, Campbell died of a ruptured dissecting aneurysm of the aorta on 30 September 1972 in Royal Adelaide Hospital and was cremated. His family holds a 1930 self-portrait and a bust by John Dowie. Campbell's work is in all State and major regional galleries; six retrospective exhibitions have been held since his death.

Art Gallery of SA, *Robert Campbell 1902-1972*, exhibition cat (Adel, 1973); Queen Vic Museum and Art Gallery (Launc), *Robert Richmond Campbell: An Australian Impressionist*, exhibition cat (Launc, 1986); J. Campbell, *Australian Watercolour Painters, 1780 to the Present Day* (Syd, 1989); Report of Art Gallery of SA, in *PP* (SA), 1951 to 1968-69; *Kalori*, 10, no 4, Dec 1972, p 3; *Art and Australia*, 11, no 2, Dec 1973, p 176; *News* (Adel), 31 Jan 1962; *Advertiser* (Adel), 2 Oct 1972; R. R. Campbell, Biog Notes (held by Art Gallery of SA); H. de Berg, Robert Campbell, taped interview (NL); information and notes supplied by Mrs J. Campbell, Rivett, Canb.　　　　　　　　CHRISTINE FINNIMORE

CAMPBELL, THOMAS DRAPER (1893-1967), professor of dentistry and anthropologist, was born on 24 March 1893 at Millicent, South Australia, son of Walter Campbell, storekeeper, and his wife Lucy, née Walters. In 1907 the family moved to Adelaide where Draper attended Prince Alfred College. He qualified with the Dental Board of South Australia in 1917 and in November joined the Australian Army Medical Corps Reserve (Dental) as an honorary lieutenant. After studying at the Elder [q.v.4] Conservatorium of Music in 1919, he entered the University of Adelaide (B.D.S., 1921; D.D.Sc., 1923). On 9 December 1927 at the Methodist Church, Archer Street, North Adelaide, he married an actress Elizabeth Jane Young; they were to remain childless. His play, *The Moon Dream*, written with librettist Trevor (Alex) Symons, was to be performed in 1932 at the Theatre Royal, Adelaide.

House surgeon at the Adelaide Hospital's dental department from 1921, Campbell became superintendent in 1926. He had taught dental anatomy at the university from 1925. Dean of the faculty of dentistry in 1938-58, he was director of dental studies from 1949 until 1954 when he was appointed foundation professor. Campbell was a competent clinician, and a skilful oral surgeon; he maintained a special interest in child dental health. Despite his gruff voice, he was a kindly, spirited and informed teacher who relished debate. He was a fellow of the Royal colleges of Surgeons, England (1948) and Edinburgh (1950), a member (1952) of the odontology section of the Royal Society of Medicine, London, and a fellow (1966) of the Australian College of Dental Surgeons.

With his colleague Frederic Wood Jones [q.v.9], Campbell had made two excursions to remote parts of South Australia in the early 1920s which developed his interest in physical and cultural anthropology. His doctoral research—published as *Dentition and Palate of the Australian Aboriginal* (1925)—noted the difference between the Aborigines' well-formed dentition and the 'ill-formed, disease-stricken' teeth common in Europeans. The book set new standards for the emerging discipline of dental anthropology.

Honorary curator (1924-40) and a board-member (1932-66) of the South Australian Museum, in 1926 Campbell helped to establish the Anthropological Society of South Australia (of which he was president, 1928-29 and 1944) and the university's Board for Anthropological Research (of which he was secretary). Between 1925 and 1939 fifteen expeditions travelled to outback South Australia and the Northern Territory; Campbell organized most of them and accompanied eight. Small teams of scientists from different disciplines contacted tribal Aborigines, often for the first time, and published their findings. Their cinematographic records of Aboriginal life and customs provided unique insights, and were later screened at universities in Europe and the United States of America. In 1939 Campbell was awarded a D.Sc. by the university for thirty-seven papers arising from his field-studies.

In 1951 he led a team of scientists to Yuendumu, an Aboriginal settlement north-west of Alice Springs, Northern Territory. Over the next decade he directed several ethnographic films about the crafts and skills of the Yuendumu people, whom he greatly admired. His significant studies of Aboriginal camp-sites and stone tools culminated in his 1963-65 investigation of archeological sites for the Australian Institute of Aboriginal Studies, of which he had been a founding member. Campbell's classification of stone tools became the typology used in Australia. Survived by his wife, he died on 8 December 1967 at his Tusmore home and was cremated. His

portrait (1959) by (Sir) Ivor Hele is in the Adelaide Dental Hospital.

C. R. Twidale et al (eds), *Ideas and Endeavours* (Adel, 1986); R. MacLeod (ed), *The Commonwealth of Science* (Melb, 1988); *Probe*, 1958-59; Aust Inst of Aboriginal Studies, *Newsletter*, 2, no 7, Apr 1968; International Assn of Human Biologists, *Occasional Papers*, 1, no 2, 1985; SA Museum, *Records*, 20, 1987; *Advertiser* (Adel), 12 Dec 1967; Aust Dental Assn (SA Branch), Minutes and papers (Goodwood, Adel); Univ Adel Archives.   TASMAN BROWN
RUTH ROGERS

CANNAN, JAMES HAROLD (1882-1976), company manager and soldier, was born on 29 August 1882 at Townsville, Queensland, sixth child of John Kearsey Cannan, a bank manager from Brisbane, and his wife Elizabeth Christian, née Hodgson, who was born on the Isle of Man. Kearsey Cannan [q.v.3] was James's grandfather. Educated at Brisbane Central Boys' and Brisbane Grammar schools, James worked for a firm of hardware merchants and for seven years with the New Zealand Insurance Co. before becoming chief agent at the Queensland branch of the Patriotic Assurance Co. From 1910 he was State manager of the Insurance Office of Australia Ltd. He married Eileen Clair Ranken on 12 December 1911 at St Matthew's Anglican Church, Sherwood; they were to remain childless.

Combining an active sporting life—he rowed, sailed and played lacrosse—with service as a citizen-soldier, on 27 March 1903 Cannan had been commissioned in the 1st Queensland (Moreton) (later 9th Infantry) Regiment. In 1912 he transferred to the 8th Infantry (Oxley Battalion) and in May 1914 took command as lieutenant colonel. On 23 September he was appointed to the Australian Imperial Force, in command of the 15th Battalion in (Sir) John Monash's [q.v.10] 4th Brigade. Tall, dark and strongly built, Cannan was an exacting leader: 'a reserved and silent man and extremely hard working', he demanded the utmost of his troops. At the Gallipoli landing on 25 April 1915 and its aftermath, he was a familiar figure in the foremost positions. In the battle of Sari Bair, his decision on 8 August to withdraw saved the remnants of the battalion from destruction; his elder brother Major D. H. Cannan, serving under him, was killed that day.

Invalided to London in October, Cannan was appointed C.B. (1915) and rejoined his unit in Egypt. He went to France in June 1916 and was soon engaged in the fighting for Pozières and Mouquet Farm. Recalled to England, he was promoted temporary brigadier in August and given the 11th Brigade. His hard training and energetic leadership prepared his soldiers for Messines and Brood-seinde, Belgium, in 1917; following these battles he was appointed C.M.G. (1918). In March 1918 Cannan's was the first Australian brigade to check the German thrust towards Amiens, France, and the 11th was specially requested by Major General E. G. Sinclair-Maclagan [q.v.11] to help the 4th Division at Hamel (July). For his performance in the victorious battles of August-September, Cannan was awarded the Distinguished Service Order and Belgian Croix de Guerre (1919). He was mentioned in dispatches six times.

Cannan saw himself as the guardian of his troops. He taught his staff that, while they were to 'obey always', they must fight against injustice. At a divisional conference he had publicly accused Monash of favouring the 10th Brigade and 'told him why'. Monash subsequently sent for him to warn him against impulsive speech and declared that, were it not for his high opinion of him, he would have sent him back to Australia. Before embarking for home, Cannan studied insurance practice in London. His A.I.F. appointment terminated on 13 December 1919 in Brisbane, where he resumed his former job. He was Queensland president of the Returned Sailors' and Soldiers' Imperial League of Australia (1920-21), and Brisbane Legacy's first president (1928). In 1932 he became manager of his company's Sydney office. Among numerous professional appointments, he presided over the Insurance Institute of New South Wales in 1936-37.

From 1920 Cannan had commanded the 2nd, then the 11th (Mixed) brigades. He transferred to the Unattached List in May 1925. Having been inspector-general to the Commonwealth Board of Business Administration for two months, in July 1940 he was promoted temporary major general and posted in command of the 2nd Division. On 24 October he was made quartermaster general and third member of the Military Board. The appointment of a militia officer to the board had been opposed by the chief of the General Staff, Lieutenant General (Sir) Vernon Sturdee [q.v.], but, when Prime Minister (Sir) Robert Menzies [q.v.] insisted, Sturdee offered the post to Cannan.

At 58, in a new war, Cannan was responsible for supply, transport and engineering services in Australia and later in New Guinea, the Solomons and Borneo. To his task he brought the skills of a businessman, capacity for command, personality, charm and 'tremendous drive'. Often working late, he co-operated closely with and kept 'a jump ahead' of the General Staff. Much of his time was spent visiting formations in Darwin, New Guinea ('about every month'), New Britain, Bougainville, Morotai and Borneo. He accompanied General Sir Thomas Blamey [q.v.]

to Hollandia in October 1944 to plan the movement of I Corps to the Philippines, only to learn that General Douglas MacArthur [q.v.] had decided not to employ the Australians.

Cannan had offered to resign in 1942 so that his post could go to a regular officer. Blamey refused the offer. He nominated him for appointment as K.B.E. in September 1943 and again in October 1945, mentioning Cannan's 'exacting and difficult duties' and the 'great diligence and outstanding success' with which he had carried them out. The government remained unmoved. Cannan relinquished his appointment on 31 December. His 'contribution to the defence of Australia [was] immense, his responsibility . . . a giant-sized burden; his acknowledgement—nil'.

In 1946 Cannan resigned from the Insurance Office of Australia Ltd and retired as honorary major general. He stayed in Sydney as director (1946-47), South-West Pacific Area, of the United Nations Relief and Rehabilitation Administration. Moved by the plight of European refugees, he called on the government to act promptly to obtain the best migrants available. Back in Brisbane, Cannan was chairman of the Queensland division of the Australian Red Cross Society (1950-51) and of the Queensland regional committee of the Services Canteens Trust (1948-57); he was also a director of several companies, including Lennons Hotel Ltd. Survived by his wife, he died on 23 May 1976 in his Wickham Terrace apartment and, after a military funeral, was cremated. His estate was sworn for probate at $294 820.

C. E. W. Bean, *The Story of Anzac*, 1, 2 (Syd, 1921, 1924), and *The A.I.F. in France, 1916-18* (Syd, 1929, 1933, 1937, 1942); T. P. Chataway, *History of the 15th Battalion A.I.F.* (Brisb, 1948); G. Drake-Brockman, *The Turning Wheel* (Perth, 1960); *Reveille* (Syd), 1 May 1933, p 8; *Courier-Mail*, 31 May 1976; Blamey papers (AWM); letters from Cannan (held by Dr D. M. Horner, Deakin, ACT).

A. J. HILL

CANTAMESSA, ETTORE GIUSEPPE (1892-1947), cane-farmer and internee, was born on 9 March 1892 at Conzano, Piedmont, Italy, son of Pietro Cantamessa, a travelling sausage-maker, and his wife Giustina, née Garrone. In 1907 Giuseppe joined his father in North Queensland and later took up sugar-farming at Ingham where there was a growing Italian community. He became a naturalized British subject in 1913. At St Monica's Catholic Church, Cairns, on 27 March 1918 he married 16-year-old, Piedmont-born Maria Alda Fiori; they were to have five sons.

Frequently called upon to represent the

Italian community, in 1925 Cantamessa gave evidence before the State royal commission which investigated the social and economic effects of increasing numbers of 'Aliens' in North Queensland. When prejudice against Italians intensified, particularly in the northern sugar districts, a 'gentlemen's agreement' between the Australian Workers' Union, the Australian Sugar Producers' Association and the Queensland Cane Growers' Association gave preference to employing British cane-cutters. Cantamessa campaigned against the definition of 'British cutters' which excluded those who were naturalized. An Italian Association of the Sugar Industry (of which he was briefly president) was formed in 1931 to protect the interests of those of Italian origin in the industry. A good organizer and a fluent speaker, he advocated moderation and conciliation, and worked to bring about industrial harmony.

Eventually producing an average cut of 2000 tons on 'the most improved sugar property' in the district, Cantamessa was chairman of the Herbert River District Cane Growers' Association and an executive-member of the Cane Prices Board at Macknade. He represented Ingham from 1929 to 1936 on the Queensland Cane Growers' Council and in 1931 was consulted over the preparation of a new Federal sugar agreement. An active member and an office-holder in most local sporting clubs, he was district vice-president of the North Queensland Life Saving Association. Cantamessa had taken part in relief work for victims of the Herbert River floods in 1927 and was associated with several charitable appeals. Elected to the Hinchinbrook Shire Council in 1936, he served on the district's first Labor administration until his forced resignation four years later.

Italy declared war on France and Britain on 10 June 1940. Next day Cantamessa was interned. In his unsuccessful appeal, heard on 24 August, he denied any interest in 'foreign politics', asserted his loyalty and pointed out that his eldest son had voluntarily enlisted in the Militia in 1938. The authorities lacked concrete evidence that he held fascist sympathies, yet a donation to Italy's Abyssinian campaign in 1936, his brief involvement in the I.A.S.I. and his leadership qualities were the grounds for his detention. Held in internment camps at Gaythorne, Queensland, Hay, New South Wales, and Loveday, South Australia, he was released on 10 November 1943, but restricted to his farm until 20 March 1945.

Survived by his wife and three sons, Cantamessa died of a cerebral tumour on 27 March 1947 in Brisbane Hospital and was buried in Ingham cemetery; his funeral cortège of two hundred cars was the largest seen in that town. The *Herbert River Express* declared that 'he discharged his duties to his adopted country faithfully and well'.

Roy Com into Aliens in North Queensland, Report, *PP* (Qld), 1925, 3, p 25 *and* PRE/A849 (QA); *Townsville Catholic News*, 1 Aug 1947; *Townsville Daily Bulletin*, 28 Apr 1931; *Herbert River Express*, 5 Apr 1947; Archbishop Duhig correspondence (Catholic Diocesan Archives, Brisb); Internment file, G. Cantamessa, CA 753, BP242/1, item Q6446 (AA, Brisb).   ILMA MARTINUZZI O'BRIEN

CANTOR, MAURICE EMANUEL HENRY (1887-1960), industrial commissioner, was born on 17 June 1887 in South Melbourne, eldest child of Henry Cantor, a Victorian-born clothier, and his wife Hannah, née Fisher, from the Cape of Good Hope. Maurice was educated at various schools in Perth before the family moved to Sydney about 1900. He attended Glenmore Road Public School and was coached by L. F. Meagher in 1903. Articled to H. E. Fulton (of Fulton & Lowe) in August 1907, Cantor was admitted as a solicitor on 30 August 1912 and joined the firm, C. A. Coghlan & Co. On 22 October that year at the Great Synagogue, Sydney, he married Beatrice Ida Langley (d. 1924). Admitted to the Bar on 2 June 1919, he soon developed a large practice in industrial law. In 1920 he became an original shareholder in Denman Chambers Ltd, a company of barristers which bought the building in Phillip Street that housed their chambers.

The Industrial Commission of New South Wales was established in December 1927 under the presidency of A. B. Piddington [q.v.11]; Cantor and (Sir) Kenneth Street [q.v.] were the other original members. The functions of the commission were to create law—by making industrial awards—and to enforce that law. During the Depression a number of Cantor's cost-of-living inquiries gained considerable publicity. He formulated many of the fundamental principles involved in industrial matters: the steel industry award that he announced in 1939 (after a hearing of more than twelve months) was still relied upon more than twenty years later.

In February 1939 Cantor had declined appointment as chief judge of the Commonwealth Court of Conciliation and Arbitration; in December 1942 he was passed over for the vacant position of president of the Industrial Commission (of which he was the senior member and had been acting-president on several occasions). After his junior colleague (Sir) John Ferguson [q.v.] declined the position, the State government let it be known that it was determined not to appoint Cantor. During World War II Prime Minister Curtin [q.v.] often conferred with Cantor on the troubled steel industry. In the turbulent industrial disputes of the postwar period Cantor presided over many highly publicized hearings, including those relating to strikes in the steel industry at Newcastle and at Port Kembla in 1945 and 1946 (he was burnt in effigy by striking ironworkers at Wollongong in January 1946). On the bench he was tolerant and patient, his judgements steeped in principle. Long before he retired from the Industrial Commission in June 1957, he enjoyed the confidence of employers and employees.

On 14 October 1939 at the district registrar's office, North Sydney, Cantor had married Lilian May Ginn, née Gill, a widow with two children. He belonged to the University Club and spent his spare time gardening and fishing. In the 1950s he moved from Wahroonga to Castlecrag. Survived by his wife, and by the son and daughter of his first marriage, he died there on 1 June 1960 and was cremated with Jewish rites; his estate was sworn for probate at £134 085. Cantor's son Henry became judge of the Supreme Court of New South Wales.

J. M. Bennett (ed), *A History of the New South Wales Bar* (Syd, 1969); *Aust Law J*, 23 June 1960, p 57; *SMH*, 5, 14, 17 Dec 1927, 3 Mar 1939, 25 Dec 1942, 5 Jan 1946, 22 June 1957, 2, 3, 8 June 1960; *Daily Telegraph* (Syd), 14 June 1957; personal information.   John Kennedy McLaughlin

CARDELL-OLIVER, Dame ANNIE FLORENCE GILLIES (1876-1965), politician, was born on 11 May 1876 at Stawell, Victoria, fifth child of Johnston Wilson, an Irish-born storekeeper, and his second wife Annie, née Thompson, from Scotland. On 26 January 1895 in Melbourne Florence married with Presbyterian forms David Sykes Boyd, a 22-year-old wool-buyer whom she accompanied to England. He died at York on 5 November 1902 from an accidental overdose of opium-based sleeping tonic. On 15 December that year Florence married Arthur Cardell Oliver (1876-1929) at St Matthias's parish church, Poplar, London; they were to have two sons.

Born on 14 April 1876 in Cardiff, Arthur served with the British Army in the South African War and subsequently established a medical practice at Hackney, London. Florence persuaded him to migrate to Western Australia where he registered as a doctor in 1912. The couple settled at York and then at Albany. An honorary captain in the (Australian) Army Medical Corps Reserve, Arthur joined the Australian Imperial Force on 7 September 1916; he was briefly based in England before his appointment terminated at his own

request on 8 August 1917 in Melbourne. He practised in South Melbourne, retired due to ill health in 1924, took his family to England and died there on 15 September 1929.

Florence had been president of the Western Australian Nationalist Women's Movement and of the Albany branch of the Women's Service Guilds, and had travelled throughout Australia addressing recruitment meetings for the armed services during World War I. After her husband's death she returned to Western Australia and became vice-president of the State branch of the Nationalist Party. In 1934 she published *Empire Unity or Red Asiatic Domination?* which outlined the economic measures she felt necessary to stave off the spread of communism. At the invitation of Mustafa Kemal Atatürk, in 1935 she attended a congress in Istanbul of the International Suffrage Alliance of Women as a delegate from the Australian Federation of Women Voters. She was, as well, a delegate to the British Commonwealth League, London. Between 1933 and 1936 she also visited the Soviet Union, the Baltic States, Germany, Spain and Italy.

Having been defeated in 1934 by John Curtin [q.v.] for the seat of Fremantle in the House of Representatives, Cardell-Oliver (as she now styled herself) was returned in February 1936 to the Western Australian Legislative Assembly as the Nationalist member for Subiaco: she defeated two other endorsed Nationalists and the Labor sitting member on preferences. A vigorous debater with independent views, in 1939 she organized a campaign to oppose the establishment of free birth-control clinics, and, in opposition to her party, on 3 September 1941 unsuccessfully moved for the abolition of the death penalty. On 26 October, during a debate on starting-price betting, she was the first woman to be suspended from any Australian parliament. She succeeded, however, with bills that required parents to be notified before a ward of the state was released and that raised the age at which children could offer goods to pawnbrokers.

On 1 April 1947 Cardell-Oliver was appointed an honorary minister without portfolio in the McLarty-Watts [qq.v.] Liberal-Country Party government and on 5 January 1948 honorary minister for supply and shipping. When she was given the additional portfolio of minister for health on 7 October 1949, she became the first woman in Australia and the oldest person in Western Australia to attain full cabinet rank. She retained these portfolios until the government was defeated in February 1953. Influenced by her experiences with undernourished children in London, she sponsored the Free Milk and Nutritional Council, and, as minister, introduced a free-milk scheme for Western Australian schoolchildren. She brought the State to the forefront of anti-tuberculosis campaigns by legislating for compulsory chest X-ray examinations.

A tall woman of imposing appearance, Cardell-Oliver wore long, flowing gowns and flower or feather-trimmed picture hats. She was a member of the Victoria League, the Royal Institute of Great Britain, and the Karrakatta and Perth clubs, was president of the Women Painters' Society of Western Australia and of the Western Australian Women's Hockey Association, and represented her Subiaco parish on the Anglican diocesan synod. Her formal education was limited, but she remembered with gratitude the care taken by her father to introduce her to learning, and developed into an accomplished linguist and an opera enthusiast. Having fulfilled her responsibilities as wife and mother, she succeeded in politics late in life through sheer hard work and force of personality. In 1951 she was appointed D.B.E.

Following her retirement in April 1956, Dame Florence visited London. Returning to Perth, she died on 12 January 1965 at Subiaco; her sons survived her. She was buried beside Arthur in St Columb Minor churchyard, Newquay, England.

D. Popham (ed), *Reflections* (Perth, 1978); M. Sawer and M. Simms, *A Woman's Place* (Syd, 1984); H. Radi (ed), *200 Australian Women* (Syd, 1988); D. Black (ed), *The House on the Hill* (Perth, 1991); *Milady*, Sept 1949; *West Australian*, 19 Feb 1936, 29 Mar 1947, 1 Oct 1949, 30 May 1959, 11 May 1963, 14 Jan 1965, 12 Mar 1977, 4 June 1981; *SMH*, 3 Apr 1947, 14 Jan 1965; M. Choules, Women in Western Australian Parliamentary Politics 1921-1968 (B.A. Hons thesis, Curtin Univ of Technology, 1988); Cardell-Oliver papers *and* Premier's Dept (WA), File 56/51 (BL); personal information.   DAVID BLACK

CARDUS, SIR JOHN FREDERICK NEVILLE (1888-1975), writer and critic, was born on 3 April 1888 at Rusholme, Lancashire, England, son of Ada Cardus (1870-1954). He never knew his father who may have been a violinist. Fred lived with his unmarried mother and aunts in the home of his maternal grandparents. His grandfather was a retired policeman and the family took in washing. By night Ada and her sisters worked as genteel prostitutes, frequenting Manchester's theatres and music-halls.

An imaginative and nervous child, Cardus attended the local board school for some five years, drifted through various jobs and in December 1904 was employed at Manchester as a clerk in a marine insurance firm. Resolving to 'live by my pen or perish', he began a rigorous scheme of self-education in literature, philosophy and the arts. In 1907 he

discovered that he could memorize whole scores without effort and added music to his curriculum. He admired the music- and theatre-critics of the *Manchester Guardian*, and set out to acquire their writing style.

Cardus dated his passion for cricket from 1901, when he saw A. C. MacLaren play at Old Trafford. He developed his own skills as a bowler and in 1912 became assistant cricket coach at Shrewsbury School, Shropshire. Rejected in 1914 for military service because of his short sight, he stayed at the school as secretary to the headmaster until 1916. Back at Manchester, Cardus briefly worked as music critic for the *Daily Citizen*. In March 1917 he was taken on by the *Manchester Guardian* as a reporter and became a writer on the editorial staff. He called himself Neville; his articles appeared over the initials, 'N.C.'

Sent by chance to report on the resumption of first-class cricket at Old Trafford in June 1919, he soon attracted a wide readership with articles which he signed as 'Cricketer'. 'Before him, cricket was reported', John Arlott wrote, 'with him it was for the first time appreciated, felt, and imaginatively described'. Cardus created folk heroes of the players; his prose was rich with allusions to music and poetry. In 1920 he became assistant to the paper's chief music critic Samuel Langford and in 1927 succeeded him. On 17 June 1921 at the register office, Chorlton, Manchester, Cardus had married Edith Honorine Walton King (1881-1968), an art teacher and an enthusiastic worker for amateur dramatics; they were to remain childless. He covered concerts in London, and in Vienna and Salzburg, Austria, and mixed with leading musicians and composers. His approach to music, as with cricket, was intuitive and personal, rather than academic and technical.

One of the heroes from his youth was Victor Trumper [q.v.12]. Late in 1936 Cardus realized an ambition to visit Trumper's home country when he covered the Marylebone Cricket Club's (England) Test tour of that season. *Australian Summer*, Cardus's fifth book on cricket, appeared in 1937. Next year he returned to Australia on a private visit.

As war in Europe approached, Cardus feared that he would lose his job. When, in December 1939, Sir Keith Murdoch [q.v.10] invited him to cover Sir Thomas Beecham's forthcoming tour of Australia, he accepted at once, arriving by flying boat in February 1940. He went to Melbourne to write for the *Herald*, but found that he could not review concerts for an evening paper and negotiated a post as music critic for the *Sydney Morning Herald*.

Making few concessions to what Lindsey Browne was to describe as the 'woefully self-important provincialism' of Sydney's cultural life, Cardus initially aroused some resentment. Yet, the humour, authority and literary craftsmanship of his reviews—written, he claimed, on the backs of telegram forms at the General Post Office's all-night counters— won him respect. He helped to lift the standard of musical criticism in Australia. In its turn, Australia, he later said, 'rejuvenated my heart and mind'.

His precise and fastidious voice, with its 'fluent but not fast, polished clergyman's tones', became familiar through radio programmes for the Australian Broadcasting Commission. His hour-long feature, 'The enjoyment of music', presented on Wednesdays in the winter of 1942 (and later on Sundays), enlarged the audience for classical music across the country. From January 1941 Cardus gave a weekly, ten-minute talk on music, illustrated by records, for the children's Argonauts' Club; in 1942-47 he also wrote regularly on music and cricket for the *A.B.C. Weekly*.

Early in 1942 Cardus rented a small flat at Kings Cross. There he wrote *Ten Composers* (Sydney, 1945), with its acclaimed essay on Gustav Mahler, his *Autobiography* (1947) and *Second Innings* (1950). In 1942 his wife joined him. Cardus described her affectionately as 'a great spirit and character, born for sisterhood not marriage'. She lived in a flat in Elizabeth Street and was soon active in local women's organizations, and in art and drama groups. Edith and Neville dined together on Tuesdays and Thursdays.

Undecided whether to remain in Australia, Cardus returned to England for a few months in 1947 and again in 1948 to cover the Test series. In April 1949 he eventually left Sydney to make his home in London. Edith followed him in June. In 1951 he rejoined the *Manchester Guardian* as its London music critic and occasional cricket writer. He revisited Australia to cover the M.C.C. tours of 1950-51 and 1954-55 for the *Sydney Morning Herald*. Appointed C.B.E. in 1964, he was knighted in 1967; he was granted honorary membership of the Royal Manchester College of Music (1968) and of the Royal Academy of Music (1972). Among his many honours, he valued most his presidency (1971-72) of the Lancashire County Cricket Club. He published eleven books on cricket and nine on music. His autobiographical *Second Innings* and *Full Score* (1970) included accounts of his time in Australia.

Slight, lean and bespectacled, with a gnome-like appearance in his last years, Cardus was a familiar sight at Lord's or the Garrick Club, pipe in mouth and book under arm. Roger Covell recalled him in Sydney as a 'marvellous raconteur and monologuist with his all-weather overcoat'. Sir Neville died on 28 February 1975 at St Marylebone, London, and was cremated.

The Essential Neville Cardus, selected and introd R. Hart-Davis (Lond, 1949); *DNB*, 1971-80; R. Daniels, *Conversations with Cardus* (Lond, 1976); K. S. Inglis, *This is the ABC* (Melb, 1983); C. Brookes, *His Own Man* (Lond, 1985); *SMH*, 26 May 1936, 11 Dec 1937, 31 Jan 1938, 31 Aug, 23 Nov 1940, 11 Jan, 15 Nov 1941, 15 May 1942, 30 Aug 1945, 11 Mar, 31 May, 30 Aug 1947, 3, 4 June 1950, 28 Nov 1954, 5 Feb 1966, 9, 10, 15 Mar 1975, 28 Dec 1976, 19 Oct 1985; *The Times*, 17 Apr 1970, 1, 7 Mar 1975; *Guardian* (Manchester and Lond), 1 Mar 1975; *Guardian* correspondence (*Guardian* Archives, John Rylands Univ L of Manchester); ABC Archives, SP 1011/0 and 1011/2 (AA, Syd); information from Mr B. Nairn, Lyneham, Canb.

SALLY O'NEILL

CARINGTON SMITH, JACK (1908-1972), artist and teacher, was born on 26 February 1908 at Launceston, Tasmania, son of native-born parents Robert Norman Smith, merchant, and his wife Muriel Matilda, née Johnstone. As a 15-year-old student at Launceston Chruch Grammar School, Jack had two water-colours accepted by the Launceston Art Society. Intent on a career as an artist, in 1925 he went to Sydney where he attended night-classes at East Sydney Technical College; he supported himself by working as a clerk for the Shell Co. of Australia Ltd and, from 1928, as a commercial artist.

On 28 September 1934 Smith married Ruth Tait Walker at St John's Anglican Church, Darlinghurst. Recognition came in the mid-1930s when he began exhibiting with the Society of Artists. In 1936 he won the New South Wales travelling art scholarship which enabled him to study at the Royal Academy of Arts, London, at the Westminster Technical Institute and in Paris. Influenced by Post-Impressionism and by the work of such contemporary British artists as Walter Richard Sickert, Carington Smith (as he now styled his surname) returned to Australia in 1939 and held his first one man exhibition in Sydney that year. He was appointed head of the art department at Launceston Technical College, but moved to Hobart Technical College in 1940. His long-held aim to transfer his department from 'the Tech' was to be achieved in 1963. Renamed the Tasmanian School of Art and relocated in the old university buildings on Queen's Domain, this new, single-discipline institution included a fine art department which he was to head until his retirement in 1970.

Drawing was the foundation of Carington Smith's art and the core of his teaching: his students were given a fine grounding in the subject. He regarded the process of composing a picture, with colours, tones, lines and forms, as being akin to musical composition. The verve and spontaneity of his technique as a water-colourist gave full expression to the medium's unique character, and made him the chief inspiration in the postwar development of a distinctive Tasmanian 'school' of water-colourists.

The subjects of his oil paintings were diverse. In the 1940s he produced a number of small, simplified compositions, depicting figures on the shores of the Derwent River near his home at Sandy Bay; with their qualities of light and apparent stillness, these works evoke a timeless character. Over the following decade Carington Smith painted haunting nocturnal scenes of a moonlit Derwent, seen through the window of the artist's studio, with vague reflections from its gloomy interior fusing with what could barely be seen in the dark outside. His 1960s work was more overtly abstract, but he continued to derive his ideas from visual experience, particularly of nature. Best known for his portraiture, he strove to portray the inner life—the essence or the spirit—of his sitters.

A thickset, quietly-spoken man, with a shy, introspective manner, Carington Smith was respected both by the artistic and the wider community. Although he travelled and painted abroad in 1964 and 1967, he preferred to live in Tasmania where he felt an artistic and a personal freedom that may have been undermined elsewhere.

While Carington Smith carried considerable teaching and administrative responsibilities from 1940 to 1970, he also participated in numerous solo and group exhibitions in Australia and overseas. He won the Sir John Sulman [q.v.12] prize (1949), the inaugural (1955) Women's Weekly prize for portraiture, the Archibald [q.v.3] prize (1963) for his portrait of James McAuley [q.v.], the Rubinstein [q.v.11] prize (1966) for his painting of Leslie Greener [q.v.], the Lloyd Jones [q.v.9] memorial prize for portraiture (1969) and the Sir Warwick Fairfax (human image) prize (1971).

A member of the Society of Artists, Sydney, and of the Australian Watercolour Institute (1948), Carington Smith belonged to the Hobart and Launceston art societies. He died on 19 March 1972 at Sandy Bay and was cremated; his wife, son and two daughters survived him. One of his self-portraits (1968) was purchased in 1982 by the Tasmanian Museum and Art Gallery; another hangs in the Carington Smith Library, Centre for the Arts, University of Tasmania. Widely considered to be the most important Tasmanian painter of the twentieth century, he is represented in every major Australian gallery. Retrospective exhibitions of his work have been held in State, university and private galleries.

Bernard Smith, *Place, Taste and Tradition* (Syd, 1945) and *Australian Painting 1788-1970* (Melb,

1971); D. H. Skinner and J. Kroeger (eds), *Renniks Australian Artists* (Adel, 1968); S. Backhouse, *Jack Carington Smith*, exhibition cat (Hob, 1976); J. Campbell, *Australian Watercolour Painters 1780-1980* (Adel, 1983); E. Gertzakis, *Quiet Records and Careful Observations* (Hob, 1985); *Who was Jack Carington Smith?* (film, Hob, 1977, scripted by M. Angus); *Art and Aust*, 10, no 3, Jan 1973, 22, no 4, June 1985.   LINDSAY BROUGHTON

CARLILE McDONNELL, ETHEL; see McDONNELL

CARMODY, SIR ALAN THOMAS (1920-1978), public servant, was born on 8 September 1920 at Malvern, Melbourne, son of Thomas James Carmody, telephone mechanic, and his wife Elsie Annie, née Ramsay, both Victorian born. A member of the ground staff of No. 3 Squadron, Australian Flying Corps, in World War I, Thomas had been awarded the Meritorious Service Medal and Bar for bravery. Alan was educated at St Patrick's College, Goulburn, New South Wales, and joined the Commonwealth Public Service on 18 March 1937 as a clerk in the central office of the Department of Trade and Customs, Canberra. He studied at Canberra University College and played Rugby Union football. In 1940 he enlisted in the Citizen Air Force of the Royal Australian Air Force; commissioned in February 1943, he specialized as a radar officer. On 25 October 1944 in St Patrick's Catholic Church, Adelaide, he married Elizabeth Mary Brennan.

Demobilized in 1945, Carmody resumed his public service career and graduated (B.A., 1946; B.Com., 1947; M.Com., 1950) from the University of Melbourne. In May 1948 he became a research officer with the Tariff Board in that city. While serving in London in 1950-52, he completed postgraduate study at the University of Leeds (M.Com., 1952). Having returned to the Department of Trade and Customs, Canberra, he rejoined the Tariff Board in Melbourne as chief executive officer in 1958. Four years later he was a deputy-secretary in the Canberra office of the Department of Trade and was earning a reputation as a protectionist. In 1964 he was appointed O.B.E. On 12 May 1966 he became comptroller-general of customs and head of the Department of Customs and Excise (later Department of Police and Customs).

Embarking on a programme of management innovation and departmental reform, Carmody overhauled and simplified procedures for customs clearance of passengers and goods entering Australia. He initiated new, uniform censorship provisions to remove many of the anomalies that existed in Commonwealth and State practices, and improved arrangements for combating the illegal import of narcotics. His department was one of the first to make extensive use of computers. He was elevated in 1971 to C.B.E. In 1975 he advocated the establishment of an agency to be known as the Australia Police, headed by himself. This body was to be formed by amalgamating the Australian Capital Territory, Northern Territory and Commonwealth police forces with sections of Carmody's existing department. Modelled on the Royal Canadian Mounted Police, the force was envisaged as having powers to deal with large-scale smuggling and white-collar crime, and was expected to centralize customs, security, narcotics surveillance and Federal police work. When Malcolm Fraser's government came to office late that year, the project was abandoned and Carmody was made secretary of the Department of Business and Consumer Affairs.

His appointment to head the Department of the Prime Minister and Cabinet in September 1976 surprised many people, among them Carmody. The *Sydney Morning Herald* claimed that the prime minister and his departmental head would make 'an odd pair. Where Mr Fraser is reserved, stilted and severe, Mr Carmody is exuberant, relaxed and jolly'. Carmody retained his buoyant and extroverted nature, despite his onerous duties and persistent angina. He worked energetically to maintain the department's high standards and to extend its capacity to provide independent advice to the prime minister across the full range of Federal government responsibilities. Lacking a background in parliamentary and cabinet practice, he concentrated on other departmental roles, particularly matters involving economics, security and the police. For recreation, he developed a grazing property near Canberra, an activity which sometimes obtruded upon his departmental responsibilities. He was knighted in 1978.

Carmody was essentially a Customs man: it took half of his total career and ten of his twelve years as departmental secretary. He had the ability to accommodate the differing personalities and styles of successive ministers. In a typical encomium, a former minister described him as 'one of the bureaucracy's ablest and most highly respected practitioners'. Carmody saw himself as a man who could get things done. His 'can do' approach invited the criticism that he occasionally acted before he had given a problem sufficient thought. About 5 ft 7 ins (170.2 cm) tall and eleven stone (69.9 kg) in weight, he was impatient of polish, disliked having to 'dress up' and was far 'too busy to publish anything'. A practising Catholic, he was conservative on social issues. Sir Alan died suddenly of coronary vascular disease on 12 April 1978 in his Red Hill home and was buried in Canberra cemetery; his wife, two daughters and three sons survived him.

Management Newsletter, 30 Jan 1968; *SMH*, 29 Mar 1975, 17, 24 Sept 1976, 13 Apr 1978; *Canb Times*, 17 Sept 1976, 13 Apr 1978; *Financial Review*, 20 Sept 1976, 13 Apr 1978; *National Times*, 20-25 Sept 1976, 3-8 Apr 1978; *Nation Review*, 28 July-3 Aug 1977; *Age* (Melb) and *Australian*, 13 Apr 1978; information from Lady Carmody, Sir G. Yeend and Mr W. Callaghan, Canb.

ROBERT HYSLOP

CARMODY, THOMAS JOSEPH (1885-1961), onion-grower and marketer, was born on 15 June 1885 at Woodford, Victoria, twin son and eighth child of Irish-born parents Edward Carmody, farmer, and his wife Catherine, née Costello, who had migrated to Victoria in 1870. Forced off their Woodford farm by the depression, in 1892 the family took to the road by wagonette, finally settling at Corunnun, near Cororooke, where large sheep- and cattle-runs on rich, volcanic soils were being subdivided for dairy-farming and potato- and onion-growing.

Although the work was laborious and demeaning, rents exorbitant, pests and diseases prevalent, and seasons capricious, the landless looked to onion-growing as the first step towards owning a farm. Leaving Cororooke State School, Thomas leased land and entered into share-farming arrangements with local landowners. He earned a reputation for his sound judgements on critical aspects of successful onion production—soils, seed and seasons—and for his diligence and skills in planting, weeding and harvesting. On 19 June 1912 at St Mary's Catholic Church, Colac, he married Margaret Goonan.

As he struggled to get established, Carmody identified with members of the Cororooke onion-growing community and began to take a lead in improving their lot by removing two of the factors that made onion-growing such a lottery—low and fluctuating prices. Looking to wartime marketing schemes for a model, in 1921 he organized a voluntary marketing pool which collapsed when a few local growers sold outside and the court judged it to be a restraint on trade.

For Carmody, the pursuit of orderly marketing was a mission, the growers' welfare became his passion, and merchant price-manipulators and black marketeers the objects of his bitter scorn. In the depressed early 1930s he stumped Victoria, urging growers to unite or face starvation. Hindered by diabetes, he was supported by his wife who travelled with him. In 1933 the Victorian Onion Corporation Ltd, based on the 'Carmody Plan', was formed, with Carmody its chairman. After E. J. Hogan [q.v.9], minister for agriculture and a former premier, steered the marketing of primary products bill (1935) through parliament as a framework for all marketing boards, Carmody was elected foundation chairman of the Victorian Onion Marketing Board. Despite legislative support for compulsory pooling, some growers continued to sell on the black market, particularly in times of abundance. With Carmody's support, vigilantes raided trucks carrying onions to clandestine destinations. Violence and tempers flared in the 'onion war'. It was not until 1958 that Carmody could claim that the black market had been obliterated. 'Tom Carmody's Board' was acknowledged to be the most persistent and successful marketing organization to grow out of the Depression.

Slight in build, Carmody was powerful in voice and personality. He became a legendary figure, a 'fighting fury' feared and respected in the produce trade. A staunch supporter (in the Scullin [q.v.11] mould) of the Australian Labor Party and president of the Cororooke branch, he stood unsuccessfully for the State seat of Polwarth in 1945. His continued allegiance to the A.L.P., following the formation of the Democratic Labor Party, raised tensions with his family and neighbours. Carmody was acknowledged, even by the many enemies of orderly marketing, as a man of high principle; he was a devout Catholic who regularly went to church to pray for guidance before meetings of the board.

Known to the press as 'the onion king', Carmody retired from the board in 1960, having been defeated in the biennial election for chairman. He retired to his 60-acre (24.3 ha) block at Coragulac, planning to expand it to a grazier's property. Survived by his wife and six of their seven children, he died on 26 September 1961 at Colac and was buried in the local cemetery.

Polwarth Elector, Nov 1945; Vic Potato Growers' Assn, Potato Grower News, 26 Sept 1958; Herald (Melb), 13, 16 Sept 1958, 22 July 1960, 27 Sept 1961; Colac Herald, 29 Sept 1961; information from Mr E. Carmody, Cororooke, and Mrs D. Ramm, Geelong, Vic.   L. LOMAS

CARR-GLYN, NEVA JOSEPHINE MARY (1908-1975), actress, was born on 10 May 1908 in Melbourne, daughter of Adolphus Benjamin Carr Glynn (d. 1923), an Irish-born vaudevillian known as 'Arthur Glynn', and his wife Marie Dunoon, née Senior, late Mola, a singer from Scotland. Travelling with her parents, Neva (aged 4) appeared as Little Willie in *East Lynne* (with her mother 'Marie Avis'), and was 'in and out of convents all over Australia'. In Sydney she learned ballet at Minnie Hooper's dancing academy. She left school at 14 and made the back line of the chorus in the Fullers' [qq.v.8] pantomime, *Dick Whittington and his Cat*, at the Majestic Theatre in December 1923, then toured until late 1924 with the *Band Box Revue*.

Given a five-year contract as a 'utility' by Sir Benjamin Fuller, Neva found the work gruelling, though 'it was wonderful training'. She was constantly busy: principal girl in *Robinson Crusoe* (1925-26), in vaudeville with Jim Gerald [q.v.] and George Wallace [q.v.12], principal boy in *Aladdin* at the Majestic (1927-28), and with Roy Rene [q.v.11] in *Clowns in Clover* (December 1929). In January 1930 she left on a tour of South Africa with the Frank Neil Company, during which she had leading roles in feathery comedies.

In London in January 1931 Neva was given the second lead in the operetta, *Nina Rosa*. She was well connected through her mother (a sister of Lady Coombe) and was a cousin of the actress 'Carol' Coombe. Imperious, with 'a dark, rather exotic grace', strong features and flashing, blue eyes, Neva temporarily dyed her raven hair because there were more parts for blondes. Joining Leslie Henson's company in 1931, she performed in such plays as *Living Dangerously* (1934), *Accidentally Yours* (1935) and *Aren't Men Beasts?* (1936). At the register office, Paddington, on 7 August 1936 she married Arthur William John, a private secretary from Australia; they were soon to be divorced. She also appeared in four films, including *The Squeaker* (1937) for (Sir) Alexander Korda.

Neva returned to Sydney in September 1937 and joined Gerald at the Tivoli. Under contract to the Australian Broadcasting Commission from mid-1938 until her release in April 1941, she worked extremely long hours and starred (often with Peter Finch [q.v.]) in countless radio plays, among them 'Toad of Toad Hall' and Max Afford's [q.v.] detective serial, 'Greyface'. She missed contact with the audience and the excitement of the theatre, but found radio to be 'a serious art with a fascination all its own', requiring 'twice the sincerity necessary in stage acting'.

At St Mark's Anglican Church, Darling Point, on 19 July 1940 Neva married a fellow actor John Paul Tate; their son Nick was born in 1942. They lived at Darling Point, acquired a cottage at Mona Vale and spent their spare time 'messing about in boats'. Developing 'fine teamwork', Neva and John appeared together in numerous radio plays (such as *Victoria Regina*) and serials (including Edmund Barclay's [q.v.] 'As Ye Sow'). A star in 'Lux Radio Theatre' and for Macquarie Broadcasting Services Pty Ltd, she won Macquarie awards for the best actress in 1950 and 1951. Throughout the 1940s Neva was also leading lady at the Minerva Theatre. The Tates toured New Zealand in 1944 with J. C.

Williamson [q.v.6] Ltd; *Arsenic and Old Lace* was in the repertoire. In August 1950 they appeared at the Theatre Royal, Hobart, for Fifi Banvard [q.v.].

In 1951-52 Neva toured Australia with the John Alden [q.v.] Company, playing—among other Shakespearian roles—Portia in *The Merchant of Venice* and Titania in *A Midsummer Night's Dream*. Her marriage ended in divorce in 1954. She appeared in *The Shifting Heart* for the Australian Elizabethan Theatre Trust in 1957 and, joining the Trust Players in 1959, was acclaimed as Oola (written for her by Peter Kenna) in *The Slaughter of St. Teresa's Day*.

Living alone from 1965, with a dog her only companion, Neva was tired of touring. In the 1960s she appeared with the Old Tote Theatre Company and the Marian Street Theatre, in films, in television programmes that ranged from 'Skippy' to 'Homicide', in the A.B.C. radio serial, 'Blue Hills', and even with a professional group that performed at clubs. She played Mrs Gillipop for four years in the children's television show, 'The Gillipops'. A battler afflicted with a severe limp, she was increasingly type-cast as 'bizarre harridan-like women', as in the film (1967) of Norman Lindsay's [q.v.10] *Age of Consent*. After missing a rehearsal for the A.B.C. television serial 'Certain Women', on 10 August 1975 she was found to have died of a cerebral haemorrhage at her Mona Vale home. Survived by her son, she was cremated. Neva Carr-Glyn was considered by her peers to be one of Australia's best actresses, able to handle both drama and sophisticated comedy with telling effect.

H. Porter, *Stars of Australian Stage and Screen* (Syd, 1965); *ABC Weekly*, 18 Jan 1941, 20 Oct 1945, 21 Aug 1948; *Listener In*, 18 June 1950, 15-21 Dec 1951; *Broadcaster*, 22 Dec, 1951; *TV Times*, 7 Aug 1971, 19 Jan 1974; *SMH*, 29 Mar, 26 Apr 1934, 15 Aug 1936, 15 Mar 1938, 17 July 1939, 28 July 1960, 11 Aug 1975; *Truth* (Syd), 19 Dec 1937; *Mercury* (Hob), 5, 8, 22 Aug 1950; *Sunday Telegraph* (Syd), 22 Sept 1957; *Australian*, 15 Jan 1965; *Sun-Herald* (Syd), 23 Mar 1969; *Daily Telegraph* (Syd), 11 Aug 1975; *Canb Times*, 12 Aug 1975; N. Carr Glyn, ABC file (AA, Syd); information from Mr R. Lane, Belrose, Syd, who holds his taped interview with Mr N. Tate and newspaper cuttings.   MARTHA RUTLEDGE

CARRODUS, JOSEPH ALOYSIUS (1885-1961), public servant, was born on 3 September 1885 at Richmond, Melbourne, third and youngest child of William Carrodus, baker, and his wife Catherine Elizabeth, née Nix, both Victorian born. Educated at St Patrick's College, East Melbourne, Joseph matriculated with honours in English, French and history. On 11 August 1904 he became a clerk in the Commonwealth Department of External Affairs. After three years he moved to its international treaties section where his knowledge of French proved valuable. He subsequently acted as private secretary to the minister, undertook considerable confidential work and was highly regarded by his superiors.

On 26 July 1915 Carrodus enlisted in the Australian Imperial Force. Although immediately accepted for officer training, he was always to emphasize that he began as a private. Reaching the Western Front in November 1916 as a lieutenant in the 37th Battalion, he was promoted captain in April 1917 and wounded in action on 12 October. His A.I.F. appointment terminated in Melbourne on 4 September 1919.

Resuming his career as a public servant, in the 1920s Carrodus headed the Papua, New Guinea and Norfolk Island branch of the Department of Home and Territories. From August to October 1923 he visited Papua and New Guinea; his report formed the basis of a review of Australian government policy on the administration of those territories. Chosen to represent Australia at the 1926 meetings of the Permanent Mandates Commission at Geneva, Switzerland, he was accompanied to Europe by his wife Mabel Florence Maud, née Waters, whom he had married on 14 March 1923 at St Silas's Anglican Church, Albert Park, Melbourne. They settled in Canberra in 1927.

Carrodus was acting-administrator of the Northern Territory for six months in 1934. He was appointed secretary, Department of Interior, on 25 November 1935. Consolidating his position as an administrator and government adviser, he played a major role in developing policies on Aboriginal affairs in the Northern Territory and on the growth of the Australian Capital Territory, and was influential on immigration issues. The failure of successive Federal governments to accept a large number of Jewish refugees in 1936-45 reflected Carrodus's persistent advice to refuse them entry, as much as it did the wishes of politicians. In his attitude to Jews suffering persecution in Europe, he showed a clear understanding of their circumstances, but shared the common indifference to their needs. He was appointed C.B.E. in 1939.

Clear sighted and single minded, Carrodus took a no-nonsense approach to administration. He was generous to, and supportive of, new and junior officers, and encouraged staff development. From May 1949 until his retirement in September 1950, he was director of civil defence. A good footballer and oarsman in his youth, he later enjoyed swimming and golf. He died on 8 April 1961 in Canberra Community Hospital and was buried in

Canberra cemetery; his wife, daughter and son survived him.

T. Wise, *The Self-Made Anthropologist* (Syd, 1985); W. D. Rubinstein (ed), *Jews in the Sixth Continent* (Syd, 1987); A. Markus, *Governing Savages* (Syd, 1990); J. P. M. Long, *The Go-Betweens* (Darwin, 1992); *Canb Times*, 8 Nov 1935; *Argus*, 2 Jan 1939; *Sun News-Pictorial*, 7 Jan 1939, 6 Mar 1942, 8 Apr 1949; *Herald* (Melb), 10 Dec 1941; CRS A571, 1904, CRS A1, 1923-38, CRS A518, 1924-26, CRS A426, 1935-36, CRS A434, 1938, CRS A433, 1940, CRS A431/2, 1949 (AA, Canb).

LYN ANNE RIDDETT

CARROLL, CECIL JAMES (1888-1970), police commissioner, was born on 8 July 1888 at Woombye, Queensland, second son of Patrick Carroll, a police constable from Ireland, and his native-born wife Margaret, née McGrath. Educated at Blackall State School, in 1904 Cecil became a pupil-teacher there and subsequently taught in schools at Petrie Terrace, West End, Cairns and Brisbane East. On 24 August 1915 he was commissioned in the Australian Imperial Force and posted with reinforcements to the 9th Battalion. Promoted captain in December 1916, he was twice wounded while serving in France, mentioned in dispatches and awarded the Military Cross. He was invalided home and his appointment terminated on 28 March 1918. At St Stephen's Catholic Cathedral, Brisbane, on 11 June that year he married a civil servant Alice Mary Fahy. Because of war-wounds in his hip and knee, Carroll abandoned teaching and joined the State Public Service as a clerk in the Land and Income Tax Office. He took two years leave of absence to engage in home-defence duties at Townsville.

Returning to the public service in 1920, Carroll rose to inspector (1922), senior inspector (1923) and chief inspector of taxation in January 1929. He was appointed royal commissioner in 1932 to inquire into the alleged payment of secret commissions in the dairying industry. About this time complaints were being voiced over problems in the administration of the police department. In 1933 Hugh Talty, secretary of the Queensland Police Union, requested a royal commission, alleging that some Labor politicians and police administrators had violated the Criminal Code. Next year public disquiet was aired about police procedures and law enforcement, while dissension was revealed within police ranks, particularly over disciplinary matters. Such concerns led the government to choose its new police commissioner from outside the force. In January 1934 the home secretary E. M. Hanlon [q.v.] selected Carroll —under whom he had served in France— in the expectation that his capacities would bring 'far greater efficiency' to police operations.

Taking office on 8 May, the commissioner began a thorough reorganization. Although many police retired, often after being examined by the medical board, Carroll increased the force's numbers, especially the ranks of non-commissioned officers. A new training system required recruits to sit an educational test. A cadet system of admission was initiated, whereby recruits entered at the clerical level at the age of 18 before undertaking regular police training. Promotion became dependent on qualifying examinations. Various lecture projects were created, among them an in-service education scheme for young detectives. The *Queensland Police Manual* was wholly revised. Despite his having taken charge without previous police experience, Carroll's reforms quickly built up efficiency and morale, and regained public confidence. In 1934 he was appointed M.V.O. He was one of three royal commissioners who investigated matters relating to racing and gaming in 1935-36.

In 1937 a consolidating Police Act changed the status of the commissioner. Previously a five-year appointee, he now headed what was virtually a separate government department, able to hold office until aged 65, with a salary equivalent to that of an under-secretary. The government argued that this new security of tenure would prevent a commissioner from being a political tool, too closely concerned with government policy. The Opposition, however, called these (and other) changes 'Hanlon's blot', while Talty condemned 'the meanest and most vicious and most tyrannical and oppressive piece of legislation ever introduced by any Parliament in the Southern hemisphere'.

Modernization was one of Carroll's notable achievements: he was 'affectionately known as the man who mechanised the Force'. When he took over, its equipment was limited to 'one or two cars, a few motor cycles and pedal cycles'. By supplying as many motor vehicles as his budget permitted, he made the force mobile. A wireless station was set up and a start made on installing receivers in motor-cars. To improve the effectiveness of the Criminal Investigation Branch, a 'modus operandi' recording system was introduced, along with the single fingerprint system and an up-to-date photography section. The firearms section was enlarged, and a scientific section established so that police could, for example, examine documents and handwriting by using ultraviolet rays or microscopy. Carroll also encouraged further specialization and planned a traffic squad at a time when motor transport was increasing and automatic signals were first installed in Brisbane. Buildings were renovated and amenities improved. New police stations included those at Fortitude Valley and Toowoomba, and barracks for recruits were built in the capital at Petrie Terrace. A police welfare club with social and recreational facilities was opened in Brisbane and police were encouraged to participate in outdoor sporting activities.

World War II greatly strained Queensland's police resources and the health of the commissioner. The movement of hundreds of thousands of Australian and American troops through the State stretched police resources to their limit. Extra duties were required by wartime emergency and security regulations, and one of Carroll's objectives was to keep out of Queensland 'undesirables' from the south. Apart from handling internees, police were invested with civil defence tasks, such as the training of air-raid wardens. The end of the war brought Carroll no relief from stress. Industrial trouble and major strikes shook the community, and police were often called upon to maintain the peace. A notorious fracas occurred on St Patrick's Day, 17 March 1948, when baton-wielding police confronted union street-marchers during a railway strike.

Although he had done much to restore the image and role of the police, the commissioner was not immune from criticism. A ballot conducted by the police union in 1942 called for a royal commission into police administration; apart from regular complaints on issues like discipline and promotion, much of the discontent was generated by Carroll's apparent preference for the detective branch to the uniformed police. In parliament there were frequent comments and questions about corruption in the force. J. F. ('Bombshell') Barnes [q.v.], aided by Tom Aikens, raised instances of brothel-keeping, starting-price betting, police abuse of power, and bribery. Barnes had no regard for Carroll whom he described as 'a bombastic little squirt'. In 1946 the commissioner came under additional attack, with insinuations that police had not fully performed their duty when T. A. Foley [q.v.], the minister in charge of police, was raided by officers from the Commonwealth Department of Trade and Customs.

On 23 July 1949 Carroll retired on the grounds of ill health: he had a nervous disability and had suffered from pernicious anaemia for fifteen months. Police and public contributed £2892 to his testimonial. Survived by his wife, son and two daughters, he died on 21 May 1970 in Brisbane and was buried in Nudgee cemetery.

R. Fitzgerald, *A History of Queensland from 1915 to the 1980s* (Brisb, 1984); *PD* (Qld), 1937, pp 318, 358, 1941, p 1091; *Courier-Mail*, 11, 12 January 1934, 7, 20 July 1949, 22 May 1970; *Truth* (Brisb), 18 May 1941; *Telegraph* (Brisb), 22 May 1970; Police Dept (Qld) staff file AF 5361 (QA).

W. ROSS JOHNSTON

CARROLL, DOROTHY (1897-1966), hospital matron, was born on 1 February 1897 at Broken Hill, New South Wales, eldest of four children of John Christopher Carroll, miner, and his second wife Mary Ann, née Panter (d. 1919). The family left Broken Hill in 1902 and successively lived at Gawler, South Australia, Parkside, Adelaide, and in the Western District of Victoria before settling at Alberton, Adelaide, where John and Mary ran a general store. On leaving primary school, Dorothy learned millinery and dressmaking, then worked for ten years as a milliner with the drapers, Wills & Co., in Rundle Street. In 1926 she began general training at the Angaston District Hospital; two years later she transferred to the (Royal) Adelaide Hospital where in 1930 her performance was laconically assessed as 'good'. She studied midwifery at the Queen's Home (later Queen Victoria Maternity Hospital), Rose Park, which was founded (1902) to provide care during confinement for 'respectable married women in need of charitable relief'.

Having completed her midwifery course, Carroll joined the hospital's staff. She helped to train about thirty nurses annually and to assist medical students in gaining experience in obstetrics. For several years she had charge of the labour ward, working a 58-hour week, with one day off a month. Efficient and humane, she lectured to student nurses who appreciated her sense of humour. After a year as deputy-matron, she resigned in 1938 to be matron of the Soldiers' Memorial Hospital, Mount Barker, but next year returned to the 'Queen Vic' as matron. In World War II difficulties in staffing and accommodation were constant. Carroll's quarters were within the main building and she was on call at all times for emergencies. Her appearance was striking. Tall and well built, she was a familiar figure in her starched, white uniform and a veil which covered most of her wavy, grey hair; her face was dominated by thick, dark eyebrows and eyes that conveyed warmth. Staff and patients alike found her approachable and ready to listen to their problems.

With increasing commitments to the wider field of nursing, in the 1950s Carroll delegated more of the hospital supervision. A member (1951-57) of the Nurses Registration Board of South Australia, she was for fifteen years one of its examiners in midwifery; she was also national president (1953) of the Florence Nightingale Committee and a fellow of the College of Nursing, Australia. In addition, she was a council-member and president (1951-52 and 1955-59) of the State branch of the Australian Trained Nurses' Association (Royal Australian Nursing Federation from 1955), and belonged to its federal council. She was appointed O.B.E. in 1955 and attended the congress of the International Council of Nurses held in Rome in 1957.

Following her retirement in 1959, Carroll joined the boards of the Royal Adelaide Hospital and the Queen Elizabeth Hospital, Woodville. She flew to meetings from Kangaroo Island where for three years she lived with her sister Daisy Zeitz and acted as matron of the hospital at Kingscote. Miss Carroll died of myocardial infarction on 18 June 1966 at Glen Ewin, near Houghton, and was cremated with Congregational forms.

I. L. D. Forbes, *The Queen Elizabeth Hospital, Woodville, 1954-1984* (Adel, 1984) and *The Queen Victoria Hospital, Rose Park, 1901-1987* (Adel, priv pub, 1988); J. Durdin, *They Became Nurses* (Syd, 1991); *News* (Adel), 13 Nov 1957; *Sunday Mail* (Adel), 12 Dec 1959; *Advertiser* (Adel), 20 June 1966; Trainee Nurse History Sheets (SA State Records Office); Nurses Bd of SA, Minutes of Bd meetings (Nurses Bd, Nth Adel); Aust Trained Nurses Assn, Minutes of council meetings *and* Florence Nightingale Cte, SA Branch, Minutes of meetings (Roy Aust Nursing Federation Archives, Kent Town, Adel); College of Nursing, Australia, SA Branch, Minutes of meetings (Roy College of Nursing, Aust, Archives, Nth Adel); information from Mrs D. Zeitz, Belair, Adel.   JOAN DURDIN

CARROLL, GARNET HANNELL (1902-1964), theatrical entrepreneur, was born on 4 December 1902 at Singleton, New South Wales, son of Roger Bede Carroll, dentist, and his wife Mildred Lorne, née Smith, both native-born. Educated at Singleton Grammar School, Garnet learned to play the cornet when the circus came to town. Rather than become a dentist, he left home at 14 and took sawmilling and fettling jobs before rejoining his family at East Maitland in 1921. While working in a menswear store, he joined the local musical society, played juvenile leads, and with his brother Bruce did supporting song-and-dance acts. In 1926 Garnet toured with Lionel Walsh's company in *No, No, Nanette* and other musical comedies. At the opening of the Empire Theatre, Sydney, on 28 February 1927 he was in the chorus line in *Sunny*. The show was bought by Sir Benjamin Fuller [q.v.8] and moved to the Princess Theatre, Melbourne. Next year, in Sydney, Carroll played Sergeant Joe Wilkins in *Rio Rita* and was stage-manager when the production toured Australasia for three years.

In New Zealand Carroll managed Fuller's Auckland theatre and married the Australian actress Catherine Stewart Elliott ('Kitty Stewart') on 11 April 1930 at the local registrar's office. Returning to Australia, he supervised the closure of the Fullers' theatrical empire and spent the Depression in Melbourne. In 1934-35 he was stage-manager for several operas directed by Charles Moore who had come from Covent Garden, London; they 'discovered' (Dame) Joan Hammond. In 1937 Fuller offered Carroll a partnership. Managing director of Fullers' Theatres Pty Ltd from 1939, Carroll had become managing director of the Carroll Fuller Theatre Co. Pty Ltd by 1946. Carroll was also a director of various other companies connected with his theatrical enterprises. He acquired the Stockton theatre at Newcastle, New South Wales, the Capital Theatre, Perth, and, after Fuller's death in 1952, bought his share of the Princess Theatre, Melbourne. Hampered by the lack of a theatre in Sydney, from 1955 Carroll worked closely with the Australian Elizabethan Theatre Trust.

After World War II Carroll brought many famous companies to Australia, including the Ballet Rambert (1947-48), the Old Vic Theatre Company with Sir Laurence (Lord) Olivier and Vivien Leigh (1948), the Shakespeare Memorial Theatre Company (1949), the Vienna Boys' Choir (1954), the Chinese Classical Theatre (1956) and the Sadler's Wells Opera Company (1960 and 1962); in addition, he brought Dame Sybil Thorndyke and Sir Ralph Richardson to open the Elizabethan Theatre, Sydney, in July 1955. Carroll was never afraid to take risks: he often staged elaborate American musicals—among them *Kismet* (which he himself produced in 1954), *The Sound of Music* (1960), *The King and I* (1960) and *Carousel* (1964)—while they were still in their early months on Broadway, and tried unknown singers and actors. He lost heavily on some productions, such as *West Side Story* and *The Diary of Anne Frank*.

Relishing his work, Carroll had helped Gertrude Johnson [q.v.] to establish the National Theatre Movement in the 1930s; he produced its first opera, *The Flying Dutchman*, at the Princess in 1938 and continued to support amateur theatre. He was appointed O.B.E. in 1949. Plump, with sleek, silver hair and heavy, tortoiseshell glasses, he kept his weight in check by dieting, and enjoyed swimming and yachting. At first nights he moved happily around and about, 'dispensing warm smiles and a pat on the back'. He belonged to the Victorian and the Green Room clubs. Having suffered from diabetes for more than ten years, Carroll died suddenly of coronary vascular disease on 23 August 1964 at his South Yarra home, Melbourne, and was cremated with Anglican rites; his wife and son survived him.

G. Coalstad (ed), *Theatre in Victoria* (Melb, 1950); H. Hunt, *The Making of Australian Theatre*

(Melb, 1960); G. Lauri, *The Australian Theatre Story* (Syd, 1960); J. West, *Theatre in Australia* (Syd, 1978); *Outdoor Showman*, Jan-Feb 1957; *SMH*, 18 Nov 1948, 13 Nov 1954, 8 Dec 1956, 24 Aug 1964; *Age*, 23, 26, 29 Aug 1964; *Australian*, 24 Aug 1964; *NT News*, 17 Aug 1985.

JULIE McKINNON

CARRUTHERS, WINIFRED ANDERSON (1890-1966), Young Women's Christian Association administrator, was born on 1 January 1890 at Ryde, Sydney, ninth child of native-born parents Rev. James Edward Carruthers, Wesleyan minister, and his wife Mary Elizabeth, née McWilliam. (Sir) Joseph Carruthers [q.v.7] was Winifred's uncle. She was educated at the Methodist Ladies' College, Burwood. Having attended a Christian students' camp, she became interested in the Y.W.C.A. and joined the Sydney branch in 1907.

Attracted to a career in the association, in 1910 Carruthers attended its first national training school; appointed as a secretary, she was involved in training and organizing members and volunteers. She travelled extensively, working as assistant-secretary (1912) at Auckland, New Zealand, and next as general secretary to the branch at Geelong, Victoria. Following World War I she returned to New Zealand before helping to establish the Y.W.C.A. in Perth in 1920-23.

As part of the Australian association's links with branches overseas, Carruthers spent some years abroad. In Britain in 1924-25 she worked first with the national holiday camps programme and then as general secretary of the Nottingham branch. Back in Australia in 1926, she joined the Y.W.C.A.'s national staff. After a further term at Nottingham as general secretary (1931-34), she resumed her post on the Australian staff and in 1935 studied part time at the University of Melbourne.

In 1940 Miss Carruthers became national training secretary and travelling secretary for the northern region. Appointed national general secretary early in 1942, she was responsible for all the Y.W.C.A.'s wartime work. Her duties included the provision of housing and recreation programmes for female munition workers and servicewomen. Although her hectic travelling schedule adversely affected her health and forced her to resign from this position in 1947, she continued to be employed by the association, initially as general secretary of the Brisbane branch and from 1949 as immigration secretary to the national body. In the latter capacity she worked with the Commonwealth Department of Immigration and the International Refugee Organization, visiting dis-

placed persons in I.R.O. assembly camps in Europe. Home again, she furthered the Y.W.C.A.'s involvement with refugees in the Australian holding and reception centres. She subsequently spent five years as general secretary to the Adelaide branch.

In 1959 Carruthers was appointed M.B.E. Next year she resigned from official service with the Y.W.C.A. Described as a 'gentle woman with a firm manner', she continued to act as a national consultant and remained available to visit different branches when needed. Despite deteriorating health, she also embarked on the vast task of assembling the records of the Y.W.C.A. of Australia. While engaged on this work in Melbourne, she died on 12 June 1966 at her Camberwell home and was cremated with Methodist forms. Her contribution to the Y.W.C.A. had been central to the consolidation and expansion of the Australian organization.

K. Reiger, *The Disenchantment of the Home* (Melb, 1985); M. Dunn, *The Dauntless Bunch* (Melb, 1991); *Aust Woman's Mirror*, 24 Feb 1931; *SMH*, 10 Feb 1931, 12 Dec 1940, 1 Sept 1942, 2 Nov 1943, 20 May, 15 Nov 1949, 15 June 1966; *Age* (Melb), 14 June 1966; K. Gray, The Acceptable Face of Feminism: the National Council of Women of Victoria 1901-1919 (M.A. thesis, Univ Melb, 1988); YWCA of Aust papers (Univ Melb Archives).

KATE GRAY

CARSON, SIR NORMAN JOHN (1877-1964), businessman, was born on 27 August 1877 at St Kilda, Melbourne, eldest child of David Carson [q.v.3], boot importer, and his native-born wife Anne Jane, née Baker. Educated at Brighton Grammar School, in 1893 Norman joined Dougharty & Tickell, stock and station agents who were associated with the Newmarket stockyards. He moved in 1896 to the woolbrokers and stock and station agents, Australasian Mortgage & Agency Co. Ltd; after some time in their wool and produce stores, he became a travelling representative. In August 1904 the firm was taken over by Australian Mortgage, (Mercantile from 1910) Land & Finance Co. Ltd. At the Independent Church, Kew, on 12 September 1911 he married Edith Riley with Congregational forms.

Like his uncle Duncan Carson [q.v.7] (a founder of the Sydney firm Winchcombe [q.v.12] Carson Ltd), Norman worked as an auctioneer. In August 1913 he was appointed A.M.L. & F.'s wool and produce manager in Melbourne. On the removal of the Australian head office to Sydney, Carson took over as Melbourne manager in January 1929. He declined appointment as Australian general manager for personal reasons and because he thought that he would be more useful to the company were he to maintain his local contacts.

Finding that his 'many outside interests' took an increasing amount of his time, in late 1945 Carson retired from A.M.L. & F. He had long been involved with the Melbourne Wool Brokers' Association (chairman 1932-35) and the National Council of Wool Selling Brokers (vice-president 1939-45). A member of the Victorian State Wool Committee in World War I and of the Central Wool Committee in World War II, he was a director (1950-54) of UK-Dominion Wool Disposal Ltd. From 1945 he served on the Australian Wool Realization Commission (chairman 1950-60) which oversaw the disposition of the wartime stockpile; for this work, he was appointed C.M.G. in 1952. Through A.M.L. & F., Carson was a director (1938-64) of Northern Assurance Co. Ltd; he was also chairman (1951-63) of Carlton & United Breweries Ltd and a director (1943-63) of the Union Trustee Co. of Australia Ltd. A long-time friend of the chairman of G. J. Coles [q.v.] & Co. Ltd, he was, as well, a board-member (1945-61) of that firm. Carson was knighted 'for services to Australian industry' in 1961.

Having moved his daughters from Methodist Ladies' College, he was involved with a group of parents and old girls in purchasing Toorak College from the Misses Hamilton in 1927, in the formation of Toorak College Ltd and in the school's relocation at Frankston. He was a foundation member (1927-63) of its council and made several generous donations to the school; the library, opened in 1960, is named after him. Interested in a wide range of hospital and welfare organizations, including the Lord Mayor's Fund and the baby health centre scheme, he sat on the board of management of the Alfred Hospital in 1940-64. A man of 'cheerful, progressive outlook', Sir Norman belonged to the Australian Club and Royal Automobile Club of Victoria, and to the Metropolitan and Kew Golf clubs. He was an active Rotarian (State president 1938-39). In his leisure time he enjoyed gardening.

Carson died on 28 January 1964 in East Melbourne and was cremated; his wife, son and two daughters survived him. His estate was sworn for probate at £101 946, and his will made provision for prizes at Toorak College and the Alfred Hospital.

J. D. Bailey, *A Hundred Years of Pastoral Banking* (Oxford, 1966); J. Robinson, *The Echoes Fade Not* (Melb, 1987); *Annual Reports*, Alfred Hospital, 1940-64, *and* Carlton & United Breweries, 1951-63, *and* G. J. Coles & Co. Ltd, 1945-61; *Pastoral Review*, 15 Dec 1945, 24 Feb 1964; *Herald* (Melb), 28 Jan 1964; *Age* (Melb) and *SMH*, 29 Jan 1964; AML&F records, 1904-45 (ANUABL).

P. A. PEMBERTON

CARSON-COOLING, GEORGE (1896-1960), headmaster, was born on 31 May 1896 at Milton, Brisbane, a twin and sixth child of John Arthur Cooling, a clerk from England, and his Irish-born wife Sara, née Kennedy. A scholarship boy at Brisbane Grammar School, in his third year there George won the Earl of Meath Challenge Cup in an essay competition open to all school students in the British Empire. Proceeding to the University of Queensland (B.Sc., 1918; M.Sc., 1920), on 7 December 1917—only days after his final undergraduate examinations—he enlisted in the Australian Imperial Force. He reached the Western Front in October 1918, by way of Egypt and England, and was posted to the 5th Divisional Artillery. Promoted to extra regimental sergeant in March 1919 and given educational duties, he taught Australian soldiers awaiting demobilization. He was discharged in Brisbane on 13 August 1919.

In 1920 Cooling was appointed to teach chemistry at Ipswich Grammar School. Two years later he returned to Brisbane Grammar. At the Church of St Michael and All the Angels, New Farm, on Christmas Day 1922 he married with Anglican rites Harriet Maud Carson, a niece of Baron Carson of Duncairn, the Irish barrister and politician; soon after, Cooling added Carson to his surname. He became in turn senior chemistry master, senior science master, senior English master and second master. Considerate and approachable, Carson-Cooling had piercing, dark eyes and a keen sense of humour. He was an inspiring and polished speaker with a fine, resonant voice. Following his appointment as headmaster in 1940, pupil numbers rose. In 1943 the Department of Public Instruction reported that 'the Headmaster rules with dignity and firmness and has the loyal co-operation of his staff. The boys are manly, courteous, well-behaved and obedient and the general tone is good'. Class discussions were commended for offering 'evidence of pleasing freedom from repression and a healthy development of self-discipline'.

That year Carson-Cooling published *Education in Post-War Reconstruction*. Having received a copy of the monograph, George Bernard Shaw responded, 'it is remarkable that my conclusions should agree so exactly with yours'. In outlining some of his ideas, Carson-Cooling explained that 'in common with many educationists throughout the world, I feel that education in its present form has failed in its duty to humanity'. He advocated extension of the school leaving age to 18 and free education to tertiary level for all. Within the school system, he proposed the abolition of external examinations and all unnecessary competition (including premierships in sport), an increase in the length of the school day to eight hours and a radically revised curriculum. These suggestions created a considerable stir and the press deemed his theories to be 'outrageous'. In a community where many were schooled to regard anything further than a basic education as an expensive luxury, he achieved little but derision, even from his colleagues.

In 1945 rumour spread at the school that Carson-Cooling was spending time with a married woman and neglecting his responsibilities. He took sick leave late in 1946, leaving the second master to present the annual report and Harriet in charge of the boarding-house. She died of cancer on 11 February 1947. In July Carson-Cooling was named as co-respondent in divorce proceedings against Freda Hazel Allan, née Blight, and the board of trustees resolved to terminate his appointment the following month. On 24 June 1948 he married Freda at Albert Street Methodist Church, Brisbane; she was a writer, aged 37. Ostracized from educational circles and from polite society, he joined the public service as a clerk. In 1949 he published an account of his life at Brisbane Grammar: interspersed with his views on education, it was wryly entitled, *Here's a Villain*. A former pupil later saw him serving behind the counter at David Jones [q.v.2] Ltd's store, Sydney.

Survived by his wife, and by the daughter and son of his first marriage, Carson-Cooling died of coronary vascular disease on 17 July 1960 at Indooroopilly, Brisbane, and was cremated with Methodist forms. Despite his occasional vanity, affectation and eccentricity, many of his pupils believed that, had he remained at Brisbane Grammar, he would have been recognized as 'one of the great headmasters and educationists of this century'.

Brisb Grammar School Mag, 1914-18, 1947; *Courier-Mail*, 9 Mar 1940, 19 July 1960; *Truth* (Brisb), 23 Nov 1947; Brisb Grammar School Archives.   MAXWELL A. HOWELL.

CARTER, LIONEL LEWIN (1890-1968), industrial advocate and employer representative, was born on 6 October 1890 at Williamstown, Melbourne, sixth child of Thomas Frederick Carter, a grocer from Ireland, and his English-born wife Emily Jane, née Knight. In 1896 the family moved to Perth where Lionel was educated at the Newcastle Street State School and Perth Technical College. Peripatetic in his early career, he worked as a clerk, blacksmith, steam-hammer driver, optician and as a trainee chemist. He studied theology, joined the Methodist Home Mission and was successively posted to Dumbleyung, Lake Grace and Menzies.

On 7 August 1915 Carter enlisted in the Australian Imperial Force and on 21 November married Amy Edith Norman in the Methodist Church, Albany. Commissioned in February 1916, he served on the Western Front with the 48th Battalion and was promoted captain in April 1917. He was the last man to withdraw when his company held ground in the face of an enemy advance near Zonnebeke, Belgium, on 12 October 1917; he was awarded the Military Cross. In April 1918 near Dernancourt, France, he was severely wounded and lost his right eye. After medical treatment in Britain, he returned to Australia, 'chock full of confidence' and ready for new challenges. His A.I.F. appointment terminated on 3 March 1919.

That year Carter stood unsuccessfully as a Nationalist against J. M. Fowler [q.v.8] and John Curtin [q.v.] for the seat of Perth in the House of Representatives. Restless and 'unfit for indoor duty', he worked as a commercial traveller before joining a real-estate firm. He was returned to the Legislative Assembly in 1921 as the member for Leederville, but was defeated in 1924 when Labor ousted Sir James Mitchell's [q.v.10] coalition government. Carter found the parliamentary system unwieldy, rued his lack of legislative training and was frustrated by the 'party wheel'. As a back-bencher, he felt that his voice 'cried in the wilderness' and he grew disillusioned, but he had been a member of the royal commission on repatriated soldiers of the A.I.F. (1923).

Already an industrial advocate, he was made executive secretary of the Western Australian Employers' Federation in 1929. With a dynamic personality, brilliant advocacy and a shoestring budget, Carter created a strong, umbrella organization that handled all local industries. Under pressure and in troubled times he regularly appeared in State and Commonwealth arbitration courts, tackling wage-fixing and awards, the 44-hour week, price pegging, negotiations with the Australian Workers' Union and other bodies, unemployment, industrial unrest and strikes.

Carter repeatedly clashed with (Sir) Walter Dwyer [q.v.8], the presiding judge of the Western Australian Arbitration Court, and was a powerful influence on the Australian Council of Employers' Federations. His most publicized and acrimonious wrangle occurred in May 1943 with E. J. Ward [q.v.], Federal minister for labour and national service, whom Carter accused of habitually, mischievously and unethically attacking employers' integrity. He cited Ward's pronouncement that, by opposing price control, employers were 'sabotaging the war effort'. Ward retorted that Mr Carter 'was not a very important person'. Backed by his W.A.E.F. principals, Carter asserted that the minister was interfering with the proper working of the arbitration process. The debate was widely covered on radio and in the press. In July the federation lost its quota for paper for the *Employers' Industrial Digest*, which did not reappear until 1947.

He left the W.A.E.F. in 1949 to establish Carter's Motors at Bunbury. In 1958 a group of Perth businessmen invited him to direct the Western Australian Trade Bureau. Carter's task was to manage a political campaign in favour of free enterprise and against the Unfair Trading and Profit Control Act (1956). Highly conservative and an experienced confrontationist, he was in his element —preparing press releases, authorizing broadcasts and initiating political cartoons. The campaign contributed to the defeat of A. R. G. Hawke's government in March 1959.

Almost six feet (182.9 cm) tall, Carter was well built and had a fair complexion. He was a gregarious man, an excellent speaker and had a wry wit. At Green Gables, his Mount Lawley home, he enjoyed tennis parties and musical evenings, and at the Charles Street Methodist Church he sang bass solo. Involved with Legacy, he also supported his wife's work for the Mofflyn Children's Home. During World War II he had been a volunteer at Western Command and sang at fund-raising concerts with Billy Edwards in a group called 'The Specialists'. Carter always marched on Anzac Day; he belonged to the Returned Services League of Australia and the 5th Military Lodge. Survived by his wife and four sons, he died on 30 March 1968 at Claremont and was cremated.

F. K. Crowley, *State Election* (Perth, 1959); *V&P* (WA), 1923, 1 (3); *London Gazette*, 14 Dec 1917; *Employers' Industrial Digest* (Perth), Apr-June 1943, Jan 1947; *Albany Advertiser*, 24 Nov 1915; *West Australian*, 14 Mar 1921, 1 Apr 1968; family papers and information from Mr D. P. Carter, Como, Perth; information from Mr F. S. Cross, Ravenswood, Western Australia, and Mr J. Cooke, Confederation of Western Australian Industry, Perth.   WENDY BIRMAN

CARTLEDGE, JACK PICKERING (1900-1966), public servant, was born on 3 July 1900 at Southwark, Adelaide, son of Herbert Cartledge, locomotive fireman, and his wife Eliza Ann, née Pickering. Educated at Petersburg (Peterborough) High School and on a scholarship at Adelaide High School, Jack won a bursary to the University of Adelaide (LL.B., 1921). He was articled to F. G. Hicks and admitted to the Bar on 15 December 1921. Next year he joined the Attorney-General's Department. Cartledge had a ruddy complexion, sleek, fair hair and, as a young

man, a toothbrush moustache. On 4 July 1923 he married Margerie Vortmann in the registrar general's office, Adelaide.

Appointed assistant parliamentary draftsman about 1927, Cartledge worked with (Sir) Edgar Bean [q.v.] on revising and consolidating more than 1200 bills passed between 1837 and 1936; they published them in nine volumes as *The Public General Acts of South Australia* (1937-40). Cartledge was appointed C.M.G. in 1947 and in 1959-65 was draftsman-in-charge of statutes. An intensely private man who belonged to no clubs, he read, played golf and devoted much of his time after 1945 to the South Australian Housing Trust.

Having been chairman (from 1934) of the Local Government Advisory Committee, in 1937-40 he chaired the Building Act Inquiry Committee which considered the need to replace insanitary or ramshackle houses with new ones. In 1938 the committee undertook Adelaide's first survey of substandard housing, classified over 25 per cent of rental housing as slums and recommended government action. Cartledge inspected the buildings which he described as 'old, damp, decayed, badly-lit, ill-ventilated and vermin-infested'. The experience affected him deeply and influenced his drafting of the Housing Improvement Act (1940).

He impressed the new premier (Sir) Thomas Playford, who was keen to expand the State's recently formed housing trust. Playford appointed him its deputy-chairman (1940) and chairman (1945), in succession to Sir William Goodman [q.v.9]; he also made Cartledge chairman (1941) of the Building Act Advisory Committee. Regarded as a 'key official', Cartledge became closely identified with Playford's use of the trust as a tool in the State's economic development. The mass construction of inexpensive houses in large estates became typical of the era; the social consequences of this development were of less concern to politicians and civil servants.

Cartledge chose the trust's staff astutely, notably Alexander Ramsay [q.v.], general manager in 1949-78. They directed a huge operation, building more than 48 000 houses, shops and factories, operating an immigration programme and constructing the satellite town of Elizabeth. Cartledge showed keen interest in the town's affairs; he first opposed, then supported its becoming a separate, local-government area. He was, as well, chairman of the State's Local Government Officers Classification Board.

After Cartledge had retired in 1965, Playford appointed him permanent chairman of the trust. Survived by his wife and son, Cartledge died of pulmonary embolism on 23 July 1966 in North Adelaide and was cremated. Ramsay praised his intellect, humanity and leadership: 'Trust developments . . . continue to pay tribute to this service to the community, and Trust policy to bear the imprint of his fertile mind'.

M. Galbreath and G. Pearson, *Elizabeth, the Garden City* (Adel, 1982); D. A. Cumming and G. C. Moxham, *They Built South Australia* (Adel, 1986); S. Marsden, *Business, Charity and Sentiment* (Adel, 1986); S. Cockburn, *Playford* (Adel, 1991); Building Act Inquiry Cte, *PP* (SA), 1940, 2 (34); *News* (Adel), 1 June 1927; *Advertiser* (Adel), 12 June 1947, 25 July 1966.   SUSAN MARSDEN

CARTWRIGHT, GEORGE (1894-1978), soldier, was born on 9 December 1894 at South Kensington, London, son of William Edward Cartwright, coach trimmer, and his wife Elizabeth, née Stracey. Migrating alone to Australia in 1912, George took a job as a labourer on a sheep-station in the Elsmore district, near Inverell, New South Wales. On 16 December 1915 he enlisted in the Australian Imperial Force and became an original member of the 33rd Battalion, formed in February 1916 as part of the new 3rd Division. In May he embarked for England where the division trained before moving to France in November. Cartwright was wounded in action on 9 June 1917 at Messines, Belgium, but remained on duty. He was one of 271 officers and soldiers from the battalion who were victims of the Germans' concentrated gas-attack at Villers-Bretonneux, France, on 17 April 1918. After being hospitalized, he rejoined his unit in June.

On 31 August 1918 the Australian Corps assaulted the enemy's formidable position at Mont St Quentin, overlooking Péronne. The 33rd Battalion attacked south-west of Bouchavesnes at 5.40 a.m. Lacking adequate artillery support at the outset, the leading troops were stopped by machine-gun fire from a post at the corner of Road Wood. Without hesitation, Private Cartwright stood up and walked towards the gun, firing his rifle from the shoulder: he shot the gunner and two who tried to replace him. Cartwright then threw a bomb at the post and, covered by the explosion, rushed forward, capturing the gun and nine German soldiers. Cheering loudly, the Australians renewed their advance. Cartwright was awarded the Victoria Cross. On 30 September, during the attack on the Hindenburg line, he was wounded in the head and left arm, and evacuated to England. Having received his V.C. from King George V, he returned to Australia and was discharged from the A.I.F. on 16 May 1919.

Cartwright lived in Sydney and worked as a motor mechanic. On 25 June 1921 he married Elsie Broker at St Stephen's Anglican Church, Chatswood; they were to have two children before being divorced. He served in the Militia's 4th-3rd Battalion and was commissioned on 25 February 1932. Mobilized for full-time service on 5 March 1940, he was promoted captain (1942) and performed training and amenities duties in Australia. Cartwright was placed on the Retired List on 11 May 1946. He found employment as an assistant-cashier and married Evelyn Mary Short on 4 September 1948 in the Congregational Church, Pitt Street, Sydney.

In 1956 Cartwright visited London for the V.C. centenary celebrations; he returned there for biennial reunions of the Victoria Cross and George Cross Association. He was a quiet, unassuming man, 5 ft 7 ins (170.2 cm) tall, with black hair and a dark complexion. Survived by his wife, and by the son of his first marriage, he died on 2 February 1978 at Gordon and was cremated. His widow presented his V.C. and other medals to the Imperial War Museum, London. He is commemorated in the New South Wales Garden of Remembrance, Rookwood.

C. E. W. Bean, *The A.I.F. in France*, 1918 (Syd, 1937); L. Wigmore (ed), *They Dared Mightily* (Canb, 1963) and second ed revised and condensed by J. Williams and A. Staunton (Canb, 1986); *Reveille* (Syd), Aug, Nov 1968; *SMH*, 19 May 1956, 15 Feb 1969, 5 June 1970, 8 July 1972, 16 Feb 1978.   ANTHONY STAUNTON

CARVER, SIR STANLEY ROY (1897-1967), statistician and economist, was born on 7 February 1897 at Goulburn, New South Wales, third child of Arthur James Carver, hairdresser, and his wife Martha Ann, née Studman, both native-born. Educated at Newcastle High School, on 6 April 1916 Stan joined the New South Wales Department of Public Instruction as a clerk. That year he enrolled as an evening student at the University of Sydney where he was to study English and economics (B.A., 1921). Carver enlisted in the Australian Imperial Force on 17 June 1918, served briefly in France after the Armistice and was discharged in Sydney on 5 September 1919. He married Frances (Fanny) Harriet Horberry on 25 November 1922 at the Methodist Church, Eastwood.

In February 1920 he had been appointed compiler, first grade, in the State Bureau of Statistics and Registry of Friendly Societies and Trade Unions. His designation was changed in 1923 to compiler and literary assistant, positions which enabled him to develop his aptitude for statistics. In the 1920s Carver contributed to successive editions of the *Official Year Book of New South Wales* which included a notable section on the State's industrial history; he was seconded in 1929 as secretary to the royal commission into the coal industry, chaired by (Sir) Colin Davidson [q.v.8]. Promoted assistant government statistician (in the renamed Bureau of Statistics and Economics) in 1933, Carver accepted varied and extensive responsibilities at a time when administrative departments employed few professional economists. He assisted (Sir) Bertram Stevens's [q.v.12] government to grapple with the financial problems of the Depression and in 1936 accompanied Stevens on a visit to Britain. There, Carver met the economists J. M. (Baron) Keynes and Colin Clark.

Carver's 'extensive unpublished research' on income distribution was used by Clark and J. G. Crawford in their work, *The National Income of Australia* (Sydney, 1938). On 5 August 1938 Carver was appointed government statistician. After World War II began, he held the additional (Federal) responsibility of acting-deputy prices commissioner in New South Wales. In 1940, while retaining his State position, he was selected to perform the duties of Commonwealth statistician in the absence of (Sir) Roland Wilson. The arrangement continued until 1946, was resumed in 1948 and was formalized in March 1951 with Carver's appointment as acting Commonwealth statistician.

Centralized wartime planning had required the development of new statistical indices of manpower, production and prices. During the 1950s Carver gave 'personal attention' to the formulation of successive retail price statistics: the 'C' Series Index, the Interim Retail Price Index and the Consumer Price Index. The use of social surveys as planning tools was inaugurated by H. P. Brown [q.v.] and D. V. Youngman, under Carver's direction. Despite his initial distrust of 'sampling methods', in the early 1950s surveys were conducted of retail establishments, and of wage and salary taxpayers.

The key involvement of the Bureau of Census and Statistics in the Federal government's economic planning led to the recognition of a need for 'a unified national organization' which would 'satisfy modern demands'. With persistence and tact, Carver convinced the separate State offices to unite with the Commonwealth. After the Statistics (Arrangements with States) Act was passed in 1956, agreements were reached with individual States for an integrated statistical service under Carver who was confirmed as Commonwealth statistician on 20 August 1957.

Sometimes listed as one of the 'seven dwarfs'—a group of Federal public servants who were influential in economic policy-making during and after World War II—Carver was essentially a statistician, 'with a statistician's respect for the value of evidence'. His professional scepticism was matched by his painstaking effort. The postwar expansion of his field was achieved without compromising his standards of 'sound and acceptable data'. Appointed O.B.E. (1954) and knighted in 1962, Carver retired from both his Commonwealth and State posts on 6 February that year. The Statistical Society of Australia made him an honorary life member in 1966.

A quiet, retiring man, Sir Stanley played golf and enjoyed the bush. He died of acute pulmonary oedema on 22 July 1967 at Ryde, Sydney, and was cremated; his wife, son and daughter survived him.

C. Forster and C. Hazlehurst, *Australian Statisticians and the Development of Official Statistics* (Canb, 1988); *Economic Record*, 43, Dec 1967; *Aust J of Statistics*, 10, no 1, Apr 1968; E. K. Foreman, Development and Co-ordination Division—Historical Note (ts, 1977, held in Deposit collection, Aust Bureau of Statistics L, Belconnen, Canb).

MARGOT KERLEY

CASCARRET, CLARE JOSEPHINE; *see* DALLEY

CASEY, GAVIN STODART (1907-1964), author and journalist, was born on 10 April 1907 at Kalgoorlie, Western Australia, second son of Frederick Arthur Casey, a native-born surveyor, and his wife Jean Stodart, née Allan, from Scotland. Gavin admired and was influenced by his father and by Frederick's mates, and was to describe them as 'strong, vigorous, hot-tempered, easy-laughing men'. Both his parents died before he was 17. Following a 'pretty sketchy State school and School of Mines education', he began a cadetship with the Kalgoorlie Electric Light Station, but left to work in Perth as a motorcycle salesman. In 1931 the Depression forced him back to Kalgoorlie where he took jobs as a surface-labourer and underground electrician at the mines, raced motorcycles and became a representative for the Perth *Mirror*. On 8 February 1933 he married Dorothy Wulff at the Anglican Cathedral of St John the Baptist, Kalgoorlie. Poverty plagued them, long after their return to Perth next year.

With aspirations to be a writer, by 1936 Casey was publishing short stories in the *Australian Journal* and the *Bulletin*. In 1938 he was foundation secretary (president 1941-42) of the West Australian branch of the Fellowship of Australian Writers. His collections of short stories, *It's Harder for Girls* (Sydney, 1942), which won the S. H. Prior [q.v.11] memorial prize in 1942, and *Birds of a Feather* (Perth, 1943), established his reputation. Realistic in their treatment of place and incident, his stories showed—beneath the jollity and assurance of his characters—inner tensions, loneliness, unfulfilled hopes, and the lack of communication between men and women.

Unpretentious and self-mocking, 5 ft 8 ins (172.7 cm) tall, with green eyes, an olive complexion, black hair and a moustache, in January 1941 Casey was employed as a reporter and feature writer by the *Daily News*. Having enlisted in the Militia in 1930, he was mobilized in February 1942 and posted to the Army Education Service in October. He was discharged in January 1943 to become a publicity censor and deputy-director of information in Western Australia. In February 1944 he joined the Commonwealth Department of Information, Canberra, as a journalist and served as a war correspondent in the South-West Pacific Area. From 1945 he headed the New York and then the London branch of the Australian News and Information Bureau; he returned to Canberra in 1947 as the bureau's chief publicity officer, a post which he held until 1950.

During his time in New York, Casey's unsteady marriage began to founder. Dorothy found it impossible to endure her husband's increasing alcoholism and they were divorced in 1947. She later wrote respectfully, but honestly, about their relationship in *Casey's Wife* (Perth, 1982). At the registrar's office, Canberra, on 31 December 1948 Gavin married his American secretary Jessie Lorraine, née Ladd, late Craigie (d. 1964), a divorcee. He had already published a novel, *Downhill is Easier* (Sydney, 1945), depicting the fatal case of a gradual slide into crime, and a novella, *The Wits Are Out* (Sydney, 1947), a light-hearted, albeit critical, account of a suburban 'keg party'.

From 1950 Casey worked as a freelance journalist in Canberra and Sydney, and published *City of Men* (London, 1950), a saga set on the goldfields. Back in Perth in 1956, he was employed by the *Daily News* as its book-review editor. He wrote further novels: *Snowball* (Sydney, 1958) examined the interaction between Aborigines and Whites in a country town, *Amid the Plenty* (Sydney, 1962) traced a family's struggle against adversity, and *The Man whose Name was Mud* (Melbourne, 1963) developed his study of character. With Ted Mayman, he produced a history of Kalgoorlie, *The Mile That Midas Touched* (Adelaide, 1964).

Although critics have observed that Casey's novels did not live up to the promise of his short stories, they have drawn comparisons between his earlier work and that of Henry Lawson [q.v.10]. Beneath 'the easy yarning style and gently melancholy tone, [there is] a consistent emphasis on hardship that is tempered, for the male at least, by the conviviality of mates'. In their perceptiveness

and in their execution, both authors rank among the finest exponents of the genre.

Lovable, gregarious and popular, Casey found 'the commonplace interesting and touching'. In debt, he died of tuberculous pulmonary fibrosis on 25 June 1964 at the Repatriation General Hospital, Hollywood, Perth, and was cremated with Anglican rites. The son of his first marriage, and two sons of his second, survived him.

J. Graham, *Perth and the South-West* (Perth, 1962); B. Bennett (ed), *The Literature of Western Australia* (Perth, 1979); Univ WA, *Critic*, 10 July 1964; *Overland*, no 30, Sept 1964; *Meanjin Q*, 23, no 4, Dec 1964; *Realist* (Syd), 16, 1964; *Aust Q*, 38, no 3, 1966; *Artlook*, no 11, 1976; *Aust Literary Studies*, 9, no 2, Oct 1979; *Weekend News*, 27 June 1964; *Kalgoorlie Miner*, 1 Oct 1976; Mss of Casey's unpublished works (NL); S. Murray-Smith papers, box 113 (LaTL).   ANTHONY FERGUSON

CASEY, RICHARD GAVIN GARDINER, BARON CASEY OF BERWICK, VICTORIA, AND THE CITY OF WESTMINSTER (1890-1976), engineer, diplomat, politician, governor and governor-general, was born on 29 August 1890 in Brisbane, eldest child of Richard Gardiner Casey [q.v.3], pastoralist and politician, and his Queensland-born wife Jane Eveline (Evelyn Jane), née Harris. Richard senior, the son of Cornelius Casey [q.v.1], worked as a jackeroo, did well as a manager of properties in New South Wales and then became a minor partner in three Queensland holdings. Partly of convict stock, and twenty years younger than her husband, Evelyn came from a notable family: her father George Harris [q.v.4] and her maternal grandfather George Thorn [q.v.6] had been Queensland parliamentarians, and an uncle George Henry Thorn [q.v.6] had been premier in 1876-77.

Poor seasons and low prices impoverished Richard senior and in 1893 he moved his family to Melbourne where he prospered as a company director, partly by drawing on connexions made in Queensland with Thomas and Walter Hall [q.v.9], major partners in the fabulous Mount Morgan Gold Mining Co. Ltd. Affluence was to free young Richard from material worries for the rest of his life, but his father was stern, dominating and misanthropic, and Richard was less privileged in emotional terms. Living in the family mansion, Shipley House, at South Yarra, he was educated as a day-boy at Cumloden School, St Kilda, and then for three years at the nearby Melbourne Church of England Grammar School. With a bent towards science rather than classics, he spent one year (1909) as an engineering student at the University of Melbourne before sailing to England and entering Trinity College, Cambridge (B.A., 1913;

M.A., 1918); he graduated with second-class honours in the mechanical sciences tripos. As a student he had been a keen debater and oarsman, rowing for Trinity at Henley, and he saw something of France and Germany. He returned to Australia and, on his father's instruction, worked at Mount Morgan (his father was now chairman of the company) until war broke out in August 1914.

Appointed lieutenant in the Australian Imperial Force on 14 September 1914, Richard junior embarked for Egypt next month. He was to serve throughout the war and rise to major, but in all those years he never commanded men. He began as an orderly officer and then aide-de-camp to Major General (Sir) William Bridges [q.v.7], commander of the A.I.F.'s 1st Division, and in August 1915 he became a staff captain with the 3rd Brigade at Gallipoli. Casey was evacuated with fever in October, but recovered in time to be appointed general staff officer, 3rd grade (intelligence), with the 1st Division, just before its move to the Western Front and the nightmare of the Somme in 1916. He observed operations, and collected and sifted information; in January 1917 he was awarded the Military Cross and was made brigade major of the 8th Brigade. This demanding position entailed regular visits to the front under trying and hazardous conditions; for his work he was awarded the Distinguished Service Order in 1918. From February that year he was G.S.O.2 (training), on the staff of the Australian Corps.

Like so many others, Casey in later life rarely referred to his war service, though letters and diary fragments make it clear that both at Gallipoli and on the Western Front he went through three distinct phases: almost boyish exuberance, followed by depression, then retreat into a detached military professionalism. Like so many, he was angered by the appalling carnage about him, and saw himself as part of a younger generation which would do better. It was perhaps unfortunate that these harrowing years of the most intense experience were, as with the previous apprenticeship to his father, spent in the service of much older and more senior men and tended to confirm his assumption that advancement came best, not from competition with equals or marshalling the support of juniors, but from nomination by seniors who rewarded courtesy, deference and industry. Twice mentioned in dispatches, he resigned his A.I.F. commission and was demobilized in London on 10 June 1919. He transferred to the Reserve of Officers and in the early 1920s served as a part-time intelligence officer at Army Headquarters, Melbourne.

Casey's brother DERMOT ARMSTRONG (1897-1977) had also served in World War I. He was born on 27 August 1897 at South Yarra, Melbourne, and educated in England at Eton and the Royal Military Academy, Woolwich. Commissioned in the Royal Horse Artillery on 23 November 1916, he was sent to the Western Front; he was awarded the M.C. (1918) for directing the fire of his battery in the face of an enemy advance. After the Armistice he worked on a number of archeological 'digs' in England. At St John's Anglican Church, Toorak, Melbourne, on 27 August 1924 he married Gwynnedd Mary Browne, a grand-daughter of A. S. Chirnside [q.v.3].

From 1929 he assisted the British archeologist (Sir) Mortimer Wheeler on sites in England. Back in Australia, Dermot was a founder of the Anthropological Society of Victoria, president (1947) of the Royal Society of Victoria and honorary ethnologist to the National Museum of Victoria for forty years. He joined Wheeler at Taxila, India (Pakistan) in 1944. Resuming fieldwork in Australia in the 1950s, he became a foundation member of the Australian Institute of Aboriginal Studies. Colleagues acknowledged his skill as an excavator and his mastery of exposition, and appreciated his modesty, good humour and generosity. Dermot died on 13 September 1977 at Mount Macedon, Victoria, and was cremated; his wife, daughter and son survived him.

With the death of his father in 1919, Richard had returned immediately to Melbourne. Although young for such positions, he virtually succeeded to his father's seats on company boards, including that of Mount Morgan. Involvement in mining employers' organizations and with groups behind the National Party followed. These affiliations, in turn, led to friendship with S. M. (Viscount) Bruce [q.v.7] who became prime minister in 1923. At this point Casey was not much interested in politics, seeing himself rather fancifully as an antipodean Henry Ford. Casey bought a small steel-manufacturing firm in Melbourne, but found that industrial greatness would not come from making cutlery. He also joined a syndicate to back the brilliant Melbourne engineer A. G. M. Michell [q.v.10] who had designed a new kind of automobile engine. Casey took the engine to America, but could not persuade the Ford Motor Co. or General Motors Corporation to accept it. He then found himself leading an incredibly busy work and social life, but it was a self-set busyness leading nowhere very obvious, and he scarcely hesitated when, in 1924, Bruce urged him to join the Commonwealth Public Service and go to London as Australia's liaison officer (in effect, as Bruce's political agent).

Casey was a great success in London. With the credentials valued by their caste, he was liked by the senior men in Westminster and

Whitehall, and he was able to report to Bruce on everything from British defence policy to club gossip. He was Bruce's eyes and ears at the Imperial centre, but he also acted for him in some political matters and for the Australian government in some League of Nations forums in 1925-30 at Geneva, Switzerland. While in London, and by now 35, he married 34-year-old Ethel Marian Sumner (Maie) Ryan on 24 June 1926 at St James's parish church, Westminster. His bride was the only daughter of Sir Charles Ryan [q.v.11], a Melbourne surgeon, and Lady Ryan (Alice, née Sumner). Maie was related by blood or marriage to leading Victorian families, among them the Clarkes, Chirnsides and Grices [qq.v.3,4,8,7,9]; a Ryan aunt had married a brother of the 6th Duke of Buccleuch and (9th Duke of) Queensberry; Maie's only brother Rupert [q.v.] had married Lady Rosemary Hay, daughter of the 21st Earl of Erroll. A lively and gregarious woman with an interest in the arts, Maie was to provide for Casey a marriage of unusually close and constant companionship. Supportive but also stimulating, she would give him strength and direction.

Because Bruce was not very interested in developing an independent Australian diplomatic service, Casey became restless in London and concerned about his future. Yet, it was only with Bruce's electoral defeat in 1929 and his replacement as prime minister by Labor's James Scullin [q.v.11]—with whom Casey could not hope to enjoy the intimate, almost filial, relationship possible with Bruce—that Casey decided to return to Australia and enter Federal politics. He left England in February 1931. At the elections later that year, and endorsed by the new United Australia Party led by Joseph Lyons [q.v.10], Casey was returned to the House of Representatives for the Victorian seat of Corio.

An indifferent orator, shy, stiff, unmoved by parliamentary ritual and irritated by what seemed to him the inexpert amateurishness of government in a democracy, Casey was poorly equipped for politics, but he worked very hard to educate himself in public finance, was prepared to live in Canberra (which he loathed), was modestly adventurous in his views (questioning protection if it did not benefit consumers), and in career terms he was successful. He became an assistant-minister at the Treasury in 1933, treasurer in 1935, and minister for supply and development in 1939. As treasurer, he had to cope with Australia's slow emergence from the Depression and, while he invested immense effort in preparing legislation and a bureaucratic structure for a national insurance scheme, the scheme was shelved because of approaching war, and he left no monuments. Encouraged initially by Bruce to see himself as a certain

prime minister, Casey was never in the race, and certainly not after the move of (Sir) Robert Menzies [q.v.] from Victorian to Federal politics in 1934. When Lyons died in 1939, Casey stood for the U.A.P. leadership, and thereby the prime ministership, but he came in behind Menzies and even old W. M. Hughes [q.v.9]. Casey did not help his cause by joining the Country Party leader Sir Earle Page [q.v.11] in appeals to Bruce to return, and, in any case, he was far too modest and too inept in organizing support for himself.

In 1939 the Menzies government decided to establish Australia's first diplomatic posts, in Tokyo and Washington. Casey was asked to head the legation in Washington. Appointed Australian minister to the United States of America, he resigned from parliament on 30 January 1940. As in London, he proved to have an extraordinary flair for diplomacy, and, despite representing a country of which Americans knew little, soon enjoyed access to President Franklin D. Roosevelt and the friendship of leading politicians, officials and servicemen. Although he was now 50, boyish charm and courteous deference opened doors to him, and he was a keen convert to the American craft of public relations.

Unable to cope with H. V. Evatt [q.v.], minister for external affairs in the Labor government which assumed power under John Curtin [q.v.] in October 1941, Casey was keen to move on, and was happily surprised when, in March 1942, (Sir) Winston Churchill offered him the position of United Kingdom minister of state in the Middle East, based in Cairo. Australia still saw itself as a British country, but this move to United Kingdom political service during war raised some Australian hackles, not least those of Curtin. It also raised hackles in Whitehall, especially in the Foreign Office. Casey's principal duties in Cairo were to contain an almost impossible range of civil problems in the region—some of it colonial and some independent, some of it occupied and some not, most of it under some form of British control but some of it ruled by the French—and to assist the theatre's military commanders at a political level. Long hours, a difficult climate, and the problems of a large and varied jurisdiction took their toll on his health, but he did the job probably as well as it could be done, and certainly well enough to satisfy Churchill who, in November 1943, offered him the governorship of Bengal, India.

On 22 January 1944 Casey took over a Bengal devastated by famine and politically sundered by nationalist agitation and communal conflict. He could (and for a time did) impose governor's rule, but ordinarily had to work with a ministry, and yet he, rather than his chief minister, would be held responsible by New Delhi and London for the good government of Bengal. He improved the civil service, fought with a measure of success for funds from New Delhi, encouraged development projects, and kept his ministries in a condition of reasonable harmony and efficiency. As in Cairo, he was shocked by British racial snobbery, and he tried to break down walls between Government House in Calcutta and the local community. Casey had his share of prejudices and assumed that everyone else had them, though he thought it ungentlemanly and politically unwise ever to show them. Again, the climate, the long hours and the frustrations of the job affected his health, but he was counted a success, and for many years to come would enjoy the affection of the politicians and officials he had known in Calcutta—more especially those who were Moslems and became Pakistanis. Casey himself was to regard his Bengal years as perhaps the most fruitful of his life.

Encouraged by some people when he was away to see himself as a successful challenger to Menzies—who now led the new Liberal Party but whose ability to woo the electorate was under question—Casey arrived home in April 1946 determined to re-enter Federal politics (with this in mind, he had refused a peerage while in Bengal). He failed to organize pre-selection in time for the elections in September that year, and was at something of a loose end until he was persuaded to become federal president of the Liberal Party in September 1947. In this position he achieved much. Although somewhat out of touch with a new generation of politicians, he had retained his old social, army and business connexions, and it was estimated that his public appeals and remorseless private solicitations raised the then extraordinary amount of £250 000 for the party in 1947-49. He also proved adept at using public relations and advertising in the Liberal interest—and in the Casey interest.

Never very happy with democratic pluralism and group strife, during World War II Casey had been both impressed by the unity of purpose achieved by a national government in Britain and appalled by the social and political conflict he had seen in the Middle East and India: he returned to Australia preaching consensus in politics and industry as vital to the country's well-being. He did what little he could to break down the barriers that faced Catholics in the Liberal Party, raged against reactionary employers and bloody-minded employees, took a close interest in the new field of industrial psychology, held a kind view of trade unionism and even urged reform of the White Australia policy.

At the elections in December 1949 Casey was returned for the outer-Melbourne seat of La Trobe and, with J. B. Chifley's [q.v.] Labor government defeated, entered the Menzies

ministry as minister for supply and development (national development from March 1950) and for works and housing. He professed to enjoy these portfolios, even though the new government was more interested in containing inflation than spending on grand public works. Casey seemed, however, to suffer a severe bout of clinical depression and it was only when he succeeded (Sir) Percy Spender in 1951 as minister for external affairs that he began to recover. His problems were many, but high among them were lack of rapport with Menzies, and impatience with party and Federal politicking. The external affairs portfolio and especially the travel that went with it allowed some removal from Menzies and domestic politics. Casey remained an indifferent performer in parliament and in cabinet, and, unlike his predecessors Evatt and Spender, was not a policy innovator. He excelled rather as a minister-diplomat, courting his overseas counterparts to the point of achieving friendship with many of them. He also took a close interest in the administration of his department and in the welfare of its officers.

In public, Casey seemed to be a devoted Cold-War warrior, fervently supportive of Britain and the U.S.A., and deeply hostile towards the Soviet Union and China; he was the minister responsible for the Australian Secret Intelligence Service. In private, his views and at times his behaviour were very different. He came out against Britain's militant reaction to the nationalization of the Suez Canal in 1956, but he could not move Menzies and said nothing against Britain in public. Again, while at ease with Americans, excessive dependence on the U.S.A. distressed him. Year after year he campaigned in cabinet for greater Australian self-sufficiency in defence, but was confronted by colleagues who preferred the financially cheaper alternative of alliance diplomacy. Totalitarianism also distressed him, but he argued in private that —whatever one thought of it—a communist China must be accommodated and urged his fellow ministers to allow diplomatic recognition; again, they turned him down.

If Casey was an innovator at all, it was in constantly preaching the importance of Asia to an Australia which had taken little interest in it. He frequently visited Asia (and thereby forced the Australian press to take an interest), kept a close eye on aid to Asian countries and urged his young diplomats to concentrate on Asia rather than Europe. Casey had also given close attention to the Antarctic since the 1920s and played a leading part in the negotiation in 1959 of a treaty covering co-operation in exploration and scientific research there. A research station and several geographical features in Antarctica were named after him. Throughout the

1950s Casey was, as well, the minister responsible for the Commonwealth Scientific and Industrial Research Organization. Although tending to be impatient with theoretical work, he was personally committed to furthering the role of the C.S.I.R.O., and few other areas of government so absorbed him or allowed him to operate with such conviction.

In January 1960 Casey was made a life peer; next month he resigned from the ministry and parliament. It was by then something of an anomaly that an Australian should be appointed to the Upper House of another country's parliament, yet, for most Australians, Britain was still the mother country and few were inclined to quibble. Lord Casey ordered his time around annual trips to London and appearances in the House of Lords, but he had no obvious constituency, he was distressed to find that British interest in the old dominions was waning fast, and he warmed to the forms of Westminster no more than he had to those of Canberra. At home, he enjoyed having a seat (1960-65) on the C.S.I.R.O. executive; he involved himself in the Australian-American Association, the Australian-Asian Association of Victoria, the Freedom from Hunger Campaign, and International House at the University of Melbourne. Then, in mid-1965, he accepted appointment, and on 22 September was sworn in, as governor-general—nominated to his grateful surprise by Menzies.

Casey was the first Australian citizen to be recommended for the governor-generalship by a non-Labor government; provided that he performed well, it was unlikely that there would be a reversion to appointees from Britain. He did perform well, mainly because he took the office seriously and because he enjoyed it. More interventionist than convention encouraged, he interposed in disputes between 'his' ministers in the interests of harmony in 'his' governments, raised policy matters with ministers and senior public servants, and questioned submissions. He was fortunate in that he had the kind of presence which, while not very impressive in cabinet rooms or parliamentary chambers, was well suited to vice-regal office. And in Maie he had an ideal wife, sharply conscious of her dignity but down-to-earth. Casey also literally civilized the office. Averse to uniforms and plumes, he chose civilian forms which made it easier for men like (Sir) Paul Hasluck to succeed him.

While not as competent and stylish a writer as Maie, and inclined at times to look to others for drafts, Casey published a good deal: *Australia's Place in the World* (Melbourne, 1931), *An Australian in India* (London, 1947), *Double or Quit* (Melbourne, 1949), *Friends and Neighbours* (Melbourne, 1954), *Personal Experience 1939-1946* (London, 1962), *The Future of the Commonwealth* (London, 1963), *Australian Father and Son* (London, 1966), and *Australian Foreign Minister* (edited by T. B. Millar, London, 1972).

Retiring in April 1969, Casey lived out his days with Maie at Edrington—a substantial house (inherited by Maie and Rupert in the 1930s) on 1000 acres (405 ha) at Berwick, outside Melbourne—and at Little Parndon, a renovated townhouse in East Melbourne. Although now moving into his eighties, Casey did not enjoy the enforced quiet of retirement. Survived by his wife, daughter and son, he died on 17 June 1976 at St Vincent's Hospital, Fitzroy, and was buried in Mount Macedon cemetery. His estate was sworn for probate at $621 560 in Victoria and £64 899 in England.

Casey was the last of a kind. Australia's evolution towards full independence, culturally as well as constitutionally, meant that no Australian could ever again enjoy the range of appointments which fell to him. An engineer by training and inclination, and always most at home with the practical (typically, his passions were cars and planes, and he and Maie took up flying in the 1930s and remained keen pilots for most of their lives), he was at times out of his intellectual depth; nervous and shy, he was often ill at ease in public life and even to some extent in domestic life; ambitious, he lacked ruthlessness; wealthy, he tried to use his freedom in public service to a society disinclined to honour his caste. He was an unusually good man, but his was the morality of Edwardian secular gentlemanliness, and there were not many Edwardian gentlemen in the worlds in which he chose to operate. Above all else, he was a trier. He looked over his own shoulder and tried to be morally good; he tried to be a good husband (and succeeded); he tried to be a good father (and did not succeed so well); he tried to do well the many different jobs which came his way (and generally succeeded). Even his demanding father could not have found fault in terms of Casey's public trophies: apart from his peerage, he was a privy counsellor (from 1939), and was appointed C.H. (1944), G.C.M.G. (1965) and K.G. (1969). A portrait by J. P. Quinn [q.v.11] is held by the National Library of Australia.

W. J. Hudson, *Casey* (Melb, 1986) and for sources; Aust Inst of Aboriginal Studies, *Newsletter*, no 9, Jan 1978; *J of Hist Soc SA*, no 9, 1981; *Aust J of Politics and Hist*, 28, no 2, 1982; *Herald* (Melb), 11 Sept 1965; Casey papers (NL *and* AA, Melb).

W. J. HUDSON

CASH, DEIRDRE ('CRIENA ROHAN') (1924-1963), novelist, was born on 16 July

1924 at Albert Park, Melbourne, elder child of native-born parents Leo Evaristus Cash, salesman, and his wife Valerie Eileen, née Walsh, an operetta principal. Indulged as a gifted son of a highly literate, musical, self-consciously Irish-Australian Catholic farming family, Leo, an aspiring poet, disappointed them by becoming a Marxist *flâneur*, active behind the scenes in the 1930s New Theatre movement in Melbourne. He and Valerie were feckless parents, admired and resented; they divorced while the children were young. Deirdre and her brother were cared for by various relations, particularly Leo's family at Calca, South Australia, and, when the Depression forced it off the land, by his selfless unmarried sisters in Melbourne. Deirdre later boarded at the Convent of Mercy, Mornington. In this unsettled upbringing she began writing occasional unpublished stories.

After matriculating, Deirdre had tuition at her mother's expense at the Melbourne (Melba [q.v.10]) Conservatorium of Music, Albert Street, East Melbourne. Her lilting, if brittle, coloratura and sensibility were attuned to informal ballad singing. A petite brunette, she was fetching, competitive, tempestuous, waspish and witty. She clung to her clan and Catholic identity while bridling against their restraints. Deirdre was pregnant when, on 4 February 1948, she married a law student Michael Damien Blackall at St Augustine's Church, Melbourne, but she was also lunging at a gentility she could not sustain. Leaving her husband and son, she earned a living as a torch-singer and ballroom-dancing teacher, occasionally on the fringe of the demi-monde. Although the autobiographical glow of her novels suggests otherwise, she was teetotal, earthy but not indecent in speech, and never in trouble with the police. Similarly, her fictional, family-based portraits are sometimes romanticized, sometimes cruel. In 1954 she met her true *inamorato*, a coastal seaman Otto Ole Distler Olsen, whom she followed to various ports. Her divorce having been granted on 18 October 1956, she married him eleven days later in the office of the government statist, Melbourne.

Hospitalization in Perth, for suspected tuberculosis, and the threat of having to take up occupational therapy, turned Cash from a scribbling raconteur into a fully-fledged writer. Rejected by several Australian publishers whom she subsequently scorned as jingoistic, Cash had *The Delinquents* (1962) launched under her Irish pseudonym ('Criena Rohan') in London, where the novel grabbed immediate attention. A compassionate tale, set in the 1950s, of defiant, street-wise, 'bodgie-widgie' teenagers oppressed by their elders and the welfare state, it was dubbed 'a back-street *Tristan and Isolde*' by London's *Daily Mail*. The *Times Literary Supplement* called the characterization of the heroine Lola 'a triumph'. In 1989 *The Delinquents* became a teenage cult film with Kylie Minogue as Lola.

Cash was dying from a now correctly diagnosed colonic carcinoma when she finalized her second novel, *Down by the Dockside* (London, 1963), which attempted a more complex characterization of alienated, working-class people in wartime Melbourne. While her often sentimental and melodramatic social realism lacks literary polish and form, this weakness is offset by Dickensian humour, sharp dialogue, throwaway gibes and a gutsy narrative style. She allegedly wrote a third novel, 'The House with the Golden Door', but, if so, the manuscript mysteriously disappeared. Survived by her husband and their daughter, and by the son of her first marriage, Cash died on 11 March 1963 at the Alfred Hospital, Melbourne, and was buried in Fawkner cemetery. Her estate was sworn for probate at £1788.

B. Reid, introductions to C. Rohan, *The Delinquents* (Melb, 1986) and *Down by the Dockside* (Melb, 1984); L. Baker (comp), *Calca 1885-1991* (Calca, SA, 1991); *Times Literary Supplement*, 16 Feb 1962, p 101; *Sun News-Pictorial*, 27 Sept 1962; information from Miss M. Cash, Hawthorn, Melb; personal information.   JAMES GRIFFIN

CASIMATY, GREGORY GEORGE (1890-1972), **ANTHONY GEORGE** (1897-1977) and **BASIL GEORGE** (1903-1962), fishermen, fishmongers and restaurateurs, were born on 6 January 1890, 15 March 1897 and 2 February 1903 at Kithira, Greece, sons of Georgios Grigoriou Kasimatis (d. 1959), farmer, and his wife Stamatina, née Kastrisios. The brothers received an elementary education and, with their father's encouragement, emigrated separately to Australia.

Gregory left Greece in 1905. Arriving in Sydney, he washed dishes at the Acropolis Café for nine months, spent several years in the fruit trade in Queensland and in 1911 came back to Sydney. In 1914 he went to Hobart where, with Peter Galanis, he established the Britannia Café in Elizabeth Street; next year he took over the business in partnership with his brother Anthony. Casimaty Brothers initially leased, then bought the premises occupied by their café and by the fish shop which they had added. By 1918 they had expanded into cray-fishing, exporting their catch to Sydney, and they later pioneered the scallop industry in Tasmania. Appointed fishmongers to the governor Sir James O'Grady [q.v.11], the brothers expanded their partnership to include Basil. In 1928 Gregory returned to Kithira, married Katina (Kathleen) Haros and brought her to Tasmania. He visited New Zealand in 1935 to open the firm's crayfish markets there. The Casimatys developed seine-fishing in Australian waters, commissioning the trawler, *Nelson*, and acquiring the *Margaret Twaits*. In 1941 the Tasmanian Fisheries Board of Enquiry investigated allegations of monopolizing and of environmental damage by Casimatys' fishermen, only to find the claims unproven. Anticipating better markets, the brothers sent the boats to Sydney, but became disillusioned when Victor Vanges, skipper of the *Margaret Twaits*, was drowned off Eden and the trawlers were commandeered for war service in New Guinea.

During the Depression the Casimatys had provided hundreds of Christmas dinners for the needy and promoted a free-milk scheme for schoolchildren. In World War II the family supported the Tasmanian branch of the Australian Red Cross Society; for his contribution to the international organization, Gregory was awarded the Red Cross medal of Greece (1946) and the Silver Cross of Phoenix (1950). In 1945 Gregory's case against the Federal government for attempting to tax and to raise loans under the national security regulations was settled out of court.

Hobart's Greek Orthodox Church of St George was built in Antill Street in 1957 on land provided by the Casimatys. The family also gave land on Kithira for an old people's home which was named Kasimateion in their honour. Among the first Greeks to settle in Tasmania, the Casimatys supported later immigrants from their homeland and fostered Greek-Australian relations.

Portly and 5 ft 6 ins (167.6 cm) tall, Gregory was known for his hospitality and for his practical jokes. He was an active member (from 1936) of the Rotary Club, Hobart, he supported the Tasmanian Society for the Care of Crippled Children and he was foundation president (1953) of the Greek Community of Hobart and Tasmania. Kathleen shared her husband's community involvement; a life member of Elizabeth Street State School Mothers' Club and of the Inner Wheel Club, she was a member of Task Force Action for Migrant Women and acted as a volunteer interpreter for many years. Ill health obliged Gregory to retire in 1965. Survived by his wife, two sons and four daughters, he died on 22 March 1972 at Sandy Bay and was buried with Greek Orthodox rites in Cornelian Bay cemetery.

Anthony sailed from Greece in 1912 and worked in Sydney cafés before joining Gregory in Hobart in 1915. Anthony returned to Greece in 1931 where, two years later, he married Adamantia (Manty) Haros, sister of Gregory's wife. Back in Hobart, he was a member of the Chamber of Commerce and often acted as spokesman for the retail fish industry. A life member of the Goulburn Street State School Mothers' Club, Manty was a volunteer medical interpreter for the Greek community for forty years. Immaculately dressed and with impeccable manners, Anthony was small and rather shy, yet he had boundless energy, enjoyed life and indulged a passion for hunting. After some fifty years in the fish shop, he retired in 1967. Survived by his wife, two sons and two daughters, he died on 14 March 1977 at Sandy Bay and was buried in the same cemetery as his brothers.

Basil joined his brothers in Hobart in 1923, but went back to Greece in 1929 to care for their ageing parents. While there, he married Panagiota (Nota) Tzoutzouris in 1935; they were to remain childless. The couple came to Tasmania in 1939. Basil soon left the partnership to open the California Fruit Co. in Hobart. During the 1940s he purchased Stockman, a property at Kempton, on which he ran cattle and sheep, while Nota managed the fruit business. Responsible for introducing Greek films to Tasmania, he was president of the Greek Community of Hobart and Tasmania (1958-60) and of the Olympia Soccer Club. Survived by his wife, he died of a coronary occlusion on 18 August 1962 at Sandy Bay and was buried in Cornelian Bay cemetery.

G. V. Brooks, *30 Years of Rotary in Hobart* (Hob, 1955); *Fisheries Newsletter*, 7, no 1, Feb 1948; *Mercury* (Hob), 27 Dec 1930, 10 Dec 1935, 23 July, 24 Dec 1941, 20 Aug 1962, 23 Mar 1972; Casimaty family papers (held by author, Cambridge, Tas).

ANNE TUCCERI

CASSIDY, SIR JACK EVELYN (1893-1975), barrister, was born on 12 June 1893 at Hargraves, New South Wales, eldest of ten children of native-born parents John Wilson Cassidy, schoolteacher, and his wife Mary Catherine, née Smith, both of Northern Irish stock. John died when Jack was 15. Mary, who had been only 16 when married, became a schoolteacher at Newcastle. She was to die, aged 99, at Muswellbrook, outliving Jack and six of her other children. Jack went to Mudgee District Public School, passed the senior public examination in 1911 and in February 1912 became a cadet draftsman in the Department of Lands. An evening student at the University of Sydney (B.A., 1917; LL.B., 1920), he paid his way by teaching at Abbotsholme College, Killara, where his pupils included Harold Holt [q.v.]. Cassidy served articles of clerkship with the Sydney solicitors Sly & Russell before being admitted to the Bar on 23 February 1922.

He established himself on the first floor of

old Selborne Chambers, Phillip Street, which, as he wrote, 'provided a collection of practitioners . . . able and colourful'. Cassidy augmented that colour by his own energetic style. On 19 December 1928 at St Martin's Anglican Church, Killara, he married Gwynneth (Gwen) Jeannie, daughter of G. A. Waterhouse [q.v.12].

A 'born trial lawyer', with 'an amazing record of forensic successes' and outstanding skill as a cross-examiner in all jurisdictions, Cassidy was one of the great advocates of his generation and took silk on 24 October 1938. He appeared in many *causes célèbres* and represented the defendant in appeals (1945-47) in the notable medical negligence proceedings, *Hocking* v. *Bell* [q.v.], before the High Court of Australia and the Privy Council. In London for that purpose, he visited Germany to observe the trials of war criminals by the International Military Tribunal at Nuremberg. Back in Sydney, in the 1940s and 1950s Cassidy held retainers for the respective proprietors of the *Daily Telegraph, Truth* and the *Daily Mirror*, and accordingly appeared in many defamation trials. He was senior counsel for the defendant in the protracted 'American Flange-Rheem' litigation (1962-63), in which his closing address occupied seventy-two days. His practice demanded most of his time, but he often surprised colleagues 'by the wide range of his interests and contacts . . . in particular with leading overseas scholars'.

Closely involved in the corporate organization of the Bar, Cassidy was a founder and chairman of Counsel's Chambers Ltd, and arranged for the construction of Wentworth and Selborne chambers as principal buildings to house the Bar. He and his wife were active in establishing the Liberal Party of Australia. Gwen was a member of its provisional executive, while Jack was vice-president (1945-56) of the New South Wales division. In 1945 he was founding chairman of the Political Research Society Ltd, set up to investigate any organization or party (especially the Communist Party of Australia) 'which appears to be deceiving the public'. He was also a founder of the Woollahra Action Committee, then influential in the selection of candidates for Woollahra Municipal Council.

A director of David Lynn Ltd, Industrial Steels Ltd, Mainguard (Australia) Ltd and other companies, Cassidy lived in the Eastern Suburbs, played golf and tennis, and belonged to the Australian, University and Royal Sydney Golf clubs. He was knighted in 1968. Gwen had been appointed M.B.E. in 1964 for her work in community services. Sir Jack retired in December 1974. Survived by his wife and son, he died on 11 June 1975 in St Luke's Hospital, Darlinghurst, and was cremated.

Aust Law J, Oct 1975, p 600; *Daily Telegraph* (Syd) and *SMH*, 12 June 1975; J. Cassidy, Selborne Chambers (ts, nd, held by NSW Bar Assn, Syd); Cassidy papers (ML); information from Lady Cassidy, Bellevue Hill, and Mr D. I. Cassidy, Syd.

JOHN KENNEDY MCLAUGHLIN

CASTELLANO, FRANCESCO (1899-1976), medical practitioner and internee, was born on 23 July 1899 at Grumo Appula, near Bari, Italy, son of Fedele Castellano, medical practitioner, and his wife Maria, née Lozito. Having graduated in medicine from the University of Naples, in 1929 Francesco migrated to Queensland. He was one of ten Italian doctors who achieved registration in the State through an Anglo-Italian treaty (1883) which provided for reciprocal recognition of British and Italian medical degrees. Castellano was appointed to an Italian community hospital at Ingham. He spent three years there in partnership with Dr Francesco Piscitelli before moving to Cairns to join Dr Angelo Vattuone. After Vattuone left for Brisbane in 1935, Castellano was the sole Italian medical practitioner at Cairns.

Following Italy's entry into World War II on 10 June 1940, the names of six Italian doctors headed the Queensland list of those who were to be interned for alleged fascist activities. The evidence submitted against Castellano was mainly based on the use made of his premises at Cairns for meetings of the Armando Diaz Society (founded by Vattuone in 1934). Vattuone's confiscated correspondence indicated that the society sought to replace the recently-defunct *fascio* at Cairns. Apart from organizing ritualistic ceremonies —to commemorate the anniversary of Benito Mussolini's march on Rome (1922)—and sponsoring poorly-attended propagandist lectures, the self-proclaimed fascist doctors achieved little. They did, however, convince Australian security officers that Mussolini's boasts about fifth columns in Italian emigrant communities were to be taken seriously. Once war hysteria abated, the absurdity of confining the doctors became obvious, especially when there was a critical need for their skills in rural areas.

On 15 June 1940 Castellano was sent to Gaythorne camp. He bore his internment in a co-operative and dignified manner, and was released in late 1943 to practise in western Queensland. On 23 October 1944 he married a 36-year-old clerk Ursula Vette Horgan (d. 1969) at St Mary's Catholic Church, South Brisbane; they were to remain childless. Next year he established a practice in the capital where the Italian community was soon to be swollen by postwar immigration. His experiences had in no way dampened his ardour to promote things Italian. At the centre of initiatives to create cultural, sporting, social and welfare institutions, he was patron of the Corale Giuseppe Verdi, the Azzurri Soccer Club, the Italian Tennis Club and the Italo-Australian Centre.

With Sir Raphael Cilento, in 1953 Castellano courageously revived the Brisbane branch of the Dante Alighieri Society, which had been suspended in 1939. (Run by a predominantly fascist committee, the society had been established by Vattuone in 1936 to promote the Italian government's purposes.) Castellano was president from 1953 until 1967. He was also foundation president (1972) of the Italian Consular Welfare Committee (later Co.As.It.). Regarded as the 'dean' of Italian communities, he lectured throughout Australia on his national culture. Castellano had a reputation for understanding, kindness and generosity: in his medical practice he sent out accounts 'once and once only'. On 26 January 1972 he married a divorcee Maria Doralice Pizzica, née de Francesco, at the general registry office, Brisbane. Survived by his wife and three stepdaughters, he died on 11 December 1976 at New Farm and was buried in Nudgee cemetery.

M. Brändle (ed), *The Queensland Experience* (Brisb, 1986); *MJA*, no 1, 1977, p 971; *Leader* (Brisb), 2 Jan 1977; M. A. Gurdon, Australian Attitudes to Italy and Italians, 1922-36 (B.A. Hons thesis, Univ Qld, 1970); D. Dignan, The Internment of Italians in Queensland (ts, held by author, Univ Qld), *and* for references to Cwlth and State government internment files.   DON DIGNAN

CASTLE HARRIS, JOHN: *see* HARRIS

CATALAN, ANSELM MARY (1878-1959), Benedictine abbot, was born on 16 November 1878 at Corella, Navarra, Spain, son of Michael Catalan. Educated at the Benedictine Abbey of Montserrat, Anselm joined the Order in 1894 and was ordained priest in 1902. At St Bede's College, Manila, he served as professor (1903-05) and rector (1909-15); he was also procurator of the Benedictine missions in the Philippines. In 1914 Dom Anselm was appointed abbot visitor to the Cassinese Congregation in Spain. Next year he was elected superior of the monastery at New Norcia, Western Australia; Pope Benedict XV made him an ordinary of this abbey nullius, giving him quasi-episcopal responsibilities for New Norcia's contingent diocese which spanned 30 000 sq. miles (77 700 km²).

He was to see his community and rural diocese affected by the social and economic repercussions of two world wars and the Depression, and by drought, rabbit plagues and isolation. The experience increased his natural caution and frugality. Nevertheless, Catalan completed the transformation of New Norcia from an Aboriginal mission—pioneered by Abbot Salvado [q.v.2]—to a monastic township wherein educational institutions, liturgy, cultural heritage and community work were fostered. He did not become embroiled in the conscription issue during World War I; while sympathetic to General Franco, he avoided partisanship at the time of the Spanish Civil War and directed his monks to follow suit. New Norcia remained relatively untouched by the centralizing policies of the chief protector of Aborigines A. O. Neville [q.v.11] and his successor F. I. Bray.

Tutored by his wide experience, Catalan planned effectively for the training of Spanish and Australian novices, and for the management of the abbey's personnel, resources and missionary endeavours. In addition, he helped to establish diocesan churches, convents and schools in the developing townships in the wheat-belt of his diocese, and supported the inception of Boys' Town, Bindoon. Buildings were added to New Norcia's schools and boarding facilities were expanded for Aboriginal pupils. Catalan recruited in Spain for nuns and in 1935 reconstituted the Sisters as Benedictine Oblates Regular to care particularly for Aboriginal children at New Norcia and Kalumburu. Their hours of schooling gradually increased and the curriculum shifted from vocational training to conventional education.

Outdoor activities for the children included participation in organized sport and in the harvesting of fruit and olives: on such outings the Benedictine Sisters allowed them to search for bush tucker. The mission, however, made limited use of Aboriginal languages, except at Kalumburu (near King Edward River) where the monks recorded and used the Pela tongue. The Japanese bombed this mission in 1943.

Dom Anselm travelled regularly and extensively throughout his diocese, and met national and international obligations. He had visited the Drysdale River Mission (established 1908) which he transferred to Pago before settling it at Kalumburu in 1937. In some respects the demands of his diocese detracted from the overall management of the abbey, but he wryly held that parishes provided safety valves for the monastic community. Devotional organizations were provided for the laity and he instituted the Benedictine Secular Oblates in 1944. To ensure that his monks and clergy were well trained, he built a seminary and also directed students to St Patrick's College, Manly, Sydney, and to institutions in Rome. (Cardinal)

James Knox was one of his protégés. Monks with artistic or musical skills were also encouraged to study interstate or overseas, and the choral and orchestral tradition of New Norcia strengthened significantly in his abbacy. In 1946, at New Norcia, Catalan hosted a national celebration of the centenary of missionary work in Western Australia.

The abbot's recreational activities ranged from music to reading, and from working in the monastery's orchards to keeping ferrets. He maintained a regular assault on the hundreds of birds that wreaked havoc in the orangery, olive groves and vineyards. The ferrets were Catalan's practical response to the rabbit-warrens on the abbey's farms and bemused unsuspecting visitors when they were shown as his pets. Well known in Perth's business circles and the Catholic community, Catalan had a reserved but hospitable manner, appreciated by many. After eight years retirement at the abbey, he died on 29 July 1959 at St John of God Hospital, Subiaco, and was buried at New Norcia.

Benedictine Community of New Norcia, *The Story of New Norcia* (New Norcia, WA, 1979), and *Pax*, 29 July 1959; D. F. Bourke, *The History of the Catholic Church in Western Australia* (Perth, 1979); *Univ Studies in Hist*, 5, no 1, 1967; *Record* (Perth), 25 Sept 1915, 6 Aug 1959; *SMH*, 11 Oct 1937.

CLEMENT MULCAHY

CATO, JOHN CYRIL (1889-1971), photographer, was born on 4 April 1889 at Launceston, Tasmania, son of Albert Cox Cato, salesman, and his wife Caroline Louise, née Morgan. An uncle, the landscape photographer J. W. Beattie [q.v.7], introduced young Jack to photography in 1896. By then he was taking classes run by Lucien Dechaineux [q.v.8] at Launceston Technical School. Having trained from 1901 under Percy Whitelaw and John Andrew, both local portrait photographers, in 1906 Cato set up his own studio in Beattie's Hobart premises. He applied to be the official photographer to (Sir) Douglas Mawson's [q.v.10] 1911 Australasian Antarctic Expedition, but was passed over in favour of Frank Hurley [q.v.9].

Disappointed at his rejection, Cato travelled that year to Europe and worked for various photographers in London, among them Claude Harris and H. Walter Barnett [q.v.7], the fashionable society and vice-regal portraitist. Cato contracted tuberculosis and left England in search of a warmer climate. From 1914 he spent six years working in South Africa. The views and portraits which he took there were suitably worked up in the atmospheric, art-photography style of the day and earned him a fellowship (1917) of the Royal Photographic Society of Great Britain. In 1920 he returned, ill, to Tasmania. He married Mary Boote Pearce (d. 1970) at the Methodist parsonage, Melville Street, Hobart, on 24 December 1921.

In 1920-27 Cato operated his own portrait-studio in Hobart before moving to Melbourne where Dame Nellie Melba [q.v.10], whom he had met in London, introduced him to society and to theatrical circles. Possessing the technical skills and the sensitivity necessary to engage the interest and confidence of the sitter, and to convey a mixture of truth and interpretation in the final image, he ran a successful portrait-studio in Melbourne for two decades. He maintained links with professional associations and amateur clubs through occasional exhibitions of his best work, and was senior vice-president (1938) and a life member of the Professional Photographers' Association. A keen stamp-collector from childhood, Cato was also president (1935) of the Royal Philatelic Society of Victoria. He was to sell his stamps for about £10 000 in 1954.

Frustrated by restrictions on materials during World War II, Cato retired from his Melbourne studio in 1946 to begin a career as an author. In addition to a large number of articles in photographic, philatelic and other magazines, he published an autobiography, *I Can Take It* (1947), a pictorial documentary, *Melbourne* (1949), and *The Story of the Camera in Australia* (1955). A racy, ebullient writer, he was chronicler for the Savage Club. In 1960-63 he was photography columnist for the *Age*. Survived by his son and daughter, he died on 14 August 1971 at Sandringham and was cremated. A collection of his photographs is held by the Australian National Gallery, Canberra.

D. M. Dow, *Melbourne Savages* (Melb, 1947); G. Newton, *Silver and Grey* (Syd, 1980); *Professional Photography in Australia*, 23, no 5, Aug-Sept 1971; *Philately from Australia*, Sept 1971; *Photofile*, 4, no 1, Autumn 1986; *Argus*, 4 May 1951; *Herald* (Melb), 5 Mar 1954; I. Cosier, Jack Cato (M.A. prelim thesis, Univ Melb, 1980).

GAEL NEWTON

CAVILL, JAMES FREEMAN (c.1867-1952), hotelier, was born at Carlton, Melbourne, according to his repeated testimony, although in 1930 he claimed to have been born about 1879 in North Sydney, son of Frederick Cavill [q.v.7], bathkeeper. Information about Jim's early life is sketchy and sometimes contradictory. According to various stories, he moved to Sydney, ran away from home at the age of 9, swam the English

Channel, was a circus acrobat, and prospected for diamonds at Kimberley, South Africa, and for gold at Coolgardie, Western Australia. In 1900 he asserted that he had married Ada Louisa Shadlow (d. 1929) at South Yarra, Melbourne, on 17 February 1890, but the event was unrecorded. They were to have five children.

Having moved to Queensland, by 1899 Cavill was living at Spring Hill, Brisbane. From 1902 he operated as a tobacconist and hairdresser at 202 Edward Street (later part of the Tattersall's Club building). In 1915 he obtained the licence of the Royal Exchange Hotel, Toowong; in 1920 he transferred to the Kedron Park Hotel, opposite the race-course owned by John Wren [q.v.12]. Relinquishing this hotel to his eldest son Richard in 1923, Cavill moved to Elston where he bought twenty-five acres (10 ha) opposite the defunct Main Beach Hotel.

At this relatively isolated place, near a long, white, surf beach, he erected a sixteen-bedroom, timber building and named it the Surfers Paradise Hotel. The enterprise was timed to coincide with the opening in 1925 of a bridge over the Nerang River which made Elston more accessible to tourists. Standing in four acres (1.6 ha) of garden, with a private zoo, Cavill's hotel quickly became popular, particularly with the 'younger set'. The district was being subdivided into seaside allotments and Cavill disposed of half his land by 1930. On 20 February that year at St Stephen's Presbyterian Church, Sydney, he married 33-year-old Elsie Elma Ronfeldt who had accompanied him to Elston; Jim said that he was 52.

Powerfully built, Cavill had 'a gravel voice and an earthy vocabulary when his temper flared, which it did often'. He was a keen sportsman who kept himself 'fighting fit' and swam daily in the surf. In his small community the flamboyant hotelier promoted civic improvements, among them a Surfers Paradise Life Saving Club (1929) and a local progress association. With others, he lobbied successfully by 1 December 1933 to have the Elston place-name changed to the more glamorous Surfers Paradise. In 1936 Cavill's original building was destroyed by fire. He then erected a brick hotel where 'sophisticated' cabaret entertainment and accommodation (incorporating a celebrated 'honeymoon tower') attracted visitors from interstate and overseas. In 1945 the South Coast Town Council named the main thoroughfare, which passed the hotel, Cavill Avenue.

Survived by his wife and their son, and by a daughter and two sons of his first marriage, Cavill (said to be aged 90) died on 5 March 1952 at Surfers Paradise and was buried in Southport cemetery with Catholic rites. His estate was sworn for probate at £79 476. In 1957 the hotel was sold to Chevron Queensland Ltd for £350 000.

A. McRobbie, *Gold Coast Heritage* (Surfers Paradise, Qld, 1991); *South Coast Bulletin*, 20 Dec 1929, 17 Sept 1937, 12 Sept 1941, 12 Mar 1952, 11 Feb 1953; R. Longhurst, The Development of the Gold Coast as a Recreational Area to 1940 (B.A. Hons thesis, Univ Qld, 1978), *and* for bibliog; family information.

PAT FISCHER

CAWTHORN, MINNIE ELIZABETH (1898-1966), headmistress and aviatrix, was born on 23 August 1898 at Prahran, Melbourne, third child of William Cawthorn, a paper merchant from England, and his Victorian-born wife Fanny Adelaide, née Williams. (Sir) Walter Cawthorn [q.v.] was her brother. Educated locally and at Melbourne Girls' High School, Minnie taught for a year at Caulfield and in 1918 entered Melbourne Teachers' College where she completed the trained primary teachers' certificate. Appointments followed as temporary assistant at Swan Hill (1919), Sea Lake (1920-22), Kingsville (1923), and in suburban West Melbourne (1924), Mont Albert (1925) and North Fitzroy (1925-27). Inspectors saw her as energetic, intelligent, forceful, painstaking and capable of maintaining excellent classroom control.

Having completed a diploma of education (conferred in 1933) at the University of Melbourne, Miss Cawthorn was an assistant-teacher at Seymour (1927-29), Wonthaggi (1929-31) and Ararat (1932-33). In 1933 she motored across the continent to Perth to take up an exchange post at Northam High School. She returned to Melbourne in April 1934 and taught at Fitzroy and Williamstown before being appointed to Wangaratta High School.

In February 1939 Cawthorn was transferred to Mildura High School as senior mistress in charge of girls. She learned to fly, qualified as a civil pilot and became a flying instructor. An enthusiastic commissioner of the Sunraysia Company of the Girl Guides' Association, she expected the same impeccable standards of behaviour and dress from her guides as from her pupils, and was said to have stood on her head to demonstrate regulation underwear to them.

In February 1948 Cawthorn was appointed headmistress of Matthew Flinders [q.v.1] Girls' School (from 1950 Matthew Flinders Girls' Secondary School) at Geelong. Dilapidated and neglected, it was a 'dumping ground' for students who left school at 14 to work in the local mills. Under her vigorous leadership two new wings were added to the school, the grounds were brought into immaculate condition and in 1950 its pupils were the first in the State to sit for the Girls' Leaving Certificate. Through the Australian Headmistresses' Association, she lobbied for a matriculation class which was eventually attained in 1960. She aimed to equip all her girls not only to run a home but to take a place in the community.

Small and rather squat, Miss Cawthorn commanded unwavering respect from staff and students. Only those teachers who met her exacting standards remained. She joined numerous community groups which she skilfully exploited to gain influential support for her school and in 1955-56 was president of the Geelong branch of the National Council of Women. Although forbidding and rather austere at work, she relaxed and indulged her sense of fun at the beach house which she shared with her deputy and companion Anne Hooper at Anglesea: there she rode a surfboard, swam out to her craypots and, occasionally, after a whisky or two, turned catherine wheels from sheer exuberance.

After Miss Hooper's death, Miss Cawthorn retired in 1958 and for some years travelled restlessly in Europe, China and South East Asia. She spent her last years at her home at Buln Buln, Victoria, and died of myocardial infarction on 10 May 1966 at Parkville. Her body was bequeathed to the University of Melbourne for scientific research.

A. Hooper, *The Story of Flinders School, Geelong, 1856-1956* (np, nd); Education Dept (Vic), *Vision and Realisation*, L. J. Blake ed (Melb, 1973); *Matthew Flinders' Log*, Dec 1966, Dec 1981; *Geelong Advertiser*, 7 Feb 1948, 12 Dec 1958, 13 May 1966; *Age*(Melb), 11, 21 May 1966; Matthew Flinders Girls' Secondary School Archives, Geelong; teaching record: M. Cawthorn, Education History Service, Ministry of Education, Melb; information from Miss I. Bromwich, Miss J. Ranson, Mrs G. W. Macmichael and Mrs E. M. McKenzie, Geelong, Vic.   DIANE LANGMORE

CAWTHORN, SIR WALTER JOSEPH (1896-1970), soldier, diplomat and intelligence chief, was born on 11 June 1896 at Prahran, Melbourne, second child of William Cawthorn, a commercial traveller from England who later entered publishing, and his Victorian-born wife Fanny Adelaide, née Williams. Educated at Melbourne High School, Walter became a schoolteacher, as did his sister Minnie [q.v.]. He enlisted in the Australian Imperial Force on 3 February 1915 and was posted to the 22nd Battalion. Arriving at Gallipoli in September, he was promoted regimental sergeant major that month and commissioned on 9 November. During his time on the peninsula he kept a diary in which he recorded his experiences.

Moved to Egypt in January 1916, the battalion was transferred to France in March.

Near Armentières, Cawthorn suffered a severe shrapnel wound to the abdomen on 27 June and was evacuated to England. He returned to the Western Front in November. Sent to England for training duties in April 1917, he was promoted captain in May. Having rejoined his unit in August, he again went to England where his A.I.F. appointment terminated when he was commissioned in the Indian Army on 13 February 1918. In the 1920s he served in India with the 16th Punjab Regiment. At Marylebone Presbyterian Church, London, on 10 March 1927 he married a widow Mary Wyman Varley, daughter of Andrew Gillison [q.v.9]; their only son Michael was to be killed (1951) in the Korean War. Walter saw active service on the North-West Frontier (1930-35) and was later a general staff officer, grade 2, at the War Office, London.

Holding the local rank of colonel, in 1939 'Bill' Cawthorn (as he was familiarly known) took charge of the Middle East Intelligence Centre in Cairo. In 1941 he became director of military intelligence at General Headquarters, India, and was later an acting (temporary) major general. From October he held the additional post of deputy-director of intelligence, South East Asia Command. Mary also performed intelligence duties in World War II and served as an officer in the Women's Army Corps, India, for four years. In 1945 her husband was a member of the Indian delegation to the United Nations Conference on International Organization, held at San Francisco, United States of America. He was appointed C.B.E. (1941), C.I.E. (1943) and C.B. (1946).

Recommended by his friend R. G. (Baron) Casey [q.v.], the governor of Bengal, Cawthorn was sent to Melbourne in 1946 as Indian representative on the Joint Chiefs of Staff in Australia. From 1948 to 1951 he was deputy chief of staff of the army of newly-independent Pakistan, and forged strong links with local political and military leaders. In 1952 he was appointed director of the Joint Intelligence Bureau, a liaison section in the Department of Defence, Melbourne. Seeking 'a better outlet for Cawthorn's talents', Casey —now minister for external affairs—selected him for a five-year posting (1954-59) as Australian high commissioner to Pakistan. During Cawthorn's term the two countries were to enjoy close ties. Casey visited Karachi in 1956 and noted that, as a result of Cawthorn's rapport with 'top Pakistanis', 'we are much better informed than the much larger diplomatic posts'. Governor-General Iskander Mirza told Casey: 'We have no secrets from Bill Cawthorn'.

Knighted in 1958, Cawthorn was appointed high commissioner to Canada next year. His stay, however, was short. In September 1960 he was back in Melbourne as head of the

Australian Secret (Intelligence) Service, after being nominated by Casey for the post. With the Cold War intensifying, the job was a demanding one and he relied heavily on his able and experienced deputy W. T. Robertson. Cawthorn took a particular interest in Indonesian affairs and expanded the Jakarta office to be A.S.I.S.'s biggest station. It has been suggested that the organization played a significant role with the U.S.A.'s Central Intelligence Agency in creating an atmosphere for the overthrow (1966) of President Sukarno. A.S.I.S. also provided instruction in clandestine operations for members of the Australian Army Training Team Vietnam.

Sir Walter retired in July 1968. He lived at Little Tocknells, at Kallista in the Dandenong Ranges. Tall and dignified, with dark hair and a military moustache, he was a quiet, unassuming man whose demeanour endeared him to many. These attributes, coupled with his discretion and ability, had enabled him to progress from private to major general, and had earned him acceptance in the highest circles. In early 1970 he was admitted to hospital following a savage attack by an unknown assailant near the Melbourne Club; survived by his wife, Cawthorn died on 4 December that year in Melbourne and was cremated.

C. E. W. Bean, *The A.I.F. in France*, 1916 (Syd, 1929) and *The Story of Anzac*, 2 (Syd, 1940); B. Toohey and W. Pinwill, *Oyster* (Melb, 1989); *Age* (Melb), 7 Dec 1970; *SMH*, 27 Jan 1983; AWM records; information from Mr R. W. Cawthorn, Glen Iris, Melb.   PETER HOHNEN

CECIL, LIONELLO (1893-1957), tenor, was born on 20 September 1893 at Waverley, Sydney, and registered as Lionel Cecil, son of Abraham Robert Sherwood, a senior sergeant of police, and his wife Kate, née Heagan, both from Ireland. Educated at Sydney Grammar School, Cecil studied singing with Hector Fleming and made his concert début on 30 September 1912. His next teacher Andrew Black encouraged him to study abroad and Cecil left for Europe in March 1914 after giving a concert at Sydney Town Hall. That year he won a scholarship to the Verdi Regio Conservatorio, Milan, Italy, and from 1916 studied with Mario Pieraccini. Adopting the stage name 'Lionello Cecil', he made his opera début in 1918 at the Storchi Theatre, Modena, as the Duke in *Rigoletto*. He rapidly established himself as a leading operatic tenor of the Italian provincial houses. In London on a concert tour, on 21 June 1923 at the register office, Paddington, he married Argia Armanda Giustina Mattioni, a ballet dancer from Trieste, Italy.

For almost fifteen years Cecil gave hundreds of performances in such places as Pisa, San Remo, Parma, Verona and Bergamo. He made occasional appearances at more famous opera houses, including the Dal Verme and the Lirico, at Milan, with seasons at La Fenice, Venice (1921, 1925) and at the Costanzi, Rome (1925). Having toured South America in 1926, he sang next year with an Italian opera company in Austria, Switzerland, Germany and Spain. In 1931 he appeared at Nice and Marseilles, France. His recording career had begun in 1919 with discs made acoustically in England for Pathé. He sang tenor lead in the first microphone recording of *La Traviata* (Italian Columbia, 1928) and in *Madama Butterfly* (Italian His Master's Voice, 1929-30), and made his last recordings in 1942 (Columbia, Australia): these discs reveal a powerful lyric tenor and singing characterized by intelligence rather than virtuosity.

Under contract to the Australian Broadcasting Commission, in September 1933 Cecil returned to Australia; in 1933-34 he sang the lead in all but one of eighteen broadcast operas. He did studio and concert work across the country for the A.B.C. until 1942, and taught his own pupils (including Ken Neate) in Sydney. After touring New Zealand in 1937, Cecil sang Alfred Hill's [q.v.9] music in Ken Hall's film, *The Broken Melody* (1938). As a military censor during World War II, Cecil interpreted for Italian prisoners of war interned at Cowra. From 1942 he appeared as 'Lionel Cecil'. At the New South Wales State Conservatorium of Music in July 1944 he sang Canio in *Pagliacci*, in what was probably his farewell to the stage.

The master of some fifty operatic roles (of which Faust in Boito's *Mefistofele* was his favourite), Cecil possessed 'great personal charm and impeccable manners', and was an amiable, unpretentious man who enjoyed playing cards; stockily built, he had dark, receding hair, somewhat heavy features and a florid complexion. In the early 1950s his health deteriorated. Predeceased by his wife and survived by their son, he died of constrictive pericarditis on 13 November 1957 at St Leonards, Sydney, and was cremated with Anglican rites.

A. Gyger, *Opera for the Antipodes* (Syd, 1990); *SMH*, 1 Oct 1912, 22 Aug 1914, 21 Oct 1916, 22 June 1918, 10 Sept 1927, 26 Sept 1933; H. Simpson, ms article on the life and career of Lionello Cecil, c.1980 (held by Mr J. Simpson, Kedron, Brisb); information from Mr and Mrs H. R. Sherwood, Carlingford, and Mr S. Riddington, Harbord, Syd.   MICHAEL P. QUINN

CERUTTY, CHARLES JOHN (1870-1941), public servant, was born on 25 November 1870 at Sale, Victoria, second son of

John Cerutty, a draper from England, and his wife Elizabeth, née Stirling. Entering the Victorian Public Service on 30 April 1888, Charles worked as a clerk in the Department of the Treasurer. On 29 March 1894 at Thorpdale South, Gippsland, he married Wilhelmina Mercer with Wesleyan forms.

In 1897 Cerutty became secretary to the Public Service Reclassification Board; he held the post until June 1901 when he joined the Commonwealth Treasury as a sub-account-ant. He assisted in the development of the Federal financial system by helping to establish the Commonwealth Bank of Australia, to raise loans, to inaugurate invalid and old-age pensions, and to introduce maternity allowances. Promoted accountant (1910) and assistant-secretary (1916), he performed the duties of Treasury secretary and director of the Commonwealth Bank's note-issue department in the absences of J. R. Collins [q.v.8].

Having acted as auditor-general for the Commonwealth from April 1926, Cerutty was formally appointed to the post on 4 June. From the outset, he was a harsh critic of government waste. In charge of scrutinizing the nation's finances during the worst years of the Depression, he recommended that public expenditure be reduced, as well as advocating cuts in private spending on luxury items and leisure pursuits. He also urged that the unemployed should be made to work for sustenance payments. In his 1932 annual report he estimated that almost one thousand cases of fraud involving pensions had occurred during the financial year 1931-32. To reduce costs, he argued for a contributory system of old-age pensions which would compel workers to provide for their retirement.

In 1933-34 Cerutty angered politicians by blocking the planned transfer of his office to Canberra. Publicly, he denied refusing to move, and claimed that the government had agreed that it would be more efficient and economical for him to remain in Melbourne. His reports regularly expressed his complaint that the treasurer's annual statements of receipts and expenditure lacked clarity. In his final report (1935) he enlivened his usual discussion of the matter with a personal attack on the acting-treasurer R. G. (Baron) Casey [q.v.]. Some members of parliament accused Cerutty of exceeding his powers and an attempt was made to deprive him of money for his accrued leave. The ploy was unsuccessful. Cerutty remained defiant, claiming that he was 'always in the right' and that he had acted in the interests of taxpayers.

A man of upright and distinguished appearance, he was a hard worker whose competence and thoroughness were admired by his colleagues. A keen golfer and shooter, and a Freemason, he regarded his job as his 'profession and hobby'. Cerutty had been ap-

pointed C.M.G. in 1927. He continued to keep a watchful eye on the state of the nation's finances after his retirement in 1935. Having suffered from angina for two years, he died of a coronary occlusion on 19 January 1941 at Caulfield and was cremated. His wife and daughter survived him.

Herald (Melb), 8 Apr 1926, 16 Dec 1927, 2 June 1933, 1 Feb 1935; *Argus*, 20 Feb, 3 Dec 1932, 20, 23 Nov 1935, 20 Jan 1941; *Sun News-Pictorial*, 26 Oct 1933, 8 Aug 1936; *Smith's Weekly* (Syd), 30 Nov 1935; *Age* (Melb), 20 Jan 1941; C. J. Cerutty, Notes on His Career (Nov 1935, held by ADB, Canb).

ELIZABETH STEWART

CERUTTY, PERCY WELLS (1895-1975), athletics coach, was born on 10 January 1895 at Prahran, Melbourne, seventh child of Harry Richard Cerutty, accountant, and his wife Emily, née Neilson, both Victorian born. When Percy was 4, Emily left her alcoholic husband and struggled alone to bring up her six surviving children. Percy left state school at the age of 12 to take a job in a hardware store. In 1910 he joined the Postmaster-General's Department as a messenger, later becoming an assistant, a mechanic and finally a technician.

A frail youth who was declared unfit for military service, Cerutty competed for Malvern Harriers until 1918, but had an undistinguished athletic career: he suffered migraines and was often violently ill after races. On 7 November 1921 he married Dorothy Clara Barwell at the East Malvern Baptist Church.

In 1939 Cerutty suffered a nervous breakdown which obliged him to take six months leave from the P.M.G. It became a period of self-examination, during which he walked, read philosophy, psychology and poetry, wrote the first of some two hundred poems, joined a weightlifting club and resolved to resume running. Contemptuous of doctors, he decided to take charge of his own health, and applied himself to alternative medicine and natural diets, boasting that he had 'completely rebuilt' his body. Weightlifting added ten lb. (4.5 kg) to a wiry, eight-stone (50.8 kg) physique.

From 1942, in his second athletic career, Cerutty applied himself to the problems of conditioning the body for intensive running. Competing once more for Malvern Harriers, he had over one hundred races. He retired from running in 1950 as State marathon champion, having set Australian records for 30, 50 and 60 miles (48, 80 and 97 km).

In 1946 Cerutty had left his P.M.G. job and bought land at Portsea. After working on the property at weekends, he retired in 1959 to his shack among the sandhills, gave it the grand name of the International Athletic Centre and devoted himself to the task of coaching. His sheer success, and the passionate, eccentric method of it, made him an international celebrity. He trained dozens of fine runners, among them Herb Elliott, John Landy, Les Perry and Dave Stephens, and helped other champions, including Betty Cuthbert, Russell Mockridge [q.v.] and Jimmy Carruthers. Cerutty worked on the bodies and the minds of his charges. He made them read Plato, poetry and the Bible, fed them raw oats and wheat germ, sent them on punishing runs through tea-tree scrub and rugged, sandy terrain, and insisted that they set goals which could be achieved only by pain and sacrifice. He made them swim year-round in the ocean and shed all their clothes in the open at least once a day. He saw it all as a process of physical and mental conditioning, based on what he called a 'Stotan' creed—his own special mix of Stoic and Spartan disciplines.

Prickly and argumentative, Cerutty sometimes attempted to taunt the best out of his athletes. He said that he needed to enter their personalities. Some, like Landy, resented the intrusion and left; Cerutty never forgave them. Although Landy achieved his greatest success after breaking away, he always acknowledged a debt to Cerutty's early inspiration and conditioning. Elliott, his greatest pupil, absorbed all the Cerutty teachings. As Herb matured, he was able to laugh at his mentor's excesses, but he also wrote: 'Percy helped me . . . by releasing in my mind and soul a power that I only vaguely thought existed'.

Cerutty saw himself as a visionary with a noble mission. Some observers accepted his own view that he was a genius of sorts; others branded him an exhibitionist, a crackpot, a nuisance and a publicity-seeker. His behaviour was often unconventional: he stood on his head at a garden party, danced a jig on championship arenas, challenged the chairman of a television panel to a fight, was evicted often from Commonwealth and Olympic games villages, and wound up in police custody as Elliott scored the triumph of his career by winning the gold medal in the 1500 metres at the 1960 Olympics in Rome.

In 1955 Dorothy divorced Percy. On 3 March 1958 he married a divorcee Ellen Ann ('Nancy'), née Keene, late Armstrong, at the Unitarian manse, East Melbourne. Between 1959 and 1967 he published six books on his training techniques. In 1969, at the age of 74, he claimed that he was sick of running up sandhills, and ceased training athletes. Cerutty was appointed M.B.E. in 1972. Survived by his wife, and by the son of his first marriage, he died on 14 August 1975 at his Portsea home and was buried in Sorrento

cemetery. In 1989 he was among the first, small group of coaches whose names were admitted to the Sport Australia Hall of Fame, Melbourne.

H. Elliott, *The Golden Mile* (Melb, 1961); H. Gordon, *Young Men in a Hurry* (Melb, 1961); G. Kelly, *Mr Controversial* (Lond, 1964); K. Dunstan, *Ratbags* (Melb, 1980); *Daily Mirror* (Syd), 23 Aug 1969; *Nation Review*, 10-16 Jan 1975; *Age* (Melb), 15 Aug 1975; *Australian*, 15-19 Aug 1975; *Bulletin*, 23 Aug 1975; personal information.

HARRY GORDON

CHAMBERLAIN, AZARIA CHANTEL LOREN (1980-1980), missing infant, was born on 11 June 1980 at Mount Isa, Queensland, third of four children of New Zealand-born parents Michael Leigh Chamberlain, Seventh Day Adventist pastor, and his wife Alice Lynne (Lindy), née Murchison. Lindy stated that the name Azaria (pronounced As-ah-ria) is from the Hebrew and means 'blessed of God'. She weighed 6 lb. 5 oz. (2.9 kg) at birth and had 'dark, violet eyes', black hair and olive skin. At nine weeks she was fit and healthy.

On 13 August 1980 the family left home in their yellow, hatchback, Torana motorcar for a holiday in Central Australia. Arriving at Ayers Rock (Uluru), Northern Territory, on Saturday 16 August, they pitched a tent next to their car at a camp-site. On Sunday 17 August at about 8 p.m. Azaria was heard to cry out. Her mother went to the tent, found the baby missing and reported seeing a dingo. Despite extensive searches by Aboriginal trackers and others, on that dark night and later, the baby was never found. Items of her bloodstained clothing were located on 24 August among boulders near the base of the Rock. It was not until 2 February 1986 that her matinee-jacket was discovered nearby. Following an inquest at Alice Springs, on 20 February 1981 the coroner Denis Barritt concluded that Azaria had met her death when attacked by a wild dingo as she slept in her family's tent, and that an unknown person or persons had helped to dispose of the body.

The case was far from closed. In November 1981 the Supreme Court of the Northern Territory quashed the findings of the inquest. In Darwin a second inquest heard new forensic evidence, particularly about bloodstains, that led the coroner Gerard Galvin on 2 February 1982 to commit the parents for trial. Lindy was charged with Azaria's murder and Michael with having assisted his wife after the crime. Sensational reporting by the media aroused intense public attention. In countless workplaces, at dinner-parties and at barbecues Australians speculated on the possibilities. Everyone, it seemed, had an opinion. Dingo jokes proliferated, as did cruel rumours, sometimes centring on the supposed meaning of the name Azaria. Found guilty by the jury on 29 October, Lindy was sentenced to imprisonment for life and was confined in Darwin Prison; Michael's eighteen-month sentence was suspended. Appeals to the Federal and High courts of Australia failed.

Interest in the matter continued almost unabated, with growing support for a further inquiry. In particular, the scientific evidence about bloodstains was challenged. On 7 February 1986, after the discovery of the matinee-jacket, Lindy's sentence was remitted and she was released from gaol. A feature film, *Evil Angels* (*A Cry in the Dark*), was made next year. The royal commission conducted by Justice Trevor Morling reported on 2 June 1987 that there were 'serious doubts and questions as to the Chamberlains' guilt', and considered new evidence to be such that a trial judge would have been obliged to direct a jury to acquit them. On 15 September 1988 both convictions were quashed. In May 1992 the Northern Territory government announced that an *ex gratia* payment of $1.3 million would be made as compensation to the parents. Long before then Azaria Chamberlain's mysterious disappearance had become a modern Australian myth.

J. Bryson, *Evil Angels* (Melb, 1985); K. Crispin, *The Crown versus Chamberlain* (Syd, 1987); Royal Commission into Chamberlain Convictions, *Report of the Commissioner the Hon. Mr Justice T. R. Morling* (Darwin, 1987); L. Chamberlain, *Through My Eyes* (Melb, 1990); *Azaria Newsletter*, no 1, Apr 1984, no 15, Oct 1989.   CHRIS CUNNEEN

CHAMBERLIN, SIR MICHAEL (1891-1972), businessman and Catholic layman, was born on 30 August 1891 at Richmond, Melbourne, eldest of nine children of Richard Chamberlin, railway employee, and his wife Julia, née Callinan, both Victorian born. Michael attended primary schools at Sale and Yarrawonga, but was educated chiefly in Geelong, at St Augustine's Christian Brothers' College and at the private Central College. Aged 15, he, too, entered the railways, and worked as a station-hand and clerk.

The young Chamberlins were encouraged in self-improvement. In 1912, in Melbourne, Michael passed the Victorian public service examination, clerical division, and entered the correspondence and accounting section of the Department of Public Works. As World War I ended, he was seconded to the State War Council and later to the Department of Public Health where he helped to establish temporary hospitals during the influenza epidemic. This experience was a turning point in his career. He studied accountancy in his spare time.

In addition, Chamberlin received training in those organizations founded by his Church to secure men's faith, improve their worldly prospects, and prepare them to defend and assist it in their turn. A keen member of the Catholic Young Men's Society, he was early marked out as a devout, active and trusted adherent. In 1921, as general president, he assisted in forming the Ozanam Club for social study, and he also initiated the C.Y.M.S. Business Institute, a commercial night-school. Neither survived, but his call in the *Advocate* of August 1917—for an organization similar to the Knights of Columbus to counter Freemasonry in the workplace—had signalled a foundation he would serve henceforward, the Order of the Knights of Francis Xavier (from 1922 the Knights of the Southern Cross). On 6 December 1924 at St Patrick's Cathedral, Melbourne, he married Veronica Christina Erck.

In 1922 Chamberlin had joined T. M. Burke [q.v.7], a real-estate agent. During the Depression he managed Burke's Sydney branch and tried to find work for the Catholic unemployed. Returned to Melbourne, he moved in March 1933 to manage another firm in which Catholics were prominent, the National Trustees, Executors & Agency Co. of Australasia Ltd. He was to be a director (from 1955) and chairman from 1969 until his death. Other directorships were held in the City Mutual Life Assurance Society Ltd and T. M. Burke Finance & Investment Co. Pty Ltd; he was also a member of the Roman Catholic Trusts Corporation for the Archdiocese of Melbourne.

He put his knowledge of finance and property at the service of numerous charitable institutions, and, as a trusted friend and later neighbour of Archbishop Mannix [q.v.10], could act as his representative on secular bodies. A member in 1944-63 and sometime chairman of St Vincent's Hospital's advisory council, and thereafter life councillor, he promoted the establishment of St Vincent's School of Medical Research as a member (from 1952) of its founding committee and was chairman from 1961. Chamberlin served on committees assisting the Mercy Private Hospital and on the committee of management (president 1951-56) of St George's Hospital, Kew. He was a council-member (1945-72) of Newman College, University of Melbourne, a member of the Mannix travelling scholarship committee and chairman of the fund-raising appeal for the Julia Flynn [q.v.8] memorial prize for children from Catholic schools; to assist the K.S.C., he sat on the Dr Horace Nowland [q.v.11] travelling scholarship committee and on the Catholic Vocational Guidance Auxiliary. A member of the committee which produced *Pattern for Peace* (1943), he became a close friend of its head B. A. Santamaria and chaired the National Civic Council's extension committee. He actively participated in the campaign for state aid to independent schools.

Appointed to the interim council and council of Monash University (deputy-chancellor 1961-68), Chamberlin took particular interest in the university's proposed religious centre and in Mannix College, of which he was made first fellow. His books formed the nucleus of its library, which was named after him. In 1969 the university bestowed on him an honorary doctorate of laws. He had also joined the La Trobe University committee in 1964, but retired when the council was formed. In 1955 Chamberlin was appointed O.B.E.; in 1964 he was knighted; in 1969 he was appointed knight of the Order of Pius.

A tall, slim, pleasant-faced man, Sir Michael was active to the end, appearing two nights before his death at a N.C.C. function—to a standing ovation. He died on 16 March 1972 at his Kew home and was buried in Boroondara cemetery. His wife survived him; they had no children.

B. A. Santamaria, *Against the Tide* (Melb, 1981) and *Daniel Mannix* (Melb, 1984); C. Jory, *The Campion Society and Catholic Social Militancy in Australia 1929-1939* (Syd, 1986); S. Priestley, *Melbourne's Mercy* (Melb, 1990); Knights of the Southern Cross, *Advance Australia*, Mar 1969; *Age* (Melb), 25 June 1965; *Herald* (Melb), 17 Dec 1970; *Sun News-Pictorial*, 17 Mar 1972; *Advocate* (Melb), 23 Mar 1972; A. W. Hannan, Victorian Catholics, State Aid and Religious Instruction in State Schools, 1901-39 (M.Ed. thesis, Monash Univ, 1974); family information.   CECILY CLOSE

CHAMBERS, CYRIL (1897-1975), politician, was born on 28 February 1897 at New Thebarton, Adelaide, son of South Australian-born Francis Bernard Chambers, railway porter, and his wife Mary Ann, née Whelan. Educated at St John the Baptist's School, Thebarton, and Hayward's Academy, Adelaide, Cyril worked as a dental-assistant for three years; in 1919 he qualified to practise dentistry. He was mayor of Henley and Grange in 1932-34 and president (1936) of the South Australian branch of the Australian Labor Party.

In March 1940 Chambers was commissioned honorary captain in the Reserve of Officers, Australian Army Medical Corps (Dental Service). Called up for full-time duty on 22 August, he served in Australia and briefly with the 3rd Field Ambulance in Port Moresby, Papua, before being invalided to Adelaide where he reverted to the reserve on 18 May 1942. At the 1943 election he won the seat of Adelaide in the House of Representatives; he was appointed minister for the army on 1 November 1946. It was partly due to his prompting that in 1947 the A.L.P. reaffirmed its 1937 decision prohibiting State branches from directing how members of Federal parliament were to vote in caucus. Supporting Prime Minister Chifley's [q.v.] stand against the communist-led Australasian Coal and Shale Employees' Federation, in July 1949 Chambers ordered troops to work the strike-bound New South Wales coalmines.

When H. V. Evatt [q.v.] became leader of the parliamentary Labor Party in June 1951, Chambers allied himself with the Victorian right-wingers. He refused to participate in his party's campaign to urge electors to vote 'No' in the referendum—initiated by (Sir) Robert Menzies [q.v.]—to amend the Constitution to give the Commonwealth powers to deal with communists and communism. Evatt had to intervene to prevent Chambers from being expelled from the A.L.P. However, for publicly attacking Evatt's leadership on 8 August 1957, Chambers was expelled from the A.L.P. on 19 September. Although readmitted in June 1958, he had been unable to contest his party's pre-selection for the seat of Adelaide in the forthcoming election and decided to retire from politics. That year the Labor Opposition nominated him as an Australian delegate to the 13th session of the United Nations General Assembly; having previously attended the 10th session in 1955, he again accepted.

Chambers tempered his austere outlook and strict Catholicism with a liberal attitude to such social issues as divorce, and was a friend and admirer of E. J. Ward [q.v.]. A good debater, with an almost demagogic style of oratory, Chambers was handsome, neatly dressed and well groomed; though kind hearted and generous, he lacked a sense of humour. His recreations included boxing, golf and racing. In 1959-62 he successively served as an immigration selection officer in Belfast, Rome and Scotland; returning to South Australia, he worked as a welfare consultant with Commonwealth Hostels Ltd. Chambers was appointed C.B.E. in 1968.

He had been married three times: on 4 May 1938 at St Ignatius's Church, Norwood, to Hilda Dorothy Mummery (d. 1943); on 23 December 1949 at St Paul's Cathedral, Melbourne, to a divorcee Salamas, née Koodak, late Rickman (d. 1954); and on 31 October 1956 at St Columba's Church, Elwood, Melbourne, to Janet Sanderson Pullen. Survived by his wife, Chambers died on 2 October 1975 at Hawthorn, Adelaide, and was buried in Centennial Park cemetery. He had no children.

R. Murray, *The Split* (Syd, 1984); T. Sheridan, *Division of Labour* (Melb, 1989); *Herald* (Melb), 8 Aug 1957; *Sun News-Pictorial*, 20 Sept 1957; *SMH*, 17 June, 21 Aug 1958; *Advertiser* (Adel), 4 Oct 1975; Chambers papers (NL).   CLYDE CAMERON

CHAN, HARRY (CHAN TIEN FOOK) (1918-1969), businessman, mayor and politician, was born on 14 June 1918 in Darwin and registered as Hen Fook, third of five children of Chin Yepp Gnee (Chan Fon Yuen), a tailor from Hong Kong, and his Darwin-born wife (Wong) Quee She (Shee). Educated at the local public school and at Oriental College, Hong Kong, Harry completed an accountancy qualification by correspondence; he was to become a fellow (1968) of the Australian Society of Accountants. Chan married a typist Lilyan Yuen on 18 January 1941 in Darwin. He worked as a tailor, and in the retail and timber industries, and participated in the affairs of the Chinese community. In 1942 he was evacuated to Sydney where he was employed by the Bank of China.

Back in Darwin after World War II, Chan established a successful grocery business, invested in real estate, became a millionaire and extended his involvement in welfare, social and sporting organizations. His efforts made him a popular figure in what was then a small and intimate town: it was said that he knew the names of almost all Darwin's residents and those of their domestic pets. Chan's gentle, cheerful and courteous nature, together with his generosity, compassion and helpfulness, served him well in seeking public office. In July 1959 he was elected to the Darwin City Council as representative for Fannie Bay Ward. He entered the Legislative Council for the Northern Territory as member for Fannie Bay in December 1962.

In 1965 Chan was unanimously chosen by his parliamentary colleagues to become the first elected president of the Legislative Council; he was to hold the office until his death. The clerk regarded him as 'the most popular person ever to sit in the Council'. Chan also continued as a city councillor (later alderman) until 1966 when he was elected mayor. Believing that his only loyalty was to his constituents, he sat as an Independent on both councils. His tenure of the two most prestigious, elected positions in the Northern Territory was a tribute to his standing and to the racial tolerance of postwar Darwin. Returned as mayor with a resounding majority in 1969, he was appointed O.B.E. that year.

Although Chan never pretended to be a consummate politician, a dynamic leader or a skilled orator, he was diligent and constructive. His character and style suited the roles of mayor and president, both of which he filled with distinction. While he favoured restricted immigration, he hoped to see a multi-racial university established in Darwin. A keen advocate of the Territory's constitutional development, he delivered a paper, 'Problems of an Anachronistic House', to the 1968 conference in Darwin of presiding officers and clerks from Australian parliaments in which he made a reasoned statement of the need for change. He died of cancer on 5 August 1969 in Darwin and was buried in the local cemetery with Anglican rites; his wife, daughter and three sons survived him. A nursing home and the Legislative Assembly building in Darwin are named after him.

D. W. Lockwood, *The Front Door* (Adel, 1968); A. Heatley, *The Government of the Northern Territory* (Brisb, 1979) and *A City Grows* (Darwin, 1986); F. Walker, *A Short History of the Legislative Council for the Northern Territory* (Darwin, 1986); *Northern Territory News*, 25 Apr 1970.   A. HEATLEY

CHANDLER, SIR GILBERT LAWRENCE (1903-1974), horticulturist and politician, was born on 29 August 1903 in North Melbourne, eldest of five children of Alfred Elliott Chandler [q.v.7], nurseryman, and his second wife Marie, née Intermann, both Victorian born. Educated at Scotch College, 'Gib' joined the family's Everson Nursery at The Basin, Bayswater, as a partner. On 22 November 1930 at Christ Church, Hawthorn, he married Thelma Alice Coon with Anglican rites.

His career followed that of his father. In 1935-55 Gilbert served on the Fern Tree Gully Shire Council (president 1938-39) and in March 1935 succeeded Alfred as a representative of South-Eastern Province in the Victorian Legislative Council. He stood as a United Australia Party candidate. At that time the minimum age for election was 30 and there was a property qualification of £1000 by municipal valuation. 'I just scraped through on both qualifications', Chandler later recalled. Following electoral redistributions, he represented Southern Province (1937-67) and Boronia Province (1967-73).

He was to spend thirty-eight years in parliament. After a short stint as minister without portfolio (1943-45) in the Dunstan [q.v.8]-Hollway [q.v.] coalition government, in June 1955 Chandler became minister of agriculture (by his own choice—the new premier (Sir) Henry Bolte had wanted him to be minister of education) and continued to serve in that portfolio until his retirement from parliament in May 1973. Under his leadership the Department of Agriculture began a remarkable development which contributed to the advancement of Victorian primary industry, especially in animal husbandry, research into animal and plant diseases, and the economic management of farms. The Gilbert Chandler

Institute of Dairy Technology at Werribee was named in his honour.

Deputy-leader of the government in the council from 1955, Chandler was leader in 1962-73. His colleagues and opponents equally admired his honest and straightforward handling of the role. I. A. Swinburne, leader of the Country Party in the Upper House, described him as one of the Victoria's 'greatest statesmen', while the Labor leader J. W. Galbally referred to him as 'a saintly man'.

Tall, with an athletic build, Chandler had been a keen sportsman in his earlier years. He played Australian Rules football (1928-29) for Hawthorn in the Victorian Football League and district cricket (1927-33) for Richmond, and subsequently served as president of football clubs in his locality. He was a member of the organizing committee for the Olympic Games in Melbourne in 1956 and a trustee of the Melbourne Cricket Ground (chairman 1973-74).

Possessing a kindly, avuncular manner, which tended to mask his deep convictions and very great capacity, Chandler undertook community service far beyond his parliamentary and ministerial duties. As chairman of the Churchill National Park's committee of management and a committee-member of the Fern Tree Gully National Park, he showed a wide-ranging interest in conservation and in preserving the beauty of the Dandenong Ranges. He chaired (1944-46) the government's bush fires relief committee and served as president of the Boronia Basin division of the St John Ambulance Brigade. Appointed C.M.G. in 1958, he was knighted in 1972.

Sir Gilbert died of a coronary occlusion on 8 April 1974 at Fern Tree Gully in the (Sir) William Angliss [q.v.7] Hospital which he had served as foundation president for thirty-five years. Survived by his wife and two sons (both of whom had joined him in the family business), he was cremated after a state funeral at the Boronia Methodist Church, of which he had been a loyal member. The officiating clergyman described him as 'a man of quiet strength who was one with the people'. Chandler's estate was sworn for probate at $495 983.

H. Coulson, *The Family of William Chandler, Horticulturist* (Kilsyth, Vic, 1978); *PD* (LC Vic), 5 Sept 1972, 12 Apr 1973, 9 Apr 1974; *PD* (LA Vic), 9 Apr 1974; *Age* (Melb), 13 Apr 1973, 9 Apr 1974; *Knox and Mountain District Free Press*, 16 Apr 1974; *Lilydale Shire Express*, 17 Apr 1974.

RUPERT HAMER

CHANDLER, SIR JOHN BEALS (1887-1962), businessman, radio entrepreneur and politician, was born on 21 February 1887 at Bunwell, Norfolk, England, posthumous son of John Chandler, bricklayer, and his wife Mary Ann, née Green. One of a large and poor family, John left school at the age of 8. He migrated to Queensland in 1907. Having worked off his government-assisted passage for two years in the cane-fields at Mossman, he was employed as a manufacturers' commission agent in Brisbane. On 24 February 1912 at the registrar's office, Red Hill, he married a nurse Lydia Isabel Parish. In 1913 Chandler opened a small general hardware store in Elizabeth Street, Brisbane. He expanded his business by dealing in household and electrical appliances, selling and installing petrol-vapour and electric-lighting systems, and entering the electrical contracting field.

In 1923 J. B. Chandler & Co. opened a store in Adelaide Street that specialized in electrical appliances and equipment. He then began to sell radio parts, eventually assembling his own 'Gloriola' wirelesses and also importing sets from America. In 1928 his company became the Queensland distributor for Amalgamated Wireless Australasia Ltd. Growing interest in radio prompted him to build and operate 4BC (BC for Beals Chandler) radio station in 1930. It was Brisbane's first, commercial broadcasting operation and, within a few days, joined in the coverage of a cricket Test played in England. Chandler subsequently established a radio network, with stations at Rockhampton, Maryborough, Toowoomba and Kingaroy; he also helped to establish stations at Ayr, Atherton and Gympie. In 1936 he exercised an option to purchase 4BH Brisbane, but the Federal government's restrictions on the ownership of broadcasting stations forced him to sell all his outlets—except 4BH—the following year.

His aggressive marketing of electrical household appliances in the 1930s, combined with his acquisition of the Australian franchise for Sunbeam Corporation Ltd products, led him to open branches of his firm throughout Queensland, in Sydney and in Melbourne, and to find distributors in other capital cities. The J. B. Chandler Investment Co. Ltd was formed in 1932 to provide hire-purchase finance and in 1938 a public company, Chandlers Pty Ltd, was established. That year the company's wholesaling, office and servicing divisions were moved to headquarters at the corner of Albert and Charlotte streets, Brisbane.

During World War II the firm was associated with A.W.A. in installing and servicing radio, radar and echo-sounding equipment in ships. Prospering in the postwar years, Chandler's operations were merged in a public company, Chandlers (Aust.) Ltd, in 1950. After losing the Sunbeam franchise, the Melbourne branch was closed, the Sydney operation converted to general wholesaling, and the group was confined to Queensland and the Northern Rivers district of New South Wales. In 1959 Chandler closed his electrical contracting supplies division in order to finance his purchase of Fame Television (Qld) Pty Ltd. Always active, he remained chairman and managing director of the Chandler group of companies until his death.

Chandler had been a councillor of Taringa shire before the creation of Greater Brisbane in 1925. In the 1940 Brisbane municipal elections he led his Citizens' Municipal Organization team to a resounding victory over the Labor administration of A. J. Jones [q.v.9]. During the first of his four consecutive terms as lord mayor (1940-52) of Brisbane, Chandler worked closely with R. H. Robinson, the assistant under-secretary of the Department of Health and Home Affairs, and also with the town clerk and city administrator J. C. Slaughter to rationalize and revitalize the city's management.

Although the C.M.O. was returned in a majority of wards in subsequent elections, Chandler's promises of extensive civic improvement were frustrated by wartime restrictions. The council had formulated a judicious wartime policy of 'Preservation, Conservation, and Preparation' which produced a five-year programme of postwar city development estimated to cost £15 million. With priorities based on pre-war assumptions, the plan's effectiveness was diminished by unforeseen inflation, population growth, and shortages of manpower and materials. In the 1952 elections Labor defeated the Chandler administration by campaigning on the inadequacies of sewerage, water-supply and transport services, and by drawing attention to the money spent on Coronation Drive. Nevertheless, Chandler's council had pointed the way to Brisbane's future development in services, town planning and urban beautification.

In 1943 Chandler had won the Queensland Legislative Assembly seat of Hamilton as an Independent. His conviction that the 'collectivism' of the Labor Party was incompatible with democracy induced him, almost immediately, to found the Queensland People's Party. It speedily absorbed the fading State section of the United Australia Party. He retired from the assembly in 1947 to concentrate on business and on developing the City of Brisbane. The People's Party later became the Queensland division of the Liberal Party of Australia.

Chandler believed that it was possible to form a government free from class consciousness and was convinced that the city council under the C.M.O. was an administration of this kind. He also held that capitalism should operate in the interests of the many rather than the few. His political views were clearly outlined in his published addresses to the Brisbane Rotary Club in 1942 (*What of the Future?*), to the Australian National Service League in December that year (*The Privileges and Responsibilities of Democracy*) and in his *Policy Speech of the Queensland People's Party* (1943). Knighted in 1952, he retired from public life after his defeat in the council election that year.

Five ft 3 ins (160 cm) tall and lightly built, but with an impressive presence, Chandler was known to his associates as 'J.B.' and to the citizens of Brisbane as the 'Little Man' who brought efficiency to the city council. A practising Anglican, he considered it his duty to repay society for the opportunities it had afforded him to become a successful businessman. He never wore the lord mayor's robes of office and, by waiving his salary and reducing his expense account, saved the city an estimated £25 000. An idealist, with the acumen, energy and courage to achieve many of his goals, he had, as well, the necessary balance and sense of humour to take success and failure in his stride. His self-assurance and tenacity were sometimes interpreted as arrogance or stubbornness, yet, while not prepared to be imposed upon, he inspired respect and loyalty in those who worked closely with him.

Twice president (1938-40) of the Brisbane Chamber of Commerce, he was a treasurer (1939-40) and life member of the Royal Automobile Club of Queensland. He founded the Australian Federation of Broadcasting Stations, and was a foundation member and president (1928-29) of the State branch of the Electrical Federation. A member of the Rotary Club of Brisbane and of the Young Men's Christian Association, he was president of the Queensland Patriotic and Australian Comforts Fund during World War II. Growing orchids and motoring were his main hobbies, though he also enjoyed golf and bowls. Sir John died on 19 January 1962 at his St Lucia home and was cremated. He was survived by his wife and two of their sons; two other sons were killed in action in World War II. Chandler's estate was sworn for probate at £326 433. A portrait by A. Baratin is held by M. N. Chandler, Beaudesert. The family's connexion with the Chandler group of companies ended in 1977.

I. K. Mackay, *Broadcasting in Australia* (Melb, 1957); G. Greenwood and J. Laverty, *Brisbane 1859-1959* (Brisb, 1959); C. Lack (comp), *Three Decades of Queensland Political History, 1929-1960* (Brisb, 1962); *Mingay's Electrical Weekly*, 4 Oct 1963; *Courier-Mail*, 29-30 Apr 1940, 14 Apr 1944, 13 Mar 1950, 14 Feb 1951, 1 Jan 1952, 20 Jan 1962; *Sunday Mail* (Brisb), 2 May 1943, 21 Aug 1949; *Cairns Post*, 18 Feb 1986; Brisb 4BC 1116, A

Dream and its Realisation (The History of 4BC), (ms, nd); Brisb City Council, Annual Reports, 1939-52, and Minutes, 1940-52 (Town Hall, Brisb); Chandlers Pty Ltd, historic file (Chandlers Appliance Stores Pty Ltd, MacGregor, Brisb).

JOHN LAVERTY

CHANDLER, LESLIE GORDON (1888-1980), ornithologist and photographer, was born on 11 January 1888 at Malvern, Melbourne, fourth child of English-born parents Robert Charles Chandler, gardener and gentleman, and his wife Ellen, née Mead(e)s. When Les was 2 the family moved to The Basin in the Dandenong Ranges. He attended the local school and, after transferring to Bayswater State School, used the three-mile (4.8 km) walk to observe nature.

Aged 15, Chandler was apprenticed to a Melbourne jeweller. Unhappy in the city, he spent weekends at home or in the bush. At 18 he began to give talks to schools. By 1907 he had become one of Australia's earliest photographers of birds. He joined the Bird Observers' Club that year, the Royal Australasian Ornithologists' Union in 1910 (life member 1961) and the Field Naturalists' Club of Victoria in 1914. During 1912 he had participated in Australia's first bird-banding scheme: skilled as a jeweller, he fashioned metal bands that were not injurious to the birds' legs.

Enlisting in the Australian Imperial Force on 8 July 1915 and promoted corporal next month, Chandler served with the 15th Field Ambulance on the Western Front. He recorded his wartime experiences with a tiny camera hidden under his uniform, and in diaries written in shorthand as was his lifelong custom. Gassed at Villers-Bretonneux, France, in April 1918, he was invalided to England; he reached Melbourne in January 1919 and was discharged medically unfit on 25 July.

Too ill for jewellery work, Chandler went to the Mallee where he roamed the countryside and regained his health. In 1921 as a soldier settler he took up a block at Red Cliffs which he converted from virgin bush to a vineyard. Next year he published *Bush Charms*, and *Jacky the Butcher-Bird* which was written by candlelight under canvas. Having founded the Nature Photographers' Club of Australia on his return from the war, in 1922 he instituted a travelling portfolio of nature photographs. Over the years his work was exhibited in London, Japan and the United States of America; he won many prizes, including the Kodak medallion. On 10 September 1931 he married Ivy Henshall at St Andrew's Presbyterian Church, Mordialloc, Victoria.

From 1909 Chandler published more than one hundred articles in such periodicals and newspapers as *Emu, Walkabout, Riverlander, Wildlife, Wildlife in Australia, Victorian School-paper*, and the *Age, Australasian, Argus, Leader, Victorian Naturalist* and *Australian Photo-Review*. As 'Oriole' he was nature correspondent for the *Sunraysia Daily*, but declined a permanent position because he wanted the freedom to 'go bush'.

In 1949 Chandler helped to form the Sunraysia Field Naturalists' Club. In recognition of his contribution as president, vice-president, treasurer and editor, he was made a life member. He was also a foundation member of the Mildura Historical Society. With other naturalists, he worked tirelessly to have the Hattah-Kulkyne area declared a National Park and succeeded in 1960.

A spare man, 5 ft 7 ins (170.2 cm) tall, with dark hair and deep-set, brown eyes, Chandler was courtly, gentle and generally silent, unless with a kindred spirit when it was difficult to stop him. He loved books, poetry and art, and enjoyed wood-carving. Survived by his wife and daughter, he died on 25 January 1980 at Mildura and was buried in the local cemetery.

H. M. Whittell, *The Literature of Australian Birds* (Perth, 1954); M. J. Chandler, *Against the Odds* (Red Cliffs, Vic, 1979) and *Tribal Lands to National Park* (Red Cliffs, Vic, 1980); L. G. Chandler, *Dear Homefolks*, M. J. Chandler comp (Red Cliffs, Vic, 1988); *Emu* (Melb), 80, pt 4, Oct 1980, p 241; *Sunraysia Naturalists' Research Trust, Seventh Report*, Apr 1970, p 63; *Geo*, 12, no 4, Dec 1990-Feb 1991, p 87; Chandler file, Roy Aust Ornithologists' Union Archives (held by author, Box Hill North, Melb).

TESS KLOOT

CHANDLER, MARGARET OLIVE; see BOGLE

CHAPMAN, GARY ARTHUR (1938-1978), swimmer and fisherman, was born on 12 March 1938 at Brighton-Le-Sands, Sydney, eldest son of Australian-born parents Arthur James Kennard Chapman, sports store proprietor, and his wife Gladys Alma, née Deller. As a youngster Gary was mischievous, even wilful, and loved outdoor life, especially tree-climbing. Told that he must learn to swim before he could boat and fish on his own, at the age of 7 he reluctantly mastered the art at Ramsgate baths and was soon coached by Steve Duff.

While still at Kogarah Boys' Intermediate High School, where he excelled at most sports, in February 1953 Chapman won the Australian 440 yards freestyle title in the record time of 4 minutes 42.6 seconds. Leaving school and coached by Frank Guthrie at the Enfield pool, in the Australian championships in early 1954 he broke the records for 440 and 880 yards freestyle. At 16 the brown-eyed, husky youngster—nicknamed 'the big horse' or 'Gazzar'—was 6 ft 2 ins (188 cm) tall, weighed 13½ stone (85.7 kg) and could wrap his hand around the handles of two tennis rackets. He swam 55 yards in thirty-seven strokes, six fewer than most of his contemporaries.

In the British Empire and Commonwealth Games at Vancouver, Canada, in August 1954 Chapman won gold medals for the 440 and 4 x 220 yards freestyle events. Resting in 1955, he kept fit by playing tennis. At North Sydney on 18 February 1956 he set a world record of 2 minutes 5.8 seconds for the 220 yards freestyle; in November he won the bronze medal at the Olympic Games in Melbourne, finishing behind his team-mates Jon Henricks and John Devitt in the 100 metres freestyle. After a lean year in 1957, in Brisbane on 3 May 1958 Chapman (with Devitt, John Konrads and Geoffrey Shipton) set a world record of 3 minutes 46.3 seconds for the 4 x 100 metres freestyle; in July at the British Empire and Commonwealth Games in Cardiff, Wales, he won a gold medal in the 4 x 220 yards and a silver in the 110 yards freestyle.

A fine sportsman, with an unaffected and happy nature, Chapman retired from competitive swimming in August 1959, despite prospects for the 1960 Olympics. 'A person who wants to be a top-line swimmer has to make too many sacrifices', he said, 'I've spent the last nine years of my life doing nothing else but eating, sleeping and swimming'. He resumed his education at St George Technical College, worked in his father's Rockdale sports store and concentrated on his great love—fishing. A member of the St George and Sutherland Shire Anglers' Club and of the Port Hacking Game Fishing Club, Chapman held many records and was New South Wales rock-fishing champion in 1964. At St Paul's Anglican Church, Kogarah, on 10 February 1962 he had married Dutch-born Audrey Bosma; they were to have three children.

On 23 September 1978 he and a friend Ronald Nelson set out in Chapman's power-boat to fish off Maroubra beach. The up-turned boat was found next day, but their bodies were never recovered: the coroner returned a finding of accidental drowning. Chapman was survived by his wife, son and a daughter; his estate was sworn for probate at $75 378.

P. Besford, *Encyclopaedia of Swimming* (Lond, 1976); *People* (Syd), 28 July 1954; *SMH*, 21, 25 Feb, 16, 27, 28 Mar 1953, 8, 11, 17 Jan, 9, 12 Feb, 26 June, 18 July, 6-8 Aug, 6 Sept 1954, 1 Aug, 20, 23 Nov, 18 Dec 1955, 1, 9, 19 Jan, 4, 19 Feb, 30 Nov, 1 Dec 1956, 21, 23 July, 16, 18, 21 Aug, 8 Sept 1958, 9 Aug 1959, 29 Aug 1969, 25, 26 Sept 1978; *Herald* (Melb), 11 Aug 1954, 23 Aug 1958, 3 Oct 1978; *Daily Mirror* (Syd), 2 Feb 1978; *Sunday Press* (Melb), 1 Oct 1978.   G. P. WALSH

CHAPMAN, JOHN AUSTIN (1896-1963), army officer, was born on 15 December 1896 at Braidwood, New South Wales, second son of (Sir) Austin Chapman [q.v.7], auctioneer and politician, and his native-born wife Catherine Josephine, née O'Brien. Educated at Christian Brothers' colleges at Waverley (Sydney) and in East Melbourne, in 1913 John entered the Royal Military College, Duntroon, Federal Capital Territory, and graduated in June 1915. Next month he was appointed lieutenant in the Australian Imperial Force and posted to the 30th Battalion. In November he embarked for Egypt where he 'helped to construct and man' Suez Canal defences.

In June 1916 Chapman moved to France and in July was promoted captain. Suffering from the effects of gas, he was evacuated to England in November. He rejoined his unit in May 1917 and held the post of adjutant until 30 October when he was promoted major and sent to a senior officers' course. A staff trainee from January 1918, he was attached to I Corps and 5th Division headquarters. While acting as brigade major of the 8th Brigade, on 28 August under heavy fire he reconnoitred the front line near the village of Estrées, France; he was awarded the Distinguished Service Order. Home again in June 1919, he continued to serve in the Permanent Military Forces. On 9 October that year in St Mary's Catholic Cathedral, Sydney, he married Chilean-born Helena Mary de Booten (d. 1961) whom he had met in London; they were to have four children.

From 1919 to 1930 Chapman occupied staff and brigade major positions. He was in England in 1930-33 where he attended the Staff College, Camberley, and underwent small-arms training. In February 1934 he became chief instructor at the Small Arms School, Sydney; he found this appointment particularly rewarding and maintained an intense interest in his 'old boys'. Described as 'a brilliant officer', he returned to England in 1938 on exchange service and taught at the Staff College. With the outbreak of World War II, in September 1939 he was posted as general staff officer, 1st grade, to the British 52nd (Lowland) Division and promoted lieutenant colonel two months later.

Back in Australia, in January 1940 Chapman assumed the duties of G.S.O.1 (training) at Army Headquarters, Melbourne. On 4 April he transferred to the A.I.F. in the rank of colonel, and went to the Middle East as chief of staff of the 7th Division. For his work during the Syrian campaign (June-July 1941) he was awarded a Bar to his D.S.O. In August 1941, as temporary brigadier, he took command of the A.I.F.'s Base Area in the Middle East. Posted to Advanced Land Headquarters, Brisbane, as deputy-adjutant and quartermaster general, he was promoted major general on 1 September 1942. He became deputy chief of the General Staff in October 1944.

In May 1946 Chapman was appointed army (and, from January 1948, defence) representative, Australian Military Mission, Washington. He went to the Balkans in 1947 as a member of the United Nations' commission of inquiry into incidents on the Greek frontier. Completing his term in the United States of America in February 1950, he returned to Australia to be general officer commanding, Central Command. His final post (February 1951 to December 1953) was quartermaster general and third member of the Military Board in Melbourne. He was appointed to the Legion of Merit (U.S.A.) in 1949 and in 1952 was appointed C.B. In retirement he retained his strong interest in army life.

A punctilious and assiduous officer, Chapman was highly regarded by his soldiers, whose names he always remembered. He was 5 ft 11 ins (180.3 cm) tall, with brown hair and a fair complexion; tone deaf, but a good raconteur, he enjoyed social gatherings. Chapman lived to the letter the tenets of Catholicism, and respected the beliefs of others. Survived by his two sons and a daughter, he died of uraemia and cancer on 19 April 1963 in his Mosman home and was buried with military honours in Northern Suburbs cemetery. Waverley College holds his portrait.

His elder brother JAMES AUSTIN (1895-1967) was also a career army officer who served in the 30th Battalion in World War I and was appointed O.B.E. (1919). After a succession of staff postings in Australia, the Middle East and Italy in World War II, he retired as honorary colonel in 1947. He was a member of the Repatriation Commission (1947-50), then worked as an associate of a judge of the Supreme Court of Victoria.

H. Sloan (ed), *The Purple and Gold* (Syd, 1938); G. Long, *Greece, Crete and Syria* (Canb, 1953); *Army J*, no 267, Aug 1971; *SMH*, 24 Oct 1938, 20 Feb 1947; AWM records; information from Mr A. Chapman, Dooralong, NSW.

ROGER C. THOMPSON

CHAPMAN, JOHN LORD (1913-1977), business administrator and trade commissioner, was born on 7 May 1913 at Balmain North, Sydney, son of Michael Ernest Chapman, a shipwright from England, and his native-born wife Clara Ellen, née Lord. Educated at Sydney Boys' High School and the University of Sydney (B.Ec., 1936; LL.B., 1950), John worked as an accountant and as assistant-secretary to the Motor Traders' Association of New South Wales Inc. He married a stenographer Helen Roy McAlpin on 4 May 1940 at Grimm [q.v.4] Memorial Church, Drummoyne, with Presbyterian forms. In 1941 he enlisted in the Citizen Air Force of the Royal Australian Air Force. Commissioned in December 1942, Chapman qualified as a navigator under the Empire Air Training Scheme and was a temporary flight lieutenant when demobilized on 10 September 1945.

Leaving the M.T.A. in 1951, he became assistant to the general manager of Clyde Industries Ltd. On 14 December 1956 he was appointed Australian government trade commissioner at Calcutta, India. He took up the post in May 1957 and in October was rebuked by (Sir) John Crawford, secretary to the Department of Trade, for his 'approach which may at times be slightly brusque in an Asian setting'. Reports, however, soon reached Canberra from Australian businessmen expressing gratitude for Chapman's assistance. At the end of his tour in August 1959, he was praised for his efforts by the governor of West Bengal, the Australian high commissioner and the British deputy high commissioner.

Chapman's next posting was as trade commissioner at Johannesburg, South Africa, where he spent two terms between December 1959 and September 1966. Again, he was attentive to the requirements of Australian businessmen who sought markets in the region. Although he had been briefed against engaging in political conversation, he did not conceal his opposition to the South African government's apartheid policy and later acknowledged the difficulty of living in that country. After returning home, he was ruled medically unfit for service in the tropics. A diabetes sufferer, he had to fight to gain admission to the Commonwealth superannuation scheme. From 1968 to 1972 he was trade commissioner at Vancouver, Canada: he found the post congenial, and succeeded in boosting Australian exports, and in fostering contacts between Australian and Canadian businessmen.

Gregarious and affable, Chapman excelled at promotional work on behalf of individual firms, but exhibited less acumen in policy and administrative matters. He was popular both with his subordinates and superiors. After an inauspicious start, he became one of his country's most highly regarded trade representatives working abroad. Of average height and well built, he wore a thick moustache in the style once favoured by air force officers. Back in Australia, ill health obliged him to retire on 1 July 1976. D. H. McKay, secretary to the Department of Overseas Trade, thanked him for his 'loyal and conscientious contribution', and noted that his knowledge and experience would not easily be replaced. Survived by his wife and son, Chapman died of cardiac infarction on 22 March 1977 in his home at Deakin, Canberra, and was cremated.

Aust Senate, Standing Cte on Trade and Commerce, *Australian Trade Commissioner Service* (Canb, 1978); A. R. Taysom, History of the Australian Trade Commissioner Service, 5 vols (ts, nd, NL); *SMH*, 26 Feb 1957, 28 Sept 1959; *Canb Times*, 25 Mar 1977; Chapman personal file (AA).

SELWYN CORNISH

CHAPMAN, LAURIE LACHLAN (1890-1978), public servant, was born on 20 April 1890 at Wodonga, Victoria, second surviving son and sixth child of Alexander John Chapman, mail guard, and his wife Rosetta Josephine, née Hickey, both Melbourne born. Educated at Moreland State School, Laurie won a scholarship to Stott and Hoare's Business College, then joined the Victorian Railways as a temporary clerk on 2 March 1906. Six-day shiftwork prevented his playing sport and his mother encouraged him to enter the public service which offered permanency and regular hours. He studied accountancy at night, but never completed any formal qualification.

Appointed clerk in the audit office, Department of the Chief Secretary, in October 1907, Chapman was promoted to the central correspondence office in 1911; owing to his ability at shorthand, he served as private secretary to successive ministers. This contact with prominent politicians led him to conclude that 'most had feet of clay' and he 'soon lost all fear or awe of them'. Under 'a talented but indolent' superior, he performed the work of two, and gained an unrivalled knowledge of the political and public service processes involved in the administration of the statutes.

On 11 May 1916 at St Mary's Catholic Church, West Melbourne, Chapman married Elsie Maud Lenehan. A tall athletic figure, he exuded authority and commanded respect in company. He was a talented cricketer who captained the Elsternwick club in the 1920s and the Public Service XI through the 1930s.

The major influence on him was his mother, a 'tiny, tempestuous, very practical, unsentimental and dominant' person and a 'severe disciplinarian who believed children should be seen and not heard and obey the ten commandments'. To his own children, Chapman was a good provider, respected and fair in his dealings, but with little time to give affection.

He was also an accomplished classical violinist.

Chapman's appointment as under-secretary on 8 April 1932 made him the State's most powerful public servant, with control over twenty varied branches and one-third of Victoria's public employees. His sound advice to governments, his ability to use his wide knowledge, his capacity to reconcile those with strongly divergent views and his acumen in initiating or accepting change made him unassailable. Not until he retired did the position of under-secretary lose its preeminence. (Sir) Daryl Lindsay [q.v.10], director of the National Gallery of Victoria, found him 'a warmly human person' with a 'dry sense of humour'. As government nominee (1947-55) on the Trotting Control Board and chairman of the Racecourses Licences Board, Chapman incurred the wrath of several Country Party members in 1954 for his tight control of the sport and was described as the 'Czar of racing in Victoria'. L. W. Galvin [q.v.], his last minister, paid tribute to his integrity and to his administration which was 'in keeping with the highest traditions of all Public Services in the British Empire'.

Appointed to the I.S.O. in 1949, Chapman retired on 19 April 1955 and devoted himself to racing, angling and maintaining his skill at billiards through his membership of the Green Room Club. He died at his Brighton home on 8 December 1978 and was buried in New Cheltenham cemetery; his wife, son and two daughters survived him.

D. Lindsay, *The Leafy Tree* (Melb, 1965); L. B. Cox, *The National Gallery of Victoria, 1861 to 1968* (Melb, 1970?); *PD* (Vic), 1954, p 2770; *Age* (Melb), 10 Dec 1954; Chapman papers, including short autobiographical notes (held by Mr J. L. Chapman, Carnegie, Melb); Museum of Vic, official files *and* minutes of Building Trustees (held by Museum of Vic, Melb); information from Mr J. L. Chapman and Mrs P. Jones, Carnegie, and Dr P. G. Law, Canterbury, Melb; personal information.

F. J. KENDALL

CHAPMAN, WILFRID DINSEY (1891-1955), engineer, was born on 16 May 1891 at Wandsworth, London, son of Frederick Chapman [q.v.7], a geologist's assistant, and his wife Helen Mary, née Dancer. In 1902 the family came to Australia where Frederick took up his appointment as palaeontologist at the National Museum, Melbourne. Educated at Camberwell Grammar School, where he was dux, Wilfrid joined the railway construction branch of the Board of Land and Works as a junior. For six years he worked as an engineering-assistant and a resident engineer, mainly in the country.

On 7 June 1915 Chapman enlisted in the Australian Imperial Force. He served with the 1st Australian General Hospital in Egypt and France. Commissioned on 29 September 1917, he was posted to the 7th Machine-Gun Company and saw action in France next year. In April 1919 he returned to Australia and his appointment terminated on 31 July. At the Collins Street Independent Church, Melbourne, on 13 December that year he married Marea Feori Anastasia Maniachi with Congregational forms.

Re-employed by the railway construction branch, Chapman was given time off to attend lectures at the University of Melbourne (B.C.E., 1923; M.C.E., 1925). Meanwhile, as assistant-engineer and engineer, he designed and constructed railways and bridges. He made his name as a pioneer in the use of electric arc welding for structural purposes, notably in widening and strengthening the rail-and-road bridge over the Murray River at Echuca in 1924.

In 1931 Chapman joined E.M.F. Electric Co. Pty Ltd as engineer in charge of research and development. He made significant advances in the theory and practice of electric welding, and did much to spread knowledge of the new technology among practising engineers. In 1936 he moved to Australian Paper Manufacturers Ltd as engineer for development and research. His investigations which preceded the establishment of the pulp-mill at Maryvale took him to various parts of Gippsland and stimulated his interest in the region's hardwoods, on which, like his father, he was already something of an authority.

When war broke out in 1939 Chapman was with the machinery firm of Malcolm Moore Ltd. Called up for part-time duty on 1 January 1940, he was appointed to the Australian Imperial Force in May. From that month, as lieutenant colonel, he commanded the 2nd/2nd Army Field Workshop which he took to Palestine. In November he became chief ordnance mechanical engineer at headquarters, I Corps, and later—as colonel—held the same post at A.I.F. Headquarters. He made some important innovations in the design of mobile workshops and was mentioned in dispatches. After he returned to Australia in May 1942, he was posted to Land Headquarters, Melbourne, as inspector of workshop services. In January 1943 he was made chief superintendent of design. Promoted temporary brigadier in August, he led a team of experts to New Guinea to investigate the effect of tropical conditions on equipment designed for temperate zones, a mission which led to major improvements for the allied armies. In November 1945 he transferred to the Reserve of Officers as an honorary brigadier and in 1946 joined the Commonwealth Department of Transport as director of civil engineering in the railway standardization division. He had been a part-time commissioner for the State Electricity Commission of Victoria since 1944 and retained that position until his death.

A founding associate-member (1920) of the Institution of Engineers, Australia, and a member from 1930, Chapman was chairman (1932) of the Melbourne division. In 1934 he wrote a seminal and widely discussed paper, 'The Future of the Engineering Profession', which advocated true professionalism based on formal tuition and study, and criticized systems such as that under which he had received early training in the field. The paper pointed to the need for the institution to control 'all matters pertaining to the profession', and to foresee and meet changing conditions. A councillor (1933-55) and president (1944-45) of the institution, in 1949 Chapman was one of three distinguished engineers upon whom the University of Western Australia conferred a doctorate of engineering *honoris causa*—a distinction in which he took such pride that he thereafter styled himself Dr Chapman.

From 1946 he had been vice-chairman of the Standards Association, on which he was the institution's representative. A member of the Institution of Civil Engineers (London), he sat on its local advisory committee in Melbourne; he was also a member (1935-39) of the faculty of engineering at the University of Melbourne and represented engineering graduates on the standing committee of convocation. He was active in the Australian National Research Council and in the Australian and New Zealand Association for the Advancement of Science. A member (from 1938) of the board of management of the Austin Hospital, Heidelberg, he took a special interest in its grounds.

Chapman died of hypertensive cerebrovascular disease on 6 May 1955 at Mount St Evin's hospital, Fitzroy; survived by his wife and son, he was buried in Coburg cemetery. Delivering the inaugural W. D. Chapman Memorial Oration in 1959 for the Victorian division of the Institution of Engineers, Sir Edmund Herring described him as 'a great and good man, who was an outstanding engineer, a fine soldier . . . and with it all a humble man, beloved of his fellows'. Other memorials include an annual award given by the Welding Technology Institute of Australia, and the Bogong gum, named *Eucalyptus chapmaniana* in 1947 after he had drawn attention to its existence.

C. Edwards, *Brown Power* (Melb, 1969); A. H. Corbett, *The Institution of Engineers, Australia* (Syd, 1973); I. V. Hansen, *By Their Deeds* (Melb, 1986); *Vic Naturalist*, 64 (1947-48), p 52; Inst of Engineers, Aust, *J*, 27, 1955, p 98, 31, 1959, p 77; *Univ Melb Gazette*, June 1955, p 33.

RONALD McNICOLL

CHARD, MARJORIE; see CONLEY

CHARLES, RICHARD STANLEY (1901-1974), spearfisherman and motor trader, was born on 23 April 1901 at Moseley, Worcestershire, England, youngest son of Edward John Charles, master builder, and his second wife Laura Jane, née Bruton. Educated at Steyne School, Worthing, Dick accompanied his family to Canada, to Mexico and in 1913 to Tasmania where Edward worked as an hydraulic engineer. After attending the Friends' High School, Hobart, Dick was apprenticed as a fitter and turner at H. Jones [q.v.9] & Co. Ltd's jam factory. Interested in flying from its early days, he obtained ground-engineer licence No. 15 and in 1921 flew from Sydney to Kingaroy, Queensland. He worked as an aircraft mechanic with Australian Aircraft & Engineering Co. Ltd at Mascot, Sydney, and as a hoist driver and motor mechanic. On 3 February 1923 at Christ Church, Bexley, he married with Anglican rites Ruth Ross Kelly, a picture-fitter; they were to have four children. About 1924 Charles moved to Hurstville and established a prospering motor-trading business there.

He tried his hand at anything and was a persuasive salesman. In the Depression Charles gave mandolin lessons, and in 1937 built and sold caravans from a factory in McEvoy Street. During World War II he joined the local National Emergency Services and was an instructor in rescue procedures. His alluvial gold prospecting company was not a success. He also bought property at Hurstville.

A founder (1927) of St George's Motor Boat Club, Charles enjoyed motorboat racing, fishing and swimming; in 1932 he had built a 10 000-gallon (37 854-litre) pool in his backyard. About 1937, before the days of fins or snorkels, he became interested in spear-fishing. Using 'an old mirror with the silver scraped off, fitted into an old tyre tube', he made his first mask and 'opened up an entirely new world'. For a spear, he 'bought some shark hooks, straightened them out and fixed them on an eight feet [2.4 m] piece of wood'. The pastime expanded after the war and attracted antagonism from shore fishermen. Fearing that disorganized activity would bring increased restrictions, Charles founded a 'Speargun Fishing Association' at a meeting at Long Reef in April 1948, the forerunner of the Underwater Skindivers' and Fishermen's Association of New South Wales of which he was president in 1948-53. Once it had overcome an unwarranted fear of sharks, skindiving surged in popularity after equipment improved and Hans Hass visited Australia in 1953. That year an inaugural meeting at

Tweed Heads elected Charles founding president of the Underwater Spearfishermen's Association of Australia. Active in promoting and defending the sport, he devised rules for interstate competitions and represented the association in negotiations with maritime authorities.

A balding, bulky, 5 ft 11 ins (180.3 cm) tall, hazel-eyed livewire, usually sporting a battered yachting cap, Charles was acknowledged as 'Australia's leading skindiver'. With a pioneer's resourcefulness, he invented cliff-rescue apparatus, a fish-bite indicator, a spear gun and a safety belt for divers. In retirement he enjoyed world travel. Survived by his wife, daughter and twin sons, he died on 11 July 1974 at his Hurstville home and was cremated. A trophy which he had presented for the Australian Underwater Federation's annual championships commemorates him. His sons were sick of fish.

E. du Cros, *Skindiving in Australia* (Syd, 1960); *Snorkel*, Dec 1954, p 12; *Aust Skindiving Digest*, Feb 1961, p 5; *Aust Skindivers Mag*, Jan 1962, p 13; *Skindiving*, 23 Aug 1974, p 5; information from the Aust Underwater Federation, Syd, Messrs M. Brown, Woonona, R. S. and W. C. Charles, Hurstville, and K. Sykes and Mrs J. Sykes, Narwee, Syd.
CHRIS CUNNEEN

CHARLESWORTH, ALAN MOORHOUSE (1903-1978), air force officer, was born on 17 September 1903 at Lottah, Tasmania, son of Edwin Moorhouse Charlesworth, a storeman from England, and his native-born wife Louisa, née Johnston. Educated at the local state school and St Virgil's College, Hobart, in 1920 Alan entered the Royal Military College, Duntroon, Federal Capital Territory: he was athletics champion (1921-23), company sergeant-major in his final year (1923) and won the sword of honour on graduating. After serving with the 2nd Light Horse Regiment in Queensland, on 27 January 1925 he was seconded to the Royal Australian Air Force and began flying training at Point Cook, Victoria. In March he was injured in an aircraft accident in which his instructor was killed.

On attaining his pilot's wings, in July 1925 Charlesworth was posted to No. 1 Squadron at Laverton; in January 1928 he transferred permanently to the R.A.A.F. and next month was promoted flight lieutenant. He married Edith Margaret Bennett on 30 April in All Saints Anglican Church, St Kilda, before embarking in May for England to attend courses at the Royal Air Force School of Photography, Farnborough. Having been attached in 1929-30 to the R.A.F. Survey Flight in British Somaliland, he returned to Melbourne. Again posted to No. 1 Squadron, in 1932 he flew around Australia with W. G. Woolnough [q.v.12] to make aerial surveys of potential oilfields; for his work, Charlesworth was awarded the Air Force Cross. While on his third posting to No. 1 Squadron (1934-39), he exercised temporary command on several occasions. In November-December 1937 he was responsible for a training flight to Queensland during which a pilot was killed; the accident was one of a series and precipitated severe criticism of the R.A.A.F.

From 1 March 1939, when he was promoted wing commander, Charlesworth held command and staff posts of increasing seniority. In September 1944, with the rank of temporary air commodore, he was posted to Darwin as air officer commanding, North-Western Area. His squadrons carried out offensive strikes to protect the southern flank of the allied drive from New Guinea to the Philippines. He was appointed C.B.E. (1946) for his skilful conduct of air operations, but a subordinate thought him 'too nice . . . to be a military man'. After being sent to England in August 1946 for instruction at the R.A.F. School of Air Support, in the following February Charlesworth became commandant of the School of Land/Air Warfare at Williamtown, New South Wales. During his tour of duty (1949-51) as chief of staff at headquarters, British Commonwealth Occupation Force, Japan, in September 1950 he briefly took charge of the base administration of No. 77 Squadron in Korea. In 1951-53 he was acting air vice marshal while A.O.C., Southern (Training) Command, Melbourne. He had charge of R.A.A.F. overseas headquarters, London, until his air force career ended on 31 December 1955; he was granted the rank of honorary air vice marshal next year.

Director of recruiting for the armed services in 1958-59, he later became an associate of a judge of the Supreme Court of Victoria. Survived by his wife and daughter, Charlesworth died on 21 September 1978 at his Glen Iris home and, after an air force funeral, was cremated.

J. E. Lee, *Duntroon* (Canb, 1952); G. Odgers, *Across the Parallel* (Melb, 1952) and *Air War Against Japan 1943-1945* (Canb, 1957); R. O'Neill, *Australia in the Korean War 1950-53*, 2 (Canb, 1985); A. Powell, *The Shadow's Edge* (Melb, 1988); C. D. Coulthard-Clark, *The Third Brother* (Syd, 1991); *Table Talk*, 10 May 1928; *Argus*, 3 June 1933; *Age* (Melb), 23 Sept 1978; information from the late Air Vice Marshal B. A. Eaton, Isaacs, ACT.　　　　　C. D. COULTHARD-CLARK

CHARLEY, SIR PHILIP BELMONT (1893-1976), dairy farmer, was born on 28 December 1893 at Belmont Park, Richmond, New South Wales, third child and eldest son of PHILIP GEORGE CHARLEY (1863-1937), a Victorian-born horse- and cattle-breeder, and his wife Clara, née Ewens, from Adelaide. Philip senior belonged to the original seven-man Broken Hill syndicate. He sold half his shares in 1886 and in 1891 purchased the historic property of Belmont at Richmond Hill, where he built an Italianate sandstone mansion, and imported, bred and exhibited Cleveland Bays, English hackney horses, Norfolk red polled cattle, and Lincoln and Shropshire sheep. The holder of extensive properties, Charley was president of the Hawkesbury District Agricultural Association, and a vice-president of the Royal Agricultural Society of New South Wales and of the Hawkesbury Benevolent Society and Hospital. He died at Rose Bay on 31 August 1937; his wife, five sons and three daughters survived him.

Philip junior attended Barker College, Hornsby, in 1908-11. A senior prefect in his final year, he was one of the cadets chosen to attend King George V's coronation in 1911. He worked at Belmont Park before accompanying (Sir) Sidney Kidman [q.v.9] on a motorcar trip in 1914 to the latter's Queensland, Northern Territory and South Australian stations. On 8 September 1915 Charley enlisted in the Australian Imperial Force and was posted to the 5th Field Artillery Brigade. From March 1916 he served in France as a driver. Following leave in England, he qualified as an observer and was commissioned in the Australian Flying Corps on 23 June 1917. He served in France at headquarters, No. 1 Wing, and returned to Australia in June 1919 where his appointment terminated on 11 August.

Charley began farming in 1919 at Clarendon Park, Richmond, a gift from his father. Constant flooding forced him to turn from market gardening to dairying. On 18 October 1923 at St Andrew's Anglican Church, Walcha, he married Norma Margaret (d. 1956), daughter of James Nivison of Ohio station. The young couple lived in old Belmont Cottage. After the sale of Belmont Park in 1936, they bought Claremont Cottage, Windsor, first occupied in 1796. Like his father, Charley was active in district affairs. President (for twenty-eight years) of the Hawkesbury District Agricultural Association, he served as an alderman (1925-28) on Richmond Municipal Council and was a director of the Hawkesbury Benevolent Society. From 1939 he supplied milk to the Royal Australian Air Force base at Richmond. During World War II he served as an acting flight lieutenant, R.A.A.F., administering the Air Training Corps, and was deputy-president of a war agriculture committee.

Elected to the council of the Royal Agricultural Society in 1938, Charley was a member of the executive, chairman (1954-65) of the horse section committee, and served on its building and works, cattle, and publicity committees. He was assistant ringmaster (1947-53) and ringmaster (1954-59) at the Royal Easter Show, Sydney, a vice-president (from 1951) of the council, deputy-president (1964) and president (1965). Universally popular, he sought to strengthen the ties between country agricultural associations and the R.A.S., as well as between the R.A.S. and the wider community. He was knighted in 1968. In July next year he sadly retired from 'his life's prime interest' and became vice-patron of the society. He belonged to the Imperial Service and Union clubs, and was president of the Richmond Ex-Servicemen's Club. At St James's Church, Turramurra, on 21 December 1957 Charley had married Myfanwy Ison Rickard, née Page, a widow and a real-estate agent. In the early 1970s they moved to Wahroonga. Survived by his wife, and by the son and three daughters of his first marriage, Sir Philip died there on 7 February 1976 and was cremated.

Richardson & Wrench, *Claremont Cottage 1796-1926* (Windsor, NSW, c1926); D. G. Bowd, *Macquarie Country* (Melb, 1969); G. Mant, *The Big Show* (Syd, 1972); S. Braga, *Barker College* (Syd, 1978); B. H. Fletcher, *The Grand Parade* (Syd, 1988); J. Oppenheimer and B. Mitchell, *Abraham's Tribe* (Walcha, NSW, 1989); Roy Agr Soc (NSW), *RAS Annual*, 1906-21, and *Official Cat of Roy Easter Show* (Syd), 1947-66; Hawkesbury Benevolent Soc and Hospital, *Annual Report*, 1936-56; *Pastoral Review*, 19 Nov 1965; *SMH*, 20 Sept 1966, 1 Jan 1968, 30 July 1969, 10 Feb 1976; *Windsor and Richmond Gazette*, 26 Oct 1923, 3, 10 Sept 1937, 20 June 1956, 10 Jan 1968, 6 Aug 1969; *Country Life*, 1 Aug 1969, 11-17 Feb 1976; personal information.   HILARY WEATHERBURN

CHARLTON, WILLIAM KENNETH (1890-1972), parliamentary officer, was born on 11 March 1890 at Balmain, Sydney, eldest son of William Apedaile Charlton, Anglican clergyman, and his wife Minnie Rose, née Day, both native-born. Educated at Sydney Grammar School, Ken enjoyed surfing. He joined the New South Wales Department of Prisons as a temporary junior clerk in 1906, transferred to the newly established Premier's Department in 1908 and in 1910 was appointed to the official staff of the governor, Lord Chelmsford [q.v.7].

In 1914 Charlton moved to the staff of the Legislative Council of New South Wales as fourth clerk. Next year he was promoted to second clerk. On 28 March 1917 he married Essie May James at St Philip's Anglican Church, Sydney. He was the first secretary (1916-19) of Taronga Zoological Park Trust when Fred Flowers [q.v.8], the president of the Legislative Council, was chairman of the zoo's trustees, and was also the first secretary of the Bronte Progress Association. A foundation member of the Organ Society of Sydney, he played at the Graham Memorial Presbyterian Church, Waverley, and tutored students of the organ. In 1924 he published a booklet, *Parliamentary Government in New South Wales,* as part of the celebrations of the centenary of legislative institutions in that State.

On 1 September 1932 Charlton was appointed clerk assistant; on 21 March 1939 he was commissioned as clerk of the parliaments and clerk of the Legislative Council, positions he held until 10 March 1954. He was also House secretary in 1933-39 and joint secretary of the State branch of the Commonwealth Parliamentary Association. A tall man, with a distinguished profile, he possessed perfect manners and 'impeccable diction' which stood him in good stead throughout his career. He was a master of parliamentary procedure and was impartial to all members who consulted him.

On his retirement, Charlton was appointed organist and choirmaster (1954-68) of St Stephen's Presbyterian Church, Macquarie Street, having formerly been the assistant-organist for many years while employed at Parliament House. In 1961 he was appointed O.B.E. He died on 6 June 1972 at his Woollahra home and was cremated. His wife and daughter survived him; his son, Pilot Officer W. R. K. Charlton, Royal Australian Air Force, had been killed in action in 1942.

PD (NSW), 31 Mar 1954; *SMH*, 10 Jan 1961, 10 June 1972; LC Special Bundles: LC Staff *and* LC Salary Register *and* LC Staff Service Register (NSW Parliamentary Archives).

ROBERT LAWRIE

CHAUNCY, NANCEN BERYL (1900-1970), author, was born on 28 May 1900 at Northwood, Middlesex, England, second of six children and elder daughter of Charles Edward Masterman, civil engineer, and his wife Lilla, née Osmond. Nan had a comfortable and conventional childhood, and was taught by governesses. In 1912 Charles suffered a business reversal and he took his family to Tasmania where he was employed as a council engineer. Nan attended the Collegiate School, Hobart.

By 1914 the Mastermans had moved to Bagdad, some twenty miles (32 km) north of the capital. There, by concerted effort, they cleared the land to grow apples and built a slab hut which Lilla named Cherry Tree Cottage. Nan, who left school at 16, was to write of her childhood as a golden age: she enjoyed the close, family teamwork, the stories told by lamplight, the discovery of fauna and flora, and the legend of a bushranger's cave nearby.

Nan's love of the outdoors stimulated her interest in the Girl Guides' Association. A small, stone-and-concrete cottage built by her brother Kay on his Bagdad property served as a meeting-house and camp-site. In 1920 she established the guides' Claremont Company and subsequently became a commissioner. Appointed welfare officer at Cadbury Fry Pascall Australia Ltd in November 1925, she travelled to England in 1930, both to advance her guiding qualifications at the training centre at Foxlease House, Hampshire, and to learn to be a writer. She lived in a houseboat on the Thames, completed an unpublished novel and in 1934 visited Sweden, Finland and the Soviet Union. Four winters were spent teaching English at Spejderskolen, a school for guides in Denmark.

Returning to Australia in the *Meliskerk* in 1938, Nan met a German refugee Helmut Anton Rosenfeld whom she married on 13 September that year at Holy Trinity Church, Lara, Victoria. They lived in Kay's cottage at Bagdad, established a Saanen stud and named their property Chauncy Vale. Although they had no running water and electricity, they were content, but wartime antagonism caused them to change their surname to Chauncy, the family name of Nan's grandmother. In 1946 Nan and Antony declared their land a sanctuary for various native and exotic animals.

Insufficient income led Nan to publish articles in *Wildlife* and to write radio scripts for the Australian Broadcasting Commission. Her first, full-length novel, *They Found a Cave*, was accepted in 1947 by Frank Eyre of Oxford University Press in England who was impressed with the freshness of its bush setting and its characterization of children. Mrs Chauncy was to publish twelve novels with Oxford. She won the Australian Children's Book of the Year award for *Tiger in the Bush* (1958), *Devils' Hill* (1959) and *Tangara* (1961), and was the first Australian to win the Hans Christian Andersen diploma of merit. A film of *They Found a Cave* was released in 1962. Her fourteen novels included the partially autobiographical *Half a World Away* (1962), *The Roaring 40* (1963), *High and Haunted Island* (1964), *Lizzie Lights* (1968) and *The Lighthouse Keeper's Son* (1969). Nan was innovative in her treatment of Aboriginal issues: *Tangara* and *Mathinna's People* (1967) are generally regarded as her finest work.

A vivacious woman, with observant, brown eyes and a sturdy figure, Mrs Chauncy dressed in practical tweeds. She was an authoritative, but unpretentious, participant at educational and cultural meetings. Her roy-

alties from publishing were small, though her books were translated into thirteen languages and set in braille. Some Australian children's authors in the 1960s and 1970s were influenced by her work and her best novels continue to appear in paperback editions. Nan was a member of the Australian Society of Authors, president (1958-59) of the Tasmanian branch of the Fellowship of Australian Writers and national correspondent (1960-63) for *The Council Fire*.

Survived by her husband and daughter, Nan Chauncy died of cancer on 1 May 1970 at Bagdad and was cremated with Anglican rites. The Children's Book Council's quinquennial award commemorates her. Chauncy Vale has been developed as a nature reserve and recreational area where her writings are displayed.

H. M. Saxby, *A History of Australian's Children's Literature, 1941-1970* (Syd, 1971); B. Niall, *Australia Through the Looking-Glass* (Melb, 1984); W. McVitty, *Authors and Illustrators of Australian Children's Books* (Syd, 1989); *Reading Time*, 36, July 1970, p 30; *PTHRA*, 25, no 4, Dec 1978, p 98; Magpies Mag, *Papers: Explorations into Children's Literature*, 1, no 3, Dec 1990, p 124; K. C. Masterman, Nan Chauncy 1900-1970 (talk to Children's Book Council seminar, Canb, 9 Mar 1975, ts held NL); Chauncy papers (TA).

BERENICE EASTMAN

CHAVE, ALFRED CECIL (1905-1971), tennis administrator, broadcaster and fruit merchant, was born on 16 August 1905 at Auchenflower, Brisbane, second child of Alfred Edward Chave, a fruit merchant from New South Wales, and his English-born wife Mabel, née Fursey. Alf was educated at Wynnum Primary and Brisbane State High schools, then joined the family fruit-business. A talented all-round sportsman, he specialized in tennis. He was a member of Queensland's team in the Linton [q.v.10] Cup from 1924 to 1926 and in 1925 was ranked second in the State behind E. F. ('Gar') Moon, a future Australian singles champion (1930). Chave was to remain one of Queensland's top ten players until 1947. At the Albert Street Methodist Church, Brisbane, on 29 July 1926 he married South African-born Raby Marie Llewellyn Davies.

From 1930, when he began reporting for the Brisbane *Telegraph*, Chave developed a career as a versatile journalist. Later known in Australia as 'the Voice of Tennis', he was a commentator on the international circuit for over forty years. He attended sixteen successive Wimbledons, reporting for the Australian Broadcasting Commission and also for the British Broadcasting Corporation. Enlisting in the Royal Australian Air Force on 13 April 1942, he was commissioned next month. He served as an intelligence officer with No. 25 Squadron in Western Australia and at headquarters, Eastern Area, Brisbane. In July 1944 he was promoted temporary flight lieutenant. On 29 December his appointment was terminated at his own request. Divorced in 1948, on 24 September 1949 Chave married a hairdresser Patricia Mary Sutherland, née Johansson, at the Presbyterian Church, Ann Street, Brisbane. After World War II he built up a successful fruit-business (Alf Chave Export Pty Ltd) at the Brisbane Markets.

Sporting administration was Chave's forte. A council-member (from 1928) of the Queensland Lawn Tennis Association, he served for many years on its management and finance committees. With the exception of the presidency, he occupied every other position on the Q.L.T.A. executive: organizing secretary (1939), vice-president (1948-49 and 1955), assistant-secretary (1950-51) and treasurer (1963-69). He was a founding member (1932) of the Umpires' Association (later the Queensland Lawn Tennis Umpires' Association) and was one of its three selectors in 1939-69.

When the United States of America played Belgium at Milton, Brisbane, in 1957 he became the first Queenslander to referee a Davis Cup inter-zone final. Chave also managed Queensland teams in the Linton Cup and took two national teams overseas. The 1961 team, which included John Newcombe, Bob Hewitt, Ken Fletcher and Fred Stolle, though declared the worst to leave Australia, returned with twenty-eight championships. In 1962 he took the first Australian team to tour the Soviet Union.

Survived by his wife, and by the son and two daughters of his first marriage, Chave died of myocardial infarction on 15 August 1971 in Brisbane and was cremated with Presbyterian forms. His estate was sworn for probate at $126 965. In 1972 the clubhouse at the Milton tennis centre was named after him.

Queensland Lawn Tennis Assn, *A Century of Queensland Tennis* (Brisb, 1988); *SMH*, 16 May 1962; *Telegraph* (Brisb), 13 Oct 1970, 16 Aug 1971; *Courier-Mail*, 16 Aug 1971, 3 Aug 1972; *Australian*, 17 Aug 1971; information from Mr T. Joseph, Robertson, Brisb, Ms T. Tambakis, Somerton Park, Adel, Mr C. and Mrs P. Wilkinson, Mermaid Beach, and Ms L. Bennett, Helensvale, Qld.

R. A. HOWELL
M. L. HOWELL

CHERRY, SIR THOMAS MACFARLAND (1898-1966), professor of mathematics, was born on 21 May 1898 at Glen Iris, Melbourne, second son of Thomas Cherry [q.v.7], bacteriologist, and his English-born wife Edith Sarah, daughter of F. J. Gladman [q.v.4]. Young Tom first attended a 'dame's school', walking four miles (6 km) each day, and became self-reliant and independent. Next came Scotch College, under the scholarly W. S. Littlejohn [q.v.10]; Tom was dux and prefect in 1914. In the senior public examinations he won exhibitions in algebra, physics and chemistry.

At Ormond [q.v.5] College, University of Melbourne (B.A. Hons, 1918), Cherry was influenced by the master D. K. Picken who emphasized algebra and by C. E. Weatherburn [q.v.12] who advocated vector analysis. In the mathematics department were Professor E. J. Nanson and J. H. Michell [qq.v.10]. Cherry was awarded the Dixson scholarship for pure and mixed mathematics, the Professor Wilson [q.v.6] prize for mathematics and natural philosophy, and the Wyselaskie [q.v.6] scholarship in mathematics. Enlisting in the Australian Imperial Force on 25 July 1918, he was posted as a cadet to the Australian Flying Corps and 'learnt telegraphy and solo whist' before his discharge on 24 December.

When Cherry began to study medicine in 1919, his godfather Sir John MacFarland [q.v.10] offered him a loan of £150 per annum to continue with mathematics at the University of Cambridge (B.A., 1922; Ph.D., 1924; Sc.D., 1950). At the end of his first year he was a Wrangler B* (starred for distinction). He was awarded an Isaac Newton scholarship, and named an undergraduate (1920-22) and a B.A. (1922-24) senior scholar at Trinity College. In 1924 he won the Smith prize for applied mathematics and was elected a fellow of Trinity College. He substituted for Professor E. A. Milne at Manchester in 1924-25 and for Professor C. G. (Sir Charles) Darwin in Edinburgh in 1927.

In 1923-28 Cherry undertook research on the ordinary differential equations of dynamics and celestial mechanics following J. H. Poincaré, with H. F. Baker and J. E. Littlewood as his local guides. He looked for integrals of these equations, periodic solutions, relations between different manifolds (families) of solutions, transitions between these families (bifurcations), and the possible complexities and pathologies of non-periodic solutions. There were eleven papers in this period and two a decade later, on this still most modern of topics. They reveal his method clearly: a general theory with pointed, illuminating examples, couched in a mixture of analysis and algebra, with applications from the classical dynamics and mathematical physics.

Cherry was a keen mountaineer and scout. After extensive experience on British mountains, he climbed the Matterhorn in Switzerland and traversed the French Pyrenees in winter. He worked easily and naturally, initially as scoutmaster and then as commissioner of the Boy Scouts in Cambridge, and founded a university rover crew in 1924. While organizing a competition for the chief scout, Lord Baden-Powell, at Cambridge, he met Olive Ellen Wright, a Girl Guide commissioner and leader of the wolf-cub pack from nearby Perse School. Having come home to Australia, he went back to Cambridge and married her on 24 January 1931 at Holy Trinity parish church. In Melbourne Cherry acted as scoutmaster of the Glen Iris troop and led various rover crews. He also founded the Melbourne University Mountaineering Club.

In March 1929 Cherry had returned to the University of Melbourne as professor of mathematics, pure and mixed, a post he held until 1952 when he reluctantly assumed the title of professor of applied mathematics. He had a heavy lecturing load of four full courses, was chairman (1929-52) of the mathematics standing committee of the university's Schools Board, and was responsible for two major reforms of the mathematics syllabi of Victorian schools.

Cherry was notorious for lecturing in the style of the French mathematician P. S. de la Place and welcomed for also lecturing in the style of the German P. G. Lejeune Dirichlet. Terse like the former, he went from mountain top to mountain top, saying: 'It is easy to show that . . .', but he knew that it would take hours to make the climbs up and down the valleys between the peaks. Yet, like Dirichlet he was well organized and made everything follow in a natural progression, building on simple foundations from first principles; again like Dirichlet, he would bring into class a mere scrap of paper with the topic or a formula on it, look at it with an index finger raised to his face in dreamy contemplation, and then proceed to fill the hour with tension and excitement. In 1930 he introduced course-notes for students and replaced the first-year practice classes of one hundred or more students with tutorial groups of twelve.

During World War II Cherry worked on aspects of military research, among them the mathematics of the klystron and of J. G. Q. Worledge's arrays of radar aerials, the use of calculating machines, detonation—pressure and temperature in nitroglycerine films under impact—and operations research. His practical, physical insight, combined with his analytical mathematical skills, made him ideal for such work, as did his army and air force background.

Outside his work for the Department of Defence in the war years, Tom produced little or no research from 1929 to 1946. His energies were devoted to school and undergraduate matters. Undergraduate examination papers consumed a whole term; undergraduate needs were put above the interests of staff, especially the latter's research; courses showed detailed dovetailing; staff workloads, in the official teaching of four year-long courses and in the extra-curricular mathematical tasks expected by Cherry, were unreasonably high. For the schools, Cherry came to occupy a dominant role: he paid detailed attention to syllabus and to teaching method—based on investigation of the underlying problems—with his natural thoroughness and his 'research' attitude; he was concerned to preserve the independence of schools and their right to hold internal examinations up to and including the Leaving certificate; he constructed syllabi suitable for students who did not go on to university, as well as for the university entrance (matriculation) examination; he produced integrated mathematics courses for secondary schools —each subject was an organized and coherent mix of algebra, geometry, trigonometry and arithmetic, linking practice and theory, and grounded on his view of what was pedagogically sound.

Devotion to this great educational machine produced graduates who knew mathematics, and who were capable and confident of producing new mathematics themselves. But his methods had their limitations: the dovetailing of the courses left no easy entry points for new mathematical topics developed after 1920; students had the tools to extend what they had learned, but remained unfamiliar with the Continental and American theories which were changing the face of mathematics. Cherry kept himself informed through wide reading and individual contacts, but very little was spent on the stock of the university library after 1929.

In 1951 the Australian National Research Council awarded Cherry the Lyle [q.v.10] medal; in 1954 he was elected a fellow of the Royal Society, London, and a foundation councillor of the Australian Academy of Science. He served the A.A.S. as secretary —in particular during the International Geophysical Year (1959) when he and a few others 'saved' Australian science's reputation —and as controversial president (1961-64), ending his term after leading a delegation to the Academia Sinica of Peking (Beijing) at a time when the Australian government did not recognize the communist government of China. He was also foundation president of the Australian Mathematical Society (1956-58) and of the Victorian Computer Society (1961-63).

The years from 1945 to 1965 saw ferment in the mathematical sciences in Melbourne. First, the university split the mathematics department by forming a department of statistics under Maurice Belz [q.v.]. Cherry's own research early in this period required vast amounts of numerical work and he read extensively on automatic computation. In 1956 the Commonwealth Scientific and Industrial Research Organization presented the university with the electronic computing machine which, after modification, became CSIRAC. Several appointments were made in computational mathematics. With his practical background, Cherry contributed to the reconstruction of the machine and to numerical methods. Once again, the university split the mathematics department, forming a department of computational mathematics (now computer science).

As a working colleague at all levels, Cherry had a single-mindedness that bordered on the ruthless. He was willing to pitch in himself, doing work of any kind, no matter how menial, but he did so as the one in control. He worked to be informed and prepared, and he was available to his staff every day at morning tea. His was a driving force: he had a very strong character, could correct behaviour with the lift of an eyebrow, and had a compelling public personality, with a kind and gentle manner. Until 1950 he was the power behind mathematics in Victoria. His research and reading drove his teaching. He was shaped in this regard by his practical, independent, Anglican family background and by his sense of responsibility in an isolated Australia. Accustomed to control, he did not find it easy to share power after 1945. While he was in some ways generous, he did not always have the background to appreciate the needs and aspirations of his colleagues for salary rises and promotions. His attitude to mathematics remained that of a practical man who was comfortable with methods based on first principles, and eventually, like others, he fell foul of David Hilbert's dictum: those who do not master and use the new, sharper and more powerful methods are destined to be left behind as mathematics progresses.

For thirty years from the time of his appointment Cherry took an active part as committee-member and president (1929-34, 1946-48) of the Mathematics Association of Victoria. He had the skill for distilling the essence of a complex situation, so much so that his frequent talks for the association made things deceptively simple, as well as elegant and precise. He was not afraid to talk about mathematics and even current research to teachers, and could do so at their levels. As a listener, he asked questions designed to bring speakers to the real point of their obscure or confused comments. The association began to lose the balance between mathematics and teaching when his influence was no longer felt.

Cherry retired from the mathematics department at the end of 1963, but continued to be involved in the A.A.S. and chaired the academic planning board of La Trobe University. In 1965 he was knighted. Soon after, he suffered a severe heart attack. He rapidly recovered and spent an academic year at the University of Washington, Seattle, United States of America, lecturing and writing his last published paper, on Hamiltonian differential equations. Survived by his wife and daughter, he died of myocardial infarction on 21 November 1966 at his Kew home and was buried in Gisborne cemetery.

Records of Aust Academy of Science, 1, no 2, Dec 1967, p 97; *Aust Mathematics Teacher*, 24, no 1, Mar 1968, pp 1, 10, 14, 18, 24, 26; *Biog Memoirs of Fellows of Roy Soc* (Lond), 14, no 2, Nov 1968, p 117; *J of Aust Mathematical Soc*, 9, 1969, p 1 *and*, Series B, Applied Mathematics, 30, 1989, pp 378, 389; Univ Melb Archives.   J. J. CROSS

CHIFLEY, JOSEPH BENEDICT (1885-1951), prime minister and locomotive engine driver, was born on 22 September 1885 at Bathurst, New South Wales, eldest of three sons of Patrick Chifley (1862-1921), a native-born blacksmith, and his wife Mary Anne, née Corrigan (1856?-1929), from Ireland. Ben owed his name to a suggestion by the Mother Superior of St Benedict's Convent, Queanbeyan, where Mary had worked as a domestic servant for the Good Samaritan Sisters. His paternal forebears were also from Ireland and belonged to the class of 'literate small farmers and cottiers . . . people of some self-esteem and position'. Chifley's origins seldom troubled or influenced him, though an outburst in 1950 was to reveal his smouldering fires and feelings: 'I am the descendant of a race that fought a long and bitter fight against perjurers and pimps and liars'.

At the age of 5 Ben went to live on his grandfather's farm at Limekilns, near Bathurst. Although his father visited him occasionally, he rarely saw his mother or brothers over the next nine years. The boy slept on a chaff-bag bed in a four-roomed, wattle-and-daub shack with whitewashed walls and an earthen floor. Cowherd, potato-bagger and general 'dogsbody', he attended a bush school which opened two days one week and three days the next. He was a 'boy alone' in a prolific Catholic community. It is probable that his isolation produced a craving for friendship and affection, but also a certain inability to display deep emotion. Chifley was fond of saying that the events of the 1890s, 1917 and the Depression 'forced the iron into [his] soul', yet his lonely existence in the formative years of childhood and adolescence were ironbark times, only relieved by his thirst for reading and knowledge.

Returning to Bathurst in 1899, he spent

two years at the Patrician Brothers' High School where he acquired some further knowledge of English, mathematics and technical subjects. Chifley's reading was a combination of the classical and the practical. He was familiar with Gibbon's *Decline and Fall of the Roman Empire* and Plutarch's *Lives*, and with a swag of familiar and obscure post-1890s Australian literature. Later, he read the work of George Bernard Shaw and corresponded with J. M. (Baron) Keynes, though towards the end of his life he read detective novels and westerns for relaxation. His fellow members of the Commonwealth Literary Fund committee, including (Sir) Robert Menzies [q.v.], were often astonished at his acquaintance with lesser-known Australian literary artisans.

The 1890s depression had moderated the financial expectations and social mobility of Chifley's father and grandfather. On leaving school, Ben found work as a cashier's assistant at John Meagher [q.v.10] & Co.'s general store, Bathurst. Aware of the disparity between his employer's profits and the wages received by juniors, he felt exploited and dissatisfied. In 1902 he became a shop-boy and subsequently a cleaner and then a fireman in the New South Wales Government Railways and Tramways. Studying four nights a week, he attended classes run by the Workers' Educational Association and the Bathurst branch technical school. By 1914 he was a first-class locomotive engine driver—the youngest in the State—and part of the 'labour aristocracy'. An instructor at the Bathurst Railway Institute, a renowned country Rugby Union footballer, and a competent boxer and cricketer, he could look forward to a settled and improving life.

In 1912 he had met his future wife Elizabeth Gibson McKenzie (1886-1962), daughter of another driver. The Chifleys had fewer financial resources than the staunch Calvinist McKenzies who had travelled to the 'old country' in 1899 and owned a De Dion-Bouton motorcar. Their wedding present to their daughter was tenancy (gifted in 1920) of the modest house at 10 Busby Street, Bathurst, which Elizabeth and Ben retained for the rest of their lives. Chifley took the brave and unusual step of defying the Papal decree, *ne temere* (effective from 1908), which forbade Catholics from marrying outside the Church. As he explained in his laconic fashion, 'One of us has to take the knock. It had better be me'. On 6 June 1914 the couple were married in the Presbyterian Church, Glebe, Sydney. Thereafter, Ben and Elizabeth worshipped in their separate churches.

While he attended Mass regularly, after 1914 Chifley believed that he was no longer a full member of the Church, nor, in his own words, could he be 'one of its model children'.

His Catholicism was strictly private and there is no evidence of religious zeal. Although he never took the agnostic position of John Curtin [q.v.], he probably came close to a humanist view in which the Australian Labor Party had a quasi-religious role; as he once said: 'I try to regard the labour movement in the same light as the leaders of the great religious faiths regard their organizations. *We* are *social* evangelists who are charged with a great responsibility'.

Chifley's marriage was one of dedication and affection. Perhaps it was the bungled aftermath of a serious miscarriage in 1915 that prevented Elizabeth from bearing children. She suffered from an arthritic or rheumatic condition and was to become a semi-invalid. While Ben was prime minister, she stayed at Bathurst, making only a few excursions to Canberra to act as hostess at The Lodge. Apart from a visit to New Zealand in 1947, she seldom travelled with him. A woman of grace, gentle nature and loyalty, she concealed her deeper feelings by 'austere self-control'. Even during the most pressing times, Ben was a devoted husband who returned to Bathurst every weekend he could manage.

In 1916 and 1917 Chifley had opposed conscription. With fellow members of the Locomotive Engine-drivers', Firemen's and Cleaners' Association, he took part in the railway strike of August-September 1917, though he counselled moderation. While expressing solidarity with the urban working class, he was never convinced of the utility or wisdom of the resulting general strike and led local negotiations for a return to work. His action did not save him from dismissal then subsequent reinstatement in the lower rank of fireman. Chifley found himself working for former subordinates (some of whom he had trained) who had been given advancement for scabbing. He later commented, 'The instructor has been fireman to his pupil' and added an oft-repeated phrase that the strike had left 'a legacy of bitterness and a trail of hate'. Premier J. T. Lang [q.v.9] restored the strikers' privileges and seniorities in 1925.

From 1912 Chifley had been a useful witness and advocate for his union in industrial tribunals. He developed a mastery of complex issues concerning wages and conditions, and dealt with evidence in a cool and reasoned manner. Usually receptive to sound advice, he modelled his approach on guidance from an old lawyer who had observed his first day in court. Chifley had gone in 'boots and all' (a favourite expression) and won the case against the employers. The old lawyer remarked, 'Son, you went very well today, but always remember that you don't start to make love to a girl by kicking her in the shins'. A man with a splendid memory for people, facts and idiosyncrasies, Chifley thenceforward built up a store of such anecdotes which he used to good effect.

After the Australian Federated Union of Locomotive Enginemen was formed in 1920, Chifley was a member of its State general committee and a delegate to federal conferences. From the 1920s he was a confirmed centralist and a determined opponent of the rights and powers of the States. In 1922 and 1924 he unsuccessfully sought Australian Labor Party pre-selection for the Legislative Assembly seat of Bathurst and in 1925 contested Macquarie for the House of Representatives. He was defeated by 903 votes, but, in 1928, at the age of 43, and with the assistance of James Scullin [q.v.11] who was to become a lifelong adviser, friend and patron, he won the seat with a majority of 3578.

In Federal parliament Chifley attacked the coal-owners of New South Wales for their handling of industrial disputes. He asserted that punitive measures against strikers had only produced martyrs and politicians, and he deplored circumstances which had always created 'one law for the nobodies and another law for the somebodies'. An admirer of H. B. Higgins's [q.v.9] approach to the settlement of disputes, Chifley supported the Commonwealth Court of Conciliation and Arbitration, and advocated the introduction of specialized arbitrators rather than judges. Echoing the early days of Federal liberalism, he believed that arbitration strengthened the social and industrial bonds that held people together. He was opposed to industrial violence and acknowledged that union leaders could be truculent—'Christ himself was able to choose only twelve good men out of thirteen', he observed—but he recognized that extenuating circumstances for strike action sometimes prevailed. To Chifley, sustained research into the economy was needed to limit industrial discontent, 'the most important problem in the economic life of Australia'.

As the Scullin government disintegrated under the pressures of the Depression and attacks from the left and right, Chifley was appointed minister for defence on 3 March 1931. He proved a competent minister, cutting expenditure, distributing surplus military clothing to the unemployed, gaining valuable experience of the Commonwealth bureaucracy and making contacts with public servants, among them (Sir) John Jensen [q.v.]. Chifley instructed the Military Board to ensure that personnel were not associated with organizations such as the New Guard, and categorically stated that 'Military Forces shall not be used in an industrial dispute' and could only be used in instances of civil disturbance if the Commonwealth agreed to a request by the States for help.

He supported the Premiers' Plan to combat the Depression. While the treasurer E. G. Theodore [q.v.12] was his fishing mate during the bleak Canberra days of 1929-31, Chif was neither as game as Curtin nor influential enough to command internal respect and back 'Red Ted's' alternative. Nor did he favour Lang's plan, a decision which cost him his membership of the A.F.U.L.E. in 1931. His cautious and conservative financial streak and his loyalty to official Labor were paramount.

In the conservative landslide of 1931 he lost Macquarie, partly as a result of the appearance of a 'Lang Labor' candidate A. S. Luchetti. Chifley resisted J. A. Lyons's [q.v.10] attempt to seduce him with an offer of the treasurership in a United Australia Party government. Back at Bathurst, he busied himself with membership of the district hospital committee (chairman 1937-44) and the Abercrombie Shire Council (1933-47). He became a director of one of the city's newspapers, the *National Advocate*, and laid the foundations for his reputation as a shrewd and effective primer of parish pumps from Oberon to Orange. For all that, at the 1934 Federal elections he polled only 10 114 votes, half those for the U.A.P. candidate J. N. Lawson [q.v.] and 4500 fewer than Luchetti.

As president (from 1934) Chifley administered the fragments of federal Labor in New South Wales, a party with only one representative from the State in Federal parliament and a handful of affiliated unions. In May 1935 he embarked on the most torrid and bitter campaign of his life, contesting Lang's personal fiefdom, the State seat of Auburn. Although beaten by 2400 votes, Chifley was in part responsible for the resurrection of the federal A.L.P. in the State—a prerequisite for government in both spheres. He had worked harder and more effectively than anyone to depose Lang and restore the unity which ensured Labor's electoral triumph in New South Wales in 1941. Here at last was his power base.

The rigours of the Auburn campaign had affected Chifley's health. His throat was reduced to 'the hopeless condition of worn-out boot leather', and his nasal Australian 'sand and gravel' drawl coarsened to resemble 'a lot of rusty old chains knocking together'. Lang, the unrelenting hater—'anxious to wound but too cowardly to strike'—was to pursue him to the end of his life. Between 1946 and 1949 the lonely black figure of the 'Big Fella', exercising 'his excessive indulgence in malevolence' in Federal parliament, was one of Menzies' best weapons against Chifley.

In 1935 Chifley had received his greatest opportunity: Federal treasurer R. G. (Baron) Casey [q.v.] arranged his appointment to the royal commission on monetary and banking systems. The commission educated and advantaged Chifley. He mastered the intricacies of government finance, and grasped that there could and should be specific remedies for economic depression, massive unemployment, stagnation and human misery. For the first time he came into contact with academic economists and other experts who, he realized, could not only put him in touch with new, Keynesian theoretical approaches, but also provide mechanical ways of solving the problems of capitalism without fundamentally changing that system.

Chifley signed the commission's report. It recommended the maintenance of a strong central bank to regulate credit, the appointment of an independent governor of a restructured Commonwealth Bank of Australia, selection of its board-members for their 'capacity and diversity of experience and contact, and not as representatives of special interests', and the cementing of ties between the government and the central bank.

Nevertheless, in a powerful declaration of dissent, reservation and addenda, Chifley parted company with his colleagues on the fundamental issue of bank nationalization. He concluded that: 'There is no possibility of . . . well-ordered progress being made in the community, under a system in which there are privately-owned trading banks which have been established for the purposes of making profit', and that 'the best service to the community can be given only by a banking system . . . entirely under national control'. Thus he was 'of the opinion that the trading section of the Commonwealth Bank should be extended, with the ultimate aim of providing the whole of the services now rendered by private trading banks'. Meantime, the profits of the trading banks should be controlled by legislation.

He became firm friends with a fellow commissioner R. C. Mills [q.v.10], whose sense of history and faith in humanity's virtues were values that Chifley, an unusually assiduous reader of the New Testament, could share. After the royal commission, Chifley's beliefs had theoretical underpinning and political potential. The comment that he 'was motivated by a personal obsession rather than deep-seated idealism' has a grain of truth in it, but his drive to make sense of adversity and, through political action, to make Australia a more humane society, raised him above this shallow judgement.

In June 1940 Jensen used his influence to have Chifley appointed director of labour supply and regulation in the Ministry of Munitions. He performed this task with ability and energy. But there was a more important evolution. A relationship of mutual respect and personal sympathy grew between Jensen, Chifley and 'the steel-master' Essington Lewis [q.v.10]. The latter were both men of iron, driven loners and outsiders, patriotically joined in wartime by a strong work ethic and dreams of a powerful, industrialized Australia. Before long, however, Chifley resigned to seek pre-selection for Macquarie in the Federal elections to be held on 21 September. After 'vigorously beat[ing] off the vultures', including H. V. Evatt [q.v.]—Chifley's 'Ivan the Terrible'—he was endorsed for and won the seat while recovering from a serious bout of double pneumonia.

When Labor gained office on 7 October 1941, Chifley had established a solid reputation for intelligence, administrative ability, dependability and durability among a small group of politicians, public servants and advisers. Outsiders were surprised that Curtin gave him the second most important portfolio, that of the Treasury, along with membership of the War Cabinet and of the production executive of cabinet. He ranked third in cabinet after Curtin and the deputy prime minister F. M. Forde. Accepting (Sir) Arthur Fadden's [q.v.] budget with few amendments, Chifley quickly made the Treasury 'one of the creative forces in the Australian war effort'. 'His quiet and obdurate strength and sound sense' rapidly became apparent as Australia, under Curtin's dynamic, sacrificial leadership, mobilized for total war.

H. C. Coombs wrote that the relationship between Chifley and his officials, even the flinty secretary S. G. ('Misery Mac') McFarlane [q.v.], was 'more effective than that achieved by any other minister [he had] known'. Chifley often sought consensus—successfully—in caucus, cabinet and the public service, and extended consultation (further than some Laborites thought desirable) to the Opposition. Yet when the arguments were delivered, he gave prompt and decisive judgement. 'A good memo', he said, 'must end with a recommendation . . . You must get off the fence'. Increasingly, as his command of issues grew, his native obduracy stiffened. The amalgam was both a political asset and, paradoxically, a liability.

Chifley's first duty was to finance the war effort. His second objective was to control inflation. In February 1942 he announced the pegging of wages and profits, the introduction of controls on production, trade and consumption to reduce private spending, and the transfer of surplus personal income to savings and war loans. On 15 April 1942 more price controls were introduced. On 23 July a uniform income tax, giving the Commonwealth a monopoly in this vital field, was attained when the States were defeated in the High Court of Australia.

In the national crisis Chifley proved himself to be his country's greatest treasurer—fiscally responsible, able to transmit the necessity for a reasonable equality of sacrifice, and capable of managing a wartime economy of complexity and difficulty. Financing the war by increased taxation, loans from the Australian public, and central bank credit, he ensured that the nation did not become burdened with overseas debt, as it had been after World War I. Every budget was accompanied by his strictures on 'vigorous self-denial', labour discipline and restriction of consumer demand with the aim of controlling a huge accumulation of purchasing power.

A cogent example of Chifley's negotiating skills was evident on 9 May 1946 when he and the American under-secretary of state Dean Acheson agreed to settle Australia's $US 27 million debt to the United States under the Lend-Lease scheme, without tariff concessions which the Americans had wanted. Chifley's speed and decisiveness produced a first-rate result for his country. So successful was his economic management that, from 1941 to 1949, government debts abroad were reduced by £117 million, and substantial external and internal reserves were created.

On 22 December 1942 Chifley had taken the additional post of minister for postwar reconstruction. His department was to lay the foundations for a new social order. In January 1943 he appointed the Rural Reconstruction Commission to rehabilitate and improve the agricultural sector. That month he selected Coombs as director-general of his new department which was staffed largely by recruitment outside the public service. Chifley's 'long-haired men and short-skirted women' quickly produced a stream of suggestions, proposals and policies, thereby setting Labor's agenda for the next seven years. His central aim was to inaugurate a policy of full employment. Through state action and controls, he hoped that Australians would achieve higher standards of living, while the disadvantaged would be provided with sufficient benefits to enable them to avoid the worst features of poverty and misfortune.

Memories of the Depression continued to gnaw at Chifley. He delivered one of his most powerful and emotional speeches in support of the referendum in 1944 which (unsuccessfully) sought to grant the Federal government fourteen new powers. In response to the claim that the proposed constitutional changes put individual liberty at risk, he observed:

In my electorate, I witnessed the freedom that was enjoyed by 2,000 men outside a factory in an attempt to secure the one job that was offering . . . the freedom to starve and to live on the dole of 8s. 9d. a week—a single man on 5s. 6d. . . . [This is] the freedom of the economic individualists whose only God was Mammon and profit . . . I would prefer regimentation to economic individualism'.

By 1944 Chifley rather than Curtin was managing the parliamentary and industrial organs of the A.L.P. Chifley had emerged from the 'industrial wing' (Curtin's phrase) of the party and Curtin from the political. As 'G.O.C. House Strategy', Chifley controlled caucus and the federal executive, using time and techniques which Curtin found onerous and debilitating. Although their backgrounds were similar, the two were temperamentally poles apart and the qualities of one complemented those of the other. The sensitive, tired leader once said, 'Come over . . . I'm spiritually bankrupt'. Chifley refreshed him. Their private relationship and political fraternalism deepened in wartime, and Evatt's absences overseas during the critical months from March to June 1942 and again from April to September 1943 allowed them to consolidate their affection. Chifley served as Evatt's replacement on the Advisory War Council and also stood in for Curtin on the council during April-July 1944. Curtin welcomed Chifley's friendship, common sense and sound advice. 'I would not like to think how I could carry on this job without what I get from old Ben', he had remarked in 1943, 'When I move on from it he is going to take my place'.

Although Chifley did well as acting prime minister from 30 April to 2 July 1945, primitive opinion polls had indicated that he was scarcely worthy of consideration for the prime ministership. Yet, after Curtin's death on 5 July, and following a brief interregnum under Forde, Chifley was sworn in as prime minister of Australia on 13 July. He had polled three times as many votes in caucus as Forde; support for the other contenders N. J. O. Makin and Evatt had been insignificant. Chifley was at first reluctant to nominate, but Scullin persuaded him to stand rather than attend Curtin's funeral in Perth. 'I couldn't go, I simply couldn't go', said Chifley, his complex honesty displaying both grief and a concern for the numbers and power.

A 'six-footer' (182.9 cm) with a spare, large-boned frame, Chifley had a strong, rough-hewn countenance which often presented a poker face. As he aged and his black hair greyed, his features increasingly resembled those of his mother. To Dame Enid Lyons, Chifley seemed like 'a Great Dane, with his rugged good looks, his immense personal dignity, and his friendly, but always slightly reserved, bearing'. He had twinkling, grey-blue eyes and great charm, was attractive to women and had an eye for a pretty girl, though he declined to take advantage of this characteristic. A long upper lip masked his teeth, the lower being invariably attached to a pipe. Like (Sir) Winston Churchill's cigars, the pipe became an invaluable political trademark and negotiating tool, consuming more matches than it did tobacco. Chifley ate sparingly, walked for exercise and was frugal with his own and the country's money. Once he and his nephew stayed at a bush hotel. Chifley had no luggage, but produced a silk pyjama coat from one pocket of his overcoat and pyjama pants from the other.

Chifley concluded Labor's wartime administration by announcing the end of the war with Japan on 15 August 1945. He favoured a soft peace treaty, arguing that, 'Unless we help Japan, we will have another war in a generation. But this is something I cannot discuss even with my colleagues'. His first trip abroad as prime minister was an unostentatious one over Christmas 1945 to Australian troops still in the South-West Pacific Area. He travelled to London in 1948, attended Commonwealth prime ministers' conferences there in 1946 and 1949, and went to Washington and Tokyo in May 1946, and to Wellington in December 1947. His visits were short, productive and inexpensive.

On 28 September 1946 Chifley's party was returned at the polls with a reduced majority, but with a mandate for social reconstruction and a further extension of the functions of the Commonwealth government. Although referenda that year on marketing and employment were defeated, one on social services was approved. This administration was among the most creative of all Australian governments. The initiatives were not socialist, or particularly radical, being constrained by Chifley's deep concern for the existing fabric of society, and by his fear of postwar inflation and unemployment. His government tightened control over the States, extended welfare services, eased ex-service personnel into civilian life (without the dislocation and suffering that had occurred after 1918), and initiated a host of liberal measures which bore fruit during the 'long boom' of the 1950s and 1960s.

Once convinced of their merits, Chifley gave such initiatives his wholehearted support. L. F. Crisp has claimed that his retention of the treasurership while prime minister was a necessary duty, and a burden that was valuable and sustainable. After 1947, however, his tenure of the two most important posts in the ministry caused physical stress and gradually became a handicap.

By his control of the Treasury he could act promptly and decisively at critical times. The best example was his personal sponsorship of (Sir) Laurence Hartnett's General Motors-Holden's [q.v.9] Ltd plan to manufacture a completely Australian-made motorcar. Through this project, Chifley envisaged that Australia's defence industry would be built up, ancillary manufacturing would be expanded, and a firm base for further corporate development, using both native and overseas capital, would be established. Private industry benefited a great deal from his support, through plant, finance and other resources allocated to it at cheap rates, and he became the political father of the local Holden car. His commitment to nationalization embraced only banking and public utilities.

Social security was extended by the Social Services Consolidation and the Pharmaceutical Benefits Acts of 1947, though the government's attempt to introduce a Commonwealth health scheme foundered on the intransigence of the British Medical Association in Australia. The National Welfare Fund, based on progressive taxation, was augmented to avoid contributory social security programmes and to offset Chifley's hard-nosed retention of relatively heavy taxation on lower income earners. There was a modest expansion into tertiary education with the funding of Commonwealth scholarships, the establishment of the Commonwealth Education Office and the setting up of the Australian National University. Nevertheless, when Chifley was asked to involve the Commonwealth in financing primary and secondary schooling, he declared that education was tied up with state aid to religion and was a State function. Advised of Commonwealth subsidies for pre-school and university education, he retorted, 'That's different—they're for kids *before* they've got souls and *after* they've lost 'em'.

The Commonwealth Conciliation and Arbitration Act of 1947 embodied many of Chifley's ideas on how industrial relations should be regulated. By then, militant unions, particularly those involving the waterside workers, seamen, coalminers and metal workers, were chafing at the government's tight controls on wages and consumption, and at its slowness in dealing with working-class grievances which had festered since the Depression and which were exacerbated by mild inflation.

Chifley often said, 'I hate bloody injustice', and, while sections of the organized working class might feel that his government was not adequately representing their aspirations, he did take pains to remedy individual problems that were brought to his attention. The former Lang supporter E. J. Ward [q.v.] had the benefit of Chifley's presence in the witness box during the royal commission into timber rights in the Territory of Papua-New Guinea (1949), and Chifley personally revived Lieutenant General (Sir) Sydney Rowell's [q.v.] career. The Council for Scientific and Industrial Research and the Australian Broadcasting Commission both enjoyed Chifley's protection.

Through A. A. Calwell's [q.v.] efforts as minister for immigration, Australia embarked on its greatest immigration endeavour. The programme was intended to preserve the

Anglo-Celtic character of the population, but ultimately transformed the composition of the nation. Chifley's government inaugurated the Snowy Mountains hydro-electric scheme. Qantas Empire Airways Ltd was converted to a successful, state-owned overseas airline. Trans-Australia Airlines was established as a viable competitor to the private carriers when nationalization of the industry proved legally impossible.

The centrepiece of the government's voluminous legislation (parallelled by fraternal Labour parties in New Zealand and Britain) was, in Chifley's mind, the Banking and the Commonwealth Bank Acts of 1945. These statutes gave the government ultimate control over monetary policy, and formally recognized the Commonwealth Bank as the nation's central bank, empowered to regulate the activities of the private trading banks.

In 1947 the Melbourne City Council challenged the validity of section 48 of the Banking Act which directed all government instrumentalities to bank solely with the Commonwealth. The High Court declared that the section was invalid. Chifley believed that attacks on more important provisions would follow and that the core of his political life's work was at risk. After securing the assent of cabinet, caucus and the federal executive, on 16 August he announced his intention to have legislation prepared for the nationalization of banking. His critics characterized the decision as sudden pique—a view which Calwell called 'the greatest piffle' he had ever heard. The need to nationalize the banks was questionable: Coombs argued that the central banking mechanism was not jeopardized, and it was to remain in place as a monument to Chifley. What is clear is that Chifley was consistent in implementing a fundamental policy of the party and standing by principles which he had held since 1935. He 'took the holy ikon of Socialism off the walls of Caucus and marched with it into the House'.

Assisted by newspapers increasingly vitriolic towards Chifley, the private banks mobilized grassroots middle-class opinion in a way that conservatives had not managed since 1932. A High Court decision (1948) to disallow the nationalization legislation, the Banking Act of 1947, was confirmed by the Privy Council in 1949. Chifley admitted to Frank Green [q.v.] that he had moved too fast on banking: 'It is a mistake to show the rooster the axe when you are going to take his head off; you should show him a bit of corn first'.

Another serious problem for Chifley had been Australia's ratification of the Bretton Woods agreement (1944) which set up the International Monetary Fund and the International Bank for Reconstruction and Development. Resolution of the issue was delayed by the A.L.P.'s distrust of international finance, by its populist tendencies and its Depression memories. Chifley was well aware of Australia's need of capital, the weakness of sterling, problems with the dollar balance and the advantages of liberalizing world trade which would eventually benefit Australia as a commodity-exporting country. In November 1946 cabinet recommended ratification to caucus, but on 4 December caucus decided to refer the issue to the party's federal conference. The rebuff was a blow to Chifley's prestige. He managed to prevent the matter from reaching conference, and finally got his way in March 1947.

In public he always asserted that the policy of the A.L.P. was the total preserve of its federal conference. 'I have fought for that principle and because I did so I lost my seat in this Parliament when the executive of the N.S.W. Labor Party resolved that each State should make its own decisions'. Yet the evidence discloses that in caucus, cabinet and conference Chifley was able to manipulate policies and personalities to a far greater extent than this profession of rectitude suggests.

With the end of World War II, international issues had demanded Chifley's attention. On many key questions he left policy to Evatt. 'Leave it to the Doc', he would say, although in November 1945 he overruled Evatt's proposal that Australia should 'play an active diplomatic role in the Netherlands East Indies' and station additional troops there. He was more sympathetic to the Indonesian nationalists than Evatt was, and tacitly supported the shipping and arms embargoes against the Dutch. He was also reluctant to involve Australia in Britain's difficulties in Malaya.

Chifley was equivocal about the new relationship between Australia and the United States of America. Sceptical of the motives behind the Americans' advocacy of trade liberalization and the demolition of Imperial preference, he was also concerned by their reluctance to tie global trade agreements to full-employment objectives. He was unwilling to facilitate American business expansion in Australia, although he was responsive to corporate investment by that country. As a counterbalance to the American connexion, he attempted to strengthen ties with Britain through defence co-operation, financial arrangements and economic agreements. He made gifts of £45 million to Britain, and agreed to keep £150 million of Australia's funds there. These measures also reflected Chifley's growing Empire loyalty.

Evatt's abrasiveness antagonized the American government, but the issue which led to a cooling of relations between the U.S.A. and Australia was growing American suspicion of the Chifley government as too radical and not entirely trustworthy. In June 1948 the U.S.A. ceased passing some categories of classified information to Australia, and the British put pressure on Chifley to create a new, federal counter-intelligence body. The establishment in 1949 of the Australian Security Intelligence Organization was the outcome.

In the 1920s Chifley had worked his return passage to the Netherlands East Indies and India. As prime minister, he took a leading part in keeping India in the British Commonwealth as a republic. Convinced that the European colonial empires were finished, he supported independence movements in South East Asia. He often argued that economic assistance rather than military action would contain the growth of communism in the region. Weakly, he delayed recognizing Communist China when Britain had already done so. His excuse was that it was ethically wrong to recognize China just before an Australian general election. The real reason was his fear that the A.L.P. would be linked with 'Yellow Communism'.

By 1948 international tensions and the emergence of the Cold War were impinging dramatically on Australia to the disadvantage of the Chifley government. At the behest of their communist leaders, the coalminers struck on 27 June 1949. The New South Wales Labor government, the Joint Coal Board (Chifley's own creation), public opinion and a growing right-wing faction in his own party led (with cabinet's concurrence) to the most drastic solution possible for a Labor leader: a virulent 'boots and all' gaoling of militant miners' leaders, the smashing of the strike by state action and, above all, the use of troops to cut coal. The strike was broken by 15 August, but popular approval of the government's firm action soon dissipated and sections of the Labor Party were alienated and demoralized.

Although tired, Chifley was undaunted. He and his team ran a complacent campaign for the 1949 general elections, never believing that the 'discredited old gang of Menzies, Fadden and Casey' would be accepted. Chifley's memories were longer than those of the swinging voter. A cartoon by E. S. Scorfield [q.v.] in the *Bulletin* (30 November), titled 'Going *my* way—on a full petrol tank?', depicted Chifley in an old model 'Marx II' car being relieved of his passenger, an elegant female voter, by the confident Menzies driving a free-enterprise Holden.

The resumption of petrol rationing on 15 November—the day after Chifley's flat policy speech lacking 'glittering promises' and predicting more tight economic controls—had been a mistake. Another was his rejection of child endowment payments for the first child:

here the prudence of the lonely boy from the bush, the childless Australian male, overcame electoral realities. Despite Calwell's confidence, Labor gained no advantage from the 1948 electoral redistribution which increased from 74 to 121 the number of seats to be contested in the House of Representatives.

In a national radio broadcast on 6 December Lang accused Ben and Elizabeth Chifley of making mortgage advances at interest rates of up to 9 per cent. The allegation hurt Chifley deeply. He had gained little personal profit from the transactions, had usually acted as a trustee and had helped borrowers who lacked security. In hindsight, however, he was politically vulnerable on the issue.

The Chifley government was destroyed on 10 December 1949. A loss of 3.7 per cent of the total vote reduced the A.L.P. to 47 voting members in the House compared with the Liberal-Country Party coalition's 74. Chifley's social faith had been rejected in favour of other priorities. On 14 November, he had said: 'It is the duty and the responsibility of the community, and particularly those more fortunately placed, to see that our less fortunate fellow citizens are protected from those shafts of fate which leave them helpless and without hope ... That is the objective for which we are striving. It is ... the beacon, the light on the hill, to which our eyes are always turned and to which our efforts are always directed'.

Chifley was not a successful leader of the Opposition. He had 'had responsibility far too long ever to be a destructive oppositionist'. While he managed to hold the party together, there were indications that even his grip on the A.L.P. was loosening. The election produced a new group of right-wing Catholic ideologues in parliament. 'Those new Melbourne fellows', he claimed, 'have a bug ... that's what's wrong with them ... the religious fanatic is worse than the political fanatic'. When the federal executive instructed the federal parliamentary party to let the Communist Party dissolution bill (1950) through the Senate, without pressing for the civil liberties safeguards that Chifley had advocated, he suffered a major defeat. 'Accept your humiliation and we can go forward; recriminate and we shall split', he said.

Nor was Chifley happy that Evatt chose to appear before the High Court to contest the validity of the Act. 'You've got to remember what Bert did for the Union after 1917. And we've got to remember that he has a brilliant mind. That's the trouble with brilliant minds. They make hellish awful mistakes'. In Chifley's last major speech on 10 June 1951 he appealed to the A.L.P. to preserve civil liberties and to contain rightist ideology. 'You cannot afford to be in the middle of the road', he declaimed. That was where he had been throughout his life in Labor politics, but, as society shifted to the right, he moved, it seemed, to the left.

On 19 March 1951 the governor-general (Sir) William McKell granted Menzies' request for a double dissolution on the grounds of parliament's failure to pass the Commonwealth Bank bill (1950). Chifley had fought the measure tooth and nail, and was surprised by the decision of McKell, whom he had appointed. The elections on 28 April were a disaster for Labor, which made a few gains in the House of Representatives but lost control of the Senate.

Chifley was physically failing. On 26 November 1950 he had suffered a coronary occlusion while driving his personal indulgence, a powerful American Buick. His convalescence was lengthy. From then on he spent more time on the couch in his office and in his bed at Canberra's Hotel Kurrajong. Towards the end of his life he lay in bed for much of the weekends, sipping tea, his favourite drink, and munching toast.

As was his custom, he refused to 'trip the light fantastic' or put on a dinner-suit (he never had one and saw no need for it) and attend the state ball on 13 June 1951 at Parliament House. That night at 7 o'clock Phyllis Donnelly, his personal secretary, confidante and affectionate companion since 1928, joined him at the Hotel Kurrajong. After listening to the A.B.C. news, he telephoned Elizabeth in Bathurst. He ate a light supper, provided as usual by Mrs Donnelly, then at about 9.20 p.m. complained of chest pains. In the throes of a massive coronary occlusion, Chifley was moved to Canberra Community Hospital. Attempts to revive him failed.

Menzies announced Chifley's death to the parliamentary merry-makers who abandoned the gathering. Chifley was given a simple and short state funeral, without eulogies, at Bathurst in the Catholic Cathedral of St Michael and St John, and was buried in the local cemetery. On his coffin lay one wreath, inscribed 'Ben, from Elizabeth'. Musical honours were provided by his favourite cultural organization, the Bathurst District Band, and 30 000 citizens watched the funeral. He had valued the freedom of the city of Bathurst (conferred on him in 1949) higher than his membership (1945) of the Privy Council. In June 1952 Evatt unveiled a grey marble obelisk over Chifley's grave, paid for by the A.L.P. federal executive and the Australian Council of Trade Unions. On the monument are words from his speech of 10 June 1951:

If an idea is worth fighting for, no matter the penalty, fight for the right, and truth and justice will prevail.

Chifley left a modest £13 400, including his half-share in 10 Busby Street which was opened by Prime Minister E. G. Whitlam in 1973 as a memorial to him. In his last three years Ben had secretly given away over £3000 to friends and relations. A posthumous portrait (1953) of Chifley by A. D. Colquhoun is held by Parliament House, Canberra.

Although he was much more than the successful, folksy, unflustered leader of popular legend, Chifley lacked Curtin's intellect, passion and deftness. Yet Jawaharlal Nehru's tribute was not exaggerated: 'Mr Chifley struck me as an outstanding personality and I was greatly attracted to him . . . Simple and straightforward . . . whatever he said . . . made an impression'. Oliver Hogue gauged his intrinsic quality when he said, 'Chifley . . . had a logical mind but he humanized all his thinking, even on politics . . . He understood the human heart, the ideals, the ambitions, the follies and the passions of men and women. Chifley put tolerance amongst the highest virtues, and he had it in large measure himself'. In Chif's own words, 'We may make mistakes because we are only human, and no political party can remake human nature. The most that we can do is to help the masses of the people and give to them some sense of security and some degree of human happiness'. This he did.

ALP (NSW) Branch), The Light on the Hill (Syd, 1951); L. F. Crisp, Ben Chifley (Melb, 1961); N. J. O. Makin, Federal Labor Leaders (Syd, 1961); L. Haylen, Twenty Years' Hard Labor (Melb, 1969); P. Hasluck, The Government and the People 1942-1945 (Canb, 1970); S. J. Butlin and C. B. Schedvin, War Economy 1942-1945 (Canb, 1977); F. Daly, From Curtin to Kerr (Melb, 1977); H. C. Coombs, Trial Balance (Melb, 1981); D. Langmore, Prime Ministers' Wives (Melb, 1992); Roy Com Appointed to Inquire into the Monetary and Banking Systems . . . in Australia, Report, PP (Cwlth), 1934-37, 5 (74); PD (Cwlth), 19 June 1951, p 61; Twentieth Century, 28, Autumn 1974, p 226; Age (Melb), 14 June 1951; SMH, 14-18 June 1951; C. Johnson, Social Harmony and Australian Labor: the ideology of the Curtin, Chifley and Whitlam Labor Governments (Ph.D. thesis, Univ Adel, 1986); Chifley papers (NL and Bathurst District Hist Soc); Chifley correspondence (AA); J. J. Dedman and D. K. Rodgers papers (NL).   D. B. WATERSON

CHINNER, NORMAN (1909-1961), organist and conductor, was born on 7 August 1909 at Malvern, Adelaide, son of Charles Williams Chinner, a South Australian-born accountant, and his wife Winifred Maud, née Cowperthwaite, a singer and violinist from Victoria. With music on both sides of his family—Norman's father, uncle and grandfather had all been organists—he was taught to play the pipe organ by Fred Pilgrim at the local Methodist church. Chinner attended Prince Alfred College and in 1928 won a scholarship for organ to the Elder [q.v.4] Conservatorium of Music; five years later he became a licentiate of the Royal Schools of Music, London. After working in a bank and being employed by a firm of woolbrokers, in 1932-39 he was musical director at his old school. While holding the posts of organist and choirmaster at Pirie Street (1939-47) and Kent Town (1932) Methodist churches, he began to make his mark as a conductor. A 'tall, dark, handsome, broad-shouldered young man', he had a modest demeanor which did not disguise the bulldoggishness of his jaw.

In 1940 Chinner joined the Australian Broadcasting Commission as musical presentations officer in South Australia. As part-time assistant to William Cade [q.v.], he conducted the Adelaide Wireless Chorus and in 1946 was to take over its successor, the Adelaide Singers. They maintained a large repertoire, and broadcast part-songs and works by Britten, Palmgren, Bartok and Holst. In 1941 Chinner also assumed direction of the Adelaide Philharmonic Choir and over the course of the next twenty years made it Australia's finest. Although deputy-conductor (from 1942) for the A.B.C., he was merely chorus master for major works, except for the first Adelaide broadcast of the *Messiah* and a charity concert for the Australian Comforts Fund, both in 1942. By 1946, however, he was in full command for *Canterbury Pilgrims, Elijah* and *Hiawatha*.

Chinner directed many early Australian performances of English choral works, as well as premieres of *Kubla Khan* and Horace Perkins's *Knight and Witchery*. From 1949 he travelled regularly to Sydney, Melbourne, Brisbane and Perth where he conducted oratorios, invariably to glowing praise from the critics. His gestures were 'free and unrestrained', but never excessively indulgent. With the Adelaide Singers he recorded W. G. James's [q.v.] carols in 1955. Three years later, he again visited Melbourne with the Adelaide Philharmonic Choir for performances to celebrate the twenty-first anniversary of its foundation.

At the Malvern Methodist Church on 1 August 1953 Chinner had married a 25-year-old actress Cecilia Patricia Halcyon Sands; they separated soon afterwards and were divorced in 1959. Having assisted Dr Robert Dalley-Scarlett [q.v.8] to make A.B.C. recordings of music to celebrate the coronation of Queen Elizabeth II, Chinner supervised musical programmes for her visit to Adelaide in 1954, and for that of the Queen Mother in 1958. His excellence with choirs was not matched by his orchestral gifts and he was given responsibility for the Adelaide Light Orchestra on country tours only. For almost ten years he directed studio broadcasts of the popular 'Moods and Melodies'. Sponsored by

the A.B.C., he twice visited England. In 1957 he was appointed O.B.E.

His name was so familiar in Adelaide that 'Chinner who conducts French' was used in 1952 as a crossword clue. He died of a coronary occlusion on 5 November 1961 in his sister's home at Netherby and was buried in Centennial Park cemetery. From 1967 the Adelaide Philharmonic Choir has commemorated him by a scholarship.

A. D. McCredie (ed), *From Colonel Light into the Footlights* (Adel, 1989); *Advertiser* (Adel), 21 Apr 1950, 4 Aug 1953, 9 Nov 1961; *SMH*, 24 Dec 1952; press-clippings, 1927-61 (held by Mrs C. Fisher, Adel).   ELIZABETH SILSBURY

CHIPPINDALL, SIR GILES TATLOCK (1893-1969), public servant, was born on 21 May 1893 at North Carlton, Melbourne, thirteenth child of Giles Tatlock Chippindall, an inspector of works from New South Wales, and his English-born wife Sarah Isaac, née Dawson. Educated at state schools and Prahran College, young Giles joined the Postmaster-General's Department on 28 September 1908 as a telegraph messenger: 'I started at the bottom of the ladder', was one of his few boasts. On 18 February 1918 he married Grace Elizabeth Bayley in the Baptist Church, Armadale. 'Chip' performed clerical work in the telegraph, mail, electrical engineer's and telephone branches, and was chief inspector (personnel) in 1936-41.

Promoted deputy-director, Department of War Organization of Industry, in 1941, Chippindall became director-general next year. He held the related post of chief executive-officer to the production executive of cabinet and was a member of numerous wartime bodies, among them the Allied Supply Standing Committee, and the Commonwealth War Commitments and Prices Stabilization committees. Responsible for co ordinating the deployment of labour, plant and material to meet essential war needs, his department was often hampered by other branches of the public service.

Some of the W.O.I.'s efforts to conserve resources were controversial: the 'Victory' suit for men was austere and unpopular, and an order curtailing Christmas advertising in 1942 occasioned derision. J. J. Dedman [q.v.] and his senior officials were accused of being ignorant of business practicalities. At times the department was over enthusiastic, but much of the criticism levelled against it was unfair. In 1945 Chippindall was appointed secretary, Department of Supply and Shipping, and chairman of the Commonwealth Disposals Commission. Although it was considered to be slow in the early years of its operation, the commission avoided malpractices that were common in similar bodies overseas.

With a reputation as a tough-minded administrator who got things done, in 1946 Chippindall returned to the Postmaster-General's Department as assistant director-general. He was appointed director-general in March 1949 and was to guide the organization through nearly ten years of growth. The number of telephones in service doubled, automatic telephone exchanges replaced manual ones, planning began for a national subscriber-dialling system, the volume of mail increased by 45 per cent, the teleprinter exchange service (telex) boomed and assets more than quadrupled to some £403 million. In 1956 television commenced in Australia: Chippindall had been influential in convincing the government that the telecommunications network could cope with a range of stations.

He restructured the post office into three streamlined divisions, implemented an extensive committee system, and fostered good relations between technical and clerical personnel. His administration had to contend with increasing public debate over capital requirements, cross-subsidization and pricing policies. In 1954 parliament's joint committee of public accounts condemned the department for emphasizing 'technical efficiency' at the expense of 'business management'.

Chippindall was proud of his organization's contribution to Australia's development. He was held in high regard in the public service, though some of his staff regarded him as a martinet. An effective lobbyist who was skilled in marshalling arguments, he approached ministers, 'Tweed suited, his briefcase conspicuously stuffed with papers, his expression earnest but mild'. (Sir) Robert Menzies [q.v.] was a personal friend. Appointed C.B.E. (1950), Chippindall was knighted in 1955. He published *The Australian Post Office: Ten Years of Progress* (Melbourne, 1958).

Following his formal retirement on 20 May 1958, Sir Giles was chairman of the Overseas Telecommunications Commission (1961-62) and of the Australian National Airlines Commission (1959-66). In the aftermath of the Airlines Equipment Act (1958) his support for the government's cross-charter arrangements displeased the staff of Trans-Australia Airlines, but they came to appreciate his 'human approach to problems and people'. Chippindall engaged in robust public exchanges with (Sir) Reginald Ansett over airline competition, and told Ansett to 'stop bleating' and 'count his blessings'.

Chairman of W. R. Rolph [q.v.11] & Sons Pty Ltd, Chippindall was also a director of many companies. In 1958, when he had joined the board of Telephone & Electrical Industries Pty Ltd (a major supplier to the Post-master-General's Department), questions were raised in Federal parliament. In 1958-69 he presided over the National Old People's Welfare Council of Australia (Australian Council on the Ageing). He was president (1946-47) and captain (1948-49) of the Kingston Heath Golf Club. An enthusiastic angler, in November 1969 he collapsed while fishing at Flinders Island, off Tasmania. Chippindall died on 20 December that year in East Melbourne and was cremated; his wife, son and daughter survived him.

P. Hasluck, *The Government and the People 1942-1945* (Canb, 1970); I. Sabey, *Challenge in the Skies* (Melb, 1979); A. Moyal, *Clear Across Australia* (Melb, 1984); *PD* (Cwlth), 1958, p 1115, 1960, p 772, 1966, p 1130; *PP* (Cwlth), 1953-54, 6, p 1147; *Telecommunication J of Aust*, 7, no 3, Feb 1949; *SMH*, 17 Apr 1958, 29 Mar 1960, 13 July 1961, 22 Dec 1969; *Advertiser* (Adel), 1 July 1966; *Age, Canb Times* and *Sun News-Pictorial*, 22 Dec 1969.

IAN CARNELL

CHISHOLM, ALEXANDER HUGH (1890-1977), journalist, ornithologist and encyclopaedist, was born on 28 March 1890 at Maryborough, Victoria, seventh of eight children of Colin Chisholm, a native-born grocer, and his Scottish-born wife Charlotte, née Kennedy. Alec attended Maryborough State School until the age of 12. During his formative years, after work and farm chores, he educated himself, learned shorthand, wrote poetry, fossicked for gold, collected stamps and cigarette cards, and enjoyed amateur theatricals. An insatiable reading appetite and an astounding memory were to serve him well.

In his autobiography, *The Joy of the Earth* (Sydney, 1969), Chisholm claimed that, from early childhood, he was aware of nature surrounding him. Whenever he could, he escaped to the bush and in 1907 commenced a diary in which the entries were almost entirely devoted to birds. That year he became a member of the (Royal) Australasian Ornithologists Union and in 1908 published six articles in *Emu*. A conservationist long before it became fashionable to be one, he attacked the plume trade in an article in the *Maryborough and Dunolly Advertiser* which won him many friends, among them (Dame) Mary Gilmore [q.v.9]; in 1911 he accepted a job as a reporter on that newspaper. An invitation to join the Bird Observers' Club led to his lifelong association with natural history societies; once nature study was accepted as a school subject, he addressed children and coached teachers.

Four major moves and the irregular hours of journalism enabled Chisholm to lead a life of varied and ceaseless activity. He often turned his experiences into books. In 1915 he moved to Queensland as a reporter on the *Brisbane Daily Mail*. There he contacted local bird-watchers, joined clubs, and became honorary advisor and lecturer (1918-22) on natural history to the Queensland government. In 1921 he promoted legislation protecting native fauna and made court appearances to prosecute offenders. Through journalism, he championed the causes of birds. His sustained efforts led to the rediscovery in 1922 of the Paradise Parrot (*Psephotus pulcherrimus*), now possibly extinct. When dignitaries went birdwatching, he was called upon to act as guide: he would count among his acquaintances Sir Philip Game [q.v.8], Lord Alanbrooke, Viscount Dunrossil [q.v.] and Sir Henry Abel Smith.

In 1922 Chisholm transferred to Sydney's *Daily Telegraph*. On 8 November 1923 at the Sacred Heart Church, Rosalie, Brisbane, he married a nurse Olive May Haseler (d. 1970). While in Sydney he chaired (1924-26) the combined meetings of the ornithological section of the Royal Zoological Society of New South Wales and the State branch of the R.A.O.U., and served as a trustee (1927-32) of (Royal) National Park. From 2UW radio on 3 July 1931 he participated in the first, live broadcast of a lyrebird's calls.

Returning to Victoria in 1933, Chisholm joined the *Argus* and *Australasian* in Melbourne. An admirer of Donald Macdonald [q.v.10], he succeeded him as nature and sports writer. Appointed editor in 1937, he resigned next year and spent eight months lecturing in Britain, the Netherlands and Germany. Again using newspapers to achieve his aims, he sought material relating to John Gould [q.v.1]. This highly successful plan, related in *Strange New World* (Sydney, 1941), led to the discovery of Gouldiana, historical documents pertaining to Australia and John Gilbert's [q.v.1] diary. Back in Melbourne, Chisholm joined the *Herald*. He was press liaison officer to the governor-general, the Duke of Gloucester [q.v.], for three months in 1945 and edited the 1947 edition of *Who's Who in Australia*.

In 1948 Chisholm resigned from the *Herald* and moved permanently to Sydney to undertake the single, largest assignment of his career—as editor-in-chief of the ten-volume *Australian Encyclopaedia* (Sydney, 1958). This achievement earned him in 1958 the O.B.E. which, with the Australian Natural History medallion (1940), became his most prized awards. He also began an association with the *Sydney Morning Herald* that lasted until his death.

As well as the hundreds of articles which he contributed to ornithological and natural history magazines, Chisholm published such monographs as: *Mateship with Birds* (Melbourne, 1922), *Birds and Green Places* (London, 1929), *Nature Fantasy in Australia* (London, 1932), *Bird Wonders of Australia* (Sydney, 1934), *The Story of Elizabeth Gould* (Melbourne, 1944), *The Making of a Sentimental Bloke* (Melbourne, 1946) and *Scots wha hae* (Sydney, 1950). After E. J. Banfield's [q.v.7] death, Chisholm had edited *Last Leaves from Dunk Island* (Sydney, 1925). He was represented in several anthologies, and his innumerable articles appeared in a wide range of newspapers and journals, as well as in the *Australian Dictionary of Biography*. His forewords, introductions, reviews and obituaries provide valuable background to Australian bird-lore, history and his own life. An excellent photographer at a time when it took herculean strength to manage the equipment, he illustrated his books and articles with his work.

President of the Queensland Gould League of Bird Lovers (1920-22), the R.A.O.U. (1934), the Royal Australian Historical Society (1959-61), the B.O.C. (1937-38) and the Field Naturalists' Club of Victoria (1937-38), Chisholm edited some of their journals. He received over twenty awards and honorary fellowships in Australia and overseas; he unveiled historic markers in three States, delivered memorial lectures and was patron of various events, notably the Maryborough Golden Wattle Festival. The price of this hectic life was bouts of ill health, and operations for gall-stones and stomach ulcers.

Chisholm was short and slight, with piercing, blue eyes and a mass of wavy hair. In later years he was a familiar figure in his hat and gabardine overcoat, carrying a suitcase and walking stick. Imperious and querulous, he gained the respect—and incurred the wrath —of many people, but remained passionately faithful to the causes in which he believed. He died on 10 July 1977 in his flat at Cremorne Point and was cremated with Presbyterian forms. His daughter survived him.

H. M. Whittell, *The Literature of Australian Birds* (Perth, 1954); *Wild Life* (Melb), Mar 1940; *Vic Naturalist*, 75, Nov 1958, p 133, 94, Sept-Oct 1977, p 188; *Emu*, 77, no 4, Oct 1977, p 232; T. Kloot, 'Alexander Hugh Chisholm: 1890-1977', *Aust Bird Watcher*, 7, no 4, Dec 1977, p 103; *JRAHS*, 63, no 3, Dec 1977, p 206; *Ibis* (Lond), 120, no 2, 1978, p 241; NSW Field Ornithologists Club, *Newsletter*, 30, Apr 1978; Chisholm file (from Roy A'sian Ornithologists Union Archives, held by author, Box Hill North, Melb); Chisholm collection (ML).

TESS KLOOT

CHISHOLM, MARGARET SHEILA MACKELLAR (1895-1969), high society beauty, was born on 9 September 1895 at Woollahra, Sydney, youngest of three children of native-born parents Harry Chisholm, grazier of Wollogorang, Breadalbane, and his wife Margaret, née Mackellar. Sheila was educated at home. Overseas when World War I broke out, she went with her mother to Egypt in 1915, planning to nurse soldiers and to see her brother John who was serving with the Australian Imperial Force. Sheila was described by an old friend Captain F. C. Aarons as being a good dancer and possessing a sense of humour, 'rather tall [5 ft 6 ins (167.6 cm)] with excellent deportment . . . not prone to cosmetics as she had a beautiful complexion'.

She met Francis Edward Scudamore St Clair-Erskine, Lord Loughborough (d. 1929), son of the 5th Earl of Rosslyn; 'Luffy' was convalescing from wounds received at Gallipoli as a first lieutenant, Royal Naval Armoured Cars. Sheila married him at the British Consulate, Cairo, on 27 December 1915. They went to England in 1916 and were to have two sons. The marriage suffered financial hardship from Loughborough's inveterate gambling, inherited from his father who was the subject of the popular song, *The Man Who Broke the Bank at Monte Carlo*. The Loughboroughs lived in Sydney in the early 1920s and were divorced in Edinburgh in 1926.

In London in the 1920s Sheila frequented the Embassy Club and was a member of the Prince of Wales's set, also known as 'The Darlings': she explained, 'we called everybody Darling and once my husband heard me calling the taxi driver Darling'. At the register office, Paddington, on 14 November 1928 she married 26-year-old Sir John Charles Peniston ('Buffles') Milbanke, 11th baronet, of Halnaby, Yorkshire. Sheila Milbanke appeared in the diaries of (Sir) Henry ('Chips') Channon, a leader of London society, who in January 1935 declared her to be 'calm, lovely, gentle, restful and perfect'. With a classic, oval face, dark brown eyes and auburn hair, she had a 'smile like a Lely court beauty'.

A friend of Evelyn Waugh, in 1947 Sheila told him about a beautiful graveyard at Los Angeles, United States of America, in which she thought that religion and art had been brought to their highest association. Waugh was intrigued and went with her to see Forest Lawn cemetery which was to inspire his novel, *The Loved One*. After Sir John died that year, Sheila ran Milbanke Travel Ltd from Fortnum & Mason Ltd, Piccadilly, London. On 29 October 1954 at the register office, St Marylebone, she married Dimitri Alexandrovitch Romanoff, Prince of Russia and a grandson of Tsar Nicholas I. They lived modestly at Belgravia. In 1967 they came to Australia, her first visit home since flying to Sydney in 1937 to see her mother. Interviewed by the press on the coincidence of all her husbands being titled, Sheila said: 'I mar-ried them all for love. None of them ever had any money'.

Princess Dimitri died on 13 October 1969 at Westminster, London; she was buried with Episcopal rites in Roslin chapel, near Edinburgh, where there is a memorial window to her younger son who had been killed on active service with the Royal Air Force in 1939. Her elder son, who succeeded as 6th Earl of Rosslyn, survived her. A woman of style and fashion, Sheila was an outstanding figure of the London social scene for half a century. A portrait by Simon Elwes and a sketch by (Sir) Cecil Beaton are held by the 7th Earl of Rosslyn.

C. Beaton, *The Glass of Fashion* (Lond, 1954); R. R. James (ed), *Chips* (Lond, 1967); C. Sykes, *Evelyn Waugh* (Lond, 1975); C. Chown (comp and ed), *Some Histories of Chisholm Families in Australia 1790-1990* (priv pub, Syd, 1990); J. Harris, 'Sheila Chisholm—An Australian Princess', RAHS, *Newsletter*, Dec 1981; *Australasian*, 26 June 1915; *SMH*, 21 Mar 1935, 3 Nov 1937, 5 Nov 1954, 10 Jan 1967; *Sunday Mirror* (Syd), 15 Jan 1967; information from and family papers held by Mrs J. Chisholm, Syd.   CAROLINE SIMPSON

CHOWNE, ALBERT EDWARD (1920-1945), army officer, was born on 19 July 1920 in Sydney, seventh child of Balmain-born parents Arthur James Chowne, grocer, and his wife Frances Ellen, née Dalziel. The Chowne and Dalziel families were well known in the Willoughby district where Bert grew up. Educated at Chatswood Boys' Intermediate High and Naremburn Junior Technical schools, he started work in 1935 as a shirt-cutter at David Jones [q.v.2] Ltd. Chowne played for Gordon Rugby Union Football Club, and also enjoyed scouting and tennis. He was 5 ft 9 ins (175.3 cm) tall, with brown hair, a fair complexion and hazel eyes.

Having served briefly in the Militia's 36th Battalion, on 27 May 1940 he enlisted in the Australian Imperial Force; he described himself as a salesman, probably to avoid reserved-occupation status. From the outset, he showed initiative, beginning in the 2nd/13th Battalion as No. 15 Platoon runner and soon advancing to company runner. Reaching the Middle East in November 1940, the battalion helped to garrison Tobruk, Libya, from April to December 1941. Chowne transferred to the carrier platoon and in September 1942 was promoted substantive sergeant. His actions in battle were always conspicuous. On 24 October at El Alamein, Egypt, he was wounded and admitted to hospital.

Returning to Australia in January 1943, the 2nd/13th moved to Papua in July. By then Chowne was mortar-platoon sergeant. Near Finschhafen, New Guinea, in the last days of

September, he twice crawled forward to direct mortar-fire on enemy positions; for his deeds he was awarded the Military Medal. A comrade wrote of his 'exceptional coolness and great courage', and of his reluctance to boast; another recalled that 'he never showed fear'. Next month Chowne was sent to Australia for officer-training. His family fondly remembered his arriving home in uniform to be godfather to his niece.

In January 1944 Chowne was appointed lieutenant. On 15 March that year at St Philip's Anglican Church, Sydney, he married a corporal in the Australian Women's Army Service, Daphne May Barton, with whom he had worked at David Jones. After training in jungle warfare at Canungra, Queensland, he had the wrenching experience of being posted to a new unit: he joined the 2nd/2nd Battalion in October, two months before its departure for New Guinea.

On 25 March 1945 in the hills south-west of Dagua, Chowne rushed a Japanese-held knoll, later to bear his name. Ascending a steep, narrow track, he hurled grenades and silenced two machine-guns. Although mortally wounded, he reached the enemy's foxholes and killed two more soldiers before he died. He was posthumously awarded the Victoria Cross. Daphne heard of his death on 29 March, her birthday. In 1946 she received his decorations from the governor-general, the Duke of Gloucester [q.v.], and subsequently presented them to the Australian War Memorial, Canberra. Chowne was buried in Lae war cemetery, New Guinea. The Lieutenant Albert Chowne, V.C., M.M., Memorial Hall at Willoughby commemorates him.

A. J. Marshall (ed), *Nulli Secundus Log* (Syd, 1946); G. H. Fearnside (ed), *Bayonets Abroad* (Syd, 1953) and *Half to Remember* (Syd, 1975); D. Dexter, *The New Guinea Offensives* (Canb, 1961); L. Wigmore (ed), *They Dared Mightily* (Canb, 1963); S. Wick, *Purple Over Green* (Syd, 1977); M. Barter, *The 2/2 Australian Infantry Battalion. The History of a Group Experience* (Ph.D. thesis, ANU, 1990); AWM records; information from Mrs H. Moxham, Whale Beach, Mrs D. Dunne, Turramurra, Mr A. Bentley, Pymble, Syd, and Mrs A. Stephenson, Marsden, Brisb.   MARGARET BARTER

CHRISTIE, GEORGE SWANSON (1917-1980), professor of pathology, was born on 9 April 1917 at Flemington, Melbourne, only child of George Christie, a painter from Scotland, and his native-born wife Anna Christina, née Swanson. Raised as a Presbyterian, young George was educated at Scotch College, Hawthorn, and at Ormond [q.v.5] College, University of Melbourne (M.B., B.S., 1941; M.D., 1949).

After a shortened period as resident medical officer at the Royal Melbourne Hospital, on 9 July 1942 Christie began full-time duty as a captain in the Australian Army Medical Corps, Citizen Military Forces. He transferred to the Australian Imperial Force on 2 February 1943 and was based in Australia. Embarking for New Guinea on 12 May 1944, he served with the 17th Field Ambulance on Bougainville from September and had short attachments to other units. On 5 November 1946 he was placed on the Reserve of Officers. As a temporary major, in 1955-64 he was deputy assistant director-general of medical services, C.M.F.

Having returned to the Royal Melbourne Hospital, Christie trained as a surgeon and became a fellow (1948) of the Royal Australasian College of Surgeons. Influenced by E. S. J. King [q.v.], he switched his interest to pathology and in 1948 was appointed assistant-pathologist. He joined the University of Melbourne's department of pathology as senior lecturer in 1951 and later that year went to England as a Nuffield dominion travelling fellow in medicine. During eighteen months in (Sir) Roy Cameron's [q.v.] department in University College Hospital Medical School, London, he acquired an abiding interest in experimental pathology, and, in collaboration with J. D. Judah, made pioneering studies into biochemical aspects of liver injury.

In 1953 Christie resumed his work at the University of Melbourne and in 1955 was promoted associate-professor. At Scotch College chapel on 20 August that year he married a secretary Stella Elizabeth Newey. After two productive years as professor of pathology at the University of Queensland, in 1966 he succeeded King as professor at Melbourne. There, in collaboration with a succession of research students, Christie continued his studies of liver injury, especially the effects of several plant toxins that were important in agriculture. He was a foundation member of and an active participant in the Australian Society for Experimental Pathology; its annual lecture was to be named in his honour.

Christie's powerful spectacles and squat, somewhat unathletic, appearance disguised considerable strength and an enormous capacity for hard work. A perfectionist and master of detail, he closely supervised all aspects of his department and found it difficult to delegate even routine matters. His administrative load severely limited his time for original work, but he maintained an active role in research until shortly before his death and published numerous papers in scientific journals. He had a high reputation as a teacher, morbid anatomist and research worker, and devoted much time and effort to his colleagues and to their welfare.

Apart from a happy family life and a delight

in tinkering, especially with his cherished Austin 10 motorcar, Christie had few interests outside his profession. Suffering from lymphoma with thrombocytopenia, he died on 19 October 1980 at Parkville and was cremated; his wife and two daughters survived him. A portrait of Christie is held by the University of Queensland; another, by his friend and colleague Professor Elsdon Storey, is in the department of pathology, University of Melbourne.

Dept of Pathology, Univ Melb, *The Melbourne School of Pathology* (Melb, 1962); K. F. Russell, *The Melbourne Medical School 1862-1962* (Melb, 1977); *Univ Melb Gazette*, 1955, p 131, 1966, p 6, 1980, p 15; *Univ Qld Gazette*, 59, 1965, p 6; *MJA*, 1980, p 647; Faculty of Medicine, Univ Melb, Minutes, Mar 1981; personal information.   JOHN V. HURLEY

CHUNG GON, JAMES (1854-1952), Chinese patriarch and businessman, was born on 23 July 1854 in Sunwui village, Kwangtung Province, China, reputedly of a once wealthy family. While working in a junk that was carrying tea to Hong Kong for transport to Australia, he heard of the gold diggings in Victoria and in 1873 made his way to Sandhurst (Bendigo). He found mining-life difficult and encountered racist sentiment, so moved to Tasmania, reaching Launceston on 16 April 1878. After being employed in the tin mines at Branxholm, and as a market gardener and woodcutter on the Lefroy goldfields, he came back to Launceston and sold vegetables.

Having learned English in the vestry of the local Baptist church, Chung Gon was naturalized on 2 November 1882. He visited China in 1885 where he married Mei (Mary) Ying Lee, daughter of a wealthy silkworm-farmer; they were to have twelve children. Next year Chung Gon sailed for Tasmania, leaving his pregnant wife with her family.

With his friend Frank Walker, Chung Gon found a rich seam of tin at South Mount Cameron; from the proceeds of its sale, he bought 200 acres (81 ha) at Turners Marsh and established a commercial orchard. In 1892 he sent for his family, including 12-year-old Rose, who had been given to them as a wedding present. They treated her as a daughter and subsequently arranged her marriage to James Chuey, a merchant and grazier of Junee, New South Wales. Chung Gon was baptized a Christian in 1893 and later became a Baptist lay preacher.

About 1904 Chung Gon sold his orchard and moved to Launceston, intending to fulfil a promise to his wife that they would return to China. When his money was misappropriated he was forced to begin again as a market gardener: he leased part of Walker's nursery at South Launceston and eventually bought 100 acres (40.5 ha) at Relbia on which to raise pigs and grow fruit and vegetables.

He sent two of his sons, JOSEPH (1895-1977) and SAMUEL (1901-1977) to China to be educated. World War I postponed the departure of the rest of the family. Joseph returned to Tasmania to help his father; Samuel stayed to study agriculture at Ling Nam University, Canton. Mary's death in 1919 led James to change his mind about living permanently in China, but he did revisit that country.

Joseph Chung Gon read constantly to keep abreast of innovations in horticulture; he is said to have pioneered the commercial use of irrigation in Northern Tasmania and to have adapted agricultural machinery. During long periods when chronic tuberculosis prevented him from working, his sisters Ann and Doris helped on the farm. Ann became well known in the late 1930s for her activities in support of the Chinese Women's Association in its appeal to help the Chinese during their war with Japan. Joseph acted as an interpreter for the local Chinese community and established a young people's club. In 1920 Samuel had returned to Launceston. There he opened the Canton Gift Store in partnership with his sister Lily before farming with Joseph at Hadspen. On 30 September 1944 Samuel married Queenie Young. He moved with his family to Sydney in 1951 to run his brother-in-law's fish business, and later owned a trading company and invested in property.

In 1937 the Launceston City Council had resumed James Chung Gon's nursery for a sportsground; he then took up nearby land. A distinguished-looking man, he was widely known as 'Daddy Chung'. Among his civic activities, he collected money from the Chinese community for the local hospital and helped to have the Chinese joss-house shifted from Weldborough to the Queen Victoria Museum and Art Gallery, Launceston. Esteemed for his probity, friendliness and generosity to those in need, he was devoted to his family. He died on 23 February 1952 at his Launceston home and was buried with Baptist forms in Carr Villa cemetery; four of his five sons and six of his seven daughters survived him.

Mercury (Hob), 21 Sept 1942, 25 Feb 1952; *Examiner* (Launc), 25 Feb 1952, 27 Oct 1977; information from Mrs Q. Chung Gon, Carlton, Syd, Mrs A. Fong and Miss D. Chung Gon, West Launc, and Dr N. Gollan, Launc.   JILL CASSIDY

CHURCH, ANN RACHEL (1925-1975), set and costume designer, was born on 7 May 1925 in South Melbourne, daughter of Seymour Church, a merchant from New Zealand, and his Russian-born wife Michlia, née

Osporat. As a child Ann travelled widely with her parents and boarded at an English school before completing her secondary education at St Catherine's School for Girls, Melbourne. She studied art privately with a daughter-in-law of Frederick McCubbin [q.v.10], and at the (Royal) Melbourne Technical College (1942-45) and the National Gallery schools (1946).

In 1949 Church was commissioned by the dancer and choreographer Rex Reid to design sets for *Les Belles Creoles* which was first presented by the new National Theatre Ballet Company at the Princess Theatre, Melbourne. For the company's 1950 season, she designed sets for *Swan Lake* (Act II), *Peter and the Wolf* and *Prasnik*. In 1951 she created decor and costumes for a full-length *Swan Lake*: her bold use of colour and fabric, and her attention to locale and period 'set new standards in Australian theatre design for ballet'.

That year Church left for London where she was commissioned by Pauline Grant as a designer for productions at the Palladium. On 30 August 1952 Ann married a medical student Raymond Hubert Michel Bury with Church of England rites at St Paul's Church, Knightsbridge; they were to remain childless. She visited Australia briefly in 1953 to supervise her decor and costumes for the premiere of Alison Lee's ballet, *En Cirque*, performed by the Victorian Ballet Guild. While in London, she also continued to design for Reid.

Returning to Melbourne in the late 1950s, Church created decor and costumes for two of the Victorian Ballet's productions, *Fête de St Valentin* (1957) and *The Night is a Sorceress* (1959): the latter was considered by many to be her most masterful work. She assisted Reid with numerous stage and television productions; from 1960 she designed for the Rex Reid Dance Players.

When the Australian Ballet was formed in 1962, Church worked for Reid on *Melbourne Cup*, creating bawdy and elegant costumes, as well as opulent, extravagant settings, to convey the rawness and romance of the running of the first race in 1861. Audiences in Australia, Britain, Paris, Copenhagen and Berlin, and throughout South America, delighted in the vitality of the production. During the 1960s *Melbourne Cup* and *The Night is a Sorceress*, both with Church's decor and costumes, were filmed for television by the Australian Broadcasting Commission. Following Reid's appointment as artistic director of the West Australian Ballet in 1970, Church redesigned several earlier works for that company. In 1973 she designed Margaret Scott's *Classical Sonata* and Mary Duchesne's production of *Grand Pas de Quatre* for the W.A.B.

Theatrical and volatile, Church presented herself with as much drama and style as she did her sets, but she took her work seriously. She was moderately tall and slightly built, and wore her thick, blonde hair in a straight, fringed, Juliette Greco style which she later exchanged for a shaggy 'chrysanthemum' cut. Her clothes were chic and *avant-garde*. Proud of her exotic Russian heritage, she included in her wardrobe a mink-trimmed, tapestry coat and several full-length furs. She lived with her husband on her beef-cattle property, Patterdale, at Main Ridge on the Mornington Peninsula, Victoria, in a home filled with antique furniture. Survived by him, she died of infective endocarditis on 17 May 1975 at Prahran and was cremated.

E. H. Pask, *Ballet in Australia* (Melb, 1982); *Ballet Annual*, 1952, 1955; *Age* (Melb), 4 Aug 1962; *Sun News-Pictorial*, 19 Feb 1963; information from Mrs L. Lawton, Nth Balwyn, Mrs A. Cousens, and Mrs R. Ryan, Sth Yarra, Melb.

REX REID

CHUTER, CHARLES EDWARD (1880-1948), public servant, was born on 11 March 1880 at Fortitude Valley, Brisbane, third child of Charles Rowe Chuter, clerk, and his wife Rosa, née Boreham, both English born. Educated at Fortitude Valley State Primary School and at Brisbane Grammar School (on a scholarship), Chuter was a short, stocky, ginger-haired young man who in his spare time enjoyed dinghy sailing. In July 1898 he joined the Home Secretary's Department as a clerk. Appointed first clerk in March 1911, he apparently dealt both with local government and health administration problems, occasionally travelling from the capital to resolve disputes between local councils. He was also active in the emerging town planning movement and was to be the honorary organizing director of the Second Australian Town Planning Conference and Exhibition, held in Brisbane in 1918.

After T. J. Ryan's [q.v.11] government took office in June 1915, Chuter was involved in research for and the implementation of Labor's programme of enlarging ('greaterising') the State's major city areas. His far-sighted conclusions, tabulations and analyses of data relevant to cities in Queensland, interstate and overseas were published in his monographs, *Local Government Administration* (1919) and *Local Government Law and Finance* (1921). In 1920 E. G. Theodore's [q.v.12] ministry reformed local government elections by replacing voluntary voting based on property qualifications with compulsory adult franchise. This change evidently prompted Chuter to conceive a radical approach to vesting powers in local government.

In 1922 he was promoted assistant under-secretary in the Home Secretary's Department. On 12 December he married Ethel May Jones at Holy Trinity Anglican Church, Fortitude Valley. The abolition that year of Queensland's Legislative Council facilitated the passage of legislation. The Hospitals Act of 1923 provided for the gradual introduction of a hospital system controlled by boards representing, and funded by, hospital subscribers, local councils and the State government. As local health authorities, councils were compelled to finance the treatment of infectious diseases by hospitals in their area. In May 1924 Chuter was appointed a government representative on the new Brisbane and South Coast Hospitals Board (chairman 1928-31).

Known as 'Mr Chuter's Bill' before its enactment, the City of Brisbane Act of 1924 established the Greater Brisbane scheme. It endowed Brisbane City Council with the unprecedented 'general competence' power to govern the city and enabled the council to respond imaginatively to unforeseen problems, without the delays and frustrations of having to seek specific authority from parliament.

Once the Greater Brisbane scheme was launched in 1925 and assisted through its first two years, Chuter turned his attention to restructuring local government elsewhere in Queensland. In March 1927 he was appointed one of three members of a royal commission to report on local government areas and boundaries. The commission recommended in May 1928 that the number of local government areas be reduced by almost half; in a minority rider to the report, Chuter proposed a larger reduction. Although the State government backed away from these recommendations in the face of widespread protest from local councils, some of the commission's proposals were adopted in piecemeal fashion over the next two decades.

Responding to complaints in local government and medical circles about aspects of hospital administration, in 1930 A. E. Moore's [q.v.10] Country and Progressive National Party government appointed a royal commission. The articulate Chuter argued forcefully before the commission that hospital board-members should represent only those who funded the hospitals; the commission subsequently described as reprehensible his conduct in mentioning certain members of the medical profession, and found a conflict of interest in his roles of chairman of B.S.C.H.'s board and assistant under-secretary. At the government's request, he resigned from the board, but was re-appointed when Labor returned to office in 1932.

From 1 January 1935 Chuter was under-secretary of his department. It was reorganized on 5 December at the direction of E. M. Hanlon [q.v.] as the Department of Health and Home Affairs: Sir Raphael Cilento was appointed director-general of health and medical services. A Hospitals Act (1936) consolidated the 1923 statute and its amendments, and also authorized hospital boards to employ full-time, salaried medical staff instead of honorary doctors. Chuter's massive consolidation of earlier legislation resulted in the acclaimed Local Government Act of 1936 wherein the 'general competence' power which Chuter had devised for Brisbane was extended to all Queensland local governments.

Both Chuter and Cilento were strong minded and clashed on a number of sensitive issues. Chuter enthusiastically supported Sister Elizabeth Kenny's [q.v.9] controversial method of treating poliomyelitis; Cilento did not. The continuing tension between the two men eventually led the government to make Chuter acting-director of local authority affairs in December 1941. Next year the office of director of local government was created, to which he was appointed on 1 January 1943.

Chuter retired on 31 December 1947. Survived by his wife, son and two daughters, he died of a coronary occlusion on 31 January 1948 in St Helen's private hospital, South Brisbane, and was cremated. Able though he had been as an administrator of hospitals, he played a more significant role in Queensland local government whose distinctive character he influenced profoundly.

D. Tucker, 'Charles Edward Chuter: An Architect of Local Government in the Twentieth Century', *Qld Geographical J*, 3, 1988; *Telegraph* (Brisb), 31 Jan 1948; J. Sinclair, My Uncle Charlie (pc of ts, held by author, Dept of Govt, Univ Qld); taped interviews with Sir Allan Sewell, 28 Oct 1977, Miss J. Sinclair, 10 Feb 1988, Mr H. Summers, 26 July 1988, and Mr N. Macpherson, 22 Aug 1989 (held by author).   DOUG TUCKER

CIANTAR, JOSEPH LAURENCE (1893-1967), Catholic priest, was born on 4 July 1893 in Valletta, Malta, and named Giuseppe Vincenzo Lorenzo Antonio, son of Giuseppe Ciantar and his wife Maria Concetta, née Buhagiar. Young Giuseppe was an aspirant at St Patrick's Salesian school, Sliema, and at the Martinetto, Turin, Italy. In 1912 he joined the Salesian congregation at Burwash, Sussex, England, and on 11 July 1920 was ordained priest at Wonersh, Surrey. He served the order at Cowley, Oxfordshire, and in 1929-37 at Macclesfield, Cheshire. From 1930 to 1938 he was also in charge of Salesian propaganda and fund-raising in Britain.

Appointed rector of Rupertswood at Sunbury, Victoria—the only Salesian institution in Australia at that time—Fr Ciantar arrived in Melbourne in 1938 and took responsibility for directing the work of the order throughout the country. In 1941 he became the first Salesian master of novices in Australia and in 1948-52 was rector of Don Bosco's Boys' Club and Hostel at Brunswick. He faced a major challenge in reducing the order's deficit of £30 000. His zest for raising money (which earned him the affectionate nickname of 'Ned Kelly' [q.v.5]) was aided by his irrepressible cheerfulness and resulted in the repayment of all debts and the commencement of a bold new era of expansion. By 1952, when he left Victoria, Ciantar had overseen the first period of growth in Salesian activity since 1927. In addition to the establishment at Brunswick, he had opened the Archbishop Mannix [q.v.10] Missionary College at Oakleigh, the Salesian School at Brooklyn Park, Adelaide, the Savio College at Glenorchy, Tasmania, and the Don Bosco's Boys' Camp at Dromana, Victoria.

From 1952 to 1964 Fr Ciantar served at Engadine, Sydney, as rector of Boys' Town, which he transformed into a large, well-equipped and modern institution; he was, as well, pastor to the local community. On retiring from Boys' Town, he served as parish priest of Engadine-Heathcote, a position which he held until his death. A photographic portrait in 1966 shows him with round, bald head, wide mouth and thin-rimmed glasses, proudly dressed in a knight's regalia of one of the unrecognized orders of St John of Jerusalem.

In 1966 Ciantar undertook his final project: he travelled to the United States of America, Malta and England to raise funds for a national shrine to St John Bosco. Opened in October 1967, the shrine served as a parish church at Engadine. Fr Ciantar died on 28 December 1967 at St Vincent's Hospital, Sydney; after a requiem Mass presided over by Cardinal (Sir) Norman Gilroy [q.v.] at the Engadine shrine, he was buried in Rupertswood cemetery. He is remembered, particularly by Maltese Australians, for his optimism, strength of faith, humility, monastic poverty and dynamism.

The First 25 Years (1921-1946) (priv pub, Sunbury, nd); E. Power, *Necrology* (priv pub, Engadine, NSW, 1968); J. Munns, *Rupertswood, A Living History* (Sunbury, Vic, 1987); B. York, *Empire and Race* (Syd, 1990); *Advocate* (Melb), 4, 11 Jan 1968; *Catholic Weekly* (Syd), 4 Jan 1968.

BARRY YORK

CLANCY, SIR JOHN SYDNEY JAMES (1895-1970), judge, was born on 30 May 1895 at Glebe, Sydney, son of John Clancy, a commission agent from Ireland, and his native-born wife Mary, née Bradshaw. Educated at Marist Brothers' High School, Darlinghurst, and at the University of Sydney (LL.B., 1925), young Clancy worked as a clerk in the Department of Public Instruction from 12 February 1913. He enlisted in the Australian Naval and Military Expeditionary Force on 11 August 1914, served at Rabaul and was discharged on 18 January 1915. Joining the Australian Imperial Force on 14 January 1916, he fought on the Western Front with the 20th Battalion until wounded in action on 3 May 1917.

Discharged in Sydney on 2 July 1918, Clancy returned to the department and to his studies. On 22 August 1922 at St Mary's Catholic Cathedral he married Ethyl Florence Christobel Buckland, a 24-year-old civil servant. Admitted to the Bar on 30 July 1925, he was attached to the Government Insurance Office in 1926-27 and soon obtained briefs to represent injured workers in compensation cases. He gained a reputation for being a level-headed, tactically shrewd and fair-minded advocate. His most notable appearance was for the relations of a young coal-miner Norman Brown at the inquest into Brown's death which occurred in the violent incident at Rothbury colliery on 16 December 1929. He also appeared for the Rothbury miners in their appeals against convictions for unlawful assembly.

When J. T. Lang's [q.v.9] government gazetted Clancy's appointment to the District Court bench on 13 November 1931, controversy erupted in the press and the legal profession. One editorialist claimed that the promotion was 'the latest manifestation of the shockingly low level to which the public life of New South Wales has been abased' and that it was 'untenable' to suggest that six years of practice was a fit qualification. Rumours were rife that Clancy's appearance for the Rothbury miners had prompted his elevation without the knowledge of the attorney-general. Senior barristers attacked the appointment as 'indefensible' and the Council of the Bar of New South Wales protested. In the Legislative Assembly on 24 November 1931 the Opposition leader (Sir) Thomas Bavin [q.v.7] argued that Clancy lacked experience, inferring that the decision was based on 'mere personal friendship' or was an example of political expedience.

Despite the hue and cry, Clancy gradually settled into a conventional, widely-respected judicial career. He served on the District Court and was chairman (from 1944) of the Crown Employees Appeal Board. Raised to the Supreme Court in July 1947, he became senior puisne judge and was acting chief justice (1964-65). His life as a judge was orthodox and conservative: he lived at the affluent North Shore suburb of Lindfield, belonged to the fashionable racing club, Tattersall's, and was prominent in the affairs of the Catholic Church and active in the Catholic Lawyers' Guild of St Thomas More. He was appointed C.M.G. (1964) and K.B.E. (1967).

Clancy made no substantial contribution to legal theory or principle. The law reports are barren of any of his judgements of enduring intellectual value. Yet, he did have the attribute of rugged common sense, in the 'no-nonsense' tradition of Sydney's Common Law Bar. Decisive, firm in his opinions and efficient in supervising the cases which came before him, he was not regarded as excessively harsh in the sentences he handed down. His stern restraint in sentencing the child kidnapper and murderer Stephen Bradley [q.v.] won praise.

In July 1949 Clancy was appointed to the first council of the New South Wales University of Technology (University of New South Wales); in 1960 he became chancellor. His stewardship began with public debate when the historian Dr Russel Ward claimed that the university's academic appointments were tainted by political discrimination and that security reports were used in vetting applications. Both Clancy and the vice-chancellor (Sir) Philip Baxter asserted that no religious or political tests were applied to appointments at the university.

Retiring from the bench on 26 May 1965, Clancy was described by Chief Justice (Sir) Leslie Herron [q.v.] as 'an unprejudiced and fearless judge', a person of simple and sincere motives, and 'a man of the people'. Sir John died on 15 October 1970 at the Prince of Wales Hospital, Randwick, and was buried in Northern Suburbs cemetery; his wife and daughter survived him.

E. Ross, *A History of the Miners' Federation of Australia* (Syd, 1970); A. H. Willis, *The University of New South Wales* (Syd, 1983); *PD* (NSW), 17 Dec 1929, p 2514, 24 Nov 1931, p 7080; *NSW State Reports* and *Weekly Notes* (NSW), 1947-65; *SMH*, 11, 15, 18 Feb, 24, 26 Sept 1930, 13, 14 Nov 1931, 17 Aug 1944, 9 July 1947, 15 Nov 1960, 27 May 1965, 17 Nov 1970; *World* (Syd) and *Sun News-Pictorial*, 12 Nov 1931; *Bulletin*, 18 Nov 1931; *Sun-Herald* (Syd), 2 Apr 1961; *Catholic Weekly* (Syd), 22 Oct 1970; *Daily Telegraph* (Syd), 27 May 1965; NSW Bar Assn, Syd, Minutes, 13 Nov 1931; information from Sir Garfield Barwick, Nth Turramurra, Syd.   J. W. SHAW

CLARE, MONA MATILDA (MONICA) (1924-1973), Aboriginal political activist and author, is said to have been born on 13 August 1924 at Dareel, near Goondiwindi, Queens-land, daughter of Daniel Herbert ('Ron') McGowan, an Aborigine, and Beatrice Scott, the blonde, blue-eyed, high-spirited daughter of English itinerant workers. Along the upper Darling and Barwon rivers where he worked, McGowan was respected as an expert shearer, despite his withered arm. A son Dan was born in 1926. After Beatrice died in childbirth in 1931, a welfare inspector removed the children as 'neglected'.

From Yasmar home for infants at Haberfield, they were fostered to Bill and Stella Woodbury, brother and sister, at their farm and orchard near Spencer on the lower Hawkesbury River. The children were given great affection, and attended a private bush school and the local Catholic church. In 1935 officials parted them, sending Monica to Redmyre Road Home, Strathfield, and Dan to a boys' training farm. She never saw him again. Monica resumed school at the home and was trained for domestic service. The racial taunts of pupils and staff made her determined to excel at study.

Monica worked for many Sydney suburban families, being paid four shillings weekly, with a rising increment of two shillings on each birthday. Her mail could be intercepted and rules were strict. Employers frequently dismissed her before the holidays fell or higher payment was due. In August 1942, no longer a ward, she accepted her final domestic position at Vaucluse, then rented a flat and obtained factory jobs. Working at W. D. & H. O. Wills (Australia) Ltd's cigarette factory, she studied typing and shorthand at night-school.

While visiting the Woodburys, who had retired to Nambucca Heads in 1946, Monica met the Aboriginal community at Bellwood reserve. She grew interested in race relations and Labor politics. Residing at Malabar, Sydney, she contacted Aboriginal families at La Perouse and in November 1949, during her campaign for Daniel Curtin (Labor's candidate for the Federal seat of Watson), enrolled them for voting. Her marriage in 1953, from which there was a daughter, ended in divorce.

On 13 August 1962 at the registrar general's office, Sydney, Monica married Leslie Forsyth Clare. Born to British parents at Waratah, Tasmania, he was a union official in the building trades. Monica joined the women's committees of the union and became a relieving clerk for the branch at Wollongong, where she and Leslie lived. Until 1970 she accompanied him on his motorcar trips four times a year to country towns where he organized on behalf of members, verified the appalling conditions on Aboriginal reserves and, through union action, fought racial discrimination.

Having direct knowledge of life on segregated reserves, Monica became secretary of the Aboriginal committee of the South Coast Labor Council. Her political activity was sustained by her shrewd understanding of human behaviour. When people presented complaints of discrimination, she bombarded shire and State politicians for improvements. Her constant correspondence had practical results: the Askin government decided to replace transitional housing for Aborigines with homes of Housing Commission standard and established low-interest loans for buying furniture.

Following the 1967 referendum which ensured Federal responsibility for Aborigines, in 1968 Monica restructured the Aboriginal committee as the independent 'South Coast Illawarra Tribe', representing the Koori people of Nowra, Orient Point, Wreck Bay, Wallaga Lake and Bega. As its secretary, she was prominent in the campaign which led to the establishment of co-operatives for re-housing the Wallaga Lake and Nowra communities with loans from Commonwealth funds. A delegate (c.1968-72) to several conferences of the Federal Council for the Advancement of Aborigines and Torres Strait Islanders, she was also active on the International Women's Day, May Day and National Aborigines' Day committees.

Described by her husband as a woman 'with strong reserves of energy and generosity', Monica had suffered from a collapsed lung, and for many years cancer took its toll. She died of subarachnoid haemorrhage on 13 July 1973 (National Aborigines' Day) at Prince Henry Hospital, Little Bay, Sydney, and was cremated. Her husband and their adopted son and daughter survived her.

Monica Clare's novel, *Karobran* (meaning 'together'), based upon her early childhood and teenage experiences as a state ward, expressed her rebellious nature, as well as her constant search for identity and family. Having attended a creative-writing course at Wollongong, Monica rewrote the manuscript many times until she was satisfied. It was published posthumously in April 1978.

M. Hill and A. Barlow (eds), *Black Australia*, 2 (Canb, 1985); T. Mayne, *Aborigines and the Issues* (Syd, 1986); *Aboriginal and Islander Forum*, June 1978; *Illawarra Mercury*, 14 July, 29 Aug 1973; *SMH*, 2 Feb, 15 Mar 1978; information from Mr and Mrs L. Donovan, Spencer, NSW; family information.   JACK HORNER

CLAREY, PERCY JAMES (1890-1960), trade union leader and politician, was born on 20 January 1890 at Bairnsdale, Victoria, fifth of six children of Francis William Clarey, general agent, and his wife Jessie Littlejohn, née Lawson (d. 1895), both native-born. When Percy was a child the family moved to Melbourne where he was educated at South Yarra State School and later at the Working Men's College. Crippled in his youth by rheumatoid arthritis, he thereafter walked with crutches. Clarey was employed as a clerk by George Pizzey & Son, leather merchants, and became involved in trade unionism: he was Victorian president of the Federated Clerks' Union of Australia at the age of 24 and federal president three years later. An organizer of the Amalgamated Food Preservers' Union of Australia and of the Federated Storemen and Packers' Union of Australia, he served as federal president of both and maintained a close relationship with them throughout his long industrial career.

At Box Hill on 31 March 1917 Clarey married a schoolteacher Catherine Mary Isabel Chambers with the forms of the Churches of Christ; they were to have two sons before being divorced in 1936. Catherine was prominent in labour and pacifist movements in the 1930s, and was a member of the Victorian central executive of the Australian Labor Party. In 1935 she was Labor candidate for the Legislative Assembly seat of Caulfield, but withdrew before the poll.

By the late 1920s Clarey had emerged as a national industrial leader through his affiliations with increasingly powerful federal unions and his work for the newly-formed Australasian (Australian) Council of Trade Unions. He presided over the A.L.P.'s Victorian branch in 1934 and next year was elected president of the Melbourne Trades Hall Council. A principal advocate for the union movement in the industrial courts, he led a protracted struggle to restore wages to the levels from which they had been cut during the Depression. In World War II he was appointed to the Victorian board of area management of the Department of Munitions (1940) and to the Manpower Priorities Board (1941). He was a delegate in 1944 to the International Labour Conference at Philadelphia, United States of America.

In 1937 Clarey had been returned to the Victorian Legislative Council as member for the province of Doutta Galla; he was to hold the seat until 1949. He was minister of labour and of public health (14 to 18 September 1943) and minister of labour and of employment (21 November 1945 to 20 November 1947) under John Cain [q.v.]. President of the A.C.T.U. (from June 1943), Clarey was criticized in parliament and the press after he accepted the ostensibly incompatible post of minister of labour in 1945. He shrugged off the protests and conducted his portfolio without any evident conflict of interest. On 21 August 1948 at the office of the government statist, Melbourne, he married a divorcee

Florence Midiam Cater, née Knowles (d. 1953).

As head of the A.C.T.U., he formed a notable partnership with the secretary Albert Monk [q.v.] who was to succeed him as president in 1949. From 1945 Clarey was involved in negotiations to resolve a wave of industrial disputes. Resisting attempts by the Communist Party of Australia to extend its influence in the labour movement, he worked with the controversial industrial groups which were linked to the Catholic Church and in 1947 defeated by thirty-eight votes a communist challenge to his leadership. Although conceding the Communist Party's right to exist, he vigorously opposed any role for it within the A.L.P. One of his final initiatives as A.C.T.U. leader was to introduce salaries for the council's president and secretary.

With a margin of only 152 votes Clarey won the Federal seat of Bendigo in December 1949; he retained it until his death. When he entered the House of Representatives there was press speculation that he would be a future leader of the federal parliamentary party. He stood for deputy-leader in 1951, but was defeated by Arthur Calwell [q.v.] by 45 votes to 36. During the A.L.P. split of 1954-55 Clarey was mentioned as a possible compromise president of the Victorian branch which bore the brunt of the internal conflict. There was also conjecture that he might replace H. V. Evatt [q.v.] as parliamentary leader. Despite Clarey's long involvement with Labor's right wing, he stuck to the official party line and in February 1955 resigned from the 'grouper'-dominated Victorian central executive. In April he moved a motion in caucus expressing complete support for Evatt, a tactic important to Evatt's survival as leader.

A man of enthusiastic artistic and literary tastes, Clarey accumulated a substantial library, and broadened his expertise in etchings and Chinese pottery. He was an innovatory publicist who built a national reputation during World War II as a radio broadcaster on patriotic, industrial and economic themes, and who became one of the first Australian politicians to appear regularly on television. His range of friends spanned the political spectrum and included (Sir) Robert Menzies [q.v.]. Clarey was a staunch advocate of industrial conciliation and arbitration, and a consistently moderating influence on trade union militancy. Although branded a 'bosses' man' and a 'strike breaker' by his opponents, he was by no means conservative in his political attitudes. At the A.L.P. federal conference of 1948 he had moved a resolution reaffirming the party's socialization objective, and he advocated trade union support for the Indonesians in their struggle against Dutch colonialism. He upheld the White Australia

policy, but urged the deletion of the term from the A.L.P. platform because it was offensive.

Clarey was described by one contemporary as a 'cripple with a fighter's face . . . a clear thinker and negotiator'. He was the country's foremost trade union leader of his generation and his presidency of the A.C.T.U. established a model for his successors. Although he was respected as a politician, his impact in Federal parliament was lessened by advancing years and failing health. In 1954 he went to New York as an Australian delegate to the United Nations General Assembly and in 1957 visited China. Survived by the sons of his first marriage, he died on 17 May 1960 at Oakleigh, Melbourne; following a state funeral, he was cremated with Methodist forms; his estate was sworn for probate at £11 425.

His younger half-brother Reynold Arthur Clarey (1897-1972) practised as an accountant and was A.L.P. member for Melbourne in the Legislative Assembly from 1955 to 1972.

R. Murray, *The Split* (Melb, 1970); A. A. Calwell, *Be Just and Fear Not* (Melb, 1972); J. Hagan, *The History of the A.C.T.U.* (Melb, 1981); K. White, *John Cain and Victorian Labor 1917-1957* (Syd, 1982); *Daily Telegraph* (Syd), 8 Dec 1945; *Herald* (Melb), 17, 18 May 1960; *The Times* (Lond), 18 May 1960; Clarey papers, 1923-59, *and* Aust Overseas Information Service (roneoed and typewritten articles, NL).

C. J. LLOYD

CLARK, ANDREW INGLIS (1882-1953), barrister and judge, was born on 6 June 1882 in Hobart, third of seven children of Andrew Inglis Clark [q.v.3], barrister, and his wife Grace, née Ross, both Tasmanian born. Young Andrew was educated at The Hutchins School and the University of Tasmania (LL.B., 1903). As an undergraduate he led his fellow students in elaborate practical jokes, and, as a commemoration prank, laid siege to the gates of Hobart Gaol with a small, muzzle-loading cannon. He was articled in turn to M. W. Simmons and A. D. Watchorn, called to the Bar on 7 December 1904 and became a partner in the firm of Finlay & Watchorn in 1910. A specialist in constitutional law, he was appointed adviser to the State government and personal adviser to the premier John Earle [q.v.8] during the constitutional crisis in 1914.

On 2 August 1915 Clark enlisted in the Australian Imperial Force and in February 1916 joined No. 4 Company, Army Service Corps, in Egypt. Moving to France in April, he transferred to the 4th Divisional Ammunition Sub-Park in August. He was attached to 1 Anzac Corps headquarters in January 1917 and to Australian Corps headquarters from November. Employed as an assistant to the court-martial officer, he was promoted temporary sergeant in January 1919 and mentioned in dispatches. Despite his educational qualifications and age, he made no apparent effort to obtain a commission and developed an extremely critical attitude towards officers, particularly English officers. He was discharged from the A.I.F. in London on 23 April 1919.

Returning via the United States of America, while in Chicago he investigated the medical qualifications of Victor Richard Ratten [q.v.11] for Finlay, Watchorn & Clark and their client, the Tasmanian branch of the British Medical Association. Clark made a report, but the dispute between the B.M.A. and Ratten simmered for years. Embittered by his war experiences and socially withdrawn, Clark dedicated himself to his legal career in Tasmania, practising mainly as a barrister. On 12 November 1926 at St Stephen's Anglican Church, Hobart, he married Vera Chancellor; they were to remain childless.

While in private practice, he was engaged in 1927 by the State attorney-general to prepare the Supreme Court civil procedure bill which was passed, with few alterations, in 1931. Appointed a judge of the Supreme Court on 31 August 1928, Clark acquired an extraordinary reputation within Tasmania for his legal knowledge and acuity. On the bench he was often testy and demanding, and somewhat pedantic. Nonetheless, the legal profession in general admired his ability, his personal and professional integrity, and his passion for justice. Some of his early judgements, including those in *Burnett* v. *Brown* (1929) and *Davies* v. *Andrews* (1930), were regarded locally as classics.

A keen gardener with a practical knowledge of fruit-growing, in 1930 Clark was chosen as a royal commissioner to inquire into the marketing of Tasmanian apples and pears. He was devoted to his profession and had little time for other pursuits, but he enjoyed social history, biography and literature. According to Frank Clifton Green [q.v.], Clark's name was submitted to Federal cabinet in the late 1930s to fill a vacancy on the High Court bench. The nomination was allegedly rejected on the grounds that Clark had not been commissioned throughout his army service. He resigned from the Supreme Court on 25 February 1952. Survived by his wife, he died on 4 July 1953 in Hobart and was buried in Cornelian Bay cemetery. In a memorial address Acting Chief Justice Sir Kenneth Green described him as the greatest lawyer the State had produced. Later observers would probably agree that the statement was right when made, subject to one exception—his father.

Tas Law Reports, 1953; *PTHRA*, 4, no 1, Jan 1955, p 5; *Mercury* (Hob), 1 Sept 1928, 6 July 1953; Clark papers (Univ Tas Archives); personal information.
         F. M. NEASEY

CLARK, CHARLES CARR (1902-1965), naval officer, was born on 21 August 1902 at East Talgai, near Warwick, Queensland, seventh child of George Carr Clark, a grazier from England, and his native-born wife Maria Gertrude, née Clark. Educated from 1911 at Toowoomba Preparatory School, Charles was a 1916 entrant at the Royal Australian Naval College, Jervis Bay, Federal Capital Territory. He graduated in 1919 with an average scholastic record and colours for cricket. Next year he sailed to England in H.M.S. *Renown*.

While undergoing sea-training with the Royal Navy, Clark was offered voluntary retirement as part of the planned reductions in Australia's armed forces, but decided to remain in the navy and to specialize in engineering. In 1923-24 he studied at the R.N. Engineering College, Devonport, played cricket in the first XI and revealed a latent academic ability which won him a place on the Advanced Engineering Course at Greenwich. He returned to Australia in August 1926 and went to sea. On 12 December 1928 he married Margaret Granville Haymen at St Andrew's Anglican Church, Indooroopilly, Brisbane. From November 1929 to June 1932 he was second assistant to the engineer manager, Garden Island Dockyard, Sydney, then again served at sea. While flotilla engineer officer in H.M.A.S. *Stuart*, Clark was promoted engineer commander on 31 December 1936.

He went back to Garden Island in January 1938 as first assistant. Involved in major refits of the cruisers *Australia* and *Adelaide*, he was plunged into a hectic round by the outbreak of war: planning *Australia*'s final fitting out and trials, readying the destroyer flotilla for deployment to the Mediterranean, preparing reserve ships for service, arming and equipping merchant vessels, overseeing civilian contractors and supporting visiting troop-ships. On 31 May 1942 the ferry, *Kuttabul*, which lay alongside the dockyard and provided accommodation for sailors, was struck by a torpedo from a Japanese midget submarine. Accompanied by the engineer manager, Clark immediately boarded and searched the vessel, wading through deep water in dark and hazardous conditions to assist the survivors.

In October 1943 he was posted to H.M.A.S. *Australia* as engineer officer. He was present at operations off Cape Gloucester, New Britain (December), Hollandia, Netherlands New Guinea (April 1944), and

Morotai Island (September). During the landings at Leyte Island in the Philippines, on 21 October *Australia* was hit by a Japanese aircraft which dived, apparently deliberately, into the foremast above the bridge. The crash occasioned damage, casualties and fires. Clark left his action station in the forward engine-room to direct fire- and damage-control parties in the bridge area; his deeds led to his being appointed O.B.E. Between 6 and 9 January 1945 at Lingayen Gulf, Luzon Island, *Australia* survived five kamikazi attacks. For his actions throughout those days, Clark was awarded the Distinguished Service Cross.

On 5 November he was promoted acting engineer captain (confirmed 31 December 1946) and appointed general manager, H.M.A. Naval Dockyard, Williamstown, Melbourne. He headed an active ship-building and refitting programme. In 1950-52 he was naval engineer officer on the staff of the Australian high commissioner, London. Posted to Navy Office, Melbourne, in September 1953 he was promoted engineer rear admiral, and appointed third naval member of the Naval Board and chief of construction. During his tenure he was responsible for the building of the Daring class destroyers. Although he fought hard to have four ships built, he was obliged to accept a political decision to reduce the number to three. He began the follow-on type-12 frigate construction programme and advocated the production in Australia of auxiliary machinery for these ships. Later, he initiated development of the Ikara anti-submarine weapon system. As a member of the Australian Shipbuilding Board, he ensured that the design of certain merchant ships embodied naval requirements. Clark was dedicated to naval technical excellence. Appointed C.B. in 1958, he retired on 21 August 1959 to a grazing property near Seymour.

Clark was a director (from 1959) of Broken Hill Proprietary Co. Ltd and a board-member of Commonwealth Aircraft Corporation Pty Ltd. He was a member (1946) of the Institution of Engineers, Australia, and the Institute of Marine Engineers, London, and vice-president (1964) of the Naval Association of Australia. Tallish and thin, with receding, dark hair, he was quiet, friendly, even tempered and very much a family man. He enjoyed tennis and trout-fishing. Survived by his wife, two sons and two daughters, he died of lymphosarcoma on 29 January 1965 at Richmond, Melbourne; after a naval funeral, he was cremated.

F. B. Eldridge, *History of the R.A.N.C.* (Melb, 1949); G. H. Gill, *Royal Australian Navy 1942-1945* (Canb, 1968); *BHP Review*, 42, no 3, Apr 1965; Navy Office (Canb) records, including Reports of Procs (Narrative of Events) HMAS *Australia*, Oct 1944, Jan 1945 (Navy Office, Canb); Roy Aust Naval College records, 1916-20 (Jervis Bay, ACT).
                                              M. P. REED

CLARK, EVE; *see* LANGLEY, EVE

CLARK, FREDERICK JOHN (1898-1970), medical practitioner, was born on 6 August 1898 in Melbourne, elder of twins born to George Clark and his wife Mary Alice, née Gray, both schoolteachers. In 1918 Frederick enlisted in the Australian Imperial Force and was medical officer (1925-28) with the 10th Light Horse Regiment. Graduating from the University of Melbourne (M.B., B.S., 1922), he was appointed resident medical officer at Fremantle Public Hospital, Western Australia. On 30 July 1925 he married a nurse Hilda Lois McDougall in the Anglican archbishop's chapel, Perth; they were to be divorced in 1945.

In 1925 Clark became honorary surgeon to (Royal) Perth Hospital and the Children's Hospital (later Princess Margaret Hospital for Children). He was a skilful general surgeon who pioneered thoracic surgery and neurosurgery in Western Australia. Ambidextrous, he was able to operate quickly, an advantage at a time when relatively unsophisticated equipment and anaesthetic techniques made speed helpful. In 1938 Clark was a member of the committee which investigated conditions at (Royal) Perth Hospital and recommended that new premises be built. Construction was delayed by World War II, but in 1948 a nine-storeyed block was opened. Having established a thoracic surgery unit at R.P.H. in 1947, Clark was appointed next year to the hospital's board of management; his appointment marked a decline in public service control over hospital management.

An attractive man, with blue eyes and a muscular frame, Clark was 5 ft 10½ ins (179.1 cm) tall, though he pretended to be taller. He joined the Australian Army Medical Corps Reserve and transferred to the A.I.F. on 8 July 1940. Promoted lieutenant-colonel, he was posted as senior surgeon to the 2nd/7th Australian General Hospital in the Middle East where he designed special, stainless-steel equipment for a mobile surgical unit which operated close to the front line. Following his return to Western Australia in February 1943, he commanded the 118th A.G.H. at Northam and held the rank of temporary colonel. His appointment terminated on 31 July 1944. Resuming private practice, he quickly re-established himself as the State's leading chest surgeon. He was to hold posts at R.P.H., Princess Margaret Hospital and the

Perth Chest Clinic, and to be closely associated with the Department of Repatriation. On 10 March 1945 he married another nurse Louise Olive Shenton in the Ross Memorial Presbyterian Church, West Perth.

In response to the Commonwealth Department of Health's call for medical teams to go to the Territory of Papua and New Guinea to treat tuberculosis sufferers, Clark served there for six weeks each year from 1955 until 1957. When the development of antibiotics reduced the need for surgery in tuberculosis cases, he turned his attention to the increasing incidence of bronchial carcinoma. He also experimented with a heart-lung machine and in 1958 performed the first open-heart surgery in Western Australia.

Beyond the medical profession, Clark gave the same meticulous care to everything he did. He was a crack duck-shooter, a scratch golfer at Lake Karrinyup club, an excellent carpenter and, in his later years, a keen gardener. Generous and sociable, he had a great sense of fun and a zest for the best things in life. He was, as well, brilliant and controversial, sensitive and reserved, proud, arrogant, determined, selfish—and lovable.

Survived by his wife, and by the two sons of his first marriage, Clark died on 9 August 1970 at Dalkeith and was cremated with Anglican rites. In 1975 a lecture theatre was named after him in the Sir Charles Gairdner Hospital, Nedlands, and in 1981 Clark's name was inscribed on a bronze tile in St George's Terrace, Perth.

G. C. Bolton and P. Joske, *History of Royal Perth Hospital* (Perth, 1982); Way '79 Commerce Cte, *A Walk Through the History of Western Australia 1829-1979* (Perth, 1980); *MJA*, 12 Dec 1970; *West Australian*, 12 Aug 1970; H. R. Elphick and J. A. Simpson, Unpublished speech notes for the opening of the F. J. Clark Lecture Theatre, Perth Medical Centre, 13 May 1975, held by Mrs L. O. Clark, Cottesloe, Perth, who also provided information.

JILLIAN MIZZI

CLARK, JAMES (1915-1944), air force officer, was born on 28 August 1915 at Waverley, Sydney, son of David Clark, carpenter, and his wife Mary McFarlane, née Kilpatrick, both Scottish born. Educated at Sydney Boys' High School, James was employed as a clerk by the Macarthur-Onslow [q.v.10] family company, Camden Park Estate Pty Ltd, at Menangle. In his spare time he studied accountancy, and played cricket (at which he had represented his school) and tennis in the Camden district. On 19 August 1940 Clark enlisted in the Royal Australian Air Force. He gave his religion as Presbyterian, and was recorded as being 5 ft 8 ins

(172.7 cm) tall, 11 st. 6 lb. (72.6 kg) in weight, with a fair complexion, blue eyes and brown hair.

After attending No. 5 Elementary Flying Training School at Narromine, in December Clark went to Canada under the Empire Air Training Scheme. He gained his flying badge at No. 4 Service Flying Training School, Saskatoon, Saskatchewan, was promoted pilot officer on 16 May 1941 and arrived in England next month for operational training at Moreton-in-Marsh, Gloucestershire. On 6 September he joined No. 458 Squadron, R.A.A.F., and flew Wellington bombers from the Royal Air Force Station at Holme, Yorkshire. His targets included Brest, Calais and Boulogne, France, Emden, Germany, and Ostend (Oostende), Belgium; he also attacked the German battle cruisers *Scharnhorst* and *Gneisenau*. In February 1942 the squadron was sent to the Middle East and in August Clark transferred to No. 148 Squadron, R.A.F.

Operating from Egypt in support of the Eighth Army, he participated in numerous sorties over Libya. He devised and pressed home new methods of attack, damaging enemy motor transport and starting fires in the dock area of Tobruk. For his deeds he was awarded the Distinguished Flying Cross (1943). By January 1943 Flight Lieutenant Clark was back in England, instructing Australian aircrew at No. 27 Operational Training Unit, Lichfield, Staffordshire. He married Ivy Eileen ('Cherrie') Cook on 10 July that year in the parish church, Normanton, Yorkshire. On 13 September he was posted to No. 460 Squadron, R.A.A.F., which was equipped with Lancaster bombers and stationed at Binbrook, Lincolnshire. Having completed navigation training, he was appointed a flight commander and subsequently assumed temporary command of the squadron.

Clark was a retiring, even shy, man, who kept most of his private life to himself. As an airman, he was popular: sincere and dedicated, he set a high example. For his later service in England, he was mentioned in dispatches, awarded the Air Force Cross (1944) and on 1 October 1944 promoted acting squadron leader. On the night of 12-13 December No. 460 Squadron took part in a 'topping-up' raid against Essen, Germany; it was 'a heavy blow' to the squadron when his aircraft went missing and he was presumed dead. His wife and infant son survived him. Eric Kennington's pastel portrait of Clark is held by the family.

P. C. Firkins, *Strike and Return* (Perth, nd); J. Herington, *Air Power over Europe 1944-45* (Canb, 1963); P. Alexander, *We Find and Destroy* (Syd, 1979); AWM records; information from Mrs C. Clark, Florey, ACT.　　　　KEITH ISAACS

CLARK, JOHN (1885-1956), entomologist, was born on 21 March 1885 at Glasgow, Scotland, son of James Souttar Clark, coach-painter, and his wife Maggie, née Scott. With little formal education, John came to Australia in 1905 and found a job with the State railways at Chillagoe, Queensland. His work enabled him to indulge in what was to become an enduring interest in ants and he collected his first specimens in North Queensland.

On 21 May 1908 Clark married Maggie Forbes at the Presbyterian manse, Cairns. They moved to Geraldton, Western Australia, where he was again employed by the railways, for some time as a wheelwright. His enthusiasm for natural history came to the attention of L. J. W. Newman [q.v.11], the entomologist with the Department of Agriculture, who took him on probation as an assistant to the entomologist on 24 February 1919. When Clark's position was confirmed on 1 October 1920, he shifted with his wife, son and two daughters to Perth, where another daughter was born. His first papers, including notes on the history of entomology in Western Australia, were published in 1921. Three years later he was promoted to assistant-entomologist.

At the Australasian Association for the Advancement of Science's congress in Perth in 1926, some visiting scientists suggested that Clark should apply for the vacant position of entomologist at the National Museum of Victoria. He was appointed to the museum on 18 November 1926 and began his duties on 24 January 1927. Finding 'museum work in Melbourne not to his liking', in 1929 he unsuccessfully applied for the post of economic entomologist in the mandated Territory of New Guinea. In March 1933 he sold his collection of ants, comprising eight thousand specimens, to the museum for £200.

Maggie died of heart disease on 5 October 1935. Clark subsequently moved from Hawthorn to Fern Tree Gully. On 1 May 1939 he married Phyllis Marjorie Claringbull at the office of the government statist, Melbourne. She bore him two daughters, but committed suicide on 26 September 1943, three months after the second daughter's birth. Unable to look after these children, Clark sent them to an orphanage.

Although generous, friendly and helpful to amateurs, Clark was intemperate in the extreme to his peers and superiors, whom he treated with contempt. This attitude, together with his lack of academic qualifications, bedevilled his career. He frequently applied for reclassification, to no avail. When R. T. M. Pescott was appointed director of the museum in August 1944, Clark immediately resigned. Having lost all his entitlements, he lived in poverty at Mooroolbark.

During his career Clark published thirty-five entomological papers. In view of his worldwide reputation as an authority on Australian ants, the division of entomology of the Council for Scientific and Industrial Research arranged in 1947 for him to undertake a comprehensive revision of the group. The first volume, published in 1951, received poor reviews and no further volumes were forthcoming. Survived by six children, he died, intestate, on 1 June 1956 at his Mooroolbark home and was buried in Burwood cemetery. His collection of ants went to the Commonwealth Scientific and Industrial Research Organization in Canberra.

Clark's second daughter Ellen (1915-1988) was also a noted naturalist. Having worked with her father at the museum, in 1940 she became secretary of the virus department of the Walter and Eliza Hall [qq.v.9] Institute, and naturalist for the *Argus* and *Australasian*. She published papers on influenza virus research—with (Sir) Macfarlane Burnett—and on crustacea, her special interest.

A. Musgrave, *Bibliography of Australian Entomology 1775-1930* (Syd, 1932); H. J. Carter, *Gulliver in the Bush* (Syd, 1933); R. T. M. Pescott, *Collections of a Century* (Melb, 1954); Dept of Agr (WA), *Annual Report*, 1919; Council for Scientific and Industrial Research, *22nd Annual Report*, 1948; *Entomological News*, 67, no 8, 1956; *Aust J of Science*, 19, 1956-57; *Sun News-Pictorial*, 2 June 1956.   MURRAY S. UPTON

CLARK, JOHN FAITHFULL (1911-1967), professor of applied psychology, was born on 20 April 1911 at Paddington, Sydney, son of native-born parents John Clark, stonemason, and his wife Mary Goodier, née Scholes. Educated at Sydney Boys' High School and the University of Sydney (B.Sc., 1931; Dip.Ed., 1932; B.A., 1940; M.A., 1948), from 1932 John taught at city and country high schools. On 28 December 1937 he married a fellow teacher Jean Olive Hutton at St Stephen's Presbyterian Church, Sydney. A dedicated lifesaver, he participated in the rescue operation on Black Sunday (6 February 1938) when some two hundred people were swept out in rough surf at Bondi and five were drowned.

After completing an arts degree and winning the university medal in psychology, in May 1940 Clark was appointed psychologist-in-charge of the vocational guidance section, Department of Labour and Industry. On 8 June 1942 he enlisted in the Royal Australian Air Force; he was then 5 ft 7 ins (170.2 cm) tall, weighed 10 st. 10 lb. (68 kg), and had blue eyes and light-brown hair. Commissioned on 11 July, he was promoted acting flight lieutenant in January 1943. On 2 December, as senior research officer, he took charge of psychological testing in the directorate of training until he was demobilized on 20 June 1946 with the rank of acting wing commander.

Appointed senior guidance officer in the technical education branch of the Department of Public Instruction in June 1945, Clark served as senior selection officer for the Commonwealth Reconstruction Scheme in 1946-47. With Squadron Leader T. G. Jones, he published *Vocational Guidance in the Royal Australian Air Force, 1942-1946* (Melbourne, 1947). In 1949 he became chief educational research officer in the Department of Technical Education. Having refined his methods of analysis, he studied at the Institute of Education, University of London (Ph.D., 1951), as a Carnegie fellow (1949-50) and Leon scholar (1950-51), and wrote his thesis on vocational aspirations.

In 1953 Clark was appointed foundation professor of applied psychology at the New South Wales University of Technology (University of New South Wales). He initially accepted the customary emphasis on general psychology in the undergraduate programme, but later promoted applied psychology—industrial and clinical—and moved increasingly towards providing professional training in that area. In recruiting his staff, he looked to expertise in this field, as well as to demonstrated teaching skills. The research he engaged in and encouraged in his large department was practical and fundamental; he was not much concerned with broad theoretical issues. In 1956-57 he chaired the Australian branch of the British Psychological Society. A fellow of the Australian Institute of Industrial Management, he brought psychology to industry and the community through extramural talks and short courses, especially on management problems.

In 1961 Clark was appointed dean of the faculty of science: he held this office while continuing as head of the school of applied psychology. As pro vice-chancellor from 1963, he liaised with the university colleges at Newcastle and Wollongong; his duties included responsibility for student facilities and overseeing student progress, and he endeavoured to blend the technological and humanistic aims of the university. He was an effective administrator, wise, patient and informed, who worked harmoniously with colleagues and subordinates. Clark died suddenly of a dissecting aortic aneurysm on 4 June 1967 at St Leonards, Sydney, and was cremated; his wife, son and daughter survived him.

D. P. Mellor, *The Role of Science and Industry* (Canb, 1958); Univ Syd Union, *Union Recorder*, 20 July 1967; *Aust Psychologist*, 2, no 2, Nov 1967; *SMH*, 10 Nov 1953, 5, 7 June 1967; *Sun-Herald*, 10 Jan 1960.

W. M. O'NEIL*

CLARK-DUFF, VICTOR WILLIAM THOMAS (1883-1974), Presbyterian clergyman, was born on 24 May 1883 at Penrith, New South Wales, son of native-born parents William George Clark (d. 1888), storekeeper, and his wife Mary Ann Larmbier, née Smith. Mary married Alexander Duff in 1890; Victor adopted his stepfather's surname. He was educated at Penrith Public School, Sydney Boys' High School (on a scholarship) and Scots College where he was strongly influenced by the headmaster A. A. Aspinall [q.v.7]. In 1901 Duff entered St Andrew's College, University of Sydney (B.A., 1904); after subsequent divinity studies, he was sent to the Hunter Valley as a preaching agent at Abermain.

Ordained in 1907, Clark-Duff (as he now styled himself) was appointed minister of Cessnock. There, he pushed along with the belated policy of the General Assembly of the Presbyterian Church of New South Wales to expand in the mining districts. Translated to Singleton in 1913, he gradually pulled together an old parish which had run into difficulties. On 18 February 1914 he married Ida Margaret Parkins at the Presbyterian Church, Mosman. Following a report presented to the assembly on future strategy in the coalfields districts, in 1921 Clark-Duff returned to Cessnock as superintendent of the Maitland Coalfields Mission. At a time of industrial unrest and pessimism, the mission proved unsatisfactory.

In 1924 the assembly thanked Clark-Duff for his 'honest, hard and efficient work', dissolved the Coalfields Mission and returned him to Cessnock-Aberdare. Faced with an increasingly arduous situation, Clark-Duff performed well, becoming something of an expert on social and economic problems, but in 1931 sought fresh experience in Sydney at the new North Shore parish of Artarmon. Despite Depression problems, Artarmon gave Clark-Duff the chance to serve the Church in a wider sphere. In addition to his parish work, he edited (1933-36) the *New South Wales Presbyterian*; he greatly reduced the paper's debts and widened its appeal. Appointed moderator in 1935, he summed up his coalfields and editorial reflections in his address, *Christianity's Challenge to Civilization.*

His election in 1936 as general secretary (a full-time post, for five years) was an indication of a Presbyterian demand for renewal. The Depression had led the Church to rethink many traditional attitudes. The Samuel Angus [q.v.7] heresy case—which divided theological liberals and conservatives, and caused immense turmoil—had reached a stalemate in 1934. Clark-Duff had dealt with it even-handedly in the *Presbyterian*. As secretary, he was able to carry on a reconstruction policy which fitted the Church to cope with the stresses of war from 1939. Re-elected in 1941, he was given a third (this time three-year) term in 1946.

Two years later, Presbyterians were startled to learn from the census that they had fallen behind the Methodists in numbers and rate of increase. With postwar issues pressing, a change seemed necessary. Clark-Duff retired, yet showed his concern for the new order by serving as a chaplain in a migrant ship from Britain in 1950. A patriarchal figure in the Church, he continued to sit on the council of Scots College and the board of the Scottish Hospital. Predeceased by his wife, son and daughter, he died on 29 June 1974 at Ashfield and was cremated.

C. A. White, *The Challenge of the Years* (Syd, 1951); Presbyterian Church of NSW, *Minutes of Procs of General Assembly*, 1921-50; *SMH*, 24 Jan 1931, 12 Jan 1935.

K. J. CABLE

CLAYTON, SIR HECTOR JOSEPH RICHARD (1885-1975), solicitor, army officer and politician, was born on 3 June 1885 at Surry Hills, Sydney, fourth child and elder of twin sons of native-born parents John Horatio Clayton, solicitor, and his wife Isabella, née Woodward. Educated at Sydney Grammar School and the University of Sydney (B.A., 1907; LL.B., 1910), Hector was articled to his father on 6 March 1907, admitted as a solicitor on 20 February 1911 and practised in partnership with his father.

Enlisting in the Australian Imperial Force on 14 August 1914, Clayton was commissioned on 9 September and posted to the 4th Battalion. He embarked for Egypt in October as a captain and took part in the landing on Gallipoli on 25 April 1915, but was wounded in action on 22 May and served in Egypt as an embarkation officer until June 1916. Transferred to the Western Front, he was promoted major in November, commanded the 4th Division Base (as temporary lieutenant colonel from October 1917) and performed administrative duties in England from June 1918. Clayton was mentioned in dispatches (1917). On 24 July 1917 he had married Phyllis Edith Midwood at the parish church, Market Drayton, Shropshire; they were to have four children.

After his appointment terminated in Sydney on Armistice Day 1919, Clayton's legal career flourished. He was a partner in Clayton & Utz (1920-24) and in Clayton, Utz & Co.

(1924-75). In 1936 he was elected to the Legislative Council; he resigned from the United Australia Party because he believed that the council should be a non-partisan house of review. On the Reserve of Officers, Clayton was mobilized on 4 September 1939. Having briefly commanded Holdsworthy Detention Camp, he was posted to staff duties and from July 1942 commanded the 1st Movement Control Group in the New South Wales Lines of Communication Area. He was placed on the Retired List as honorary colonel in August 1945.

His political ambitions and achievements were modest. As a solicitor and councillor of the Incorporated Law Institute of New South Wales (1933-43), Clayton was effective in ensuring that the Legislative Council protected the interests of other professional groups. His infrequent speeches were invariably characterized by 'gentlemanly behaviour', although his critics accused him of pedantry. His most significant achievement lay in his resourceful contribution to frustrating the Australian Labor Party's attempts to abolish the Upper House. In 1959-60 he led the resistance through the Supreme Court and the High Court of Australia; in April 1961 the people of New South Wales voted in a referendum for the council's retention.

In 1960 Clayton had allowed himself to be appointed 'Principal Representative of Members who are not supporters of the [Labor] Government', a position he held in the council for two years. Dismayed by the Liberal Party's methods of selecting leaders, he arranged for Brigadier T. A. J. Playfair [q.v.11] to nominate him in August 1966 as president of the Upper House. Aged 81, mustachioed, heavily jowled and somewhat corpulently proportioned, Colonel Clayton was about to attain the peak of his political career, but, on the morning of the crucial council meeting, Playfair suffered a fatal heart attack. Stunned, and grieving for his old friend, Clayton declined to contest the election. He was knighted in 1968 and retired from the council in 1973.

Influential in commercial circles from the 1930s, he had been a director of several insurance companies and of Australian Guarantee Corporation Ltd (1942-73). As its chairman, he presided over Australia's largest finance company at a time when the 'use of instalment credit spread almost like a contagion in Australia'. With G. K. Bain [q.v.], Clayton was enthusiastic about the rise in 'consumer demand' for this type of financial service and in 1957 led the firm into a profitable relationship with the Bank of New South Wales. During the 1961 credit squeeze he was able to announce that A.G.C. had built one of Sydney's first skyscrapers and had still made a net profit of £1 285 244. He remained an implacable opponent of other drains on working-class finances, such as poker machines.

Sir Hector's recreations included bowls and gardening. He was a member of the Australian, University and Royal Sydney Golf clubs, and a trustee of the War Widows' Guild of Australia. Survived by his two sons and a daughter, he died on 18 July 1975 at Paddington and was cremated.

K. Turner, *House of Review?* (Syd, 1969); G. Whitwell, *Making the Market* (Melb, 1989); *SMH*, 25 Apr 1958, 14 July 1961, 15 Nov 1972, 9-11 Aug 1966, 19 July 1975; *Sun* (Syd), 4 Aug 1961; *Daily Telegraph* (Syd), 10 Aug 1966.

ANDREW MOORE

CLEARY, GLORIA DAWN; *see* DAWN

CLEGG, WILLIAM EDWARD (1886-1957), industrialist, was born on 9 April 1886 at Douglas, Isle of Man, eldest child of William Henry Clague, greengrocer, and his wife Margaret Jane, née Kewley. In 1890 the family migrated to New South Wales where William Henry established a milk-vending business at Newcastle. Young William was educated at Wickham Superior Public School, but spent most afternoons assisting on the milk run. In 1901 he was apprenticed as a fitter and turner to A. Goninan [q.v.] & Co. Ltd; in the evenings he attended Newcastle Technical College, and later undertook correspondence courses in metallurgy and accounting. He regularly travelled throughout the State for Goninans, installing winding machines and boilers. At St James's Anglican Church, Wickham, on 21 May 1912 he married Elsie Parsons, daughter of an engine driver.

In 1916 Clegg established engineering works at Cowra, before returning briefly to Newcastle in 1919 to manage Goninans. In March 1921 he was appointed engineering consultant at Commonwealth Steel Products Co. Ltd (Commonwealth Steel Co. Ltd after the Broken Hill Proprietary Co. Ltd purchased a controlling interest in 1935). He became manager in September 1921 and general manager in 1925. Under his stewardship the company expanded: new shops were built, modern plant was installed and employees increased from 170 in 1921 to 2283 in 1951. He visited the United States of America, England and Europe in 1926, 1929, 1935 and 1939 to keep abreast of developments.

Clegg's lifelong hatred of trade unions— whose leaders, he believed, were 'false prophets . . . leading the men [into] a desert' —underpinned the company's policy of vigorous and pertinacious anti-unionism. On the job, he tempered his hardline approach with heartfelt paternalism; he knew many workers personally, but did not hesitate to dismiss troublesome employees. When he retired in December 1951, he was made a director of Commonwealth Steel, honoured with numerous testimonial dinners and presented with the deeds to the company-owned mansion, Braeside, Waratah, where he had lived since 1921.

President (1936-55) of the Newcastle Technical Education Advisory Council, Clegg served on the council of the New South Wales University of Technology (University of New South Wales). From 1951 he represented the university on the Newcastle University College advisory committee and was awarded an honorary D.Sc. in 1955. The University of Newcastle has annually awarded the W. E. Clegg memorial prize in mechanical engineering since 1958.

A foundation member (1926) of the Rotary Club of Newcastle, in 1932 Clegg helped to establish the Newcastle and District Association for Crippled Children and insisted that classes be held in his dining-room until its school was completed in 1936. He was involved with the Newcastle Chamber of Commerce and with local branches of the Chamber of Manufactures (president 1924-29), Metal Trades Employers' Association, Institution of Engineers, Australia, Australasian Institute of Cost Accountants, Standards Association of Australia, Australian Institute of Management and the Royal Empire Society. Lawn bowls was his abiding passion and the source of graphic tales of exploits: he was president (1922-51) of Islington Bowling Club and patron (from 1935) of the Newcastle District Bowling Association.

Holding an extensive share portfolio, Clegg was a wealthy man and one of the last Edwardians. His housekeeper and two maids lived at Braeside until old age forced them into nursing homes (an expense he happily bore). Meals were events with the best silver and china; fruit could not be eaten unless the appropriate knife and fork were used. His wife laid out his suits every day. He was barely more than five feet (152.4 cm) tall, and had a fetish about punctuality and day-to-day routine. An Anglican, he attended church regularly. He was devastated by the deaths of his daughter Marion and, in April 1955, of his wife; without her support, his regimented world began to crumble. Survived by his son and two daughters, he died on 23 July 1957 at Braeside and was cremated.

BHP Review, Apr 1937, p 5, June 1937, p 5, Mar 1952, p 14; *Newcastle Morning Herald*, 10 Dec 1923, 20 Mar 1926, 30 Nov 1929, 24 Sept 1938, 28 Apr 1950, 29 Nov 1951, 24 July 1957; *SMH*, 24 July 1950; BHP papers (BHP Archives, Melb); Univ Newcastle papers (Univ Newcastle Archives); Univ

NSW papers (Univ NSW Archives); family papers held by and information from Mrs B. Bates, Kotara Heights, NSW.   WARWICK EATHER

CLEGGETT, ELLA (1884-1960), schoolteacher and welfare worker, was born on 18 December 1884 at Mount Barker, South Australia, fourth of six daughters of native-born parents John Cleggett, farmer, and his wife Louisa, née Capner, a former schoolteacher. Ella attended the local public school and—like three of her sisters—was trained as a teacher. From 1906 she spent nineteen years with the South Australian Education Department. She taught at Flinders Street Model School, Adelaide, at Moonta, at Burra and at Mount Barker. There she contracted scarlet fever which left her with a permanent loss of hearing that eventually made her abandon classroom work. Transferring from Thebarton Public School to the Correspondence School, in 1924 she was assessed by an inspector as being 'enthusiastic, patriotic, a strong influence, critical'.

During World War I Cleggett had been active in the Schools' Patriotic Fund. Her visits to Bedford Park Sanatorium provided opportunities to meet returned servicemen suffering from tuberculosis. In 1921 the Tubercular Sailors', Soldiers' and Airmen's Association formed the Tubercular Soldiers' Aid Society of South Australia, a fund-raising and welfare organization, of which Ella became honorary secretary. The association was only concerned with pensions; the society was to seek additional benefits and gainful employment for those weakened by the effects of the disease. In 1924 Cleggett took leave from the Education Department to raise money for the T.B.S.A.S., but was told that she could not do so again; next year she resigned to be the society's full-time, paid secretary.

Her joking, almost frivolous, manner gave former diggers the impression that she was 'just a girl', but Cleggett was a woman of energy and determination who was devoted to her cause. She often sat up each night for weeks, reading by candlelight to a dying man; she looked after orphans; she tramped the city seeking light work for the afflicted. Tall and slim, with auburn hair and smoky-blue eyes, she treated tubercular soldiers as if they were her brothers, offering hope and reassurance to her charges and their families who called her 'Auntie Cleggett'. Intent on counteracting the stigma attached to 'the shadow of T.B.', she named the society's newsletter the *Optimist*.

Cleggett petitioned councils, doctors and prominent business firms for contributions, and attended fund-raising balls and concerts. She established Angorichina Hostel in the warm, dry Flinders Ranges where patients learned to craft fine furniture from the offcuts of red-gum railway sleepers. The workshop was transferred to Adelaide in the 1930s, but the hostel was retained (until 1973) and remained her main concern.

In 1951 Miss Cleggett was granted honorary life membership of the Returned Sailors', Soldiers' and Airmen's Imperial League of Australia and was appointed M.B.E. She was an Anglican. On 26 March 1960 she died in Rua Rua Private Hospital, North Adelaide, and was buried in Mitcham cemetery; a commemorative plaque was unveiled there three years later. Although she had raised over £250 000 for the society, her estate was sworn for probate at only £1325. She bequeathed her small collection of Australian paintings to her nieces.

G. Ralph, *Thebarton Primary School 1879-1979* (Adel, 1979); F. J. Cleggett, *From Kent to South Australia* (Adel, 1985); *Observer* (Adel), 14 Nov 1925; *Advertiser* (Adel), 28 Mar 1960; information from Mrs B. Duke, TBSAS, Adel, who holds a copy of N. Dugdale, A Tribute to Miss Ella Cleggett, ms, nd.   SUSAN MARSDEN

CLELAND, SIR DONALD MACKINNON (1901-1975), soldier and administrator, was born on 28 June 1901 at Coolgardie, Western Australia, eldest son of Adelaide-born Elphinstone Davenport Cleland, mine-manager, and his second wife Anne Emily, née Mackinnon, from Scotland. After a childhood on the goldfields of Kalgoorlie, from 1912 Don attended the Church of England Grammar School, Guildford, where he was captain (1919). Excluded on medical grounds from the Royal Military College, Duntroon, Federal Capital Territory, he enlisted in the Militia in July 1919 and rose to captain in the 3rd Field Artillery Brigade before resigning in 1928. On 18 December that year he married Rachel Evans at St George's Anglican Cathedral, Perth.

Appointed to the Australian Imperial Force on 13 October 1939 as staff captain, 6th Divisional Artillery, Cleland arrived in the Middle East in February 1940. He was promoted temporary major in November. For his work as deputy assistant quartermaster general, I Corps, during the campaigns in Libya, Greece and Syria in 1941, he was appointed M.B.E. (1942) and mentioned in dispatches.

After a brief period in Australia early in 1942, Cleland was appointed temporary colonel and posted as D.A.Q.M.G., Australian New Guinea Administrative Unit, Port Moresby. In October he was promoted temporary brigadier and from March 1943 held the additional position of chairman of the Australian New Guinea Production Control

Board. Effectively chief of staff, Cleland was responsible for the day-by-day civil administration of Papua and New Guinea, for the running of the pre-war plantations and for A.N.G.A.U.'s operational commitments. The military administration raised standards of health care and labour supervision, and began a new education scheme. Again mentioned in dispatches, Cleland was elevated to C.B.E. in 1945 and transferred to the Reserve of Officers on 12 May. He was to be made honorary colonel of the Pacific Islands Regiment in 1958.

Before World War II Cleland had worked as an articled clerk, qualified as a solicitor and barrister in 1925, and practised as a partner with Villeneuve, Smith & Keall. Active in conservative politics, he was president (1936-38) of the National Party of Western Australia and thrice stood unsuccessfully for the Legislative Assembly (1933, 1936 and 1939). On his return to Perth in mid-1945, he was elected vice-president of the State branch of the Liberal Party. When John Curtin [q.v.] died, Cleland—showing 'an itch for public service and a gaucherie of platform manner' —was defeated in the by-election for the seat of Fremantle in the House of Representatives. In October he was appointed director of the federal secretariat of the Liberal Party, and in that position organized the effective 1949 campaign.

An applicant to be administrator of Papua and New Guinea in 1945, he believed that he was rejected for (Sir Jack) Murray [q.v.] on political grounds, yet Cleland's appointment as assistant-administrator in 1951 was denounced as being 'political', and the 'howl' increased when Murray was asked to resign and Cleland became acting-administrator, then administrator in 1953. (Sir) Paul Hasluck, minister for territories, pointed to Cleland's record in A.N.G.A.U. where Murray had been junior to Cleland. In their twelve-year partnership Hasluck was the public figure, but he was dependent on Cleland's assiduous administration and both men crossed roles, with Cleland setting policy and Hasluck forcing action from the bureaucracy. According to Hasluck, Cleland was 'cool-headed, firm and decisive', with a 'clear view of his loyalties', though he did not always get prompt action from his officers. Under Hasluck's less influential successor Charles Barnes, Cleland resisted direction from Canberra.

Cleland was pragmatic, balancing commercial, mission and government interests against what he thought was primary: the orderly development of the indigenous people. Publicly, he measured success in terms of building roads, bridges and airstrips, the increase in government revenue and the expansion of the public service. He chaired the Legislative Council, his 'pride and joy', until 1964 and directed the introduction of the first House of Assembly elected by full adult franchise; he restructured the public service so that it would be dominated by Papua New Guineans, paid at a rate the country could afford; and he continued the elimination of discriminatory legislation, most obviously ending the liquor ban in 1962. While his reports were methodical, in his diary he made quick, shrewd judgements of people and events. He was knighted in 1961. When he retired in 1967 he regarded talk of Papua New Guinea becoming a seventh State of Australia as 'completely impractical' and cautioned against premature independence. Energetic, with broad interests and deft social skills, Rachel complemented his dour, sometimes gruff, manner, and eased contact with diverse people. She was to be appointed D.B.E. in 1981.

In retirement Cleland lived in Port Moresby, the only administrator of either territory to choose to stay there. He was pro-chancellor and chancellor (from 1971) of the University of Papua New Guinea, and chancellor (from 1967) of the Anglican diocese of Papua New Guinea. Survived by his wife and two sons, Sir Donald died on 27 August 1975 in Port Moresby; accorded a state funeral, he was buried in the cemetery at Bomana. Cleland won the trust of ambitious lieutenants, he was stoic in the face of criticism, and his integrity and judgement were undoubted. He did not court popularity, but was widely respected, and remembered with affection.

The History of Melanesia (Port Moresby, 1969); P. Hasluck, *A Time for Building* (Melb, 1976); I. Downs, *The Australian Trusteeship* (Canb, 1980); R. Cleland, *Papua New Guinea* (Perth, 1983); *PIM*, June 1952, Mar 1953, Feb 1967; *SMH*, 15 Aug 1945; personal papers (held by Dame Rachel Cleland, Perth).   II. N. NELSON

CLEWS, HUGH POWELL GOUGH (1890-1980), surveyor and army officer, was born on Christmas Day 1890 at Rotherham, Yorkshire, England, son of William Henry Clews, restaurateur, and his wife Helen Powell, née Sharp. After a basic education, Hugh completed a two-year apprenticeship as a surveyor. At 5 ft 6¼ ins (168.3 cm), he was considered too short for the Royal Engineers, so he enlisted in the Sherwood Foresters in July 1909. He left the British Army in 1911 and migrated to Western Australia.

On 1 August 1912 Clews joined the Permanent Military Forces as a sergeant in the survey section of the Royal Australian Engineers. He was employed as a mapmaker in South Australia and—with the new (Royal) Australian Survey Corps—in Victoria and

Western Australia. In December 1917 he transferred to the Australian Imperial Force. Before embarking for England, on 10 January 1918 he married Alice May Reeves with Anglican rites at Holy Trinity Church, Balaclava, Melbourne. Clews served in France from June 1918 to April 1919. Back home, he reverted to the P.M.F. in July and next year was posted to New South Wales where he carried out topographical surveys and established survey control for mapping.

Commissioned lieutenant and made officer commanding No. 3 Survey Section in November 1933, he took command of No. 2 Field Survey Company in October 1940 and was promoted major next month. From successive headquarters at Strathfield and Kyogle, and Childers and Ingham in Queensland, he supervised coastal triangulation, geodetic control and topographic mapping. 'Iron Man' Clews endeared himself to his subordinates by his feats of endurance, and by his humanity and charm. In June 1944 he reluctantly gave up field-work for staff duties in Sydney. Placed on the Retired List on 29 July 1949 as an honorary lieutenant colonel, he established a home in the bush at Bell.

In early 1950 Clews entered into an initial five-year contract as a senior surveyor with the Snowy Mountains Hydro-electric Authority. Wiry and white haired, he wore a battered hat and loved being the first into new territory. His reconnaissance surveys, carried out on foot through harsh terrain, preceded the construction of roads and tunnels, and anticipated the work of hydrologists, other surveyors and blasting teams as the vast water-diversion project took shape. 'The Major's' courage and leadership made him a legend among fellow workers, many of whom were European refugees. He retired in February 1958 to a forty-acre (16.2 ha) lease at Indi, near Khancoban, where he built a pisé house. Eccentric but by no means a recluse, he enjoyed the *Illustrated London News*, the works of Rudyard Kipling, the music of Sibelius, gardening, a pipe and a drink of rum. He wrote *Strzelecki's Ascent of Mount Kosciusko* (Melbourne, 1970).

Until the 1970s 'Clewsie' continued to march on Anzac Day in Sydney and was a regular visitor to the army's School of Survey at Bonegilla, Victoria. Increasingly frail, he moved to Khancoban, then to Frankston, Melbourne. Survived by his son and two daughters, he died there on 22 August 1980 and was cremated. A granite cairn at Indi commemorates him.

L. Fitzgerald, *Lebanon to Labuan* (Melb, 1980); S. McHugh, *The Snowy* (Melb, 1989); B. Collis, *Snowy* (Syd, 1990); *Aust Surveyor*, 6, no 7, Sept 1937, 23, no 7, Sept 1971; *National Bulletin of Survey Corps Associations*, Nov 1966, Sept 1975, Nov, Dec 1980, Dec 1981; Survey Ex-Servicemens Assn (NSW), *Bulletin*, 66, 1980, 67, 1981; *Sabretache*, 31, Oct-Dec 1990; information from Mr H. Clews, Chelsea, Melb, Brig D. Macdonald and Mr L. N. Fletcher, Syd, and Col J. Hillier, Canb.

JOHN ATCHISON

CLIFT, CHARMIAN (1923-1969), writer, was born on 30 August 1923 at Kiama, New South Wales, third and youngest child of Sydney Clift, a fitter and turner from England, and his native-born wife Amy Lila, née Currie. Although Charmian attended Kiama Public and Wollongong High schools, she attributed her education to her parents' love for books, and to the wild beach and little valley that bounded her home. After passing the Intermediate certificate in 1938, she worked at odd jobs around Kiama. Tall, with an athletic build, Clift was growing into the beauty that would become one of her best-known attributes. In May 1941 she won the New South Wales title in *Pix* magazine's Beach Girl Quest and escaped to Sydney. There she became an usherette at the Minerva Theatre, Kings Cross.

Enlisting in the Australian Women's Army Service on 27 April 1943, Clift served with the 15th Australian Heavy Anti-Aircraft Battery in Sydney. She was commissioned lieutenant in August 1944 and worked as an orderly officer at Land Headquarters, Melbourne. While editing an army magazine, she began to write and publish short stories. Having transferred to the Reserve of Officers on 11 May 1946, she joined the *Argus* and met the war correspondent George Henry Johnston [q.v.]. Their employers disapproved of their relationship and three months later both were summarily dismissed. Clift and Johnston left for Sydney and, following his divorce, were married on 7 August 1947 at the courthouse, Manly. They collaborated on the novel, *High Valley* (1949), which won the *Sydney Morning Herald*'s £2000 prize for 1948.

Early in 1951 Charmian, George and their son and daughter went to London where Johnston was in charge of the Associated Newspaper Service's office. Clift completed little in the way of writing until the family moved to the Greek island of Kálimnos late in 1954. She then wrote *Mermaid Singing* (Indianapolis, 1956), a semi-autobiographical account of life in Greece. In her second travel book, *Peel me a Lotus* (London, 1959), she described their move to Hydra (Ídhra) and the birth of their second son.

Clift next turned her lyrical talent to the landscape of Kiama in her first solo novel, *Walk to the Paradise Gardens* (London, 1960). A slow and painstaking writer, she spent the next four years on the romantic novel,

Honour's Mimic (London, 1964). While struggling with this book, she began an autobiographical novel about her childhood ('The End of the Morning'), and acted as the sounding-board for Johnston during his writing of *My Brother Jack* (London, 1964). He returned to Australia in February 1964 for its release; Clift and the children followed in August.

Her four books had received glowing reviews in Britain and the United States of America, but had barely been distributed in Australia. Back in Sydney, Clift was a literary nonentity—or worse, the wife of a literary celebrity. She soon achieved recognition in her own right: her weekly column in the *Sydney Morning Herald* and the Melbourne *Herald* immediately attracted a large and devoted readership. Originally commissioned to produce 'real writing from a woman's point of view', she in fact wrote essays. Although her form was traditional and her style exquisite, her subject matter often included topical issues such as the Vietnam War, conscription, the Greek junta and world hunger. In 1965 thirty-six of these essays were anthologized in *Images in Aspic* (Sydney). The acclaimed ten-part television series of *My Brother Jack*, which Clift had scripted for the Australian Broadcasting Commission, went to air in August-October that year. Funding never eventuated, however, for her subsequent film and television projects.

Over the next few years Clift met the deadline for her weekly column. She also carried the main burden of housework and parenting, for Johnston was seriously ill and spent many months in hospital. Little time remained for writing books. Receiving a six-month Commonwealth Literary Fund fellowship in late 1968, she again turned to 'The End of the Morning', but it remained a fragment. The combination of work pressure and personal pain had become too great by mid-1969. On the night of 8 July, while considerably affected by alcohol, Charmian Clift took a fatal overdose of sleeping tablets at her Mosman home; survived by her husband and three children, she was cremated. Since her death, her reputation has grown. In 1970 a second anthology of essays, *The World of Charmian Clift*, was compiled by George and illustrated by their elder son Martin. Her other essays were collected in two volumes, *Trouble in Lotus Land* (1990) and *Being Alone With Oneself* (1991), and all her early books were republished in a uniform edition (1989-90). Ray Crooke's portrait of Clift is held by the National Library of Australia, Canberra.

C. Clift, *Images in Aspic*, G. Johnston introd (Syd, 1965), and *Trouble in Lotus Land*, N. Wheatley ed and introd (Syd, 1990); D. Foster (comp and introd), *Self-Portraits* (Canb, 1991); *Walkabout*, Jan 1969; *Aust Women's Weekly*, 3 Sept 1969; *SMH*, 8 May 1948; *Sun* (Syd), 6 July 1966; *Australian*, 23 Nov 1968; Clift papers *and* G. Johnston papers (NL).

NADIA WHEATLEY

CLIFTON, MARSHALL WALLER GERVASE (1903-1975), architect and artist, was born on 11 September 1903 at Wokalup, Western Australia, second of five sons of Gervase Clifton, farmer, and his wife Florence Mabel, née Knowles, and great-great-grandson of Marshall Waller Clifton [q.v.3]. The family took up land at Northampton in 1910. Young Clifton's drawings at primary school so impressed H. J. Hughes, the visiting inspector, that he invited him to stay with his family in order to complete his education at Northam High School. A good student, with a flair for mathematics, Clifton planned to study engineering at the University of Western Australia, but in March 1922 began a four-year cadetship in architecture at the Public Works Department, Perth. Elected an associate (1926) of the Royal Institute of Architects of Western Australia, he remained in the department as a junior assistant architect (1926-27) and assistant architect (1927-29), before joining the practice of George Herbert Parry.

In 1930 Clifton sailed for England to further his career. From September he was employed in London by E. Vincent Harris, and helped with designs for the Manchester Central Library and the Leeds Civic Hall. He also attended classes at the Royal Academy's school of architecture from January 1931. Having visited Europe, he returned to Perth in December 1932 and next year formed a partnership with Parry. At St Paul's Presbyterian Church, Northam, on 28 April 1934 Clifton married Nancy Millicent Hughes, with whose family he had lived as a youth. He was honorary architect and artist to the Royal Western Australian Historical Society in 1936-75.

A gifted and largely self-taught water-colourist, Clifton belonged to a generation which considered that the ability to draw and a knowledge of the history of art and architecture were essential to an architect's training. He was inspired by the English water-colourists and painted 'with as little fuss as possible', endeavouring to capture a scene with spontaneity, economy and restrained colour harmonies.

Influenced by Mediterranean vernacular building forms, Clifton's 'romantic' response to his European travels was evident in such early work as the Captain Stirling Hotel, Nedlands (1935). In June 1937 he established his own practice and concentrated on domestic architecture. The Clifton house, Johnston Street, Mosman Park (1937), and Day house, Victoria Avenue, Claremont (1939), exemplified his mature design. He favoured a 'Spanish style', with its courts and loggias, seeing it as ideally suited to the climate and casual lifestyle of Perth's suburbs. These projects established his reputation.

Fine featured, clean shaven and 5 ft 10 ins (177.8 cm) tall, Clifton was appointed lieutenant in the Militia on 23 June 1941 and posted in January 1942 to Western Command where he performed engineering staff duties. He was transferred to the Australian Imperial Force on 8 September and confirmed in the rank of captain in July 1943. Continuing to serve in Australia, he was demobilized in Perth on 19 September 1944.

In 1946 he formed a partnership with his former pupil Eric Leach, an able and articulate exponent of the cause of modern architecture. Clifton was attracted to modern architectural design because its approach was based upon a careful assessment of climate and site in order to make the most effective use of sun and shade. He re-established his own practice in 1953. The University of Western Australia's faculty of arts building (1962) is characteristic of his later work. A fellow (1952) of the Royal Australian Institute of Architects, he was president of its Western Australian chapter (1956-58) and a fellow (1959) of the Royal Institute of British Artists. As honorary architect to the State branch of the National Trust of Australia (1965-72), he was responsible for restoration work at Strawberry Hill Farm, Albany (1966), and Woodbridge, Guildford (1970).

Clifton died on 3 December 1975 at Mosman Park and was buried with Anglican rites in Australind cemetery; his wife and two daughters survived him. A modest and unpretentious man, best known as a designer of houses, he had done much to develop a regional architecture appropriate to its social surroundings and climatic conditions.

B. Chapman (ed), *Marshall Clifton: Watercolours and Drawings 1931-1973*, exhibition cat (Perth, 1986); B. van Bronswijk and D. Richards (eds), *Marshall Clifton: The Art of Building*, exhibition cat (Perth, 1989); B. Chapman and D. Richards, *Marshall Clifton: Architect and Artist* (Perth, 1989); D. Richards, 'Puzzles and Problems: The Architecture of Marshall Clifton', *Fremantle Arts Review*, 2, no 12, Dec 1987, p 18, and 'The Spanish Scene: Some 1930s Houses of Marshall Clifton (1903-1975)', *Architect* (Melb), 28, no 3, Dec 1988, p 16; R. Green, Marshall Clifton, Man, Manner and Mannerist (1986, research report, copy held in Resource Center, School of Architecture, Univ WA).   DUNCAN RICHARDS

CLINT, WILLIAM ALFRED (1906-1980), Anglican clergyman, was born on 8 January 1906 in Wellington, New Zealand, son of English-born parents John William Clint,

commercial traveller, and his wife Lilian Lancaster, née Cawdery. The family came to Sydney in 1910. Alfred attended Balmain Public and Rozelle Junior Technical schools, but left early because his father was unemployed. Radicalized by his family's poverty, he worked for the Balmain Co-operative Society Ltd's store, joined the Australian Labor Party and studied Marxism, while also teaching in Sunday School at the Anglican church where his devout, Low Church parents worshipped.

After several visits to Christ Church St Laurence, Clint was converted to the High Church Christian Socialism of Fr John Hope [q.v.], with whose assistance he entered St John's College, Morpeth. He studied there for three years under the guidance of (Bishop) E. H. Burgmann [q.v.]. Made deacon in 1929, Clint joined the Brotherhood of the Good Shepherd, one of the Bush Brotherhoods whose mission was to bring Christianity to the outback. He agreed to enter the ministry on the condition that he could retain his trade union and Labor Party affiliations, and remained a member of the A.L.P. and the Australian Workers' Union throughout his life. Graziers were angered by his support for the workers, small farmers and unemployed in western New South Wales, and by his activities on the organizing committee of the 1930 Brewarrina shearers' strike.

On 18 December 1932 Clint was ordained priest. He completed his term with the Brotherhood in 1935, was rector (1935-41) at Weston in the diocese of Newcastle, then served at Portland, near Lithgow (1941-48). A better speaker at the pit-top than in the pulpit, he was popular with the miners and cement workers in these towns, but some parishioners objected to his radicalism and his High Church practices. At the invitation of Philip Strong, bishop of New Guinea, he became co-operative adviser at Gona, Papua, in 1948. Appointed priest warden next year, he walked from village to village helping to organize Christian co-operatives. In 1951 he spent months in a Sydney hospital with severe dermatitis and was advised against returning to the tropics. He worked briefly in the Bathurst diocese before being rescued from 'parish respectability' by his appointment in 1953 as director of co-operatives, Australian Board of Missions.

Convinced by his Papuan experiences that co-operatives were a non-exploitative and culturally consistent way of integrating indigenous people into the dominant society's political and economic system, Clint travelled to the A.B.M.'s Aboriginal missions. He helped to establish co-operatives at Lockhart River Mission, North Queensland (1954), Moa Island, Torres Strait (1956), and Cabbage Tree Island, New South Wales (1959).

At Glebe, Sydney, in 1958 he founded Tranby Co-operative College, a centre for training Aborigines to run their own co-operatives.

By 1959 the Lockhart River co-operative was in a state of undeclared bankruptcy due to the collapse of the trochus-shell market. S. J. Matthews, the new bishop of Carpentaria, saw Clint as a destabilizing influence and in 1961—with the support of members of the Queensland government who considered Fr Clint a communist—prohibited his entry to Anglican missions in Carpentaria. These problems led the A.B.M. to review its co-operative department: in 1962 it was replaced by an autonomous body, Co-operative for Aborigines Ltd, of which Clint became general secretary. His subsequent efforts met with little success and a disappointing lack of government support. He also assisted the Aboriginal-Australian Fellowship to lobby politicians on Aboriginal issues.

Stocky and curly haired, Alf Clint was generous, humorous, hard working and idealistic, with a simple theology in which God's plan for a co-operative society was opposed to the interests of 'monopoly capitalism'. Kylie Tennant, who wrote an appreciative account of his work, *Speak You So Gently* (London, 1959), called him 'the only remaining link between the Church of England and the working class'. He supported Aboriginal self-reliance, cultural self-determination and land rights at a time when these ideas were not endorsed by most White Australians. Although his vision was not realized, his greatest legacy is the success of Tranby College, with which he continued to be involved. He died, unmarried, on 21 April 1980 at Glebe and was cremated after a service at Christ Church St Laurence attended by almost five hundred Aboriginal and non-Aboriginal admirers.

I. Southall, *Parson on the Track* (Melb, 1962); L. C. Rodd, *John Hope of Christ Church* (Syd, 1972); R. A. F. Webb, *Brothers in the Sun* (Adel, 1978); K. Tennant, *The Missing Heir* (Melb, 1986); F. Dandler, *Turning the Tide* (Canb, 1989); *Goorialla*, 2, Summer 1980-81, p 12; *SMH*, 12 Aug 1960, 4 Feb 1966, 20 July 1974, 22, 25 Apr 1980; *Tribune* (Syd), 28 May 1980; N. Loos and R. Keast, 'The Radical Promise' (forthcoming). EWAN MORRIS

CLINTON, FRANCES MALLALIEU; *see* PAYNE

CLISBY, LESLIE REDFORD (1914-1940), air force officer, was born on 29 June 1914 at McLaren Vale, South Australia, second of four children of native-born parents Albert Edward Clisby, carpenter, and his wife Mabel Eliza, née Chapman. The Clisbys were a music-loving, Methodist family. Educated at Nailsworth Junior Technical School, Les attended night-classes in engineering at the South Australian School of Mines and Industries, Adelaide; earnest and thorough, he gained reasonable results. In 1935 he enlisted as a mechanic in the Royal Australian Air Force and was soon accepted for flying training at Point Cook, Victoria. A good sportsman, he was 5 ft 9 ins (175.3 cm) tall, slim in build, with light-brown hair.

Convinced that his aircraft was out of control while practising formation flying on 24 April 1936, Clisby parachuted safely. His plane was destroyed. A court of inquiry attributed the mishap to his inexperience. Graduating in 1937, he was one of twenty-five pilots immediately sent to England. On 26 August he was granted a five-year commission in the Royal Air Force. Clisby was posted to No. 1 Squadron, based at Tangmere, Sussex. There he gained a thorough knowledge of the workings of a fighter unit as part of a larger air force; he also enjoyed the sporting and social life open to an officer in the R.A.F. He informed his family that he had become engaged to a young woman in Adelaide, though he had not seen her since leaving home.

The squadron was equipped with new Hawker Hurricanes, armed with eight .303-inch (7.70 mm) machine-guns; its commanding officer, Squadron Leader Patrick Halahan, defied regulations and ordered the guns to be sighted so that the eight streams of bullets converged at 250 yards (228.6 m), increasing their effectiveness. Britain declared war on Germany on 3 September 1939 and five days later No. 1 Squadron flew to Le Havre, France. During the 'phoney war' in Western Europe, the airmen engaged in a series of small clashes with the *Luftwaffe* and endured the harsh winter of 1939-40. Well trained and confident, Clisby wrote reassuring letters to his parents.

On 1 April 1940 he experienced his first aerial conflict and more action followed that month. The German blitzkrieg began on 10 May. Outnumbered, the R.A.F. and French squadrons were rapidly overwhelmed, although the modification to the guns of No. 1 Squadron's aircraft ensured that its pilots had considerable success. Clisby flew each day and was credited with destroying fourteen enemy aeroplanes; the number may have been twenty, but insufficient records survived for the true figure to be known. In one exploit he shot down a German bomber, landed beside it in a field and captured its crew at pistol-point. The squadron diarist quipped: 'He wanted their autographs!'

To maintain his national identity, Flying Officer Clisby wore a R.A.A.F. uniform on operations and was Australia's first fighter ace of World War II. On 14 or 15 May 1940 he was killed in combat with Messerschmitt 110s in the vicinity of Reims. Clisby was awarded the Distinguished Flying Cross while listed as missing. He was buried in Choloy war cemetery, near Nancy.

N. Monks, *Squadrons Up!* (Lond, 1940); P. Richey, *Fighter Pilot* (Lond, 1941); M. Shaw, *Twice Vertical* (Lond, 1971); V. Bingham, *'Blitzed'* (New Malden, Surrey, Eng, 1990); L. McAulay, *Six Aces* (Melb, 1991).   LEX MCAULAY

CLOWES, CYRIL ALBERT (1892-1968), army officer, was born on 11 March 1892 at Warwick, Queensland, eldest child of Albert Clowes, a dentist from England, and his New Zealand-born wife Beatrice Hall, née Odling. A captain in the Militia, Albert was appointed an area officer under the universal training scheme of 1909. Cyril was educated at Toowoomba Grammar School. In 1911 he and his brother Norman entered the Royal Military College, Duntroon, Federal Capital Territory. Twice decorated in World War I, Norman transferred to the British Army in 1931 and rose to major general. His stepbrother Kenneth served in World War II; another stepbrother Trevor attended Duntroon, fought in the Papuan campaign and was killed in action in 1942.

Graduating on 14 August 1914, Cyril was appointed lieutenant in the Australian Imperial Force, posted to the 1st Field Artillery Brigade and commissioned in the Permanent Military Forces. He embarked for Egypt in October. At Gallipoli from 25 April 1915, he directed naval support-fire as a forward observation officer. Although wounded—and rendered partially deaf for the rest of his life—he quickly established a reputation for thoroughness and competence. In Egypt in January 1916 he was made staff captain, 2nd Divisional Artillery.

Next June, as divisional trench-mortar officer at Bois Grenier, France, Clowes assisted raiding-parties while under heavy shell-fire and was awarded the Military Cross. He was promoted major in January 1917. For successfully positioning nine brigades of artillery at Villers-Bretonneux in August 1918, he won the Distinguished Service Order; he was also awarded the Serbian Order of the White Eagle and twice mentioned in dispatches. He returned to Australia in April 1919 and his A.I.F. appointment terminated on 28 June.

Promoted captain and brevet major, P.M.F., in 1920-25 Clowes was an instructor at Duntroon. On 17 December 1925 at Jeir station, near Yass, New South Wales, he married with Catholic rites Eva Florence Magennis. He performed staff, training and command duties in Brisbane (1926-30), Sydney (1931-33) and Darwin (from 1933).

Advanced to lieutenant colonel in January 1936, he sailed for England that year to undertake a gunnery staff course. Repatriated in 1938, he became chief instructor at the School of Artillery, Sydney, and in August 1939 took charge of the 6th Military District (Tasmania). He was promoted substantive colonel on 2 November. Seconded to the A.I.F. as temporary brigadier and appointed commander, Royal Australian Artillery, I Corps, on 4 April 1940, he arrived in the Middle East in December. His contemporaries thought that he or Brigadier (Sir) Sydney Rowell [q.v.] would become the first Duntroon graduate to lead Australia's army.

In northern Greece in 1941 Clowes demonstrated his capacity for command. On 14-16 April three fast-moving German battalions, opposed only by the New Zealand 21st Battalion, threatened the Anzac Corps' eastern flank. Lieutenant General Sir Thomas Blamey [q.v.] sent Clowes to the Pinios (Tempe) Gorge to retrieve the situation. Calm, taciturn—his nickname was 'Silent Cyril'—pipe-smoking, organized and organizing, and able to convey a point simply, Clowes told the 21st that it was to stay put until reinforcements arrived, 'even if it meant extinction'. He rallied the flank, allowing the main force time to withdraw.

One of a number of senior officers brought back to Australia to sharpen the leadership of the home forces, on 7 January 1942 Clowes was promoted temporary major general and given command of the 1st Division which was positioned to defend the Sydney-Newcastle region. On 21 July the Japanese landed in Papua at Gona and Buna. Although gazetted to command New Guinea Force, Clowes was ordered to Port Moresby as commander, 'C' (later Milne) Force. He flew to Milne Bay and on 22 August assumed command, four days before the arrival of an enemy invasion force.

Clowes fought the ensuing battle of Milne Bay with considerable advantages. Most of the fighting took place within the range of his field artillery. Aircraft from his two Royal Australian Air Force fighter squadrons intercepted and destroyed a secondary assault, and also shattered Japanese amphibious logistics. The civilian population assisted his soldiers. His Militia and A.I.F. infantry were well disciplined; their training, if not complete, was thorough; for the most part, they were capably, even superbly, led.

Nevertheless, it was Clowes who had to realize this potential. The situation was complex. By sea and by land, many options were open to the Japanese, and the fog of battle left the Australian commander uncertain of their intentions. Rain, low cloud and mist reduced observation, and mud slowed movement to a 'dead crawl'. Milne Force lacked a coherent signal network. Clowes was further hampered by poor maps, disagreement in the field, and continuous and gratuitous tactical interference by General Douglas MacArthur [q.v.], who was in Brisbane.

By 7 September Clowes had won a prestigious battle which broke the spell of Japanese invincibility. His rewards were meagre. MacArthur disparaged him and dismissed the efforts of his six battalions. Blamey added his own criticisms. As a friend of Rowell, Clowes seems to have fallen under suspicion, especially after Blamey's bitter quarrel with Rowell in Port Moresby in late September. Rendered friendless in high places, Clowes obtained leave. After his return to duty, he suffered from malaria. On 7 December Milne Force was renamed the 11th Division, but by January 1943 Clowes's command had become a backwater. He commanded the Victorian Lines of Communication Area in 1943-45 and, following several short postings, had charge of Southern Command from 1946. On 1 June 1949 he transferred to the Retired List as honorary lieutenant general. For his service in World War II he had been awarded the Greek Military Cross, appointed C.B.E. (1943) and twice mentioned in dispatches.

In retirement he spent his time gardening and playing golf. He had been an outstanding sportsman. Predeceased by his wife and survived by their daughter, Clowes died on 19 May 1968 at the Repatriation General Hospital, Heidelberg, and was buried with full military honours and Anglican rites in Springvale cemetery.

G. Long, *To Benghazi* (Canb, 1952), and *Greece, Crete and Syria* (Canb, 1953), and *The Final Campaigns* (Canb, 1963); D. McCarthy, *South-West Pacific Area—First Year* (Canb, 1959); D. Horner, *Crisis of Command* (Canb, 1978); *Age* (Melb), 23 May 1968; AWM records; information from Mrs E. Blake, Sth Melb, Mr P. Clowes, Toowoomba, Qld, and Mrs E. Wood, Galston, Syd.

DAVID DENHOLM

CLUNE, FRANCIS PATRICK (1893-1971), author, journalist and accountant, was born on 27 November 1893 at Darlinghurst, Sydney, son of George Clune, a labourer from Ireland, and his Victorian-born wife Theresa Cullen. Educated in Sydney at St Colombkille's and St Benedict's Catholic schools, Frank grew up at Redfern and took a job as a newsboy. He left school at 14, and claimed to have worked as a messenger-boy in the government printer's office, to have run away to become an itinerant bush labourer and to have had twenty-five different jobs by the age of 17. After joining the United States Army in Kansas on 26 October 1911, he subsequently deserted and was a seaman when he enlisted in the Australian Imperial Force on 10 May 1915. Serving with the 16th Battalion at Gallipoli from 2 August, he was wounded in both legs five days later and evacuated to a hospital in Cairo; he returned to Sydney in November and was discharged on 29 March 1916. At Woollahra in a civil ceremony on 31 October that year he married a tailoress Maud Elizabeth Roy; they were divorced in 1920.

Employed as a commercial traveller, Clune married a 21-year-old saleswoman Thelma Cecily Smith on 9 May 1923 at the district registrar's office, Waverley; she was to appear in his columns as 'Brown Eyes' and to become the proprietor of an art gallery. At night he studied accountancy and in 1924 established a tax consultancy, registering Clune Accounting Systems Ltd in 1928. He lived at Vaucluse from 1930 and belonged to the New South Wales Golf Club. His adventures at sea, as a trooper in the American cavalry, at Gallipoli, bootlegging in Canada, touring Queensland in the chorus of an opera company, and as a mouse-trap salesman provided the basis of his first book, *Try Anything Once* (1933). It was an immediate success and sold tens of thousands of copies.

From 1933 to 1936 Clune developed the formula which he was to use for many other books: *Rolling Down the Lachlan* (1935) and *Roaming Round the Darling* (1936) were speedily-written accounts of his travels as a tax-consultant in western New South Wales and of an expedition to Coopers Creek, Queensland. His combination of historical detail, narratives of explorers and contemporary political observations found an eager market. Following the example of Ion Idriess [q.v.9], Clune used a rough-and-ready prose style and expressed his sense of nationalism. His travel books, again employing his trusted formula, covered Europe, the Pacific, the Middle East, Asia and North America. By 1952 he estimated that his twenty-three books had sold over a half a million copies.

Clune (and his supporters) took his writing seriously, seeing it as an expression of simple Australian virtues and unvarnished Australian speech. Others were more sceptical. Kenneth Slessor [q.v.] met him in Cairo in 1942 and wryly noted that Clune, although an honorary commissioner of the Australian Comforts Fund, spent most of his time arranging free travel and collecting guide books as sources for *Tobruk to Turkey* (1943); Clune donated the royalties (£750) to the fund. He 'left a very bad impression' on General Sir Thomas Blamey [q.v.]—as much for his self-conferred rank of major as for his 'irregular methods and indiscreet utterances' about the British 'only playing at war'. Blamey ensured that Clune was subject to military censorship and, when Clune managed to get to New

Guinea in 1943 through the help of the U.S. Army, had him smartly returned to Australia.

With a strong sense of his public, Clune did not confine his enthusiasm for travel, adventure and history to books. When he had been auditioned, officials of the Australian Broadcasting Commission found that his 'voice is not all good', but from 1936 he badgered (Sir) Charles Moses (on a golf course) to arrange for him to give a series of radio talks. Clune wrote for newspapers and magazines, including *Smith's Weekly* and the *A.B.C. Weekly*, and continued to broadcast; his regular show on the A.B.C., 'Roaming Round Australia' (1945-57), boasted an audience of one million.

There were more critical responses to Clune's apparent insouciance with evidence when he wrote what purported to be orthodox history rather than travelogue. Starting with *Dig* (1937), an account of Burke and Wills [qq.v.3,6], he worked his way through Australian history, writing accounts of bushrangers, 'crooks' and other romantic figures. *The Viking of Van Diemen's Land* (1954), its narrative full of action and dialogue, was thought to have more in common with historical novels than history; Clune and his collaborator P. R. Stephensen [q.v.12] were taken to task for passing off conjecture as fact in the life of Jorgen Jorgenson [q.v.2]. The book had come from notes which Clune had made over eighteen years and from the work of researchers employed on contract, and was written up in a dramatic manner. With its impressive bibliography, it illustrates Clune's strengths and weaknesses: an ability to ferret out information, but a desire to embroider it. Nevertheless, in books such as *Dig* and *Wild Colonial Boys* (1948), where he took care, he handled complex narrative and evidence comparatively well.

While his defects as a historian and a literary stylist are obvious, Clune's readability and his capacity to sound like an enthusiastic representative of the ordinary traveller brought him wide popularity. He wrote in a pre-television era when men, in particular, read for entertainment and vicarious adventure. As he said in the first number of his short-lived *Frank Clune's Adventure Magazine* (1948), 'We don't want stories of snoopy sex, written by anaemic lounge lizards and pub-crawlers. Action is the password to these pages. This is reading for men with red blood in their arteries'.

Although his fifty-ninth (and last) book appeared in 1968, he had continued to practise as a tax consultant, in partnership with his elder son from about 1959. (Sir) William Dargie and (Sir) William Dobell [q.v.] painted portraits of Frank Clune and he bought examples of their work, as well as paintings by other artists. Dobell's portrait emphasizes the bluff, steel-coloured, short-cropped hair, and the energy, confidence and humour in his eyes. Clune was appointed O.B.E. in 1967. Survived by his wife and two sons, he died on 11 March 1971 at St Vincent's Hospital, Darlinghurst, and was buried with Catholic rites in South Head cemetery. The travel books remain valuable social records and the histories, although contentious, gave rise to some Australian mythologizing; *Jimmy Governor* (1959) was the inspiration for Thomas Keneally's novel, *The Chant of Jimmie Blacksmith* (1972). The portraits of Clune are held by the family.

B. Adamson, *Frank Clune* (Melb, 1943); K. Slessor, *The War Diaries of Kenneth Slessor* (Brisb, 1985); *ABC Weekly*, 23 Dec 1939, p 8; *People* (Syd), 12 Apr 1950, p 21; *Walkabout*, 1 Mar 1953, p 40; *PTHRA*, 3, nos 2 and 3, 1954, pp 28, 52; *Biblionews*, 8, no 2, Feb 1955, p 4, no 4, Apr 1955, p 11, no 7, July 1955, p 22; Clune papers (NL); Clune files, especially SP 1558/2/0 box 36 (AA, Syd) *and* 244/1/463 (AA, Melb); F. Clune, mss and working papers of several unfinished books (Univ NSW L); information from Mr T. Clune, Elizabeth Bay, Syd.

JULIAN CROFT

CLUNIES ROSS, SIR WILLIAM IAN (1899-1959), veterinary scientist and administrator, was born on 22 February 1899 at Bathurst, New South Wales, fourth and youngest son of William John Clunies Ross [q.v.8], teacher, and his wife Hannah Elizabeth, née Tilley. William's father Robert was a sea captain from Scotland and a brother of John Clunies Ross who settled on the Cocos-Keeling Islands in 1827 and 'founded a tiny Malay kingdom'. Hannah's father, an evangelist, was born of farming stock in England; Hannah's mother came from the distressed Irish Protestant gentry and shared her husband's evangelism. Born in Australia, Hannah was a schoolteacher before her marriage. Her brother was W. H. Tilly [q.v.12].

Resident master at Bathurst branch technical school, William combined enthusiasm for science with an egalitarian disposition. He was 48 when his fourth son was born, and Ian's feelings towards him were more those of respect than affection. Ian was especially close to his mother, who taught him in his early years and imbued him with a sense of social decorum and a keen, progressive drive. Home life was warm and supportive, although Ian seems to have been acutely conscious of the marked differences in style and temperament between his parents.

In 1903 the family moved to Summer Hill, Sydney, and four years later to the outer suburb of Ashfield where Ian developed a keen interest in the plentiful local fauna. With his brother Rob, he devised an elaborate game based on the sale, at fanciful prices, of captured animals to zoos around the world. Educated at Newington College, Ian was an average student, and it was a surprise when he gained second-class honours in English in passing the Leaving certificate. His father's death in 1914 left the family in reduced circumstances. Rob and the elder brothers, Allan and Egerton, joined the Australian Imperial Force. In October 1918 news arrived that Egerton had died from pneumonic influenza and that Rob had been killed in action. It appears that Hannah exercised her legal right to prevent Ian from enlisting.

In 1917 Clunies Ross had enrolled in agricultural science at the University of Sydney, but in 1918 switched to veterinary science (B.V.Sc., 1921). By his own account he was a moderate scholar who was pleased to complete the course with second-class honours.

Despite the difficulty of establishing a practice, the times were opportune for an energetic veterinary graduate: the transformation of biological science and of human medicine before and during World War I was beginning to leave its mark on veterinary science. Clunies Ross spent 1921 as a temporary lecturer in veterinary anatomy at the university; next year he was appointed a Walter and Eliza Hall [qq.v.9] research fellow. In England he studied parasites at the Molteno Institute, Cambridge, and at the London School of Tropical Medicine. It marked a crucial phase of his life. For the next fifteen years the seemingly prosaic subject of parasitology was to enable him to build a national reputation as an applied scientist and one of Australia's best scientific communicators.

After a short visit to Poland, Clunies Ross returned to Australia in 1923 via the United States of America. In 1925 he tried unsuccessfully to start a veterinary practice in the heart of Sydney. He resumed research on parasites and undertook some part-time teaching at the university's veterinary school. The outlook was far from promising. Then, in 1926, the new Council for Scientific and Industrial Research decided to give its highest priority to research into the health and nutrition of animals, particularly sheep. Clunies Ross was appointed C.S.I.R. parasitologist. He continued to work at the veterinary school until the F. D. McMaster [q.v.10] Animal Health Laboratory, built adjacent to the school, was officially opened in November 1931. Clunies Ross became officer-in-charge. After a lengthy courtship, on 6 October 1927 at the Catholic Apostolic Church, Redfern, he had married Janet Leslie Carter, an honours graduate in English.

As a scientist and a public figure, Clunies Ross showed special strength in exploring the interconnections between disparate phenomena. His early work involved an understanding of the relationship between host and parasite. He soon broadened his interest to the links between applied science and the pastoral industry, to the nexus between science and society, and to Australia's place in international affairs. Using his experience of science and industry, he sought to build a richer, more diverse and better educated society, and one that would enjoy a closer involvement with other countries.

Clunies Ross was primarily concerned with the application of science, less with science for its own sake. His early research focussed on two of the most severe health problems of the pastoral industry, the liver fluke, *Fasciola hepatica*, and the hydatid parasite, *Echinococcus granulosus*. In co-operation with graziers, he established field-stations to test ways of controlling parasites and to gather information about the incidence of disease. Research was also undertaken to investigate the dog tick, *Ixodes holocyclus*, prevalent in the bush around Sydney, and a reasonably effective method of immunizing dogs was developed. He was extension worker as much as scientist, and played an important part in building the reputation of C.S.I.R. in the pastoral districts of New South Wales. The university awarded him a D.V.Sc. (1928) for his work on hydatids, and, during his career as a researcher, he published over fifty scientific papers. With H. McL. Gordon, he wrote *The Internal Parasites and Parasitic Diseases of Sheep* (1936).

One of Clunies Ross's outstanding qualities was that of leadership. Able to identify and nurture the strengths of those around him, he influenced the careers of such prominent wool researchers as H. B. Carter, M. R. Freney, Menzie Lipson, F. G. Lennox, E. H. Mercer and Helen Newton Turner. Clunies Ross was also responsible for expanding the research interests of the McMaster laboratory to encompass genetics, a neglected field in a country relying heavily on animal production.

As part of C.S.I.R.'s policy of enabling its young scientists to gain experience abroad, Clunies Ross had spent almost a year from June 1929 studying parasites at the Government Institute for Infectious Diseases at Tokyo Imperial University, an experience that deepened his interest in Japan and Asia generally. He was an active member of the Australian Institute of International Affairs, and, under its auspices, edited *Australia and the Far East* (1935). With the support of several pastoralists' organizations, for five months in 1935-36 he studied sheep and wool production in China, Japan, Korea and Manchuria. He concluded that Asian wool-growers did not present an early threat to their Australian counterparts.

In 1937 Australia, New Zealand and South

Africa established the International Wool Publicity and Research Secretariat, based in London. Clunies Ross, by then well known as a publicist for the wool industry, was selected as Australia's representative, and made chairman. The secretariat had some success in the U.S.A., and the foundations were laid for its achievements in research and promotion in the postwar period. In November 1939 the University of Sydney appointed Clunies Ross professor of veterinary science, but he remained in London until July 1940 to complete his term at the secretariat.

World War II saw widening horizons and ambitious planning for the future. University teaching did not occupy Clunies Ross fully: the Australian Broadcasting Commission used him as a news commentator; in 1941 he was elected president of the Australian Institute of International Affairs; and, at the request of the Sydney *Daily Telegraph*, he prepared a booklet, *Should We Plan for Peace?* (1941). Next year he became adviser on scientific and technical personnel in the Commonwealth Manpower Directorate, a task that enabled him to widen his understanding of Australia's scientific resources.

In the final months of the war he devised a scheme for research and development in support of the wool industry. Because of the large stockpile and the growing threat from synthetics, the industry's prospects appeared gloomy. Clunies Ross put forward a scheme for a national wool industry council which would combine science, technology, publicity, economic research and education. He advocated research into all aspects of sheep and wool production, among them wool biology, nutrition, physiology (particularly reproduction), genetics, agrostology, economics and statistics, supported by a strong extension service. The grand plan did not survive the scrutiny of special interest groups and the concern about duplication, but many of the ingredients were adopted by the government, by C.S.I.R. and by its successor, the Commonwealth Scientific and Industrial Research Organization.

On 1 January 1946 Clunies Ross was appointed a full-time member of C.S.I.R.'s executive-committee, with general responsibility for the agricultural and biological divisions. He moved to Melbourne that year. In 1947-48 the institution came under intense political scrutiny because of allegations that it was lax in regard to security. C.S.I.R. underwent a minor reorganization, including the change in name to C.S.I.R.O. in 1949. The chairman Sir David Rivett [q.v.11] retired and Clunies Ross replaced him on 19 May. He was selected for his breadth of vision, public prominence and his capacity to project the Enlightenment ideal of the unity of science and society.

Clunies Ross was at the height of his powers in his early years as head of C.S.I.R.O. Tall, with a full head of black hair, parted in the centre, and a handsome and mobile face, he was a figure of elegance and distinction. Reflecting C.S.I.R.O.'s dominance of Australian science and the sound foundations laid by Rivett, he was able to reap the benefits of a series of glittering successes. Radio astronomy, the discovery of the role of minor elements in animal and plant physiology, the dissemination of myxomatosis virus for the control of rabbits, and improvements in wool processing combined to propel the organization to national prominence. Clunies Ross played a personal role in the success of myxomatosis by selecting Francis Ratcliffe [q.v.] as officer-in-charge of the wildlife survey section; he supported him in the face of Dame Jean Macnamara's [q.v.10] aspersions against C.S.I.R.O.'s professionalism and injected himself with the virus to demonstrate that it was harmless to humans.

As a visionary, Clunies Ross was mostly concerned with C.S.I.R.O.'s broad strategy. The organization received strong support from the minister-in-charge R. G. (Baron) Casey [q.v.]. Clunies Ross maintained a relentless round of public-speaking engagements and rarely refused an invitation. His oration on the occasion of the centenary of the University of Sydney drew attention to the serious under-financing of higher education. He was genuinely concerned about the future of the university system, but also wished to deflect criticism of C.S.I.R.O.'s superior funding. In 1957 he served as a member of Sir Keith Murray's committee on Australian universities and was largely responsible for the first draft of its report.

Towards the end of his career Clunies Ross was showered with honours. He was appointed C.M.G., elected a foundation fellow of the Australian Academy of Science and knighted—all in 1954. At the University of Melbourne, he was first chairman of International House and deputy-chancellor (1958). Clunies Ross was troubled by angina in the late 1940s and in 1957. He suffered a cerebral haemorrhage and coronary attacks in September 1958, but continued as C.S.I.R.O. chairman. In April 1959 he began a diary, later published in his *Memoirs and Papers* (Melbourne, 1961). Survived by his wife, three sons and adopted daughter, Sir Ian died of atherosclerotic heart disease on 20 June 1959 in Melbourne and was buried in Box Hill cemetery.

After his death the Sheep Biology Laboratory at Prospect, New South Wales, was named the Ian Clunies Ross Animal Research Laboratory. When issued in 1973, the $50 note celebrated the achievement of two Australian scientists, Sir Ian Clunies Ross and

Baron Florey [q.v.]. The Ian Clunies Ross Memorial Foundation was established in 1959. The National Science Centre at Parkville, Melbourne, was designated Clunies Ross House in 1968: the building featured a majestic mural by Robert Ingpen (commissioned by the Australian Veterinary Association) which depicted the three main phases of Clunies Ross's life—as scientist, administrator and public figure. All these tributes were indications that he, more than any other Australian scientist, symbolized the hopes and aspirations of a generation.

C. B. Schedvin, *Shaping Science and Industry* (Syd, 1987); *Aust Veterinary J*, Oct 1968, p 467; *Records of Aust Academy of Science*, 3, no 3-4, 1977.　　　　　　　　　　C. B. SCHEDVIN

COALDRAKE, FRANK WILLIAM (1912-1970), Anglican priest and missionary, was born on 12 March 1912 in Brisbane, second child of native-born parents Thomas John Coaldrake, insurance superintendent, and his wife Eliza Rose, née Smith. After attending Sandgate State School and Brisbane Grammar School, Frank enrolled at the Teachers' Training College, Brisbane, and, during a short teaching career, became an external student at the University of Queensland.

His meeting with members of the Bush Brotherhoods led Coaldrake to Anglo-Catholicism and to an interest in the Church's ministry in the Australian outback. In 1932 he went to the pastoral town of Charleville in south-west Queensland as warden of the boys' hostel run by the Brotherhood of St Paul. There, for four years, despite meagre resources, his enthusiasm, talent for community work and rapport with the young turned the hostel into a hive of purposeful activity. Deeply influenced by the Brothers, he found his vocation to the ministry.

In 1936 Coaldrake returned to study full time at the university (B.A., 1938; M.A., 1944) in the school of mental and moral philosophy. A tall, striking figure, he threw himself into university life, excelling at inter-varsity debating, winning a Blue for rowing while at St John's College and editing the student newspaper, *Semper Floreat*. In 1937 he represented his student union at a meeting in Adelaide at which the National Union of Australian University Students was formed; as a postgraduate student, he was its third president (1940). Yet, it was within the Australian Student Christian Movement that he found spiritual and intellectual affinities which stimulated him to apply his Christian faith to what he saw as the great moral issues confronting his generation. During his term as travelling secretary (1938-39) for the A.S.C.M. he grew convinced that, for a true

Christian, pacifism was imperative. Three weeks after Australia's declaration of war in 1939, he founded the *Peacemaker*, a monthly paper to inform and assist men who conscientiously objected to military service.

That year Fr Gerard Tucker [q.v.12] recruited Coaldrake to the Brotherhood of St Laurence to work in the inner-Melbourne suburb of Fitzroy. His personality and gifts as a community worker made him a dynamic member of the chapter. He supervised a hostel for homeless youth, lobbied local councils and State ministers, served as a probation officer, and organized non-violent protests against the injustices of the landlord and tenant legislation. Sleeping only sparingly, he completed his M.A. thesis on 'A Theory of Evil' and obtained his licentiate from the Australian College of Theology (1942). Made deacon in 1942 and ordained priest in 1943, he served as curate at St Cuthbert's, East Brunswick, and was assistant to the dean at St Paul's Cathedral, Melbourne.

Coaldrake's presidency (1943-46) of the Federal Pacifist Council of Australia and his prominence in radical social protest were viewed with concern by many in the Church's hierarchy and by the Australian security service. He fervently believed that the Christian response to Japanese aggression should be to build a 'bridge of reconciliation' between Australia and Japan. His offer to serve as a missionary in Japan was supported by Bishop George Cranswick [q.v.], chairman of the Anglican Church's Australian Board of Missions. During fifteen months of preparation, Coaldrake studied Japanese language and culture at the University of Sydney and was assistant priest to Rev. John Hope [q.v.] at Christ Church St Laurence.

Mastering the language and overcoming daunting physical and cultural barriers, from June 1947 Coaldrake served in the battered and demoralized Japanese Episcopal Church, initially assisting a Japanese priest at Odawara in the diocese of Yokohama. Early in 1949 he embarked on what was to be his most remarkable achievement as priest in charge of the mountainous Izu peninsula, south of Tokyo. There he employed the methods of the Bush Brotherhoods to penetrate the isolated villages of a region which had never been evangelized by Christian missionaries. On furlough, Coaldrake married a Tasmanian diocesan youth organizer Maida Stelmar Williams on 3 December 1949 at Christ Church St Laurence. She was to share with him the creation of an Izu mission community centred on the city of Ito, Japan. On being offered the chairmanship of the Australian Board of Missions in 1956, Coaldrake returned with his wife and two children to Sydney.

For the next fourteen years, with his clear vision of the Church's responsibility for mission and his formidable capacity for administration, Coaldrake sought to shape the A.B.M.'s policies to meet the rapidly changing world of the 1960s. While remaining a devout Anglo-Catholic, he encouraged the development of ecumenical ties between missionary bodies of all denominations through his roles in the National Missionary Council of Australia and the Australian Council of Churches. More than a decade in advance of the world Anglican communion's advocacy of 'partnership in mission', he argued that Western concepts of mission were untenable in the post-colonial era and held that indigenous Christians in 'emerging' nations should be assisted to conduct missionary exchange with the 'home' churches on a basis of equality.

In 1960 Coaldrake was made a canon of All Souls Quetta Memorial Cathedral, Thursday Island. Convinced that, in mission work with Aborigines, the goal of 'assimilation' was harmfully racist, he persuaded the A.B.M. to adopt 'acceptance' as a guiding principle and to appoint an Aborigine as policy adviser in 1969. Although the privations of his early years in Japan had left Coaldrake less robust than in his exuberant youth, an inner asceticism enabled him to sustain a punishing administrative workload and to withstand the rigours of constant travel to mission stations. He relaxed at home in his workshop with carpentry and bookbinding, and he smoked a pipe.

Celebrated in the Church as 'a great missionary statesman [of] prophetic vision', on 10 July 1970 Coaldrake became the first Australian-born priest to be elected archbishop of Brisbane. Before he could be consecrated, he suffered an intragastric haemorrhage and died of myocardial infarction on 22 July in Royal North Shore Hospital, Sydney. His funeral was held at Christ Church St Laurence and he was buried in Northern Suburbs cemetery; his wife, son and two daughters survived him.

J. Handfield, *Friends and Brothers* (Melb, 1980); *ABM Review*, 60, no 4, Aug-Sept 1970; *Peacemaker*, Aug-Sept 1970; *Courier-Mail*, 11 July 1970; *Australian, Canb Times* and *SMH*, 23 July 1970; P. Wilson, A Question of Conscience: Pacifism in Victoria 1938-1945 (Ph.D. thesis, La Trobe Univ, 1984); Aust Bd of Missions Archives (ML); Aust Student Christian Movement Archives (NL).

LAURIE O'BRIEN

COATES, SIR ALBERT ERNEST (1895-1977), surgeon, was born on 28 January 1895 at Ballarat, Victoria, eldest of seven children of Arthur Coates, letter carrier, and his wife Clara Annie, née Eustice, both Victorian born. Although their worldly possessions were few, Arthur and Clara raised their family in an affectionate atmosphere and instilled in them the virtues of honesty, industry and education. They were strong supporters of the Methodist Church. Albert loved reading and had a thirst for knowledge, even as a child. His formal education at Mount Pleasant State School ended when he obtained his Merit certificate, aged 11. He began work as a butcher's apprentice, but at 14 was indentured to a bookbinder, which afforded opportunities to read widely.

Encouraged by (Sir) Leslie Morshead [q.v.] who had opened a night-school at Ballarat, Coates passed the junior public examination with distinctions in five subjects, including French and German. He had decided to study medicine, but first took a job in the Postmaster-General's Department to earn some money.

On 17 August 1914 Coates enlisted in the Australian Imperial Force and became a medical orderly in the 7th Battalion. He served on Gallipoli and was one of the last to leave the peninsula on the night of 19/20 December 1915. His battalion was transferred to France in March 1916 and fought in the battle of the Somme. His skill as a linguist came to the attention of his superiors and in February 1917 he was attached to the intelligence staff, I Anzac Corps. Sir John Monash [q.v.10] and British authorities recognized his ability and, at the end of the war, he was invited to apply for a commission in the British Army. Coates preferred, however, to go home to Australia where he found employment in the office of the Commonwealth censor in Melbourne.

Late in 1919 he returned to the P.M.G. where he continued to work night-shifts, while studying medicine at the University of Melbourne (M.B., B.S., 1924; M.D., 1926; M.S., 1927). Coates was one of the top students in his year, gaining second place in anatomy with first-class honours, and the exhibition in pathology in fourth year. At the final examinations he finished fourth in the class, with first-class honours in all subjects. On 26 March 1921 he had married Harriet Josephine Hicks (d. 1934) at the Methodist Church, Camberwell; they were to have a son and three daughters.

In 1925 Coates was a resident at (Royal) Melbourne Hospital where he came under the guidance of Hamilton Russell and (Sir) Sidney Sewell [qq.v.11]. He then worked with Professor Richard Berry [q.v.7] in the university's department of anatomy, first as a Stewart lecturer (1925-26) and next as acting-professor (1927). Back at (Royal) Melbourne Hospital, he was appointed honorary surgeon to out-patients in 1927 and to inpatients in 1935. Following his wife's death he visited surgical centres in Britain, Europe and North America; shortly after his return he was asked to establish the neurosurgical unit at the R.M.H. On 31 December 1936 at St Paul's Anglican Cathedral, Dunedin, New Zealand, he married Catherine Martha Anderson. From 1936 to 1940 he was part-time lecturer in surgical anatomy at the University of Melbourne.

Appointed lieutenant colonel, Australian Army Medical Corps, on 1 January 1941, Coates joined the Australian Imperial Force next day. He was posted to the 2nd/10th Australian General Hospital and stationed at Malacca, Malaya. After the Japanese invaded on 8 December, the 2nd/10th A.G.H. fell back to Singapore; Coates was ordered to join a party which sailed on 13 February 1942 for Java, Netherlands East Indies. The convoy was bombed and the survivors reached Tembilahan, Sumatra, where Coates saved many lives with his surgical skill. He made himself responsible for treating all British casualties, and felt duty-bound to stay with them, though he could have left on several occasions. On 28 February he arrived at Padang which was occupied by the Japanese three weeks later.

In May 1942 Coates's captors moved him to Burma. At the Kilo-30 and Kilo-55 camps on the Burma-Thailand Railway he cared for hundreds of prisoners of war under deplorable conditions. He subsequently described his medical practice at Kilo-55 to the International Military Tribunal for the Far East: in a bamboo lean-to, with his only instruments a knife, two pairs of artery forceps and a saw (used by the camp butchers and carpenters), his daily work consisted of 'segregating the sick from the very sick . . . curetting seventy or eighty ulcers during the morning . . . and, in the afternoon, proceeding to amputate nine or ten legs'.

In December 1943 the Japanese sent Coates to Thailand. There, from March 1944, he was chief medical officer of a prisoner-of-war hospital (10 000 beds) at Nakhon Pathom (Nakompaton). Through 'his initiative, resource and enthusiasm he was responsible for many improvisations which provided artificial limbs, transfusions and surgical appliances'. (Sir) Edward Dunlop was to recall that Coates's 'short, upright figure with a ghost of a swagger, a Burma cheroot clamped in his mouth, and his staccato flow of kindly, earthly wisdom became the object of hero-worship and inspiration'. With the cessation of hostilities, Coates returned to Melbourne in October 1945, transferred to the Reserve of Officers on 6 December and was appointed O.B.E. in 1946.

He resumed work as honorary surgeon to in-patients at R.M.H. In 1949-56 he was Stewart lecturer in surgery at the university; with Sir Alan Newton [q.v.11] he played a

major role in the establishment of chairs of medicine and surgery. In 1946 Coates was a medical witness at the war crimes tribunal in Tokyo and in 1951 a delegate to the signing of a peace treaty with Japan at San Francisco, United States of America. He was president (1941 and 1947) of the Victorian branch of the British Medical Association, a delegate (1951) to the International Red Cross at Monte Carlo, Monaco, president (1955-61) of the War Nurses Memorial Centre, Melbourne, and an influential member (1949-76) of the board of management of the Fairfield Infectious Diseases Hospital (chairman 1956-57). In 1953 he was elected a fellow of the Royal College of Surgeons, London.

Knighted in 1955, Coates was president (1954-55) of the Melbourne Rotary Club and a council-member (1953-57) of the University of Melbourne which in 1962 awarded him an honorary doctorate of laws. In 1971 he retired from medical practice. He was elected to the International Mark Twain Society in 1976 as successor to (Sir) Alexander Fleming.

Despite his height of 5 ft 5½ ins (166.4 cm), Coates was a distinguished figure, and was proud to be involved in great causes as a soldier and citizen. He enjoyed company and conversation, and had a deep love of the English language. In 1977, with Newman Rosenthal, he published *The Albert Coates Story*. He was a gifted orator, and equally compelling in the lecture theatre or teaching at the bedside. As a surgeon, he was bold and resourceful, and a favourite with patients. Although he was one of the last of the old-fashioned general surgeons, he was aware of advances in medical and allied sciences, and of their impact on surgical practice; he encouraged his juniors in research and in acquiring specialized skills.

At times Coates could be blunt, but he was always straight and to the point; he despised pretentiousness and any deviation from honourable behaviour. Intensely loyal by nature, he received great loyalty in return. He was simple and uncomplicated in his tastes and recreations, and had a happy home life. Coates hosted tennis parties and regularly played golf with his close friend Sir John Latham [q.v.10]. Survived by his wife and their son, and by the children of his first marriage, Sir Albert died on 8 October 1977 at Royal Melbourne Hospital and was cremated with Anglican rites. A portrait by Murray Griffin is held by the Australian War Memorial, Canberra; two others, by Aileen Dent and Louis Kahan, are in the family's possession.

A. S. Walker, *Clinical Problems of the War* (Canb, 1952) and *Middle East and Far East* (Canb, 1953); E. E. Dunlop, *The War Diaries of Weary Dunlop*

(Melb, 1989); *MJA*, 7 Apr 1979; *Aust and NZ J of Surgery*, 58, 1988, p 419; *Herald* (Melb), 1 Dec 1943, 17 Apr 1953; *Age*(Melb), 8 July 1954, 10, 13 Oct 1977; *Sun News-Pictorial*, 9 June 1955, 24 Feb 1971.
ROWAN WEBB*

COBB, WILTON WINSTANLEY (1917-1942), army officer and grazier, was born on 6 June 1917 at Albion, Brisbane, second child of Frederick Cobb, a grazier from New Zealand, and his Queensland-born wife Hannah Belle, née Lloyd. Educated by correspondence and at All Souls' School, Charters Towers, Wilton completed the junior public examination in 1932. Known as 'Bill', he worked on his father's station, Frensham, near Winton, and on other properties in the district. He was commissioned lieutenant in the Militia on 19 August 1939.

Transferring to the Australian Imperial Force on 1 May 1940, Cobb joined the 2nd/15th Battalion. On 29 June that year he married Cynthia Mary Molle at St Andrew's Presbyterian Church, Southport. Two days later he was sent to Darwin, but was back in Brisbane for three months before he embarked from Sydney on 26 December, bound for Egypt. After training in Palestine, in March 1941 his battalion moved to Marsa Brega, Libya. Cobb took part in the withdrawal eastwards, arrived at Tobruk in April and was promoted captain that month.

On 16 May he organized and led a patrol deep into enemy territory, capturing a machine-gun position, inflicting casualties and taking a prisoner; he was awarded a commander-in-chief's card. During the five weeks (June-July) that the 2nd/15th was under fire at the Salient, his personal example 'infused . . . confidence in his men which maintained their morale at a high level and cultivated an aggressive spirit'. Cobb's planning of night-operations assisted his company to advance its line some 500 yards (457 m). For his leadership over the period March to July, he was awarded the Military Cross. From August to October he attended the Middle East Tactical School, then returned to the battalion as second-in-command of 'A' Company. Having been deployed (from late 1941) in Palestine and Syria, the 2nd/15th occupied positions at Tel el Eisa, near El Alamein, Egypt, in August 1942.

On the night of 4-5 August Cobb took a fighting patrol of twelve men behind enemy lines. About 1500 yards (1372 m) north of Point 25 (Baillieu's Bluff), the party was challenged and went to ground. When some Germans inadvertently disclosed the location of their nearby post, Cobb attacked. A bullet from a machine-gun hit him in the leg, but he silenced the weapon with a grenade. Attempting to withdraw with a prisoner, he was wounded in the arm by an enemy gunner who also killed the prisoner. Cobb shot his adversary, removed identifying material from the dead man and, suffering from loss of blood, retired with the help of his troops. He was awarded a Bar to his M.C. Evacuated to hospital, he sent a telegram to his mother: 'Nothing serious. Don't worry'.

A tall, lean man, with a cheerful, outgoing disposition, Cobb was a quick thinker and a natural leader. He rejoined his battalion in September as 'A' Company commander, but was killed in action on 23 October 1942, the first day of the battle of El Alamein, and was buried in the local war cemetery. His wife survived him; they had no children.

B. Maughan, *Tobruk and El Alamein* (Canb, 1966); *Winton Herald*, 30 Aug 1939, 12 Aug, 11 Nov 1942; *Age* (Melb), 29 Aug 1942; *Argus*, 18 Sept 1943; AWM records; information from Mr G. Kennedy, Winton, Mrs C. Douglas, Hope Island, Qld, and Major R. F. Cowie, Ashgrove, Brisb.
MARGARET PULLAR

COCHRAN, SAMUEL FOGO (1898-1972), public servant and administrator, was born on 30 May 1898 at Glasgow, Scotland, son of David McGilvray Cochran, journeyman ironturner, and his wife Agnes Clelland, née Fogo. The family migrated to Queensland in 1910. Educated at Glasgow and at Ipswich, in January 1914 Sam joined the Queensland Railway Department and worked as a clerk at Ipswich. He enlisted in the Australian Imperial Force on 14 February 1917, served in France with No. 4 Railway Section, was promoted lance sergeant in November 1918 and was discharged in Brisbane on 3 January 1920. After he rejoined the railway department, he studied accountancy. On 15 December 1921 he married 17-year-old Pearl Isobel Lupton in the Presbyterian Church, Booval.

From May 1923 Cochran was based in Brisbane as a shorthand reporter in the Department of Justice. In 1927-37 he served as secretary to a number of royal commissions, including those on railways, the wheat and flour industries, racing and gaming, transport, and electricity. He was appointed assistant under-secretary in the Premier's and Chief Secretary's Department in September 1937. Chairman of the State Electricity Commission of Queensland in 1938-50, he was its sole commissioner in 1948-50. His leadership and enterprise, personality and irrepressible energy, ensured a reorganization in the provision of electricity to southern Queensland and the establishment of a decentralized system of supply.

Cochran's experience, knowledge and enthusiasm ensured that his skills were in demand during World War II. His political awareness, capacity to identify issues and ability to make decisions were reinforced by his command of administrative detail. A member of several State wartime committees, he was deputy-director of rationing for Queensland and temporarily (in 1943) director of rationing in Australia. When the Federal government assumed emergency control of electricity supply, Cochran was appointed regional controller for Queensland. He was also a member (from 1944) of the Commonwealth Secondary Industries Commission.

On 10 July 1950 he was appointed chairman of the Commonwealth and New South Wales Joint Coal Board, and moved to Sydney. The board had been set up in 1947 to control the production and distribution of coal, and to develop the industry. Cochran tackled the serious problems, promoted mechanization and advocated better labour relations. Once sufficient quantities had been produced for local requirements, he identified and developed overseas markets for high quality coal. Charm, diplomatic tact and negotiating skills lay behind his forceful leadership. In 1957 he was appointed C.B.E. He retired in May 1963, having made a notable contribution to an efficient and prosperous industry.

Although something of a loner, Cochran was good company, a keen golfer and a talented pianist. A fellow of the Australian Society of Accountants, in his retirement he took up directorships of Thiess Holdings Ltd and Evans Deakin Industries Ltd, but in 1968, following a stroke that left him completely disabled, he returned to Queensland. He died on 24 January 1972 at the Broadbeach Nursing Centre and was buried in the Allambee Garden of Memories, Nerang. His wife and two daughters survived him.

M. I. Thomis, *A History of the Electricity Supply Industry in Queensland*, 2, 1938-1988 (Brisb, 1990); J. Priest, *The Thiess Story* (Brisb, 1981); *Aust Coal, Shipping, Steel and the Harbour*, 1 Aug 1950; *Sunday Mail* (Brisb), 16 Jan 1944, 11 June 1950; *SMH*, 18 July 1950, 28 Oct 1958; personnel records, held by Qld Dept of the Premier, Economics and Trade Development, Brisb; information from Mr H. Neil Smith, Longford, Tas, Justice R. Else-Mitchell, Deakin, Canb, and Mrs S. Clare, Nth Turramurra, Syd.   JACK WATSON

COCKETT, CHARLES BERNARD (1888-1965), Congregational minister, was born on 24 February 1888 at Marrickville, Sydney, son of Frank Cockett, a draper from England, and his Scottish-born wife Rebecca, née Bowles, both of whom were members of the Rockdale Congregational Church. After attending Bexley Public and Fort Street Model schools, Bernard worked as a clerk with the Australian Gas Light Co. In 1910 he enrolled at the University of Sydney (B.A., 1913;

M.A., 1915); he was Lithgow [q.v.2] scholar in logic and mental philosophy, and won the Carslaw prize for astronomy and the (Sir) Francis Anderson [qq.v.7] prize for philosophy. A fine athlete, in 1913 Cockett held the State title for the one-mile (1.6 km) walk. He studied theology at Camden College, Sydney, under Rev. Dr G. W. Thatcher [q.v.12].

On 23 March 1915 Cockett married Florence Champion at the Congregational Church, Camberwell, Melbourne. Ordained seven days later, he served his first pastorate at Rockhampton, Queensland (1915-17), and was successively minister of the Wyclif Church, Surrey Hills, Melbourne (1917-20), and of the Memorial Church, Hobart (1920-25). His 1917 Livingstone lectures, 'Sex and Religion', raised some eyebrows in Congregational circles, as did his publication, *Sex and Marriage* (Sydney, 1920). He attended the International Congregational Council's meeting at Boston, United States of America, in 1920 and the Universal Christian Conference on Life and Work held in Stockholm in 1925.

As minister (1925-31) of Bunyan Meeting House, Bedford, England, Cockett developed an abiding interest in John Bunyan, on whom he published a monograph (London, 1928), and about whom he subsequently delivered many sermons and lectures. From 1931 he served at the Vine Memorial Church, Ilford, London, before returning to Sydney in 1939 to become minister at Pitt Street Church, the traditional seat of Congregationalism in New South Wales. He was active in religious and civic affairs, and in ministering to armed services' personnel. Foundation president (1941-46) of the Australian Council of Churches, honorary secretary (1946) of the Australian section of the World Council of Churches, and president (1941-46) of the Congregational Union of Australia and New Zealand, he was awarded an honorary doctorate of divinity in 1943 by the Pacific School of Religion, Berkeley, California, U.S.A.

In November 1946 Cockett embarked for England where he lectured for the Colonial Missionary Society and in 1948-51 served at the Chapel-in-the-Fields, Norwich. Following Florence's death, he returned again to Australia and became secretary to the Congregational Union of Western Australia, an office he was to hold until 1954. On 29 September 1952 he married Grace Edna Beal at Dalkeith, Perth. His last pastorate (1955-59) was at Haslemere, Surrey, England. Retiring to Australia, he died on 24 November 1965 in East Melbourne and was cremated. His wife survived him, as did the son and daughter of his first marriage.

C. Bernard Cockett, as he was formally known, was noted for the ebullient enthusiasm that characterized his varied activities.

He had been acquainted with notable Church leaders in Britain and North America, and gave significant leadership to the ecumenical movement in Australia. As a preacher, he stressed the Gospel's relevance to contemporary social and theological issues.

J. A. Garrett and L. W. Farr, *Camden College, a Centenary History* (Syd, 1964); *Congregationalist* (Syd), Jan 1966, p 8; Congregational Union of NSW, *Year Book*, 1967, p 19; C. B. Cockett, The Wheel of Life (ms autobiog, Melb, 1965, La Trobe Univ L).

GEOFFREY BARNES

COE, PAUL JOSEPH (1902?-1979), drover and buckjumper, was an Aborigine born at Cowra, New South Wales, son of Thomas Coe, drover, and his second wife Jessie Mary, née Waggerah (Crow). Paul spent his first years on what later became the Erambie Aborigines' Reserve. Jessie died in 1907. Because he was frequently away droving, Thomas then arranged for his three younger sons to be cared for at Canowindra, but the children were sent to the government's Farm Home for Boys at Mittagong under the 1909 Aborigines Protection Act.

A ward of the state, from the age of 14 Paul was placed in several jobs as dairyhand and farm labourer. Although he stated in an interview that he was treated well, privately he remained bitterly resentful of his removal. At 18 he returned to Cowra to begin droving with his father in Queensland and New South Wales. He enjoyed telling droving yarns, and believed that his father's party was the first to drive sheep from Cooma to Bega via Tantawangalo Mountain. Based at Erambie, he established his own droving business in the late 1920s and became as widely known and respected as his father. On 19 July 1927 at St Raphael's Catholic Church, Cowra, he married 17-year-old Edith Murray; they were to have five children.

Attached to touring rural shows, Coe was engaged throughout New South Wales as a buckjumper. These shows functioned on the same lines as the boxing troupes in offering opportunities to Aboriginal youths. Buckjumping was less physically damaging and better paid, and enabled him to establish his reputation. Known as 'Jimmy Callaghan' after the former, noted rider Jack Callaghan, Coe worked with troupes in Queensland and New South Wales, where his co-ordination and small frame brought him particular fame as a 'high jumper'. At this time, he recalled, he enjoyed a 'wonderful life' and formed close relationships with several show proprietors. In World War II he worked in the Small Arms Factory at Lithgow, and was later involved in a variety of droving and rural activities.

The managers of Erambie station allowed his White friends to visit him, an unusual privilege in the 1940s and 1950s. While mixing frequently with Whites, Coe remained proud of his Koori identity, chose to live on the Cowra Aboriginal station, played football with and coached several 'all-black' teams, and on one occasion defied the rule of a particularly autocratic Erambie manager. Survived by two sons and a daughter, he died on 3 August 1979 at Cowra District Hospital. Paul Coe was of the generation of self-made Aboriginal men and women which valued the respect won in Koori and White society. He saw what was best in each, and criticized what he saw as the shortcomings of both. The esteem he had gained allowed him to drink, unofficially, in country hotels, even though the sale of alcohol to Aborigines was illegal in New South Wales until 1963. His descendants are prominent in the Aboriginal community, among them his grandson, the lawyer Paul Coe.

P. Read (ed), *Down There with Me on the Cowra Mission* (Syd, 1984); *Aboriginal History*, 4, pt 1, 1980, p 97.

PETER READ

COHEN, IDA (1867-1970), charity worker, was born on 27 August 1867 at Tamworth, New South Wales, eldest child of native-born parents Nathan Cohen, stock and station agent, and his wife Esther, née Solomon. Nathan and his siblings—including twin brothers Henry [q.v.3] and George—had been born at Port Macquarie. Esther died in 1881; next year Nathan, who was mayor (1882-84) of Tamworth, married her sister Deborah. Ida was small and slight, with dark hair and eyes. Although a deeply religious Jewess, she was educated at St Dominic's Convent, and was foundation president (1925-46) and patron (1946-70) of the Tamworth Dominican Old Girls' Union. On 4 December 1901 at her father's Tamworth home she married George's son, her cousin Victor Isaac Cohen (d. 1935), managing director (from 1912) of Nathan Cohen & Co. Ltd. The ceremony, conducted by Rabbi Landau of Sydney, was believed to be Tamworth's first Jewish wedding. Ida and Victor were to have three sons.

In 1914 Mrs Cohen became a foundation member of the Tamworth branch of the British Red Cross Society; her sister Alice was secretary. Soon afterwards Ida began fundraising. She was regularly to be seen on the post office corner—equipped with a small table, a chair and a large Union Jack suspended from the railing—gently urging passers-by to make donations, or to buy buttons, miniature tin hats or poppies. Cohen collected there for Red Cross and other charities until she was 89, protected in summer by 'a yellowing panama hat' and in winter by one rug around her shoulders and another across her knees. Her dignified, gracious manner, unfailing kindness, tolerance and genuine interest in the welfare of others won her the admiration and respect of her fellow citizens.

Disapproving of women who spent their days 'wiping marks off mirrors', Mrs Cohen preferred to invest her time and talents in 'every charitable and patriotic appeal in her district'. She was a justice of the peace, foundation member and president (1916-62) of the Tamworth Ladies' Benevolent Society, a member of the Tamworth and District Ambulance committee (1927-52) and president of its ladies' committee. Involved in the Country Women's Association, she also belonged to the women's auxiliaries of Tamworth Hospital and of the Returned Sailors', Soldiers' and Airmen's Imperial League of Australia. In 1948 she received a certificate of appreciation from the State executive of the R.S.L. Awarded the Red Cross long service medal and bar, she was appointed M.B.E. in 1955: in deference to her 87 years, Governor Sir John Northcott [q.v.] travelled to Tamworth for the investiture.

Keenly interested in history, Ida was foundation president (1952-61) of the Peel Valley Historical Society and a member of the Australian Jewish Historical Society. In 1959, aged 91, she delivered the Anzac Day commemorative address at Tamworth and was given State-wide radio coverage. Her interest in charities continued until she was 96. Survived by two sons, she died, aged 102, on 18 April 1970 in St Elmo Private Hospital, Tamworth, and was buried in the local cemetery.

Dominican, 1, 1937, p 50, 10, 1946, p 88; *Aust Women's Weekly*, 11 May 1955, p 20; *Aust Jewish Hist Soc J*, 1970, p 552; *Tamworth Observer*, 7 Dec 1901; *Northern Daily Leader*, 26 Apr 1959, 26 Aug 1967, 20 Apr 1970; information from Mr A. Cohen, Tamworth, NSW.   SHEILA TILSE

COHEN, RIEKE (1887-1964), Zionist leader, was born on 8 October 1887 at Newtown, Sydney, fifth child of Jacob Selig, a pawnbroker who came to Australia in 1863 from Friedrichstadt, Schleswig (then part of Denmark), and his English-born wife Sarah Rebecca, née Solomon. Jacob and Sarah became dedicated workers for the Jewish community. Rieke assisted her mother in the pawnshop, and studied and taught elocution at the New South Wales State Conservatorium of Music. At the Great Synagogue, Sydney, on 14 February 1912 she married a clothing manufacturer Harris Cohen (d. 1944); he was a Polish widower, twenty-five years her

senior, who was to support her community work.

A foundation member (1923) of the (National) Council of Jewish Women of New South Wales, Cohen met ships from Europe, escorted Jewish immigrants to the N.C.J.W. hostel at Pyrmont and helped them to find employment. In 1930 she travelled overseas with her husband: she saw the degradation of the Jews in Poland and the pioneering efforts of Jews in Palestine which strengthened her resolve to work for the Zionist cause. State president (1931-33) of the N.C.J.W., she formed a branch in the Eastern Suburbs. Despite its success, in December 1934 the federal president Dr Fanny Reading [q.v.11] and her executive decided to close the branch. The action was partly the result of a clash between Reading and Cohen, and partly the outcome of their differing opinions over the importance of Zionist work.

Alienated by the decision, Cohen immediately resigned from all N.C.J.W. activities. In January 1935 she called a public meeting to form a new organization, Ivriah, with the aims of supporting the development of a Jewish homeland in Palestine and promoting Jewish education; in March she began a monthly journal, also named *Ivriah*, which she continued to publish until her death. She bought a property at 640a Old South Head Road in 1936 and converted it at her own expense into the Ivriah headquarters. This centre served as the first place of worship of the Mizrachi congregation. In January 1937 Ivriah was directly affiliated with the Women's International Zionist Organisation and from 1939 was officially called the Australian Federation of W.I.Z.O.

During World War II Cohen founded the New South Wales Jewish War Memorial Red Cross Sewing Circle and was a member of the executive-committee responsible for raising funds for the Sir John Monash [q.v.10] Hut Anzac Buffet. After the war her continued efforts for the reception of immigrants made her loved and respected by the survivors of the Holocaust. She was federal president (1949-54) of W.I.Z.O., an executive-member of the State Zionist Council, the Zionist Federation of Australia and New Zealand, and the Jewish National Fund, and an elected member of the New South Wales Jewish Board of Deputies. In recognition of her work she was appointed an honorary life member of the Australian federation, and the world executive, of W.I.Z.O.

An accomplished orator, Cohen was a radical champion of Zionism at a time when the cause was unfashionable. She was aided by her close friend and confidante Elsa London, a domestic science teacher who was vice-president of Ivriah, and State vice-president and later national treasurer of W.I.Z.O.

Childless herself, Cohen made the W.I.Z.O. community—including many Holocaust survivors—her family. For much of her life she suffered from diabetes and necrosis of the skin. She died on 13 August 1964 at Prince Henry Hospital, Little Bay, and was buried in Rookwood cemetery. From her estate, sworn for probate at £82 918, she made substantial donations to W.I.Z.O.'s children's home at Haifa, to the Hebrew University of Jerusalem and to the Jewish National Fund, Israel.

L. Cohen, *Beginning with Esther* (Syd, 1987); W. D. Rubinstein (ed), *Jews in the Sixth Continent* (Syd, 1987); *WIZO Review*, Oct-Nov 1964; S. D. Rutland, The Jewish Community in New South Wales, 1914-1939 (M.A. Hons thesis, Univ Syd, 1978) and The History of Australian Jewry, 1945-1960 (Ph.D. thesis, Univ Syd, 1989); Minutes and correspondence, WIZO Archives, Syd; information from Mr A. Selig, Bellevue Hill, Syd.   SUZANNE D. RUTLAND

COHEN, SAMUEL HERBERT (1918-1969), politician and barrister, was born on 26 October 1918 at Bankstown, Sydney, elder child of Max Lazarus Cohen, tailor's cutter, and his wife Fanny Dinah, née Fagelman, both Russian born. Having spent his childhood at Leeds, England, Max had come to Sydney as a young man and married there. In 1925 he moved with his family to Melbourne, where Sam was educated at Elwood Central School, Wesley College and the University of Melbourne (B.A., LL.M., 1942). A gifted student, he achieved his education through scholarships.

At university Sam entered student life enthusiastically: he was president of the Students' Representative Council, a founding member of the National Union of Australian University Students and active in the theatre. On 11 May 1942 he enlisted in the Militia and was posted to Major Alfred Conlon's [q.v.] research section at Land Headquarters, Melbourne. Cohen was subsequently seconded to the (Australian) Universities Commission in Sydney. He was discharged as a sergeant on 29 April 1943.

Influential in Jewish communal affairs in Melbourne, Cohen was a founding member (1942) and later president of the Jewish Council to Combat Fascism and Anti-Semitism. This body became embroiled in the politics of the Cold War and many—both in the Jewish community and outside—castigated it as a communist-front organization. Cohen strenuously rejected the criticism. In 1948 he was secretary of the first United Israel Appeal. His interests also extended to Jewish welfare, the Montefiore Homes and the Friends of the Hebrew University of Jerusalem.

In 1946 Cohen had been admitted to the Victorian Bar. He practised in common law, became a specialist in industrial law and took silk in September 1961. On 3 May 1953 at the Great Synagogue, Sydney, he had married Judith Jacqueline Selig, a solicitor and niece of Rieke Cohen [q.v.]. A member (from 1946) of the Australian Labor Party, in 1961 he was chosen for a safe position on Labor's Victorian ticket for the Senate in preference to Maurice Ashkanasy [q.v.]. Cohen took his seat on 1 July 1962. His political opponents tried to ambush him by instigating a debate in the Upper House on 18 October on the persecution of Jews in the Soviet Union: Cohen's response resulted in widespread controversy.

Skilled, persuasive and eloquent, he soon made his mark in the chamber where he became party spokesman on education, legal issues and matters relating to science, radio, television and culture. In 1962-63 he was prominent on the much-publicized Senate select committee on the encouragement of Australian productions for television. Elected deputy-leader of the Opposition in the Senate in 1967, Cohen was appointed shadow minister on education, science, communications and the arts. He served as a council-member of the Australian National University and as an executive-member of the Commonwealth Scientific and Industrial Research Organization. That year, at the University of Western Australia, he delivered the Curtin [q.v.] memorial lecture, 'Education in the 1970's', in which he laid the blueprint of the education policy later implemented by the Whitlam government. Cohen played a crucial role in the A.L.P.'s policy change to assist all schools on the basis of need.

An ebullient man of unfailing courtesy and great integrity, Cohen consistently demonstrated his clarity and strength of argument. He never resorted to guile or invective, and made no enemy in the parliament. Although he was a member of the left faction of the A.L.P., he was respected as a healer and as one who endeavoured to achieve consensus. After addressing an election meeting in Adelaide, Cohen collapsed and died of cardiac infarction on 7 October 1969 at Queen Elizabeth Hospital, Woodville; he was accorded a state funeral and buried in Melbourne general cemetery. His wife and two daughters survived him. A portrait by Louis Kahan hangs in the Hebrew University of Jerusalem; another by the same artist is in the family's possession. In 1970 Cohen was posthumously given the Maurice Ashkanasy award for Australian Jew of the Year (1969). A Senator Cohen memorial lecture was established; the first was delivered by R. J. L. Hawke on 6 October 1971.

Alfred Conlon (priv print, Syd, 1963); R. J. L.

Hawke, 'Masada, Moscow and Melbourne', *The Inaugural Senator Cohen Memorial Lecture* (Melb, 1967); P. Y. Medding, *From Assimilation to Group Survival* (Melb, 1968); Parliament of Cwlth of Aust, *A Tribute to the Memory of Senator Samuel Cohen, Q.C.* (Canb, 1969); C. Holding, 'The Labor Case for Israel', *Senator Cohen Memorial Lecture* (Melb, 1975); Jewish Museum of Aust, *Diversity and Development*, exhibition cat (Melb, 1985); S. D. Rutland, *Edge of the Diaspora* (Syd, 1988); W. D. Rubinstein, *The Jews in Australia*, 2 (Melb, 1991); Aust Jewish Hist Soc, *J*, 10, no 6, May 1989, p 524, no 7, Nov 1989, p 598, 11, no 1, Nov 1990, p 160; information from Mrs J. Cohen, Kew, Sir Zelman Cowen, East Melb, and Mr L. Jedwab, Brighton, Melb; personal information.   JULIAN PHILLIPS

COLE, ADRIAN LINDLEY TREVOR (1895-1966), air force officer, was born on 19 June 1895 at Glen Iris, Melbourne, fourth child of Robert Hodgson Cole, barrister and medical practitioner, and his wife Helen Helmsley, née Hake, both native-born. Educated at Geelong and Melbourne Church of England grammar schools, Adrian excelled at rowing and was a member of the contingent of cadets from Victorian public schools which went to London in 1911 for the coronation of King George V. Cole obtained a commission in the Australian Military Forces in August 1914, but resigned in order to enlist in the Australian Imperial Force on 28 January 1916. As he wanted to become a pilot, he was posted to No. 1 Squadron, Australian Flying Corps, and in March embarked with it for Egypt; he was promoted second lieutenant in June and began flying training in August.

Operating in support of the Egyptian Expeditionary Force's advance to Palestine, on 20 April 1917 Cole and another pilot attacked and disorganized six enemy aircraft about to bomb a cavalry formation near Gaza; for his skill and courage, Cole was to be awarded the Military Cross. Next day, while he was reconnoitring Tel el Sheria, the motor of his Martinsyde was hit by anti-aircraft fire and he came down behind Turkish lines: Captain (Sir) Richard Williams [q.v.12] was able to land and rescue him. In June, when returning from a strike against Turkish Fourth Army headquarters on the Mount of Olives, Jerusalem, Cole landed in hostile territory near Beersheba to help stricken comrades. Because the undercarriage of his aircraft broke during his attempted take off, he and his companions had to walk across no man's land to safety. In December Captain Cole was posted to England.

In May 1918 he was sent to No. 2 Squadron, A.F.C., one of three squadrons of an elite British offensive force which had been formed on the Western Front in April. On 17 July Cole helped to destroy a Fokker triplane in aerial combat over Armentières, France, and in August shot down two Fokkers in the Lys region. In the 7 October mass raid on roads and railway stations at Lille, he led his flight with initiative and determination, and was awarded the Distinguished Flying Cross for his part in the action. Having downed another enemy aircraft later that month, Cole returned to Melbourne where his A.I.F. appointment terminated on 20 June 1919. He briefly entered business as an importer, before taking a permanent commission on 31 March 1921 in the (Royal) Australian Air Force. On 30 November at St Peter's Chapel, Melbourne Grammar School, he married a cousin Katherine Shaw Cole. Completing studies at the Royal Air Force Staff College, Andover, England, in 1923, he commanded No. 1 Flying Training School, Point Cook, Victoria, in 1926-29, and was air member for supply on the Air Board in 1933-36. Wing Commander Cole had been deputy-chairman of the sub-committee that planned the international air race (conducted for the 1934 Victorian centenary celebrations) and did much of the organizing for the event. He was promoted group captain on 1 January 1935 and appointed C.B.E. in 1937.

Commanding officer (1936-37) of R.A.A.F. Station, Richmond, New South Wales, Cole attended the Imperial Defence College, London, in 1938, and was in command of the base at Laverton, Victoria, on the outbreak of World War II. His promotion to temporary air commodore in December 1939 complemented his increasingly important postings to staff and operational duties in New South Wales and Victoria. In September 1941 Cole was attached to the R.A.F.'s Western Desert Air Force, North Africa, where he briefly commanded No. 235 Wing. Transferring to headquarters, No. 11 Group, England, in May 1942, he sailed in the destroyer H.M.S. *Calpe* to co-ordinate air support for the 19 August raid on Dieppe, France. Cole was on the bridge of the *Calpe* when German fighters strafed the ship; fragments from an exploding cannon-shell lodged in his jaw, neck and back, and he underwent facial plastic surgery. On 15 October he became air officer commanding, Northern Ireland, with the rank of acting air vice marshal. He was awarded the Distinguished Service Order for his performance during the assault against Dieppe.

Repatriated in May 1943, Cole was posted as A.O.C., North-Western Area, on 21 July. From his headquarters in Darwin he organized the air defence of the region and launched strikes against Japanese shipping and shore facilities. Later in the year his forces bolstered the Allies' offensive in New Guinea by reducing enemy strength in the Netherlands East Indies. Appointed air member for personnel on the Air Board in October 1944, he left for India in January 1945 to assume the post of R.A.A.F. liaison officer on the staff of the supreme allied commander, South East Asia. Cole was at Rangoon on 26-27 August for peace negotiations and was senior Australian representative when the Japanese formally surrendered in Singapore on 12 September. Retiring on 17 April 1946, he was promoted substantive air commodore and granted the rank of honorary air vice marshal that day. He stood as a Liberal candidate in the 1946 Federal election, unsuccessfully contesting the Victorian seat of Maribyrnong against A. S. Drakeford [q.v.], his former minister.

Athletic in build and 6 ft 4½ ins (194.3 cm) tall, 'King' Cole enjoyed company, convivial occasions and playing golf; he was a director of Pacific Insurance Co. Ltd and Guinea Airways Ltd. He died of chronic respiratory disease on 14 February 1966 in Heidelberg Repatriation Hospital; after an air force funeral in the Anglican chapel, R.A.A.F. Station, Laverton, his body was interred in the family vault at Camperdown cemetery. His wife, two sons and two daughters survived him.

F. M. Cutlack, *The Australian Flying Corps* (Syd, 1923); J. Herington, *Air War Against Germany and Italy 1939-1943* (Canb, 1954); G. Odgers, *Air War Against Japan 1943-1945* (Canb, 1957); D. N. Gillison, *Royal Australian Air Force 1939-1942* (Canb, 1962); C. D. Coulthard-Clark, *The Third Brother* (Syd, 1991); *Herald* (Melb), 21 Apr 1934; Cole papers (AWM); AWM records.   BRIAN EATON*

COLE, GEORGE RONALD (1908-1969), headmaster and politician, was born on 9 February 1908 at Don, near Devonport, Tasmania, one of the five children of George Cole, labourer, and his wife Alice, née Rutter, both native-born. Alice was a staunch Methodist who imbued her children with the work ethic and a sense of social values. Educated at Devonport High School, young George became a student-teacher in 1925 and later studied at the University of Tasmania. While playing for New Town, in 1928 he won the Wilson J. Bailey trophy for best and fairest in the Tasmanian Australian National Football League; he also represented his State at the 1930 carnival in Adelaide. Cole's earnings from the game helped his family during the Depression.

On 28 March 1932 he married a hairdresser Kathleen Mary Cuttriss at St Mary's Catholic Cathedral, Hobart. By this time Cole was converted to Catholicism. A successful and popular teacher and headmaster, he became a certificated assistant (1938) and subsequently first assistant at West Devonport Practising School. He enlisted in the Citizen Military Forces in March 1939 and was posted to the 12th-50th Battalion; promoted lieutenant in April 1941, he transferred to the Australian Imperial Force on 18 September 1942. Next year he briefly had charge of a prisoner-of-war camp near Darwin where he formed an amicable relationship with the inmates, most of whom were Italian. Cole later carried out instructional duties in Australia until his appointment terminated on 7 September 1944.

Returning to Devonport, he was successively headmaster of primary schools at Strahan (1946), Longford (1947) and Latrobe (1948-49). He joined local sporting teams and was an organizer for the Australian Labor Party. Cole's earlier interest in politics intensified after World War II and he won Labor pre-selection for the Senate in 1949. Supported by his wife and children, who helped him with electioneering, he was returned that year. The choice of a Senate seat would prove significant after the A.L.P. 'split' in 1955.

Although the debates within the party over the industrial groups and the convulsions in Victoria of the early 1950s had little effect in Tasmania, Cole's anti-communist spirit distanced him from his colleagues. Believing that Arthur Calwell would have the numbers to defeat H. V. Evatt [qq.v.], at the federal caucus meeting on 13 October 1954 Cole moved that all leadership positions be declared vacant. He was the lone Tasmanian to vote for the motion which was defeated by 52 votes to 28. In March 1955 he joined the right-wing boycott of the A.L.P.'s federal conference in Hobart. These actions did not diminish his standing with the rank and file, and a week later he topped the poll for places on the Tasmanian executive. Evatt's supporters, however, were in the majority on the executive and Cole's party membership was immediately suspended.

On 24 August 1955 Cole announced that henceforward he would represent the Australian Labor Party (Anti-Communist) in the Senate. That party was to become the Democratic Labor Party in 1957. The Menzies [q.v.] government outraged the A.L.P. by granting Cole status as a party leader. In 1956 F. P. McManus joined him in the Upper House, where they held the balance of power and were able to influence the government's welfare and housing policies. Cole went to Melbourne to launch the D.L.P. campaign for the 1958 election. He stressed that his party's differences with the A.L.P. were to do with anti-communism and foreign policy rather than domestic issues. When Evatt offered to stand down as A.L.P. leader in exchange for D.L.P. preferences, Cole countered by insisting that the A.L.P. take up the fight against communism in the unions and ban unity tickets. He was re-elected that year with 16.98 per cent of the Tasmanian vote.

Cole's Catholic affiliations do not seem to have been the sole determinant of his political actions: while he admired B. A. Santamaria's world view, he opposed the National Civic Council's attempt to take over the D.L.P. His attitude to foreign affairs led him to support British atomic-bomb testing in Australia and the Vietnam War. In domestic affairs he believed in European immigration, the importance of the family as a unit, universal home ownership, and in an Australia free from social strife and committed to 'a fair go' for all. Late in 1964 he collapsed in parliament with appendicitis and was in poor health thereafter. Having lost the Senate election that year, he unsuccessfully endeavoured to maintain the Tasmanian branch of the D.L.P. Cole died of chronic renal failure on 23 January 1969 at Latrobe and was buried in Mersey Vale Memorial Park cemetery, Devonport; his wife, three sons and two daughters survived him.

R. Murray, *The Split* (Melb, 1970); P. Ormonde, *The Movement* (Melb, 1972); *Mercury* (Hob), 14 Sept 1928, 24 Jan 1969; *Examiner* (Launc), 24 Jan 1969; *Advocate* (Hob), 24 Jan 1969; information from Mr M. Cole, Brisb, and Mrs J. Westwood, Hob.   R. J. K. CHAPMAN

COLE, LESLIE GEORGE (1892-1978), magician, was born on 5 March 1892 at Alexandria, Sydney, son of native-born parents George Cole, driver, and his wife Sarah Catherine, née Chapman, late Reid. The family moved to Wangaratta, Victoria, where George bred trotters and ran a dairy-farm. Educated locally, Les found a job driving a baker's cart. At 17 he went to Melbourne and worked as a billiard-marker and barman at the Vine Hotel, Richmond. There he met the showman Tom Selwyn and became his protégé; Selwyn gave him the stage-name 'Levant' (an 'e' was later added for effect, though the vowel was silent). Cole spent two years playing bit parts in repertory before embarking on a career as a professional magician.

Having earned a pittance entertaining in the intervals between silent films in city cinemas, 'The Great Levante' appeared at Luna Park, Melbourne, and at White City, Sydney, then took to the road in Queensland. He was inspired by the feats of Harry Houdini and, as an escapologist, tantalized audiences by the light of kerosene lamps at remote shearing sheds. The life was rough, the rewards a few shillings and a meal. During World War I he worked in propaganda and recruiting. In Brisbane on Armistice Night 1918 he saw a 19-year-old clerk Gladys Pretoria Costin and was introduced to her three days later. They were married on 7 June 1919 with Methodist forms at her father's Kelvin Grove home; their only child Esme was born in 1921. In Western Australia the Coles acquired a Dodge bus and travelled the outback, performing from Broome to Birdsville, Queensland.

The trio began a world tour in 1927 that was to last thirteen years, during which they played before princes and peasants in Asia and Europe. Through the bustle of ships and trains, hotels and living out of suitcases, with his wife and daughter as assistants, Les gradually perfected his legerdemain, pulling rabbits from hats, aces from ears, golf balls from every respectable orifice, and endlessly sawing Gladys and Esme in halves. Weighed down by manacles and chains, he hurled himself into the Thames from Lambeth Bridge, London. He also struggled from straitjackets, often suspended high above city streets. The unexpected is the expected with magicians.

In 1935 the Institute of Magicians, London, named Levante's trunk trick the 'Mystery of Mysteries'; the Inner Magic Circle awarded him its gold star; and in 1939 the International Brotherhood of Magicians invited him to the United States of America where he was elected the world's number one magician. He declared that the worst patrons he faced were those in Russia and at the Imperial Court Theatre, Japan; the best were the English and the Indian. Les also tackled the most acute of observers—children— and thought that the secret of success was never to play down to them. While in England he devised *How's Tricks*, a magical revue that incorporated comedy, chorus girls and animals galore. It had a cast of forty. In one extravagant piece, members of his troupe dressed as nuns sang *Ave Maria* and, as a climax, he made a choirboy materialize from an organ-pipe. Returning to Australia in November 1940, Les subsequently entertained troops in Queensland. He settled in New South Wales, visited South America in 1954 and continued to tour Australia for nine months each year for much of that decade. In 1977 he retired.

On stage, Levante was a suave and imposing figure. Tall and ramrod-backed, with a flowing cape, top hat, cane, white tie and tails, he wore his hair plastered back and, later, as a mane. His smile was cold and knowing, his light-brown eyes intense and eldritch. Away from the limelight, he was unaffected, genial and modest. Believing that 'the hand is quicker than the eye', he held that his fame was simply due to hard work. He maintained a ramshackle, weatherboard cottage at Old Guildford, at the rear of which stood his 'Fun Factory', a grim, black Nissen hut in which he kept all the paraphernalia of illusion. Within that den he built, renovated and painted his equipment and props; therein he stored seventeen boxes of costumes, many of which were designed and made by Gladys. By such means, and by his genius, he brought excitement to millions, bewildering onlookers for some sixty-five years in theatres, halls and tents throughout the world.

To Les Cole, show business was as much about business as about show. He combined drive and purpose with frugal habits. After World War II he had saved enough to invest shrewdly and to buy an eleven-room house at Bellevue Hill where he lived with his wife, daughter, son-in-law and grandson. At home, he relaxed, smoked, sipped whisky and grew orchids; he collected sixty water-colour paintings and engravings by Norman Lindsay [q.v.10], and added more books on magic to his library; W. L. Gresham's *Nightmare Alley* (New York, 1946) continued to fascinate him. He was a Freemason and attended Lodge No. 519. His hobbies included bowls, trout-fishing, chess and exposing spiritualists as frauds. Gifted with a marvellous memory, he concealed his sense of power over the credulity of his fellow human beings and kept close-mouthed about the secrets of his craft. Magic explained is no longer magic. Survived by his wife and daughter, Cole died on 20 January 1978 at his Sydney home and was cremated.

N. Bridges, *Curtain Call*, (Syd, 1980); *People* (Melb), 24 Feb 1954; *Pix/People*, 22 Jan 1976; *Daily Telegraph* (Syd) and *Sun* (Syd), 21 Jan 1978; *SMH*, 24 Jan 1978; information from Dr F. B. Smith, Turner, Canb, and Mr P. Purtell, East St Kilda, Melb.   JOHN RITCHIE

COLECHIN, LAWRENCE DICKENS (1895-1951), optician, was born on 23 November 1895 at Fitzroy, Melbourne, eighth and youngest child of English-born parents William Henry Colechin, tea merchant, and his wife Annie Maria, née Howson (d. 1898). William was a Collingwood city councillor (1895-1904) and a Labor member of the Legislative Assembly (1904-07). He remarried in 1901. After attending Cambridge Street State School, Collingwood, Lawrence trained with an optician, E. Wood, in Melbourne.

On 19 August 1914 Colechin enlisted in the Australian Imperial Force. He was then 5 ft 8¾ ins (174.6 cm) tall, with blue eyes and fair hair. Posted as lance corporal to the 6th Battalion, he embarked on 19 December. At the Gallipoli landing on 25 April 1915 he was wounded in the leg. Invalided to England, he returned to Melbourne where he was discharged on 20 February 1916. He was appointed temporary lieutenant in the Australian Military Forces on 1 September and served with the cadets until 15 March 1920

when he resigned his commission. On 3 April 1917 at the Richmond Congregational Church he had married Florence Isabel Freeman.

On leaving the army, Colechin joined an optical business established by his brother Albert, but rivalries led Lawrence to found the Victorian Optical Co. Pty Ltd in 1921. His business skill was such that by 1928 it had a staff of seventy, with branches in Sydney and at Newcastle. In 1928 he formed the Australian Optical Co. Ltd which absorbed the assets of the V.O.C. He was chairman and managing director. Branches were established in Perth (1928), Brisbane (1931), Adelaide (1933) and at Townsville (1935). Bifocal blanks were made in Sydney and in 1933 a factory was opened in Melbourne to manufacture spectacle cases. In 1949 the A.O.C. took over the Precision Optical Co. Ltd of Wellington, New Zealand.

During World War II the Directorate of Ordnance Production, advised by T. H. Laby [q.v.9] and his Optical Munitions Panel, asked Colechin to work on optical munitions (especially telescope lenses) when the supply from Britain ceased following the fall of Dunkirk. The A.O.C. made more than one-quarter of the 27 000 instruments produced in Australia in the war. With the return of peace, the Australian Universities Commission called for tenders for microscopes, then in short supply due to the high number of ex-service students. Colechin submitted a design which was not successful, sold it in Ceylon and then reverted to optometry.

President of the Association of Optical Manufacturers of Australia, he had a strong — if not dominant—personality and a single-minded desire to promote a well-developed optical industry. He was a fellow of the Australian Institute of Management, and a member of the Navy, Army and Air Force, the Victoria Racing, the Victoria Golf and the Royal South Yarra Tennis clubs. Colechin died of a coronary occlusion on 2 April 1951 at Wahroonga, Sydney, and was buried with Anglican rites in Warrandyte cemetery, Victoria. He was survived by his wife, from whom he was estranged; there were no children. His estate, sworn for probate at £148 407, included large bequests to longstanding employees of his company. In 1952 his widow unsuccessfully contested his will.

J. S. Rogers, *History of the Scientific Instrument and Optical Panel Initially Optical Munitions Panel July 1940 to December 1946* (Melb, 1946); D. P. Mellor, *The Role of Science and Industry* (Canb, 1958); Aust Optical Co. Ltd, *Prospectus*, Sept 1937; *J of Opticians and Optometrists Assn of NSW*, 1 May 1951; *Aust Physicist*, 27, 1990, p 31; *Herald* (Melb), 6 Apr, 20 Sept 1951, 27 Nov 1952; *Sun News-Pictorial*, 22 Sept 1951; information from Mr L. D. Colechin, Brighton, Melb.   H. C. BOLTON

COLEMAN, EDITH (1874-1951), naturalist, was born on 29 July 1874 at Woking, Surrey, England, daughter of Henry Harms, carpenter, and his wife Charlotte, née Edmunds. Edith was educated at Holy Trinity and St Mary's National School, Guildford, Surrey, and, after her family arrived in Melbourne in 1887, at Camberwell State School. From 1889 to 1898 she taught at six state schools in Gippsland, Maryborough and suburban Melbourne. On 7 April 1898 at Christ Church, South Yarra, she married with Anglican rites James George Coleman, a salesman and pioneer motorist.

Joining the Field Naturalists' Club of Victoria in 1922, Edith Coleman immediately delivered a paper, 'Some Autumn Orchids', which exemplified the knowledge, love of nature and pleasing style that were to characterize the contributions she sent from her Blackburn home to the *Victorian Naturalist* for twenty-nine years. Her prolific output of natural history notes and papers was also published in the press, popular nature magazines, and in one or two scientific journals.

Through a series of papers (1927 to 1933) in the *Victorian Naturalist,* Coleman recorded her discovery of the pollination of three *Cryptostylis* orchid species by the Ichneumon wasp, *Lissopimpla semipunctata*, via the insect's pseudo-copulation with the orchid flower that resembles the female Ichneumon. Her descriptions 'created enormous world interest', and confirmed and extended overseas research on orchid pollination by insects. A member of the Australian Orchid Society, she published in its journal, as well as in the London periodicals, *Orchid Review* and *Journal of Botany*.

Other botanical subjects in which Coleman was interested ranged from the description of new species to the pollination of yucca in Australia by hive bees, and from medicinal and culinary herbs to the movements of plants and the spread of mistletoe. Her article, 'The Romance of Kipling's Dittany' (1940), was a delight of botanical folk-lore and herbal history. She studied animal life with equal ease and precision. While sometimes anthropocentric in expression, her observations were never without a naturalist's quest for truth, whether touching 'the graceful courtship parades' of huntsman spiders, or the habits of the mountain grasshopper, pipe fish, lizards, phasmids, bats, case moths or her engaging echidnas. In addition, she compiled ornithological observations on the clustering of woodswallows, the pre-roosting flocking of common mynahs, the feeding habits of the tawny frogmouth, the use of herbs by birds and the nocturnal singing of budgerigars during rain after drought. Her daughter Dorothy regularly assisted her with drawings and observations.

The first woman to receive the Australian Natural History medallion (1949), Coleman generously helped beginners in natural history. Although English by birth, in her *Come Back in Wattle Time*(1935) she wrote—as an Australian—of the many soldiers in World War I who had received a tiny spray of wattle that 'whispered something deeper than "Come Back"'. During World War II she raised money for the Australian Red Cross Society through sales of *Angelica* seeds from her garden. She died on 3 June 1951 at Sorrento, Victoria, and was buried in the local cemetery; her husband and two daughters survived her.

J. A. Baines (comp), *The Victorian Naturalist Author Index*, 1884-1975 (roneoed, Melb, 1976); R. Desmond, *Dictionary of British and Irish Botanists and Horticulturalists*(Lond, 1977); *Vic Naturalist*, 67, Sept 1950, p 99, 68, July 1951, p 46; *Woman's World*, 1 Aug 1927, p 450; *Wild Life*, May 1950, July 1951; *NZ J of Botany*, 17, 1979, p 467; *Age*, 15 Apr 1950; *Herald* (Melb), 4 June 1951.

ALLAN McEVEY

COLEMAN, JOHN DOUGLAS (1928-1973), Australian Rules footballer and publican, was born on 23 November 1928 at Port Fairy, Victoria, fourth child of Victorian-born parents Albert Ernest Coleman, manager, and his wife Ella Elizabeth, née Matthews. John first began to kick a football at the Port Fairy Higher Elementary School; after his family moved to Melbourne in the early years of World War II, he attended Ascot Vale West State and Moonee Ponds Central schools. At the age of 12, he was already playing in a local under-18 team. In 1943 Ella and her children moved to Hastings while her husband remained in Melbourne to look after his business. Coleman divided his time between Melbourne, where he attended University High School, and Hastings, where he played in the Mornington Peninsula League. In 1946 he was invited to train with the Essendon Football Club, but was unable to force his way into the first-grade side. He returned to Hastings and in 1947-48 kicked a total of 296 goals. By the beginning of the 1949 season, word of his prowess had spread to several clubs in the Victorian Football League and Essendon immediately rushed him into its senior team.

From his first game, when he kicked twelve goals against Hawthorn, Coleman was a star. Six ft 1 in. (185.4 cm) tall, pale and slightly built, he appeared almost listless as he stood in the goal square, a yard or so behind the full-back, his guernsey (number 10) rolled to the elbows. Then, with explosive speed, he would slip the guard of his opponent and soar, sometimes waist-high above the pack, to mark the ball. His uncanny ability to make position and his prodigious leap immediately caught the public imagination. Although his leads often left him with difficult shots for goal, he converted a high proportion of his opportunities with long, flat punts.

The first postwar V.F.L. player to kick a hundred goals in a season, and the only one to do so in his first, Coleman kicked his hundredth goal in the last quarter of Essendon's victory over Carlton in the 1949 grand final. Next year he recorded his best seasonal total (120) to help Essendon win the premiership against North Melbourne.

Opposing coaches and full-backs were hard put to curb Coleman's brilliance. Close-checking, spoiling players fared best; but few could outrun, and none outmark, him. He often faced two, or even three, opponents and was constantly needled, jostled and punched behind the play. In the last home-and-away round of the 1951 season, Coleman exchanged blows with the Carlton backman Harry Caspar. Both were reported. Despite a boundary umpire's evidence that Coleman had retaliated only after two unprovoked punches from Caspar, each was suspended for four weeks. Coleman was distraught. Disconsolate supporters blamed his suspension for Essendon's failure to win its third successive premiership.

In the next few years Essendon dropped down the ladder, yet Coleman continued to head the V.F.L. goal-kicking table, scoring 103 goals in 1952 and 97 in 1953. In the seventh game of the 1954 season he kicked his biggest ever tally, 14 goals, but in a match a week later fell heavily and dislocated his knee. Despite surgery, he was forced to retire, aged 25, having kicked an average of almost 5½ goals a game in his 98 V.F.L. appearances.

Coleman was a capable businessman who understood the commercial potential of his fame. His studies for a degree in commerce at the University of Melbourne were curtailed in 1949 by the greater attractions of football and business. While his match-winning feats brought no increase in his Saturday pay-packet (all Essendon players received £4 per game), Coleman was given management of the Auburn Hotel by one of the club's vice-presidents, Ted Rippon. Their association continued when Coleman became licensee of the Essendon Hotel, but he subsequently went into business on his own account at the West Brunswick Hotel. From 1954 he also wrote for the *Herald* newspaper. On 3 March 1955 at St Thomas's Anglican Church, Essendon, he married Reine Monica Fernando.

In 1961, following the retirement of Dick Reynolds, Coleman returned to Essendon as coach. A clever tactician, he eschewed the histrionics of rival coaches, concentrating his efforts instead upon quietly harnessing the individual talents of his players. In 1962 he coached 'the Bombers' to their first premiership for twelve years and they won the flag again in 1965. During his playing days Coleman had developed a special loathing for umpires and they were often the target of his venomous tongue as a coach.

By 1966 Coleman's health had begun to cause him concern. His knee injury now prevented him from actively participating in training and he suffered from thrombosis. He agreed to return for the 1967 season; at its end, he retired to concentrate on his hotel business at Dromana. There, on 5 April 1973, he died suddenly of coronary atheroma; survived by his wife and two daughters, he was cremated. His estate was sworn for probate at $280 270. Coleman's reputation is commemorated by the annual award of the John Coleman medal to the highest goal-kicker in the Australian Football League.

R. S. Whitington, *The Champions* (Melb, 1976); M. Maplestone, *Those Magnificent Men, 1897-1987* (Melb, 1988); W. Brittingham, *Essendon Football Club Premiership Documentary, 1949 and 1950* (priv print, Melb, 1991); *Herald* (Melb), 17 Sept 1949, 5 Apr 1973, 23 Mar 1979; *Age* (Melb), 3, 7 Sept 1951; information from Mr W. Brittingham, Glenroy, and Mr K. Fraser, Lower Plenty, Melb.

GRAEME DAVISON

COLEMAN, LOYD RING (1896-1970), advertising manager, was born on 18 November 1896 at Brockport, New York, United States of America, third child of Arthur Coleman, Post Office inspector, and his wife Mabel, née Ring. Known as 'Deke' (his friends thought that he looked like a deacon), Loyd attended the Normal School, Brockport, and the University of Rochester (A.B., 1918); he also studied in 1918-19 for a master's degree in English while employed by several small companies and as assistant advertising manager for North East Electric Co. In 1917 he had served with the naval reserve, 'scrubbing hospital floors'. He taught at East High School and in May 1921 married a journalist Emily Tyler Holmes, of Hartford, Connecticut. Having given birth to their son in January 1924, Emily suffered puerperal fever and was confined in a mental asylum for three months before convalescing in Europe. Coleman reacted by studying psychology in 1925-26 for a doctorate at Columbia University; he co-authored *Psychology, a Simplification* (New York, 1927) and joined Emily in Paris.

Appointed to the staff of the advertising firm, J. Walter Thompson Co., in London in 1928, he became manager of the branch at Antwerp, Belgium, in 1931. Emily stayed in France. Following his divorce, on 30 April

1932 Coleman married a Frenchwoman Henriette Louise Jamme. From 1935 he controlled Thompson's European operations from Paris. After the outbreak of World War II he made a survey of German propaganda methods for British intelligence and left Paris just ahead of the German army; he and Louise remained in France until December 1940.

Back in New York, Coleman was persuaded to take over as managing director of the Australian office and reached Sydney in July 1941. Over the next nineteen years the Sydney branch became the third largest overseas member of the Thompson organization and one of the largest advertising agencies in Australia. Coleman avoided the direct approach, relying on gentle but relentless persistence. Despite his slow voice, 'soft as a kitten's fur', he 'ran his business with almost military precision'. Among the big accounts he acquired for the firm were those of the Australian Consolidated Press Ltd, Broken Hill Proprietary Co. Ltd, Andersons [q.v.] Meat Industries Ltd, the Colonial Sugar Refining Co. Ltd and the Coca-Cola Co.

A principal speaker at congresses of the International Chamber of Commerce in Berlin (1937), Copenhagen (1939), Montreal (1949) and Tokyo (1955), Coleman was a committee-member of the Australian Association of Advertising Agencies, and belonged to the Australian and American National clubs in Sydney. He relinquished the managing directorship in 1958, when he became a director, and wrote of his experiences and opinions in *The Practice of Successful Advertising* (1959). Firmly believing in free enterprise, he criticized price control and restricted shopping hours.

Influential in Sydney's literary and social circles, Coleman lived at Rose Bay in a two-storey house overflowing with books. His only exercise was to take his poodles for a walk. He and E. J. (Ted) Moloney edited some of William Wallace Irwin's recipes for French home-cooking, *The Garrulous Gourmet* (1947). With his idiosyncratic sense of humour, Coleman contributed 'a bubbling fountain of dogma' to another cookery book, their acclaimed *Oh, for a French Wife!* (1952), illustrated by the cartoonist George Molnar.

In 1960 Coleman returned to Paris, the city he and Louise loved, to reap the benefits of retirement. Survived by his wife, and by the son of his first marriage, he died on 23 March 1970 at his home in the 16e Arrondissement.

People, 6 Oct 1954, p 35; J. Walter Thompson Co, *Aust News* (priv pub), 1, no 3, 1960, *News* (NY, priv pub), 25, no 11, 1970; *SMH*, 18 July, 8 Aug 1941, 7 May 1949, 20, 26 Apr 1952, 26 June 1954, 10 May 1957, 29 May 1958, 19 Sept 1959, 13 Mar 1960; information from Univ Rochester, NY, USA, *and* Mme R.-P. Jeanneret, Paris.

LICIA CATTANI

COLEMAN, PATRICK EUGENE (1892–1950), public servant and army officer, was born on 8 December 1892 at Malvern, Melbourne, son of John Coleman, hotelkeeper, and his wife Ellen, née Shanahan, both Victorian born. Educated at the local state school and at South Melbourne College, Patrick—known from childhood as 'Johnny'—was a good scholar. On 1 July 1910 he entered the Commonwealth Public Service as a clerk in the Department of Defence. Enlisting in the Australian Imperial Force on 16 August 1914, he was promoted staff sergeant and posted to 1st Division headquarters for clerical duties.

Having taken part in the landing at Gallipoli on 25 April 1915, Coleman transferred in July to the headquarters of the 2nd Division, then forming in Egypt, and was promoted warrant officer. He was returning to Gallipoli in the *Southland* when she was torpedoed on 2 September; though the ship remained afloat, he narrowly escaped drowning in a lifeboat accident. Promoted honorary lieutenant in March 1916 and appointed superintending clerk at I Anzac Corps headquarters next month, he moved to France and in October became the A.I.F.'s deputy assistant adjutant-general. From January to August 1917 he filled the same post at A.I.F. administrative headquarters, London, before resuming duty on the Western Front. Described as a 'quiet spoken, courteous, and efficient young staff officer, always reliable and conscientious', Coleman was twice mentioned in dispatches. He was appointed O.B.E. in June 1918 and promoted major on 1 November; following the Armistice, he occupied several staff positions in London. On 21 April 1920 in St Robert's Catholic Church, Harrowgate, he married Doris Smith; they were to remain childless. His A.I.F. appointment terminated in Melbourne on 3 October.

Selected from 101 applicants, on 1 January 1921 Coleman was appointed secretary both to the Air Board and to the Air Council. He ensured that R.A.A.F. Headquarters functioned smoothly and enjoyed warm relationships with his uniformed colleagues. In time he became thoroughly identified with the running of the air force. His significant role was recognized in 1934 when he was nominated to attend the Imperial Defence College, London. On 13 November 1939 the War Cabinet decided to appoint a separate minister for air and to make Coleman permanent head of the new department; two weeks later, however, the position was given to M. C. Langslow [q.v.] and Coleman took the assistant-secretaryship. In September 1941 he accompanied Australia's special representative Sir Earle Page [q.v.11] to England and remained in London as secretary to Page's committee of military advisers. By mid-1943 Coleman was back in Melbourne. He transferred to the Department of Defence in September 1946 and became one of Sir Frederick Shedden's [q.v.] assistant-secretaries. Coleman was promoted first assistant-secretary in July 1948 and occasionally acted as permanent head.

A kindly man, with a keen sense of humour, he was 5 ft 8½ ins (174 cm) tall and had blue eyes, dark hair and a fresh complexion. Survived by his wife, he died of hypertensive renal disease on 13 April 1950 at his Elsternwick home and was buried in Brighton cemetery. Air Marshal Sir Richard Williams [q.v.12] paid tribute to his hard work, ability and experience.

C. E. W. Bean, *The A.I.F. in France*, 1916 (Syd, 1929); D. N. Gillison, *Royal Australian Air Force 1939-1942* (Canb, 1962); E. Page, *Truant Surgeon*, A. Mozley ed (Syd, 1963); W. J. Hudson and H. J. W. Stokes (eds), *Documents on Australian Foreign Policy 1937-90*, 5 (Canb, 1982); C. D. Coulthard-Clark, *The Third Brother* (Syd, 1991); *Reveille* (Syd), 1 Sept 1934; *Stand-To*, Apr 1950; *Argus*, 14 Apr 1950.

C. D. COULTHARD-CLARK

COLES, Sir GEORGE JAMES (1885-1977), businessman and philanthropist, was born on 28 March 1885 at Jung Jung, near Murtoa, Victoria, second of ten children and eldest son of George Coles, storekeeper, and his first wife Elizabeth, née Scoular, both Victorian born. The family moved frequently, establishing several stores; George was educated at various state schools and as a boarder at Beechworth College.

In 1910, after working in Melbourne and in the country, George bought his father's store at St James. Three years later he decided to travel to the United States of America and Britain to observe the methods and style of retailing. He was greatly impressed by what he saw, particularly in the '5 and 10 cent stores', common in the U.S.A. In April 1914, in partnership with his brothers Jim and (Sir) Arthur, he opened a store in Smith Street, Collingwood.

Enlisting in the Australian Imperial Force on 18 June 1917, George fought in France as a lance corporal in the 60th Battalion. In April 1918 at Villers Bretonneux he was shot in the knee and evacuated to England. He was discharged on 1 March 1919 in Melbourne. His brothers Arthur, Jim and David had also served in the A.I.F.; Jim was killed in action (1916) and David died from wounds (1917). On 7 February 1920 George married Margaret Gertrude Herbert with Anglican rites at Holy Trinity Church, Kew; they were to have five children.

After the war George and Arthur sold their store to an uncle and in June 1919 opened another in larger premises in Smith Street. The success of the partnership encouraged them to establish G. J. Coles & Co. Pty Ltd on 1 July 1921, with George as managing director. By 1924 their brothers (Sir) Edgar and (Sir) Kenneth, and half-brother (Sir) Norman had also become involved. They began to use the slogan 'nothing over 2/6' which became a by-word for the business.

Expansion was swift. During the 1920s G. J. Coles & Co. acquired further stores and in 1924 opened one in Bourke Street, in the heart of Melbourne's central business district, diagonally opposite the Myer [q.v.10] Emporium. It contained what was said to be Australia's first self-service cafeteria. On 31 October 1927, with nine stores operating in Victoria and total sales of £840 000, the company went public. Next year it purchased Cole's [q.v.3] Book Arcade, Bourke Street, and opened an Art Deco store there. Suffering poor health in 1931, George handed over the managing directorship to Arthur, but remained as chairman. His autocratic style of leadership led to an abortive attempt by his brothers to oust him in 1935 amid public controversy. G. J. Coles & Co. continued to expand despite the Depression, and on the eve of World War II operated eighty-six stores nationally.

Finding that the less onerous role of chairman enabled him to pursue other interests, in 1934 George had become president of the Melbourne Rotary Club. In the previous year he had taken on the honorary position of treasurer to the Alfred Hospital and was soon advocating expansion and improvement. He was appointed chairman of a sub-committee to develop a ten-year building plan which in 1936 proposed a multi-storey development. George contributed some £10 000. As president (1939-42) of the board, he made good use of knowledge acquired since his appointment (1935) to the Victorian Hospital and Charities Commission. George made a further substantial contribution to the Alfred Hospital to enable the construction of a much-needed wing. It opened in 1943 as the Margaret Coles Maternity Wing (from 1955 Margaret Coles House) in honour of his wife who had joined him in energetically supporting several charities, among them the Melbourne District Nursing Society.

After World War II the retailing sector of G. J. Coles grew rapidly. Dominated by a few family dynasties, retailing was highly concentrated and Coles acquired many of the smaller chains. In the 1950s Selfridges (Australasia) Ltd, Penneys Ltd, F. & G. Stores Ltd and

Manton & Sons Ltd all succumbed to Coles' aggressive expansion policies.

In 1956 George retired as chairman and continued as a director. He remained comparatively aloof from the family business, concentrating more of his energy on political and philanthropic causes. He belonged to the Royal Melbourne and the Peninsula golf clubs (president 1954-58), as well as to the Athenaeum, the Victoria Racing and the Melbourne Cricket clubs, but his family and other intellectual interests took up most of his time. A committed Christian, he was a warden of St John's Anglican Church, Toorak.

George's support of conservative political ideas had helped to promote the foundation of the Institute of Public Affairs in 1943. Coles was president until 1957, but was not a significant financial backer and preferred to keep behind the scenes. He appears to have maintained a similar role at the National Bank of Australasia where he was a director (1946-68) and vice-chairman (1966-68).

Appointed C.B.E. in 1942, Coles was knighted in 1957 in recognition of his charitable activities. In his later years he gave money for building the Howard Florey [q.v.] Institute of Experimental Physiology and Medicine, opened at the University of Melbourne in 1963. Survived by his wife, son and three daughters, Sir George died on 4 December 1977 at his Toorak home and was cremated. His estate was sworn for probate at $986 486. The family business continued to expand, forming a partnership in 1968 with an American company in the establishment of K-Mart (Aust.) Ltd. With the takeover of the Myer operation in 1985, Coles Myer Ltd became the largest private employer in Australia.

A. M. Mitchell, *The Hospital South of the Yarra* (Melb, 1977); W. Ives, *Arthur William Coles* (Melb, 1982); J. McLaughlin, *Nothing over Half a Crown* (Main Ridge, Vic, 1991); *Nautilus*, Winter 1968, *Aust Women's Weekly*, Oct 1985; *Herald* (Melb), 6 Feb 1957, 12 Jan 1971; *Age* (Melb), *Australian*, *SMH* and *Financial Review*, 6 Dec 1977.

DIANE SYDENHAM

COLLEANO, CON (CORNELIUS) (1899-1973), tightwire artist, was born on 26 December 1899 at Lismore, New South Wales, third of ten children of native-born parents Cornelius Sullivan, showman, and his wife Vittorine Julia, née Robinson. Julia's father came from the Isle of St Thomas, West Indies, and her grandmother was an Aborigine; boxing and gambling were among her husband's sources of income. About 1907 the family settled at Lightning Ridge where the children received schooling and learned circus skills. By 1910 the family's little circus was travelling the State, but in hard times the 'Collinos' worked for other circuses, including Ashton's [q.v.7] in 1913 and Eroni Bros in 1914-15. Late in 1915 the family again started out on its own. From late 1918 Colleano's All Star Circus toured Queensland by special train. With their 'sable' features, the children endeared themselves as 'The Royal Hawaiian Troupe'. Practising up to seven hours a day, young Con endeavoured to perfect the almost impossible feet-to-feet forward somersault on the tightwire: one afternoon in 1919 he brought it off. In 1922 he was engaged by the Tivoli vaudeville circuit for £60 a week. Next year he performed at Fuller's [qq.v.8] New Theatre while other members of his family appeared at the Tivoli as 'Eight Akabah Arabs'.

Con went abroad with his fiancée Winifred Constance Stanley Trevail, a vaudeville soubrette who claimed descent from the earls of Derby. At Johannesburg, South Africa, in April 1924 Colleano adopted the Spanish costume that became his trademark. After a successful American début at the Hippodrome, New York, in September, he was soon engaged by Ringling Bros and Barnum & Bailey Combined Circus. Entering the centre ring, he made the traditional passes of a bullfighter; on mounting the wire, he gracefully performed tangos, jotas and fandangos; he concluded his twelve-minute act with the dangerous forward somersault. On 10 July 1926 at Detroit, Michigan, he married Winifred with Methodist Episcopal forms; they were to remain childless. She taught Colleano elements of style, dress and dancing, and was eventually his compere.

Billed as 'The Australian Wizard of the Wire', Colleano remained Ringlings' principal star into the 1930s, drawing a salary of $US1000 a week, with the privilege of his own apartment in the long circus train. Each winter he toured the vaudeville houses of Europe. The Spanish flavour of his act, as well as his Latinate appearance and name, beguiled many into presuming that he was a Spaniard. On one of his few visits to Sydney, he appeared at the Tivoli in 1937. He continued working in American circus and vaudeville, and gave television appearances on the Texaco Star Theatre programme in 1952. Con and the other Colleanos used his farm in Pennsylvania as a holiday retreat and practice ground.

Although he had become a naturalized American citizen in 1950, six years later Colleano came back to New South Wales where he ran the Albion Hotel at Forbes. Returning to the United States, he resumed work on the wire, giving his final performance, unnoticed, in Honolulu in 1960. He died on 13 November 1973 in his home at Miami, Florida. Winifred returned to Sydney where she died in 1986.

Colleano's name had been included in the Circus Hall of Fame, Sarasota, Florida, in 1966.

R. Croft-Cooke and W. S. Meadmore, *The Sawdust Ring* (Lond, 1951); A. D. H. Coxe, *A Seat at the Circus* (Lond, 1951); *Theatre* (Syd, Melb), 1 May 1923; *Variety*, 1 Oct 1924; *Pix*, 29 Jan 1938; *Warialda Standard*, 28 Nov 1910; *Western Star*, 10 Feb 1917; *SMH*, 28 May 1921, 19 Mar 1923, 29 June 1937, 10 Nov 1955; *NY Times*, 28, 30 Mar 1925, 13 Apr 1930; *Detroit Free Press*, 10 July 1926; *Miami Herald*, 31 Jan 1966, 15 Jan 1973; *Daily Mirror* (Syd), 3 Sept 1979; Colleano family papers (held by author, Glebe, Syd); information from Mr F. Braid, Ballina, NSW; family and personal information.
                                MARK VALENTINE ST LEON

COLLIER, JAMES DOUGLAS ARCHER (1893-1970), journalist and librarian, and **JOHN STANLEY GORDON** (1895-1968), architect, were born on 17 April 1893 at Hamilton-on-Forth, Ulverstone, Tasmania, and 2 May 1895 at Zeehan, sons of James John Collier, Congregational clergyman, and his wife Rosa Mabel, née Tomlins. Both boys were educated at Leslie House School (later Clemes [q.v.8] College), Hobart.

Five ft 9½ ins (176.5 cm) tall, with fair hair and hazel eyes, in 1909 Archer joined the Commercial Bank of Tasmania. From 1911 he was employed as a journalist on the Hobart *Mercury* and attended lectures at the University of Tasmania where he acquired a lifelong interest in literature. Enlisting in the Australian Imperial Force on 23 July 1915, Collier reached France in June 1916 as a corporal in the 47th Battalion. He was commissioned on 28 June 1917. At Passchendaele, Belgium, on 12 October he was wounded and made a prisoner of war; for some weeks he was believed to have been killed. Released from Germany, he arrived in England in February 1919 and was given leave to study journalism at the Polytechnic Institution, London. In September he embarked for Australia where he had the mixed pleasure of reading his own obituary. When his A.I.F. appointment terminated on 18 December, he rejoined the *Mercury* and served as Tasmania district president (1921-22) of the Australian Journalists' Association.

Although he lacked professional qualifications, in 1922 Archer Collier was appointed librarian of the Tasmanian Public Library. On 28 February 1923 he married Vivien Erskine Copeland Dean in St David's Anglican Cathedral, Hobart. A regular contributor of literary articles and reviews to newspapers and periodicals, he edited the second volume of R. W. Giblin's [q.v.8] *The Early History of Tasmania* (1939), to which he also contributed several chapters.

Archer Collier was a member (president 1944-46) of the Australian Institute of Librarians (later the Library Association of Australia) from its foundation in 1937. In 1943 Kenneth Binns [q.v.7], librarian of the Commonwealth National Library, praised his 'able and untiring efforts in the face of continued discouragement and difficulty' in providing library services for the people of Tasmania. Next year Collier was appointed Tasmania's first State librarian; he was to hold the post until his retirement in 1954. He was actively involved in his work and under his aegis much progress was made. His most important contribution was in developing a State-wide children's library service, later used as a model by overseas librarians.

Under the auspices of the British Council, the Carnegie Corporation of New York and the Tasmanian government, Collier spent nine months in 1951 studying library developments in Britain and the United States of America. He was a council-member (1943-50) of the University of Tasmania, and served on the Adult Education Board and on the central committee of the Associated Youth Clubs. A founding member of the Hobart Remembrance Club, he was State president of the Workers' Educational Association, and belonged to the Tasmanian Theatre and Fine Arts Society and to the Hobart Orchestral Society. The Collier Room at the State Library was named in Archer's honour. Survived by his wife, son and three daughters, he died on 9 July 1970 in Hobart and was cremated.

John Collier enrolled at the University of Tasmania in 1913, then enlisted in the A.I.F. on 20 August 1914. Sent to Egypt with the 7th Battalion, he was discharged in April 1915 on being commissioned in the British Army. He saw action in the Middle East and on the Western Front with the East Lancashire Regiment. Returning home in 1919, he resumed his studies, graduating B.A. (1922) from the University of Tasmania and B.Arch. (1924) from the University of Sydney.

In 1925 Collier entered the New South Wales Public Service and from February 1937 worked as an architectural draftsman in the Department of Works and Local Government. Mobilized in November 1940, he was posted to the Militia's 54th Battalion and served in Western Australia. By September 1942 he had risen to lieutenant colonel and had command of the battalion. His appointment terminated on 30 June 1944. Returning to Sydney that year, he joined the Housing Commission of New South Wales as deputy chief architect, a position he held until his retirement in 1955. Five ft 8½ ins (174 cm) tall, with a dark complexion, hazel eyes and brown hair, John was a member of the Legacy Club of Sydney. He died, unmarried, on

27 October 1968 at Rose Bay, Sydney, and was cremated with Anglican rites.

Cyclopedia of Tasmania (Hob, 1931); R. Munn and E. R. Pitt, *Australian Libraries* (Melb, 1935); K. Binns, *Library Services in Tasmania* (Hob, 1943); Lib Assn of Aust (Tas Branch), *Library Opinion*, 2, no 11, Nov 1954; *Mercury* (Hob), 5 June 1951, 17 May 1954, 29 Oct 1968, 10 July 1970.

JOHN LEVETT

COLLIER, MARIE ELIZABETH (1927-1971), dramatic soprano, was born on 16 April 1927 at Ballarat, Victoria, daughter of THOMAS ROBINSON COLLIER (1894-1962), railway employee, and his wife Annie Marie, née Bechaz, both Victorian born. Thomas enlisted in the Australian Imperial Force on 14 July 1915, was commissioned in January 1917 and was attached to the 8th Brigade as signal officer. For maintaining communications under fire near Ypres, Belgium, in October, he was awarded the Military Cross. At Corbie, France, on 23 April 1918, though shelled and almost blinded by gas, he kept his lines open, winning a Bar to his M.C. Twice mentioned in dispatches, he returned to Australia where his appointment terminated on 19 November 1919. He resumed work with the Victorian Railways and was in turn a porter, station master, train controller, staff superintendent (from 1946) and chief traffic manager (from 1956). During World War II he had served at Land Headquarters, Melbourne, becoming director of transportation and rising to honorary colonel. He died on 3 April 1962.

Marie was educated at Camberwell High School. A choir-member at St John's Anglican Church, Camberwell, she was involved in the Youth Operatic Society's Gilbert and Sullivan productions. On leaving school she worked as a pharmacist's assistant. When a broken arm prevented her from playing the piano, she began to train as a singer. In 1948 she won a scholarship to the University Conservatorium of Music and completed the first year of a diploma. Short of money, and discouraged by the formality of the conservatorium's teaching methods, she joined the chorus of a J. C. Williamson [q.v.6] Ltd production of *Oklahoma*. She turned for tuition to Katherine Wielaert who, after eighteen months of private lessons, sent her to classes with Gertrude Johnson [q.v.], director of the National Theatre Movement's opera school.

On 18 March 1952 Collier made her operatic debut as Santuzza in Mascagni's *Cavalleria Rusticana* with the National Theatre Opera Company. She was an instant success. So many offers were received that Wielaert advised her to make singing her career. On 10 December that year she married a civil engineer Victor Benjamin Vorweg in the chapel of Melbourne Church of England Grammar School.

Her first dramatic success came in 1953 as Magda Sorel in Menotti's *The Consul* at the Melbourne Arts Festival organized by Johnson's N.T.M. On 1 March 1954 Collier appeared as Giulietta in Offenbach's *Tales of Hoffmann* at the Princess Theatre in the presence of Queen Elizabeth II; late that year she also appeared as Helen of Troy in a disastrously miscast production of Offenbach's *La Belle Hélène.*

Assisted by a grant from the Hawthorn City Council, in early 1955 Collier left for Milan, Italy, where she studied with Ugo Benevenuto-Giusti. The 7th Earl of Harewood, artistic director of the Royal Opera House, Covent Garden, London, heard her sing at Milan and recommended her to Rafael Kubelik, the local musical director. In 1956 she entered into a contract with the Royal Opera Company and won a three-year scholarship for advanced study offered by the Worshipful Company of Musicians. Her early roles at Covent Garden included Giulietta in *Tales of Hoffmann*, the First Lady in Mozart's *The Magic Flute*, Polyxena in Berlioz's *The Trojans* and Musetta in Puccini's *La Bohème.* In May 1960 Evan Senior described her Musetta as 'the most astonishing and effective playing and full-voiced singing of the role I have ever heard or seen'.

On loan to Sadler's Wells for the 1959-60 season, Collier performed with the regular company and the New Opera Group. In 1960 she sang three title roles for the first time: Madam Butterfly, Katya Kabanova and Tosca. She also appeared in lighter parts for the group, notably Concepcion in Ravel's *L'Heure Espagnol* in 1961.

Back at Covent Garden, Collier sang Santuzza in Franco Zeffirelli's production of *Cavalleria Rusticana*, Cio-Cio San in *Madama Butterfly*, Marie in *Wozzeck* and Elizabeth in *Don Carlos*. In 1962 she toured South America with the Royal Opera Company, appearing in the first performance of Britten's *Midsummer Night's Dream* at the Teatro Colon, Buenos Aires. Later that year she created the role of Hecuba in Tippett's *King Priam*, singing it at Covent Garden and at Coventry Cathedral. In January 1963 Collier sang her first Tosca at Covent Garden, with Tito Gobbi as Scarpia. Harold Rosenthal wrote: 'she was vocally in thrilling form . . . There is no denying that this Australian soprano possesses one of the most vibrantly exciting and "Italianate" voices now to be heard'.

Collier's international reputation was established when she sang both the title role in the first Western performance of Shostakovich's *Katerina Ismailova* at Covent Garden on 2 December 1963 (in the presence of the composer) and the role of Emilia Marty in Janacek's *The Makropulos Case* at Sadler's Wells in February 1964. At the end of that month she returned to Australia to appear— at the composer's request—in Walton's *Troilus and Cressida* at the Adelaide Festival of Arts.

From that time Collier was in demand not only for modern roles, but for the regular, lyric-dramatic parts. She appeared in Vienna, at the Metropolitan Opera House, New York, and at San Francisco, with considerable success. In May 1964 she again sang Tosca at Covent Garden: her performance was compared with that of Maria Callas who had sung the role there only a few months before, and Arthur Jacobs declared that Collier's was the better. When Callas cancelled three performances as Tosca scheduled for 1965, Collier replaced her. After a representative of La Scala had heard only one rehearsal, a contract was offered for Collier to sing at Milan. Reviewers everywhere sounded her praises. In 1966 she was awarded the Harriet Cohen international musical medal. The pace, however, increased season by season, with international tours and the filming of *Tosca* and of *Il Tabarro* with Gobbi. During 1967, while singing in twenty major opera houses, she was under doctor's orders to rest, but the pressure to consolidate her career was too tempting.

International stardom was not, for Collier, a synonym for success. She made no secret of her loneliness and was once reported as saying: 'When rehearsals are over and you leave the theatre, there's nothing'. It was this public statement that led to rumours of suicide when her sudden death was announced on 8 December 1971. She had died of intercranial haemorrhage and a fractured skull in Charing Cross Hospital, London, after falling from a window of her London flat. Her blood-alcohol level was .28. The coroner returned a verdict of accidental death. Survived by her husband, daughter and three sons, Marie Collier was cremated.

B. and F. Mackenzie, *Singers of Australia* (Melb, 1967); J. Cargher, *Opera and Ballet in Australia* (Syd, 1977); D. Arundell, *The Story of Sadler's Wells 1683-1977* (Lond, 1978); A. Saint et al, *A History of the Royal Opera House Convent Garden 1732-1982* (Lond, 1982); *People* (Syd), 15 July 1953; *Age* (Melb), 5 Nov 1960, 5 Apr 1962, 26 Nov 1964, 9, 16 Dec 1971; *The Times*, 29 Jan 1963, 22 Feb, 9 Dec 1971; *SMH*, 3 July 1965, 9 Dec, 14 Dec 1971; *Canb Times*, 13 Jan 1967, 9, 17 Dec 1971; *Herald* (Melb), 19 Jan, 20 Mar 1967, 8 Dec 1971.

MAUREEN THÉRÈSE RADIC

COLLINS, SIR ARCHIBALD JOHN (1890-1955), consultant physician, was born on 19 June 1890 at Lismore, New South Wales, fourth child of James Patrick Collins, a schoolteacher from Ireland, and his native-born wife Annie Maria, née Long. Educated at Manly Public and Fort Street Model schools, he graduated with first-class honours from the University of Sydney (M.B., Ch.M., 1913). Although he was awarded a Walter and Eliza Hall [qq.v.9] travelling scholarship, he did not take it up, becoming instead a resident medical officer at Royal Prince Alfred Hospital.

Appointed captain in the Australian Army Medical Corps, Australian Imperial Force, on 18 November 1915, Collins served in Egypt and on the Western Front. While with the 12th Field Ambulance in 1918, he was awarded the Military Cross for attending wounded at the front line and the Distinguished Service Order for evacuating casualties under fire. Promoted major and mentioned in dispatches, he returned to Australia where his appointment terminated on 27 October 1919. At St Francis's Catholic Church, Melbourne, on 31 July 1920 he married a nurse Clotilde Donnelly.

That year Collins returned to R.P.A.H. as medical superintendent. On being appointed honorary assistant physician in 1923, he began private practice as a consultant in Macquarie Street. He subsequently obtained appointments at several other hospitals, but R.P.A.H. remained his main base as a physician and teacher. There he became honorary physician (1934-50), honorary consulting physician (1950-55) and a member (1935-55) of the board of directors. As a physician he was sound, conservative and thorough. His teaching was orthodox, clear and practical.

At the University of Sydney, Collins was lecturer in therapeutics (1935-50) and in clinical medicine (1940-50), as well as a fellow (1939-54) of the senate. He had been elected a foundation fellow of the Royal Australasian College of Physicians in 1938. A consulting physician (from 1941) to the Royal Australian Navy, in 1947 he received the rank of honorary surgeon captain.

Collins was a leading figure in the British Medical Association in Australia, and a councillor (1930-55) and president (1934) of the State branch. As a member (1945-55; president 1951-55) of the federal council, he was involved in the long-running battle between the B.M.A. (representing an unusually united medical profession) and the Chifley [q.v.] government over Labor's attempts to nationalize health services. When Sir Earle Page [q.v.11], minister for health in the Menzies [q.v.] government, established his National Health Service in 1953, Collins was appointed to chair two of its influential advisory committees. He was knighted in 1955.

Tall and straight, Collins appeared dignified and imposing, but his ready smile and habit of blinking made him approachable. He was respected and well liked, and affectionately known as Archie. In public life he was determined; in private he was relaxed and sociable. He enjoyed playing bridge with friends and was intensely proud of his family. Sir Archibald died of acute myocardial infarction on 24 June 1955 at his Killara home and was cremated with Presbyterian forms; his wife and two sons survived him. A portrait by his colleague Grant Lindeman is held by Collins's family.

G. E. Hall and A. Cousins (eds), *Book of Remembrance of the University of Sydney in the War 1914-1918* (Syd, 1939); G. L. McDonald (ed), *Roll of the Royal Australasian College of Physicians*, 1, 1939-1975 (Syd, 1988); *MJA*, 13 Aug 1955, pp 38, 266, 432; Univ Syd, *Gazette*, Nov 1955; Collins file (Roy A'sian College of Physicians Archives, Syd).

G. L. McDONALD

COLLINS, HAROLD HENRY (1887-1962), farmer and politician, was born on 9 August 1887 at Alexandra, Victoria, fourth child of native-born parents George William Collins, farmer, and his wife Mary Anne Sophia, née Coster. Harold was educated at Kings College, Clifton Hill, Melbourne. Having travelled in New South Wales and New Zealand, he arrived in Queensland in 1909 on horseback with all his belongings in a swag. He took various jobs, serving as overseer and bookkeeper for the Queensland Federal Shearing Co. and as manager of a sheep-station in the Hughenden district, before settling in 1913 as a dairy-farmer and maize-grower on the recently opened Atherton tableland. There, at Rowan Lodge, on 16 February 1915 Collins married with Presbyterian forms Barbara Catherine Annie McCraw (d. 1958); they were to remain childless.

He rose through the usual rural *cursus honorum*. Elected to the Tinaroo Shire Council in 1916, he was president (1922-25) of the Atherton Agricultural Show Society, a member (from 1923) of the maize marketing board, president (1928-29) of the Atherton Hospital Board and a member (1932-35) of the Cairns Harbour Board. With this record Collins was just the sort of successful local identity whom the Forgan Smith [q.v.11] government hoped to recruit as a parliamentary candidate. Endorsed by the Australian Labor Party, on 11 May 1935 he won the seat of Cook in the Queensland Legislative Assembly; following a redistribution in 1950, he held Tablelands until 1957. His speeches—thoughtful, well prepared and prolix—were mostly based on his farming experience. He was an advocate of co-operative societies and orderly marketing. Appointed secretary for agriculture and stock in 1946, he held the portfolio for what was then a record period of

eleven years. Collins presided over the post-war expansion of Queensland's agriculture soundly, and on the whole efficiently, despite one or two failures—such as the British-funded Peak Downs project for raising sorghum and pigs, and the establishment of irrigated tobacco-growing at Clare, on the Lower Burdekin.

During his term of office the Department of Agriculture oversaw a largely successful soldier-settlement scheme, fostered increased grain production (especially of sorghum) and encouraged the bulk handling of sugar for export during a period of great expansion. His own constituency saw the construction of Queensland's second largest reservoir at Tinaroo in the mid-1950s, which brought temporary benefit to local tobacco-growers. A successful fighter in cabinet for departmental funding, Collins was a gentlemanly and popular member of parliament; described as 'a placid unruffled debater', he spoke slowly, 'in weighty, measured tones with a somewhat precise and pedantic manner'.

The even tenor of his career was eventually destroyed by the Labor 'split' of 1957. Like all but one of his cabinet colleagues, Collins sided with V. C. Gair [q.v.] in forming the Queensland Labor Party, and lost his seat in the election that year. He died on 12 July 1962 in Brisbane; after a state funeral, he was buried with Anglican rites in Hemmant cemetery. Tall and strapping when young, in his later life photographs show him as bald, bespectacled and burly, virtually a clone of half the Queensland cabinet ministers of that period.

C. Lack (comp), *Three Decades of Queensland Political History, 1929-1960* (Brisb, 1962); *Qld Agr J*, Apr 1946; *Courier-Mail*, 13 July 1962.

G. C. BOLTON

COLLINS, THOMAS JOSEPH (1884-1945), politician and stock and station agent, was born on 6 April 1884 at Yass, New South Wales, eighth child of John Collins, storekeeper, and his wife Mary, née Hartigan, both Irish born. Educated at a local Catholic school, in 1902 Tom enlisted in the 5th Battalion, Australian Commonwealth Horse, to fight in the South African War. The unit embarked in May, but hostilities ended before its arrival and he was back in Australia by August.

About 1906 Collins went to Young where he worked in the office of C. H. Ellerman & Co., stock and station agents. In February 1911 he started his own agency with a capital of £7. The business prospered. By the mid-1920s his firm, Collins, Ellerman & Co., was one of the largest stock and property businesses in the State, with connexions in

Queensland, Victoria and South Australia. He also operated various sheep- and cattle-runs. Collins had married Ruby Violet Summerhayes with Catholic rites on 17 February 1914 in her father's house at Young; Blair Athol, a nearby property, was to be their home for many years.

Long interested in politics, he had contested the Federal seat of Newcastle in 1913 and was a close associate of Charles Hardy [q.v.9], leader of the Riverina Movement. In the elections of December 1931 Collins defeated P. J. Moloney [q.v.10] (Australian Labor Party) for the seat of Hume and entered the House of Representatives as a Country Party member. Although Collins could be an entertaining orator, he was never an important parliamentary performer. His speeches were mainly on rural issues, such as postal and telecommunications services to country regions, and on the development of the Northern Territory, which he visited in 1935. A tactful presiding officer, he served as a temporary chairman (1934-40) and deputy-chairman (1940) of committees. He was, as well, a member (1937-40) of the joint standing committee on public works.

Collins was involved in the conflict between (Sir) Robert Menzies [q.v.] and Sir Earle Page [q.v.11] over the leadership of the United Australia Party-Country Party coalition, following the death of J. A. Lyons [q.v.10] on 7 April 1939. To prevent Menzies from becoming prime minister, Page tried to exploit divisions within the U.A.P. On 19 April Collins heightened speculation about Page's intentions by a radio broadcast in which he praised the accomplishments of Page, a man who had been 'five times Acting Prime Minister'. Next day Page attacked Menzies in parliament, dismaying his own supporters and causing (Sir) Arthur Fadden and B. H. Corser [qq.v.] to resign from the Country Party. Collins, too, dissociated himself from Page's comments. A few days later he and Albert Badman announced that they would not attend meetings of the parliamentary party while Page remained leader.

On 26 April 1939 Menzies formed a U.A.P. ministry. Page resigned in September as leader of the Country Party. In the election to choose his successor, Collins and his three breakaway colleagues were not permitted to vote. As a result, Page's supporter Archie Cameron [q.v.] became leader, prolonging the breach with Menzies and the division within the Country Party. Collins and the others returned to the party in November, but the coalition was not restored until 14 March 1940. When Menzies reconstructed his government in October, he made Collins minister assisting the prime minister (dealing with external territories) and minister assisting the minister for the interior. On 26 June

1941 Collins was appointed postmaster-general and held office until Labor took power on 7 October. He lost his seat in the 1943 general elections.

In his home town Collins was known for his charitable outlook, gifts as an entertainer, skill as a judge and breeder of livestock, and support of football, cricket, tennis and polo. He considered again standing for parliament, but died suddenly of coronary sclerosis on 15 April 1945 at Young and was buried in the local cemetery. His wife and daughter survived him.

P. Hasluck, *The Government and the People 1939-1941* (Canb, 1952); U. Ellis, *A History of the Australian Country Party* (Melb, 1963); *Argus*, 28 July 1934, 24, 25 Apr, 6 May, 15 Nov 1939, 19 Aug 1940; *Canb Times*, 19-21, 28, 29 Apr, 4, 5 May 1939, 17, 20 Apr 1945; *Age*, 22 Apr, 5, 6 May 1939; *SMH*, 14 Sept 1939, 17, 20 Apr 1945; *Young Witness*, 17 Apr 1945.   H. M. BOOT

COLLINS, VERNON LESLIE (1909-1978), medical practitioner, was born on 10 November 1909 at Nhill, Victoria, third child of John Collins, farmer, and his wife Susan Alice, née Hann, both Victorian born. Vernon was educated at Horsham High School and the University of Melbourne (M.B., B.S., 1933; M.D., 1936). After residencies at Royal Melbourne Hospital (1934-36) and the (Royal) Children's Hospital (1936), he was medical superintendent at the latter institution in 1937-39. He published a monograph, *Infant Feeding* (1939), which became a standard text.

In London, in 1940 Collins was elected a member of the Royal College of Physicians and awarded a diploma of child health by the Royal College of Surgeons. At St Joseph's Catholic Church, Highgate Hill, on 20 July that year he married a nurse Mary Josephine O'Shea. He worked at North Middlesex County Hospital until 1946 as full-time physician to adults and also had responsibility for the children's ward.

Returning to the (Royal) Children's Hospital, Melbourne, Collins was honorary physician to out-patients (from 1946) and then to in-patients (from 1948). Experience had convinced him that the hospital's medical administration needed restructuring if modern advances in knowledge, training methods and clinical research were to be successfully implemented. His views were shared by the new lady superintendent Lucy de Neeve and the president Lady Latham [qq.v.]. In 1949 Collins was appointed first medical director, responsible for all medical and ancillary services, and able to control and initiate policy.

The three objects of the (Royal) Children's

Hospital, as Collins saw them, were patient-care, research and teaching. His prime achievement in the area of patient-care was to substitute a senior, salaried staff for the time-honoured system of honorary medical officers. Clinical assistants were replaced by senior specialists on a salaried, sessional basis. The large departments were administered by paid, full-time specialists with a salaried staff. The existing clinical research unit was able to expand. Closely integrated with the hospital, it comprised a small research ward with an independent nursing staff and adjacent laboratories. On the teaching side, Collins insisted that undergraduates receive instruction from salaried, senior doctors, both in the wards and the clinics.

In 1959 Collins became the first occupant of the Stevenson chair of child health (later paediatrics) at the University of Melbourne. He remained in close contact with the R.C.H. and represented the university on its committee of management, reinforcing the hospital's teaching role. At the university he was a fellow of Queen's College.

Honorary consulting paediatrician to the Alfred, the Royal Women's, the Mercy and the Prince Henry hospitals, Collins was president of the Paediatric Society of Victoria (1955) and of the Australian Paediatric Association (1969-70). He was a councillor (1952-59) of the British Medical Association in Australia and a member (1960-65) of the National Health and Medical Research Council, whose child-health committee he chaired (1966-69). His recreations were gardening and tennis; in his early years he had played the violin, and music consoled him when in 1969 he developed Parkinson's disease. Appointed C.B.E. in 1973, he retired in 1975. He died on 24 March 1978 at his Hawthorn home and was cremated; his wife and two sons survived him.

L. Gardiner, *Royal Children's Hospital Melbourne 1870-1970* (Melb, 1970); K. F. Russell, *The Melbourne Medical School 1862-1962* (Melb, 1977); H. Williams, *From Charity to Teaching Hospital* (Melb, 1989); *Univ Melb Gazette*, Oct 1959, p 11; *Herald* (Melb), 6 Jan 1975; information from Dr K. Collins, Balwyn, and Mr D. Collins, Blackburn, Melb.

LYNDSAY GARDINER

COLLOCOTT, ERNEST EDGAR VYVYAN (1886-1970), missionary, scholar and peace activist, was born on 7 June 1886 at Northcote, Melbourne, son of Victorian-born parents Alfred John Collocott, a Methodist minister who had recently returned from Fiji, and his wife Alice Jane, née Bickford. Educated from 1898 at Geelong College (dux 1902) and at the University of Melbourne (B.A., 1907; M.A., 1909; Litt.D., 1928),

Edgar graduated with honours in classical philology. On 29 December 1909 at Randwick, Sydney, he married a cousin Edith Idabelle Bickford; they were to have five sons. After a stint of schoolteaching, he entered the Methodist ministry in 1911.

That year Collocott sailed with his wife to Tonga. He served as a missionary in the Ha'apai circuit before becoming principal of Tupou College, Nuku'alofa, in 1915. While there he completed a bachelor of divinity (1916) by correspondence with the University of London, and began a study of the traditional history and culture of the Tongan people. From 1920 to 1921 he entertained E. W. Gifford and W. C. McKern, anthropologists employed by the Bernice P. Bishop Museum in Honolulu, providing them with valuable contacts and ethnographic material. In 1921 he began teaching in English at the college's new site at Nafualu. An ardent educationist, cricketer and tennis player, he had left his mark on the institution when his family's ill health led him to return with them to Melbourne in 1924. Collocott's reputation as a scholar increased with the publication of *Koe Ta'u'e Teau . . .* (London, 1926) and *Tales and Poems of Tonga* (Honolulu, 1928), and with his doctorate of letters.

Financial secretary (1924-29) of the Albury district of the Methodist Church of Australasia, Collocott was chairman (1929-30) of the Cootamundra district while he was based at Temora, New South Wales. From 1931 he was successively minister at Bowral, Strathfield, Stanmore, Kiama, East Maitland and Dural; he retired to Epping in 1952. A widower, he had married Dorothy Miriam Williams on 7 May 1949 at the Methodist Church, Dural.

Although he lectured on Tongan affairs, worked on an English-language history of Tonga and taught philosophy to divinity students, Collocott devoted much of his later years to the cause of peace. He was president (1933) of the Peace Pledge Union, chairman (1953-55) of the New South Wales Peace Council, a member of the Fellowship of Reconciliation and an editor of the pacifist journal, *Peacemaker*. Sometime president of the Democratic Rights Council in New South Wales, he took a leading role in the Methodist Christian Socialist Union and joined the Australian Labor Party in 1957.

In 1938 at the Railway Institute, Sydney, he had made his first public speech on international friendship. Vice-president (1939-45) of the Wollongong branch of the Friendship with Russia League, he was active in the Medical Aid to Russia movement. Collocott was national chairman in 1953 of the Australia-Soviet Friendship Society (later the Australia-U.S.S.R. Society), and visited the Soviet Union that year and in 1962. Survived by his wife and by two sons of his first marriage, he died on 9 October 1970 at Dundas and was cremated.

PIM, Aug 1937, May 1944, July 1953; Aust-USSR Soc, *Friendship*, 1, no 7, Aug 1957, 7, no 2, Autumn 1963, 13, no 1, Jan 1971; *Pambu*, no 9, Apr 1969, p 6; *SMH*, 4 Oct 1924, 22 June 1929, 23 Mar 1959; *Methodist* (Syd), 8 Dec 1962, 7 Nov 1970; Collocott papers (ML *and* Alexander Turnbull L, Wellington, NZ).   NIEL GUNSON

COLMAN, SIR GEORGE STANLEY (1884-1966), businessman, was born on 10 May 1884 at Narrandera, New South Wales, son of George Colman, a selector from Ireland, and his Australian-born wife Mary, née Cambage. Raised as an Anglican, Stanley was educated at St John's Grammar School, Parramatta. He began his business career as a youth in 1900, in the shipping department of G. S. Yuill & Co. Ltd, Sydney, before transferring in 1905 to Yuill's Melbourne office as assistant-manager and to the Brisbane office in 1907 as manager. Next year he moved to its branch in Manila, Philippine Islands, where he managed (from 1910) the shipping, cold storage and merchandising operations.

In 1913 Colman returned to Brisbane as general manager of the Queensland Meat Export Co. Ltd; he was also general manager and director of the Australian Stock Breeders' Co. Ltd. At St John's Anglican Cathedral on 27 April 1916 he married a nurse Marion Dalrymple. In 1926 he joined the prominent, London-based pastoral and sugar enterprise, Australian Estates & Mortgage Co. Ltd (later Australian Estates Co. Ltd), as assistant general manager in Melbourne. The Australian general manager N. C. Clapperton had assured the London principals that Colman would fulfil the business duties and social obligations with 'ability and dignity'. Colman became joint general manager in 1928 and sole general manager in 1931. His executive responsibilities spread to associated companies of Australian Estates. He was managing director of Amalgamated Sugar Mills Ltd (Queensland), chairman of directors of Meredith, Menzies Co. (Melbourne), and a director of the Trustees, Executors & Agency Co. Ltd, the National Mutual Life Association of Australasia Ltd and Spicers (Australia) Ltd.

Colman held public office as vice-consul (1923-26) for Argentina in Brisbane, chairman (1930) of the Woolbrokers' Association and member of the Council for Scientific and Industrial Research. He sat on a committee appointed in 1932 by the assistant-treasurer S. M. (Viscount) Bruce [q.v.7] to examine unemployment and on a royal commission appointed in 1941 by the Fadden [q.v.]

government to inquire into hire purchase. He was, as well, a council-member of the Melbourne Chamber of Commerce and served on the University of Melbourne's appointments board. As a founding member and deputy-chairman of the Business Archives Council of Australia (Victorian branch), he promoted belief in the values of historical inquiry, understanding and enlightenment.

From the late 1950s Colman's formal business commitments contracted, leaving him more time for his recreations of golf and tennis. A president (1949) of the Melbourne Club, he was also a member of the Australian (Melbourne), Queensland, Union (Sydney) and Reform (London) clubs, and belonged to Round Table. He was known to his associates and to his family as a warm, sympathetic and encouraging man. Appointed C.B.E. in 1937, he was knighted in 1965. Sir Stanley died on 4 February 1966 in East Melbourne and was buried in Melbourne general cemetery; his wife, daughter and two sons survived him.

L. Foster, *High Hopes* (Melb, 1986); *SMH*, 5 July 1926, 1 Mar 1928, 1 Jan 1931, 11 May 1937, 30 Sept 1940, 1 Apr 1947, 15 July 1950, 12 June 1965; *Age* (Melb) and *Sun News-Pictorial*, 7 Feb 1966; Aust Estates Co records (Univ Melb Archives); information from Mr J. S. and Dr R. D. Kerr, St Lucia, Brisb.   FRANK STRAHAN

COLSON, EDMUND ALBERT (1881-1950), explorer and bushman, was born on 3 June 1881 at Richmans Creek, near Quorn, South Australia, eldest of eight children of Peter Errick Colson (Carlsen), a farmer from Sweden, and his second wife Ellen Amy, née Lines, who was English born. Educated at Yatina Public School, Ted became a voracious reader and developed a retentive memory. In 1896 he and his father sailed to Western Australia and walked 150 miles (241 km) to the Norseman goldfields. Ted stated that he was a contractor when he married a domestic servant Alice Jane Horne on 7 December 1904 at the Christian Chapel, Kalgoorlie; they were to remain childless. He took a job at Brunswick Junction in the south-west of the State before moving in 1917 to Victoria, where he worked on the construction of the Maroondah dam and in 1926 began a motor transport service between Healesville and Melbourne. Next year he was employed in extending the railway north of Oodnadatta, South Australia. In 1931 he leased Blood Creek station at Abminga, north-west of Oodnadatta; there he ran sheep, tended the government bore and kept a store.

In 1928 Colson had explored west of the Goyder River for 300 miles (483 km) beyond Mount Irwin station. Familiar with the Musgrave Ranges, he opened the route north from Moorilyanna Hill and Ernabella Creek to Kelly Hills and Opparinna Creek. He was cameleer and guide on Michael Terry's 1930 expeditions to the Petermann and Tomkinson ranges, and conducted A. P. Elkin [q.v.] on his anthropological investigations west of Charlotte Waters. Colson understood the rites, customs and dialects of several Aboriginal tribes. Over camp fires he sang, told yarns and indulged his talent for mimicry. Equally resourceful with camels and motorcars, he had a genius for mending and adapting equipment. He was burly and strong, with a shock of hair and a bristling moustache. Gentle, cheerful and unassuming, he was trusted both by Aborigines and by Whites. He was a Freemason and a district master of the Loyal Orange Institution of South Australia.

The triumph of Colson's explorations was his crossing of the Simpson Desert, which had previously defeated Charles Sturt and David Lindsay [qq.v.2,10]. Prompted by an exceptionally wet season and accompanied only by young Eringa Peter of the Antakurinya tribe, Colson set out from Blood Creek on 26 May 1936. He led a train of five camels eastward along the 26th parallel, clambering over a thousand steep, red sand-ridges, and naming Alice Hills, Glen Joyce and Lake Tamblyn. Navigating by compass, he reached his goal, Poeppel's Corner, the point where the Queensland, Northern Territory and South Australian borders met. Ted and Peter walked into the Birdsville pub, Queensland, on 11 June. Three days later they headed back, nailing a tin plate—bearing the date and Colson's initials—to the peg at Poeppel's Corner. After making a detour southwards, they arrived home on 29 June, having traversed more than 550 miles (885 km) in thirty-five days. In that exceptional season, the desert, said Colson, was 'one vast field of herbage, grass and shrubs'.

He continued to pioneer routes through Central Australia and to study Aboriginal culture. The South Australian Museum holds his manuscript, 'Legend of the Innja', and his 1931-32 correspondence with N. B. Tindale about Antakurinya legends. Ted moved to Finke in the Northern Territory where he established Colson Trading Co. Driving from Adelaide in a new Land Rover, he hit an electricity pole near Balaklava and died from injuries on 27 February 1950. He was buried in Centennial Park cemetery, Adelaide. A memorial cairn was erected at Birdsville in 1973.

M. Terry, *Untold Miles* (Lond, 1932); M. Shephard, *The Simpson Desert* (forthcoming); *Geog J*, 78, 1931, p 341; *PRGSSA*, 41, 1939-40, p 10; *Sth Australiana*, 18, no 1, Mar 1979, p 3; *Sun News-Pictorial*, 20 June 1936; *Advertiser* (Adel), 16-19 June, 15 July 1936, 28 Feb 1950; *Chronicle* (Adel), 8 Aug 1940; *Herald* (Melb), 9 July 1956, 11 June 1986; M. Terry, Log of Expedition to the Petermann and Tomkinson Ranges, ms, 1930 (RGSSA, Adel); Colson papers (Mort L *and* Anthropology Archives, SA Museum); file DL 2841/35 (SA Dept of Lands, Adel).
C. J. HORNE

COLVIN, GEORGE EDWARD (1903-1975), army officer, company manager and community worker, was born on 22 April 1903 in Melbourne, son of native-born parents George Edward Colvin, labourer, and his wife Hannah Victoria, née Sweetingham. Educated at Victoria Park State School, at the age of 12 George junior joined the cadets. The family moved to Sydney in 1919 where he served part time with the 1st Cavalry Division Signals from 1921. Commissioned lieutenant on 1 July 1925 and promoted captain in 1930, he transferred to the Reserve of Officers in November 1931; meanwhile, he continued to work as a salesman. On 29 December 1934 he married Florence Hannah Williams at St Jude's Anglican Church, Randwick; they were later to be divorced.

Resuming his Militia service in 1939, Colvin was appointed to the Australian Imperial Force on 3 March 1940 and posted to the 2/13th Battalion in May. The unit arrived at Suez in November. While engaged in the defence of Tobruk, Libya, he was promoted major in September 1941. After Lieutenant Colonel F. A. Burrows [q.v.] was wounded at Ed Duda on 1 December, Colvin took temporary command of the battalion. He was second-in-command to Lieutenant Colonel R. W. N. Turner when the battle of El Alamein, Egypt, began on 23 October 1942. The following day Turner was mortally wounded and the battalion, which had suffered heavy losses, was disorganized and pinned down. Colvin took over, advanced with his soldiers and held firm against a counter-attack. Promoted lieutenant colonel and confirmed in command, on 28 October he conducted a successful assault across unknown, booby-trapped ground to the Fig Orchard and beyond. Next morning he was concussed by a shell-blast and evacuated. For his deeds he was awarded the Distinguished Service Order.

Back in Australia, from February to July 1943 the battalion trained in New South Wales and North Queensland before moving to Milne Bay, Papua. On 4 September it landed at Yellow Beach for the offensive against nearby Lae, New Guinea, and eighteen days later took part in the amphibious assault on Finschhafen. Always well forward when his troops were in action, Colvin directed the decisive attack at Kakakog on 1 October which led to the fall of Finschhafen. His enthusiasm ensured a high *esprit de corps* in his unit. Following engagements on the Sattelberg Road and in the advance up the Huon Peninsula, the battalion returned home in March 1944. Colvin was awarded a Bar to his D.S.O.

Having left Queensland in April 1945, he and his men embarked from Morotai and landed in Brunei on 10 June. They were deployed north of the Brooketon-Brunei Road, then in the Lutong-Miri region until hostilities ceased in August. From elements of the 9th Division, Colvin formed the 66th Battalion which he commanded in Japan between February 1946 and June 1947. He transferred to the Reserve of Officers on 16 December in Sydney and was active in the Citizen Military Forces in the 1950s. On 22 November 1952 he married a widow Alma Beryl ('Pat') Bolger, née Ryan, at St Stephen's Presbyterian Church, Sydney.

Colvin was State manager (1952-68) of Kelvinator Australia Ltd and served on the council of the Electrical and Radio Development Association of New South Wales. Presiding (1960-63 and 1965-75) over the State branch of the Royal Commonwealth Society, he was elected national president in 1966. Pat chaired the local auxiliary for twenty-five years and was appointed M.B.E. (1973). Vice-president of the Royal New South Wales Institution for Deaf and Blind Children, in 1968 Colvin was appointed C.M.G. for his community services. He died on 6 December 1975 in the Repatriation General Hospital, Concord, and was cremated; his wife survived him, as did the son of his first marriage.

G. H. Fearnside (ed), *Bayonets Abroad* (Syd, 1953); D. Dexter, *The New Guinea Offensives* (Canb, 1961); G. Long, *The Final Campaigns* (Canb, 1963); B. Maughan, *Tobruk and El Alamein* (Canb, 1966); AWM records; information from Mrs A. B. Colvin, Frenchs Forest, Syd.

GRAHAM MCLENNAN

COMPSTON-BUCKLEIGH, EDMUND; *see* BARCLAY, EDMUND

COMPTON, GEORGE SPENCER (1891-1971), geologist, metallurgist, soldier and historian, was born on 6 May 1891 at Southern Cross, Western Australia, son of Edward Alfred Frederick Compton, civil servant, and his wife Agnes Maria, née Mitchell. Edward worked as a mining registrar under J. M. Finnerty [q.v.8]. Spencer attended primary schools at Coolgardie and Guildford, proceeded to Perth Boys' School, qualified as an assayer at Perth Technical School and was awarded an associate diploma in metallurgy (1913) by the Western Australian School of Mines. He was employed at mines at Norse-

man, Laverton, Ravensthorpe, Sandstone and Youanmi. On 2 January 1914 he married Elizabeth Jane Cobley with Anglican rites at All Saints Church, Sandstone.

Lithe and slim, with light brown hair and grey eyes, Compton was 5 ft 5½ ins (166.4 cm) tall and a good sportsman. He enlisted in the Australian Imperial Force on 9 August 1915 and was commissioned in October. Joining the 28th Battalion on the Western Front in June 1916, he was three times wounded in action. From 8 October 1917 he was treated in a series of hospitals, but remained permanently lame in one leg; he returned to Australia where his appointment terminated on 15 July 1918.

After assisting the Geological Survey of Western Australia, Compton lectured at Perth Technical School and studied part time at the University of Western Australia (B.Sc., 1923). In 1924 he was the State's representative to the mineral section of the British Empire Exhibition at Wembley, London. Early in 1934 he was appointed lecturer in mining and geology, and curator of the mineral museum, at the Western Australian School of Mines, Kalgoorlie. During his leave in 1937-39 he was consultant to the Lady Shenton and First Hit mines at Menzies, and subsequently managed Spargo's Reward mine. Appointed temporary captain in the Militia on 22 June 1940, Compton performed staff and training duties in Western Australia, was attached to the Anti-gas School, Narrogin, in 1942, and from March 1943 worked in the directorate of military operations, Land Headquarters, Melbourne. He was placed on the Retired List on 10 November 1944.

Having returned to the School of Mines in 1946, Compton taught an increasing number of ex-service students and ran a rehabilitation course on prospecting; that year he also helped to found the Eastern Goldfields Historical Society. He retired from the school in 1949, and worked as a consultant to Paringa Mining & Exploration Co. Ltd and Gold Mines of Kalgoorlie (Aust.) Ltd. In 1956 he headed an oil-exploration expedition to the remote Rudall River for Westralian Oil Ltd.

Moving to Perth, Compton continued to write newspaper articles, publish booklets and indulge his love of poetry. He spent much time researching goldfields history at the Royal Western Australian Historical Society and contributed to its journal. In 1967 he was made a freeman of the shire of Kalgoorlie; in 1971 he was appointed M.B.E. Compton died on 23 July that year at the Repatriation General Hospital, Hollywood, and was buried in Karrakatta cemetery; his wife, two sons and two daughters survived him.

Dept of Mines (WA), *Annual Report*, 1934-44; *Kalgoorlie Miner*, 1 Jan 1958, 26 Aug 1961, 1 Jan

1964, 24 July 1971; *Daily News* (Perth), 26 Sept 1961, 7 May 1971; *West Australian*, 24 July 1971; A'sian Inst of Mining and Metallurgy, member records (held at Clunies Ross House, Parkville, Melb); WA School of Mines, Student records; PR 7148 *and* 2198A/52 (BL); information from Mr G. S. Compton, Kalgoorlie, WA.

M. K. QUARTERMAINE

CONDE, HAROLD GRAYDON (1898–1959), engineer and public servant, was born on 18 June 1898 at West End, Brisbane, son of English-born parents Alfred Conde, carter, and his wife Ann, née Hinchcliffe. Harold received his early engineering training in New Zealand. In 1925 he was sponsored by the Auckland Power Board to take courses of special training with the Thomson Houston Co. Ltd in England and the General Electric Co. in the United States of America. Conde came back to New Zealand in 1929 and later that year joined the Electric Light and Power Supply Corporation Ltd (also known as the Balmain Co.) in Sydney as distribution engineer. He rose to chief assistant engineer in 1934 and general manager of the company in 1938.

In June 1945 J. B. Chifley [q.v.] appointed Conde chairman of the War Establishments Investigating Committee which was convened to accelerate the process of releasing from the army 30 000 servicemen urgently needed in industry. Next year the prime minister asked him to investigate alleged irregularities in the disposal of army equipment; Conde found no evidence to support the charges.

Having returned in 1947 to manage the Balmain Co., in 1949 Conde became emergency electricity commissioner, charged by the State government with responsibility for overcoming widespread and frequent failures in power supply. He soon recognized the inadequacy of existing generating capacity and devised a scheme whereby particular regions in Sydney were blacked out on a roster system. A 'blackout bureau' was established to inform consumers of projected power cuts. The immediate postwar power problems, and his efforts to alleviate them, drew attention to the need for more fundamental reform. In May 1950 the Electricity Commission of New South Wales was set up. Conde was appointed full-time chairman and chief executive officer; he had four part-time commissioners to support him.

The Electricity Commission endeavoured to eliminate power shortages by planning additional generating stations and improved transmission facilities. Seven 'package' steam-generating stations were ordered from the U.S.A. and in May 1951 Conde flew there to expedite delivery. He returned to Australia in September and secured approval for immediate installation of the new plant. On 25 May 1953 all restrictions on the use of power in New South Wales were lifted. That year Conde was appointed to the interim advisory council which reported to Federal and State governments on the Snowy Mountains hydro-electric scheme.

In 1954 the Electricity Commission of New South Wales announced cuts in bulk energy charges. Between 1950 and 1960 the commission more than trebled power capacity, from 490 megawatts to 1800. It expanded units at Bunnerong, White Bay and Balmain, developed the Pyrmont 'B' station, and established new stations at Tallawarra, near Port Kembla (1954), Wangi, at Lake Macquarie (1956), and Wallerawang, near Lithgow (1957).

Conde was a tall man of sturdy build. Shy and self-contained, he never married. He enjoyed swimming and gardening, and was a keen apiarist. In 1955 he was appointed C.M.G. He died of pneumonia complicating rheumatic heart disease on 5 October 1959 at Mosman and was cremated with Anglican rites; his estate was sworn for probate at £86 752. In 1961 the New South Wales Local Government Electricity Association and the Electricity Commission established two awards to commemorate Conde's contribution as chairman of the commission.

Electricity Comm of NSW, *A Decade of Progress* (Syd, 1960) and *Network*, Oct 1959, May, July, Nov 1961; *SMH*, 11 June 1945, 6 Oct 1959, 17 Dec 1981; information from Mr J. Conde, Pacific Power (ELCOM NSW), Syd.   SARAH VALLANCE

CONDON, DORIS CATHERINE (1908–1979), mayor, was born on 28 September 1908 at Richmond, Melbourne, daughter of William Arthur Lennox Forsyth, a Scottish-born cordial-waggon driver, and his wife Dora Jane, née Barnden, from South Australia. In 1917, when William was granted a fourteen-acre (5.7 ha) soldier-settlement block, the family moved to the Mildura district and lived at first in 'two tents and a hessian kitchen'.

On 16 September 1928 Doris married Arthur Edmund Condon at the Methodist manse, Berri, South Australia. Settling in Victoria, the Condons ran a bus service between Mildura and Bendigo; after it closed in 1942, they shifted to South Melbourne where Arthur became a taxi driver. In 1957 Doris was appointed a justice of the peace. She joined the women's committee of the Honorary Justices Association.

Active in the Australian Labor Party, Mrs Condon was treasurer of the South Melbourne branch, a member (1964–65) of the State central executive, an executive-member of the women's central organizing committee and a regular broadcaster over radio station 3KZ. In August 1962 she was elected as an A.L.P. candidate to the South Melbourne City Council. She immediately became the council's representative on the Baby Health Centre, the Pre-School, and the Day Nurseries and Crèches associations.

Elected mayor of South Melbourne in 1969, during her year of office Condon spoke out against proposals that the council be amalgamated with that of the City of Melbourne. Relations with the latter body were not helped when she was asked to nominate a male colleague to attend in her stead its traditional lord mayor's dinner. Her assertion, 'I think the first citizen of a city is the first citizen regardless of sex', received support from the press. In 1970 she joined with three other South Melbourne Labor councillors in a public letter to the national executive of the Labor Party, advocating federal intervention in the organization of the Victorian branch.

A persuasive speaker who was hard to deflect from a course to which she was committed, Condon was always aware of the problems of the underprivileged. She was particularly sympathetic to the needs of women, whether recent immigrants or residents of the new, high-rise, Housing Commission flats. In her mayoralty the council decided to proceed with Victoria's first, municipal, family-planning clinic, which she strongly supported, particularly in light of the report on battered babies submitted by the medical officer Dr Dora Bialestock. Condon saw family planning as part of the council's preventative health measures.

Lacking the advantages of social position and formal education, Condon came comparatively late to public life. With its tradition of municipal welfare services fostered under the town clerk Harold Alexander, South Melbourne provided fertile soil for her ideas. Before it was common for women to be outspoken in public affairs, she projected a pioneer image—bluff, direct, honest, hard working and sensible, but ever aware of the less fortunate. Her concern for world peace led her to serve on a committee of the United Nations Association as a co-opted (1970-71) and an elected (1971-73) member. A former State president (1968) of the Australian Local Government Women's Association, Condon was national president in 1971-72. She retired from the council in 1974 and was appointed A.M. in 1975. Survived by her husband and four sons, she died of hypertensive coronary vascular disease on 25 March 1979 at her South Melbourne home and was cremated.

A. V. Smith, *Women in Australian Parliaments and Local Governments, Past and Present* (Canb,

1975); *Age* (Melb), 25 Sept, 2 Dec 1969, 14, 27 May 1970; *Herald* (Melb), 28 May 1970; *Emerald Hill and Sandridge Times*, 29 Mar 1979; *Record* (Sth Melb), 3 Apr 1979; Biographies of members of Vic Labor Womens' Executive *and* Letter to Federal Executive ALP, in Papers of Vic Labor Party (LaTL); information from Mrs E. McCallum, Kew, Justice H. Nathan, St Kilda, Mr W. Monagle, Sth Melb, Mr D. Bethke, East Melb, and Mrs J. Manning, Hawthorn, Melb.   B. MARGINSON

CONLEY, MARJORIE MARGARET (1931-1959), soprano, was born on 24 June 1931 at Stanmore, Sydney, second daughter of Henry Conley, baker, and his wife Evelyn, née Wightman, both Queensland born. Educated at Mascot and Gardeners Road public schools, Marjorie learned the piano at Our Lady of the Sacred Heart Convent, Kensington. She had sung a great deal at home, and was 'the star turn' at school functions and at recitals by Marjory Robinson's dancing school where she acquired her assured stage presence. Aged 16, she began lessons with Thelma Houston, wife of Roland Foster [q.v.8]. At the New South Wales State Conservatorium of Music, Conley learned singing under Foster, undertook advanced vocal work with Florence Taylor and studied piano. During her student days she regularly sang at the Australia Hotel on Sunday evenings.

From 1950 to 1955 Conley competed annually in the Mobil Quest. In 1952 she won the national vocal section of the Australian Broadcasting Commission's competition and the *Sun* aria award at the City of Sydney Eisteddfod. Her numerous other prizes included the Bathurst aria contest of 1953 and the Mobil Quest in 1955. These successes placed her in demand as a concert, oratorio and opera singer. She toured widely in 1952 for both the Mobil Quest and the A.B.C. Tall and dark eyed, in 1953 she sang leading operatic roles for Clarice Lorenz's National Opera of Australia (including the first performance of John Antill's *Endymion*) and in performances with the Conservatorium opera school under (Sir) Eugène Goossens [q.v.] of Gluck's *Orfeo ed Euridice*, Debussy's *Pelléas et Mélisande*, and Gounod's *Roméo et Juliette* and *Faust*. She also sang under Goossens in 1954 in the première of his oratorio, *The Apocalypse*.

At St Mark's Anglican Church, Darling Point, on 5 May 1956 Marjorie married the Sydney baritone Geoffrey William Chard. They joined the Australian Elizabethan Theatre Trust's company for its inaugural Mozart opera season which opened in Adelaide in July; Marjorie sang Pamina (*The Magic Flute*) and Fiordiligi (*Così fan tutte*). Although some critics found her performances cool and passionless, others were fulsome in praising her 'golden promise'. The critic Martin Long wrote: 'A porcelain figurine in pink satin called Marjorie Conley who sang in a voice as liquid and slithery as satin and with as fine a finish as porcelain'. After the birth of their son in 1957, Marjorie and Geoffrey left the company and concentrated on radio, television and concert work.

In late July 1959, while holidaying at Surfers Paradise after a 6000-mile (10 000 km) Queensland tour, Marjorie collapsed with a cerebral haemorrhage. Survived by her husband and 2-year-old son, she died on 11 August in Brisbane Hospital and was buried in Woronora cemetery, Sydney. The subject of a Brisbane *Telegraph* placard, Marjorie Conley's early death was a tragic loss for Australian music. If, as she said herself, singing 'enthralled' her, her singing enthralled the public. One of her colleagues said that she 'was a remarkable lyric singer with a serene, classical stylishness, great accuracy and flawless pianissimo'.

Aust Musical News, Nov 1951, p 9, Dec 1951, p 17, Aug 1952, p 37, Nov 1952, p 33, Oct 1955, p 6, Aug 1959, p 9, Sept 1959, p 21; *Telegraph* (Brisb), 11 Aug 1959; *Courier-Mail* and *SMH*, 12 Aug 1959; press-clippings, concert and opera programmes (held by Mr G. Chard, Hunters Hill, Syd); information from Mr E. Clapham, Chatswood, Syd, Mr G. Chard, and Dr V. O'Hara, Kenmore, Brisb.   JOHN CARMODY

CONLON, ALFRED AUSTIN JOSEPH (1908-1961), army officer and medical practitioner, was born on 7 October 1908 in East Sydney, son of native-born parents Arthur George Conlon, tram conductor, and his wife Esther Mary, née Hayes. Educated at Fort Street Boys' High School and the University of Sydney (B.A., 1931), Alf helped to found the National Union of Australian University Students.

From youth, Conlon moved with precocious ease among his intellectual elders, made acceptable to them by his wide learning, unobtrusive manner and sardonic wit. It was his *métier* to operate outside the formal apparatus and hierarchy of power. This characteristic rendered him elusive and mysterious —impressions he did nothing to discourage; he was, and consciously desired to be, an exemplar of Dr Johnson's dictum that 'the mystery of Junius increases his importance'.

After studying medicine in 1932 at the University of Sydney, Conlon worked as a law clerk. On 24 January 1936 at the district registrar's office, Waverley, he married a hairdresser Willna Georgina Catherine Macpherson; they were to have two sons. Returning to the university in 1937, he represented undergraduates on the senate in 1939-43. He also served as the university's manpower officer in 1940-41, processing the selection of students for, or their exemption from, military training. Although this experience was his first taste of power, and he liked the flavour, he rarely used his influence for personal advantage.

From 1942 he chaired the prime minister's committee on national morale, which carried some vestige of the authority of John Curtin [q.v.], whom Conlon knew. On 7 April he was appointed major in the research section of the Directorate of Military Intelligence, Land Headquarters, Melbourne. The intelligence attachment was short-lived, but it created a spurious 'cloak-and-dagger' aura which clung to him. In February 1943 he assumed charge of L.H.Q.'s new research section which in October became a directorate (later retitled the Directorate of Research and Civil Affairs). Promoted temporary lieutenant colonel on 1 January 1944, he was to be elevated to temporary colonel in September 1945.

At D.O.R.C.A. Conlon assembled around him an exceptional group of talented people, among them (Sir) John Kerr, (Sir) James Plimsoll, James McAuley [q.v.], Harold Stewart, Camilla Wedgwood [q.v.], H. I. P. Hogbin, W. E. H. Stanner and Ida Leeson [q.v.10]. Conlon reported direct to the commander-in-chief, General Sir Thomas Blamey [q.v.]. The directorate prepared studies which Blamey had ordered and provided reports on a broad range of topics which Conlon judged to be of national importance. His staff dealt with such subjects as army health and nutrition, the study of terrain, dietary standards for Papuans and New Guineans employed by the army, trends in allied, Imperial and international relations, and a host of other matters great and small.

One of D.O.R.C.A.'s chief roles was to provide policy advice on the military government of Papua and New Guinea. Conlon's imaginative enterprise extended far beyond the needs of day-to-day military exigency and anticipated the country's independence. Work of enduring value was performed: the Territories were placed under one administration; their laws were consolidated and codified; and the L.H.Q. School of Civil Affairs, established in Canberra in 1945 to train service personnel to be colonial administrators, became in peacetime the Sydney-based Australian School of Pacific Administration.

Blamey sought his advice in handling the intricate political relationship between the high command and the Federal government. Conlon's propensity for informal contacts, deliberate avoidance of regular channels of communication and command, and neglect of proper administrative procedures and records led to his activities and his directorate

479

being suspected by some official bodies. Members of the Opposition—notably (Sir) Thomas White and Archie Cameron [qq.v.]—attacked D.O.R.C.A. in parliament. On the other hand, Sir Paul Hasluck and Gavin Long [q.v.] underrated Conlon's influence and achievement in their official histories of Australia in the war of 1939-45.

Conlon's judgement was on occasions seriously flawed, as in his hare-brained scheme for Australia to take over British Borneo after its recapture from the Japanese. The devious methods he used to delay the arrival of British civil affairs officers in the colony caused further distrust and he was increasingly denied access to top-level government material. People of irreproachable good faith denounced him as a charlatan. Yet, he remained Blamey's confidant. The creation of the Australian National University drew impetus from Conlon's vision and he persuaded Blamey to support the concept of a national centre of learning. Among senior A.N.U. scholars, (Sir) Keith Hancock held Conlon in deepest detestation, but (Sir) Mark Oliphant maintained cordial relations with him.

Relinquishing his appointment on 8 October 1945, Conlon spent 1948-49 as an unsuccessful and unhappy principal of A.S.O.P.A. He resumed his medical degree at the University of Sydney and qualified (M.B., B.S., 1951) with difficulty, and despite opposition from members of the faculty. Having worked at Newcastle (1952) and in Melbourne (1953-54), he conducted a chiefly psychiatric practice from his North Sydney home. In his last years his prestige dwindled, though he tried hard to maintain contact with scholarship, with affairs and with the counsels of influence.

Conlon was rather tall and of bulky build. Beneath dark hair, worn stiffly *en brosse*, his face was pallid and fleshy. He wore horn-rimmed spectacles, from behind which his grey eyes gazed unblinking for disconcertingly long periods. His smile had the power to charm. He spoke softly, using his pipe in conversational gestures. Quite unconcerned by personal appearance, when he put on uniform he cut a most unmilitary figure.

Johnsonian in the range of his discourse, Conlon at times demonstrated superficial knowledge, but withal knew more than most of his peers. He was a patriotic man who, when he had power, tried to use it for his country's good; he never expected or wanted public recognition. His acts of private kindness were countless and he served as a board-member (from 1956) of the Benevolent Society of New South Wales. He smoked, drank and ate liberally, avoided fresh air and shunned exercise; he declared that he was not interested in a long life, and he did not have one. Survived by his wife and one son, Conlon died of cardiovascular disease on 21 September 1961 in Sydney and was cremated with Anglican rites.

Alfred Conlon (priv pub, Syd, 1963); G. Long, *The Final Campaigns* (Canb, 1963); J. Thompson, *Five to Remember* (Melb, 1964); P. Hasluck, *The Government and the People, 1942-1945* (Canb, 1970); R. Hall, *The Real John Kerr* (Syd, 1978); personal information.   PETER RYAN

CONLON, PATRICIA ANNE (1939-1979), feminist, labour movement activist and public servant, was born on 2 November 1939 at Neutral Bay, Sydney, eldest of five children of Sydney-born parents John Hoare Carden, woolclasser, and his wife Patricia Anne, née de Coque. Young Anne was educated at St Joseph's Convent School, Neutral Bay, Monte Sant' Angelo College, North Sydney (dux 1956), and—on a teacher's scholarship—at the University of Sydney (B.A., 1961; M.A., 1973) where she became senior student at Sancta Sophia College. Renowned for her soprano voice, she competed in the City of Sydney Eisteddfod, and performed in choral and musical productions at school and university.

Disappointed at missing first-class honours in history, Carden taught in public high schools (which she found unrewarding) before and after spending 1964-65 on a postgraduate scholarship at the University of Saskatchewan, Canada. At St John's College, Sydney, on 29 September 1967 she married Telford James Conlon, a physicist belonging to a Labor-connected family. In 1968 she became research assistant to John Manning Ward, professor of history at the University of Sydney, and in 1973 completed her master's thesis, Eyewitness Accounts of Australia—1815-1850. Her son was born in 1971 and her daughter in 1974.

A founding member (1972) of the Women's Electoral Lobby, Conlon stood unsuccessfully as the Australian Labor Party candidate for Mosman at a by-election for the Legislative Assembly in July 1972. Next year she was a convener of W.E.L.'s first national conference in Canberra. She helped to produce submissions on conciliation and arbitration legislation to the Federal government, on the disadvantaged position of single mothers to R. F. Henderson's commission of inquiry into poverty, and—with Edna Ryan—on the minimum wage for women to the 1974 national wage case.

Awarded a grant by the Australian National Advisory Committee of International Women's Year 1975, Conlon and Ryan expanded their research into a book, *Gentle Invaders* (1975), which was notable both for the depth and quality of its evidence, and for its pioneering work on the history of women and labour in Australia. Conlon published articles on issues involving women in the Electrical Trades Union's *E.T.U. News*, *Catholic Weekly* and *Australian Quarterly*. An article based on her thesis had appeared in 1970 in the *Journal of the Royal Australian Historical Society*. In 1976 she was appointed lecturer at the Australian Trade Union Training Authority.

A founding member (1977) of the New South Wales Women's Advisory Council, Conlon became special projects officer with the government's Women's Co-ordination Unit in February 1978 and transferred next year to the Premier's Department. She worked on the Anti-Discrimination Act (1977), on an amendment to the maternity-leave provision and on the welfare of women prisoners. Her achievements impressed the premier Neville Wran.

Tall and striking, auburn haired and freckled, Conlon was witty, energetic, compassionate and extremely loyal. At Sancta Sophia she had been volatile and chronically unpunctual. Although she retained her Catholic faith, she broke for a time with the institutional Church because, she believed, it had failed to respond to the women's cause. She was a good debater, and had presence and authority, but did not seek the limelight, preferring to be a 'backroom operator' and to rely on an impressive network of friends and supporters. Politically astute, she was one of the few women in W.E.L. who belonged to the A.L.P.; she disavowed the prevailing philosophy that women should remain lobbyists and not join political parties.

To her profound grief, her marriage collapsed and in January 1979 she was divorced. Six months later she was diagnosed as suffering from cancer. Survived by her children, she died on 13 December 1979 at Mater Misericordiae Hospital, North Sydney. Hundreds of people packed a requiem Mass at nearby St Mary's Church; typically, she had meticulously arranged her own funeral, even the hymns sung by the choir of her old school. She is commemorated by an annual memorial lecture sponsored by the W.A.C. and by a building at Mulawa Training and Detention Centre for Women which bears her name.

E. Ryan and A. Conlon, *Gentle Invaders* (Syd, 1975); Women's Advisory Council, *Proceedings: Anne Conlon Memorial Lecture*, 24 Nov 1980 (Syd, 1980); Monte Sant' Angelo College, *Register of Ex-Students* (Syd, 1988); RAHS, *J*, 55, pt 1, Mar 1969, p 43; *Aust Q*, Sept 1977, p 11; Women's Electoral Lobby, *Newsletter*, 1972-80.

ELIZABETH WINDSCHUTTLE

CONNAL, NORMAN SCOTT (1888-1969), headmaster, was born on 11 February 1888 at Walcha, New South Wales, only child of native-born parents John Scott Connal (d. 1891), grazier, and his wife, Frances Margaret, née Rutledge. After Frances remarried, Norman was educated in Sydney. His brains, so his mother insisted, came from her. He attended St Mark's Crescent School, Darling Point, Fort Street Model School and the University of Sydney (B.A., 1910), and from 1901 was a chorister at his stepfather's church, St Mark's, Granville. Connal taught briefly at Mowbray House, a preparatory school at Chatswood, before being appointed in 1911 to Maryborough Grammar School, Queensland. There he taught English and Latin, and coached both boys and girls at sport; promoted senior master in 1913, he was acting-headmaster that year. On 2 July 1914 he married Elsie Marjorie Mackenzie (d. 1955) at St Stephen's Presbyterian Church, Maryborough; they were to have four children. From 1915 he was English teacher and sportsmaster at Brisbane Grammar School and in 1918 became secretary of the Queensland Great Public Schools Association.

In 1929 he was appointed headmaster of the somewhat neglected Church of England Boys' Preparatory School, Toowoomba. While espousing traditional concepts of upright behaviour and learning, the revitalized 'Toowoomba Prep' was conducted along unusually liberal lines and in a distinctively Australian way. Connal taught mathematics and English, transmitting his love of literature and regularly reading aloud to the boarders in the evenings. The number of boarders (some of them from remote stations in the bush) rose over thirty years from 27 to 160 and dayboys increased from 40 to 83. Although shy and often unwell, Marjorie Connal acted as the school's unpaid and devoted housekeeper, and was as much a mother to many small boys as Connal was a father.

In an institution run always on a shoestring, Connal struggled manfully with problems of finance and building, particularly during the Depression and World War II. The Australian army occupied the Toowoomba site in 1942-43, forcing the school's evacuation to Southport; there, as at Toowoomba, opportunities abounded to make cubby-houses, hobbies were fostered, and groups could hike and 'boil the billy' in the adjacent bush.

Colleagues throughout Australia and clergy of several denominations saw in Connal a philosopher and a friend; he was the confidant of whole families and of successive Anglican archbishops of Brisbane, especially J. W. C. Wand [q.v.12] and R. C. Halse [q.v.]. Connal was a member of the Brisbane diocesan synod, and clergy summer schools were regularly held at 'the Prep'. In 1952 he became foundation chairman of the Junior Schools' Association of Australia; at its conference in 1958, he spoke of discipline as 'consecrated commonsense' and received a standing ovation. He preferred traditional wisdom to modern psychology. Known as 'Boss' (but to earlier pupils as 'Jelly'), he inspired respect, trust and deep affection. Connal was candid and convincing, wise in his understanding of his charges, ebullient, humorous and, on occasion, earthy. His monumental body (he loved food), rich voice (equally compelling whether preaching or leading the choir), sagacious eyes and aroma of pipe smoke made him larger than life to adults and children alike. Naturally dignified and humble, he remained a well-loved legend for decades after his retirement in 1958.

On 11 December 1958 Connal married a divorcee Flora Margaret Armitage, née Dunn, at St Thomas's Anglican Church, Toowong; they later visited Britain, the fulfilment of his lifelong dream. Survived by his wife, and by three daughters of his first marriage, he died on 13 April 1969 at his St Lucia home and was cremated. A new wing of the school had been named after him in 1966.

J. Somerville, *Boss of Toowoomba Prep* (Toowoomba, Qld, 1985); P. McNally (ed), *School Ties* (Toowoomba, 1990); C of E Boys' [Preparatory] School, Toowoomba, *St Aidan*, 1929-58 *and* Archives; Maryborough Boys' State High School, *Palma*, 1956, and *Centenary*, 1981; family and personal information.

MICHAEL D. de B. COLLINS PERSSE

CONNELL, CYRIL JOHN (1899-1974), university registrar and Rugby League administrator, was born on 6 June 1899 in Sydney, son of John Maurice Connell, a saddler from Victoria, and his American-born wife Sadie, née Hanley. Educated at Brisbane Central Boys' and Brisbane Grammar schools, in February 1916 Cyril joined the office of the Queensland Public Service Board as a clerk. On 19 May 1917 he enlisted in the Australian Imperial Force and saw action in France with the 26th Battalion; he was discharged in Brisbane on 6 October 1919 and returned to the public service. On 5 January 1927 he married Honora Fitzgerald (d. 1936) at St Joseph's Catholic Cathedral, Rockhampton.

During the 1920s Connell qualified in accountancy and secretaryship; as an external student, he later graduated from the University of Queensland (B.Com., 1936). At the Church of Christ, Albion, Brisbane, on 19 December 1940 he married Coral Enchelmaier, a public servant. In that year he had been appointed secretary and accountant of the Queensland Government Printing Office;

he was seconded to civil defence in 1942 and transferred to the Public Service Commissioner's Office in 1944. Having taught commercial subjects in technical colleges at Charters Towers, Rockhampton and Brisbane in 1921-40, he became supervisor of the new Brisbane Technical Correspondence School in 1945. In March 1947 he was made assistant under-secretary of the Department of Public Instruction and in January 1949 became principal of the State Commercial High School where he completed *Essentials of Bookkeeping* (Sydney, 1954).

Deputy-registrar (from 1954) of the University of Queensland, Connell was appointed registrar in 1957. He began with an octogenarian vice-chancellor J. D. Story [q.v.12] and few senior assistants; over the next nine years he managed to find the accommodation, equipment and staff needed for an average annual increase of one thousand students, and to make the practical arrangements essential for new courses and specializations. He was also involved in the establishment (1960) of the University College of Townsville, the preparation of a site for Griffith University and completing the transfer of the University of Queensland from the city to St Lucia. Connell's administrative ability, prodigious work and organizational leadership lay behind these achievements. Modest and reticent, he was respected for his care, judgement and gentle strength. In 1965 he was appointed C.B.E. When he retired in 1969, the university conferred on him an honorary doctorate of philosophy.

An outstanding Rugby League footballer in his youth, the 5 ft 4 ins (162.6 cm) Connell had been a half-back in the first Queensland team to defeat New South Wales in 1922. He toured with State representative teams to Sydney in 1922-23 and New Zealand in 1925. During twenty years as an officer of the Queensland Rugby League, he was its president (1953-59), selector (1939-52), treasurer (1943-47) and acting-secretary. He was a member (1945-57) and treasurer of the Australian Board of Control, a national selector, and co-manager of the 1956 Kangaroo team that toured England and France.

Survived by his wife, son and daughter, and by the son and two daughters of his first marriage, Connell died on 25 October 1974 in his home at Chapel Hill, Brisbane, and was cremated.

P. James, *100 Years of Grammar Rugby* (Brisb, 1988); Univ Qld, *Univ News*, 7 Nov 1974; *Courier-Mail*, 18 Mar 1958, 26 Oct 1974; S. A. Rayner, *Cyril John Connell (1899-1974)* (ts, 1991, held by ADB), *and* for bibliog; Connell's staff cards, History Unit, Qld Dept of Education, Brisb; Qld Rugby League, Annual Reports, 1921-23, 1938-59 (held by Qld Rugby Football League, Milton, Brisb); Juvenile Employment Bureau file, 1938-39 *and* Brisb

Technical correspondence file, 1944-49 (QA); Univ Qld Archives.   S. A. RAYNER

CONNELL, ROBERT (1867-1956), police commissioner, was born on 19 December 1867 at Waterville, County Kerry, Ireland, youngest son of Lot Connell, coastguard, and his wife Anne, née Burliegh. After two years at sea, Robert came to Western Australia in September 1886 and almost immediately joined the police force. In February 1887 he was transferred to the criminal investigation department as a detective and served at Albany, Coolgardie, Fremantle and in Perth. At St George's Anglican Cathedral, Perth, on 3 June 1889 he married Alice Maud Dobbie. Rapidly promoted, Connell became a sub-inspector in September 1899. He was 5 ft 9 ins (175.3 cm) tall, with an aquiline nose, a prominent chin and a military bearing. That month he was sent to deal with unrest among miners at Kalgoorlie. Transferred to Albany, he took charge of the Plantagenet district and carried out surveillance on political activists during the turbulence that led to Federation.

Next year Connell was appointed officer-in-charge, Central Police Station, Perth. He dealt with problems associated with gambling, liquor and prostitution. In 1902 he sailed for England. There he studied the methods of the police in London; on his return, he successfully advocated the adoption of the fingerprint system of identification. In February 1904 he became chief of the criminal investigation department and was promoted to inspector in August. Elevated to chief inspector in July 1911, he supported the formation of a non-political police association. In January 1912 he won King George V's police medal for 'special skills displayed in the execution of duty'. He was made acting-commissioner of police on 1 April, an appointment which created antagonism among some of his fellow officers. In putting forward his own candidacy for the commissionership, Connell pointed to his long service, his experience, and his plan to effect economy and efficiency in the force's hierarchy. Appointed commissioner of police on 1 April 1913, he was to hold the post for twenty years.

A man of strong convictions and considerable energy, Connell used his annual reports to convey his misgivings about government inaction in responding to such social issues as child abuse, the plight of deserted mothers and illegal street-betting. He opened the police force to women in 1917, introduced car radios for police patrols in the remote North West in 1931 and recommended the installation of traffic lights operated by detection pads in the capital. His concern for his officers' welfare was evident in his push for a superannuation scheme to replace the gratuity system. He raised standards of recruitment and training, and advocated promotion by merit (based partly on successive examinations) rather than by seniority.

Connell argued strongly that the C.I.D. should provide a self-contained promotion and career structure, and succeeded in separating that branch from the uniformed police. In supporting the unpredictable detective Stephen Condon at the expense of the ill-fated J. J. Walsh [q.v.12] to head the C.I.D. in August 1920, Connell aroused the curiosity of the press. No revealing evidence about the affair has survived, nor do any retired policemen recall that carefully guarded web of intrigue.

On the whole, Connell presided effectively over a period marked by change and tumult. In the Depression the police were used to suppress political extremists and to control demonstrations by strikers, but in these actions they had considerable public support. Connell retired on 31 March 1933 and lived at Albany where he served as a special constable in World War II. Predeceased by his wife and survived by their son, he died on 11 June 1956 in Perth and was cremated. His estate was sworn for probate at £17 621.

J. S. Battye (ed), *Cyclopedia of Western Australia*, 1 (Adel, 1912); R. M. Lawrence, *Police Review 1829-1979 since the Days of Stirling* (Perth, 1979); Police Dept, Annual Report, *V&P* (LA WA), 1913-33; *Police Review* (Perth), Oct 1913, Oct 1917; *Police News* (Perth), 31 July, 31 Oct 1930, 18 Mar 1934; *Kalgoorlie Miner*, 21-27 Nov, 1 Dec 1899; *Western Mail* (Perth), 6 Apr 1912; *West Australian*, 12 June 1956; Police Dept (WA), Personnel files: S. Condon, R. Connell, D. Hunter (closed access, held WAA); information from Mrs E. Moody, East Malvern, Melb.   T. J. MCARTHUR

CONNELLY, SIR FRANCIS RAYMOND (1895-1949), businessman and lord mayor, was born on 1 September 1895 in East Melbourne, fourth child of John Connelly, butcher, and his wife, Susan, née Rooney, both Victorian born. Educated at twelve schools, including Christian Brothers' School, North Melbourne, and Xavier College, Kew, Raymond gained experience as a jackeroo in Queensland before joining the family business, the Moreland Grain & Free Stores Pty Ltd, at Brunswick.

Over six feet (182.9 cm) tall and weighing 16½ stone (104.8 kg), with a warm and outgoing personality, he was a resourceful businessman and a natural leader. During World War I Federal and State governments introduced the Australian Wheat Pooling Scheme which continued until the 1920-21 crop was marketed. A keen observer of international trends, Connelly made the first of many trips abroad in 1922 to study the bulk handling of grain and wheat. He also established La Trobe Motors Pty Ltd which introduced hire-cars to the city. On 17 November 1927 at St Patrick's Cathedral, East Melbourne, he married Lurline Marie (d. 1944), a daughter of Sir David Hennessy [q.v.9].

Returned by the electors of Smith Ward as a non-Labor representative to the Melbourne City Council in 1934, Connelly became chairman of the abattoirs and markets committee. That year he sponsored and organized for the Melbourne centenary celebrations a musical pageant, *Hiawatha*, which was staged at the Exhibition Building. He served three terms as lord mayor (1945-46, 1946-47 and 1947-48). A widower, he nominated his sister-in-law Valerie, wife of (Sir) Bernard Heinze, to be lady mayoress. Connelly was a progressive reformer who supported a Greater Melbourne planning authority. Seeking a 'brighter' metropolis, he urged the relaxation of laws on liquor and Sunday entertainment. He advocated longer shopping hours, the opening of an international airport and the training of hotel staffs to encourage tourists. An ardent Empire loyalist and charity-worker, he was prominent in the Food for Britain campaign, and in the development of the Lord Mayor's Camp at Portsea which in summer provided accommodation as well as free dental and health care for poor children from the country.

In 1948 Connelly was knighted. On 29 April that year at St Mary's Catholic Church, West Melbourne, he married 27-year-old Patricia Anne Holschier. They travelled to London where Connelly began the campaign which was to secure the Olympic Games for Melbourne (in 1956). While in London he staged at his own expense a banquet for three hundred people. With Sir Frank Beaurepaire [q.v.7], he subsequently toured Europe, interviewing delegates. One of Connelly's last official acts was to light a replica of the Olympic torch on 29 April 1949, following the announcement that Melbourne had been awarded the Games.

Throughout his political career Connelly had aspired to a seat in State or Federal parliament. He thrice stood unsuccessfully for the Victorian Legislative Assembly: for Grant as a Nationalist candidate in 1927, and for Toorak as an Independent United Australia Party candidate (1941) and as an Independent (1943). At the time of his death he was seeking Liberal preselection for the Senate. A keen sportsman, he belonged to the Peninsula and Metropolitan golf clubs, the Victoria Racing Club and the Melbourne Cricket Club.

Survived by his wife, Sir Raymond died of coronary vascular disease on 4 May 1949 in Mount St Evin's Hospital, Fitzroy. He had no children. Two thousand people attended a requiem Mass at St Patrick's Cathedral celebrated by Archbishop Mannix [q.v.10]; a mile-long cortège followed the hearse to Brighton cemetery in what was reputedly the biggest funeral procession since that of Sir John Monash [q.v.10]. Connelly's estate was sworn for probate at £41 750. A bust by Arthur Fleischmann is at the Mercy Hospital where a wing built by public subscription is named after Connelly; the gates at the Lord Mayor's Camp, Portsea, were built as another memorial.

G. Lomas, *The Will to Win* (Melb, 1960); *Herald* (Melb), 25 Nov 1940, 27 Aug, 6 Oct 1945, 5 Oct 1946; *Argus*, 16 Feb, 8 Dec 1945, 5, 7 May 1949; *A'sian Post*, 9 May 1946; *Age* (Melb), 11 June 1946, 6 July 1948, 5 May, 15 Oct 1949; *Sun News-Pictorial*, 5, 7 May 1949; information from Lady Connelly, Sth Yarra, Melb.   DAVID DUNSTAN

CONNELY, HAROLD FREDERICK (1921-1976), air force officer, was born on 26 March 1921 at Breakfast Creek, Brisbane, son of Frederick Henold McCoomb Connely, draper, and his wife Theresa Maud, née Saltrick, both Queensland born. A Catholic, he was educated at St Joseph's College, Gregory Terrace. Harry worked as a clerk and from 24 January 1940 was employed as a wireless operator with the Royal Australian Air Force. Six feet (182.9 cm) tall and solidly built, he enlisted as aircrew on 16 August, trained in Australia and Canada, and was a sergeant air observer on his arrival in England in July 1941.

Posted to No. 97 Squadron of the Royal Air Force's Bomber Command, in November Connely was promoted flight sergeant. On 20 April 1942 he went on his first sortie, a strike against Rostock, Germany. In an attack on Gennevilliers, Paris, on 29-30 May, his Lancaster aircraft was repeatedly hit by light anti-aircraft fire which wounded a gunner and damaged two engines and the tail. On the following night Connely participated in a 1000-bomber raid against Cologne. His plane flew low over the city while the crew took photographs: Connely's close view of the destruction was seared in his memory. Promoted warrant officer that month, he was designated navigator in July. He was awarded the Distinguished Flying Medal (1942) for his work.

On completing his tour, Connely volunteered for a second and was sent to No. 207 Squadron. His Lancaster crew-members, among whom he was the only Australian, became known throughout Britain after a team from the British Broadcasting Corporation accompanied them on a raid against

Berlin on the night of 3-4 September 1943. The dramatic coverage of the flight was interrupted by an enemy fighter which attacked the bomber as it approached its target. Tension eased on the return journey and next day listeners heard the tape-recording on which Connely sang *Annie Laurie* 'because he felt happy'. It had been his fiftieth sortie.

He experienced his worst moments in the air on his fifty-fourth trip. Cannon-shells from a night-fighter wounded the wireless operator and a gunner, put two turrets out of action and started fires; burning incendiary bombs had to be jettisoned; Connely attended to the wireless operator and probably saved his life. Connely was awarded the Distinguished Flying Cross (1944). Having completed fifty-seven missions, he was transferred to an operational training unit as an instructor and subsequently commissioned on 1 December 1943. He returned to Australia on 21 October 1944, was posted to the General Reconnaissance School at Laverton, Victoria, and later flew on transport operations in the South-West Pacific theatre.

Remaining in the R.A.A.F., Connely was promoted flight lieutenant in September 1948. From February to November 1951, during the Malayan Emergency, he served in Singapore with No. 38 Squadron. Ill health necessitated his transfer in 1955 to the Special Duties Branch as an air-traffic control officer; he was placed on the Retired List on 4 April 1962. Connely never married. He lived in Brisbane where he served as an Australian Rules football and surf life-saving administrator. A diabetic, while holidaying in Scotland he died of myocardial infarction on 18 November 1976 in Edinburgh and was cremated. His medals were presented to the Australian War Memorial, Canberra.

F. Johnson (ed), *R.A.A.F. over Europe* (Lond, 1946); AWM records; information from Mr K. Beavis, Mayne, Brisb.　　　PETER BURNESS

CONNOLLY, PATRICK ANDREW (1866-1946), racecourse owner, was born on 20 October 1866 at Ophir, New South Wales, fourth child of Irish-born parents Patrick Connolly, farmer, and his wife Agnes, née Graham. Little is known of Paddy's early life, save that his mother apparently ran a bush pub. He rode his family's horses at local racetracks and had a stint as an itinerant stockman in Queensland before joining the gold rush to Kalgoorlie, Western Australia, in 1894. There he entered the carrying trade with such success that in 1900 he purchased a large property on the outskirts of Perth, leased an inner-city hotel and moved to the capital. On 7 February 1898 he had married Alice Julia Hide at St George's Anglican Cathedral, Perth; they were to be divorced in 1924. He invested in a string of hotels, tin-mines and pastoral stations, but his first love was horses.

In 1903 in Sydney Connolly bought for 155 guineas Blue Spec, the horse that was to make his name. Victorious in the Kalgoorlie and Perth cups in 1904, next year Blue Spec won the Moonee Valley Cup and the Melbourne Cup (as a 6-year-old, in record time, at odds of 10/1), bringing Connolly more than £30 000 in prize-money and bets. By 1910 his horses had won six Perth Cups, the Western Australian Derby three times and a host of other races. At one stage he owned or leased 120 horses. 'Lucky Connolly' was known throughout the country as an astute breeder, a canny owner and a big punter. Tall and well built, he had a determined jaw and eyes that told nothing. Few shared his confidence; fewer claimed him as a friend.

Before World War I he bought a controlling interest in Helena Vale racecourse which he kept in operation for nearly thirty years. The trials of running a race club forced Connolly into the public world. He engaged in battles with the Western Australian Turf Club over his share of meeting dates, with politicians over the extent of horse-racing in the State and with starting-price bookmakers over the threat they allegedly posed to the sport. Partly from self-interest and partly from his devotion to horse-racing, Connolly regularly urged governments to suppress the 'illegals'. Yet, unlike the turf club, he was prepared to take risks to attract punters to his course: in the Depression—when horse-racing's survival seemed threatened—he reduced admission prices and arranged with the railways department to reduce the cost of fares.

As he aged, Connolly became reclusive and eccentric; he built a barricaded shack for himself behind his beloved Kalamunda Hotel because he was convinced that his enemies were trying to kill him. He could also be irascible and often enlivened turf club meetings with intemperate attacks on jockeys, trainers and the state of racing in general. A lonely man, he had an unrequited affection for children. He was a generous benefactor, known as 'The Prince of Givers'. Connolly died on 28 December 1946 in St Omer's Hospital, West Perth, and—despite his atheism—was buried with Anglican rites in Karrakatta cemetery. His estate was sworn for probate at £149 332: he bequeathed over £100 000 to children's charities and almost £30 000 to country hospitals, with the specification that none of it go to any with a religious connexion.

D. L. Bernstein, *First Tuesday in November* (Melb, 1969); J. Tomlinson, *Born Winners. Born Losers* (Perth, 1990); Select Cte of the Legislative

Council and the Legislative Assembly to consider the Question of Horse Racing within the State, *V&P* (WA), 1915, 2; *Age* (Melb), 8 Nov 1905, 30 Dec 1946; *West Australian*, 8 Nov 1905, 30, 31 Dec 1946, 1 Dec 1947; *Punch* (Melb), 4 Nov 1909; *Daily News* (Perth), 31 Dec 1946; *Western Mail* (Perth), 19 Dec 1959. CHARLIE FOX

CONNOLLY, ROY NEVILLE (1893-1966), journalist and author, was born on 18 January 1893 at Gympie, Queensland, third of five children of Peter Joseph Connolly, a native-born bank clerk, and his wife Mary Dora, née Herbert, from Ireland. Roy was employed as a cadet journalist on the *Gympie Miner*, then worked on newspapers at Bundaberg, in Brisbane and at Toowoomba. After moving to Melbourne as representative for the Sydney *Sun*, he joined the *Daily Telegraph* and the *Sunday Times* in Sydney. On 29 August 1919 he married a typist Eileen Alice Stanislaus Searle at St Stephen's Catholic Cathedral, Brisbane; they were to have two children before being divorced in 1934. Connolly was editor (1923) of the short-lived Sydney *Daily Mail* and from April 1924 managing editor of the paper when it reappeared as the *Labor Daily*. Despite compulsory subscriptions from trade unions, working capital was so scarce that Connolly frequently had to draw the cartoons. His efforts to improve declining circulation by resorting to sensationalism, as well as his 'intemperance and obstinacy and contumacious disregard of the directions given to him', led to his sacking in September that year.

Sometime associate-editor of the *Sunday Guardian*, in 1931 Connolly became news editor of another short-lived Labor paper, the *World*. Next year he visited Ireland. While freelancing in London, he collaborated with Frank McIlraith on a dystopian novel, *Invasion from the Air* (London, 1934). It argued that future European warfare, if conducted by intensive bombing of civilian populations, would lead to political anarchy and bring down any government involved.

Back in Brisbane in 1934, Connolly became book reviewer for the *Sunday Mail* and a freelance writer for other papers, among them *Smith's Weekly*. He later contributed features to the *Sunday Mail*, occasionally using the pseudonym 'Neville de Lacy', and wrote columns for the Brisbane *Truth*. On 10 October 1940 at the general registry office, Brisbane, he married a 32-year-old school-teacher Edna Alice Perkins. That year he published *Southern Saga* (London, 1940; Sydney 1944, 1945 and 1946), a novel based on careful research into the history of the Gayndah district where his Irish great-grandfather had settled. Its romantic plot is underpinned with considerable humour and sharp insights into race-relations. In 1941 and 1960 he was awarded Commonwealth Literary Fund fellowships, but two subsequent novels remained unpublished.

Despite—or because of—his experiences with the radical press, he developed a strong aversion to Labor politics and in 1946 became press secretary to (Sir) Arthur Fadden [q.v.]. For the 1949 election campaign, Connolly wrote *You won't vote Labor when you've read this story!*, a pamphlet denouncing state-enterprise in Australia. Friendship with the Drysdale [q.v.4] family led him to write *John Drysdale and the Burdekin* (Sydney, 1964). Independent, gregarious, but somewhat litigious, Connolly exasperated his employers and fell out with his publishers. He was attracted to investigative journalism: though sometimes luridly presented, his work was tempered by a respect for history. In 1942 he had criticized inadequate surveillance of foreign nationals in northern Australia and was fined for refusing to divulge his sources of information.

Survived by his wife, and by the son and daughter of his first marriage, Connolly died on 13 September 1966 in Brisbane and was cremated with Anglican rites.

R. B. Walker, *Yesterday's News* (Syd, 1980); *NSW State Reports*, 1925, p 398; *Newspaper News*, 1 Sept 1931; *Courier-Mail*, 14 Sept 1966; Connolly papers (NL). CHRIS TIFFIN

CONNOR, REGINALD FRANCIS XAVIER ('REX') (1907-1977), motor dealer and politician, was born on 26 January (Australia Day) 1907 at Wollongong, New South Wales, elder child of Peter Francis Connor, labourer, and his wife Ethel, née Deegan, both native-born. Winning a scholarship to Wollongong High School, Rex worked towards a career as an analytical chemist, but contracted pneumonia in his final year; largely through self-tuition, he matriculated well and was named honorary dux of the school. When his father died in 1925, Connor abandoned academic aspirations to support his mother and sister. In February 1926 he was articled to the solicitor Charles Morgan, and handled industrial and workers' compensation cases. Morgan dismissed him in 1931, possibly because of Connor's association with another firm. Although he excelled in his final examination, without Morgan's support he was twice rejected by the Solicitors' Admission Board.

This setback, and perhaps his inability to maintain payments on a land purchase, seem to have embittered Connor. In 1931 he was acquitted on a charge of fraud involving £80 worth of motorcar parts. On 14 August that year he married a 30-year-old nurse Grace Amelia Searl with Catholic rites at the bishop's house, Maitland. Despite the Depression, he developed a flourishing motor dealership, winning sales awards and employing a staff of ten. Although settled and successful, he frequently clashed with the police over traffic and licensing matters, and was twice convicted of assault: in 1935 he pulled a ladder from the feet of a council employee who was disconnecting his electricity; in 1938 he felled a customer who complained about the price of a car.

At 17 Connor had joined the Australian Labor Party, but was not active in politics until the late 1930s. Having stood unsuccessfully as an Independent for the Wollongong Municipal Council in 1937, he was elected in May next year with trade union endorsement. By February 1939 he was a member of the breakaway Industrial Labor Party led by Robert Heffron [q.v.]; Connor was elected to the central executive, became an enthusiastic socialist and moved closer to the Communist Party of Australia. Shifting to the left-wing State Labor Party of M. J. R. Hughes and W. P. Evans, in 1940 he gained pre-selection for the seat of Werriwa in the House of Representatives and ran third with 12.6 per cent of the vote. He considered himself a State Labor candidate when re-elected to the Wollongong council during World War II, but rejoined the A.L.P.'s Wollongong branch in 1944.

In the late 1940s Connor established a local ascendancy in the A.L.P. which lasted until his death. He narrowly won the State seat of Wollongong-Kembla in June 1950, following a torrid campaign in which he was accused of communist sympathies and dishonesty. His thirteen years in the Legislative Assembly were frustrating, although Labor held office throughout. A leader of the minority left-wing faction, he was excluded from the ministry by the dominant right. He tried to mitigate Wollongong's industrial pollution, dramatizing his case for new legislation by producing in parliament a 'pathetic specimen of a cabbage', 'the unrecognizable foliage of a cauliflower' and other withered flora from the district. His efforts ushered in the State's Clean Air Act (1961). In 1963 he successfully led a revolt in caucus against government proposals to increase housing-commission rents.

Disappointed in State politics, Connor switched to Federal parliament, winning the seat of Cunningham at the 1963 elections. He distanced himself from the left and became a close ally of deputy-leader E. G. Whitlam, whose gratitude he earned by undeviating support in several, bitter party battles. When

Whitlam became the A.L.P.'s federal leader in February 1967, Connor was promoted to the parliamentary executive and appointed shadow minister for energy, resources and secondary industry. He lost his place on the executive in 1969, but was selected for cabinet when Labor came to power in December 1972. Whitlam appointed him to the new portfolio of minerals and energy.

In almost three years of pugnacious and often controversial administration Connor transformed public policy on energy and resources. The export of all minerals was subjected to controls and Connor intervened in negotiations to insist on higher prices. Producers were encouraged to deal collectively with foreign cartels to obtain longer contracts and protection against inflation and currency revaluations. Markets for iron ore were opened with China, mining companies' taxes were increased and the quarrying of uranium was facilitated. The Commonwealth assumed jurisdiction over resources on the continental shelf. Connor established the Pipeline Authority to bring natural gas from South Australia's Cooper Basin to south-eastern Australia. Seeking 'to buy back for Australia what is part of Australia's birthright', he tried to ensure at least 51 per cent Australian investment in new minerals ventures. His creation of the Petroleum and Minerals Authority sparked a notable political and constitutional battle after the bill was blocked in the Senate. Having survived the election that followed the double dissolution in April 1974, the government had the legislation approved on 7 August by an unprecedented joint-sitting of both Houses, but the High Court of Australia subsequently pronounced the Act invalid.

In May Connor had been elevated to third position in cabinet and was later, briefly, acting prime minister. At its federal conference in February 1975, the party acclaimed his policies and his assertive Australian nationalism. Connor's rapid political downfall in the ensuing months stemmed from plans he had sponsored to borrow petrodollars for the exploitation of Australian resources during the world energy crisis of the mid-1970s. In December 1974 he obtained Executive Council authority to solicit a loan of $US4 billion (reduced in January 1975 to $US2 billion). News of the proposed borrowing was leaked to the Opposition and the scheme was abandoned in May. By then, the government had lost control of the 'Loans Affair' which flared into high political drama with allegations of impropriety, illegality and incompetence. Much of the controversy concerned Tirath Khemlani, an obscure commodities dealer who had been encouraged by Connor to sound out possible lenders. Whitlam recalled Parliament for a special sitting on 9 July to defend the attempted transaction. In a defiant speech Connor invoked a little-known Australian poem:

Give me men to match my mountains,
Give me men to match my plains,
Men with freedom in their vision,
And creation in their brains.

The tumult subsided, but the 'Loans Affair' simmered and erupted again in October 1975 with allegations that Connor had attempted to raise money after his authority had been revoked. He fought back, denying the charges until confronted with evidence that he had at least once sought to revive the negotiations. Whitlam demanded his resignation. Connor capitulated on 14 October only after caucus had sanctioned his departure. This incident provided the 'reprehensible circumstance' which the Opposition used to justify its blocking of supply in the Senate. Thus began the great constitutional crisis of October-November 1975 which culminated in the dismissal of the Whitlam government and its decisive defeat at the Federal elections in December. Connor remained in parliament, but did not attempt to return to the caucus executive. Predeceased by his wife (d. 10 April 1977) and survived by their three sons, he died of a coronary occlusion on 22 August 1977 at Canberra Hospital and was buried in Lakeside Memorial Park cemetery, Dapto, New South Wales.

During Connor's long political career, his imposing bulk and quirkish personality earned him a range of allusive sobriquets: 'Bulger', 'Al Capone', 'the High Priest of Wollongong Politics', 'King Kong', 'the Abominable Snowman' and, most commonly, 'the Strangler'. He dressed characteristically in a dark suit, white shirt, dark tie, braces and a wide-brimmed felt hat. A massive yet subtle and complex man, he could be chillingly abrupt and sometimes bellicose. Suspicious and strongly inclined to be secretive, he could also be courtly, patient, persuasive, and enthusiastic, especially when speculating about advanced technology or expatiating on a prized project. Connor was respected in Wollongong for the attention he gave his electorate and for his role in developing the local university. He epitomized his career in a rare aphorism: life, said Rex Connor, was 'an equation in hydrocarbons'.

C. J. Lloyd and A. Clark, *Kerr's King Hit* (Syd, 1976); G. Freudenberg, *A Certain Grandeur* (Melb, 1977); M. Sexton, *Illusions of Power* (Syd, 1979); E. G. Whitlam, *The Whitlam Government* (Melb, 1985); *National Times*, 8-13 Oct 1973, 29 Aug-3 Sept 1977; *SMH*, 6 Aug 1982; Strangler or Strangled? (unpublished procs of the Connor Conference, 24 July 1982, Dept of Politics and Hist, Univ Wollongong); R. F. X. Connor, official papers (Univ Wollongong Archives).   C. J. LLOYD

CONRAD, ARNOLD HENRY (1887-1979), architect, was born on 6 January 1887 at Clifton Hill, Melbourne, second son of Henry Ferdinand Conrad, a surveyor from Prussia, and his native-born wife Ellen, née Bower. Articled to the architect Edwin J. Ruck, Arnold attended the Working Men's College, Melbourne, and remained with him after qualifying. In 1911 he moved to Queensland and entered the Department of Public Works as a temporary draftsman; next year he joined the Brisbane firm, H. W. Atkinson & C. McLay.

From 1912 Conrad taught at the Central Technical College, imparting his considerable structural and constructional knowledge to a generation of Brisbane architects. He shifted to Warwick in 1917 to establish his own practice and was commissioned by the Presbyterian Church to design new secondary schools. Next year he rejoined his former firm which became Atkinson & Conrad. Highly successful, the partnership undertook numerous projects that ranged from residential and educational to commercial and industrial buildings: foremost among them were the Trades Hall, the 'Spanish mission'-style Craigston (Brisbane's first high-rise apartment block) and a warehouse for W. D. & H. O. Wills Ltd, a multi-storey building with a complete concrete frame.

Following their appointment in 1926 as architects to the Brisbane and South Coast Hospital Board, the practice was merged with Lange L. Powell as Atkinson, Powell & Conrad. On 22 December 1927 Conrad married 26-year-old Hilda Mary Scorer at Scots Church, Melbourne. While he was overseas investigating hospital design, controversy over the erection of the firm's initial building at the hospital led to a royal commission into public hospitals in 1930. The commission recommended that, to avoid architectural fees, the design of public hospitals should revert to the Department of Public Works, but the commission's chairman submitted a minority finding which favoured the firm. Without Powell, Atkinson and Conrad subsequently retained the patronage of the board. They designed Brisbane General Hospital, and hospitals at South Brisbane and Chermside.

Credited with popularizing the 'Spanish mission' style in Brisbane, Conrad may have acquired his interest from his former master Ruck who pioneered the style in Melbourne. Craigston predated Conrad's visit to California, United States of America, in 1928, as did the work of other local exponents such as E. P. Trewern. With Atkinson, Conrad was to apply the style to many large projects, including the B.G.H. nurses' quarters, Tristram's soft-drink factory and the Greek Orthodox Church. Another of their important projects —designed in association with (Sir) Arthur

Stephenson [q.v.12] and Percy Meldrum [q.v.]—was the *Courier-Mail* newspaper headquarters, the first modern office-building erected (1936) in the capital.

When Atkinson died in 1938, T. B. F. Gargett entered the partnership and the firm dominated architectural practice in Brisbane for another thirty years. Shortly before his retirement in December 1974, Conrad designed and drafted proposals for an organ loft in St John's Cathedral, Brisbane. He was appointed C.M.G. in 1977. A councillor (1920-25) and fellow of the Queensland Institute of Architects, he was a life fellow and vice-president (1934) of the Royal Australian Institute of Architects. Survived by his wife, son and daughter, he died on 13 February 1979 at Auchenflower and was buried with Anglican rites in Pinaroo lawn cemetery.

Roy Com into Public Hospitals, Report, *PP*(Qld), 1929-30, 2nd S, 1; *Architecture and Building J of Qld*, 10 Nov 1928, p 60; *Qld Architect*, May-June 1971, no 2, p 4; *Courier-Mail*, 14 Feb 1979; Dept of Public Works, Staff file on A. H. Conrad (QA); A. H. Conrad, unpublished memoir (held by Mr W. A. H. Conrad, Conrad & Gargett Pty Ltd, Brisb).

DON WATSON

CONYBEARE, ALFRED THEODORE (1902-1979), judge, was born on 30 April 1902 at College Park, Adelaide, only child of Alfred Henry Conybeare, salesman, and his wife Marion Forrest, née Eglinton. In 1907 the family moved to Sydney where Alfred senior was employed at David Jones [q.v.2] Ltd's store. Theo was educated at North Sydney Boys' High School and the University of Sydney (B.A., 1924; LL.B., 1927). Although he entered articles of clerkship to a solicitor, he was admitted to the Bar on 6 June 1928. At the district registrar's office, Chatswood, on 28 December 1929 he married Ena Myra Rice, a schoolteacher whom he had met at university.

Conybeare's practice involved extensive work in damage cases in the Supreme and District courts, and before the Workers' Compensation Commission of New South Wales. His most notable brief was as junior to F. A. Dwyer, K.C., who appeared for (Sir) William Dobell [q.v.] when the award to Dobell of the 1943 Archibald [q.v.3] prize was challenged.

Soon after Conybeare took silk in 1951, he was appointed chairman of the Workers' Compensation Commission from 8 October. As a judge, he was unpretentious, courteous, and a stickler for gentlemanly conduct and legal technicality. He took pains to understand the facts (including the complex medical evidence involved in many cases) and awarded compensation under the statutory provisions which were often quite technical. During his term the commission's work increased enormously and the number of judges rose from three to six. In 1966 he presided over the move to new premises in Macquarie Street, overlooking Sydney Harbour. Funded by a levy on workers' compensation insurance, these superior quarters created some envy.

Taking long service leave in 1962, Conybeare visited North America and Europe. He described how 'the scales were struck' from his eyes as he realized the inadequacy of mere monetary awards in compensation cases without provision for rehabilitation; he was also impressed by the Canadian system where insurance companies were not involved in these cases. On his return, he called for more attention to be given to the rehabilitation of injured workers. In 1969 he began an official inquiry into the feasibility of establishing such a system in New South Wales that led to a major report, delivered in December 1970. Yet, his proposals to terminate common law rights (notably to sue employers for negligence) and to increase compensation payments were criticized by the legal profession and by the Labor Council of New South Wales. To Conybeare's profound disappointment, this opposition ensured that no action was taken, apart from the establishment of the commission's vocational rehabilitation department.

At his farewell ceremony in April 1972 Conybeare was praised as a 'wise and kindly judge'. Disenchanted, he declared that compensation law had been 'stagnant for too long' and lacked 'freshness, innovation, initiative'. After his retirement he was inaugural chairman (1973-75) of the State committee on discrimination in employment and occupation. He belonged to the University Club, continued his interest in literature and tended the garden at his Lindfield home. Survived by his wife and three sons, he died on 27 November 1979 at Greenwich and was cremated. His portrait had been painted by H. Hanke for the Workers' Compensation Commission.

Aust Law J, Oct 1951, p 403, Feb 1980, p 107, May 1992, p 276; *SMH*, 17, 18 Feb 1971, 28 Apr 1972, 29 Nov 1979; *Australian*, 29 Apr 1972.

MICHAEL KIRBY

COOK, EMMA JANE; *see* CALLAGHAN

COOK, FRANCIS WILLIAM (1918-1967), army officer, was born on 12 May 1918 at West-End, Hampshire, England, son of Second Lieutenant Frederick Francis Cook, Royal Garrison Artillery Special Reserve, and his wife Honor Selina, née Copp. Frederick won the Military Cross in World War I and brought his family to Adelaide when Francis was a child. Aged 14, Francis began work as a laboratory cadet at the Waite [q.v.6] Agricultural Research Institute.

Having risen to sergeant in the Militia's 27th Battalion, on 3 November 1939 Cook enlisted in the Australian Imperial Force and was posted to the 2nd/10th Battalion. He was commissioned lieutenant in March 1940, sailed for Britain in May and arrived in the Middle East in December. His battalion reinforced the garrison at Tobruk, Libya, in April 1941. On the night of 3-4 May the defenders mounted a counter-attack. Cook was given command of two platoons and ordered to mop up enemy positions bypassed in the main thrust. When his men came under heavy machine-gun fire, he led them in a bayonet charge and captured an enemy post without loss; he then assailed another post, taking equipment and two prisoners. For his actions he was awarded the Military Cross.

Relieved at Tobruk in August, the 2nd/10th was sent to Palestine and Syria. Cook was accidentally injured at Aleppo in January 1942 and came home to recuperate. On 13 June that year at St David's Anglican Cathedral, Hobart, he married a hairdresser Joan Marlene Alderson; they were to have a son before being divorced in 1947. In July 1942 he rejoined the battalion which sailed to Papua next month. Promoted captain in October, by early 1943 he had command of 'A' Company. At Sanananda on 19 January, although outnumbered, his soldiers followed him in a daring assault on a Japanese position that had been thwarting the advance. The enemy broke and fled. Cook was awarded the Distinguished Service Order.

Returning to Queensland in March, he became chief instructor at the Junior Leaders' School, South Australia, in October. In April 1944 he returned to the 2nd/10th and was promoted major in May 1945. Following the landing at Balikpapan, Borneo, on 1 July, Cook's 'C' Company dashed inland and took 'Parramatta' ridge. He was mentioned in dispatches. Transferring to the Reserve of Officers on 1 November, he became sales manager of the Adelaide branch of Cooper Engineering Co. Pty Ltd. At the Baptist Church, North Adelaide, on 4 October 1947 he married a stenographer Elizabeth Wyly.

Resuming his military career on 26 February 1951, Cook served with the Australian Ancillary Unit Korea (1951-52) and the Pacific Islands Regiment (1952-54). He then performed command and staff duties in Australia as lieutenant colonel. After attending the Armed Forces Staff College at Norfolk, United States of America, he was assistant Australian army representative, Washington, in 1962-64. He was appointed deputy-director of military training at Army Headquarters, Canberra, in May 1966 and promoted colonel in July.

Six ft 1½ ins (186.7 cm) tall, with a lined, weather-beaten face and an open expression, Cook was an enthusiastic sportsman who had excelled at lacrosse. He died of coronary thrombosis on 26 June 1967 at his Watson home and was buried with Methodist forms in Canberra cemetery; his wife, and their son and two daughters, survived him. Geoffrey Mainwaring's portrait of Cook is held by the Australian War Memorial, Canberra.

F. Allchin, *Purple and Blue* (Adel, 1958); D. McCarthy, *South-West Pacific Area—First Year* (Canb, 1959); G. Long, *The Final Campaigns* (Canb, 1963); B. Maughan, *Tobruk and El Alamein* (Canb, 1966); *Advertiser* (Adel), 8 Mar 1961, 27 June 1967; AWM records; CSIRO Archives, Canb; information from Mr A. Kunnick, Beaumont, Adel.

ROBIN PRIOR

COOKE, EDGAR ERIC (1931-1964), murderer, was born on 25 February 1931 at Victoria Park, Perth, eldest of three children of Vivian Thomas Cooke, a native-born shop-assistant, and his wife Christian, née Edgar, from Scotland. Educated at five different schools, including Perth Junior Technical and Forrest High, from the age of 14 Eric took a succession of semi-skilled jobs. Having served in the Citizen Military Forces, he joined the Permanent Military Forces on 27 May 1952, but was discharged on 28 August when it was discovered that—before enlistment—he had a series of convictions for theft, breaking and entering, and arson. On 14 October 1953 at the Methodist Church, Cannington, he married Sarah (Sally) Lavin, a 19-year-old waitress; they were to have seven children.

In the early hours of 27 January 1963 a series of random shootings with a .22 inch (.55 cm) rifle occurred in the suburbs of Perth. The victims were a couple who were wounded in a parked car at Cottesloe, a male accountant, fatally wounded by a single shot to the head while asleep in a flat nearby, an 18-year-old student (John Sturkey), killed by a single bullet to the head while sleeping on the verandah of a boarding house at Nedlands, and a retired grocer who was similarly murdered when answering the bell of his front door in the next street. Public anxiety was exacerbated by a series of murders a fortnight later, for which Brian William Robinson was arrested, tried and hanged.

January's pattern and fears returned in August when an 18-year-old female student was killed by a single shot to the head while babysitting at Dalkeith. It was for this murder that Cooke was captured by police on

1 September when he attempted to retrieve the hidden weapon. In addition to the four who died by Cooke's marksmanship, he was acknowledged by the state to be responsible for the murders of a South Perth beautician, stabbed on 30 January 1959, and of a female social worker, strangled in West Perth on 16 February 1963.

Brought to trial on 25 November 1963 for the murder of Sturkey, through his counsel Cooke sought a verdict of not guilty on the grounds of insanity. Evidence revealed that this short, dark-haired man with a quick temper and a retentive memory had been brutalized by a father for whom he had never formed affection; he had further been tormented at school for the impediments of a cleft palate and hare lip, hospitalized frequently for head injuries, suspected brain damage and recurrent headaches, and admitted to an asylum. Life's blows extended to the next generation: the eldest of his children was mentally retarded, while another was born with a deformed arm. Dr A. S. Ellis, director of mental health services, rejected the defence's claim that Cooke suffered from schizophrenia. The state permitted no other psychiatric specialist to examine him. The death sentence was pronounced on 27 November.

With six convictions for minor crimes at the time of his arrest for murder, Cooke later claimed to have committed more than two hundred thefts, five hit-and-run offences against young women, and the two murders for each of which Darryl Raymond Beamish and John Button were already imprisoned. These confessions led to unsuccessful appeals. Little credence was placed in Cooke's testimony by the court: the chief justice Sir Albert Wolff called him a 'villainous unscrupulous liar'. There were inconsistencies in Cooke's testimony, but in confessions to his chaplain and in sworn statements he re-affirmed his guilt in each case. The circumstances in which confessions were originally obtained from Beamish and Button, together with arguable flaws in judicial procedure and judicial reasoning in their appeals, leave open the possibility that each suffered a miscarriage of justice which Cooke sought to overturn.

Although opponents of capital punishment had organized protest in several previous cases, there was little public dissent from the sentence imposed on Cooke. Only one woman kept vigil outside Fremantle Prison on the morning of his execution, 26 October 1964. He was buried in an unmarked grave at Fremantle cemetery; his wife, three daughters and three of his four sons survived him. Cooke was the last person to be hanged in Western Australia for wilful murder before the State abolished capital punishment in 1984.

In the period when his crimes had remained unsolved there was a discernible change in Perth's attitude towards personal and household security. Police and politicians were widely criticized; gunsmiths, locksmiths and the dogs' refuge did a brisk trade; and the breezy habits of an informal town in a hot climate were no longer innocently enjoyed. The social impact of Cooke's crimes and the atmosphere in which he was tried are imaginatively but faithfully reflected in Tim Winton's novel, *Cloudstreet* (Melbourne, 1991).

P. Brett, *The Beamish Case* (Melb, 1966); M. Hervey, *Violent Australian Crimes* (Melb, 1978); J. Coulter, *With Malice Aforethought* (Perth, 1982); *West Australian*, Jan, Feb, Aug, Sept, 26-28 Nov 1963, 16, 17 Jan, 27 Oct 1964; *Daily News* (Perth), Jan, Aug, Sept, Nov 1963, Oct 1964; *SMH*, 25 Oct 1964; *Living Today* (Perth), June 1977; N. Mattingley, The Abolition of Capital Punishment in Western Australia, 1960-1984 (B.A. Hons thesis, Murdoch Univ, 1990); Supreme Court of WA, R. v Cooke, no 280, 25-27 Nov 1963 (unpublished transcript); Dept of Corrective Services (formerly Prisons Dept) files (WAA).   HUGH COLLINS

COOKSON, ISABEL CLIFTON (1893-1973), botanist and palaeobotanist, was born on Christmas Day 1893 at Hawthorn, Melbourne, third and youngest daughter of English-born John Cookson, gentleman, and only child by his second wife Elizabeth, née Somers, from Adelaide. Educated at Methodist Ladies' College, Kew, Isabel gained honours in anatomy, physiology and botany in the senior public examination. She also developed skills as a pianist, was a prefect and played in the school's first tennis team. At the University of Melbourne (B.Sc., 1916; D.Sc., 1932) she graduated with exhibitions in zoology and botany. Tennis remained an interest and she competed in intervarsity matches.

Appointed demonstrator in botany (1916), in 1916-17 Cookson was awarded a government research scholarship (for work on the flora of the Northern Territory), the MacBain [q.v.5] research scholarship in biology, a first-class honours scholarship in botany and other grants. She tutored at the university and pursued botanical research on the longevity of cut flowers and on crown rot in walnut trees. Visiting England in 1925-26, she continued her work at the Imperial College of Science and Technology, London, and, on a return visit in 1926-27, at the University of Manchester.

Back in Melbourne, in 1929 Cookson turned her attention to fossil plant studies, which brought her international recognition and acclaim. Collaborating with Professor

W. H. Lang, of the University of Manchester, she published several important papers on some of the oldest-known vascular land plants that occurred in Victoria during the latest Silurian and Early Devonian times (c.370-410 million years ago). She collected many of the specimens herself from rocks exposed in rugged terrain near Walhalla and at other localities in the upper reaches of the Yarra River. From this work, theories have been developed on early land-plant evolution. Cookson also researched more recent fossil plants (c.10-20 million years old) from coal deposits at Yallourn. Her research showed that Huon pine and several other conifers and flowering plants—which now occur in the vegetation of austral regions—grew within the coal-forming flora. In 1930 she was appointed lecturer in botany at the University of Melbourne, a post she was to hold until 1947; she was responsible for the evening course in first year botany.

During the 1940s Dr Cookson began working on microscopic fossil-plant remains. Her studies of spores, pollen and phytoplankton, and of fossil woods, leaves and fruits, provided a wealth of evidence on the composition of Australia's past vegetation. Moreover, she demonstrated the usefulness of plant microfossils in geological correlation and in oil exploration. The significance of this pioneering work was recognized by the Council for Scientific and Industrial Research, by the State Electricity Commission of Victoria, and by the University of Melbourne which established in 1949 a pollen research unit under her leadership. In 1952 she was appointed research fellow in botany.

Cookson had been a keynote speaker at the official opening in 1947 of the Birbal Sahni Institute of Palaeobotany, Lucknow, India. She held a Leverhulme research grant at the University of Manchester in 1948-49. Elected a corresponding member (1957) of the Botanical Society of America, she was a life member (from 1959) of the Royal Society of Victoria. In 1959-62 she acted as honorary associate in palaeontology to the National Museum of Victoria, to which she had donated her collection of palaeobotany in 1950. Papers given at a symposium held at the University of Queensland in 1971 to honour her outstanding contributions to palaeobotany were published by the Geological Society of Australia. In her research career of fifty-eight years she published eighty-five papers, fifty-two of them in collaboration with seventeen other scientists. Thirty were published after her retirement in 1959.

Known affectionately as Cookie by her colleagues, she had a close circle of friends with whom she shared her interests in music and travel. Although she was an entertaining conversationalist, her thoughts were never far

from her research. In later years she organized her working hours so as to be free to listen to the Australian Broadcasting Commission's 'Blue Hills' and the 'Argonauts'. As a young woman she had been left to nurse her mother through a long illness under strained financial circumstances. After World War II, when her university salary increased, Isabel developed skills as an investor on the stock exchange; she used the profits to support her research in retirement and her trips abroad. She died on 1 July 1973 at her Hawthorn home and was cremated; her estate was sworn for probate at $169 112. Her name is commemorated by an award for the best palaeobotanical paper presented at the annual meeting of the Botanical Society of America.

R. T. M. Pescott, *Collections of a Century* (Melb, 1954); J. E. Glover and G. Playford (eds), *Mesozoic and Cainozoic Palynology* (Canb, 1973); F. Kelly, *Degrees of Liberation* (Melb, 1985); H. Radi (ed), *200 Australian Women* (Syd, 1988); *Review of Palaeobotany and Palynology*, 16, no 3, Nov 1973, p 133; *Univ Melb Gazette*, May 1983.

MARY E. DETTMANN

COOPER, CAROLINE ETHEL (1871-1961), letter-writer, traveller and musician, was born on Christmas Day 1871 in North Adelaide, daughter of Arthur Bevan Cooper (d. 1874), deputy surveyor general, and his native-born wife Harriette Isabella, née Woodcock (d. 1879), a music teacher. Ethel's great-uncle was Sir Charles Cooper [q.v.1]. Educated by a governess and at Miss Annie Montgomerie Martin's progressive school at Norwood, Ethel and her younger sister Emmie were raised by their maternal grandmother and formed a close friendship with Harriet Stirling's [q.v.] family. After studying music under I. G. Reimann [q.v.11], Ethel taught piano in rooms in King William Street.

By 1896 her sister was married and Ethel felt free to travel. She was to visit Germany five times between 1897 and 1936. Having furthered her musical studies at Leipzig in 1897-1906, she returned to Adelaide. Emmie was beautiful. Ethel's face had character. She was a small, slim woman with soft, brown hair; her voice was authoritative, her words carefully chosen and precise, salted with trenchant humour; she was described as eccentric, highly intelligent and an individualist. Wearing a black jacket and tie, she played trombone for visiting orchestras at the Theatre Royal and also formed her own Women's Orchestra. In 1911 she went back to Germany.

Her 227 letters to Emmie from Leipzig,

written in English, one a week between 31 July 1914 and 1 December 1918, described living conditions in wartime Germany and people's reactions to news from the Western and Eastern fronts. The letters of an observant and literate woman, they depicted the constant struggle for food and heating, the lazarettes where she played music for the patients, the deaths of friends and their relations, and the extremes of patriotism in the war's early years. The first fifty-two were smuggled to Switzerland and posted from Interlaken; the remainder were hidden, first between the pages of scores of Beethoven's string quartets and later in the cavity of a friend's dining-table. Ethel sent them from England when she was repatriated in 1918. Emmie subsequently deposited them in the archives of the State Library of South Australia.

Early in World War I most aliens had been required to move from German towns where there were fortifications, airship sheds or army installations, yet Cooper received a pass which stated that her presence 'was agreeable to the military authorities'. Throughout 1917 she made several attempts to leave, but was prohibited 'for military reasons'. Her premises were often raided and searched by police, but she had a wide circle of loyal friends who shared her love of music. She kept a pet crocodile ('Cheops') in her apartment. Back in Adelaide in 1921-22, Cooper soon returned to Europe. While not a Quaker, she joined a relief-team of the Society of Friends to work in Poland. Her fellow workers nicknamed her 'Pharaoh'.

At Salonica (Thessaloniki), Greece, Cooper did further relief-work in 1924-28, resettling refugees from Turkey: the society recorded its appreciation of her 'initiative, powers of organisation and her knowledge of the Greek language'. She bought a donkey and named it 'Agamemnon', and offered insects as sacrifice on her altar to Pan. For three and a half years she travelled in eastern Europe and the Mediterranean, indulging her passion for archaeology.

Finally settling in Adelaide with the widowed Emmie in 1936, Ethel worked as a translator and censor during World War II; one colleague deemed her 'a wicked gypsy'. Cooper drove an A-model Ford, sometimes regardless of other vehicles, and invariably with a cigarette in her mouth. In old age she suffered from arthritis and Parkinson's disease. She never married. Survived by Emmie, who lived to be 100, Ethel died on 25 May 1961 at Malvern and was buried in North Road cemetery.

S. Bowen, *Drawn from Life* (Lond, 1941); D. Denholm (ed), *Behind the Lines* (Syd, 1982).

DECIE DENHOLM

COOPER, FRANK ARTHUR (1872-1949), clerk and premier, was born on 16 July 1872 at Blayney, New South Wales, seventh child of Charles Cooper, a miller from England, and his Irish-born wife Mary Ann, née Scott. Educated at Blayney Public School, Frank was employed as a clerk in a Sydney warehouse until 1890 when he moved to the Church of England's Sydney diocesan registry and eventually rose to chief clerk. In 1900 he joined the Westinghouse Brake Co. Ltd. After postings to New Zealand, Melbourne and Sydney, he was sent in 1909 to Ipswich, Queensland, where the State's main railway workshops were located.

A member of the Brisbane Clerical Union, Cooper became vice-president, president and secretary of the Ipswich Workers' Political Organisation, and secretary of the Ipswich and West Moreton Eight Hour Day Union. He was a founding member of the local branch of the Workers' Educational Association, and was active in repertory theatre and the debating society. After publicly expressing support for coalminers in the general strike of 1912, he was sacked by Westinghouse. With enhanced standing in the labour movement, he worked as a journalist for several years.

In May 1915 Cooper won the Queensland Legislative Assembly seat of Bremer and joined the first majority State Labor government under T. J. Ryan [q.v.11]. Intelligent, well read, energetic and popular, Cooper held his seat for more than thirty years. He sat on royal commissions into the administration of the railways (1917-18) and public works (1922-32), and was temporary chairman of committees in 1920-32. In addition, he was an alderman (1924-27) and deputy-mayor of Ipswich City Council. On 29 June 1925 he had married 23-year-old Agnes Maisie Hardy at All Saints Anglican Church, Booval.

The Labor government was defeated at the elections in May 1929, but Cooper survived narrowly. During A. E. Moore's [q.v.10] administration, he distinguished himself in the Opposition with hard-hitting, well-researched speeches. Following Labor's return under William Forgan Smith [q.v.11], Cooper was secretary for public instruction and assistant-treasurer (1932-38). The priorities of this government, which led Queensland out of the Depression, lay in public works and improvements in health and agriculture. While neither side of the House saw any need to extend secondary education, Cooper presided over a restoration of Moore's budget cuts, some expansion in technical and rural education, and a steady increase in government scholarships.

Elected to the Queensland central executive of the Australian Labor Party in 1938, he joined its executive-committee in November 1939. Having also been appointed treasurer in Forgan Smith's government on 12 April 1938, Cooper concerned himself with careful management and his second budget was the first to show a surplus since 1927. He was elected deputy-leader of the State parliamentary party in September 1940. During World War II he served on the four-member Council of Public Safety which wielded overriding powers. Japan's entry into the war on 7 December 1941, only two months after the formation of the John Curtin [q.v.] Federal Labor government, introduced a new element of urgency and Queensland mobilized its resources behind the war effort.

In May-June 1942 the Commonwealth government introduced uniform taxation. Queensland was one of four States which immediately but unsuccessfully challenged the measure in the High Court of Australia. Although Queensland accepted the decision, Forgan Smith decided to resign and on 9 September Cooper was elected leader. He became premier on 16 September 1942; he was, at 70, the oldest person to take this office for the first time. Cooper co-operated closely with Curtin, supporting him at A.L.P. and premiers' conferences, even when the Queensland central executive opposed the decision taken by the A.L.P. federal conference in January 1943 to permit the Militia to serve in the South-West Pacific Area. After a conference of Federal and State governments, in November the Commonwealth called for a referral of powers for the duration of the war and five years thereafter. In the following months only Queensland and New South Wales passed the necessary draft amending bill. Cooper subsequently campaigned, with his Federal colleagues, in the unsuccessful referendum held on 14 August 1944.

Preparing for the 1944 State election, Cooper travelled throughout Queensland, revitalizing party organization and delivering his policy speech—a comprehensive programme for postwar reconstruction—at Ipswich. His government was returned with a reduced majority on 15 April and E. M. Hanlon [q.v.] took over the treasurership. In March 1945 Cooper departed on a tour of Britain. As acting-premier, Hanlon carried legislation to establish a Queensland Housing Commission and to approve agreements with the Commonwealth for housing and hospital benefits. Cooper resumed his duties on 5 November 1945, but was prepared to make way for Hanlon: he resigned as party leader on 6 March 1946 and as premier next day.

Appointed lieutenant-governor on 24 April 1946, Cooper was acting-governor until Sir John Lavarack [q.v.] was sworn in on 1 October. Cooper was a member (from 1946) of the senate of the University of Queensland and of the Anglican synod; he was also president of the Church Army and of the Brisbane City Mission. Survived by his wife and daughter, he died on 30 November 1949 at his Kedron home and, after a state funeral, was cremated. His constructive role as a wartime premier has been overshadowed by the achievements of his vigorous predecessor Forgan Smith and by those of his able successor Hanlon. Widely respected for his sincerity, great charm of manner and quiet dignity, Cooper was a capable politician and a gifted speaker, blessed with a delightful sense of humour.

C. Lack (comp), *Three Decades of Queensland Political History, 1929-1960* (Brisb, 1962); P. Hasluck, *The Government and the People 1942-1945* (Canb, 1970); D. J. Murphy *et al* (eds), *Labor in Power* (Brisb, 1980); *Herald* (Melb), 10 Sept 1942, 7 Mar 1946; *Sun News-Pictorial*, 20 July 1943; *Courier-Mail*, 1 Dec 1949; *Worker* (Brisb), 5 Dec 1949; Anglican Church Diocesan Archives, Brisb.

MANFRED CROSS

COOPER, HAROLD MORE (1886-1970), wireless operator, archaelogist and historian, was born on 29 December 1886 in North Adelaide, eldest son of Robert Cooper, accountant, and his wife Mary Antill, née Osborne. Educated locally at Queen's School and through travel in Europe, from the age of 18 Harold was employed by the Eastern Extension Australasian & China Telegraph Co. Ltd, Adelaide; he resigned in 1926 after spending years of exhausting shiftwork transmitting and receiving morse code. From his Glenelg home he operated an amateur, experimental wireless station. He made worldwide contacts, participated in research (including the effects of climatic conditions and sunspot disturbances on long-distance, short-wave communication) and provided a radio link between the magnetic observatory at Watheroo, Western Australia, and Washington, D.C., United States of America.

Becoming interested in Aboriginal stone culture in 1934, Cooper discovered at Hallett Cove, eight miles (12.9 km) south of Adelaide, 'a vast camp-site of ancient people' whose large, crude, stone implements he found on ground exposed by recent ploughing. These implements resembled some previously collected on Kangaroo Island which had been uninhabited when visited by Matthew Flinders [q.v.1]. Despite his slight, almost frail appearance, this gentle, generous man had the stamina and spirit to work hard and long in the field. Over the succeeding thirty-six years he made more than two hundred visits to the site, meticulously documenting his finds and observations. He also explored Kangaroo Island, locating ancient camp-sites and collecting hundreds of implements, products of an early culture which N. B. Tindale named 'Kartan'. Several of the twenty papers that Cooper published in the *Records of the South Australian Museum,* the *Transactions of the Royal Society of South Australia* and other journals were devoted to Kartan implements which he continued to find on the mainland.

Appointed assistant-ethnologist at the South Australian Museum in 1941, Cooper was praised by Tindale, the curator of anthropology, for his painstaking work which ensured that the tools were recognized as 'the handiwork of the first Australians'. In addition to archaelogical items, Cooper brought back numerous specimens, among them new species of land snails and insects (two of the former and three of the latter were named after him). His recreations were sailing and deep-sea fishing, and he secured many rare fishes, including two new species.

In World War II, during Tindale's absence, Cooper packed half of what was the world's largest collection of Aboriginal artefacts and stored them in a disused railway tunnel in the Adelaide Hills. He later supervised their return to the museum. In April 1944 he joined the Naval Auxiliary Patrol as a staff skipper and patrolled Gulf St Vincent. With three others in Adelaide, working six-hour shifts, he maintained a constant radio monitoring service to detect any indication of enemy action. He published *Australian Aboriginal Words and their Meanings* (1949), *Naval History of South Australia* (1950), *French Exploration in South Australia* (1952), *The Unknown Coast* (1953) and *The Unknown Coast—a Supplement* (1955). The last two discussed Flinders' 1802 exploration of Australia's southern coast.

Cooper retired from his position at the museum in 1957, but continued as honorary associate in anthropology until his eighty-third year. In his seventies his field-work had still ranged from Hallett Cove to the Flinders Ranges. He died, unmarried, on 14 May 1970 at Waterworth Hospital, Glenelg, and was buried in St Jude's Anglican churchyard, Brighton.

SA Museum, *Hallett Cove—a Field Guide* (Adel, 1970); P. G. Jones, *A Bibliography of Aboriginal Archaeology in South Australia* (Adel, 1985); H. Mincham, 'Harold More Cooper', *Friends of the SA Museum Newsletter,* 2, June 1966, p 4; *Advertiser* (Adel), 28 Sept 1963, 18 May 1970.

HANS MINCHAM

COOPER, MARIEN; *see* DREYER

COOPER, SIR WALTER JACKSON (1888-1973), soldier, grazier and politician, was born on 23 April 1888 at Cheetham, near Manchester, Lancashire, England, son of Joseph Pollitt Cooper, salesman, and his wife Sarah, née Jackson. Educated at Bedford Grammar School and Wyggeston Boys' School, Leicester, Walter served as a reservist in the Leicestershire Imperial Yeomanry and in the Royal Horse Artillery, Territorial Force. In 1910 he migrated to Western Australia and worked his way to Brisbane where he set himself up as an indent agent. Having helped to rescue bathers from the surf at Southport on 28 December 1912, he was awarded a certificate of merit by the Royal Humane Society of Australasia. At a land ballot in June 1914 Cooper drew a 28 000-acre (11 331 ha) block from Llanrheidol station in the Middleton district, 132 miles (212 km) west of Winton. He eventually acquired neighbouring properties to raise sheep on a consolidated holding which he named Brackenburgh and retained until 1950.

Enlisting in the Australian Imperial Force, Cooper was commissioned on 12 June 1915 and joined the 15th Battalion on Lemnos in October. He served at Gallipoli, moved to Egypt and was promoted captain in April 1916. Two months later he arrived in France. At Mouquet Farm on 10 August he was so badly wounded that his leg had to be amputated. After convalescing in England, in January 1918 he became acting-adjutant of No. 6 Training Squadron, Australian Flying Corps. On 14 February that year he married Louie Dorothy Marion Crick at St Peter's parish church, Leicester; they were to remain childless. Cooper returned to France in September as recording officer of No. 4 Squadron, A.F.C., and was appointed M.B.E. (1919) for his work in the unit. From early 1919 he attended textile classes at the University of Leeds. His A.I.F. appointment terminated in Brisbane on 31 March 1921.

Cooper joined a number of service organizations, including the Brisbane Legacy Club and the Queensland branch of the Returned Sailors' and Soldiers' Imperial League of Australia. In seeking Country Party endorsement for the Senate in 1928, he made what (Sir) Arthur Fadden [q.v.] was facetiously to dub, 'the worst speech I ever heard', but was elected in November. Defeated in 1931, he was returned again in 1934. During a lengthy parliamentary career, he was a member of the joint standing committee on public works (1937-43) and of the joint committee on social security (1941-46); in 1947-49 he was leader of the Opposition in the Senate and in 1949-60 he led the Country Party in that chamber.

In 1949 he had been appointed minister for repatriation in the Liberal-Country Party coalition government of (Sir) Robert Menzies [q.v.]. Known as 'the diggers' friend', Cooper directed his efforts to improving conditions for ex-service personnel, especially through pensions, hospital benefits and housing; he even tried out the artificial legs developed in his department's factories. As minister, he maintained close, informal ties with leaders of the R.S.L. and was granted life membership in 1961. He was a member of the cabinet committee on ex-servicemen's affairs which Menzies had established in 1949 and to which the R.S.L.'s national executive alone had access. From 1949 to 1951 Cooper also sat on the interim council of the Australian National University.

Tall and slender, he was modest, unassuming and unfailingly courteous to all, qualities which earned him the sobriquet of cabinet's 'first gentleman'. Cooper was knighted in 1959. He resigned from the ministry in 1960 and retired from the Senate in 1968, the longest-serving parliamentarian of his contemporaries. Survived by his wife, Sir Walter died on 22 July 1973 at the Repatriation General Hospital, Greenslopes, Brisbane; following a state funeral, he was cremated.

E. J. Richards (comp), *Australian Airmen* (Melb, 1918); T. P. Chataway, *History of the 15th Battalion A.I.F.* (Brisb, 1948); G. L. Kristianson, *The Politics of Patriotism* (Canb, 1966); *Townsville Daily Bulletin*, 24 Nov 1966; *Courier-Mail*, 29 Mar 1967, 14 Sept 1968, 23, 25 July 1973; LAN/P510 (QA); Cooper papers, 1931-68 (NL); AWM records.

MARGARET BRIDSON CRIBB

COPELEY, JOSEPH HERBERT (1897-1977), rabbiter, was born on 8 April 1897 at Spring Creek, near Young, New South Wales, fourth son of native-born parents Thomas Copley, miner, and his wife Jane, née Shoard. He attended Burrangong Heights Public School where he admired the fighting prowess of his fellow pupil (Sir) Vernon Treatt. Joe's upbringing was strict: 'I was trained to tell the truth when I was a boy. If I was caught out telling a lie I was thrashed'. On leaving school, the Copeley boys became labourers and lived at Little Spring Creek.

For fifty years Joe and a younger brother Ken trapped rabbits for skin and carcase in many parts of New South Wales and Queensland. Their usual method was to drive their truck as far as possible into the bush and then push on farther with bicycles strung with steel (gin) traps. After setting their traps, they inspected them at sunset, by lantern in the evening, and at dawn. When trapping for the freezing works, they gutted the rabbits and hung them in pairs in a hessian screen in a shady place for collection. Although Joe warned that rabbiters 'tell tales like fishermen', he reckoned that he and his brother had caught well over half a million rabbits in their

careers. The most they ever caught in a night was 288 (when the price was threepence a pair); the most in a fortnight was 1080.

From the early 1960s the brothers camped on Tara station, sixty-eight miles (109.4 km) north-west of Condobolin, New South Wales. There, with their dogs and junk, they inhabited a collection of dirt-floored, tattered tents and tin sheds. They lived frugally and rarely went into town, except on special occasions like Anzac Day. Joe was famous locally for his ability to solder aluminium and for the makeshift repairs he carried out on his battered vehicles.

Of medium height and wiry build, with a weather-beaten, wrinkled face, Joe was very critical of modern life when interviewed at the age of 72. He reflected that he could have married 'on four occasions', but added philosophically, 'when I saw men during the depression, with wives and children, who were absolutely out of their minds because they couldn't feed their families, I didn't feel too bad about not having married'.

In his last years Copeley suffered from diabetes and heart disease. He died on 17 August 1977 in Condobolin District Hospital and was buried in the local cemetery with Anglican rites. Joe was typical of many rural workers. Of humble origins and with limited prospects, he found his purpose in the rough but free bush life, combating Australia's worst introduced pest. Whatever the state of the economy, there was always the rabbit to trap, sell and eat: thousands in both town and country have depended on it for their sustenance or livelihood.

Sun-Herald (Syd), 23 Nov 1969.

G. P. WALSH

COPLAND, SIR DOUGLAS BERRY (1894-1971), academic, economist, bureaucrat and diplomat, was born on 24 February 1894 at Otaio, near Timaru, New Zealand, thirteenth of sixteen children of Alexander Copland and his wife Annie Morton, née Loudon, both Scottish-born Presbyterians. Alexander and Annie were pioneer farmers who grew wheat, raised sheep and bred horses. Educated at Esk Valley Primary School and Waimate District High School, Douglas qualified as a secondary schoolteacher at Christchurch Teachers' Training College and studied concurrently at Canterbury College, University of New Zealand (B.A., 1915; M.A. Hons, 1916).

Upon graduation, Copland tried to enlist in the New Zealand Expeditionary Force, and subsequently in the reserve, but was rejected as medically unfit. Greatly unsettled, he spent the summer of 1915-16 as a compiler at the

Census and Statistics Office in Wellington before becoming a mathematics master (1916-17) at Christchurch Boys' High School and a graduate research assistant in economics (1917) at Canterbury College. In addition, in 1915-17 he lectured in economics for the Workers' Educational Association, both in Wellington and at Christchurch.

From 1917 Copland pioneered the development of the economics profession in Australia. That year he took up a joint appointment as lecturer in history and economics at the University of Tasmania and tutor with the State branch of the W.E.A. of Australia. By the end of his seven years in Hobart, he enjoyed an established reputation as professor of economics (from 1920) and dean of the new faculty of commerce (which he had helped to inaugurate in 1920), and as director of tutorial classes for the Tasmanian branch of W.E.A. (he was the organization's federal president in 1921-22). He had given advice to successive Tasmanian governments on economics and education, and become a prolific writer and controversial public speaker. The University of New Zealand awarded him a D.Sc. in 1925 for his study of the wheat industry in that country. Each of these achievements, although pleasing to him, merely stimulated him to look for a wider field of activity, either in his homeland or in Melbourne. Initially, he favoured New Zealand because of family ties. On 28 January 1919 he had married Ruth Victoria Jones with Presbyterian forms in her father's house at Waimate. Ruth and Douglas had known each other from their schooldays. She was reluctant to leave New Zealand, but Copland's applications for chairs at Canterbury College and the University of Otago were unsuccessful.

Supported by leaders of the business community, the University of Melbourne established a faculty of commerce and in 1924 appointed Copland to the foundation Sidney Myer [q.v.10] chair. He was to occupy the post for twenty years until 1944 when he accepted the new Truby Williams chair of economics. From 1924 to 1939 (with the exception of 1933) he was also dean. His energetic and efficient leadership ensured the rapid expansion of the faculty and brought him control (from 1930) of the school of economics in the faculty of arts. The majority of commerce scholars were part-time or external students. Employed in industry, the public service or education, or enrolled externally if they lived in rural areas, they differed from the usual undergraduates. It was Copland's mission to see that they were at least equally esteemed. To this end, they were 'bred to the world of affairs, public policy and applied economics'.

Never did Copland interpret the professorial role in a narrow sense. He had been a founding member and first president (1925-28) of the Economic Society of Australia and New Zealand. As editor-in-chief (1925-45) of the society's journal, the *Economic Record*, he aimed to give the profession a cohesive focus and to raise the level of public debate. His insistence that governments take professional advice on economic problems had two obvious effects: the public service, at State and Federal levels, was gradually opened up to graduates, and academics were increasingly consulted on policy matters. Many demands were placed on him. At the invitation of the Commonwealth Development and Migration Commission, he evaluated a series of investment projects and wrote 'The Control of the Business Cycle with Special Reference to Australia', Appendix 1 to the commission's *Report on Unemployment and Business Stability in Australia* (Melbourne, 1928). The Federal government sought his views on tariff policy. Although his book, *The Australian Tariff: An Economic Enquiry* (Melbourne, 1929), co-authored with J. B. Brigden, E. C. Dyason, L. F. Giblin and C. H. Wickens [qq.v.7,8,12], was not acted upon, it achieved lasting fame in academic circles in Australia and abroad.

With the onset and deepening of the Depression, Copland publicly recommended exchange-rate depreciation, and, as an expert witness before the Commonwealth Court of Conciliation and Arbitration, advocated a reduction in the basic wage. In 1931 he chaired a committee of economists and under-treasurers which reported to the Australian Loan Council on means of restoring financial stability. The resulting Premiers' Plan (first called the Copland Plan) featured budgetary cuts and the conversion of internal debt to a lower rate of interest. It underscored the need for Australia to retain viability as a borrower and to spread the income losses of the Depression across the community.

Then, and later, these measures proved highly controversial. Encouraged by J. M. (Baron) Keynes's public assessment in 1932 that 'the Premiers' Plan last year saved the economic structure of Australia', Copland vigorously explained and defended the strategy adopted. In particular, the publication of *Australia in the World Crisis 1929-1933* (Cambridge, 1934)—the Alfred Marshall Lectures he had delivered in England at the University of Cambridge in 1933—roused international debate on Australian policies and earned Copland a Litt.D. (1935) from the University of Melbourne. From 1932 the Victorian government had regularly asked for his advice on financial relations with the Commonwealth and chose him in 1938 to chair the State Economic Committee. The premier of New South Wales (Sir) Bertram Stevens [q.v.12] retained his services as an unofficial adviser (1932-39); so, too, after 1932, did the businessmen whose firms constituted the Collins House Group, their principal contact with Copland being W. S. Robinson [q.v.11].

Copland's influence was not confined to Australian affairs. Having been selected in 1925 by the Rockefeller Foundation as its Australian and New Zealand representative on the Laura Spelman Rockefeller memorial (fund), he forged links with the international community of economists. In 1926, as guest of the foundation, he visited key universities, business schools, agricultural colleges, research institutes, government departments and banks in the United States of America, Canada, Britain and Europe. Opportunities were thus created for overseas scholars to visit Australia and for Australians to study abroad. Australia thereby became locked into an international study of quantitative aspects of the business cycle, which the foundation sponsored and which continued through the 1930s.

In 1932 Copland was one of four members of the Economic Committee which reported to the New Zealand government on Depression policies. In 1933 he was an Australian delegate to the fourteenth session of the League of Nations, held at Geneva, Switzerland, and that year gave advice—especially on the problems of wheat marketing—to S. M. (Viscount) Bruce [q.v.7] at the Monetary and Economic Conference, London. In 1935 he lectured at universities in Japan as a guest of the Japanese government. In 1938, representing the Australian Institute of International Affairs, he was a delegate to the second British Commonwealth Relations Conference, held at Lapstone, New South Wales. Increasingly concerned with the consequences of autarky and totalitarianism, he campaigned in favour of industrial mobilization for the defence of Australia.

As Copland grew in public stature, his role at the University of Melbourne expanded. He became increasingly involved in finance and administration. In his opinion there was much room for reform—through increased State grants, financial support from the private sector, the appointment of a paid vice-chancellor, and the recognition of academic initiative and opinion in the direction of university affairs. As chairman of the professorial board (1935-37) and acting vice-chancellor (1936-37), he vigorously pursued these ends. On the resignation of the first salaried vice-chancellor (Sir) Raymond Priestley [q.v.11], Copland was the choice of a committee of the university council, and a majority of the professorial board, for the post. Influential members of the council sought an alternative candidate, however, and (Sir) John Medley [q.v.] was selected in March 1938 by a vote of 15 to 14. Severely embarrassed by the rebuff, Copland

began to seek employment elsewhere. He did not formally resign from the university until late 1945, but he increasingly withdrew from Melbourne, accepting secondment to Canberra as Commonwealth prices commissioner (1939-45) and as economic consultant to the prime minister (1941-45).

Copland's national and international experience fitted him for the work of a wartime bureaucrat. As prices commissioner, he was outstandingly successful. He aimed to control rather than to fix prices. In early 1943 he initiated a comprehensive policy of stabilization, which provided for price ceilings and subsidies to ensure adequate production and equitable distribution of basic articles of consumption at reasonable prices. The Australian system was recognized as one of the most effective in the Western world. In the role of economic consultant, Copland maintained liaisons with appropriate departments. He was concerned with the development of social security, and with Australia's external economic relationships in the light of the government's full employment policy and its attitude towards the Bretton Woods agreement (1944).

A break in Copland's career came in 1946 when he was appointed Australian minister to China. The power of the Kuomintang (Nationalist Party) government was fading. Copland's dispatches revealed a quick disillusionment with the Nationalists, who appeared inefficient, corrupt and intractable, and destined to be displaced by the communists. His time in China was that of an itinerant. He travelled widely, attended the first session of the United Nations General Assembly (1946) and participated in preliminary negotiations for drafting a peace treaty with Japan.

In 1948 Copland returned to Canberra and to academic life as founding vice-chancellor (from 11 May) of the Australian National University. His pioneering activity entailed gruelling demands, for the university existed as little more than an idea and a name, supported by the services of an interim council and an academic advisory committee. The construction of buildings was made difficult by shortages of supplies. Potential staff and scholars were apt to be repelled by Canberra's relative isolation. Relationships with the State universities, eager for funds, were delicate. In the five years of his tenure he presided over the establishment of University House (the residential college), the research schools of physical sciences, social sciences and Pacific studies, and the John Curtin [q.v.] School of Medical Research. Eminent expatriate scholars and promising younger Australians were attracted to the staff. By publicly stressing A.N.U.'s research role and by taking a leading part in the Commonwealth committee of inquiry into the universities (1950), Copland did much to allay the fears of State universities.

When accepting appointment as vice-chancellor, he had stipulated that he retain his role as economist. He was outspoken on Federal policy; in particular, he warned in 1949 that Australia could develop a 'milk-bar economy' if the balance of production were not moved to basic industries; he was also critical of the management of the wool boom. Copland began a long association (1949-68) with the Immigration Planning Council, gave advice concerning the Snowy Mountains Hydroelectric Authority and urged closer economic ties with the U.S.A. While his efforts to influence public policy were not always popular with the Federal government, he was appointed K.B.E. in 1950.

In 1953 Sir Douglas accepted the post of high commissioner to Canada, a move which gave scope to his skills as diplomat and economist. Apart from his duties in Canada, where he was a popular appointee, he represented Australia at sessions of the United Nations General Assembly. As a member (president 1955) of the United Nations Economic and Social Council, he chaired the fifth session of the Intergovernmental Committee on European Migration (1953) at Geneva and attended the World Population Conference (1954) in Rome.

He greatly enjoyed his work in Canada, but resigned after three years to undertake a new venture. During the 1950s there was in Australia a growing recognition of the need to develop managerial and administrative skills. In 1956 a group of prominent businessmen established the Australian Administrative Staff College and considered Copland the obvious choice for its founding principal. He accepted, seeing the post as a new frontier in education. Very soon the college, wonderfully housed at Mount Eliza, Victoria, was conducting its first programmes, with participants living-in for a fixed session. Demand for its services was brisk, and the principal had a new forum as economist. He tirelessly preached the 'adventure of growth', and became the inaugural chairman of the National Obsolescence Council (1958) and of the Australian Productivity Council (1959). Alert to the future educational possibilities of business archives, in 1957 he had been chosen as first president of the Victorian branch of the Business Archives Council of Australia.

In 1960 his term at Mount Eliza ended and he was invited to lead a group of Australian industrialists and manufacturers on a trade mission to Canada and the U.S.A. It was well received. On his way home, he visited Geneva. There he advised the director-general of the International Labour Organization on setting up an international institute for labour studies, using the institutional methods adopted at Mount Eliza. Offered a three-year appointment as director, Copland took the job. He quickly became convinced that he was being used as a figurehead, rather than as a working director, and resigned. Back in Melbourne, it was necessary to make a new start, but that was not difficult. He became first chairman of the board of trustees of the Committee for Economic Development of Australia, accepted a number of directorships with private industry and was economic consultant to Walter P. Ham & Co., stockbrokers. Retirement came only with illness.

Copland was a big man, with immediate presence. He dressed immaculately. His large face was usually set in an expression of bland determination or urbane geniality, without which it looked somewhat aloof. Although athletic and energetic, he had been rejected for military service because of a lesion in the heart valve. In 1922 overwork resulted in a general breakdown of health and the development of a stomach ulcer which proved troublesome for the rest of his life, particularly at times of stress. He was hospitalized in 1932 after his exertions of the previous two years. Gregarious by nature, he evoked affection and loyalty, or dislike and hostility, but seldom indifference. He was admired for his optimism, forthrightness, warmth and courage, but criticized for his aggressiveness, naive vanity and occasional irritability—criticism which he accepted without malice.

An outstanding administrator, Copland was often 'first in the freshest field'. He chose his staff carefully, built up a feeling of solidarity, and delegated well. As an economist, he concentrated on the application of theory rather than on its advancement. His writings were abundant and various: books, monographs, articles in a wide range of scholarly journals, and contributions to popular magazines and newspapers. His skills as an editor encouraged other scholars; as a radio commentator, he was in constant demand. Among many overseas universities, he lectured at Harvard, U.S.A. (for its Tercentenary in 1936 and as Godkin lecturer in 1945), Oxford, England (Sidney Ball Lecture 1953), Dublin, Ireland, and McGill, Canada. He was a member (1948) of the American Philosophical Society.

Public recognition was not lacking. He had been appointed C.M.G. (1933) and received honorary doctorates from the A.N.U. (1967), as well as other universities in Australia, the U.S.A. and Canada. For his sixty-fifth birthday, the Economic Society of Australia and New Zealand devoted the March 1960 issue of the *Economic Record* to 'Essays in Honour of Sir Douglas Copland'. Survived by his wife and two daughters, he died on 27 September

1971 at Kyneton, Victoria, and was buried in Springvale cemetery. His name is perpetuated by a lecture theatre at the University of Melbourne, a building at A.N.U., a secondary college in the Canberra suburb of Melba and by a series of lectures sponsored by the Committee for Economic Development of Australia. Charles Wheeler's [q.v.12] portrait of Copland is held by the University of Melbourne; another by Paul Fitzgerald is at the Australian Management College, Mount Eliza.

Economic Record, vol 36, no 73, Mar 1960, pp 1, 124, and for pubs, p 173, vol 47, no 120, Dec 1971, p 465; *Aust Economic Hist Review*, 32, no 2, Sept 1983, p 193; H. Bourke, Worker Education and Social Inquiry in Australia (Ph.D. thesis, Univ Adel, 1981); Copland papers (NL).   MARJORIE HARPER

COPPEL, ELIAS GODFREY (1896-1978), barrister, was born on 7 October 1896 at South Yarra, Melbourne, eldest of four children of Albert Coppel, financier, and his wife Alice, née Abraham, both Victorian born. Educated at Melbourne Church of England Grammar School, in 1914 he began law at the University of Melbourne (LL.B., 1921; LL.M., 1925; LL.D., 1937) before enlisting in the Australian Imperial Force on 9 June 1915. After nine months in Egypt, he was sent in August 1916 to the Western Front where he served with the 5th Field Ambulance and (as a medical detail) with the 2nd Divisional Ammunition Column. He was discharged in Melbourne on 22 June 1919.

Admitted to the Victorian Bar on 2 May 1922, 'Bill' Coppel established a good practice, notably in commercial and constitutional matters. On 18 December 1925 at the registrar's office, Collins Street, Melbourne, he married MARJORIE JEAN SERVICE (1900-1970), a graduate from the university (B.A., 1922; LL.B., 1925) who had made a name as an actress and as a speaker on public affairs.

In 1935 Coppel published *The Law relating to Bills of Sale, Liens on Crops, Liens on Wool, Stock Mortgages and the Assignment or Transfer of Book Debts* which earned him his doctorate. He subsequently wrote a number of articles on legal subjects. In 1945 he took silk. He was admitted to the Tasmanian Bar in 1956. His practice took him into the highest courts, and he appeared before the Privy Council in 1948, 1949 and 1950. He was appointed to conduct several inquiries, including investigations of companies (1949 and 1962), and was a royal commissioner who examined third-party insurance (1959) and the Queen Victoria Market (1960). He also served as an acting-justice of the Supreme Court of Victoria (1950-52) and of Tasmania (1956 and 1958).

Following a sharp illness, Coppel retired from the Bar in 1965 and thereafter acted as consultant to Phillips [q.v.11], Fox & Masel, a leading firm of Melbourne solicitors. In 1950-59 he was warden of convocation of the University of Melbourne; in 1959-67 he was a member of its council and of its faculty of law. He was, as well, a vice-president of the Medico-Legal Society of Victoria and a music-lover.

Marjorie Coppel had long been active in the Council for Civil Liberties. After World War II she campaigned for day-care centres for children of working mothers. She published a study of nutrition, *Food and Health* (1941), and, with Mary Lazarus, a textbook, *The Making of the Modern World* (1960). Marjorie also wrote radio plays. She died on 18 August 1970.

A leading member of the Victorian Bar, Coppel proved an able and learned lawyer. In style and character he was a man of contrasts: at times courteous, gracious and urbane, at others sharp, relentless, wounding and abrasive. Particularly on the bench, he seemed on occasions to show antagonism and hostility to counsel and to others who appeared before him. He was appointed C.M.G. in 1965. Survived by two of his three sons, he died on 4 October 1978 at his East Malvern home. His body was willed to the anatomy department, University of Melbourne.

K. Anderson, *Fossils in the Sandstone* (Melb, 1986); *Aust Gazette*, 1, no 5, July 1965; *MCEGGS Mag*, Dec 1970; *Herald* (Melb), 13 Feb 1953, 24 June 1957; *Mercury* (Hob), 24 Oct 1956; *Age* (Melb), 8 May 1957, 5 Jan, 26 July 1960; *Sun News-Pictorial*, 5 June 1957, 20 Apr, 19 June 1959, 7 Feb 1962.   ZELMAN COWEN

CORBETT, ARTHUR BROWNLOW (1877-1970), engineer and administrator, was born on 18 February 1877 at New Shoreham, Sussex, England, son of George Frederick Corbett, collector, and his wife Susan Ellen, née Kerr. Arthur was educated at Ardingly College, Sussex. The family migrated to Queensland in 1890 where he attended Christian Brothers' College, Brisbane, and passed the junior public examination in 1892. After completing his indentures, in March 1899 he joined the Post and Telegraph Department as a junior clerk and was based at the General Post Office, Brisbane. Enlisting in the 5th (Queensland Imperial Bushmen) Contingent, he reached South Africa in April 1901 and was promoted sergeant on 10 July. The contingent fought in the Cape and Orange River colonies and the Transvaal before returning to Brisbane in April 1902. Employed by the Postmaster-General's Department next month, Corbett served in the accounts branch at the G.P.O. prior to becoming an assistant-engineer, electrical engineers branch, in December 1913. At St Stephen's Catholic Cathedral, Brisbane, on 4 October 1905 he had married a clerk Evelyn Mary Byrne.

In 1914 Corbett carried out the first survey of telephone requirements for the city. He was subsequently district engineer (1914-15) at Rockhampton and engineer-in-charge (1915-25), metropolitan line construction, Brisbane. In 1924 he was commissioned to investigate the possibilities of introducing mechanical mail-handling to the Brisbane Mail Exchange. Built locally from Corbett's plans, the original machine for sorting packets and newspapers was installed in December 1925. He then designed and commissioned the installation in Melbourne and Sydney of larger systems which were the forerunners of more advanced machinery. In January 1926 he transferred to Melbourne as inspector, central staff. Promoted superintendent of mails in Sydney in 1927, he introduced a simplified process of mail-sorting. He was an enthusiastic modernizer who also reorganized mail branches, introduced staff-training schemes and proposed amendments to postal regulations. Known to his staff as 'ABC', from 1933 he was deputy-director of posts and telegraphs, Queensland.

In April 1939 Corbett was appointed director-general of the new Commonwealth Department of Civil Aviation which was located in Melbourne. His technical and administrative abilities were regarded as vital qualifications for the reorganization of a previously confused and problem-ridden branch of the Department of Defence. He promptly divided D.C.A. into seven sections. During World War II he arranged for the conversion of all available civil aircraft to military use, personally supervised an airlift of servicemen from Papua and took an early interest in postwar planning. His term was extended repeatedly before he retired in August 1944. He then established a plantation at Montville, Queensland. In 1945 he chaired the provisional executive formed to create a State branch of the Liberal Party.

An associate member (1923) of the Institution of Engineers, Australia, Corbett had published a paper on the mechanical handling of mails in its journal in 1933. He was a member of Rotary and of the Queensland branch of the Professional Officers' Association. In 1938 he was appointed M.B.E. Survived by his daughter and three of his five sons, he died on 20 March 1970 at Kangaroo Point and was buried in Toowong cemetery.

C. A. Butler, *Flying Start* (Syd, 1971); R. L. Whitmore (ed), *Eminent Queensland Engineers* (Brisb, 1984); *Brisb Courier*, 14 July 1933; *SMH*, 16 Mar 1939, 18 Jan 1941, 4 Apr 1945; personal information.　　　　　　　　　　S. A. PRENTICE

CORBETT, THOMAS GODFREY POLSON; see ROWALLAN

CORKILL, ARTHUR BASIL (1898-1958), medical researcher, was born on 28 October 1898 in North Melbourne, son of Isaac Corkill, a native-born clerk, and his wife Louisa Marie, née Donnecker, from New Zealand. Basil was educated at Melbourne High School and the University of Melbourne (M.B., B.S., 1922).

Appointed a resident medical officer at the Alfred Hospital, Corkill showed sufficient promise to be seconded to work with Professor Maclean at St Thomas's Hospital, London; his expenses were underwritten by Dr J. F. Mackeddie, a powerful member of the Alfred board who was pressing for the establishment of a department of biochemistry. Returning to Australia in 1924, Corkill became the hospital's first biochemist. Insulin (discovered in 1922) and carbohydrate metabolism was his principal area of research. As the first physician in charge of the Alfred's diabetic clinic, with Ewen Downie [q.v.] he adopted an enlightened policy of patient-public education, using clearly written brochures which were widely distributed.

In 1926 the hospital's biochemistry department was absorbed into the new Baker [q.v.7] Medical Research Institute. At the Cairns Memorial Church, East Melbourne, on 9 April 1927 Corkill married Mona Ross Scott with Presbyterian forms. Two years later he was given leave to work on adrenalin and insulin with (Sir) Henry Dale at the National Institute for Medical Research, Hampstead, London. He had a further year with Dale, supported by a Rockefeller Foundation fellowship (1931-32).

In 1935 Corkill was appointed acting-director of the Baker Institute when Dr W. J. Penfold [q.v.11] was incapacitated by illness; on Penfold's retirement in 1938, he succeeded him as director. During World War II obligations to the Department of Defence and to the chemical warfare section of the Department of Munitions preoccupied him and robbed him of the chance to develop his research. In 1948 he helped and encouraged Joseph Bornstein when he began his career at the institute. Although Corkill's work was never properly recognized, he was awarded a D.Sc. (1935) by the University of Melbourne and was a foundation fellow (1938) of the Royal Australasian College of Physicians.

With the postwar enlargement of the Baker Institute, both in funding and staff, Corkill established close collaboration with the Alfred Hospital's departments of biochemistry and pathology, and also with the honorary staff. Balcombe Quick [q.v.11] wrote of 'his essentially kindly nature' which was manifest in the way he assisted younger colleagues. A man of very considerable scientific capacity, Corkill undertook research which laid a foundation for advances by others, but circumstance prevented him from fulfilling his promise.

Illness had slowed him down. Golf and fishing no longer were possible, and the toll of liver disease, which was to prove fatal, led to his resignation from the directorship in 1949. Corkill had a quiet retirement at his Kilsyth home. Survived by his wife and daughter, he died there of chronic hepatitis on 30 October 1958 and was cremated with Anglican rites. In the next two decades the Baker Institute developed into a leading Australian biomedical research centre, with many distinguished researchers who had first trained under Corkill.

T. E. Lowe, *The Thomas Baker, Alice Baker and Eleanor Shaw Medical Research Institute* (Melb, 1974); A. M. Mitchell, *The Hospital South of the Yarra* (Melb, 1977); G. L. McDonald (ed), *Roll of the Royal Australasian College of Physicians*, 1, 1938-1975 (Syd, 1988); *MJA*, 11 Oct 1958; information from Prof J. Bornstein, Kew, Melb.

R. R. ANDREW

CORNWALL, EDWARD SATCHWELL (1886-1954), engineer and administrator, was born on 9 November 1886 at Ballinlough, County Roscommon, Ireland, son of William Cornwall, farmer, and his wife Fanny, née Satchwell. The family migrated to Queensland when Edward was a child. Educated at Mount Morgan Primary School, he served an engineering apprenticeship with Mount Morgan Mines Ltd. He consolidated his knowledge of mechanical and electrical engineering in several posts before becoming a marine engineer, first with (William) Howard Smith [q.v.6] & Co. Ltd and then with the Australasian United Steam Navigation Co. Ltd. His friendship with Daniel Evans [q.v.8]—formed about 1910—was to lead to lasting co-operation between Evans's engineering firm and the Queensland electricity industry.

After supervising installation of the first alternating-current generating plant for the City Electric Light Co. Ltd, Brisbane, in January 1914 Cornwall joined C.E.L. as superintendent of its power station in William Street. On 3 February 1916 he married Tasmene Louise Turnidge (d. 1945) in St Martin's Anglican Church, Killara, Sydney. Transferred to head office in Brisbane as engineer of construction in 1919, he quickly mastered an operation which comprised a substantial direct-current network, including part of the tramways system, and a rapidly developing alternating-current system. He was successively promoted chief assistant-engineer, assistant-manager and, in 1937, manager and chief engineer of C.E.L.

In 1936 Cornwall had presented to the royal commission on electricity a proposal to extend electrification in Queensland. In the following year the State Electricity Commission of Queensland was established and in 1939 he negotiated an agreement with that body for a co-ordinated development of electricity supply for coastal, south-east Queensland. A complicated project, it involved interconnection with the Brisbane City Council's system, as well as absorption of Ipswich Electric Supply Co. Ltd and a number of individual country undertakings. Cornwall married Lottie Forster on 5 January 1946 at St Mary's Anglican Church, Kangaroo Point. He became a director of C.E.L. in 1948 and next year was appointed managing director.

During its postwar expansion Cornwall guided C.E.L. through serious engineering, administrative and financial difficulties. He anticipated the problems inherent in further development of the region by private industry, and his initiative influenced the concept and structuring of the Southern Electric Authority of Queensland, the successor to C.E.L. In 1952 he was appointed general manager and chief engineer of the newly formed S.E.A. Cornwall was sought after as an adviser. He was chairman (1938-39) of the Brisbane division of the Institution of Engineers, Australia, and twice president of the Electricity Supply Association of Australia. A high-principled, hard-working disciplinarian, with a deep and clever sense of humour, he was comfortable enough in his relations with his staff to draw the remark, 'Ted, you are a cranky old devil, but we still love you'.

Survived by his wife, and by the daughter of his first marriage, Cornwall died of a cerebral haemorrhage on 12 July 1954 in South Brisbane and was cremated with Presbyterian forms. In 1956 the E. S. Cornwall memorial scholarship for engineering graduates was established at the University of Queensland.

R. L. Whitmore (ed), *Eminent Queensland Engineers* (Brisb, 1984); *Southern Electricity Authority News*, no 1, 1954; *Courier-Mail*, 13 July 1954.

HORACE B. MARKS

CORONES, HARALAMBOS (HARRY) (1883-1972), hotelier and businessman, was born on 17 September 1883 at Kithira, Greece, son of Panayiotis Coroneos, fisherman, and his wife Stamatea, née Freeleagus. From 1904 to 1906 Harry completed national service as a first-aid orderly. Having unsuccessfully applied to enter the United States of

America, he emigrated to Australia, disembarking in Sydney on 10 August 1907. Six weeks later he went to Brisbane where he worked in the Freeleagus [q.v.8] brothers' oyster-saloon in George Street. About 1909 he moved to Charleville and took over a café. In 1911 he opened the Paris Café on the corner of Wills and Galatea streets; from its rear premises he operated a silent-picture cinema and staged vaudeville shows with performers brought from Brisbane and Sydney.

In 1912 Corones acquired the lease of the Charleville Hotel. Reputedly, Paddy Cryan—a commercial traveller for the Castlemaine Perkins Brewery—had visited the Paris Café for a meal and was so impressed with Harry's conviviality that he suggested he move into the hotel business. Harry told him that he didn't know anything about hotels and didn't have any money. Cryan persuaded him that he could learn the trade, and the brewery would help to finance the deal. Corones was naturalized in June 1912. At Holy Trinity Church, Surry Hills, Sydney, on 29 April 1914 he married with Greek Orthodox rites Eftehia, daughter of Fr Seraphim Phocas [q.v.11]. Fire had destroyed the Charleville Hotel in 1913, but it was rebuilt and Corones ran it until the lease expired in 1924.

An enthusiastic supporter of air transport as the means to end the isolation of Queensland's west, in 1922 Corones bought 100 original shares in Queensland and Northern Territory Aerial Services Ltd. He catered for the airline, supplying picnic hampers and sit-down meals for transit passengers in a converted hangar at Charleville airport. He has also been credited with suggesting the names for the airline's first five aircraft—*Hermes, Atlanta, Apollo, Diana* and *Hippomenes*—drawing on the classical mythology of his native Greece.

In July 1924 Corones leased another hotel (the Norman) at Charleville. After purchasing the freehold, he demolished the building to begin construction of the Corones Hotel: built in stages, it was completed in 1929 at a cost of £50 000. By then, Charleville was the centre for a booming wool industry. The hotel, with its jazz hall, embossed plaster ceilings and en-suite bathrooms, was an oasis for graziers, wool-buyers and commercial travellers. Charleville became a scheduled stopping-off point for the fledgling aviation industry, bringing a host of visiting celebrities who passed through the hotel. They included the Duke of Gloucester [q.v.], Gracie Fields and Peter Dawson [q.v.8], and the aviators Amy Johnson, Elly Beinhorn and Sir Charles Kingsford Smith [q.v.9].

At Quilpie, Corones ran three additional hotels under the management of his nephews. He had purchased the Quilpie Hotel in 1921 and four years later built the Imperial Hotel.

In 1934 he leased the Club Hotel from the Castlemaine Perkins Brewery. His other business interests included a 17 000-acre (6880 ha) station, Whynot, near Thargomindah, and a half-share in an importing firm that operated from Sydney until the Depression.

To commemorate his membership (1916-69) of the Charleville Hospital Board and his sometime chairmanship of its works committee, the nurses' quarters were named the Harry Corones Block. He was a member of the original committee (1919) of the ambulance centre and was involved in its affairs until 1958. In addition, he served on the local fire-brigade board for over twenty years. Corones was a foundation member and major developer of the golf and bowling clubs, and a foundation patron and life member (1966) of the All Whites Football Club. His 'perennial youthful exuberance and impishness' made him the focus of many stories. He was a Freemason. In 1965 he was appointed M.B.E.

Survived by his wife, two daughters and by two of his three sons, Corones died on 22 March 1972 at Charleville and was buried with Anglican rites in the local cemetery.

Architecture and Building J of Qld, 10 Sept 1930, p 16; Qld Ambulance Transport Brigade Hospital, Charleville Centre, *Annual Report*, 1958; Charleville Hospitals Bd, *Annual Report*, 1964-65, p 4; *Fourex News*, no 6, Aug 1978, p 4; *Courier-Mail*, 24 Apr 1952, 12 June 1965; *Western Times* (Charleville), 17 June 1965, 23, 30 Mar 1972; *Sunday Mail* (Brisb), 15 Sept 1991.   DIANNE BYRNE

CORRAN, ALEXANDER (1861-1940), printer and newspaper editor, was born on 17 November 1861 at West Derby, Lancashire, England, son of William Corran, printer, and his wife Margaret, née Gill, both from the Isle of Man. Having learned his trade, Alexander migrated to New South Wales in 1883 and subsequently shifted to Queensland. At East Brisbane on 3 June 1885 he married Manx-born Mary Ann Kelly with the forms of the Churches of Christ; they were to have four children. A first-class printer, he worked in various Brisbane offices until 1893 when the bank crashes and the depression forced him into bankruptcy. He moved north and was briefly editor of the *Gladstone and Port Curtis Advertiser* before settling on Thursday Island in 1896. Corran took over the *Torres Straits Pilot and New Guinea Gazette*, a four-page weekly newspaper. From 1914 he gradually replaced it with the daily *Pilot*, a single quarto sheet, printed only on one side, said to be 'the smallest newspaper in the world'. He continued to edit it until his death.

In 1897 Corran gave evidence before a Queensland parliamentary commission inquiring into the regulation of the pearl-shell and bêche-de-mer fisheries. His submission directly attributed economic depression at Thursday Island to the introduction of Japanese workers about 1892. Although the shelling industry had prospered, wages once spent locally were now largely sent to Japan, and, in what was to be his reiterated refrain, Corran declared that 'money is sent out of the country which should be spent here'. He advertised in the *Pilot* to undertake all classes of job printing 'to stop Work being sent away from the Island, and Money leaving the District'. By mid-1899 he had been appointed a magistrate and a licensing justice for the Somerset district. He was also a member of the committees of management of the Torres Strait Hospital and the local state school, but he failed dismally to win a seat on the Torres Divisional Board.

The pearl-shelling industry began to suffer from a labour shortage after the Immigration Restriction Act (1901) was passed and many luggers moved to the Aru Islands. Corran criticized the consequent recruitment of Papuan crews on the same grounds as he had opposed Japanese labour: having to be paid in Papua, they spent no part of their wages in Torres Strait. In 1909 Corran was elected to the Torres Shire Council. When Thursday Island was constituted a municipality in 1912, he became a member of the first town council. After failing to be elected in 1914, he rejoined the council in 1917 and next year was elected mayor. By 1936 he was indefatigably addressing the Brisbane *Courier-Mail* on the 'decline of Thursday Island as a business centre'.

In July 1938 Corran discovered that he was ineligible—as an undischarged bankrupt—to hold civic office. Having been the island's longest-serving mayor, he resigned on 11 August and obtained his discharge from bankruptcy in Brisbane in June 1939. Slender, neatly bearded and with a Shavian elegance of appearance, in his later years he was accorded the status of the island's 'grand old man'. He died on 17 October 1940 at his home on Thursday Island and was buried with Anglican rites in the local cemetery; his wife, son and two daughters survived him.

Commission into the pearl-shell and bêche-de-mer fisheries, Report and Procs, *PP* (Qld), 1897, 2, p 1273; *Torres Straits Pilot and New Guinea Gazette*, 27 Feb 1897-21 Mar 1914; Government Resident at Thursday Island, *Annual Report*, 1905, p 2; *Courier-Mail* and *Herald* (Melb), 25 Oct 1940; Thursday Island Federal Hotel Register (held by RHSQ, Brisb).   MARGARET LAWRIE

CORSER, BERNARD HENRY (1882-1967), farmer, grazier and politician, was born on 4 January 1882 at Maryborough, Queensland, fourth child of Edward Bernard Cresset Corser, a merchant who had emigrated from England as a boy, and his native-born wife Mary Jane, née Brown. Educated at the Christian Brothers' School, Maryborough, St Ignatius' College, Riverview, Sydney, and Queensland Agricultural College, Gatton, young Corser became a dairy-farmer in the Burnett district, near Gayndah. In his twenties he chaired Rawbelle Shire Council. He married Marie Glissan on 22 May 1912 at St Stephen's Catholic Cathedral, Brisbane.

That year Corser won the seat of Burnett, joining his father, who then represented Maryborough, in the Queensland Legislative Assembly; both were Ministerialists. In his maiden speech Bernard stated: 'I come from the land, and I do not come from the stump. I come as a member representing the agricultural industry . . . as a fair man, in the interests of every section of the community'. A founder (1920) of the parliamentary Country Party in Queensland, he was its deputy-leader in 1923-24. He also served on the royal commission on public works (1923-28) and was joint Opposition whip (1926-28). In 1915 'E.B.C.' had entered Federal parliament as member for Wide Bay, a seat which he held until his death in 1928; Bernard then immediately resigned from the assembly. Unopposed, he won his father's seat in the House of Representatives and held it from 1928 to 1954.

Putting principle before party ties, in the late 1930s Corser voted against the national insurance scheme proposed by the United Australia Party-Country Party coalition government of J. A. Lyons [q.v.10]. Following Lyons's death in April 1939, the Country Party leader Sir Earle Page [q.v.11] tried to prevent the U.A.P.'s (Sir) Robert Menzies [q.v.] from becoming prime minister. On 20 April Page made an intemperate attack on Menzies in parliament. Corser dissociated himself from Page's remarks and, with (Sir) Arthur Fadden [q.v.], resigned from the Country Party. Albert Badman and Tom Collins [q.v.] joined the rebels, all of whom returned to the party in November, after Page had been replaced as leader. Corser was joint government whip (1940-41), joint Opposition whip (1941-43) and Country Party whip (1943-51), and a member (1946-49) of the joint committee on the broadcasting of parliamentary proceedings.

An articulate speaker, he had a good sense of humour and a penchant for playing practical jokes on fellow politicians. At times of stress during his prime ministership in World War II, Menzies would send for Corser and Collins whose light-hearted company enabled him to relax. Corser's constituents found him enthusiastic, obliging, courteous and efficient. A tall, dark-haired man with grey eyes, Bernie was a popular local member. His combination of Catholicism and conservatism was then unusual in Australian politics. He retired for reasons of health in 1954.

Retaining his interest in agricultural and pastoral pursuits, Corser had acquired what remained of Wetheron station in 1931, a farm at Cobargo, New South Wales, in 1933, and later a grazing property, Yandra, at Nimmitabel. In retirement he lived in Sydney. A widower, he died on 15 December 1967 at Killara and was buried in Northern Suburbs cemetery. His son and daughter survived him.

C. A. Bernays, *Queensland Politics During Sixty (1859-1919) Years* (Brisb, nd, 1919?); E. Page, *Truant Surgeon*, A. Mozley ed (Syd, 1963); R. G. Menzies, *The Measure of the Years* (Melb, 1970); *PD* (Qld), 1912, p 259, 1928, p 265; *Maryborough Chronicle*, 1, 14, 16, 17 Aug 1928, 22 Jan, 22 May 1954, 16 Dec 1967; *Courier-Mail*, 16 Dec 1967; *SMH*, 29 Apr, 10 Nov 1939; information from Mrs M. Anderson, Middle Dural, NSW.

ELAINE BROWN

CORY, GILBERT ERNEST (1906-1977), solicitor and army officer, was born on 23 December 1906 at Saumarez, near Armidale, New South Wales, fourth child of native-born parents Frederick Ernest Cory, schoolteacher, and his wife Blanche, née Hicks. Educated at Maitland East Boys' High School, Gilbert worked on the land for a year before being articled (1926) to a Moree solicitor William A. Cole (later Moodie, Cole & Co.) and joining the Militia. On 17 February 1931 in St Thomas's Anglican Church, North Sydney, he married Helen Louie Annie Vaughan. He was admitted as a solicitor on 13 March.

In early 1939 a friend who had lent him money abruptly asked for repayment in full. Unable to comply, Cory was issued with a bankruptcy notice. Without disclosing his financial affairs, he obtained a loan from a client of his employers. Rather than defending his conduct in court, Cory fled to Canberra and adopted the alias 'Graham'. He was struck off the roll of solicitors on 18 May. During this period his marriage broke down. After working as a motorcar salesman at Uralla, New South Wales, on 2 November he enlisted in the Australian Imperial Force. He was posted to the 2nd/3rd Battalion and on 9 January 1940 embarked for the Middle East. From February to July 1941 he saw action successively in North Africa, Greece and Syria, and was mentioned in dispatches.

Returning to Australia as a sergeant, in September 1942 he went with his unit to Papua. On 28 October at Eora Creek he led No. 14 Platoon in an assault against a strongly-defended Japanese position. When the platoon lost most of its non-commissioned officers, Cory moved between sections and directed operations. Although shot in the face and temporarily blinded, he continued to take charge until he was evacuated. Awarded the Distinguished Conduct Medal, he was promoted lieutenant on 1 February 1943. His wound required extensive plastic surgery in Australia and it was not until July that he rejoined the battalion at Wondecla, Queensland. By January 1945 he was involved in the fighting east of Aitape, on the north coast of New Guinea. At Long Ridge on 1 February Cory commanded two platoons in a daring raid on a Japanese camp; the attack disorganized the enemy and inflicted heavy casualties. For his deeds he was awarded the Military Cross.

Cory was 5 ft 8½ ins (174 cm) tall, with blue eyes and brown hair. His bravery and outgoing personality made him popular with his comrades. Promoted temporary captain in June 1945, he transferred to the 67th Battalion in October; he served on Morotai Island and from February 1946 with the British Commonwealth Occupation Force at Kure, Japan. He was repatriated in May due to ill health. Following postings in the Sydney area, he left the army in February 1949 with a disability pension.

A divorcee, on 16 September 1950 Cory married Florence Alvin Joy Pugh with Methodist forms at Concord West. They lived at Bondi. He had found a job as a managing clerk in a solicitor's office, but was bitterly disappointed when his application for readmission as a solicitor was rejected in November 1960. With his wife, he retired to South West Rocks in 1972. Survived by her, he died of emphysema on 4 September 1977 at Kempsey and was cremated with Anglican rites.

D. McCarthy, *South-West Pacific Area—First Year* (Canb, 1959); G. Long, *The Final Campaigns* (Canb, 1963); K. Clift, *War Dance* (Syd, 1980); *SMH*, 19 May 1939, 18 Nov 1960; AWM records; information from Mrs M. Noble, Castle Hill, Syd.

IAN GRANT

COSGROVE, SIR ROBERT (1884-1969), grocer, trade unionist and premier, was born on 28 December 1884 at Tea Tree, Tasmania, son of Michael Thomas Cosgrove, a farmer from Ireland, and his wife Mary Ann, née Hewitt. Educated at Campania, Sorell and Richmond state schools, and at St Mary's School, Hobart, Robert entered the grocery trade and was soon actively involved in the fledgling Labor Party and the United Grocers' Union. He was a founder of the Shop Assistants' and of the Storemen's and

Packers' unions. From 1906 he spent three years in New Zealand where he held office on the Trades Hall Council, Wellington.

On 10 January 1911 at St Mary's Catholic Cathedral, Hobart, Cosgrove married GERTRUDE ANN Geappen (1882-1962); they were to have four children. President of the local Trades Hall Council, in 1916 he stood unsuccessfully in the Denison electorate for the House of Assembly. He supported the temperance movement in its campaign for the 6 p.m. closing of hotels and opposed conscription in 1916-17.

Returned in 1919 as a member for Denison, Cosgrove promoted legislation on shop trading hours and workers' compensation. At the 1920 State conference of the Australian Labor Party he was elected president of the Tasmanian branch. Although he lost his parliamentary seat in 1922, he worked pragmatically with J. A. Lyons and A. G. Ogilvie [qq.v.10,11] to temper socialist doctrine and win Catholic support.

Regaining a seat in Denison in 1925, he became Labor's whip under Lyons and was a member (1926-27) of the select committee which inquired into civil law reform. Defeated again in 1931, he returned to his grocery business in Liverpool Street, Hobart. He kept aloof from the party's ideological confusion and its threats to secede from the federal body over the next three years.

Led by Ogilvie, on 9 June 1934 Labor won power with the support of an Independent. In August Cosgrove was given the portfolios of agriculture, forests and the Agricultural Bank. Travelling widely in the State, he built a reputation for common sense, won the confidence of the predominantly rural community and reorganized the Department of Agriculture.

Following Ogilvie's sudden death on 10 June 1939, E. J. C. Dwyer-Gray [q.v.8], aged 69, was elected premier on the understanding that he would resign after six months. Cosgrove defeated T. G. De L. D'Alton [q.v.] for the deputy-leadership. As treasurer, Cosgrove introduced his first budget late that year and co-operated fully with the Commonwealth in putting the economy on a wartime footing. He also favoured control of prices and rents under the National Security Act (1939) and took steps to set up fair-rents boards. Tasmania's economy was emerging from the Depression and there were plans for further hydro-electrical development. Exchanging offices with Dwyer-Gray, Cosgrove became premier on 18 December. His style of leadership lulled the Opposition and the Legislative Council into underestimating his intellectual ability and strength of character. Yet, while Cosgrove was calm in temper and approach, he was determined to govern effectively and to have his way. Giving

whole-hearted support to the war effort, he advocated Eire's active participation in World War II 'as an ally of Great Britain in defence of their common liberties and those of the Empire'.

Having refused to placate the party's left wing in 1941, Cosgrove was criticized by Bill Morrow of the Trades Hall Council, Launceston, but quietly prepared for the State election. On 13 December Labor won 20 of the 30 seats in the assembly, with Cosgrove topping the poll in Denison. During 1942 he co-operated with John Curtin and J. B. Chifley [qq.v.]; he refused to join four other States in challenging uniform taxation proposals in the High Court of Australia, and received an increased reimbursement grant for Tasmania. In the same year, when the States opposed H. V. Evatt's [q.v.] move to extend the Federal government's powers for post-war reconstruction, Cosgrove proposed that certain rights be 'referred' to the Commonwealth for five years after the war. To Cosgrove's annoyance, Evatt's plan was blocked by the Legislative Council in Tasmania. About this time Cosgrove came to distrust Evatt's arrogance.

In August 1944 lack of manpower almost halted construction of the hydro-electric dam at Butlers Gorge. Cosgrove pressed the Commonwealth for labour through the Allied Works Council. As premier, he presided over a smooth transition from war to peace amid Commonwealth controls and many shortages. In 1946 the Tasmanian government was obliged to appoint a royal commission to inquire into allegations of bribery in timber deals; the former minister for forests D'Alton was charged with corruption, but acquitted. In November Cosgrove won the election with 16 seats in the assembly to the Liberals' 12, though his own vote dropped considerably.

Cosgrove now dominated his government and saw Tasmania recover slowly, but soundly, in the postwar period. Orderly and punctual in his daily routine, he appeared calm and unruffled, and graciously received visitors—however lowly—in the executive chamber. He was shrewd in transacting business, and quick to recognize and promote talent; he faced problems with courage, doggedness, and with a clear understanding of other people's weaknesses and of his own limitations. A political survivor, against all odds he gained a reputation for electoral invincibility. Each Saturday he relaxed by dining and dancing with his wife at the Wrest Point Hotel.

Gertrude was a staunch companion to her husband in his political career and a devoted mother to their children. Their elder son Robert was killed in 1940 while serving with the Royal Air Force. Mrs Cosgrove was treasurer of the West Hobart women's branch of the A.L.P. and active in the Australian Comforts Fund, the Country Women's Association, the Australian Red Cross Society and the Victoria League. From 1916 she worked devotedly for Elizabeth Street State School; her leisure activities included gardening and crochet. Appointed D.B.E. (1947), she was invested at Buckingham Palace, London, by King George VI in 1949.

Resigning as premier on 18 December 1947, Cosgrove appeared before Chief Justice Sir John Morris [q.v.] on 10 February 1948, charged with bribery, corruption and conspiracy. He spent ten hours in the witness box and was acquitted on all counts on 22 February. Three days later caucus re-elected him premier.

On 8 July the Legislative Council, by a vote of 13 to 3, agreed to grant only two months' supply, provided that the government agreed to call a general election. Following a campaign fought on constitutional issues, on 21 August the voters returned 15 Labor, 12 Liberal and 3 Independent members to the assembly. Cosgrove polled well in Denison. A chastened Legislative Council saw his government continue with the support of an Independent W. G. Wedd. Cosgrove entered the most difficult period of his career. The turbulence of Federal politics—the defeat of Chifley in 1949, (Sir) Robert Menzies' [q.v.] move to ban the Communist Party of Australia, Evatt's leadership of the A.L.P. and eventually the Labor 'split'—spilled over into Tasmania, despite Cosgrove's efforts to prevent its so doing.

A good, though never too obvious Catholic, Cosgrove disliked and distrusted communists; he said that the world was well rid of Joseph Stalin on his death in 1953. On radio Cosgrove boldly advocated forward defence against communist insurgency in Malaya until the A.L.P. federal executive ruled against it. From the referendum campaign in 1951 to Labor's 'split' in 1955, he used his diplomacy to avoid any breakaway in Tasmania. He steered clear of Evatt's meetings, smoothed over ideological differences, meticulously accepted party decisions and made compromises at party conferences. In the end, he just failed to prevent a 'split' and some of the disaffection within the Labor Party was to bedevil the Tasmanian branch for the next twenty years.

Tasmanian politics remained in the doldrums. Cosgrove's party had no majority in parliament and he faced and survived elections in 1950 and 1955. Next year one of his ministers C. A. Bramich crossed the floor and gave the Opposition a majority. Cosgrove obtained a dissolution and was again returned to office with the support of an Independent. His tribulations continued when his treasurer R. J. D. Turnbull repeatedly breached cabinet solidarity, and was also tried and acquitted on charges of bribery and corruption in 1958.

Despite such political instability, Cosgrove had piloted Tasmania to prosperity in the 1950s. Well regarded by Menzies, he obtained good financial grants, enabling rapid expansion of the hydro-electricity scheme and attracting industries to the State. As minister for education (1948-58), Cosgrove introduced an extensive school-building programme. His popularity reached its meridian at the time of the visit of Queen Elizabeth II and Prince Philip in 1954: 'Cossie', as he was affectionately known, and his wife appeared everywhere, benign, tireless, immaculately groomed, and widely respected.

In July 1958, amid the Turnbull crisis, Cosgrove became ill; after undergoing surgery in Melbourne, he retired on 25 August. Except for two months in 1947-48, he had been premier for a continuous and record term of almost nineteen years. On leaving parliament, he quietly pursued a new interest in real estate as chairman of Willowdene Development Co. Pty Ltd. Cosgrove was knighted in 1959. He continued to attend State party conferences until 1968: in that year he failed to bridge a gap between his generation and Young Labor which was convinced that the old man had organized a Catholic voting-bloc with Brian Harradine. Among his many interests, Cosgrove was chairman of the Tasmanian Tourist Council and of the Southern Tasmanian Trotting Association; he was, as well, a member of the council of the University of Tasmania (1940-46 and 1948-55) and of the local branch of the St Vincent de Paul Society, and president of the Royal Hobart Golf Club.

Although his political reputation went into an eclipse, in his prime Cosgrove had some of the qualities of a statesman. Survived by a son and two daughters, Sir Robert died on 25 August 1969 in Hobart; he was accorded a state funeral and buried in Cornelian Bay cemetery.

Cyclopaedia of Tasmania (Hob, 1931); R. Davis, *Eighty Years' Labor* (Hob, 1983); T. Newman, *Tasmanian Premiers 1856-1988* (Hob, 1988); W. A. Townsley, *Tasmania* (Hob, 1991); *Mercury* (Hob), 1 Jan 1947, 23 Feb 1948; information from Justice H. E. Cosgrove, Hob.   W. A. TOWNSLEY

COTTER, TIMOTHY JOHN PATRICK (1900-1972), medical practitioner and pathologist, was born on 13 October 1900 at Richmond, Melbourne, first surviving child and elder son of Timothy Cotter, railway employee, and his wife Margaret Mary, née Crowley, both Irish born. Educated at Xavier College, Kew (1915-18), young Tim entered the University of Melbourne (M.B., B.S.,

1924) and in 1926 commenced practice in a partnership at Ripponlea. On 19 January 1927 he married Lesley Beatrix Hennessy at St Patrick's Catholic Cathedral, Melbourne; they were to have one son and were later divorced.

Attracted by the opportunity to study bacteriology, he joined the laboratories of the Commonwealth Department of Health, under J. H. L. Cumpston [q.v.8]. In 1933 Cotter was transferred to the department's branch at Townsville, Queensland, as pathologist-in-charge, to investigate tropical diseases and fevers. Next year he went to Ingham to examine a disease which had caused serious illness and some deaths among canecutters in the sugar industry. Assisted by Gordon Morrissey, a local doctor, and William Sawers from the School of Public Health and Tropical Medicine, Sydney, Cotter found spiral-shaped organisms resembling those responsible for Weil's disease in the urine of some patients and succeeded in isolating the leptospira. The leptospirosis was carried by rats whose numbers were increasing rapidly in the havens provided by cane-fields. Discovery of the disease had serious economic consequences for the sugar industry. Because baits were not effective as a method of controlling the rats, the cane had to be burnt. But burnt cane incurred a penalty of one shilling per ton (at a time when the canecutter's rate of pay was only five shillings per ton). In addition, the manufacture of sugar from burnt cane was more difficult and it was also necessary to ensure that stale cane was not supplied. After prolonged negotiations involving a review of industrial awards, the burnt-cane solution was accepted and the suppression of the disease was ensured.

With Cumpston's support, in May 1936 Cotter was appointed medical superintendent of Innisfail Hospital. Following an aircraft crash near Mundoo aerodrome in 1938, an 18-year-old passenger was brought to the hospital with forty-seven fractures; after nine months she was able to leave without a blemish due to Cotter's skilful surgery. Late the same year, when a serious typhoid outbreak occurred, he obtained newly-released sulphur drugs and used them for the first time in North Queensland. On 21 May 1940 he resigned from the hospital to take up a private practice at Innisfail. He was appointed M.B.E. in 1956. From 1958 until 1972 he was a government-nominated member of the local hospitals board. On 26 August 1961 at his Innisfail home he married with Presbyterian forms Nita Nell Wentzel, a 30-year-old nurse.

In 1972 Cotter retired to Brisbane. Survived by his wife and their two daughters, and by the son of his first marriage, he died there on 23 May that year and was buried in Pinaroo lawn cemetery with Catholic rites; his estate was sworn for probate at $387 099. Innisfail Hospital holds his portrait.

R. Patrick, *A History of Health and Medicine in Queensland 1824-1960* (Brisb, 1987); J. H. L. Cumpston, *Health and Diseases in Australia* (Canb, 1989).   A. L. MARTINUZZI

COTTON, FREDERICK SIDNEY (1894-1969), aviator and businessman, was born on 17 June 1894 at Allensleigh, near Bowen, Queensland, third child of Alfred John Cotton, a grazier from the Channel Islands, and his native-born wife Annie Isabel Jane, née Bode. Educated at the Southport School and in England at Cheltenham College, Sid worked as a jackeroo at Cassilis, New South Wales. In England on 26 November 1915 he was appointed temporary flight sub-lieutenant in the Royal Naval Air Service. After only five hours solo, he was flying B.E.2c aircraft from Dover on Channel patrols.

With No. 5 Wing, Cotton piloted a Bréguet on night-bombing sorties from Coudekerque, France. He next joined No. 3 Wing at Luxeuil and bombed targets in southern Germany. In the winter of 1916-17 he devised the cold-resistant 'Sidcot' flying-suit which was to be widely used by civilians and the military until the 1950s. He flew Sopwith Pups with No. 8 Squadron until temporarily grounded for medical reasons and sent to England. Promoted flight lieutenant in June 1917, he helped to prepare the Handley Page bomber which attacked Constantinople in July, but he soon conflicted with his seniors and resigned his commission. On 16 October that year he married a 17-year-old actress Regmor Agnes Joan Morvaren Maclean at the register office, Camberwell, London; they were to have a son before being divorced in 1925.

Back home, Cotton ran his father's apple-drying factory in Tasmania, then returned to England in 1919. In February 1920 he unsuccessfully attempted to fly from Hendon to Cape Town and in July he destroyed his D.H.14a in the English Aerial Derby. He was based for three years in Newfoundland, Canada, where he worked as an airborne spotter for sealing companies, an aerial photographer, an air-mail operator and a supplier of timber. Giving his occupation as landowner, on 20 February 1926 at the register office, St George, Hanover Square, London, Cotton married Millicent Joan Henry, an 18-year-old schoolgirl whom he had met in Newfoundland and whose education he fostered in England; they were to have a daughter, but the marriage ended in divorce in 1944.

From the late 1920s Cotton was engaged in various business activities, including the transfer of patents from the United States of America to Britain. Although his attempt to promote the French-invented, colour-photographic process, 'Dufaycolor', ended in failure, he eventually made a substantial capital gain. In 1927 he was engaged by members of the Dupont family to search over Newfoundland for the French aviators Charles Nungesser and François Coli; in 1931 he supervised the operation that rescued Augustine Courtauld from the ice in Greenland.

Directed by the British Secret Intelligence Service in his civilian capacity, in 1939 Cotton carried out clandestine flights over Germany and the Middle East, photographing military installations, and, only days before the outbreak of World War II, obtaining valuable naval intelligence. He improved the Royal Air Force's photographic-reconnaissance capability: made honorary wing commander on 22 September and head of the new Photographic Development Unit at Heston, England, he operated a force of converted Blenheims and, later, of camera-fitted Spitfires. In June 1940, after again coming into conflict with senior officers, he was removed from his post. For his work he was appointed O.B.E. (1941). He also assisted Air Commodore William Helmore to produce an airborne searchlight, designed to illuminate enemy bombers.

From 1945 Cotton continued to combine audacity and adventure with an eye for profitable commercial ventures. Employing a fleet of Lancastrians, in 1948 he organized an airlift of arms to Hyderabad, India; he was accused of gun-running and fined the nominal sum of £200. His involvement in securing oil concessions in the Middle East was largely defeated by local politics. At the British consulate-general, Nice, France, on 1 August 1951—now calling himself a company director—he married 25-year-old Thelma Olive ('Bunty') Brooke-Smith, his former secretary. He recorded his life in *Aviator Extra-ordinary: The Sidney Cotton Story as told to Ralph Barker* (London, 1969). Survived by his wife, and by their son and daughter, Cotton died on 13 February 1969 at East Grinstead, Sussex, and was cremated with Anglican rites.

Cotton had been an unconventional individualist who was often right when well-placed opponents were wrong. Somewhat arrogant and conceited, he made powerful enemies easily, which cost him recognition and financial rewards. Yet, he was a man of considerable courage and energy, with a sharp mind and a flair for improvisation. In another age he would have made a splendid buccaneer.

D. Mondey (ed), *The International Encyclopaedia of Aviation* (Lond, 1977); C. B. Smith, *Evidence in Camera* (Lond, 1958); *The Times*, 21 Feb 1969.

JOHN MCCARTHY

COTTON, LEWY (1894-1972), waiter, was born on 6 November 1894 at Odessa, Russia, and named Loca, son of Joseph Andreus Cotton (Xotton), and his wife Mary. After three years in France, Loca arrived in England. In London he attended a school for waiters in 1907 and two years later became a dummy waiter, fetching and carrying at the Hotel Russell. In 1914, as a ship's steward, he joined a Russian four-master bound for Australia, jumped ship at Fremantle and became known as Lewy Cotton. He worked as a logger before taking a job at the Palace Hotel, Perth. Lewy claimed to have gained experience at the Savoy restaurant, Melbourne, and the Pier Hotel, Glenelg, Adelaide. In Perth on 8 June 1916 he enlisted in the Australian Imperial Force; he was 5 ft 8 ins (172.7 cm) tall, with a fresh complexion, brown eyes and dark hair. Posted to the 16th Battalion, he saw action in France in 1917-18.

After being discharged on 21 March 1920, Cotton was engaged by Adelaide's leading hotel, the South Australian, a three-storeyed, bluestone building with broad balconies, on North Terrace, opposite the railway station. A grand cedar staircase rose from the foyer with its plush furnishings and crystal chandeliers. The establishment was patronized by snobs, the rich and the famous. As head waiter from 1928, Cotton found an autocratic niche and continued in it when Mrs Louisa O'Brien [q.v.] acquired the premises. Despite his marriage to a machinist Ivy Gertrude Jenkins on 15 September 1924 at the Catholic presbytery, Goodwood, and the birth of a son, Lewy only spent Sundays at his Westbourne Park house. The hotel 'is my home and my life', he remarked. His day began by overseeing breakfast and ended late at night; but he took an afternoon nap in a room he rented across the lane from the hotel.

The major-domo enforced correct dress, even at breakfast (eventually a cravat was permitted) and luncheon. Incomplete gentlemen were asked, 'Have we a tie, sir?' and persuaded to leave if they had not. Cotton went to an excellent tailor and wore a morning suit, then white tie and tails at night. Patrons savoured his European background and counted his smile or nod an accolade. Lewy's manner was discreet, his bearing lofty; he reputedly gained substantial tips, though was apparently never wealthy. His supervision of the gilded dining-room, where drunks never disturbed his aplomb, ensured that his and the hotel's reputation remained untarnished. This 'Prince of Head Waiters' relished meeting the great, among them Pavlova. While he claimed to treat everyone equally, whether high or low, some less well-born or well-heeled guests found him disdainful. His staff, however, he managed kindly.

Lewy grew stout, his hair thinned and

receded, but his memory remained infallible and his smile enigmatic. Although suffering from emphysema, and hospitalized in 1968, he did not resign from his hotel until 31 December 1970. Next year 'The South' was demolished. Perhaps its destruction broke his spirit: survived by his wife and son, he died on 27 December 1972 in the Repatriation Hospital, Daw Park, and was buried in Centennial Park cemetery.

Hotel Gazette of SA, Jan 1970, Jan 1971, Jan 1973; *News* (Adel), 31 Jan 1958; *Sunday Mail* (Adel), 23 May 1959; *Advertiser* (Adel), 1 Jan 1971, 12 Jan 1973.
SUZANNE EDGAR

COTTON, THOMAS RICHARD WORGAN (1907-1970), soldier and intelligence officer, was born on 14 November 1907 at Dover, Kent, England, son of Captain Frederick William Cotton, Royal Army Medical Corps, and his wife Muriel May, née Pictor. Tom began an officer-training course with the Dorsetshire Regiment before migrating with his parents to Western Australia. In the 1930s he worked as a jackeroo. With the outbreak of World War II, he enlisted in the Australian Imperial Force on 7 November 1939 and was posted to the 2nd/11th Battalion.

Rising rapidly through the ranks, in May 1940 he was commissioned lieutenant. By June he was in England where he transferred to the 72nd Battalion (which was redesignated the 2nd/33rd Battalion in October and allotted to the 7th Division's 25th Brigade). Engaged against Vichy-French forces in Syria, on 8 June 1941 Cotton led his company in an attack against Fort Khiam. His men silenced a machine-gun in one of the fort's bastions, enabling a party to scale the wall and open a breach from the inside. Under cover of mortar fire, Cotton put more men through the hole. That night the French abandoned the fort. The Australians took the high ground and occupied the nearby village. Cotton was awarded the Military Cross.

After the Japanese entered the war in December, the 7th Division was recalled to Australia. Reluctant at leaving his British comrades in the Middle East, Cotton arrived home in March 1942. He was promoted major and, as second-in-command of the battalion, embarked for Port Moresby in September. In the arduous advance across the Owen Stanley Range and on to Gona, Cotton co-ordinated the provision of rations and ammunition to his unit, and the removal of casualties from the front line. At each location of an air-drop, he prepared a clearing, set up a rear headquarters, and supervised the collection and distribution of supplies. He was mentioned in dispatches for his efforts in the Papuan campaign.

From January 1943 he recuperated with his battalion in Queensland and trained for forthcoming battles against the Japanese. He took command of the 2nd/33rd in May and next month was confirmed in the rank of lieutenant colonel. After the battalion reached Port Moresby in July, plans were made to air-lift it on 7 September into enemy territory around Nadzab in the Markham Valley, New Guinea. At 4.20 that morning an American Liberator aircraft, loaded with bombs and petrol, crashed into five trucks containing men of the 2nd/33rd. Cotton witnessed the carnage: 59 of his soldiers died and 92 were injured. Despite the disaster, Cotton reorganized the unit, landed with his troops near Nadzab and on 14-15 September successfully attacked a Japanese position at Edwards's plantation. In extremes of weather the battalion fought until December over difficult country in the Ramu Valley and the Finisterre Range. Cotton led his men well, remained cool under fire and personally made reconnaissances. He was awarded the Distinguished Service Order.

In February 1944 Cotton returned with his soldiers to Queensland. Moving to Morotai, in June 1945 they embarked in a flotilla of landing craft for the invasion of Balikpapan, Borneo, and began operations on 2 July. The Australians had plentiful air and naval support, and outnumbered the Japanese. On 6 July enemy shells hit the battalion's command post and Cotton was wounded. From December 1945 to May 1946 he held administrative command of the 25th Brigade, then became a general staff officer, 2nd grade, at Southern Command headquarters, Melbourne. He married a 40-year-old Englishwoman Pamela Levett-Scrivener on 23 August 1946 at St Philip's Anglican Church, Sydney; they were to remain childless.

Cotton transferred to the Reserve of Officers in April 1947 and was active in the Citizen Military Forces. Fond of the quick riposte and the odd classical quotation, he was a 'tough, dour' and 'decisive' leader who was inspiring in action, meticulous in his planning and ruthless in dealing with inefficiency. He joined the Australian Security Intelligence Organization, for which he worked in Perth in the 1950s and as Victorian director until he retired in the late 1960s. Survived by his wife, he died of chronic bronchitis and emphysema on 26 September 1970 at South Yarra, Melbourne, and was cremated.

G. Long, *Greece, Crete and Syria* (Canb, 1953) and *The Final Campaigns* (Canb, 1963); D. Dexter, *The New Guinea Offensives* (Canb, 1961); W. Crooks, *The Footsoldiers* (Syd, 1971); J. Robertson, *Australia at War 1939-1945* (Melb, 1981);

L. McAulay, *Blood and Iron, the Battle for Kokoda 1942* (Syd, 1991); AWM records.   DAVID LEE

COUGHLAN, FRANK JAMES (1904-1979), jazz musician, was born on 7 June 1904 at Emmaville, New South Wales, third son of native-born parents William Kershaw Coughlan, tinminer, and his wife Elizabeth, née Parr. William became master of the Glen Innes and District band in 1912 and taught his five sons to play brass instruments. Educated at local public schools, in 1922 Frank went to Sydney where he heard recordings of the White-American trombonist 'Miff' Mole which revolutionized his approach to music.

Having found work in 1923, playing in Will James's dance band at the Bondi Casino, two years later Coughlan joined 'The Californians' at J. C. Bendrodt's [q.v.] Palais Royal, and gained valuable experience in style, feel, arranging and instrumental configuration. The band performed extensively in Sydney and Melbourne. On 20 November 1926 Coughlan married Agnes Helen Waddington at St Martin's Anglican Church, Kensington, Sydney; they were to be divorced in 1938. He went abroad in December 1928, toured Europe with Jack Hylton and joined Fred Elizalde's group at the Savoy Hotel, London. Returning home next year, he played in restaurant and 'palais' bands in Brisbane, Sydney and Melbourne.

In April 1936 Coughlan led the thirteen-piece orchestra at the opening of the Trocadero, Sydney. This 'palais' band was one of the finest in Australia and the public looked to him for the latest styles in jazz and dance music. With his trim physique and pencil-thin moustache, he cut a dashing figure in formal attire. The band's formation coincided with the advent of swing music: it played swing, as well as commercial favourites, and, from September 1938, some of its members gave renditions of traditional or Dixieland jazz. A feature film, *The Flying Doctor* (1936), had included the Trocadero band in a nightclub sequence, and the band made several records. Elected president of the Sydney Swing Music Club in March 1936, Coughlan wrote articles (1936-37) on the history of Australian jazz in the *Australian Music Maker and Dance Band News*. He married a professional vocalist Margaret Rose Grimshaw on 18 March 1939 at St John's Anglican Church, Darlinghurst.

From August 1939 Coughlan appeared with smaller ensembles in Sydney, Brisbane and Melbourne, before taking over the Melbourne Trocadero band. He played in Sunday afternoon jam sessions at Fawkner Park Kiosk, South Yarra, a key venue for contemporary jazz. Mobilized in the Militia in November 1942, he transferred to the Australian Imperial Force on 26 September 1943. He performed with the 9th Division Concert Party in Queensland in 1944 and with the 10th Entertainment Unit on Bougainville in 1945-46. Promoted sergeant on 30 August 1945, he was discharged on 25 March 1946. Coughlan went back to the Sydney Trocadero in October and directed the band until July 1951. After two years at its Melbourne namesake, he was maestro at the Sydney Trocadero from September 1954 until the nightclub closed on 31 December 1970. He then retired.

One of the most influential musicians in the development of jazz in Australia, Coughlan was an outstanding trombonist—in traditional and mainstream styles—a trumpet-player and an arranger. He advanced the careers of many spirited young performers and was an indefatigable advocate of jazz. Survived by his wife and their son, and by the daughter of his first marriage, he died on 6 April 1979 at Randwick and was cremated with Catholic rites.

A. Bisset, *Black Roots, White Flowers* (Syd, 1979); B. Johnson, *The Oxford Companion to Australian Jazz* (Melb, 1987); J. Mitchell, *Australian Jazz on Record, 1925-80* (Canb, 1988).

ANDREW BISSET

COUGHLAN, WILLIAM GEORGE (1902-1979), Anglican clergyman and social reformer, was born on 27 December 1902 at Armidale, New South Wales, son of native-born parents Benjamin Singleton Coughlan, draper, and his wife Minnie Maria, née Chapman. George was educated at Sydney Boys' High School and the University of Sydney (B.A., 1923) where he graduated with first-class honours in German. Although he intended to study law, he turned to the ministry while teaching at Trinity Grammar School, Summer Hill.

In 1926 Coughlan was made deacon and appointed curate at Dulwich Hill; next year he took first-class honours in the licentiate of theology and was ordained priest on 16 December. At St Matthew's Anglican Church, Bondi, on 11 February 1928 he married Norma Olive Bishop; they were to remain childless. In 1928-32 he ministered in turn at Bondi, Manly and Marrickville, and in 1934-43 at Holy Trinity, South Kensington (Kingsford from 1936); he also served as assistant-director of the board of education of the Sydney diocese. Beyond Sydney, he had ministered in the coal-mining district of Corrimal where, in 1932-34, he saw suffering caused by the Depression.

Widely read in British Christian social thought, Coughlan was influenced by (Archbishop) William Temple and the Malvern

Conference of 1941, Gerald Studdert-Kennedy and the Industrial Christian Fellowship, and George Macleod and the Iona Community. As secretary of the Sydney diocesan social problem committee, as a memorialist in *A Plea for Liberty* (1938), as a member of the social questions committee of the general synod of Australia, as editor (1935-36) of the *Church Times*, as well as in the Christian Socialist Movement and the United Christian Peace Movement, Coughlan expressed his belief that the Church must be concerned with all aspects of life, social as well as personal.

During World War II he pressed for Church guidance of postwar reconstruction. When the social questions committee established the Christian Social Order Movement for this purpose, Coughlan was appointed its director in September 1943. He plunged into an ambitious programme to bring Christian influence to bear on all aspects of life—through local branches, public meetings and a wide range of contacts in the community, and also through pamphlets, press and radio, particularly the movement's radio programme and its journal, *New Day*. With his wife he travelled throughout Australia, helping to organize branches and encourage local initiatives, such as the Aboriginal Children's Aid Committee at Wellington, New South Wales, and the Christian Co-operative Credit Union in Brisbane. To maintain dialogue with communist sympathizers, he and Bishop George Cranswick [q.v.] joined the Australian-Russian Society, but resigned in 1948 in protest at perceived communist domination.

Within the C.S.O.M. the Coughlans pioneered marriage guidance counselling; in 1951-67 he was director of the Marriage Guidance Council of New South Wales. Coughlan developed it as an open, self-governing organization, subsidized by government, with non-judgemental, non-directive counselling. He campaigned for liberalizing divorce law and for the establishment of family courts. In 1969 he became president of the Abortion Law Reform Association.

Coughlan was appointed A.M. in 1976. A man of enormous energy and of keen mind, he was a voluble speaker and debater, and a capable and resourceful administrator; stimulating and provocative, persuasive and abrasive, he was to many a sympathetic counsellor of humanity and compassion. He died on 26 May 1979 at Castle Hill and was cremated; his wife survived him.

Christian Social Order Movement (Syd), *New Day*, Sept-Nov 1948, Dec 1950; *People* (Syd), 16 July 1952; Marriage Guidance Council of NSW (Syd), *Annual Report*, 1952, 1953, 1966-67, 1968-69; J. Mansfield, 'The Social Gospel and the Church of England in New South Wales in the 1930s', and 'The Christian Social Order Movement 1943-51', *J of Religious Hist*, 13, no 4, Dec 1985, p 411, *and* 15, no 1, June 1988, p 109; *SMH*, 7 Apr 1928, 9 Feb 1937, 20 July 1938, 20, 24 Aug 1948, 29 Dec 1950, 17 Feb 1951, 6 Jan 1968, 26 Feb 1969, 28 May 1979; J. Mansfield, Social Attitudes in the Church of England in New South Wales, 1929-1951, with special reference to the Christian Social Order Movement (M.A. thesis, Univ Syd, 1979).

JOAN MANSFIELD

COULL, JAMES (1900-1972), trade unionist and orator, was born on 8 March 1900 at Upper Kinmonth, Kincardineshire, Scotland, son of James Coull, seaman, and his wife Margaret, née Drummie. Young Jim served in the British Army during World War I and was demobilized in 1919. On his return to Scotland, he met the socialist John McLean.

Six feet (182.9 cm) tall and solidly built, with a ruddy complexion and strong, thick hair, Coull was already a skilled debater and public speaker when he migrated to Australia in 1922. He found employment in Melbourne as an electrician, and became active in the Electrical Trades Union and the Victorian Socialist Party. Elected an executive-member (1924), president (1927) and vice-president (1929) of the Victorian branch of the E.T.U., and a delegate (1926) to the Trades Hall Council, in 1930 he was defeated for the union's presidency in a right-wing push to drive the socialists and other revolutionaries from the leadership. He lost again in 1931.

On 17 November 1928 Coull had married with Catholic rites Kathleen Veronica Lucas in the vestry of the Carmelite Church, Middle Park. That year he began working as an electrician for Carlton and United Breweries Pty Ltd, and, while retaining his E.T.U. membership, joined the Federated Liquor and Allied Trades Employees' Union of Australasia which briefly returned him as a delegate to the T.H.C. in 1931. He maintained his presence on the council by becoming the representative of the Ballarat Trades and Labor Council in 1932.

In 1928 Coull had established his own speakers' corner on Friday nights at Albert Park. 'Red Square' or 'Moscow Square', as his pitch was quickly dubbed, grew in notoriety. He also spoke at the Yarra Bank on Sunday afternoons. Some contemporaries judged him a better speaker than Tom Mann [q.v.10], with 'more of the Australian approach to things, yet lightened with Scottish humour'. Jimmy's oratory—particularly fiery and colourful in his descriptions of the 'enemies of socialism' (among whom he included Australian Labor Party politicians and their trade union supporters)—soon incurred the wrath of his opponents. Although the Liquor Trades Union secretary Morgan Murphy succeeded in having him expelled from the union in 1934, Coull had the decision overturned within two months. A remark he made at 'Red Square' about the T.H.C. being run by a 'secret junta' brought expulsion from that body in 1935. He was not readmitted for three years.

Having won a position as delegate to the federal council of the L.T.U. in 1936, Coull refused to accept office. Next year his 'Rank and File' team scored a convincing win. He was elected his union's vice-president (1937-49), federal councillor and delegate to the T.H.C., and was to hold the last two positions for nearly thirty years. In 1943 he stood unsuccessfully for the Legislative Assembly as the Socialist Party of Australia's candidate for the seat of Albert Park, addressing crowds of up to four thousand at 'Red Square'. Defeated again in 1945, he joined the Communist Party of Australia that year.

Elected assistant-secretary (1944) and secretary (1949) of the Victorian branch of the L.T.U., Coull led the union through the bitter years of anti-communism in the 1950s. The Australian Security Intelligence Organization began a file on him in 1947. Among union members, however, he won a personal following and a reputation for energetic leadership, especially in the long-running conflict with (Sir) Reginald Fogarty, the general manager of C.U.B.

Ill health forced Coull to resign as secretary in 1963, but he continued on the union's management committee. In retirement, he was in demand for radio and television appearances, and in 1965 toured the Soviet Union. He died on 13 December 1972 at Caulfield and was cremated. His wife survived him; they had no children.

B. Walker, *Solidarity Forever* (Melb, 1972); A. Best, *The History of the Liquor Trades Union in Victoria* (Melb, 1990); *Liquor and Allied Industries Union J*, July-Sept 1963, June 1966, Mar 1973; Labour Hist, Melb, *Recorder*, Feb 1973, p 2; *Tribune* (Melb), 18 Dec 1972, 16 Jan 1973; Liquor Trades Union (Vic Branch) archives (Univ Melb Archives); ASIO, CRS A6119/73, item 434 (AA, Canb).   ALLEYN BEST

COURTICE, BENJAMIN (1885-1972), farmer, sugar-industry leader and politician, was born on 28 March 1885 at Bundaberg, Queensland, sixth of twelve children of English immigrants Francis Courtice, labourer, and his wife Elizabeth, née Hamilton. Francis's difficulties in finding employment during the 1890s depression left a deep impression on Ben. Educated at Bundaberg South State School, at the age of 12 he began work as a 'juice boy' in the laboratory of the Millaquin sugar refinery; he also cut cane on local farms and was active in the labour movement. With his elder brother Frederick, in 1905 he helped to form the Bundaberg and District Workers' Union; it later merged with the Australian Workers' Union.

Employed in Henry Axelsen's bakery at Maryborough, Courtice met William Demaine [q.v.8], whose daughter Bertha (d. 1925) he married with Methodist forms on 31 August 1910 in her father's Maryborough home; they were to have four children. Handsome, well built and a fine athlete, Courtice had recently won a professional footrace at Bundaberg and with the £90 prize-money bought a sugar-farm, Hillside, which he developed in partnership with Fred. They subsequently moved to a property at Barolin Road; with a younger brother Sydney, Ben acquired another farm, Sunnyside. A founder of the United Cane Growers' Association, in 1926 Ben was elected to the Millaquin Mill Suppliers' Committee and to the Bundaberg District Cane Growers' Executive. In 1930 he became chairman of the executive and a member of the Queensland Cane Growers' Council; he was also a member (1933-37) of the Sugar Experiment Stations Advisory Board.

On 13 June 1936 Courtice married a 44-year-old nurse Elsie Dora Maud Joyner (d. 1966) at St John's Anglican Cathedral, Brisbane; they had met through his involvement with the Bundaberg Hospitals Board. In September 1937 the Queensland government selected him to fill a casual vacancy in the Senate; he was to be re-elected five times as an Australian Labor Party candidate. Throughout his parliamentary career he maintained his commitment to the sugar industry. He was Opposition whip (1937-41), a member of the Senate standing committee on regulations and ordinances (1937-38 and 1940-43), and chairman of committees (1943-46). Making it known that he wanted a man of undoubted honesty for the job, in late 1946 Prime Minister J. B. Chifley [q.v.] chose Courtice to be minister for trade and customs; he held the portfolio from 1 November 1946 until 19 December 1949. As a Labor representative, he visited London in 1953 for the coronation of Queen Elizabeth II. He retired on 30 June 1962, and thereafter lived in Brisbane and at Bundaberg.

Described as 'one of the original Labor men', 'a good unionist of the old school' and 'one of Labor's elder statesmen', Courtice was respected for his intelligence, integrity, courtesy and capacity for hard work. He kept himself well informed and had the ability to see all sides of an issue. Survived by the son and three daughters of his first marriage, he died on 7 January 1972 at Bundaberg; after a state funeral, he was cremated.

J. Kerr, *Southern Sugar Saga* (Bundaberg, Qld, 1983); *PD* (Cwlth), 22 Feb 1972, p 3; *Aust Sugar J*, Jan 1972; *Courier-Mail*, 8, 12 Jan 1972; information from Mrs E. Clay, Bundaberg, and Mr B. Courtice, Parliament House, Canb.   ELAINE BROWN

COURTNEY, VICTOR DESMOND (1894-1970), journalist, was born on 27 May 1894 at Raymond Terrace, New South Wales, seventh child of Henry Courtney, a newspaper proprietor from England, and his native-born wife Katie, née O'Connor. The family moved to Western Australia where Henry was managing editor of the *Greenbushes Advocate* and the short-lived *Sunday Press* (Perth). On leaving school in 1909, Victor entered the State public service before taking a cadetship in 1911 with the *Sunday Times*. In 1918, in partnership with J. J. Simons [q.v.11], he became managing editor of a sporting weekly, the *Call*, soon gaining publicity from a libel suit brought by the lord mayor of Perth, Sir William Lathlain. The partners also acquired a struggling Saturday-evening paper, the *Mirror*, and built its circulation during the 1920s to over 10 000, largely through racy reporting of scandals and divorces.

By 1935 Courtney and Simons were able to take over Western Press Ltd, publishers of the *Sunday Times*. They abandoned its crusade for Western Australian secession, but retained most of its other populist features, including the bush balladry of E. G. ('Dryblower') Murphy [q.v.10]. On 8 February 1937 Courtney married Thela Pearl Richards (d. 1962) in St Patrick's Catholic Church, West Perth. When Murphy died in 1939, Courtney took over as topical versifier, writing under the pen-names 'The Hobo' and 'Veecee'. He published *Random Rhymes* (1941) and *Cold is the Marble* (1948). Although few have stood the test of time, Courtney was pleased enough with his verses to name his only child Veecee.

Politically, Courtney favoured many Labor attitudes and denounced capital punishment, conscription and knighthoods. In July 1942 he stood as endorsed Nationalist candidate at a by-election for the Metropolitan-Surburban province in the Legislative Council: his views caused disquiet among members of the National Union who funded the anti-Labor coalition parties. Defeated by the unendorsed Nationalist (Sir) Frank Gibson, Courtney vigorously attacked the National Union and prominent Nationalist politicians at the 1943 Federal and State elections. Despite Courtney's personal friendship for John Curtin [q.v.], his newspapers never explicitly supported Labor and backed the Liberals under (Sir) Robert Menzies [q.v.].

Managing editor of the *Sunday Times*, Courtney also assumed the roles of chairman and managing director after Simons died in 1948. He built up a chain of thirty country newspapers, and successfully developed the *Sunday Times* as an advertising medium which enjoyed monopoly Sunday circulation. Yet, its format appeared increasingly old-fashioned and, in 1955, he sold Western Press to the young Rupert Murdoch's News Ltd.

Following his retirement to North Beach, Courtney published a biography of Simons and two books of reminiscences, *All I May Tell* (1956) and *Perth—and All This* (1962). These works present the Perth of the 1920s and 1930s as an easygoing, largely consensual community, free from many of the class or sectarian rancours of eastern Australia. This image is consistent with the tone of the *Sunday Times* under Courtney, though it is harder to reconcile the salacity of the *Mirror* with his sober, Catholic, family principles. Survived by his daughter, Courtney died on 1 December 1970 in St Anne's Hospital, Mount Lawley, and was buried in Karrakatta cemetery.

West Australian, 2 Dec 1970.

G. C. BOLTON

COUSENS, CHARLES HUGHES (1903-1964), army officer and radio broadcaster, was born on 26 August 1903 at Poona, India, son of Lieutenant (later Colonel) Robert Baxter Cousens, artillery officer, and his wife Esther, née Cummins. Educated in England at Wellington College, Berkshire, and the Royal Military College, Sandhurst, Charles was commissioned on 31 January 1924 and posted to the 2nd Battalion, Sherwood Foresters, in India. The battalion served on the North-West Frontier. Tall and bespectacled, Cousens was good at languages (he taught himself Urdu), navigation, boxing, cricket and polo. Unable to afford the expensive lifestyle of the Foresters, he resigned his commission on 29 June 1927 and worked his way to Sydney.

With jobs hard to find, he took employment as a wharf labourer and picked up a few pounds as a boxer in preliminary bouts at a suburban stadium. He then moved into newspaper advertising. On 20 May 1929 at St John's Anglican Church, Darlinghurst, he married an advertising representative Dorothy May Allan; they were to have a daughter before being divorced. Cousens found his true niche by reading some of his own copy over radio station 2GB. The quality of his voice and his pleasing personality soon made him a popular announcer. His best-known programme was 'Radio Newspaper of the Air' which encouraged even very young children to take an interest in selected news events. While uncommitted to any political viewpoint, he delivered a number of anti-communist broadcasts. He married a divorcee Winifred Grace James, née Dettmann, on 23 December 1938 at the registrar-general's office, Sydney; they were to have a son.

Appointed captain in the Australian Imperial Force on 1 July 1940, Cousens was posted to the 2nd/19th Battalion. He had command of a rifle company in Malaya when Japan entered the war in December 1941. Badly burnt when demolishing a village, he rejoined his battalion for the fighting on Singapore Island. His commanding officer and the troops commended his leadership in action, and he was promoted temporary major on 13 February 1942.

Soon after the capitulation on 15 February, A.I.F. headquarters in Malaya inadvertently revealed to the Japanese that Cousens had been a radio announcer. He refused to broadcast on their behalf while in Changi prison. Taken alone from a prison-camp in Burma, he was shipped at the end of July to Japan. There, under threat and fear of torture and death (as he would always claim), he wrote propaganda scripts, 'coached' English-speaking Japanese announcers and made short-wave broadcasts over Radio Tokyo. He maintained that the broadcasts were of minimal use to the Japanese, and that he had frequently sabotaged them by subtle ridicule and by inserting information useful to the Allies. Cousens also worked on a propaganda programme, 'Zero Hour', and chose as its main presenter an American woman of Japanese parentage—Iva Toguri (later d'Aquino), the misnamed 'Tokyo Rose'—who tried to help him undermine the broadcasts.

Following the Japanese surrender, Cousens was interrogated and brought home to Sydney under arrest. Because no Commonwealth legislation covered treasonable acts committed abroad, he was charged in New South Wales under the English statute, 25 Edw.III (1351). The gravest crime of all, treason was a capital offence. A magistrate's inquiry began in Sydney on 20 August 1946. Although Cousens had his critics, support for him firmed with the news that the Crown was depending heavily on the evidence of two Japanese who had worked with him. He was committed for trial, but the State's attorney-general C. E. Martin [q.v.] dropped the charge on 6 November.

Commonwealth legal and military authorities then considered court-martialling Cousens, only to reject the plan lest it 'would have the appearance of persecution and would thus be politically inexpedient'. They decided,

nonetheless, to strip Cousens of his commission. Their action, carried out on 22 January 1947, was widely regarded as vindictive. Three months later the men of the 2nd/19th Battalion elected Cousens to lead them on the Anzac Day march through Sydney. He was welcomed back to 2GB, and in 1957-59 worked as a television newscaster with ATN-7. In 1949 at San Francisco, United States of America, he had been a defence witness for Iva d'Aquino who, despite his assistance, was gaoled for treason.

The Cousens case was never properly resolved. Official historians of Australia in the war of 1939-1945 avoided the question of the degree of physical and mental endurance that could have been expected from prisoners of war. The army had shirked the issue in the first place by not ordering an immediate military court of inquiry or a court martial. Many years later Sir Garfield Barwick (who had been a member of the prosecution team at the magistrate's inquiry) thought that a jury trial would have been fairer and would probably have resulted in acquittal. Cousens died of cardiac disease on 9 May 1964 at his Greenwich home and was cremated with Christian Science forms; his wife and the children of both his marriages survived him.

2/19 Battalion A.I.F. Assn, *The Grim Glory of the 2/19 Battalion A.I.F.* (Syd, 1975); I. Chapman, *Tokyo Calling: The Charles Cousens Case* (Syd, 1990) *and* for bibliog, including Japanese publications; *Honolulu Star-Bulletin*, 10 Dec 1945; War diaries, 2nd/19th Battalion *and* 8th Division, AIF, 1941-42 *and* Brigadier A. Varley war diary *and* Lt Col R. Oakes, ms on 1941-42 Malayan campaign, 1947, *and* ms autobiog, 1984 (AWM); Lt Cdr G. H. Henshaw wartime diary (AA); Cwlth *and* NSW Attorney-General files, 1942-47 (AA *and* NSWA); correspondence and oral hist interviews with Aust, Japanese and American participants by author (Wentworth Falls, NSW).   IVAN CHAPMAN

COUSIN, ALLAN PATERSON (1900-1976), naval officer, was born on 29 March 1900 at Mount Pleasant, Back Plains, near Clifton, Queensland, seventh child of John McLean Cousin, a farmer from Scotland, and his Victorian-born wife Jane, née McLean. In 1914 Allan entered the Royal Australian Naval College, Geelong, Victoria, and next year moved to Jervis Bay, Federal Capital Territory, when the college was relocated there. He was awarded colours for cricket and graduated in 1917.

Promoted midshipman in January 1918, Cousin was sent to Britain and appointed to H.M.S. *Agincourt.* In 1919 he returned home and served in several ships, including H.M.A.S. *Marguerite.* Back in Britain for courses in 1921, he was promoted lieutenant in October and embarked for Australia in

November 1922. Cousin resigned his commission on 23 April 1923. He joined the Union Steam Ship Co. of New Zealand Ltd in 1924 and plied the trans-Pacific route to North America. Appointed lieutenant, Royal Australian Naval Reserve (Seagoing), on 1 April 1925, he was promoted lieutenant commander in 1930 and commander on 30 June 1936.

Cousin was mobilized for full-time service in March 1941 and took command of H.M.A.S. *Katoomba* on 17 December. She joined the 24th Minesweeping Flotilla at Darwin and participated in the action in which the Japanese submarine I 124 was sunk on 20 January 1942. Three days later *Katoomba* was rammed by the American tanker, *Pecos*, and was towed to Darwin and placed in the floating dock. The corvette was still out of the water on 19 February when Japanese aircraft raided the town. Cousin used her guns to harass one plane which attacked the ship and dock.

Deployed under Cousin on escort duties in northern Australian and Papuan waters, in August 1942 *Katoomba* rescued the crew of the United States Navy submarine S 39 from Rossel Island Reef. With a sister-ship, *Ballarat*, she was targeted by dive-bombers, off Buna-Gona, on 28 November; neither ship suffered damage or casualties, and one bomber was shot down. *Katoomba* was again attacked by aircraft in January 1943, near Oro Bay, but was unscathed.

On 27 January 1944 Cousin was appointed to command H.M.A.S. *Manoora*, a landing ship, infantry. As senior naval officer, Australian landing ships, he also had charge of *Kanimbla* and *Westralia*. The L.S.I.s supported the offensive in the South-West Pacific Area. Between April 1944 and July 1945 *Manoora* landed troops in Netherlands New Guinea at Tanahmerah Bay, Wakde and Morotai, in the Philippines at Leyte and Lingayen Gulf, Luzon, and in Borneo and Brunei at Tarakan, Labuan and Balikpapan. Cousin was awarded the Distinguished Service Order (1945) for his 'gallantry, fortitude and skill' during the amphibious assaults.

The efficiency of the Australian L.S.I.s drew widespread praise. Tropical service in the vessels was arduous: they lacked air-conditioning and were usually crowded. Cousin had found a three-week break in Sydney's cooler weather (July 1944) 'a veritable Godsend' and the crew's spirits lifted. After hostilities ceased in 1945, *Manoora* repatriated prisoners of war and transported personnel of the British Commonwealth Occupation Force to Japan.

Promoted acting captain in February 1945 and confirmed in the rank on 30 June 1946, Cousin was a skilful seaman, respected by those who served with him. Although tall,

robust and rugged in appearance, he had a retiring nature. He remained with the L.S.I.s until he was demobilized on 10 May 1949. Settling in Brisbane, he worked as a clerk in the war service homes division of the Commonwealth Department of Social Services. On 22 December 1949 at Mowbraytown Presbyterian Church, East Brisbane, he married a divorcee Cena Ethel Gundry, née Christesen (d. 1974). He died on 7 January 1976 at his Norman Park home and was cremated.

F. B. Eldridge, *A History of the Royal Australian Naval College* (Melb, 1949); G. H. Gill, *Royal Australian Navy 1939-1942* and *1942-1945* (Canb, 1957, 1968); I. Nesdale, *The Corvettes* (Adel, 1982); J. J. Atkinson, *By Skill and Valour* (Syd, 1986); *SMH*, 27 Jan 1945, 27 Jan 1947.

L. M. HINCHLIFFE

COVERDALE, PERCIVAL GEORGE (1882-1963), yachtsman and boatbuilder, and FREDERICK MYLES (1885-1958), sculler and shipwright, were born on 20 March 1882 and 12 April 1885 at Holbrook Place, Hobart, second and third sons of Norrison John Coverdale, clerk, and his wife Mary Elizabeth Gawan, née Hinsby, and grandsons of John Coverdale [q.v.1]. Educated at the state school, Macquarie Street, they grew up at Battery Point near the boatbuilding yards that had made the area famous. Norrison bequeathed to his sons 'the love of the river' and encouraged their aquatic pursuits. On leaving school, both boys were apprenticed to Hobart shipbuilders.

Fred first raced as an oarsman in a 'short four' for the Hobart Rowing Club in the Boxing Day regatta at New Norfolk in 1902. Over the next decade he developed into a champion stroke in both IVs and VIIIs, but it was in the single scull that he excelled. Champion of Hobart (1906-12) and of Launceston (1909-13), Fred won the Australian single sculls title in 1913 before retiring from championship rowing. He credited his successes to instruction by Alec Young and the Bayes brothers, and to physical fitness developed from hard training. For relaxation, he enjoyed hunting and fishing in the steep hills between the Lachlan and Huon rivers.

On 8 November 1915 Fred married Nina Grace Dixon with Presbyterian forms at her aunt's home in Hobart. A founding member (1910) of the Sandy Bay Rowing Club, he contributed much to his sport as a coach and supporter, and returned at the age of 37 to stroke the club's VIII. In the early 1920s Fred leased his brother Percy's boatyard at Battery Point, but moved by 1925 to Adamsfield where he prospected for osmiridium. Returning to the capital, he worked as a shipwright during the 1930s and 1940s for the Marine Board of Hobart and for Purdon & Featherstone. He coached the Buckingham and the Lindisfarne clubs, and trained several interstate crews, including the Tasmanian VIII in 1949. Predeceased by his wife and survived by two of his three daughters, Fred Coverdale died on 15 July 1958 at his Battery Point home and was buried in Cornelian Bay cemetery.

At 15, Percy Coverdale was employed by Robert Inches in his slipyard at lower Cromwell Street, Hobart. On 15 February 1910, at the nearby Anglican Church of St John the Baptist, Percy married Frances Minnie Rodgers (d. 1959); they were to remain childless. In 1914 he took over Inches's business. A keen oarsman and competitive cyclist in his youth, Percy became known throughout Australia as a yachtsman and master boatbuilder. Devoted to the native timbers of Tasmania, he avoided plans and constructed his boats from hand-sculptured 'half-models', producing some of the finest craft on the Derwent.

Four times in the 1930s Percy won the Royal Yacht Club of Tasmania's Bruni Island race. His best-known yacht was *Winston Churchill*, in which he finished third in the inaugural Sydney to Hobart race in 1945; in other hands she continued to be a force in sailing for many years. He also built *Landfall, Windward, Chloe, Telopea* and *Frances*, the last of which he built for himself in 1961. Percy Coverdale was a great raconteur who addressed his listeners as 'mate'. Lean and wiry, with a pipe perpetually clenched between his teeth, and a reputation for being touchy, he welcomed those who shared his passion for boats and sailing. He died on 29 March 1963 at New Town and was cremated.

E. H. Webster and L. Norman, *A Hundred Years of Yachting* (Hob, 1936); Roy Yacht Club of Tas, *Sailing On* (Hob, 1980); J. Muir, *Marine Reminiscences* (Hob, 1991); *News* (Hob), 14 Nov 1924; *Mercury* (Hob), 17 July 1958, 30 Mar 1963; information from Mrs J. Harvey, Hob. A. J. HARRISON

COWAN, SIR DARCY RIVERS WARREN (1885-1958), medical practitioner, was born on 8 August 1885 at Norwood, Adelaide, one of eight children of James Cowan, a merchant from Ireland, and his wife Sarah Ann, née Warren. Darcy attended Prince Alfred College and the University of Adelaide (M.B., B.S., 1908) where he won a triple Blue in lacrosse, football and tennis, and also played cricket. On 19 April 1910 at the Hahndorf home of Alfred von Doussa [q.v.12] he married Effie Hewitt Cox with Catholic rites; they were to remain childless. The Cowans were in England at the outbreak of World War I and

on 5 November 1914 Darcy was appointed temporary lieutenant in the Royal Army Medical Corps. Returning to South Australia, on 22 May 1916 he joined the Australian Army Medical Corps Reserve as an honorary captain.

In 1924-35 Cowan served as honorary physician to the (Royal) Adelaide Hospital where he became increasingly absorbed with the problem of tuberculosis and concerned with the toll that the disease was taking of young people, particularly those nurses and doctors occupationally exposed to it. Cowan's mission was threefold: prevention, patient care, and convincing his colleagues and government that the matter could and should be successfully tackled. In 1937 he visited the United States of America to investigate methods of control. President (1935-36) of the South Australian branch of the British Medical Association, he became a foundation fellow of the Royal Australasian College of Physicians in 1938.

His constant pressure and forthright statements resulted in the establishment at (Royal) Adelaide Hospital of a chest clinic, with a ward for tuberculous patients, of which Cowan was physician-in-charge (1938-50). In 1943 he criticized one tuberculosis ward in Adelaide for being located next to a dusty coal-dump and with a full view of the hospital mortuary. That year he founded the South Australian Tuberculosis Association, devoted to the welfare of patients, to public education and to the study of the disease. In 1947 in London he emphasized the importance of providing economic and psychological relief for sufferers and for their families. Returning to Adelaide, he introduced the use of *Bacillus Calmette-Guérin* vaccine which was prepared by Dr Nancy Atkinson. Next year he helped to form the National Association for the Prevention of Tuberculosis in Australia and forged links with kindred societies in Britain and America.

Virtually single-handedly, Cowan founded Bedford Industries, a new factory (opened in 1950 at Panorama, Adelaide) which offered opportunities for the rehabilitation of those afflicted with tuberculosis; it developed into a broad-based enterprise and the main building was named after him. Assisted by Sir Josiah Symon [q.v.12], Cowan had earlier set up Northcote Home, a residence for children whose parents were in hospital with tuberculosis. Although he found the task 'stupendous' and 'almost frightening', he never allowed politicians to forget the tuberculosis issue and maintained his relentless advocacy until the success of the National Campaign Against Tuberculosis was assured. In 1947-57 he assisted the James Brown Memorial Trust which owned and managed Kalyra Sanatorium and Estcourt House, Grange.

Cowan's obsession and his public pronouncements earned him opposition, even occasional enmity, from some professional colleagues, public servants and politicians. Rather belatedly, he was knighted in 1955. Plump, bald and bespectacled, with a benign, quizzical smile, he possessed an equanimity which calmed his patients' fears and showed a concern for their condition which extended beyond the province of medicine.

Despite a busy life, Sir Darcy enjoyed gardening and was an office-holder in the South Australian Lawn Tennis Association; he had helped to organize the Davis Cup challenge rounds at Memorial Drive in 1952 and 1956. He belonged to the Adelaide Club (from 1929) and was a life member of the B.M.A. Survived by his wife, Cowan died on 9 June 1958 at Calvary Hospital, North Adelaide, and was buried in Payneham cemetery. The Australian Laennec Society commemorated him by the Sir Darcy Cowan prize for research into respiratory disease.

G. L. McDonald (ed), *Roll of the Royal Australasian College of Physicians*, 1, (Syd, 1988); A. J. Proust (ed), *History of Tuberculosis in Australia, New Zealand and Papua New Guinea* (Canb, 1991); *MJA*, 2 May 1959; *SMH*, 20 May 1943, 16 Sept 1946, 12 July 1947, 17 Oct 1969; *Advertiser* (Adel), 11 July 1947, 9 June 1955, 9 June 1958.

PHILIP WOODRUFF

COWAN, RONALD WILLIAM TRAFFORD (1914-1964), educationist, was born on 10 April 1914 at Unley Park, Adelaide, third child of William James Trafford Cowan, pastoralist, and his wife Ethel Hilda Hedwig, née Hantke. Educated first by governesses on his father's property, Fernleigh, at Lucindale, Ron spent two years at boarding-school in England before entering the Collegiate School of St Peter in 1928 and then St Mark's College, University of Adelaide (B.A., 1936). He excelled as an all-rounder, gaining colours in athletics and football, and a first in history and political science; G. V. Portus [q.v.11] recalled him as 'perhaps the wisest' of his students. Selected as Rhodes Scholar for South Australia for 1936, Cowan went to England and entered New College, Oxford, where he took a good second in Modern Greats in 1938 and a B.Litt. in 1939 with a thesis on Australian federalism.

Returning to St Mark's that year, Cowan enlisted in the Australian Imperial Force on 3 June 1940 and was posted to the 2nd/27th Battalion. He fought in Syria in 1941, was commissioned in September and served in Papua in 1942-43, chiefly as an intelligence officer. Promoted temporary major on 18 October 1943, he taught at the Royal Military College, Kingston, Canada, in 1944. Back in Australia, in January 1945 he was appointed senior instructor at the Land Headquarters School of Military Intelligence; he transferred to the Reserve of Officers on 30 October. On leave in Adelaide he had married Mary Josephine Dawson on 18 July 1942 in the chapel of his old school. Late in 1945 he stood unsuccessfully as a member of the Liberal Country League at a by-election for the seat of Victoria in the South Australian House of Assembly.

Appointed warden of Trinity College, University of Melbourne, Cowan took office on 2 June 1946. Unlike his aloof predecessor (Sir) John Behan [q.v.7], he was a direct and forceful warden. Stocky and bespectacled, he was unbending in discipline but nevertheless convivial, risking his dignity in the college billiards-room the more easily because he usually won. He demanded high standards, admitted students on the basis of academic performance and expelled them for failure, with no favours for the sons of former members. Cowan observed his students keenly, and counselled wisely those who sought his advice. An exceptionally efficient man, he left his predecessor's elaborate files untouched and ran Trinity with a minimum of paper: the only instruction found by his successors was an outdated reminder to hire a bull for the college cows. (His nickname was, inevitably, 'The Bull'.) Sharing Cecil Rhodes's admiration for the residential college as an educational environment, he fostered a strong tutorial programme. He believed that the best colleges were small, but accepted the inevitability of growth and carried through a building programme sufficient to serve Trinity for some decades. In 1961 he skilfully negotiated the separation from Trinity of Janet Clarke [q.v.3] Hall.

An excellent committee man, Cowan made himself 'virtually indispensable' in academic Melbourne. He served twice on the university council, discreetly led his fellow heads of colleges, helped to found International House and the Overseas Service Bureau, and served as president of the university football club and vice-president of the staff association. He sat on the councils of Melbourne Church of England Grammar School and the Boy Scouts' Association, presided over Melbourne Rotary and was secretary of the association of Rhodes scholars in Victoria. Appointed to the interim and first councils of Monash University, he won praise from its founding vice-chancellor for his vision and plain speaking.

Cowan was vice-president of the Australian Council for Educational Research. In a series of outspoken addresses, including the Sir Richard Stawell [q.v.12] oration of 1961, he called for the transfer to the Commonwealth of sole responsibility for education, and for a doubling of expenditure. He edited a symposium, *Education for Australians* (1964), but, before it appeared, fell ill with bacterial endocarditis. Survived by his wife, two sons and two daughters, he died on 26 June 1964 in Royal Melbourne Hospital and was cremated with Anglican rites. A portrait by L. Scott Pendlebury is in Trinity College.

J. Grant, *Perspective of a Century* (Melb, 1972); *Univ Melb Gazette*, Sept 1964; *Age* and *Advertiser* (Adel) and *Herald* (Melb), 27 June 1964; Archives of Trinity College, Univ Melb; Univ Melb Council Minutes (Univ Melb Archives); personal information.   J. R. POYNTER

COWPER, ANDREW KING (1898-1980), air force officer, was born on 16 November 1898 at Bingara, New South Wales, fifth child of Henry Percival Cowper, a native-born surveyor, and his wife Amy Fraser, née Farquhar, from Guernsey, Channel Islands. Andrew was a fourth-generation descendant of William Cowper and P. G. King [qq.v.1,2]. Educated in England at Eastbourne College, Sussex, on 10 May 1917 he was appointed temporary second lieutenant in the Royal Flying Corps. He qualified as a pilot and in August joined No. 24 Squadron in France.

Flying D.H.5 and subsequently S.E.5a aeroplanes, Cowper operated from the Amiens and Dunkirk districts against German air and ground forces. In November 1917 he was credited with shooting down two enemy planes. On 26 February 1918 he skilfully shepherded a Pfalz west of the lines and forced it to land at a British aerodrome. Between 18 February and 6 March he destroyed two aircraft by solo effort and a further four in conjunction with other pilots; for his actions he was awarded the Military Cross.

Having acted as flight commander for some weeks, on 24 March 1918 Cowper was confirmed in the post and promoted temporary captain. In aerial engagements from the 8th to the 29th he accounted for another eight enemy aeroplanes by himself and two with the assistance of his comrades; he won a Bar to his M.C. Between 21 March and 1 April he flew twenty ground-attack sorties and caused 'great havoc and confusion' among German troops. Although his aircraft was repeatedly hit by enemy fire, he escaped injury. His 'magnificent dash and determination' earned him a second Bar to his M.C. Posted to England in April, he transferred to the Royal Air Force that month. After the Armistice he served in Germany and India before retiring on 13 February 1920.

Returning to Australia, Cowper took over Wiliga, his parents' sheep-property near Coonamble, New South Wales. On 28 April 1924 he married Miriam Goldberg at the district registrar's office, Randwick, Sydney; they were to have two sons Leon and Henry. Drought forced the Cowpers off the land and they moved to Sydney. Miriam opened a florist's shop in the city; Andrew became proprietor of Henderson & Co., seed and plant merchants; their business enterprises eventually included a gladioli-farm at Mona Vale. Cowper enlisted in the Royal Australian Air Force on 23 February 1942, rose to squadron leader in the Administrative and Special Duties Branch, and was demobilized on 2 March 1945.

Horticulture was Cowper's hobby as well as his living and he established a fine garden at his Bellevue Hill home. He was a member of the Australian Jockey and the Sydney Turf clubs. Fair minded and even tempered in outlook, he participated in Jewish festivals for his wife's and children's sake, but retained his allegiance to Anglicanism. The deaths of Miriam (1963), Leon (1971) and Henry (1972) saddened his later years. Cowper died on 25 June 1980 at the Prince of Wales Hospital, Randwick, and was cremated.

A. E. Illingworth, *A History of 24 Squadron* (Lond, nd, c1920); *SMH*, 28 June 1980; information from RAF Personnel Management Centre, Innsworth, Gloucester, Eng, *and* from Mrs F. Cowper, Vaucluse, Syd.   DARRYL BENNET

COX, GEOFFREY SOUTER (1914-1964), army officer, real-estate agent and politician, was born on 4 December 1914 at Bondi, Sydney, third and youngest son of Fred Fabian Cox, a property agent from England, and his native-born wife Mary, née Cameron. Educated at Sydney Grammar School, Geoff worked as a clerk with the Bankers' and Traders' Insurance Co. Ltd, played football, and enjoyed sailing and billiards. He joined the Citizen Military Forces in 1936, became an artilleryman in the 16th Heavy Battery at South Head and rose to sergeant in 1939. On 10 November he enlisted in the Australian Imperial Force and was appointed lieutenant in the 2nd/2nd Battalion next month.

Embarking as a platoon commander, Cox arrived in the Middle East in February 1940. He was wounded on 3 January 1941 during the attack on Bardia, Libya. After the ill-fated Greek campaign, he was posted in July to the 2nd/1st Battalion which was re-forming in Palestine. Promoted temporary captain in August, he accompanied the unit to Syria as adjutant. In March 1942 the 2nd/1st was sent to Ceylon and in July sailed for Australia. On 14 August that year at St John's Anglican Church, Toorak, Melbourne, he married Irma Robina Hitchins who had served as a Sister with the Australian Army Nursing Service in the Middle East; they were to have a son and two daughters, but were later divorced.

The battalion left for Port Moresby in September 1942 and was soon in action on the Owen Stanley Range. Before dawn on 23 October Cox guided a company of troops safely across the first bridge over Eora Creek; he was awarded the Military Cross for his courage and calm bearing. Invalided to Australia in December, he rejoined the battalion in July 1943 in Queensland. He was promoted major in December and in November 1944 transferred to the 2nd/7th Battalion, which he took to New Guinea as administrative commander before reverting to second-in-command. On 5 April 1945 he was promoted lieutenant colonel and nine days later assumed command of the 2nd/4th Battalion.

From the field headquarters which he had developed to a 'spartan standard of efficiency', Cox planned his battalion's attacks on Wewak Point (10 May) and Wirui Mission (14-15 May). In these engagements he 'was with his forward troops continually, and personally controlled and directed them'. For the brilliant success of both operations he won the Distinguished Service Order. Slim and taut, he was regarded by some as austere and aloof, but those who worked closely with him appreciated his loyalty and enthusiasm, and the empathy he had with his soldiers. Cox gave the same attention to detail in training as in battle. Junior officers saw him as the epitome of the infantry officer.

Transferring to the Reserve of Officers on 22 December 1945, Cox joined his brother Alan in the family firm, Alldis & Cox Pty Ltd, real-estate agents of Bondi. Their other brother John had served in the A.I.F. and died in 1943 while a prisoner of the Japanese. Geoff continued his involvement in the C.M.F. He commanded the St George Regiment in 1948-52 and the 8th Brigade in 1952-56. Promoted substantive brigadier on 31 August 1953, he was a member of the Eastern Command Officers Staff Group in 1958-62.

In August 1957 Cox had been elected to the New South Wales Legislative Assembly as Liberal member for Vaucluse. He married a widow Vivienne Yvonne, née Lylian, on 11 December 1961 at St Andrew's Scots Church, Rose Bay. Experiencing mounting business pressures, on 16 November 1964 he shot himself through the head in his room at Parliament House; he was cremated with Presbyterian forms. His wife and the daughters of his first marriage survived him. In 1970 the debts of his estate were found to exceed its assets by $8552.

A. J. Marshall (ed), *Nulli Secundus Log* (Syd, 1946); 2nd/4th Battalion Assn, *White over Green* (Syd, 1963); E. C. Givney (ed), *The First at War* (Syd, 1987); *Bulletin,* 23 July 1952, 4 Sept 1957; *Daily Telegraph* (Syd), 17 Nov 1964; *SMH,* 17, 20 Nov 1964, 15 Jan, 3 Sept 1965, 9 Oct 1970; information from Mrs M. Fitzhardinge, Barton, Canb, Maj Gen G. L. Maitland, Warrawee, and Maj Gen P. A. Cullen, Darling Point, Syd.

PETER BURNESS

COX, HENRY DANIEL BLANDFORD (1875-1979), pharmacist, was born on 10 June 1875 in Sydney, eldest of seven children of Nadir Cox, a painter from England who became a tramway guard, and his Irish-born wife Jane, née Sullivan. Educated at Redfern Public and Fort Street Model schools, at 13 Harry was employed in the dispensary at (Royal) Prince Alfred Hospital. In 1891 he was apprenticed to W. V. Bond, a chemist and tooth-drawer. After passing the Board of Pharmacy's preliminary examination, Cox voluntarily attended evening classes run by the Pharmaceutical Society of New South Wales; he passed examinations in botany, inorganic chemistry and materia medica in 1896; he was to be registered on 14 October next year under the Pharmacy Act (1897).

Having worked in pharmacies at Queanbeyan and in Sydney, in 1896 Cox returned to the Prince Alfred as assistant-dispenser on £150 a year. By 1903 he had chemist shops in Oxford and Waverley streets, but in 1907 moved to North Sydney and a partnership with A. R. Joscelyne. In 1908 Cox set up the North Sydney Pharmacists' Association to act against price-cutting on patent medicines and to promote early closing—he was 'fed up' with not being able to get to the football.

A councillor (c.1903-05) of the Pharmaceutical Society, Cox was a founder in 1903 and a director of the Proprietary Articles Trade Association of New South Wales which attempted to save chemists from price competition in patent medicines at the cost of shoring up small, unprofitable pharmacies. The P.A.T.A. was suspended in New South Wales under the Profiteering Prevention Act of 1920, but was re-established in 1923; Cox gave up his retail interests to become its full-time secretary. Retiring in 1950, he served as honorary general secretary until the organization was outlawed by the Trade Practices Act in 1971. He was also vice-president of the Master Pharmacists' Association, a director of Pharmaceutical Defence Ltd for fifty years and chairman of the Sydney Fire Office Ltd until 1965.

In partnership with his brothers in a Queensland dairy-farm, Cox had bought Jersey cattle because of their top-quality milk. He joined the Australasian Jersey Herd Society in 1919 and was co-opted to its executive. As president of the Australian Cattle Research Association, he was prominent in campaigns to eradicate such cattle diseases as piroplasmosis, brucellosis and mastitis. Later, he was president of the Australian Dairy Produce Board.

A bachelor, Cox spent his last active years with his niece at Artarmon. He was a Freemason and president of the local branch of the Liberal Party. With discernment, quick judgement and a remarkable memory, he was clear and careful in speech. Even in old age he showed no signs of the effects of a terrible motorcar accident in which he had been involved in 1917. Pushed by his mother to attend St John's Anglican Church, Glebe, as a youth he had been more interested in debating than in religion, and gained confidence in his ability to frame motions, draft regulations and write constitutions. Harry Cox outlived those who remembered his energies and his service: 104 years old, he died on 27 August 1979 at Wahroonga and was cremated.

G. Haines, 'Three Grains and Threepenn'orths of Pharmacy' (Kilmore, Vic, 1976) and Pharmacy in Australia (Syd, 1988); Chemist and Druggist of A'sia, 1 June 1904; Aust J of Pharmacy, June 1975, Oct 1979; SMH, 4 Dec 1918, 22 Mar 1939, 3 Apr 1940, 9 Aug 1971, 7 Sept 1979; Primary Producer (Syd), 23 Oct 1970; taped interview and correspondence with H. D. B. Cox, 1974 (held by author, Croydon, Syd).   GREGORY HAINES

COX, LEONARD BELL (1894-1976), neurologist and art collector, was born on 29 August 1894 at Prahran, Melbourne, fifth child of Victorian-born Rev. Edward Thomas Cox and his wife Isabella, née Bell, from England. Edward was an Anglican clergyman who became a Methodist. Leonard was educated at Wesley College (where he formed a lasting friendship with (Sir) Robert Menzies [q.v.]) and at the University of Melbourne (M.B., B.S., 1916; M.D., 1920). Following a brief residency at (Royal) Melbourne Hospital, on 3 May 1917 he was commissioned captain, Australian Army Medical Corps, Australian Imperial Force. From October 1917 he served on the Western Front, mainly at headquarters, 5th Divisional Engineers, until April 1919 when he took leave in Britain.

Admitted that year as a member of the Royal College of Physicians, Edinburgh, Cox returned to Melbourne where his A.I.F. appointment terminated on 20 December. He took up a position as Beaney [q.v.3] scholar in pathology at the university, but illness caused him to retire temporarily and he convalesced at a cottage which his father had built at Olinda. On 23 December 1925 at St Andrew's Anglican Church, Brighton, he married Nancy Compson Trumble.

Struggling to establish a consultant practice in neurology, Cox supplemented his income by working as an anaesthetist. At the same time he pursued his interests in neuropathology and research. In 1932-51 he was honorary part-time lecturer in neurological pathology at the university and in 1937 Stewart lecturer. As honorary neurologist (1934-55) to the Alfred Hospital, he persuaded its authorities to permit the formation of the first department of neurology in Melbourne and by 1936 had encouraged his brother-in-law H. C. Trumble [q.v.] to devote his surgical skills to neurosurgery: their partnership was also the first of its kind in Melbourne.

Throughout his years at the Alfred Hospital, at the Baker [q.v.7] Medical Research Institute and at the university, Cox made important contributions to neurological literature. His lectures in the medical faculty were fully attended and students received a synopsis of each lecture. At the bedside, his clinical skills and strength were evident. He was a superb teacher who had the gift of perceiving the problem from the history, and his examination of the patient went straight to the point. To Cox, the basis of clinical medicine came from an understanding of pathology and anatomy. In World War II he was a part-time neurologist with the Royal Australian Air Force and rose to acting wing commander. The initiator and one of eight founding members of the Australian Association of Neurologists, he was its foundation president (1950-62).

Early in life Cox had become a collector. He made his first purchase—a Battersea enamel box bought on a sudden impulse from a second-hand dealer—in 1917 while he was stationed on Salisbury Plain, Wiltshire, England. A fellow officer, a collector of Chinese art, encouraged him to view the Oriental antiquities in the British Museum. Cox continued to collect discriminatingly in Australia after the war. During this period he studied his subject in depth and learned Chinese characters to further his knowledge.

In 1937 the collection of H. W. Kent [q.v.], which had been assembled in Asia, was presented to the public and became the nucleus of the National Gallery of Victoria's department of Oriental art. Cox later succeeded Kent as honorary curator. Although Chinese art was his major delight, he had also acquired selected prints, etchings, Australian paintings, a collection of rare books, woodcuts by old and modern masters, and samples of English eighteenth- and early nineteenth-century cabinet-making. Nothing, however, surpassed his collection of Chinese ceramics, which was held to be the finest private collection in the country and made him internationally known. In 1953 a Rockefeller grant for medical research made possible a world trip on which Cox contacted many notable private collectors. He was a member of a cultural delegation to China in 1956 and next year returned there as leader of a medical delegation, at the request of the Chinese government.

In 1947 Cox had helped to establish the National Gallery Society of Victoria (president 1952). He was chairman of the trustees of the gallery (1957-65) and of the National Gallery and Cultural Centre committee (1957-64). In 1958 he was appointed a member of the Felton [q.v.4] bequest committee. When the new gallery was being designed, he partly withdrew from medical practice to devote more time and effort to the detailed planning. In 1970 he published *The National Gallery of Victoria 1861 to 1968*. For his contribution to culture and to the N.G.V. he was appointed C.M.G. in 1968. The gallery invited him in 1972 to mount a special exhibition of his own collection; the catalogue was entitled *Hundred Treasures*. Subsequently, the Felton trustees purchased a blue-and-white stem cup in his honour. Following his retirement in June 1965, he regularly attended gallery meetings.

In 1962 Cox had moved with his wife to the family cottage at Olinda, the grounds of which he had further developed by Edna Walling [q.v.]. There, in his glasshouse, he propagated and cultivated rhododendrons and camellias, and gathered rare species. He helped to form the National Rhododendron Garden at Olinda, providing many specimens from his beautiful garden. Survived by his wife and daughter, he died on 24 July 1976 at his home and was buried in Box Hill cemetery. From his estate, sworn for probate at $372 456, he bequeathed books and items of Chinese art to the N.G.V.

Procs of Aust Assn of Neurologists, 12, 1975; *MJA*, Jan 1977, p 37; *SMH*, 22 Jan, 8 Feb 1957, 8 June 1968; information from Sir Sydney Sunderland, Melb, Prof K. Bradley, Toorak, and Dr R. Anderson, Middle Brighton, Melb.

ARTHUR SCHWIEGER

CRACE, SIR JOHN GREGORY (1887-1968), naval officer, was born on 6 February 1887 at Gungahleen, New South Wales (Gungahlin, Australian Capital Territory), eighth child of Edward Kendall Crace, an English-born grazier, and his wife Kate Marion, née Mort, a Queenslander and niece of T. S. Mort [q.v.5]. Having attended The King's School, Parramatta, Jack sailed for England in October 1899 for further private schooling. In May 1902 he joined the Royal Navy's training ship H.M.S. *Britannia* on a colonial cadetship.

Pursuing a career with the R.N., in 1911

Crace specialized as a torpedo officer. He returned to his native land for tours of duty in 1908-10 and 1913-14, the second while serving in H.M.A.S. *Australia*. On 13 April 1920 he married Carola Helen Baird with Episcopalian rites in St Mary's Cathedral, Glasgow, Scotland. For the next nineteen years he served at sea and in instructional and staff duties ashore, advancing from commander (1920) to captain (1928). Promoted rear admiral in August 1939, next month Crace was appointed commander of the Australian Squadron. He arrived in Sydney and found that the government had committed most of his ships to theatres outside Australia. The few vessels remaining in home waters performed escort and counter-raider operations for the succeeding two years. Although he was appointed C.B. in July 1941, he was frustrated by the low level of local activity and by the Naval Board's interference in operational matters. He sought to be replaced and, in October, tried to resign his post.

After Japan had entered the war, in February 1942 Crace became commander of the allied naval squadron, Anzac Force. During operations in New Guinea waters with a carrier task force of the United States Navy, he was dissatisfied with the minor supporting role given to his ships. In April command arrangements in the Pacific were reorganized and Crace's squadron was renamed Task Force 44, but, despite his seniority, he was made subordinate to the U.S.N. tactical commander.

On 1 May 1942 Crace's force was ordered from Sydney to join two U.S.N. carrier groups that were deployed to the Coral Sea in anticipation of a major Japanese move southwards. The squadron was detached on 7 May to intercept troop-ships heading for Port Moresby. Lacking air cover, it came under heavy enemy attack and the flagship, H.M.A.S. *Australia*, narrowly escaped being bombed. Crace received no further orders and knew little of the crucial carrier battle which was fought next day, east of his position. He withdrew on 10 May when fuel was running low and it was obvious that the enemy's advance had been checked. The battle of the Coral Sea marked the end of Japanese expansion in South Pacific waters.

Handing over his command on 13 June 1942, Crace returned to England. As vice admiral, then admiral, on the Retired List, he superintended Chatham naval dockyard until July 1946. Appointed K.B.E. in 1947, he retired to Hampshire. Sir John died on 11 May 1968 at Liss and was cremated; his wife and three sons survived him.

C. Coulthard-Clark, *Action Stations Coral Sea* (Syd, 1991), and for bibliog.

C. D. COULTHARD-CLARK

CRAIG, DAVID ALEXANDER (1887-1950), businessman, was born on 18 August 1887 at Dunedin, New Zealand, son of John Craig, an Otago-born storeman, and his wife Martha Clark, née Marshall, from Ireland. Educated locally, David became a greengrocer's assistant. He was a warehouse manager when he married Margaret Bennie (d. 1925) on 29 November 1910 at St John's Church, Wellington; they were to have one son. By 1917 Craig was in Sydney working as a manufacturer's agent and merchant. In 1917-19 he registered trademarks for soap and salt, and in 1921-22 (as assignee for an American firm) patents for batteries.

Regarding real property as a bad use of capital, for some years Craig chose to live at the Australia Hotel with his family. His preferred entrepreneurial strategy was to help in introducing an overseas brand to Australia, but to sell out rather than develop the product. He frequently travelled to the United States of America and Europe. In 1925 he held sales contracts for Life Savers sweets, and is claimed to have been involved (about 1931) in setting up Smith's Potato Crisps. At All Souls parish church, St Marylebone, London, on 5 December 1928 he had married Marina Graciela de Lopez, from San Salvador; they were to have two daughters. With homes in Paris and London, his three children received some of their education in Switzerland.

In the 1930s Craig and his associates secured, from the U.S.A., local patent rights for an industrial process to manufacture fibreboard from woodchips. A director of the Masonite Corporation (Australia) Ltd, which was registered on 3 September 1937, he resigned in 1939, after the company had built a plant at Raymond Terrace, but before defence orders during World War II helped it into profit. From 1939 he led a consortium seeking approval to manufacture bitumen in Sydney from imported crude oil. In 1940 the Advisory Committee on Capital Issues rejected the application. He appealed to (Sir) Arthur Fadden [q.v.], but, following a Tariff Board inquiry, the proposal was again rejected. It was not until 4 March 1946 that Bitumen and Oil Refineries (Australia) Ltd was incorporated under Craig's chairmanship. With part-owners California Texas Oil Co. Ltd supplying the crude product, a bitumen and oil refinery was opened in March 1947 at Matraville on Botany Bay, despite opposition from oyster-farmers and others who feared oil pollution. Craig seems to have been reimbursed up to £20 000 for expenses incurred in preparing for the company's formation. In October he resigned in ill health. The firm later sold its oil interests and, as Boral Ltd, became one of the country's largest manufacturers of building materials.

In October 1942 he had been appointed to the Central Cargo Control Committee by R. V. Keane [q.v.], the Federal minister for trade and customs. Among other mineral-development ventures, Craig had a property at Thuddungra, near Young, which produced magnesite for the making of steel at Broken Hill Pty Co. Ltd's Newcastle plant.

Craig was a big man, with blue-grey eyes, who enjoyed playing the piano. He played bridge and belonged to the Bowral and New South Wales golf clubs, and to the Australian Jockey and Elanora Country clubs. From 1936 the family lived at Darling Point. Craig suffered from diabetes. He died on 30 September 1950 in Nassau, in the Bahamas; his wife, son and daughters survived him.

Jobson's Investment Digest, 1 July 1925, p 342; *Stock Exchange Official Record*, Mar 1947, p 78; '*Wild Cat' Mthly*, 4 May 1946, p 101; *SMH*, 29 Aug 1941, 27 Oct 1942, 2, 12 July 1946; information from Mr D. J. Craig, Syd, and Mrs J. Ridd, Lond.

CHRIS CUNNEEN

CRAIG, ELINOR FRANCES (1888-1969), headmistress, was born on 8 February 1888 at Swansea, Tasmania, eldest child of Rev. William Waters Craig, Presbyterian clergyman, and his wife Frances Jane, née Morris. After William was called to Singleton, New South Wales, young Frances completed her primary schooling there and attended Casino Grammar School, but her father, who taught classics, made an invaluable contribution to her education. Frances began her teaching career in 1912 at a private school at Newcastle and later enrolled at the University of Sydney. In 1917 she was appointed resident mistress at Brisbane High School for Girls (Somerville House from 1920, a private school run by the Presbyterian-Methodist Schools Association). She graduated from the University of Queensland (B.A., 1919) to which she had transferred in 1917.

Having taken leave to complete the final year of her arts course, Craig returned to the school as senior resident mistress in 1919. Absent on leave in Europe from November 1925 to February 1927, she spent her time mostly in France; at the Sorbonne, Paris, she qualified for a diploma in French language and literature. In England she studied the work and methods of schools for girls, particularly Cheltenham Ladies' College. On her return to Brisbane, she was acting-principal of Somerville House while its joint-principals, Constance Harker [q.v.9] and Marjorie Jarrett, were overseas. In 1928 Craig was appointed principal of Ravenswood Methodist Ladies' College, Gordon, Sydney.

In 1932 she accepted an invitation to become vice-principal of Somerville House, following Harker's retirement which had left Jarrett as sole principal. Jarrett retired in 1940 and Craig took over as principal in January 1941. Somerville House was commandeered by the Australian Military Forces in February 1942 and later used as headquarters by a supply section of the United States Army. Pupils from north of the Brisbane River were transferred to Raymont Lodge, Auchenflower, while those from the south went to the former Queen Alexandra Home, Coorparoo; boarders were sent to Moiomindah at Stanthorpe which became the school's administrative centre. Based at Stanthorpe, Craig held together the three dispersed centres and frequently commuted by rail to maintain a presence in Brisbane. Due to her efforts, the school resumed its former premises with minimal inconvenience in January 1945 and classes commenced on 6 February.

Now able to bring to fruition the plans she had long formulated, Craig introduced a course, independent of public examination requirements, to prepare senior girls for careers in business. The school was also divided into houses to create opportunities for healthy competition in art, music and drama, as well as in sport. Miss Craig retired in 1953 but, due to the unexpected early retirement of her successor, returned in 1956 as caretaker principal until a new headmistress began duty in 1957. Frances Craig was tall, elegant and dignified in appearance; her administration was marked by breadth of vision and by a sense of proportion. She died on 16 January 1969 at Mosman, Sydney, and was cremated.

P. G. Freeman (comp), *History of Somerville House* (Brisb, 1949); R. Goodman, *Secondary Education in Queensland, 1860-1960* (Canb, 1968); *Somerville House Mag*, 1953, 1969; *Courier-Mail*, 17 Jan 1969; family information.   K. E. GILL

CRAIG, LESLIE (1892-1966), soldier, farmer and politician, and FRANCES EILEEN (1896-1974), community worker, were husband and wife. Leslie was born on 23 November 1892 at York, Western Australia, fourth son of Scottish-born parents, Francis Craig, hotel proprietor, and his wife Hannah Elford, née Taylor. Educated at the High (later Hale [q.v.4]) School, Perth, and at Melbourne Church of England Grammar School, he worked briefly on his father's property, Golden Valley, Balingup. After serving for two years as a second lieutenant in the 25th Light Horse Regiment, Citizen Military Forces, on 28 October 1914 Craig transferred to the Australian Imperial Force. On 7 August 1915 at Gallipoli he was shot in the left ankle. His leg was amputated and he was admitted in October to the 3rd London General Hospital where he met a nurse Frances Eileen Boyd.

Born on 9 July 1896 at Lifford, County Donegal, Ireland, daughter of John Boyd, medical practitioner, and his wife Phyllis Constance, née Sutcliffe, Frances attended Calder Girls School, Seascale, Cumberland, England, before joining a Voluntary Aid Detachment. Leslie married her on 22 September 1917 at the parish church, Clonleigh, Donegal, with the rites of the Church of Ireland. In October 1917 Captain Craig brought his wife to Western Australia where his A.I.F. appointment terminated on 21 January 1918.

Having studied accountancy, he joined the firm of James Paterson, in which he was soon admitted to partnership. Craig also became a member of the State government's Land Purchase Board, which classified and evaluated areas for soldier settlement. In 1923 he acquired Prinsep Park at Dardanup and moved there with his wife and four children next year. Despite his wooden leg, he worked hard on his property and played competitive cricket, using a runner between wickets. He was an agricultural representative at the British Empire Exhibition, Wembley, London, in 1924, and president (1937-38) of the Royal Agricultural Society of Western Australia. In 1928-51 he served on the Dardanup road board (chairman 1947-51). As a Nationalist and Liberal in turn, Craig represented South-West Province in the Legislative Council in 1934-56 and was a member (1940-41) of the royal commission into the provisions of the companies bill.

Frances had adapted quickly to country life. In 1928 she joined the Western Australian branch of the Country Women's Association, and rose to be president of the southern division (1936-39) and State president (1939-44). In 1938 she was appointed M.B.E. Next year she was a delegate to the fourth triennial conference of the Associated Country Women of the World, held in London; in 1947, in Amsterdam, she was elected a vice-president of the international association.

When their son Frank took over the management of the family property in 1951, the Craigs moved to Perth. Leslie was chairman of the State branch of several companies, among them the Perpetual Executors, Trustees & Agency Co. Ltd (1947-57), the Australian Mutual Provident Society (1960-62) and Goldsbrough Mort [qq.v.4,5] & Co. Ltd (1950-62). A councillor of Fairbridge [q.v.8] Farm School and of Chandler [q.v.7] Farm Boys Settlement, he was also a board-member (from 1940) and chairman (1957-62) of Hale School: he was instrumental in the school's relocation at Wembley Downs and in its return to the Anglican Church. Craig belonged to the Weld, West Australian and South Western clubs. Six feet (182.9 cm) tall and well proportioned, he carried himself with dignity, in spite of his cane and his uneven gait, and was known for his fairness and for his ability to work with a range of people. In 1966 he was appointed C.M.G. He died on 9 February that year in St John of God Hospital, Subiaco, and was cremated; his estate was sworn for probate at $170 660.

Inspired by the C.W.A.'s sponsorship of refugee children, in 1947 Frances had supported the introduction of the Save the Children Fund to Western Australia. She was its State chairman (1953-57) and national president (1968-69). An attractive, tall and strongly-built woman, she had a flair for leadership and administration, and served on such community bodies as the Travellers' Aid Society, the Friends of Royal Perth Hospital, the State advisory committee of the Australian Broadcasting Commission and the board of St Mary's Anglican Girls School which named Craig House after her. She was a member (from 1929) of the Karrakatta Club (president 1952-59 and 1962-64), and played bridge and golf. Survived by her daughter and three sons, she died on 10 October 1974 at Subiaco and was cremated. In 1975 a plaque in her honour was placed at the S.C.F. memorial wishing-well in King's Park, Perth.

D. Popham, *Reflections* (Perth, 1978); B. Neary, *Irish Lives* (Perth, 1987); *Old Haleian*, May 1962; *West Australian*, 11 Apr 1962, 1 Jan, 10 Feb, 4 Aug 1966, 18 Oct 1967; Craig papers (BL); family papers (held by Dr J. Craig, Claremont, Perth); information from Dr J. Craig and Mr F. Craig, Mosman Park, Perth.   JAN RYAN

CRANSWICK, GEOFFREY FRANCEYS (1894-1978), Anglican bishop, was born on 10 April 1894 at Petersham, Sydney, third and youngest son of Edward Glanville Cranswick, Anglican clergyman, and his wife Edith, née Harvard, both English born. George Harvard Cranswick [q.v.] was his elder brother. Geoffrey was educated at Hayfield preparatory school, The King's School, Parramatta, Sydney Church of England Grammar School (Shore) and the University of Sydney (B.A., 1916). An active member of the Australasian Student Christian Movement, he was State representative on its general committee and president (1915) of the men's branch of the Sydney University Christian Union. He was appointed tutor at Moore Theological College in March 1916 and became the S.C.M.'s travelling secretary next year; he joined the Rejected Volunteers' Association and worked on the land in his spare time.

In 1918 Cranswick sailed for England where he entered Ridley Hall, Cambridge. Made deacon in 1920 and ordained priest on 2 October 1921, he became curate at West Ham under Canon Guy Rogers. The parish continued to support him as its 'own missionary' after his appointment in 1923 to King Edward's School, Chapra, India, a vocational training institution run by the Church Missionary Society. On 7 December 1927 at St Paul's Cathedral, Calcutta, he married Rosamund Mary Robotham; their only child Peter was born in 1933.

Cranswick returned to England in 1938 and was employed as organizing secretary for the C.M.S. in the dioceses of Canterbury, Chichester and Rochester. Later that year he took over responsibility for some three hundred missionaries in India and Iran. He served as an air-raid warden at Orpington, Kent, during World War II. His work for the C.M.S. brought him into contact with the archbishop of Canterbury, William Temple, and with the bishops William Wilson Cash and Horace Crotty; in 1943 they selected him as the eighth bishop of Tasmania. He was consecrated in Westminster Abbey on 25 January 1944 and enthroned in St David's Cathedral, Hobart, on 16 May.

Described as 'direct and vital', Cranswick held liberal theological and political views which embroiled him in controversies in the conservative Tasmanian diocese. He soon overcame opposition to participation in the Tasmanian Council of Churches and, by October, had introduced pulpit exchanges between Anglican and other Protestant clergy. His support for ecumenism in Southern India caused division at his first synod, leading him to describe the ignorance of his clergy as 'pathetic'. A further row followed his repeated criticism of the local Catholic Church's insistence on denominational commemorative services on Anzac Day.

An ardent proponent of the United Nations Organization and of the World Council of Churches, in 1947 Cranswick attended the general synod of the Anglican Church in China as a member of a delegation led by Archbishop Halse [q.v.]; a second visit in 1956, in the depths of the Cold War, would lead him to endorse communist rule in China as a great improvement on what he had seen in 1947. He visited England for the Lambeth Conference in 1948 and later that year was a delegate at the first assembly of the World Council of Churches. In 1950 he sponsored a controversial visit to Tasmania by Bishop Yashiro, the presiding bishop in Japan.

In 1956 Cranswick was drawn into the events surrounding the summary dismissal of Sydney Sparkes Orr [q.v.] from the University of Tasmania. A former member (1945-52) of the university council, he had been Orr's spiritual adviser since 1953, and seemed initially to support the dismissal. By November 1959, however, he was convinced that a miscarriage of justice had occurred and made a public call for a new inquiry. Although the university rejected his request, and despite trenchant criticism of his position by the press and the Southern Law Society, Cranswick was supported by the Catholic archbishop (Sir) Guilford Young and other church leaders.

Cranswick retired in 1962, well satisfied with his ecumenical achievements. A slender, erect man, with an abiding commitment to ending religious and secular divisions, he continued to live in the local diocese. He was president of the Australia-Soviet Friendship Society (1946-62) and the Australia-China Society (1968-73); he was also an opponent of conscription and the war in Vietnam, a critic of the White Australia policy and an advocate of the formal recognition of the People's Republic of China. Survived by his wife and son, Cranswick died on 19 July 1978 in Hobart; after a service at St David's Cathedral, he was cremated. His portrait by Alfred Reynolds is in Church House, Hobart.

W. H. C. Eddy, *Orr* (Brisb, 1961); C of E in Tas, Synod, Diocesan Council, *Year Book*, 1943-62; *Church News* (Hob), 133, no 7, Aug 1978; Minutes of Tas Council of Churches, *and* Congregational Assembly, council and executive, *and* Methodist Church Assembly and executive, *and* Aust Church Union, Tas Branch (TA), *and* Society of Friends (NL); L. V. Daniels, Cranswick the Ecumenist (B.A. Hons thesis, Univ Tas, 1974).

LOUIS V. DANIELS

CRANSWICK, GEORGE HARVARD (1882-1954), Anglican bishop, was born on 26 November 1882 at Ecclesall Bierlow, Yorkshire, England, son of Edward Glanville Cranswick, Church of England clergyman, and his wife Edith, née Harvard. Geoffrey Franceys Cranswick [q.v.] was his younger brother. The family sailed to Australia in 1883 where Edward took up an appointment in the diocese of Sydney. George was educated at The King's School, Parramatta, and at St Paul's College, University of Sydney (B.A., 1904).

While at university, Cranswick was president of the Sydney branch of the Christian Union. In 1904 he led a delegation to a student conference at Ormond [q.v.5] College, University of Melbourne, at which he was deeply influenced by the visiting American evangelist John R. Mott. Cranswick was assistant-master (1904-05) at Geelong College, Victoria, and housemaster (1905-06) at The Armidale School, New South Wales, before he left for England to study theology at Wycliffe Hall, Oxford. Made deacon in 1907

and ordained priest on 20 December 1908 for the diocese of Chichester, he served his curacy at St Margaret's parish, Brighton.

In 1910 Cranswick was appointed vice-principal and professor of English at Noble Hall (College) at Masulipatam, India, and in 1911 became headmaster of Bezwada (Ghandi) High School, Kijayawada. On furlough that year, he preached at St Paul's Church, Chatswood, Sydney, where he met and on 29 April married Olive Carr Hordern. Next year he was appointed chaplain to Bishop Azariah of Dornakal, India. Cranswick suffered some censure from his compatriots for being willing to serve under a 'coloured' leader and in a subservient role.

In 1914, when his wife was ill with malaria, Cranswick returned with his family to Sydney. Attributing her survival to prayer, he began his involvement in the ministry of healing. After short appointments at Chatswood (1914), and at Bendigo, Victoria (1915), he was elected second bishop of Gippsland in 1917. Consecrated in St Paul's Cathedral, Melbourne, on 1 November by Archbishop H. L. Clarke [q.v.8], on 15 November Cranswick was enthroned in St Paul's Cathedral, Sale. He came to a diocese of great expanse, poor public transport, sparse population, scarce manpower and practically no finance.

At the 1920 Lambeth Conference, London, Cranswick was a member of the commission on women in the Church. Back at Sale, he brought thirteen men from England to serve as licensed lay readers in remote parts of his diocese. He also brought out five women: one was a deaconess; the others were 'ordained' as deaconesses according to the ordinal; they were later accorded seats with the house of clergy in the diocesan synod. In 1923 Cranswick established a deaconess house and next year founded St Anne's Primary School, Sale (from 1934 St Anne's Church of England Girls' Grammar School). In addition, he opened hostels for girls from outlying districts.

Thirty-two new churches were established under Cranswick's guidance, nine were restored and seventeen other buildings erected. He published four books, including one based on his Moorhouse [q.v.5] lectures of 1923, and was president (1926-36) of the Church of England Men's Society in Australia. Retiring as bishop in 1942, he went to Sydney and served as chairman of the Australian Board of Missions until 1949. He had chaired the first meeting (1946) of the World Council of Churches (Australian section) and in 1950-54 was commissioner for its Australian council. A strong advocate after 1945 of the Australia-China and the Australian-Russian societies, he resigned from the latter in 1948 with Rev. W. G. Coughlan [q.v.] in protest at communist control. His association with these societies brought him under suspicion in certain political circles, as did his friendship with Dr H. V. Evatt and Eddie Ward [qq.v.].

A moderate Evangelical, Cranswick was tolerant of other viewpoints within the Church. He was concerned that his clergy should be well educated, grounded in their faith, and able to defend it and interpret it—however they practised it. Although he was charged with being autocratic in disciplining his clergy, his strictures against their marrying were based on the inadequacy of the stipend to support a wife and children. His commitment to racial equality remained with him: in the last year of his life he chaired a W.C.C. committee which was set up to help Asian students. Survived by his wife, two sons and four daughters, he died on 25 October 1954 at Stratford, Victoria, and was cremated.

A. E. Clark, *Church of Our Fathers* (Melb, 1947); *C of E Messenger*, Nov 1954; *Aust Intercollegian*, Dec 1954; *SMH*, 8 Dec 1941, 16 Dec 1946, 24 Aug 1948; *Age, Argus, Herald* (Melb) and *Sun News-Pictorial*, 26 Oct 1954; information from Mrs T. G. Littleton, Sth Yarra, Melb.

ALBERT B. MCPHERSON

CRANWELL, JOSEPH ARCHIBALD (1889-1965), trade unionist, was born on 22 February 1889 at Braybrook, Melbourne, eldest child of Victorian-born parents George Cranwell, grocer, and his wife Joan Ann, née McLeod. In 1905 Joseph was apprenticed as an ironturner at H. V. McKay's [q.v.10] Sunshine Harvester Works. He married 29-year-old Alice Caroline Lynch on 17 December 1913 at the Presbyterian Church, Sunshine. In September 1916 he went to England as a munitions worker, and was employed at Tinsley, Yorkshire, and at the Austin Motor Co., Birmingham, Warwickshire. There, for patriotic reasons, he worked during a strike in May 1918. He was discharged in Melbourne on 2 March 1919.

A shop steward for the Amalgamated Engineering Union, in 1922 Cranwell represented the Fitzroy No. 2 and Sunshine branches on the union's Melbourne district council, of which he was president in 1923-30. He also served in Victoria as a delegate to the Melbourne Trades Hall Council, to the State Labor Party conferences and to the wages board for engineers and skilled brassworkers. In 1930 his dedication to union duties helped him to win a vacant, full-time position in Sydney, representing Victoria, South Australia and Tasmania on the Commonwealth Council of the A.E.U.

With the retirement of A. S. Evernden, Cranwell was elected council chairman in 1934. Although only allowed a casting vote if a councillor were absent, the chairman represented the union in important dealings with employers, other unions and the government. Cranwell was the most respected and perhaps the most competent chairman the A.E.U. ever had. He fiercely defended the status and conditions of members, and was prepared to take militant action to achieve union objectives, even if it meant clashing with other sections of the labour movement.

During World War II he questioned the ability of the Australasian Council of Trade Unions to represent A.E.U. members. Ignoring an A.C.T.U. boycott, he chaired the Trade Union Advisory Panel, established in 1940 by (Sir) Robert Menzies [q.v.]. Cranwell resisted pressure from the Federal and Victorian Labor governments, and the A.C.T.U., to limit and end the metal trades dispute of 1946-47. He did, however, serve as an A.E.U. delegate to A.C.T.U. conferences on numerous occasions and was A.C.T.U. vice-president (1945-47). In addition, he was president (1943-54) of the Metal Trades Federation of Unions.

Following the conflict between pro-Lang [q.v.9] and anti-Lang forces in the 1930s, Cranwell had been elected president of the New South Wales branch of the Australian Labor Party in August 1939 and played a critical role in stabilizing the party at a unity conference in Sydney. Although not a member of parliament, he chaired a parliamentary Labor Party meeting on 5 September at which (Sir) William McKell defeated Lang in a leadership ballot. Deposed as president, Cranwell supported intervention by the federal A.L.P. in August 1940 and remained on a provisional executive established by the federal party. He also represented the State on the A.L.P. federal executive in 1939-40.

After retiring as chairman of the Commonwealth Council of the A.E.U. in 1954, Cranwell was briefly company secretary for a printing firm. He died on 26 November 1965 at his Hurlstone Park home and was cremated; his wife and daughter survived him.

T. Sheridan, *Mindful Militants* (Cambridge, 1975); P. Weller and B. Lloyd (eds), *Federal Executive Minutes, 1915-1955* (Melb, 1978); B. Nairn, *The 'Big Fella'* (Melb, 1986); M. Easson (ed), *McKell* (Syd, 1988); ACTU records (ANUABL); AEU records (ANUABL *and* Univ Melb Archives); Munitions Workers dossiers, MT 1139/1 (AA, Melb); information from Mrs A. Burns, Beverly Hills, Syd.

GREG PATMORE

CRAWFORD, JOHN WILSON (1899-1943), army officer and solicitor, was born on 8 July 1899 at Paddington, Sydney, and baptized John, son of John Crawford, produce merchant, and his wife Emily, née Wilson, both Irish born. Educated at Sydney Church of England Grammar School (Shore) and the University of Sydney (B.A., 1922; LL.B., 1926), young John joined the school cadets and served with the Sydney University Scouts, in which unit he was appointed lieutenant on 16 February 1922. He had added Wilson to his name in 1919.

Admitted to practice as a solicitor on 2 June 1926, he soon formed a partnership with H. C. Ellison Rich. Crawford married Gladys Marjory Lyndon Clay on 28 January 1928 at St Stephen's Presbyterian Church, Sydney. During the Depression he was associated with the Old Guard, a paramilitary group of predominantly middle-class men who organized to prevent an anticipated socialist revolution. The Old Guard mobilized when the Labor premier J. T. Lang [q.v.9] came to power in 1930. Crawford was group clerk for quota 1 headquarters of the Old Guard's Pacific Highway nucleus—architects, lawyers, orchardists and businessmen who lived in the suburbs of Hornsby and Warrawee. After Governor Sir Philip Game [q.v.8] dismissed Lang on 13 May 1932, the Pacific Highway nucleus continued to collect intelligence on communists and others whom its members considered to be subversives.

Maintaining his connexion with the Citizen Military Forces, in July 1933 Crawford was promoted lieutenant colonel and given command of the renamed Sydney University Regiment. From July 1937 he performed staff duties at 2nd District Base. Called up for full-time duty in August 1939, he briefly commanded the 4th Battalion before transferring to the Australian Imperial Force on 18 March 1940. Next month he was appointed to establish and command the 2nd/17th Battalion. The unit sailed for Palestine in October and in March 1941 arrived at Marsa Brega, Libya. A German and Italian advance compelled British forces to retreat to Tobruk where, by 9 April, they had taken up defensive positions.

The siege began on 11 April 1941 and that day Crawford's men withstood one of the first armoured and infantry attacks against the fortress. Before dawn on 14 April the Germans mounted a major assault in the sector held by the 2nd/17th Battalion: some forty tanks and large numbers of troops broke through the line, but Crawford directed counter-attacks which helped to rout the enemy. He was awarded the Distinguished Service Order (1942) and mentioned in dispatches. Regarded as a committed Anglophile, he was a stickler for discipline. At Tobruk his soldiers initially resented having to use scarce water for regular shaving. Crawford had been nick-named the 'Cake Eater' because he insisted on strict formalities at official social occasions. In October the battalion was relieved

and returned to Palestine; Crawford relinquished command in December.

After a brief attachment to headquarters, I Corps, in the Middle East, he returned to Australia. On 11 April 1942 he was promoted temporary brigadier and placed in charge of the 11th Brigade, based at Townsville, Queensland. He also commanded Yorkforce. On 7 March 1943 a Royal Australian Air Force aircraft in which he was travelling crashed at Freshwater Gorge, near Cairns. Crawford died from a fractured skull and was buried in Cairns war cemetery; his wife and 8-year-old daughter survived him.

A History of the 2/17 Australian Infantry Battalion 1940-1945 (Balgowlah, NSW, nd); B. Maughan, *Tobruk and El Alamein* (Canb, 1966); *SMH*, 20 Mar 1943; *Herald* (Melb), 19 Mar 1953; P. V. Vernon papers (ML); AWM records.

FRANK CAIN

CRAWFORD, SIDNEY (1885-1968), businessman and philanthropist, was born on 4 November 1885 at Warrnambool, Victoria, son of James John Crawford, a brewer from South Australia, and his New Zealand-born wife Ruth, née Harding. James's father Edward had operated a large brewery at Hindmarsh, Adelaide, in the 1840s, but James was poor and his children sold rags, bones and papers. The experience may have strengthened Sidney's determination to gain education, wealth and influence, as well as contributing to his growing social conscience. A scholarship to Surrey College, Surrey Hills, Melbourne, at the age of 14 provided an opportunity to escape from poverty. After being employed by the English, Scottish, & Australian Bank Ltd, he worked as a manager at Tarrant [q.v.12] Motors, Melbourne.

On 23 February 1917 Crawford enlisted in the Australian Imperial Force and became a motor transport driver, serving in France in 1918, mainly with the 4th Australian Motor Transport Company. He was discharged in Melbourne on 27 October 1919. At St Philip's Anglican Church, Abbotsford, on 10 September 1920 he married English-born Elsie Mary Allen. In 1922 they moved to Brighton, Adelaide, where he promoted junior and intermediate Legacy clubs.

That year he founded Adelaide Motors Ltd and in 1930 was appointed to the State's first Transport Control Board. Four years later he established Commercial Motor Vehicles Pty Ltd and Commercial Finance Pty Ltd, of which he was chairman and managing director until his death. In 1934-38 C.M.V. replaced the South Australian Fire Brigade's engines with about forty Diamond Ts, 'fast and spectacular' new American trucks, which were also popular as goods carriers and buses. In its first year of trading C.M.V. paid bonuses to its workers, but no dividends to its shareholders. Staff continued to receive the greater share of the firm's profits, which enhanced Crawford's rapport with his employees and lessened the possibility of industrial disputes. He dedicated *Hauling for Profit* (1939), his handbook on the economics of road transport, to truck drivers, whom he described as 'Knights of the Road'. It sold widely.

Crawford advised Federal and State governments on economic matters. During World War II he was a member of the Commonwealth War Workers' Housing Trust. With J. W. Wainwright [q.v.12], Tom Garland (a prominent communist) and Alex Ramsay [qq.v.], in 1942 he formed the Common Cause movement to develop public co-operation in winning the war, and, once peace was attained, to work for improved social conditions and to promote international harmony. Crawford served on the executive-committee. Despite criticism from conservatives, the movement attracted some three thousand members. It provided a wide-ranging programme of lectures, study groups and public meetings on issues that included substandard housing, adult education and the Commonwealth's emergency powers. Believing that community work was 'the only visible answer to totalitarianism', he helped to set up a community centre at Nuriootpa and to produce the Common Cause publication, *A Township Starts to Live* (1944). He resigned soon afterwards. The movement disbanded in 1949.

Another business venture in wartime demonstrated his initiative. Crawford habitually smoked a pipe and burnt a hole through one within days. Because import restrictions had created a shortage, he asked his workshop staff to make some pipes and was eventually to employ forty-eight people in their manufacture. Having experimented with Australian woods, he sent examples to Prime Minister Chifley [q.v.].

In 1947 Crawford established the C.M.V. Foundation, a charitable trust which fostered educational and cultural activities for children by supporting kindergartens and library services, like those at Brighton and Noarlunga. In the 1960s he and his son Jim (who succeeded him in the family's conglomerate of companies) donated money and vehicles for South Australia's first mobile libraries in such rapidly-growing suburbs as Marion and Tea Tree Gully, and at rural Millicent. An agent for Iron & Steels Disposals Ltd, London, Sidney was also chairman of the local branch of British Motor Industries.

Tall, well built and energetic, he spoke his mind, regardless of the consequences. This attitude characterized his relationship with Heinerich Meyer who in 1950 succeeded Hugh Angwin [q.v.] as commissioner of the South Australian Harbors Board, on which Crawford had served since 1930. As chairman (1946-65), Crawford often spent more time on its business than on that of his own companies, but he found it difficult as an outsider 'to stand up to' sub-engineers, and frequently complained of the department's inefficiency and failure to collaborate with him.

Travelling abroad in 1948 and 1953, Crawford had inspected harbour facilities in Britain and South Africa. On the first trip he conceived a scheme to redevelop the upper reaches of the Port Adelaide River and later urged the S.A.H.B. to undertake the Greater Port Adelaide Plan. Large areas of swampland and sandhills on Lefèvre's Peninsula were reclaimed for wharfs, industry and public housing. Yet, when Crawford retired from the board in 1965, he regretted that the plan had made slow progress. Although the major housing redevelopments were to be carried out by private companies, Jack Cartledge [q.v.], chairman of the South Australian Housing Trust, praised Crawford's imagination, his persistence in keeping the scheme alive, his creative intelligence and his social concern.

Crawford was a vestryman of St Jude's Anglican Church, one of Brighton's earliest buildings. When the church was damaged by an earthquake in March 1954, he successfully fought to prevent the trustees from demolishing it by taking the case to the Supreme Court. Survived by his wife, son and two daughters, he died on 14 May 1968 at Brighton and was buried in St Jude's churchyard.

R. Parsons, *Hindmarsh Town* (Adel, 1974); C. Bridge, *A Trunkful of Books* (Adel, 1986); *JHSSA*, 16, 1988; *Advertiser* (Adel), 16 June 1950, 16 May 1968, 25 Feb 1984; Crawford papers (Mort L); information from Mr J. A. Crawford, Hahndorf, SA.
                                        SUSAN MARSDEN

CREAGHE, EMILY CAROLINE; *see* BARNETT

CREMEAN, HERBERT MICHAEL (1900-1945), politician, was born on 8 May 1900 at Richmond, Melbourne, eldest son of native-born parents Timothy Cremean, carpenter, and his wife Hannah Cecelia, née O'Connell. Educated at St Ignatius' School, Richmond, St Patrick's College, East Melbourne, and Hassett's Coaching and Business College, Prahran, Bert was employed in turn as a clerk, timberworker, machinist and tram driver. On 6 September 1924 he married Alice Nora Mosley at St James's Catholic

Church, Richmond. He was a Trades Hall Council delegate (1925-27) for the Timber Workers' Union and by 1927 had acquired accounting qualifications.

The Cremeans were prominent in Richmond Labor politics. In 1925-26 Cecelia acted as mayoress when her brother Geoff O'Connell served as mayor. A member (1926-30) of Richmond City Council, Cremean was mayor in 1928-29, serving effectively in a period when the council was rent by factionalism. In 1929 he failed narrowly—in controversial circumstances—to gain pre-selection for the seat of Richmond in the Legislative Assembly.

At the State election that year Cremean won Dandenong for the Australian Labor Party. Defeated in 1932, he worked as a purchasing officer and union organizer before being returned to the assembly in August 1934 at a by-election for Clifton Hill: although unopposed, he had first to win an acrimonious battle for pre-selection. Cremean was an acquisition in a party not notable for its parliamentary talent. He was a fluent speaker, a cool and logical debater, and a hard worker. His 'tact' and 'business-like acumen' brought him the deputy-leadership in 1937. In the previous year he had been elected to the A.L.P.'s State executive. A devout Catholic and long-time friend of John Wren [q.v.12], Cremean had an uneasy relationship with his leader John Cain [q.v.], but he was not personally compromised by his friendship with Wren. The party relied on his moderation and ability to keep its various factions working together.

It was Cremean who first suggested the co-ordination of Catholic trade union groups to combat communism; from this idea 'the Movement' emerged. It was he who put forward the idea, adopted in 1940, that Australian Catholic bishops should publish an annual statement on social problems. His one brief taste of ministerial office was as chief secretary and deputy-premier in the four-day Cain government of September 1943. Cremean took on a broad range of responsibilities, especially during the war years. He was secretary (from 1935) of the Fire Brigade Employees' Union, a member of select parliamentary committees on widows' pensions (1936) and child endowment (1937-40), a member (from 1939) of the Patriotic Funds Council (vice-chairman from 1940), vice-chairman (from 1940) of the State War Council and deputy-chairman (from 1942) of the State Evacuation Committee. In 1942 he was appointed vice-chairman of the Commonwealth Board of Business Administration. He also belonged to 'innumerable other charitable and patriotic committees', and was described as 'the octopus-armed wonder of the Labor movement'. Of strong physique, he worked 16 to 18 hours a day and gave up watching football, cricket and films.

Following an operation for a long-standing colonic fistula, Cremean died of peritonitis on 24 May 1945 in Mount St Evin's private hospital, Fitzroy; after a state funeral he was buried in Melbourne general cemetery. His wife and adopted daughter survived him. B. A. Santamaria judged him the 'finest man' in Labor politics. Frank McManus acknowledged Cremean's 'outstanding ability and great personal charm', and suggested that, 'if he had lived, the split of 1955 might never have happened'. A brother John Lawrence Cremean (1902-1982) held the Clifton Hill seat (1945-49) and was a member of the House of Representatives for Hoddle (1949-55); he joined the Anti-Communist Labor Party (later Democratic Labor Party) in the 'split'. Another brother Francis William Cremean (1912-1987) was an outstanding hospital administrator.

R. Murray, *The Split* (Melb, 1972); F. McManus, *The Tumult and the Shouting* (Adel, 1977); B. A. Santamaria, *Against the Tide* (Melb, 1981); K. White, *John Cain and Victorian Labor 1917-1957* (Syd, 1982); J. McCalman, *Struggletown* (Melb, 1984); *Sun News-Pictorial*, 10 Jan 1942.

GEOFF BROWNE

CREMIN, ERIC JAMES (1914-1973), professional golfer, was born on 15 June 1914 at Mascot, Sydney, fifth child of William Cremin, a bricklayer from Brisbane, and his Sydney-born wife Theresa Evelyn, née Coffey. At the age of 14 Eric left Gardeners Road Public School to work as a full-time caddy at the Australian Golf Club where his elder brother was employed on the greens staff. Sympathetic members provided Eric with his first full set of clubs and he dedicated himself to practice. After several years without a regular wage, in 1935 he was appointed assistant-professional at the Australian which made him eligible to play in professional tournaments two years later.

Small and slight, 5 ft 7 ins (170 cm) tall and weighing 10 st. 1 lb. (64 kg), Cremin built his game around fine putting skills, accurate iron play and timing, rather than big hitting and brute strength. He was naturally balanced, with a leisurely swing and upright stance. In 1937 he won the first professional event in which he entered, then went on to take the Professional Golfers' Association's New South Wales and Australian titles; in the latter he defeated V. S. Richardson at Royal Sydney Golf Club. Cremin won both events again next year. On 18 February 1939 at St Mary's Catholic Cathedral, Sydney, he married Kathleen Marie Whiteford, a waitress. When

World War II broke out he tried to enlist, but was rejected because he had flat feet.

Between 1946 and 1962 Cremin was seven times runner-up in the Australian professional title, losing to such players as 'Ossie' Pickworth [q.v.], Norman von Nida, Kel Nagle and Bill Dunk; nonetheless, he was Australia's leading money winner in 1949. That year he won the Australian Open, scoring birdies at four of the last five holes. He wrote for the *Sydney Morning Herald* and published *Par Golf* (1952). When his tournament wins started to dwindle, he took a position as professional at Roseville Golf Club in 1955.

Having played in the Philippines Open in 1939, from the early 1950s Cremin helped to develop the Asian professional circuit. In 1960 he became the professional at the Valley Golf Club, Manila, and travelled throughout Asia conducting clinics as a member of Precision Golf Forging Pty Ltd's promotional staff. Renowned as a golf teacher, he numbered kings, presidents and prime ministers among his pupils. In 1971 he accepted the professional's position at Singapore Island Country Club. Among other benefits, he felt that he was treated as an integral part of the club and not as a servant—which, he considered, was too often the case in many Australian golf clubs. 'Impeccable and precise in attire', he was good-humoured, 'always wearing that puckish little smile'. Cremin collapsed on the first tee at the Sine Road golf course, Singapore, and died of myocardial infarction on 29 December 1973. His wife and two sons survived him.

N. von Nida, *Golf Is My Business* (Syd, 1956); J. Pollard, *Australian Golf* (Syd, 1990); NSW Golf Assn, *NSW Golf*, 9, no 2, Feb 1974; *SMH*, 18 Sept, 6 Oct 1937, 17 Nov 1938, 30 Oct 1960, 31 Dec 1973; *Sunday Herald*, 2 Oct 1949; *Herald* (Melb), 4 Oct 1949, 25 Sept 1965, 25 Mar 1972; *Age* (Melb), 16 Mar 1971, 31 Dec 1973; *Advertiser* (Adel) and *Australian*, 31 Dec 1973; *Daily Mirror* (Syd), 10 Feb 1978, 3 Mar 1986.   BRIAN STODDART

CREMOR, WILLIAM EDWARD (1897-1962), army officer and schoolteacher, was born on 12 December 1897 at Sandringham, Melbourne, son of William Edward Cremor, railway porter, and his wife Jane, née Phelan, both Victorian born. Educated at Footscray State School, Hyde Street, in April 1914 young William entered the Victorian Public Service as a clerk and transferred next year to the Commonwealth Department of Trade and Customs. He enlisted in the Australian Imperial Force on 11 December 1917, embarked for England in July 1918, served briefly in France with the 3rd Field Artillery Brigade and was discharged in Melbourne on 8 November 1919. Cremor obtained a commission in the Militia in November 1920 and in 1921-23 studied law, arts and education at the University of Melbourne (B.A., 1945).

On 1 January 1923 he had been appointed as an English teacher at Footscray Technical School. He assumed the additional duty of sportsmaster and devoted much of his private time to students' welfare. From about 1926 he was prominent in the rivalry between qualified teachers and vocational instructors in technical schools. As secretary (1927-29) and president (1930-31) of the Victorian Teachers' Union, Cremor advanced the cause of the teachers and attacked the narrow, vocational focus of the technical curriculum, arguing that students destined for working-class jobs needed a liberal education. His stand brought him into conflict with Donald Clark [q.v.8] and probably resulted in Cremor's being passed over for promotion. He resigned in 1934 to become secretary of the Victorian Dried Fruits Board. The children of deceased servicemen benefited from his dedicated work with Melbourne Legacy (of which he was president in 1936) and the Baillieu [q.v.7] Education Trust.

Continuing his Militia service, on 1 May 1936 Cremor was promoted lieutenant colonel and given command of the 10th Field Brigade, Royal Australian Artillery. He joined the A.I.F. in October 1939 and sailed for the Middle East in April 1940 as commanding officer of the 2nd/2nd Field Artillery Regiment. For his part in operations in the Western Desert from December 1940 to February 1941, he was appointed O.B.E. Cremor led his regiment during the campaign in Greece and Crete (March-May 1941) and returned to Australia in August 1942. Promoted temporary brigadier that month, he was made commander, Royal Australian Artillery, 3rd Division. In the 1943 Federal election he stood for the seat of Fawkner as an Independent: advocating the formation of one army for service anywhere, he polled 22 per cent of the vote. Cremor held the headquarters' posts of commander, Corps of Royal Australian Artillery, I Corps (October 1943-May 1944) and II Corps (October 1944-April 1945), and of brigadier, Royal Australian Artillery, New Guinea Force (May-October 1944). Transferred to the Reserve of Officers on 12 April 1945, he was appointed C.B.E. for his services in the South-West Pacific Area.

In 1945 'Old Bill' accepted the position of guidance officer for ex-service students at the University of Melbourne. Through his column in the *Argus*, he gave advice to returned servicemen; he championed their cause in public addresses and in newspaper articles. He was a member of the Soldiers' Children Education Board of Victoria, administered by the Repatriation Commission. In 1949 the Victorian government appointed him its representative on the Teachers' Tribunal, an office he was to hold until his death. A member (from 1927) and sometime committeeman of the Naval and Military Club, he was also secretary of the Fitzroy Cricket Club in 1953. Cremor was general editor of the 2nd/2nd Field Artillery Regiment's history, *Action Front* (1961).

'The Brig' was 5 ft 10½ ins (179.1 cm) tall, with fair hair, blue eyes and a ruddy complexion. Forthright, humane, generous and loyal, he would not tolerate humbug or incompetence. His leadership in battle and charitable works in peacetime earned him affection and respect. Cremor never married. He died of aortic stenosis on 11 April 1962 in the Repatriation General Hospital, Heidelberg; following a Masonic service, he was cremated.

W. Perry, *The Naval and Military Club, Melbourne* (Melb, 1981); C. Rasmussen, *Poor Man's University* (Melb, 1989); *Melb Legacy Weekly Bulletin,* 17 Apr 1962; *Thirtyniner* (Melb), 5, nos 3 and 6, May and Aug 1962; *Univ Melb Gazette,* July 1962; *Action Front,* Apr 1963; AWM records.

NEIL SMITH

CRESPIN, IRENE (1896-1980), geologist and micropalaeontologist, was born on 12 November 1896 at Kew, Melbourne, daughter of Godwin George Crespin, auctioneer, and his wife Eliza Jane, née Kitchen, both Victorian born. Educated at Mansfield Agricultural High School where her interest in geological sciences was stimulated by the headmaster Charles Fenner [q.v.8], Irene cherished unfulfilled hopes for a career as a musician. Intending to become a teacher, she enrolled at the University of Melbourne (B.A., 1919). Her decision to read geology brought her under the influence of Frederick Chapman [q.v.7], palaeontologist at the National Museum of Victoria and a lecturer at the university. President of the Students' Representative Council in 1918, Crespin undertook further studies after graduating and worked for the Geological Survey of Victoria.

In December 1927 she became Chapman's assistant. He had been appointed Commonwealth palaeontologist in the Department of Home and Territories as part of the Federal government's effort to discover oil and minerals. Crespin conducted palaeontological investigations in the national museum's inadequate quarters, made field-trips to east Gippsland, and appreciated contact with visiting scientists who were also engaged in the search for oil. On 1 January 1936 she succeeded Chapman as palaeontologist in the Department of the Interior; the appointment entailed her transfer to Canberra to be in contact with the Commonwealth's geological adviser W. G. Woolnough [q.v.12]. Because she was female, her salary was fixed at about half that previously paid to Chapman; she again had to make do with inadequate office space and inferior equipment.

Visiting Java and Sumatra in the Netherlands East Indies in 1939, Crespin consulted with micropalaeontologists and petroleum geologists regarding the problems of Tertiary correlation in the Indo-Pacific region. She travelled widely in Australia to collect fossils and to see the location of the sediments she examined. In the 1940s at Lakes Entrance, Victoria, a shaft was dug to a depth where oil-bearing strata should have been found; Crespin descended the 1200-ft (366 m) shaft in a kibble to inspect the sequence of Tertiary rocks. From 1946 her post was attached to the Bureau of Mineral Resources. She went to Roma, Queensland, in 1947-48, and to the Carnarvon Basin, Western Australia, in 1950. A regular participant in national and international scientific conferences, she toured the United States of America in 1951.

Crespin received a blow in 1953 when many of her books and specimens were destroyed as a result of a fire in the Canberra offices of the B.M.R. That year she received Queen Elizabeth II's coronation medal. She chaired (1955) the Canberra branch of the Territories Division of the Geological Society of Australia and was president (1957) of the Royal Society of Canberra; both institutions were to grant her honorary life membership. In 1957 she was awarded the (W. B.) Clarke [q.v.3] medal of the Royal Society of New South Wales; in 1960 she was made an honorary fellow of the Royal Microscopical Society, London, and received a D.Sc. from the University of Melbourne in recognition of her publications. During her career she published some ninety papers—including notable work on foraminifera—as sole author and more than twenty in collaboration with other scientists. She retired in 1961. The Commonwealth Professional Officers' Association presented her with its award of merit in 1962 and she became an honorary member (1973) of the Australian and New Zealand Association for the Advancement of Science, but her autobiographical pamphlet, *Ramblings of a Micropalaeontologist* (Canberra, 1975), showed that she took most pride in her appointment as O.B.E. (1969). The Bureau of Mineral Resources, Geology and Geophysics published its *Bulletin,* No. 192 (1978), in her honour.

With her enthusiasm and drive, wide range of interests, good humour and extensive circle of friends, Crespin led an energetic life outside her scientific endeavours. She delighted in her frequent trips abroad. A charter member and president (1957) of the Soroptimist Club of Canberra, she was granted life membership in 1971. She played tennis and in 1942 had a handicap of fifteen in golf. An avid follower of Test cricket, she presented the Crespin cup to be contested annually by the 'hard-rocks' and 'soft-rocks' teams within the B.M.R.; in her old age she continued to support the 'soft-rocks' side. Miss Crespin died on 2 January 1980 in Royal Canberra Hospital and was cremated with Anglican rites.

H. Radi (ed), *200 Australian Women* (Syd, 1988); Bureau of Mineral Resources, Geology and Geophysics (Canb), *Bulletin,* no 192, 1978; *Canb Times,* 6 Feb 1960, 28 Oct 1964, 28 Nov 1968, 5 Jan 1980; Crespin papers (NL).

MARGARET E. BARTLETT

CRESWICK, ALICE ISHBEL HAY (1889-1973), Red Cross commandant and kindergarten administrator, was born on 21 September 1889 at Aberdeen, Scotland, daughter of William Reid Reid, advocate, and his wife Jeannie Georgina Farquharson, née Begg. Alice was educated in private schools at Tonbridge, Kent, England, at Geneva, Switzerland, and at Hanover, Germany. During the winter sports at Grindelwald, Switzerland, she met Henry Forbes Creswick, son of Australian pastoralist Alexander Creswick [q.v.8]; Henry had read law at the University of Oxford. Forbidden to wed until she was 21, she married him on 30 November 1910 at the Scottish National Church, Chelsea, London.

Henry took his bride to Liewah (one of his father's many stations) in the Riverina district of New South Wales. After making a resourceful adjustment to outback life, in 1914 Alice sailed for Britain with her husband and newborn son; she stayed with her parents while Henry served as an officer with the King Edward's Horse in World War I.

Back in Australia, the Creswicks remained at Liewah until about 1928 when they came to Melbourne to care for the elderly Alexander. The mother of four children, Mrs Creswick served on the committee (president 1928-38) of the Lady Northcote [q.v.11 Northcote] Free Kindergarten. Henry Creswick was killed in a traffic accident in 1935. Impressed by her financial acumen, Alice's father-in-law made her a director of the family properties, a position she was to hold for the rest of her life. In her bereavement she flung herself into public activity: she joined the executive of the Free Kindergarten Union and became president in 1939.

A capable and forceful leader, Mrs Creswick was diverted from her activities with the F.K.U. in 1940 when the Australian Red Cross Society asked her to be its principal commandant. In this capacity she travelled widely each year, inspecting the work of existing Red Cross Emergency Service companies and establishing new ones. She organized conferences of divisional commanders, and held courses for hospital visitors attached to the army and for personnel selected to assist prisoners of war. In addition, she visited Britain and Europe where she conferred with the International Red Cross about arrangements for Australian prisoners of war, and for the sick and wounded.

When she resigned from her position in 1946, the national Red Cross paid tribute to her 'skill in choosing and inspiring the women who served in Field Force'. Next year she was appointed a dame of grace of the Order of St John. Mrs Creswick continued her wholehearted involvement with the Red Cross as vice-chairman (1946-49) of the national council and national executive, as honorary life member (from 1949) and as a member of the national council to 1959. She represented the Australian Red Cross at conferences in Stockholm (1948) and Oslo (1954).

In 1946 Mrs Creswick had resumed her presidency of the F.K.U. She persistently lobbied the State government for greater support for pre-school training and succeeded in setting the union's finances on a sound basis. In 1947 she gained State government help for the extension of buildings and facilities at the Kindergarten Training College, Kew, where a new wing was named in her honour. She called frequently on the forty-two free kindergartens under her direction and in 1949 visited pre-schools in England, France and Sweden. While ill health forced her to resign as president of the F.K.U. in April, she was made a life vice-president.

Mrs Creswick also retained a close interest in the Australian Association of Pre-School Child Development (later Australian Pre-School Association), of which she was a foundation vice-president (1939); she was subsequently a vice-chairman of its Victorian branch and a life vice-president. In 1953 she established the Colombo Plan pre-school standing committee of the A.P.A. which sent training officers to Ceylon (Sri Lanka). Concerned with the need for professional leadership in the pre-school movement, in 1955 she founded a scholarship fund: she contributed £4000 herself and £4000 which she had obtained from donors in Victoria. The Alice Creswick (now the Alice Creswick and Sheila Kimpton) scholarship enabled its first recipient to visit the United States of America in 1956. Mrs Creswick was appointed O.B.E. in 1958.

Although vigorous and practical, she had a Celtic regard for religion and superstition.

She was conservative and conventional, with a strong sense of duty. Her active working life left little time for her other interests which included opera and ballet, 'a spot of golf', growing camellias, and collecting old china, furniture and flower prints. In retirement she had more leisure to devote to these hobbies, and to her country home near Flinders where she worked off 'excess energy' in the garden and orchard. At her Toorak home she held an annual exhibition of floral arrangements to raise funds for Victorian kindergartens and pre-schools.

Survived by a son and daughter, Alice Creswick died on 24 October 1973 at Armadale and was buried in Boroondara cemetery. Her will made generous bequests to the Anglican Church, the Australian Red Cross and the F.K.U.

L. Gardiner, *The Free Kindergarten Union of Victoria, 1908-80* (Melb, 1982); *Aust Pre-School Q*, Feb 1967; *Age* (Melb), 19 Aug 1935, 2 Apr 1945, 9 Nov 1954, 21 Oct 1959; *Herald* (Melb), 29 Nov 1941, 1 Jan 1949, 14 Nov 1956; *Sun News-Pictorial*, 15 Aug 1947, 6 Apr 1949; information from Mrs S. Kimpton, South Yarra, and the Archivist, Aust Red Cross Soc, Melb.   DIANE LANGMORE

CROFT, IDA LUCY (1878-1957), pharmacist, was born on 6 February 1878 at Terowie, South Australia, eldest of four surviving children of John Thomas Davey Croft, a pharmacist from England, and his native-born wife Lucy Nixon, née Wardle (d. 1913). The family lived in Adelaide when Ida was young, but about 1891 moved to Broken Hill, New South Wales, where for twenty years her father ran a pharmacy. Ida probably helped in the shop and began her apprenticeship under her father's guidance before the passage of the 1897 Pharmacy Act. On 12 July 1900 she was one of the last three women in the State to gain registration without passing the Board of Pharmacy's examinations. She gained her poisons licence in August and was a dispenser for her father until his death in 1911. Executrix of his will, Miss Croft handled his affairs and maintained the pharmacy until 1914 when she went to live and work at Semaphore, Adelaide.

Returning about 1921 to Broken Hill, where her married sister Cordelia was living, Croft was employed by the Broken Hill United Friendly Societies' Dispensary Ltd and managed its South Broken Hill branch in Patton Street until it was closed about 1927. The years spent working with her father, and a thriving friendly society membership, ensured that she was well known and widely respected in the community: a passenger on a Broken Hill bus claimed that 'We ALWAYS used to go to her for father's asthma powders'. Croft later had her own business in Patton Street, near the old shop, but in the mid-1930s was dispensing for Dr Ian MacGillivray.

By 1941 Croft had moved to Balaklava, South Australia, where she worked in C. F. Martindale's pharmacy. Although she resigned in 1942, suffering from pneumonia and pleurisy, she registered in that State in July and managed R. W. Goldsack's pharmacy at Victor Harbor while he served (1942-45) with the Royal Australian Air Force. After the war she bought a small business at Semaphore; she retired about 1955, but remained a registered practitioner.

A small, serious woman with dark hair, large, grey eyes and a fair complexion, Croft was 'very fond' of literature. Her strong character was evidenced by her choice of a profession in which women were uncommon at the time of her entry and in which she exhibited considerable competence. Although unable to attend meetings because of ill health, she was a loyal member of the Women Pharmaceutical Chemists' Association of South Australia. She died on 5 June 1957 in Le Fevre Community Hospital, Semaphore, and was buried in the graveyard of St Jude's Anglican Church, Brighton. Father and daughter had dispensed for the Broken Hill populace for nearly fifty years of the town's pioneering days.

A'sian J of Pharmacy, 44, no 526, Oct 1963, pp 929, 38, no 450, June 1957, pp 747, 855, no 452, Aug 1957, p 959; *Chemist and Druggist of A'sia*, no 8, Aug 1900, p 209, no 9, Sept 1900, p 238, no 13, Dec 1915, p 468; *Barrier Miner*, 27 Sept 1911; *Observer* (Adel), 30 Sept 1911; *Advertiser* (Adel), 8 June 1957; Pharmaceutical Soc of NSW, miscellaneous papers (NSWA).

HILARY WEATHERBURN

CROMBIE, CHARLES ARBUTHNOT (1914-1945), air force officer, was born on 16 March 1914 in Brisbane, son of David William Alexander Crombie, a Queensland-born grazier, and his Indian-born wife Phoebe Janet, née Arbuthnot. Charles's grandfathers were James Crombie [q.v.8] and Sir Charles Arbuthnot, a general in the British Army; John Cameron [q.v.7] was Charles's great-uncle. Educated at Sydney Church of England Grammar School (Shore), Charles worked as a jackeroo, initially at Mountside, the family property near Warwick, Queensland. He loved life on the land. From 1934 to 1938 he served in the Militia, attaining sergeant's rank in the 11th Light Horse Regiment.

Hearing that young men 'who have done a bit of machine-gun work and can ride a horse' were considered good pilot material, Crombie took civil flying-instruction to enhance his prospects; he enlisted on 24 May 1940 in the Citizen Air Force of the Royal Australian Air Force and was selected for aircrew. Dark complexioned, with blue eyes and brown hair, he had an ideal physique for the cramped cockpits of fighter aircraft: he was 5 ft 6½ ins (168.9 cm) tall and weighed 9 st. 3 lb. (58.5 kg). On 20 September 1940 in his school's chapel he married Betty Deane-Butcher before embarking within two weeks for training in Canada. Commissioned on 17 January 1941, he arrived in Britain next month. In May he joined the Royal Air Force's No. 25 Squadron as a Beaufighter pilot. Transferring to No. 89 Squadron in the Middle East in October, he operated from bases in Egypt and Malta; by the end of the year he had destroyed six enemy aircraft and probably another two. His next posting was to No. 176 Squadron, stationed in India.

On the evening of 19 January 1943 Crombie intercepted a formation of four Japanese bombers near Calcutta. Enemy fire set his Beaufighter's starboard motor ablaze, but he persisted with the attack and shot down one plane. When flames from the burning motor swept back, he ordered his navigator to parachute to safety and pressed on alone. Crombie destroyed a second bomber and damaged a third, then his fuel tank exploded and he was forced to bale out with his clothing alight. His typically modest and laconic account of the combat in a letter to his wife made no mention of his success, merely relating that he had been shot down and 'landed in the most God awful swamp'. For his courage and determination in this 'magnificent lone-hand action', he won the Distinguished Service Order; a Distinguished Flying Cross, awarded in May, recognized the leadership and fighting spirit which he had displayed in earlier engagements. At the end of his operational tour he had been credited with the destruction of twelve enemy aircraft and probably an additional four.

Repatriated on 27 September 1943, Crombie was promoted temporary flight lieutenant in October and acting squadron leader in November. He was posted in December to No. 5 Operational Training Unit, based at Tocumwal, New South Wales. During a test flight on 26 August 1945 he was killed when his Beaufighter crashed at Williamtown. Crombie's popularity had been such that the entire unit stood down for his funeral; he was buried with Anglican rites in Sandgate war cemetery; his wife and 1-year-old son survived him.

G. Odgers, *Air War Against Japan 1943-1945* (Canb, 1957) and *The RAAF* (Syd, 1989); L. McAulay, *Against All Odds* (Syd, 1989); B. Crombie, The Man I Knew: The Story of Charles Arbuthnot Crombie (ms, 1987, held by Mrs B. Crombie, Durack, Brisb); AWM records.
ALAN STEPHENS

CRONIN, DEVERICK JOHN ('MICK') (1911-1979), Australian Rules footballer and commentator, was born on 18 March 1911 at Wagin, Western Australia, son of native-born parents Michael Henry Cronin, farmer, and his wife Nellie Agatha, née Dawson. Although of Methodist background, Mick completed his primary education at a convent-run boarding-school at Toodyay, then worked as a delivery-boy and as an apprentice to a butcher at Harvey. In 1930 he was recruited by East Perth Football Club which found him a job with a grocer in Perth. Cronin was later employed at Whitty's lottery agency and at Boans Ltd department store. In the 1930s he was also a middle-order batsman with the Subiaco Cricket Club.

Excelling in Australian Rules as an agile half-forward flanker and centreman with a penetrating, left-foot kick, Cronin played 164 games for East Perth between 1930 and 1940, and in 1931 received its fairest and best award. In 1936, the first of his five consecutive years as captain, he took the team from fourth place at the start of the finals to win the premiership. He regularly represented Western Australia and won the inaugural Tassie medal in the interstate carnival in 1937. After coaching East Perth (1939-41), he was made a life member of the club in 1941.

On 6 April 1940 Cronin had married a stenographer Roma Chipper at St Andrew's Presbyterian Church, Perth. That year he opened a confectionery shop at the Hurlingham Picture Theatre, South Perth. Mobilized in the Citizen Military Forces in January 1942, he served at home in the Australian Imperial Force for the duration of the war, engaged mostly in anti-aircraft activities. He was discharged with the rank of sergeant in October 1945, after which he ran snack shops in central Perth.

Returning to football, Cronin umpired twenty-five Western Australian Football League games in 1947-48 and officiated at the 1947 interstate carnival in Hobart. Well known for his didactic style, he taught football to juniors in Perth colleges and the South Perth district, and coached East Perth again (1951-55) and the State team in 1951. He was to be a successful agent for the Scottish Amicable Insurance Co. in 1966-79.

Benefiting from a football boom in Perth, Cronin became a dominant figure on TVW-7's weekly 'World of Football' television programme from 1965 until his death; he earned respect for his sincerity and knowledge, but aroused controversy by his frankness and dogmatism. Meanwhile, he also broadcast football matches over radio 6IX and contributed through a ghost writer to a weekly column, 'On the Back Page', in *Sports Review*.

A man of natural wit and bubbly charm, sincere, honest and forthright in his manner, Cronin was popular in sporting circles and esteemed for his community work. He was a Freemason, and a lifelong non-smoker and teetotaller; he enjoyed punting on the horses and liked a game of golf. Cronin died suddenly of a ruptured aortic aneurysm on 1 September 1979 at Royal Perth Hospital and was cremated; his wife and son survived him.

M. Glossop (ed), *East Perth 1906-1976* (priv pub, Perth, 1977); G. Christian, *The Footballers*, R. Jordan ed (Perth, 1985); *Sports Review* (Perth), 28 Aug 1964; *Daily News* (Perth), 3 Sept 1979; *West Australian*, 4 Sept, 5 Oct 1979; Cronin papers and press-cuttings (held by Mrs R. Cronin, Sth Perth); information from Mr S. H. Briggs, Floreat Park, Mr D. S. Cronin, Ardross, Mrs R. Cronin, Sth Perth, Mr E. D. Smith, Dianella, Mr F. V. Sparrow, Kingsley, and Mr J. Sweet, Sth Perth.

LYALL HUNT

CRONIN, MICHAEL JOSEPH (1892-1970), surveyor, valuer and administrator, was born on 21 July 1892 at Glebe, Sydney, second son of Irish-born parents William Cronin, policeman, and his wife Brigid, née Keogh. Joe attended the Patrician Brothers' school, Glebe, and Cleveland Street Public School, leaving early, like his elder brother, to assist in paying for the education of five younger siblings. He joined the Department of Lands as a clerk on 10 December 1909, became a draftsman, went into the field in 1913 (based at Dubbo) and in 1916 was appointed a licensed surveyor. Working closely with Francis Peter 'Valuation' Brown, head of the Forbes Land Board, Cronin established his expertise as a valuer after 1920. At St Brigid's Catholic Church, Dubbo, on 30 September 1922 he married Beatrice Mary Kathleen Digges, daughter of a Coonamble grazier.

Secretary and treasurer of the New South Wales Staff Surveyors' Association in 1924-25, Cronin remained active on that body until 1931. He advocated the early resumption of land adjacent to the incomplete Wyangala dam at current value. Both he and Brown urged surveyors to adopt a provable 'sales' or market approach in order to present a more professional image before the Land and Valuation Court. In 1931 a royal commission into the Western Division praised his thoroughness which had assisted in establishing the incompetence of the Western Lands commissioner and two of his officers. With Brown, Cronin became a member of the Closer Settlement Advisory Board in 1931 (chairman from 1944) and moved his family to Chatswood, Sydney. In 1942 he was promoted assistant under-secretary for lands. On 23 April 1946 Cronin was appointed

Western Lands commissioner. His task was to implement Labor government policy on soldier and closer settlement in the Western Division, and to break up stations into smaller holdings. Despite widespread belief that the areas were too small, by 1957—after the Korean War and the wool boom—204 soldier settlers in the division were reported as generally being in a sound position; 59 of the 91 who had borrowed from the Crown had repaid loans. The combination of the State's new legislation and price-control introduced by the Federal government gave Cronin what appeared to be formidable power as administrator: he was zealous, meticulous and, when questioned, unyielding. A number of large landholders felt that he was waging a vendetta against them. To achieve land redistribution, some title-holders (frequently women who had been bequeathed interests by their fathers) were required to divest themselves of equity and title. Cronin's adherence to the government's objectives was seen as too extreme by his successor, who applied some policies more flexibly.

An active Catholic, Cronin was a member of the Knights of the Southern Cross and belonged to the superior council of the Society of St Vincent de Paul in Australia. He was appointed to electoral boundary commissions in 1952, 1957 and 1960. Having retired in 1957, he set up as a valuer and registered land agent, but in 1961 suffered a cerebral haemorrhage which left him largely speechless, though alert. He died on 16 June 1970 at Darlinghurst and was buried in Northern Suburbs cemetery; his wife, son and two daughters survived him. The daughters recalled his integrity, egalitarianism, public-speaking skill, patience and, particularly during his lengthy incapacity, his inner peace.

Report of the Western Lands Commissioner, 1949 and 1957, *PP* (NSW), 1948-50, 1, and 1956-57, 1; *SMH*, 19 June 1952, 19, 20 July 1957, 20 Oct 1960; *Catholic Weekly* (Syd), 25 June 1970; NSW Staff Surveyors' Assn, Annual Report, 1929, 1932 (ML); Western Lands Comm files (NSWA); information from Mrs M. Stackpoole, Pymble, Mr B. Stapleton, Gymea, and Mr H. Kilby, Dee Why, Syd.

JAN COOPER

CROSBY, JOSEPH ALEXANDER ('MARSHALL') (1882-1954), actor, was born on 18 February 1882 at Caltowie, South Australia, twelfth of thirteen children of Walter Thomas Crosby, a labourer from Scotland, and his native-born wife Ann, née Cameron. At age 10 Alex moved with the family to Port Pirie where he finished his schooling, then worked as a clerk in the local post office and rose to telegraphist. He married Teresa King on 25 April 1907 in St Patrick's Catholic Cathedral, Melbourne.

Although he had sung at school and won at an eisteddfod, Crosby had no thoughts of a theatrical career until he auditioned as a baritone and joined Leslie Harris's company as 'Marshall' Crosby. He appeared at the Theatre Royal, Adelaide, in August 1907 before touring with Henry Clay and Harry Rickards [q.v.11] in vaudeville. While performing at the Tivoli, Sydney, Crosby sang a patriotic song, *Australia's Bonny Boys in Navy Blue*, on 4 August 1914; next day Australia was at war.

Having starred in musicals in the early 1920s for J. C. Williamson [q.v.6] Ltd, from 1925 Crosby toured in revues and in the burlesque operetta, *His Royal Highness*, with George Wallace [q.v.12]; their collaboration was to continue, intermittently, for nearly twenty years until vaudeville faded out. In their heyday the Wallace revues took over local cinemas in the Sydney area for one or two nights at a time. In 1932 Crosby appeared with Wallace in *His Royal Highness* for F. W. Thring's [q.v.12] Efftee Film Productions. Between that year and 1949 Crosby had character parts in over fifteen films, among them *Dad and Dave Come to Town* (1938), *Smithy* (1946) and *Eureka Stockade* (1949). He also broadened his skills, taking roles in straight plays such as *Queer Cargo* (1935) and *Three Men on a Horse* (1936).

Politically, Crosby supported trade unions and the Labor Party. He was vice-president (from 1942) and president (1945-48) of the Actors' and Announcers' Equity Association of Australia when it was controlled by members of the Communist Party of Australia. In spite of his more moderate views, he worked with the radicals to improve conditions for performers and to protect the jobs of Australian artists.

In the 1940s Crosby took leading roles in radio serials which included 'Digger Hale's Daughters' (1944), 'Officer Crosby' and 'Hagen's Circus' (1949) for commercial networks. He also featured in plays for the Australian Broadcasting Commission and was Josh Roberts in Gwen Meredith's long-running serial, 'Blue Hills'. His two hobbies were cooking and fund-raising for St Margaret's Hospital with his racing friends Billy Cook, Lachie Melville and George Moore. Survived by his wife, daughter and four sons, Crosby died on 1 January 1954 at Port Macquarie and was buried in Botany cemetery, Sydney. Marshall Crosby's role was written out of 'Blue Hills', but was later revived by his son Don, who also inherited his father's commitment to Actors' Equity.

ABC Weekly, 27 Aug 1949; *Critic* (Adel), 14, 28 Aug 1907, 5 Jan 1925; *SMH*, 7 Aug 1914, 3 July, 27 Oct 1945, 23 Feb 1948, 2 Jan 1954; Actors' Equity of Aust, Minutes (ANUABL); information from Miss P. Crosby, Waverley, Syd.   GILL E. VALE

CROSS, SIR RONALD HIBBERT (1896-1968), governor, was born on 9 May 1896 at Pendleton, Lancashire, England, son of James Carlton Cross, master cotton spinner, and his wife Marian Gertrude, née Hibbert. The Crosses were wealthy mill-owners. Educated at Ludgrove Preparatory School and at Eton, Ronald subsequently learned German as a commercial asset before taking up a career as a merchant banker. During World War I he served with the Duke of Lancaster's Own Yeomanry and as a pilot with the Royal Flying Corps. On 7 January 1925 at St Peter's parish church, Pimlico, Middlesex, he married Louise Marion Green-Emmott; they were to have four daughters, and a son who died at the age of 2.

Embarking on a political career, in October 1931 Cross was elected to the House of Commons as Conservative member for Rossendale. His vigorous support of the cotton interest led to rapid promotion: he was a government whip (1935), junior lord of the treasury (1937), vice-chamberlain of the royal household (1937-38) and parliamentary secretary to the board of trade (1938-39). Appointed minister of economic warfare on 3 September 1939, he became well known for his efforts to bring about the economic isolation of Germany. Cross was sworn of the Privy Council on 7 June 1940 and became minister of shipping in Churchill's coalition government. Following press criticism of his performance, he was removed from his portfolio on 1 May 1941.

That year he succeeded Sir Geoffrey Whiskard as British high commissioner to Australia. Cross arrived in Sydney in July and immediately became embroiled in controversy. Because of his allegedly adverse remarks about the 'Russian system', he was censured by W. M. Hughes [q.v.9] and some trade unionists demanded his recall. He was created baronet of Bolton-Le-Moors, Lancaster, on 15 August. More controversy with unionists occurred in October, yet, for the most part, Sir Ronald spent his term promoting the Empire's war effort. Questions about his prolonged absence prompted him to visit his Lancashire electorate in 1944 and again in May 1945, but he was unseated in the July general elections. After his Australian appointment was terminated by the Attlee Labour government, he became London chairman of the Australian Express Food Parcels Scheme.

In February 1950 Cross was again elected to the House of Commons. Appointed chairman of the public accounts committee, he resigned his Ormskirk seat a year later. In 1951 he was chosen as governor of Tasmania and began his term on 23 August. He was appointed K.C.V.O. (1954) and K.C.M.G. (1955). Following C. A. Bramich's resignation from the Labor Party, on 12 September 1956 the Cosgrove [q.v.] government was defeated in the House of Assembly. Arguing that the governor was bound to follow his advice, Cosgrove asked Cross to dissolve parliament. Although he did not accept that his discretion was either limited or affected by the deadlocks clause of the Constitution Amendment Act (1954), Cross nevertheless granted the dissolution because he believed it 'proper' that the electorate express its will.

Six ft 4 ins (193 cm) tall, 'blond, bony, dressy, charming', and addicted to 'fat cigarettes', Sir Ronald was essentially a family man. He enjoyed shooting and fishing, raced Beau Gene with the Tasmanian Racing Club and was a Freemason who belonged to Lodge Fidelity. Having presented his African hunting trophies to Government House, Cross retired on 4 June 1958 and returned to England. Survived by his wife and daughters, he died on 3 June 1968 at Westminister. Mount Ronald Cross in western Tasmania is named after him.

W. A. Townsley, *The Government of Tasmania* (Brisb, 1976); *PP*(Tas), (59), 1956; *Mercury*(Hob), 10 May 1940, 12 Mar 1941, 13 Sept 1956, 5 June 1968; *Argus*, 18 July 1941, 2 Jan 1943, 26 May 1945; *Age* (Melb), 19 Feb 1944, 15 Nov 1952; *The Times*, 4 June 1968.   HILARY KENT

CROSS, STANLEY GEORGE (1888-1977), cartoonist, was born on 3 December 1888 at Los Angeles, California, United States of America, third son of English-born parents Theophilus Edwin Cross, builder and architect, and his wife Florence, née Stanbrough. The family settled in Perth in 1892. An outstanding student, Stan attended the High School, Perth, on a scholarship, but, because of his father's ill health, turned down a scholarship to the University of Adelaide in order to 'help at home'. At 16 he began work as a cadet clerk with the railways while studying art part-time at Perth Technical School.

In 1912, with the help of a 'more or less affluent brother', Cross resigned from the railways to study in London. His first published cartoons appeared in *Punch*. Returning home, he began freelancing with several newspapers and magazines, among them the *Sunday Times* and the *Western Mail*. In 1918 Claude McKay [q.v.] requested samples of his work and offered him a position with *Smith's Weekly* at £5 a week; Cross accepted and arrived in Sydney in 1919. At the Waverley Methodist Church, Bondi Junction, on 17

November 1924 he married a 25-year-old clerk Jessie May Hamilton (d. 1972); they were to have a son and a daughter.

During twenty years with *Smith's*, Cross developed into one of Australia's finest black-and-white artists and the country's foremost 'single-panel' cartoonist. His bold comic-art presented an array of 'typical' Australians, from farmer and jackeroo to digger and doctor. Cross's first collection of cartoons appeared in *Australian Humour in Pen and Ink* (c.1921). He created many and varied features, such as 'Things that Make Stan Cross', 'Famous Australian Places that We Have Never Seen' and '"Smith's" Australian History'. Other output included some of Australia's earliest comic strips, 'Story of the Man who Faked his Income Tax Return' (31 July 1920) and 'You and Me' (7 August 1920). The latter, taken over in 1940 by Jim Russell, became 'The Potts' and is the longest surviving comic strip in Australian newspapers. '"Smith's" Vaudevillians' and 'Adolf and Hermann' were further comic strips created by Cross.

On 12 August 1933 *Smith's Weekly* 'reprinted by request' Cross's celebrated cartoon of 29 July, affectionately known by its caption, 'For gorsake, stop laughing—this is serious!', and took the unprecedented step of publishing a print on 'high-class art paper' for sale at 2s. 6d. (or 3s. posted). The cartoon touched the 'funny bone' of the Australian public as no other before or since. Cross's popularity was such that he reputedly earned £100 a week during the Depression.

On Christmas Eve 1939 Cross resigned from *Smith's Weekly*. In 1940 he accepted an offer from Sir Keith Murdoch [q.v.10]— to work for the Melbourne *Herald*—that allowed him to remain in Sydney. For the *Herald*, he created 'The Winks' which by July 1940 had evolved into 'Wally and the Major'. Over the next thirty years in newspapers throughout Australia, New Zealand and Fiji, and in eighteen annual comic books (c.1943-60), readers were able to enjoy the extraordinary, knock-about adventures and lifestyle of Wally Higgins, Major Winks, Pudden Bensen and a company of comedy players—in the army in World War II and afterwards—and on their North Queensland sugarcane plantation. After Cross retired in 1970, 'Wally and the Major' was continued by Carl Lyon.

An imposing man, 6 ft 2 ins (188 cm) tall, with a pencil-thin moustache, Cross had a birthmark on his left cheek and wore spectacles. He was loquacious and enjoyed being funny in company as well as on paper. Regarded by his colleagues as proud, and by himself as energetic (in spurts), he acknowledged that he had a temper which needed to be kept under control. He was the second and longest serving president (1939-70) of the

Black and White Artists' Club, Sydney. An 'erudite man of quirky knowledge', he wrote (but did not publish) books on his main interests outside the art world—accountancy, economics and English grammar.

Survived by his daughter, Stan Cross died on 16 June 1977 at Armidale and was buried with Anglican rites in the local lawn cemetery. His humour was that of everyday life, the humour of ordinary Australians. In November 1985 his legendary cartoon was produced in three-dimensional form by the German-born sculptor Eberhard Franke as the statuette for the national awards ('Stanleys') made by the *Bulletin* and the Australian Black and White Artists' Club.

G. Blaikie, *Remember Smith's Weekly* (Adel, 1966); V. Lindesay, *The Inked-in Image* (Melb, 1970); J. Ryan, *Panel by Panel* (Syd, 1979); *Punch* (Lond), 25 Nov 1914; *Smith's Weekly* (Syd), 5 Apr 1919, 12 Aug, 25 Nov 1933; *Bulletin*, 12 Nov 1985; *Herald* (Melb), 20 Apr 1940, 8 June 1957; *Australian*, 29 Nov 1980; *Age* (Melb), 19 Nov 1981; H. de Berg, Stan Cross (taped interview, 1969, NL); information from Mrs S. Cross, Armidale, NSW, Mr V. Lindesay, Ripponlea, Melb, and Mr J. Russell, Sylvania, Syd.   JAMES KEMSLEY

CROWLEY, GRACE ADELA WILLIAMS (1890-1979), painter, was born on 28 May 1890 at Forrest Lodge, Cobbadah, New South Wales, elder daughter and fourth child of native-born parents Henry Crowley, grazier, and his wife Elizabeth, née Bridger. By 1900 the family had moved to nearby Glen Riddle, Barraba. When Grace was about 13 her parents sent one of her pen-and-ink drawings to the magazine, *New Idea*, which awarded her a prize. Taught by governesses at the homestead, in 1907 she had a year at boarding-school in Sydney and attended Julian Ashton's [q.v.7] Sydney Art School one day a week.

Back in the bush, she 'did no more drawing' once her mother sacked the maid and introduced Grace to 'household duties'. Her interest revived following Ashton's painting trip to Glen Riddle about 1910. She studied full time at the Sydney Art School from 1915 and in 1918 became an assistant-teacher there. Grace shared a flat and later a cottage at Vaucluse with her best friend Anne Dangar [q.v.]. Having exhibited (from 1916) with the Society of Artists, Crowley resigned her teaching position in 1923 and prepared for the society's travelling scholarship. She went to Glen Riddle on holidays, completed several rural subjects and 'longed to "do a thing" of men shearing, but my father vetoed that'. Crowley did not win the scholarship, but visited Melbourne and worked briefly in Bernard Hall's [q.v.9] classes. Her parents

grudgingly gave her the fare to Europe, and her brother Wilfred sent her an annual stipend. In February 1926 she left with Dangar for France, intending to study at the Slade school in London.

Crowley's four years in Paris were the most enjoyable of her life. Grace and Anne worked at Colarossi's without a teacher, acquired their own studio-home at Montrouge in October and from early 1927 were enrolled at André Lhote's academy at Montparnasse (where Crowley spent three years). Lhote's academic cubism was a revelation, as were geometric systems like Dynamic Symmetry and the Golden Section. An occasional writer, Crowley had contributed a chapter to *The Julian Ashton Book* (Sydney, 1920) and was to send letters from France and lectures on cubism for publication in the Sydney Art School's journal, *Undergrowth*. After they had attended Lhote's summer school at Mirmande, near Montélimar, Dangar sailed for Sydney in 1928. Next year Crowley spent some weeks at Mirmande, attended Albert Gleizes's classes in Paris and visited museums in Paris, Italy, The Netherlands and Britain. Her Académie Lhote paintings were exhibited in various Parisian salons in 1928 and 1929. Learning of her mother's illness, Grace returned to Glen Riddle in February 1930 to find her easel thrown upon a rubbish tip and Anne about to settle in France. By then Crowley was probably the most experienced modernist painter in Australia.

In March 1930 her French work was seen in the Group of Seven exhibition at the Macquarie Galleries, Sydney; a modernist portrait of her cousin Gwen Ridley was a startling sight in the 1930 Archibald [q.v.3] prize competition. Crowley came to Sydney in 1932 to help Dorrit Black [q.v.7] with exhibitions, art classes and a sketch club at her short-lived Modern Art Centre where Crowley held her first solo exhibition, chiefly showing work from France. Obtaining a studio at 215a George Street, she and 'Rah' Fizelle [q.v.8] established the Crowley-Fizelle school, the principal centre for modernist painting. When it closed in 1937, she impulsively invited Ralph Balson [q.v.] to continue his weekend painting in her studio-flat at 227 George Street, a pleasant, rooftop terrace, shaded with a grapevine.

Exhibition 1, at David Jones's [q.v.2] Art Gallery in August 1939, was a climax for the Sydney semi-abstract movement, showing work by Balson, Crowley, Fizelle, Frank Medworth, Gerald Lewers [qq.v.] and others. In the 1940s and early 1950s Balson's and Crowley's body of abstract 'Constructive Paintings' were unique in Australia. They participated in group exhibitions at the Macquarie Galleries and David Jones, but, because neo-romanticism in Sydney and expressionism in Melbourne had become the fashion, their work lost prominence. In 1949 Crowley taught abstract painting at East Sydney Technical College before handing over to Balson.

In 1954 Crowley bought High Hill, a house at Mittagong. Balson painted there at weekends and decorated the ceiling of the living-room with a large, constructivist design; he later lived in the garden-studio. Her own painting virtually ceased as she watched over him. She only half-heartedly followed Balson's new, loose direction in several isolated paintings to which she turned her hand in England and France in 1960-61 while travelling with him. Grace was content to be at High Hill: the 'garden and the house and their care seemed to take up my time'.

After Balson died in August 1964, Crowley gave her energy to ensuring his place in art history. Her own work was reassessed and her paintings were suddenly acquired for art museum collections. A major exhibition, Balson, Crowley, Fizelle, Hinder (1966), and a retrospective exhibition of her work (1975) were mounted by the Art Gallery of New South Wales. The feminist movement, as well as the growth of Australian art history, brought admirers in Crowley's late years. Janine Burke featured her art and reminiscences (beginning 'Me voici reflecting upon la vie passée') in an exhibition (1975) and book, Australian Women Artists, One Hundred Years: 1840-1940 (Melbourne, 1980). Burke was to draw upon Crowley for a Frenchified Australian painter Margeurite Dance in her novel, Company of Images (Melbourne, 1989).

Small and very slight of build, Grace was somewhat vague in manner and self-effacing in promoting Balson's work. Yet she was strong-willed in her own self-liberation from housework in the bush to painting in Sydney and Paris (and in her insistence on the pronunciation of the name Crowley, to rhyme with 'slowly'). She dressed with chic, favouring the simplest, cream, linen dresses and silk scarves. She lived in immaculate, sparsely decorated, light-filled spaces, with pots by Dangar and paintings by Balson.

High Hill was sold in 1966. Next year Grace bought a modern flat at Manly (she kept her George Street studio until 1971). Fizelle's widow also moved to a flat on a different floor of the same building. They both received research students and museum curators, planned the disposition of the works still in their care, and complained about each other. Crowley died at her home on 21 April 1979 and was cremated. Her estate was sworn for probate at $318 441; she bequeathed her remaining paintings to Australian art museums and her papers to the Mitchell [q.v.5] Library, Sydney. Balson's

portrait (1939) of Crowley is in the Art Gallery of New South Wales.

Her teaching and single-minded nurturing of Balson's reputation might seem as important as her own rather small body of work. However, her painting, like her dress and living spaces, was consciously pared down. Crowley knew that the twenty-five paintings and twelve drawings gathered together in 1975 were enough. Seeing her life's work summed up, she was 'Appalled, and thrilled'.

D. Thomas, Project 4: Grace Crowley, exhibition cat (Syd, 1975); Art Gallery of NSW Q, Oct 1966; H. de Berg, Grace Crowley (taped interview, Feb, 1966, NL); Australia Council archival film interview, 1975 (A.F.I. Distribution Ltd, videocassette); Crowley papers (ML).   DANIEL THOMAS

CUDMORE, SIR COLLIER ROBERT (1885-1971), lawyer and politician, was born on 4 June 1885 at Avoca station, near Wentworth, New South Wales, second son of Daniel Henry Cudmore [q.v.8], pastoralist, and his second wife Martha Earle, née McCracken. Educated in Adelaide at the Collegiate School of St Peter and the University of Adelaide, and in England at Magdalen College, Oxford (B.A., 1909), Robert won a gold medal in rowing as a member of the British IV at the 1908 Olympic Games. He was called to the Bar at the Inner Temple, London, in 1910, and, after returning home, to the South Australian Bar next year. Cudmore joined the Adelaide Club and the Liberal Union, serving as a branch secretary and as a member (from 1912) of that party's State executive. With (Sir) Stanley Murray [q.v.], he established the firm Murray & Cudmore, in which he was to practise as a solicitor until 1955.

Commissioned in the Royal Field Artillery Special Reserve in France on 11 August 1915, Cudmore commanded a battery and was twice severely wounded; thereafter he wore a back-brace and used a walking-stick. His brother Milo was killed in action in 1916. Invalided home in 1919, Cudmore was a member of the State Repatriation Board, an administrator (1919-36) of the Soldiers' Fund, and deputy-chairman (1936-44) of the South Australian Sailors and Soldiers' Distress Fund. On 27 April 1922 in St Peter's college chapel he married Phyllis Miriam Wigg (d. 1964). He was a member (1926-43) of the Anglican diocesan synod, a governor (1932-57) of his old school, and patron of the Adelaide City and University boat clubs. A director of North British & Mercantile Insurance Co. Ltd, Esperance Land Co. Ltd, and Elder, Smith [qq.v.4,6] & Co. Ltd, in 1947-56 he organized Elder's takeovers of De Garis, Sons & Co. Ltd, Commonwealth Wool &

Produce Co. Ltd, Nenco Ltd and Moreheads Ltd. As vice-president of the South Australian Liberal Federation, he promoted its fusion with the Country Party in 1932 to form the Liberal and Country League. He was its president in 1934-36.

In 1933 Cudmore had been elected to the Legislative Council as a member for Adelaide Central District No. 2. An able speaker and committee-man, he led his party in the Upper House from 1939 until his retirement in 1959. He defended the council's role as a house of review, and insisted that L.C.L. councillors convene separately and refain from attending party meetings with their colleagues in the Legislative Assembly. He has been seen as a reactionary because of his opposition in 1945-46 to (Sir) Thomas Playford's nationalization of the Adelaide Electric Supply Co. Ltd when he once called Playford a 'Bolshevik'. Cudmore's antagonism may have owed something to his professional and family links with Murray, the company's chairman. Yet, Cudmore also mistrusted any large increase in the public debt when resources were required for postwar reconstruction. He was later to praise Playford's action.

A liberal conservative, steeped in the writings of Aristotle, Burke, Brougham and Adam Smith, Cudmore sponsored bills of his own and hundreds of his amendments were passed. From 1933 he had campaigned for a parliamentary public accounts committee, more liberal lottery and gaming legislation, and later hours for hotel trading. These proposals were anathema to Playford, but they became law soon after Labor won office in 1965. While demanding stiffer penalties for those who sexually abused children, Cudmore was too radical for many of his contemporaries in expressing approval of a properly controlled 'red light' district. He secured pensions for Supreme Court judges, better traffic laws, compulsory tuberculosis examinations, protection of circus animals, more humane methods for slaughtering livestock, and the introduction of racing and trotting meetings on Anzac Day. Although critical of soldier-settler and organized marketing schemes, of state capitalism and H. V. Evatt's [q.v.] plans for the Federal parliament's aggrandizement, Cudmore also insisted that the 'rights' of private property should be 'necessarily circumscribed in the interests of others'.

As a council-member (1933-53) of the University of Adelaide, Cudmore obtained changes to allow the appointment of a salaried vice-chancellor, and one who was not already a member of the university; he also gained pensions for the staff. He championed John Henry Newman's ideas on university education and fought for adequate funding of the humanities, especially history, quoting

the dictum of the American patriot Patrick Henry: 'I know of no way of judging the future but by the past'.

During World War II Cudmore had been a battalion commander in the Volunteer Defence Corps and chairman of the Australian War Service League which proposed conscription of 'Manpower, Womanpower, Wealth and all other Resources' to promote 'equality of sacrifice'. He was knighted in 1958. While he cherished relics of the 'gracious living' of the late nineteenth century, he was a spender, not an accumulator, of wealth. Sir Collier was confined to a wheelchair in his last years. Survived by his son and daughter, he died on 16 May 1971 in North Adelaide and was cremated.

E. J. R. Morgan, *The Adelaide Club, 1863-1963* (Adel, 1963); *PD* (SA), 1933-58; *Advertiser* (Adel), 7 May 1958, 17 May 1971; Univ Adel, *Calendar* and Council Minute-books, 1933-53 (Univ Adel Archives); SA Sailors and Soldiers' Distress Fund, *Reports*, 1937-44; Cudmore papers (Mort L); information from Mr M. C. Cudmore and Mrs F. F. Shaw, Walkerville, Adel.   P. A. HOWELL

CUMMING, WILLIAM GORDON (1894-1972), woodcarver, was born on 24 October 1894 at Launceston, Tasmania, youngest of nine children of Thomas Girdwood Cumming, an ironworker from Scotland, and his wife Thirza Martha, née Cruse. Educated at Invermay State School, Gordon was apprenticed to W. Coogan & Co., furniture manufacturers, and studied carving and modelling under Hugh Cunningham at Launceston Technical College. He exhibited carved furniture with the Arts and Crafts societies of Northern Tasmania (1911), Victoria (1912) and Tasmania.

On 21 August 1915 Cumming enlisted in the Australian Imperial Force; he served with the 13th Field Ambulance in Egypt and on the Western Front. Embarking for Australia as a lance corporal in May 1919, he was discharged in Tasmania in September and was re-employed by Coogans. On 27 September 1922 at Oakleigh, Melbourne, he married with Methodist forms Elsie May Tranter (d. 1968) whom he had met in France. He taught carving, modelling and repoussé work on a part-time basis at Launceston Technical College in 1922.

Having lost his job in the Depression, in 1930 Cumming established a woodcarving business at his home. There he took commissions, and taught school children and adult pupils, to whom he imparted his crisp and decisive technique and his eclectic approach. He excelled when working in collaboration with the architects Alexander North [q.v.11] and Frank Heyward, and with the cabinet-makers J. & T. Gunn Pty Ltd and Hinman,

Wright & Manser Ltd, and was frequently employed to furnish and ornament Tasmanian churches. In 1932 he carved the monumental cover for the font in Holy Trinity, Launceston, which was designed by North in a combined Gothic Revival and Arts and Crafts style that incorporated gum leaves and nuts. Next year Cumming completed the furnishings, with exquisite fretwork-carving of stylized, eucalypt motifs, for the chapel of Launceston Church Grammar School. He was also proficient at repoussé metalwork and cement modelling: he executed the foliated, cement-column capitals (c.1934) in St John's, Launceston, and decorated commercial buildings in that medium, including a set of panels (c.1932) depicting contemporary life for the Tasmanian Farmers' Co-operative Association Ltd's premises at Burnie.

Five ft 10 ins (177.8 cm) tall, wiry and balding, Cumming was deeply religious, honest and gentle; his wry sense of humour and enthusiasm for nature expressed itself in his love of his craft and of his garden. He played the violin and flute, and was a Freemason who belonged to the Army and Navy Lodge. On 21 March 1970 he married a widow Margery Joyce Butterworth, née Forward, at Christ Church, Launceston, with Congregational forms. Survived by her, and by the two daughters of his first marriage, he died on 13 June 1972 at Launceston and was cremated. After his death, Cumming's final carvings for the furnishings of Scotch College chapel, Launceston, were found completed on his workbench.

C. Miley, *Beautiful and Useful* (Launc, 1987); K. Dimmack, *Woodcarving in Tasmania* (Launc, 1988).   CAROLINE MILEY

CUMMING THOM, WILLIAM;
see THOM

CUMMINS, ALICE MARY (1898?-1943), businesswoman, was born probably on 31 March 1898 in Adelaide, only child of James Hurtle Cummins, a publican from Victoria, and his wife Mary, née Ryan. James moved to Kalgoorlie, Western Australia, but Alice attended Loreto Convent, Norwood, Adelaide, where she did well in languages, drawing and music. She studied at the Elder [q.v.4] Conservatorium and played the cello in local ensembles. Weakened by severe influenza in 1923, she abandoned both her musical activities and her ambition to study medicine. Instead, she read law at the University of Adelaide (LL.B., 1928) and served her articles with the solicitor Percy Hague; although admitted to the South Australian

(1928) and Western Australian (1930) Bars, she never practised.

Beginning as a ledgerkeeper in her father's Kalgoorlie Brewing & Ice Co. Ltd, Cummins soon mastered the financial, engineering, refrigeration and marketing aspects of the brewing industry. In the early 1930s she urged her father to turn from the production of English-style beer and introduce the top-fermentation process of German lager. He thought her brilliant and made her director of the Merredin brewery. Hoping to reconcile her parents who were divided on the issue of alcohol, Alice designed a substantial and elegant residence at Merredin for the Cummins family. She installed Mollie Redvers-Bate as housekeeper, and briefly employed her husband Charles, an ex-British army officer and failed Burracoppin farmer, to manage the brewery.

When James Cummins died in London on 19 March 1936, Alice became managing director and the major shareholder of his enterprises. With support for the old-style beer flagging, rival breweries expanding and hotels being progressively 'tied' by competitors, her situation was critical. Undaunted, she installed new plant and equipment, and boosted Kalgoorlie Brewing's outlets by acquiring hotel freeholds and leases—for the company and in her own right—at Kalgoorlie, Merredin, Moorine Rock, Sandstone, Boyanup, Tammin, Yellowdine, Wagin and Meckering. She triumphed when the instant popularity of Hannan's lager in September 1937 was reflected in its escalating consumption figures. Despite her success, wealth and confidence, Alice retained her quiet, generous and kindly nature. Her rift with the Catholic Church over her father's cremation and the removal of his ashes to Merredin remained permanent.

Of average height, with dark eyes and hair, Miss Cummins was demure, yet rather modish as a young woman; in maturity, she wore tailored coats and skirts, plain blouses and flat-heeled shoes. Accompanied by her secretary, she regularly visited Kalgoorlie, Merredin and Perth, driving Lincoln or Chrysler black limousines. About 1934 she had taken Mollie on a world cruise, then brought her to live at The Bend of the Road, her home at Crawley, where Alice again took up the cello, installed a radio transmitter and spent hours modelling miniature galleons. There she entertained visiting celebrities, such as the violinist Jeanne Gautier.

On Mollie's departure for Melbourne in early 1943, Alice was bereft. For a few months she continued to oversee her empire, warding off attempted takeover bids from Swan Brewery Co. Ltd. She died of a coronary occlusion on 27 June that year at her Kalgoorlie home and was cremated with Anglican rites. Her estate was sworn for probate at £109 903, much of which she bequeathed to Mollie and her two daughters.

S. Welborn, *Swan* (Perth, 1987); *Black Swan*, May 1971; *Chronicle*(Adel), 22 May 1930; *Kalgoorlie Miner*, 21 Mar 1936, 28 June 1943; *Sunday Times* (Perth), 29 Aug 1937; *West Australian* and *Daily News* (Perth), 28 June 1943; *Herald* (Melb), 29 June 1943; *Merredin Mercury*, 1 July 1943; papers and clippings held by Miss D. Day, Mount Lawley, Perth.   WENDY BIRMAN

CUMPSTON, GLADYS MAEVA (1887-1975), community worker, gardener and Braille transcriber, was born on 31 May 1887 at Rosedale, Victoria, second of five children of George Albert Walpole, a medical practitioner from Ireland, and his London-born wife Margaret, née Andrews, a nurse. As a child Gladys lived with relations in London and Ireland while her brother Stanley attended boarding-school in England and their parents remained in Australia. Reunited in 1895, the family lived first in Melbourne and then in turn at Strahan, Queenstown and Gormanston, Tasmania. Gladys was educated mainly by governesses, but also briefly attended Shirley College, Brighton Beach, and Presbyterian Ladies' College, Melbourne.

In 1905 Gladys travelled to Dublin, planning to become a nurse, but she found the training disappointing and returned to Australia. On 2 January 1908 she married a family friend John Howard Lidgett Cumpston [q.v.8] at St John's Anglican Church, Fremantle, Western Australia. Having lived in Perth, Brisbane and Melbourne, the Cumpstons moved to Canberra in 1928.

They built Greystones, renowned for its excellent garden, in Wilmot Crescent, Forrest. A life member of the Horticultural Society of Canberra, Mrs Cumpston regularly exhibited in its shows, winning the Ormond Cup in 1936 and the Lady Gowrie [q.v.9 Earl Gowrie] Challenge Cup in 1949. In the 1960s Gladys was an active member of the Society for Growing Native Plants. She also made artificial flowers of stiffened and shaped silk and velvet, a skill learned in the 1950s at St Martin's School of Art, London.

In 1943 she had helped the Canberra Mothercraft Society to gain Lady Gowrie's patronage for the establishment of the Canberra Nursery Kindergarten Society and was a vice-president on both the provisional committee and the first elected council. During World War II Gladys was prominent in the Voluntary Aid Detachments, the Lady Gowrie Services Club, Manuka, and the Australian Red Cross Society; she single-handedly raised over £700 for charity by the sale of home-grown flowers at the Hotel

Canberra. She also made camouflage nets, draping them across the fireplace in her home and inviting visitors to add to them. The Cumpstons joined the Canberra and District Historical Society as foundation members (1953). In addition to accompanying her husband on his trips abroad, she also helped him to trace the journeys of early Australian explorers. Following Howard's death in 1954, she promoted the posthumous publication of his historical research.

In her seventies and eighties Gladys transcribed fiction, non-fiction and school texts into Braille with the aid of a primer from the Royal National Institute for the Blind and a Stainsby machine. After she had completed fifty volumes (including books by her daughter Mrs Margaret Spencer) the Queensland Braille Writing Association recorded her name on its honour board. Gladys's correspondence with her family contains fascinating descriptions of Canberra. Survived by three sons and four daughters, she died on 18 June 1975 at Red Hill and was cremated.

H. Crisp and L. Ruddock, *The Mothering Years* (Canb, 1979); Canb and District Hist Soc, *Newsletter*, Aug 1975; M. Spencer, John Howard Lidgett Cumpston, 1880-1954: A Biography (ts, 1987) *and* Canb Nursery Kindergarten Soc (ts, 1945) *and* I. M. Cumpston papers (NL); information from Mrs M. Galloway, Forrest, Miss I. M. Cumpston, Deakin, and Mrs H. Cumpston, Aranda, Canb, and Mrs M. Spencer, Tenterfield, NSW.

JILL WATERHOUSE

CUNI, LUKE (1911-1980), Albanian community leader, was born on 31 August 1911 at Prizren, Kosovo-Metohija, son of Albanian parents John Cuni and his wife Marta. During his secondary schooling he improved his knowledge of Albania's history, literature and language; he later studied Latin and classical Greek, graduated from the faculty of philosophy at Skopje, Yugoslavia, and is reputed to have become a professor at that institution. On 1 July 1936 he married Filomena Marko (d. 1979) at Skopje.

After witnessing the suffering of the Albanians under the Kosovan authorities, Cuni and two of his university friends began to organize festivities to celebrate the Albanian National Day (28 November)—against the wishes of the Yugoslav government. In World War II Italy took over the Kosovo district on behalf of Albania. Supported by Josip Broz Tito's Yugoslav forces, in 1944 Albanian partisans defeated the local nationalists and carried out a policy of repression against anti-communists. With his wife, son and daughter, Cuni sought refuge in Austria (1944-45) and Italy (1945-49) where they lived in refugee camps before sailing for

Australia. They arrived in Melbourne on 27 March 1950.

Life as immigrants was not easy. The family was forced to separate: Luke was employed at the migrant hostel, Williamstown, while Filomena found a job as a housemaid at Croydon and the two children boarded at separate schools. Reunited in 1954, they settled at Yarraville. Cuni was naturalized on 24 July 1957, one of the proudest days of his life. He worked at Spartan Paints Pty Ltd, Footscray, as a storeman for the State Electricity Commission and part time in a delicatessen. In his spare hours he taught English privately and in migrant hostels.

An active member of the community, Cuni was associated with the Australia Day Council, the Captive Nations Association, the Yarraville Community Centre, the Good Neighbour Council and the Catholic Family Welfare Bureau. As a talented linguist who spoke eight languages, he helped newly-arrived immigrants; as an interpreter, he worked for the police, in the law courts and in prisons; as a devout Catholic, he preached and conducted funeral services. Successful in mixing with members of many different migrant communities, he was a familiar and respected figure in the Yarraville and Footscray districts. In 1979 the Rotary Club of Footscray named him citizen of the year.

A leader in the Albanian community in Victoria, Cuni was widely known as presenter of the Albanian language programme on radio 3ZZ (1975-77) and on 3EA (1977-80). Like his kinswoman Mother Teresa, he was a pacifist. Shortly before his death, he broadcast on the topic of law and order, and spoke of the pointlessness of vengeance and the virtue of forgiving one's enemies. On 21 May 1980, while working as an interpreter at the Supreme Court, Melbourne, Luke Cuni, with four others, was shot by a man who had threatened to kill anyone associated with a particular hearing. Survived by his daughter and son, he died next day in Royal Melbourne Hospital and was buried in Footscray cemetery.

S. Baldwin (ed), *Unsung Heroes and Heroines of Australia* (Melb, 1988); *Herald* (Melb), 22 May 1980; *Sun News-Pictorial* and *Mail* (Footscray), 23 May 1980.   BAHRI BREGU

CUNNINGHAM, KENNETH STEWART (1890-1976), educationist, was born on 3 February 1890 at Sebastopol, Victoria, second of twelve children of native-born parents Rev. William Richard Cunningham and his wife Amy, née Stephenson. William was a Methodist minister who was later received into the Presbyterian Church. Owing to the peripatetic nature of his father's calling, Ken-

neth attended at least seven different schools in Tasmania and Victoria before completing his matriculation in 1907 at St Andrew's College, Bendigo.

When Cunningham's ambition to study medicine was frustrated by his parents' inability to afford the fees, he turned to schoolteaching. Because of the shortage of teachers, he qualified as a junior teacher in 1909 after only six-months training at a local primary school. In the next two years he took charge of schools in five remote locations, ranging from the Murray River district to the Gippsland hills. Gaining varied experience, the young teacher carted a tin trunk full of books around the countryside and studied at length each evening. At the competitive examination in 1912 he won a studentship to the Melbourne Training College (Melbourne Teachers' College from 1913).

In the course of his three-year stint at M.T.C., Cunningham displayed a spark of high academic potential. On being exposed to the theories of the 'new education' movement and intelligence testing, he developed a voracious appetite for reading about overseas trends. He also came under the influence of the principal Dr John Smyth [q.v.12] who permitted him to transfer to secondary teacher training during his second year and to study at the University of Melbourne (B.A., 1919; M.A., Dip.Ed., 1922). Late in 1914 Smyth also persuaded him to accept an appointment at the Bell Street Special School for mentally handicapped children, which had opened in 1913 at Fitzroy under the headmastership of Stanley Porteus [q.v.11]. Cunningham taught there for eight months, during which he assisted Porteus with research and testing programmes.

On 6 August 1915 Cunningham enlisted in the Australian Imperial Force. He trained with the Australian Army Medical Corps before embarking in April 1916 for the Western Front where he served with the 5th Field Ambulance as a stretcher-bearer. His extensive diaries recorded his observations of conditions in the trenches and highlighted his belief in the futility of war. Commissioned on 23 November 1918, he returned to Australia next May and transferred to the Reserve of Officers on 1 January 1920.

At the Presbyterian Church, South St Kilda, on 3 January 1920 Cunningham married a fellow schoolteacher Ella Myrtle Tuck; they were to have three children. He resumed his university course, completing both his bachelor's and master's degrees, and his diploma of education, with first-class honours, and winning the Dwight [q.v.4] prize. Accepting Smyth's offer of a lectureship, Cunningham taught courses in educational psychology and experimental education at the college and the university. Throughout the

1920s he directed the work of a 'psychological laboratory' at M.T.C. where he devised intelligence tests suitable for local use and conducted clinical work with 'problem' children. After receiving a Macy scholarship, he studied at the Teachers' College, Columbia University, New York, in 1925-27 under such leading educationists as John Dewey and Edward Thorndike. His doctoral thesis (1926) was published as *The Measurement of Early Levels of Intelligence* (New York, 1927).

In 1930 Cunningham was appointed foundation chief executive officer (director from 1939) of the Australian Council for Educational Research. In this post he exerted a significant influence on the development of Australian educational research for almost a quarter of a century. He supervised the construction of standardized tests for Australian schools, took chief responsibility for the distribution of research and travel grants, selected material for the A.C.E.R.'s vigorous publication programme and organized a successful New Education Fellowship conference in 1937.

A voluminous writer on educational subjects, Cunningham made considerable contributions to the development of Australian libraries and the social sciences in general, and championed the use of tests for vocational purposes during World War II. He was a member of the Australian National Research Council and chaired (1943-52) its social science research committee. In addition, he was a founder of the Australian branch of the British Psychological Society and a postwar president of the Eugenics Society of Victoria.

Cunningham's working life spanned an era when psychology was being applied more readily to the problems of education. The study of individual differences and mental measurement became fashionable in Australian schools. With other advocates of the testing movement, he shared a vision that education would eventually be elevated to the status of a science. Objective testing—although controversial—was seen as a means of eliminating much of the educational wastage caused by outdated teaching methods based on tradition or mere opinion.

Undemonstrative, cautious and diplomatic, Cunningham steered the A.C.E.R. to institutional permanence by carrying out the continuing negotiations throughout the 1940s which secured the grants needed for its survival. His insistence on high academic standards established the council's credibility as a research authority and enabled him to elicit the necessary co-operation from Australia's centralized systems of educational administration.

Following his retirement in 1954, Cun-ningham remained actively devoted to education. He accepted an invitation from the United Nations Educational, Scientific and Cultural Organization to work in Indonesia in 1955-56 as a consultant on teacher-training and he continued to publish widely. He remained in excellent health until 1973, when a stroke left him partly paralysed. Survived by his son and a daughter, he died on 27 June 1976 at Fairfield, Melbourne, and was cremated. In 1965 Monash University had named a chair of education after him.

W. F. Connell, *The Australian Council for Educational Research* (Melb, 1980); C. Turney (ed), *Pioneers of Australian Education*, 3 (Syd, 1983); *Aust Lib J*, 25, Oct 1976, p 349; *Aust Psychologist*, 12, July 1977, p 204; *J of Aust Studies*, 31, 1991; Cunningham personal papers (held by Miss L. Cunningham, Kew, Melb); Cunningham's war diaries (AWM); ACER Archives, Hawthorn, Melb.

BRIAN WILLIAMS

CUNNINGHAM, LUCIEN LAWRENCE (1889-1948), farmer and politician, was born on 4 June 1889 at Inverell, New South Wales, tenth child of Eugene Cunningham, farmer, and his wife Mary, née Edgeworth, both Irish born. Eugene had been a policeman and hotelkeeper; the family was well known in the Inverell district and the site of their property is still called Cunninghams Hill. Educated at Goonoowigall Public School, Lou helped his father on the farm and eventually ran it; he also worked intermittently as a wool-presser and was an organizer for the Australian Workers' Union.

As president of the local branches of the No-Conscription League and of the Australian Labor Party, Cunningham was one of the younger activists whose political prospects were enhanced after the departure of the conscriptionists from the party during World War I. Having failed in 1917 to win the Legislative Assembly seat of Gough, in 1919 he defeated William Webster [q.v.12] for Gwydir in the House of Representatives. In parliament Cunningham's approach was influenced by his rural orientation, devout Catholicism, fierce hostility to communism and dislike of the A.L.P.'s socialist objective. His ability was soon recognized and caucus promoted him to the executive in 1921. He paid 'the closest attention to the interests of his electors' and, with A.W.U. backing, seemed to have a promising future, but he lost Gwydir to C. L. A. Abbott [q.v.] in 1925.

While out of parliament, Cunningham farmed at Leeton. On 3 September 1927 he married a typist Catherine Crosby at St Brigid's Catholic Church, Coogee, Sydney. He stood unsuccessfully for Gwydir in 1928, but regained it next year when James Scullin [q.v.11] became prime minister. The government's disintegration in the face of daunting economic and political problems created opportunities for advancement. In March 1931 caucus nominated Cunningham for Deputy-Speaker and chairman of committees: the move failed because D. C. McGrath [q.v.10] refused to stand aside and Scullin was so unsure of the government's majority that he avoided a vote in the House.

Unlike some of his colleagues, Cunningham defended the demoralized government; he entered cabinet as an assistant-minister on 26 June. Tall and about 17 stone (108 kg), he was described as 'the Goonoowigall Giant' and 'Australia's biggest cabinet minister'. The government was routed at the elections in December and Cunningham lost his seat. As the federal A.L.P. candidate, in February 1932 he polled poorly in a by-election for East Sydney, a stronghold of J. T. Lang's [q.v.9] party.

Although he lived at Coogee for the rest of his life, Cunningham maintained his links with primary industry as secretary of the Amalgamated Milk Vendors' Association of New South Wales. In the struggle for control of the State A.L.P. he continued to oppose the 'Langites' and—following Lang's removal as leader in 1939—stood for the assembly as A.L.P. candidate for Coogee, traditionally an anti-Labor electorate. His unlikely success in the 1941 elections was due to his political skills and standing in the community, as well as to Labor's rejuvenation under (Sir) William McKell. Cunningham retained the seat in 1944 and 1947. Survived by his wife and two sons, he died of a coronary occlusion on 23 March 1948 at Coogee and was buried in Randwick cemetery.

P. Weller (ed), *Caucus Minutes 1901-1949*, 2, 1917-1931 (Melb, 1975); E. Wiedemann, *World of its Own* (Inverell, NSW, 1981); R. McMullin, *The Light on the Hill* (Melb, 1991); *Labor News*, 6 Dec 1919; *SMH*, 9 Dec 1922; *Aust Worker*, 25 Dec 1929; P. Cook, The Scullin Government (Ph.D. thesis, ANU, 1971). ROSS MCMULLIN

CURLEWIS, FREDERICK CHARLES PATRICK (1876-1945), cane-grower and administrator, was born on 10 December 1876 at Bellarine, Victoria, fifth child of Alfred Claribeaux Curlewis, a native-born inspector of schools, and his wife Ellen Jessie, née Curlewis, from England. Educated at Brighton Grammar and Melbourne Church of England Grammar schools, Frederick worked for a shipping agent before becoming a vigneron near Rutherglen. He moved to North Queensland in 1909, reputedly for his health, but two of his uncles had explored the colony's frontier in the 1860s. Curlewis grew sugar-

cane for the Mulgrave and Hambledon mills and became active in the Hambledon Cane Farmers' Association. On 23 August 1910 he married a nurse Harriet Ethne O'Brien with Anglican rites at Corowa, New South Wales. As secretary (from 1912) of the Cairns Canegrowers' Association, he wrote on industry matters for the *Cairns Post*. He sold his farm in 1924, following his appointment as northern industrial representative for the Australian Sugar Producers' Association which acted on behalf of growers as well as millers.

The A.S.P.A. competed with the United Cane Growers Association (formed in 1914) and antagonism was commonplace. Ill feeling intensified when the latter body, renamed the Queensland Cane Growers Association, used the provisions of the Primary Producers Organization and Marketing Act (1926) to force compulsory membership on all cane-growers. While officially apolitical, the A.S.P.A. was aligned with right-wing politics and the Q.C.G.A. with the left. The Cairns Canegrowers' Association, however, contrived to represent both the A.S.P.A. and the Q.C.G.A. —an achievement attributed to Curlewis's diplomacy and integrity.

After the death of its foundation secretary G. H. Pritchard, the A.S.P.A. took nearly a year to select Curlewis from 238 applicants for the post. He left Cairns for Brisbane and began his duties on 13 May 1931. Unlike his extroverted and confrontationist predecessor, he was pronounced by the Innisfail delegate to be 'the most painstaking man he had ever met'. Curlewis's practical knowledge of sugar politics was of exceptional value in preparing submissions and in briefing A.S.P.A. representatives. A member of the Commonwealth sugar inquiry committee (1929-31) and of the Queensland royal commission on sugar peaks (1938-39), he was respected for his balanced approach. He was a conciliator in an industry where growers and millers had common, and competing, interests.

Curlewis worked well with the Q.C.G.A.'s secretaries Bill Doherty and Ronnie Muir, and seldom raised his voice, although he regarded the flamboyant Muir as something of a playboy. As a matter of principle, Curlewis strongly supported the Bureau of Sugar Experiment Stations in disciplining farmers to prevent the spread of diseased cane; he also advocated increased funding for the bureau and persuaded the industry to augment the salary of the bureau's director (a public servant). With lean features and a pensive expression, Curlewis was a quiet perfectionist who expected and received devotion from his staff; politically conservative, he was well read, and enjoyed classical music and golf.

During World War II, when vital staff enlisted, Curlewis carried a heavy workload which was increased by wartime regulations and shortages. Survived by his wife, son and daughter, he died of a coronary occlusion on 12 March 1945 at Kelvin Grove, Brisbane, and was cremated.

Aust Sugar J, Aug 1931, p 87, Mar 1932, p 679, Mar 1945, p 439; *Queenslander*, 23 Apr, 14 May 1931; *Courier-Mail*, 12, 13 Mar 1945; information from Dr H. W. Kerr, St Lucia, and Mrs N. A. Gutteridge, Ascot, Brisb.　　　　JOHN D. KERR

CURMI, HENRY FELIX VINCENT CASIMIR CRENI (1890-1967), diplomat, was born on 2 October 1890 at Sliema, Malta, eldest of eight children of Giorgio Curmi, civil servant, and his wife Paolina, née Decelis. Educated at the Royal University of Malta, Henry served in various civil service departments, among them the lieutenant-governor's office, before taking up a commission in the King's Own Malta Regiment of Militia in 1910. After being mobilized in the Royal Malta Artillery in 1915, he served from 8 September at Gallipoli where he was mentioned in dispatches. He was also stationed on Lemnos, in Egypt and in Palestine, and was promoted lieutenant in 1917. During the war he met Bessie Evelyn Simmonds, an English nurse stationed in Malta. She converted to Catholicism and they were married on 23 April 1919 at St Polycarp's Church, Farnham, England.

Captain Curmi's interest in Maltese emigration was stimulated by his successive appointments as secretary (1921) to the minister for labour, posts and agriculture (who had responsibility for migration) and as secretary (1922) of Malta's emigration committee. In 1928 he was made commissioner for labour and in 1929 was appointed to Australia as Malta's first commissioner for migration. His arrival coincided with the Depression which provoked intense anti-immigrant feeling. Having undertaken gruelling trips from Perth to Cairns (Queensland) and Melbourne, in 1930 he returned in ill health to Malta. He was replaced by H. W. Potts [q.v.11] and then by the Melbourne solicitor Frank Corder.

In June 1936 Curmi came back to Australia as commissioner for Malta. Next year he was appointed O.B.E. His office at 108 Queen Street, Melbourne, became a focal point for Maltese settlers throughout the country, as well as a base for the Malta Relief Fund, which raised money and food for the besieged Mediterranean island during World War II. A central and recurring issue for Curmi was the Federal government's refusal to recognize the Maltese as 'white British subjects'. He worked patiently to alter Australian policy and attained formal success in 1944. In addition, he played a key role in negotiations which led to the Malta-Australia Assisted Passage Agreement in 1948. During Curmi's second period as commissioner, the Maltese in Australia increased from some 3000 to about 10 000. He retired in 1952 and was appointed C.B.E. that year.

Curmi's strong and charming personality was born of a sense of personal worth which carried over into his dignified representation of Malta. While fully Maltese, he was very aware of things British. In Malta he had been general secretary of the Boy Scouts' Association. He was an avid reader of European and Church history; in his retirement, he indulged his interest in wood, leather and ivory work, and was secretary of the Arts and Crafts Society of Victoria. Predeceased by his wife, and survived by their three daughters and two sons, he died on 5 March 1967 at Kew and was buried in Springvale cemetery.

B. York, *Empire and Race* (Syd, 1990); *Advocate* (Melb), 9 Mar 1967; *Maltese Herald* (Syd), 19 Apr 1967; information from Ms M. Curmi, Box Hill, and Mr E. Curmi, Surrey Hills, Melb.　　　BARRY YORK

CURR, FRANCIS LAWRENCE (1920-1944), air force officer, was born on 21 June 1920 at Clayfield, Brisbane, third son of Frederick Carlton Curr, grazier, and his wife Maude Alice, née Rogers, both Queensland born. Educated at Downlands College, Toowoomba, Frank worked as a jackeroo, studied accountancy and obtained a private pilot's licence. He enlisted in the Royal Australian Air Force on 26 April 1940, one of the first to be selected under the Empire Air Training Scheme.

Graduating as a pilot, Curr was promoted sergeant in December 1940 and sent to the Middle East where he joined No. 38 Squadron, Royal Air Force, in April 1941. He took part in fifty bombing sorties before moving to England in April 1942. From August to October he flew Wellingtons of No. 75 Squadron, Royal New Zealand Air Force. For pressing home attacks from low altitudes, he was awarded the Distinguished Flying Medal (1942). In November he transferred to the R.A.F.'s No. 156 Squadron, Pathfinder Force, which operated Lancasters. His determination and fearlessness in raids over Italy and Germany won him a Bar to his D.F.M. (1943): he was one of only two R.A.A.F. airmen to be so decorated. Although an exceptionally experienced and successful captain of heavy bombers, he was not commissioned until 18 October 1942. Australian newspapers had criticized his lack of advancement.

Back in Australia in July 1943, with some seventy-five operations to his credit, Curr was employed on instructional duties. Following an unenthusiastic performance, he was posted in March 1944 to No. 33 Squadron, R.A.A.F., to fly Dakota transports from Milne Bay, Papua. He continued to be discontented by R.A.A.F. policy which generally debarred those with extensive operational experience elsewhere from postings to combat units in the South-West Pacific Area. On 28 August, while ferrying a Tiger Moth from Australia to Milne Bay, he was stranded on Daru Island off the south coast of Papua; he remained there for several weeks awaiting a spare propeller.

On 24 September 1944 the aircraft was again serviceable. Against the advice of local army authorities, and accompanied by a soldier who did not have permission to travel with him, Curr took off at 6.20 p.m., apparently intending to fly back across Torres Strait to Horn Island. In failing light and adverse weather, and in a single-engined, light aircraft, with no radio, dinghy or extra fuel, he embarked on a risky venture. The Tiger Moth did not arrive. Despite extensive searches, no trace of it or its occupants was found. Frederick Curr offered a reward of £500 for his son's rescue. A court of inquiry attributed the accident to Curr's making 'an unauthorized flight at night without adequate night flying equipment, safety equipment or an escort'.

A Catholic and a bachelor, Curr was 5 ft 11 ins (180.3 cm) tall and 12 stone (76.2 kg) in weight, with brown eyes and hair. He was an outspoken and high-spirited young man, never amenable to authority, but very well liked by his contemporaries. His somewhat turbulent character probably accounted for the delay in granting him a commission. The refusal of the R.A.A.F. to approve his requests to return to bombing operations resulted in a deterioration in his flying performance and morale, and, considering the circumstances of his last flight, his judgement.

J. F. Mooney, *Downlands, the First Fifty Years* (Toowoomba, Qld, 1981); *Courier-Mail*, 9 Oct 1944; AWM records; AT2010/4, file 166/8/663 (AA, Canb); information from the RAAF Historical Section, Canb, from Mr J. J. Curr, Goodna, and Mr P. Murphy, St Lucia, Brisb, Mr D. Delaney, Oatley, Syd, and Wg Cdr P. Isaacson, Toorak, Melb.

ALAN FRASER

CURREY, CHARLES HERBERT (1890-1970), educationist and legal historian, was born on 25 May 1890 at Ulmarra, New South Wales, fifth child of Frederick Charles Currey, a schoolteacher from Maryland, United States of America, and his Australian-born wife Alice, née Garven. Attending a school where his father taught Aboriginal children, Charles received—through Frederick's American-inspired views—a sense of the importance of liberty in civilized societies. He did well at Grafton and Ballina Superior public schools, and in 1904 won a bursary to Sydney Boys' High School.

In 1908 Currey began a lifetime's association when he entered Teachers' College, Sydney, where K. R. Cramp [q.v.8] thought him his best student. Currey attended the University of Sydney (B.A., 1912) on a scholarship, graduating with first-class honours in English and history, and the Frazer [q.v.4] scholarship. He obtained his M.A. (1914) with first-class honours in history and the Nathan prize (1915) for his essay, 'British Colonial Policy from 1783 to the Present Time', a modified form of which he published in 1916. Like Cramp, he was drawn to Australian history by Professor G. A. Wood [q.v.12], who, as Professor J. M. Ward observed, 'enlivened [Currey's] passionate belief in liberty—and in history as the story of liberty'. Unlike Cramp, Currey went on to study law at university; his 1917 Beauchamp [q.v.7] prize essay, 'Industrial Arbitration in New South Wales', was seminal. He graduated LL.B. (1922) and attained Sydney's rare LL.D. (1929) by thesis, his 'Chapters on the Legal History of New South Wales' entering a previously unexplored field.

In 1912 Currey had succeeded to Cramp's Teachers' College lectureship, eventually as senior lecturer in charge of history and political science. Eschewing academic administration, he devoted himself to teaching, research and writing. Although he became an inspector of schools, he only briefly taught children. Similarly, although admitted to the Bar on 1 September 1922, he did not practise law. His powerful influence over the exposition of history in New South Wales schools was achieved not only by devising new teaching methods, but also through writing numerous 'primers' that dealt with notable figures, European history, the British Commonwealth and the growth of Australia. In 1930 he offered a weightier methodological dissertation, *Study and Teaching of History and Civics*. He presided over the Teachers' College Lecturers' Association and, as president (1933-34) of the Teachers' Federation, tried unsuccessfully to turn back waves of political activity that would soon alter the federation's course.

On 10 January 1916 at St Anne's Anglican Church, Strathfield, Currey had married Linda Wise; they lived at Strathfield and were to remain childless. He was fond of gardening and 'motoring', and enjoyed his Blue Mountains retreat at Mount Wilson. Actively involved in local affairs, he published *Mount Wilson* in 1968.

Having been a member (from 1925) of the Royal Australian Historical Society, he served as a councillor, contributed numerous lectures and papers, and was made a fellow in 1945. Currey was president (1954-59) in turbulent times, exacerbated by his own argumentative temperament. He fell out with many councillors over a proposed sale of the society's Sydney premises, while disputes raged over such other issues as the composition of the council and the filling of honorary offices. His public, 'viperine' clashes with M. H. Ellis [q.v.] were remarkable, alike for venom and want of ratiocination.

Interested in international affairs, Currey belonged to the Sydney group of Round Table. After retiring from Teachers' College in 1951, he continued until 1961 his part-time lecturing, begun in 1933, at Sydney University Law School. His domain, English and Australian legal and constitutional history, led naturally to his major books. *The Irish at Eureka* (1954), *The Transportation . . . of Mary Bryant* [q.v.1] (1963) and *The Brothers Bent* [qq.v.1] (1968) were important, if relatively small, studies. His greatest work, *Sir Francis Forbes* [q.v.1] (1968), a monumental review of the early social, political and legal history of New South Wales, vindicated Chief Justice Forbes's constitutional position in his relations with Governor Darling [q.v.1]. Currey's wit as a lecturer rarely showed in his books where he preferred a stilted and ponderous vocabulary. He contributed to the *Australian Dictionary of Biography*. Professor Douglas Pike [q.v.] wrote to him: 'good men are very scarce and we are very keen to have the distinction of your name and mark'.

At work on a life of Sir William Denison [q.v.4], Currey died on 2 March 1970 at Mount Wilson; his wife survived him. He willed half his residuary estate to the Public [State] Library of New South Wales 'to promote the writing of Australian history from the original sources'; his bequest endowed the library's annual C. H. Currey memorial fellowship.

L. Foster, *High Hopes* (Melb, 1986); J. and J. Mackinolty (eds), *A Century Down Town* (Syd, 1991); *Canb and District Hist Soc J*, 1970, pt 2, p 13; *Hist Studies*, 55, Oct 1970, p 480; *RAHS Newsletter*, 91, Apr 1970, p 4; *JRAHS*, v 73, 1988, pp 243, 267, v 76, 1990, p 190; *SMH*, 7 Mar 1970; Currey papers *and* file (ML); RAHS Archives (Syd); Currey letters, Syd Teachers' College papers (Univ Syd Archives).　　　　　　　　　　J. M. BENNETT

CURTHOYS, ROY LANCASTER (1892-1971), journalist, was born on 4 October 1892 at Ballarat, Victoria, son of native-born parents Alfred George Curthoys, pharmaceutical chemist, and his wife Ada Marion, née Willetts. Educated at the High School, Perth, Roy learned typing and shorthand at John Wardrop's business school and in 1910 joined the literary staff of the *Daily News*. He transferred to the *West Australian* in 1916 and, moving to Melbourne in 1919, joined the *Herald*. From 1912 Curthoys was a leading member of the Australian Journalists' Association. He was largely responsible for setting up a course for journalists at the University of Western Australia in 1919 and was also involved in the establishment of a diploma in journalism at the University of Melbourne in 1922.

In 1920 Curthoys had transferred to the Melbourne *Argus* and two years later travelled to the United States of America and Europe. Commissioned by the A.J.A. federal executive as its special representative, he reported on the higher education of journalists in the countries he visited. In 1925 he was appointed assistant-editor to (Sir) Edward Cunningham [q.v.8], whom he succeeded as editor in 1929. The school of journalism of the University of Missouri in 1934 conferred its medal of honour on the *Argus* as a 'distinguished exponent of the best traditions of journalism'; on a world tour that year, Curthoys received the award personally.

Following disagreement with the *Argus* management over the paper's content and format, Curthoys resigned his editorship in 1935. He had been since 1927 chief Australian correspondent for *The Times*, though on assuming editorship of the *Argus* he delegated the reporting jobs and kept a supervisory role. *The Times* commitment now became his primary occupation: on a substantial salary (£600 per annum) he took over as chief correspondent, responsible for Melbourne and Canberra, and for co-ordinating the work of correspondents in Sydney and Brisbane. He was also employed as Australian correspondent (1935-57) for the *New York Times*. Sir Keith Murdoch [q.v.10] gave Curthoys free accommodation in the offices of the Melbourne *Herald* and employed him as occasional leader writer. In 1938 and 1939 Murdoch offered Curthoys the London editor-managership of Australian Associated Press Ltd at a salary of £1750, but *The Times* connexion was more congenial and remained the focus of Curthoys' professional life until his retirement in 1958.

Appreciation of Curthoys' journalistic skills and integrity was universal. Cunningham wrote enviously of his clarity, judgement and learning, and his 'gift of exposition in lucid English'. Sir James Darling remembered him as 'charming and lovable, a great conversationalist, knowledgeable and informed, witty and occasionally caustic, a loyal friend, but not a notably forgiving antagonist who without asserting himself personally enlarged the culture of Australia at the time of its rebirth'.

A bachelor and a member of the Savage Club, Curthoys was active in the Institute of International Affairs and served on the council of the Brotherhood of St Laurence. He declined an offer of appointment as O.B.E. in 1951, feeling 'bound by the longstanding tradition that members of the editorial staff of *The Times* do not accept honours'. In 1958 he was appointed C.M.G. He died on 24 September 1971 at Prahran and was cremated, according to his request, without religious rites. His estate was sworn for probate at $103 254.

Newspaper News, 2 Jan 1929; *Journalist*, Apr 1972; *Age, SMH*, and *The Times*, 28 Sept 1971; Curthoys papers (NL); information from Sir James Darling, Armadale, Melb.   A. W. MARTIN

CURTIN, JOHN (1885-1945), prime minister and journalist, was born on 8 January 1885 at Creswick, Victoria, eldest of four children of Irish-born parents John Curtin (1854?-1919) and his wife Catherine (Kate) Agnes, née Bourke (1859?-1938). John senior worked as a warder at Pentridge Gaol, served as a soldier, was a policeman at Creswick (1881-90), then was employed in hotels, sometimes as manager, in Melbourne and at Dromana, Charlton, Macedon and elsewhere. The family eventually settled, in poverty, at Brunswick.

Jack had erratic education at several Catholic and state schools. He became a copy-boy on the *Age*, page-boy at a city club, office-boy on the *Rambler* and a labourer at a pottery, before finding steady work from September 1903 with the Titan Manufacturing Co., on £2 a week as an estimates clerk. Night after night at the Public Library he read 'serious books': political works, poetry, novels and essays. He played much cricket and football, eventually for Brunswick. A sturdy backman, about 5 ft 11 ins (180 cm) tall and almost twelve stone (76 kg), he was subsequently active in football administration.

Curtin joined the Political Labor Council, gained a reputation as a 'Labor boy-orator' on the Yarra Bank and at the Eastern Market, and lost his Catholic faith; he allegedly played cornet in a Salvation Army band.

He probably first met his local State member Frank Anstey [q.v.7] in 1902 and, with his great mate Frank Hyett [q.v.9], soon joined Anstey's Sunday-morning study circle. Throughout an enduring friendship Curtin was to acknowledge Anstey's dominant influence. He also attended Tom Mann's [q.v.10]

Economic Study Circle with Hyett, Don Cameron [q.v.7], John Cain and E. J. (Jack) Holloway [qq.v.].

Curtin's first publications were in 1906 in the *Socialist*, edited by Mann for the Victorian Socialist Party; he was by then tutor at its speakers' classes. In 1907-08 he was president, then secretary, of the Brunswick branch of the P.L.C. His activities, however, came to centre on the V.S.P. in its halcyon days of utopian revolutionary socialism. He wrote extensively for the *Socialist* on industrial organization and in 1909 asserted that 'Australian defence policy was part and parcel of the international war policy played by the international gang of capitalists'. Visitors from overseas such as Ben Tillett and Keir Hardie led him later to recall that he was 'brought up among the great international socialists'.

Socially, the V.S.P. was a delight, with its Sunday-night lectures, picnics, choir, orchestra, dances, 'Sunday School', and the growth of lasting friendships with the Bruce family, Jack Gunn [q.v.9] and R. S. (Bob) Ross [q.v.11]. For about three years Curtin wrote to Gunn's young sister Jessie in the country, confiding in her and struggling to improve his self-expression. In 1909-10 he was honorary secretary of the V.S.P. which was already breaking down in factional disputes.

In February 1911 Curtin became organizing secretary of the sawmillers' (timberworkers') union, Victorian branch, and threw himself into consolidating scattered local groups and improving working and accommodation conditions. His *Timber Worker* appeared from February 1913 as a vehicle of industrial agitation and socialist propaganda. In 1914 he became first federal president of the union. He also led the campaign for the Workers' Compensation Act (1914) and sat on the Trades Hall Council's disputes committee. As John Joseph Ambrose Curtin, in September he stood for the House of Representatives seat of Balaclava; though defeated, he polled surprisingly well.

In April 1912 Curtin had helped to re-establish his union's Tasmanian branch. He struck up a warm friendship there with Abraham Needham and was attracted to his daughter Elsie (1890-1975). When she was leaving for a long, family visit to South Africa in 1914, Jack proposed to her on St Kilda beach, Melbourne, and was accepted.

Curtin's friends admired him for his idealization of the working class, his intellectual grasp, deep knowledge of the international socialist movement and his broad reading, but were concerned by his drinking. By 1914 his problem was conspicuous. In November 1915 he resigned his union post, mentioning his health and the 'stress and storm of trade union responsibility'. He became an

Australian Workers' Union organizer, but by June 1916 was drying out in hospital.

Such was their trust, in August the Australian Trades Union Anti-Conscription Congress appointed Curtin organizer (later secretary) of its national executive to oppose conscription for overseas service. His attitude blended pacifism, traditional socialist anti-militarism and the Marxist analysis that war was essential to the capitalist system. 'Socialism is the only way—it will end war, even as it will conquer poverty'. He had led local support for the Hardie-Vaillant resolution at the Socialist International in 1910 which called for a general strike in the event of war. Yet there is inconclusive evidence that he volunteered for the Australian Imperial Force only to be rejected because of inadequate eyesight. Nonetheless, he had no doubts about conscription and worked closely with Holloway, Hyett and Ross in preparation for the plebiscite on 28 October 1916. Their anti-conscription manifesto was seized by the police.

Under W. M. Hughes's [q.v.9] ill-judged ordering of single men to camp, Curtin was charged with failure to enlist, convicted in his absence (interstate) to three months imprisonment, and gaoled for three days, but released when such prosecutions were tardily withdrawn. Meanwhile Hughes and his followers were being expelled from the Australian Labor Party.

Seeking a fresh start and a salary which would enable him to marry, Curtin was appointed editor of the A.W.U.'s *Westralian Worker*. In February 1917 his friends emotionally farewelled him with the traditional purse of sovereigns. Elsie joined him in Perth and they were married on 21 April in the district registrar's office, Leederville. For ten years Jack abstained from alcohol.

The 'red-ragger from the East' turned out to be a 'mild bespectacled man', quiet, affable and earnest. In 1917 the local Labor Party was in a state of collapse; working closely with Alex McCallum [q.v.10], his chief sponsor, Curtin fought hard through a disastrous year. Labor lost every Western Australian seat in Federal parliament and won only 15 out of 50 State seats, but in the second conscription plebiscite considerably reduced the 'Yes' majority. Curtin was convicted and fined for some remarks about revolution. At the June 1918 federal party conference he supported the successful, moderate resolution 'encouraging the Imperial Government to openly declare its war aims and its readiness to negotiate'. He was elected to the State executive, unwillingly stood for Perth at the 1919 Federal election, and was badly beaten. Suffering from neurasthenia and veering between optimism and melancholy, he had to have six months complete rest; both his father

and Hyett had died that year. Curtin supported adoption of the socialist objective in 1921.

Writing hundreds of articles and editorials over a decade, he made the weekly *Westralian Worker* probably the best Australian Labor paper. He was State district president (1920-25) of the Australian Journalists' Association and strongly supported the Workers' Educational Association. Professors (Sir) Walter Murdoch and Edward Shann [qq.v.10,11] became his good friends.

Marriage gave Curtin stability and a degree of serenity. A daughter and son were born, and in 1923 the family moved into a red-brick bungalow at Cottesloe. He enjoyed bringing up the children, surfed with them, often walked on the beach, cheerfully did household chores, pottered in the garden and kept a dog. Perth came to be very congenial to him, not least because of the fervent idealism and friendship of so many in the labour movement. According to Victor Courtney [q.v.], everyone liked him for his tolerance and kindliness; he was no wowser, but did not tell *risqué* stories and 'bloody' was almost his only swearword.

Curtin soon struck up a close friendship with Phil Collier [q.v.8] who owed much to him as adviser and confidant. While still an international socialist, Curtin was modifying his views. 'Soap-boxing' on street corners remained essential; oratory was 'the great instrument of conversion', backed by education in the *Worker*. But he was realistically concluding that parliamentary action by the Labor Party, from which communists had to be excluded, was the only practical means of social change. 'Incessant strikes' were of dubious advantage.

In mid-1924 Curtin was an Australian delegate to the annual conference of the International Labour Organization at Geneva, Switzerland. He met many interesting people and returned with moderate enthusiasm for the League of Nations as a force for peace. In 1927-28 he served on the Commonwealth royal commission into the possibility of introducing child endowment, spending long periods away from Perth, living in hotels and drinking again. He was angered by his inability to impress his views on the conservative members of the commission and, with Mildred Muscio [q.v.10], produced a forceful minority report.

Having stood unsuccessfully for the marginal Federal seat of Fremantle in 1925, Curtin won it with substantial majorities in 1928 and 1929. Few members have entered parliament with more extensive grassroots experience or better intellectual preparation. He had been reading the works of J. M. (Baron) Keynes, A. C. Pigou and others, and talking to academic economists. He developed his own views—'I have attended the funeral of so many economic theories'. Anstey welcomed him warmly as an ally and in February 1929 Curtin was elected to caucus executive: 'the Labor party had added to its ranks an orator whose worth as a fighting force seemed incalculable'. But he was humiliated when he was not elected to Scullin's [q.v.11] ministry and blamed E. G. Theodore [q.v.12].

Thus Curtin was frustrated, underemployed, morose, lonely and drinking. When the ministry was reconstructed in March 1931, he withdrew his candidature after Anstey was 'dumped'. Meanwhile his speeches outshone those of the ministers floundering in the depths of the Depression. On 10 June 1930 he spoke strongly for Theodore's unsuccessful central reserve bank bill. He was prominent in the 'caucus revolt' in protest at the Melbourne Agreement following Sir Otto Niemeyer's recommendations. J. T. Lang's [q.v.9] adoption of 'repudiation' and the imposition of his policy on New South Wales Labor members led to the expulsion, moved by Curtin, of the State branch in March 1931. Curtin was now convinced that the impotent Scullin government should resign and fight an election. It could not govern in the face of hostility by the Commonwealth Bank of Australia, the Senate's rejection of all important legislation, the resignation of J. A. Lyons and J. E. Fenton [qq.v.10,8], and Lang's sabotage. Curtin's motion at federal executive to reject the Premiers' Plan was only just lost. At the December election he was badly beaten.

Curtin settled down to enjoy home life, freelancing for daily, interstate and country newspapers. He corresponded irregularly with Theodore who wrote: 'I have long believed that you are destined for great things, if you keep hold of yourself, and if that old hag, Fate, is not too relentless'. And about this time Curtin permanently gave up the drink. He appealed to Theodore to rally the movement—but Theodore was fed up. At successive federal conferences Curtin took the lead in holding firm against Lang.

In mid-1932 the Perth Trades Hall Council appointed Curtin publicity officer and he returned to the *Worker* as a sporting writer who gave racing tips; he was a student of racing form but hardly ever betted, apart from an annual £1 on the Melbourne Cup. Collier soon appointed Curtin full-time chairman, on £12 a week, of the advisory council to prepare the Western Australian case before the new Commonwealth Grants Commission. Curtin had been totally opposed to secession, but considered that the A.L.P. should abandon its policy of unification because of opinion in the 'smaller' States. In fruitful collaboration with (Sir) Alexander Reid [q.v.], he worked hard for a year on preparing the case and presenting it.

Curtin was determined to recapture Fremantle, as he did comfortably in September 1934. He again immediately impressed people by the quality of his speeches, especially in recommending expansion of credit to reduce unemployment. Scullin's health was precarious and he resigned as leader on 1 October 1935. Curtin had not considered that he stood any chance, but when Holloway approached him—and gained his pledge that he would totally abstain from alcohol—agreed to stand. He was elected by one vote over Frank Forde who was staggered, as was Scullin, but proved a good, loyal loser. The pressmen were astounded. Curtin was elected as an opponent of the Premiers' Plan, with a union background; it was unique for any party to have a Western Australian leader.

Allan Fraser [q.v.] recalled: 'Curtin found he was a much better leader than he ever dreamt he could be'. Now 'John' Curtin, he dressed the part—good, plain suit, a black bowler for a time, occasional bow-tie, laces well tucked into boots—and insisted that Labor candidates be well turned out. He won general respect. In October 1938 a journalist remarked that 'Few men are so deeply liked all round the House'.

To build unity, Curtin immediately toured State executives and local centres. His sense of urgency, 'quiet steadiness' and 'incisive clarity' were effective. Sydney was the key. In October 1935 the federal executive, on Curtin's motion, had agreed to call a unity conference with New South Wales Labor. As a result, in February 1936 J. A. Beasley, E. J. Ward [qq.v.] and other 'Langites' joined caucus. Lang's power was declining after crushing electoral defeat. Curtin still had to endure insults and intimidation at New South Wales conferences until the machine-men and racketeers were overcome by federal authority. Then, in 1940, New South Wales briefly split into three groups and Beasley and others again left caucus, for ten months.

Foreign policy and defence issues dominated the later 1930s. Curtin struggled to find compromise policies among the isolationists, pacifists, international socialists, communists, Catholics and opportunists who made up the movement. As leader, he had to defend the policies arrived at, whatever his own beliefs. Abyssinia (Ethiopia) and Spain were irreconcilable issues on which he deliberately decided not to lead. To have endorsed the actions of the British and Australian governments in applying sanctions against Italy would have further divided the party. Recognizing the depth of conflict in the community over the Spanish Civil War, both Curtin and Lyons evaded positive policies. Curtin knew that 'although he sympathized with the Spanish government, he only had to say one word to split Labor from top to bottom'.

Labor was stirred at last to pay some attention to defence. On 5 November 1936 Curtin argued in parliament that 'The dependence of Australia upon the competence, let alone the readiness, of British statesmen to send forces to our aid is too dangerous a hazard upon which to found Australia's defence policy'. Japan was in his mind. More funds should be allocated to the air force and less to naval rearmament; self-reliance was essential, as were closer links with the United States of America. The basis of defence was industrial strength, increased migration and a contented people. Curtin was in touch with the heretical views of Colonel H. D. Wynter [q.v.]. But Curtin's interest in development of air power dated back as far as 1909 to speculation with Anstey.

At the October 1937 elections Curtin could not evade the charge of isolationism. He fought powerfully, but was hampered by A.L.P. disunity which had caused him to declare the referendum on marketing and aviation (March) a non-party issue. Labor gained only two seats in the House, though it had a striking victory in the Senate. Appeasement of the dictators continued: Labor backed the government in its support for British Prime Minister Neville Chamberlain in September 1938; caucus, in ignorance of what Nazism meant, unanimously declared that 'no man must be sent out of Australia to participate in another war overseas'. Curtin and the A.L.P. disagreed with the waterside workers' provocation of Japan in refusing to load pig-iron. All parties, however, now recognized the need for increased armament. In May 1939 the government introduced a manpower survey. Fearing industrial conscription, Labor had opposed the legislation, but Curtin dissuaded the Australasian Council of Trade Unions from a boycott: 'I would not allow the bankers or the Chamber of Manufactures to disobey the law were a Labor Government in power'.

Deep schisms remained, yet on the declaration of war in September 1939 Curtin was confidently able to approve Labor participation. The party opposed reintroduction of compulsory military training, but only mildly attacked the dispatch to the Middle East of the 6th Division, A.I.F., and of airmen under the Empire Air Training Scheme. During the 'phony war' Curtin, like many others, recommended a last attempt at peace negotiations. The German offensive in mid-1940 brought firmness of determination to the A.L.P., as to Australia in general, marked by willingness to reinforce troops in the Middle East. Prime Minister (Sir) Robert Menzies [q.v.] suggested to Curtin in June that Labor should join in a national government. Consistent with his long-standing policy, he dismissed the proposition.

At the September 1940 elections Labor almost wiped out the government's majority, while suffering a major defeat in the Senate. Gains were made in New South Wales where Curtin campaigned vigorously. He neglected Fremantle and seemed to have lost it, but he was declared safe even before the arrival of most servicemen's votes. The narrow squeak brought home to the party his vital importance. Curtin and caucus again brusquely refused Menzies' offer of a national government; the only thing worse than a two-party government would be a three-party one—if carried, it would create a large left-wing opposition. Menzies accepted Curtin's compromise suggestion of an Advisory War Council of senior party representatives, with an understanding that the government would look favourably on such Labor social policies as child endowment, together with an assurance that Labor would co-operate in a bipartisan war policy.

The talented H. V. Evatt [q.v.] was pressing hard to bring down the government, asserting that Curtin was a weak leader, while exploring the personal possibility of joining a national government. Caucus resolved to attack the budget; Curtin took the matter to the A.W.C., won concessions, and caucus finally complied. Experience on the council was to increase considerably Curtin's grasp of war issues.

Both Menzies and Curtin were beset by treacherous back-benchers, but the relationship between the two leaders was impeccable. Menzies had been passing on all important information about the war and they also met regularly and chatted on 'Bob and John' terms. Nevertheless, Curtin remarked once, 'Ah, poor Bob, it's very sad; he would rather make a point than make a friend'.

In February 1941, with Menzies overseas, Curtin made a detailed assessment at the A.W.C. of Australia's circumstances. Japan had recently concluded its Axis Pact with Germany and Italy, and seemed to be increasingly menacing. (Sir) Arthur Fadden [q.v.] and (Sir) Percy Spender agreed with him that the public needed to be shocked into recognizing the 'utmost gravity' of the situation. Curtin concurred in the dispatch of the 8th Division to Malaya and made strong efforts to persuade union officials of the needs of the war crisis.

Menzies returned in May, determined to intensify the war effort. He repeatedly implored Labor to join a national government, eventually offering to serve under Curtin with half Labor representation. Wise Labor moderates held out against Evatt and would not be tempted by the prospect of uncertain majorities in both Houses. Curtin's problem had been to judge whether and when Labor was sufficiently united organizationally and on war policy to be fit for office. The view of some contemporaries and historians that lack of confidence and timidity governed him is probably astray; he knew his fate and judged the moment very well. Menzies was conspicuously failing to hold party loyalty and resigned on 28 August. Fadden could be no more than a stopgap: the government parties had disintegrated, and Fadden was defeated when the Independents (Sir) Arthur Coles and Alexander Wilson [q.v.] crossed the floor.

Curtin was sworn in on 7 October 1941 as prime minister and minister for defence coordination (defence from 14 April 1942). J. B. Chifley [q.v.] as treasurer ranked third in cabinet behind Forde, and was followed by Evatt and Beasley. The ministerial tail was long. The inner War Cabinet numbered eight. (Sir) Frederick Shedden [q.v.] was Curtin's chief adviser. Curtin immediately displayed decisiveness, imperturbability and confidence in his capacity to lead, a change in outward personality which surprised many. On 6 November he replied brilliantly to Menzies in the budget debate. That day the formation of a production executive of cabinet, chaired by J. J. Dedman [q.v.], was announced. Essington Lewis [q.v.10] was soon to be appointed as director-general of aircraft production, as well as of munitions.

The Japanese attack on Pearl Harbour (7 December 1941) was in some ways a relief, for the U.S.A. was now totally involved. Curtin made a broadcast next day: 'We Australians have imperishable traditions. We shall maintain them . . . We shall hold this country and keep it as a citadel for the British-speaking race and as a place where civilisation will persist'. Unlike in 1939, the government made a separate declaration of war. All leave was cancelled and the call-up for military training was urgently accelerated. The *Prince of Wales* and *Repulse* were lost on 10 December. Accidentally, a routine article for the Melbourne *Herald*, probably drafted by Don Rodgers [q.v.] but worked over by Curtin, enraged Prime Minister (Sir) Winston Churchill. It included the famous words: 'Australia looks to America, free of any pangs as to our traditional links or kinship with the United Kingdom'. Curtin was merely stating the obvious, though it might have been worded more tactfully. Agreement was reached on bringing back the A.I.F.'s 6th and 7th divisions to the Far East theatre.

Meanwhile the Philippines had been invaded; Ambon and Rabaul were taken; Singapore fell on 15 February 1942; four days later Darwin was bombed and Timor invaded. On the 16th Lieutenant General (Sir) Vernon Sturdee [q.v.], on behalf of the chiefs of staff,

had recommended that the two divisions be diverted to Australia. Curtin had received strong formal advice from Sturdee and Shedden; War Cabinet and caucus were firmly behind him. He now had to withstand the full pressure of the British and American governments to redirect the 7th Division to the defence of Burma—Churchill actually turned the convoy north before submitting. Thus the 7th Division was saved from almost certain destruction. Curtin suspected that Churchill regarded Australia as expendable. He was briefly ill from the strain.

Menzies and the Opposition parties had supported Churchill. Never had the division between those backing supposed Imperial and Australian interests been so exposed; Curtin's decision was a landmark in Australian history.

As invasion appeared imminent, both government and people began to develop the jitters. Yet basic military and economic measures were carried out efficiently; army generals, despite slender resources, maintained a proper offensive attitude. The government had already pressed for the appointment of an American commander-in-chief for the region and General Douglas MacArthur's [q.v.] arrival in mid-March boosted morale immensely. It is futile to deplore the loss of Australian sovereignty and the subservience involved. Australia was to be the base from which an American-led counter-attack would be launched; the Americans were saving Australia only incidentally. Curtin had pressed in vain for Australian participation in the supreme authority conducting the Pacific war. As a very minor power, dependent, anxious and insecure, Australia could not influence high policy. The government fully learned only in May 1942 of the 'beat Hitler first' policy which had been confirmed by Churchill and President Franklin D. Roosevelt in December-January. MacArthur might ensure adequate reinforcements and supplies, and be a channel for high policy.

Curtin saw all this clearly, as did MacArthur. For at least eighteen months they worked closely together, with warm mutual respect and regard. The prime minister was wise enough not to be an amateur strategist, and knew that MacArthur had to have his way on almost everything. Curtin agreed to leave the 9th Division temporarily in the Middle East, but had to fight hard for its eventual extraction; when it came home in early 1943 under weak naval escort, he endured sleepless nights pacing around Canberra, dwelling on the ships' safe arrival, as he had done when the 6th and 7th divisions returned.

General Sir Thomas Blamey [q.v.] had been appointed commander-in-chief of the Australian Military Forces and commander of the Allied Land Forces. Unlikely though it seemed, Curtin and Blamey soon developed a warm relationship. In September 1942 MacArthur persuaded Curtin to send Blamey to Papua to take direct command. Blamey subsequently relieved Major General (Sir) Sydney Rowell [q.v.] of his duties, and a damaging feud ensued; Curtin later had to order Blamey to give Rowell a senior posting. For all that, Curtin strongly supported Blamey, at least until late 1944, despite the many bitter attacks on him. He took the advice of MacArthur and Blamey on military matters and 'quasi-political problems', and confined his own military decisions to permission to use Australian troops for particular purposes. Furthermore, he helped to smooth the MacArthur-Blamey relationship.

The Coral Sea battle in May 1942, the success of Midway in June and Australian victory in Papua at Milne Bay in September had relieved fears of invasion. MacArthur knew that Japan currently did not intend to invade, but the possibilities remained of strong raids on the mainland and of the course of the war turning against the Allies. Curtin's pleas for more aircraft from Britain and America were usually ignored; he was frequently in conflict with Roosevelt as well as with Churchill. By mid-1942 Australia's defences had been transformed and by the end of the year it was clear that immediate danger was past. Curtin had played on the nation's fears—elementary politics in order to maintain the war effort.

Conversion of the economy to the needs of total war was a massive achievement. Manufacture of aircraft, weapons and ammunition replaced production of many consumer goods. More senior businessmen took administrative posts; the public service was swollen with temporary recruits; women joined the workforce in huge numbers. Clothing and food rationing, and high income taxation, were imposed, vast war loans were over-subscribed. Direction of labour—industrial conscription—was introduced, not without agony in cabinet. The Allied Works Council, under Theodore, and its Civil Constructional Corps were operating by April 1942. The government lifted the ban on the Communist Party of Australia which used its substantial influence in some unions to further the war effort. Coalminers were continually in conflict with management; by a mixture of threats, conciliation and compromise they were jollied along without a major strike. In isolated cases, watersiders and seamen yielded to the threat of sending in troops.

Curtin was distressed that a minority of unionists did not give a damn that the country was fighting for its life. Similarly, when he introduced his sustained austerity campaign, he was saddened by the difficulty of influencing those whose lives were centred on beer and betting, as well as the black marketeers and their customers. The puritan in him came out in his scolding. Nonetheless, the vast majority of Australians responded to his broadcasts, supporting his preaching of equality of sacrifice. 'By his earnestness and his honesty of purpose and his innate integrity, John Curtin has dominated Parliament and the country', Nelson Johnson, the American ambassador, reported.

Caucus allowed Curtin to make war decisions at his discretion. The leadership was never in doubt. The brotherly Chifley was sheet-anchor, chief confidant, protector. The ambitious Evatt was 'neither intimate nor easy' but knuckled down. Beasley, potentially dangerous, warmed to Curtin. Irreconcilably hostile, Ward sometimes contradicted Curtin's calls for a greater war effort and challenged cabinet decisions in caucus: he once emerged exclaiming, 'He's done it again—the humbug'. A. A. Calwell [q.v.], not elected to the ministry until 1943, frustratedly sniped at the government.

At a federal conference in November 1942 Curtin loosed a bombshell by requesting a change of policy to enable the Militia to serve in a limited area of the South-West Pacific. Calwell, Cameron and others bitterly attacked him on traditional anti-conscriptionist grounds, the matter was referred to State executives, and in January 1943 was narrowly carried. Curtin acted primarily for strategic and diplomatic reasons: the Japanese were still on the advance, a two-army situation was indefensible in the presence of American conscripts, and MacArthur had requested removal of all constraints. The change in policy was diplomatically effective but came at great personal cost: Curtin survived party turmoil, vicious attacks by Ward and Calwell, and the outrage of old friends. At Christmas he had suffered from skin trouble. In March Calwell accused him of preparing to lead a national government, Curtin offered his resignation, Calwell apologized and caucus unanimously confirmed the leadership.

Immensely experienced, Curtin could pitch his speeches to diverse audiences, with intellectual command and compelling expository force. His voice, after decades of open-air speaking, was raspy. He used few gestures, but was sometimes theatrical and could bring a tear to the eye, even of hard-boiled politicians and pressmen. Frank Green [q.v.] ranked him as the best orator parliament had known. Menzies also considered him a good orator, if given to too many abstract nouns and Latinisms. Curtin's most famous speech lasted only two or three minutes when he told the House that the Coral Sea battle was in progress. He asked the people of Australia 'to make a sober and realistic estimate of their duty to the nation . . . Men are fighting for

Australia today; those who are not fighting have no excuse for not working'. His intensity and passion made a profound impact. He was at his forceful best on his home ground—party conferences. Curtin began his wartime broadcasts, 'Men and Women of Australia' and concluded 'God bless you'. His eloquent broadcast to the people of the United States in March 1942 was effective; his 1943 Australia Day talk was heard by millions in Britain and America. He was a master of the graceful impromptu on less formal occasions.

The 'press circus' had been greatly impressed when on request, early in his prime ministership, Curtin spontaneously surveyed the world strategic situation for one and a half hours. His daily press conferences 'usually consisted of him relaxing in a swivel chair, lighting a cigarette . . . and "thinking out loud"' (his A.J.A. badge on his watch-chain). He trusted the press by giving them off-the-record information—and few ever betrayed his confidence. In contrast, he was on terms of enmity with the newspaper-proprietors Sir Keith Murdoch [q.v.10] and (Sir) Frank Packer [q.v.], especially after their vilification during the 1943 elections. Later in the war he became disillusioned with many journalists, yet remained staunch in his belief in press freedom, and made no attempt to constrain criticism of his government (except in personal protest at misrepresentation). Throughout, he supported the independence of the Australian Broadcasting Commission.

Ward had been pursuing his unverifiable claim that the Menzies and Fadden governments had adopted a plan, known as the Brisbane Line, for concentration of forces in east-central Australia. As the 1943 election drew nearer, the inflamed Opposition moved to the attack and used its weight in the Senate. Curtin was conciliatory, but would not deny Ward's charges outright. Harmony was lost in the A.W.C. Parliament became chaotic. Curtin called elections for 21 August, suspended Ward from the ministry and conceded a royal commission.

Curtin proudly defended his government's war planning and outlined its idealistic schemes for postwar reconstruction. His campaign was triumphant. Fadden recognized the 'biggest thrashing' his side had ever had: 49 seats to 24 as well as all 19 contested Senate seats, an A.L.P. vote of 50 per cent, and over 60 per cent of the armed-services vote, to 33 per cent for the Opposition parties.

From mid-1943 war policy became increasingly uncertain. Official historians were to criticize the government's inability to clarify plans for future effort. The chief problem was allocation of manpower between the services and industry, including production of food and supplies for Britain and the American troops.

As the war moved on, Curtin's dependence on MacArthur markedly declined; the latter could not, or would not, decide on future use of Australian forces and eventually excluded them from expected operations in the Philippines. The government believed that Australia's participation at the peace table would partly depend on the extent of its military involvement. Moreover, throughout 1944 discussions about a possible large-scale British operation based on Australia complicated the situation. For the government, the late years of the war were 'a time of frustration rather than of mastery'.

Still a socialist, Curtin was 'always looking forward to the reconstructive aspects of his work'. Fairer distribution of wealth began with drastic taxation reform. In December 1942 Chifley took charge of a new ministry of postwar reconstruction, with H. C. Coombs as director and a talented staff of planners of a 'new social order'. In 1942-44 widows' pensions, maternity allowances, funeral benefits, and unemployment and sickness benefits were introduced. The Keynesian planning for a full-employment economy came to fruition in the 1945 white paper which Curtin, having seen the British model, had demanded. He totally supported Chifley's intention to reform the Commonwealth Bank and to take control of the monetary system, and he favoured development of immigration, establishment of the Australian National University and more university scholarships. The attempt to gain increased powers for the Commonwealth for five years was badly handled. Curtin was seemingly outvoted by Evatt who foolishly insisted on presenting the transfer of the fourteen powers on 19 August 1944 in a single question. Curtin took little part in the referendum campaign.

Curtin was a natural Australian, impervious to Imperial ideology. Nor did he care anything for his Irish heritage, regarding its claims as bogus. Labor and Australia were his twin causes. Manning Clark was to use him to represent 'the young tree green'.

On lonely weekends Curtin used to visit the governor-general Lord Gowrie [q.v.9] and his wife; despite Curtin's 'smoking his interminable cigarettes', a warm friendship developed. Gowrie gave him staunch support during dark days of war. In 1943 Curtin sounded out Scullin as Gowrie's possible successor, then in November announced the appointment of the Duke of Gloucester [q.v.]. Curtin convinced his colleagues that a gesture of Empire solidarity was timely: it might encourage greater British participation in the late stages of the Pacific war, and the appointment would be short-term.

During the 1943 election campaign Curtin suggested development of machinery for Imperial co-ordination of policy: the Empire/

Commonwealth was more of a potential force for good than he had believed. The proposals were pushed aside at the 1944 prime ministers' conference and it was some twenty years before a Commonwealth secretariat was formed. Curtin was not closely involved in the formulation of the agreement for mutual collaboration between Australia and New Zealand in January 1944 and allowed Evatt his head.

Curtin had to go overseas in April-June. In Washington he had several days in bed with high blood pressure and neuritis. His meetings with Roosevelt and Cordell Hull were embarrassing: Evatt's activities and the 'Anzac' agreement were not appreciated. Roosevelt concluded that it was best to 'forget the whole incident', and they otherwise got on well. Curtin persuaded his wife to stay in Washington and endured a dangerous flight from Bermuda to Ireland—he feared flying.

England was a disappointment; he was unwell. At the prime ministers' conference, without any adviser from External Affairs, he was out of touch with the department's current inclinations. But he endeavoured to soften the hostility to Australia of the high-handed Churchill and other politicians, while affirming his country's intention to rely primarily on the Commonwealth in defence and foreign-policy matters—on the basis of equality and full consultation. When the City of London granted him its freedom, (Sir) Anthony Eden (1st Earl of Avon) was impressed by his daring to improvise a fine speech without notes. Cambridge conferred on him a doctorate of laws. He had been appointed to the Privy Council in 1942. On his return trip, he addressed the Canadian parliament and had further discussions in Washington. He was still able to comport himself as a man of stature.

His associates, however, believed that Curtin was never the same man again. He became more irritable, markedly more inclined to resent criticism, ever more lonely. Dame Enid Lyons implored him to retire. Curtin was well aware of the sin of self-pity and struggled to retain his ability to laugh at himself. In early November he suffered a coronary occlusion and was confined to hospital in Melbourne for two months. Returning to duty in late January 1945, he made only one major parliamentary speech and, to the distress of his colleagues, was unable to cope with work. He recognized his situation, yet seemed stubbornly determined to be a martyr. Curtin was searching his conscience. Had he shown adequate dedication? Where had he failed the Australian people?

He was also groping towards religious consolation. Although he had long been a tolerant rationalist, in his last years he tended to invoke God in his speeches, and paid some attention to the Moral Rearmament movement. To his friends he confided that he had striven to 'live a decent straight clean life as near to Christ's as humanly possible' and that he believed there was an afterlife in which he would have to answer for his misdeeds.

Late in April 1945 Curtin's lungs became congested. After several weeks in hospital he insisted on returning to The Lodge. 'I'm not worth two bob', he told his driver, Ray Tracey, but kept up a cheerful front with Elsie, and summoned old friends for a chat. He died peacefully on 5 July, a war casualty if ever there was one. His state funeral was attended by large crowds in Canberra and Perth; Royal Australian Air Force planes escorted the body; he was buried in the Presbyterian section of Karrakatta cemetery; Elsie and the children were among those present. Curtin had asked his good Presbyterian friend and neighbour Rev. Hector Harrison [q.v.] to conduct his funeral. He spoke nobly, recalling Curtin's 'transparent simplicity', 'downright honesty' and 'singular humanity'. A memorial service was held in Westminster Abbey. Numerous memorials remain, notably at Cottesloe and in Canberra. A posthumous portrait by Dattilo Rubbo [q.v.11] is in the Parliament House art collection.

Jack and Elsie Curtin had enjoyed a happy, stable marriage; her support is incalculable. 'Dad' and 'Nippy' they called each other. In early 1942 he wrote: 'The war goes very badly & I have a cable fight with Churchill almost daily . . . But enough, I love you, & that is all there is to say'. When the children had grown up, she undertook the long journey to Canberra about twice yearly, staying for a month or two, dutifully entertaining at The Lodge, launching corvettes and working for the Australian Red Cross Society. She was with him for his last six months. There were many good reasons why, by mutual agreement, she did not move to Canberra, despite her husband's loneliness. Elsie was a well-read Labor woman, musical, outspoken and unguarded in public, who had a nice turn of phrase in bringing her husband or anyone else down to earth. She worked as a magistrate and prison visitor and was appointed C.B.E. in 1970.

Curtin was often described as shy, moody, sad-looking, awkward, aloof, not a good mixer in company or an enjoyer of the limelight, complex, mercurial. Even his admirer Reg Pollard remarked that 'You couldn't get close to him'. It was partly a consequence of his misleading stare, the cast in his left eye. He was gregarious around the fire at the Hotel Kurrajong in Canberra, or at the football. He was always good for a yarn, talking books and history, not politics. He conversed easily with

waiters, waitresses, maids, liftmen, tram conductors; the staff at the Victoria Palace, Melbourne, were devoted to him. Curtin loved
vaudeville and musical comedy, was a film-
addict, particularly fond of Claudette Colbert
and Greer Garson, and read westerns for
relaxation; his favourite songs were 'Sweet
Genevieve' and 'Little Grey Home in the
West'. He enjoyed bridge on those interminable train journeys. He was a crossword
enthusiast and billiards player. Plebeian
tastes, intellect and good manners were an
attractive combination.

After Curtin's death Gowrie wrote of 'one
of the most selfless men I have ever met'.
Viscount Bruce [q.v.7], who from London had
been a major private adviser, recalled him as
'extraordinarily receptive and perceptive . . .
I'd never desire to work under a better man'.
Menzies singled out his 'broad and pragmatic
mind' and his 'great human relations'; he had
'received many wounds from John Curtin but
none of them . . . in the back'. Fadden's was
the most remarkable eulogy: 'The best and
fairest I ever opposed in politics . . . one of the
greatest Australians ever . . . he gave me . . .
his mateship'. Bishop Burgmann [q.v.] called
him the 'authentic voice of Australia'. (Sir)
Douglas Copland [q.v.] remembered what a
'constant inspiration' he was, Holloway
mourned 'such a mate in the fight for the
underdog' and Tracey 'that good man . . . who
considered everybody'.

The great justification of Curtin as prime
minister is that there was no viable alternative government in 1941-45; his contemporaries acknowledged that no other politician
was fit for the task. For a time his government
was impressively decisive, and he successfully projected himself as national leader,
inspiring respect from cynical Australians as
few prime ministers have. His unassuming

dignity, simplicity, straightforwardness, absence of vanity and refusal of any personal
privilege got through to many of his compatriots. Curtin took full responsibility for grave
decisions and made no major blunders. He
grew in wisdom and character. His coercion
of his party to his will was an astounding
achievement. He sought national consensus,
not by abandoning Labor policies, but by
pushing them to the limits of acceptability,
and was masterly in gauging those limits. The
succession of international and domestic
party crises in 1942-43 and the consequent
strain were more than such a vulnerable man
could bear. Thereafter he began to lose his
grip.

When Curtin died the general, Australia-
wide remark, confirmed by posterity, was
'He did a good job'. The inscription on his
gravestone reads:

> His country was his pride
> His brother man his cause.

W. Denning, *Caucus Crisis* (Syd, 1937; P. Has-
luck, *The Government and the People 1939-1941*
(Canb, 1952), *1942-1945* (Canb, 1970), and *An
Open Go* (Melb, 1971) and *Diplomatic Witness*
(Melb, 1980); V. Courtney, *All I May Tell* (Syd,
1956); J. Thompson (comp), *On Lips of Living Men*
(Melb, 1962); R. G. Menzies, *Afternoon Light*
(Melb, 1967); A. Fadden, *They Called Me Artie*
(Brisb, 1969); A. A. Calwell, *Be Just and Fear Not*
(Melb, 1972); L. Ross, *John Curtin* (Melb, 1977);
W. Denning, *Caucus Crisis* (Syd, 1982); H. C.
Coombs, *John Curtin—A Consensus Prime Minis-
ter?* (Canb, 1984); C. M. H. Clark, *A History of
Australia*, 6 (Melb, 1987); G. Souter, *Acts of Parliament* (Melb, 1988); D. Langmore, *Prime Ministers' Wives* (Melb, 1992); *Woman*, 12 Mar-9 Apr
1951; *Argus* and *SMH*, 6-9 July 1945; E. J. Holloway memoirs *and* H. Harrison papers *and* L. Ross
papers (NL); information from the late T. M. Fitzgerald, Centennial Park, Syd.

GEOFFREY SERLE

D

DACOMB, BEATRICE ELIZA (1863-1947) and CLARA THURSTON (1867-1946), co-inventors of Dacomb shorthand, were born on 22 November 1863 and 15 October 1867 at Portland, Victoria, sixth and eighth children of Edmund Dacomb, merchant, and his wife Eliza, née Evans, both English born. Beatrice matriculated with honours, taught at Kilmore Ladies' College, obtained registration as a teacher of shorthand in 1914 and practised privately. Educated at Holstein House Ladies' College, South Yarra, Clara matriculated with honours in 1886 and gained a Pitman shorthand diploma. In 1899-1914 she worked as a matriculation coach and commercial teacher at Methodist Ladies' College, Lilydale High School and various secretarial colleges before becoming in 1914 proprietor of the School of Shorthand, Block Arcade, Melbourne.

In 1918 a friend called upon the sisters' well-known expertise to help him prepare for a shorthand examination in three months. His failure prompted them to invent a simpler form of shorthand. In 1921 they published a book on their system, *Web Speed*. From 1922 they taught it at the Australian Commercial College, Collins Street. It was tested in Essendon High School (1923), University High School (1928) and several private schools (1928-29) with satisfactory results. Following a formal trial against the Pitman system at Coburg High School in 1933, it was widely used in private and government schools, and was officially adopted by the Department of Education in 1943.

Meantime, the Dacomb College had been established in 1936 in the Presgrave Building, 279 Little Collins Street, with the sisters as co-principals. Handsome, strong-looking women, they were strikingly different in appearance and personality. Beatrice was a big woman, difficult to get to know and rather forbidding in manner; Clara was smaller, vivacious, a good mixer, outgoing and persuasive. Between them, they successfully pioneered a new system, secured its wide acceptance and challenged the longstanding dominance of the Pitman system. Clara died on 19 October 1946 at their South Yarra flat where Beatrice also died on 12 February 1947; both were cremated.

After their deaths the Dacomb College was run by Mrs Jean Joy whom Clara and Beatrice had chosen as their successor. Under her management a Dacomb college was established at Geelong, with G. A. H. Lang as principal. The last barriers to the system fell in 1955 when a Dacomb student was admitted as a court reporter and in 1972 when two students were appointed Hansard reporters for State parliament. Basically phonetic in form, Dacomb shorthand was adaptable to foreign languages and was introduced in Buenos Aires, Argentina, in 1956 and in Tonga in 1974.

When Joy retired in 1977, the Melbourne college continued in other hands until it closed in 1984. Ownership of the Geelong college was transferred to Lang. Although Dacomb shorthand is still taught there, as well as in some technical colleges, it was generally in decline from the 1970s, largely due to the emergence of a simplified form of Pitman shorthand which was adopted in high schools and colleges of advanced education from 1975.

J. Joy, *The Dacomb Sisters and How They Changed My Life* (priv pub, Geelong, 1990); *Age* (Melb), 28 Nov 1971, 25 Feb, 26 Nov 1974; *Herald* (Melb), 12 July 1972; *Geelong Advertiser*, 21, 23 Feb 1976; teacher registration files, C. T. *and* B. E. Dacomb (PRO, Vic); special case file, VPAS 892/1266, Dacomb shorthand in State schools (Vic Education Dept Archives, Fawkner, Melb); closed schools file, Dacomb College 1936-84, Geelong 1968-77 (Registered Schools Bd, Melb); Univ Melb Archives; information from Miss E. E. Brame, Glen Iris, Melb, and Mr G. A. H. Lang, Clifton Springs, Vic.

MOLLIE MISSEN

DADSWELL, HERBERT ERIC (1903-1964), wood scientist, was born on 5 March 1903 at Newtown, Sydney, only child of Herbert Edward Dadswell, a native-born clerk employed by the *Sydney Morning Herald*, and his wife May, née Walton, from England. Herbert senior rose to be secretary of John Fairfax [q.v.4] & Sons Pty Ltd and was a prominent member of the Congregational Union of New South Wales. Educated at Newington College and the University of Sydney (B.Sc., 1925; M.Sc., 1927), Eric studied organic chemistry, and played tennis, golf and cricket.

In 1926 the recently established Council for Scientific and Industrial Research (Commonwealth Scientific and Industrial Research Organization from 1949) selected Dadswell as one of its first overseas research students. He sailed for the United States of America in November, entering the Forest Products Laboratory at Madison, Wisconsin, then the world's leading institution of its kind. On 4 June 1928 in a civil ceremony at River Falls he married Inez Margaret Williams, a biochemist at the University of Wisconsin.

Returning to Australia in April 1929, Dadswell was appointed to C.S.I.R.'s division of forest products. Initially attached to the Australian Forestry School in Canberra and based in Melbourne from June 1930, he embarked on investigations into the anatomy, chemistry, identification and utilization of wood which became his life's work. He studied many genera of the south-west Pacific region, particularly the genus, *Eucalyptus*, on which he published more than one hundred papers. In 1931 he was placed in charge of the division's research into wood structure. The University of Melbourne awarded him a D.Sc. in 1941 for a thesis and published work on the structure, identification and properties of Australian timbers.

Widely respected for the breadth and depth of his knowledge, Dadswell lectured at North American universities and in 1955 was Walker-Ames professor of forestry at the University of Washington, Seattle. His laboratory in Melbourne attracted guest-workers and students from abroad. From 1935 he had been an Australian delegate at international congresses, on forestry as well as forest products. An office-bearer in learned and technical societies, he was a foundation member (president 1950) of the Australian (and New Zealand) Pulp and Paper Industry Technical Association, and a council-member (president 1962) of the Royal Australian Chemical Institute. For his contribution to forest products research, he was awarded Queen Elizabeth II's coronation medal in 1953. Next year he was appointed assistant-chief of C.S.I.R.O.'s division of forest products and was promoted to chief in 1960.

In his later years Dadswell found recreation in gardening and trout-fishing. His social life revolved around his family and professional colleagues, and he was a generous host to visitors from overseas. Survived by his wife and their two adopted sons, he died suddenly of hypertensive coronary vascular disease on 19 December 1964 at East Ringwood and was cremated.

Foreword to H. E. Dadswell, *The Anatomy of Eucalypt Woods* (Melb, 1972); *CSIRO Forest Products Newsletter*, no 315, Jan-Feb 1965, p 1, no 350, Apr-May 1968, p 4; CSIRO Archives, Canb; information from Mr G. Dadswell, Warragul, Vic.

L. T. CARRON

DAHLENBURG, EDWARD WALTER (1882-1970), wheat farmer, and ALFRED ERNEST (1886-1973), stud breeder and stock-and-station agent, were born on 18 September 1882 and 23 June 1886 at Winiam, near Nhill, Victoria, second and fourth of nine children of Heinrich Ernst Dahlenburg, farmer, and his wife Rosalie, née Harders, both South Australian born. Educated at the local state school, they worked on their father's Wimmera property, Oakdene. On 14 October 1908 Edward married Marie Caroline Bertha Liemering (d. 1942) with Methodist forms in her father's home at Noorak; Alfred married Martha Weir at the Methodist Church, Winiam, on 30 March 1911.

Edward Walter ('Watty') inherited Heinrich's interest in scientific agriculture. After acquiring his own property, Ellerslie, at nearby Salisbury, from 1920 he conducted cereal experimental plots in association with the Department of Agriculture. Pasture demonstrations and field-days attracted many visitors from overseas. He published a booklet, *Wheat Growing in the Wimmera* (1926), and represented west Wimmera on the executive of the Victorian Wheat and Wool Growers' Association.

Keenly involved in local affairs, Watty was a committee-member (1921-48, president 1927-28) of the Nhill Agricultural Society. He was, as well, a Lowan shire councillor (1931-50, president 1934), a commissioner of the Nhill Waterworks Trust, and sometime chairman and a member of the Nhill Hospital management committee. Instrumental in the formation of rural fire brigades, he captained the Noorak brigade for several years. During World War II he was associated with the Commonwealth government's Manpower Committee. Woodworking was his favourite hobby and, according to his family, he could make anything, though the finish usually smacked of bush carpentry. He was also a keen photographer.

A quiet, kindly man who endeared himself to all who knew him, Edward was a devoted husband and father. On 24 June 1954 he married a widow Olive Blake, née Banfield, with Methodist forms at Collingwood, Melbourne. They lived at Brunswick, but his son Eric continued his cereal experiments at Ellerslie until the property was sold in 1967. Survived by his wife, and by the three sons and six daughters of his first marriage, Edward died on 12 May 1970 at Nhill and was buried in the local cemetery; his estate was sworn for probate at $77 041.

After their marriage, Alfred took his wife to New Zealand where they settled on their first dairy farm at Thornbury, in the Southland region. In 1921 they returned to Winiam East, bringing their best, purebred, Friesian cattle, a new breed in the district. His father had been the first to introduce Clydesdale horses locally and Alf also showed an avid interest in these active, strong and hardy animals which were eminently suited to work in the wheatlands of the Wimmera and Mallee. A founder of the Nhill horse parades and foal shows, he exhibited horses and cattle with much success and in 1934 won first prize for a two-year-old filly, Dalholme Coreen, at the Melbourne Centenary Royal Show. In 1936 he was nominated to the council of the Royal Agricultural Society as the representative of Clydesdale breeders. He became chief steward and an active member of the horse and arena committee, and was prominent on the farm produce committee. An honorary life member of the R.A.S. from 1960, he attended every Royal Melbourne Show for thirty-six years.

In 1942 Alf gave up farming and became a partner in a stock and station agency at Nhill. Retaining his interest in every aspect of farming, he judged stock at numerous shows and also judged the Victorian ploughing competitions. As president of the draughthorse memorial committee, he was largely responsible for the bronze statue that was unveiled in 1968 in Goldsworthy Park, Nhill, as a reminder of the important role the breed had played in the Wimmera. In addition, he was president of the local hospital committee and of the original committee of the Nhill Lake Development Scheme.

Despite being confined to a wheelchair in later years following the amputation of his leg, Alf retained his keen sense of humour and love of the land. Survived by his two sons and two daughters, he died on 22 October 1973 at Nhill and was buried in the local cemetery with Presbyterian forms; his estate was sworn for probate at $30 588.

L. Blake, *Land of the Lowan* (Maryborough, Vic, 1976); A. P. Dahlenburg (ed), *Dahlenburg Australia 1849-1981* (Adel, 1981); F. H. Noble and R. Morgan, *Speed the Plough* (Melb, 1981); *J of Agr* (Vic), Jan 1969; *Nhill Free Press*, 10 Oct 1968, 14 May 1970.   MARJORIE WAITE

DALE, MARGUERITE LUDOVIA (1883-1963), feminist and playwright, was born on 22 October 1883 at Boorowa, New South Wales, eldest of four daughters of Charles Ludovia Hume, a local grazier and nephew of Hamilton Hume [q.v.1], and his wife Celia Annie, née Maltby, who was born at Calcutta, India. Marguerite spent her childhood on her parents' station and was educated by governesses before being sent to Ascham School, Sydney. Although clever and ambitious, she ran the family home after her mother's death in 1904. Attractive, vivacious and energetic, on 16 January 1907 at St Philip's Anglican Church, Sydney, she married a solicitor George Samuel Evans Dale (d. 1944); they lived at Chatswood and were to have two daughters.

Mrs Dale supported the campaign in 1916 for early closing of hotels and was prominent in the movement that resulted in the Women's Legal Status Act (1918). She soon developed a reputation for being 'learned and bright, a good speaker with a quick flow of language and a rich vein of humour'. Active in the Women's Reform League of New South Wales under Laura Luffman [q.v.10], she became president of the reconstituted Women's League in 1923. In addition, she worked for the Workers' Educational Association, the National Council of Women and the Australian Federation of Women's Societies (later Women Voters). An office-bearer in the North Sydney branch of the Housewives' Association, she belonged to the Lyceum, Feminist and Women's clubs.

In 1922 Dale was appointed an alternate delegate to the third general assembly of the League of Nations at Geneva, Switzerland, and addressed the assembly on the White slave traffic. On her return she spoke on the league's work to enthusiastic audiences across Australia. In 1924 she wrote that she was 'practically retiring from public life because of poor health' and spent eighteen months in a sanatorium at Geneva.

Well known in Sydney's literary and theatrical circles, Dale had also written plays: her *Secondary Considerations* was produced by Gregan McMahon [q.v.10] for the Sydney Repertory Theatre Society in December 1921. She ambitiously took her comedy, *The Mainstay*, to London where it was read at the Lyceum Club and subsequently performed in Sydney on 8 August 1923 to raise funds for delegates to the International Woman Suffrage Alliance's congress in Rome. Following her association with the Swedish writer Hedwig af Petersens (whose memoir, 'A Year in Australia', she had edited in 1921), *The Mainstay* was translated into Swedish and produced at Uppsala in 1929. Other plays by Dale, *Paris in the Air* and *Meet as Lovers*, were staged in Sydney at Carrie Tennant's Community Playhouse in 1930 and produced by May Hollinworth [q.v.] at the Savoy Theatre in October 1934. Despite Dale's 'gift for characterisation and a rare natural sense of theatrical requirements', her career as a playwright faded.

An intrepid traveller, in 1935 Dale flew to Britain. Back in Sydney, she remained interested in the women's movement and in the arts, and wrote occasional articles under the pen-name, 'Femina'. Survived by her daughters, she died on 13 May 1963 at Neutral Bay and was cremated.

B. M. Rischbieth, *March of Australian Women* (Perth, 1964); *Woman's World*, 1 Aug 1929, p 530; *BP Mag*, 4, no 2, Mar 1932; *SMH*, 1, 11 Sept 1922, 29 Aug, 17 Oct 1923, 22 Oct 1930, 11, 17 Oct 1934, 17, 24 Oct 1935; M. A. Foley, The Women's Movement in New South Wales and Victoria,

1918-1938 (Ph.D. thesis, Univ Syd, 1985); Dale papers (ML); information from Mrs H. Brewster, Macmasters Beach, NSW.   AUDREY TATE

DALEY, DANIEL ALEXANDER (1916-1949), grazier and soldier, was born on 6 August 1916 at Moree, New South Wales, only son and youngest of four children of James Joseph Daley, labourer, and his wife Ethel Maud, née Smith, both native-born. James established himself as a grazier and acquired two properties, The Point, and Springfield, near Biniguy, on which the family lived. Educated at Pallamallawa Public School and The King's School, Parramatta, Dan left in December 1932 to work with his father. Tall and dark, a good boxer and a skilled horseman, young Daley became widely known in show rings and at rodeos in the State's north-west. He was a 'very popular man in the community'.

In March 1939 he joined the 24th Light Horse Regiment (Militia) and on 27 June 1940 enlisted in the Australian Imperial Force. With other light horsemen, Daley volunteered for the 20th Infantry Anti-Tank Company in July and in October sailed for Palestine. In February 1941 his unit moved to Cyrenaica, Libya, where it was involved in the withdrawal to and the defence of Tobruk. There Daley knocked out several enemy tanks and was appointed lance corporal.

After returning to Palestine in September, his company was absorbed into the 2nd/3rd Anti-Tank Regiment. Daley was made lance sergeant in April 1942. Back in the Western Desert in July, he had charge of a 2-pounder (0.9 kg) gun at El Alamein. On 17 July he supported the 2nd/32nd Infantry Battalion in the fighting for Makh Khad Ridge. Through heavy shelling and machine-gun fire, he kept his gun and crew in action, but suffered a slight wound. German tanks then attacked. Although under a hail of armour-piercing bullets which seriously wounded him and his gunlayer, he put six of the tanks out of action. 'By his courage and determination he materially assisted in breaking up the counterattack, and in no small degree inspired the gunners of the troop in rear of him.' While recovering in hospital, Daley was awarded the Distinguished Conduct Medal. He rejoined his regiment on 27 October during the climactic battle of El Alamein.

Promoted acting sergeant, Daley arrived in Sydney with the 9th Division in February 1943. He served in Papua and New Guinea from August, but, as there were no Japanese tanks, his battery was used as labour and in coastal defence near Finschhafen. The great days were over. At home, his father (whose health was failing) struggled to keep the properties going. Obtaining release on compassionate grounds, Daley returned to Australia in April 1944 and was discharged on 22 May. He then took over management of Springfield and The Point.

Dan Daley's enjoyment of life as a grazier in the postwar boom was brief. In the early hours of 20 August 1949, while driving five friends to Moree, he and four of his companions were killed when the motorcar failed to take a bend. Daley was buried in Moree cemetery with Anglican rites. He was unmarried.

'Silver John' (J. N. L. Argent), *Target Tank* (Parramatta, 1957); B. Maughan, *Tobruk and El Alamein* (Canb, 1966); AWM records; newspaper-cuttings from Moree *Champion* and Warialda *Standard*, nd Aug 1949 (held by ADB); information from Mr R. Daley, Gravesend, and Mrs M. Coppock, Moree, NSW.   A. J. HILL

DALEY, HENRIETTA JESSIE SHAW (1890-1943), community worker, was born on 17 May 1890 at Malvern, Melbourne, second daughter of Thomas Pryce Obbinson, real-estate agent, and his wife Rosa Phillis, née Caudwell, both Victorian born. Educated at Presbyterian Ladies' College, East Melbourne, and Rosbercon College, Brighton, Jessie studied science at the University of Melbourne. On 27 January 1917 at the Australian Church, Flinders Street, she married a public servant Charles Studdy Daley [q.v.8]; they were to have five children.

In August 1926 the family moved from Caulfield to Canberra. Mrs Daley was soon prominent among the small band of women who were determined to improve life in the 'bush capital'. Joining the Canberra Society of Arts and Literature, she performed in a number of early productions, assisted backstage and served as wardrobe mistress. She became a member (later president) of the Canberra Golf Club Associates, was first president of the Canberra Ladies' Choir, belonged to the Canberra Women's Hockey Club and was active in school associations.

Although deeply saddened in 1930 by the death of her 6-year-old son, Daley continued her involvement in community life. That year she accepted the presidency of the local Girl Guides' association and in 1931-32 was district commissioner. From 1930 she had been vice-president of the Canberra Mothercraft Society. In March 1935 she was elected president, but immediately became embroiled in factional squabbles. Faced with staunch and bitter opposition over a staffing issue, she resigned and failed to be re-elected.

Undeterred, Daley turned her energies to

the Young Women's Christian Association, putting her skills as a hostess, her competence as an organizer and her experience in sporting and cultural activities to good use. Her frequent 'at-homes' and card-afternoons provided a welcome for newcomers to the city and raised funds for charity. In 1937 she became vice-president of the Y.W.C.A.'s Canberra branch and a non-resident member of the national board. During World War II she was involved with the association's hospitality centre and 'Leave House' which helped to make the capital 'a home away from home' for service personnel.

In a further attempt to enhance life for Canberra families, Jessie used her influence in the Y.W.C.A. to form an Australian Capital Territory branch of the National Council of Women. On 4 July 1939 she was elected its founding president. Under her leadership the A.C.T. division brought representatives of community organizations and public-spirited individuals together, enabling them to co-ordinate their activities. In particular, the N.C.W. took up the cause of the Canberra Relief Society which assisted the needy.

A generous, strong-willed woman who worked tirelessly to promote the welfare of Canberra's citizens, Jessie still found time to be a steady helpmate to her husband. Survived by him, three daughters and a son, she died of cancer on 10 November 1943 at Mosman, Sydney, and was cremated with Christian Science forms.

Principal Women of the Empire, 1 (Lond, 1940); *Canb Times*, 2, 9, 10, 15-18 Apr 1935; ACT Local Assn of Girl Guides, Minutes (Girl Guides Hall, Manuka, Canb); Canb Mothercraft Soc, Annual Reports, A1928/1, 680/23 Sec 1 *and* Annual General Meetings, A659, 1943/1/5/06 (AA); National Council of Women, ACT Branch, Executive Minute-Book, Book 1, M121/1 vol 1 (AA); YWCA of Canb, Minutes of Meetings of Bd of Directors, *and* Minute-Book, 1941-47 *and* Annual Reports, 1929-50 (YWCA Office, Kingston, Canb).

KATHLEEN DERMODY

DALGARNO, ANN(E) PATRICIA (1909-1980), politician, community leader and nurse, was born on 6 July 1909 at Wrentham, Suffolk, England, daughter of Henry Patrick Smith, farmer, and his wife Mabel Christina, née Edwards. Cardinal Patrick Moran [q.v.10] was Anne's great-uncle. Educated by governesses and at the Convent of the Holy Family, Littlehampton, Sussex, at the age of 16 she migrated to Western Australia with her parents and seven siblings. She trained at the Children's and Perth hospitals, becoming a registered nurse in 1933, then qualified in midwifery at the Women's Hospital, Crown Street, Sydney. On 1 June 1937 at St Mary's Cathedral, Sydney, she married a civil engineer Kenneth John Dalgarno. They had two children and moved to Canberra in 1948.

In 1954 Anne established the Nurses' Club (later the Nursing Service Agency) which provided nurses for patients in their own homes and for those needing special care in hospital. Believing that a mother's place is in the home as long as she is needed there, she was to run the service from her Red Hill residence until 1979. Mrs Dalgarno was a board-member (1954-59) of Canberra Community Hospital and president (1965-66) of the Australian Capital Territory branch of the Royal Australian Nursing Federation. Standing as a Liberal (1958) and an Independent (1966), she unsuccessfully contested the seat of the A.C.T. in the House of Representatives.

In 1959 Dalgarno had been elected as an Independent to the A.C.T. Advisory Council; apart from a break of three years after her defeat at the 1967 polls, she remained a member until her retirement in 1974, and chaired the council's recreation and culture committee in 1970-74. The only female on the council, she urged women to seek election, declaring that they 'had ignored politics for too long'. She was prominent in the A.C.T. Debating Union which she represented in national championships. In 1974 she submitted a strongly-argued case against self-government to the Federal parliamentary joint committee on the A.C.T., advocating instead that a lord mayor was appropriate 'for the dignity and well being' of Australia's capital city.

Dalgarno devoted considerable time to counselling her constituents and to interceding with government or private bodies on their behalf. Having prepared a report for the council in 1965 on facilities needed for the Territory's youth, she presided (from 1972) over the Foundation for Youth Ltd which aimed to develop leisure activities for young people. She established the A.C.T. Emergency Housing Committee in 1973. The 'most active woman in public life in Canberra', she was at one time a member of twenty-two organizations. In 1977 she was appointed M.B.E.

Tall, slim, fair haired and blue eyed, she was a confident public speaker whose voice made clear her English upbringing. She upheld conventional Christian values and was an outspoken opponent of abortion. Mrs Dalgarno died of chronic asthma and its complications on 6 May 1980 at Royal Canberra Hospital and was buried in Canberra cemetery; her husband, son and daughter survived her.

A. Lofthouse (comp), *Who's Who of Australian Women* (Syd, 1982); *Canb Times*, 10 June 1965, 19 Mar 1966, 28 Aug 1970, 4 Oct 1972, 16 Nov 1974, 8 May 1980; *Canb Post*, May 1968; *Canb News*,

9 Sept 1970; Dalgarno papers *and* biog-cuttings file *and* Foundation for Youth Ltd papers (NL); information from Marjorie Dalgarno, Brisb.

PATRICIA CLARKE

DALLEY, MARIE ('MA') (1880-1965), scrap-metal merchant and mayor, and CASCARRET, CLARE JOSEPHINE (1902?-1977), city councillor, were mother and daughter. Marie was born on 4 June 1880 at Kewell, near Minyip, Victoria, and registered as Minnie Mary, fifth child of German immigrants Carl Heinrich Fimmel, farmer, and his wife Matilda, née Baum. On 18 July 1897 in her parents' home at Kewell she married with Wesleyan forms John Thomas Francis Moroney, a carpenter.

Styling herself Marie Dalley and declaring herself a widow, in 1905 she found a job in Melbourne as a part-time packer for a tea firm; after work she sewed oatmeal bags at four pence per thousand. She later bought three hundred fire-damaged chairs for thirty shillings, repaired them and sold them for five shillings each. Learning that greater profits were to be made from reselling scrap metal, she obtained a dealer's licence and operated from a South Melbourne hardware business, purchased for £600, one-sixth of which she had borrowed. In 1914 she bought out a hardware business in Elizabeth Street, Melbourne.

World War I 'turned old iron into gold' and Ma Dalley's business expanded. In 1915 she bought the wreck of the schooner, *Rio*, which insurance assessors wrote off after it had run aground off King Island. Camped overnight in an abandoned hut, she found the sails, winches and cargo that had been hidden by beachcombers, and made £80 profit on the deal. She travelled widely, buying plant from the goldfields and hunting for items on order. Indefatigable and reluctant to waste time, she journeyed to and from Sydney on the overnight train.

Having rented the premises, in 1925 Dalley paid £25 000 for the freehold of a three-acre (1.2 ha) site in Bedford Street, North Melbourne. Her business, M. Dalley & Co. Pty Ltd, grew to be one of the largest scrap-dealers in the country. She presided over apparent chaos with precision. Sewing-machines, coppers, bath screens, coils of wire, telephones, petrol bowsers, wheels, boxes, rods, garden rollers, ships' boilers, machines for corrugating iron and grinding gravestones, two-ton vats, stoves and chains were offered for sale.

Dalley subsequently bought the bankrupt Shepparton Freezing Works for £15 000, reorganized the business, opened a butcher's shop next door and by 1946 was exporting 20 000 lambs annually to Britain. She pioneered a system of pre-cooling fruit for local growers and canneries, holding it green until ready for market. In addition, she began to manufacture margarine, owned and supervised a farm near Horsham, and acquired city properties.

From 1918 Dalley had assisted many ex-servicemen to start in business, often as their guarantor. She and her daughter Clare bought food at the Victoria Market which they distributed in North Melbourne and they kept open house for visiting sailors. Ma was an active participant in and contributor to such charities as the North Melbourne Boys' Club, the Mooroopna Bush Hospital and the City Free Kindergarten. During World War II she supervised the Red Cross Waste Products Depot which made profits of more than £70 000. She was patron of the Ravenswood old people's home at Ivanhoe and in 1948 tried to develop a settlement for elderly women on her property near Bendigo.

A justice of the peace (from 1935) and honorary secretary of the Women Justices' Association, Dalley served every Wednesday as special magistrate of the North Melbourne Court where she displayed firm views on drunkenness. In 1949 she was appointed O.B.E. She later sat on the bench of the Children's Court, through which she met Katherine Trahan who became her ward and worked in the ironmongery yard. Neighbours set their watches as Kay drove Ma from their Kew home at 7.30, six mornings a week; regardless of the weather, Ma wore a fur coat. A firm but generous employer, Dalley believed in equal pay for equal work. She favoured the reduction of the working week to forty hours as the only way to maintain high levels of employment. Some of her workers were with her for thirty years and she introduced a scheme to provide her staff with shares in the business.

In 1948 Dalley was elected to the Kew City Council; in 1954 she was its first woman mayor. An active member of the public works and health committee, she broke convention by insisting that money collected for the mayoral gift should be donated to the St George's Hospital Appeal. In 1951 she was a delegate to the Jubilee Women's Convention in Canberra. She was narrowly defeated at the council elections in 1963.

Survived by her two daughters, Ma Dalley died on 8 May 1965 at Kew and was buried with Anglican rites in Minyip cemetery. Her estate was sworn for probate at £148 442. Her daughters lost a bitter court case when a former employee won an appeal to the High Court of Australia overturning a Supreme Court ruling on the status of employee shares.

Clare was born probably in 1902 at Minyip. After leaving school she worked for her mother. On 16 February 1929 at the Congregational Church, Bourke Street, Sydney, she married Alfred Percy Withers, a garage manager. Divorced on 11 November 1948, she married Jean Cascarret, an officer in the French merchant navy, on 25 January 1949 at the office of the government statist, Melbourne. He retired from the sea and worked for M. Dalley & Co. of which Clare and her sister Ida became joint managing directors.

Involved in community affairs, Mrs Cascarret was a life governor of the Alfred Hospital and of the Royal Victorian Institute for the Blind, a committee-member of the Business and Professional Women's Association, and president of the Royal Overseas League. After thrice standing unsuccessfully for Kew City Council, she was elected to the Melbourne City Council in 1967 (on her second attempt) and entered what she described as an 'exclusive men's club'. Her stated aim was to have women on every city council, but, unlike Doris Condon [q.v.], she did not wish to attend the all-male lord mayor's dinner. She weathered controversy over irregularities in voting for the 1968 council elections when some of her supporters were convicted and fined.

In 1969 the scrap-metal business was sold: the site—on which the Old Melbourne Hotel was to be built—fetched $500 000, the contents $51 000. Retiring from the council in 1976, Clare Cascarret died on 8 April 1977 at Mount Eliza and was buried in Fawkner cemetery. Predeceased by her husband, she was survived by the daughter of her first marriage. Her estate was sworn for probate at $220 699.

Kew City Council, *Minutes of Ordinary Meetings*, Feb 1949-June 1955; *People* (Syd), 20 Dec 1950; *New Idea*, 24 Feb 1960; *Herald* (Melb), 16 Sept 1940, 27 June 1953, 14 Aug 1964, 11 May 1965, 25 May 1968; *Sun News-Pictorial*, 4 Mar 1946; *Argus*, 14 Sept 1948; *Kew Advertiser*, 20 Apr, 11 Oct 1951; *Age* (Melb), 31 Oct 1967, 1 Jan 1969; *Daily Mirror* (Syd), 22 Aug 1973; information from Mrs J. Withers, Mornington, Vic, and Mrs J. Woodward, Kew, Melb.   DEIRDRE MORRIS

DALRYMPLE-HAY, MARGARET FORDYCE; *see* HAY

DALTON, GEORGE CLIFFORD JAMES (1916-1961), engineer, was born on 20 May 1916 at Te Awamutu, Waikato district, New Zealand, second of three sons of New Zealand-born parents George Dalton, carpenter, and his wife Jessie, née Robson, a schoolteacher. George became a successful builder; Jessie died while their boys were still at school. Having completed his schooling at Auckland Grammar School, Clifford read engineering at Auckland and Canterbury colleges, University of New Zealand (B.Sc. 1937; B.E., 1939). He was awarded a Rhodes scholarship for 1937. Stricken by poliomyelitis which ended his career as a Rugby Union footballer, he eventually entered Oriel College, Oxford, in 1939.

On 17 October 1941 Dalton was commissioned in the Royal Air Force Volunteer Reserve. Allocated to the Technical Branch, he was to carry out radar research until the end of the war. Late in 1941 he met a radar-operator in the Women's Auxiliary Air Force, Catherine Robina, daughter of the writer Robert Graves, then known by her mother's maiden name of Nicholson. To the chagrin of a Danish girl who had thought Dalton's Rhodes scholarship an insuperable impediment to matrimony, Clifford and Catherine were married on 31 January 1942 at the register office, Aldershot.

Dalton was demobilized with the rank of squadron leader. He returned to Oxford and obtained his doctorate of philosophy in engineering in 1947. Allowed a 'semi-bachelor life' by his wife, he found time to coach Rugby, swim, and row despite a lame right leg. He eschewed industrial employment and joined the Atomic Energy Research Establishment at Harwell. A paper he produced examining options for the development of the elusive fast-fission reactor impressed his new friend Klaus Fuchs and led to Dalton's appointment by Sir John Cockcroft as head of a fast-reactor group in the engineering division. The major design problems were quickly solved, but Britain faced a long delay before it would have enough plutonium to justify constructing the reactor.

In 1949 Dalton moved with his family to New Zealand where a chair in mechanical engineering at Auckland University College offered more challenge, 'more sunshine and better food'. Shortly after his appointment he took over as dean of engineering. He inherited an unhappy faculty situated at a desolate airfield site. His financial acumen, crisp administrative style, commitment to staff interests, rapport with students and considerable research reputation did much to restore morale. Continuing international consultancies, membership of the New Zealand Defence Scientific Advisory Council and friendship with the vice-chancellor brought growing influence. Impressed by his commanding personality and warmed by his 'equable temperament and a sense of humour that rarely deserted him', Dalton's colleagues were evidently oblivious to the regime of parsimony and neglect to which his wife alleged that she and their five children were subjected.

In 1955 Dalton was appointed chief engineer and deputy chief scientist of the Australian Atomic Energy Commission. He brought his family to Sydney. Soon after, he took them to England where he joined the chief scientist, fellow New Zealander Charles Watson-Munro, and sixty other A.A.E.C. staff who were seconded to Harwell for training. Always open minded about reactor systems, Dalton was now converted from fast reactors to high-temperature, gas-cooled systems. He advised Dutch authorities and industry on their research-reactor programme before returning with his family to Sydney. At the newly-built Research Establishment at Lucas Heights he worked closely with Watson-Munro from September 1957 on developing the high-flux, heavy-water-moderated reactor (HIFAR).

By late 1957 symptoms of the cancer from which Dalton was to die were apparent. As early as 1955 his wife had also been distressed by what she later claimed to have diagnosed as his schizophrenic behaviour. According to her, Dalton's 'indomitable nature', forthright utterance and 'obvious integrity' to which his colleagues attested were accompanied by caprice and violence in his private life. Although convinced of Clifford's infidelity and concerned for her children's safety, Catherine would not divorce or abandon a husband whose sickness she attributed to poisoning by malevolent elements of the intelligence community.

When he succeeded Watson-Munro as director of the Research Establishment in March 1960, Dalton brought to the task what the A.A.E.C. deputy executive commissioner M. C. Timbs was to call 'the full powers of a singularly lucid, penetrating and scientifically sophisticated mind'. Survived by his wife, two sons and three daughters, Dalton died on 17 July 1961 at Sutherland District Hospital, Caringbah, and was cremated. Sir Mark Oliphant noted that few men trained in traditional applied science had 'so readily adapted themselves to the new engineering of electronics and nuclear power'.

Dalton's contribution to radar and atomic-power research cannot be assessed until official archives are open. His widow's conviction that he was murdered for refusing to stop helping the Dutch to break the American monopoly on nuclear-enriched fuel is rejected by informed contemporaries. But it would not be surprising if the Western nuclear establishment and its associated intelligence community had been apprehensive about so powerful a mind allied to the 'abnormal political innocence' to which Catherine Dalton testified.

J. Bassett, *The School of Engineering, University of Auckland, 1906-1969* (Auckland, 1969); C. R. Dalton, *Without Hardware* (Canb, 1970); G. Hartcup and T. E. Allibone, *Cockcroft and the Atom* (Bristol, 1984); *Atomic Energy*, 4, no 3, July 1961, p 2; *Atom*, no 59, Sept 1961, p 14; *Aust J of Science*, 24, no 5, Nov 1961, p 232; *Auckland Univ Engineers' Assn Annual Bulletin*, vol 18, 1981, pp 27, 46, vol 19, 1982, p 24; *Hist Records of Aust Science*, 8, no 3, 1991, p 183; *The Times*, 18 July 1961; correspondence from Mr M. C. Timbs, Prof C. M. Segedin, Dr J. A. Goedkoop, Prof A. G. Bogle, Dr J. Bretherton and Ms L. Arnold, *and* taped reminiscences of Prof A. Titchener, Aug 1992, and Mr F. N. Kirton, Sept 1992 (held by author, Qld Univ of Tech).   CAMERON HAZLEHURST

DALTON, LIONEL SYDNEY (1902-1941), naval officer, was born on 26 October 1902 in South Melbourne, second son of Edward Lisle Dalton, a clerk from Adelaide, and his Victorian-born wife Annie Myra, née Oliver. Educated at Middle Park State School, in 1916 Syd entered the Royal Australian Naval College, Jervis Bay, Federal Capital Territory. He did reasonably well academically, won colours for cricket and Rugby Union football, and gained a reputation as a good 'all rounder' who was prepared to 'have a go'. In January 1920 he was promoted midshipman and sent to sea in H.M.A.S. *Australia*.

Based in England for further training from 1921, Dalton served in several Royal Navy ships. He was promoted lieutenant in December 1924, graduated from the R.N. Engineering College at Keyham, Devonport, in 1925, and returned to Australia that year. After postings to H.M.A.S. *Anzac* and *Adelaide*, he went back to England in 1927 to commission the new vessel, *Australia*. On 24 March 1928 he married Margaret Mary Anderson at St Andrew's parish church, Plymouth. Home again, in 1931 he was posted to the seaplane-carrier, *Albatross*. While an instructor (1932-34) at the engineering school, H.M.A.S. *Cerberus*, Westernport, Victoria, he was promoted engineer lieutenant commander. In 1934 he found himself once more in England, standing by the six-inch-gun cruiser, *Sydney*, then under construction at Wallsend, Northumberland. He sailed in her to Australia and in 1937 transferred to H.M.A.S. *Adelaide*.

Promoted engineer commander on 31 December 1937, Dalton rejoined *Sydney* in June 1939 as engineer officer. In May 1940 the ship was deployed for service in the Mediterranean. On 19 July, while patrolling off Cape Spada, Crete, a flotilla of British destroyers sighted two Italian cruisers, the *Bande Nere* and *Bartolomeo Colleoni*. Some forty nautical miles (74 km) to the north, *Sydney* changed course to lend assistance: she pursued the Italian vessels at high speed down the west coast of Crete, destroyed the *Bartolomeo Colleoni* and damaged the *Bande Nere*. Dalton's steadfastness and professionalism ensured that *Sydney*'s machinery performed faultlessly throughout the engagement. He was awarded the Distinguished Service Order.

Sydney's action against a superior force was widely regarded as Australia's most significant naval victory. Dalton recorded the ship's arrival in Alexandria harbour, Egypt, next day: '[We] . . . steamed down the line of battleships and cruisers, receiving a welcome that was wonderful. All ships cleared lower deck and gave us three cheers as we proceeded, and anyone would have imagined that we had won the war'. In 1940 the demands made on Dalton and his staff were enormous, with the ship steaming a total of 66 000 nautical miles (122 300 km). *Sydney* returned to Australian waters in February 1941.

On 19 November 1941, about 150 nautical miles (278 km) south-west of Carnarvon, Western Australia, *Sydney* challenged a disguised merchant vessel, later known to have been the German raider, *Kormoran*, which lured the cruiser closer then opened fire. Both ships were lost in the action, *Sydney* with her entire complement of 645 men. Dalton was survived by his wife and son David who became an engineer officer in the R.A.N. and rose to captain.

F. M. McGuire, *The Royal Australian Navy, its Origin, Development and Organization* (Melb, 1948); G. H. Gill, *Royal Australian Navy 1939-1942* (Canb, 1957); J. Collins, *H.M.A.S. Sydney* (Syd, 1971); *Roy Aust Naval College Mag*, 1916-19; MP 1185/8 file 2026/3/351 (AA, Vic).   ALAN HINGE

D'ALTON, THOMAS GEORGE DE LARGIE (1895-1968), boilermaker and politician, was born on 8 December 1895 at Warracknabeal, Victoria, fourth surviving and youngest child of William Duncan Vincent De Largie D'Alton (d. 1905), millwright, and his second wife Ruth, nee Bell, both native-born. In 1899 the family moved to Queenstown, Tasmania. Tom attended the local state school and at 13 was employed as a boilermaker's offsider. In 1911, during a strike at Mount Lyell, he moved to Sydney (where he won a boxing championship) before returning to Tasmania and working as a painter. D'Alton gave his occupation as labourer on 10 February 1915 when he married Eliza Letitia Barwick (d. 1964) with Catholic rites at Queenstown. From 1917 he was a boilermaker. Sturdy, 5 ft 8 ins (172.7 cm) tall, and an all-round sportsman, he captained a football team and umpired major games. His dark good looks, and skills such as juggling and fire-eating, led him into local theatricals. He later claimed to have chosen politics over the stage on the toss of a coin.

Quick, personable and persuasive, D'Alton proved an excellent negotiator as president (1928) of the Queenstown branch of the Amalgamated Engineering Union. In 1929 he unsuccessfully contested the House of Representatives seat of Darwin for the Australian Labor Party. He was returned for Darwin to the Tasmanian House of Assembly in May 1931 and steadily increased his vote in successive elections. On 22 June 1934 D'Alton joined A. G. Ogilvie's [q.v.11] Labor cabinet as minister for agriculture and for railways, but his major portfolio was that of chief secretary (which he held until December 1939) with charge of social welfare and thus of unemployment relief. His kindness to men on public works became well known.

After Ogilvie's death on 10 June 1939, E. J. C. Dwyer-Gray [q.v.8] became premier on the understanding that he would hold the office until the end of the year. D'Alton, president (1937 and 1939-43) of the State branch of the A.L.P., was narrowly beaten by (Sir) Robert Cosgrove [q.v.] for the deputy-leadership of the parliamentary party. On 18 December Cosgrove formed his ministry. D'Alton received the portfolios of forestry, commerce and agriculture, and held them until 30 November 1943. At first his career continued to flourish. He enthused his public servants, though he worked closest with a tight band of confidants whose help extended to political campaigning. In 1941 he became deputy-premier, but by mid-1943 questions were being asked in parliament about bribery in the Forestry Department, his pet scheme for building wooden ships was failing and even the success of his 'Dizzy-Doo' fund-raising revue raised eyebrows.

In November 1943 D'Alton was appointed Tasmania's first high commissioner to New Zealand. Boasting his ownership of the best diplomatic cellar in Wellington, he was proud of his social successes, but his involvement in a fist-fight at a theatre was embarrassing. When a royal commission was appointed in Tasmania in 1945 to investigate forestry administration, he refused to give evidence on the ground of cost. In May 1946 the commission dismissed two charges of corruption, but found that D'Alton had twice accepted bribes. His New Zealand post had quietly lapsed in March. Although he was acquitted by a criminal-court jury in September, his political career seemed beyond repair, and he spoke privately of taking a touring show to the mainland.

Salvation came through the death on 17 October 1947 of James McDonald, the member for Gordon, a Legislative Council seat based on Queenstown. D'Alton persuaded the heir apparent to step aside and in November was elected with 489 votes. An assiduous local member who was passionately loyal, he was re-elected unopposed in 1952, 1958 and 1964.

In the Legislative Council, where the bribery allegations had been first and most bitterly aired, D'Alton could not even muster the traditional two supporters when he took his seat. Yet he quickly became effective. From early 1948 he was leader for the government in the council; he was to become a champion of the Upper House. In person he disarmed the most unlikely members, and his famous drinking and sometimes questionable associations were regarded as mere marks of a 'lovable rogue'.

Soon, however, D'Alton was largely the cause of two successive general elections. In 1950, when Cosgrove attempted to appoint D'Alton agent-general in London, the Independent speaker W. G. Wedd forced a dissolution of the hung House. In 1955, following ill-advised tampering with Queenstown patronage by the minister for housing C. A. Bramich, a row erupted that resulted in Bramich crossing the floor and the government again going to the people. During the reshuffles surrounding Cosgrove's resignation in 1958, D'Alton was no longer able to muster party support.

Having helped to set up the Spastic Children's Treatment Fund in 1954, D'Alton was increasingly identified with its Miss Tasmania Quest. His skills as an impresario and wide contacts were central to its success. On 12 May 1967 he married a widow Nancy Rachel Denholm, née Tilyard, at St Mary's Catholic Cathedral, Hobart; his religious ties never extended to regular churchgoing. Still government leader in the council, D'Alton died on 7 May 1968 at his South Hobart home; he was accorded a state funeral and was buried in Cornelian Bay cemetery. His wife survived him, as did the son and daughter of his first marriage.

R. Davis, *Eighty Years' Labor* (Hob, 1983); W. A. Townsley, *Tasmania: From Colony to Statehood, 1803-1945* (Hob, 1991); *PP* (Tas), (39), 1945-46, (1), 1946; *Mercury* (Hob), 5 Sept 1946, 8, 10 May 1968, 21 Aug 1985, 8 Dec 1990; *Examiner* (Launc), 8, 10 May 1968; *Advocate* (Burnie), 8-10 May 1968; W. A. Townsley, Tasmania. Microcosm of the Federation or Vassal State? 1945-1982 (ms held by author, Hob); information from Sir Angus Bethune, Sandy Bay, and Messrs P. Fletcher, Moonah, B. K. Miller, Lenah Valley, B. G. Murphy, Howrah, and E. E. Reece, Claremont, Tas.

ALAN HAIG

DALZIEL, ALLAN (1887-1956), marine engineer and shipbuilder, was born on 22 July 1887 at Carronbridge, Dumfriesshire, Scotland, sixth of seven children of Hugh Dalziel, railway pointsman, and his wife Johnan, née Rae, a domestic servant. In 1890 the family moved to Kirn on the Firth of Clyde where Allan was introduced to shipbuilding. After leaving school he was apprenticed (1903-08) as a fitter to David Rowan & Co., Glasgow, builders of ships' engines. He joined Cayser, Irvine & Co. as a junior engineer and spent two years on trading voyages (mainly to India) before returning in 1911 to Glasgow where he obtained his Board of Trade second-class certificate. His next ship, the *Clan Campbell*, was sent to Australia under charter to the Adelaide Steamship Co. Ltd which bought the vessel and renamed her *Camira*; Dalziel remained with the *Camira* and settled in Melbourne.

At the Presbyterian Church, Yarraville, on 12 November 1913 he married Annie Jean Ross, a saleswoman. In 1917 he received his first-class engineer's certificate. Following further sea service, he briefly worked at the Newport power station and in 1919-23 assisted Thompson [q.v.12] & Co. at Williamstown to install engines in D and E class vessels of the Commonwealth Government Line of Steamers. In 1923 three of these ships were sold to Broken Hill Proprietary Co. Ltd and Dalziel became chief engineer of the company's *Iron Master*. Within two years he was promoted superintendent engineer of the firm's ships at Newcastle, New South Wales. B.H.P. had acquired a fleet to bring its various steelmaking components from around Australia and to transport the finished products, but these vessels were bought or chartered from other companies. By 1935 B.H.P. planned ships of its own, specifically suited to its needs. Dalziel supervised the construction of four of them in Scotland and came back to Australia in 1938.

The company's managing director Essington Lewis [q.v.10] was keen to resuscitate Australian shipbuilding and responded before World War II to the British Admiralty's request for B.H.P. to build warships. Whyalla, South Australia, was chosen as the site: this port was less vulnerable than the eastern seaboard to naval or air attack, and had a recently-dredged harbour, ample space for a shipyard, a burgeoning township and other amenities. Dalziel was appointed superintendent of shipbuilding. He recruited from Scotland executives and artisans to train the shipyard workers, most of whom came from South Australia's farming districts and quickly mastered the craft. Dalziel admired the Australian working man. Big in stature and in mind, he led and did not drive; he knew most of his employees by name, listened to their troubles and counselled them in their personal problems. They thought the world of him and industrial unrest was rare under his stewardship. An advocate of immigration, he believed that the old world was finished and that his adopted land was the country of the future.

By 1942 four naval vessels of the mine-sweeper-corvette type had been completed at Whyalla. There followed a programme of merchant shipbuilding which, by Dalziel's retirement in 1952, comprised seventeen ships. The last of these, of the Yampi class, were—at 12 500 tons d.w.—the largest ships then built in Australia. The yard's workforce numbered more than nine hundred. Like many of his origin and generation, work was Dalziel's passion, though he enjoyed a rich family life, played bowls and golf, and was a Freemason. Survived by his wife, daughter and four of his six sons, he died of coronary vascular disease on 13 June 1956 at Whyalla and was buried in Brighton cemetery, Melbourne.

Aust Shipbuilders' Assn, *Shipbuilding in Australia* (Canb, 1968); G. Blainey, *The Steel Master* (Melb, 1971); S. J. Butlin, *War economy 1939-42* (Canb, 1955) and with C. B. Schedvin, *War Economy 1942-1945* (Canb, 1977); A. Trengove, *What's Good for Australia . . . .!* (Melb, 1975); M. Page, *Fitted for the Voyage* (Adel, 1975); B. Pemberton, *Australian Coastal Shipping* (Melb, 1979); *Whyalla News*, 15 June 1956; Nautical Assn of Aust, *Log*, 1, no 5, 1968; information from Mr D. J. Dalziel, Toorak, Melb, and Mr J. McLaren, Glenelg, Adel.

GERALD DONAGHY

DALZIEL, ALLAN JOHN (1908-1969), social reformer and political secretary, was born on 29 December 1908 at Pymble, Sydney, son of William Dalziel, a ship's officer from Scotland, and his native-born wife Florence Mary Annie, née Barbour. Educated at Cleveland Street Intermediate High School, Allan successively worked as a clerk, in an advertising agency, in the motor trade, as a butcher and as a freelance journalist. In the 1930s his strong Presbyterian beliefs were tempered by growing secular concerns. While living above his uncle's butcher's shop at Redfern during the Depression, he became secretary of the Legion of Christian Youth, founded by his close friend (Bishop) E. H. Burgmann [q.v.] to awaken community interest in the need for better housing. In 1936 the State government appointed Dalziel to the Housing Conditions Investigation Committee. His articles on slum reform brought him to the attention of intelligence officials who deemed him to be 'an opponent of constituted authority'.

Possibly through his friendship with Burgmann, Dalziel was appointed as H. V. Evatt's [q.v.] electoral secretary for the Federal seat of Barton in 1940. Although he was promoted private secretary to the attorney-general (Evatt), he publicly criticized repressive aspects of the government's regulations under the National Security Act. In 1946 he was condemned by the press for undertaking electoral duties for Evatt while technically a public servant. He looked after the Barton electorate during Evatt's long absences abroad. Dalziel's tall, 'spare figure, usually in sombre grey or black', became familiar in Sydney. In 1947 anti-communist Catholics informed British and American intelligence that Dalziel was a 'Communist sympathiser'. Australian intelligence held a similar view, noting Dalziel's close association with J. F. Hill, a diplomat, and John Burton, secretary of the Department of External Affairs.

Having toured Australia early in 1947 to promote the government's commitment to the United Nations, Dalziel and Hill represented Australia at a conference of the United Nations' Commission on Human Rights in New York. Dalziel censured American materialism and political repression, but expressed admiration for Eleanor Roosevelt, Henry Wallace, Charlie Chaplin and Paul Robeson.

In 1954 Dalziel, Hill, Burton and others were named as alleged contacts of Soviet intelligence in 'G Documents' before the royal commission on espionage. Evatt created immense controversy when he appeared as counsel for Dalziel and others on his staff. Dalziel was questioned for over one hundred days about his appointment to Evatt's staff of a young typist Frances Bernie who belonged to the Communist Party of Australia and about a tenuous claim that he had sought a military pass in 1945 for the communist writer Rupert Lockwood. Dalziel was exonerated.

After Evatt retired from parliament in 1960, Dalziel worked as a field officer for the New South Wales Council of Churches. In 1968 he was appointed full-time general secretary of the New South Wales Temperance Alliance and campaigned vigorously against moves to introduce hotel trading on Sundays. He published *Evatt the Enigma* (Melbourne, 1967), a defence of his chief, in which he implied that the commission which followed the defection of Vladimir Petrov was a conservative conspiracy to destroy Evatt and the Labor Party. Dalziel died of a staphylococcal infection on 5 October 1969 at Royal North Shore Hospital and was cremated with Presbyterian forms. He was unmarried. L. C. Haylen [q.v.], Dal's closest friend, described him as 'one of the most effective social workers and workers for socialism in this country'.

NSW Temperance Alliance, *Allan John Dalziel* (Syd, 1969); K. Tennant, *Evatt* (Syd, 1970); *SMH*, 6 Oct 1969; RG 59, Records of Dept of State, US Embassy in Canb, 1947, file on Aust *and* central decimal file 847.008/6-2347 (National Archives, Washington, DC); RG 25, Records of Dept of External Affairs, box 325, file 9629-40C (National Archives, Ottawa, Canada); CRS A6335/3, file 15 (AA).

GREGORY J. PEMBERTON

DANGAR, ANNE GARVIN (1885-1951), painter and potter, was born on 1 December 1885 at Kempsey, New South Wales, fifth child of native-born parents Otho Orde Dangar, auctioneer and member (1889-93) of the Legislative Assembly, and his wife Elizabeth, née Garvin. Called Nancy by her family, she attended East Kempsey Public School and in 1906 took art lessons in Sydney under Horace Moore-Jones. She joined Julian Ashton's [q.v.7] Sydney Art School before 1916 and taught there from 1920; meantime, she worked at Angus & Robertson [qq.v.7,11] Ltd by day. An adventurous reader, she discovered Cézanne and exchanged modernist ideas with her colleagues Dorrit Black, 'Rah' Fizelle [qq.v.7,8] and Grace Crowley [q.v.]. Dangar shared a cottage at Vaucluse with Crowley who became her dearest friend—yet they were never to meet after 1930.

In February 1926 they sailed for France where Dangar was overwhelmed by Cézanne's work. Seeking instruction in the principles and techniques of modern painting, they studied at André Lhote's academy in Paris and in 1928 attended his summer school at Mirmande, near Montélimar. Dangar visited Italy with Crowley before returning alone to Australia. While assisting at the Sydney Art School in 1929, she met opposition when she attempted to introduce ideas about cubism and modern art, and was further frustrated by the parochial attitude of her family. Early in 1930 she travelled to the south of France where she joined an artists' commune, Moly-Sabata, which had been set up at Sablons by the cubist Albert Gleizes and his wife Juliette, née Roches.

Apart from the Gleizeses (intermittently resident nearby), Dangar became the central figure at Moly-Sabata. Chronically short of money, she grew fruit, flowers and vegetables, kept bees and cleaned for the commune. She worked with local peasants at their potteries, re-introducing and revitalizing traditional techniques, and basing her decorations on Gleizes's theories about the relationship of art to Catholicism and medieval mysticism. In the 1930s she made three shipments of her pots to Australia, and sent instructions from Gleizes and reports of discussions to the Sydney modernists. She recorded her life in letters to Grace and continued to hope that her darling 'Smudgie' would join her in France. Respected as a teacher of drawing and design, Dangar successfully exhibited her pottery in France; in 1939 she spent six months in Morocco, based at Fez, as 'monitress' to local potters, and was in turn influenced by their traditional Islamic designs.

Back in France in January 1940, Dangar was confined to Sablons during World War II. She taught English to survive. Apart from enduring loneliness, cold and hunger, she found the absence of soap and matches hardest to bear. In March 1943 she was sent to a concentration camp at Grenoble, but released five days later. Despite the difficulties in filling commissions because of the scarcity of essential materials, she decided to remain in France and in 1947 her own kiln was built. In March 1951 Dangar was converted to Catholicism. Monks from a nearby monastery tended her in her last months. She died of cancer on 4 September 1951 at Moly-Sabata and was buried in the Roches family vault at Serrières, Ardèche.

One of the few Australian artists whose work has been acclaimed more in the country of her adoption than at home, Anne Dangar is best known in Australia for her pottery although she thought of herself as a painter throughout her life. Examples of her work are in several collections in France, including the Musée National d'Art Moderne, Paris, as well as in the Australian National Gallery, Canberra, and in the art galleries of New South Wales and South Australia.

E. Bénézit, *Dictionnaire Critique et Documentaire des Peintres, Sculpteurs, Dessinateurs et Graveurs* (Paris, 1976); I. North, *The Art of Dorrit Black* (Melb, 1979); J. Burke (ed), 'Grace Crowley's Student Years', *Australian Women Artists* (Melb, 1980); M. Eagle, *Australian Modern Painting* (Syd, 1990); H. Maxwell, 'Profile of Anne Dangar', *Art and Aust*, 26, no 3, Autumn 1989; *SMH*, 14 Dec 1933; *Sunday Sun* (Syd), 18 Mar 1945; Grace Crowley papers (ML).   HELEN MAXWELL

DANN, GEORGE LANDEN (1904-1977), playwright and draughtsman, was born on New Year's Day 1904 at Sandgate, Brisbane, second child of English-born parents George William Dann, gardener, and his wife Mildred Challis, née Pearman. Young George was educated at Brisbane Grammar School. He entered the survey office of the Queensland Lands Department in 1920, trained as a draughtsman and in 1924 joined the Brisbane City Council.

Having written plays for the amateur dramatic society at Sandgate, in 1931 he won the Brisbane Repertory Theatre's competition with *In Beauty It Is Finished*. Set at a remote island lighthouse, it explored the lightkeeper's indifference to the effects of isolation on his long-suffering family. Burdened himself with caring for a widowed mother and an invalid sister, Dann wrote bitterly against duty and self-sacrifice, and feelingly about the yearning for escape. His representation of the liaison between a White prostitute and a part-Aborigine led *Smith's Weekly* to denounce the play as a 'Sordid Drama of Miscegenation'.

Minor deletions and the support of such leading citizens as Gerald Sharp [q.v.11], the Anglican archbishop of Brisbane, allowed production to proceed: despite continuing public controversy, the play opened on 16 July.

In his best-known and most acclaimed play, *Fountains Beyond*, Dann returned to the issue of race relations. First staged and broadcast in 1942, and published two years later, it told the story of an Aboriginal community leader Vic Filmer, a character based on the athlete and Fraser Island identity Freddy Ross. In the play Vic refuses the demeaning request of the local shire chairman to stage a sacred corroboree for a visitor, and also leads opposition to a proposal to close the Aboriginal settlement because it can be seen from newly-built beach houses; another Aborigine stages the ceremonial dance which becomes a drunken disaster; the play ends in tragedy when Vic accidentally shoots his wife. *Fountains Beyond* was placed second to Douglas Stewart's *Ned Kelly* [q.v.5] in the Australian Broadcasting Commission's radio-drama competition in 1942. It was staged throughout Australia, and in London and Wales in 1950.

Keen-eyed, shy and somewhat reclusive, Dann was a prolific playwright, even though he only wrote part time. His works won prizes, were widely performed by amateur companies and were presented regularly by the A.B.C. *The One Clear Harp* and *The Young Disciple* had biblical subjects. Australian history contributed to *Monday Morning* (about a bushranger condemned on false evidence) and to one of Dann's most popular works, *Caroline Chisholm* [q.v.1], produced in 1939 and published in 1943. Dann portrayed women either as saintly, or as weak and corruptible. His most successful female character is old Carrie, the arthritic recluse of *The Orange Grove*, a radio play produced in 1958.

Dann's writing was appreciated for its social realism. His early ambition to become a pastor is reflected in the high moral seriousness of his plays and in their central characters who are mostly drawn from the fringes of White society—several of them were based on acquaintances he met during his trips to the outback. In December 1954 Dann retired from the city council and moved to the relatively isolated Maroochydore-Noosa region of the Sunshine Coast. He never married. His last work, *Rainbows Die at Sunset*, drew on a riot at Nambucca Heads in 1958 when White residents prevented the sale of a house to Aborigines. Although somewhat dated in its style and language, it was highly commended in a competition in 1975 at Newcastle, New South Wales. Dann died on 6 June 1977 at Eumundi, Queensland, and was cremated with Anglican rites. In 1992 the *Courier-Mail* and the Royal Queensland Theatre Company

inaugurated an award in his honour that is presented to young playwrights.

L. Rees, *Towards an Australian Drama* (Syd, 1953); D. Carroll, *Australian Contemporary Drama 1909-1982* (NY, 1985); *Meanjin Papers*, 4, no 1, 1945, p 65; *Smith's Weekly*, 4 July 1931; *Courier-Mail*, 19, 26 Mar, 7 June 1977; *National Times*, 21-26 Mar 1977; *Bulletin*, 30 Apr 1977; D. Rasmussen, The Plays of George Landen Dann (B.A. Hons thesis, Univ Qld, 1976); Dann papers (Fryer L, Univ Qld). RICHARD FOTHERINGHAM

DARBYSHIRE, PHILLIP ARTHUR (1898-1969), radio scriptwriter, was born on New Year's Day 1898 at Stratford, Victoria, second son of James Arthur Christian Darbyshire, stationmaster, and his wife Blanche, née Marie, both native-born. When Phillip was 5 his parents moved to Western Australia where he was educated at Perth Modern School and won a State junior piano championship. He served in the Militia, but was rejected on medical grounds for the Australian Imperial Force; after World War I he worked as an articled clerk and book-keeper. On 20 February 1926 at the Anglican parish church, Victoria Park, he married Marjorie Nesta Helene Hopkins. With his father, he had acquired a pastoral station, Coolabong, near Moulamein, New South Wales; he became a shire councillor, justice of the peace and coroner. In the early 1930s he was involved with the New Guard.

From an early age Darbyshire had written short stories. His work appeared in the *Home* and the *Bulletin*; one story gained first prize in a London *Daily Mirror* competition and another, 'Mr Platapan's Roof', was published in 1935 in London's *Evening Standard*. Forced off the land by the Depression and drought, and with a wife and five young children to support, he found a job as a radio announcer at Deniliquin. Next year he moved to Melbourne and took up full-time scriptwriting for commercial radio in association with the producer Hal Percy [q.v.]. Darbyshire's literary interests led him to join J. K. Moir's [q.v.] Bread and Cheese Club.

In 1941 Darbyshire secured a position in the Australian Broadcasting Commission's light entertainment section, then based in Melbourne, and began a long career of writing scripts for A.B.C. variety, comedy and drama programmes, among them 'Words and Music', the 'A.B.C. Victory Show', 'Happy Go Lucky', the 'Modern Minstrel Show', 'Screen Serenade' and 'Souvenirs of Song'. He also wrote shows for the armed forces during World War II. Many of his plays were presented on A.B.C. radio, such as 'The Egotist' which went to air in April 1945 on the 'Over to Youth Session'.

From May 1942 to March 1971 Darbyshire's musical variety programme, 'The Village Glee Club', was broadcast. One of the longest-running, weekly shows on Australian radio, it had a distinctly British flavour, presenting old songs and mild comedy set in an Australian country choir. Backed by the A.B.C. Wireless Chorus, its singers included Sylvia Fisher, Kathleen Goodall and Lorenzo Nolan. Local actors Colin Crane, Agnes Dobson, Kathleen Goodall and Patricia Kennedy spoke such roles as Mr Crump, Mrs Sharpp-Shott, Miss Coy and Miss Crump. The programme's combination of genteel comedy and sentimental music outlived many changes in radio entertainment.

Phil Darbyshire was a tireless, prolific writer, able to create up to six radio shows per week. Colleagues remembered him as generous and likeable. He retired in 1960, but continued to write 'The Village Glee Club', and made several trips abroad to pursue his musical and theatrical interests. Survived by his wife, two daughters and five sons, he died on 16 November 1969 at his Oakleigh home and was cremated. A large collection of his scripts is held in the State Library of Victoria.

K. S. Inglis, *This is the ABC* (Melb, 1983); *Listener In*, 18 Dec 1937, 12 Aug 1942, 16-22 Jan 1954, 20-26 Mar 1971; *ABC Weekly*, 9 May 1942, 25 Nov 1944; *Radio Active*, Jan 1960; Darbyshire scripts (La Trobe Collection SLV); information from Mr D. Darbyshire, Melb.   MIMI COLLIGAN

DARKER, WALTER BRUCE (1878-1950), colliery proprietor and company director, was born on 11 September 1878 at North Ipswich, Queensland, seventh of twelve children of Richard Thomas Darker, a locomotive foreman from England, and his Scottish-born wife Williamina, née Forbes. Educated at North Ipswich Primary School, Walter briefly worked with P. L. Cardew & Simpson, solicitors, before being employed by the local branch of the Royal Bank of Queensland Ltd. In 1904 he joined his brother Thomas in a book-selling business in Brisbane Street, Ipswich, and later began to take an interest in the coal-mining industry. One of his aunts, Johanna, was married to the colliery-owner Joseph Stafford, in whose mining operations Richard Darker had invested. When Stafford died in 1917, Johanna formed a partnership with Richard and his son Walter in order to continue running the Stafford Bros collieries. Following Richard's death in 1921, his place in the partnership was filled by Walter's brother, Tom. Johanna Stafford died in 1925. Walter then became chairman of the Darkers' mining interests which were floated as the Whitwood Collieries Pty Ltd.

Formidable commercial, negotiating and consultative skills made Walter Darker a leading figure in the State's business community. He was president of the Queensland Colliery Proprietors' Council (1921), of the Ipswich Chamber of Commerce (1919-23) and of the Associated Chambers of Commerce of Queensland (1924-29, 1931, 1933); the first Queenslander to be president (1929-30) of the Associated Chambers of Commerce of Australia, he was also chairman (1929-30) of the Australian national committee of the International Chamber of Commerce. Chairman of the South Brisbane Gas & Light Co. Ltd, the Royal Insurance Co. Ltd (Brisbane branch) and of Allan & Stark Ltd, he was a director of several other enterprises, among them the Brisbane Permanent Building & Banking Co. Ltd. Darker was a tireless contributor to community activities and a generous philanthropist; he was, as well, a prominent Rotarian and a Freemason. During World War II he chaired (1940-43) State division of the Australian Red Cross Society.

In the 1920s Darker, who never married, had joined other members of the family at Woodston, their home at Clayfield, where he lived for the remainder of his life. A self-educated man with simple tastes, he enjoyed gardening, boating and occasional fishing. He possessed a rare combination of business acumen, an instinct for community leadership and the knack of getting on with people, which he honed into a powerful commercial tool. While attending a Masonic function at Ipswich he died on 25 March 1950 and was cremated with Anglican rites. His estate was sworn for probate in Queensland at £115 592; his benefactions included the endowment of undergraduate scholarships in the faculty of engineering at the University of Queensland.

R. L. Whitmore (ed), *Eminent Queensland Engineers* (Brisb, 1984) and *Coal in Queensland*, 2 (Brisb, 1991); *Notable Men of Qld* (Brisb, 1950); *Qld Times*, 28 June 1898, 21 Mar 1905, 26 Mar 1907, 27 Mar 1950; *Brisb Courier*, 9 Apr 1938, 27 Mar 1950; information from Mr W. I. George, St Lucia, Brisb.   RAYMOND L. WHITMORE

DARWIN, DONALD VICTOR (1896-1972), civil engineer, was born on 11 October 1896 at Redhill, South Australia, son of Henry Darwin, a native-born bank manager, and his wife Jessie Louise Cleta, née Gmeiner. Educated at the Collegiate School of St Peter, Adelaide, and the University of Melbourne (B.C.E., 1920; M.C.E., 1926), he enlisted in the Australian Imperial Force on 3 January 1916. He reached France in November as a sapper in the 10th Field Company, Engineers. From 28 March to 1 April 1918 at Buire, near

Albert, he reconnoitred front-line posts while under heavy fire and was awarded the Military Medal. He was discharged in Melbourne on 25 May 1919.

Joining the infant Country Roads Board of Victoria, Darwin was appointed assistant-engineer in 1920 and bridge engineer in 1924. One of his major projects was to design the Princes Highway's crossing of the Barwon River. In 1929 he was promoted to assistant chief engineer. He contributed significantly to the C.R.B.'s plan to meet the needs of the automobile era by constructing a system of 'low cost' motor roads. That task involved systematic experiments on the road-building qualities of a wide variety of locally-occurring soils and rocks, and the development of efficient machinery and streamlined techniques for the construction of bitumen surfaces on arterial motor routes.

On 1 March 1930 Darwin married a 24-year-old music teacher Evelyn Hope Scott at the Presbyterian Church, Malvern. Appointed chief engineer in 1940, he brought his versatility to the building requirements of munitions facilities and airfields in Victoria, and to defence-related constructions in the Northern Territory (including the Stuart Highway). His appointment to the three-member board of the C.R.B. in 1945 reflected respect for his engineering and administrative capacities.

During the stressful period of postwar reconstruction, in 1949 Darwin became chairman of the C.R.B., while continuing to lecture and examine in civil engineering at his old university. He supervised a major upgrading of the State's roads and bridges system, and helped the C.R.B. to plan for the advent of high-density, urban, motor traffic and heavy-duty freeways to link major population centres.

Articulate and dedicated, with uncommon intellectual ability and a prodigious memory, Darwin was a demanding administrator, capable of visionary and encouraging leadership. He was not, however, a master of the arts of political compromise or expediency, and some blamed him for a decline in C.R.B. influence. One protégé described him as 'an academic person . . . quite shy but humorous . . . a hard person to get to know'. That painful shyness, a notoriously clammy and limp handshake, and a devout Anglican's moral scrupulousness contributed to Darwin's difficulties in relating to State and municipal politicians.

Having retired in 1962, he assisted the Australian Road Research Board. That year he won the Kernot [q.v.5] medal. He was appointed I.S.O. in 1963 and awarded the (Sir) Peter Nicol Russell [q.v.6] medal in 1966 by the Institution of Engineers, Australia, an organization he had served as president in

1957. Survived by his wife and daughter, Darwin died on 8 March 1972 at Malvern and was cremated. His estate was sworn for probate at $123 692.

Sun News-Pictorial, 5 Jan 1945, 2 Sept 1950, 11 Sept 1953; *Argus*, 22 Mar 1949; *Herald* (Melb), 10 July 1950, 1 Feb 1956; *Age* (Melb), 17 Apr 1957, 24 July 1962, 10 Mar 1972; *SMH*, 8 June 1963, 25 Nov 1966; D. Chambers, From Bullock Tracks to Bitumen (ms, LaTL); Country Roads Bd (Vic) Archives (PRO, Laverton, Vic); information from Mr P. McCullough, Tyabb, Vic.

DON CHAMBERS

DAVEY, GEOFFREY INNES (1906-1975), civil engineer and priest, was born on 27 November 1906 at Double Bay, Sydney, eldest surviving son of Joseph Innes Davey, a law clerk from England, and his native-born wife Caroline, née Hurley. Geoffrey was educated at Marist Brothers' High School, Darlinghurst, and won an exhibition to the University of Sydney (B.E., 1929). Joining the Metropolitan Water, Sewerage and Drainage Board, he became assistant construction engineer for the Woronora dam. Two years later Davey began his own business in Queensland where he pioneered the manufacture of concrete roofing tiles. Employed by Australian Iron & Steel Ltd in 1933, he oversaw the installation of its mill at Port Kembla, New South Wales. He worked in turn in Papua as a consulting engineer on hydraulic and mining investigations, and in Tasmania on the construction of a rock pile dam. At St Mary's Cathedral, Sydney, on 6 February 1935 he married an architect Elsa Annette Isabel Hazelton.

That year Davey went into partnership with Gerald Haskins. Their commissions included the Morning Star dam, Tasmania, and sewerage works in New South Wales. They amalgamated with A. Gordon Gutteridge in 1939 and received contracts for Commonwealth munitions factories during and after World War II. Davey was sole principal (1942-49) of the firm and governing partner (1949-64). In 1946 he had unsuccessfully contested the House of Representatives seat of Hume for the Liberal Party—a breach of his school's strong Labor tradition. A founder and president (1956-57) of the Association of Consulting Engineers, Australia, he was a councillor (1962 and 1964-65) of the Institution of Engineers, Australia, which he represented on the National Capital Planning Committee in Canberra. He was appointed C.B.E. in 1966.

Already a knight commander (1960) of the Order of St Gregory the Great, Davey was a 'lieutenant' of the all-weather ecclesiastic Monsignor T. O. Wallace, as well as building adviser to the expanding Catholic school system in Sydney and a director of St Vincent's Hospital, the Mater Misericordiae Hospital and the *Catholic Weekly* newspaper. On retiring from his firm in 1964, he became executive-director of the Sydney Catholic Schools Building and Finance Commission.

In 1967, three years after Elsa died, Davey began theological studies in Rome at the Pontifical Beda College, a seminary for mature-age students. He was ordained priest on 10 July 1971 by Cardinal Sir Norman Gilroy [q.v.] at the Holy Name Priory, Wahroonga, Sydney, a church designed by Davey's wife. At the ceremony he was photographed blessing his six children and seven grandchildren. The new priest was sent as curate to the parish of Strathfield, but he remained close to the inner working of the archdiocese and served for a time as general manager of the *Catholic Weekly*. Survived by his four sons and two daughters, he died of a coronary occlusion on 12 February 1975 at the Strathfield presbytery and was buried beside his wife in Mona Vale cemetery.

Marist Brothers' High School, Darlinghurst, *Blue and Blue*, 1960, p 10, 1966, p 27; *SMH*, 29 Apr 1946, 13 Apr 1960, 11 June 1966, 14 Feb, 27 Mar, 12 Apr, 12 July 1971, 14 Feb 1975; National Memorials Cte information sheet (copy held by ADB).   EDMUND CAMPION

DAVEY, JOHN ANDREW (1907-1959), radio entertainer, was born on 8 February 1907 at Auckland, New Zealand, son of Arthur Henry Davey, mariner, and his wife Ella May, née Hunter, both New Zealand born. Arthur became a ship's captain on the trans-Tasman run. Educated (1918-22) at King's College, Auckland, Jack took various jobs and was briefly an assistant stage manager at a local theatre.

Shortly after arriving in Sydney, in 1931 Davey performed on radio as a crooner with the Australian Broadcasting Co. (2BL) and Macquarie Broadcasting Services Pty Ltd (2GB). Ten months later he was employed as an announcer on 2GB and quickly had his own shows, the first of which was a breakfast session. His opening 'Hi, Ho! Everybody!' was to be his enduring call sign. He began to develop the techniques of spontaneity—'ad-libbing' and quick-witted humour—that were to ensure his popularity, and he exploited this style when he took on extra work as a commentator (1933-57) for Fox Movietone News. On 17 July 1936 at the registrar general's office, Sydney, he married Dulcie May Mary Webb, a book-keeper; they were to be divorced in 1942.

The quiz and variety shows on radio in the 1940s and 1950s established Davey's fame. He had formed his own company, Jack Davey Productions Pty Ltd, in the late 1930s, but it closed in 1940. Next year Colgate-Palmolive Pty Ltd and the advertising agency, George Patterson [q.v.] Pty Ltd, set up their own radio production unit. As director of productions, Davey wrote, produced and compered variety and quiz shows for the Colgate-Palmolive Radio Unit. The 'Youth Show' and 'Stage Parade' (from September 1942 'Calling the Stars') were recorded at the Trocadero's ballroom in Sydney before audiences of some two thousand people each week. For several months from the end of 1941 the unit also recorded at the Comedy Theatre, Melbourne.

In December 1943 Davey joined the American National Red Cross as a field-entertainer in the South-West Pacific Area. Having toured Australia to promote the first Victory Loan, in mid-1944 he rejoined the Colgate-Palmolive unit (which was to transfer its productions from 2GB to 2UE in 1946). He published a book of anecdotes, *Hi, Ho! Everybody!* (Melbourne, 1945). His shows now included 'Leave Pass', the 'Colgate Cavalcade' and 'Calling the Stars'. In 1950 he returned to Macquarie as director of productions; his personality reversed its ailing fortunes.

Davey was earning a large salary, and spending far more. His extravagance, reckless gambling, expensive cars and big-game fishing meant that he was perpetually in debt. At St Columba's Presbyterian Church, Woollahra, on 24 May 1947 he married a divorcee Dorothy Daisy ('Diana') Lush, née Richmond. Marriage had little effect on his way of life.

He was chubby and small, 'quite out of keeping with his big voice'. In addition to his radio work, Davey engaged in much-publicized, if unprofitable, business ventures —motorcar auctions at Kings Cross, the Stork Club restaurant at Sylvania where he sang and danced, and a real-estate agency. As well as dispensing largesse during his shows, he visited hospitals, entertained disabled children in his cruiser, *Sea Mist*, and lent his name to charitable appeals, especially the Children's Medical Research Foundation.

The first Redex Reliability Trial in 1953 gave Davey the opportunity to indulge his enjoyment both of cars and of publicity. With co-driver Lou Moss he took part in the 6500-mile (10 460 km) race and sent constant, humorous reports back to Sydney to be published in his regular newspaper column in the *Sun-Herald*. Soon after the trial it collapsed. Next year, however, he again took part in the Redex trial—9600 miles (15 450 km) around Australia—and made nightly reports on radio.

A McNair-Anderson [qq.v.] survey in 1955 reported that the quiz was Australia's most popular type of radio programme. Jack Davey competed with his friend and rival Bob Dyer to be the most successful compere. Although the shows increasingly emphasized the questions and the prizes rather than the vaudeville style of Davey's 1940s programmes, he continued to have an immense following. In contrast to Dyer's carefully-written scripts, Davey's spontaneity and wit, delivered in the warm, rich voice, for which he was so well known on radio, did not attract television audiences. He began with three programmes in 1957, broadcast simultaneously on television and radio, but the television shows were cancelled about a year later.

Jack's health was rapidly deteriorating. Survived by his wife, and by a daughter, he died of cancer on 14 October 1959 in St Vincent's Hospital, Darlinghurst, and was cremated after a service at St Andrew's Anglican Cathedral. Between 100 000 and 150 000 people stood in pouring rain to pay tribute to him. His life was, and continues to be, surrounded by myth-making, and he had ensured that stories and anecdotes were continually disseminated as central to any public version of that life. Davey was a showman, a consummate performer, at all times. His capacity to project his personality into the living-rooms of his listeners and the extraordinary agility of his 'wise-cracking' humour made him known as 'Mr Radio'.

L. Wright, *The Jack Davey Story* (Syd, 1961); N. Bridges, *Wonderful Wireless* (Syd, 1983); J. Kent, *Out of the Bakelite Box* (Syd, 1983); *Wireless Weekly*, 4 May 1934; *Commercial Broadcasting*, 12 Sept 1940, 3 July 1941; *People* (Syd), 24 May 1950; *Aust Letters*, Apr 1958; *SMH*, 17 Nov, 13 Dec 1943, 14 Apr 1944, 17 Oct 1959; *A'sian Post*, 19 Nov 1953, 14 July 1955; *Age*(Melb), 5 Jan 1985; information from Messrs B. Wright and C. Dexter-Palmer, Avoca Beach, NSW.
                                           LESLEY JOHNSON

DAVID, CAROLINE MARTHA (1856-1951), community worker, was born on 26 April 1856 at Southwold, Suffolk, England, daughter of Samuel Mallett, fisherman, and his wife Pamela, née Wright. Orphaned early, Cara was raised by her grandmother and trained as a teacher at Whitelands College, London. She was appointed principal of Hurlstone Training College for women teachers and reached Sydney on 27 November 1882 in the *Potosi*. Tall, slim, warm hearted and dark eyed, she had met (Sir) Tannatt William Edgeworth David [q.v.8] on board ship. They were married on 30 July 1885 at St Paul's Anglican Church, Canterbury.

While David was mapping the coalfields of Maitland, Cara lived in camp with her infants Margaret [q.v. McIntyre] and Mary (Molly).

Eventually, she took a house at Maitland. Pregnant for the third time, alone in the house and armed only with an unloaded revolver, she challenged a burglar. He fled. After her son William was born in 1890, she settled at Ashfield with the children. Next year David was appointed to the chair of geology at the University of Sydney.

Accompanying her husband on the 1897 Royal Society's expedition to bore coral reefs at Funafuti, Ellice Islands (Tuvalu), Cara cheerfully suffered constant rain, mouldy clothes and lack of privacy, while forging close friendships with Funafuti women. She treated the expedition's members and the locals for illness and injury, kept the expedition records, collected cultural artefacts and botanical and zoological specimens, and traced tattoo patterns from the bodies of older islanders. In return for English lessons, she was taught Samoan. Becoming ill, she convalesced in Samoa and Fiji.

Back home, Cara wrote 'Mission work in Funafuti' for the *Australian Christian World* (1897), declaring that she had studied 'the biological specimen called "missionary" in his own habitat'. To her delight, John Murray published her book, *Funafuti* (London, 1899; abridged edition, 1913), an 'unscientific account of a scientific expedition'. She wrote to a friend, 'If I could afford it I would publish all the indelicate facts—because they are full of teaching which is needed'.

The Davids accepted responsibility for the education of a Fijian princess Adi Elanoa, aged 11. She became a much loved member of the household, but was to die of influenza while holidaying in Fiji. In the early 1900s the family moved to Woodford in the Blue Mountains. Strong willed and receptive to new ideas in religion, diet and health, Cara refused to allow her children to attend Sunday School. She prepared them for confirmation herself, as 'she held very strong anti-hell opinions and was afraid we might be introduced to the devil and church doctrine relating to him'. Her health regime involved chest-expanders and dumb-bells, the avoidance of tight lacing, and removing glass from the bedroom windows of their Blue Mountains home. A migraine sufferer for many years, she found relief in vegetarianism.

Following the success of *My Brilliant Career* (London, 1901), Cara offered Miles Franklin [q.v.8] advice on her shortcomings as a writer and invited her to Woodford to broaden her experience of life. An excellent public speaker, Mrs David regularly addressed meetings on topics such as 'Complete womanhood' and 'Housewifery schools'. In 1913 she became president of the Bush Book Club of New South Wales and served on its committee until 1922. She was also president of the Girls' Realm Guild.

During World War I Cara turned the Woodford house into a Red Cross convalescent home for soldiers. As president of the Women's National Movement for social reform, she advocated sex education for the young and the eradication of venereal disease. She believed in prohibition and, as a means to that end, spoke passionately in favour of six-o'clock closing of public houses. When David enlisted in the Australian Imperial Force in 1916, Cara went to England to be near him and their son William, a regimental medical officer. Fervently patriotic, she insisted on sailing in a British ship. The Davids returned to Sydney and moved to Hornsby where Cara again indulged her 'passion for building additions'.

An original divisional commissioner (from 1920) of the New South Wales branch of the Girl Guides' Association, Lady David was State commissioner in 1928-38. She organized the purchase of Glengarry at Turramurra for its training headquarters and in 1934 was invested with the Order of the Silver Fish, the highest guiding award. Following her husband's death in August that year, she went to live with Molly. Throughout World War II Cara knitted hundreds of socks for servicemen, often spinning the wool herself. Survived by her son and one daughter, she died on Christmas Day 1951 at Hornsby and was cremated. In 1907 David had observed: 'Whatever success I may have achieved in life, is due chiefly to my wife'.

M. E. David, *Professor David* (Lond, 1937) and *Passages of Time* (Brisb, 1975); Girl Guides Assn (NSW Branch), *Waratah*, 32, no 9, Mar 1952, p 2; C. Cantrell and K. A. Rodgers, 'Australia and the Funafuti connection: 2. An all Australian Assault', *Search*, 20, no 1, 1989, p 27; Bush Club of NSW, *Annual Report*, 1913-50; *Evening News*, 9 Dec 1907; *SMH*, 27 Aug 1909, 9 Dec 1914, 18 July 1916, 18 May, 16 June 1933, 28 Mar 1934, 2 Jan 1952; T. W. Edgeworth David papers (Fisher L, Univ Syd); David family papers (ML).

CAROL CANTRELL

DAVIDSON, BESSIE ELLEN (1879-1965), artist, was born on 22 May 1879 in North Adelaide, second of five children of David Davidson, mining secretary, and his wife Ellen, née Johnson, both from Scotland. Bessie was educated in Adelaide, studied art in 1899 under Rose McPherson (who was later to be known as Margaret Preston [q.v.11]) and exhibited with the South Australian Society of Arts in 1901-03. After her mother's death, in July 1904 Bessie left for Europe with Rose and studied briefly at the Künstlerinner Verein, Munich, Germany. They moved to Paris in November. At the Académie de la Grande Chaumière her teacher was René-Xavier Prinet. She was also taught by Raphael Collin, Gustave Courtois and Richard Miller. Davidson formed a wide circle of artistic and literary friends, and particularly admired the work of Vincent van Gogh, Pierre Bonnard, Edouard Vuillard and Paul Cézanne. Next year she exhibited her 'Petite Marie' at the Salon de la Société des Artistes Français; in 1906 two of her paintings were shown at the Société Nationale des Beaux-Arts. She became a founding member of and exhibited with the Salon des Tuileries.

Back in Adelaide in December, she leased a studio with McPherson and they held a combined show in March 1907. Davidson exhibited regularly with the S.A.S.A., her work including still lifes, portraits and landscapes. In 1908 the National Gallery of South Australia bought her portrait of her friend Gladys Reynell [q.v.11]: typical of her early work, it was informed by Prinet's classical style and reflected contemporary interest in tonal values. Her self-portrait (1909) shows her mass of swept-up, chestnut hair, expressive, brown eyes and her favourite smock; it also reveals her independent spirit, restraint and dignity. A slight woman, who dressed in a rather severe style, she was a good-humoured and stimulating companion.

Davidson returned to Paris in 1910, exhibited annually, and travelled through Europe and Russia. Home again in 1914, she completed the delightful, light-filled 'Mother and Child' which depicts her sister and infant niece seated on their verandah. When World War I began she sailed immediately for Paris. There she joined the French Red Cross Societies and worked as a nurse, eventually running a hospital for the wounded.

After the war Davidson showed her paintings frequently in Paris, winning praise from the critics. She was an associate (1920), member and secretary (1922) of the Société Nationale des Beaux-Arts, and is said to have studied under Rupert Bunny [q.v.7]. In 1930 she became vice-president of La Société Femmes Artistes Modernes; she was also a founding member of the Société Nationale Indépendentes. With her career approaching its zenith, Bessie sent a message to her father: 'I can sell as many pictures as I can paint. I was born under a lucky star . . . never worry about me'. In 1931 she was appointed to the Légion d'honneur. She contributed to L'Exposition du Groupe Feminin at the Petit Palais de la Ville de Paris in 1938. Davidson was later represented in the annual International Exhibition at the Carnegie Institute of Technology, Pittsburgh, and exhibited at St Louis and New York, United States of America, in Edinburgh, and with the International Society of Sculptors, Painters and Gravers, in London and at Venice, Italy.

Like Anne Dangar [q.v.], Davidson remained in France during World War II. Friends sheltered her at Grenoble where she continued to paint. In 1945 she returned to her studio-apartment in the Latin Quarter, Paris, which was her base for the rest of her life. Often she stayed on her farm at Buchy, near Rouen; every year she visited relations in Scotland; and she returned to Adelaide once, in 1950.

Davidson died on 22 February 1965 at Montparnasse and was buried in a cemetery at St Saëns, Normandy. In 1967 an exhibition of her work was held at the Osborne Art Gallery, Adelaide. Her early paintings showed the influence of Margaret Preston; by the 1910s and early 1920s her style broadened to become freer and somewhat Impressionistic; from the 1930s onward her still lifes and interiors were vigorous, modernist compositions characterized by deep and dramatic colouring. Davidson's freely-painted and finely-composed landscapes, ranging from coastal scenes to snow-filled views of mountains and buildings, show her lifelong interest in and ability to capture light and atmosphere. Her work is held by several State galleries and by the Australian National Gallery, Canberra.

Dictionnaire Critique et Documentaire des Peintres, Sculpteurs, Dessinateurs et Graveurs (Paris, 1976); R. Biven, *Some Forgotten, Some Remembered* (Adel, 1976); N. Ioannou, *Ceramics in South Australia 1836-1986* (Adel, 1986); R. Butler, *The Prints of Margaret Preston* (Melb, 1987); S. C. Wilson, *From Shadow into Light* (Adel, 1988); *News* (Adel), 3 Sept 1931; *Advertiser* (Adel), 25 Feb, 1 June 1967; *Financial Review*, 28 Apr 1988; Art Gallery of SA correspondence; Art Gallery Bd of SA, papers.   JANE HYLTON

DAVIDSON, DAVID LOMAS (1893-1952), town planner, was born on 7 July 1893 in Sydney, eldest son of native-born parents George Thom Davidson, police constable, and his wife Florence, née Taunton. Said to have attended Fort Street Model School, David was trained as a draughtsman. At Newtown on 3 June 1912 he married an 18-year-old typist Daisy May Paynter with the forms of the Churches of Christ; they were to have a son and two daughters. Davidson studied in the department of military science at the University of Sydney in 1914. Enlisting in the Australian Naval and Military Expeditionary Force on 11 August, he took part in the campaign in German New Guinea and was a lance sergeant when discharged in Sydney on 4 March 1915. He was to be commissioned in the Militia in 1933 and transferred to the Reserve of Officers in December 1940.

Having served two years in Malaya as a licensed surveyor, Davidson was registered to practise in New South Wales in June 1920 after nine months work under the supervision of H. F. Halloran [q.v.9], his mentor in town planning. An associate member of the American Society of Civil Engineers and of the Royal Sanitary Institute of Great Britain, Davidson was employed in 1920-29 as a surveyor and architect by the Metropolitan Water, Sewerage and Drainage Board. In 1928 he became president of the Town Planning Association of New South Wales and lobbied for improved legislation so that the mistakes made in planning Sydney's growth should not be repeated in smaller towns. On 4 February 1929 the senate of the university chose him to be Vernon [q.v.12] memorial lecturer in town planning (a post previously held by Sir John Sulman [q.v.12]), but Davidson did not take it up, possibly because the faculty of architecture protested against the 'unfortunate appointment'. On 30 July he accepted instead the newly created commissionership for town planning in Western Australia. Matrimonial difficulties may also have encouraged the move; divorced on 2 April 1935, he married a 25-year-old stenographer Esme Mary Powell on 6 July that year in the Church of Christ Chapel, Lake Street, Perth.

He arrived at a time when W. E. Bold [q.v.7] and Harold Boas [q.v.] had given Western Australia's town planning movement considerable momentum, but, due to the Depression and World War II, Davidson had little opportunity of implementing the ideas he had formed in Sydney, though he did design the plan for the township of Walpole (gazetted 1932). He was soon at odds with municipal authorities—especially the Perth City Council—which further impaired his chances of constructive policy-making. His opportunity came in planning for postwar reconstruction. In 1943 he chaired the State government's six man advisory committee on postwar housing. It recommended the erection of 20 000 houses in five years under the system operating for the Workers Homes Board, the improvement of sub-standard housing, and rent subsidies for low-income earners and Aborigines. In a reserved submission Davidson additionally proposed that each new house should have a hot-water system, a refrigerator, and flyproof doors and windows; he urged the establishment of a state housing authority and a co-operative credit scheme similar to that operating in New South Wales.

These enlightened ideas were not followed by postwar performance. Between 1945 and 1951 Davidson and his staff were reportedly working on a master plan for the Perth metropolitan region, yet it did not materialize. Public servants in neighbouring departments found him secretive and choleric, perhaps because of his deteriorating health, and his relations with local authorities remained poor. The Western Australian government continued to support him, fortified by favourable comments from visiting authorities such as Sir Patrick Abercrombie and Professor William (Baron) Holford. Late in 1951 the government legislated for the creation of a Metropolitan Region Planning Authority on which Davidson would play a leading role, and his performance was inconclusively debated in parliament. He never had the chance of responding to this development: he died of hypertension and uraemia on 20 June 1952 at Harrow Hospital, Subiaco, and was cremated; his wife and their son survived him, as did the children of his first marriage. Davidson was remembered as a forceful administrator handicapped by a cranky temperament. Throughout his period in Western Australia he apparently never owned a home.

Report of the State Advisory Committee on Postwar Housing (Perth, 1943); *PD*, 1951-52, p 1084; *SMH*, 4 Aug 1927, 24 July, 27 Nov 1928, 10 Jan, 11 Feb, 18 Apr, 18, 31 July, 1 Aug, 3 Sept 1929, 8 Feb 1932; *West Australian*, 12 Sept, 30 Oct, 10, 14, 16, 18, 31 Dec 1929, 20 July 1936, 21 June 1952; H. Boas, The Evolution of Town Planning in Western Australia (ms, Perth, 1956, BL); Town Planning press-cuttings, 1929-35, *and* Town Planning Assn, Minutes, Apr 1931-Nov 1935, *and* Davidson papers (BL); Univ Syd Archives; personal information. G. C. BOLTON

DAVIDSON, EDWIN JOHN (1899-1958), Anglican bishop and publicist, was born on 12 February 1899 at Goulburn, New South Wales, only son of William Andrew Davidson, a native-born storekeeper, and his wife Edith Amy, née Quartly, from London. Edwin was educated at Petersham Superior Public School, passed the junior public examination in 1914 and joined the State taxation department. Encouraged by Bishop A. W. Pain, in 1916 he entered the divinity hostel at Sale, Victoria. He enlisted in the Australian Imperial Force on 17 May 1917, fought on the Western Front as a gunner in the 13th Field Artillery Brigade and was discharged in Sydney on 15 June 1919.

In 1920 Davidson enrolled at the University of Sydney (B.A., 1924); he played representative Rugby Union football and was president of the Student Christian Movement. After a year at Moore Theological College and as catechist at Erskineville and Picton, he was made deacon on 19 December 1924 and ordained priest by the archbishop of Sydney on 18 December 1925. He served his curacy at St Clement's, Marrickville. At the invitation of Rev. P. T. B. Clayton, founder of

Toc H, he spent 1926-27 in England as a chaplain based at Manchester. Davidson was subsequently Toc H padre for New South Wales (1928-30). He married Doris Evelyn Whatmore on 26 November 1930 at St Thomas's Church, North Sydney. That year he entered the Bathurst diocese where he officiated as curate, canon residentiary of the cathedral (1932), acting-rector of Orange (1934) and rector of Carcoar (1935). In 1936 he became curate to E. H. Lea at St Mark's, Darling Point, Sydney.

His appointment in February 1938 by Archbishop Mowll [q.v.] as the first Australian-born rector of St James's, Sydney, in succession to P. A. Micklem [q.v.10], occasioned a trial of strength between the Anglo-Catholic parishioners and the Evangelical diocese. Davidson's immediate 'simplification' of ritual incited protests from the wardens and worshippers, and culminated in the memorial of fifty clergy to the archbishop in July.

Davidson's eloquence as a preacher, his appreciation of the parish's inner city mission and, above all, his newspaper articles and radio broadcasts, gradually erased memories of the controversy that surrounded his appointment. From early 1942 he wrote frequently for the *Sydney Morning Herald* on such subjects as 'Faith and Freedom' (1942), 'Japan and Justice' (1945), 'Obstacles to Peace' (1946) and 'Why the Down and Outs?' (1947); he also contributed regularly to its 'Religion and Life' series (1946-58). In August 1948 he resigned as chairman of the Australian-Russian Society and in November criticized ministerial censorship of religious broadcasts. An honorary canon (from 1949) of St Andrew's Cathedral, he chaired the Sydney Diocesan Synod's social problem committee, and belonged to the Rotary Club of Sydney, the State executive of the Australian Board of Missions, the editorial board (1952) of the *Anglican* and various experimental theatre groups.

In January 1955 Davidson was elected bishop of Gippsland and was consecrated on 29 June at St Paul's Cathedral, Melbourne. Survived by his wife and two daughters, he died of cancer on 1 April 1958 at Epworth Private Hospital, Richmond, and was cremated. With G. M. Long [q.v.10], E. H. Burgmann and J. S. Moyes [qq.v.], Davidson represented a line of native-born bishops of country sees who led opinion on national and social issues in a way that contemporary, English-born archbishops never matched in Australia.

K. J. Cable, *St James' Church, Sydney* (Syd, 1982); *SMH*, 7 Sept 1928, 3 Nov 1937, 7, 8, 18 Feb, 27 Aug 1938, 15 July, 5 Aug, 29 Nov 1948, 2 Apr 1958; *Anglican*, 11 Apr 1958. RUTH TEALE

DAVIDSON, ELIZABETH; see McMILLAN, ELIZABETH

DAVIDSON, JAMES WIGHTMAN (1915-1973), historian, was born on 1 October 1915 in Wellington, New Zealand, son of George Wightman Davidson, an Australian-born commercial traveller, and his wife Edith Mabel, née Brown, a New Zealander. Educated at Waitaki Boys' High School and Victoria University College (B.A., 1936; M.A., 1938), Jim proceeded to St John's College, University of Cambridge, in 1938 where he was Holland Rose student and Bartle Frere exhibitioner in 1940. His doctoral thesis, 'European penetration of the South Pacific, 1779-1842', was accepted in 1942. During the next two years Davidson worked for the Naval Intelligence Division of the Admiralty, contributing historical sections to the four-volume geographical handbook, *Pacific Islands* (London, 1943-45). Returning to Cambridge as a fellow of St John's in 1944, he was university lecturer in colonial studies from 1947.

He was in Western Samoa in 1949, reporting to the New Zealand government and advising the high chiefs on independence negotiations, when he accepted the foundation chair of Pacific history in the Research School of Pacific Studies at the Australian National University; his tenure began next year. Having assisted in a survey of administration in the Territory of Papua and New Guinea, Davidson settled permanently in Canberra in December 1951. Commitment to political advancement for all Pacific Islanders shaped the rest of his career.

Championing indigenous history, Davidson placed Pacific societies at the centre of the scholarly stage. On accepting the chair, he had cautioned the vice-chancellor (Sir) Douglas Copland [q.v.] against allocating Pacific politics to any other department. 'I could not study the past satisfactorily without an interest in the structure of contemporary society, nor would I feel happy about studying contemporary politics divorced from their historical setting'. By example and precept, he encouraged participants to write history and historians to participate.

Spending much of a decade advising Samoans on constitutional matters, Davidson provoked the vice-chancellor Sir Leslie Melville to regret his frequent absences and the paucity of his publications: 'While he is certainly taking part in the making of history, such activities are perhaps marginal as academic activities of a History Professor'. Davidson's own priorities were clear from his subsequent involvement in drafting constitutions for the Cook Islands (from 1963), Nauru (from 1967), Micronesia (from 1969)

and Papua New Guinea, whose constitutional planning committee he joined shortly before he died of a coronary artery occlusion on 8 April 1973 in Port Moresby. His body was returned to Canberra and cremated.

Davidson was extrovert but enigmatic, gregarious but unmarried. Wealthy, and 'even patrician' in style, he enjoyed literature and music, laughter and informality. He was a social democrat, best remembered for advising Western Samoan *matai* title-holders who restricted the franchise, Nauruans who became idly rich through nitrate royalties and Cook Islanders who accepted incomplete independence from New Zealand. He wrote more words in newspapers than in books, producing only one—the perceptive classic *Samoa mo Samoa* (Melbourne, 1967)—in twenty-three years as professor. Preferring field-work and political action to contemplation, he was nonetheless an effective dean until the school appointed a full-time director. Davidson supported the creation of the *Journal of Pacific History* (1966) and other research tools (which he endowed with his outside earnings), but he had not altered his will since 1947 when he named his old Cambridge college his residual legatee, once his surviving sister's needs had been met.

NZ J of Hist, 7 no 2, 1973, p 211; *J of Pacific Hist*, 8 1973, p 5; *Hist Studies*, 16, no 62, Apr 1974, p 157; archives of Dept of Pacific and Sth East Asian Hist, *and* of Registrar, ANU.

DONALD DENOON

DAVIES, CYRIL WALTER (1889-1971), solicitor, was born on 13 April 1889 at Malvern, Melbourne, son of Walter Davies, solicitor, and his wife Adelaide Frances Emily, née Fox, both Victorian born. Walter was a half-brother of (Sir) John, George, Joseph and (Sir) Matthew Davies [qq.v.4]. Educated at Melbourne Church of England Grammar School and the University of Melbourne (LL.B., 1911), Cyril won a Blue for lacrosse and was admitted as a barrister and solicitor in 1913. Having worked in his father's practice, on 2 March 1914 he joined the Commonwealth Attorney-General's Department as a clerk in the crown solicitor's office. On 18 May 1920 in his school chapel Cyril married Sigrid Elise Margrette (d. 1964), daughter of H. K. Dannevig [q.v.8]; they were to remain childless.

Promoted senior clerk (property) in 1924, Davies represented his office that year at the auction of land-leases in the Federal Capital Territory. In 1925 he transferred to Canberra to open an office of the crown solicitor. His principal duties were to provide legal advice to the Federal Capital Commission, to review and draft ordinances, and to act as registrar of titles. By 1927 he had returned to private practice: through successive partnerships, his firm was to become Davies Bailey & Cater, one of the largest in Canberra. Davies was appointed a notary public in 1929, and lectured part time at Canberra University College in 1931 and 1934. An accomplished legal draftsman, he formulated documents relating to conveyancing, wills and companies which continue to provide useful precedents.

In April 1933 Davies was one of the founders of the Law Society of the Territory for the Seat of Government (Law Society of the Australian Capital Territory). The society was established with the objectives of improving the quality of legislation and facilitating the professional business of solicitors practising in the territory. Davies served as vice-president (1933) and president (1936-64). He was a charter member of the Canberra Rotary Club and acted as honorary solicitor to a number of service organizations, among them the Canberra Returned Soldiers' Club. A foundation member (1954) of the Commonwealth Club, he also belonged to the Canberra Club (president 1953), of which he was made a life member. In the 1950s he deputized at meetings of the A.C.T. Advisory Council.

Davies was a slim, active man who enjoyed tennis, parties and snooker. A doyen of the territory's private legal profession, he loved his work and was devoted to it. After his formal retirement in 1965 he continued as a consultant with his firm for six years. He died on 18 December 1971 in Canberra Hospital and was buried in Canberra cemetery.

H. E. Renfree, *History of the Crown Solicitor's Office* (Canb, 1970); J. Gibbney, *Canberra 1913-1953* (Canb, 1988); *Canb Times*, 21 Dec 1971; Federal Capital Com, *Annual Report*, 1925, 1926; R. J. Linford, History of the Law Society of the A.C.T. (1933-1983) (ts held by Law Soc of ACT, Canb).   R. G. BAILEY

DAVIES, ELLIS HARVEY (1882-1942), engineer and wartime public servant, was born on 26 June 1882 at Warwick, Queensland, eldest child of Australian-born parents Henry Michael Davies, grazier of Rosenthal Creek, and his wife Alice Louise Rubelle, née Skyring. At the age of 14 Ellis was sent to Melbourne where he continued his education at Brighton Grammar School and the Working Men's College; he then served an apprenticeship with Austral Otis Engineering Co. Ltd. As a young man, he was a keen cross-country runner.

In association with Bewick, Moering & Co., Davies travelled to Western Australia to work on the goldfields as a mining engineer. On 4 March 1909 at Christ Church, Claremont, he married Christmas Mildred Ridge with Angli-

can rites; they were to have a son before being divorced in 1923. Returning to Melbourne during World War I, Davies joined the Richmond works of Charles Ruwolt [q.v.11] Pty Ltd: rising to chief engineer, he was responsible for the firm's extensive contracts for the design and supply of machinery to mines throughout Australia, and in New Zealand, Fiji and the mandated Territory of New Guinea. He also designed equipment for the newsprint industry in Tasmania. Davies married 19-year-old Mary Isabel Maclean on 9 April 1923 at Scots Church, Melbourne; they were to have a son and were later divorced.

Complementing his professional standing, Davies became a respected member of the Athenaeum Club and the Austral Temple Masonic Lodge. An element of adventurousness caught public notice when in 1935 he toured a number of mines in Western Australia by motorcar, covering considerable distances and inspecting one of his 'most notable achievements'—a new milling and flotation plant for the Great Boulder goldmine. He then sailed for England and America to visit business connexions of his firm. At the register office, St Marylebone, London, on 4 April 1935 he married 22-year-old Patricia Lilian Allan Officer.

Following the outbreak of war in the Pacific, in early 1942 Davies was mobilized on the staff of the Allied Works Council, and appointed director of mechanical equipment and materials supply. He was responsible for the impressment and census of all earth-moving plant in Australia (a task which involved notifying over 40 000 owners of equipment), for importing additional plant, and for its classification and allocation to the construction of facilities required by the armed services. According to E. G. Theodore [q.v.12], director-general of the A.W.C., Davies displayed 'extraordinary judgement' in these duties. While taking a weekend break, he died of a rupture of the heart on 2 October 1942 at Frankston and was cremated. His wife and their two sons survived him; the sons of his previous marriages had predeceased him. His estate, including the family home at Toorak, was sworn for probate at £10 043. In a tribute to Davies, Essington Lewis [q.v.10], director-general of munitions, praised his 'sterling personal qualities', recalled the respect accorded him by fellow engineers and spoke of a 'tremendous loss' to the nation.

Herald (Melb), 5 Feb 1935, 3 Oct 1942; *Argus* and *SMH*, 5 Oct 1942.   NICHOLAS BROWN

DAVIES, HAROLD WHITRIDGE (1894-1946), professor of physiology, was born on 27 June 1894 in Adelaide, eldest of five children of Edward Harold Davies [q.v.8], musician and music teacher, and his wife Ina Jane, née Deland. Educated at Prince Alfred College, Harold graduated from the University of Adelaide (M.B., B.S., 1917) and on 5 July 1917 was appointed captain, Australian Army Medical Corps, Australian Imperial Force. He served on the Western Front with the 3rd Division. From late 1919 Davies spent three terms as an advanced student at New College, Oxford. He then worked at the Ashurst War Hospital as a research-assistant to J. S. Haldane, a leading respiratory physiologist. Davies's first scientific papers were in this field, which was to be his major research interest throughout the rest of his career.

After his A.I.F. appointment terminated in Adelaide on 12 August 1920, Davies followed Professor J. C. Meakins, with whom he had worked at Oxford, to the University of Edinburgh. As a research-assistant and lecturer, Davies continued to publish papers mainly concerned with the influence of circulatory disturbances on the gaseous exchange of the blood. His monograph with Meakins, *Respiratory Function in Disease* (London), appeared in 1925. He also published with C. G. Lambie [q.v.9] and others on the use of insulin in diabetic patients. Having been appointed a Rockefeller Foundation fellow (for one year) in 1923, Davies worked with C. A. L. Binger at the Hospital of the Rockefeller Institute of Medical Research in New York and was associated with some of the leading respiratory physiologists in the United States of America. In 1926 he moved from Edinburgh to the University of Leeds, England, as lecturer in physiology and pharmacology.

In 1930 Davies was appointed professor of physiology at the University of Sydney. On his arrival he found that the academic staff of the department had remained largely unchanged since World War I. The small amount of research that was being done was generally reported only in Australian journals. Davies arranged for two staff members—H. S. Wardlaw in 1930 and F. S. Cotton [q.v.8] in 1933—to be awarded Rockefeller fellowships to work in the U.S.A.

In 1933 and 1934 Davies made two expeditions to Central Australia to study the possibility that Aborigines living in the hot, arid conditions there could have become especially adapted to water deprivation. The first expedition, with Wardlaw and three students, was to Hermannsburg, 70 miles (113 km) south-west of Alice Springs, Northern Territory. The second, which included T. G. Strehlow [q.v.], was to Mount Liebig, 155 miles (250 km) north-west of Alice Springs. They concluded that there was no significant difference between the Black and the White man's adaptation to water deprivation.

Faced with formidable difficulties in building up the department of physiology, Davies proved unable to sustain his initial impact. When he had come to Sydney the Depression was at its worst and there was little possibility of making new staff appointments. In addition, the department was responsible for teaching both biochemistry and physiology, and from 1935 classes in pharmacology became an added burden. In the face of these difficulties, he began drinking heavily.

Unmarried, 'Pete' Davies was a kind and generous man who was held in affectionate regard by his many friends. He was a competent cellist and a bon viveur. An honorary consultant physiologist at three teaching hospitals, he became a foundation fellow of the Royal Australasian College of Physicians in 1938. That year a complaint from the medical students' society about the teaching of physiology and pharmacology was upheld by an investigatory sub-committee of the university's senate. In consequence, pharmacology was removed from the department of physiology and a separate department of biochemistry was established.

The outbreak of World War II provided Davies with a diversion from the cares of his department. An army reservist from 1920, he was mobilized as lieutenant colonel in June 1941 and commanded the 9th Field Ambulance for seven months; he was bitterly disappointed not to be sent overseas and relinquished his post in January 1942. Reports of his excessive drinking obliged the vice-chancellor to suspend him from duty at the university in May 1946. A committee of senate appointed to inquire into the suspension decided on 24 May to recommend that Davies be informed that the university no longer required his services. He died of a cerebral haemorrhage on 7 June that year, as a result of falling down the stairs in the Imperial Service Club, Barrack Street, Sydney, and was cremated with Anglican rites.

J. A. Young et al (eds), *Centenary Book of the University of Sydney Faculty of Medicine* (Syd, 1984); G. L. McDonald (ed), *Roll of the Royal Australasian College of Physicians*, 1, 1938-75 (Syd, 1988); C. Turney et al, *Australia's First* (Syd, 1991); *Aust J of Science*, 9, no 1, Aug 1946; *SMH*, 21 Aug 1923, 15 Oct 1929, 2 Mar, 22 Dec 1933, 5 Apr 1934, 10 June 1946.   P. O. BISHOP

DAVIES, JOHN GRIFFITHS (1904-1969), agricultural scientist, was born on 10 May 1904 at Aberystwyth, Cardiganshire, Wales, son of William Davies, grocer, and his wife Margaret, née Griffiths. Brought up by an aunt on her farm near Borth, Jack was educated at local county schools and at the

University College of Wales, Aberystwyth (B.Sc., 1924; Ph.D., 1927), where he studied under Professor (Sir) George Stapledon who led the development of grassland improvement in Britain. In 1927 Davies took up an appointment as assistant-agrostologist at the Waite [q.v.6] Agricultural Research Institute, University of Adelaide, under A. E. V. Richardson [q.v.11]. As a somewhat unwilling guest at one of Mrs Richardson's musical events, he met Kathleen Michell Gryst whom he married on 23 December 1929 at St Bede's Anglican Church, Semaphore.

In 1938 Davies moved to Canberra to direct the pasture research section of the division of plant industry, Council for Scientific and Industrial Research (Commonwealth Scientific and Industrial Research Organization from 1949). His study of the poor response of native pastures to superphosphate led to four formative ideas in grassland science: greater scope for improving productivity through the use of exotic species; the role of annual legumes in the accretion of nitrogen to the ecosystem; the need to assess the value of pastures by their effects on the production of the animals which grazed on them; and the importance of statistical controls in experimentation. One noteworthy grazing experiment exposed the false claims made for the benefits of rotational grazing, and a simpler management system was promoted in which paddocks were to be occupied by animals throughout the year, albeit with seasonal variation in their density. Davies showed energy and acumen in establishing pasture research groups in Perth and Brisbane, and at Deniliquin, Armidale and Trangie, New South Wales. By 1950 his section encompassed more than half the staff employed by the division of plant industry.

Following the retirement in 1949 of the divisional chief B. T. Dickson and of Davies's mentor Richardson (who had joined C.S.I.R. in 1938), Davies advocated the establishment of a separate division of pasture research. A review committee recommended strengthening genetics and physiology within the existing division and (Sir) Otto Frankel was appointed chief in 1951. Davies found that Frankel's temperament, scientific emphases and approach differed radically from his own. He fled to Brisbane. There, as associate chief (1952-59) and officer-in-charge of the plant and soils laboratory, he concentrated on the improvement of tropical pastures. The Queensland Department of Agriculture and Stock (later Primary Industries) had already made notable advances in this field, but lacked a critical research base.

Davies's vision led to Queensland becoming a recognized international centre for this disciplinary area, and transformed the nature and productivity of millions of acres of grazing land. The distinguished plant-breeder E. M. Hutton and the legume bacteriologist D. O. Norris left Canberra to join him. This refugee nucleus group promoted a revolution in tropical pasture science. Davies soon gathered a multidisciplinary body of scientists about him. With the support of Sir Ian Clunies Ross [q.v.], in July 1959 a new division of tropical pastures was established in Brisbane, of which Davies was foundation chief. The C.S.I.R.O.'s Cunningham Laboratory was built at the University of Queensland where he trained students in agricultural science.

Appreciating the regional diversity of agricultural problems, Davies recognized that their solution required the integration of field-experiments with laboratory and controlled environment studies. Research centres were set up at Samford and Beerwah in the coastal lowlands of south-east Queensland; in 1962 the Pastoral Research Laboratory, near Townsville, was developed; in 1966 the Narayen Research Station, near Mundubbera, was inaugurated; and research was also undertaken on farming properties. By 1969 the division comprised fifty-three scientists whose research was concentrated in the humid and sub-humid zones.

Shortly after arriving in Queensland, Davies had courageously declared to a large meeting of cattlemen at Rockhampton: 'Your natural pastures are no b--- good!' His proposals focussed essentially on the introduction and improvement of well-adapted pasture legumes from other tropical regions (which fixed nitrogen from the atmosphere, and whose nutritive value was superior to that of the grasses). Of equal importance was the identification of mineral deficiencies and —where feasible—the replacement of native grasses with African grasses more responsive to improved soil fertility. This system was further enhanced by determining the rates of stocking to synchronize pasture availability and animal needs. He eschewed the feed-lot fattening systems in vogue in North America and Europe, and sought the solution to difficulties of feeding in dry months by growing suitable plants in the wet season.

Davies's stature as a scientist derived more from the organization and leadership he gave to research than his publications. Capable of analysing the problems of an agricultural industry in a holistic way, he designed research programmes which benefited industry when adopted. Teams of interacting scientists from different disciplines were able to study the soil-plant-animal complex. They were recruited from agronomy and plant ecology, plant nutrition and physiology, biochemistry, plant-breeding and plant-introduction, legume bacteriology and animal nutrition. He gave special attention to developing a young and promising staff, but did not appoint women. His close association with successive meetings of the International Grassland Congress was strengthened by his membership (1960-64) of its continuing committee. Scientists from overseas were encouraged to visit his division, while his own assignments in tropical countries helped to develop its international status.

At ease with people in all walks of life, Jack Davies was noted for his conviviality: the resources for his work were sometimes derived from his cultivation of community leaders. In his youth he had played hockey and helped to organize the Amateur Sports Association of South Australia. He was short and slightly built, usually charming and confident, but occasionally morose. Fiercely emotional and graphically expressive in defending his friends or a point of view, he could be a teasing devil's advocate, ever determined to extract central conclusions from a discussion. Having once asked a visiting dignitary whether their meeting was formal or informal, and being reassured that it was the latter, Davies removed an uncomfortable upper denture before resuming business.

He was federal president (1951), a medallist (1957) and a fellow (1958) of the Australian Institute of Agricultural Science. The University of New England conferred on him an honorary doctorate of science in 1958; he won the Britannica Australia award in natural and applied science in 1964; and he was appointed C.B.E. in 1967. Survived by his wife and two daughters, Davies died of cardiac infarction on 15 March 1969 in South Brisbane and was cremated.

Aust J of Science, 32, no 2, 1970, p 45; *Tropical Grasslands*, 4, Mar 1970, p 1, *and* for publications; A. G. Eyles, Factors influencing the nature and extent of the research program of the CSIRO Division of Tropical Crops and Pastures (M.Sc. thesis, Griffith Univ, 1979); information from Mrs J. Gibson, Surrey Hills, Melb, Dr L. Gillbank, Univ Melb, Dr C. S. Christian, Forrest, Mr W. Hartley, Deakin, and Dr W. M. Willoughby, Cook, Canb, Dr E. F. Henzell, Corinda, Mr A. G. Eyles, Dr E. M. Hutton and Mr N. H. Shaw, Indooroopilly, Brisb, and Dr R. J. Jones, Townsville, Qld.

L. R. HUMPHREYS

DAVIES, NATALIA (1907-1951), schoolteacher and defence worker, was born on 25 January 1907 at Lampeter, Cardiganshire, Wales, only surviving child of Latimer Morgan Davies, divinity student, and his South Australian-born wife Florence Germain, née Morgan. A precocious reader, Natalia attended St David's College School, Lampeter, and immersed herself in British and military history. Having separated from her husband, in 1919 Florence brought her daughter to South Australia where they spent a year at Warrow, the Morgans' property near Coulta on Eyre Peninsula. Natalia studied privately and learned to ride. Solitary and regarded as odd, she entered Adelaide High School in 1921 and became a probationary teaching student next year. Her mother worked at dressmaking. After Florence died in 1923, Natalia boarded at hostels and took her holidays at Warrow.

She attended Adelaide Teachers' College in 1924-25 and enrolled at the University of Adelaide (B.A., 1930; Dip.Ed., 1940). Slight but erect, with dark eyes and a deep voice, she wore her light-brown hair in an Eton crop and dressed in blazer, collar and tie: fellow students dubbed her the 'Card'. Nat 'hated being a woman'; she retained her boyish hairstyle, always wore tailored clothes, and had a passion for mastering facts and acquiring practical skills.

From 1926 Miss Davies taught at Uraidla Public School until April 1928 when, possibly protecting a pupil, she claimed responsibility for deliberately lit fires at the school. She remained calm while she was arrested, charged with arson and taken into custody. Police confiscated the .22-inch (5.5 mm) calibre revolver she used to practise shooting. Although she was suspended from duty, the director of education W. T. McCoy [q.v.10] offered to provide bail and vouched for her 'unimpeachable' record. Eight weeks later the prosecution entered a *nolle prosequi*. Davies resumed teaching at Pennington Public School. Following her appointment in 1939 to Croydon Central (later Junior Technical) School, she taught only in girls' technical schools, ending her career as senior mistress (1949-51) at Port Adelaide. Ruth Gibson [q.v.] consistently found her to be meticulous and thorough, and noted a mellowing in her brusque, commanding manner.

Davies had been treasurer (1934-37) of the Women Assistants' Association. In February 1937 she drafted and presented a detailed motion to the South Australian Public School Teachers' Union to admit women's associations—with the object of facilitating equal-pay negotiations. When her motion was defeated, female unionists resigned *en masse* and formed the Women Teachers' Guild under Phebe Watson [q.v.12]. Davies was its liaison officer (1938-42), delegate (from 1938) to the National Council of Women and vice-president (1945-49). As the guild's advocate before the Education Salaries Board, she gained substantial pay increases, particularly in 1947.

Foreseeing that Nazism would mean war, in February 1933 Davies had founded the Defence Society. Its initial membership of twelve increased to 130 by the time World War II began. As president, Davies obtained current information from the British Home

Office, and lectured on air-raid and poison-gas precautions. From 1940 she organized and often taught evening classes on first aid, home nursing, motor engineering, elementary electrical work and fire drill. The society's members were predominantly women, without uniform and drawn from all walks of life. Natalia's full-time, voluntary staff officer Amylis Laffer became her close friend. Charging a shilling an hour, the society taught hundreds of women to shoot and maintain a rifle. In 1942, after Japan entered the war, classes extended to pistol shooting, map-reading and unarmed defence. Each night members went on duty at a roof-watching post in the city.

The sole, female, civil-defence area officer in Adelaide, Davies advised the Education Department; military authorities accepted her camouflage designs; and at Keswick Barracks society members made snipers' suits from hessian. In 1940 Davies had been appointed deputy-commandant of the State's Women's Air Training Corps and next year joined the Women's War Service Council. Despite her intensity, women found her an inspiring leader.

After the war Davies wrote historical plays for the Australian Broadcasting Commission's educational programmes. In 1947 she became a national quiz champion on radio. She died of septicaemia on 29 April 1951 at the Willard Guest House, Wakefield Street, Adelaide, and was buried with Anglican rites beside her mother in North Road cemetery. Miss Laffer subsequently endowed the Natalia Davies prize for first-year history at the University of Adelaide.

Port Adel Girls' Technical School Mag, 1951; Women Teachers' Guild (SA), *Guild Chronicle*, June 1947, p 11; *SA Teachers' J*, Feb 1937, p 10; *Advertiser* (Adel), 11 Apr 1928, 29 Aug 1939; *News* (Adel), 11 Apr 1928; *Register* (Adel), 12 Apr 1928; SA Education Dept, Teachers' hist sheets, N. Davies, *and* Director of Education, Correspondence files (SRSA); Univ Adel, Student records, N. Davies, *and* Correspondence files, no 510, 1951-82 (Univ Adel Archives); Davies papers (Mort L); information from Mrs B. G. Griffiths, Coffin Bay, SA.   HELEN JONES

DAVIES, ROBERT IAN (1923-1941), naval officer, was born on 13 November 1923 at Greenwich, Sydney, son of Thomas Robert Davies, a native-born clerk, and his wife Mabel Irene, née Saville, from England. 'A friendly, fresh-faced lad', Bob attended North Sydney Boys' High School. In 1937 he entered the Royal Australian Naval College, Flinders Naval Depot, Westernport, Victoria. He gained colours for athletics and for Rugby Union football, a game in which he also showed 'strong, determined running'. Gradu-

ating near the top of his class in 1940, he was promoted midshipman on 1 January 1941 and sent to England for sea-training. On 8 March he joined the battle cruiser, H.M.S. *Repulse*. Although involved in little action, the ship spent long periods at sea and Davies demonstrated his mettle as an officer of quarters of close-range guns.

In October 1941 the British government decided to deploy a battle fleet to Singapore with the aim of deterring Japan from entering the war on the side of the Axis powers. It was intended that the principal units of the new Eastern Fleet would be *Repulse*, the battle-ship, *Prince of Wales*, and—to provide 'all-important self-contained air cover'—the aircraft-carrier, *Indomitable*. The fleet was not to have *Indomitable*'s services, however, as she ran aground in the West Indies in November. An 'unbalanced token force' of two capital ships and their escort of destroyers arrived at Singapore on 2 December.

On 8 December the Japanese landed troops in Malaya and Thailand. That afternoon *Prince of Wales*, *Repulse* and four destroyers sailed, as Force Z, to intercept enemy transports and their escorts at Singora, Thailand, which was thought to be the main invasion point. Because the Royal Air Force could not provide cover at Singora, Force Z's only hope was to make a surprise attack and withdraw. Next day Japanese aircraft were seen shadowing the force. The operation was abandoned and the ships altered course for Singapore. At dawn on the 10th they approached the Malayan coast at Kuantan to investigate a report of a new landing. The information proved to be false and they turned east, steaming towards the Anambas Islands. About 10 a.m. Japanese aircraft were sighted.

Force Z could have had air support on 10 December 1941. Yet Admiral Sir Tom Phillips, the commander-in-chief, did not request it. His reasons for not doing so are unknown. He died that day. Shortly after 11 a.m. high-level bombers attacked, causing minor damage to *Repulse*. Twenty minutes later a formation of torpedo-bombers appeared. *Repulse* evaded the torpedoes, but *Prince of Wales* was hit and stricken. Although a second assault by conventional bombers proved as ineffectual as the first, two more waves of torpedo-bombers destroyed both ships. Struck five times, *Repulse* rolled over and sank at 12.33 p.m. Davies's shipmates last saw him 'firing an Oerlikon gun at enemy aircraft when he and the gun mounting were slowly submerging'. He was posthumously mentioned in dispatches.

F. B. Eldridge, *A History of the Royal Australian Naval College* (Melb, 1949); G. H. Gill, *Royal Australian Navy 1939-1942* (Canb, 1957); D. Gillison,

Royal Australian Air Force 1939-1942 (Canb, 1962); M. Middlebrook and P. Mahoney, *Battleship* (Lond, 1977); *Roy Aust Naval College Mag,* Dec 1940, Dec 1943; information from Hist Collection Officer, H.M.A.S. *Creswell,* Jervis Bay, ACT, and Mr W. T. Sykes, Moruya, NSW.

DARRYL BENNET

DAVIES, STELLA MARGUERITE (1885?-1965), hospital almoner, was born probably in 1885 at Ashfield, Sydney, eldest of three children of Henry Roberts Davies, post office clerk, and his first wife Annie Elizabeth (d. 1889), née Walkley, both Sydneysiders. Stella was educated at Sydney Girls' High School. Her father had remarried in 1890; after his death in 1910, she lived with her half-sister Violet at Neutral Bay. By 1925 Stella was a social worker and two years later was secretary of the Sydney Day Nursery Association, which she represented in July 1928 at a meeting convened by the National Council of Women to establish a course in social work in Sydney.

Invited in 1930 by (Sir) Robert Wade [q.v.12] to set up the almoners' department at the Royal Alexandra Hospital for Children, next year Davies received the certificate of the Board of Social Study and Training of New South Wales (founded in 1929). In January 1932 she arrived in London to undertake further training at St Thomas's Hospital and on 8 February 1933 received the certificate of the Institute of Hospital Almoners. One of the first qualified medical social workers practising in Sydney, she belonged to the small, pioneering coterie of English-trained almoners who were to influence hospital social work for the next two decades. In the 1930s Davies and Katharine Ogilvie, who assisted in training students, criticized the quality of the course offered by the B.S.S.T. and agitated for local, specialist, medical training for almoners. Their objective was realized with the founding of the New South Wales Institute of Hospital Almoners in 1937; Davies was a member (1937-42) of its executive-committee.

Patients at R.A.H.C. had increased from 480 in Davies's first year to 2378 in 1940, but by 1947 its almoners' department had difficulty in attracting and retaining staff. Davies had a formidable reputation as 'the world's rudest and worst tempered woman'. Nonetheless, although she was suspicious of newer methods of 'non directive' social work imported from North America, she earned the respect and even the affection of her clients, and of many of her colleagues. Practising through the wretched years of the Depression and the family disruption of World War II, she identified systematic child-abuse well before it was acknowledged in research literature, and dealt with it in an authoritarian manner, having no compunction in notifying the police and placing vulnerable children in care. Nancy Keesing, a fledgling social worker, heard her snap: 'Almost any child is better off alive than dead. Almost any parent is better off free than serving a sentence for murder'. Keesing concluded that, 'First and last she was a realist'. Davies remained in charge at R.A.H.C. until she retired in 1950.

To Keesing, Stella Davies appeared 'little and frail and [generally] gently spoken', with faded, blue eyes; she wore her 'dusty-half-grey brown hair in a very sparse bun and wisps of it flew around her head. She had a sweet smile that was pathetic because so uncertain'. Familiar with the back streets of Sydney, Miss Davies drove from her Cremorne home in an old Morris, 'confidently, competently and slowly, yet dreadfully' because she ignored other road-users. She died on 16 October 1965 in hospital at Mosman and was cremated with Anglican rites.

R. J. Lawrence, *Professional Social Work in Australia* (Canb, 1965); D. G. Hamilton, *Hand in Hand* (Syd, 1979); N. Keesing, *Riding the Elephant* (Canb, 1988); Bd of Social Study and Training, NSW, *Annual Report,* 1927-28; N. Parker, Address to NSW Branch of Aust Assn of Social Workers, Fiftieth Annual General Meeting, Syd, 1982 (ms held by author).

ELSPETH BROWNE

DAVIES, WILLIAM (1895-1966), professor of chemistry, was born on 2 February 1895 at Prestwich, Lancashire, England, son of Joe Senior Davies, a cotton-goods salesman, and his wife Clara, née Sheard. After attending the Standard Grammar School, Whitefield, William entered the Victoria University of Manchester (B.Sc., 1917; M.Sc., 1918; D.Sc., 1929) where he studied under Professor Arthur Lapworth, a pioneer of mechanistic organic chemistry. During World War I Davies investigated the chemistry of mustard gas and nitrophenyl hydrazine. In 1918 he moved to Lincoln College, Oxford (D.Phil., 1921), as a Ramsay research fellow. There he was associated with W. H. Perkin junior and developed an enduring interest in heterocyclic chemistry.

In 1924 Davies was appointed lecturer at the University of Melbourne. From the outset, he realized that a strong research base was essential for the growth of organic chemistry, and spent some £2000 on chemicals and apparatus. He cherished an Oxford tradition that laboratory research took priority over teaching duties. Dissatisfied with the still-inadequate laboratory conditions and with the syllabus (no organic chemistry was taught to first-year students), he investigated other possible posts while overseas in 1928, but returned to Melbourne to concentrate on his own research and training his research students. He was promoted to associate-professor in 1935. With his team he investigated the properties of sulphonyl fluorides. In the late 1930s, when his interest turned to biochemical development, he studied vitamin chemistry, particularly the vitamin A content of Australian fish, work for which he won the Grimwade [q.v.9] prize.

Davies had an idiosyncratic, exasperating, but endearing lecturing style, and was forthright and totally undevious in his views. A resident tutor at Queen's College until 1936, he married Lucy Gardner on 10 March that year at the Methodist Church, Middle Park. In World War II Davies's major work was on drug synthesis and toxic gas production. He was a member (from 1942) of a sub-committee of the Chemical Defence Board.

In 1953 Davies became the university's first professor of organic chemistry. As well as furthering his research in heterocyclic chemistry, he branched out into the area of carcinogenic compounds. From the late 1950s he and his associates investigated possible links between high temperatures in cooking processes and the production of small amounts of cancer-causing agents. Following his retirement in 1961, he was appointed a senior fellow of the Anti-Cancer Council.

Beyond the university, Bill Davies was a strong supporter of the chemical profession and an active participant in the organic chemistry group of the Royal Australian Chemical Institute. He was a keen fly-fisher and gardener, and was widely read. His later years were saddened by the deaths of his wife and their two daughters, but he was able to recover from these blows and worked in the laboratory almost until his death on 20 October 1966 at Malvern. He was buried in Brighton cemetery. His estate, sworn for probate at $67 313, included a bequest to the Methodist Ladies' College for a literature prize named in honour of his daughter Dorothy Clare Davies.

J. Radford, *A History of the Chemistry Department of the University of Melbourne* (Melb, 1978); *Univ Melb Gazette*, Dec 1966; *Herald* (Melb), 20 Oct 1954; *Age* (Melb), 10 Aug 1962.

Q. N. PORTER

DAVIS, HERBERT NELSON (1899-1963), organist, choirmaster and conductor, was born on 21 April 1899 at Coburg, Melbourne, sixth child of native-born parents William Bulmer Davis, tailor, and his wife Letitia Ellen, née Calder. Educated at St Paul's Cathedral School, Melbourne,

Herbert received his early choir training under Ernest Wood, and studied piano with Harold Smith, and organ with Claude Kingston at the Collins Street Baptist Church. Davis's first appointment as organist was in 1918 at the Presbyterian Church, Richmond. In 1923 he moved to the Australian Church, Russell Street, then to Wesley Church (1924-25), to the Independent Church, Collins Street (1925-30), and finally in 1930 to the adjacent Scots Church where he and the choir recorded *Beloved Hymns of the Presbyterian Church*. As a church musician he was noted for his innovative approach to repertoire and for the high standard of his choirs.

During the 1920s Davis also moved to the forefront in the wider musical community until, in 1939, the *Herald* wrote that he 'bids fair to rival Sir James Barrett [q.v.7] as champion holder of presidencies and other leaderships around town'. Davis was president of the Musical Society of Victoria (1935-63) and of the Society of Organists (Victoria), vice-president of the St Paul's Cathedral Old Choir Boys' Association, and an active member of the Choral Association of Victoria, the Victorian Music Teachers' Association and the National Theatre movement. He was a popular organ recitalist, accompanist, examiner and adjudicator, as well as a conductor of amateur operatic productions.

Davis's principal secular sphere of influence as a conductor was that of the suburban choral societies. Founder and conductor (1925-54) of the Malvern Choral Society, he was involved with choral societies at Mentone, Mitcham and Box Hill, and with the Australian Boys' Choir, the Orpheon Choristers and the Presbyterian Oratorio Choir, many of which appeared together at the spectacular massed-choir performances of sacred oratorios presented from the mid-1930s to the early 1950s.

In 1933-59 Davis conducted the Zelman [q.v.12] Memorial Symphony Orchestra. The link thus established between his choirs and a stable, if amateur, orchestral group led to performances of a large repertoire of sacred oratorios and the introduction to Australia of major choral works by such English composers as Ralph Vaughan Williams, Gustav Holst and Sir Hubert Parry. Between 1928 and 1959 Davis gave forty performances of Handel's *Messiah*. His special feeling for the music of Handel was further reflected in his concerts with the strings of the Z.M.S.O. and in his organ recitals. In 1937 Davis was appointed organ and piano teacher at the Melbourne (from 1956 Melba [q.v.10] Memorial) Conservatorium of Music, Albert Street, where he subsequently served as director (1955-63). On Christmas Day 1947 he married Lorna Beatrice Mauger at St Giles's Presbyterian Church, Murrumbeena.

Davis was a major figure in Melbourne's musical life: 'If it was music, Herbert was in it'. He was held in affection for his humour, compassion, ideals and selflessness. It is said that he was 'devastated' when driven out of Scots Church by intrigue in 1960. Later that year he suffered a sudden illness, but continued his teaching and other activities. He died of coronary vascular disease on 17 July 1963 at Burwood and was cremated. His wife survived him; they had no children. The M.S.V. established three scholarships that bear his name.

S. Nemet, *History of the Musical Society of Victoria, 1861-1981* (Melb, nd, c1981); D. Fairweather, *Your Friend Alberto Zelman* (Melb, 1984); L. Marsi, *Index to the Australian Musical News 1911-1963* (Melb, 1990); *Herald* (Melb), 28 Oct 1937, 27 June 1939; *Age*, 18 July 1963; Malvern Choral Soc papers (LaTL); Musical Soc of Vic papers (LaTL *and* Performing Arts Museum, Vic Arts Centre, Melb); National Theatre Movement papers (Performing Arts Museum); Zelman Memorial Symphony Orchestra papers (Grainger Museum, Univ Melb).   KAY DREYFUS

DAVIS, LESLIE DAVID (1885-1973), businessman and philanthropist, was born on 10 October 1885 in Sydney, son of native-born parents George Henry Davis, general manager of S. Hoffnung [q.v.4] & Co. Ltd, import merchants, and his wife Katie Victoria Eugenie Lydia, née Davis. Leaving Sydney Grammar School at the age of 16, Leslie was employed by Hoffnungs as a junior on five shillings a week and pursued his interest in cabinet-making at night-school. He worked as a country traveller, then as a warehouse-manager in Sydney. On 5 June 1912 he married Daisy Victoria Goldstein in the Great Synagogue.

Elevated to the company's Australian board in 1917, Davis soon joined the London board. In 1936 he became managing director and chairman of the Australian board. Against the opposition of a majority of the directors in London, Davis advocated diversification into local manufacturing to counteract high protectionist tariffs: he achieved limited success in the production of gramophones, custom-moulded plastics and flexible packaging. He was chairman of Tallerman & Co. Pty Ltd (from 1929), Commonwealth Moulding Co. Pty Ltd (from 1935) and the wholesale grocers Davis & Penney Pty Ltd (from 1937).

Having served on several wartime committees established by the Curtin [q.v.] government, in 1959 Davis was nominated to the Consultative Committee on Import Policy by his acquaintance Prime Minister (Sir) Robert Menzies [q.v.]. At the recommendation of the State Labor government, next year Davis was appointed O.B.E. Although

politically conservative, in letters to Sydney newspapers he had often criticized policies of the United Australia Party and Liberal governments, especially in relation to fiscal impositions and the size of the Federal bureaucracy. He was a member of Lloyd's, London, and president (1955-57) of the Sydney Chamber of Commerce. In the mid-1960s he persuaded the London board to enter the retail hardware business in Australia and chaired Hoffnung's subsidiary companies, among them B.B.C. Hardware Pty Ltd (following the acquisition of Benjamins Building Centre at Chatswood which provided the initials).

A founding member of the liberal synagogue, Temple Emanuel, Davis was a director (1937-71) and vice-president (1957-65) of Sydney Hospital, and active on the board of the Royal Alexandra Hospital for Children. After serving as joint-chairman (1960-63) of the Hospital Contribution Fund of New South Wales, he chaired (until 1970) the Medical Benefits Fund of Australia. He generously supported the Civilian Maimed and Limbless Association.

Devoted to his wife and their two sons, 'L.D.D.' (as he was widely known) played bowls and tennis; he was fond of contract bridge, on which he wrote a pamphlet in the 1940s. He usually spent his lunchtimes over dominoes at the Millions (later Sydney) Club; he also belonged to the University and American National clubs. His gardening activities are commemorated in the variety of dahlia, *Finchley*, named after his Woollahra home. Survived by his wife and sons, he died on 15 July 1973 at Woollahra and was cremated. Sydney Hospital's audiology unit (opened 1963) bears his name.

SMH, 5 July, 6 Aug 1953, 31 Dec 1960, 9 Nov 1962; family papers held by Mr G. Davis, Mosman, Syd; information from Mr G. Davis, and Mr A. Davis, Lond.   JOHN PERKINS

DAVIS, NORMA LOCHLENAH (1905-1945), poet, was born on 10 April 1905 at Glenore, Tasmania, second of three daughters of Samuel Davis, farmer, and his wife Alice Laura, née Plane, both Tasmanian born. Norma attended the state school at nearby Whitemore, but, like Helen Power [q.v.11] who grew up in the same district, gained much of her education from her own reading. With loving scrutiny she came to know the bush and farmland surrounding her home and was to write not only of birds, trees and flowers, commonly accepted as beautiful, but also of bats, insects, snakes and the scaly surface of rocks, rough with 'flaxen moss . . . as harsh as jute'.

About 1914 Davis moved with her parents and younger sister to Glenarvon in the township of Perth. There, only 14 miles (23 km) from her birthplace, she continued to explore the countryside, for which she possessed a spiritual affinity. While recuperating after falling from a tree, she began to write to occupy her time. Living quietly with her family at Glenarvon, she played the piano, painted in water-colour, and contributed nature poems to the *Australian Woman's Mirror* and the *Bulletin*. She used such pseudonyms as 'Glenarvon' and 'Malda Norris'.

It was only in the early 1940s, shortly before her death, that Miss Davis concentrated fully on writing. In 1943 Angus & Robertson [qq.v.7,11] Ltd published *Earth Cry*, her collection of sixty-one poems. Most reviewers, including Douglas Stewart, were enthusiastic, though A. D. Hope was to publish a corrosive critique in 1945. Other poems by Davis appeared in *Meanjin Papers* and the South Australian periodical, *Poetry*; Flexmore Hudson, editor of the *Jindyworobak Anthology* (1943), singled out her contribution, 'Awakening', for special commendation. The public response, expressed in a flow of admiring letters, was equally warm. Davis's nature poetry went beyond precise, imaginative descriptions of places and animals. Her work, agreeable and competently crafted, was filled with hints of love betrayed and images of creatures lost, mocked and destroyed: it reflected the qualities both of the land she knew and her own seemingly placid life, darkened by pain and isolation.

Although she was suffering from cancer, Davis went on to complete *I, The Thief* (Melbourne, 1944), an extended dramatic monologue describing the release of Barabbas and Christ's crucifixion through the eyes of the felon who was nailed to the cross at Jesus's right hand. She produced a poem of private religious experience which, despite its Victorian mannerisms, was a moving representation of physical agony and ultimate, mystical vision. Davis died on 5 November 1945 at Glenarvon and was cremated; according to her request, her ashes were scattered in the bush near her home.

D. Stewart, *The Flesh and the Spirit* (Syd, 1948); M. Giordano and D. Norman, *Tasmanian Literary Landmarks* (Hob, 1984); L. Hergenhan (ed), *The Penguin New Literary History of Australia* (Melb, 1988); *Southerly*, 5, no 4, 1944, p 58; *Poetry*, 15, 1945, p 31; *Bulletin*, 10 May 1944; *Examiner* (Launc), 6 Nov 1945.   MARGARET SCOTT

DAVISON, ALEXANDER NICHOLAS (1923-1965), racing motorist, was born on 12 February 1923 at Moonee Ponds, Melbourne, only child of Victorian-born parents Alexander Ambrose Davison, manufacturer, and his wife Elizabeth, née Nolan. Educated at Xavier College, Kew, in 1941 Lex captained the athletics team, rowed stroke, played in the first XVIII, and was heavyweight boxing champion and vice-captain of the school.

In December that year Davison was called up for Militia service. The family company, Paragon Shoes Pty Ltd, was a major supplier to the armed forces. Because of his father's ill health, Lex was discharged on 10 August 1942 to assist in the business. When his father died in September 1945, Lex assumed control of the firm and inherited his father's fine collection of motorcars. On 2 October 1946 at St Peter's Catholic Church, Toorak, he married Diana Margery Crick, a dental nurse.

Three days later Davison began his formal motor-racing career in the New South Wales Grand Prix at Bathurst, but his Alfa Romeo proved uncompetitive. In 1947 he returned there for the Australian Grand Prix with a huge, supercharged Mercedes Benz 38/250: he recorded the fastest time and was placed third on handicap. Soon acknowledged as one of Australia's leading drivers, he competed successfully in races, hill climbs and reliability trials.

During the 1950s Davison's business interests prospered and included Monte Carlo Motors (a General Motors Holden [q.v.9] dealership), Killara Park (an Aberdeen Angus stud and dairy at Lilydale), as well as Paragon Shoes and an associated tannery. The profits enabled him to pursue a busy racing programme throughout Australia and overseas, using some of the best equipment available. He won the Australian Grand Prix in 1954 (driving a Jaguar), 1957, 1958 (both in Ferraris) and 1961 (in a Cooper-Climax), the Australian Hill Climb championship in 1955, 1956 and 1957, and the Victorian Trophy in 1955, 1957 and 1963. In 1957 the Confederation of Australian Motor Sport awarded him the gold star as champion Australian racing driver. He assisted Donald Campbell in his land-speed record attempt in 1964 at Lake Eyre, South Australia, driving *Bluebird* at more than 160 miles (257 km) per hour on the dry saltpan.

Over six feet (182.9 cm) tall, prematurely balding, with broad shoulders and an athletic build, Davison was generous, cheerful and friendly—totally unspoiled by money and fame. He showed a keen interest in spearfishing and water-skiing, and was a competent clarinet player. A natural leader with a gift for words and conversation, he was a founder of the Victorian division of the Vintage Sports Car Club of Australia, president (1956-59) of the Light Car Club of Australia, and a member of the Melbourne Swimming Club and of the founding council of the Museum of Modern Art, Melbourne.

On 20 February 1965 at the Sandown Park circuit near Springvale, while driving his 2.5 litre Brabham Climax in practice for the International 100, Davison suffered a heart attack. The car, travelling at over l00 m.p.h., left the road, hit a culvert, somersaulted and crashed through a railing fence. Davison sustained severe head injuries and was dead when officials reached him. Survived by his wife, five sons and two daughters, he was buried in Box Hill cemetery. His estate was sworn for probate at £234 686. Gay Dutton's portrait of Davison is held by the author.

Aust Motor Sport, Mar 1953, p 20, Apr 1953, p 16, Apr 1965, p 34; *People* (Syd), 30 June 1954, p 35; *Wheels*, July 1954, p 18; *Cars*, May 1956, p 14; *Sports Car World*, Jan 1962, p 40, Aug 1964, p 16, Apr 1965, p 12; *Aust Autosportsman*, Mar 1965, p 25; *Racing Car News*, Mar 1965, p 28; *Herald* (Melb), 20, 23 Feb 1965, 29 Apr 1967.

JOHN B. BLANDEN

DAVISON, FRANK DALBY (1893-1970), writer, was born on 23 June 1893 at Hawthorn, Melbourne, and registered as Frederick Douglas, eldest child of Victorian-born parents FREDERICK DAVISON (1868-1942), printer, and his wife Amelia, née Watterson. Frederick senior was raised at Sandhurst (Bendigo) where he was apprenticed to a printer. In 1890 he opened a printing business in Melbourne and subsequently joined the Australian Natives' Association whose journal, *Advance Australia*, he edited and published in 1897-99. He was a dynamic and opinionated 'Progressive' with a fervent belief in the White Australia policy, the British Empire, national development and private enterprise. During the 1920s he set up as a real-estate agent in Sydney and published two short-lived magazines in which he championed 'men, money and markets' and expounded his militantly entrepreneurial ideology. In the 1930s he published several didactic novels.

Frederick junior grew up at Gardenvale, Melbourne, and attended Caulfield State School, but left in 1905 to work as a farm labourer. In 1909 his father took the family to the United States of America where young Frederick was apprenticed to a Chicago printer and published the ephemeral broadsheet, *Roo Thuds*. He served in a Caribbean cargo ship in 1914—and was to publish a reminiscence as *Caribbean Interlude* (Sydney, 1936)—then went to New York shortly after the outbreak of World War I. Travelling via Canada to England, Davison enlisted as a trooper in the 2nd Dragoon Guards. He served on the Western Front from October 1915. Commissioned on 25 September 1918, he transferred to the Hertfordshire Regiment before returning to England in April 1919. While doing his initial training at Aldershot, he had met Agnes (later known as 'Kitty' or 'Kay') Ede whom he married on 7 August 1915 at the register office, Farnham, Surrey.

In May 1919 Davison brought Kitty and their son and daughter to Australia where he took up a selection on a soldier-settlement subdivision near Injune, Queensland. The selection failed disastrously, and in 1923 a penniless Davison moved to Sydney. He joined his father's real-estate business (though he later set up on his own) and became advertising manager for Frederick's latest venture in magazine publishing, the *Australian*. In 1920-21, while labouring on his selection, Davison had written a number of poems, sketches and short stories for the *Australian Post*. He now produced a torrent of such material, most of it to illustrate and promote his father's views.

The Depression destroyed his real-estate business and forced him towards writing as a means of survival. He recovered two sets of related stories he had written for the *Australian*, revised them, and in 1931 published them as two novels—*Man-Shy* and *Forever Morning*—which he bound in wallpaper and hawked from door to door. Next year *Man-Shy* won the Australian Literature Society's gold medal for the best novel of 1931. Its literary success encouraged Davison to consider himself a professional writer and to think that he might make a living by his pen. He took the forenames Frank Dalby and produced a mass of short stories, plays and a novel, little of which was published or survives. The only significant work from this period was *The Wells Of Beersheba*, a short 'prose epic' commissioned by Angus & Robertson [qq.v.7,11] for Christmas 1933. In the early 1930s Davison was extremely poor, working at several casual jobs and accepting the dole until finally achieving precarious security as a regular reviewer for the *Bulletin*.

A decisive change in Davison's life and outlook began in 1934. Desperate for cash, he planned to write a conventional travel book and made a trip to Queensland with an amateur naturalist. Instead of scenic beauties, he discovered soil erosion, deforestation and man-made ugliness, and realized that the sort of entrepreneurship he had championed in the 1920s was ruining Australia's environment. He suffered a nervous breakdown when he returned to Sydney. His book, *Blue Coast Caravan* (1935), was a scathing critique of national development policies. Davison worked successfully at short stories after this catharsis, but never recovered his complacency and continued to regard his society with increasingly critical eyes. His first mature short story, 'The Wasteland' (1935), and his next important published work, *Children of the Dark People* (1936), were explicitly conservationist replies to the scenes he had criticized in *Blue Coast Caravan*.

Davison's 'political awakening' (as he referred to it) was further advanced by his concern with authoritarian trends in Australia and the spread of fascism abroad. Active in the increasingly left-wing Fellowship of Australian Writers since the Egon Kisch affair and president in 1936-37, he formed a close working relationship with Marjorie Barnard and Flora Eldershaw [q.v.] whose 'salon' became a forum in which debates about politics and literature could be thrashed out. They worked together to turn the F.A.W. into a trade union of professional writers and to ensure that it adopted progressive positions on political questions. Within literary circles the three were known as 'the triumvirate'. Davison himself took strong public stands on numerous issues, especially literary and political censorship, the integrity of Australian literature, the policy of appeasement and local threats to civil liberties. For his services to literature he was appointed M.B.E. in 1938. The most striking fruit of this phase was his anti-fascist pamphlet, *While Freedom Lives*, which he wrote that year in order to clarify his political ideas as a prelude to writing a working-class play in the agitprop genre. The play did not eventuate, but his concern with democratic values was patent in many of the short stories collected in his next publication, *The Woman at the Mill* (1940), a volume which contains some of his finest work.

From the mid-1930s Davison's marriage had been breaking up. He had brief affairs with a number of women in Sydney's social and literary circles, and a more enduring, though secret, liaison with Marjorie Barnard. World War II brought them particularly close. Both became pacifists, largely through fear that war would occasion an authoritarian crackdown which would destroy civil liberties. Davison's short story, 'Fathers and Sons', dramatizes some of the issues then at stake. Although he was never a communist, he found himself closely aligned with the Communist Party of Australia—particularly when it was banned (1940-42) under wartime emergency powers—and made several public appearances in defence of its right to operate legally. With the successive entry of Russia and Japan into the war, Davison's pacifism softened, but he refused to seek work as a war correspondent or as a publicist for the war effort.

Earning a living remained a problem. In 1939-40 Davison was awarded a Commonwealth Literary Fund fellowship. He found work as a clerk at the Commonwealth Aircraft Factory, Mascot, and next as a journalist in the publications section of the Department of Labour and National Service, a position which removed him to Melbourne in 1943. A year earlier he had met Edna Marie McNab; they decided that they wanted to live together; once the divorce from Kay was secured, they were married on 8 December 1944 at the district registrar's office, Paddington, Sydney. By this time Davison was living in Melbourne and hard at work on his next book, *Dusty* (1946), which won first prize in the *Argus* competition for novels. At one level the story of a half-kelpie, half-dingo sheepdog which becomes in turn a champion worker, a killer and a wild dog, *Dusty* has also been read as a meditation on many of the political issues which animated Davison in the early 1940s, among them his fascination with the rebel and his ambivalent attitude towards the promised new social order following victory over fascism.

Davison continued to work for the Department of Labour and National Service. With their savings and the proceeds of the *Argus* prize, he and Marie bought a 61-acre (24.7 ha) farm at Arthur's Creek which they named Folding Hills and on which they worked at weekends. In 1951 Frank resigned from the department so that they could move there and make a living from mixed farming. He had written a rural column in the *Argus* for a few months in 1950, and in 1964 revised a number of his short stories for a new collection, *The Road to Yesterday*. Most of his creative energy, however, was reserved for a book which he had been trying to write since the late 1930s: a study of human relationships, particularly sexual behaviour, among the generation he had known in Sydney between the wars, and of the harmful effects which repression and guilt could have on sexual and emotional desires. The work grew far beyond the length of anything Davison had previously written, and was eventually completed in 1967 and published as *The White Thorntree* (1968). It drew widely divergent assessments from critics and the novel's status remains controversial.

In 1960 John Hetherington described Davison as having grey hair fringing a high-domed, bald head, a clipped moustache, a strong voice, and eyes which, behind his glasses, were still bright and young. Despite failing health, he retained a mental alertness that was evident in the lengthy interviews conducted by Owen Webster for the Australian Broadcasting Commission in 1969. Davison died on 24 May 1970 at Greensborough, Melbourne; a lifelong atheist, he was cremated after a secular funeral. His wife, and the two children of his first marriage, survived him.

A man of broad tolerance, Davison mistrusted authority and particularly despised that which perverted or blocked natural human tendencies. In his writings he sought to tell the truth as he saw it, to reveal the Australian situation and to promote liberal, democratic values. He saw literature as a means by which people might be helped to know themselves and their society as a necessary prelude to reform. If any symbol sums up his life and character, it is his beloved dingo: an animal which can snap viciously when threatened, but which can also be playful and loving.

J. A. Hetherington, *Forty-two Faces* (Melb, 1962); H. Dow, *Frank Dalby Davison* (Melb, 1971); O. Webster, *The Outward Journey* (Canb, 1978); L. E. Rorabacher, *Frank Dalby Davison* (Boston, US, 1979); *Meanjin Q*, 27, no 3, 1968; R. Darby, While Freedom Lives: Political Preoccupations in the Writing of Marjorie Barnard and Frank Dalby Davison, 1935-1947 (Ph.D. thesis, Univ NSW, 1989); Angus & Robertson *and* Fellowship of Aust Writers papers (ML); Davison *and* Palmer *and* Owen Webster papers (NL); information from Mrs M. Davison, Folding Hills, Vic, Mr P. Davison, Neutral Bay, Syd, and Mrs D. Price, Campbelltown, NSW.   ROBERT DARBY

DAWES, ALLAN WESLEY (1900-1969), journalist, was born on 22 June 1900 at Camberwell, Melbourne, youngest of five sons of native-born parents Robert Wesley Dawes, printer, and his wife Rosina, née Fletcher. Allan was educated at state schools and at Scotch College, Hawthorn, where he edited the *Scotch Collegian*, won the J. D. Burns and Alexander Morrison [q.v.5] prizes, and at the 1917 Leaving examinations gained honours in English and French. He was to be one of an editorial committee of seven which produced (1927) a celebratory history of the school. Matriculating at the University of Melbourne, Dawes was awarded the W. T. Mollison [q.v.2] scholarship for the study of Japanese, but did not graduate. On 23 June 1921 he married Hazel Tasma Ward (d. 1925) at St John's Anglican Church, Camberwell. At St Patrick's Cathedral, Melbourne, on 9 April 1928 he married with Catholic rites Agnes Mary McPhail.

Having begun his journalistic career at the *Age* in 1918, the 'restless genius' later worked for the *Argus*, the Sydney *Sun* and the Melbourne *Star*. Employed by the Commonwealth government, Dawes visited the mandated Territory of New Guinea in 1928 and 1929 to compile an official handbook: it was not completed, but his information provided the basis for the detailed volume published in 1937. When the *Star* closed in 1936, he joined the Sydney *Daily Telegraph* and its talented team put together by the new owner (Sir)

Frank Packer and editor Sydney Deamer [qq.v.]. Dawes wrote on a variety of topics, from crime to international affairs. He was one of the early journalists to cover Australian politics from Canberra and he travelled to Rabaul, New Britain, to write on the 1937 volcanic eruption. From 1938 he was a public-relations officer for the government, lasting just 'a few days' as spokesman for W. M. Hughes [q.v.9]. In 1941 Dawes returned to Melbourne as a special writer on the *Herald*.

Best known as a war correspondent, he wrote for the *Herald* from Darwin and often from 'somewhere in New Guinea'. He flew in air-raids over Rabaul and Wewak, went north with Americans towards Tambu Bay, and was with the Australian infantry during the advance on Salamaua and the assaults on Lae and Finschhafen. Later he reported from Netherlands New Guinea and Morotai, and saw conditions in Malaya and Java after the Japanese surrendered. Dawes deliberately played down conflict between the Australian Imperial Force and the Militia, and between Australian and American troops; he emphasized that the loyalty of New Guineans was a result of benign Australian policies; and he propagated digger characteristics that Australians wanted to read about—shop-assistants and stockmen transformed into tough, independent soldiers, 'lean and hard and muscular'. Moreover, he fostered the Australians' belief in themselves as jungle fighters, men in loose, 'faded, sweaty, mud-stained green', with Owen guns slung. And, he laughed at himself: 'I was the last war correspondent to enter Lae ...'. His focus on individuals, together with his vital prose, breadth of reference, wit and literary tricks made him an excellent writer for afternoon newspapers, but when sustained over *Soldier Superb* (Sydney, 1944), illustrated by (Sir) Russell Drysdale, his writing is contrived and jingoistic.

In 1944 Dawes was selected by John Curtin [q.v.] as one of three press delegates to visit Canada at that country's invitation. Don Whitington [q.v.] saw him as 'a born thespian and an enthusiastic drinker ... an enormous attraction in the faded war correspondent's uniform he wore throughout the tour'. In the postwar years Dawes wrote a column, 'It strikes me', for the *Herald*, then worked free-lance and as public-relations officer for the Royal Agricultural Society of Victoria. In 1948 he helped to organize the Liberal Party of Australia's press office.

Slender and effervescent when young, Dawes was about 17 stone (108 kg) by the time he was 40—'witty and weighty'. He quoted and wrote poetry and irreverent verses, published short stories and had the co-operation of (Sir) Robert Menzies [q.v.] to write his biography. Dawes, however, was drinking heavily and unable to meet deadlines. Admired as a journalist, he did not produce the lasting work that his facility with language might have allowed. He died of cerebral thrombosis on 7 September 1969 at Northcote and was buried in Fawkner cemetery; his wife and their two sons survived him.

History of Scotch College, Melbourne, 1851-1925 (Melb, 1926); *Official Handbook of the Territory of New Guinea* (Canb, 1937); C. Edwards, *The Editor Regrets* (Melb, 1972); D. Whitington, *Strive to be Fair* (Canb, 1977); *SMH*, 25, 27 Mar 1941, 8, 12 Sept 1969; *Age* (Melb) and *Sun News-Pictorial*, 8 Sept 1969.   H. N. NELSON

DAWES, EDGAR ROWLAND (1902-1973), trade unionist, politician and broadcasting commissioner, was born on 28 November 1902 at Stepney, Adelaide, son of George Dawes, carpenter, and his wife Gertrude Ellen, née Lockett, a shop-assistant. Known in his boyhood as Tom, he attended East Adelaide Public and Norwood High schools before being apprenticed to A. W. Dobbie & Co. Ltd, engineers. He gave his occupation as millwright on 28 August 1926 when he married a shop-assistant Adeline Melba Hurcombe with Congregational forms in the Stow [q.v.2] Memorial Church, Adelaide. In 1927, while employed at the Islington railway workshops, he became secretary of the South Australian branch of the Australasian Society of Engineers. He also attended classes at the Workers' Educational Association and served two years as its president.

In April 1930 the Australian Labor Party won government in South Australia and Edgar Dawes was returned for the seat of Sturt to the House of Assembly. Although seen by the visiting Sir Otto Niemeyer as 'a nervous youth, crammed with undigested economics', Dawes developed into a 'big, vigorous man' with a 'strong platform style'. After the labour movement split over the Premiers' Plan and L. L. Hill [q.v.9] and his cabinet were expelled from the A.L.P. in August 1931, Dawes led the official parliamentary party until the 1933 election at which he lost his seat. He unsuccessfully contested the Senate in 1934 and the House of Representatives seat of Adelaide in 1940. President (1937) of the State branch of the A.L.P., he had long been active in its industrial wing as secretary of the Metal Trades Council of South Australia, president of the United Trades and Labor Council and as an industrial advocate.

In 1941 Dawes resigned as secretary of the A.S.E. to concentrate on war-work. A member (1940-45) of the South Australian board of area management, Department of Munitions, he was controller of gun ammunition and ordnance production, and chief technical officer.

In December 1944 Dawes was appointed to the post which was to be his great love: vice-chairman of the Australian Broadcasting Commission. His pre-war association with the A.B.C. dated from 1932 when he had spoken on wireless about politics and international affairs; in addition, he had been a member of the South Australian talks advisory committee. His connexion with the A.L.P. was rewarded by the Curtin [q.v.] government which placed him on the commission, but he was reappointed by later Liberal-Country Party governments and spent a record twenty-two years as vice-chairman.

For sixteen of those years he was deputy to the chairman (Sir) Richard Boyer [q.v.]. While absorbing much of his chief's idealistic outlook, Dawes brought a practical approach to the partnership. A 'shrewd and practised negotiator' in industrial affairs, he was 'confident, down-to-earth, and painstaking . . . a good foil for Boyer'. In 1956, when Boyer was considering an appointment overseas, they discussed the chairmanship. Dawes hoped to be chairman for a short term, but knew that he was not acceptable to many of the people with whom Boyer dealt. Acting-chairman after Boyer died in 1961, Dawes was disappointed not to succeed him, though he continued happily under (Sir) James Darling. Both were removed in 1967, to their chagrin.

A board-member (1933-72) of the Royal Adelaide Hospital, Dawes was a commissioner (from 1938) of its charitable funds (chairman from 1967); he served, as well, on the board of the Queen Elizabeth Hospital, Woodville. He was a councillor (from 1940) of the Institute of Medical and Veterinary Science. In 1965 he joined the board of governors of the Adelaide Festival of Arts and from 1970 chaired its executive-committee. Between 1951 and 1955 he had been a council-member of the Australian National University, Canberra. In 1963 he was a delegate to the United Nations conference on the application of sciences and technology, held at Geneva, Switzerland.

Dawes had numerous business interests. From the 1950s he was managing director of the South Australian engineering firm, Charles Richardson & Sons Ltd; he was also chairman or director of various other companies. His property, Coonalpyn Downs, was managed by his son. Dawes was appointed C.M.G. in 1958.

In 1965 he suffered a heart attack. That year his wife died. On 3 March 1966 he married a 42-year-old secretary Patricia Margaret Henderson with Catholic rites in the Good Shepherd Church, Clearview,

Adelaide. Survived by her, and by the son and daughter of his first marriage, Dawes died of cerebrovascular disease on 4 August 1973 at Royal Adelaide Hospital and was cremated. His estate was sworn for probate at $96 784. The E. R. Dawes research fellowship at R.A.H. commemorates him.

J. E. Hughes, *A History of the Royal Adelaide Hospital* (Adel, 1982); K. S. Inglis, *This is the ABC* (Melb, 1983); *Hist Studies*, 20, no 79, Oct 1982; *Herald* (Melb), 21 Nov 1961; *News* (Adel), 16 Dec 1965; *Advertiser* (Adel), 30 June 1967, 6 Aug 1973; E. R. Dawes oral hist transcript (ABC Radio Archives, Syd).   JAN BRAZIER

DAWN, GLORIA (1929-1978), entertainer, was born on 26 February 1929 in Port Melbourne and baptized Gloria Dawn, only child of William Edward Evans, a Melbourne-born theatrical artist, and his wife Zilla Emma Edith, née Odling (d. 1993), who was born in Bangkok. Gloria travelled with her parents, itinerant vaudeville performers known as Billy 'Andross' and Zilla 'Weatherly', and began her stage career in infancy. By the age of 13 she had progressed from doing Shirley Temple imitations at picture theatres to taking soubrette roles. Before performing at night, she attended the local convent by day wherever the family happened to be working. Her theatrical training was gained through experience. A brilliant mimic with a retentive memory, she mastered pantomime, vaudeville, cabaret, revue, musical comedy and drama, but she would never, in her words, work 'blue or nude'.

On 15 January 1947 at the Presbyterian Church, Indooroopilly, Brisbane, Gloria married Francis (Frank) Patrick Cleary, a variety artist. Their three children lived with them in a caravan through years of travel. When the family settled into a modest house at Rosebery, Sydney, in the mid-1960s, it was Gloria's first permanent home. She later moved to Darling Point. Although she separated from Frank about 1970 after the birth of their fourth child in 1969, she valued family traditions and never sought a divorce.

In the 1950s Gloria Dawn had endeared herself to a wide audience as the golden-haired *ingénue* in Sorlie's [q.v.12] travelling tent-show. She played the lead in the pantomime, *Goody Two Shoes* (1957-58), and in the musical comedies, *Once upon a Mattress* (Melbourne, 1959) for Garnet Carroll [q.v.] and Albert Arlen's version of C. J. Dennis's [q.v.8] poem, *The Sentimental Bloke* (1962). Dawn consolidated her position as 'Australia's First Lady of Revue' in popular satirical shows at the Phillip Theatre, Sydney, notably *A Cup Of Tea, A Bex and A Good Lie Down* (1965). From revue and pantomime Gloria had

learned timing and command of the audience. Although diminutive, 'five foot nothing' (152.4 cm), she had a powerful voice, 'vitality, toughness and singleminded professionalism'. In her first serious role, as Oola in Peter Kenna's *The Slaughter of St. Teresa's Day*, she was voted the best actress of 1972 by the Sydney Theatre Critics' Circle. Her performances next year in Bertolt Brecht's *Mother Courage* for the Melbourne Theatre Company and in Kenna's *A Hard God* were acclaimed. She also appeared in two films, *They're a Weird Mob* (1966) and *The Mango Tree* (1977).

Considerate and unassuming off stage, Gloria took up her knitting in spare moments during a production. She was the model for the businesslike and motherly Doris in Kenna's *Furtive Love*. At the height of her stage success she was happy to appear at a club and in a television advertisement. Treatment for cancer obliged her to forfeit the demanding role of Rose in the musical, *Gypsy* (1975), and to abandon her show at the Music Loft, Manly (1977). Once the nature of her illness became generally known, fellow actors held a benefit night which raised $8000. Survived by her two sons and two daughters, she died on 2 April 1978 in King George V Memorial Hospital, Camperdown, and was buried with Catholic rites in Botany cemetery.

ABC, *Women in Question*, television documentary series (Syd, 1978); K. Brisbane, *Entertaining Australia* (Syd, 1991); *Listener In-TV*, 21-27 July 1972; *Australian Women's Weekly*, 5 Mar 1975; *Theatre* (Syd, Melb), July 1977, May 1978; *Australian*, 28 Oct 1972, 10 Oct 1975, 6 Apr 1978; *Herald* (Melb), 20 May 1974, 1 May 1975; *Sunday Telegraph* (Syd), 12 Jan 1977; H. de Berg, Gloria Dawn (taped interview, 18 Mar 1977, NL).

SUSAN HOGAN

DAWS, CHARLES KINGSTON (1903-1980), Methodist minister, was born on 29 October 1903 at Llanelly, Victoria, second son of native-born parents Thomas Daws, miner, and his wife Emily Agnes, née Gansberg. Educated at Eaglehawk State School, Charles won a scholarship to the Bendigo School of Mines, but transferred to the Bendigo Business College. There he studied accountancy while working as a clerk and subsequently as accountant at a local grocery store.

Following a conversion experience on 24 May 1924 at Charlton, Daws became Sunday School superintendent and trust-secretary at the Methodist Church, Eaglehawk West, where he married Edith Isabel Dunstan on 15 May 1926. He was accepted as a candidate for the Methodist ministry in 1928, sent to Foster that year and ordained in 1933. In turn, he was appointed to circuits at Belgrave (1929), Diamond Creek (1931), Pyramid Hill (1934) and Wycheproof (1938).

Appointed chaplain in the Militia in November 1939, Daws transferred to the Australian Imperial Force on 14 January 1941. He was posted to 9th Division headquarters and served in the Middle East in 1941-42 before returning to Australia as deputy-assistant chaplain-general (Methodist), III Corps. In 1944-45 he was assistant chaplain-general (Protestant), New Guinea Force, then deputy-assistant chaplain-general (Protestant), Northern Territory Force. Transferred to the Reserve of Officers in March 1945, he succeeded T. C. Rentoul [q.v.11] in the part-time post of chaplain-general (Methodist) on 30 January 1946. His immediate task was to resettle chaplains in the civilian ministry. He visited Australian troops in Japan (1947), Korea (1951) and Malaya (1958), and was a staunch advocate of character guidance and training in moral leadership. Retiring on 1 July 1963, he was appointed C.B.E. in 1966.

Concurrent with his service as chaplain-general, Daws had held important positions in the Church in Victoria. As superintendent (1945-52) of the North Melbourne Christian Community Centre, he inherited an innovative attempt to make the Church more accessible by establishing outlets for its mission in shop-front premises. After two years (1952-54) at Moonee Ponds, Daws was appointed managing secretary of the Methodist Church in Victoria, responsible for the direction of finance and property. He was president (1957) of the Victoria and Tasmania Conference, and president-general (1969-72) of the Methodist Church of Australasia. In 1966-72 he served on the joint-constitution committee for the formation of the Uniting Church in Australia.

A wartime colleague described Daws as one who 'earned the reputation among combatant officers and other ranks with whom he served as having the qualities of a statesman and the strength to be firm'. This reputation was sustained as he assumed increasing responsibilities within the army and the Church, but he was sometimes displeasing to those who held different opinions or who sought favours from him. He made good use of his accounting qualifications (F.A.S.A., F.I.C.S.) and his experience in business, enabling the Methodist Church on 22 June 1977 to unite with Congregationalists and Presbyterians with its house in sound order.

Daws was an exceedingly busy, yet orderly man. With neat handwriting, cryptic to the point of illegibility, he was in the habit of personally typing many letters which flowed with advice, admonition and friendly discourse. He aimed to clear his desk by the end of each day.

As a preacher he was practical and forceful. He had confidence in the orderly processes of the Church and its ability to be effective in the world.

Well built, open featured, with a bearing and composure consistent with his long military association, Daws encouraged conversation and friendship, though he was occasionally formidable. In his youth he aspired to be a professional cyclist; his later pursuits included fishing and gardening, and an unswerving loyalty to the players of the Collingwood Football Club. In 1974 he became a supernumerary minister. Survived by his wife, son and two of his three daughters, he died on 28 December 1980 at Blackburn and was cremated.

Methodist Church of A'sia, *Minutes of Vic and Tas Conference*, 1928, 1957, and *Minutes of General Conference*, 1963, 1972; *Herald* (Melb), 12 Feb 1946, 2 Feb, 16 May 1947; *Age* (Melb), 1 Mar 1955, 28 Feb 1957; *Spectator* (Melb), 27 Feb 1957; *Church and Nation*, 28 Jan 1981; information from Uniting Church in Aust, Synod of Vic Archives, Melb, *and* from Mrs H. O'Rourke, Blackburn, Melb, and Mrs V. Blacker, Hastings, Vic.

AUBREY QUICK

DAWSON, CLAUDE CHARLES (1902-1945), journalist, was born on 7 January 1902 at Geelong, Victoria, only child of Thomas Charles Dawson, gardener, and his wife Emma Mary, née Sceney, both native-born. Known as 'Dick', he was schooled locally. He completed theological training at the Churches of Christ College of the Bible, Glen Iris, but, rather than becoming a pastor, enrolled at the University of Melbourne (B.A., 1927) where he studied philosophy. Joining the literary staff of the *Argus*, he was later its Federal political roundsman. On 1 June 1929 at the Church of Christ, North Melbourne, he married a schoolteacher Elizabeth May Woodbridge.

In the early 1930s Dawson was a regular preacher at the Church of Christ, Swanston Street. Approached by Joseph Lyons [q.v.10], he moved to Canberra in 1938 to take up the post of Commonwealth publicity officer (prime minister's press secretary). He worked closely with Lyons, who relied heavily on him for speeches, and was present when Lyons died on 7 April 1939 in Sydney. Dawson was then appointed press secretary to (Sir) Robert Menzies [q.v.]. In August 1941 Dawson succeeded C. E. Sayers [q.v.] as editor in the Department of Information, which had been established to influence public opinion during World War II. He had the sensitive task of disseminating material that was authoritative and factual, yet consistent with the requirements of official propaganda.

Following the outbreak of war in the Pacific in December 1941, the Australian government increased its efforts to publicize the country's contribution to the allied cause, especially in the United States of America and Britain. At H. V. Evatt's [q.v.] request, in 1943 Dawson reported on the operation of the Australian News and Information Bureau in New York. On Dawson's return, Prime Minister John Curtin [q.v.] asked him to open a similar office in London; in December the minister for information A. A. Calwell [q.v.] announced the appointment. The London bureau aimed to be 'an organised centre of reference on Australian problems, and a distributing house for Australian official statements, photographs and films', with the intention of making 'Australia and Australians better known to people overseas'.

Dawson and his wife arrived in London in early 1944. While he ran the bureau, she lectured on the Australian war effort. A brilliant writer and speaker, Dawson had not accepted a permanent appointment in the public service. His passion was writing, and he wanted to earn his living as an independent political journalist whose work would be syndicated to various newspapers. In building up the Australian information service, he was an effective consolidator, more at home with the British approach than the American.

Contracting a severe cold which complicated an existing kidney condition, Dawson died of acute pyelonephritis on 16 October 1945 in North Western Hospital, Hampstead. He was survived by his wife and two sons, one of whom (Sir) Daryl was appointed a justice of the High Court of Australia in 1982.

SMH, 16 Sept 1938, 28 Aug, 17 Oct 1941, 27 July, 18 Dec 1943, 18 Oct 1945, 9 Oct 1946; *Argus*, 18 Oct 1945; *Canb Times*, 19 Oct 1945; information from Mrs E. Dawson, Deakin, Canb.

R. E. NORTHEY

DAWSON, DOROTHY; *see* BRUNTON

DAWSON, GERALD MACADAM (1905–1979), carpenter and trade union leader, was born on 15 July 1905 in South Brisbane, fifth child of Cress Dawson, a labourer from New Zealand, and his Queensland-born wife Annie Maria, née Ott. Cress was secretary of the Brisbane branch of the Waterside Workers' Federation. Gerry was educated locally at St Laurence's (Christian Brothers') College. He entered the Ipswich Road workshop, Department of Public Works, as an apprentice and remained there as a tradesman. In 1924 he joined the Amalgamated Society of Carpenters and Joiners, of which he was elected shop delegate. At the Vulture Street

Congregational Church, South Brisbane, on 18 February 1928 he married 19-year-old Gladys Pokarier, a waitress. Unemployed for almost four years during the Depression, with a wife and child to support, he was to be conditioned by the experience for the remainder of his life.

An active member of the Dutton Park branch of the Australian Labor Party, Dawson was a well-informed and widely-read debater. He was a delegate to the South Brisbane electorate's executive-committee and in 1932 was campaign director when V. C. Gair [q.v.] won the seat in the Legislative Assembly. From 1942 until 1969 Dawson was his union's State secretary; he was also secretary of the Queensland Building Trades Group and edited the *Building Workers' Journal* for more than twenty-one years. He was able to weld the union's numerous provincial city branches into an effective, State-wide organization. The relationships that he developed with smaller unions, such as the plasterers, bricklayers and painters, led to later amalgamations. Following the formation of the Building Workers' Industrial Union in 1945, he was its State secretary and later federal president (1955–68).

At a time of steadily growing support for communism in the Queensland trade union movement, Dawson had joined the Communist Party of Australia in 1940. His union subsequently withdrew its affiliation from the A.L.P. Due to his strategic position, he was elected to the Queensland committee of the C.P.A., but his role was essentially industrial. He was a union delegate (1935–71) to and vice-president (1943–48) of the Trades and Labor Council of Queensland. In July 1948 he succeeded H. J. Harvey [q.v.] as president, and for nine years worked alongside the energetic communist secretaries Michael Healy and Alex Macdonald [q.v.]. In this period Dawson developed into an uncompromising negotiator and outstanding advocate in the State Industrial Court; he was especially concerned with basic-wage and safety issues, and campaigned for the provision of public housing.

The T.L.C.Q. played an unprecedented role in the railway strike of 1948 and in the pastoral industry strike of 1956. By then the reduced power of the C.P.A. encouraged an attempt to broaden the leadership of the trade union movement in Queensland and to preserve Macdonald's position as secretary of the T.L.C.Q. In July 1957 (Sir) John Egerton was elected president of the T.L.C.Q., but Dawson remained as an executive-member and was a delegate to the powerful interstate executive of the Australian Council of Trade Unions; he also continued to act as chairman of the basic wage committee and as the council's advocate.

From the mid-1960s he suffered so severely from Parkinson's disease that he was barely able to complete his term as union secretary. Survived by his two sons and two daughters, he died on 18 May 1979 at Annerley and was cremated. Dawson was a sincere and honest representative of working people: his personal prestige allowed him to pursue an independent line in the trade union movement and enabled him to steer the T.L.C.Q. through some of its most difficult times.

Building Workers' J(Brisb), 1942-69; *Qld Guardian*, 1943-54, 1960-66; *Telegraph* (Brisb), 18 May 1979; *Courier-Mail*, 19 May 1979; TLCQ, Minutes, 1935-79 (Fryer L, Univ Qld). MANFRED CROSS

DAWSON, WILLIAM SIEGFRIED (1891-1975), psychiatrist, was born on 27 April 1891 at Skipton, Yorkshire, England, son of William Harbutt Dawson, newspaper editor, and his wife Anna Clara Augusta, née Gruetz. Will was educated at Skipton Grammar School (1898-1903), Sedbergh School (1903-06), Dulwich College (1906-10) and Trinity College, Oxford (B.A., 1914; M.B., B.Ch., 1916; M.A., 1918; M.D., 1923). Commissioned lieutenant in the Royal Army Medical Corps Special Reserve on 20 May 1914, he served in East Africa and Egypt in 1916-19 and was promoted captain in January 1917; he contracted filariasis, which left him with a permanent gross oedema in his leg.

Returning to England, Dawson became a physician at St Thomas's Hospital, London. In 1920 he joined the mental hospitals service of London County Council. Next year he obtained his diploma of psychological medicine from the Royal colleges of Physicians and Surgeons, and was appointed senior assistant at Maudsley Hospital and lecturer in psychiatry at the University of London. He gained a reputation as one of England's most promising psychiatrists and was awarded the Gaskell gold medal, a bronze medal and prizes of the Royal Medico-Psychological Association. In 1925 he was a Rockefeller fellow and worked with Adolf Meyer at the Johns Hopkins Hospital, United States of America. While there, he developed continuing interests in medical education, delinquency, child guidance, and the links between psychiatry and social work. He wrote a widely respected textbook, *Aids to Psychiatry* (London, 1924), which ran to eight editions.

Dawson married Gladys Lyle Paton with Church of England rites at St Matthew's Church, Denmark Hill, Lambeth, on 29 January 1927; they were to remain childless. Appointed professor of psychiatry at the University of Sydney, he took up his post in March for a seven-year term. As well as teaching, he was honorary adviser (from 1928) to the Australian Institute of Industrial Psychology; he was also consultant to the psychiatric clinics at Broughton Hall and Royal Prince Alfred Hospital, under the control of the Department of Public Health. In 1934 Dawson was unable to reach agreement with the university over his right to private clinical practice. Against the wishes of the government, the university advertised a lectureship to which Dawson was appointed in 1935; he was then allowed to pursue private practice. The university eventually agreed to allow the professor to treat referred patients as part of his consulting practice and in 1937 he was appointed to the chair for a further seven years. He was re-appointed in 1944 and retired in 1951.

Elected a fellow of the Royal College of Physicians, London, in 1933, Dawson was a foundation fellow (1938) of the Royal Australasian College of Physicians. In 1946 he was elected inaugural president of the Australasian Association of Psychiatrists and in 1964 was made honorary fellow of the Royal Australian and New Zealand College of Psychiatrists.

A captain (from 1940) in the Reserve of Officers, Australian Army Medical Corps, on 25 August 1941 Dawson was appointed lieutenant colonel and consultant psychiatrist in the Australian Imperial Force. He embarked for the Middle East in September and served as medical psychiatrist at A.I.F. Headquarters. His leg proved debilitating and he returned to Sydney where he transferred to the Reserve of Officers on 7 July 1942.

Six ft 2 ins (188 cm) tall, with blue-grey eyes and dark hair, Dawson was regarded by his colleagues as shy and retiring. Others found that, in his later years as professor, the bright, dynamic psychiatrist had become cynical and disillusioned with his work. After Gladys died, in 1964 he returned to England and lived with his sister at Oxford. He died there on 13 March 1975.

Aust and NZ J of Psychiatry, 9, 1975; *MJA*, 24 Jan 1976, p 98; Univ Syd Archives; information from the late Prof W. M. O'Neil. STEPHEN GARTON

DAY, ARCHIBALD JOHN SHEPERDSON (1901-1975), organist and music teacher, was born on 10 November 1901 at Red Hill, Brisbane, son of John William Day, a bootmaker from England, and his Welsh-born wife Annie, née Lewis. Educated at Ithaca Primary School, in 1919 Archie won a travelling scholarship to Trinity College of Music, London, where he qualified as a fellow in 1923 with piano and organ as his principal studies. While in London he gave two piano recitals at Steinway Hall and was an accompanist for recitals in the city and the provinces. He returned to

Brisbane that year and, for the next decade, was to perform in concerts at Albert Hall, both as accompanist and as a duo-pianist (with Percy Brier [q.v.7] or Jack Ellis).

In 1923 Day was appointed church organist and choirmaster at the Ann Street Presbyterian Church. He moved in 1933 to the Albert Street Methodist Church and remained organist there for the rest of his life. On 6 February 1942 he enlisted in the Militia and was posted to the 8th Motor Ambulance Convoy; he transferred to the Australian Imperial Force in July. He served at headquarters, Queensland Lines of Communication Area, as a lance sergeant, and from August 1944 was attached to the Army Education Service.

Discharged on 6 September 1945, he resumed his career as church organist, and as a teacher of piano and organ; he also examined for the Australian Music Examinations Board. Following George Sampson's [q.v.11] death, in 1950 Day was appointed city organist, a part-time position which required him to play in the Brisbane City Hall at official functions and to give public recitals. As a member of the Brisbane City Council's advisory committee, he was largely responsible for establishing civic concerts and recitals at city hall, designed primarily to encourage young musicians. An excellent organist, Day was renowned for his ability to extemporize. His thirty-minute, Sunday-evening recitals before the service at Albert Street Church were notable in the city's musical life, as were his recitals in the 'Organists of Australia' series for the Australian Broadcasting Commission. The University of Queensland holds the manuscript of *Carillon,* his only extant composition for organ; in addition, he wrote choral settings for three psalms for the Albert Street choir. In 1974 he was appointed M.B.E.

Quick-witted, and extremely perceptive as a musician, Day was capable of conducting a conversation with a visitor while simultaneously correcting errors in an organ student's playing. Besides collecting fine furniture and china, he had a passion for owning and driving 'sporty' cars, including a Daimler coupé in the late 1950s. He enjoyed fishing and playing tennis, and watching Test cricket matches and tennis tournaments. Although he never married, he was fond of children and related easily to young people. Lean and fit, with a head of thick, grey hair, he was distinguished in appearance and in manner. He died of coronary atherosclerosis on 25 February 1975 at Paddington, Brisbane, while waiting for a bus, and was cremated with Methodist forms.

P. Brier, *One Hundred Years and more of Music* (Brisb, 1971); *Queenslander,* 3 Jan 1920, 29 July 1922; *Sunday Mail,* 26 Sept 1976; family papers and photographs (held by Mrs G. Kynaston, Ascot, Brisb); information from Rev G. Nash, and Mr J. Stehbens, Brisb.   GORDON D. SPEARRITT

DEACON, JAMES HUNT (1901-1968), numismatist, was born on 9 February 1901 at Charlton, near Woolwich, London, son of James Thomas Deacon, journeyman carpenter, and his wife Eliza, née Hunt. The family migrated to South Australia in 1912. Educated at Westbourne Park Public and Unley High schools, in 1918 young Jim applied for and was appointed assistant to the keeper of coins in the art department of the Public Library, Museum and Art Gallery of South Australia, Adelaide. Two factors influenced his decision. His only brother, a coin collector, had been killed in World War I, and Jim had no left arm below the elbow which limited his choice of a career. Although he never used an artificial limb, he cycled, played tennis and became a rover scout.

At a time when the institution was rapidly developing, Deacon was art gallery assistant (1925-32), working with H. B. S. Van Raalte and L. A. A. Wilkie [qq.v.12]. Deacon accessioned, classified and catalogued prints, did clerical work and answered inquiries about coins. In 1932, when he was promoted keeper, there were 26 248 coins in the collection, reputedly the largest in the Southern Hemisphere. He began a project to illustrate the 'Evolution of Coinage'. The catalogues needed updating and detailed research was required; the coin-room was overcrowded and poorly lit; and there was a shortage of display cabinets and fittings. From 1938 he was also keeper of the gallery's historical section, responsible for displays, pictures and relics of the State's past. In 1940 the National Gallery of South Australia became an independent, semi-statutory body. Despite his knowledge of ancient history in relation to coins, his honesty and his hard work, Deacon's position was never reclassified.

On 19 January 1932 at St George's Anglican Church, Magill, Deacon had married a schoolteacher Dulcie Fay Benger; they were to have two children. Although their home boasted no luxuries, they were a devoted family. A foundation member (1926) and thrice president (1929-30, 1950-51 and 1958-59) of the Numismatic Society of South Australia, Deacon edited its journal in 1951-65. He was also a fellow of the Royal Numismatic societies of London (1948) and New Zealand (1961), and the first district secretary in Australia for the American Numismatic Association. A frequent contributor to these and similar societies, he published *The 'Ingots' and 'Assay Office Pieces' of South Australia* (Melbourne, 1954) and, with K. J. Irons,

Catalogue of the Australian Commonwealth Coinage (Adelaide, 1961).

Slightly built, lantern jawed and bespectacled, Deacon wore his hair brushed back and smoked a well-matured pipe. He provided a service for those who were fascinated by medals, tokens, coins and notes—a fascination fostered by soldiers bringing back foreign money from two world wars and by the advent of decimal currency on 14 February 1966, the year of his retirement. He was never interested in the commercial value or the grading of coins, and he did not overly care for modern currency. Towards the end of his career he devoted much time to his hobby, genealogy, and drew up a 66-ft (20 m) family tree. Known to be hypertensive, he died of a coronary occlusion on 18 July 1968 and was cremated; his wife, son and daughter survived him.

Bd of Governors of Public L, Museum and Art Gallery of SA, *Annual Report*, 1917-18, 1924-25, 1931-32, 1935-36; National Gallery of SA, *Annual Report*, 1940, 1949, 1966-69; *Aust Numismatic J*, Oct 1959, July/Sept 1968; National Gallery of SA, *Bulletin*, 24, no 3, Jan 1963; information from Mrs D. Pope, Hawthorn, Mr R. Appleyard, Brighton, Adel, and Mr M. Keain, Norton Summit, SA.

JOYCE GIBBERD

DEAKIN, VERA; *see* WHITE

DEAMER, SYDNEY HAROLD (1891-1962), newspaper editor, was born on 1 December 1891 at Avondale Square, off the Old Kent Road, London, son of Rhoda Deamer. After Rhoda emigrated to North America, Syd was brought up by an aunt and educated at the British School, Hitchin, Hertfordshire. Having worked briefly as a provincial journalist, he emigrated to Australia in 1912 and spent the next two years in the far north-west of Western Australia, as a railway navvy at Marble Bar, and butcher, storekeeper and gold prospector at Bamboo Creek.

Enlisting in the Australian Imperial Force on 26 October 1914, Deamer served at Gallipoli and in Egypt. From August 1916 he was attached to the A.I.F. War Chest Club in London. He married Martha Clara Jones on 30 September 1916 at the parish church, Bishopwearmouth, Durham. On completing pilot training, he was commissioned in the Australian Flying Corps on 2 May 1918 and served in France with No. 3 Squadron from September. Lieutenant Deamer was shot in the calf while flying an R.E.8 artillery spotter over German lines near Bellicourt on 29 September. In January 1919 he returned to Australia with his wife; his appointment terminated in Sydney on 24 April.

A small, assertive man with limited formal education but considerable intellect and pungent wit, Deamer became one of Australia's most prominent and mobile journalists, equally at home in the reporters' room, board-room and bar-room. Following a year on the new *Smith's Weekly*, he moved successively to the Sydney *Sun*, Melbourne *Sun News-Pictorial* and Melbourne *Herald*. In 1926 he was elected general president of the Australian Journalists' Association, but three years later his employer (Sir) Keith Murdoch [q.v.10] lured him away from the union and into the editor's chair of the moribund Adelaide *Register*. Deamer revived it sufficiently to scare Advertiser Newspapers Ltd into selling a controlling interest to the Herald and Weekly Times Ltd, though not sufficiently for the *Register News-Pictorial* to survive. With its closure in 1931, Deamer was put in charge of the Melbourne *Herald* and fought off a threat posed by the *Star*, a rival afternoon newspaper.

He spent some months in London in 1935 with the new cable service, Australian Associated Press Pty Ltd, then went to Sydney next year as editor of the resurgent *Telegraph* which had been acquired by Consolidated Press Ltd, a company controlled by the young (Sir) Frank Packer [q.v.]. Under a new masthead, the *Daily Telegraph* became a brighter and more profitable broadsheet. Deamer got on well with his talented and often hard-drinking journalists, one of whom described him as 'a scintillating, Bohemian type of man, possibly too much so [but] a fine editor nonetheless'. Deamer's relations with Packer were less harmonious: during the 1936 abdication crisis in Britain he tartly corrected his proprietor's dinner-table reference to 'morgantic marriage'—'Morganatic, old dear, morganatic!'

Deamer resigned in 1939 to edit the new *A.B.C. Weekly* for four years. He was an accredited war correspondent and, as controller of public relations for the Australian Broadcasting Commission, gave evidence of political interference to the Parliamentary Standing Committee on Broadcasting in 1944. Packer welcomed him back as associate-editor (1944-46) of the *Daily Telegraph* and a director of Consolidated Press.

Moving to the *Sydney Morning Herald*, from 1947 to 1961 Deamer was founding editor of 'Column 8', a daily, front-page feature of miscellaneous paragraphs under a symbolic drawing of 'Granny Herald' whose waspish features bore a resemblance to his own. He retired in February 1961, only a month before the death of his wife. Next year, while travelling to England in the *Orion*, he suffered a heart attack. When the ship docked he was transferred to hospital at Billericay, Essex, and died there on 30 October 1962. He was survived by two sons, Tom and Adrian, the latter of whom was to edit the *Australian*.

F. M. Cutlack, *The Australian Flying Corps* (Syd, 1923); R. S. Whitington, *Sir Frank* (Melb, 1971); D. Zwar, *In Search of Keith Murdoch* (Melb, 1980); D. Horne, *Confessions of a New Boy* (Melb, 1986); *A'sian Journalist*, 15 Apr 1926; *SMH*, 16 May 1939, 29 Nov 1944, 8 Mar 1945, 21 June, 6, 13, 20, 27 Sept, 4, 11 Oct 1958, 1 Apr 1961, 1, 3 Nov 1962.　　　　　　　　　　　GAVIN SOUTER

DEAN, SIR ARTHUR (1893-1970), judge, was born on 25 May 1893 at Merino, Victoria, eldest of seven children of John Henry Dean, schoolteacher, and his wife Alice, née Macgugan, both Australian born. Arthur's was a country childhood, but far from settled, as his father's career within the Victorian state school system meant frequent moves from town to town. In February 1907, when the family were living at Chiltern, Arthur entered Scotch College, East Melbourne. Modest and studious, in 1910 he won an exhibition to the University of Melbourne (LL.B., 1915; LL.M., 1927).

Postponing his entry into the legal profession, on 26 July 1915 Dean enlisted in the Australian Imperial Force. In December he sailed for Egypt with reinforcements for the 7th Battalion. By March 1916 the battalion was on the Western Front where it was to see some of the bloodiest fighting of the war. Dean found the battle of Pozières, France, in July the worst: 'it lives to-day in the memory of many a man as a dreadful nightmare'. He was commissioned in September and promoted lieutenant in July 1917. Wounded in action on 4 October at Passchendaele, Belgium, he was invalided to England; shortly after his return to France he was gassed in late December and again hospitalized. Towards the end of his service he undertook legal work to do with courts martial and intelligence. He was something of a 'trench poet', contributing light verse to army magazines; his delight in composing 'doggerel' was to continue all his life. Arriving back in Melbourne in April 1919, he was demobilized on 22 June. With E. W. Gutteridge, he wrote his unit's history, *The Seventh Battalion, A.I.F.* (1933). Dean rose to lieutenant colonel in the Reserve of Officers and in 1939-42 served as the 3rd Division's legal officer. He was a member of the 1942 court of inquiry into events that followed the Japanese invasions of New Britain, Timor and Ambon.

On 1 June 1919 Dean had been admitted to the Victorian Bar. He built up a substantial practice, principally in the fields of Equity and industrial property, of which he was the Bar's acknowledged leader. On 12 April 1922 at Prahran Presbyterian Church he married

Dorothy Muriel Bolle. While at the Bar, he published two legal monographs which long remained standard practitioners' texts: *The Law relating to Estate Agents and Auctioneers* (1925) and *The Law relating to Hire Purchase in Australia* (1929).

Appointed K.C. in March 1944, Dean became a judge of the Supreme Court of Victoria in February 1949. His qualities of learning, industry, fairness, humility, independence of mind and moral courage were seen as admirably fitting him for the position. Given the nature of his practice at the Bar, he was most comfortable in the Equity and commercial work of the court. He was admired, too, for his mastery of practice and procedure, and for his expedition in court business. His many reported judgements are marked by clarity, a direct style, a firm grasp of legal principle, skilful use of case-law, concentration on the major issues and strong common sense. Chairman of the Council of Law Reporting (1950-65) and of the Country Libraries Committee, he was also involved in the work of the Chief Justice's Law Reform Committee. Dean was knighted in 1960.

In 1961-62 Sir Arthur found himself at the centre of enormous public attention for the only time in his life because of his role in 'the Tait Case', a celebrated and highly controversial prosecution for murder. Dean was the trial judge and presided over two further applications in relation to the matter, the second involving a late evening hearing only two days before Robert Peter Tait was due to be hanged. The controversy over the case (legal issues apart) turned on the general question of capital punishment and the role of the executive; the State government finally commuted Tait's sentence to one of life imprisonment. While Dean's role was crucial to the whole affair, his own handling of the case was never the subject of criticism. At his farewell from the bench in 1965, he doffed his wig and gown, stepped down from the bench, and shook hands with the dozens of barristers and solicitors who had come to say goodbye—an action regarded as 'the most spectacular thing he ever did in court'.

Dean gave years of service to the university. Lecturer in Equity (1929-39), he was a member (1931-39) of the standing committee of convocation (warden 1944-50), a member (1950-69) of council, deputy-chancellor (1953-54) and chancellor (1954-66). He was a 'working chancellor' and loved the position, giving himself to all its duties with unflagging dedication. With Lady Dean, he took particular interest in the establishment of International House. He presided over the university during a demanding period in which it doubled its student numbers and commenced a massive rebuilding programme. While some of his senior colleagues doubted whether he ever fully came to grips with the complex and subtle culture of the university, all acknowledged his integrity, his hard work and his genuine devotion to the institution. In 1963 the universities of Melbourne and Western Australia conferred upon him honorary doctorates of laws.

An elder of the Malvern Presbyterian Church, Dean was for sixteen years superintendent of its Sunday School. As chairman (1945-58) of the council of the Presbyterian Ladies' College, he oversaw its move from East Melbourne to Burwood. In retirement he found his greatest fulfilment in writing the official history of the Victorian Bar, *A Multitude of Counsellors* (1968). The book, which reflects the man, is direct, thorough, honest, highly readable, rich in information and a treasury of good stories.

Stocky in figure, with square, rather severe features, Dean exhibited a serious manner which tended to hide both his essential kindliness and his droll, old-fashioned humour. His principal recreations were tennis, golf, bowls and reading. Survived by his wife and their two daughters, he died on 25 September 1970 in East Melbourne and was cremated. The University of Melbourne holds his portrait by Paul Fitzgerald.

C. Burns, *The Tait Case* (Melb, 1962); A. Dean, *A Tribute to the Memory of the Late Sir Norman O'Bryan* (priv print, Melb, nd, 1968?); *Aust Law J*, 17 Feb 1949; *Law Inst J*, Mar 1949, July 1965, Nov 1970; *Who Was Who*, 1961-1970; *Univ Melb Gazette*, May 1963, June 1966; *Aust Bar Gazette*, July 1965; Scotch College (Melb) Archives; cuttings relating to the Tait case (held by author, Law School, Univ Melb); information from Mrs I. Tulloch, Kew, and Mrs M. Whiteside, Malvern, Melb; personal information.   R. L. SHARWOOD

DEARTH, HENRY ALAN (1908-1964), radio producer, was born on 12 August 1908 at Fulham, London, son of Henry Dearth and his wife Edith Eliza Eleanor, née Bristow, well-known singers. Young Harry attended (1917-23) Cranleigh School, Surrey, passed the Oxford and Cambridge examination, and claimed to have spent six months in the 20th Middlesex (Artists) Rifle Volunteers in London. Reaching Sydney in the *Largs Bay* on 31 May 1926, sponsored by the Big Brother Movement, he worked as jackeroo on Garangula and Cunningar stations, near Harden, and later at Wingadee, Coonamble. Early in 1929 he sought theatrical work in Sydney. Engaged by J. C. Williamson [q.v.6] Ltd, he progressed from the chorus to minor roles in musical comedies, among them *Our Miss Gibbs* (Melbourne, 1933).

On 15 June 1935 at St Philip's Anglican Church, Sydney, Dearth married a soubrette Mona Potts. He had found a stable position with the Australian Broadcasting Commission. Late in 1934 he moved to Macquarie Broadcasting Services Pty Ltd's 2GB as an announcer and 'personality', presenting programmes such as 'Melody and Mirth with Harry Dearth'. Gifted with a 'fine, resonant voice', he took singing lessons to learn correct breathing. He occasionally played supporting roles with the 'B.S.A. Players' (Broadcasting Services Association Pty Ltd) and developed his interest in producing radio drama. In addition, he sometimes took roles under (Dame) Doris Fitton at the Independent Theatre and was later a director of the John Alden [q.v.] Company.

In April 1939 Dearth joined J. Walter Thompson (Australia) Pty Ltd as producer of an Australian version of the popular American programme, 'Lux Radio Theatre', for broadcasting nationally over the Macquarie network. He also produced 'Australia's Amateur Hour'. In December 1941 the company transferred 'Lux Radio Theatre' to station 2UW, owned by M. F. Albert's [q.v.7] Commonwealth Broadcasting Corporation Pty Ltd. Dearth continued its production until he enlisted in the Royal Australian Air Force on 18 September 1942. He was commissioned on 18 December. As flying-officer (from June 1943) attached to various R.A.A.F. headquarters, he was in charge of an entertainment party which gave performances on the mainland and in operational areas of New Guinea. His appointment terminated on 19 December 1945.

Dearth returned to J. Walter Thompson as producer of the 'Lux Radio Theatre' and remained until the programme ended in 1951. Back at 2GB, he was producer-compere of 'Leave It to the Girls' and the 'General Motors Hour' (1952-54), before moving to 2UW for 'Harry Dearth's Playhouse'. Involved in television as producer of (ultimately disappointing) simulcasts for 2GB/ATN-7, he was appointed production manager at ATN in 1960. He produced and appeared in the television series, 'Jonah' (1962).

Tall, slim and athletic, Dearth loved his golf and belonged to the Lakes club. Ever conscious of his image, he dressed extremely well. He brought showmanship to live radio drama and was reputedly the only producer to leave the panel-operator's booth and 'direct' the cast from centre-stage. He had a great respect for actors—he wished to be one himself—and tried to give them further recognition by introducing a 'curtain call' for live radio productions. While he was overseas in 1963 studying television techniques, his respiratory illness worsened. Survived by his wife, son and daughter, Dearth died of cancer on 7 July 1964 in his home at Cammeray, Sydney, and was cremated.

J. Kent, *Out of the Bakelite Box* (Syd, 1990); *Wireless Weekly*, 10 June 1938, p 33; *Listener In*, 19-25 Jan 1946, p 3, 16-22 Mar 1946, p 3, 6-12 Apr 1946, p 20; *Herald* (Melb), 19 Apr 1933; *SMH*, 4 Sept 1954, 8 July 1964; *Sun-Herald* (Syd), 28 July 1957; information from Messrs A. Dearth, Chatswood, R. Lane, Belrose, and S. Macoboy, Neutral Bay, Syd.

DIANA R. COMBE

DEASE, CONLY JOHN PAGET (1906-1979), broadcaster and actor, was born on 26 May 1906 at Bhamo, Burma, son of Conly Edward Dease, a lieutenant in the 91st Punjabi Regiment, and his wife Ida Ferley, née Vogt. The family returned to England and Jack attended Monkton Combe School, Somerset, matriculating at the age of 16. When he refused to enter a military college, he was indentured as a farm apprentice by his mother. One of the 'Barwell [q.v.7] Boys', he reached Adelaide in the *Barrabool* on 29 April 1923. He worked at Clare for E. H. Mattner who found him 'a very spoiled lazy boy . . . always reading—novels' and commented on 'his clever and mischievous tongue'. Apprenticed to Hunter Bros at Montacute from December that year, Dease was released from his agreement on 7 November 1925. After various jobs, in 1928 he was taken on as a junior master at Scotch College, Adelaide, and enrolled at the university. Next year he taught at Tudor House, Moss Vale, New South Wales, and from February 1930 at Scots College, Sydney.

Leaving Scots in August 1933, John Dease studied drama with (Dame) Doris Fitton at the Independent Theatre. He was engaged by J. C. Williamson [q.v.6] Ltd and appeared in musical comedies, among them *The Dubarry* (January 1934), before touring New Zealand with the company. In mid-1935 he joined Macquarie Broadcasting Services Pty Ltd's principal radio station, 2GB, as an announcer. Its management concentrated on promoting such personalities as Jack Davey, Charles Cousens and Harry Dearth [qq.v.]. For twenty-five years Dease presented the musical programme 'World-Famous Tenors'. He married a clerk Margaret (Greta) Mary Mildred Lofberg on 15 December 1938 at St Mary's Catholic Cathedral, Sydney; they were to remain childless and to be divorced in 1944. Dease's programmes included 'Radio Newspaper of the Air', 'World's Best in Music' and 'Reflections in a Wineglass', as well as game shows such as 'Mathematical Jackpots'. He became 2GB's chief announcer, read the news and was to record some two hundred talking-books for the blind.

The 'Quiz Kids'—which grew to be Dease's best-known programme—began in 1942, continued on radio every Sunday night until 14 October 1962 (with an abortive attempt in 1956-57 to run concurrently on ATN-7 television) and transferred to Australian Broadcasting Commission television in March 1964. Based on a popular American programme, it had a regular panel of five, aged between 11 and 15 years, who answered questions sent by listeners. If the 'Quiz Kids' failed to answer, the senders received a small cash prize. In promotional material and on television the quizmaster and panel always wore mortar boards and academic gowns. The word 'avuncular' could have been coined for Dease who was both dignified and enthusiastic.

In 1946 Dease had helped his friend Peter Finch [q.v.] to establish the Mercury Theatre; among his sundry roles was Henry Higgins in *Pygmalion*. That year he also appeared in the film, *Smithy*. On 2 January 1948 he married a divorcee Raukura Margery De Villiers Walmsley, née East, at St Stephen's Presbyterian Church, Sydney. Some months after denying that he was a communist, he resigned in November 1948 as vice-president of the Actors' and Announcers' Equity Association of Australia.

After the 'Quiz Kids' was seen for the last time on 29 December 1968, Dease took character roles in television series, including 'Number 96' and 'Young Doctors', and in the films *Ned Kelly* (1970) and *Colour Me Dead* (1970). In 1972 he was in the 'It's Time' advertisement for the Australian Labor Party, but contested the Federal seat of Evans for the Australia Party; he joined the A.L.P. in 1974. His chief enjoyment was watching cricket. He emerged from semi-retirement in 1978 to play Ken, a newsreel commentator in the film, *Newsfront*. Survived by his wife, daughter and two sons, he died on 1 February 1979 at Ashfield and was cremated. Dease and the 'Quiz Kids' were featured on an 85-cent stamp issued by Australia Post in 1991.

R. R. Walker, *The Magic Spark* (Melb, 1973); K. S. Inglis, *This is the ABC* (Melb, 1983); J. Kent, *Out of the Bakelite Box* (Syd, 1983); L. Johnson, *The Unseen Voice* (Lond, 1988); *Wireless Weekly*, 26 July 1935, 9 July 1937, p 2; *ABC Weekly*, 27 July 1957, p 9; *TV Times*, 4 Mar 1964; *SMH*, 7 July, 13 Nov 1948, 17 Aug 1964, 27 Oct, 29 Nov 1972, 3 Feb 1979; *Sunday Telegraph* (Syd), 22 Aug 1971; *Australian*, 12 Nov 1976; *Sun-Herald*, 7 Aug 1977; *Daily Telegraph* (Syd), 3 Feb 1979; Immigration Dept, farm apprentices, file no 779 SRSA.

BARRY O. JONES

DEASEY, MAUDE KATHLEEN (1909-1968), teacher, army officer and administrator, was born on 26 May 1909 at Collingwood, Melbourne, second of six children of Rev. Denis Murrell Deasey, an Anglican clergyman, and his wife Maude Williamson, née Watt, both Victorian born. Educated at Geelong Church of England Girls' Grammar School and the University of Melbourne (B.A., 1931; M.A., 1933; Dip.Ed., 1935), Kathleen proceeded in 1935 to Newnham College, Cambridge (B.A., 1937; M.A., 1946), and graduated in the theological tripos. She visited Poland for a conference of the International Federation of University Women and made two tours of the Continent with the National Union of Students.

Back in Australia, Miss Deasey taught for a year at Frensham, Mittagong, New South Wales, then in 1940 became lady superintendent at Methodist Ladies' College, Melbourne. Following the formation of the Australian Women's Army Service in August 1941, she was recruited to be one of its officers. Appointed assistant-controller, A.W.A.S., Southern Command, in November, she received the rank of major on 28 January next year. She established the service's structure in Victoria and in 1942 supervised the enlistment and training of over five thousand recruits. From May 1943 she was assistant-controller at First Army headquarters, Toowoomba, Queensland.

Seconded to the Australian Army Chaplains' Department, Land Headquarters, Melbourne, in October, Deasey acted as adviser to the chaplains-general and ensured that servicewomen—wherever they were stationed —were able to maintain contact with their churches. She compiled a booklet, *Readings and Prayers for Members of Army Women's Services*, which the chaplains' department published in 1944. Her duties entailed considerable travel in Australia and the South-West Pacific Area. In 1946 she represented the A.W.A.S. in the Victory march in London. After returning to Australia, she drafted a history of the service. She transferred to the Reserve of Officers on 25 January 1947.

In the late 1940s Deasey helped to place migrant families for the Department of Immigration. She was in Europe in 1950-52 and studied at the Sorbonne, Paris, for a year. Home again, she administered an agency sponsorship scheme for the World Council of Churches to assist intending immigrants who had no friends or relations in Australia. In 1958-59 she travelled in the United States of America on a Ford Foundation grant and was a teaching fellow in the faculty of education, New York University. Having been a senior tutor in education at the University of Melbourne in 1960-61, she was principal of St Ann's College, University of Adelaide, until 1966. Next year she returned to Melbourne and joined the staff of Larnook Domestic Arts Teachers' College, Armadale.

Deasey was 5 ft 5 ins (165 cm) tall and slim in build, with blue-grey eyes; sincere, studious and determined, she loved music, and was gifted with sympathy, understanding and outward tranquillity. Her conversation was stimulating, she had a good sense of humour, made friends easily and was a dedicated Anglican. She died of a cerebral haemorrhage on 6 September 1968 at Prahran and was buried in Boroondara cemetery, Kew.

L. Ollif, *Women in Khaki* (Syd, 1981); A. Howard, *You'll be Sorry!* (Syd, 1990); *Advertiser* (Adel), 10 Sept 1968; information from and papers held by Archdeacon R. Deasey, Hawthorn, Melb.

EILEEN MACINTYRE

DEBENHAM, FRANK (1883-1965), Antarctic scientist and geographer, was born on 26 December 1883 at Bowral, New South Wales, younger of twins and third child of English-born parents Rev. John Willmott Debenham (d. 1898), an Anglican clergyman, and his wife Edith, née Cleveland. Frank had a happy childhood and youth, camping in the bush and attending the little school run by his father. Sent to The King's School, Parramatta (1900-02), he was dux and excelled at Rugby football and cricket. After reading English and philosophy at the University of Sydney (B.A., 1906), he joined the staff of The Armidale School; there he taught himself some science and introduced compulsory classes in that subject. Back at university in 1908, Debenham studied geology under (Sir) Edgeworth David [q.v.8] and became Deas Thomson [q.v.2] scholar in geology.

In 1910 he and T. G. Taylor [q.v.12] joined Captain Robert Falcon Scott's Antarctic expedition as geologists. Debenham's first scientific work was done on the western side of McMurdo Sound. A knee injury, from playing football in the snow, prevented his going on the ill-fated Polar journey, but he investigated the geology of the Granite Harbour region in the summer of 1911-12. Impressed with his expertise in large-scale, plane-table mapping, Scott wrote that he was 'a well-trained, sturdy worker, with a quiet meaning that carries conviction; [he] realises the conceptions of thoroughness and conscientiousness'.

In 1913 Debenham entered the University of Cambridge (B.A., 1919; M.A., 1922) to work up his field-notes. Next year he visited Australia with the British Association. On the outbreak of World War I, he returned to England and was commissioned lieutenant on 27 October 1914. Posted to the 7th Battalion, Oxfordshire and Buckinghamshire Light Infantry, he served in France and at Salonika, Greece, where he was severely wounded and shell-shocked in August 1916. At St Philip's parish church, Kensington, London, on 27 January 1917 he married Dorothy Lucy Lempriere of Melbourne. Remaining in England, he was demobilized as a major and appointed O.B.E. in 1919.

Lecturer in cartography and surveying (from 1919) at Cambridge, in 1920 Debenham was elected a fellow (tutor 1923-28) of Gonville and Caius College. In 1921, with (Sir) Raymond Priestley [q.v.11] and others, he produced two reports on the geology of Antarctica; in 1923 he published his *Report on the Maps and Surveys* of the *Terra Nova* expedition (1910-13). Debenham was appointed founder-director of the Scott Polar Research Institute at Cambridge in 1925. Reader in geography (from 1928), in 1931 he accepted the first chair of geography at the university. That year he began the *Polar Record* and was its founding editor.

Modest, approachable and friendly, Deb was essentially a practical man. He took a keen personal interest in the design and equipment of his new premises, and rejuvenated the teaching of his subject by emphasizing field-work, vacation camps and laboratory sessions. During World War II he trained service cadets, lectured to Royal Air Force navigators and devised relief-model techniques for briefing commandos. A much-loved, highly successful departmental head, he had, according to Lord McNair, 'a very warm heart under the control of a sound judgement'. Debenham wrote easily and well. In addition to numerous papers, he published *The Polar Regions* (1930) and *Map Making* (1936), and edited *The Voyage of Captain Bellingshausen to the Antarctic Seas, 1819-1821*, for the Hakluyt Society in 1945.

Debenham retired from the Polar Institute in 1946 and from his chair in 1949. He travelled extensively in Africa, and published on such subjects as the water resources of arid regions, the construction of small earthen dams, the ecology of the Kalahari, and on David Livingstone. Among his later publications were *The Use of Geography* (1950), *Seven Centuries of Debenhams* (Glasgow, 1957) and *Antarctica: the Story of a Continent* (1959).

A fellow (1914) and vice-president (1951-53) of the Royal Geographical Society of London, Debenham received its Murchison grant (1926) and Victoria medal (1948), as well as the American Geographical Society's David Livingstone centenary medal (1948); in 1952 he was president of the Geographical Association. He was awarded honorary doctorates of science by the universities of Western Australia (1937), Durham, England (1952), and Sydney (1959). In his last years Debenham suffered from heart disease and deafness, but continued to write, and, with the assistance of Mrs Deb, to offer hospitality to former students and Polar travellers. Survived by his wife, a son and four daughters, he died on 23 November 1965 at Cambridge. His elder son had been killed in World War II. Debenham is commemorated by two buildings at Cambridge and by a mountain and a glacier in Antarctica. His portrait by H. A. Freeth is held by the Scott Polar Research Institute.

R. F. Scott, *Scott's Last Expedition* (Lond, 1923); G. Taylor, *Journeyman Taylor* (Lond 1958); G. E. Hall and A. Cousins (eds), *Book of Remembrance of the University of Sydney in the War 1914-1918* (Syd, 1939); *DNB*, 1961-70; *Geog J*, 132, 1966, p 173; *Geog Review*, 56, 1966, p 596; *Geography*, 51-52, 1966-67, p 150; Inst of British Geographers, *Trans*, no 40, Dec 1966, p 195; *J of Glaciology*, 6, no 45, 1966, p 455; *Polar Record*, 13, no 83, 1966, p 215; *SMH*, 14 Apr 1959; *The Times*, 25 Nov 1965; The King's School, Parramatta, Syd, Archives.

G. P. WALSH

DE BURGH, ERNEST CHARLES (1892-1977), journalist, was born on 30 March 1892 at Battersea, London, second son of Henry Augustus de Burgh, farmer and grazier, and his wife Annette Elizabeth (Bessie), née Lefroy, both of whom belonged to Western Australia's established landed families. Ernest was educated first by a tutor and then at Guildford Grammar School, Perth, where he was captain, stroke of the boat crew and senior lieutenant in the cadet corps. After leaving school in 1911, he worked for two years as a cadet reporter on Perth's *Daily News* and for a time managed the family property, Cowalla, at Moore River near Gingin, for his brother Sidney.

On 10 May 1917 de Burgh enlisted in the Australian Imperial Force. He reached France in April 1918 and was posted to the 5th Divisional Signal Company. While mending communication lines near Amiens on 9 July, he was gassed and invalided to England. He returned briefly to France after the Armistice and was discharged on 26 August 1919 in Western Australia.

Although he again tried farming at Cowalla, de Burgh found that his health was unsatisfactory and joined the *West Australian* newspaper in 1922. He married Cecil Molyus Hungerford on 30 May 1928 at St Mary's Anglican Church, West Perth. Working principally as an agricultural reporter, he became a leader-writer in 1933 under H. J. Lambert and editor-in-chief on 21 August 1946. He held this post until his retirement on 1 July 1956. As editor-in-chief, he continued his interest in agricultural matters and campaigned for the development of sand-plain farming, notably in the Esperance area where he influenced the establishment of an agricultural research station.

Politically conservative, de Burgh was a Western Australian patriot who believed that the State should generate its own economic development and financial independence, but he nonetheless supported increased Federal income tax. He was also concerned with strengthening Australia's defences, following the experience of Japanese raids on northern Western Australia during World War II, and advocated the establishment of a naval base at Fremantle. Unlike most of his contemporaries, he took a sympathetic interest in Aboriginal issues, as did his younger colleague (Sir) Paul Hasluck. Using *The Times* as his model, and maintaining strict standards of accuracy and expression in his carefully crafted editorials, de Burgh never adapted to the tabloid format necessitated by postwar shortages of newsprint. He also resisted pressure from his managing editor James Edward Macartney [q.v.] to liberalize and popularize the newspaper.

A pleasant and widely-respected man, de Burgh was steeped in English literature and the Bible. He was essentially a private person who kept aloof from the more robust side of journalistic life. Interested in local history, he was a stalwart of the Royal Western Australian Historical Society. While he was appointed O.B.E. in 1955, he was never a public figure and remained a farmer at heart. He died on 18 June 1977 in Perth and was cremated; his wife, son and daughter survived him.

Guildford Grammar School, *Swan*, June 1911; *West Australian*, 28 June 1977; W. de Burgh, Cowalla Part 1: 1896 to 1922 (mimeograph 1983) *and* Cowalla Part 2: 1922 to 1947 (mimeograph 1986); de Burgh papers (BL); personal information.

R. H. W. REECE

DE CASTELLA, FRANCOIS ROBERT (1867-1953), viticulturist, was born on 16 January 1867 at South Yarra, Melbourne, son of Swiss-born Charles Hubert de Castella [q.v.3], vigneron, and his wife Frances Alice, née Jenkins, from Sydney. In 1879-82 François was educated at Xavier College, Kew; there, at his father's insistence, he was served wine with meals. He left Australia in 1883 to study natural science at Lausanne, Switzerland, and vine-growing and wine-making in France.

On his return in 1886, de Castella managed St Hubert's vineyard at Yering, owned by his father in partnership with Andrew Rowan [q.v.6]. After Rowan purchased Hubert's share in 1890, François joined the Victorian Department of Agriculture as a viticultural expert. He travelled throughout the State, advised vignerons and wrote the influential *Handbook on Viticulture for Victoria* (1891). Retrenched in 1892, he purchased Tongala vineyard and in 1896 became manager of Chateau Dookie for the Bank of Victoria.

Following the outbreak of grape phylloxera at Bendigo, in 1894 de Castella condemned the Victorian government's policy of vineyard eradication. He supported regional quarantine and the introduction of phylloxera-resistant American rootstocks, as had been done in Europe. Although he was aware of the latest methods adopted by the French in combating the pest, his advice was ignored.

In 1907 the Victorian wine industry verged on collapse. At the behest of Hans Irvine [q.v.9], de Castella was again appointed viticultural expert with the Department of Agriculture. That year he was sent to Europe to obtain further information on the control of phylloxera. This journey, fully documented (1907-09) in the Victorian *Journal of the Department of Agriculture* (to which he was a frequent contributor), was the basis for the reconstitution of affected vineyards in central and northern Victoria. At Rutherglen de Castella cultivated varieties of rootstocks for Australian needs and developed the technique of field-grafting. His tour also led to the introduction of cultures of flor yeasts for producing delicate, dry sherries of the fino type.

Dark bearded, energetic, intelligent and purposeful in his youth, and silver-haired and sprightly in old age, de Castella was known to his departmental colleagues as Cas. To the wine merchant Samuel Wynn [q.v.12], he combined the 'lively cultivated manners of a European aristocrat' with the 'honesty, matiness and deep practicality of the true Australian'. Fluent in French, de Castella was a prolific writer in English, and also an active broadcaster and educationist. His friends considered him a confirmed bachelor and were surprised when, on 31 January 1923, at St Patrick's Cathedral, East Melbourne, he married a 33-year-old nurse Phyllis Yvonne Van Hemert Silvestre (d. 1936). Following his retirement in 1936, the Phylloxera Board of South Australia commissioned him to report on the grape varieties of that State. His achievements, especially in ampelography, were recognized abroad. He was appointed to the French Ordre du Mérite Agricole in 1937.

De Castella enjoyed life and was a regular at Camillo Triaca's [q.v.12] restaurant, 'the Latin'. He coined the term 'eubiotics' for the science of good living, and was foundation president (1936) of the Victorian branch of the Wine and Food Society. Survived by his three sons, he died on 12 May 1953 at Charterisville, his Heidelberg home, and was buried in nearby Warringal cemetery. A portrait by Will Rowell [q.v.11] is held by the family.

A. Wynn, *The Fortunes of Samuel Wynn* (Melb, 1968); *Aust Vigneron and Fruit Grower's J*, 1 Dec 1892, 1 Mar, 2 Aug 1894, 25 July 1908, 28 Apr

1923; *People* (Syd), 28 Feb 1951; *Aust Brewing and Wine J*, 20 May 1953; *J of Agr* (Vic), June 1953; *Argus*, 24 May 1890, 17 Jan 1939; *Herald* (Melb), 13 May 1953; de Castella papers (Univ Melb Archives).   DAVID DUNSTAN

DECHAINEUX, EMILE FRANK VERLAINE (1902-1944), naval officer, was born on 3 October 1902 at Launceston, Tasmania, son of Florent Vincent Emile Lucien Dechaineux [q.v.8], an artist from Belgium, and his native-born wife Isabella Jane, née Briant. The family moved to Hobart where Emile was educated at the Friends' High School. In 1916 he entered the Royal Australian Naval College, Jervis Bay, Federal Capital Territory. An average scholar and sportsman who was popular with his peers, he graduated in 1919 and was promoted midshipman in January 1920.

After cruises in H.M.A.S. *Australia* and *Anzac*, Dechaineux was sent to Britain for sea- and shore-training with the Royal Navy. He returned to Australia in 1924, joined H.M.A.S. *Brisbane* and was promoted lieutenant before transferring to *Melbourne* in 1925. Back in England in 1926-29, he qualified as a torpedo officer and a naval (air) observer, and was awarded the Ogilvy medal (1929) for gaining first place in the advanced torpedo course. In 1929-34 he served in turn in H.M.A.S. *Anzac* and *Australia*, and in H.M.S. *Kempenfelt*. Promoted lieutenant commander (September 1932), in 1935-36 he was squadron torpedo officer in H.M.A.S. *Canberra*. On 20 November 1936 he married Mary Grant Harbottle in St David's Anglican Cathedral, Hobart.

In 1937 Dechaineux travelled to England to attend the R.N. Staff College. His promotion to commander on 30 June that year, ahead of all his contemporaries, marked him out for advancement to high rank. Between December 1937 and April 1940 he worked in the Admiralty's Tactical and Minesweeping divisions. During the evacuation of Dunkirk, France, from 29 May to 3 June 1940, he had temporary command of the destroyer, H.M.S. *Vivacious*, and completed five trips. He subsequently commanded the destroyer flotilla-leader, H.M.S. *Eglinton*, in which he patrolled the North Sea and conducted successful searches for German E-boats. For 'outstanding zeal and devotion to duty', he was awarded the Distinguished Service Cross (1941).

Home again, in October 1941 Dechaineux became director of operations at Navy Office, Melbourne. He commissioned the Tribal-class destroyer, H.M.A.S. *Warramunga*, in November 1942. In June 1943 he was appointed commander, Task Group 74.2, and had tactical control of a formation of de-stroyers which included ships of the United States Navy. *Warramunga* operated in Australian and New Guinea waters. From November the vessel took part in bombardment and escort duties, supporting allied landings at Arawe and Cape Gloucester, New Britain, Saidor, New Guinea, and the Admiralty Islands. Again selected early, Dechaineux was promoted captain on 31 December that year.

On 9 March 1944 he took command of the flagship of Task Force 74, the heavy cruiser, H.M.A.S. *Australia*. In adapting to the much larger vessel, he realized the need to rely on the expertise of specialist officers; he appreciated the merit of his staff, and endorsed proposals to improve the equipment and armament of the ship through unofficial American channels. Between April and September *Australia* supported landings at Hollandia, on the north coast of Netherlands New Guinea, and at the nearby islands of Biak, Noemfoor and Morotai; she also participated in the bombardments of Wakde Island and of Aitape, New Guinea. By October *Australia* was in the Philippines.

Tall, with a misleadingly remote bearing, Dechaineux was regarded by his officers as an approachable, generous and humane captain; his sailors found that he held high expectations of them and that he was fair—quick to praise performances out of the ordinary, though hard on wrongdoers. He kept the ship's company informed of impending actions and their likely outcomes, and constantly tried to foster the men's welfare and to maintain their morale.

At dawn on 21 October 1944, while supporting the U.S. landings at Leyte Gulf, *Australia* was attacked by a Japanese Navy dive-bomber. Her anti-aircraft guns engaged the plane, but it deliberately crashed into the ship's foremast, causing an explosion and an intense fire on the bridge. Dechaineux was mortally wounded and died some hours later. He was buried at sea that night, along with twenty-nine officers and sailors who had also perished. The U.S. government posthumously appointed him an officer of the Legion of Merit for his seamanship, professional skill, leadership and devotion to duty. In 1990 the Federal government announced that a Collins-class submarine was to be named after him. His portrait is in the Tasmanian Art Gallery, Hobart. Dechaineux was survived by his wife, daughter, and son Peter who joined the R.A.N.

F. B. Eldridge, *A History of the Royal Australian Naval College* (Melb, 1949); G. H. Gill, *Royal Australian Navy 1942-1945* (Canb, 1968); *Roy Aust Naval College Mag*, 1916-19; *Mercury* (Hob), 27 Oct 1944; AWM records; information from Cmdr R. P. Middleton, Giralang, Canb, Cdre J. L. W.

Merson, Clifton Gardens, Syd, Vice Adm Sir Richard Peek, Chakola, NSW, and Mr C. G. Hopping, Blackburn, Melb.   JANE PEEK

DEDMAN, JOHN JOHNSTONE (1896-1973), politician, was born on 2 June 1896 at Knowe, Kirkcudbrightshire, Scotland, son of James Baillie Dedman, schoolteacher, and his wife Mary, née Johnstone. John was taught by his father in village schools and imbued with the precept: 'whatever thy hands find to do, do it with all thy might'. After attending Ewart Boys' High School, Newton Stewart, he entered the faculty of science at the University of Edinburgh in 1914 and planned to study engineering.

On 19 March 1915 Dedman was commissioned in the British Army and posted to the 10th Battalion, Border Regiment. He fought at Gallipoli, in Egypt and in France where he was wounded in action in 1917. Transferring to the Indian Army that year, he saw active service in Afghanistan and Iraq. In 1922 he resigned and joined a schoolboy friend Walter McEwen in Victoria; in April they purchased a dairy-farm near Launching Place. Dedman bought out his partner's share and on 24 June 1925 married McEwen's sister Jessie Lawson at the Presbyterian Church, Surrey Hills, Melbourne.

Dedman produced milk for the Melbourne market. In an attempt to break a wholesalers' cartel, he joined the Country Party and in 1927 stood unsuccessfully for the seat of Upper Yarra in the Legislative Assembly. When the Country Party helped to block the milk board bill (1927) in the Legislative Council, he became a member of the Australian Labor Party in 1928. Two years later he moved to a smaller property at Millgrove, but the Depression forced him to abandon farming and in 1934 he took local work with the Forests Commission of Victoria.

During the early 1930s Dedman read widely in economics and emerged as one of Labor's more radical voices on banking reform. In 1932-34 he contested one Federal and two State seats. He was more successful in local government polls and served on the Upper Yarra Shire Council from 1926 to 1939 (president 1931 and 1937). In 1938 he enrolled as a part-time student at the University of Melbourne, hoping to increase his understanding of Keynesian economics. Having won Corio in a crucial by-election in March 1940, he soon established himself in the House of Representatives as an unrelenting debater on financial affairs. His principles were, and remained, socialist, but were tinged with healthy pragmatism and robust Christianity.

With the formation of the Labor government on 7 October 1941, John Curtin [q.v.] helped to secure Dedman's elevation to cabinet. He was appointed minister in charge of the Council for Scientific and Industrial Research, minister for war organization of industry and chairman of the production executive of cabinet. In December 1941 he was also appointed to the War Cabinet. His main responsibilities were to co-ordinate the Commonwealth's production departments and to reorganize industry so that resources were diverted to military needs and essential services.

The general public saw Dedman as the minister for 'austerity', or even 'morbidity'. He not only ignored the controversies which his decisions created, but even enjoyed the lampooning that he received from cartoonists. In their zeal for imposing controls, Dedman and his department were identified—often mistakenly or unfairly—with limiting everything from bread to bungalows. He deprived men of their waistcoats and shirt tails (hence the nickname 'Lumbago Jack'), brides of pink icing on their wedding cakes (white was the mandatory colour) and children of Father Christmas (restrictions on seasonal advertising in 1942). Yet he also won admirers, among them vice-chancellors and university students who appreciated his introduction of means-tested scholarships. At the end of World War II his achievement was acknowledged, but his style was remembered. As one journalist observed, he had discharged his duties 'like a born dominie . . . with all the bleakness of the kirk'.

While retaining his C.S.I.R. portfolio, on 2 February 1945 Dedman succeeded J. B. Chifley [q.v.] as minister for postwar reconstruction. The department's principal concerns were to implement Labor's full-employment objective, to retrain ex-service personnel and to foster a balanced peacetime economy based on manufacturing, exports and a national works programme. Dedman had responsibility for the white paper on employment, the Commonwealth and State Housing Agreement and the Snowy Mountains' scheme, as well as for legislation to promote wool, and to establish the Joint Coal Board, the Universities Commission and the Australian National University.

He enjoyed shaping initiatives that removed the spectre of the hard times of the 1930s, but was frustrated when new programmes were transferred to other departments, or to the States, where they lost much of their vitality. Although sometimes at odds with Prime Minister Chifley, who increasingly urged financial caution, he remained his 'indispensable henchman' in national and international planning. Dedman, however, could be his own worst enemy, not least because of his rash remarks.

In forums abroad Dedman was more the

statesman. A leading participant in the World Conference on International Trade and Employment, held in Cuba in 1947-48, he proved a tough but flexible negotiator. He insisted that his advisers leave an expensive Havana hotel for a rented house in the suburbs. In July 1949 he deputized for Chifley at the conference of British Commonwealth finance ministers in London.

From 1 November 1946 Dedman had also been minister for defence. Less committed to this portfolio, he nonetheless maintained strong ties with the British Commonwealth and helped to inaugurate the British-Australian Joint Guided-Weapons Project. As minister in charge of C.S.I.R., he encouraged the institution's expansion, though he insisted that, for reasons of public direction and internal security, its governing council be replaced by an executive. The renamed Commonwealth Scientific and Industrial Research Organization was inaugurated in 1949.

After barely losing Corio in December 1949, Dedman narrowly failed to regain the seat in 1951 and 1954. Unable to find employment, he eventually acquired a small sheep-property at Apollo Bay. In 1955 he became Australian director of the resettlement of refugees department of the World Council of Churches. Retiring to Canberra in 1962, he was appointed to the council of the A.N.U. in 1966 and graduated (B.A.) that year. The university had awarded him an honorary doctorate of laws (1964) and decided in 1970 to name a building after him.

Dedman wrote about his ministerial experiences during the war and was a frequent visitor to Parliament House. He retained his membership of the A.L.P., served as an elder of St Andrew's Presbyterian Church, Forrest, and lived long enough to see the Whitlam government introduce some of the policies he had championed. Dedman died on 22 November 1973 in Canberra; he was accorded a state funeral and was cremated. His wife, son and two daughters survived him.

A. Spaull, 'John Johnstone Dedman: Australia's "First Federal Minister for Education" (1941-1949)', *History of Education Review*, 21, no 1, 1992; *Canb Times*, 23 Nov 1973; G. T. Peterson, The Honourable J. J. Dedman, Political Democrat and Economic Socialist (B.A. Hons thesis, Univ NSW (Duntroon), 1980); Dedman papers (NL); H. de Berg, J. J. Dedman (taped interview, 6 Oct 1967, NL); information from Mrs R. Rodgers, Canb.   ANDREW SPAULL

DEEN, FAZAL (1898?-1963), hawker, battery-operator and entrepreneur, was born probably on 19 June 1898 at Mehron, near Moga, in the Punjab, India, son of Foth Deen, hawker, and his wife Umri Bebe, both Mus-

lims of the Rajput clan. Educated at Mathra Das College, Moga, at the age of 16 Fazal married Burkit Bebe; they were to have six children. In 1922 he left his immediate family to join his father at Blackall, Queensland. Foth and Fazal hawked throughout Central Queensland, selling drapery, hosiery, fancy goods, confectionery and jewellery from a Bedford truck specially fitted with shelves and drawers on either side of the body. Fazal had brought gems from India and peddled these to miners in the region.

In 1933 he moved to Tennant Creek, Northern Territory, where he set up a general store and extended credit to hopeful gold-miners. Next year, on a site south of Mount Samuel and adjacent to the Stuart Highway, he erected a battery to treat gold ore. Initially a two-stamper, it was enlarged to a four-stamper, with a crusher. From 3630 tons of ore, the plant produced 1890 oz. (53.6 kg) of gold valued at £13 375 in 1935-36. Although Deen engaged apprentices to work at the battery, many were discouraged by his practice of paying a portion of their wages in goods from his store. He acquired rights to a nearby government bore and charged a fee to passing drovers for the water he pumped to drinking troughs. Running goats, cattle and horses, he killed his own meat in accordance with Islamic rites.

By 1936 his four sons had joined him. They lived in a large house with ant-bed floors, galvanized-iron walls and a roof supported by mulga beams; incorporating an inner room surrounded by verandahs, the isolated home was supplied with running water and electricity. Well groomed and dignified in bearing, Deen was an excellent cook and host who conversed with people from all walks of life, and kept a supply of wines and spirits for his guests. He was a devout Muslim and observed the prayer ritual five times daily; he did not drink alcohol, nor did he smoke. With the onset of World War II the battery's engines were removed, the plant was rendered inoperable and he left Tennant Creek in 1944.

A diabetic who needed two injections of insulin each day, Deen shifted to Brisbane where he bought and managed cafés. In 1949 he visited India. While staying in a Hindu village near Moga, he narrowly escaped death in the violence that continued after the 1947 partition. Forced to hide in a cellar for thirty days, he was smuggled to a refugee camp and interned for a month before being moved to Pakistan. In March 1949 he returned with his wife and daughters to Brisbane and settled at Wynnum. Deen invested in the Chelmsford Hotel at Southport and in a Holiday Inn on the Gold Coast. Government agencies made use of his skills as an interpreter and he came to be regarded as an unofficial representative of Pakistan. Survived by two daughters and three sons, he died of a coronary occlusion on 29 December 1963 at Southport and was buried in Mount Gravatt cemetery, Brisbane. Following his death, litigation continued over £29 000 worth of gold bars alleged to have been left by Deen with a Brisbane company and lost in 1953.

D. Carment, R. Maynard and A. Powell (eds), *Northern Territory Dictionary of Biography*, 1 (Darwin, 1990); *Courier-Mail*, 30 Dec 1963.

JUDITH CHURCH

DEERING, HAROLD HASTINGS (1896-1965), engineer and businessman, was born on 22 August 1896 at Ashfield, Sydney, second son of Harold Deering, clerk, and his wife Edith Lilian Marian Australia, née MacCulloch, both Sydney born. Harold attended Hayfield and Sydney Grammar schools; he represented the latter in football and rowing. In England on 27 February 1917 he was commissioned in the British Army. Transferring to the Royal Flying Corps on 30 April and to the Royal Air Force on 1 April 1918, he served as a pilot in England and France, and flew in the same squadron as (Sir) Charles Kingsford Smith [q.v.9].

After the war Lieutenant Deering tested new aircraft for the R.A.F. until he was placed on the Unemployed List on 7 May 1919. He claimed to have enrolled in classics at Jesus College, Oxford, and later returned to Oxford to lecture in aerial strategy. An associate-fellow of the Royal Aeronautical Society, London, he joined the Associated Equipment Co., a firm of bus manufacturers associated with the London Transport Group. Back in Sydney, on 6 April 1920 at St Anne's Anglican Church, Strathfield, he married Constance Ellie, daughter of H. J. Rose [q.v.11]; their daughter died in childhood and they were to separate in the 1950s. By 1922 he had formed his own business, Deering Engineering Co., and established an agency, A.E.C. (Australia) Pty Ltd, of which he was managing director; he was, as well, managing director (1927) in Australia for Associated Daimler. In 1933 the London Transport Group sent him to Europe and North America to investigate diesel traction and trolley buses.

Hastings Deering Pty Ltd, a private company which he set up in 1935, became the sole metropolitan distributor for the Ford Motor Co. Interested in architecture and classics, Deering oversaw the design of the company's spectacular head office on the corner of William and Crown streets. The Art Deco building had six storeys linked by a system of one-way, concrete ramps for cars. At one stage he was the largest individual Ford dealer in the world, handling 7000 new and 12 000 used cars a year. Deering often

proclaimed his belief in 'National Service, National Development and National Defence', and in the 'Seven Pillars of Wisdom for Australia'—transport, roads, water, food, coal, steel and defence. In 1940, when he indicated to the New South Wales board of area management of the Department of Munitions that he was willing to assist in ordnance production, his offer was accepted by the prime minister.

Realizing the potential for franchising, in 1947 Deering obtained heavy earthmoving equipment by acquiring the Caterpillar agency at Alice Springs, Northern Territory. He expanded to Darwin (1948), the Territory of Papua-New Guinea and the British Solomon Islands (1949), and to Queensland (1952). Spending time in the 1950s on developing the beef industry in the north and the inland, he established the Hastings Deering experimental station—covering 2600 square miles (6734 km²) at Palmer Valley in the MacDonnell Ranges—where he built large dams to show that stations in Central Australia could be made drought-proof. He acquired a further 4000 square miles (10 360 km²) at Henbury.

His 'financial empire' encompassed sixteen companies: Deering held a controlling interest in each of them, and was involved in detailed design-work and financial matters. Using war-surplus hangars, in 1947-48 he had developed an assembly plant at Lidcombe, Sydney, in which he manufactured A.E.C. chassis for buses and trucks, crane carriers and ground-support equipment for all types of aircraft, in addition to carrying out extensive engine reconditioning and repairs to cars and trucks. He also established the Australian Atlas Co. Pty Ltd in 1949 to produce rock-drills, compressors, and pneumatic tools and loaders.

A keen photographer, Deering supervised advertising campaigns and his company's monthly magazine for which he wrote a column, 'Faith in the Future'. He was 6 ft 2 ins (188 cm) tall and weighed 17 stone (108 kg); he was known to his friends as Hastings; he liked smoking a pipe, racing cars and trout-fishing. Deering often told his staff: 'You can buy expertise, but you can't buy loyalty'. He kept a penthouse atop the company headquarters in William Street, a home at Homebush, a 70-acre (28 ha) farm at Castle Hill and a holiday house in the Blue Mountains. Survived by his wife, Deering died of cardiac disease on 16 June 1965 at Homebush and was cremated. His estate was sworn for probate at £581 544, much of which he left to his secretary and members of his corporate staff.

Rydge's, Feb 1951; *People* (Syd), 4 Nov 1953; *Hastings Deering News*, Dec 1960, p 46; *SMH*,

19 Apr 1917, 6 July 1927, 4 Sept 1934, 16 Aug 1940, 4 Nov 1949, 17 June 1965; information from Mrs S. A. Knight, Hurstville, Syd, and Mr C. W. Horsley, Tarragindi, Brisb.   PETER SPEARRITT

DE GRUCHY, GORDON CARL (1922-1974), physician, was born on 24 February 1922 at Coburg, Melbourne, son of Victorian-born parents Thomas Bernard de Gruchy, chemist, and his wife Norma Christine, née Ehrenstrom. Educated at three Christian Brothers' schools and at Xavier College, Kew, Carl entered the University of Melbourne (M.B., B.S., 1944; M.D., 1948) where he was Beaney [q.v.3] scholar in 1946. Next year he became a member (later fellow) of the Royal Australasian College of Physicians. After serving his residence at St Vincent's Hospital, de Gruchy specialized in haematology. From 1949 he worked in Professor J. V. Dacie's department at the Postgraduate Medical School of London. A member (1950, fellow 1966) of the Royal College of Physicians, London, in 1951 he was a Rockefeller fellow in medicine in the United States of America.

Returning to Melbourne in 1952, de Gruchy began a distinguished career, based at St Vincent's and at the university. He was physician to out-patients, university research scholar in haematology and, from 1958, first-assistant to Professor John Hayden [q.v.] in his new department of medicine at St Vincent's Hospital Clinical School. That year de Gruchy published *Clinical Haematology in Medical Practice* (Oxford). In 1962 he succeeded Hayden in the chair of medicine at St Vincent's.

President (1964-66) of the International Society of Haematology, de Gruchy won early fame for his investigation of haemolytic anaemias, and subsequent renown for the study of glycolytic enzymes in white blood cells and platelets. Most of the work was carried out in the first-rate laboratory he had established at St Vincent's. De Gruchy wrote well, and could judge fairly and explain clearly the research of others. In his department he established an alcoholism clinic which later fell under the hospital's responsibility.

De Gruchy was a good clinician, an excellent teacher and speaker, and an administrator who would have preferred to be engaged in research or treating patients. Burdensome administrative duties, which he met with ability and care, troubled him, as did occasional lapses by colleagues in meeting his demands. His usual charm and cheerfulness would then suffer and he found onerous his later years as professor of medicine. Such difficulties, coupled with his developing a malignant melanoma, made easier his decision to retire from his chair in 1970. He was awarded the Eric Susman prize for medical research in 1971. Although he completed a significant monograph, *Drug-Induced Blood Disorders* (Oxford, 1975), further achievements were prevented by his illness.

A devout Catholic, de Gruchy was one of the most distinguished graduates of St Vincent's, yet he was unwilling to be identified only as a son of the hospital. In his last year, when he sat for his portrait, courageous and cheerful but haggard and weary, he chose to wear the blue, silk tie of London House, a residential institution in England with which he was associated. He was a reserved man but a sociable host who remained unmarried. De Gruchy died of cancer on 13 October 1974 at his Kew home and was buried in Boroondara cemetery. His portrait by Sir William Dargie is in the board-room of St Vincent's Hospital.

K. F. Russell, *The Melbourne Medical School 1862-1962* (Melb, 1977); *Roll of the Royal Australasian College of Physicians*, 1, 1938-1975 (Syd, 1988); *Univ Melb Gazette*, Mar 1962, Mar 1970; *MJA*, 28 June 1975; information from Miss D. de Gruchy, Kew, Melb; personal information.
BRYAN EGAN

DELAMOTHE, SIR PETER ROYLANCE (1904-1973), medical practitioner and politician, was born on 29 June 1904 at Spring Hill, Brisbane, fourth child of Charles Joseph de la Mothe, a chemist from France, and his Queensland-born wife Anna Mary, née Oliver. 'Bobby', as the family called him, was educated at St Francis School, Hughenden, and Mount Carmel College, Charters Towers; he finished third in the State in his final examinations, won an open scholarship and entered the University of Sydney (M.B., B.S., 1926) where he augmented his funds by tutoring. He served as junior (1927-28) and senior (1929-30) resident medical officer at Sydney Hospital, spending time as an ophthalmological surgeon before entering private practice. On 23 April 1931 Delamothe (as he now styled his surname) married Myrtle Eunice Lois Bussell at the Methodist Church, Ashfield.

In January 1933 he was appointed medical superintendent of the hospital at Collinsville, North Queensland. Hard working and popular, he performed seventy-seven operations in his first seven weeks there. According to one report, the hospital's 'popularity . . . increased tenfold' after his arrival. In early 1936 he set up his own practice at Bowen. Delamothe was involved in numerous organizations at Bowen and Collinsville, and stood unsuccessfully as an Independent for the Bowen mayoralty in 1939. Appointed probationary flight lieutenant, Royal Australian

Air Force, on 12 March 1940, he served in various R.A.A.F. hospitals and medical receiving stations during World War II. He was promoted temporary wing commander in October 1942 and transferred to the reserve on 26 October 1944.

Returning to Bowen, Delamothe resumed his practice and in April 1946, again standing as an Independent, was elected mayor. A divorcee, on 17 May 1947 at the Australian Inland Mission Hall, Broome, Western Australia, he married with Presbyterian forms Joan Patricia Milner, a 28-year-old clerk. Although unable to achieve the construction of a major highway diversion to Bowen in the course of his twelve-year term, he saw sewerage works begun and the first co-ordinated attempts made to attract tourists to the region. He served simultaneously as mayor and doctor (with his surgery also for a time located in the municipal chambers); his efforts were meticulously recorded and favourably publicized in the *Bowen Independent*. In April 1958, while the town was being devastated by a cyclone, the mayor operated 'with calm intensity by torchlight' on a desperately ill patient in an unroofed hospital. For Delamothe, a week of virtual twenty-four-hour days followed as he supervised the beginning of the town's reconstruction. Next year he was appointed O.B.E.

In 1960 Delamothe accepted Liberal endorsement for the new seat of Bowen in the Legislative Assembly. The electorate encompassed many strong Labor areas, including the militant and heavily unionized Collinsville, but his personal following enabled him to win Bowen that year and to hold the seat narrowly until 1971. He was more persuasive than most backbenchers at extracting government funds: in his first term Bowen's high school was completed and a new hospital built. Following the closure and sale of the state-owned coalmine at Collinsville in 1961, he negotiated with local employers to redeploy the retrenched workers. Soon after, the introduction of a major dam and power-station project eliminated unemployment at Collinsville.

On 26 September 1963 Delamothe was appointed minister for justice and attorney-general. In the eight years he held the portfolio he acted to ease the backlog of cases in Queensland courts, and oversaw the establishment of the Law Reform Commission and the Legal Aid Bureau. By introducing weekend detention and work-release schemes for minor offenders, and by persuading the government to begin an extensive building programme, he significantly alleviated prison overcrowding. His reform of the State's drinking laws resulted in the provision of new types of liquor licences which allowed Brisbane hotels to remain open on Sundays and permitted women in public bars. He also introduced Queensland's first consumer-protection laws. According to an enthusiastic journalist, 'The Doc' 'probably put forward more compassionate and humane legislation than any other politician in the state's history'. From June 1967 he was deputy-leader of the Queensland Liberal Party.

Following an electoral redistribution, the seat of Bowen was abolished. On 20 December 1971 Delamothe took up his appointment as Queensland agent-general in London. He was knighted in June 1973. Already seriously ill, he resigned on 30 September. Sir Peter died of cancer on 26 October that year at St Mary's Hospital, Paddington, England, and was cremated; his ashes were scattered on Bowen harbour. His wife, their son and two daughters, and four sons of his first marriage survived him.

J. Delamothe and B. Stevenson, *The Delamothe Story* (Brisb, 1989).   BRIAN F. STEVENSON

DELANEY, COLIN JOHN (1897-1969), police commissioner, was born on 28 February 1897 at Pyramid Hill, Victoria, seventh child of Cornelius Delaney, a farmer from Ireland, and his Victorian-born wife Bridget Vera, née Irwin. After schooling at Bendigo, Colin worked as a stationary engine driver. He was a buttermaker when he married Gladys Viola Thirza Frances Meyers (d. 1966) on 19 September 1918 at the Congregational parsonage, Richmond. Moving to Sydney, he found employment as a tram conductor and remarried his wife at St Mary's Catholic Cathedral on 23 January 1919.

On 29 April that year Delaney joined the New South Wales Police Force. Appointed constable in 1920, he carried out his duties in the inner city; in 1922 he was transferred to criminal investigation and based at the Regent Street station. In 1927 he moved to police headquarters. Promoted detective constable (1928) and detective sergeant (1933), he 'proved an acute and skilful investigator', but, at his own request, was returned to the uniformed branch in 1939. Delaney worked in the licensing and traffic sections, helped to establish the State's police-cadet system and served on the Police Appeal Board, becoming inspector (February 1943) and superintendent (September 1946). While at Tamworth in 1947-50, he was in charge of the northern police district. In the course of his career Delaney took several exchanges with interstate police, and probably had some involvement with security and intelligence work during World War II. His progress was enhanced by a close association, at critical stages, with Commissioner W. J. MacKay [q.v.10]. Deputy-commissioner from May

1952, Delaney was appointed commissioner of police on 14 October that year, the first Catholic to hold the position. Relations between the police and the public were at a low ebb, with allegations of bribery and of assaults by police.

Initiating major and essential reforms, Delaney modernized his force by increasing the number of police stations in Sydney (from 53 in 1952 to 92 in 1962) and the number of four-wheel police vehicles in the State (from 272 to 773), by encouraging the use of new technologies and by decentralizing decision-making. For all that, his attempts to introduce promotion by merit rather than by seniority met with rebuffs from the Crown Employees' Appeal Board and he never really solved the problem of institutionalized corruption within the force. Several royal commissions and investigations indicated police involvement in this area, and later revelations concerning Delaney's successors Norman Allan and Frederick Hanson [qq.v.] suggest that corruption had existed at the highest levels of the force for a considerable time.

Regarding homosexuals as Australia's 'greatest menace', Delaney made their surveillance and prosecution a major priority. On his recommendation, legislation was introduced in the 1950s which promulgated new homosexual crimes. Police methods of entrapment (using 'good-looking young C.I.D. officers') were ethically dubious. Because of his obsession, scarce police resources were diverted from areas where they might have been more usefully deployed.

Delaney's nine commendations, several medals and appointments to C.V.O. (1954) and C.B.E. (1962) attested to his bravery, drive and ability. He had greying, wavy hair and a bulky frame, wore double-breasted suits when out of uniform, supported the Federation of New South Wales Police-Citizens Boys' Clubs and belonged to the City Bowling Club. After retiring in February 1962, he visited Britain and Europe with his wife. Survived by his son, Delaney died on 5 July 1969 at his Wahroonga home and was buried in Northern Suburbs cemetery. His estate was sworn for probate at $73 409.

F. Cain, *The Origins of Political Surveillance in Australia* (Syd, 1983); A. Moore, *The Secret Army and the Premier* (Syd, 1989); *People* (Syd), 14 July 1954, p 11; *NSW Police News*, Aug 1990, p 17; *Bulletin*, 22 Oct 1952; *SMH*, 19 Feb 1954, 11 June 1958, 2, 28 Feb 1962, 6, 9 July 1969, 7 Nov 1981, 11 Nov 1991; *Australian*, 26 Aug 1969.

GARRY C. WOTHERSPOON

DE LA RUE, HIPPOLYTE FERDINAND (1891-1977), merchant seaman and air force officer, was born on 13 March 1891 at Auburn, Sydney, second son of Edmond Emile De La Rue, jeweller, and his wife Ellen Georgina, née Brown, both native-born. Known as 'Bill' in his youth, he received a limited education. In 1908 he went to sea in the merchant navy and by 1914 was a second officer.

Soon after World War I broke out, De La Rue was engaged in transporting soldiers and equipment from England to France. As navigator of the troop-ship, *Huntsgreen*, he was present at the Gallipoli landing on 25 April 1915 and served off the peninsula until the evacuation in December. In London on 30 July 1916 he was appointed temporary flight sub-lieutenant in the Royal Naval Air Service. He gained his pilot's wings at Cranwell, Lincolnshire, in November, undertook seaplane training at Calshot, Hampshire, and in February 1917 was sent to Fishguard, Wales. While patrolling coastal waters, he attacked and apparently destroyed a German submarine in St Georges Channel, but the sinking could not be confirmed.

In January 1918 De La Rue was promoted flight lieutenant (honorary captain, Royal Air Force, from April) and joined No. 6 Wing at Otranto, Italy. A member and later commander of No. 223 Squadron, he took part in long-distance bombing, sea patrols and escort duties. On a raid against the Austrian-held port of Durazzo (Durrës, Albania), he piloted one of two Short torpedo-carrying seaplanes protecting the bombers. Both escorts were fired upon and the second was forced to put down in the enemy harbour. De La Rue rescued the pilot and observer, and returned to base, though it had been 'extremely doubtful if his machine would rise from the water with four on board'. For this action he was awarded the Distinguished Flying Cross (1918). He also received the Italian Silver Medal for Military Valour (1919). In January 1919 he joined No. 64 Wing, R.A.F., at Alexandria, Egypt, where he commanded No. 270 (Seaplane) Squadron. Despite being granted a permanent commission in August, he decided to return to Australia and seek employment as a naval aviator.

Appointed captain in the Australian Air Corps in May 1920, De La Rue transferred as flight lieutenant to the (Royal) Australian Air Force on its formation in March 1921; he was the service's only experienced seaplane pilot. His early postings (1921-29) were to units at Point Cook, Victoria, and to R.A.A.F. Headquarters, Melbourne. On 1 October 1923 he married Clara Constance Stone with Presbyterian forms at Scots Church, Melbourne. Sent to England on exchange in 1929 to familiarize himself with aircraft-carrier work, he also performed administrative duties in No. 201 (Flying-Boat) Squadron at Calshot. Back home, he commanded the Seaplane

Squadron at Point Cook (1931-33) and No. 1 Flying Training School (from 1933). Promoted wing commander in December 1932, he advanced to group captain in January 1937. Twelve months later he took command of the R.A.A.F. station at Richmond, New South Wales.

With the onset of World War II, on 9 October 1939 De La Rue was chosen to lead an air expeditionary force abroad. The plan was cancelled, however, in favour of Australia's participation in the Empire Air Training Scheme. In October 1940 he became senior air staff officer at headquarters, Central Area. Next month it was decided that a R.A.A.F. base depot should be established overseas and De La Rue was chosen to take a nucleus staff to England. This scheme was also abandoned, and the Australian authorities rejected a British suggestion that De La Rue proceed to the Middle East instead. On 9 January 1941 he was promoted acting air commodore and made air officer commanding, Western Area, with headquarters in Perth. He took the post of inspector of administration at Air Force Headquarters in January 1943, and was appointed C.B.E. in 1944.

Stocky in build and energetic in temperament, 'Kanga' De La Rue was a rigid disciplinarian with a short temper; he ended telephone conversations which displeased him by throwing the handset out of the window. Yet, there was another side to his nature, revealed in his kindness, generosity and reticence, and also in his work as a watercolourist. He retired on 1 April 1946 and was granted the honorary rank of air commodore in 1956. Survived by his daughter, he died on 18 May 1977 in his home at Kew, Melbourne, and was cremated; his estate was sworn for probate at $148 104.

J. Herington, *Air War Against Germany and Italy 1939-1943* (Canb, 1954); D. Gillison, *Royal Australian Air Force 1939-1942* (Canb, 1962); C. D. Coulthard-Clark, *The Third Brother* (Syd, 1991); A. W. Stephens, *Power Plus Attitude* (Canb, 1992); *Reveille* (Syd), July 1937, Nov 1939; *Herald* (Melb), 10 Oct 1939; information from Mrs Y. C. Bonwick, Mt Martha, Vic.   C. D. COULTHARD-CLARK

DELLIT, CHARLES BRUCE (1898-1942), architect, was born on 7 November 1898 at Darlington, Sydney, son of Albert Dellit, a furniture manufacturer from Victoria, and his second wife Agnes Gertrude, née Mack, who was born in New South Wales. On leaving Christian Brothers' College, Waverley, Bruce was employed by the architect John L. Berry, studied at Sydney Technical College in 1912-18 and attended Leslie Wilkinson's [q.v.12] lectures at the University of Sydney in 1919-20.

Moving to Queensland in 1920, Dellit became chief draftsman for Hall [q.v.9 F. R. Hall] & Prentice, architects, and worked on the design of a town hall for Brisbane. He married Victoria Sara Miller on 15 October 1921 at St Andrew's Anglican Church, South Brisbane. Back in Sydney, after joining the firm of Spain [q.v.12] & Cosh in 1922, he registered under the Architects Act on 23 June 1923 and worked on city buildings. He began private practice in 1928 and completed his first major project, Kyle House, in Macquarie Place, an office building which rejected period stylism and introduced a characteristic Dellit motif, the monumental entrance arch.

In 1929 he won a design competition for an Anzac memorial in Hyde Park, Sydney, from 117 entries. With significant contributions from the sculptor Rayner Hoff [q.v.9], Dellit completed the Anzac Memorial in 1934. Built of Bathurst granite, with a striking, 'stepped' silhouette, it has been claimed as Australia's finest example of monumental Art Deco architecture. Commercial and domestic work followed throughout the 1930s, including renovations to the Australia Hotel (1933), funeral parlours (1933) in Oxford Street for Charles Kinsela [q.v.], and the Liberty Theatre (1934). Dellit's finest commercial building, the Bank of New South Wales in O'Connell Street, was completed in 1940. Contrasting with his commercial work, his own house, Aleuria (c.1928), in Fox Valley Road, Wahroonga, was a free interpretation of the Mediterranean idiom introduced by Wilkinson.

Breaking from his conservative architectural education, Dellit pioneered the Art Deco style. He looked for inspiration to American skyscrapers and to new technology, new materials and new uses for traditional materials. He believed that architects should 'go to work in a healthy way in sympathy with scientific progress' and 'by the aid of modern science reach beyond our present dreams to artistic creations as yet undreamt of'.

A large man—seldom seen without his 'fearsome sombrero'—Dellit was described as 'a human dynamo', 'arresting and vital' and 'supremely confident'. He was an exceptionally talented draftsman and renderer. A gifted painter in oils, he associated with Norman Lindsay and 'Rah' Fizelle [qq.v.10,8]. He spared neither himself nor his staff: in busy times, working days began at 5.30 a.m. and ended at midnight, six days a week. When a job was completed, he spent a night on the town, 'blowing the cobwebs away'. Survived by his wife, son and two daughters, Dellit died of cancer on 21 August 1942 in hospital at Hornsby and was cremated.

The Anzac Memorial, Hyde Park, Sydney (Syd, nd); H. Tanner (ed), *Architects of Australia* (Melb,

1981); *Architecture*, 20 Mar 1920, 1 Aug 1929, 1 Aug 1930; *Building* (Syd), 12 July 1930, 12 Mar 1931, 13 Mar, 12 Apr 1933, 24 July 1940, 24 Aug 1942; *Art in Aust*, 15 Aug 1934; *SMH*, 26 Aug 1942; *Bulletin*, 2 Sept 1942; A. Stuart-Robertson, Charles Bruce Dellit, Architect: 1900-1942 (research paper, Power Institute of Fine Arts, Univ Syd, 1976).

PETER REYNOLDS
RICHARD E. APPERLY*

DE NEEVE, LUCY (1906-1976), nurse and administrator, was born on 25 October 1906 at Darwen, Lancashire, England, daughter of Nathaniel Walmsley, auctioneer, and his wife Ada, née Duckworth. Lucy trained at Royal Liverpool Children's Hospital in 1926-29, then worked with children for four years before undertaking general training at University College Hospital, London. Focussing her interest on paediatrics, she became a home sister and a theatre sister at the Princess Elizabeth of York Hospital for Children, also in London. On 1 July 1937 she married Gerald Alexander Auguste Sechiari at the register office, Westminster; they were to be divorced in 1949.

During World War II Mrs Sechiari organized plastic-surgery theatres at the Ministry of Pensions Hospital, Roehampton, and at Stoke Mandeville, Buckinghamshire. Having joined Queen Alexandra's Imperial Military Nursing Service, she was matron of several hospitals in India from 1943 to 1946 and completed her war service in February 1947. She was briefly employed at Lord Mayor Treloar's Orthopaedic Hospital for Children at Alton, Hampshire, and returned to the Queen Elizabeth Hospital for Sick Children (previously the Princess Elizabeth). In August 1947 she was appointed lady superintendent of the (Royal) Children's Hospital, Melbourne. She arrived in November. At Scots Church, Russell Street, on 23 January 1953 she married a divorcee Josef Anton de Neeve, an airlines liaison officer.

At the Children's Hospital Lucy had found obsolete methods, inadequate training and morale at a low ebb. After her initial inspection she remarked that she felt as if she had been 'transported to the middle ages'. Insufficient staffing (248 in 1947) was blamed on shortage of accommodation. Lucy demanded, and got, additional staff to cope with non-nursing duties, and, eventually, a new home was built to accommodate 315 nurses. She treated her staff well: their uniform was redesigned, their meals improved and their hours on duty were adjusted. Preliminary training was extended from two to four weeks, and in 1950 to eight. An advanced course in paediatric nursing was also established. The old 'starch curtain' was torn aside when a sisters' council and a student nurses'

executive were formed. To all, she was unfailingly courteous and tolerant, and she upheld the rights and position of her staff against the often dictatorial demands of the medical staff who were prone to regard themselves as demi-gods. At ward level, Lucy's overriding concern was for the patient. Numerous traditional and disruptive practices—such as baths and bed-making at 9 p.m.—were abolished; a mandatory 'quiet hour' was introduced; children who were well enough were allowed greater freedom of movement and more interesting activities; and restrictions on visiting hours were gradually abolished.

In each of her reforms directed to child care, nursing conditions and standards, and the better integration of nursing with general hospital administration, Lucy worked closely with the medical director Dr V. L. Collins [q.v.]. Beyond the hospital, she was an influential member of the Nurses' Board of Victoria (1950-59) and the council of the Royal Victorian College of Nursing (vice-president 1950-59; president 1959-61). Paediatric nursing in Australia benefited immeasurably from her experience, intelligence and confident leadership. She retired in 1962 and went with Anton to Bali, Indonesia, where she died on 19 July 1976. Her husband survived her. She had no children.

L. Gardiner, *Royal Children's Hospital Melbourne 1870-1970* (Melb, 1970); H. Williams, *From Charity to Teaching Hospital* (Melb, 1989); *UNA*, July-Aug 1976, p 3; *Herald* (Melb), 4 Aug 1947, 20 Nov 1948, 23 Jan 1953, 5 June 1962; *Sun News-Pictorial*, 7 Aug 1947, 14 Sept 1962; *Age*, 26 July 1952, 4 Aug 1976; Roy Children's Hospital, Melb, Archives; personal information.

LYNDSAY GARDINER

DENNING, ARTHUR (1901-1975), educationist, was born on 23 April 1901 at Glebe, Sydney, second child of Australian-born parents Benjamin Reuben Denning, schoolteacher, and his wife Florence, née Duffin. Arthur was educated at Sydney Boys' High School and the University of Sydney (B.Sc., 1922; Dip.Ed., 1923). Entering the Department of Public Instruction in 1923, he taught at Wagga Wagga (1924), Armidale (1924-28) and Canterbury Boys' (1928-36) high schools. He was a council-member of the New South Wales Public School Teachers' Federation and secretary (1934-36) of the Secondary Teachers' Association. Having begun teaching mathematics part time at Sydney Technical College in 1930, he was promoted head teacher of mathematics in 1935 and deputy-principal next year. On 23 December 1938 in his brother's house at Cronulla he married with Methodist forms Margaret Cecily Mordaunt; they were to have three children.

Believing that technical education was an essential ingredient of any effective national policy to make industries more efficient and internationally competitive, and to improve Australia's economy and standard of living, Denning endorsed the efforts in 1936 of D. H. Drummond [q.v.8], the minister for education, to obtain Commonwealth support. He was disappointed with funding provisions in Drummond's Technical Education Act (1940) and relieved that the incoming Labor government nullified the Act's proclamation in 1941.

During World War II Denning was responsible—under the Commonwealth Reconstruction Training Scheme—for projects which included co-operation with the United States Army in establishing the correspondence teaching centre for the South-West Pacific Area (42 000 students), setting up courses for the Australian armed services (30 000 students) and arranging the training of munitions workers.

While deputy-principal (assistant-superintendent from 1945) at S.T.C., Denning introduced policies aimed at increasing the number of highly-qualified technologists. The standard of diploma courses was upgraded, and the range of diploma and post-diploma courses was increased to cover new areas such as radio and television. He sought co-operation from the University of Sydney to gain recognition of improved standards. When credits for diploma courses, approved by the university senate, failed to achieve wide recognition at home and abroad, Denning persistently recommended the establishment of an institution with authority to award degrees, like the Massachusetts Institute of Technology, United States of America. With the support of Robert Heffron and Wallace Wurth [qq.v.], respectively minister for education and chairman of the Public Service Board, a developmental council was set up in 1947. Next year an 'Institute of Technology', with Denning acting as director and using the facilities of S.T.C., began enrolling students in degree courses.

Heffron made provision for the institute to be a university through the Technical Education and New South Wales University of Technology Act (1949). On 1 July 1949 Denning was named director of the new university (his appointment was renewed annually) and appointed deputy-director of technical education. On the retirement of Percy Riddell [q.v.] in January 1950, Denning became director of technical education and permanent head of the department, while continuing as director of the university.

Many of the professors whom he had recruited, such as R. M. Hartwell, objected to working under public service regulations and resented having a public servant as their director. For his part, Denning regarded academic attitudes and irregular working hours as a handicap to good communication and administration. While he recognized that a university, once it had own facilities, should be independent and separate from a government department, some academic staff thought that he wanted to keep the university and the Department of Technical Education together indefinitely. Eventually, his dream of maintaining a close working relationship between the department and the staff responsible for the broad spectrum of vocational courses provided by the university was shattered.

In June 1951 four professors, among them A. E. Alexander [q.v.], signed a 'prayer' to the university council recommending that immediate steps be taken to separate the university from the department and the board. In November 1952 the university council took swift action after its sub-committee had reported in favour of autonomy (from 1 July 1954). Denning was left no option but to resign as director when Professor (Sir) Philip Baxter was elected by council to that office from January 1953. As an ordinary member of council from the end of 1952, Denning was not able to contribute greatly to the university's future, but his founding achievements were recognized by the conferring of an honorary doctorate of science in 1957. He was elected a fellow of the Royal Society of Arts (1952) and appointed C.B.E. (1962).

As director of technical education (until 1958), Denning endeavoured to meet a growing need and demand: five new technical colleges were established between 1953 and 1959. He was chairman of the Australian Committee for Study and Training in the U.S.A., a director of the United States Educational Foundation in Australia (Fulbright Board), an executive-member of the American Australian Association and —with Sir Owen Dixon [q.v.]—a founder of the Australian Canadian Committee, of which Denning was secretary-treasurer.

In 1958 Denning was appointed commissioner for New South Wales in the U.S.A. Based in New York, he assisted American firms to set up subsidiaries in Australia by promoting joint-ventures and arranging licensing agreements. Back in Sydney in 1967, he became a management consultant, a director of several companies, and chairman and chief executive of Value Search Pty Ltd. He belonged to the Australian Golf, Double Bay Bowling and American National clubs, and enjoyed playing bridge and chess. Survived by his wife, daughter and one son, Denning died on 27 March 1975 in Royal

Prince Alfred Hospital and was cremated. His portrait by H. A. Hanke is held by the University of New South Wales.

D. H. Drummond, *Technical Education in Australia* (Syd, 1936); A. H. Willis, *The University of New South Wales* (Syd, 1983); Technical Education Comm, Report, *PP* (NSW), 1935-36, 1, p 311; *Technical Gazette of NSW*, 24, pt 2, 1936, p 21; *SMH*, 8 May 1936, 21 Feb 1948, 11 June 1949, 6 Aug 1958, 28 Mar 1975; A. Denning, curriculum vitae (copy held by ADB); Dept of Education (NSW), teachers' records (NSWA); Univ NSW Archives; information from Mrs M. Denning, Darling Point, Syd.　　　　　　　　　　　　HUGH KING

DENNING, WARREN EDWIN (1906-1975), journalist, was born on 14 October 1906 in South Perth, eldest child of Arthur Feldwick Denning, a boot salesman from New South Wales, and his Victorian-born wife Minnie Ellen, née Warren. The family moved to Sydney when Warren was 7. As a boy, he dreamed of boarding-school and Oxford, but his parents' financial circumstances forced him into a working career at 16 as a cadet-journalist on the *Cumberland Times*, Parramatta. He graduated to the *Labor Daily* in 1926 and, after promotion to senior journalist, covered the opening of Parliament House in Canberra in 1927.

A member of the Federal Parliamentary Press Gallery by 1928, Denning was appointed senior Canberra correspondent for the Melbourne *Argus* in 1931. During the mid-1930s he worked in Sydney and Melbourne, and gained a diploma in journalism from the University of Melbourne in 1935. He returned to Canberra in 1937 as local manager of Australian United Press. On 8 May 1939 he became the first staff-correspondent in the news service of the Australian Broadcasting Commission. As manager of the A.B.C.'s Canberra bureau, he supported moves for a fully independent news service.

In 1937 Denning had published *Caucus Crisis* (Sydney), a vibrant and informed account of the downfall of the Scullin [q.v.11] government in 1931. Although it was criticized for largely ignoring the role of the Depression, the book became a classic, partly because of its revelation of caucus in-fighting, and partly because it carried political and moralizing messages for subsequent Labor governments.

Denning had two other notable publications. *Inside Parliament* (Sydney, 1946) was designed to give 'the man in the street' a notion of what parliament was and did, and how it was important in Australian life. For many years Denning's book served as a school and university text. *The Road to Canberra* (Sydney, 1947) recorded a trip in March 1944 from Sydney to Canberra. Drawing upon research into people, buildings and places, it was also a whimsical account of what a short, overweight and normally well-groomed journalist saw—when red-faced and puffing—from 'the lowly elevation of a bicycle-seat'.

Denning loved the Canberra where he spent his most productive years. He wrote several sketches of the new capital and, in 1953, published an article on Walter Burley Griffin [q.v.9] in *Meanjin*. His favoured spot was Parliament House where he participated in and observed political intrigue, and where he liked to impart wisdom to the younger members of his profession.

He was always a Labor man. The Depression had convinced him of the ruinous consequences of capitalism, and his political outlook was cemented by moral and religious conviction. Born an Anglican, Denning converted to Catholicism shortly before marrying Constance Helen Fergus (d. 1953) on 11 March 1931 in St Christopher's Church, Canberra. While denying that he experienced a Pauline awakening, Denning became a devout Catholic, anxious to reconcile Labor's socialist principles with the Church's teachings on the rights to private property and on the individuality of the soul.

The good Labor man feared that the party had lost its idealism. Yet, he maintained, 'in some queer but compelling way of its own', Labor stood for the best things in politics, exemplified by his hero John Curtin [q.v.] whose whole life seemed to confirm the possibility of peace and justice for everyone who lived under the Southern Cross. Denning was not, however, narrowly partisan. He made several friends on the other side of politics, including Archie Cameron [q.v.], and his numerous unpublished profiles of political figures, composed in the mid-1940s, were balanced, shrewd and sympathetic. Like many of his contemporaries, he paid homage to Charles Hawker [q.v.9], respected J. A. Lyons [q.v.10] for his integrity and thought highly of (Sir) Robert Menzies [q.v.] for his intellectual capacity.

After leaving Canberra in 1946, Denning went to Sydney. He was the A.B.C.'s news editor in Queensland (1948-49), a chief sub-editor of national evening bulletins in Sydney (1949-57) and news editor in Tasmania (from 1957), before taking the post of federal cadet counsellor in Sydney in 1966. At St Joseph's Church, Edgecliff, on 1 June 1957 he had married a widow Esther Josephine Hollingworth, née Bang. He retired in 1971 and was appointed M.B.E. in 1972. Having suffered from diabetes for thirty years, Denning died of myocardial infarction on 24 March 1975 in St Vincent's Hospital, Darlinghurst, and was buried in Botany cemetery. His wife, two stepdaughters and the son of his first marriage survived him.

A. Reid, 'Memoir', in W. Denning, *Caucus Crisis* (Syd, 1982); K. S. Inglis, *This is the ABC* (Melb, 1983); *Journalist*, Mar 1966, Apr 1975; *Radio Active*, Oct 1971; *SMH*, 26 Mar 1975; Denning papers (NL).   I. R. HANCOCK

DENNIS, CLARA (1916-1971), swimmer, was born on 7 March 1916 at Burwood, Sydney, third of six children of native-born parents Alexander Miller Dennis (d. 1931), police constable, and his wife Susan Violet, née Efford. In the early 1920s the family moved to Clovelly. Clare, as she was known, attended the local public and Randwick Domestic Science schools. By a determined splash across Clovelly Bay at the age of 7, she had persuaded her father to let her join her elder sister Thora at the Sydney Ladies' Swimming Club. Inspired by Thora's selection in the Australian team for the Olympic Games in 1928, Clare was soon competing in interclub events and left school at 14.

In the 1930 State championships Dennis discovered that breast-stroke was her forte. She won her first New South Wales and Australian 220 yards breast-stroke titles in 1931. On 18 January 1932 at the Domain baths she broke the world record—swimming 200 metres breast-stroke in 3 minutes 8.6 seconds. Her achievement brought automatic selection for the 1932 Olympics at Los Angeles, United States of America, but it was only through various donations that Dennis was able to attend.

In the heats she was almost disqualified for showing 'too much shoulder blade' in her regulation, silk, Speedo swim-suit. Following protracted official negotiations the charge was dismissed and Dennis went on—with a new Olympic and world record time of 3 minutes 6.3 seconds for the 200 metres breast-stroke—to become the first Australian woman, since Fanny Durack [q.v.8] in 1912, to bring home an Olympic gold medal. The Australian press admired Dennis's speed, strength and, not least, her 'femininity'. Engaged in the 'graceful', no 'muscles-or-sweat' sport of swimming, she avoided the opprobrium often cast on female athletes.

After returning from Los Angeles, Dennis began work for Anthony Hordern [q.v.4] & Sons Ltd in Sydney and devoted her spare time to swimming. In February 1933 she broke Australian and world records with a 100 metres breast-stroke swim of 1 minute 24.6 seconds and set a new Australian record of 3 minutes 9.2 seconds for the 220 yards breast-stroke. Next year, in London, she became the first Australian woman to win a gold

medal in the British Empire Games (with a time of 2 minutes 50.2 seconds for the 200 yards breast-stroke). In 1936, amid much controversy, she was passed over for the Berlin Olympics. Disappointed, she retired from amateur competitive swimming, although she continued to swim for pleasure and was to be involved in professional coaching.

On 12 December 1942 at the Presbyterian Church, Randwick, Dennis married George Augustus Golding, a detective in the police force and a former Olympic track athlete; they were to remain childless. She was then a masseuse and owned two hairdressing salons, at Clovelly and Henley. George taught her to shoot, and they enjoyed frequent hunting trips. Having lived in several Sydney suburbs —thanks to George's hobby of building houses—the Goldings eventually settled at Manly. Clare died of cancer on 4 June 1971 at a local private hospital and was cremated. In 1981 she was honoured by the Swimming Hall of Fame at Fort Lauderdale, Florida, U.S.A., and in 1985 she was listed in the Sport Australia Hall of Fame, Melbourne.

G. Atkinson, *Australian and New Zealand Olympians* (Melb, 1984); R. and M. Howell, *Aussie Gold* (Brisb, 1988); A. Clarkson, *Lanes of Gold* (Syd, 1990); *SMH*, 19 Jan 1931, 11 Aug 1932, 10, 15 Feb 1933, 8 Aug 1934, 6 Apr 1936; *The Times*, 7 Aug 1934; *Sun* (Syd), 6 June 1984; V. Raszeja Wood, A Decent and Proper Exertion: The Rise of Women's Competitive Swimming in Sydney to 1912 (B.A. Hons thesis, Univ NSW, 1990); information from Ms A. Dennis and Mr G. Golding, Manly, Syd.

V. M. RASZEJA

DENNY, CHARLES KEITH (1888-1975), lavender farmer, was born on 23 February 1888 at Kingston, Surrey, England, only son of Charles Denny, corn merchant, and his wife Ada Ellen, née Lampard. Educated at Charterhouse, young Charles was admitted to the Institute of Chartered Accountants in England & Wales on 2 August 1911. At the parish church, Bridestowe, Devon, on 8 April 1913 he married Blanche Ellen Francis. During World War I he was seconded to munitions production.

From 1919 Denny was manager of F. S. Cleaver & Sons Ltd, Twickenham, a soap and perfumery business half-owned by his family. When the firm was sold to Lever Brothers Pty Ltd in 1921, he decided to emigrate. He planned to establish a farm in a climate suitable for growing 'true lavender' (*Lavandula augustifolia*), an unhybridized shrub then found only in the higher altitudes of a small region of the southern French Alps. Its oil was used as a base for the finest scent and for medicine.

Arriving in Tasmania in November 1921,

Denny settled with his family at North Lily-dale, near Launceston, in April 1922. To honour Blanche's birthplace, he named their farm Bridestowe Estate. He sowed the 'true lavender' seeds which he had brought from France on a quarter-acre (0.1 ha) plot, and was confident that the strain would remain pure. Picked by hand in 1924, his first harvest yielded 11 lb. (5 kg) of flower-heads from which a minute amount of oil was extracted. In England the oil was analysed as having promise, but, like new wine, its final quality could not be assessed until it had matured.

With limited planting stock and no appro-priate machinery, Denny sowed 5 acres (2 ha) of the same lavender in 1927 and 1928. He designed and built a distillery on his property in 1930 and exported his first batch of oil five years later. By 1939 he had 50 acres under cultivation and began to recoup his outlay. The cessation of lavender-oil imports during World War II advantaged Denny, Australia's only significant lavender-grower. His two sons returned from the war and rejoined their father's business. The Dennys bought a sec-ond farm near Nabowla, planted it in 1948 and began prolonged testing. Next year they adapted an old harvester by equipping it with a special header, but lost out to foreign com-petitors when the French franc was devalued. In 1950 they sought tariff protection to avoid ruin.

Charles handed over management of his properties to his sons in 1956; it took them until 1974 to perfect their stock. Patriotic, somewhat eccentric and a man of dogged per-severance, Denny remained an active gar-dener. He died on 2 June 1975 at St Luke's Hospital, Launceston, and was buried in Lily-dale cemetery; his sons survived him. By 1981 the estate produced 15 per cent of the world's supply of lavender oil. Tourists visited the property to see 100 acres of beautifully contoured crops in bloom. The family retained the business until 1990 when it was acquired by Natural Extracts International Pty Ltd.

Bridestowe Estate, *Jubilee Season 1921-22 to 1981-82* (np, Launc?, 1981); J. McLeod, *Lavender, Sweet Lavender* (priv pub, Syd, 1989); Trans Aust Airlines, *Transair,* Oct 1981; *Aust Country Style,* Dec-Jan, 1990-91, p 46; *Mercury* (Hob), 8 June 1950; personal information. R. A. FERRALL

DERBYSHIRE, MAXWELL (1915-1980), soldier, was born on 27 June 1915 at Laun-ceston, Tasmania, son of Adye Russell Derbyshire, labourer, and his wife Louisa Sarah, née Pinnington, both Tasmanian born. When Max was a boy the family moved to Wagga Wagga, New South Wales, where he received further schooling and worked as a

coach and motorcar trimmer. In 1933-39 he served in the 56th Battalion of the Militia and rose through the ranks to lieutenant.

Transferring to the Australian Imperial Force on 9 April 1940, Derbyshire joined the 2nd/2nd Battalion in Egypt in October. Dur-ing the offensive in the Western Desert, in January 1941 he saw action in Libya in the battle of Bardia and the capture of Tobruk. Moved to Egypt, his unit was then sent to Greece where it disembarked on 22 March and took up defensive positions in the north. On 16 April the battalion withdrew to the Piniós Gorge and engaged in fierce fighting against German armoured forces. Driven from their positions, the Australians made their way south in fragmented groups. Derbyshire was one of those taken prisoner. After two attempts, he escaped on 30 June.

Befriended by Greeks in the Athens-Piraeus region, Derbyshire joined the nascent underground movement. The genial Aus-tralian—dark haired, slim and 5 ft 11 ins (180.3 cm) tall—became an almost legendary figure. He took part in daring acts of sabotage and set 'a striking example of tenacity and cool courage' for which he was awarded the Military Cross (1943). His exploits became known to the Gestapo and he was forced to change locations frequently. In December 1942 he joined nine others who planned to leave Greece. For three days and two nights he marched on bleeding feet, through mud and snow, to a rendezvous north of Athens. Having been rowed (by two drunken boat-men) across the strait to Euboea, he em-barked in a small caique. Although twice sighted by the enemy, his party reached Turkey whence he travelled to Egypt. He returned to Australia in January 1943.

Rejoining the 2nd/2nd in North Queensland in June, Derbyshire was promoted captain on 21 June 1944. The battalion arrived in New Guinea in December. Derbyshire led 'A' Company throughout the Aitape-Wewak cam-paign (February to August 1945). For his bravery and resourcefulness he won a Bar to his M.C. From October to December his company was detached to Merauke, Nether-lands New Guinea, to counter anticipated trouble from Indonesian nationalists.

Back home, Derbyshire decided to re-main in the army. On 19 January 1946 at St Andrew's Presbyterian Church, Wagga Wagga, he married Belle Amy Edney who was to predecease him. Employed mainly in train-ing duties in Australia, he also had postings as an observer with the Far East Land Forces in Malaya (1950-52) and with the 1st Battalion, Royal Australian Regiment, in Japan and Korea (1955-56). He was promoted major in 1955 and ended his service at the In-fantry Centre, Ingleburn, New South Wales, where he was briefly officer commanding.

On 28 June 1962 he was placed on the Retired List as lieutenant colonel.

Settling at Lurnea, Derbyshire ran a cleaning business before working for Fair Deal Real Estate Pty Ltd. He died of coronary vascular disease on 24 December 1980 at Liverpool and was cremated. His wife June survived him, as did the two sons of his first marriage.

G. Long, *Greece, Crete and Syria* (Canb, 1953) and *The Final Campaigns* (Canb, 1963); S. Wick, *Purple Over Green* (Syd, 1977); AWM records; information from Mrs J. Derbyshire, Liverpool, Syd.

A. J. SWEETING

DERHAM, FRANCIS PLUMLEY (1885-1957), soldier and lawyer, and ALFRED PLUMLEY (1891-1962), soldier and physician, were born on 15 May 1885 and 12 September 1891 at Camberwell, Melbourne, first and fourth sons of Thomas Plumley Derham, a solicitor from England, and his Victorian-born wife Ellen Hyde, née Hodgson. Frederick Thomas Derham [q.v.4] was the brothers' uncle and Enid [q.v.8] their sister.

Alfred was educated at Scotch College and the University of Melbourne (M.B., B.S., 1918; M.D., 1923), but interrupted his medical studies when World War I broke out. Formerly a subaltern in the Melbourne University Rifles, he enlisted in the Australian Imperial Force on 26 August 1914 and was posted to the 5th Battalion. He was commissioned next month and sailed for Egypt in October. On 25 April 1915 he landed at Gallipoli as a platoon commander. Wounded that day, he refused to be evacuated until the 30th, and conducted himself in the meantime with such gallantry and energy that he was awarded the Military Cross and mentioned in dispatches. Derham transferred to the staff of the 2nd Brigade in August. He left the peninsula in December, moved from Egypt to France in March 1916 and was permitted to embark for Australia in November to complete his degree. On 10 July 1917 he married a schoolteacher Frances Alexandra Mabel Letitia Anderson at St Mary's Anglican Church, Caulfield, Melbourne.

Francis completed the articled clerks' course at the University of Melbourne and on 1 August 1906 was admitted as a solicitor. In 1907 he was commissioned in the Australian Field Artillery. He married Adeline Matilda Bowden on 7 October 1909 at the Presbyterian Church, Hawthorn; they were to remain childless. Promoted major in January 1915, he transferred to the A.I.F. in October, embarked for Egypt next month and by March 1916 was on the Western Front. For his service as a battery commander in the 4th Field Artillery Brigade he was awarded the Distinguished Service Order and mentioned in dispatches. He commanded the 14th F.A.B. as lieutenant colonel in 1917-19. Awarded the French Croix de Guerre and thrice more mentioned in dispatches, he was repatriated in July 1919.

Between the wars the brothers lived in Melbourne and continued their careers as citizen-soldiers: Alfred rose to lieutenant colonel in the Australian Army Medical Corps and commanded field-ambulances in the Militia in the 1930s; Francis was promoted colonel in December 1930, and commanded artillery and infantry brigades. Establishing a private practice at Preston in 1920, Alfred moved his premises to the city in 1922. He specialized in children's diseases, was honorary physician to the Children's Hospital and held the post of medical officer for the city of Kew. Francis practised as a solicitor with Moule, Hamilton & Derham, of which he was co-founder. He appears, as well, to have been involved in the leadership of the 'White Army', a clandestine, right-wing organization.

On 10 April 1940 Alfred was appointed colonel in the A.I.F. Made assistant director of medical services to the 8th Division, he organized and trained its medical units and flew to Malaya in April 1941. That month he was appointed A.D.M.S., A.I.F. headquarters, Malaya. In the campaign which followed the Japanese invasion in December, Derham inspired his staff while supervising the evacuation of medical units across the Causeway to Singapore. Captured when Singapore fell on 15 February 1942, he was incarcerated in Changi prisoner-of-war camp for six months, and subsequently shipped to Formosa and then to Manchuria. He arrived home in September 1945 and his A.I.F. appointment terminated on 26 March 1946. That year he was appointed C.B.E. Alfred's period of captivity ruined his health. Survived by his wife and four of their five sons, he died of myocardial infarction on 26 June 1962 at the Repatriation General Hospital, Heidelberg, and was cremated. His son David became professor of jurisprudence and later vice-chancellor of the University of Melbourne.

Francis enjoyed higher rank than Alfred, but had no opportunity for active service. Promoted temporary major general on 2 May 1940, he held command of the 4th Division (1940-42), and of the 1st Division (1942-43) which functioned purely in a training role in New South Wales. He transferred to the Reserve of Officers on 7 November 1943 and was appointed C.B. in 1944. Resuming his legal practice in Melbourne, he appeared regularly in the Commonwealth Court of Conciliation and Arbitration for employers' groups. Francis was a director of G. J. Coles [q.v.] & Co. Ltd and of numerous other companies; he was founding president (1935) of the Victorian Society for Crippled Children and served on the Royal Melbourne Hospital's committee of management. Survived by his wife, he died on 22 October 1957 in East Melbourne and was cremated with Anglican rites.

C. E. W. Bean, *The Story of Anzac*, 1 (Syd, 1921); A. S. Walker, *Middle East and Far East* (Canb, 1953); M. Cathcart, *Defending the National Tuckshop* (Melb, 1988); G. L. McDonald (ed), *Roll of the Australasian College of Physicians*, 1 (Syd, 1988); *Sun News-Pictorial*, 22 Apr 1947; *Herald* (Melb), 24 Oct 1957, 26 June 1962; A. P. Derham papers (Univ Melb Archives).   JEFFREY GREY

DERHAM, FREDERICK JOHN WALCOTT (1900-1953), businessman, was born on 21 July 1900 at Armadale, Melbourne, second child of Victorian-born parents Frederick John Derham, stockbroker, and his wife Muriel Isabel, née Fosbery. F. T. Derham [q.v.4] was his grandfather. Young Derham attended Melbourne Church of England Grammar School where he did not excel scholastically, but rowed in the VIII that won the 'Head of the River' in 1918. Known as John or Jack, from the age of 16 he talked business with his father and much of his later shrewdness came from his mother who invested in the stock market. He began work as a salesman with James Hardie & Co. Pty Ltd, importers and exporters, and in 1921 joined with a friend Robert Corbett to form Corbett Derham & Co., merchants. On 22 March 1922 he married Mary Travers in the chapel of his old school. They bought a fine house at Toorak.

Although Derham's early commercial career was marked by periodic financial crises, he was always bailed out by his prosperous family who had built their fortune largely from Swallow [q.v.6] & Ariell Ltd. One of his ventures, Tunafone Wireless Pty Ltd, which manufactured receivers, stimulated his interest in plastics. Bakelite, a hard plastic, was used for wireless knobs, mountingboards and cases, as well as for electrical fittings and such items as buttons, bangles and ashtrays. Derham launched Victoria's first plastics firm, Australian Moulding Corporation Pty Ltd, in September 1927. One of 'Ma' Dalley's [q.v.] best customers, he excelled in adapting second-hand machinery for use in making plastics. The firm specialized in short runs and rapid response to market opportunities.

During a period of intense competition and takeovers in the industry in the early 1930s, Derham was forced out for a short time, but he was soon called back to help his competitors get their businesses in order. In 1936 he bought out the Dunlop plastics interests, Moulded Products (Australasia) Pty Ltd, and became managing director. It was floated as a public company in 1939. Demand for plastics grew rapidly in World War II when rubber was scarce. Bolstered by Derham's forceful managerial leadership and his firm belief in scientific and technical knowledge, the company tackled wartime problems and provided many innovative solutions, among them insulating telephone and other cables with plastics. Most products were marketed under the brand name Nylex, registered in 1941. After the war Moulded Products (Australasia) Ltd switched rapidly to manufacturing such articles as garden hoses and raincoats.

Derham lived a hectic life, with a fondness not only for work, but also for good food, spirits, wines and cigarettes—smoking sixty a day. He made few adjustments following a series of heart attacks, the last of which proved fatal. Survived by his wife, daughter and two sons, he died on 12 May 1953 at his Toorak home and was cremated. In 1967 the firm was renamed Nylex Corporation Ltd.

T. Hewat, *The Plastics Revolution* (Melb, 1983); *Herald* (Melb), 13 May 1953; *Age* (Melb), *Argus* and *Sun News-Pictorial*, 14 May 1953.

BRIAN CARROLL

DERRICK, EDGAR MARSH (1905-1976), child welfare worker and scout commissioner, was born on 10 July 1905 at Hawthorn, Melbourne, seventh child of Victorian-born parents Albert James Derrick, architect and founding secretary of the Central Methodist Mission, and his wife Martha Evelyn, née Finlay. Educated at Swinburne Technical College, Edgar initially worked as a commercial artist, but his great love was scouting. A founding member of Victoria's first cub pack (1st Camberwell), he rose to be scoutmaster of the Armadale troop. His enthusiasm for hard work earned him the nickname of 'Bus' (short for 'bus-horse') which stayed with him for the rest of his scouting career. In 1927 he was employed as quartermaster at State headquarters until he contracted tuberculosis. On his recovery he was advised by doctors never to return to indoor work.

In 1929 Derrick accepted a voluntary position as assistant-commissioner for leader training in the scouts; he was to hold the post for twenty years. Tally Ho, a farm at Burwood for homeless and delinquent boys founded by the Central Methodist Mission in 1903, had been going through turbulent times since the death of its founder Rev. George Cole [q.v.8] in 1919. In July 1930 Derrick informed the mission's executive-committee of his interest in the institution; with Rev. (Sir) Irving Benson's [q.v.] support, he was installed as superintendent that month.

In his twenty-seven years at Tally Ho, Derrick earned a reputation as an innovator. He believed that a bad boy was made, not born. Hence reformation was possible 'by removal from his old environment, the formation of new and more wholesome friendships . . . and the development of an ambition to succeed'. Using the ideas of Homer Lane, an American, Derrick created a society in miniature, with its own courts and parliament constituted by the boys, all of whom had jobs for which they were paid; the money was used to buy food and clothing, to pay for entertainment and to meet fines imposed by the courts for misdemeanours. Good behaviour was rewarded with stars which could be redeemed for extra privileges. While the system was not without its faults, it was a revolutionary change in an institution where corporal punishment had been the norm.

On 31 March 1934 at Wesley Church, Melbourne, Derrick married Hazel May Dalton, a fellow staff member who then took on the role of matron. During their tenure the institution expanded to include a training farm, Woodlands, at Lilydale. Never content with the traditional model, Derrick was an early advocate of both campus and scattered cottages, co-education in juvenile institutions, as well as secondary education and city-based hostels for boys unsuited to farm work. After World War II he was able to bring some of these ideas to fruition in the reconstruction of Tally Ho on the cottage system which allowed a more family-like atmosphere and greater recognition of individual needs.

Through his membership of a range of child-welfare organizations, Derrick helped to change the way in which the state cared for its wards. He was particularly influential in the establishment of training courses for child-care workers. A member of the committees of the Child Welfare Advisory Council, the National Fitness Council and the Victorian Council of Social Service (president 1954-56), he was vice-chairman of the Australian Social Welfare Council and chairman of the Youth Council of Victoria. In 1958 he was appointed M.B.E.

Derrick had continued to be involved in scouting. Appointed full-time commissioner for training and development in 1957, he became national secretary in 1965. He was also a prolific contributor to *Victorian Scout* and received a series of awards culminating in the silver kangaroo in 1971. Although he relinquished the national secretaryship in 1973, he maintained his interest in the movement and was a much-loved guest at troop meetings and camps. He died on 25 September 1976 at Glen Waverley and was cremated; his wife, daughter and son survived him.

E. W. King, *Dreams Become Deeds* (Melb, 1986); Central Methodist Mission, *Annual Report*, 1931-57; *Vic Scout*, Mar 1973, Oct 1976; *Spectator* (Melb), 27 Sept 1950, 30 July 1952, 1 Dec 1954; *Age* (Melb), 15, 25 July 1957, 1 Jan 1958, 24 Aug 1963; *Sun News-Pictorial*, 15 July 1957, 27 Sept 1976; Tally Ho records (Wesley Central Parish Mission Archives, Wesley Central Mission, Melb).

SHURLEE SWAIN

DERRICK, EDWARD HOLBROOK (1898-1976), medical practitioner, was born on 20 September 1898 at Blackwood, Victoria, second of four children of Clement Herbert Derrick, a native-born schoolteacher, and his wife Elizabeth Mary, née Sweetman, from England. Educated at Wesley College, Edward entered Queen's College, University of Melbourne (M.B., B.S., 1920; M.D., 1922). On 14 June 1918 he enlisted in the Australian Imperial Force, but, as a medical student, was not called up for service. He was appointed resident medical officer at the (Royal) Melbourne Hospital in 1920 and next year was Sir John Grice [q.v.9] cancer research scholar at the Walter and Eliza Hall [qq.v.9] Institute of Research in Pathology and Medicine. Having been awarded a free passage to England, in 1922-23 he worked as a pathology assistant at London Hospital. Derrick's programme of postgraduate training, directed at preparing himself for work as a medical missionary, was interrupted by illness: one brother had already died of tuberculosis, and Edward's own battle with that disease had a major influence on his life.

He returned to Australia in February 1924. While 'in search of a curative climate', he spent over ten years in country practice, holding brief locum-tenencies at Yea, Victoria, Curramulka, South Australia, Broken Hill, Tibooburra and Coolamon, New South Wales, and at Killarney, Mareeba and Innisfail, Queensland; he was also employed at the Austin Hospital, Melbourne. He settled for several years in North Queensland, at Irvinebank and then at Mount Mulligan. On 11 March 1930 at the Methodist Church, Irvinebank, he married a nurse Margaret Gina Quadrio. With his health restored, he resigned from Mount Mulligan in 1934 to begin a private practice in Brisbane.

In June 1935 Derrick was appointed director of the Queensland Department of Health Laboratory of Microbiology and Pathology. His investigation of a series of unexplained fevers in abattoir workers defined a disease entity not previously described which he named Q (for Query) fever. He succeeded in transmitting the infectious agent of that disease to guinea-pigs and collaborated with (Sir) Macfarlane Burnet to identify it as a rickettsia later named *Coxiella burnetii*. Subsequent studies showed survival of the organism in bandicoots and the tick *Haemaphysalis humerosa*, but it was left to scientists in the United States of America to discover the major source of human infection in bovine placenta. Derrick and his laboratory staff studied other agents of febrile disease in Queensland, and made several contributions, including the first isolation of *Leptospira pomona*. Both it and *Coxiella burnetii* proved to be of worldwide importance.

Heavy routine commitments and the dispersal of staff during World War II hindered research. In 1944, in his annual report to the secretary for health, Derrick suggested the creation of a research unit to explore disease problems in Queensland. Next year he was appointed chairman of an advisory committee whose recommendations led to the establishment of the Queensland Institute of Medical Research, Brisbane. In 1947 he became its deputy-director; he succeeded I. M. Mackerras [q.v.] as director in 1961. Derrick continued to investigate fevers of unknown origin in North Queensland, taking a key role in studies based at Innisfail which led to the discovery of many new serotypes of leptospires, and greatly extended knowledge of leptospirosis and scrub typhus in that area. Responsible for establishing a virology unit at the institute, he fostered its growth until the major part of its programme was concerned with viruses or virus diseases. The appearance of epidemic Q fever in shearers in western Queensland allowed further studies of that disease.

Interested from 1960 in the epidemiology of asthma in Queensland, Derrick carried out a long series of studies, especially of two annual seasonal peaks of incidence. He retired as director in July 1966, but continued to work as an honorary research fellow at the institute and published a further twenty-one papers. Director (1966-73) of the Queensland Asthma Foundation's research bureau, he maintained an association with that organization until his death.

Derrick's achievements were widely recognized. Among his many honours, he was appointed C.B.E. (1961). In 1939 he had shared the Commonwealth Department of Health's Cilento medal with Macfarlane Burnet; he also received the Britannica Australia Award for Medicine (1965) and the medal of the Australian and New Zealand Association for the Advancement of Science (1969). In 1948 he was Bancroft [q.v.3] orator of the Queensland branch of the British Medical Association and in 1962 Elkington [q.v.8] orator of the Queensland Society of

Health. In 1966 he received an honorary doctorate of science from the University of Queensland. He was a fellow of the Australian Academy of Science (1955), the Australian Medical Association (1968) and the Australian Postgraduate Federation in Medicine (1971). Almost half of his 126 scientific papers were published in the *Medical Journal of Australia*, including his classic paper (1937) on the discovery of Q fever. The journal published a *festschrift* issue in his honour in December 1967. His last published work—on his own experience with angina pectoris—appeared in 1976. A complete list of Derrick's publications was compiled by Mackerras in 1978.

Survived by his wife and two sons, Derrick died on 15 June 1976 in Brisbane and was cremated. Much of his career and his studies was identified with Queensland, and he had a great influence on two generations of researchers there. Modest, gentle and deeply religious, he was a meticulous scientist and a dedicated medical practitioner. His portrait by Graeme Inson hangs in the foyer of the Queensland Institute of Medical Research, Brisbane.

R. Patrick, *A History of Health & Medicine in Queensland 1824-1960* (Brisb, 1987); Dept of Health and Home Affairs (Qld), Health and Medical Services Branch, Annual Report, 1959-60, *PP* (Qld), 1960 (34), p 103; *MJA*, 9 Dec 1967, p 1067, *and* R. L. Derrick, 'E. H. Derrick—his published record and its background', *MJA*, 9 Dec 1967, p 1069, *and* 'Obituary: Edward Holbrook Derrick', *MJA*, 6 Nov 1976, p 731, *and* Bancroft Oration: part 1, 'The Bancroft tradition in infectious disease research in Queensland', *MJA*, 2 Dec 1978, p 560, *and* part 2, *MJA*, 16 Dec 1978, p 591; *Records of the Aust Academy of Science*, 4, no 1, 1978, p 83, *and* for Derrick's publications; *Courier-Mail*, 13 Dec 1966, 16 June 1976; E. H. Derrick, Fragments of an Autobiography (nd, Basser L, Academy of Science, Canb).   R. L. DOHERTY

DERRICK, THOMAS CURRIE (1914-1945), vineyard worker and soldier, was born on 20 March 1914 in the Salvation Army hospital at Medindie, Adelaide, eldest son of David Derrick, a labourer from Ireland, and his native-born wife Ada, née Whitcombe. The Derricks were battlers. Tom walked, often barefooted, to two primary schools in succession—Sturt Street Public School in the city and Le Fevre Peninsula School, Port Adelaide. He left school as soon as he could, aged 14. By then he was a bit of a larrikin around the Port, venturesome and quick-witted, keen on boxing, Australian Rules football, cricket and gambling. During the Depression his cheeriness found him odd jobs, fixing bikes, selling newspapers and working for a local baker. Early in 1931 he and some mates rode their bikes about 140 miles (225 km) to Berri, on the Murray River, chasing work. 'Diver', as he was now nicknamed, did long spells in the local 'susso' camp, once living on grapes for a week, but in late 1931 talked his way into work on a vineyard at Winkie. He stayed nine years.

In the presbytery of St Laurence's Catholic Church, North Adelaide, on 24 June 1939 Derrick married Clarance Violet ('Beryl') Leslie. As with C. J. Dennis's [q.v.8] Ginger Mick, whom in peace and war Derrick so much resembled, marriage gave his life a more serious purpose. He did not volunteer for the Australian Imperial Force until 26 June 1940 and enlisted on 5 July. Although never overtly religious, he became a convert to Catholicism (his wife's religion) in early 1945. When Tom was at the war, Beryl walked almost every day to the post office, hoping for news of him.

On 17 November 1940 Derrick had embarked for the Middle East with the 2nd/48th Battalion, which was to be the most decorated unit in the A.I.F. In that distinguished company Derrick was outstanding. At Tobruk, Libya (April to October 1941), his enthusiasm and aggression in patrolling enemy positions brought him promotion to corporal, and he was probably recommended for a Military Medal on 1 May 1941. An officer at this time described him as 'resourceful, brave, aware, humane, forever bending over backwards for his men'.

At Tel el Eisa, Egypt, on 10-11 July 1942 Derrick ran forward through a barrage of grenades, destroyed three machine-gun posts and captured over a hundred prisoners. He then inspired the defence against a counter-attack, wrecking two tanks with sticky grenades. Awarded the Distinguished Conduct Medal, he was promoted sergeant on 28 July. At El Alamein in late October he showed his customary leadership and daring during a week of violent battle. Only forty-one of his battalion still stood at the end of that week, and Diver had been slightly wounded, but he destroyed three more machine-gun posts, and those who saw him were certain he had earned a Victoria Cross.

The 2nd/48th returned to Australia in February 1943 and trained in North Queensland and Papua before helping to capture Lae, New Guinea, in September. By 24 November the battalion was attacking the heights of Sattelberg, overlooking Finschhafen. Late that afternoon, while leading the advance platoon, Derrick confronted an almost vertical slope of thick jungle hiding Japanese machine-guns, and above that an open patch stretching menacingly 100 yards (90 m) towards the crest. Diver was told to withdraw, but he decided to go on. Covered by his mates, he scrambled hands and feet up the cliff, hurling grenades into enemy posts and clearing them out with his rifle. Even in peacetime the climb is barely possible, yet Derrick cleared ten machine-gun posts, stopping just short of the crest as dusk fell. It was one of the most astonishing feats of the war. He was awarded the V.C. (22 March 1944). In North Africa he had remarked that his D.C.M. had come in a Comforts Fund parcel; now he said that his achievement was due mainly to his mates.

In February 1944 the 2nd/48th again returned to Australia, and in August Derrick was posted to an officer-training unit. On being commissioned lieutenant in November, he became one of the few second A.I.F. men promoted from the ranks who rejoined their old battalions. On 1 May 1945 the 2nd/48th took part in the landing at Tarakan, Borneo, and soon pushed inland. On the 22nd/23rd Derrick led his platoon against a small hill, code-named Freda, thick with enemy defences. His skill and courage that day might easily have won him another V.C., but by night the enemy still held the highest knoll. Derrick spread out his men, then lay down on the jungle track to rest. At about 3 o'clock next morning a Japanese light machine-gun, on a fixed line, fired a burst down the track. Diver sat up to see that his men were O.K., the gun fired again, and five bullets caught him in an arc from his left hip to his right chest. He lay back quietly, and, after a time, said to a mate, 'I've had it. That's that. Write to Beryl'. He continued to direct operations until mid-morning. Then they carried him back, his grin and his courage never deserting him. He died on 24 May 1945 and was buried in Labuan war cemetery, plot 24, row A, grave 9. His wife survived him. (Sir) Ivor Hele's portrait of Derrick is held by the Australian War Memorial, Canberra.

Derrick looked the archetypal digger: a fine photo of him on the dustjacket of Allan Dawes's [q.v.] 'Soldier Superb' (Sydney, 1944) became one of the best-known Australian images of the war. It shows a man fit, strong and stocky (he was 5 ft 7 ins [170 cm] tall), a deep tan matching his dark hair, a cocky grin stoking the laughter lines around his brown eyes. It suggests both the larrikin and the professional, both the man who stuck by his mates and the born leader. It leaves unstated the man with such brilliant tactical judgement, such concern for his men, such modesty, such courage, such flair for being a soldier. It does not reveal the man who collected butterflies, who wrote poetry and kept a wartime diary, who liked rhyming slang. It does not say that here is one of the finest fighting soldiers of the war.

Derrick displayed the most fearless bravery throughout four years of battle. When he might honourably have quit the field he insisted on going back. Very few soldiers can compare with him. War gave him distinction, but he gave life honour. He was an extraordinary man.

J. G. Glenn, *Tobruk to Tarakan* (Adel, 1960); M. Farquhar, *Derrick VC* (Adel, 1982); Derrick diary *and* interview with T. C. Derrick, 1 Dec 1943, Gavin Long's note-books *and* Derrick citations *and* M. Farquhar papers (AWM).   BILL GAMMAGE

DE TISNE, FIFI; *see* BANVARD

DEVANEY, JAMES MARTIN (1890-1976), poet, novelist, journalist and teacher, was born on 31 May 1890 at Sandhurst, Victoria, fourth child of Patrick Devaney, a labourer from Ireland, and his native-born wife Mary, née Conroy. Educated at Bendigo and at St Joseph's College, Hunters Hill, Sydney, in 1904 James entered the college's Marist Brothers' juniorate. In 1915 he made his final vows and took the religious name Fabian Joseph. Trained as a teacher, from 1911 he successively served in schools in Sydney, South Australia and New Zealand. Brother Fabian contracted severe tuberculosis and returned to Sydney in 1919 to teach at Darlinghurst. His Superior so relentlessly opposed adequate medical treatment that, driven to the point of despair, Devaney left the Order in July 1921. He recuperated in a sanatorium near Rockhampton, Queensland, and at the Diamantina Hospital, Brisbane. On 29 November 1924 at the Church of Mary Immaculate, Annerley, he married his nurse Phyllis Norah de Winton; they were to remain childless.

Living mostly in the Brisbane district, and at times in Sydney and at the Blue Mountains, Devaney established a career as a freelance journalist. Under the pen-name 'Fabian', from 1924 to 1943 he contributed a nature column to the Brisbane *Courier* (*Courier-Mail* from 1933) which was syndicated in other Queensland newspapers. He had a long association with the *Catholic Leader* as editor of its literary page and on occasions was acting-editor.

His volumes of verse, *Fabian* (Melbourne, 1923), *Earth Kindred* (Melbourne, 1931), *Dark Road* (Melbourne, 1938) and *Where the Wind Goes* (Sydney, 1939), established him as a fine lyric poet, well regarded by contemporary critics. *Poems* (Sydney, 1950) brought together selections from his earlier works and from *Freight of Dreams* which had been printed in Melbourne, but not released, in 1946. In *Poetry in Our Time* (Melbourne, 1952) he confronted modernism and forcefully expounded his own beliefs, but was seen by many critics as reactionary. Although his two historical novels, *Currency Lass* (Sydney,

1927) and *Washdirt* (Melbourne, 1946), were less successful, a volume of vivid and imaginative stories based on Aboriginal lore, *Vanished Tribes* (Sydney, 1929), enjoyed popular success; it was later used in schools and was an influence in the formation of the Jindyworobak movement. *The New Law* (Brisbane, 1955), a dramatic dialogue set in biblical times, received little critical attention.

Devaney played a leading role in the vigorous local literary community of the 1930s and 1940s: he provided a focus for the Catholic Poetry Society and was president (1944-45) of the Queensland Authors' and Artists' Association. While John Shaw Neilson [q.v.10] convalesced in Devaney's Brisbane home in 1941, Devaney helped to transcribe his poems. His spirited defence of Neilson's painstaking craftsmanship—*Shaw Neilson* (Sydney, 1944)—disposed of criticism of Neilson as an 'instinctive warbler' and a 'thoughtless mystic'. In 1947 he edited the *Unpublished Poems of Shaw Neilson* (Sydney). That year he delivered lectures under the auspices of the Commonwealth Literary Fund, from which he subsequently received a pension. He supported the writing community through lectures and workshops, encouraged writers such as Oodgeroo Noonuccal (Kath Walker) and assisted others financially in the publication of their works. In 1958, in company with Professor Manning Clark and Judah Waten, he represented Australian writers on a visit to the Soviet Union.

Having interrupted his journalism, Devaney found it difficult to obtain the same work after World War II. In 1946 he had returned to teaching, first in Victoria and then at pastoral stations in Queensland. He resigned from his last post in February 1962 to nurse his wife. She died from a drug overdose in July. Her addiction had resulted in their virtual separation from the mid-1940s, but he had continued to hope for the eventual restoration of their domestic life. Tall, spare, gentlemanly and modest, Devaney was a humanitarian with a deep-rooted sense of justice. He remained a staunch Catholic, but no sectarian, who opposed intolerance and narrow-mindedness within the Church. Never afraid to speak his mind, he supported the Labor Party, advocated 'a democracy free from the monarchy' and was reputed to have declined appointment as M.B.E. in 1968. He died on 14 August 1976 in Brisbane and was buried in Redcliffe cemetery.

Walkabout, 1 Feb 1952; *Meanjin Q*, June 1965; Archbishop James Duhig papers (Catholic Church Diocesan Archives, Brisb); Martin Haley papers (Fryer L, Univ Qld); J. Devaney papers (Fryer L *and* OL); J. Davis, The Southwellians, 1938, and the Catholic Poetry Society (M.Litt. thesis, JCU, 1986); information from Br M. Naughtin, Marist Bros Archives, St Joseph's College, Hunter's Hill,

Syd, Mrs M. Stewart, Moonee Ponds, and Dr C. B. Christensen, Eltham, Melb, and Mrs M. Freer, Bardon, Brisb.   M. D. O'HAGAN

DEVANNY, PATRICIA (1913-1980), political activist, was born on 5 November 1913 at Puponga, New Zealand, second of three children of Francis Harold Devanny, miner, and his wife Jane [q.v.8], née Crook, both New Zealand born. Jane and Hal were active in the New Zealand Labour Party. In August 1929 the family emigrated to Sydney only to encounter the crisis of the Depression. Having taken part in demonstrations of the unemployed, the Devannys became involved in the communist movement. Patricia joined the Young Communist League and in November 1930 was arrested for participating in an unauthorized street demonstration and sentenced to fourteen days imprisonment. While she was in Long Bay gaol, a hunger strike was mounted by the Communist Party of Australia to support several men (the 'Clovelly Boys') imprisoned for burning the house of a landlord who had evicted an unemployed family. Patricia joined a number of other young women in this protest until her sentence ended eight days later.

Her resilience and courage, as well as her militant family connexions, recommended Devanny to the C.P.A. Early in 1931 she was selected to study at a communist international school in Moscow, where she was trained in Marxist-Leninist theory, organization and propaganda. This education was part of a worldwide reconstruction (bolshevization) of communist parties, directed towards creating a new cadre of party workers and leaders. On her return to Australia early in 1933, Devanny became national secretary of the Young Communist League. Despite having to contend at times with remarkable directives from the Young Communist International, including that of 'liquidating the bourgeois youth organisations', she maintained a discreetly critical detachment. Under her leadership the Y.C.L. changed from a semi-secret, street-cell formation to an open system of suburban clubs, with a sporting and social life, as well as political activity and discussion.

Early in 1939, with her husband Ronald William Jackson Hurd, a seaman who had fought with the British Battalion, XVth International Brigade, in the Spanish Civil War, she went to New Zealand where their only son was born. After the family returned to Sydney during World War II, Ron went back to sea and Pat assisted in establishing a women's auxiliary of the Seamen's Union which provided a club for seamen in Pitt Street, near Circular Quay. Following some years at Fremantle, Western Australia, in the late 1950s she broke with the communist movement and the family moved to Townsville, Queensland, where her parents were living. There she joined the Australian Labor Party, chaired its local women's branch and campaigned for Aboriginal rights. She later helped to form a women's crisis centre and to provide community assistance for overseas students at the James Cook University of North Queensland.

Devanny's early experience of the misery of unemployment and the harshness of police methods in the Depression made her a committed fighter for the underprivileged. Only 5 ft 2 ins (157.5 cm) tall and fundamentally gentle in nature, she could be roused by injustice to towering rage. She drowned on 5 December 1980 in a neighbour's swimming pool at Townsville and was cremated with Anglican rites; predeceased by her husband, she was survived by her son.

J. Devanny, *Point of Departure*, C. Ferrier ed (Brisb, 1986); *Labour Hist*, 45, Nov 1983, p 94; family information.   JACK STEPHENS

DEW, SIR HAROLD ROBERT (1891-1962), professor of surgery, was born on 14 April 1891 at Reservoir, Melbourne, eldest child of Victorian-born parents Joseph Dew, schoolteacher, and his wife Alice Lucy, née Steed. Educated at the Melbourne Continuation School and at Scotch College, in 1909 Harold entered Ormond [q.v.5] College, University of Melbourne (M.B., B.S., 1914). After a year as resident medical officer at (Royal) Melbourne Hospital, he sailed for England where he was commissioned temporary lieutenant in the Royal Army Medical Corps on 14 April 1915. He served in France with the 57th Field Ambulance and in Egypt with the 146th. From January 1918 Captain Dew was officer commanding the cholera laboratory at the 3rd Egyptian Stationary Hospital, Kantara; there he also performed general and clinical pathology, and surgery. He assembled a fine collection of pathological specimens of endemic Egyptian diseases, particularly those that illustrated dysentery and bilharziasis. The French government had awarded him the *médaille d'honneur des épidémies* in August 1917.

His appointment having terminated in April 1919, Dew went to London for postgraduate study and hospital experience, and in 1920 was admitted a fellow of the Royal College of Surgeons, England. Back in Melbourne, he became resident tutor in surgery and anatomy at Ormond College. As an honorary associate (first-assistant 1922-25) at the Walter and Eliza Hall [qq.v.9] Institute, he collaborated with (Sir) Neil Fairley [q.v.] on such topics as dysentery, malaria and schistosomiasis, and—in what was to become his outstanding work—hydatid disease and testicular tumours. Concurrent with his research, Dew's clinical work also developed, with an appointment in 1922 as a clinical-assistant and in 1923 honorary surgeon to out-patients at Melbourne Hospital. On 27 February 1925 at Christ Church, South Yarra, he married with Anglican rites Doreen Lorna Beatrice Lawrance.

In 1924 Dew had won the R.C.S.'s Jacksonian prize for his essay on malignant disease of the testicle; next year he expanded the essay into a book. He shared the university's David Syme [q.v.6] research prize in 1927 for work which was to be published in 1928 as *Hydatid Disease* and which rapidly became an international classic. Secretary (from 1923) of the Surgical Association of Melbourne, he was a fellow (1928) of the (Royal) Australasian College of Surgeons.

Appointed in February 1930 to the new Bosch [q.v.7] chair of surgery at the University of Sydney, Dew received glowing tributes to his intellectual, professional and personal qualities from his referees, among them Professors Sir Charles Martin and W. A. Osborne [qq.v.10,11]. Dew spent seven months abroad and was Hunterian professor of the R.C.S. On taking up his duties in Sydney in September, he collaborated with Charles Lambie [q.v.9], Bosch professor of medicine, in reorganizing the clinical curriculum. The pair, who have been characterized as 'like chalk and cheese, Lambie a fussy little man and Dew a plain man with no airs and graces', complemented each other admirably. Dew also oversaw the construction of the new medical school. Determined that the university should derive the fullest benefit from a substantial grant from the Rockefeller Foundation, he attempted to have equipment for the building exempted from sales tax, a cause which he furthered through protracted correspondence with his old Melbourne friend (Sir) John Latham [q.v.10] and other Federal politicians.

While the physician R. Scot Skirving [q.v.11] was not alone in scorning his prosaic lecturing style, Dew was a popular teacher with students. In his very didactic way 'he made the subject as understandable as possible by placing great emphasis on the practical'. He was an honorary at Royal Prince Alfred Hospital where, despite a certain 'crustiness', he was liked by his patients. His major clinical achievement, apart from stressing surgical pathology as the basis for surgical practice, was that he began neurosurgery in Sydney, after observing in 1930 the work of Harvey Cushing at Boston, United States of America. Previously only very limited cranial exploration had been undertaken by general surgeons. By backing his gifted protégés Rex Money and Gilbert Phillips [q.v.], Dew

ushered in a new era. One colleague described him as coming like 'a breath of fresh air into the static, insular and self-satisfied medical world of Sydney'. Dew was, himself, a poor operative surgeon which limited his effectiveness, especially in postgraduate education, because he was never accepted by (Sir) Herbert Schlink [q.v.11], the doyen of R.P.A.H. Although some colleagues considered that Dew's move into administration seriously limited his professional potential, accounts of his periods as dean of medicine and as a fellow (1936-38 and 1940-52) of the senate have emphasized his fairness and 'good-heartedness', as well as his battles with wartime difficulties and large enrolments after 1945.

Dew did no research himself once he had arrived in Sydney, but he introduced the B.Sc. (Med.) degree in 1949 and promoted a post-war flowering of research by providing facilities and encouragement. In 1937-56 he had represented the R.A.C.S. on the National Health and Medical Research Council; he was a foundation member of the N.H. & M.R.C.'s executive-committee and foundation chairman (1946-56) of its medical research advisory committee. He emphasized 'the importance of initiating a national scheme . . . to encourage young medical graduates to take up medical research as a career' and urged the Commonwealth government to provide 'a definite annual sum' to ensure continuity.

A council-member (1940-54) of the R.A.C.S., Dew was vice-president (from 1948) and president (1953-54). During World War II he had been a member of the Royal Australian Air Force Flying Personnel Research Committee. Despite numerous commitments, he sat on the editorial committees of the British and Australasian journals of surgery, the New South Wales Rhodes scholarship committee and the Nuffield Foundation advisory committee for Australia. In 1953 he was Sims Commonwealth travelling professor for the R.C.S. and again Hunterian professor in London. He was awarded an honorary Sc.D. by the University of Cambridge (1953) and knighted in 1955.

With an abiding love of the Snowy mountains, for most of his life Dew belonged to the Waterfall Farm Fly-Fishers' Club which held land on the Geehi River; he was its secretary for more than twenty years. J. T. Lang [q.v.9] had denounced the group as a 'conservative cabal'. Its members included Dew's close friends Latham, (Sir) Thomas Bavin and (Sir) John Harvey [qq.v.7,9], but there is no evidence of overt political activity on Dew's part. He also belonged to the Australian Club.

Lady Dew was active in the affairs of the Sydney University Settlement and the Royal Alexandra Hospital for Children where a lecture theatre is named after her. With her husband, who was a bon viveur, she was known in Sydney for her hospitality. Following his retirement in 1956, they lived at Wheelers Hill, on the outskirts of Melbourne. Sir Harold never really recovered from the destruction by a fire of his uninsured home, paintings and library only a year after they had moved to Victoria. Survived by his wife (d. 1993) and two daughters, he died on 17 November 1962 at Wheelers Hill and was cremated.

G. H. Hall and A. Cousins (eds), *Book of Remembrance of the University of Sydney in the War 1914-1918* (Syd, 1939); J. A. Young et al (eds), *Centenary Book of the University of Sydney Faculty of Medicine* (Syd, 1984); A. Macintosh (ed), *Memoirs of Dr Robert Scot Skirving 1859-1956* (Syd, 1988); *Lancet*, 8 Dec 1962; *British Medical J*, 1 Dec 1962; *SMH*, 15 Apr 1924, 5 Feb 1930, 10, 11 Oct 1952, 15 July 1953, 9 June 1955; *Smith's Weekly* (Syd), 22 Feb 1930; *Herald* (Melb), 17 June 1958; Sir John Latham papers (NL); Roy A'sian College of Surgeons Archives (Melb); Univ Syd Archives; information from Sir Douglas Miller, Neutral Bay, Dr M. Joseph, Killara, Syd, Emeritus Prof P. Bishop, Avoca, Dr W. Neild, Newcastle, NSW, and Mr J. Dew, Mont Albert, Melb.

JOHN CARMODY

CORRIGENDA

to accompany volume 13

Australian Dictionary of Biography

This list includes only corrigenda discovered since the Index volume was published in 1991. In making these corrections it is assumed that previous corrigenda have been noted.

Only corrections are shown; additional information is not included; nor is any reinterpretation attempted. The exception to this procedure occurs when new details about parents, births, marriages and deaths become available.

Documented corrections are welcome from readers. Additional information, with sources, is also invited and will be placed in the appropriate files for future use.

Volume 1: 1788-1850 A-H

42b AUSTIN
lines 2-4 *for* was a . . . where *read*
was baptized on 13 August 1776 at
Baltonsborough, Somerset, England, son of John Austin and his wife
Sarah. He was a farm labourer at
Baltonsborough when

63b BARTLEY
line 2 *for* a *read* born on 22 September 1803,

124b BOLDEN
lines 55-56 *for* a Miss . . . sons. *read*
Henrietta Travers on 26 January
1860 at Kilmany Park; they had at
least eight children.

419b FROST
line 32 *for* Zephania *read* Zeph-
aniah

437a GELLIBRAND
line 1 *for* 1786 *read* 1792?

439b GIBSON
line 1 *for* 1780? *read* 1778?
lines 2-3 *for* in Perth, Scotland. *read*
at Aberuthven, Perthshire, Scotland, and baptized on 26 April 1778,
son of John Gibson and his wife
Giles, née Binning.

472a GREENWAY
line 42 *for* reign *read* rein

524a HAWDON
line 2 *for* born *read* baptized on
15 December 1813
line 3 *for* Walkerfield *read* Wacker-
field
line 9 *for* By the time that *read*
After
line 10 *delete* had
line 31 *delete* alone,
line 35 *delete* and then Lake Alexan-
drina
line 37 *for* Captain *read* Lieutenant
lines 47-48 *for* depasturing licence
read crown lease
line 49 *after* he *insert* returned to
England. In 1863 he
lines 53-55 *for* on . . . attend. *read*
was a member of the Legislative
Council in 1866-71.
line 58 *for* Melbourne *read* Durham
on 19 January 1842

Volume 2: 1788-1850 I-Z

5a IRWIN
line 40 *for* in *read* on 31 March

9b JACKSON
line 12 *after* Swanston *insert* [qq.v.]
line 13 *delete* [qq.v.]

360b RAINE
line 6 *for* Rainbarn *read* Rainham

394a ROSE, T.
line 1 *for* 1749? *read* 1754?
line 2 *for* England. *read* England,
and baptized on 24 November
1854, son of Christopher Rose and
his wife Mary, née Belben.
line 3 *for* There *read* On 8 August
1779 at Sturminster Newton

410b RUSSELL
line 45 *for* dageurreotype *read*
daguerreotype

507a TERRY
line 1 *after* was *insert* baptized on
17 March 1771,
line 2 *for* Ralph *read* John
line 5 *for* He *read* On 12 July 1797
at Hornby he
line 7 *for* of Hornby Castle *read* , a
farmer of Hunters Hill

522b THOMSON
line 11 *for* 1837 *read* 1836

613a WILTON
line 9 *after* 1820. *insert* On 1 January 1823 in the parish of Awre,
Gloucester, he married Elizabeth
Plaistowe.

Volume 3: 1851-1890 A-C

xiva AUTHORS
line 38 (Moyle) *for* U *read* V

33a ANDREW
line 6 *for* Jones *read* Job
lines 10-12 *for* Tasmania . . . in 1858
read Melbourne. His father had
arrived in Melbourne in 1853, resigned from the ministry,

266b BROWNE
line 28 *for* Martha Elizabeth *read*
Elizabeth Martha Ann

301b BURING
line 19 *for* U *read* V

335a CAMBRIDGE
lines 46-47 *for* 27 April *read* 19
July

Volume 4: 1851-1890 D-J

143a EVANS, M.
line 5 *after* two *insert* surviving
line 6 *for* schoolmaster *read* oilman,

and his wife Elizabeth Ann, née Jacob
line 9 *for* a son *read* two sons

143b line 3 *for* 26 *read* 18
line 11 *for* 1861 *read* 1859
line 17 *for* years *read* hours
lines 23-24 *for* Soon afterwards *read* In 1882
line 30 *for* Lowe *read* Low
line 46 *for* collected short stories *read* collection

308b GUNTHER
line 3 *for* 25 *read* 28 (correcting corrigenda issued with volume 5)

Volume 5: 1851-1890 K-Q

xvb AUTHORS
line 6 *for* McKillop *read* MacKillop

122a MCARTHUR, D.
line 2 *for* 1810 *read* 1808 *and after* born *insert* on 20 September 1808

122b line 47 *after* Wright *insert* , whom he had married on 3 April 1835 at St Cuthbert's parish church, Edinburgh

174a MCKILLOP, M.
line 1 *for* McKILLOP *read* MACKILLOP
line 5 *for* McKillop *read* MacKillop

203b MANNING
line 39 *for* 1890- *read* 1893

262b MITCHELL, Sir W.
line 9 *for* Clyde *read* Sir Thomas Munro *and for* June *read* January

323b MURRAY-PRIOR
line 45 *for* Clarissa *read* Clarina
line 49 *for* eleven *read* twelve

376b OSBORNE, P.
line 9 *for* Garley *read* Earley

429b PENFOLD
line 3 *after* vigneron, *insert* was born on 2 August 1811,
line 5 *for* June *read* Jane

Volume 6: 1851-1890 R-Z

xviiib AUTHORS
line 9 *for* ZAIN'UDDIN *read* ZAINU'DDIN

190a STEPHEN, J.
line 9 *for* ZAIN'UDDIN *read* ZAINU'DDIN

254b TENISON-WOODS
line 38 *for* McKillop *read* MacKillop

Volume 7: 1891-1939 A-Ch

1a ABBOTT
line 12 *for* McKillop *read* MacKillop

36b ALLAN, P.
line 10 *delete* As a *insert* A *and for* Warrigal *read* Newtown

99b ARNOLD, R.
line 11 *for* Association *read* Club

170a BARBOUR
line 6 *for* -81 *read* -84

170b line 5 for *Record* read *Chronicle*
line 7 *for* 1889- *read* 1888-

209a BATES
line 15 *delete* [q.v.]

237a BEAUREPAIRE
line 39 *for* 1936 *read* 1934

253b BELL, G.
lines 16-17 *delete* with Hugh Ramsay [q.v.]

382b BRADFIELD
line 4 *for* all *read* most

385b BRADY
line 16 *for* That year *read* In 1884

480a BUNNY
line 48 *for* him *read* his

482b BURDETT
line 13 *for* Vassilief *read* Vassilieff

548b CAMPBELL
line 2 *after* Fraser *insert* Stewart

612b CHAPMAN, F.
line 46 *for* Wilfred *read* Wilfrid

Volume 8: 1891-1939 Cl-Gib

125b COWAN
line 15 *for* Academia *read* Accademia

128a COX
line 8 *for* State *read* colonial

236b DAVIS, A.
line 1 *for* 1933 *read* 1934
line 2 *delete* next year

379a DUNSTAN, A.
line 41 *for* NSW *read* Melb

411b EDKINS
line 1 *before* , pastoralist *insert* [q.v.4]

465b FALKINER
line 4 *for* Edith *read* Ethel

478a FEEZ
line 12 *for* When young, *read* In 1885

line 13 *for* several times *read* twice

521a FLEGG
line 6 *for* About 1888 *read* In 1884

646a GIBBS (Cross Reference)
line 1 *for* SYBIL *read* SIBYL

646a GIBLIN
lines 12-13 *for* All-England *read* England

Volume 9: 1891-1939 Gil-Las

xia AUTHORS
line 48 *for* BERGMANN *read* BERG-MAN

78b GRANT
line 15 *for* appointed K.C.B. *read* knighted.

82b GRATTON
line 6 *for* May *read* Cay
line 8 *for* 12 *read* 18

188a HANNAN
line 1 *for* 1843 *read* 1840
line 2 *for* October 1843 *read* April 1840
line 3 *for* Patrick *read* John
line 4 *for* Catherine, née Gleeson *read* Bridget, née Lynch

262a HENNESSY
lines 15-18 *for* represented . . . 1902. *read* toured New Zealand in 1901, and represented New South Wales against Queensland in 1904.

359b HOOD
line 26 *for* two *read* 11
line 27 *before* ewes *insert* 33
line 30 *delete* on its dispersal
line 31 *delete* part of
line 40 *for* 1877 *read* 1878
line 49 *for* the younger Robert *read* his son Alec
line 55 *for* Robert *read* Alec

360a line 11 *for* thirty-four *read* thirty-three

461b JACOBS, J.
line 3 *for* BERGMANN *read* BERG-MAN

473a JEFFERIES
line 18 *after* Mallalieu *insert* [q.v. Willmore]

513a JONES, Sir H.
line 3 *for* eldest *read* second
line 6 *for* Smith *read* Matheson (Mapperson)

656b LANE
line 30 *after* Turley *insert* [q.v.]

666a LANG
line 45 *for* 6 *read* 5

Volume 10: 1891-1939 Lat-Ner

xvia AUTHORS
line 55 *for* O'KEEFE *read* O'KEEFFE

4a LATHAM
line 37 *for* Solomon *read* Abraham

26b LAWTON, T.
lines 2-3 *for* Congumbogan, *read* Cungumbogan, near Waterford,

184b LYONS
line 55 *for* an 18- *read* a 17-

290a MACKAY, D.
line 14 *for* 1931 *read* 1930
line 17 *for* 1931 *read* 1930

317b MCKIVAT
line 10 *delete* next year

Volume 11: 1891-1939 Nes-Smi

326b RAMSAY
line 3 *for* fourth *read* sixth

385b RICHARDSON
line 63 *for* Evonne *read* Yvonne

409a ROBERTS, T.
line 8 *for* 1868 *read* 1869

472b ROYSTON
line 29 *for* After a *read* On the

490a RUWOLT
line 1 *for* 1873? *read* 1873
line 3 *for* probably in . . . in *read* on 19 March 1873 at Mieckenhagen,

Volume 12: 1891-1939 Smy-Z

ix COMMITTEES
line 22 *after* Cross; *insert* J. C. H. Gill;

16a SOMMERLAD
line 45 *before* member *insert* life-

88a STEWART
line 53 *before* suspended *insert* to be *and after* suspended *insert* in 1944

121a STREETON
lines 35-36 *for* appointed K.B.E. *read* knighted.

137a SULMAN
line 11 *for* Giles *read* George